U.S.
INDUSTRY
PROFILES
The Leading 100

HIGHLIGHTS

The second edition of *U.S. Industry Profiles: The Leading 100* covers the current status and predicted future for 100 significant U.S. industries, including:

- Advertising Agencies
- Book Publishing and Printing
- Computer Software
- Engineering Services
- Motion Pictures
- Petroleum Refining
- Security and Commodity Exchanges
- Telecommunications

USIP also includes some "hot" industries, including:

- Catalog and Mail-Order Services
- Travel and Tourism

PROVIDES INDUSTRY INFORMATION SOURCES

Each chapter provides a directory of additional sources of industry data, complete with full contact information. Listings include associations and societies, periodicals and newsletters, databases, general works, and statistics sources.

INCLUDES HUNDREDS OF CHARTS AND GRAPHS

USIP contains over 400 charts and graphs representing industry trends and forecasts for occupations, establishments, and compensation; state-level data, illustrated with state and regional maps; lists of top companies; and market share statistics.

EASY TO USE

Organized in alphabetical order by industry, *USIP* contains a Table of Contents and two indexes. The Industry Index provides access to industries by Standard Industrial Classification (SIC) code; and the General Index references all companies, associations, publications, key government agencies, and specific legislation cited in the book.

ISSN 1082-9798

U.S. INDUSTRY PROFILES

The Leading 100

SECOND EDITION

JOSEPH C. TARDIFF, EDITOR

GALE

DETROIT · NEW YORK · TORONTO · LONDON

Joseph C. Tardiff, *Editor*

Jennifer L. Carman and Susan J. Cindric, *Assistant Editors*

Scott Heil, Christine Kelley, Jane A. Malonis, Rebecca Marlow-Ferguson, Terrance W. Peck, Stephen Thor Tschirhart, and Mike Weaver, *Contributing Editors*

Diane Maniaci, *Managing Editor*

Mary Beth Trimper, *Production Director*
Deborah L. Milliken, *Production Assistant*

Cynthia Baldwin, *Production Design Manager*
Pamela A.E. Galbreath, *Art Director*

Theresa A. Rocklin, *Manager, Systems and Programming*
Charles Beaumont, *Programmer/Analyst*

Gary Leach, *Desktop Publisher*

☞™ This book is printed on acid-free paper that meets the minimum requirements of the American National Standard for Information Sciences—Permanence Paper for Printed Library Materials, ANSI Z39.48-1984.

ISBN 0-7876-0856-4
Printed in the United States of America

TABLE OF CONTENTS

PREFACE VII

A

Accounting, Auditing, and Bookkeeping
  Services 1
Adhesives and Sealants 8
Advertising Agencies 13
Agricultural Production—Crops 19
Agricultural Production—Livestock 28
Air Transportation, Passenger 36
Aircraft 43
Apparel, Men's and Boys' 50
Apparel, Women's and Girls' 57
Appliances, Household 65
Asphalt Paving and Roofing Materials 72
Audio and Video Equipment, Household 76

B

Banks and Savings Institutions 81
Beverages, Alcoholic 91
Beverages, Malt 99
Book Publishing and Printing 106

C

Cable and Other Pay Television Services 114
Catalog and Mail~Order Houses 121
Cereal Breakfast Foods 127
Chemicals, Agricultural 130
Chemicals, Industrial Inorganic 137
Chemicals, Industrial Organic 147
Coal Mining 156
Computer Peripheral Equipment 163
Computer Programming Services 169
Computers, Electronic 174
Concrete, Gypsum, and Plaster Products 184

Construction, Building 191
Construction, Heavy 198
Cotton Broadwoven Fabric Mills 203

D

Data Preparation and Processing 209
Defense and Armaments 216

E

Educational Services 222
Electric and Gas Services 229
Electric Lighting and Wiring Equipment 238
Elevators and Moving Stairways 245
Engineering Services 248

F

Fishing, Commercial 253
Flour and Other Grain Mill Products 257
Flour and Other Grain Mill Products 257
Forestry 267
Furniture, Household 272

G

Glass Products 277

H

Hardware and Hand Tools 283
Hospitals 288
Hotels and Motels 299

I

Insurance, Accident and Health 305
Insurance, Life 313
Iron and Steel Foundries 321

J

Jewelry 327

L

Legal Services 331

M

Machinery and Equipment, General Industrial . . 338
Machinery, Refrigeration and Service Industry . . 344
Machinery, Special Industry 350
Management Consulting Services 357
Medicinals and Botanicals 365
Metal, Fabricated Structural 371
Metal Mining 375
Motion Pictures 383
Motor Vehicles and Motor Vehicle Equipment . . 394
Motors and Generators 405

N

Newspaper Publishing and Printing 409

O

Office Machines 415
Oil and Gas Field Services 419
Ophthalmic Goods 425

P

Paints and Allied Products 431
Paper Mills 438
Paperboard Mills 446
Perfumes, Cosmetics, and Toiletries 450
Periodical Publishing and Printing 457
Petroleum and Natural Gas 465
Petroleum Refining 472
Pharmaceutical Preparations 481
Photographic Equipment and Supplies 489
Plastics Materials and Resins 495
Plastics Products 503

Postal Services 510
Printing, Commercial 514
Pulp Mills 520

R

Radio and Television Broadcasting Stations . . . 529
Railroad Transportation 536
Real Estate Agents and Managers 542
Restaurants 548
Retail Department Stores 554
Rubber Products 560

S

Search and Navigation Equipment 567
Security and Commodity Exchanges 574
Semiconductors and Related Devices 581
Soft Drinks 588
Software, Prepackaged 594
Sporting and Athletic Goods 603
Steel Works and Blast Furnaces 609
Sugar and Confectionery Products 614
Surgical and Medical Instruments and
   Apparatus 622

T

Telecommunications 629
Telephone and Telegraph Apparatus 635
Tobacco Products 644
Travel and Tourism 650
Trucking and Courier Services 657

W

Water Transportation of Freight 663

INDUSTRY INDEX **669**

GENERAL INDEX **673**

PREFACE

U.S. Industry Profiles: The Leading 100 (USIP) is a key business reference source covering 100 significant industries or industry groups in the United States. This second edition is an indispensable tool for students, professional researchers and writers, and business people. Organized alphabetically by industry, each chapter covers the current status and predicted future of each industry. *USIP* is illustrated with over 400 statistical charts, graphs, and maps.

USIP patterns its coverage on the Standard Industrial Classification (SIC) code system. The SIC system was established by the U.S. government's Office of Management and Budget to provide a uniform means of collecting, presenting, and analyzing economic data. These codes are widely used by federal, state, and local government agencies; trade associations; private research organizations; librarians; and business professionals to promote comparability in the presentation of statistical data.

In 1994, after 35 editions, the U.S. Department of Commerce discontinued publication of *U.S. Industrial Outlook (USIO),* the standard industry forecasting tool in the United States. *U.S. Industry Profiles: The Leading 100* is designed to follow in the footsteps of *USIO*. *USIP* adds a wealth of information sources; coverage of "hot" industries not discretely covered in the SIC system; several hundred charts, graphs, and maps; and two easy-to-use indexes.

ENTRY CONTENT

Each chapter in *U.S. Industry Profiles* contains textual material that originally appeared in Gale's *Encyclopedia of American Industries (EAI)* and was custom-edited to serve the needs of *USIP* readers. *EAI* covers every four-digit SIC classification (1,004 in total).

Where an industry was thought to be too narrow for *USIP*'s coverage, a number of essays contained in *EAI* were combined into one general essay for use in *USIP*. For example, *EAI* covers 20 separate four-digit classifications dealing with Agricultural Crop Production in as many essays. *USIP* provides broader coverage, combining these into one chapter under the heading "Agricultural Production—Crops," SIC 0100. For easy understanding of the full coverage of industries, the Industry Index in *USIP* links four-digit classifications to the appropriate chapter. This index is discussed later in this section.

An overall summary of the current state and predicted future of the industry prefaces each chapter. Other sections of coverage may include the following:

- Industry Snapshot: Provides a concise overview of the industry and its status in the mid-1990s.

- Industry Outlook: Discusses the trends and predicted future for each industry.

- Organization and Structure: Details the configuration and functional aspects of the industry.

- Work Force: Contains information on the size, diversity, and characteristics of the industry's work force.

- Research and Technology: Provides information on major technological advances, areas of research, and their potential impact on the industry.

- America and the World: Discusses the United States' standing in the industry's global marketplace, as well as trade issues and key international developments and competitors.

INDUSTRY INFORMATION SOURCES

A convenient listing of information sources selected from Gale's *Encyclopedia of Business Information Sources* (with the exception of the Further Reading section, which was taken from the *Encyclopedia of American Industries*) is provided for each chapter. Each is designed to reduce the time spent by librarians, students, and business professionals in searching for key sources of information on specific industries. Each citation contains an address, phone number and, where available, URL information. Coverage may include the following:

- Associations and Societies
- Periodicals and Newsletters
- Databases
- Statistics Sources
- General Works
- Further Reading

STATISTICAL CHARTS AND GRAPHS

Over 400 charts, graphs, and maps have been culled from Gale's *Business Rankings Annual; Finance, Insurance, and Real Estate USA; Manufacturing USA; Market Share Reporter;* and *Service Industries USA*.

The types of graphic information appearing in the book include:

- General Statistics: Contains U.S. statistics for the years 1982-1998 on such topics as companies, establishments, employment, compensation, and production (including the cost of materials, value added by manufacture, value of shipments, and capital investments).

- Occupations: Covers those occupations that represent one percent or more of total employment in the specific industry. Data are shown for 1994 in percent of total employment for a three-digit SIC grouping. Also shown is the Bureau of Labor Statistics' projection of the growth or decline of the occupation to the year 2005.

- Map Graphics: Two maps titled "Location by State" and "Regional Concentration" indicate the specific industry's concentration in the United States.

- Industry Data by State: Provides ten data elements in which the industry is active. The data are drawn from the most recently available *Census of Manufactures* state-level data. Data elements include: the number of establishments; shipments, including the total number of shipments, percent of U.S. shipments, and shipments per establishment; employment, including the total number, the percent of U.S. employment, the number of employees per establishment, and wages; cost as percent of shipments; and investment per employee.

- Market Share Reports: Includes a variety of formats, including pie charts, bar graphs, and lists of information. Market share reports may fall into one of four broad categories: corporate market share; institutional share; brand market share; and product, commodity, service, and facility share.

INDEXING

U.S. Industry Profiles provides two indexes to aid the user. The Industry Index lists more than 250 cross-references to four-digit SIC codes contained in the essays. The General Index contains alphabetical references to all companies, associations, publications, key government agencies, and significant legislation cited in the book. This index also includes inversions on significant keywords in the citations.

COMMENTS AND SUGGESTIONS

Questions, comments, and suggestions regarding *U.S Industry Profiles: The Leading 100* are welcomed. Please contact:

The Editor
U.S. Industry Profiles: The Leading 100
Gale Research
645 Griswold St.
Detroit, MI 48226-4094
Telephone: (313) 961-2242
Toll-free: (800) 877-GALE
Fax: (313) 961-6083
URL: www.gale.com

Accounting services are increasingly global businesses. Leading U.S. industry participants, known widely as the "Big 6," also have worldwide concerns in such activities as consulting, legal services, and public relations. While the industry is generally healthy, some of its domestic markets are mature and consequently the industry is expected to see continued consolidation of companies and personnel to maximize profits. Growth for top firms will also come from further overseas expansion, especially in Africa, Asia, and Latin America.

ACCOUNTING, AUDITING, AND BOOKKEEPING SERVICES

SIC 8721

A large and relatively stable industry, accounting services will continue to post healthy albeit modest growth in terms of revenues and employment into the twenty-first century. Finding niche markets, diversifying services, and catering to global markets are key growth strategies for companies in the industry.

 **TOP U.S. ACCOUNTING FIRMS**

Ranked by: Fee income in 1995, in millions of dollars.

1. Andersen Worldwide, with $3,860 million
2. Ernst & Young, $2,974
3. Deloitte & Touche LLP, $2,570
4. KPMG LLP, $2,289
5. Coopers & Lybrand LLP, $1,905
6. Price Waterhouse, $1,771
7. Grant Thornton, $240
8. McGladrey & Pullen, $230
9. BDO Seidman, $202.5
10. Crowe Chizek, $76

Source: *Accountancy,* February, 1996, p. 9.

Industry receipts grew by roughly 30 percent from 1992 to 1996, when they surpassed the $50 billion milestone. Annual growth in the 1990s has been slower, however, than the double-digit percentage increases of the late 1980s. In the mid-1990s accounting firms moved toward confronting ethical and legal problems of their clients, including such issues as corporate governance and accountability, according to *Oregon Business.*

Large international firms, including the Big 6, have branched out into management consulting services. However, according to *The CPA Journal,* the attractive consulting fees may have led many firms to ignore potential conflicts of interest in serving as an auditor and as a management consultant to the same client. The profession's standards were also said to be jeopardized by the entrance of non-CPA partners and owners in influential accounting firms. Many companies facing these problems, like Arthur Andersen, split their accounting and management consulting operations into separate divisions or companies to avoid accusations of impropriety.

During the mid- to late 1990s, accounting firms have evolved by restructuring their services and offering new services such as attestation and other assurance services, according to *The CPA Journal*.

ORGANIZATION AND STRUCTURE

Accounting firms have multiple specialties and functions. Public accountants run their own businesses or are employed by accounting firms to meet the particular accounting needs of their clients, who may include the general public. Accountants employed by companies to record and summarize financial data are known variously as management, industrial, corporate, or private accountants. Internal auditors are employed by companies to check records for signs of inefficiency, mismanagement, or fraud. Accountants and auditors employed in government not only produce and check government financial records but also audit persons or businesses regulated and taxed by government. Each of these broadly defined fields is further subdivided by choices of specialization, yielding a wide variety of niches for accountants to fill.

ASSOCIATIONS

Numerous organizations within the accounting profession cater to the specialized needs of different groups of accountants, ranging from the Association of Black CPA Firms to the American Women's Society of Certified Public Accountants to the National Association of Accountants. By far the largest and most important of the organizations within the profession, however, has been the American Institute of Certified Public Account-

ants (AICPA), which not only represents over 330,000 CPAs but also serves as a self-regulating body within the profession that is recognized by the Securities and Exchange Commission (SEC). The AICPA's three special member divisions neither monitored competency nor provided accreditation but served as outlets for volunteer members with particular interests; they were the Federal Tax Division (dating from 1983), and two divisions created in 1986—Personal Financial Planning, and Management Advisory Services.

In addition to the standards established by the ASB (the AICPA's Auditing Standards Board) and by other standards boards, the standards that have governed the accounting profession are those known by the acronym GAAP—Generally Accepted Accounting Principles.

WORK FORCE

In 1996 accounting firms employed some 580,000 persons, more than half of whom were women, according to the U.S. Department of Labor. Average salaries in the industry range from $24,000 to $29,000; however, experienced accountants and managers usually earn substantially more.

Because every state establishes its own licensing requirements, there are some differences in the type of education and experience required of a person seeking to become a CPA. Typically, the requirements consist of a four-year college degree, one or two years of on-the-job experience, and a passing grade on the CPA examination.

The shortage of teachers with doctoral degrees in accounting—largely attributable to the higher pay available to talented accountants in public and industrial accounting—presented a major hurdle to those who advo-

SIC 8721 - Accounting, Auditing & Bookkeeping
Industry Data by State

State	Establishments			Employment			Payroll			Revenues - 1992 ($ mil.)			% change 87-92	
	1987	1992	% of US 92	1987	1992	% of US 92	1987 ($ mil.)	1992 ($ mil.)	$ Per Empl. 92	Total ($ mil.)	Per Estab.	$ Per Empl. 92	Revenues	Payroll
California	10,297	11,082	47.8	70,553	76,251	52.5	1,692.6	2,085.2	27,346	5,366.2	0.5	70,375	35.4	23.2
New York	4,929	5,382	23.2	45,826	55,794	38.4	1,212.2	1,634.6	29,297	4,242.1	0.8	76,032	38.5	34.8
Texas	5,427	5,949	25.7	31,418	36,808	25.3	721.8	987.7	26,833	2,309.0	0.4	62,731	29.0	36.8
Illinois	2,942	3,461	14.9	23,479	27,590	19.0	605.9	919.1	33,311	2,219.2	0.6	80,434	54.9	51.7
Florida	4,377	5,661	24.4	23,203	26,250	18.1	517.2	682.6	26,005	1,572.7	0.3	59,911	33.8	32.0
Pennsylvania	2,533	2,803	12.1	18,160	21,730	15.0	413.5	598.7	27,552	1,506.2	0.5	69,312	49.8	44.8
New Jersey	2,256	2,511	10.8	15,402	16,236	11.2	373.1	537.1	33,080	1,305.5	0.5	80,410	39.4	44.0
Ohio	2,407	2,767	11.9	16,967	18,922	13.0	359.5	494.6	26,136	1,159.8	0.4	61,292	34.4	37.6
Massachusetts	1,615	1,767	7.6	13,134	14,683	10.1	343.2	474.3	32,303	1,127.9	0.6	76,819	39.5	38.2
Michigan	2,187	2,568	11.1	14,754	16,306	11.2	350.5	467.9	28,693	1,060.4	0.4	65,031	34.7	33.5

Source: Census of Service Industries, 1987 and 1992, Bureau of the Census, U.S. Department of Commerce. Data are sorted by 1992 revenues and, if revenues are unavailable, by establishments in 1992. (D) indicates that data are withheld by the source to avoid disclosure of competitive information. A dash (-) indicates that data are not available. Percentage changes between 1987 and 1992 are calculated using numbers that have *not* been rounded; hence they may not be reproducible from the values shown.

SIC 8721
Occupations Employed by SIC 8721 - Accounting, Auditing, and Bookkeeping

Occupation	% of Total 1994	Change to 2005
Accountants & auditors	35.8	15.2
Bookkeeping, accounting, & auditing clerks	10.8	1.7
Secretaries, ex legal & medical	8.2	23.4
Management support workers nec	7.2	35.6
General managers & top executives	5.2	28.6
General office clerks	4.9	15.6
Clerical supervisors & managers	2.8	38.7
Data entry keyers, ex composing	2.4	0.0
Receptionists & information clerks	2.2	35.5
Typists & word processors	2.0	-32.2
Financial managers	1.8	35.5
Professional workers nec	1.5	103.3
Computer operators, ex peripheral equipment	1.3	-64.4
Administrative services managers	1.2	62.7
Systems analysts	1.1	92.5

Source: *Industry-Occupation Matrix*, Bureau of Labor Statistics. These data relate to one or more 3-digit SIC industry groups rather than to a single 4-digit SIC. The change reported for each occupation to the year 2005 is a percent of growth or decline as estimated by the Bureau of Labor Statistics. The abbreviation nec stands for 'not elsewhere classified'.

cated the desirability of requiring a fifth year of education for CPAs, and prompted the AICPA to institute a financial aid program for doctoral candidates, in hopes of boosting the numbers of faculty in accounting.

Through the year 2005, job growth in accounting was predicted to be higher than the average for all occupations tracked by the U.S. Department of Labor. Meanwhile the annual number of accounting graduates has remained essentially stable, which means students capable of meeting the existing educational requirements face good prospects in the U.S. accounting industry.

Though CPAs were expected to have a better choice among a greater range of employment activities, other accountants and accountants without college degrees could be expected to find niches in a growing market. Moreover, accountants of all levels of training and experience could take confidence from the fact that downturns in the national economy seldom had an adverse impact on their chosen profession, because even a poorly performing economy still generated data that had to be analyzed and interpreted.

The target employers for most new graduates were the Big 6. Flexible working hours and a liberal promotion system are among the incentives U.S. accounting firms increasingly offer their personnel.

AMERICA AND THE WORLD

The largest of the accountancy firms in the United States conduct extensive and often highly profitable business overseas. Some of the smaller firms worked in conjunction with similar outfits overseas by associating with them in cooperative networks. With the increasing trend toward a global economy apparent at the end of the twentieth century, the importance of such international transactions is sure to increase, stressing the desirability of essentially uniform worldwide accounting standards in making cross-border financial data as accurate and useful as possible.

Because the American way of doing business exerted a powerful influence on the rest of the world throughout the twentieth century, and because American accounting standards, building on British precedent, have established a level of sophistication and authority recognized around the world, international accounting standards to a great degree conform to the American model.

Asia, particularly China, represents a significant and growing market for accounting services. Such firms as Arthur Andersen anticipated doubling their business in China during the late 1990s. The firm's Chinese operations enjoyed yearly growth of more than 30 percent in the mid-1990s and resulted in more than $100 million in revenues. Similarly, industrial growth in Africa and Latin America, as well as in eastern Europe and the former Soviet Union, is expected to stimulate demand for accounting, auditing, and related services in those areas.

ASSOCIATIONS AND SOCIETIES

AMERICAN ACCOUNTING ASSOCIATION
5717 Bessie Dr.
Sarasota, FL 34233-2399
Phone: (813) 921-7747
Fax: (813) 923-4093

AMERICAN INSTITUTE OF CERTIFIED PUBLIC ACCOUNTANTS
1211 Avenue of the Americas
New York, NY 10036-8775
Phone: (800) 862-4272 or (212) 596-6200
Fax: (212) 596-6213

ASSOCIATION FOR ACCOUNTING ADMINISTRATION
136 S. Keowee St.
Dayton, OH 45402
Members are accounting and office systems executives. Includes an Information Management Committee.

ASSOCIATION OF GOVERNMENT ACCOUNTANTS
2200 Mount Vernon Ave.
Alexandria, VA 22301-1314
Phone: (703) 684-6931
Fax: (703) 548-9367
Members are employed by federal, state, county, and city government agencies. Includes accountants, auditors, budget officers, and other government finance administrators and officials.

EDP AUDITORS ASSOCIATION
3701 Algonquin Rd.
Rolling Meadows, IL 60008
Phone: (708) 253-1545
Fax: (708) 253-4010

FINANCIAL ACCOUNTING FOUNDATION
401 Merritt, No. 7
Norwalk, CT 06851
Phone: (203) 847-0700
Fax: (203) 849-9714

INFORMATION SYSTEMS AUDIT AND CONTROL ASSOCIATION
3701 Algonquin Rd., Ste. 1010
Rolling Meadows, IL 60008
Phone: (708) 253-1545
Fax: (708) 253-1443

INSTITUTE OF INTERNAL AUDITORS
249 Maitland Ave.
Altamonte Springs, FL 32701-4201
Phone: (407) 830-7600
Fax: (407) 831-5171

INSTITUTE OF MANAGEMENT ACCOUNTANTS
10 Paragon Dr.
Montvale, NJ 07645

Phone: (800) 638-4427 or (201) 573-9000
Fax: (201) 573-8185

NATIONAL SOCIETY OF PUBLIC ACCOUNTANTS
1010 N. Fairfax St.
Alexandria, VA 22314-1574
Phone: (800) 966-6679 or (703) 549-6400
Fax: (703) 549-2984

TAX ANALYSTS
6830 N. Fairfax Dr.
Arlington, VA 22213
Phone: (800) 955-3444 or (703) 533-4400
Fax: (703) 533-4444
An advocacy group reviewing U.S. and foreign income tax developments. Includes a Tax Policy Advisory Board.

PERIODICALS AND NEWSLETTERS

ACCOUNTING REVIEW
American Accounting Association
5717 Bessie Dr.
Sarasota, FL 34233
Phone: (813) 921-7747
Quarterly. Free to members; non-members, $190.00 per year.

ACCOUNTING TODAY: THE NEWSPAPER FOR THE ACCOUNTING PROFESSIONAL
Faulkner & Gray, Inc.
11 Penn Plz.
New York, NY 10001
Phone: (212) 967-7000
Fax: (212) 967-7155
Biweekly. $96.00 per year. Provides news of accounting and taxes.

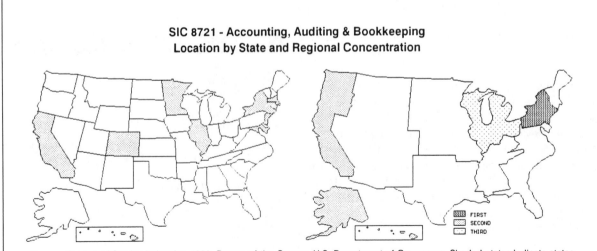

SIC 8721 - Accounting, Auditing & Bookkeeping
Location by State and Regional Concentration

FIRST
SECOND
THIRD

Source: Census of Service Industries, 1992, Bureau of the Census, U.S. Department of Commerce. Shaded *states* indicate states which have proportionately greater representation in the industry than would be indicated by the state's population; the ratio is based on revenues or establishments in 1992. Shaded *regions* indicate where the industry is regionally most concentrated.

BOWMAN'S ACCOUNTING REPORT

Hudson Sawyer Professional Services Marketing, Inc.
950 E. Paces Ferry Rd., No. 2425
Atlanta, GA 30326-1119
Phone: (404) 264-9977
Fax: (404) 264-9968
Monthly. $215.00 per year. Newsletter. Provides information and news relating to the accounting profession, with emphasis on certified public accounting firms.

THE CPA JOURNAL

New York State Society of Certified Public Accountants
530 5th Ave., 5 Fl.
New York, NY 10036-5101
Phone: (212) 973-8300
Fax: (212) 972-5710
Monthly. $42.00 per year.

CPA MARKETING REPORT

Strafford Publications, Inc.
Drawer 13729
Atlanta, GA 30324-0729
Phone: (800) 926-7926 or (404) 881-1141
Fax: (404) 881-0074
Monthly. $197.00 per year. Newsletter. Contains strategies for practice development.

CPA PERSONNEL REPORT

Strafford Publications, Inc.
Drawer 13729
Atlanta, GA 30324-0729
Phone: (800) 926-7926 or (404) 881-1141
Fax: (404) 881-0074
Monthly. $197.00 per year. Newsletter. Provides advice on human relations and personnel procedures for accounting firms.

INTERNAL AUDITOR

Institute of Internal Auditors
249 Maitland Ave.
Altamonte Springs, FL 32701-4201
Phone: (407) 830-7600
Fax: (407) 831-5171
Bimonthly. $60.00 per year.

JOURNAL OF ACCOUNTANCY

American Institute of Certified Public Accountants
1211 Avenue of the Americas
New York, NY 10036-8775
Phone: (800) 862-4272 or (212) 596-6200
Fax: (212) 575-3846
Monthly. $52.00 per year.

MANAGEMENT ACCOUNTING

Institute of Management Accountants
10 Paragon Dr.
Montvale, NJ 07645-1760
Phone: (800) 638-4427 or (201) 573-6269
Fax: (201) 573-0639
Monthly. $130.00 per year.

NATIONAL PUBLIC ACCOUNTANT

National Society of Public Accountants
1010 N. Fairfax St.
Alexandria, VA 22314
Phone: (703) 549-6400
Fax: (703) 684-0540

Monthly. Free to members; non-members, $18.00 per year. For accounting and tax practitioners.

THE PRACTICAL ACCOUNTANT: ACCOUNTING AND TAXES IN EVERYDAY PRACTICE

Faulkner and Gray, Inc.
11 Penn Plz., 17 Fl.
New York, NY 10001
Phone: (212) 967-7000
Fax: (212) 967-7162
Monthly. $60.00 per year. Covers tax planning, financial planning, practice management, client relationships, and related topics.

PUBLIC ACCOUNTING REPORT

Strafford Publications, Inc.
Drawer 13729
Atlanta, GA 30324-0729
Phone: (800) 926-7926 or (404) 881-1141
Fax: (404) 881-0074
Semimonthly. $247.00 per year. Newsletter. Presents news and trends affecting the accounting profession.

DATABASES

ACCOUNTING AND TAX DATABASE

UMI/Data Courier
620 S. 3rd St.
Louisville, KY 40202
Phone: (800) 626-2823 or (502) 583-4111
Fax: (502) 589-5572
Provides indexing and abstracting of the literature of accounting, taxation, and financial management from 1971 to date, with weekly updating. Primarily covers accounting, auditing, banking, bankruptcy, employee compensation and benefits, cash management, financial planning, and credit. Inquire as to online cost and availability.

MANAGEMENT CONTENTS

Information Access Co.
362 Lakeside Dr.
Foster City, CA 94404
Phone: (800) 227-8431 or (415) 378-5000
Fax: (415) 358-4759
Covers a wide range of management, financial, marketing, personnel, and administrative topics. About 140 leading business journals are indexed and abstracted from 1974 to date, with monthly updating. Inquire as to online cost and availability.

NAARS

American Institute of Certified Public Accountants National Automated Accounting Research System
201 Plaza 3
Jersey City, NJ 07311-3881
Phone: (201) 938-3248
Financial statements, authoritative accounting literature, most current five years online, 1972 to present offline. Inquire as to online cost and availability.

TAX ANALYSTS' HOME PAGE

Tax Analysts
Information for tax professionals includes notices of events, a list of the organization's publications and databases, daily Tax

Court news, and archives of several discussion groups. Time span: 1982 to date. Updating frequency: Daily. Fees: Free.

- URL: http://205.177.50.2/default.htm

TAX PLANNING

Markle Stuckey Hardesty & Bott, Certified Public Accountants, CPA
Covers cutting-edge fields, such as software and multimedia licensing, and independent contractors. Time span: Current information. Updating frequency: Irregularly. Fees: Free.

- URL: http://www.hooked.net/cpa/plan/index.html

WILSONLINE: WILSON BUSINESS ABSTRACTS

H. W. Wilson Co.
950 University Ave.
Bronx, NY 10452
Phone: (800) 367-6770 or (718) 588-8400
Fax: (718) 590-1617
Indexes and abstracts 350 major business periodicals, plus the Wall Street Journal *and the business section of the* New York Times. *Indexing is from 1982, abstracting from 1990, with the two newspapers included from 1993. Updated daily. Inquire as to online cost and availability. (Business Periodicals Index without abstracts is also available online.)*

GENERAL WORKS

ACCOUNTING: THE BASIS FOR BUSINESS DECISIONS

Walter B. Meigs and Robert F. Meigs
McGraw-Hill
1221 Avenue of the Americas
New York, NY 10020
Phone: (800) 722-4726 or (212) 512-2000
Fax: (212) 512-2821
1995. 10th edition. $66.25.

ACCOUNTING INFORMATION SYSTEMS: CONCEPTS AND PRACTICE FOR EFFECTIVE DECISION MAKING

John Wiley & Sons, Inc.
605 3rd Ave.
New York, NY 10158
Phone: (800) 225-5945 or (212) 850-6000
Fax: (212) 850-6088
1990. $24.95. Fourth Edition

ADVANCED ACCOUNTING

Andrew Haried
John Wiley & Sons, Inc.
605 3rd Ave.
New York, NY 10158
Phone: (800) 225-5945 or (212) 850-6000
Fax: (212) 850-6088
1993. $50.00. Fifth edition. Reflects recent pronouncements of the Financial Accounting Standards Board (FASB) and the Governmental Accounting Standards Board (GASB).

AUDITING

Jack C. Robertson
Richard D. Irwin
1333 Burr Ridge Pky.
Burr Ridge, IL 60521

Phone: (800) 634-3961 or (708) 789-4000
Fax: (800) 374-7946
1992. $68.95. Seventh edition.

AUDITING: AN INTEGRATED APPROACH

Alvin A. Arens and James K. Loebbecke
Prentice-Hall
200 Old Tappan Rd.
Old Tappan, NJ 07675
Phone: (800) 922-0579
Fax: (800) 445-6991
1994. $75.00. Sixth edition.

AUDITING: INTEGRATED CONCEPTS AND PROCEDURES

Donald H. Taylor and G. William Glezen
John Wiley & Sons, Inc.
605 3rd Ave.
New York, NY 10158-0012
Phone: (800) 225-5945 or (212) 850-6000
Fax: (212) 850-6088
1993. Sixth edition. Price on application.

FINANCIAL REPORTING: AN ACCOUNTING REVOLUTION

William H. Beaver
Prentice-Hall
200 Old Tappan Rd.
Old Tappan, NJ 07675
Phone: (800) 922-0579
Fax: (800) 445-6991
1988. Second edition. Price on application. (Contemporary Topics in Accounting Series)

FUNDAMENTAL ACCOUNTING PRINCIPLES

Kermit D. Larson and others
Richard D. Irwin
1333 Burr Ridge Pky.
Burr Ridge, IL 60521
Phone: (800) 634-3961 or (708) 789-4000
Fax: (800) 374-7946
1993. $66.95. 13th edition.

MANAGEMENT ACCOUNTING

Don R. Hansen and Maryanne M. Mowen
South-Western Publishing Co.
5101 Madison Rd.
Cincinnati, OH 45227
Phone: (800) 543-0487 or (513) 271-8811
Fax: (513) 527-6956
1994. $60.95. Third edition.

PORTFOLIO OF ACCOUNTING SYSTEMS FOR SMALL AND MEDIUM-SIZED BUSINESSES

National Society of Public Accountants
Prentice-Hall
200 Old Tappan Rd.
Old Tappan, NJ 07675
Phone: (800) 922-0579
Fax: (800) 445-6991
1977. $64.95. Revised edition.

FURTHER READING

Demery, Paul. "The Changing Demographics of Accounting Firms." *The Practical Accountant,* March 1996.

Kelly, Jim. "The People Who Really Count." *The Financial Times,* February 22, 1995.

Oliverio, Mary Ellen, and Bernard H. Newman. *Auditing in Public Accounting Firms: A Preliminary Look to 1999.* February 1996.

"Professional Services: Global State of The Industry." *Oregon Business,* May 1996.

ADHESIVES
AND
SEALANTS

SIC 2891

A *resurgence in markets, including construction, automobile manufacturing, and a relatively-resistant packaging segment, may translate into overall improvement for the $5.4 billion industry, which has typically seen growth rates exceeding the gross national product by 2 percent. Concurrent with these developments, stricter environmental regulation accelerated the development of new technologies. The industry will continue to grow by approximately 3 percent per annum to 2000. The value of product shipments is expected to increase to $7.3 billion by 1998, while the total employment figure is forecast to grow to 22,500.*

The adhesives and sealants industry includes two chemically similar but functionally different groups of formulated products. Adhesive products are used to create a bond between two different or similar materials. Sealants are used to create an impenetrable barrier to gas or moisture. Adhesives and sealants are made from precise blends of petroleum-derived plastic resins, synthetic rubber elastomers, and agents or additives. The final formula ultimately depends on the end use. Industries that use adhesives and sealants include construction, consumer products, assembly, packaging, labeling, and transportation.

The industry serves two broad markets: firms that formulate products for their own use and the merchants that create products to sell to end users. The merchant market comprises about two-thirds of total shipments.

Top 6 **TOP SEGMENTS OF THE ADHESIVES MARKET, 1995**

1. Construction, 20%
2. Packaging, 16%
3. Transportation, 15%
4. Textile, 13%
5. Primary wood bonding, 10%
6. Other, 26%

Source: *Chemicalweek*, March 27, 1996, p. 29, from Kusumgar & Nerlfi.

Packaging holds the biggest share of the manufacturing adhesives market, with $1.1 billion in annual sales and a growth rate of 1.5 percent. Construction-related sectors, including forest products and wood-working, generate an $675 million in annual sales. The construction equipment market claims approximately $430 million in annual sales.

The growth rate of the formulated adhesives market is forecast at 4 percent throughout the decade according to some industry analysts. The waterborne adhesives market, estimated at about 64 percent of the total adhesives market, should post a 4 percent increase. For hot melts, representing about 18 percent of the total market, a growth rate of 5 percent is projected. The solvent-based sector of the manufacturing adhesives market claimed about 12 percent of the total and was expected to have flat growth. Specialty technologies, including reactives, experienced a growth rate of less than 10 percent.

The aerospace industry is an important sealant market, dominated by polysulfide, which constitutes 80 per-

Adhesives Market by Type

The market was valued at $9.4 billion.

Waterborne	38.0%
Hot melt	16.0
Solventborne	16.0
Other	30.0

Source: *Chemicalweek*, March 27, 1996, p. 28, from ChemQuest.

cent of the products sold. It is also a diverse market, with numerous varieties of polysulfide sealants and about 1,500 products. Because this market shrunk in the 1990s, manufacturers aggressively sought new markets and product applications. About 60 percent of the industry's business in the aerospace market is dependent on commercial aircraft. The remaining 40 percent of the market depends on military spending, a sector in decline since the early 1990s when the Cold War ended.

Compound manufacturers are adapting to regulations and their customers changing priorities, such as recyclability and the demand for higher-quality products. New specifications are forcing compound manufacturers to use more complex processes and advanced equipment. Indeed, compounds themselves have become more complex because they combine difficult-to-mix components, as in the case of stainless-steel-reinforced compounds. This type of high technology manufacturing drives capital requirements higher and makes it more difficult for small, entrepreneurial ventures to stay profitable.

In 1996, the adhesives and sealants industry was comprised of more than 700 U.S. establishments and employed approximately 12,000 people. Product shipments were valued at $6.8 billion, an increase of 26 percent over 1990.

INDUSTRY OUTLOOK

In the latter half of the 1990s, the sealants industry continued to suffer from the vagaries of the construction market, especially in maintenance and repair. Growth was expected to continue at 3 percent per year, especially if the construction market continued to pick up as predicted. Automobile manufacturers continued to show an interest in using corrosion-resistant adhesives to replace welding.

Having undergone some fundamental changes, the adhesives and sealants industry matured, with adhesives having penetrated the mechanical fasteners markets. The development of environmentally acceptable alternatives to products containing high levels of volatile organic compounds represented a growth opportunity for the industry.

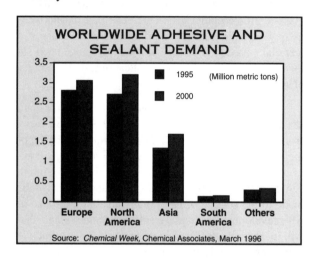

WORLDWIDE ADHESIVE AND SEALANT DEMAND

Source: *Chemical Week*, Chemical Associates, March 1996

Despite raw materials pricing and environmental pressures, producers expect the adhesives industry to grow by about 4 percent per year through the year 2000. The adhesives industry struggled to contain costs in spite of strong sales. The North American pressure-sensitive adhesives market, valued at $1.86 billion per year, was expected to grow at 5.4 percent per year through 2000. The nonpressure-sensitive adhesives industry, valued at $7.5 billion, was expected to climb by 3.7 percent per year.

RESEARCH AND TECHNOLOGY

Adhesives and sealants manufacturers are counting on proactive research and development to keep them one step ahead of environmental regulators and market demands. Among the challenges faced are regulation compliance—aimed at reducing volatile organic compound emissions—and bolstering pollution prevention measures.

Technological advances have contributed to the growing use of adhesives by car makers to build lighter and more fuel-efficient vehicles. Corporate Average Fuel Economy (CAFE) standards have driven the weight of automobiles down. To lighten automobiles, adhesives are replacing mechanical fasteners and are increasingly taking the place of spot welds. They are also reducing the corrosion problems associated with traditional bonding methods.

The biggest growth area for adhesive technology has come as a result of changes in the materials used in auto body parts. The most significant of these new materials is sheet molded compound (SMC). Many opportunities for weight reduction with sheet molded compounds have not been fully explored however.

Other technological challenges include the use of glass-reinforced polyesters. One emerging plastic technology is resin transfer molding (RTM), a polyester material, based on resin, currently being used in lower-volume auto and truck applications, such as sporty or upscale car models.

A growing number of players in the adhesives and sealants industry have expressed a desire to move away from the use of primers in adhesive systems because of their flammability and volatility. Such a change, however, presents difficulties in getting the right adhesion to certain materials. Physical and chemical changes can be made to the surface of these materials, but the focus of new development is to make adhesives and sealants that will incorporate the function of a primer. Environmental mandates on chlorofluorocarbons, volatile organic compound emission standards, and other ecological considerations are thus forcing adhesive formulators to remove from their product line, and find alternatives for, solvents. Research continues on meeting high-performance parameters, such as water resistance, durability, and humidity resistance without using such solvents.

In addition, a number of large users of solvent-borne adhesives have already installed equipment to recapture and recycle, or properly incinerate solvents, and are less likely to change to solventless products. Already, adhesive manufacturers have moved production of industrial adhesives away from solvents to 100 percent solids, epoxies, and urethanes. With respect to pressure sensitive adhesives, such as duct tape and heavy duty industrial tapes, manufacturers have raised solid content to 65 percent, from as low as 35 percent.

AMERICA AND THE WORLD

The 1990s began with demand for global compounds of 700,000 metric tons annually, and a relatively flat growth rate of one to 1.5 percent. Industry experts estimated that worldwide annual growth rates of 6 to 7 percent would prevail through the middle of the decade and product demand would grow to an estimated one million tons during this time period. By the end of the century, total global demand is estimated to reach 1.3 million tons annually.

Numerous mergers and acquisitions indicated higher levels of foreign participation in the domestic industry in recent years. As industry-wide restructuring drew to a close in the United States, consolidation of the European industry continued, with a few highly diversified multinational corporations purchasing small privately-held firms. Companies in Japan, the United Kingdom, and Germany have emerged as major competitors of U.S. firms in the world arena.

SIC 2891 - Adhesives & Sealants
General Statistics

Year	Com-panies	Establishments		Employment			Compensation		Production ($ million)			
		Total	with 20 or more employees	Total (000)	Production Workers (000)	Hours (Mil)	Payroll ($ mil)	Wages ($/hr)	Cost of Materials	Value Added by Manufacture	Value of Shipments	Capital Invest.
1982	517	683	233	18.2	10.9	20.7	365.5	8.36	1,699.9	1,150.2	2,856.7	72.4
1983		676	238	18.2	10.8	20.9	384.5	8.84	1,909.8	1,209.0	3,118.5	42.0
1984		669	243	18.5	11.4	22.3	415.8	8.94	2,075.0	1,428.5	3,488.2	55.8
1985		662	248	18.4	11.4	22.1	420.6	9.26	2,147.4	1,528.7	3,672.0	74.3
1986		664	259	19.3	11.6	22.4	441.8	9.45	2,233.3	1,596.4	3,838.3	82.8
1987	537	714	274	20.9	11.8	24.2	552.8	10.59	2,694.8	1,996.1	4,678.1	111.7
1988		722	295	21.2	11.8	23.9	579.0	11.05	2,875.6	1,994.8	4,859.9	118.4
1989		729	290	22.1	12.3	25.6	612.7	11.02	3,128.8	2,169.1	5,285.7	136.2
1990		710	294	22.1	11.9	24.6	633.3	11.50	3,167.9	2,333.2	5,485.1	127.1
1991		706	283	20.9	11.7	25.1	645.5	11.43	3,181.3	2,297.5	5,483.4	139.4
1992	517	685	271	21.1	11.6	24.5	677.8	12.41	3,016.9	2,643.0	5,659.0	189.6
1993		680	276	20.9	11.5	24.6	684.0	12.57	3,131.2	2,746.0	5,859.3	182.8
1994		709P	299P	19.2	11.3	23.7	687.1	13.41	3,338.5	2,503.2	5,848.9	204.2
1995		711P	304P	21.8P	11.9P	25.7P	761.3P	13.52P	3,730.8P	2,797.4P	6,536.2P	208.1P
1996		714P	308P	22.0P	11.9P	26.1P	792.0P	13.93P	3,886.6P	2,914.2P	6,809.2P	221.0P
1997		717P	313P	22.3P	12.0P	26.4P	822.7P	14.33P	4,042.4P	3,031.0P	7,082.1P	233.8P
1998		719P	318P	22.5P	12.0P	26.7P	853.5P	14.74P	4,198.2P	3,147.8P	7,355.1P	246.7P

Sources: 1982, 1987, 1992 *Economic Census; Annual Survey of Manufactures*, 83-86, 88-91, 93-94. Establishment counts for non-Census years are from *County Business Patterns*; establishment values for 83-84 are extrapolations. 'P's show projections by the editors. Industries reclassified in 87 will not have data for prior years.

ASSOCIATIONS AND SOCIETIES

ADHESIVE AND SEALANT COUNCIL
1627 K St. NW, Ste. 1000
Washington, DC 20006-1707
Phone: (202) 452-1500
Fax: (202) 452-1501

ADHESIVES MANUFACTURERS ASSOCIATION
401 N. Michigan Ave., 24 Fl.
Chicago, IL 60601
Phone: (312) 644-6610
Fax: (312) 321-6869

GUMMED INDUSTRIES ASSOCIATION
5 Darrow Ct.
Greenlawn, NY 11740
Phone: (516) 261-0114

PERIODICALS AND NEWSLETTERS

ADHESIVES AGE
Argus, Inc.
6151 Powers Ferry Rd. NW
Atlanta, GA 30339-2941
Phone: (800) 443-4969 or (404) 955-2500
Fax: (404) 955-0400
Monthly. $52.00 per year. Includes annual Directory.

THE COMPOSITES AND ADHESIVES NEWSLETTER
T/C Press
PO Box 36006
Los Angeles, CA 90036-0006
Phone: (213) 938-6923
Bimonthly. $150.00. Presents news of the composite materials and adhesives industries, with particular coverage of new products and applications.

INTERNATIONAL JOURNAL OF ADHESION AND ADHESIVES
Elsevier Science Publishing Co.
660 White Plains Rd.

Tarrytown, NY 10591-5153
Phone: (914) 524-9200
Fax: (914) 333-2444
Quarterly. $414.00 per year. Published in England.

JOURNAL OF ADHESION
Gordon and Breach Science Publishers, Inc.
Riverfront Plaza Sta., PO Box 200029
Newark, NJ 07102-0301
Phone: (201) 643-7500 or (215) 750-2642
Fax: (201) 643-7676 or (215) 750-6343
16 times a year. Price varies.

U.S. GLASS, METAL, AND GLAZING
Key Communications, Inc.
PO Box 569
Garrisonville, VA 22463
Phone: (540) 720-5584
Fax: (540) 720-5687
Monthly. $35.00 per year. Edited for glass fabricators, glaziers, distributors, and retailers. Special feature issues are devoted to architectural glass, mirror glass, windows, storefronts, hardware, machinery, sealants, and adhesives. Regular topics include automobile glass and fenestration (window design and placement).

DATABASES

CA SEARCH
Chemical Abstracts Service
2540 Olentangy River Rd.
Columbus, OH 43210
Phone: (614) 447-3731
Fax: (614) 447-3751
Guide to chemical literature, 1967 to present. Inquire as to online cost and availability.

SIC 2891 - Adhesives & Sealants
Industry Data by State

State	Establish-ments	Shipments			Employment				Cost as % of Shipments	Investment per Employee ($)
		Total ($ mil)	% of U.S.	Per Establ.	Total Number	% of U.S.	Per Establ.	Wages ($/hour)		
Ohio	53	817.2	14.4	15.4	3,100	14.7	58	12.94	50.0	5,419
Illinois	48	598.9	10.6	12.5	1,700	8.1	35	12.41	55.0	6,294
New Jersey	53	457.0	8.1	8.6	1,500	7.1	28	12.89	56.5	7,467
California	75	400.9	7.1	5.3	2,100	10.0	28	13.91	49.1	4,238
Kentucky	9	400.7	7.1	44.5	800	3.8	89	14.25	65.3	34,000
Michigan	36	337.1	6.0	9.4	1,300	6.2	36	13.69	51.0	5,154
Missouri	22	285.0	5.0	13.0	1,200	5.7	55	10.67	47.5	15,333
Georgia	38	262.9	4.6	6.9	700	3.3	18	13.13	52.8	7,143
Pennsylvania	40	231.0	4.1	5.8	700	3.3	18	14.50	52.8	7,000
Texas	38	207.8	3.7	5.5	700	3.3	18	10.13	52.5	7,714

*Source: 1992 Economic Census. The states are in descending order of shipments or establishments (if shipment data are missing for the majority). The symbol (D) appears when data are withheld to prevent disclosure of competitive information. States marked with (D) are sorted by number of establishments. A dash (-) indicates that the data element cannot be calculated; * indicates the midpoint of a range.*

PAPERCHEM DATABASE

Information Services Div. Institute of Paper Science and
Technology
500 10th St. NW
Atlanta, GA 30318
Phone: (404) 853-9500
Fax: (404) 853-9510
*Worldwide coverage of the scientific and technical paper indus-
try chemical literature, including patents, 1967 to present.
Monthly updates. Inquire as to online cost and availability.*

WORLD SURFACE COATINGS ABSTRACTS [ONLINE]

Paint Research Association of Great Britain
Waldegrave Rd.
Teddington, Middlesex, England TW11 8LD
Phone: 181-9 77-4427
Fax: 181-9 43-4705
*Indexing and abstracting of the literature of paint and surface
coatings, 1976 to present. Monthly updates. Inquire as to online
cost and availability.*

STATISTICS SOURCES

U.S. INDUSTRIAL OUTLOOK: FORECASTS FOR SELECTED MANUFACTURING AND SERVICE INDUSTRIES

Available from U.S. Government Printing Office
Washington, DC 20402
Phone: (202) 512-1800
Fax: (202) 512-2250
Annual. $37.00. (Replaced in 1995 by U.S. Global Trade
Outlook.*) Issued by the International Trade Administration, U.S.
Department of Commerce. Provides basic data, outlook for the
current year, and "Long-Term Prospects" (five-year projec-
tions) for a wide variety of products and services. Includes high
technology industries.*

- Gopher://gopher.umsl.edu:70/11/library/govdocs/
  usio94

GENERAL WORKS

ADHESIVES

International Plastics Selector, Inc.
D.A.T.A. Digest
D.A.T.A. Business Publishing
PO Box 6510
Englewood, CO 80155-6510
Phone: (800) 447-4666 or (303) 799-0381
Fax: (303) 799-4082
*Annual. $180.00. Describes over 7,800 commercially available
adhesives, sealants, primers, and related products. Includes
trade name index.*

ADHESIVES AGE DIRECTORY

Communication Channels, Inc.
6151 Powers Ferry Rd. NW
Atlanta, GA 30328
Phone: (404) 955-2500
Fax: (404) 955-0400 or (404) 250-0590
Annual. $51.95. Formerly Adhesives Red Book.

ADHESIVES AND SEALANTS

ASM International
6939 Kinsman Rd.
Materials Park, OH 44073
Phone: (216) 338-5151
Fax: (216) 338-4634
1990. $130.00. (Engineered Materials Handbook Series).

FURTHER READING

D'Amico, Esther. "Squeezing Out Profits: Adhesives Makers
Get Set For Growth." *Chemical Week,* 27 March 1996, 24.

Murphy, Elena Epatko. "Soft Market Unglues Possibility of
Price Hikes." *Purchasing,* 9 November 1995, 81. ◀━

ADVERTISING AGENCIES

SIC 7311

Advertising agencies are responsible primarily for two functions. The first is the production of advertising materials in the form of written copy, art, graphics, audio, and video. The second is the strategic placement of the finished creative product in various media outlets, such as periodicals, newspapers, radio, and television. Agencies generally receive compensation for production costs from the client, plus a standard 15 percent commission from the media source for the ad placement.

Advertising agencies can be found throughout the United States, with the greatest percentage located in large cities. Many have headquarters in New York and field offices in Chicago, Los Angeles, San Francisco, Atlanta, Detroit, and other major areas of commerce in order to be close to clients. Although the larger agencies are most frequently mentioned in the media and trade publications, the industry actually is dominated by smaller agencies, many with only one or two principals, for the past few years. Industry observers credit lower overhead, diversified services, willingness to accommodate change, and an entrepreneurial attitude for the success of smaller, boutique agencies.

As many clients began to focus on a variety of forms of marketing communications, advertising agencies had to look beyond conventional media-based advertising to sustain industry growth. Advertising budgets began to reflect this shift, with additional dollars earmarked for point-of-sale promotions and public relations—and a major entry into the Internet. Changing demographics and a savvy American consumer were the driving forces behind these forms of alternative marketing communications.

Ranked by: Domestic gross income in 1995, in millions of dollars.

1. DDB Needham Worldwide, with $474.8 million
2. Young & Rubicam, $472.0
3. BBDO Worldwide, $460.1
4. J. Walter Thompson Co., $388.3
5. Leo Burnett Co., $370.6
6. Saatchi & Saatchi Advertising, $365.8
7. Grey Advertising, $354.6
8. Foote, Cone & Belding Communications, $339.4
9. McCann-Erickson Worldwide, $321.4
10. D'Arcy Masius Benton & Bowles, $320.2

Source: *Advertising Age,* Agency Report (annual), April 15, 1996, p. S-34.

Some industry leaders projected that advertising agencies would not only need to augment their primary line of work, but also change their long-standing commission compensation system. Realizing the need for "integrated marketing services," many agencies responded by adding public relations, direct mail, promotional departments, and Internet services.

INDUSTRY OUTLOOK

The total dollar value of U.S. advertising spending rose by 7.7 percent in 1995 according to the *McCann-Erickson Insider's Report.* This increase followed a 5.2 percent gain in 1993 and a 3.9 percent gain in 1992. The recovery seen in the early 1990s was broad-based, spreading across all media and market categories. Stronger than expected growth for the second year in a row seemed to provide a strong indication that the full recovery in advertising was well in place. McCann-Erickson expected total U.S. advertising to reach $174.1 billion in 1996, for a gain of 7.8 percent over 1995.

However, the advertising depression that began in 1988 had not left the memories of agency executives or their clients. Many industry observers suggested that the recession of the early 1990s only emphasized the diminished power of traditional advertising to sell products and services. Industry analysts suggested several explanations for why advertising apparently lost its effectiveness. First of all, consumers became less receptive to the continual assault of commercials, and also became more price conscious and less brand loyal. The days of a "Colgate family" or "Crest family" effectively ended, as large numbers of shoppers bought primarily on the basis of price.

At the same time, technological advancements and the proliferation of alternative communication tools transformed the way advertisers reached their customers. For example, computerized market research allows manufacturers to collect detailed information about their customers. Direct marketing increased in usage and popularity, along with in-store promotions and price discounts. Advertising agencies have had to respond to these changes by expanding their services into new areas and developing new specialties like direct marketing or Internet services.

The increased variety of television stations also took its toll on the advertising industry. The networks of ABC, CBS, and NBC used to account for 93 percent of the U.S. homes watching TV. In 1993, the big three maintained only a 60 percent share, while cable television and alternative networks claimed the difference. Network television stations began cutting their ad rates in an attempt to draw back advertisers. But since agencies obtained most of their commissions from placing media ads, they lost money with the implementation of rate reductions.

In addition, as clients searched for greater creativity and lower costs, many began to diversify their accounts by assigning media and creative work to different agencies. Larger companies even began to bring some of their

**SIC 7311 - Advertising Agencies
General Statistics**

	Establish-ments	Employment (000)	Payroll ($ mil.)	Revenues ($ mil.)
1982	10,225	106.8	2,654.7	5,919.8*
1983	-	-	-	8,196.0
1984	-	-	-	9,248.0
1985	-	-	-	11,100.0
1986	-	-	-	11,748.0
1987	12,335	134.0	4,399.4	12,019.0
1988	12,048	135.7	4,906.3	13,154.0
1989	11,005	138.5	5,127.9	13,627.0
1990	11,068	137.4	5,351.9	16,326.0
1991	11,044	132.1	5,306.7	15,542.0
1992	13,879	132.0	5,649.1	16,636.0
1993	13,578	133.3	5,785.3	17,650.0
1994	13,071P	142.9P	6,348.0P	18,708.5P
1995	13,283P	145.3P	6,641.4P	19,625.9P
1996	13,495P	147.6P	6,934.8P	20,543.2P

Sources: Data for 1982, 1987, and 1992 are from *Census of Service Industries*, Bureau of the Census, U.S. Department of Commerce. Revenue data are from the *Service Annual Survey* or from the Census. Revenue data from the Census are labelled with *. Data for 1988-1991 and 1993, when shown, are derived from *County Business Patterns* for those years from the Bureau of the Census. A P indicates projections made by the editor.

marketing, advertising, and promotional needs in-house. Smaller advertising agencies appeared to be more capable of adjusting to the evolving marketing needs of their clients. A lack of bureaucracy and emphasis on creativity helped smaller agencies become the fastest-growing segment of the industry by capturing large accounts.

ORGANIZATION AND STRUCTURE

The activities within an advertising agency typically are divided into four broad groups: account management, the creative department, media buying, and research. These divisions are usually physically separated from each other, although all four areas work closely together to produce an advertising campaign in its entirety. Account managers usually have daily interaction with a counterpart at the client's office and coordinate the activities of the other departments according to the client' wishes. The creative department designs original themes or concepts for ads, while the media department places finished ads within the media where they receive the most exposure to a target audience. Research provides data about consumers to help the agency and the client make informed advertising decisions.

Recently added to advertising agencies' roster of services are public relations, direct marketing, and promotional services. Other activities that used to be completed by outside vendors, such as photography and high-tech print work, also were brought inside many agencies.

WORK FORCE

Similar to other industries, the field of advertising is traditionally dominated by large, public corporations, many a collection of independent agencies. However, most professionals who work in the industry are employed at small agencies. In fact, the average firm has only 11 employees, and nearly 4 out of every 5 agencies employed fewer than 10 people. Workers in smaller agencies might be responsible for a variety of tasks, while those in larger agencies would find their job duties to be more defined.

SIC 7311
Occupations Employed by SIC 7311 - Advertising

Occupation	% of Total 1994	Change to 2005
Sales & related workers nec	20.1	28.2
Artists & commercial artists	9.2	20.3
Marketing, advertising, & PR managers	7.6	19.4
Secretaries, ex legal & medical	6.1	-12.2
General managers & top executives	5.9	3.0
Writers & editors, incl technical writers	4.3	8.5
General office clerks	4.3	-7.4
Bookkeeping, accounting, & auditing clerks	3.7	-18.6
Clerical supervisors & managers	2.8	11.0
Production, planning, & expediting clerks	2.4	8.5
Marketing & sales worker supervisors	2.4	2.8
Purchasing agents, ex trade & farm products	2.3	1.0
Painters & paperhangers	2.3	8.5
Professional workers nec	2.3	62.8
Financial managers	2.2	8.5
Receptionists & information clerks	2.1	8.5
Public relations specialists & publicity writers	2.0	8.5
Producers, directors, actors, & entertainers	1.8	55.0
Accountants & auditors	1.2	8.6
Managers & administrators nec	1.1	8.4

Source: Industry-Occupation Matrix, Bureau of Labor Statistics. These data relate to one or more 3-digit SIC industry groups rather than to a single 4-digit SIC. The change reported for each occupation to the year 2005 is a percent of growth or decline as estimated by the Bureau of Labor Statistics. The abbreviation nec stands for 'not elsewhere classified'.

The advertising industry is highly competitive in terms of entry. Most entry-level applicants earned at least a bachelor's degree and many participated in internships or gained some kind of previous work experience. Advertising is a predominately white-collar industry, as managers, executives, sales people, and administrative support workers account for 9 of every 10 jobs.

Due to the projected growth of new products, increased competition, and industry deregulation, employ-

ment in the advertising industry was marked to grow nearly 45 percent over the 1990-2005 period. Nonetheless, job competition should remain brisk due to the industry's ever-present pool of qualified applicants.

RESEARCH AND TECHNOLOGY

Advances in computer technology dramatically changed work habits within the advertising industry. Although some companies were initially resistant to change, most agencies adopted personal computers once they saw the cost-effectiveness and time-management benefits of automation. Those agencies that embraced computerization became increasingly capable of going "head-to-head" with larger competitors.

"Back-shop" operations remained the most popular functions for computerization. Almost all agencies relied upon computers for word processing, spreadsheets, revenue/income analysis, customer billing, and client record-keeping. A majority of media buying and trafficking also was automated, including market analysis. The use of personal computers was only the beginning. The impact of the Internet on the advertising industry has been tremendous, with agencies having to quickly develop expertise in this area to compete with smaller, specialty firms.

Most agencies acknowledged the necessity for not only computerization, but complete office automation. For example, Leo Burnett invested close to $2 million to install fiber-optic cable necessary to link the 1,200 computers in the agency to each other. At Ogilvy & Mather, 90 cents out of every dollar spent on capital investment in 1990 went toward technology. The goal was to bring all of its departments online and respond to client needs in a more integrated fashion. Accordingly, a big technological problem facing agencies was how to connect computers within the office to the computer systems of clients and outside vendors.

Some of the smaller agencies opened their doors with fully automated, connected, and portable offices. For example, in 1987, the agency of Messner, Vetere, Berger, Carey, and Schmetterer was established with no secretaries or administrative staff. Instead, everyone had a Macintosh computer with an electronic mail system (e-mail) and various software packages, including graphics, drawing, and desktop-publishing tools. Employing a full-time network manager, the agency began setting up connections with its clients' internal e-mail systems to facilitate direct online communication. In addition, remote access to e-mail via notebook computers, complete with a fax modem and access to files on the

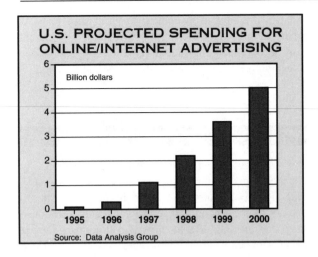

U.S. PROJECTED SPENDING FOR ONLINE/INTERNET ADVERTISING

Billion dollars

Source: Data Analysis Group

Another new term used in back-office agency operations was "workflow technology." This kind of software program let the employees automate their work procedures by breaking down a complex set of human interactions into four steps: client request, vendor agreement, vendor reports completion, and customer satisfaction verified. Nicolas Rudd, chief information officer at Young & Rubicam, indicated in *PC Week* that the process of breaking down interactions helped the agency and its client jointly develop a process most efficient for completing projects. According to Rudd, "the agency was able to reduce overtime by 50 percent and eliminate miscommunications by two-thirds just six months after the pilot program began."

corporate network, created completely portable and time-efficient agency operations.

Other advances in office automation included the development of second-generation "back office" software programs. For example, McCann-Erickson offices throughout the world began testing a new software package designed to collect, standardize, and consolidate advertisers' media budget data and generate customized reports. The system allowed staff members to input information in their native language and currency. The information then was sent to a processing unit to be converted into a standard format. Financial information included actual and estimated ratings and the client's original, revised, and current budgets.

AMERICA AND THE WORLD

As major U.S. manufacturers of consumer products ventured into overseas markets, American advertising agencies followed. International advertising growth became stagnant in 1991, however, due to weak economies in major markets throughout the world, but began an upward trend in 1992. All indicators showed strong long-term growth of advertising in overseas markets relative to growth in the United States. Two hot areas tapped were China and the former Soviet Union. Other promising regions included eastern Europe, Latin America, and the Asia/Pacific region.

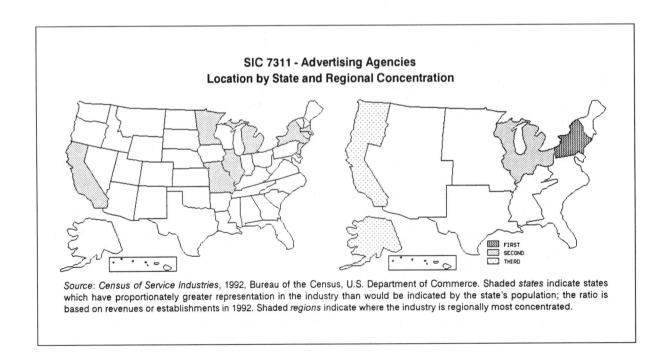

SIC 7311 - Advertising Agencies
Location by State and Regional Concentration

FIRST
SECOND
THIRD

Source: Census of Service Industries, 1992, Bureau of the Census, U.S. Department of Commerce. Shaded *states* indicate states which have proportionately greater representation in the industry than would be indicated by the state's population; the ratio is based on revenues or establishments in 1992. Shaded *regions* indicate where the industry is regionally most concentrated.

In fact, some agencies began gearing up for entry into Vietnam, a country touted as the next boom market in Asia. With 68 million people—half under the age of 19—Vietnam held tremendous potential for marketers of consumer goods. Latin America also was expected to be a popular destination for marketers during the 1990s. This region should provide an overwhelming market of young consumers, as 65 percent of its population of 450 million were under 30 years old, and 37 percent were between 10 and 29. These age groups were successful target markets for consumer products.

Compared to the mature U.S. market, international markets such as Asia and Latin America offered tremendous growth. After lagging for decades, overseas advertising grew at a faster rate than U.S. advertising from 1985 to 1992. In fact, by 1988 the total dollar value of foreign advertising, at $164.7 billion, surpassed ad spending in the United States at $132.1 billion, according to McCann-Erickson research. Thus, marketers and ad agencies viewed international expansion as an essential part of their future growth. Total worldwide advertising expenditures were expected to rise by 7.3 percent to $377 billion in 1996.

ASSOCIATIONS AND SOCIETIES

AMERICAN ASSOCIATION OF ADVERTISING AGENCIES
666 3rd Ave., 13 Fl.
New York, NY 10017
Phone: (212) 682-2500
Fax: (212) 682-8136

ASSOCIATION OF NATIONAL ADVERTISERS
155 E. 44th St.
New York, NY 10017
Phone: (21) 697-5950
Fax: (212) 661-8057

LEAGUE OF ADVERTISING AGENCIES
2 S. End Ave., No. 4-C
New York, NY 10280
Phone: (212) 945-4314

MUTUAL ADVERTISING AGENCY NETWORK
25700 Science Park Dr.
Cleveland, OH 44122
Phone: (216) 292-6609
Fax: (216) 292-6780

PERIODICALS AND NEWSLETTERS

ADVERTISING AGE: THE INTERNATIONAL NEWSPAPER OF MARKETING
Crain Communications, Inc.
2200 E. 42nd St.
New York, NY 10017-5806
Phone: (800) 992-9970 or (212) 210-0100
Fax: (212) 210-0799
Weekly. $79.00 per year. Includes supplement Creativity.

ADVERTISING AGENCIES: WHAT THEY ARE, WHAT THEY DO, HOW THEY DO IT
American Association of Advertising Agencies
666 3rd Ave.
New York, NY 10017-4056
Phone: (212) 682-2500

AMERICAN ADVERTISING MAGAZINE
American Advertising Federation
1101 Vermont Ave. NW, Ste. 500
Washington, DC 20005
Phone: (202) 898-0089
Fax: (202) 898-0159
Quarterly. Membership.

JOURNAL OF ADVERTISING RESEARCH
Advertising Research Foundation
641 Lexington Ave., 11 Fl.
New York, NY 10022
Phone: (212) 751-5656
Fax: (212) 319-5265
Bimonthly. $100.00 per year.

MEDIA INDUSTRY NEWSLETTER
Phillips Publishing, Inc.
7811 Montrose Rd.
Potomac, MD 20854
Weekly. $345.00 per year. News of advertising, broadcasting, and publishing. Reports on the number of advertising pages in major magazines.

DATABASES

ABI/INFORM
UMI/Data Courier
620 S. 3rd St.
Louisville, KY 40202
Phone: (800) 626-2823 or (502) 583-4111
Fax: (502) 589-5572
Provides online indexing to business-related material occurring in over 800 periodicals from 1971 to the present. Inquire as to online cost and availability.

ADVERTISER AND AGENCY RED BOOKS PLUS
National Register Publishing Co.
Reed Reference Publishing
121 Chanlon Rd.
New Providence, NJ 07974
Phone: (800) 521-8110 or (908) 464-6800
Fax: (908) 665-6688

Quarterly. $1,195.00 per year. The CD-ROM version of Standard Directory of Advertisers, Standard Directory of Advertising Agencies, Standard Directory of International Advertisers and Agencies.

INFORMATION BANK ABSTRACTS
New York Times Co.
229 W. 43rd St.
New York, NY 10036
Phone: (212) 556-3575
Fax: (212) 556-1629
Provides indexing and abstracting of current affairs, primarily from the final late edition of The New York Times *and the Eastern edition of* The Wall Street Journal. *Time period is 1969 to present, with daily updates. Inquire as to online cost and availability.*

MARKETING AND ADVERTISING REFERENCE SERVICE
Information Access Co.
Foster City, CA 94404
Phone: (800) 321-6388 or (415) 358-4643
Fax: (415) 358-4643

STATISTICS SOURCES

ADVERTISING AGE: NATIONAL EXPENDITURES IN NEWSPAPERS
Crain Communications, Inc.
220 E. 42nd St.
New York, NY 10017-5806
Phone: (800) 9929970 or (212) 210-0100
Fax: (212) 210-0799
Annual.

GENERAL WORKS

ADVERTISING AGE-LEADING NATIONAL ADVERTISERS
Crain Communications, Inc.
740 N. Rush St.
Chicago, IL 60611-2590
Phone: (312) 649-5200
Fax: (312) 446-0347
Annual. $5.00. List of the 100 leading advertisers in terms of the amount spent on national advertising.

ADVERTISING AGENCY BUSINESS
Herbert S. Gardner, Jr.
NTC Publishing Group
4255 W. Touhy Ave.
Lincolnwood, IL 60646-1975
Phone: (800) 323-4900 or (708) 679-5500
Fax: (708) 679-6375
1990. $39.95. Second edition. A guide for business people who need to know more about successful advertising practices.

ADVERTISING PURE AND SIMPLE
AMACOM American Management Association
135 W. 50th St.
New York, NY 10020
Phone: (800) 538-4761 or (212) 586-8100
Fax: (212) 903 8168
1990. $21.95. Second Edition. A discussion of what makes advertising effective.

FURTHER READING

Goldman, Kevin. "IBM Combines Ad Accounts In One Agency." *Wall Street Journal,* 25 May 1994.

"McCann-Erickson Insider's Report." 4 December 1995.

"Standard & Poor's Industry Surveys." 20 July 1995.

The agricultural production of crops in the United States consists of cash grains, field crops, vegetables and melons, and fruits and tree nuts. The major crops in these categories include: corn, wheat, soybeans, cotton, tobacco, sugarcane and sugar beets, citrus fruit such as oranges and grapefruit, grapes, and deciduous fruit such as apples, apricots and pears. Graced with vast natural resources, a stable economic history, and cutting edge agricultural technology, the U.S. farming industry is a significant contributor to the global production of these and numerous other crops.

CASH GRAINS

The United States is the world's leading producer and exporter of corn, growing about two-thirds of the world's supply. Although it is grown in all 50 states, approximately three-fourths of U.S. corn comes from the section of the Midwest known as the Corn Belt, which consists of parts of Illinois, Indiana, Iowa, Michigan, Minnesota, Missouri, Nebraska, Ohio, South Dakota, and Wisconsin. The leading corn-producing states are Iowa and Illinois. In the late-1990s, corn was the number one U.S. crop in terms of acreage, with over 70 million acres devoted to it. Corn was a major source of livestock feed, and approximately half the annual harvest of corn was fed to chickens, hogs, and cattle.

Wheat farms in the United States produced over 2.5 billion bushels of grain annually, harvesting approximately 60-70 million acres with yields ranging from 35-40 bushels per acre. In terms of acres planted, wheat ranks second behind corn. Average prices for the several classes of American wheat fluctuated between $2.50 and $3.50 per bushel and depended on an enormous range of environmental, political, economic, and technological factors. Devoting almost half of its harvest to exports, the United States accounted for over 30 percent of the world wheat trade on average. Due to the importance of U.S. wheat in international trade and the integral role the U.S. Department of Agriculture (USDA) played in every sector of the agricultural economy, wheat farmers were in many ways more affected by shifts in the political climate than by actual weather conditions.

Soybeans were the third largest cultivated crop in the United States, behind only corn and wheat, with about 60 million acres harvested annually. They were also the largest U.S. export crop. The United States grew more soybeans than any other country in the world, supplying about two-thirds of the world's total production. Iowa, Illinois, Minnesota, Indiana, Missouri, and Ohio were the leading states in production of this crop. Soybeans, which possess high quantities of protein, and

AGRICULTURAL PRODUCTION— CROPS

SIC 0100

Agricultural exports will continue to rise in the late 1990s—especially to Mexico—as the farming industry benefits from the favorable market conditions surrounding the North American Free Trade Agreement (NAFTA). Farmers will also seek to take advantage of new market opportunities that arise from the passage of the Federal Agriculture Improvement and Reform Act of 1996 (FAIR), in which the federal government will gradually reduce farm subsidies and open the agriculture sector to the free market by 2002. Released from government restrictions, farmers are likely to increase crop exports and focus more closely on high-revenue crops. Look for family and small, independent agricultural operations to take the biggest economic hit from both federal subsidy reductions and increased competition from large agricultural operations.

LEADING CROP PROTECTION PRODUCT MANUFACTURERS

Ranked by: Sales, in millions of dollars.

1. Ciba Crop Protection, with $917 million
2. DuPont, $872
3. American Cyanamid, $867
4. Dow Elanco, $738
5. Monsanto, $716
6. Zeneca, $540
7. Rhone-Poulenc, $363
8. BASF, $263
9. Sandoz, $262
9. Bayer, $262

Source: *Agri Marketing*, February, 1996, p. 15.

soybean products are used in a wide range of food and industrial products. Soy products have three major divisions: soy oil products, whole bean products, and soy protein products. Food products include baby food, cereal, diet foods, imitation meats, processed meats, soy sauce, tofu and miso, salad dressings and margarine, cooking oil, candy, and baked goods. Soybeans are used in pet foods and as the leading source of protein meal for U.S. livestock. Industrial uses for soybeans include wallboard and plywood, medicines, soaps and disinfectants, pesticides, fertilizers, candles, linoleum, and varnish, fire extinguisher fluid, and paint.

FIELD CROPS

The United States has been a leading producer of cotton since the eighteenth century. Because cotton requires warm conditions for germination and growth, it has always been grown in the southern regions of the United States, from Virginia to California. For three centuries, U.S. cotton production was centered in the area stretching from the Atlantic coast westward to central Texas. However, the increasing availability of irrigation facilities has allowed western growers to produce cotton that is more consistent in color and weight. By 1995, the largest producers of cotton were Texas and California, with annual harvests of about 4.5 million and 2.5 million bales respectively. Although California growers plant approximately one-quarter the number of acres as Texas growers, their yield per acre has often been triple that of Texas growers.

Sugarcane and sugar beets—two other major U.S. crops—are grown mainly to produce table sugar and sucrose. Although refining processes for sugar sources are similar, cultivation and harvesting techniques are quite different. Sugarcane is planted using stalk cuttings, and matures between eight and sixteen months, depending on the region. A crop of sugarcane may produce acceptable yields for two to three years before being replanted and, in the case of Hawaii, where there is no danger of frost, can be harvested year round. Sugarcane is most often harvested mechanically, with specially-designed harvesters that cut the stalk at the bottom, strip the unneeded leaves and top, and transfer the cane to a wagon. Sugar beets are harvested annually and have benefited from the attention of agricultural specialists who devised seed types and planting methods which encourage maximum yields. Still, great care must be taken to ensure adequate distance between plants, weed control, planting depth, and proper fertilization. However, mechanical cultivation and harvesting equipment makes labor costs in sugar beet production negligible. Both sugar industries have attained yields that are among the highest in the world: the average yield for sugar cane was 32.81 tons per acre in 1995-96, while it was 19.74 tons per acre for sugar beets.

The tobacco segment, which is composed of approximately 62,000 tobacco farmers in the United States, grows and sells tobacco to cigarette companies and other tobacco product retailers. Warnings issued by the government and medical authorities about the relationship between smoking and heart disease, cancer, and a number of major respiratory ailments continue to impact the industry. Nonetheless, the U.S. Department of Agriculture indicated that U.S. farmers intended to plant 10 percent more acres of tobacco in 1997 than were planted in 1996.

VEGETABLES AND FRUIT

Vegetables and fruit are the second largest food group in the United States by volume and consumption, behind milk and dairy products. California, Florida, Texas, Arizona, and New York are the largest truck farming states, producing such crops as asparagus, beans, broccoli, cabbage, cantaloupe, cauliflower, celery, sweet corn, cucumber, green peas, lettuce, onions, peppers, squash, and tomatoes. Produce is sold directly to processors, wholesalers, retailers, or consumers by truck farmers. Large truck farms usually specialize in one or two crops for shipment to the rest of the country, while smaller farms may grow a large variety for sale at local farmers' markets, stands, and stores. Smaller farms may also market their produce together through a cooperative in order to negotiate better prices.

Citrus fruits, a $2.26 billion industry, include oranges (about 65 percent of total worldwide citrus production); tangelos, temples, and tangerines (15 percent); lemons and limes (10 percent), and grapefruits (10 percent). In the United States, oranges and grapefruit account for approximately 90 percent of the country's citrus production. With more than 20,000 producers of all sizes, no one grower is dominant in the production phase, and the industry itself governs its own marketing orders. Growers heed marketing factors as they specify grade and standard of crop leaving the region; control amount of product leaving the region during marketing season; designate periods when no new product can be shipped; provide market support such as research and price information; and provide market development programs.

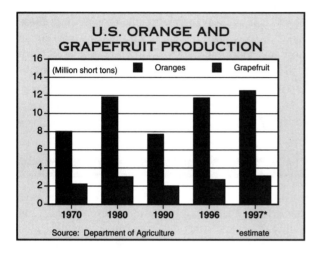

U.S. ORANGE AND GRAPEFRUIT PRODUCTION

Source: Department of Agriculture   *estimate

Grape production has consistently constituted one of the largest U.S. non-citrus fruit crops, usually competing with apples for the greatest amount of total fruit produced. However, in the general fruit category, grapes have always trailed oranges. The farm value of the grape crop totaled approximately $1.5 to $2 billion each year since the mid-1980s. The two types of establishments engaged in the production of grapes in the United States are grape farms and vineyards. Grapes are grown for table use, processed into wine or juice, canned or frozen, and dried for raisins. California, Washington, and New York lead the country in grape production, although California alone produces over 90 percent of the country's grapes.

The deciduous fruit industry consists of farms and orchards that maintain and harvest a variety of fruits, specifically apples, apricots, cherries, nectarines, peaches, pears, persimmons, plums, pomegranates, prunes, and quinces. In the late 1990s, crop production for these fruits was valued at several billion dollars. The apple crop alone constitutes the country's third largest fruit crop, trailing grapes and oranges. More than 1 million acres of farmland were devoted to the growth of major deciduous fruits in the United States.

INDUSTRY OUTLOOK

During the mid- to late 1990s, there was a trend toward less government involvement in the agricultural sector as a whole. Most notable was the U.S. Congress's passage of the Federal Agriculture Improvement and Reform Act of 1996 (FAIR), also known as the "Freedom to Farm" Bill. This legislation would curtail federal government involvement by gradually reducing farm subsidies over a seven year period and finally ending the program in 2002. Further, it would allow farmers to sow as many acres as the market dictates, without having to rely on government planting stipulations. Still, the government plans to maintain some control to avoid surplus or shortage crises. The bill was also expected to promote more sound business practices through the alleviation of surplus production, making U.S. producers more competitive. Some producers in the agricultural sector— cash grain and cotton producers, for example—viewed this bill optimistically in that they stood to reap greater profits for their high-demand products on the international market. Other sectors such as sugar producers— who have traditionally relied on government subsidies as insurance in a typically volatile industry—lobbied hard against the passage to the Freedom to Farm Bill.

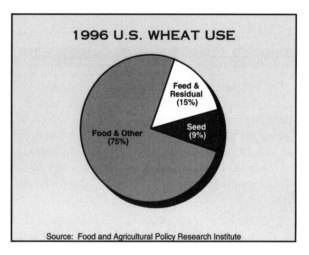

1996 U.S. WHEAT USE

Feed & Residual (15%)

Seed (9%)

Food & Other (75%)

Source: Food and Agricultural Policy Research Institute

The United States has also continued to dominate the export market, in part because of production efficiency, but also because the market conditions of the North American Free Trade Agreement of 1993 (NAFTA) continue to favor the export of American-grown crops. For example, NAFTA has brought the U.S. corn industry increased access to the Mexican grain market. Corn exports to Mexico have risen, because the trade accord has reduced support for Mexican corn growers, forcing the country to rely on imported corn. In its first year of implementation, Mexico imported 2.5

million metric tons (98.5 bushels) of corn. Another emerging key importer of U.S. corn was the Pacific Rim in Asia. The USDA has predicted that exports would rise to 2.9 billion bushels by 2004. However, controversy and drops in exports ensued in 1996 when U.S. producers tried to sell a mixture of regular and genetically engineered soybeans to the European market. Though U.S. policy did not require labeling of genetically engineered products, European customers demanded to receive only soybeans that were not tampered with genetically. This controversy cost producers $150 million, almost 10 percent of their European exports.

Despite the overall market success that the agriculture sector has enjoyed, the increase of crop yield has been taking a toll on the nation's water supplies. Pesticides and fertilizers have contaminated ground water in major agricultural areas and have invaded the drinking water of people who depend on wells for their water. The nation's fertile topsoil has continued to erode: as farms have expanded, erosion has become more of a problem because larger fields are more vulnerable to topsoil erosion. Use of heavy farm equipment has also contributed to the erosion problem. As the United States and other nations began to deal with environmental issues more intensely, erosion and pollution caused by farming received more attention.

WORK FORCE

An estimated 3.8 million people are employed on at least a part-time basis in the U.S. agricultural industry. Career opportunities include jobs in production, processing, and marketing. Wages vary widely according to the size and structure of the farm, the nature of the job held, and the education level of the employee. Predictably, college graduates with a degree in agriculture-related

fields can expect annual salaries significantly higher than farm laborers without a college education. Many farm operators hold non-farm, part-time jobs to earn money to supplement their farm income. This trend has been in effect since the 1950s, a result of both higher farming costs and the increased cost of living. In addition, the number of farmers that report farming as their principal occupation is also diminishing.

In recent years, another significant development was the aging of the agriculture industry's work force. The largest numbers of farmers are between the ages of 55 and 64. Moreover, while the number of farmers over 64 years of age was increasing, the proportion of those under 35 was decreasing. As the industry has grown more and more mechanized, young people in agricultural communities have had to find other types of employment.

RESEARCH AND TECHNOLOGY

Researchers in the agricultural sector have always tried to find the best ways to increase crop yield and quality. They knew that the size of their crop depended on the seed they used; to that end, they have worked to engineer larger and healthier seeds. Moreover, researchers carefully observed the results of their seed selection and learned to develop strains adapted for certain locations and conditions. Ultimately, farmers could increase the quality of their crop and the bushels per acreage yield by simply selecting a scientifically engineered seed. Scientists and farmers began to apply knowledge of hybrid seed breeding, which involved fertilizing one kind of seed with another to produce seeds with particular growing characteristics.

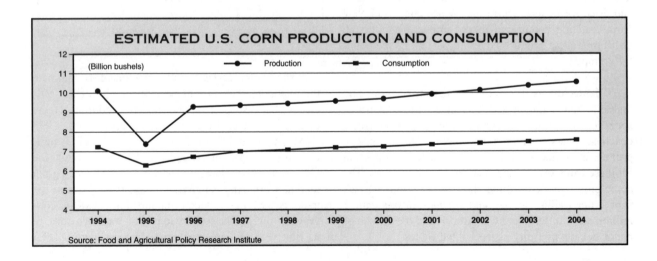

ESTIMATED U.S. CORN PRODUCTION AND CONSUMPTION

Source: Food and Agricultural Policy Research Institute

Seed Corn Market - North America

Shares are for 1994.

Pioneer Hi-Bred	44.9%
DEKALB Genetics	8.7
Northup-King (Sandoz)	4.1
Cargill	3.4
ICI	3.3
Mycogen(TM) brand seed corn	2.0
Other	33.6

Source: *Investext,* Thomson Financial Services, December 14, 1995, p. 3, from Pioneer Hi-Bred.

international nonprofit research efforts for enhancing productivity, profitability, and sustainability of wheat and corn and developing a wheat hybrid that is more heat resistant. Theoretically, such a wheat hybrid would alleviate some of the capriciousness of growing wheat.

U.S. Crop Plantings

Data are shown in millions of acres.

Corn	79.2
Wheat	70.3
Soybeans	61.7
Cotton	13.7
Sorghum	9.8
Sunflowers	3.6
Rice	3.4

Source: *Agricultural Outlook*, May 1996, p. 2, from United States Department of Agriculture.

Some industry observers predicted that by the beginning of the next century, biotechnologists would be able to engineer seeds genetically to produce specific traits such as modified proteins, oils, or starches, as well as resistance to disease and insects. To that end, for example, the National Corn Growers Association (NCGA) implemented the National Corn Genome Initiative (NCGI)—a program to create a comprehensive gene map of corn in an effort to realize the corn industry's goals of creating corn hybrids for different environments and reduce reliance on pesticides and fertilizers.

Land grant universities like Texas A&M and Kansas State University performed a great deal of research that has been successful in developing stronger strains of grain and more effective chemical fertilizers. Yields were expected to continue to rise as a result of this work. Increasingly, however, concerns for the environment were pushing researchers away from sheer yield growth projects. Researchers have been working to develop ways to maintain farmers' profitable yields while lessening their dependence on chemicals. In addition, droughts and sun-scorched farms have prompted the

AMERICA AND THE WORLD

In recent years, the U.S. has continued to experience increased pressure from such competing agricultural producers as China and Russia. In an effort to maintain their influence in consumer markets in Japan, Canada, Korea, and other nations, the U.S. federal government has passed legislation which will make it easier for farmers to produce higher crop yields and offer competitive prices for crops sold overseas. During the late 1990s, it is expected that American agriculture will generate more than $40 billion dollars in export trade annually. Major crop products include animal feeds, cotton, tobacco, corn, wheat, soybeans, and horticultural products.

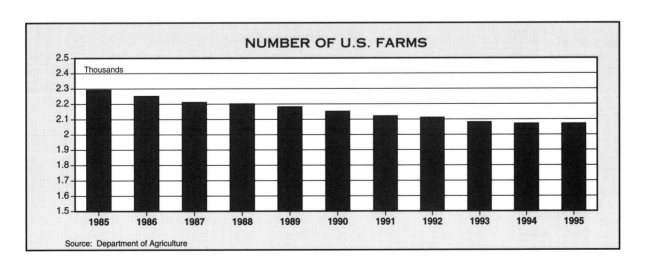

NUMBER OF U.S. FARMS

Thousands

Source: Department of Agriculture

Some industry analysts predict that the demand for U.S. products on the international market may decline as other nations develop their own farming industries. Low labor costs in some countries may enable them to produce crops more cheaply than could be accomplished in the United States. In addition, improved technology, such as the availability of advanced irrigation systems, is increasing the ability of some countries to grow crops.

ASSOCIATIONS AND SOCIETIES

AGRICULTURAL RESEARCH INSTITUTE
9650 Rockville Pike
Bethesda, MD 20814
Phone: (301) 530-7122
Fax: (301) 530-7007

AGRICULTURE COUNCIL OF AMERICA
3 McPherson Sq.
927 15th St., Ste. 800
Washington, DC 20005
Phone: (202) 682-9200
Fax: (202) 289-6648

AMERICAN FARM BUREAU FEDERATION
225 Touhy Ave.
Park Ridge, IL 60068
Phone: (312) 399-5700
Fax: (312) 399-5896

AMERICAN SOCIETY OF AGRICULTURAL ENGINEERS
2950 Niles Rd.
St. Joseph, MI 49085-9659
Phone: (616) 429-0300
Fax: (616) 429-3852

AMERICAN SOCIETY OF AGRONOMY
677 S. Segoe Rd.
Madison, WI 53711
Phone: (608) 273-8080
Fax: (608) 273-2021

COTTON INCORPORATED
1370 Avenue of the Americas
New York, NY 10019
Phone: (212) 586-1070
Fax: (212) 265-5386

NATIONAL ASSOCIATION OF STATE DEPARTMENTS OF AGRICULTURE
1156 15th St. NW, Ste. 1020
Washington, DC 20005
Phone: (202) 296-9680
Fax: (202) 296-9686

NATIONAL ASSOCIATION OF WHEAT GROWERS
415 2nd St. NE, Ste. 300
Washington, DC 20002
Phone: (202) 547-7800
Fax: (202) 546-2638

NATIONAL CORN GROWERS ASSOCIATION
1000 Executive Pky., Ste. 105
St. Louis, MO 63141-6397
Phone: (314) 275-9915
Fax: (314) 275-7061

U.S. WHEAT ASSOCIATES
1620 Eye St. NW, Ste. 801
Washington, DC 20006
Phone: (202) 463-0999
Fax: (202) 785-1052

PERIODICALS AND NEWSLETTERS

AGRICULTURAL OUTLOOK
Available from U.S. Government Printing Office
Washington, DC 20402
Phone: (202) 512-1800
Fax: (202) 512-2250
Monthly. $40.00 per year. Issued by the Economic Research Service of the U.S. Department of Agriculture. Provides analysis of agriculture and the economy.

AGRICULTURAL RESEARCH
Available from U.S. Government Printing Office
Washington, DC 20402
Phone: (202) 512-1800
Fax: (202) 512-2250
Monthly. $28.00 per year. Issued by the Agricultural Research Service of the U.S. Department of Agriculture. Presents results of research projects related to a wide variety of farm crops and products.

AGRONOMY JOURNAL
American Society of Agronomy, Inc.
677 S. Segoe Rd.
Madison, WI 53711
Phone: (608) 273-8080
Fax: (608) 273-2021
Bimonthly. Members, $64.00 per year; non-members, $108.00 per year.

AGRONOMY NEWS
American Society of Agronomy, Inc.
677 S. Segoe Rd.
Madison, WI 53711
Phone: (608) 273-8080
Fax: (608) 273-2021
Monthly. Free to members; non-members, $12.00 per year.

JOURNAL OF AGRICULTURAL AND FOOD INFORMATION
Haworth Press, Inc.
10 Alice St.
Binghamton, NY 13904-1580
Phone: (800) 342-9678 or (607) 722-5857
Fax: (607) 722-1424
Quarterly. $50.00 per year. A journal for librarians and others concerned with the acquisition of information on food and agriculture.

JOURNAL OF SUSTAINABLE AGRICULTURE
Haworth Press, Inc.
10 Alice St.

Binghamton, NY 13904-1580
Phone: (800) 342-9678 or (607) 722-5857
Fax: (607) 722-1424
Quarterly. $90.00 per year. An academic and practical journal concerned with resource depletion and environmental misuse.

KIPLINGER AGRICULTURE LETTER
Kiplinger Washington Editors, Inc.
1729 H St. NW
Washington, DC 20006
Phone: (202) 887-6400
Fax: (202) 778-8976
Biweekly. $54.00 per year. Newsletter.

NATIONAL FARMERS UNION WASHINGTON NEWSLETTER
Farmers Educational and Cooperative Union of America
600 Maryland Ave. SW, Ste. 202
Washington, DC 20024
Phone: (202) 554-1600
Fax: (202) 554-1654
18 times a year. $10.00 per year.

WASHINGTON AGRICULTURAL RECORD
Georgetown Sta., PO Box 25001
Washington, DC 20007
Phone: (202) 333-8190
Weekly. $65.00 per year. Newsletter.

WHEAT GROWER
National Association of Wheat Growers
415 2nd St. NE, Ste. 300
Washington, DC 20002
Phone: (202) 547-7800
Fax: (202) 546-2638
Eight times a year. $20.00 per year.

WHEAT LIFE
Washington Association of Wheat Growers
109 E First St.
Ritzville, WA 99169-2394
Phone: (509) 659-0610
11 times a year. $12.00 per year. Covers research, marketing information, and legislative and regulatory news pertinent to the wheat and barley industries of the Pacific Northwest.

DATABASES

AGRICULTURAL WASTE DATABASE
Auburn University
Research-based information concerning solutions to agricultural waste management and by-product utilization. Time span: 1978 to date. Updating frequency: As needed. Fees: Free.

- Gopher: gopher.acenet.auburn.edu; Choose: Agriculture and Natural Resources
- URL: gopher://gopher.acenet.auburn.edu:70/11/ waste_mgt/ag

BIOTECHNOLOGY INFORMATION CENTER
U.S. Dept. of Agriculture
National Agricultural Library
Biotechnology Information Center

Contains educational resources, legislation and regulation, selected full texts of agricultural biotechnology patents, biotechnology videos, bibliographies, reports and studies, and the full text of biotechnology newsletters, as well as links to other biotechnology resources on the Internet. Updating frequency: As needed. Fees: Free.

- Gopher: gopher.nalusda.gov; Port: 70; Choose: NAL Information Centers/ Biotechnology Information Center (BIC)
- URL: http://www.inform.umd.edu/EdRes/Topic/ AgrEnv/Biotech

CAB ABSTRACTS
CAB International North America
845 N. Park Ave.
Tucson, AZ 85719
Phone: (800) 528-4841 or (602) 621-7897
Fax: (602) 621-3816
Contains 46 specialized abstract collections covering over 10,000 journals and monographs in the areas of agriculture, horticulture, forest products, farm products, nutrition, dairy science, poultry, grains, animal health, entomology, etc. Time period is 1972 to date, with monthly updates. Inquire as to online cost and availability. CAB Abstracts on CD-ROM also available, with annual updating.

CRIS
U.S. Dept. of Agriculture Cooperative
State Research Service
Beltsville, MD 20705
Phone: (301) 504-6846
Fax: (301) 504-6272
Descriptions of research projects related to agriculture, 1974 to present. Inquire as to online cost and availability.

U.S. DEPARTMENT OF AGRICULTURE MARKET WIRE REPORTS
U.S. Department of Agriculture
University of Kentucky, College of Agriculture
Provides information about weekly arrivals and shipments with terminal prices for agricultural products, and weekly summaries of market activities. Fees: Free.

- Gopher: shelley.ca.uky.edu; Choose: Ag Markets.Agricultural Marketing Info
- URL: gopher://shelley.ca.uky.edu:70/11/agmkts/ market_wire

WILSONLINE: BIOLOGICAL AND AGRICULTURAL INDEX
H. W. Wilson Co.
950 University Ave.
Bronx, NY 10452
Phone: (800) 367-6770 or (718) 588-8400
Fax: (718) 590-1617
Indexes a wide variety of agricultural and biological periodicals, 1983 to date. Weekly updates. Inquire as to online cost and availability.

STATISTICS SOURCES

AGRICULTURAL STATISTICS

Available from U.S. Government Printing Office
Washington, DC 20402
Phone: (202) 512-1800
Fax: (202) 512-2250
Annual. $21.00. Produced by the National Agricultural Statistics Service, U.S. Department of Agriculture. Provides a wide variety of statistical data relating to agricultural production, supplies, consumption, prices/price-supports, foreign trade, costs, and returns, as well as farm labor, loans, income, and population. In many cases, historical data is shown annually for 10 years. In addition to farm data, includes detailed fishery statistics.

AGRICULTURE FACT BOOK

Available from U.S. Government Printing Office
Washington, DC 20402
Phone: (202) 512-1800
Fax: (202) 512-2250
Annual. $8.00. Issued by the Office of Communications, U.S. Department of Agriculture. Includes data on U.S. agriculture, farmers, food, nutrition, and rural America. Programs of the Department of Agriculture in six areas are described: rural economic development, foreign trade, nutrition, the environment, inspection, and education.

CROP PRODUCTION

Available from U.S. Government Printing Office
Washington, DC 20402
Phone: (202) 512-1800
Fax: (202) 512-2250
Monthly, with annual summary. $49.00 per year. Issued by the Agricultural Statistics Board, U.S. Department of Agriculture. Contains reports on current production, market trends, crops in storage, acreage, prices, etc. Includes statistical tables.

INTERNATIONAL WHEAT COUNCIL WORLD GRAIN STATISTICS

International Wheat Council, Haymarket House
1 Canada Sq.
Canary Wharf, England E14 5AE
Phone: 0171 513 1122
Fax: 0171 712 0071
Annual. $125.00. Text in English, French, Russian and Spanish.

UNITED STATES CENSUS OF AGRICULTURE

U.S. Bureau of the Census
Washington, DC 20233-0800
Phone: (301) 457-4100
Fax: (301) 457-3842
Quinquennial. Results presented in reports, tape, CD-ROM, and diskette files.

WHEAT FACTS

National Association of Wheat Growers
415 2nd St. NE, Ste. 300
Washington, DC 20002
Phone: (202) 547-7800
Fax: (202) 546-2638
Annual. Price on application.

GENERAL WORKS

ADVANCES IN AGRONOMY

Academic Press, Inc.
525 B St., Ste. 1900
San Diego, CA 92101-4495
Phone: (800) 321-5068 or (619) 231-0926
Fax: (800) 336-7377 or (619) 699-6715
Irregular. Price on application.

CORN ANNUAL

Corn Refiners Association
1100 Connecticut Ave. NW
Washington, DC 20036
Phone: (202) 331-1634
Fax: (202) 331-2054
Annual. Single copies free.

YEARBOOK OF AGRICULTURE

U.S. Department of Agriculture
Available from U.S. Government Printing Office
Washington, DC 20402
Phone: (202) 512-1800
Fax: (202) 512-2250
Annual. $14.00.

AGRIBUSINESS MANAGEMENT

Walter D. Downey and John K. Trocke
McGraw-Hill Cos.
1221 Avenue of the Americas
New York, NY 10020
Phone: (800) 262-4729 or (212) 512-2000
Fax: (609) 426-5924
1987. Second edition. Price on application.

AGRICULTURAL RESEARCH POLICY

Vernon W. Ruttan
Books on Demand
300 N. Zeeb Rd.
Ann Arbor, MI 48106-1346
Phone: (800) 521-0600 or (313) 761-4700
Fax: (313) 665-5022
1982. $109.50.

EXPLORING AGRIBUSINESS

Ewell Paul Roy Interstate Publishers
PO Box 50
Danville, IL 61834-0050
Phone: (800) 848-4774 or (217) 446-0500
Fax: (217) 446-9706
1980. $29.95. Third edition.

FURTHER READING

American Soybean Association. ''ASA Positive on New Farm Bill.'' St. Louis: ASA, 4 April 1996. Available from http://www.oilseeds.org/asa/fb_signd.htm

Burns, Greg, and Dave Lindorff, et. al. ''The New Economics of Food'' *Business Week,* 20 May 1996.

Florida Department of Citrus. Economic and Market Research Department. ''Citrus Reference Book, 1996.'' Florida. April

1996. Available from: http://www.fred.ifas.ufl.edu/citrus/r1.html#t12

Ibrahim, Youssef M. ''Genetic Soybeans from U.S. Alarm Europeans.'' *New York Times*, 7 November 1996.

National Corn Genome Initiative. ''The National Corn Genome Initiative.'' St. Louis, MO, National Corn Growers Association, May 1995. Available from http://www.inverizon.com/ncgi/early/NCI_NCI.html

National Corn Growers Association. ''World of Corn On-line.'' St. Louis, MO, 1996. Available from http://www.ncga.com/02world/page02.html

United States Department of Agriculture. National Agricultural Statistics Service. ''Agricultural Statistics 1995-1996.'' Washington, DC, 1996. Available from http://www.usda.gov/nass/pubs/agr95_96/agr95_5.pdf

U.S. Department of Agriculture. *Tobacco Yearbook*. Washington: Economic Research Service, 6 May 1997.

United States Department of Agriculture. ''Wheat Yearbook.'' Washington, DC, 29 February 1996. Available from http://usda.mannlib.cornell.edu/reports/erssor/field/whs-bby/wheat_yearbook_02.29.96

United States Feed Grains Council. ''The Impact of NAFTA.'' Washington, DC, 3 June 1996. Available from http://www.grains.org/policy/nafta.htm ◆

AGRICULTURAL PRODUCTION— LIVESTOCK

SIC 0200

Despite surging competition from poultry and pork producers, beef continues to reign as the most popular meat for American consumers. In terms of both edible and dollar amounts, beef far surpasses the other meats and will continue to do so for the foreseeable future. Nevertheless, the poultry market continues to grow at an impressive rate of more than 5 percent per year; in fact, some industry analysts speculate that per capita consumption of chicken will sky rocket from current levels of around 48 pounds to 95 pounds by 2000. Recent federal legislation—such as the USDA's Hazard Analysis and Critical Control Points (HACCP) system and the Federal Agriculture Reform and Improvement Act (FAIR)—have added a regulative burden to the livestock industry in an effort to protect consumers from meat contamination and unfair price controls. How the industry adjusts to these regulations will no doubt impact their profits in the years to come.

Totaling some $33.9 billion, the sale of cattle and calves is the largest segment of the American agricultural economy. This market comprises 16 percent of the gross national product and accounts for almost one quarter of the country's farm and ranch cash receipts. Beef cattle are one of the few agricultural commodities produced in all fifty states, and in 34 states the population of beef cattle producers exceeds 10,000. In fact, there are 1.064 million independently owned farms and ranches producing beef cattle for breeding and for feeding in the United States.

Poultry has recently made inroads into beef's long-held position as America's most popular meat. Much of poultry's popularity has been attributed to price and to the low-fat content of its meat. In 1996, the average price of a three-ounce serving of beef was 50 cents, whereas the average price for a three-ounce serving of chicken was 42 cents. Despite the many advances of the poultry industry, the production of beef continues to top all other forms of meat production in the United States. In terms of economic value, the production of beef is still four times greater than its nearest competitor.

Top 10 TOP STATES FOR CATTLE INVENTORY, JANUARY 1, 1997

Ranked by: All cattle inventory (1,000 head).

1. Texas, 14,100
2. Kansas, 6,550
3. Nebraska, 6,550
4. Oklahoma, 5,400
5. California, 4,550
6. Misouri, 4,450
7. Iowa, 3,900
8. South Dakota, 3,800
9. Wisconsin, 3,700
10. Colorado, 3,150

Source: USDA-NASS, Historic Data: 1996 Livestock Rankings by Species.

With gross annual sales of about $11 billion, the pork industry represents another vital part of the American livestock market. In 1995, over 180,000 pork producers nationwide raised an annual average of 17.8 billion pounds of the meat, garnering $10.5 billion in sales. The pork herd reached its highest level in over a decade, with the U.S. Department of Agriculture estimating that American producers maintained about 49 million hogs on farms and feedlots in May of 1995 and slaughtered 96.5 million throughout the year.

Dairy farming is another leading agricultural activity with dairy cash receipts totaling over $20 billion a year. Because of scientific advances increasing milk production, the total number of dairy cows in the United States has been declining steadily since 1970, while the total output and the output per cow have increased significantly. Milk sales constitute about 12 percent of all money made from agricultural activities.

NEW MEAT INSPECTION POLICY

In 1996, President Clinton announced a new, expanded meat inspection program that would require the participation of the private sector as well as the U.S. Department of Agriculture (USDA). The USDA implemented the Hazard Analysis and Critical Control Points (HACCP) system to replace the look-touch-smell meat inspection system that began in 1907. The new system requires companies to use new technology, anti-microbial chemical sprays, and irradiation to combat meat contamination hazards and to determine where in the production process contamination takes place. Companies must also submit meat samples to the USDA for inspection.

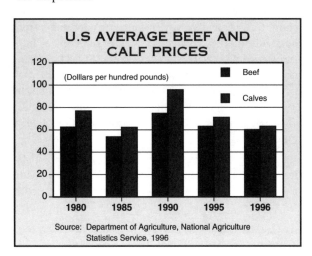

U.S AVERAGE BEEF AND CALF PRICES

(Dolllars per hundred pounds)

■ Beef

■ Calves

Source: Department of Agriculture, National Agriculture Statistics Service. 1996

INDUSTRY OUTLOOK

BEEF INDUSTRY

Although beef consumption leveled off in the 1990s, a combination of factors contributed to its decline as the premier meat for American consumers. Intense competition from other meat producers got the attention of beef producers as the poultry industry challenged beef's position as "The King of Meats." In the early 1990s, the poultry industry proudly announced that more

chicken was consumed per person in the United States than beef. This development marked the first time in the industry's history that beef was displaced from its position as the most consumed meat, in terms of poundage, in the country. Cattlemen like to point out, however, that beef at the retail level is a 94 percent boneless product, while chicken is only 69 percent boneless. On an edible meat basis, therefore, Americans still ate more beef than chicken in 1996—66.7 pounds versus 48.1 pounds. On a dollar basis the difference is more dramatic. Americans spent $189.9 per person on beef in 1996 compared with $108.85 on pork and $125.42 on chicken. As the largest dollar volume item sold in grocery stores, beef represents more than 6 percent of all grocery store sales. Consumers tended to prefer cuts of beef over ground beef in 1980s and 1990s. In 1995, Americans consumed 38.8 pounds of beef cuts compared to 28.6 pounds of ground beef.

In the early 1990s, beef producers faced a challenge from the outbreak of a strain of the E. coli bacteria in ground beef. Ground beef is the product most affected by the bacteria because E. coli tends not penetrate the inner muscling of steaks and roast and is easily destroyed when the outside meat is heated, seared or barbecued. The safety hazard occurs when the E. coli are ground up with the hamburger, and the meat is not cooked at temperatures high enough to destroy the bacteria. The result of these outbreaks were new labeling laws on meat products that urged consumers to follow proper cooking instructions and to not eat rare hamburger. New studies on irradiation and acid rinses of beef carcasses were also implemented.

Concern for Bovine Spongiform Encephalopathy (BSE), popularized as "Mad Cow Disease," came to a head in 1995 as producers in the United Kingdom continuously found escalating numbers of afflicted cattle throughout the country. BSE is a fatal disease that affects the central nervous system of cattle. However, the United States government and the USDA have conducted studies showing that no cases of BSE existed in the United States. As a precautionary measure, the United States does not import cattle from countries with reported cases of BSE. Moreover, many scientists contend that the disease is not transmissible through an infected cow's meat or through physical contact.

POULTRY INDUSTRY

The poultry industry held a strong economic position in the mid-1990s. Increased national and international demand for chicken and chicken products fueled steady growth within the industry of about 5 percent per year since the early 1960s. In 1995, chicken producers raised about 7.33 billion birds with sales of over $11.4

billion. Total broiler production was forecasted to continue increasing, surpassing 1995's approximately 34 billion pound level of production. About 50 percent of chickens were sold directly to consumers, another 40 percent were sold to restaurants, and 10 percent went for export or pet food.

Despite a sustained drop in the price of chickens in 1994 and 1995, wholesale prices for broilers climbed to about 60 cents per pound in 1996, while broiler parts held at roughly $1.92 a pound for boneless breasts and about 96 cents for breasts with ribs on. Retail prices ranged from 98 cents a pound for fresh whole broilers to about $2.05 for bone-in breasts.

In 1996, per capita consumption of chicken stood at 72.9 pounds and was expected to continue increasing, particularly if prices remained competitive. From another perspective, however, the consumption level was somewhat less. On an edible basis (boneless) Americans only ate about 48.1 pounds of chicken. Some estimates predicted that consumption could reach 95 pounds (retail weight) per head by the year 2000. A key to the industry's future profitability will be its ability to meet this growing demand. Under current population growth assumptions, simply to satisfy the present level of demand for chickens, farmers will have to increase their output by 10 percent by the year 2000. If demand increases by just 10 percent, the industry will have to increase its productivity by 70 percent by the year 2000. Throughout the mid-1990s, chicken production increased prompted by escalating foreign and domestic demand.

PORK INDUSTRY

The National Pork Producers Council (NPPC) estimated that 764,080 jobs and $26 billion in personal income were directly and indirectly linked to the U.S. pork industry in 1995. Sales of pork earned U.S. farmers $10.5 billion, while retailers sold this pork for over $30 billion to consumers. Counting these and other sectors, from production through processing, the NPPC calculated that the hog producing industry and its satellite industries had a total economic value-added impact of more than $66 billion. Pork consumption in the United States held at 52.3 pounds in retail weight for 1995, constituting the country's third most popular meat after beef and chicken.

DAIRY INDUSTRY

In 1995, U.S. dairy farmers produced more than 154 billion pounds of marketed milk. Dairy products accounted for 60 percent of this amount. Butter production claimed 1.26 billion pounds of the total marketed milk, while cheese (excluding cottage cheese) accounted for 6.94 billion pounds. In addition, cottage cheese production claimed about 700 million pounds of the total. Other leading dairy products included ice cream, sherbet, frozen yogurt, and dry milk. Per capita consumption of fluid milk and cream was 226 pounds per person in 1994, while for cheese the level of consumption was 26.8 pounds and for ice cream it was 16.1 pounds.

The United States remains the largest producer of milk with 69.6 million metric tons in 1994; however, production of this volume required a third fewer cows than India, who also produced only about 60 million metric tons. This disparity in milk per cow stems from the ability of U.S. cows to yield 7.3 kilograms of milk per cow, while India's cows only averaged 1.9 kilograms per cow. The United States exported about 201,800 metric tons of dairy products in 1994. Industry analysts predicted that the trend of larger dairy farms with fewer cows would persist, followed by a concentration of dairy processing as well.

In 1996, the dairy industry was impacted by legislation known as the Federal Agriculture Reform and Improvement Act (FAIR). This legislation addressed a

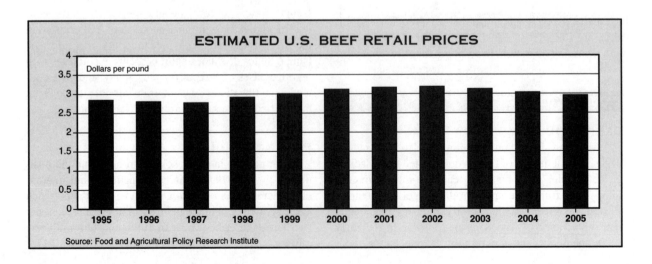

ESTIMATED U.S. BEEF RETAIL PRICES

Source: Food and Agricultural Policy Research Institute

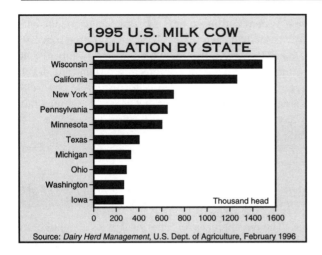

1995 U.S. MILK COW POPULATION BY STATE

Wisconsin
California
New York
Pennsylvania
Minnesota
Texas
Michigan
Ohio
Washington
Iowa

Thousand head

0   200   400   600   800   1000   1200   1400   1600

Source: *Dairy Herd Management*, U.S. Dept. of Agriculture, February 1996

number of concerns that had existed for decades about milk price regulation, price supports, and market orders. For years, critics had demanded changes in these dairy-management policies. FAIR called for the elimination of the milk price support program effective in 2000. Furthermore, the price support amount was scheduled to decrease from $10.35 to $9.90 over the period leading up to 2000. After that, the subsidy will become a recourse loan—an inventory loan from the government—for processors who have butter or cheese in storage. The government hoped this move would get rid of the floor on dairy products.

WORK FORCE

Approximately 98 percent of all American cattle producers are considered small or mid-sized (under 500 cattle) by the National Cattlemen's Association. These ranchers raise the majority of the nation's beef cattle. While the cattle feeding and meat packing industries continue to become more concentrated in the hands of fewer and larger corporations, the beef cow herds remain in the hands of small or mid-sized producers. Often cattle are run as a sideline, a hobby, or in conjunction with a farming operation. In addition, they are often used to consume what is left after crops have been harvested.

On many ranches all of this work is done by the owner or his family, but on larger ranches a crew of cowboys is employed. Typically they are given a house, a ration of beef per year, a pick-up truck, and a monthly salary that ranges from $650 to $2,000. The National Cattlemen's Association estimated that the industry produced some 186,000 full-time jobs.

Approximately 73 percent of chicken farms employed under four workers in the 1996, and over 9 percent employed between five and nine workers. About

4.5 percent of operations employed over 100 people, while 2 percent employed between 10 and 14, and 3 percent, between 20 and 49. Approximately 1 percent employed between 15 and 19 and between 50 and 99 workers. The National Pork Producers Council (NPPC) estimated that 764,080 jobs and $26 billion in personal income were directly and indirectly linked to the U.S. pork industry in 1995.

Leading Pork Producers

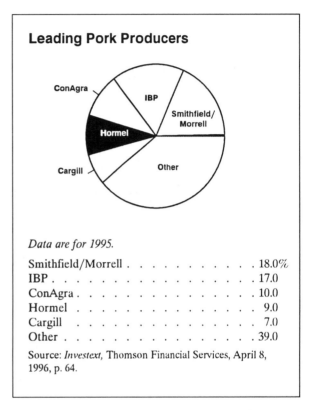

ConAgra
IBP
Smithfield/Morrell
Hormel
Cargill
Other

Data are for 1995.

Smithfield/Morrell 18.0%
IBP 17.0
ConAgra 10.0
Hormel 9.0
Cargill 7.0
Other 39.0

Source: *Investext,* Thomson Financial Services, April 8, 1996, p. 64.

Dairy farmers and workers put in long hours with few days off since the cows must be milked twice a day every day. Farmers must also keep the barns and pens cleared out, clean milking equipment, and keep track of each cow's food consumption and milk production. Most dairy farmers also plant crops to provide feed for their cattle in the winter. Many smaller dairy farms have been in the same family for a few generations, and very few new family farms have been started in recent years because the costs of land, equipment, and a dairy herd are prohibitive. But the increase in larger dairies is changing the landscape of dairy-related employment. On Braum's Dairy Farm in Oklahoma, for example, employees earn $8 to $9 per hour, working in six-day intervals punctuated by two days off. The dairy also provides benefits and a savings plan. However, such wages and amenities are not feasible for smaller farms.

RESEARCH AND TECHNOLOGY

Cattle numbers in the 1990s stood at around 100 million head, yet the industry was producing as much beef as it did in the 1970s when its cattle inventory numbered 120 million head. Such efficiency was made possible by the use of scientific technology, new breeds, computerization, and increased mechanization. Output per man hour in agriculture increased twice as fast as that in manufacturing industries. American beef cattle producers were producing nearly 25 percent of the world's beef supply with just 10 percent of the world's cattle population.

These advances in productivity were largely due to the introduction of new genetics and the rapid acceptance of breed improvement programs. As recently as the 1970s, ten pounds of grass or feed were required to put on one pound of beef; however, modern day cattle could put on the same weight with as little as six pounds of grass or feed. Many cattle are gaining up to five pounds per day in the feedlot and are reaching marketable weights in half the time of their predecessors.

Leading Cattle Producers

Market shares for feed cattle production are shown in percent for 1995.

IBP	35.0%
ConAgra	21.0
Cargill	20.0
Other	24.0

Source: *Investext,* Thomson Financial Services, April 8, 1996, p. 64.

Many dairy farms have joined the computer age, enabling farmers to keep track of food consumption and milk production to better manage their herds and their finances. Computerized systems also allowed farmers to design better feeding programs for their herds. Computer controlled trolley systems allowed some dairy farmers to deliver just the right food mix to each individual cow, based on the cow's current milk production, age, weight, overall health and its stage in the lactation cycle. A personal computer in the farmer's home is linked with a programmable controller in the barn. Boards in the controller correspond with the various mechanical hardware in the barn. The correct amount of feed, with the correct ratios of forage (corn and hay), grain, soybean meal, and minerals, is measured out for each cow. This computer-ized system can make any necessary adjustments, as a cow's needs change daily based on its milk-producing cycle. The system then delivers the custom-mixed feed to the appropriate cow. Before this system was developed, farmers had no easy way to custom-design a diet for each cow and deliver that diet as much as three times a day. Computers also allow farmers to keep track of milk production.

AMERICA AND THE WORLD

Though there have been difficulties in marketing beef during the 1980s and 1990s, there have also been some stunning success stories. The most economically significant success for the industry has been the increased international demand for American beef. The United States produced 24.9 percent of the world's beef supply in 1994, with exports representing 9 percent of the value of all U.S. beef production. From 1980 to 1990, there was a four-fold increase from $493 million to $2.145 billion in beef sales. It is estimated that between 10 percent and 12 percent of the value of every steer produced domestically comes from the added demand created by the export market. Consequently, the National Cattlemen's Association was very much in favor of the North American Free Trade Agreement (NAFTA) due to the fact that Mexico proved to be a lucrative market for American beef.

Much of the export success story was a direct result of lowered tariffs on American beef in Japan. Japanese consumers have shown a marked preference for American grain fed beef over grass fed beef from Australia and other beef exporting nations. When tariffs were lowered, exports of beef to Japan increased 167 percent from 1985 to 1992. By 1996, 25 percent of the beef consumed in Japan came from the United States. Exports are also increasing to Canada, South Korea, Mexico, Taiwan and many other countries around the world. In all, the United States exported $5.4 billion worth of beef in 1995.

Similar to the beef industry, the poultry sector has enjoyed enormous success abroad, exporting chicken to important markets in western Europe, the Caribbean, Mexico, and the Pacific Rim. Demand for U.S. chicken has also increased in Russia and Former Soviet Union countries. The USDA estimated that Russia imported more than 4.6 billion pounds of broilers in 1996, and imports of U.S. broilers were predicted to continue rising. Because of Hong Kong's reversion to Chinese rule, its imports of U.S. chicken have been somewhat uncertain, though still strong. China drastically increased its imports of U.S. chicken, making it one of the largest customers in 1996. South Africa also imported 50 percent more U.S. chicken in 1996 than in 1995. In addition, exports to Mexico, Canada, and Japan rose significantly in 1996, and are expected to remain high through the end of the decade. Soaring to record highs in all sectors, total poultry exports amounted to 5.4 million pounds with a value of $2.5 billion.

The top customers for U.S. pork exports in the mid-1990s were: Japan (131,700 metric tons), Russia (46,786 metric tons) Mexico (20,902 metric tons), Canada (17,528 metric tons), and South Korea (12,035 metric tons). The National Pork Producers Council (NPPC) attributed 1996's $1 billion in U.S. pork exports in part to the implementation of the General Tariffs and Trade Agreement (GATT) and to the North American Free Trade Agreement (NAFTA).

ASSOCIATIONS AND SOCIETIES

AMERICAN SOCIETY OF ANIMAL SCIENCE
c/o Carl D. Johnson
309 W. Clark St.
Champaign, IL 61820-4690
Phone: (217) 356-3182
Fax: (217) 398-4119

INTERSTATE PRODUCERS LIVESTOCK ASSOCIATION
1705 W. Luthy Dr.
Peoria, IL 61615
Phone: (309) 691-5360

LIVESTOCK MARKETING ASSOCIATION
7509 Tiffany Springs Pky.
Kansas City, MO 64153-2315
Phone: (800) 821-2048 or (816) 891-0502

NATIONAL CATTLEMEN'S ASSOCIATION
PO Box 3469
Englewood, CO 80155
Phone: (303) 694-0305
Fax: (303) 694-2851

NATIONAL LIVE STOCK PRODUCERS ASSOCIATION
4851 Independence St., No. 200
Wheatridge, CO 80033
Phone: (303) 423-4792

TEXAS LONGHORN BREEDERS ASSOCIATION OF AMERICA
2315 N. Main St., Ste. 402
Fort Worth, TX 76106
Phone: (817) 625-6241
Fax: (817) 625-1388

PERIODICALS AND NEWSLETTERS

BEEF
Intertec Publishing Co.
Webb Div.
7900 International Dr., Ste. 300
Minneapolis, MN 55425
Phone: (612) 851-4710
Fax: (612) 851-4601
13 times a year. $25.00 per year.

CATTLEMAN
Texas and Southwestern Cattle Raisers Association, Inc.
1301 W. 7th Ave.
Fort Worth, TX 76102
Phone: (817) 332-7155
Monthly. $25.00 per year.

DOANE'S AGRICULTURAL REPORT
Doane Information Services
11701 Borman Dr.
Saint Louis, MO 63146
Phone: (314) 569-2700
Fax: (314) 569-1083
Weekly. $88.00 per year. Newsletter. Covers farm marketing and management.

JOURNAL OF ANIMAL SCIENCE
American Society of Animal Science
309 W. Clark St.
Champaign, IL 61820-4690
Phone: (217) 356-3182
Fax: (217) 398-4119
Monthly. Institutions, $160.00 per year.

LARGE ANIMAL VETERINARIAN: COVERING HEALTH AND NUTRITION
Watt Publishing Co.
122 S. Wesley Ave.
Mt. Morris, IL 61054-1497
Phone: (815) 734-4171
Fax: (815) 734-4201
Bimonthly. $36.00 per year. Services the large animal veterinary (food animal) field. Formerly Animal Nutrition and Health.

LIVESTOCK MARKET DIGEST
Livestock Market Digest, Inc.
PO Box 7458
Albuquerque, NM 87194
Phone: (816) 531-2235
Weekly. $20.00 per year.

LIVESTOCK PRODUCTION SCIENCE
Elsevier Science Publishing Co., Inc.
Madison Square Sta., PO Box 882
New York, NY 10159
Phone: (212) 989-5800
Fax: (212) 633-3900
Monthly. $662.00.

LIVESTOCK WEEKLY
Southwest Publishing, Inc.
PO Box 3306
San Angelo, TX 76902
Phone: (915) 949-4611
Fax: (915) 949-4614
Weekly. $25.00 per year.

DATABASES

AGRICULTURE VIRTUAL LIBRARY
North Carolina State University, National Integrated Pest
Management Network
*Contains documents, collections, directories, and information
about organizations related to agronomy, animal husbandry,
fisheries, forestry, horticulture, industrial applications, range
management, veterinary medicine, and wildlife management.
Includes mirror sites for European users. Time span: Current
information. Updating frequency: As needed. Fees: Free. URL:
http://ipm_www.ncsu.edu/cernag/cern.html*

CAB ABSTRACTS
CAB International North America
845 N. Park Ave.
Tucson, AZ 85719
Phone: (800) 528-4841 or (602) 621-7897
Fax: (602) 621-3816
*Contains 46 specialized abstract collections covering over
10,000 journals and monographs in the areas of agriculture,
horticulture, forest products, farm products, nutrition, dairy science, poultry, grains, animal health, entomology, etc. Time period is 1972 to date, with monthly updates. Inquire as to online
cost and availability. CAB Abstracts on CD-ROM also available, with annual updating.*

CITIBASE (CITICORP ECONOMIC DATABASE)
FAME Software Corp.
77 Water St., 9 Fl.
New York, NY 10005
Phone: (212) 898-7800
Fax: (212) 742-8956
*Presents over 6,000 statistical series relating to business, indus-
try, finance, and economics. Includes series from* Survey of
Current Business *and many other sources. Time period is 1947
to date, with daily updates. Inquire as to online cost and avail-
ability.*

WILSONLINE: BIOLOGICAL AND AGRICULTURAL INDEX
H. W. Wilson Co.
950 University Ave.
Bronx, NY 10452
Phone: (800) 367-6770 or (718) 588-8400
Fax: (718) 590-1617
*Indexes a wide variety of agricultural and biological periodi-
cals, 1983 to date. Weekly updates. Inquire as to online cost and
availability.*

STATISTICS SOURCES

AGRICULTURAL STATISTICS
Available from U.S. Government Printing Office
Washington, DC 20402
Phone: (202) 512-1800
Fax: (202) 512-2250
*Annual. $21.00. Produced by the National Agricultural Statis-
tics Service, U.S. Department of Agriculture. Provides a wide
variety of statistical data relating to agricultural production,
supplies, consumption, prices/price-supports, foreign trade,
costs, and returns, as well as farm labor, loans, income, and
population. In many cases, historical data is shown annually for
10 years. In addition to farm data, includes detailed fishery
statistics.*

BUSINESS STATISTICS
Available from U.S. Government Printing Office
Washington, DC 20402
Phone: (202) 512-1800
Fax: (202) 512-2250
*Biennial. $20.00. Issued by Bureau of Economic Analysis, U.S.
Department of Commerce. Shows annual data for 29 years and
monthly data for a recent four-year period. Statistics correspond
to the* Survey of Current Business.

LIVESTOCK AND POULTRY SITUATION AND OUTLOOK
Available from U.S. Government Printing Office
Washington, DC 20402
Phone: (202) 512-1800
Fax: (202) 512-2250
*Bimonthly. $16.00 per year. Issued by the Economic Research
Service of the U.S. Department of Agriculture. Provides current
statistical information on supply, demand, and prices.*

LIVESTOCK, MEAT, WOOL, MARKET NEWS
U.S. Dept. of Agriculture
Washington, DC 20250
Phone: (202) 720-2791
Weekly.

LIVESTOCK SLAUGHTER
Available from U.S. Government Printing Office
Washington, DC 20402
Phone: (202) 512-1800
Fax: (202) 512-2250
*Monthly. $35.00 per year. Issued by the Agricultural Statistics
Board, U.S. Department of Agriculture. Provides data on cur-
rent production and market trends, with statistical tables.*

GENERAL WORKS

ANIMAL HEALTH YEARBOOK
Food and Agriculture Organization of the United Nations
Available from UNIPUB
4611-F Assembly Dr.
Lanham, MD 20706-4391
Phone: (800) 274-4447 or (301) 459-7666
Fax: (301) 459-0056
Annual. $60.00.

FURTHER READING

Cattle and Beef Handbook, Englewood, CO: National Cattlemen's Association, 1996. Available from: http://www.cowtown.org/library/nca4700.html

"Cowculations." Englewood, CO: National Cattlemen's Association, 1996. Available from http://www.cowtown.org/library/nca4400.html

The Facts Machine, Englewood, CO: National Cattlemen's Association, 1997. Available from http://www.cowtown.org/library/nca4300.html

Freese, Betsy. "Pork Powerhouses." Agriculture Online. Successful Farming, 1996. Available from http://www.agriculture.com/contents/sf/porkpwr/pp.html

Looker, Dan. "The Milk Meisters." *Agriculture Online.* June 1996. Available from http://www.agriculture.com/

National Technical Information Service. "USDA Modernizes 90-year Old System of Meat inspection Final Rule." Springfield, IL: November 1996.

Pork Facts, 1996-1997. Des Moines, IA: National Pork Producers Council (NPPC), 1996.

U.S. Department of Agriculture. "Layers and Egg Production." Washington, D.C.: 31 January 1997. Available from http://usda.mannlib.cornell.edu/reports/nassr/poultry/pec-bbl/layers_and_egg_production_annual_01.31.97.

———. *Poultry Outlook.* Washington, D.C.: 18 November 1996. Available from: http://usda.mannlib.cornell.edu/reports/erssor/livestock/ldp-pbb/1996/poultry_outlook_11.18.96

AIR TRANSPOR-TATION, PASSENGER

SICs 4512, 4522

Recent statistics projected to the year 2000 indicate that enplanements on major carriers will reach 573 million annually. The Federal Aviation Association (FAA) has also predicted that aircraft fleet will total nearly 6,000 jets and that the industry will reach 8.2 million departures annually. Mergers are a likelihood for major airlines who want to maximize profits and cut costs during this period of growth; however, any potential consolidation will meet resistance from industry unions and anti-trust regulations.

The passenger air transportation industry has provided air travel to both domestic and international destinations. What once began as a mode of transport for the U.S. mail has become a multi-billion dollar industry. According to a 1997 *Fortune* magazine article, total revenues for the 10 largest U.S. airlines reached $81.2 billion and total profits reached $2.8 billion. Passenger air travel has continued to dominate all other modes of transportation in the commercial inter-city market. In fact, air travel has become so commonplace that, according to an Air Transport Association (ATA) Gallup poll, nearly 75 percent of all Americans have flown on a commercial airliner at least once.

From the third quarter of 1995 through the second quarter of 1996, revenue passenger miles were approximately $399.8 billion in domestic scheduled passenger service, as estimated by the U.S. Bureau of Transportation Statistics. A revenue passenger mile represents one fare-paying passenger transported one mile. Airline industry revenue continues to account for approximately one percent of the nation's gross domestic product.

The leading airport entering the mid-1990s in terms of volume was Chicago O'Hare Airport, with approximately 70 million passengers transported in 1996. Atlanta Hartsfield International transported approximately 63 million passengers, Los Angeles International Airport transported 58 million passengers, and Dallas/Fort Worth International transported 55 million passengers in 1996. Total revenue passenger enplanements—the total number of revenue passengers boarding aircraft—has reached more than 554 million annually. The load factor (the percentage of seating that is utilized) increased to 68 percent in the second quarter of 1996, up from 67 percent a year earlier. The average domestic trip length in the mid-1990s was 855 miles.

Three carriers have historically dominated the industry. American Airlines, United, and Delta have become the most well-known domestic carriers and, in total, have captured more than 50 percent of the market share. These carriers and others have experienced significant financial improvements since the early 1990s, for economic conditions in the United States and operating costs in the industry have all improved. Of the ten leading U.S. airlines, only one—Southwest—posted a profit in 1992. American, United, and Delta combined lost approximately $2.5 billion that year, despite revenues of more than $37 billion. However, the industry in three year's time turned around to the point that American, United, and Delta made approximately $46.6 billion in revenues and $1.6 billion in net profits in 1996.

Top 10 MOST POPULAR AIRLINES

Ranked by: Revenue in 1995, in thousands of dollars.

1. American Airlines, with $15,501,000 thousand
2. United Airlines, $14,943,000
3. Delta Air Lines, $12,194,000
4. Northwest Airlines, $9,080,000
5. USAir, $7,474,000
6. Continental Airlines, $5,825,000
7. TWA, $3,320,000
8. Southwest, $2,872,751
9. America West Airlines, $1,600,000
10. Alaska, $1,417,500

Source: *Business Travel News*, Business Travel Survey (annual), May 27, 1996, p. 32.

According to *Ward's Business Directory of U.S. Private and Public Companies 1996,* the U.S. nonscheduled air transportation industry was made up of at least 112 companies that generated $2.68 billion in revenue, employing 13,600 workers. This nonscheduled segment of the air transportation industry included all companies that provided charter service, airlines carrying passengers and/or cargo, and helicopter services. One major characteristic of the nonscheduled industry was that companies operated on the basis of full plane sales. Using this procedure, the total aircraft capacity was sold to an organization, such as a ticket wholesaler. In general, these wholesalers were tour operators, military and governmental agencies, specialty charter customers, and sponsors of incentive travel packages. Most charter carriers, either passenger or cargo, were small operations working within a niche market. According to the U.S. Department of Transportation (DOT), for the 12-month period ending June 1996, total charter flights by all U.S. airlines represented approximately 2.9 percent of all available seat miles (ASMs) flown within the United States.

INDUSTRY OUTLOOK

The passenger air transportation industry has made an unprecedented turnaround in profitability, traffic, and price stability. The industry had flourished from the late 1950s through the early 1970s, as U.S. airline passenger traffic grew at 13 percent a year. By the early 1990s, however, the industry had been hit hard by the Gulf War, rising fuel prices and other operating costs, fare wars, rising debt service costs, and the slowdown of the American economy. On average, the industry's annual growth in traffic was less than one percent from 1987 through

1992, and even this dismal rate was achieved by selling seats below cost. "In short, there has been little or no true growth in revenue passenger miles since 1986 . . ." reported *Forbes* in 1993. However, *Valueline* reported in its March 1997 outlook that industry revenues reached $69.9 billion with an average load factor of 65 percent and net profits of $2.7 billion in 1996. Net profit margins reached 3.9 percent in 1996, and net worth increased to $12.6 billion.

Business and vacation travel were strong in 1995 and 1996, causing a turnaround in capacity, for unlike the mid- to late 1980s, it grew more slowly than traffic, as some airlines eliminated routes, disposed of aircraft, and slowly grew their fleets. In 1996, the available seat miles in the United States grew slowly by 3.5 percent, positively affecting the load factor, or the percentage of seats sold. Most importantly, unit costs, excluding fuel, rose less than inflation in 1996.

Consolidation in the industry was forecast to pick up again. In late 1996, American and British Airways, Continental and Delta, and USAir and United toyed with the idea of joining forces. None of these happened in 1996, but Wall Street sources indicate it is likely that attempts will be made again. On the other hand, pilots, unions, and government anti-trust sentiments hamper these merger prospects.

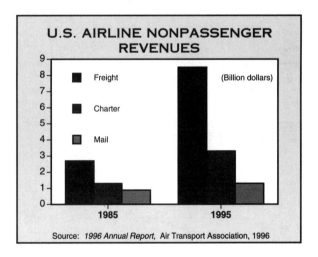

U.S. AIRLINE NONPASSENGER REVENUES

- Freight
- Charter
- Mail

(Billion dollars)

1985   1995

Source: *1996 Annual Report,* Air Transport Association, 1996

Successful nationals provided service to a niche market, did not interfere with the majors, and operated from airports with minimal competition. Examples included Southwest Airlines at Dallas Love Field, Midway Airlines at Midway Airport in Chicago, and America West in Phoenix. Alaska Airlines has remained the only large, successful national airline in operation, with more than 50 percent market share of the Pacific Northwest/Alaska market.

Regional airlines have continued to flourish for two reasons. First, in an effort to cut costs, the majors have "handed over" to affiliated regional airline routes that were not profitable for them. Customers were attracted to fly on the regional line with the enticement of gaining frequent flyer miles. With this arrangement, the major airline maintained its name recognition without having to run an unprofitable route.

The majors' withdrawal of jet service to certain markets also presented opportunities for non-affiliated regional airlines. Defying negative trends, several small airlines such as Reno Air Inc., Skybus Corp., and Kiwi International Air Lines Inc. started operations during the early 1990s. Tapping into the glut of planes and unemployed workers created by the industry shake-out of the late 1980s, 17 airlines had applied to become certified for chartered service by the end of 1991.

During the early 1990s, carriers put forth a serious effort to control operating costs by cutting personnel, reducing salaries, trimming flight schedules, and retiring older aircraft. The industry benefited from 1994 through 1996 as the capacity glut diminished.

Overall, traffic on U.S. airlines was estimated to increase 4.7 percent annually from 1993 to 2002. This continual industry growth is based on assumptions of higher load factors, larger seating capacities on aircraft, and longer passenger trip lengths. Figures projected to the year 2000 have suggested enplanements on major carriers will reach 573 million annually. The FAA has also predicted that aircraft fleet will total nearly 6,000 jets and that the industry will reach 8.2 million departures annually.

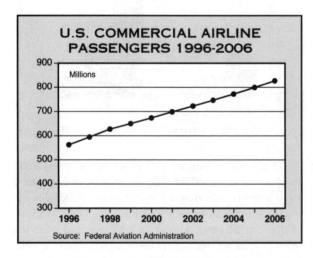

U.S. COMMERCIAL AIRLINE PASSENGERS 1996-2006

Millions

Source: Federal Aviation Administration

This growth is dependent to some extent on the continued globalization of the airline industry. Presidents of some of the world's largest airlines have agreed that the industry has been headed toward greater consolidation with fewer, but larger, carriers. Some potential alliances have included British Airways and US Air, Continental and Air Canada, Northwest and KLM, Australia and Quantas, and the acquisition of a major interest in Sabena and CSA by Air France.

Thus far, advances in communications technology have benefited the airline industry in nearly every aspect of operations, and the technological advancements in global communications has not lessened the need for air travel. Information that travels via fax or modem already has become commonplace, and teleconferencing has not replaced air travel.

At the beginning of 1996, profits and traffic in the airline industry were affected by the expiration and reinstatement of a 10 percent federal excise tax on domestic airline tickets. Congress let the tax expire at the end of 1995, but reinstated it on August 17, 1996. The airlines lowered prices during this time and traffic increased—as did profits. However, the tax expired again at the end of 1996, and was reinstated in March 1997. This time, most airlines (except Southwest) raised prices after the reinstatement. Wall Street analysts are betting that strong airline traffic and lower fuel costs will have a more positive effect on the industry, despite the reinstatement of the federal excise tax and any threat of future price wars.

CHARTER AIRLINES

Charter airlines have struggled to improve their image with the flying public. When the largest charter carrier, American Trans Air (ATA), began operations in 1973, the industry had a reputation for "rusty planes, lousy in-flight service and long delays," said George Mikelsons, chairman of Amtran, the parent company of ATA, in *Travel Weekly*. "It has been a very slow process to get people comfortable with the fact that you can buy a charter flight that is at least the equal of coach class on a good scheduled carrier."

The charter industry continued to face stiff competition from the major scheduled carriers in the mid-1990s. As the major airlines reorganized, some industry leaders predicted a three-tier system of scheduled operations, with the third level being packaged tours, reported Howard Banks in *Forbes*. Yet John Tague, senior vice president of sales and marketing for ATA, defended the charter industry, claiming that the charters can become a viable alternative for leisure travel in the United States. "Charters are a more economic product because we sell on the basis that the customer will use 80 to 100 percent of the product," he commented in Travel Weekly, contending further that scheduled airlines cannot do the same.

WORK FORCE

Following deregulation in 1978, employment in the airline industry increased from 340,000 jobs to more than 530,000 jobs in the early 1990s. In 1997, total employment by the 10 major carriers was 450,753 workers. James Landry, president of ATA, stated in a 1993 editorial in the *Dallas Morning News* that ''Despite...layoffs and salary cuts, airline employees remain one of the best paid work forces in the United States, with the average wage and compensation package exceeding $51,000 per year, nearly twice the national average.'' A popular way to reduce wages in 1995 and 1996 was the use of employee stock payments. TWA, United, Northwest, and Southwest all reached agreements with their labor unions to exchange equity for wage increases.

Deregulation, though, also created differences between the airlines and various unions, which at the end of the 1970s filled 90 percent of all industry jobs. New airlines were able to operate with much lower labor costs than established outfits, and the industry giants soon decided that they had to reduce their labor costs in order to compete. While at some airlines unions and management were able to reach agreements (equity for wage concessions, etc.), other companies resorted to measures that brought turmoil across the industry. Braniff Airlines and Continental Airlines both utilized Chapter 11 bankruptcy regulations in the early 1980s to nullify existing labor contracts. Chapter 11 regulations enabled the companies to return to business without union employees if they so desired. In Continental's case, they fired their employees after filing for bankruptcy, then re-hired them as non-union employees at wages that were in some cases more than 50 percent lower than prior to Chapter This maneuvering galvanized unions across the industry, spurring them to protect themselves legally.

With the exception of American Airlines, company relationships with labor unions significantly improved in 1995 and 1996 from earlier years. Management of major carriers such as United Airlines and American Airlines demanded concessions from unions to cut costs, while unions dug in their heels; but both airlines resolved the issues, United with an employee buyout and American with the flight attendants—but only after a costly strike. Northwest Airlines was able to reach an agreement with labor in July 1993 with wage reductions and other concessions in exchange for 30 percent of the airline's preferred stock and an increased voice in operations. United's successful employee stock ownership plan (ESOP) was touted as a model of employer-employee relationships by the Clinton administration, and other carriers with higher labor costs may try similar employee buyouts to solve the problem of high labor costs.

Future trends in hiring airline industry employees will always be contingent on the strength and pace of the industry's economic outlook. While airlines are making good money, job security will probably always be tenuous, especially at the less-profitable carriers. The prospect of future airline mergers may also have a negative effect on industry employment. The emergence of new regional airlines has provided some opportunity for employment, but wages have been lower than the industry standard due to the large number of experienced unemployed airline workers. Computer-related jobs, such as systems analysts and reservations and keyboard operators will continue to be in demand as companies become increasingly automated.

RESEARCH AND TECHNOLOGY

From improved reservations computer systems to high-tech amenities for business travelers to advances in aircraft design, computer software technology is expected to have a tremendous impact on the future of the airline industry.

High-tech amenities for the business traveler may be the next battleground for customer service among the major domestic carriers. Satellite-based telephone systems capable of handling calls to and from anywhere in the world have been placed on board planes, and in-flight faxes, computer, and data transmission services are commonplace.

The most significant advances in communications technology continue to be in the design, development, and operation of the airplane itself. ''Satellite-guided landings have marked more addition to the panoply of technologies that allow airplanes virtually to fly themselves. Hands-off piloting, navigation, and landing of aircraft have become a routine part of civil aviation,'' reported *Scientific American* in 1991.

Computer technology will continue to refine the cockpit. By 1980, instrumentation and control systems had created the autopilot and ''blind flying'' instruments, which allowed a plane to fly straight and level even if the pilots removed their hands from the controls. By 1988, aircraft automation took a further step with the introduction of the Airbus A320. The flight control computers on board actually told the pilot how to fly the plane and could prevent the pilot from exceeding the aircraft's structural limitations.

Modern aircraft have become so automated that some pilots and even some aircraft manufacturers have grown concerned about excessive reliance on the automated systems. New training programs have been established to combat this fear of over-reliance. Although advances in technology will continue to assist in the creation of safer and more fuel-efficient planes, the captain of a plane cannot be eliminated or automated out of the cockpit.

Additionally, according to an Airports Council International survey, "The new generation of large aircraft currently on the drawing boards of aircraft manufacturers could reduce airport capacity and have considerable cost implications for the world's airports." Approximately $105 million in infrastructure modifications may be needed to accommodate these new planes. The 600-plus passenger aircraft lower the unit operating costs and increase capacity for the airlines, but the modifications to runways, taxiways, and aprons could cost an average of $62 million per airport. Changes to passenger terminals and operational facilities could add another $43 million in costs.

AMERICA AND THE WORLD

The U.S. Department of Transportation's Office of International Aviation reported that 48.7 million passengers traveled by air between the United States and the rest of the world during the first half of 1995. This was a 6 percent increase in passenger traffic compared to the first half of 1994. In June 1995, approximately 9.3 million passengers traveled by air in U.S. international markets, which was about 7 percent greater than the same period in 1994. In the first half of 1995, New York, Miami, Los Angeles, Chicago, and Honolulu were the top five U.S. international gateways. Miami recorded an 11 percent increase, with 674,000 passengers. The greatest passenger loss was felt in Boston, where a drop of 6 percent, or 88,000 passengers, occurred in the first half of 1995. The top five country markets for U.S. international travel were Canada, Japan, the United Kingdom, Mexico, and Germany.

More than 1.25 billion passengers per year rely on the world's airlines for business and vacation travel. The world's airline industry transports approximately a quarter of the manufactured exports by value. In the early 1900s, approximately 22 million jobs were in the world airline industry, producing approximately $1 trillion in annual gross output.

Between 1994 and 2010, passenger and freight traffic were expected to increase at an average annual rate of 5 to 6 percent, which is significantly greater than the growth in global GDP. Estimates are that by the year 2005, there could be in excess of 2.5 billion air travelers per year. By the year 2010, the world airline industry

could exceed $1.7 trillion with over 30 million jobs provided.

Growth in international travel will be contingent on the successful application of Open Skies legislation and other agreements with foreign governments and carriers. Open Skies agreements have offered airlines from foreign countries almost unlimited access to the U.S. market and freedom to set prices. The first-ever Open Skies aviation agreement was signed on September 4, 1992, between the United States and the Netherlands. The agreement allowed the integration of the operations of KLM Royal Dutch Airlines, the Netherlands flag carrier, and Northwest Airlines, in which KLM would own a major interest.

The European Community (EC) has been working on its own version of Open Skies deregulation. The initial resolution, effective January 1993, abolished the web of government-to-government agreements, which allocated routes within the EC and fixed fares. The 12 EC community nations and their 7 partners in the European Free Trade Area (EFTA) have been trying to create a common market within Europe and to develop a cohesive group in order to gain access in the U.S. market.

The impact that the EC liberation policy will have on U.S. carriers has yet to be determined. But as *Air Transport World* noted, "Whether they view competition from U.S. carriers as threat or potential opportunity, all are adamant that Washington open up the U.S. market before Europe makes a move. And none appear to feel particularly hampered by having to continue bilateral negotiations with the U.S., for lack of a united position."

Charter airline service in Europe, as opposed to that in the United States, offers significant competition to the scheduled airline industry for passenger traffic to leisure destinations. In fact, charter airlines have traditionally carried slightly more than half of all European travelers. The charter industry's success has been due in part to the fact that charter carriers have been subject to fewer regulations than the scheduled airlines. Thus the European market has been of interest to American charter companies like ATA simply because charter services are well known and well liked throughout Europe. But this situation was changing rapidly in the early 1990s.

In January 1993, the European version of Open Skies legislation was enacted, removing government restrictions on air fares and on cabotage throughout the European Community member countries. This program has allowed airlines to set fares at any level. By April 1997, carriers also were able to offer services on domestic routes in other member states. Such legislation was expected to have the same effect on the European charter industry that deregulation had on the U.S. charter industry. Industry leaders predicted that the charter carriers will lose market share as the scheduled airlines become free of capacity and price restraints, thus reducing possibilities for American firms to expand into European markets.

ASSOCIATIONS AND SOCIETIES

AIR TRANSPORT ASSOCIATION OF AMERICA
1301 Pennsylvania Ave., Ste.
1100 Washington, DC 20004-7017
Phone: (202) 626-4000
Fax: (202) 626-4166

AMERICAN ASSOCIATION OF AIRPORT EXECUTIVES
4212 King St.
Alexandria, VA 22302
Phone: (703) 824-0500
Fax: (703) 820-1395

NATIONAL AIR CARRIER ASSOCIATION
1730 M St. NW, Ste. 806
Washington, DC 20036
Phone: (202) 833-8200
Charter Airlines.

NATIONAL AIR TRANSPORTATION ASSOCIATION
4226 King St.
Alexandria, VA 22302
Phone: (703) 845-9000
Fax: (703) 845-8176

PERIODICALS AND NEWSLETTERS

AIR TRANSPORT WORLD
Penton Publishing, Inc.
600 Summer St.
Stamford, CT 06904
Phone: (203) 348-7531
Fax: (203) 4023
Monthly. $50.00 per year.

AIRPORT BUSINESS
Johnson Hill Press
PO Box 803
Fort Atkinson, WI 53538-0803
Phone: (800) 547-7377 or (414) 563-6388
Fax: (414) 563-1702
Bimonthly. $40.00 per year.

AIRPORT PRESS
P.A.T.I.
15 Lakeside Dr.
Katonah, NY 10536
Phone: (718) 244-6788
Fax: (718) 995-3432
Monthly. $32.00 per year.

AVIATION DAILY
McGraw-Hill, Inc.
Information Services
1156 15th St. NW, Ste. 600
Washington, DC 20005
Phone: (202) 822-4600
Fax: (202) 293-2682
Daily. $1,275.00 per year. Newsletter. Covers current developments in air transportation and aviation manufacturing.

BUSINESS TRAVEL NEWS
CMP Publications, Inc.
600 Community Dr.
Manhasset, NY 11030
Phone: (516) 562-5000
Fax: (516) 365-4601
36 times a year. $40.00 per year.

DATABASES

ABI/INFORM
UMI/Data Courier
620 S. 3rd St.
Louisville, KY 40202
Phone: (800) 626-2823 or (502) 583-4111
Fax: (502) 589-5572
Provides online indexing to business-related material occurring in over 800 periodicals from 1971 to the present. Inquire as to online cost and availability.

MANAGEMENT CONTENTS
Information Access Co.
362 Lakeside Dr.
Foster City, CA 94404
Phone: (800) 227-8431 or (415) 378-5000
Fax: (415) 358-4759
Covers a wide range of management, financial, marketing, personnel, and administrative topics. About 140 leading business journals are indexed and abstracted from 1974 to date, with monthly updating. Inquire as to online cost and availability.

NEWSNET
NewsNet, Inc.
945 Haverford Rd.
Bryn Mawr, PA 19010
Phone: (800) 345-1301 or (215) 527-8030
Fax: (215) 527-0338

NEXIS SERVICE
LEXIS-NEXIS
PO Box 933
Dayton, OH 45401
Phone: (800) 543-6862 or (513) 865-6800
Fax: (513) 865-6909
Makes available the full text of a wide variety of periodicals and some major newspapers, including the New York Times.

TRADE & INDUSTRY INDEX
Information Access Co.
362 Lakeside Dr.
Foster City, CA 94404
Phone: (800) 227-8431 or (415) 378-5000
Fax: (415) 358-4759

Provides indexing of business periodicals, January 1981 to date. Daily updates. (Full text articles from some periodicals are available online, 1983 to date, in the companion database, Trade & Industry ASAP.) Inquire as to online cost and availability.

STATISTICS SOURCES

AIR CARRIER FINANCIAL STATISTICS QUARTERLY
U.S. Dept. of Transportation
John A. Volpe
National Transportation Systems Center
Center for Transportation Information
Kendall Sq.
Cambridge, MA 02142
Phone: (617) 494-2450
Fax: (617) 494-2497
Quarterly. Contains profit and loss and asset information for specific airlines.

AIR CARRIER TRAFFIC STATISTICS MONTHLY
U.S. Dept. of Transportation
John A. Volpe
National Transportation Systems Center
Center for Transportation Information
Kendall Sq. Cambridge, MA 02142
Phone: (617) 494-2450
Fax: (617) 494-2497
Monthly. Provides passenger traffic data for large airlines.

AIRPORT ACTIVITY STATISTICS OF CERTIFICATED ROUTE AIR CARRIERS
U.S. Department of Transportation
Available from U.S. Government Printing Office
Washington, DC 20402
Phone: (202) 783-3238
Annual.

FAA AVIATION FORECASTS
Federal Aviation Administration
Available from U.S. Government Printing Office
Washington, DC 20402

Phone: (202) 512-1800
Fax: (202) 512-2250
Annual. $15.00.

FAA STATISTICAL HANDBOOK OF AVIATION
Federal Aviation Administration
Available from U.S. Government Printing Office
Washington, DC 20402
Phone: (202) 512-1800
Fax: (202) 512-2250
Annual. $11.00.

NATIONAL TRANSPORTATION STATISTICS
Available from U.S. Government Printing Office
Washington, DC 20402
Phone: (202) 783-3238
Annual. $17.00. Issued by Bureau of Transportation Statistics, U.S. Department of Transportation. Provides data on operating revenues, expenses, employees, passenger miles (where applicable), and other factors for airlines, automobiles, buses, local transit, pipelines, railroads, ships, and trucks.

FURTHER READING

The Air Charter Journal. March 1996. Available from http://www.guides.com/acg/nlmar96.htm.

''Air Transport Industry.'' *Valueline,* March 1997.

Airports Council International. ''The Economic Benefits of Air Transport.'' May 1997.

Bureau of Transportation Statistics May 1997. Available from http//www.bts.gov/oai/indicators/top.html.

U.S. Department of Transportation. *Federal Aviation Administration Forecasts, Fiscal Years 1991-2002.* Washington, GPO.

Ward's Business Directory of U.S. Public and Private Companies 1997. Detroit: Gale Research, 1997.

Woods, Lynn. ''Pay Now, Fly Later: Just Make Sure You're Not Left High and Dry.'' *Kiplinger's Personal Finance Magazine,* March 1997. ◄►

The aerospace industry consists of space vehicles, space propulsion parts, guided missiles, aircraft, aircraft engines, and aircraft parts. The total value of all products and services for the aerospace industry was $101.5 billion in 1995, estimated to be $112 billion in 1996, and projected to become $125 billion in 1997. The value of all products and services of the aircraft industry alone is nearly one-half that of the aerospace industry total. The production and sale of aircraft further constitutes about 50 percent of the total aircraft industry's value.

According to the International Trade Administration (ITA), the total value of all products and services in the aircraft industry was estimated to be $48.5 billion in 1995, down slightly from the previous year, representing 49 percent of shipments for the total aerospace industry.

AIRCRAFT

SIC 3721

Aircraft *manufacturing has historically been one of the most consistently profitable and successful of American industries, and by all indications this trend is likely to continue. The growth of the commercial market over the military market, increased foreign competition, and continuing mergers and acquisitions are some of the major factors that will drive the industry during the next few years.*

Top 5 TOP AIRPLANE MANUFACTURERS, 1996

Ranked by: 1996 revenues, in millions of dollars.

1. Lockheed Martin Corporation, $26,900
2. The Boeing Company, $22,700
3. McDonnell Douglas Corporation, $13,800
4. Airbus Industrie (France), $8,800
5. Northrup Grumman Corporation, $8,100

The Aerospace Industries Association of America (AIAA), states that there were 1,677 shipments of civilian (transports, general aviation, and rotocraft) aircraft valued at $22.19 billion in 1996. There were a total of 431 aircraft accepted by U.S. military agencies in 1995 (down from 775 in 1994) at a flyaway value of $11.76 billion. The number of shipments of complete U.S. aircraft in 1995, according to ITA, was estimated to be 2,275 with a predicted value of $28.39 billion. This number has dropped from a peak of 19,381 in 1978, when the total value of shipments was $10.1 billion. The greatest drop in production occurred in general aviation (primarily due to product liability) from peaks of 17,800 units in 1978 to an estimated 1,077 in 1995. The Teal Group predicts 25,537 aircraft valued at $655.5 billion will be built throughout the world during the decade 1997-2006.

Commercial aircraft deliveries are expected to rise from 400 in 1996 to over 700 by the year 2000. The commercial jet fleet was estimated to be 11,500 by the end of 1996 and 23,600 by the year 2016, 7,000 of which were expected to be Boeing aircraft. The industry entered 1997 with $96 billion in orders. Boeing alone had $7.5 billion in new orders in September 1996, was hiring 1,000 new workers a month for its wide body and jumbo jet production, and entered 1997 with a backlog of orders for 1,239 aircraft. Business jet deliveries rose from 307 in 1995 to 330 in 1996 and are estimated to reach 400 by 1998. Business jet sales are expected to be $14-28 billion over the next 15 years. Aircraft deliveries are expected to crest in the year 2000.

Industry earnings rose to $7.6 billion in 1996, the highest in three decades, as a result of downsizing and increased productivity that boosted stock market interest. Military sales were predicted to decline from 1996 to 1997 by 6 percent. The military market is still active in some parts of Europe and the Far East. Central European nations could buy more than 200 planes worth $8 billion in the next five years according to *Business Week*.

Passenger Jet Producers

Shares are shown based on new passenger jet orders.

Boeing	70.0%
Airbus Industrie	15.0
McDonnell Douglas	10.0
Other	5.0

Source: *Financial Times*, May 31, 1996, p. 12.

INDUSTRY OUTLOOK

Aircraft industry analysts expect that the 1990s will see a period of great change in aircraft manufacturing. For years the industry had been propelled by ever-increasing military budgets and ever-increasing numbers of commercial airline passengers, but both of those stimuli changed in the 1990s. Government military expenditures peaked in 1987, when aircraft manufacturers supplied over 1,200 planes. In 1994, U.S. manufacturers shipped only 755 military aircraft or $7.9 billion in sales, approximately two-thirds the number shipped in 1987. By 1995 the number of military aircraft had dropped to 410 although the value had risen to $11 billion, generally reflecting budget cuts with corresponding reductions in employment by military aircraft manu-

facturers. The increased competition for scarce military dollars is expected to reduce the number of military aircraft providers or possibly force industry consolidation.

Commercial Jet Suppliers

Airplane orders have increased from $18.8 billion in 1994 to $48.8 billion in 1995.

	1994	1995
Boeing	41.0%	70.0%
Airbus Industries	41.0	20.0
McDonnell Douglas	8.0	10.0

Source: *Purchasing*, March 7, 1996, p. 7.

While military aircraft manufacturers struggled to adjust to changing military budgets, commercial aircraft manufacturers had to adjust to declining demand for aircraft by major carriers, production overcapacity, and government-supported foreign competition in the first half of the 1990s. These challenges were made all the more pressing in 1991, when for the first time in history, the number of passengers riding on commercial airlines declined. This drop in air travel prompted many airlines to cancel or postpone orders for aircraft, leaving manufacturers with an excess of inventory. Fortunately, by 1996 the industry had begun to recover.

According to *Interavia* contributor John Crampton, ''Aerospace manufacturers are learning to live with a whole new set of rules brought about by the industry-wide recession and the peace dividend.'' Manufacturers were adjusting to this changed marketplace in a number of ways. Most notable has been a trend toward industry consolidation and cooperation. Many of the smaller manufacturers in the industry were eliminated by the recession, and those that survived have increasingly banded together to share the risk of developing new products. Industry analysts believed that those manufacturers best able to form working partnerships would be the ones to succeed in the 1990s. In this spirit of pulling together, 1996 saw many mergers, primarily precipitated by the effects of deregulation and the decline in military contracts. Technological advances will also pave the way for cost reduction as manufacturers increasingly turn to computer-assisted design mock-ups and paperless workplaces as ways of reducing costly experimentation and excess paperwork.

Other positive signs for the industry include Boeing's "exclusive supplier" relationship with several airline companies and the new F-22 Raptor single seat fighter. At $70 million per unit, the F-22 was designed to secure dominance over any adversary aircraft. Original plans called for the U.S. military to purchase 438 of these planes at more than $71 billion.

The decline in the general U.S. aviation market—from 17,817 shipments of its aircraft in the late 1970s to 780 in the early 1990s—has been blamed primarily on tough American product-liability laws requiring manufacturers to purchase costly insurance in case their products are implicated in accidents. Rising fuel costs and the decreasing cost of flying on commercial airlines also contributed to the decline of this segment of the industry. Another impact of general aviation litigation was to escalate the market for used aircraft, due to the scarcity of new planes and the export demand for old planes.

In an effort to offset the litigation, the General Aviation Revitalization Act of 1994 forbade any civil actions against manufacturers for death or injury from an incident in a less than 20-passenger aircraft more than 18 years old (the 18 year limitation is superseded by states having lesser periods; 13 states have absolution from liability after six to 12 years). This eliminated the devastating impact that product liability suits had upon the industry and revitalized single engine propeller aircraft manufacturing.

The world market for helicopters is recovering from a four year downturn and is expected to grow modestly. Strong, stable worldwide economies and a resurgence of off-shore drilling are setting the stage for the helicopter industry in 1997. Membership in Helicopter Association International has grown by 25 percent in the past four years, indicating a growing interest. Other indications: Japan conducted its first flight of a tandem seat light helicopter in 1996; Sikorsky developed a helicopter with better performance and a reduced crew load, the S-76C; and Eurocopter sold 228 new helicopters valued at $2.26 billion in 1996.

ORGANIZATION AND STRUCTURE

American aircraft companies provide airplanes for three distinct markets: the military, commercial aviation, and general aviation, which includes business aviation. From the end of World War II until the collapse of the Soviet threat in 1989, American military services had a voracious appetite for sophisticated aircraft, which American firms sought to satisfy. This 49-year boom in military spending not only guaranteed the health of many manufacturers, but it also allowed those manufacturers to devote resources to research and development, ensuring that American aircraft would be the most technologically advanced in the world. The end of the Cold War, which reduced military spending in the United States and around the world, has provided the greatest challenge for American aircraft manufacturers who had grown accustomed to lucrative Department of Defense contracts. As a result, the military aircraft industry appears to be shrinking. Although the U.S. government has sought to guarantee its technological dominance through continued funding of research and development, funds are declining.

The development of commercial aircraft poses far greater risks than that of military aircraft. The development process for a passenger airliner capable of carrying several hundred people is both lengthy and costly, requiring manufacturers to anticipate the needs of airlines far in advance and to gamble vast amounts of money on the product's success. The *Economist* estimated that a new medium-sized airliner costs over $2 billion to develop, with engines costing another $1.5 billion, and noted that "aerospace companies bet their futures on each product."

As a result of the risks involved, commercial aircraft manufacturers have been rather conservative, pursuing modifications on existing airframes rather than reinventing complete aircraft, and most existing commercial airliners have changed little in recent history. However, some exciting new aircraft developments are taking place in the areas of speed, range, capacity and efficiency. Given the tremendous financial risks associated with developing new aircraft, many manufacturers today work cooperatively, jointly developing a design and dividing work among partners if the design is successful. The development of a new aircraft might involve many dozens of companies, each contributing some portion of a plane that they have perfected.

Though military and commercial aircraft manufacturers dominate the industry, American companies also produce a number of aircraft for the general aviation and the helicopter market segments, which include fixed wing aircraft and rotorcraft for business transportation, regional airline service, recreation, specialized uses such as ambulance service and agricultural spraying, and training. American manufacturers have historically produced about 60 percent of the world's general aviation aircraft and 30 percent of the helicopters.

Most aircraft manufacturers derive a significant proportion of their profits from the production of replacement and upgrade parts for their airplanes. Since large commercial jets represent such a large investment—a new twin-engine passenger jet may cost several hundred million dollars—airlines try to keep them in the air for many years. Moreover, the Federal Aviation Administration (FAA) sets stringent guidelines on repair and replacement procedures for passenger aircraft.

WORK FORCE

The total aircraft industry employment was 259,600 in December 1996, with 103,900 employed as production workers at an average wage close to $20 per hour. The aerospace industry employed 465,000 total. With the backlog of orders at several manufacturers, the potential for employment should remain good until the year 2000.

Although there have been reductions in defense spending, cuts in aircraft purchases by troubled commercial airline carriers, and the elimination of thousands of jobs in the industry prior to 1996, the industry seems to be improving with commercial orders making up for the deficit from the military sector.

RESEARCH AND TECHNOLOGY

Recent technological advances include: augmented reality, a variation of virtual reality that allows the user to ''see'' the world as an overlay of information so that it appears attached to a work piece; a thin-film skin of nearly imperceptible ridges to reduce surface turbulence and cut fuel burn; and a digital airframe factory using a laser tracking system.

AMERICA AND THE WORLD

The value of aircraft exports declined slightly during the five year period from 1990-1995 (from a high of $26.4 billion to $13.6 billion). There was a corresponding decline in aircraft imports from $3.9 to $3.5 billion during the same time period. Japan, the United Kingdom, South Korea, Canada and the Netherlands were the top export markets in 1995. France, the number one market in 1991 and number two or three until 1994, was not among the most recent top five, but has consistently remained the number one importer to the U.S. for the same period.

While the worldwide market for military aircraft was a tepid one in the early 1990s because of overcapacity and diminished demand, the market for commercial aircraft rebounded somewhat in 1996. As *U.S. Industrial Outlook 1994* noted, ''demand in world commercial markets, particularly the expanding economies of Asia and the Pacific Rim, is expected to show increases over the next 10 to 15 years.'' In fact, the larger share of the commercial transport market is now overseas. The U.S. share, as a percentage of the world market, will shrink. Airline traffic, especially international traffic, is expected to show strong growth throughout the rest of the decade requiring more aircraft over the next 20 years.

Overseas aviation projects include the development of a 90-140 seat twin-jet by Aviation Industries of China; the AN-70 transport, a joint Russian-Ukrainian project; and Brazil's Embraer, which delivered two EMB-145 50-seat regional jets, out of an ordered 25, to Continental Express in December of 1996. Chinese enterprises are expected to buy 1,200 aircraft costing $90 billion in the next two decades. And although the Korean Aircraft Industry saw plans for a 100 seat jet collapse,

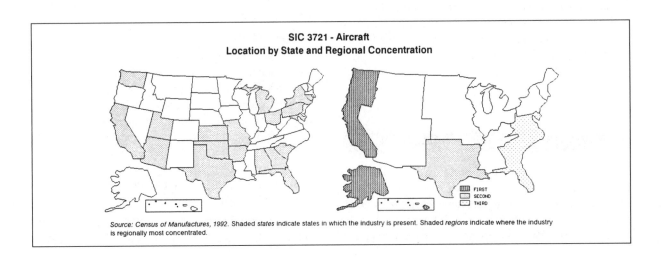

SIC 3721 - Aircraft
Location by State and Regional Concentration

FIRST
SECOND
THIRD

Source: *Census of Manufactures, 1992.* Shaded *states* indicate states in which the industry is present. Shaded *regions* indicate where the industry is regionally most concentrated.

Daewoo Heavy Industries has developed fuselages and panels for F-16 fighters.

ASSOCIATIONS AND SOCIETIES

AERONAUTICAL REPAIR STATION ASSOCIATION
121 N. Henry St.
Alexandria, VA 22314
Phone: (703) 739-9543

AEROSPACE INDUSTRIES ASSOCIATION OF AMERICA
1250 Eye St. NW
Washington, DC 20005
Phone: (202) 371-8400
Fax: (202) 371-8573

AMERICAN INSTITUTE OF AERONAUTICS AND ASTRONAUTICS
c/o Michael Lewis
370 L'Enfant Promenade SW
Washington, DC 20024
Phone: (202) 646-7400
Fax: (202) 646-7508

FLIGHT SAFETY FOUNDATION
2200 Wilson Blvd., Ste. 500
Arlington, VA 22201
Phone: (703) 522-8300
Fax: (703) 525-6047

GENERAL AVIATION MANUFACTURERS ASSOCIATION
1400 K St. NW, Ste. 801
Washington, DC 20005
Phone: (202) 393-1500
Fax: (202) 842-4063

NATIONAL BUSINESS AIRCRAFT ASSOCIATION
1200 18th St. NW, 2 Fl.
Washington, DC 20036
Phone: (202) 783-9000
Fax: (202) 331-8364

PERIODICALS AND NEWSLETTERS

AEROSPACE AMERICA
American Institute of Aeronautics and Astronautics, Inc.
370 L'Enfant Promenade SW
Washington, DC 20024
Phone: (202) 646-7471
Fax: (202) 646-7508
Monthly. Free to members; non-members, $75.00 per year. Provides coverage of key issues affecting the aerospace field.

AEROSPACE ENGINEERING MAGAZINE
Society of Automotive Engineers
400 Commonwealth Dr.
Warrendale, PA 15096-0001
Phone: (412) 776-4841
Fax: (412) 776-5760
Monthly. $48.00 per year. Provides technical information that can be used in the design of new and improved aerospace systems.

AIR MARKET NEWS
General Publications Co.
PO Box 480
Hatch, NM 87937-0408
Phone: (505) 267-1030
Fax: (505) 267-1920
Bimonthly. Controlled circulation. Subject matter is news of aircraft products and services.

AVIATION DIGEST: THE NEWS MAGAZINE EDITED FOR AIRCRAFT OWNERS
Aviation Digest Associates
288 Christian St., No.16
Oxford, CT 06478-1038
Phone: (203) 264-4333
Fax: (203) 264-4511
Monthly. $30.00. Formerly Aviation.

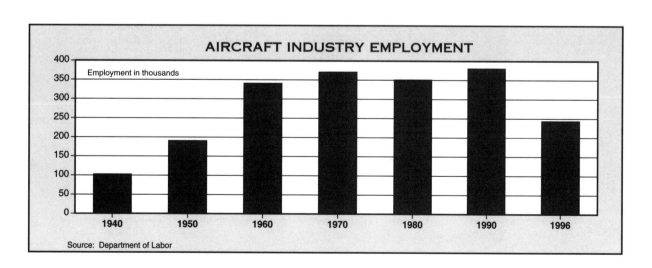

AIRCRAFT INDUSTRY EMPLOYMENT

Employment in thousands

Source: Department of Labor

AVIATION EQUIPMENT MAINTENANCE

Phillips Business Information, Inc.
1201 Seven Locks Rd., Ste. 300
Potomac, MD 20854
Phone: (301) 424-3338
Fax: (301) 309-3487
Monthly. $30.00 per year.

AVIATION WEEK AND SPACE TECHNOLOGY

McGraw-Hill
1221 Avenue of the Americas
New York, NY 10020-1095
Phone: (800) 722-4726 or (212) 512-2000
Fax: (212) 512-4256
Weekly. Individuals, $85.00 per year; libraries and government agencies, $105.00 per year.

DATABASES

AEROSPACE/DEFENSE MARKETS AND TECHNOLOGY

Information Access Co.
362 Lakeside Dr.
Foster City, CA 94404
Phone: (800) 321-6388 or (415) 358-4643
Fax: (415) 358-4759
Abstracts of commercial aerospace/defense related literature, 1982 to date. Also includes information about major defense contracts awarded by the U.S. Department of Defense. International coverage. Inquire as to online cost and availability.

CITIBASE (CITICORP ECONOMIC DATABASE)

FAME Software Corp.
77 Water St., 9 Fl.
New York, NY 10005

Phone: (212) 898-7800
Fax: (212) 742-8956
Presents over 6,000 statistical series relating to business, industry, finance, and economics. Includes series from Survey of Current Business and any other sources. Time period is 1947 to date, with daily updates. Inquire as to online cost and availability.

MANAGEMENT CONTENTS

Information Access Co.
362 Lakeside Dr.
Foster City, CA 94404
Phone: (800) 227-8431 or (415) 378-5000
Fax: (415) 358-4759
Covers a wide range of management, financial, marketing, personnel, and administrative topics. About 140 leading business journals are indexed and abstracted from 1974 to date, with monthly updating. Inquire as to online cost and availability.

PREDICASTS FORECASTS: U.S.

Information Access Co.
362 Lakeside Dr.
Foster City, CA 94404
Phone: (800) 321-6388 or (415) 378-5000
Fax: (415) 358-4759
Provides numeric abstracts of a wide range of published forecasts relating to specific U.S. products, markets, and industries. Monthly updates. Time period is 1971 to date. Inquire as to online cost and availability.

SCISEARCH

Institute for Scientific Information
3501 Market St.
Philadelphia, PA 19104
Phone: (800) 523-1850 or (215) 386-0100
Fax: (215) 386-2911

SIC 3721 - Aircraft
General Statistics

| Year | Com-panies | Establishments | | Employment | | | Compensation | | Production ($ million) | | | |
		Total	with 20 or more employees	Total (000)	Production Workers (000)	Hours (Mil)	Payroll ($ mil)	Wages ($/hr)	Cost of Materials	Value Added by Manufacture	Value of Shipments	Capital Invest.
1982	137	166	87	275.4	138.8	272.7	7,750.1	12.91	15,716.6	15,717.4	28,047.4	840.3
1983		168	85	250.9	120.6	238.9	7,562.0	13.60	14,910.0	14,012.5	30,522.0	621.8
1984		170	83	232.5	115.5	228.2	7,456.9	14.05	1,577.2	15,498.2	28,453.2	860.8
1985		173	80	241.8	121.9	238.6	8,006.8	14.60	17,482.1	17,096.3	34,976.5	1,013.3
1986		151	77	256.7	135.3	269.5	8,983.9	14.71	22,167.9	15,160.7	38,184.3	1,108.2
1987	137	155	79	268.2	141.5	282.3	9,679.5	15.38	23,140.9	17,311.0	39,092.7	1,052.1
1988		163	85	274.2	140.0	274.3	10,015.2	16.16	26,140.8	18,218.6	41,493.7	1,029.6
1989		169	81	287.7	140.3	272.0	10,468.6	16.40	29,723.8	20,363.6	43,338.9	1,269.6
1990		181	90	300.0	139.7	268.1	11,224.7	17.02	33,171.2	20,235.4	51,369.6	1,020.9
1991		198	94	258.3	125.3	244.8	10,324.1	17.82	36,077.2	23,090.6	58,090.2	1,046.1
1992	151	182	103	264.9	122.1	227.0	11,498.9	19.98	36,133.3	25,157.1	62,980.8	1,661.3
1993		260	116	241.2	104.4	198.7	10,790.0	19.90	33,206.4	22,903.3	55,119.8	1,154.4
1994		211P	103P	217.9	92.8	172.7	10,312.1	20.77	25,778.3	23,606.4	50,944.0	872.2
1995		216P	105P	255.0P	114.0P	214.4P	11,848.0P	20.93P	31,599.8P	28,937.4P	62,448.6P	1,280.7P
1996		221P	107P	254.4P	112.3P	210.0P	12,177.1P	21.58P	32,985.6P	30,206.4P	65,187.2P	1,314.8P
1997		226P	109P	253.9P	110.5P	205.6P	12,506.3P	22.23P	34,371.4P	31,475.5P	67,925.9P	1,348.8P
1998		232P	111P	253.3P	108.8P	201.2P	12,835.4P	22.87P	35,757.2P	32,744.5P	70,664.6P	1,382.9P

Sources: 1982, 1987, 1992 Economic Census; Annual Survey of Manufactures, 83-86, 88-91, 93-94. Establishment counts for non-Census years are from County Business Patterns; establishment values for 83-84 are extrapolations. 'P's show projections by the editors. Industries reclassified in 87 will not have data for prior years.

Broad, multidisciplinary index to the literature of science and technology, 1974 to present. Inquire as to online cost and availability. Coverage of literature is worldwide, with weekly updates.

STATISTICS SOURCES

AEROSPACE FACTS AND FIGURES
Aerospace Industries Association of America
1250 Eye St. NW
Washington, DC 20005
Phone: (202) 371-8400
Fax: (202) 371-8473
Annual. $25.00. Includes financial data for the aerospace industries.

BUSINESS STATISTICS
Available from U.S. Government Printing Office
Washington, DC 20402
Phone: (202) 512-1800
Fax: (202) 512-2250
Biennial. $20.00. Issued by Bureau of Economic Analysis, U.S. Department of Commerce. Shows annual data for 29 years and monthly data for a recent four-year period. Statistics correspond to the Survey of Current Business.

FAA STATISTICAL HANDBOOK OF AVIATION
Federal Aviation Administration
Available from U.S. Government Printing Office
Washington, DC 20402
Phone: (202) 512-1800
Fax: (202) 512-2250
Annual. $11.00.

GENERAL AVIATION STATISTICAL DATABOOK, 1992
EDITION
General Aviation Manufacturers Association
1400 K St. NW
Washington, DC 20005
Phone: (202) 393-1500

STANDARD & POOR'S STATISTICAL SERVICE
Standard & Poor's Corp.
25 Broadway
New York, NY 10004
Phone: (800) 221-5277 or (212) 208-8000
Fax: (212) 412-0040
Monthly. $640.00 per year. Includes 10 Basic Statistics sections, Current Statistics Supplements, and Annual Security Price Index Record.

GENERAL WORKS

A/C FLYER
McGraw-Hill, Inc.
1221 Anenue of the Americas
New York, NY 10020
Phone: (800) 722-4726 or (212) 512-2000
Fax: (212) 512-2281

$54.00 per year. Lists used aircraft for sale. Also includes Maintenance Directory (aircraft service centers) and FBO Facility Directory (fixed base operators).

ABD - AVIATION BUYER'S GUIDE
Air Service Directory, Inc.
105 Calvert St.
Harrison, NY 10528
Phone: (914) 835-7200
Fax: (914) 835-2323
Quarterly. $25.00 per year.

AIRCRAFT TRANSACTION LISTINGS
Aviation Consulting Inc.
90 Moonachie Ave.
Teterboro, NJ 07608
Phone: (201) 288-4900
Bimonthly. $275.00 per year. Tabulation of aircraft type, parties involved, data and price of current commercial transport aircraft sale and lease transactions.

AVIATION BUYER'S GUIDE
Dabora, Inc.
1211 E. Lane St.
Shelbyville, TN 37160
Monthly. $10.00 per year. Lists used aircraft for sale.

AVIATION LAW REPORTS
Commerce Clearing House, Inc.
4025 W. Peterson Ave.
Chicago, IL 60646
Phone: (800) 248-3248 or (312) 583-8500
$1,670.00 per year. Four looseleaf volumes. Periodic supplementation.

FURTHER READING

Aboulafia, Richard. "Flat Market for Business Aircraft." *Aviation & Space Week Technology*, 13 January 1997.

"Boeing Projects Healthy Airplane Demand Over Next 20 Years." Available from http://biz.yahoo.com/prnews/97/03/04/ba_y0002_1.html.

"Boeing 777 Breaks Speed and Distance Records." Available from http://biz.yahoo.com/finance/97/04/02/ba_y0002_1.html.

U.S. Department of Commerce. Economics and Statistics Administration. Bureau of the Census. *Statistical Abstract of the United States 1996*, 116th ed. Washington: GPO, 1996.

U.S. Department of Labor. Bureau of Labor Statistics. *E&E: Employment and Earnings*, December 1996.

U.S. Department of Labor. Bureau of Labor Statistics. *Occupational Outlook Handbook: 1996-97*, ed. Washington: GPO, 1996.

Ward's Business Directory of U.S. Private and Public Companies, Detroit: Gale Research, 1996.

APPAREL, MEN'S AND BOYS'

SICs 2310, 2320

The outlook for the men's and boys' apparel industry was being shaped by a number of processes in the mid-1990s, including cyclical changes in the broader economy, a changing retail structure, and the impact of imports produced with cheap labor. These factors and the long range effects of implementing the North American Free Trade Agreement (NAFTA) and the Agreement on Clothing and Textiles (ACT) created a climate of uncertainty in the industry. Most industry projections indicated that the trend toward downsizing will continue into the next century.

The value of men's and boys' apparel production dropped 2 percent in 1996; however, retail sales of men's apparel climbed 7.3 percent, almost twice the growth in 1995, and retail consumption of boys' apparel grew 4.4 percent.

A new World Trade Organization (WTO) was established in 1995, and the Multifiber Arrangement (MFA), which allowed importing countries to limit the flow of imports from lower cost, developing countries, was replaced by the Agreement on Textiles and Clothing (ATC) which required the phasing out of MFA quotas over a ten-year period. According to Linda Shelton in an *Industry, Trade, and Technology Review* report, ''The elimination of MFA quotas likely will have a significant impact on the U.S. textile and apparel sector given the level of protection that such restrictions have provided domestic producers over the past two decades.'' Since the U.S. has until 2005 to implement the ATC, the legislation's impact on the men's and boys' apparel industry may not be realized for several years.

In the mid-1990s, output and employment in the men's and boys' suit and coat industry continued the long-term pattern of contraction that had begun over two decades earlier. In 1979, industry sources estimated that, of the 25 million suits sold in the U.S., approximately 80 percent were U.S.-made; in 1994, by contrast, according to Department of Commerce figures, U.S. manufacturers accounted for a much smaller share—55 percent—of the much smaller number of suits, just 13 million, sold in this country. The number of people employed making suits and coats had fallen from well over 100,000 in the late 1960s to just 34,000 by 1994. The outlook of this branch of production was being shaped by a number of processes—cyclical changes in the broader economy, a changing retail structure, the impact of imports produced with cheap labor—that were having similar effects across the entire apparel industry. One key factor, however—changing dress habits among American men— was having an especially acute impact on the suit and coat industry.

Like the suit and coat sector, the 1990s were an up-and-down period for the men's and boys' nightwear and underwear industry. Two years of increases in the value of shipments of these products in 1992 and 1993 were followed by two years of decline, in 1994 and 1995. Results from the first three quarters of 1996 indicated, however, that shipments were once again on the rise.

About 130 establishments were engaged in the manufacture of men's and boys' neckwear in the United States in the early 1990s. All told, shipments of neck-

TOP MEN'S WEAR COMPANIES

Ranked by: Sales, in millions of dollars.

1. Polo/Ralph Lauren Corp., with $4,400 million
2. Phillips-Van Heusen, $1,464
3. Oxford Industries Inc., $656
4. Hartmarx Corp., $595
5. Salant Corp., $502

Source: *Apparel Industry Magazine,* Top 100 Sewn Products Companies (annual), June, 1996, p. 26.

wear from these businesses in 1994 were just over $700 million, which represented a steady rise from the 1990 total of $500 million. A climate of uncertainty, however, surrounded the industry in the mid-1990s, in large part due to changing conditions of international trade, with the implementation of the North American Free Trade Agreement (NAFTA) and the Agreement on Clothing and Textiles (ACT). The progressive growth of the import share of the U.S. neckwear market during the 1980s and early 1990s generated considerable alarm and prompted calls for protectionism among members of the Neckwear Association of America (NAA), the principal trade association representing U.S. neckwear manufacturers. In the NAA's opinion, any further reduction in current import duties would only exacerbate a trend that had already wreaked havoc upon U.S. domestic producers.

During the first half of the 1990s, the value of shipments by U.S. companies making men's and boys' trousers and slacks rose steadily, while employment levels remained flat. If aggregate statistics suggested stable conditions, these years were in fact, however, a period of substantial transformation in this industry.

Pressures for change in the industry came from a number of different sources. First, shifts in the nature of consumer demand, especially a growing preference for casual clothes, led manufacturers to introduce new lines and new products in the early 1990s. Second, concentration in the U.S. retail industry meant that manufacturers of pants had fewer potential retailers with whom to deal, and this process, consequently, gave greater leverage to those powerful chains that remained. In response to retailers' demands for cheaper goods and faster replenishment, manufacturers invested in new communications technologies and developed new methods of production. Finally, U.S. manufacturers had to compete for space on retailers' shelves with cheaply produced imported pants—a trend likely to intensify in the aftermath of the implementation of new international trade agreements in the mid-1990s. One response to pressure from

foreign competitors was to downsize domestic production and base an increasing share of production off-shore.

About 225 establishments active in the manufacture of men's and boys' work clothing accounted for an inflation adjusted value of total product shipments of $1.2 billion in 1992. This figure, though up by 6.1 percent from the previous 1991, remained in line with the five year declining trend, which peaked during 1987 and 1988 and was some 13.2 percent below the peak period's level of performance. When viewed over a five year period covering 1987-1992, the annual percentage change in the inflation adjusted value of total product shipments fell by an average of 2.2 percent. Total product shipments reached $1.7 billion in 1994. In 1995, the industry employed roughly 26,500 individuals, down from 28,500 in 1994, and down even further from 30,000 in 1993.

INDUSTRY OUTLOOK

The persistent downward trend in U.S. production of suits and coats, which began in the 1970s, continued in 1995. U.S. manufacturers produced 9.6 million suits in 1995, valued at $930 million, and 11.6 million tailored coats, valued at $737 million. For these two classes of products, which make up the vast majority of goods produced by this branch of the apparel industry, these figures represented a significant drop in quantity and value from 1994 (when 11.2 million suits and 13.5 million tailored coats were produced). Industry analysts explained the continued contraction of this industry, during a period of overall growth, as a result of two major factors: competition from inexpensive imported clothes, and an acceptance of more casual dress in settings where suits were once required. A central part of this trend was relaxed dress-codes at large corporations, most famously IBM, which instituted "dress down" days on which employees could show up for work in casual clothes.

In 1995, Census Bureau statistics estimated the value of nightwear and underwear shipments (including robes) by U.S. manufacturers at $1.81 billion. This figure was up from the total of $1.67 billion in 1991, but below the peak of $1.84 billion in 1993. Throughout the 1990s, nightwear shipments made up a very small share of the total, just $119 million in 1995, or roughly seven percent. Of the $1.45 billion in men's and boys' underwear shipments in 1995, the two largest categories were knit shorts and briefs, at $562 million, and undershirts, at $510 million. The remaining shipments were made up of woven boxers ($205 million) and thermal underwear ($172 million).

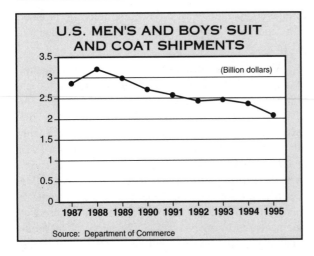

U.S. MEN'S AND BOYS' SUIT AND COAT SHIPMENTS

(Billion dollars)

Source: Department of Commerce

ates executive, for example, estimated that by the year 2000, one-half of all U.S. corporations would no longer require formal dress at all. In order to capitalize, major manufacturers like Levi Strauss and Haggar Corp. planned to introduce new lines of pants in the mid-1990s that would straddle the division between casual and formal wear.

Third quarter 1996 figures revealed a decline in the productions of all segments of the men's and boys' work clothing industry. Production of work jackets fell 21 percent from third quarter 1995; production of work shirts dropped 7 percent; production of work pants declined 4 percent; and production of washable service apparel tumbled 10 percent.

The first half of the 1990s witnessed a major shift in tie styles. In the 1990s, American men preferred to wear ties, when they wore them at all, that made more personal and colorful statements. Out of fashion were the conservatively patterned yellow and red power ties which set the tone in the 1980s. In the 1990s ties tended to be wider and more brightly colored, and had bolder abstract patterns. Exemplifying these trends was the line of ties designed by the late Grateful Dead leader Jerry Garcia, which were introduced in 1992 and enjoyed record sales after his 1995 death. These ties, perhaps, were as appealing to women—who continued to buy the majority of ties sold in the U.S.—as to men.

The value of shipments of men's and boys' trousers and slacks by U.S. manufacturers stood at $7.23 billion in 1994, according to Census Bureau statistics. This figure marked a substantial rise from 1990, when shipments were valued at $5.66 billion. By 1998 shipment values were expected to increase further to about $7.87 billion. In the longer run, growth in output appeared less impressive, as 1990 represented a low-point after several years of decline, from a total of $6.01 billion in 1987, the first year statistics were recorded for this category of apparel.

The two major product categories in this industry fared very differently over the early 1990s. Annual unit shipments of dress and sport trousers declined between 1991 and 1995, from 103 million to 92 million, while the value of these garments fell from $1.57 billion to $1.54 billion. Shipments of jeans and jean-cut casual pants, on the other hand, climbed steadily, from 237 million to 311 million units, and shipment values increased from $3.47 billion to $4.49 billion. These changes were the result of attempts by American pants manufacturers to adapt to the shifting clothing habits of American men, in a society where informal dress was increasingly common in both business and leisure contexts. This was a trend that showed every sign of continuing: a Levi Strauss Associ-

WORK FORCE

The suit and coat industry employed 34,000 people in 1994, 28,700 of whom were production workers. At Hartmarx, the largest producer, most production workers were covered by contracts with the Union of Needletrades, Industrial and Textile Employees (UNITE). For the industry as a whole, production workers' wages averaged $7.97 per hour in 1992, among the highest for the apparel industry, but well below the $11.55 average for all manufacturing industries in that year. Sewing machine operators, mostly women, were the largest group in the work force.

Men's and boys' underwear industry employment data from 1987 to 1994 reflected a trend of steady job losses. In 1987 the number of production workers stood at 16,200 and by 1994 had fallen to 10,100. Underlying this trend were automation in the industry and the tendency of U.S. producers to relocate apparel establishments abroad or to outsource to foreign locations work formerly performed within U.S. borders. Wages for production workers in the industry averaged $7.03 per hour in 1994, as compared to an average of $12.09 for all manufacturing industries.

Employment in the men's and boys' neckwear industry, despite annual fluctuations, remained relatively flat for the period from 1982 to 1994. Total employment in the neckwear industry in 1994 was estimated at about 6,200 workers, approximately 4,600 of whom were classified as production workers. These figures were down considerably from 1992, when total employment stood at 7,500 total workers, and 5,800 production workers. Projections based on Census Bureau figures predicted an increase to 6,800 total workers in 1995, after which employment was expected to remain flat for several years. The average hourly wage for production workers in the men's and boys' neckwear industry in 1994 was

$9.21. This was a relatively high figure for the apparel industry as a whole, but still far below the average of $12.09 per hour for manufacturing industries in general.

Total employment in the men's and boys' trousers and slacks industry stood at 82,200 people in 1994, 71,900 of whom were production workers. These figures represented a continuation of the trend of flat employment levels through the first half of the 1990s, following a steep decline in the late 1980s. Projections for the second half of the 1990s, based on Census Bureau statistics, predicted a new round of sharp reductions in employment. Employment was expected to drop to 68,800 by 1998. Average hourly wages for production workers in this industry in 1994 were $7.03, up from $5.88 in 1987, but still far below the average of $12.09 for all manufacturing jobs. Wages were only expected to increase to $7.81 per hour by 1998. Major employers in this industry reported that only small minorities of their workers were covered by collective bargaining agreements.

Total employment in the men's and boys' work clothing industry was 33,000 in 1987, of which 29,000 were classified as production workers. By 1992, total employment had fallen to 31,100, of which 27,300 were production workers. For the entire period total employment fell by 5.8 percent while production employment declined slightly more by 5.9 percent. From 1987-1992 industry real wages had fallen without interruption, while value added per production worker rose, though not in a dramatic manner, suggesting that productivity improvements and real wages were moving in opposite directions. In 1993, the number of individuals employed in the industry rose slightly to 32,500.

RESEARCH AND TECHNOLOGY

Following World War II, improvements in the sewing machine eliminated the need to stitch button holes, pockets, belt loops, and lapels by hand. New technology introduced since the 1960s has also increased productivity, although some promising technologies were later abandoned. In the 1960s, some manufacturers replaced reciprocating blade cutting machinery with lasers. However, the lasers tended to fuse layers of synthetic fabrics. Computer-controlled spreading, marking, and cutting systems were introduced in the late 1970s and early 1980s. Sewing machines also became more sophisticated beginning in the late 1960s, eliminating much of the manual labor involved in handling and positioning garments as they moved from one sewing-machine operator to another. These advances led to significant increases in productivity, and employment has dropped

significantly faster than the value of output since the early 1980s.

By the mid-1990s, the most aggressive industry response to its economic condition was to step up its investment in state-of-the-art communication systems that facilitate the rapid transmission of sales information back to the producers, so as to immediately adjust production to consumer preferences. Referred to as the "quick response" system, this consumer-driven process more finely integrates various phases of the production cycle, shortening the duration of various production steps and reducing inventory levels to a bare minimum.

In addition to the quick response system, firms active in this industry directed major investments at computer controlled machinery. Such purchases were undertaken in an effort to increase productivity, to minimize waste, and to secure efficiencies in traditional apparel areas such as design, cutting, embroidery, sewing, finishing, ticketing and distribution operations. Independent of the particular area of operation, the overall investment goal was intended to reduce the amount of labor-time per task, which remained high when compared to other non-apparel group industry standards.

AMERICA AND THE WORLD

Imported goods met a substantial share of U.S. consumers' demand for suits and coats in the mid-1990s. In 1994, for example, 70 percent of tailored coats and 45 percent of suits bought by U.S. consumers were imports. The value of imported suits and coats rose rapidly in the first half of the 1990s: between 1991 and 1994, for example, imports of men's and boys' wool suits rose from $258 million to $354 million.

With the passage of the North American Free Trade Agreement (NAFTA) and the Agreement on Clothing and Textiles (ACT) in the mid-1990s, competition from foreign manufacturers and pressures to downsize domestic operations were likely to increase. The former lifted quotas and removed some tariffs on apparel imports from Mexico. The latter called for accelerated growth in quota levels for apparel imports from other countries and for the eventual elimination of quotas by the year 2005.

ASSOCIATIONS AND SOCIETIES

AMALGAMATED CLOTHING AND TEXTILE WORKERS UNION
15 Union Sq. W
New York, NY 10003
Phone: (212) 242-0700
Fax: (212) 255-8169

AMERICAN APPAREL MANUFACTURERS ASSOCIATION
2500 Wilson Blvd., Ste. 301
Arlington, VA 22201
Phone: (703) 524-1864
Fax: (703) 522-6741

BUREAU OF WHOLESALE SALES REPRESENTATIVES
1801 Peachtree St. NW, Ste. 200
Atlanta, GA 30308
Phone: (800) 877-1808 or (404) 351-7355
Fax: (404) 352-5298

CHAMBER OF COMMERCE OF THE APPAREL INDUSTRY
570 7th Ave., 10 Fl.
New York, NY 10018
Phone: (212) 354-0907
Fax: (212) 768-4732

CLOTHING MANUFACTURERS OF THE U.S.A.
1290 Avenue of the Americas, Ste. 1061
New York, NY 10104

COUNCIL OF FASHION DESIGNERS OF AMERICA
1412 Broadway, Ste. 1714
New York, NY 10018
Phone: (212) 302-1861
Fax: (212) 768-0515

INDUSTRIAL ASSOCIATION OF JUVENILE APPAREL MANUFACTURERS
1430 Broadway, Ste. 1603
New York, NY 10018
Phone: (212) 244-2953

INFANT AND JUVENILE MANUFACTURERS ASSOCIATION
575 Lexington Ave., 19 Fl.
New York, NY 10022-6102
Phone: (212) 754-3100
Fax: (212) 371-2980

MENSWEAR RETAILERS OF AMERICA
2011 Eye St. NW, Ste. 300
Washington, DC 20006
Phone: (202) 347-1932

TEXTILE INSTITUTE
10 Blackfriars St.
Manchester M3 5DR, England
Phone: 161-8 34-8457
Fax: 161-8 35-3087
Members from more than 100 countries are involved with textile industry management, marketing, science, and technology.

UNITED GARMENT WORKERS OF AMERICA
4207 Lebanon Rd.
Hermitage, TN 37076
Phone: (615) 889-9221
Fax: (615) 885-3102

UNITED INFANTS' AND CHILDREN'S WEAR ASSOCIATION
1430 Broadway, Ste. 1603
New York, NY 10018
Phone: (212) 244-2953

PERIODICALS AND NEWSLETTERS

BABY AND JUNIOR: INTERNATIONAL TRADE MAGAZINE FOR CHILDREN'S AND YOUTH FASHIONS AND SUPPLIES
Meisenbach GmbH
Hainstrasse 18
Bamberg, Germany 96047
Phone: 0951 861 135
Fax: 0951 861 158
Monthly. 60.00 per year. Text in English, French and German.

APPAREL INDUSTRY MAGAZINE
Shore Communications, Inc.
6225 Barfield Rd. NE, Ste. 200
Atlanta, GA 30328-4300
Phone: (404) 252-8831
Fax: (404) 252-4436
Monthly. $54.00 per year.

NEEDLE'S EYE
Union Special Corp.
1 Union Special Plz.
Huntley, IL 669-3209
Phone: (708) 669-4334
Fax: (708) 699-3543
Bimonthly. Free. Text in English; summaries in several languages.

TEXTILE HI-LIGHTS
American Textile Manufacturers Institute, Inc.
1801 K St. NW, Ste. 900
Washington, DC 20006-1301
Phone: (202) 862-0500
Fax: (202) 862-0570
Quarterly. $75.00 per year. Monthly supplements.

TEXTILE WORLD
Maclean Hunter Publishing Co.
Textile Publications
4170 Ashford-Dunwoody Rd., Ste. 420
Atlanta, GA 30319
Phone: (404) 847-2770
Fax: (404) 252-6150
Monthly. Free to qualified personnel; others, $42.00 per year.

DATABASES

CITIBASE (CITICORP ECONOMIC DATABASE)
FAME Software Corp.
77 Water St., 9 Fl.
New York, NY 10005
Phone: (212) 898-7800
Fax: (212) 742-8956
Presents over 6,000 statistical series relating to business, industry, finance, and economics. Includes series from Survey of Current Business *and many other sources. Time period is 1947 to date, with daily updates. Inquire as to online cost and availability.*

F & S INDEX
Information Access Co.
362 Lakeside Dr.
Foster City, CA 94404
Phone: (800) 321-6388 or (415-358-4643
Fax: (415) 358-4759
Contains about four million citations to worldwide business, financial, and industrial or consumer product literature appearing from 1972 to date. Weekly updates. Inquire as to online cost and availability.

TEXTILE TECHNOLOGY DIGEST [ONLINE]
Textile Information Center
Institute of Textile Technology
2551 Ivy Rd.
Charlottesville, VA 22903-4614
Phone: (804) 296-5511
Fax: (804) 977-5400
Contains indexing and abstracting of more than 800 worldwide journals and monographs in various areas of textile technology, production, and management. Time period is 1978 to date, with monthly updating. Inquire as to online cost and availability.

WORLD TEXTILES
Elsevier Science, Inc.
655 Avenue of the Americas
New York, NY 10010
Phone: (800) 457-3633 or (212) 989-5800
Fax: (212) 633-3680
Provides abstracting from 1983 and indexing from 1970 of worldwide textile literature (periodicals, books, pamphlets, and reports). Includes U.S., European, and British patent information. Updating is monthly. Inquire as to online cost and availability.

STATISTICS SOURCES

BUSINESS STATISTICS
Available from U.S. Government Printing Office
Washington, DC 20402
Phone: (202) 512-1800
Fax: (202) 512-2250
Biennial. $20.00. Issued by Bureau of Economic Analysis, U.S. Department of Commerce. Shows annual data for 29 years and monthly data for a recent four-year period. Statistics correspond to the Survey of Current Business.

FAIRCHILD'S TEXTILE AND APPAREL FINANCIAL DIRECTORY
Fairchild Books
Fairchild Publications, Inc.
Seven W. 34th St.
New York, NY 10001
Phone: (800) 247-6622 or (212) 630-3880
Annual. $85.00. Provides statistical and analytical marketing data, including industry concentration, materials consumed, import/export sales, value of shipments, retail sales by outlet type, advertising expenditures, consumer buying habits, and industry trends.

MONTHLY RETAIL TRADE: SALES AND INVENTORIES
Available from U.S. Government Printing Office
Washington, DC 20402
Phone: (202) 512-1800
Fax: (202) 512-2250
Monthly, with annual summary. $57.00 per year. Issued by Bureau of the Census, U.S. Department of Commerce. Includes Advance Monthly Retail Sales.

SURVEY OF CURRENT BUSINESS
Available from U.S. Government Printing Office
Washington, DC 20402
Phone: (202) 512-1800
Fax: (202) 512-2250
Monthly. $41.00 per year. Issued by Bureau of Economic Analysis, U.S. Department of Commerce. Presents a wide variety of business and economic data.

U.S. MERCHANDISE TRADE: SELECTED HIGHLIGHTS
Bureau of the Census, U.S. Department of Commerce
Available from U.S. Government Printing Office
Washington, DC 20402
Phone: (202) 512-1800
Fax: (202) 512-2250
Monthly. $25.00 per year. Formerly Highlights of the United States Export and Import Trade.

GENERAL WORKS

FASHION MERCHANDISING: AN INTRODUCTION
E. Stone and J. Samples
McGraw-Hill, Inc.
1221 Avenue of the Americas
New York, NY 10020
Phone: (800) 722-4726 or (212) 512-2000
Fax: (212) 512-2821
1989. $27.25. Fifth edition.

FASHION MERCHANDISING AND MARKETING
Marian H. Jernigan and Cynthia R. Easterling
200 Old Tappan Rd.
Old Tappan, NJ 07675
Phone: (800) 223-2336
Fax: (800) 445-6991
1990. Price on application.

THE U.S. APPAREL INDUSTRY: INTERNATIONAL
CHALLENGE-DOMESTIC RESPONSE
Jeffrey S. Arpan and others
Georgia State University
Business Press University Plz.
Atlanta, GA 30303
Phone: (404) 658-4253
Fax: (404) 651-4256
1982. $24.95.

FURTHER READING

Apparel Industry Trends. Arlington, VA: American Apparel Manufacturers Association, March 1997.

Darnay, Arsen J., ed. *Manufacturing USA*. Detroit: Gale Research, 1996.

Dunlop, John T., and David Weil. "Diffusion and Performance of Modular Production in the U.S. Apparel Industry." *Industrial Relations,* July 1996.

Focus: An Economic Profile of the Apparel Industry. Arlington, VA: American Apparel Manufacturers Association, 1996.

Shelton, Linda and Robert Wallace. "World Textile and Apparel Trade: A New Era." *Industry, Trade, and Technology Review,* October 1996. Available from http://www.usitc.gov/ittr.htm. ◂▬▸

More than 900 companies were engaged in the manufacture of women's and girls' apparel in 1992. This figure marks a considerable drop in the industry, for ten years earlier there were more than 1,800 companies engaged in this area of manufacturing. Much of the drop can be attributed to anemic product demand and the increased market share enjoyed by international competitors. In 1994 establishments in the industry accounted for an inflation-adjusted value of total product shipments estimated at $4.1 billion. In 1996 total product shipments for the industry had only increased to $4.4 billion. These figure were consistent with an overall declining industry trend which began in 1982 and with only minor aberrations, continued through the mid-1990s.

In addition to the loss of market share to foreign companies, the domestic industry also felt the sting of a declining trend in middle class discretionary incomes. The decline was particularly important since in former times the personal consumption expenditures of this income strata were a cornerstone of the industry target market, responsible for a major portion of apparel purchases of all types. The lingering overhang of takeover debt accumulated from the takeover frenzy of the late 1980s also imparted a growth inhibiting effect on company profits. To a lesser extent, other significant factors contributing to the industry's decline included a stabilization in the number of women entering the work force, as well as a change in consumer buying habits to discounters and off-price stores.

One positive business trend in recent years for women's apparel manufacturers has been an increased ability to take advantage of overseas opportunities. The long term decline in the value of the dollar spurred the export sales of women's and misses' blouses and shirts. In the early 1990s industry watchers remained enthusiastic about the prospects for export growth as a cure for the industry's economic woes. Their optimism was further buoyed with the 1993 passage of the North American Free Trade Agreement (NAFTA) and the elimination of significant world trade barriers as specified under the General Agreement on Tariffs and Trade (GATT).

The clothing industry, particularly women's apparel, is sensitive to changes in economic conditions. In the 1980s, consumers were wearing designer labels and $100 jeans. The economic downturn in the early 1990s, however, caused consumers to look for value and savings. Consumer preferences shifted from fancy dressing to basic apparel at home as well as at work. As a result of this shift, manufacturers moved to the extremes of the industry: discounters and high fashion designers. Consequently, the number of women's apparel manufacturers

APPAREL, WOMEN'S AND GIRLS'

SICs 2330, 2340

A report issued by the U.S. Department of Commerce projected moderate growth for the U.S. apparel industry through the mid-1990s. This forecast, based on a favorable long-term outlook for consumer spending, housing starts, and new car purchases, also noted the increasingly competitive nature of the industry as foreign producers work to increase their share of the U.S. market. The elimination of the Multifiber Arrangement (MFA) quota program in 1995 bodes well for domestic women's and girls' apparel manufacturers who have suffered from intense foreign competition for years.

TOP WOMEN'S WEAR COMPANIES

Ranked by: Sales, in millions of dollars.

1. Liz Claiborne, with $2,081 million
2. Jones Apparel Group, $776
3. Cygne Designs Inc., $540
4. Donna Karan, $510
5. Avon Products, $501

Source: *Apparel Industry Magazine,* Top 100 Sewn Products Companies (annual), June, 1996, p. 21.

declined. An increase in imports further increased the competition in this already volatile and difficult industry. Although imports increased by only 5 percent per year between 1988 and 1991, they jumped 15 percent in 1992, and again in 1993, slowing to 12 percent in 1994, 1995, and 1996. According to *Apparel Industry Magazine,* ''Weak consumer demand (prompted by factors that include consumers' anxiety about their jobs, the tendency of Baby Boomers to spend more on furniture and less on clothing, and casual Fridays)'' was to blame for sluggish apparel imports.

These events created increased competition and a reluctance on behalf of manufacturers and retailers to raise prices on apparel. Many small players were forced to close their doors, and the strength of the remaining manufacturers during the mid-1990s depended on an end to worldwide recessionary conditions. Between 1992 and 1997, average annual apparel employment decreased by 160,000 workers. In 1996, dress production fell 9 percent.

The women's apparel industry consists of several specific segments. There were more than 3,500 manufacturers of women's, juniors', and misses' dresses in the United States in 1993. In 1994, this industry generated over $6 billion in total shipments, representing nearly 25 percent of the $22 billion women's and misses' outerwear category. In 1995, women's, misses', and juniors' dress shipments reached nearly $6.2 billion. Over 1,000 companies produced women's suits, coats, skirts, and jackets in 1993. The value of shipments of women's suits, coats, skirts, and jackets in 1995 fell to $3.92 billion from $3.93 billion in 1994 and $4.2 billion in 1993, continuing a decade and a half-long downward trend. Factors such as the increase in imports and a general shift toward more casual office wear had a negative impact on this segment of the U.S. market.

There were more than 1,700 manufacturers of women's, misses', and juniors' outerwear in the United States in 1993. In 1994, total shipments of women's, misses' and juniors' outerwear not elsewhere classified totaled $8.1 billion.

About 340 establishments were engaged in the manufacture of women's, misses', children's, and infants' underwear in 1993. These establishments were collectively responsible for an inflation adjusted value of total product shipments estimated at $1.9 billion. This figure was in line with a long term declining trend which, beginning in 1984, had fallen without interruption. When tracked over the five year period covering 1987-1992, the annual percentage change in the value of the total product shipments averaged a negative 6.1 percent. The industry grew slightly from 1993 to 1995 with total product shipments for the industry valued at $2.2 billion in 1995. The U.S. bra and allied garment industry shipments were valued at $1.8 billion in 1995.

INDUSTRY OUTLOOK

According to the American Manufacturers Association, apparel imports grew only 10 percent in 1995. Imports of cotton apparel grew 1 percent; man-made fiber apparel imports increased 7 percent; and wool apparel imports rose 8 percent. Imports of fibers covered by the Multi Fiber Arrangement (MFA) fell 18 percent. In keeping with these overall industry trends, imports of women's knit shirts and blouses fell 12 percent in 1996, while import figures for women's shirts and blouses, not knit, remained similar those of 1995. Although import growth was down and domestic production dropped in 1996, U.S. apparel consumption grew 5.8 percent. Retail sales of women's apparel grew 5.1 percent in 1996 compared to a 1 percent growth in 1995.

A new World Trade Organization (WTO) was established in 1995, and the Multifiber Arrangement which allowed importing countries to limit the flow of imports from lower cost, developing countries was replaced by the ATC which required the phasing out of MFA quotas over a ten-year period. According to Linda Shelton in an *Industry, Trade, and Technology Review* report, ''The elimination of MFA quotas likely will have a significant impact on the U.S. textile and apparel sector given the level of protection that such restrictions have provided domestic producers over the past two decades.'' Since the U.S. has until 2005 to implement the ATC, the legislation's impact on the women's apparel industry may not be realized for several years.

The value of women's wear shipments declined gradually through the 1990s. One of the many reasons included a leveling-off of the number of women entering the work force. Historically, women's apparel accounted for half of all clothing sold, and it was sold primarily to working women, who by 1990 comprised 45 percent of

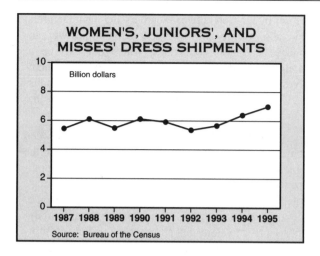

WOMEN'S, JUNIORS', AND MISSES' DRESS SHIPMENTS

Billion dollars

Source: Bureau of the Census

the U.S. work force. In addition, office wear became more casual, and this particularly affected the sales of women's suits. And as the U.S. population aged, people often became less concerned with up-to-the-minute fashions than with saving for mortgage payments and children's educations. The market stabilized in 1996 and 1997 as manufacturers adjusted their lines to meet the demands of the more casual workplace. Nearly 63 million women were in the labor force in 1997, and they represented almost 50 percent of managerial and professional positions.

Retailers themselves sought to cut costs and become more efficient as the market became more competitive. Retailers often looked to the larger apparel manufacturers that were providing merchandise that consumers recognized and respected. By limiting the number of manufacturers supplying them, retailers could reduce overhead expenses—thus favoring the larger manufacturers over the smaller ones.

ORGANIZATION AND STRUCTURE

The apparel industry was composed of three types of producers: contractors, jobbers, and manufacturers. Contractors were independent firms performing specialized work, such as sewing a garment, for a number of competing firms. Contractors were hired by producers who either did not have their own sewing apparatus or whose own capacity had been exceeded. Contractors were not involved in the retail sale of merchandise. Over one-half of the plants making women's coats and suits were run by contractors.

Jobbers were design and marketing businesses that were hired to perform specific functions. For example, jobbers might purchase materials, design patterns, create samples, cut material, and hire contractors to manufacture the product. Most jobbers, however, did not sew

garments, but instead hired contractors to sew and finish the products. These contracted sewing-machine operators completed specific parts of the garment, which were provided by the manufacturer. Through this system of piece work, operators could work more quickly and efficiently because they did not have to switch or adjust their machines.

Jobbers often had their own design staffs to create seasonal lines, or they might hire free-lancers to do design work. A jobber bought the materials needed to produce the pieces, and then created the patterns for different sizes. The cut material was then sent to contractors to be sewn and finished. Orders were taken for the garments, and the finished garments were then shipped to retailers.

Manufacturers were those establishments performing all functions involved in creating apparel from purchased materials. The manufacturer had a staff that produced designs, or it bought work from free-lancers. It then purchased the needed materials (fabric and trimmings). Generally the cutting and sewing of the garment was done in the manufacturer's factories. However, when demand for an item exceeded the manufacturer's ability to supply it within shipping deadlines, outside contractors might be hired. The manufacturer's own sales and shipping staff took orders and sent them out.

When a manufacturer handled all stages of a garment's assembly, it clearly had greater control over the quality of the product. Nevertheless, the advantages to using contractors were numerous. For example, those companies without the capital to update machinery would find the system advantageous. Manufacturers who relied upon contractors also avoided the responsibility of hiring and training workers. And the contractor system was flexible—providing manufacturing capacity when needed at busy periods without having to meet payroll obligations at off-peak periods.

WORK FORCE

In 1982 total employment in the women's and girls' apparel industry stood at 92,300, of which 79,400 were classified as production workers. By 1991 total employment had fallen to 55,900, of which 46,900 were production workers. During those ten years total employment fell by 39.5 percent and production worker employment dropped by 41 percent. Over the same period the annual total value added by production workers either stayed about the same or increased as their average weekly hours steadily increased from 34 hours in 1982 to 36.4 hours in 1991. From 1982 to 1990 the industry's value added per production worker climbed almost continuously from $23,200 to $36,000. For the same period movements in the real wage indicated a mostly downward trend, suggesting that productivity gains were not being matched by increases in the real wage. In 1995, the industry's work force dropped 10 percent and wages increased to approximately $7.30 per hour for women's apparel workers.

Compared against the measures of employment by gender, race and Hispanic origin for the U.S. manufacturing sector as a whole, women, black, and Hispanic workers active in the apparel work force far exceeded their national counterparts. According to American Apparel Manufacturers Association estimates for 1995, women accounted for 70.1 percent of the apparel work force, a figure considerably higher than the overall manufacturing average of 31.6 percent. Black apparel workers accounted for 15 percent of the work force total—the total manufacturing average is 10.4 percent—and Hispanic workers accounted for 24 percent of the employee work force, compared to the national average of 10.2 percent.

The number of workers involved specifically in the manufacture of women's, juniors', and misses' dresses fell from a high of 122,000 in 1983 to less than 100,000 by 1993. In that same time period, average wages rose from $5.18 per hour to close to $7.00 per hour. In 1995, average wages reached $7.29 per hour. There were approximately 40,400 workers involved in the manufacture of women's suits, coats, skirts, and jackets apparel in 1995, down from 45,900 five years earlier. The majority (approximately 30,900) were production workers. Wages averaged $8.09 an hour, up more than $1 an hour from wages in 1990. In 1995 the total number of individuals employed by women's and children's underwear and nightwear manufacturers fell to 31,200, with 27,100 classified as production workers. The average hourly wage in 1995 was $6.75, only $.24 more than the previous year and well below the industry average. Manufacturers of bras and allied garments employed approximately 14,100 workers in 1996, 10,500 of whom were involved in production activities. Average hourly earnings within the industry were projected at $8.15 in 1995, up from $7.22 in the previous year.

New York was the state with the largest number of employees in the women's apparel industry, while Pennsylvania, New Jersey, California, and Massachusetts also had significant concentrations of workers.

RESEARCH AND TECHNOLOGY

Despite being caught up in ongoing grip of establishment downsizing, major technological changes began to impact on the industry in the late 1980s that led to a closer integration between retailers and manufacturers. New labor saving and lower cost technologies were introduced at larger companies, which only served to widen the competitive cost differentials between themselves and the middle and lower tier firms in the industry. Unless rectified, this situation could also stoke the industry's downsizing trend.

A significant development in recent years between retailers and the industry's manufacturers has been the implementation of the quick response system, a computerized strategy that provides for the quick and precise replenishment of "hot-selling" garments. By means of electronic data interchange, participating apparel producers are privy to an instant and continuous flow of information concerning retail sales by styles, sizes, and colors, along with the level of retail inventory. With this information in their possession, manufacturers plan further production rounds on a more precise basis by discarding slow-moving styles and devoting their efforts towards fast selling items. As a result, they avoid costly markdowns and increase turnover. In most instances quick response systems have been formed between large volume manufacturers and retailers with the high level of funds necessary to purchase these costly systems.

Internal to the establishments, new automated technologies were being installed to speed up the manufacturing process and reduce the labor time required per garment. Examples included automated marker and patternmakers, computer inspection of fabrics, scanning and measurement of fabric width variance, and shade recognition apparatus, which have all become automated parts of a fully integrated quality enhancing system. New programmable sewing units that utilize microprocessors were also instrumental in reducing sewing labor costs. Prior to their introduction the sewing of a garment accounted for the largest portion of an article's labor cost, while anywhere from 70 to 80 percent of its in-process production time was spent handling and positioning a garment. To reduce in-process handling new automatic conveyor systems are being developed, along with robotics systems and automated warehouse facilities.

AMERICA AND THE WORLD

IMPORTS

Overseas markets have become increasingly important to U.S. apparel manufacturers, particularly in the developing markets of the former Soviet Union and Eastern Europe. An economic newsletter published by the American Apparel Manufacturers Association paid particular attention to trends in Asia that suggested opportunities for domestic apparel manufacturers. Japan, for example, had huge stores of foreign exchange but the public's living standard is below that of U.S. citizens. The cultural climate in Japan was changing in the early 1990s and Japan's citizens were beginning to enjoy more leisure time. It was anticipated that such time would lead to an increase in the consumption of personal goods and services. Likewise, the opening of trade doors to China and the increasing interest in Western goods offered tremendous growth opportunities for U.S. apparel manufacturers.

A new World Trade Organization (WTO) was established in 1995, and the Multifiber Arrangement (MFA), which allowed importing countries to limit the flow of imports from lower cost developing countries was replaced by the Agreement on Textiles and Clothing (ATC), which required the phasing out of MFA quotas over a ten-year period. According to Linda Shelton in an *Industry, Trade, and Technology Review* report, "The elimination of MFA quotas likely will have a significant impact on the U.S. textile and apparel sector given the level of protection that such restrictions have provided domestic producers over the past two decades." Since the United States has until 2005 to implement the ATC, the legislation's impact on the women's apparel industry may not be realized for several years.

Ever since the end of World War II, the domestic producers of women's and misses' blouses and shirts have been vulnerable to import penetration. Although they still account for the largest share of U.S. imports, the market share of the "Big Four"—the People's Republic of China, Taiwan, Hong Kong, and Korea— actually declined after the early 1980s dropping from 63 percent in 1984 to 41 percent in 1992. Shipments from all of these countries declined with the exception of China, which recorded an increase of more than 100 percent. The "Big Four" continued to lose market share to new players such as Bangladesh, Indonesia, and Thailand, and represented only 28 percent of apparel imports in 1995. This was due in part to increased implementation of "quick response" and U.S. apparel manufacturers ability to react more quickly to fluctuating consumer demands. By far the largest gains in import market share occurred were enjoyed by the Caribbean countries and Mexico. These countries increased their market share from 20 percent in 1992 to approximately 54 percent in 1996.

EXPORTS

Exports of apparel grew from 2 percent of total U.S. product shipments in 1987 to more than 7 percent in 1992. Total U.S. exports in that year were nearly $4 billion. Although much of this growth represented expansion of existing or new markets, a large portion of

this gain was due to semi-finished garments sent abroad for finishing and then returned to the United States under the provision of Harmonized Tariff Schedule of the United States (HTSUS) code 9802, formerly 807. Although section 807 existed since the Tariff Act of 1790, it only gained importance during the 1980s, as apparel imports dramatically increased. In the decade from 1980 to 1990, apparel imports increased 202 percent.

The 9802 program allows a manufacturer to pay duty only on the value added to the garment abroad, not the total value of the product. In 1992, HTSUS 9802 trade was slightly more than 14 percent of total imports, and nearly $900 million worth of HTSUS 9802 imports were produced in the Dominican Republic. Mexico produced approximately $700 million, followed by Costa Rica with $400 million in apparel production.

In addition, the North American Free Trade Agreement (NAFTA), which created a free-trade zone between the United States, Mexico, and Canada by gradually eliminating tariffs over 15 years, took effect January 1, 1994. Since a similar agreement was already in effect between the United States and Canada, analysts expected NAFTA to increase trade with Mexico. Apparel-industry executives supported NAFTA. The ILGWU and the ACTWU, by contrast, sought to stem the loss of jobs in the apparel industry by limiting the imports allowed into the country. However, their arguments did not succeed in challenging the free-market philosophy that ultimately triumphed in the passage of NAFTA.

ASSOCIATIONS AND SOCIETIES

AFFILIATED DRESS MANUFACTURERS
500 7th Ave.
New York, NY 10018
Phone: (212) 819-1011

AMALGAMATED CLOTHING AND TEXTILE WORKERS UNION
15 Union Sq. W
New York, NY 10003
Phone: (212) 242-0700
Fax: (212) 255-8169

AMERICAN APPAREL MANUFACTURERS ASSOCIATION
2500 Wilson Blvd., Ste. 301
Arlington, VA 22201
Phone: (703) 524-1864
Fax: (703) 522-6741

AMERICAN CLOAK AND SUIT MANUFACTURERS ASSOCIATION
450 7th Ave.
New York, NY 10123
Phone: (212) 244-7300

ASSOCIATED CORSET AND BRASSIERE MANUFACTURERS
1430 Broadway, Ste. 1603
New York, NY 10018
Phone: (212) 354-0707
Fax: (212) 221-3540

BUREAU OF WHOLESALE SALES REPRESENTATIVES
1801 Peachtree St. NW, Ste. 200
Atlanta, GA 30308
Phone: (800) 877-1808 or (404) 351-7355
Fax: (404) 352-5298

CHAMBER OF COMMERCE OF THE APPAREL INDUSTRY
570 7th Ave., 10 Fl.
New York, NY 10018
Phone: (212) 354-0907
Fax: (212) 768-4732

CLOTHING MANUFACTURERS OF THE U.S.A.
1290 Avenue of the Americas, Ste. 1061
New York, NY 10104

COUNCIL OF FASHION DESIGNERS OF AMERICA
1412 Broadway, Ste. 1714
New York, NY 10018
Phone: (212) 302-1861
Fax: (212) 768-0515

INDUSTRIAL ASSOCIATION OF JUVENILE APPAREL MANUFACTURERS
1430 Broadway, Ste. 1603
New York, NY 10018
Phone: (212) 244-2953

INFANT AND JUVENILE MANUFACTURERS ASSOCIATION
575 Lexington Ave., 19 Fl.
New York, NY 10022-6102
Phone: (212) 754-3100
Fax: (212) 371-2980

INTERNATIONAL ASSOCIATION OF CLOTHING DESIGNERS
475 Park Ave. S, 17 Fl.
New York, NY 10016
Phone: (212) 685-6602

INTERNATIONAL LADIES' GARMENT WORKERS' UNION
1710 Broadway
New York, NY 10019
Phone: (212) 265-7000

INTIMATE APPAREL MANUFACTURERS ASSOCIATION
1430 Broadway, Ste. 1603
New York, NY 10018
Phone: (212) 354-0707
Fax: (212) 221-3540

NEW YORK COAT AND SUIT ASSOCIATION
500 7th Ave.
New York, NY 10018
Phone: (212) 814-1011

TEXTILE INSTITUTE
10 Blackfriars St.
Manchester M3 5DR, England
Phone: 161-8 34-8457
Fax: 161-8 35-3087
Members from more than 100 countries are involved with textile industry management, marketing, science, and technology.

UNITED GARMENT WORKERS OF AMERICA
4207 Lebanon Rd.
Hermitage, TN 37076
Phone: (615) 889-9221
Fax: (615) 885-3102

UNITED INFANTS' AND CHILDREN'S WEAR ASSOCIATION
1430 Broadway, Ste. 1603
New York, NY 10018
Phone: (212) 244-2953

PERIODICALS AND NEWSLETTERS

APPAREL INDUSTRY MAGAZINE
Shore Communications, Inc.
6225 Barfield Rd. NE, Ste. 200
Atlanta, GA 30328-4300
Phone: (404) 252-8831
Fax: (404) 252-4436
Monthly. $54.00 per year.

BABY AND JUNIOR: INTERNATIONAL TRADE MAGAZINE FOR CHILDREN'S AND YOUTH FASHIONS AND SUPPLIES
Meisenbach GmbH
Hainstrasse 18
Bamberg, Germany 96047
Phone: 0951 861 135
Fax: 0951 861 158
Monthly. 60.00 per year. Text in English, French and German.

BODY FASHIONS: INTIMATE APPAREL
Advanstar Communications, Inc.
7500 Old Oak Blvd.
Cleveland, OH 44130
Phone: (800) 346-0085 or (216) 243-8100
Fax: (216) 891-2726
Monthly. $25.00 per year.

INTIMATE FASHION NEWS
MacKay Publishing Corp.
307 5th Ave.
New York, NY 10016
Phone: (800) 886-6677 or(212) 679-6677
Fax: (212) 679-6374
Semimonthly. $25.00 per year. Provides essential information on the intimate apparel industry.

NEEDLE'S EYE
Union Special Corp.
1 Union Special Plz.
Huntley, IL 669-3209
Phone: (708) 669-4334
Fax: (708) 699-3543

Bimonthly. Free. Text in English; summaries in several languages.

TEXTILE HI-LIGHTS
American Textile Manufacturers Institute, Inc.
1801 K St. NW, Ste. 900
Washington, DC 20006-1301
Phone: (202) 862-0500
Fax: (202) 862-0570
Quarterly. $75.00 per year. Monthly supplements.

TEXTILE WORLD
Maclean Hunter Publishing Co.
Textile Publications
170 Ashford-Dunwoody Rd., Ste. 420
Atlanta, GA 30319
Phone: (404) 847-2770
Fax: (404) 252-6150
Monthly. Free to qualified personnel; others, $42.00 per year.

WOMEN'S WEAR DAILY: THE RETAILER'S DAILY NEWSPAPER
Fairchild Fashion and Merchandising Group
7 W. 34th St.
New York, NY 10001
Phone: (800) 247-6622 or (212) 741-4000
Fax: (212) 630-4879
Daily. $89.00 per year.

DATABASES

CITIBASE (CITICORP ECONOMIC DATABASE)
FAME Software Corp.
77 Water St., 9 Fl.
New York, NY 10005
Phone: (212) 898-7800
Fax: (212) 742-8956
Presents over 6,000 statistical series relating to business, industry, finance, and economics. Includes series from Survey of Current Business *and many other sources. Time period is 1947 to date, with daily updates. Inquire as to online cost and availability.*

F & S INDEX
Information Access Co.
362 Lakeside Dr.
Foster City, CA 94404
Phone: (800) 321-6388 or (415-358-4643
Fax: (415) 358-4759
Contains about four million citations to worldwide business, financial, and industrial or consumer product literature appearing from 1972 to date. Weekly updates. Inquire as to online cost and availability.

TEXTILE TECHNOLOGY DIGEST [ONLINE]
Textile Information Center
Institute of Textile Technology
2551 Ivy Rd.
Charlottesville, VA 22903-4614
Phone: (804) 296-5511
Fax: (804) 977-5400
Contains indexing and abstracting of more than 800 worldwide journals and monographs in various areas of textile technology,

production, and management. Time period is 1978 to date, with monthly updating. Inquire as to online cost and availability.

WORLD TEXTILES
Elsevier Science, Inc.
655 Avenue of the Americas
New York, NY 10010
Phone: (800) 457-3633 or (212) 989-5800
Fax: (212) 633-3680
Provides abstracting from 1983 and indexing from 1970 of worldwide textile literature (periodicals, books, pamphlets, and reports). Includes U.S., European, and British patent information. Updating is monthly. Inquire as to online cost and availability.

STATISTICS SOURCES

BUSINESS STATISTICS
Available from U.S. Government Printing Office
Washington, DC 20402
Phone: (202) 512-1800
Fax: (202) 512-2250
Biennial. $20.00. Issued by Bureau of Economic Analysis, U.S. Department of Commerce. Shows annual data for 29 years and monthly data for a recent four-year period. Statistics correspond to the Survey of Current Business.

FAIRCHILD'S TEXTILE AND APPAREL FINANCIAL DIRECTORY
Fairchild Books, Fairchild Publications, Inc.
Seven W. 34th St.
New York, NY 10001
Phone: (800) 247-6622 or (212) 630-3880
Annual. $85.00. Provides statistical and analytical marketing data, including industry concentration, materials consumed, import/export sales, value of shipments, retail sales by outlet type, advertising expenditures, consumer buying habits, and industry trends.

MONTHLY RETAIL TRADE: SALES AND INVENTORIES
Available from U.S. Government Printing Office
Washington, DC 20402
Phone: (202) 512-1800
Fax: (202) 512-2250
Monthly, with annual summary. $57.00 per year. Issued by Bureau of the Census, U.S. Department of Commerce. Includes Advance Monthly Retail Sales.

SURVEY OF CURRENT BUSINESS
Available from U.S. Government Printing Office
Washington, DC 20402
Phone: (202) 512-1800
Fax: (202) 512-2250
Monthly. $41.00 per year. Issued by Bureau of Economic Analysis, U.S. Department of Commerce. Presents a wide variety of business and economic data.

U.S. MERCHANDISE TRADE: SELECTED HIGHLIGHTS
Bureau of the Census, U.S. Department of Commerce
Available from U.S. Government Printing Office
Washington, DC 20402
Phone: (202) 512-1800
Fax: (202) 512-2250

Monthly. $25.00 per year. Formerly Highlights of the United States Export and Import Trade.

GENERAL WORKS

FASHION MERCHANDISING: AN INTRODUCTION
E. Stone and J. Samples
McGraw-Hill, Inc.
1221 Avenue of the Americas
New York, NY 10020
Phone: (800) 722-4726 or (212) 512-2000
Fax: (212) 512-2821
1989. $27.25. Fifth edition.

FASHION MERCHANDISING AND MARKETING
Marian H. Jernigan and Cynthia R. Easterling
200 Old Tappan Rd.
Old Tappan, NJ 07675
Phone: (800) 223-2336
Fax: (800) 445-6991
1990. Price on application.

THE U.S. APPAREL INDUSTRY: INTERNATIONAL CHALLENGE-DOMESTIC RESPONSE
Jeffrey S. Arpan and others
Georgia State University
Business Press
University Plz.

Atlanta, GA 30303
Phone: (404) 658-4253
Fax: (404) 651-4256
1982. $24.95.

FURTHER READING

Apparel Import Digest. Arlington, VA: American Apparel Manufacturers Association, 1997.

Apparel Industry Trends. Arlington, VA: American Apparel Manufacturers Association, March 1997.

Brady, Jennifer L. "Analysts: Apparel on Slow Road to Recovery." *Women's Wear Daily,* 13 May 1996.

Focus: An Economic Profile of the Apparel Industry. Arlington, VA: American Apparel Manufacturers Association, 1996.

"Import Growth Slowing, AAMA Says." *Apparel Industry,* June 1996.

Shelton, Linda, and Robert Wallace. "World Textile and Apparel Trade: A New Era," *Industry, Trade, and Technology Review,* October 1996.

Statistical Abstract of the United States, Washington DC: U.S. Department of Commerce, 1996.

A uniquely American innovation, electric and gas household appliances became commonplace in U.S. homes during the post-war economic expansion of the 1950s, 1960s, and 1970s. By the early 1980s, miscellaneous appliance makers in the United States were shipping about $1.5 billion worth of goods each year and employing a work force of more than 14,000. Continued rapid growth in the 1980s, moreover, pushed industry sales past $3.2 billion by the early 1990s. In the mid-1990s, renovations of homes reached a record $69.5 billion, reflecting the increasing trend for home-improvement and bolstering the U.S. replacement market.

The North American Free Trade Agreement may also help expand U.S. exports of home appliances to Mexico. In terms of five-year growth, shipments were projected to increase about 2 percent every year due in part to the fact that appliances are a mature industry. Most appliances are purchased for new housing, replacement, or remodeling.

By the beginning of the 1990s, decades of consolidation had left an industry with little room for growth domestically. There were no smaller companies left for the large corporations to buy. According to *Appliance* magazine, the industry was mature with 99.9 percent of American households possessing refrigerators; about 40 percent of homes contained a freezer. In 1996 freezer sales totaled $1.69 billion, and sales of refrigerators totaled $8.67 billion. Most companies sold appliances under many brand names, which have been around since home refrigeration became feasible in the late 1920s.

Although mechanical washing contraptions existed before the start of the twentieth century, only since the 1950s have gas and electric-powered laundry equipment achieved widespread use. By the early 1990s, over 70 percent of all U.S. homes had both a washer and a dryer. In 1996, 6.92 million washers and 5.24 million dryers (both electric and gas) were shipped. Laundry equipment was the second largest home appliance market, following refrigeration. With commercial laundry appliances, the total number of shipments in the industry was 12.165 million units in 1996.

Electric housewares and fans comprise a major portion of the widely diverse products of the general housewares category, ranking third in shipments—refrigeration is first and laundry equipment second. In 1997, the industry shipped an estimated 16 billion units, totaling $3 billion worth of product and employing 20,000 workers. Like the other sectors of the housewares industry, the economic success of this industry is tied to

APPLIANCES, HOUSEHOLD

SIC 3630

Although manufacturers suffered during an economic recession in the early 1990s, sales began to pick up entering the mid-1990s. Export growth was augmenting the domestic recovery and promised to provide an avenue for long-term expansion. Furthermore, positive demographic trends and U.S. replacement markets were expected to buoy domestic revenues throughout the decade. Challenges faced by competitors in the early 1990s included federal regulations designed to address environmental concerns and a lack of major new product lines.

BEST SELLING APPLIANCE BRANDS

Ranked by: Sales in 1994, in billions of dollars.

1. Whirlpool, with $8.1 billion
2. GE Appliance, $5.9
3. Frigidaire, $4.4
4. Maytag, $3.3
5. Amana, $0.5

Source: *Brandweek,* Superbrands: America's Top 2,000 Brands, October 9, 1995, p. 118.

the health of the housing industry and to general consumer confidence levels.

Following solid industry growth during the 1960s and 1970s, the household vacuum cleaner industry realized steady expansion during the 1980s. Prodded by new product introductions and positive demographic trends, vacuum cleaner sales rocketed from $775 million in 1982 to $1.87 billion in 1990, reflecting an average annual growth rate of more than 10 percent. Stick and handheld vacuums were the fastest growing product segments during this period. Economic recess sent industry revenues tumbling below $1.7 billion in the early 1990s. A recovery entering the mid-1990s, however, buoyed earnings and promised to revive struggling manufacturers. Overall unit shipments were forecast to rise with stick and upright vacuums leading industry growth.

INDUSTRY OUTLOOK

Sluggish economic conditions, which suppressed housing starts and replacement sales, battered manufacturers of miscellaneous appliances in 1990. Home building and consumer expenditures picked up in 1992, though, prodded by low interest rates and pent-up demand. After plunging to $3.1 billion in 1990, industry revenues climbed to $3.3 billion in 1991 and grew about 4 percent annually during 1992 and 1993. Unit sales volume climbed even faster. Dishwasher shipments, for example, jumped almost 8 percent in 1993, and water heater orders increased by about 6 percent.

Although appliance makers lacked major new product offerings that could broaden their industry, they were having some success enticing new buyers to the market by adding new features to established products. Manufacturers were also benefitting from generally positive demographic trends. In addition, large numbers of appliances sold in the early 1980s were rapidly approaching replacement age. Although the strong growth that miscellaneous appliance makers enjoyed during the 1980s was unlikely to occur throughout the 1990s, observers expect steady modest growth for the next several years. In addition, some industry niches, such as portable dishwashers, may realize periods of faster growth. Furthermore, continued gains in manufacturing productivity should boost bottom-line profits.

In an effort to exceed forecasts, producers in the mid-1990s were striving to accelerate replacement sales by developing more energy-efficient, convenient, and versatile machines. They also hoped to expand export sales. Encouraging industry participants was the likelihood of continued low interest rates, diminishing inventories, steady annual growth in consumer spending, and the potential of completely new product introductions.

New government environmental regulations were one of the greatest hurdles facing appliance makers in the mid-1990s. The U.S. Department of Energy's (DOE's) National Appliance Energy Conservation Act of 1987, for example, set new standards that limit energy consumption by new appliances. The act requires manufacturers to cut energy consumption in their products by 25 percent every five years.

The refrigerator and freezer industry was also under pressure to find an alternative coolant to chlorofluorocarbons (CFCs), which were believed to cause depletion of the ozone layer that protects the planet from dangerous cancer-causing ultraviolet rays. An agreement called the Montreal Protocol called for complete elimination of the use of CFCs by the year 2000; however, officials and environmentalists from many countries were pushing for elimination of CFCs sooner because of evidence that the level of CFCs in the stratosphere over North America was even worse than originally reported.

Laundry industry sales grew about 2 percent per year from 1990 to 1997. Unit volume grew annually at a steady 2-3 percent. Increased sales were largely the result of an uptick in housing starts and escalating consumer expenditures following the recession. The replacement market for washers and dryers was a constant; for example, in 1996, 3.396 million washing machines were replaced.

ORGANIZATION AND STRUCTURE

Both the manufacturers and appliance distributors were busy consolidating in the 1970s and 1980s. As the distributors became larger, they wanted more pricing and service concessions. This put pressure on manufacturers as they had to accept smaller profit margins. The manufacturers were better able to provide concessions through their own consolidation, which streamlined operations. This consolidation enabled them to produce more efficiently and maintain tight profit margins despite large volume discounts to giant distributors and mega-retailers. The suppliers of the manufacturers—especially the steel industry—rose to the challenge in the early to mid-1990s improving processes and the ability to deliver more finished and more flexible products and processes. Gains in such procedures as powder painting and custom steel cutting made for faster turn-around and further cuts in the cost of manufacture.

About 98 percent of all major appliances, except microwave ovens, are American-made. Smaller appliances like coffee makers, food processors, and toasters, however, are imported from Europe. Some cooking equipment sold in the United States is also manufactured overseas.

The appliance industry can be differentiated from other manufacturing sectors by its production characteristics. Appliance manufacturing is essentially an assembly-line process whereby ready-made components are assembled. Because it has low fixed costs and is labor intensive, appliance production offers abundant opportunities for manufacturing efficiency gains. This characteristic contributes to a high weight-to-value ratio that limits overseas appliance imports into the United States, and caused prices to remain effectively fixed during the 1980s and early 1990s.

Appliance sales are driven primarily by three factors: replacement sales; product market penetration, particularly in the case of completely new appliances; and new construction, which generates demand by builders that perform first-time installations. Because most product categories have achieved almost full market penetration, miscellaneous appliance sales are highly dependent upon replacement sales and new construction, and are closely linked to housing starts and economic growth.

About 26 percent of industry revenues in the early 1990s was garnered from individual consumer purchases. Residential builders consumed about 20 percent of aggregate output, while commercial and institutional developers made up approximately 24 percent of the market. Roughly 5 percent of production was exported. The remaining 25 percent of sales were made to the armed forces, state and local governments, mobile home builders, and other sectors.

Household laundry equipment represented about 17 percent of the overall U.S. household appliance industry in the 1990s. Nearly 80 percent of all household laundry equipment is purchased by individuals for home use. An additional 6 percent of industry output is consumed by laundromats, dry cleaners, and other services that use domestic laundry equipment. The remainder of the U.S. market is comprised of state, local, and federal government institutions, such as the armed forces and prisons. Over 7 percent of U.S. production in the early 1990s was exported.

SIC 3631 - Household Cooking Equipment
General Statistics

Year	Com-panies	Establishments		Employment			Compensation		Production ($ million)			
		Total	with 20 or more employees	Total (000)	Production Workers (000)	Hours (Mil)	Payroll ($ mil)	Wages ($/hr)	Cost of Materials	Value Added by Manufacture	Value of Shipments	Capital Invest.
1982	71	88	59	23.7	17.0	31.4	402.1	8.11	1,408.3	941.4	2,414.9	51.5
1983		87	58	26.5	19.7	39.4	488.7	8.22	1,862.0	1,276.9	3,075.8	69.4
1984		86	57	27.7	21.5	42.9	544.8	8.64	2,161.4	1,528.8	3,578.5	86.3
1985		85	56	24.2	18.5	35.9	492.4	9.02	2,006.7	1,236.5	3,297.3	76.6
1986		82	55	22.2	16.9	32.6	461.9	9.51	2,089.8	1,305.3	3,328.7	88.6
1987	65	78	47	21.9	16.9	33.3	475.8	9.72	2,118.3	1,267.9	3,395.8	79.6
1988		75	52			33.3	463.8		2,382.3	1,404.7	3,699.4	
1989		77	48	21.5	15.9	31.3	440.7	9.77	1,940.0	1,087.6	3,094.5	63.2
1990		79	48	20.2	15.3	30.2	442.2	10.03	1,821.7	1,138.9	2,994.0	84.7
1991		90	53	18.4	14.8	28.0	401.5	9.95	1,801.0	1,091.2	2,890.7	95.7
1992	80	89	43	18.8	15.0	29.9	437.0	9.81	1,811.7	1,141.4	2,950.0	82.9
1993		98	42	18.6	14.9	29.6	461.1	10.34	1,741.5	1,330.7	3,010.2	82.6
1994		87P	42P	18.6	15.0	30.2	491.2	10.69	1,922.1	1,908.0	3,813.9	101.6
1995		87P	41P			27.6P	447.1P		1,675.7P	1,663.4P	3,325.0P	
1996		88P	39P			26.8P	445.0P		1,685.0P	1,672.6P	3,343.4P	
1997		88P	38P			26.1P	442.9P		1,694.3P	1,681.9P	3,361.9P	
1998		88P	37P			25.3P	440.8P		1,703.6P	1,691.1P	3,380.4P	

Sources: 1982, 1987, 1992 *Economic Census*; *Annual Survey of Manufactures*, 83-86, 88-91, 93-94. Establishment counts for non-Census years are from *County Business Patterns*; establishment values for 83-84 are extrapolations. 'P's show projections by the editors. Industries reclassified in 87 will not have data for prior years.

WORK FORCE

Although productivity gains allowed manufacturers to boost shipments, revenues, and earnings during the 1980s, the workforce suffered cutbacks as a result of those gains. Continued advances in efficiency combined with the movement of manufacturing facilities overseas during the 1990s could significantly curtail industry job prospects in the future. In fact, most blue-collar workers will realize cutbacks of 20 to 40 percent by 2005, according to the U.S. Bureau of Labor Statistics.

SIC 3639
Occupations Employed by SIC 363 - Household Appliances

Occupation	% of Total 1994	Change to 2005
Assemblers, fabricators, & hand workers nec	31.2	-16.9
Helpers, laborers, & material movers nec	4.1	-16.9
Machine assemblers	3.9	-25.2
Inspectors, testers, & graders, precision	3.1	-41.9
Blue collar worker supervisors	3.0	-25.4
Electrical & electronic assemblers	2.7	-25.3
Industrial truck & tractor operators	2.6	-16.9
Plastic molding machine workers	2.6	-0.3
Machine forming operators, metal & plastic	2.5	-58.5
Freight, stock, & material movers, hand	1.9	-33.6
Electrical & electronic equipment assemblers	1.7	-16.9
Machine operators nec	1.5	-41.4
Welding machine setters, operators	1.5	-25.2
Sales & related workers nec	1.5	-17.0
Maintenance repairers, general utility	1.5	-25.2
Janitors & cleaners, incl maids	1.2	-33.6
Tool & die makers	1.2	-32.9
Material moving equipment operators nec	1.2	-16.9
General managers & top executives	1.1	-21.2
Machine tool cutting & forming etc. nec	1.1	-33.6

Source: Industry-Occupation Matrix, Bureau of Labor Statistics. These data relate to one or more 3-digit SIC industry groups rather than to a single 4-digit SIC. The change reported for each occupation to the year 2005 is a percent of growth or decline as estimated by the Bureau of Labor Statistics. The abbreviation nec stands for 'not elsewhere classified'.

In 1972, the average production worker in the electric housewares industry earned $3.03 per hour and added $11.58 worth of value to the product for each production hour. By 1996, that wage had jumped to $8.14 per hour. According to the 1987 *Census of Manufactures,* workers in this industry earned 71 percent of the average industrial hourly wage. In 1996 there were 20,000 people employed in this industry, a number expected to slowly but steadily decline through the turn of the century.

RESEARCH AND TECHNOLOGY

Technological advancements in the mid-1990s centered around compliance with environmental regulations and the development of more efficient appliances. Producers were striving to retain the cleansing power of dishwashers, for example, while reducing water usage. Meanwhile, water heater manufacturers continued to search for more efficient heating, insulation, and distribution technology. Advancements related to all types of appliances were being achieved through the increased use of plastics. New thermoplastics, for example, were being used to reduce heat loss that occurs in appliances encased in metal. Other plastics were helping manufacturers reduce shipping weight and increase the strength and durability of their products.

The five big companies of this industry all instituted programs to improve productivity. The industry was considered one of the most efficient in the country—leaving little room for foreign products to take any significant market share as they had in the car and electronics industries. In addition, prices of American refrigerators and freezers remained reasonable. Several stylish European appliances found a small market in the United States, but they were unlikely to take any significant market share because of their expense. The mid-1990s also saw domestic appliance manufacturers increasing their focus on a stylish product.

U.S. manufacturers were under serious environmental pressure in the 1990s to increase recyclability of refrigerators, reduce energy consumption, and eliminate chlorofluorocarbons as the refrigerant in refrigerators and freezers. Chemical companies, refrigerator makers, and environmentalists were involved in development of alternative refrigerants. One of the alternative refrigerants being suggested was a hydrofluorocarbon (HFC). Use of an alternate substance such as this would allow refrigerator makers to retain the current technology of the vapor-compressor refrigerator. One of the other proposed refrigerants was said to be dangerous because it posed a risk of fire or toxic fumes, while environmentalists claimed that another posed an environmental threat because, although it was not harmful to the ozone, it might contribute to the greenhouse effect. Furthermore, because chlorofluorocarbons (CFCs) were also used in refrigerator insulation, several possible replacements would require new liner materials.

Another approach was represented by the work of U.S. physicist, Steven L. Garrett, who was developing a thermo-acoustic refrigerator that used sound instead of CFCs to transfer heat. This technology, which was first designed for military satellites, would be less harmful to the environment than any substance in a vapor-compressor refrigerator. Even so, thermo-acoustics would require manufacturers to retool their facilities or send their production workers back to school to learn a new technology. Alternative refrigerants would not require these changes.

Capital investments during the mid-1990s were being used to develop more efficient production and distribution methods and to achieve compliance with environmental regulations and pressures. They were also being used to create better and less-expensive products. For example, control software that was being incorporated into machines optimized wash and dry cycles for different types of laundry, adjusted temperature and water levels during a cycle, and allowed machines to talk to users. These microprocessors were also making possible many advanced features, such as self-diagnostic systems, delayed-start timers, and touch controls with cycle programming. New features were also being designed to maximize energy efficiency—an improvement that could expedite replacement sales.

AMERICA AND THE WORLD

The United States is the largest consumer and producer of appliances in the world. It produces and consumes more than 30 percent of global output of most product segments and maintains the highest level of market saturation in virtually every major line of appliances. While 50 percent of U.S. households had a dishwasher in 1993, for example, only 35 percent of French homes were so equipped, and just 15 percent of households in the United Kingdom had dishwashers. Generally low penetration of major appliances in comparison to the United States reflects higher energy costs, less space, and lower living standards characteristic of other countries.

Because manufacturers have achieved close to maximum market penetration with most miscellaneous appliances in the United States, they have increasingly focused their expansion efforts in the 1990s on foreign markets that offered a greater potential for growth. Europe proffered the greatest prospects for profits. Appliance industries on that continent were still fragmented, leaving the market open for massive U.S. conglomerates.

While opportunities prevailed in rapidly unfurling Asian markets, U.S. producers were largely avoiding that region. Three successful Japanese conglomerates established a strong grip on much of the Asian market and posed formidable entry barriers to even the most savvy American competitors. Likewise, Japanese producers were avoiding North American markets for fear of their U.S. counterparts, which maintained a lead in production efficiency, distribution, and marketing know-how—U.S. producers supplied over 75 percent of domestic demand for all types of appliances in 1993. Japanese companies succeeded in penetrating the sewing machine market, though, and were supplying over 70 percent of global demand for that appliance going into 1994.

Imports and exports of appliances increased at nearly the same rate, according to the *U.S. Industrial Outlook 1994*—about 7 percent to $4.1 billion for imports and 6 percent to $2.5 billion for exports. American appliance manufacturers formed joint partnerships with foreign companies to make stoves and microwave ovens overseas for the American market. Many of these foreign-made appliances then come under an American label. The *U.S. Industrial Outlook* stated that "Mexico is expected to increase its lead because of the growing integration of its appliance industry with that of the United States." Countries with traditionally lower wages, like South Korea and China, will continue to be major suppliers of small appliances. Microwave ovens

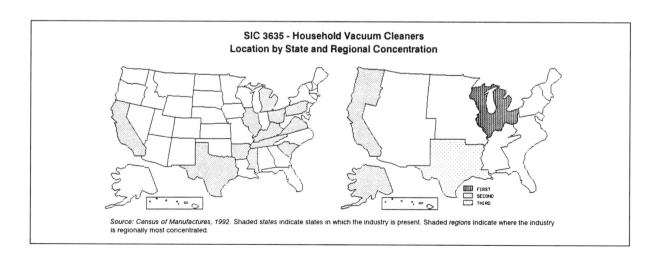

SIC 3635 - Household Vacuum Cleaners
Location by State and Regional Concentration

FIRST
SECOND
THIRD

Source: Census of Manufactures, 1992. Shaded *states* indicate states in which the industry is present. Shaded *regions* indicate where the industry is regionally most concentrated.

still represent the majority of imported appliances, but in recent years, demand for microwaves has tapered off.

ASSOCIATIONS AND SOCIETIES

APPLIANCE PARTS DISTRIBUTORS ASSOCIATION
228 E. Baltimore St.
Detroit, MI 48202
Phone: (313) 872-3658
Fax: (313) 872-5312

ASSOCIATION OF HOME APPLIANCE MANUFACTURERS
20 N. Wacker Dr., Ste. 1500
Chicago, IL 60606
Phone: (312) 984-5800
Fax: (312) 984-5823

NATIONAL APPLIANCE SERVICE ASSOCIATION
9240 N. Meridan St., Ste. 355
Indianapolis, IN 46260
Phone: (317) 844-1602
Fax: (317) 844-4745

NATIONAL ASSOCIATION OF RETAIL DEALERS OF AMERICA
10 E. 22nd St.
Lombard, IL 60148
Phone: (708) 953-8950
Fax: (708) 953-8957

NATIONAL HOUSEWARES MANUFACTURERS ASSOCIATION
6400 Shafer Ct., Ste. 650
Rosemont, IL 60018
Phone: (708) 292-4200
Fax: (708) 292-4211
Members are manufacturers of housewares and small appliances.

PERIODICALS AND NEWSLETTERS

APPLIANCE
Dana Chase Publications, Inc.
1110 Jorie Blvd., CS-9019
Oakbrook, IL 60522-9019
Phone: (708) 990-3484
Fax: (708) 990-0078
Monthly. $60.00 per year.

APPLIANCE MANUFACTURER
Business News Publishing Co.
5900 Harper Rd., No. 105
Solon, OH 44139
Phone: (216) 349-3060
Fax: (216) 248-0187
Monthly. $55.00 per year.

APPLIANCE SERVICE NEWS
Gamit Enterprises, Inc.
110 W. Saint Charles Rd.
Lombard, IL 60148
Phone: (708) 932-9550
Fax: (708) 932-9552
Monthly. $15.25.

DEALERSCOPE MERCHANDISING: THE MARKETING MAGAZINE FOR CONSUMER ELECTRONICS AND MAJOR APPLIANCE RETAILING
North American Publishing Co.
401 N. Broad St.
Philadelphia, PA 19108-9988
Phone: (800) 777-8074 or (215) 238-5300
Fax: (215) 238-5457
Free to qualified personnel; others, $65.00 per year. Formed by the merger Dealerscope *and* Merchandising.

DATABASES

CITIBASE (CITICORP ECONOMIC DATABASE)
FAME Software Corp.
77 Water St., 9 Fl.
New York, NY 10005
Phone: (212) 898-7800
Fax: (212) 742-8956
Presents over 6,000 statistical series relating to business, industry, finance, and economics. Includes series from Survey of Current Business *and many other sources. Time period is 1947 to date, with daily updates. Inquire as to online cost and availability.*

STATISTICS SOURCES

BUSINESS STATISTICS
Available from U.S. Government Printing Office
Washington, DC 20402
Phone: (202) 512-1800
Fax: (202) 512-2250
Biennial. $20.00. Issued by Bureau of Economic Analysis, U.S. Department of Commerce. Shows annual data for 29 years and monthly data for a recent four-year period. Statistics correspond to the Survey of Current Business.

MAJOR HOME APPLIANCE INDUSTRY FACT BOOK: A COMPREHENSIVE REFERENCE ON THE UNITED STATES MAJOR HOME APPLIANCE INDUSTRY
Association of Home Appliance Manufacturers
20 N. Wacker Dr.
Chicago, IL 60606
Phone: (312) 984-5800
Fax: (312) 984-5823
Biennial. $35.00. Includes statistical data on manufacturing, industry shipments, distribution, and ownership.

MAJOR HOUSEHOLD APPLIANCES
U.S. Bureau of the Census
Washington, DC 20233-0800

Phone: (301) 457-4100
Fax: (301) 457-3842
Annual. (Current Industrial Reports MA-36F.)

GENERAL WORKS

APPLIANCE - APPLIANCE INDUSTRY PURCHASING DIRECTORY
Dana Chase Publications
1110 Jorie Blvd., CS-9019
Oakbrook, IL 60522
Phone: (708) 990-3484
Fax: (708) 990-0078
Annual. $45.00.

APPLIANCE MANUFACTUER BUYER'S GUIDE
Corcoran Communications, Inc.
29100 Aurora Rd.
Solon, OH 44139
Phone: (312) 472-8116
Annual. $25.00.

FURTHER READING

Darnay, Arsen J., ed. *Manufacturing USA.* 5th Ed. Detroit: Gale Research, 1997.

Jiambalvo, John R. "The Skinny On Small Appliances." *Appliance,* January 1997.

Le Blanc, Jenny. "1997: Slow Growth Ahead." *Appliance,* January 1997, 38.

Magid, Lawrence J. "Home, Sweet, Automated Home." *Los Angeles Times Syndicate,* MNSBC, 1997. Available from http://www.msnbc.com/news/6966.asp.

"Portrait of the U.S Appliance Industry." *Appliance,* September 1996.

"Small Electric Appliances." 1997. InterCenter Company Website. Available from http://www.intercenter.com/cgi-local/webSession/store=home_store/department.

ASPHALT PAVING AND ROOFING MATERIALS

SIC 2950

Industry sources predict modest growth for the asphalt industry as government spending for road projects and a robust construction industry continue to fuel sales. Future employment prospects in this industry are not promising due to increased automation and a decrease in the growth of demand for some asphalt-based products. Positions for the mostly blue-collar work force were expected to decline by 10 to 20 percent between 1990 and 2005.

INDUSTRY SNAPSHOT

Asphalt is a compound made of hydrogen and carbon, with minor proportions of nitrogen, sulfur, and oxygen. It exists in forms ranging from a black liquid to a glassy solid. Most asphalt is obtained as a byproduct of the distillation of petroleum or other natural materials. Some natural asphalt, however, is extracted from organic mineral deposits in the early stages of their breakdown into petroleum.

Asphalt is used most often in the construction of roads, parking lots, walkways, and other paved surfaces. Of the 2.27 million miles of paved road in the United States, 94 percent of them are surfaced with asphalt, including 65 percent of the interstate system. Asphalt is also commonly utilized in reservoir linings, dam facings, and other harbor and sea applications. When formed into felts and coatings, asphalt provides a reliable protectant and sealant. It is extremely water-repellent, tolerates temperature fluctuations, and resists the breakdown and decay caused by exposure to the elements. These characteristics make asphalt ideal for roofs, coatings, floor tilings, and waterproofing. Asphalt coatings and sheets are also popular soundproofing materials. Roofing shingles represented 40 percent of the total industry output during the 1990s, and all roofing and siding fabrics combined made up 75 percent of production. Roofing cements and coatings accounted for an additional 15 percent of sales.

The primary advantages of asphalt—over concrete, for example—are cost and flexibility. Because it softens when heated and is comparatively elastic, asphalt offers a high degree of adaptability in construction applications. Its physical properties also make it less susceptible to cracking and weathering. Furthermore, asphalt is easier to remove and costs much less than either concrete or natural paving materials.

INDUSTRY OUTLOOK

The total number of paving, surfacing, and tamping equipment operators in the United States in the mid-1990s was 73,000. The main asphalt paving product is hot mix asphalt; the Hot Mix Asphalt (HMA) Industry employed about 300,000 people in 1996. Another 600,000 jobs revolved around the HMA Industry. Organizations involved in this industry are the National Asphalt Pavement Association (NAPA) of Lanham, Maryland, and the Asphalt Institute's National Asphalt Training Center II in Lexington, Kentucky.

A concern to the asphalt industry, revealed in 1992 by the U.S. Department of Labor's Occupational Safety and Health Administration (OSHA), was 500,000 workers potentially exposed to asphalt fumes that could cause headache, skin rash, fatigue, reduced appetite, throat and eye irritation, and cough. OSHA was developing an action plan to reduce exposures to this hazard but had not initiated any further action.

In the early 1990s, asphalt paving mixture producers used over 50 million barrels of asphalt per year, selling more than $4 billion worth of mixtures and blocks annually. By 1996, sales increased to nearly $5.0 billion. During the period from 1987 to 1996, asphalt sales increased 12 percent.

WORK FORCE

The asphalt paving mixture industry employed about 14,000 workers in the early 1990s—down from 15,000 a decade earlier. Most employees were blue-collar laborers, such as truck drivers and machine operators. By 1996, 13,500 people were employed, which represented a decrease of 7 percent from the 1987 level. The average hourly wage for asphalt workers in 1996 was $15.86, an increase of 24 percent over the $12.76 average wage of 1987. The *Occupational Outlook Handbook,* published by the Bureau of Labor Statistics, projected the employment change to be faster than usual from 1994 to 2005, with most occupations decreasing. Similarly, employment in the asphalt felts and coatings industry declined from about 14,000 in the 1980s to 10,900 in 1996 as manufacturers boosted productivity through automation and layoffs. Depressed

construction markets in the late 1980s and early 1990s further reduced earnings. The average hourly wage in 1987 was $11.75, which increased 30 percent to $15.24 by 1996.

RESEARCH AND TECHNOLOGY

Among the most prominent technological breakthroughs in the industry in the 1990s was stone mastic asphalt (SMA). Developed in Europe, SMA incorporates cellulose fibers that make it stronger than conventional asphalt. Efforts to use recycled rubber tires as an asphalt ingredient were encouraged by 1991's Intermodal Surface Transportation Efficiency Act (ISTEA), which mandated the use of scrap tires in federally funded state roads.

In 1996, Superpave also represented a breakthrough in asphalt technology. This breakthrough was a method of custom-designing asphalt cements, which are used to mix hot mix asphalt and was expected to be in steady use by the year 2000.

ASSOCIATIONS AND SOCIETIES

ASPHALT EMULSION MANUFACTURERS ASSOCIATION
3 Church Cir., Ste. 250
Annapolis, MD 21401
Phone: (410) 267-0023

SIC 2951 - Asphalt Paving Mixtures & Blocks
General Statistics

Year	Companies	Establishments		Employment			Compensation		Production ($ million)			
		Total	with 20 or more employees	Total (000)	Production Workers (000)	Hours (Mil)	Payroll ($ mil)	Wages ($/hr)	Cost of Materials	Value Added by Manufacture	Value of Shipments	Capital Invest.
1982	569	1,034	202	15.2	11.1	22.2	340.5	10.32	2,162.4	925.9	3,098.6	76.1
1983		1,032	188	15.0	10.7	22.1	343.4	10.43	2,242.1	1,005.2	3,237.4	48.1
1984		1,030	174	14.4	10.3	22.6	358.3	10.19	2,445.9	1,072.5	3,515.9	111.2
1985		1,027	161	14.6	10.6	23.7	375.4	10.07	2,811.9	1,164.9	3,971.8	144.1
1986		1,032	169	14.7	10.6	22.1	404.7	11.56	2,644.0	1,330.9	4,024.1	102.9
1987	542	1,101	199	14.6	10.0	20.9	430.1	12.76	2,758.2	1,602.9	4,346.2	123.4
1988		1,068	146	15.5	10.6	21.8	475.2	13.24	2,730.1	1,771.3	4,509.2	108.5
1989		1,061	149	12.2	9.7	21.1	430.4	12.53	2,535.9	1,469.1	4,001.1	178.6
1990		1,063	154	12.6	10.4	22.9	466.9	13.34	2,784.0	1,449.8	4,213.8	128.0
1991		1,085	153	13.9	10.0	21.0	461.0	13.43	2,524.5	1,306.1	3,794.4	105.8
1992	539	1,150	168	13.2	9.3	20.0	433.8	14.24	2,405.2	1,416.1	3,835.8	111.4
1993		1,105	162	13.4	9.7	20.9	451.0	14.57	2,802.2	1,568.2	4,362.6	130.5
1994		1,122P	148P	14.4	10.4	20.3	500.7	16.37	2,852.4	1,763.8	4,617.6	199.9
1995		1,130P	145P	13.1P	9.7P	20.4P	504.8P	15.87P	2,817.3P	1,742.1P	4,560.7P	164.7P
1996		1,139P	142P	13.0P	9.6P	20.2P	516.8P	16.35P	2,869.9P	1,774.6P	4,646.0P	171.0P
1997		1,147P	138P	12.8P	9.5P	20.0P	528.8P	16.83P	2,922.6P	1,807.2P	4,731.3P	177.3P
1998		1,156P	135P	12.7P	9.4P	19.8P	540.8P	17.30P	2,975.3P	1,839.8P	4,816.6P	183.6P

Sources: 1982, 1987, 1992 *Economic Census; Annual Survey of Manufactures,* 83-86, 88-91, 93-94. Establishment counts for non-Census years are from *County Business Patterns;* establishment values for 83-84 are extrapolations. 'P's show projections by the editors. Industries reclassified in 87 will not have data for prior years.

ASPHALT INSTITUTE
Research Park Dr.
PO Box 14052
Lexington, KY 40512-4052
Phone: (606) 288-4960
Fax: (606) 288-4999

ASPHALT ROOFING MANUFACTURERS ASSOCIATION
6288 Montrose Rd.
Rockville, MD 20852
Phone: (301) 231-9050

ASSOCIATION OF ASPHALT PAVING TECHNOLOGISTS
400 Selby Ave., Ste. 1
St. Paul, MN 55102
Phone: (612) 293-9188
Fax: (612) 293-9193

NATIONAL ASPHALT PAVEMENT ASSOCIATION
NAPA Bldg.
5100 Forbes Blvd.
Lanham, MD 20706-4413
Phone: (301) 731-4748
Fax: (301) 731-4621

PERIODICALS AND NEWSLETTERS

ASPHALT
Asphalt Institute
PO Box 14052
Lexington, KY 40512-4052
Phone: (606) 288-4960
Fax: (606) 288-4999
Three times a year. Free.

***HMAT* (HOT MIX ASPHALT TECHNOLOGY)**
National Asphalt Pavement Association NAPA
5100 Forbes Blvd.
Lanham, MD 20706-4413
Phone: (301) 731-4748
Fax: (301) 731-4621
Quarterly. Free to qualified personnel. Formerly Paving Forum.

MARKETING NEWSLETTER
National Asphalt Pavement Association
5100 Forbes Blvd.
Lanham, MD 20706
Phone: (301) 731-4748
Monthly. Membership.

DATABASES

F & S INDEX
Information Access Co.
362 Lakeside Dr.
Foster City, CA 94404
Phone: (800) 321-6388 or (415-358-4643
Fax: (415) 358-4759
Contains about four million citations to worldwide business, financial, and industrial or consumer product literature appearing from 1972 to date. Weekly updates. Inquire as to online cost and availability.

STATISTICS SOURCES

MINERALS YEARBOOK
Bureau of Mines, U.S. Department of the Interior
Available from U.S. Government Printing Office
Washington, DC 20402
Phone: (202) 512-1800
Fax: (202) 512-2250
Annual. Three volumes.

GENERAL WORKS

ASPHALT AND PRODUCTS
Available from FIND/SVP, Inc.
625 Avenue of the Americas
New York, NY 10011
Phone: (800) 346-3787 or (212) 645-4500
Fax: (212) 645-7681

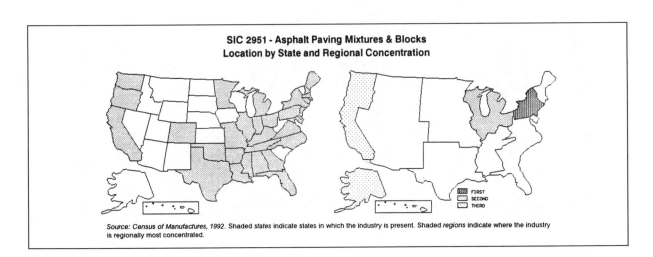

SIC 2951 - Asphalt Paving Mixtures & Blocks
Location by State and Regional Concentration

FIRST
SECOND
THIRD

Source: Census of Manufactures, 1992. Shaded *states* indicate states in which the industry is present. Shaded *regions* indicate where the industry is regionally most concentrated.

1990. $1,900.00. Published by the Freedonia Group. Market data with forcasts to 1994 and 2000. Includes information on paving, coating, and roofing asphalt products.

ASSOCIATION OF ASPHALT PAVING TECHNOLOGISTS-PROCEEDINGS
Association of Asphalt Paving Technologists
1444 Concordia Ave.
St. Paul, MN 55104
Phone: (612) 642-1350
Annual. $50.00. Includes research papers.

FURTHER READING

Darnay, Arsen J., ed. *Manufacturing USA.* 5th ed. Detroit: Gale Research, 1996.

''Reshaping the Basics of Hot Mix Asphalt: Wholesale Change Readies HMA for the Twenty-first Century.'' *ENR.* 2 December 1996.

U.S. Department of Labor. ''Paving, Surfacing, and Tamping Equipment Operators.''

U.S. Department of Labor Occupational Safety and Health Administration. ''Asphalt Fumes.'' Available from http://www.osha/gov/oshinfo/priorities/asphalt.html. ◀▬▶

Audio and Video Equipment, Household

SIC 3651

Since the 1980s, foreign competition—especially from Japan—has taken an enormous toll on the household audio and video equipment industry in the United States. As a result of this intense competition, the industry lost more than 9,000 employees during the decade of the 1990s. However, some industry sources believe that U.S. electronics companies have the competitive edge in the burgeoning market for Internet television equipment. Analysts predict that sales of this equipment will increase from $2.3 billion in 1995 to more than $25 billion by 2002.

In 1996 U.S. manufacturers of household audio and video equipment reported sales of $10.8 billion. The industry employed 56,000 workers—including approximately 34,000 production workers. U.S. manufacturers focused almost exclusively on producing audio speakers and advanced technology televisions. Virtually all other consumer electronic components sold in the United States were manufactured abroad or manufactured in the United States by foreign owned companies. Video equipment—televisions, videocassette recorders, and camcorders—accounted for more than 65 percent of 1995 sales in this industry, while audio equipment—radios, cd players, tape recorders and players, and car audio units—accounted for nearly 35 percent of sales.

Top 10 BEST-SELLING VIDEOCASSETTE RECORDERS

Ranked by: Market share in 1995, in percent.

1. Thomson Corp., with 16%
2. NAP, 10%
3. Matsushita, 8%
4. Emerson, 7%
5. JVC, 5%
5. Mitsubishi, 5%
5. Sanyo Fisher, 5%
5. Sony, 5%
5. Zenith, 5%
10. Goldstar, 4%

Source: *Appliance Manufacturer*, April, 1996, p. 33.

Approximately 210 companies manufactured household audio and video equipment in the United States in 1996, down 40 percent from a peak of more than 350 companies in the early 1990s. This dramatic decline was due in large measure to intense foreign competition, primarily from Japan and South Korea, which forced many U.S. manufacturers to abandon consumer electronics altogether.

In 1989 the New York attorney general charged Matsushita, whose products sold in the United States under the Panasonic and Technics brand names, with price fixing. Although the company denied any wrongdoing, it agreed to pay an $18 million fine. This action indicated to some industry analysts that Japanese manufacturers, having virtually eliminated American competition through predatory pricing policies, now intended to squeeze larger profit margins from the U.S. market.

However, a lingering recession was also affecting the industry. Many of the same Japanese companies that established U.S. manufacturing facilities in the 1970s to avoid restrictions on imports were beginning to move their operations to Mexico, where labor costs were considerably lower. Televisions made in Mexico by foreign companies went almost exclusively into the U.S. market.

In 1993 several major corporations, including Zenith and General Instruments, were waiting for the Federal Communications Commission to set technological protocols for High Definition Television (HDTV) in the United States. These companies—and a third partnership led by Thomson, Philips, and NBC—were hopeful that HDTV would help revitalize the U.S. electronics manufacturing industry. However, after considerable activity, interest in HDTV appeared to be waning. To maximize profits, U.S. based manufacturers were beginning to concentrate on large screen televisions and home theater units, leaving low margin color televisions to be manufactured elsewhere.

ORGANIZATION AND STRUCTURE

The U.S. household audio and video manufacturing industry was dominated in the early 1990s by American subsidiaries of Japanese companies who used technolo-

gies developed by American companies. These subsidiaries assembled color televisions and high fidelity audio equipment from components imported from Japan or from Japanese-owned manufacturing facilities in other countries. The exception was speaker systems, where U.S. owned companies were recognized as market leaders worldwide. Only one major U.S.-owned company still manufacturing color televisions in the mid-1990s.

WORK FORCE

In the 1990s, the work force in the household audio and video equipment industry continued to decline dramatically. This trend was largely due to the fact that U.S. companies were increasingly exiting the market sector because of stifling foreign competition. In fact, the industry lost more than 9,000 employees since 1989. This trend may slow or possibly reverse depending upon the success of Internet TVS in the United States. In 1996 the electronics industry employed 56,000 workers—including approximately 34,000 production workers.

RESEARCH AND TECHNOLOGY

In early 1994, the HG Digital Conference—a committee representing 50 electronics companies in Europe, Asia, and the United States—agreed on a proposed standard for VCRs that will use digital technology. The

SIC 3651 - Household Audio & Video Equipment
General Statistics

| Year | Companies | Establishments | | Employment | | | Compensation | | Production ($ million) | | | |
		Total	with 20 or more employees	Total (000)	Production Workers (000)	Hours (Mil)	Payroll ($ mil)	Wages ($/hr)	Cost of Materials	Value Added by Manufacture	Value of Shipments	Capital Invest.
1982	435	458	182	48.4	35.4	65.3	862.3	8.36	3,967.2	2,010.6	6,063.9	140.9
1983		430	173	45.3	32.5	64.8	935.9	9.17	4,648.4	2,096.6	6,772.8	166.7
1984		402	164	47.5	35.9	68.9	1,038.0	9.85	5,642.5	2,868.0	8,216.9	255.9
1985		374	156	45.1	33.7	64.6	1,033.2	10.47	6,333.9	2,323.1	8,888.1	252.9
1986		354	156	44.9	33.7	65.6	1,067.9	10.48	6,994.6	2,539.2	9,363.9	240.5
1987	352	378	150	30.9	23.6	45.2	583.9	8.02	4,247.8	1,702.1	5,911.2	124.9
1988		368	149	31.6	24.2	47.1	659.2	8.54	4,709.3	1,553.4	6,326.8	127.7
1989		376	164	34.0	24.9	50.1	704.1	8.54	5,532.1	1,904.3	7,360.2	139.0
1990		395	173	33.7	22.5	45.2	704.3	9.00	5,592.9	1,892.0	7,520.5	255.7
1991		401	170	31.1	21.7	41.9	732.4	9.36	5,893.8	2,122.4	7,993.6	277.5
1992	400	427	163	31.2	22.3	44.3	736.6	9.52	6,444.2	2,280.1	8,769.3	252.9
1993		439	164	31.2	22.6	45.0	774.8	9.60	6,596.7	2,567.4	9,159.3	211.5
1994		398P	161P	30.5	23.3	46.6	798.2	9.64	7,617.4	2,756.3	10,285.6	225.8
1995		398P	160P	25.6P	18.4P	37.5P	667.6P	9.38P	6,830.9P	2,471.7P	9,223.7P	237.8P
1996		398P	160P	24.0P	17.1P	35.3P	646.1P	9.39P	6,971.5P	2,522.6P	9,413.5P	242.4P
1997		397P	159P	22.3P	15.9P	33.0P	624.6P	9.41P	7,112.1P	2,573.5P	9,603.3P	247.1P
1998		397P	159P	20.6P	14.6P	30.7P	603.2P	9.42P	7,252.7P	2,624.3P	9,793.5P	251.7P

Sources: 1982, 1987, 1992 Economic Census; Annual Survey of Manufactures, 83-86, 88-91, 93-94. Establishment counts for non-Census years are from County Business Patterns; establishment values for 83-84 are extrapolations. 'P's show projections by the editors. Industries reclassified in 87 will not have data for prior years.

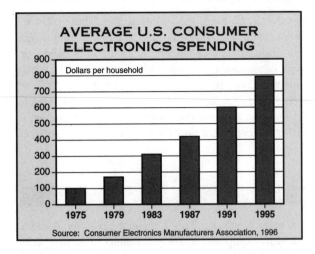

AVERAGE U.S. CONSUMER ELECTRONICS SPENDING

Dollars per household

Source: Consumer Electronics Manufacturers Association, 1996

agreement was reached in part to avoid future format battles such as the one that took place in the 1980s between Beta and VHS systems. This new technology, which is expected to provide manufacturers with the ability to increase image quality, involves storing tape images with ones and zeroes of binary computer codes rather than the current wave-like form. These new VCRs are expected to use video tapes that are one-quarter inch wide—one-half the width of existing VHS tapes. As noted in the *New York Times,* ''some industry experts think it will take a few years for costs to come down enough for such machines to become popular. Initial estimates range up to $3,000, which is up to 10 times the cost of some current VCR models.''

Arguably the greatest innovation in the industry revolves around the production of Internet TV equipment, which took off in late 1996. Industry sources believe that sales of software/Internet TV equipment will increase from $2.3 billion in 1995 to more than $25 billion by 2002, when an estimated 33 percent of all American households will own such devices. Internet TVS and set top units will allow television users to access the Internet without having to use a personal computer. Among the potential drawbacks of Internet TV is that the average American views television from 8-12 feet away, making script on the screen difficult to see.

ASSOCIATIONS AND SOCIETIES

AMERICAN VIDEO ASSOCIATION
2885 N. Nevada St., No. 140
Chandler, AZ 85225
Phone: (800) 926-8358 or (602) 892-8553
Fax: (602) 926-8358
Members are independent retailers of consumer video products.

ELECTRONIC INDUSTRIES ASSOCIATION
2500 Wilson Blvd.
Arlington, VA 22201
Phone: (703) 907-7500
Fax: (202) 457-4985
Includes a Solid State Products Committee.

PROFESSIONAL AUDIOVIDEO RETAILERS ASSOCIATION
9140 Ward Pkwy.
Kansas City, MO 64114
Phone: (816) 444-3500
Fax: (816) 444-0330
Members are retailers of high quality equipment.

PROFESSIONAL FILM AND VIDEO EQUIPMENT ASSOCIATION
PO Box 9436
Silver Spring, MD 20906
Phone: (301) 460-8084
Members are manufacturers and distributors of professional recording equipment.

PERIODICALS AND NEWSLETTERS

THE ABSOLUTE SOUND
Harry Pearson, editor
Pearson Publishing Enterprises
PO Box 360
Sea Cliff, NY 11579
Phone: (516) 676-2830
Fax: (516) 676-5469
Eight times a year. $49.95 per year.

AUDIO
Hachette-Filipacchi Magazines
1633 Broadway
New York, NY 10019
Phone: (800) 274-4027 or (212) 767-6000
Fax: (212) 767-5633
Monthly. $24.00 per year.

AUDIO WEEK: THE AUTHORITATIVE NEWS SERVICE OF THE AUDIO CONSUMER ELECTRONICS INDUSTRY
Warren Publishing, Inc.
2115 Ward Ct. NW
Washington, DC 20037
Phone: (202) 872-9200
Fax: (202) 293-3435
Weekly. $554.00. Newsletter. Provides audio industry news, company news, and new product information.

ELECTRONICS NOW: TECHNOLOGY, AUDIO, VIDEO, COMPUTERS, PROJECTS
Gernsback Publications
500 Bi-county Blvd.
Farmingdale, NY 11735
Phone: (516) 293-3000
Fax: (516) 293-3115
Monthly. $19.97 per year. Formerly Radio Electronics.

HIGH PERFORMANCE REVIEW: DEFINITIVE
MAGAZINE FOR AUDIOPHILES AND MUSIC LOVERS
David H. Tarumoto, editor
High Performance Review Publishing, Inc.
PO Box 346
Woodbury, CT 06798
Phone: (203) 273-5826
Fax: (203) 273-5826
Quarterly. $20.97 per year.

STEREO REVIEW
Hachette-Filipacchi Magazines, Inc.
1633 Broadway
New York, NY 10009
Phone: (800) 274-4027 or (212) 767-6000
Fax: (212) 767-5633
Monthly. $17.94 per year.

STEREOPHILE: FOR THE HIGH FIDELITY STEREO
PERFECTIONIST
Stereophile
PO Box 5529
Santa Fe, NM 87502
Phone: (505) 982-2366
Fax: (505) 989-8791
12 times a year. $35.00 per year. Review of high-end audio
products.

TELEVISION DIGEST WITH CONSUMER ELECTRONICS
Warren Publishing, Inc.
2115 Ward Ct. NW
Washington, DC 20037
Phone: (202) 872-9200

TWICE: THIS WEEK IN CONSUMER ELECTRONICS
Cahners Publishing Co.
249 W. 17th St.
New York, NY 10011
Phone: (800) 662-7776 or (212) 645-0067
Fax: (212) 337-7066
28 times a year. $85.00 per year. Free to qualified personnel.
Contains marketing and manufacturing news relating to a wide
variety of consumer electronic products, including video, audio,
telephone, and home office equipment.

VIDEO BUSINESS
Capital Cities
825 7th Ave.
New York, NY 10019
Phone: (212) 887-8400
Weekly. $70.00 per year.

VIDEO MAGAZINE
Reese Communications, Inc.
460 W. 34th St.
New York, NY 10001
Phone: (212) 947-6500
Fax: (212) 947-6727
Monthly. $12.00 per year.

VIDEO REVIEW
Viare Publishing
902 Broadway
New York, NY 10010
Phone: (212) 477-2200
Monthly. $15.97 per year. Covers audio and video hardware.

STATISTICS SOURCES

EARLY WARNING REPORT
Warren Publishing, Inc.
2115 Ward Ct. NW
Washington, DC 20037
Phone: (202) 872-9200
Monthly. $975.00. Analyzes sales trends and inventory figures
for the retail video industry.

HOUSEHOLD AUDIO AND VIDEO EQUIPMENT
Current Industrial Reports
Bureau of the Census
U.S. Department of Commerce
Washington, DC 20233

GENERAL WORKS

DIRECTORY OF CONSUMER ELECTRONICS
Chain Store Guide
Information Services
3922 Coconut Palm Dr.
Tampa, FL 33619
Phone: (800) 925-2288 or (813) 664-6700
Fax: (813) 664-6810
Biennial. $230.00. Includes retailers and distributors.

SOUND AND RECORDING: AN INTRODUCTION
Francis Rumsey and Tim McCormick
Butterworth-Heinemann
225 Wildwood Ave.
Woburn, MA 01801
Phone: (800) 366-2665 or (617) 928-2500
Fax: (617) 928-2620 or (617) 933-6333
1994. $29.95. Second edition. Covers the theory and principles
of sound recording and reproduction, with chapters on ampli-
fiers, microphones, mixers, and other components.

VIDEO CAMERAS AND CAMCORDERS
Available from FIND/SVP, Inc.
625 Avenue of the Americas
New York, NY 10011
Phone: (800) 346-3787 or (212) 645-4500
Fax: (212) 645-7681
1990. $495.00. Published by Simmons Market Research Bureau,
Inc. Provides consumer market data.

VIDEO PLAYERS-RECORDERS
Available from FIND/SVP, Inc.
625 Avenue of the Americas
New York, NY 10011
Phone: (800) 346-3787 or (212) 645-4500
Fax: (212) 645-7681
1990. $495.00. Published by Simmons Market Research Bureau,
Inc. Provides consumer market data.

VIDEO RECORDER DEALER DIRECTORY
American Business Directories, Inc.
5711 S. 86th Circle
Omaha, NE 68127
Phone: (402) 593-4600
Fax: (402) 331-1505

Annual. $410.00. Lists over 12,000 dealers. Compiled from U.S. Yellow pages.

VIDEO STORE
Entrepreneur Group, Inc.
2392 Morse Ave.
Irvine, CA 92714
Phone: (714) 261-2325
$45.00. Looseleaf.

VIDEO TAPE RECORDERS MARKET
Industrial Marketing Research, Inc.
140 Burlington St.
Clarendon Hills, IL 60514
Phone: (708) 654-1077
Quarterly consumer market survey.

FURTHER READING

Elstrom, Peter. ''The Angry Angels at Zenith.'' *Business Week,* 12 August 1996, 32.

Krantz, Michael. ''The Biggest Thing Since Color.'' *Time,* 12 August 1996.

Lazich, Robert S., ed. *Market Share Reporter.* Detroit: Gale Research, 1997.

Markoff, John. ''Zenith Plans TV Set That Can Access Internet Without PC.'' *The New York Times CyberTimes,* 10 May 1996. Available from http://www.nytimes.com/web/docsroot/ library/cyber/week/051zenith.html.

Morri, Aldo. ''ITV Hardware and Software Market Showing Signs of Maturity.'' *News & Views,* March 1996. Available from http://165.247.175.190/mmp/mmp_mar96/ dep_news.html.

The banking and savings institutions industry is broad in scope and complex in nature. Modern commercial banks and savings institutions, or thrifts, provide both individual and corporate customers with an increasing number of financial services. Banks are constantly seeking to improve service to customers by expanding the quality and number of their services. Recent innovations in this industry include the introduction of credit cards, accounting services for corporate firms, factoring, leasing, trade in Eurodollars, lock box banking, and security investment.

Commercial banks perform at least eight major functions in the U.S. economy. First, banks facilitate the elastic credit system that is necessary for economic progress and steady growth. Second, they allow the efficient transfer of money between firms and individuals. Third, they encourage the pooling of savings, making these savings available for lending. Fourth, banks extend credit to credit worthy borrowers, increasing production and capital investment. Fifth, banks facilitate the financing of foreign trade by converting various currencies. Sixth, they act as trust administrators and advisors. Seventh, they aid in the safekeeping of valuables. Finally, banks have recently been allowed to engage in brokering activities, buying and selling securities for customers.

Commercial banking was among the first industries to develop in the United States. Today, it is the most important segment of the American financial industry in terms of aggregate assets, which exceed $1 trillion. The 50 largest banking companies alone employed more than 1 million people. In 1996, 9,586 commercial banks were in the United States, with nearly $4.5 trillion in assets.

Due to its importance, banking has developed into one of the most regulated industries in America. In addition to the federal regulatory bodies which oversee national banks, each state has a system of supervisory bodies charged with the chartering and regulation of state commercial banks. These diverse structures and organizations are responsible for regulating the state's banking industry in a manner most appropriate for the financial, economic, and social environment of the state.

A small minority of commercial banks are private—neither federally nor state chartered. These banks are sometimes owned by a small group of partners who assume unlimited liability, in effect, insuring the bank themselves. These banks tend to focus on global custody and private banking, two growth sectors of banking in the 1990s. Traditional global custodian services include paying for a security in local currency, minimizing settlement problems; collecting dividends and interest; han-

BANKS AND SAVINGS INSTITUTIONS

SICs 6020, 6030

The *forces that have reshaped commercial banking since the early 1980s— deregulation, competition, and technological advance—continued their transformation in the mid-1990s. Booming profits and a looser regulatory environment were leading to a blurring of the regulatory borders between various branches of the financial services world. Meanwhile, changes in computer technology have radically altered the role of banks and savings institutions in American society.*

Top 10 LARGEST COMMERCIAL BANKS

Ranked by: Revenue in 1995, in millions of dollars.

1. Citicorp, with $31,690 million
2. BankAmerica Corp., $20,386
3. NationsBank, $16,298
4. Chemical Banking Corp., $14,884
5. J. P. Morgan, $13,838
6. Chase Manhattan Corp., $11,336
7. First Chicago NBD Corp., $10,681
8. First Union Corp., $10,583
9. Banc One Corp., $8,971
10. Bankers Trust New York Corp., $8,600

Source: *Fortune,* Fortune 500 Largest U.S. Corporations (annual), April 29, 1996, p. F-45+.

dling safekeeping and tax reclamation; and taking care of bookkeeping for stock splits and rights issues.

Private banking involves offering banking services to very wealthy individuals. These services are generally more personalized and flexible than services offered by other types of commercial banks. Private banks usually set net worth or minimum deposit requirements that vary from $250,000 to $2 million. One reason that U.S. banks are chartered is to impose discipline on the individual banks. In private banks, discipline is imposed by the need for consensus, the unlimited liability of the partners, and the limitation of capital. This structure also has the benefit of allowing the partners, who often serve for many decades, to take a long-term view of their business.

Savings institutions can be classified in three ways: by type of ownership (stock or mutual), by type of institution (savings and loan association or savings bank), and by type of charter (state or federal). Since the mid-1980s, the state-chartered portion of the thrift industry has been characterized by a greater rate of insolvencies. Because they were governed by fewer regulatory safeguards than federal thrifts, state thrifts were able to make risky investments with depositors' funds. Also, there was increasing defection to federal charters amongst savings and loans, with similar but less widespread charter flipping among savings banks.

As of December 1996, more than 1,900 thrift institutions were in the United States, down from 2,500 in 1991. These thrifts held more than $1.0 trillion in assets, employed about 250,000 people, and operated from some 14,500 offices. Of these thrifts, 1,334 were federally chartered, with total assets of $789 billion. The remaining 590 thrifts were state chartered and held some $259 billion in assets. This trend reflected regulatory changes that saw some thrifts convert to commercial banks. It also reflects the wave of mergers and acquisitions that continued to alter the nation's entire financial services world.

Of the nation's thrifts, more than 1,500, including virtually all the federally chartered institutions, were insured by the Savings Association Insurance Fund (SAIF). The remaining few hundred thrifts were insured by the Bank Insurance Fund (BIF). Of the industry's total $1.028 trillion assets on December 31, 1996, some $502 billion, or 50 percent, were in 1 to 4 family mortgages. That was a sharp decline from the 76 percent level for these small mortgages just five years earlier—another reflection of the growing diversification of the financial services industry. Of thrifts other assets, some $262 billion were held in securities, while $59 billion were in multifamily residential properties and $50 billion were in commercial real estate loans. Although the number of institutions continued to shrink, the industry's level of assets, deposits, and other measures stabilized in the mid-1990s after undergoing major restructuring and shrinkage in the early 1990s.

INDUSTRY OUTLOOK

The banking industry enjoyed record profits in 1996, thanks to strong income from management investments and other non-lending businesses and by cutting costs. Some banks also raised their earnings on a per-share basis by buying back their own stock. Credit card losses continued to plague many banks, though, as more consumers stopped paying their bills.

Some felt the U.S. banking system was unsound and might experience a disaster similar to that experienced by the savings-and-loan industry in the mid- and late 1980s. Bank deregulation under the Reagan administration was blamed for the failures of hundreds of savings-and-loans, which would cost American taxpayers as much as $500 million in repayments to depositors. Those seeking lessons from the fiasco tended to suggest that banks needed more rather than less regulation. Some felt the federal government did a poor job of examining the books of banks and thrifts. The Comptroller of the Currency, Charles Bowsher, indicated he felt the regulatory agencies did not adequately ensure that unsafe banking practices were uncovered.

The trend in banking in the mid-1990s was to offer more services to attract customers. The fiercely competitive market forced banking institutions to offer a greater range of services, and this competitive atmosphere also encouraged a merger mania. Some analysts interpreted these developments in a Darwinian manner, suggesting the consolidation in the banking industry would result in fewer, but stronger financial institutions.

In the second quarter of 1996, commercial banks reported $13.8 billion in profits; 95.9 percent of all commercial banks were profitable, 2 percent less than the first quarter of 1996. Noninterest income was the main source of earnings in the second quarter, according to Federal Deposit Insurance Corporation (FDIC) Chairman Ricki Helfer. For the eighteenth straight quarter, the number of banks losing money dropped, and only three banks failed.

ORGANIZATION AND STRUCTURE

Banking is one of the most regulated parts of the U.S. financial system. The industry operates under the supervision of three regulatory agencies: the Federal Reserve System, the Office of the Comptroller of the Currency (OCC), and the Federal Deposit Insurance Corporation (FDIC). The Federal Reserve System, created in 1913, is the United States' central bank and is responsible for monetary policy. Its operations are carried out by its 12 regional banks. The OCC has wide discretionary authority, which it uses in routine examinations of all national banks' books to identify unsafe or unsound banking practices. This agency is the most involved with national bank regulation. The OCC has

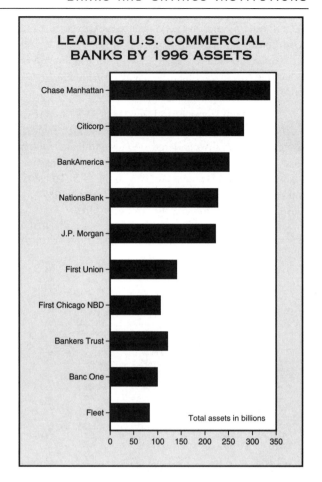

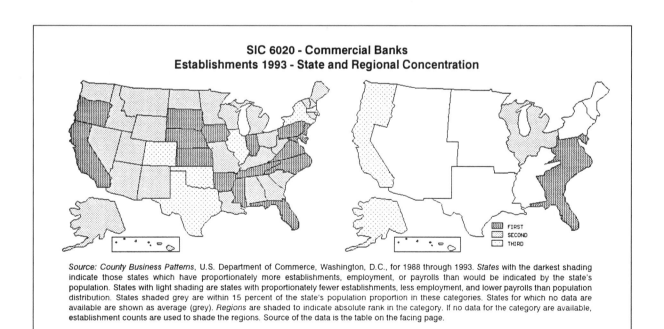

Source: County Business Patterns, U.S. Department of Commerce, Washington, D.C., for 1988 through 1993. *States* with the darkest shading indicate those states which have proportionately more establishments, employment, or payrolls than would be indicated by the state's population. States with light shading are states with proportionately fewer establishments, less employment, and lower payrolls than population distribution. States shaded grey are within 15 percent of the state's population proportion in these categories. States for which no data are available are shown as average (grey). *Regions* are shaded to indicate absolute rank in the category. If no data for the category are available, establishment counts are used to shade the regions. Source of the data is the table on the facing page.

the authority to take any actions necessary to correct the conditions resulting from violations of law or sound and safe banking practices. Finally, the FDIC was created to reduce the risk of making deposits by insuring the deposits of member banks, both national and state.

The Federal Home Loan Bank (FHLB) System is to thrifts what the Federal Reserve is to banks. It provides liquidity to federally chartered savings and loans, which must join it, and to any state chartered institutions that wish to join. FHLBs have credit with the U.S. Treasury and issue government agency debt bonds, much the way that the Federal Reserve sells Treasury bills.

SIC 6020 - Commercial Banks
Establishments, Employment, and Payroll

	Estab-lish-ments	Mid-March Employ-ment	1st Q. Wages (annualiz. $ mil.)	Payroll per Empl. 1st Q. (annualiz.)	Annual Payroll ($ mil.)
1988	49,567	1,454,561	33,983.8	23,364	32,120.0
1989	51,284	1,463,412	35,982.0	24,588	33,620.7
%	3.5	0.6	5.9	5.2	4.7
1990	52,303	1,472,304	37,903.8	25,745	35,567.3
%	2.0	0.6	5.3	4.7	5.8
1991	61,395	1,606,240	42,661.1	26,560	39,720.3
%	17.4	9.1	12.6	3.2	11.7
1992	65,049	1,576,334	44,325.8	28,120	42,518.2
%	6.0	-1.9	3.9	5.9	7.0
1993	62,629	1,528,258	42,770.8	27,987	42,099.7
%	-3.7	-3.0	-3.5	-0.5	-1.0
% 88-93	26.4	5.1	25.9	19.8	31.1

Source: County Business Patterns, U.S. Department of Commerce, Washington, D.C., for 1988 through 1993. Payroll per employee is calculated using mid-March employment and 1st Quarter wages, annualized. Annual payroll, also shown, may not equal the annualized 1st Quarter wages. Rows headed by a percent sign (%) indicate change from the previous year. na stands for not available. The symbol (D) indicates that data are withheld by the source to avoid disclosure of competitive information. A dash (-) indicates that data are not available or cannot be calculated.

All national banks are required to be members of the Federal Reserve bank of their district and to invest in the capital stock of the bank as required by the Federal Reserve Act of 1913, which requires that 6 percent of the national bank's capital and surplus must be pledged and three percent deposited as payment. National banks are further required to be insured by the Federal Deposit Insurance Corporation (FDIC). In all states, federal deposit insurance coverage is a necessary condition to obtain and keep a state charter. All depository institutions, both state and federal and including thrifts, must hold a certain amount of deposits as reserves. The current reserve requirement is 3 percent of all savings deposits up to $42.2 million in deposits, and then 10 percent of all savings deposits above $42.2 million. The

Federal Reserve imposes this "reserve requirement" as a hedge against bank runs.

National banks have 20 enumerated, general powers that are effective upon the execution and filing of the articles of association and the organization certificate. Such powers include the obvious—receiving and loaning money—as well as the obscure—providing travel services for customers. National banks are granted general corporate powers, which include making contracts, suing and being sued, electing and appointing directors, and prescribing by-laws, and are allowed to establish branch offices in the United States and abroad, under specified conditions. They are also allowed a range of activities involving real estate, U.S. government securities, the establishment of trusts, and other financial activities. Such broadly construed powers enable national banks to engage in far more than strictly commercial banking.

Commercial banks may be classified as either unit or branch banks. In the United States, unlike other countries, banks of both types exist. Historically, however, unit banking has been the most common. Under unit banking, services are provided by a single office or institution. Branch banking is a system under which a single banking firm operates at two or more locations. There are different degrees of branch banking across the country. In general, the more densely populated areas, such as the East and West Coasts, have adopted branch banking, while more sparsely populated areas have maintained unit banking.

The many failures in the thrift industry, beginning in the late 1980s, brought savings institutions under great scrutiny and regulation, along with banks. The Office of Thrift Supervision (OTS), an agency within the U.S. Treasury Department, became the chief regulator of the thrift industry with the bailout law of 1989. Since the bailout law, thrifts are tightly regulated, mainly because the deposits of their customers are federally insured. It is to the taxpayer's advantage that thrifts be profitable. The OTS decides if a thrift is healthy and profitable enough to do normal business, and it charters, regulates, and examines the operations of federally chartered savings and loans.

Whereas the OTS is the chief regulator of thrifts and is concerned with overall operations, with an emphasis on the asset side of the balance sheet, the FDIC regulates deposits at thrifts and conducts investigations to the effect of securing deposits. The FDIC works closely with the Resolution Trust Corporation (RTC) in administering the affairs of failed thrifts. The RTC seizes the assets of Group IV thrifts and attempts to either sell the institutions or liquidate them and pay off depositors with federal insurance money, as provided for in the 1989 bailout law.

SIC 6030 - Savings Institutions
Establishments, Employment, and Payroll

	Estab-lish-ments	Mid-March Employ-ment	1st Q. Wages (annualiz. $ mil.)	Payroll per Empl. 1st Q. (annualiz.)	Annual Payroll ($ mil.)
1988	20,158	383,698	7,786.1	20,292	7,727.3
1989	21,953	434,730	9,186.5	21,132	8,997.3
%	8.9	13.3	18.0	4.1	16.4
1990	21,689	416,571	9,049.6	21,724	8,791.9
%	-1.2	-4.2	-1.5	2.8	-2.3
1991	22,211	393,715	9,066.6	23,028	8,809.5
%	2.4	-5.5	0.2	6.0	0.2
1992	21,089	355,035	8,850.2	24,928	8,758.8
%	-5.1	-9.8	-2.4	8.2	-0.6
1993	19,330	318,553	7,983.4	25,062	8,254.4
%	-8.3	-10.3	-9.8	0.5	-5.8
% 88-93	-4.1	-17.0	2.5	23.5	6.8

Source: County Business Patterns, U.S. Department of Commerce, Washington, D.C., for 1988 through 1993. Payroll per employee is calculated using mid-March employment and 1st Quarter wages, annualized. Annual payroll, also shown, may not equal the annualized 1st Quarter wages. Rows headed by a percent sign (%) indicate change from the previous year. na stands for not available. The symbol (D) indicates that data are withheld by the source to avoid disclosure of competitive information. A dash (-) indicates that data are not available or cannot be calculated.

Thrifts offer two types of loans: fixed-rate loans and adjustable-rate mortgages (ARMs). About 30 percent of the thrift industry offers mainly fixed-rate loans, most of which are the traditional 30-year mortgage, though some other time periods are available. About 30 percent of thrifts offers both kinds of loans, and 40 percent of the industry offers mainly ARMs. Many thrifts prefer to offer ARMs because they pose less risk to the institution by not locking into a low rate. ARMs are adjusted either monthly or yearly and may be tied to either the Office of Thrift Supervision's cost-of-funds index for monthly adjustments or to the rate of the one-year Treasury bills for annual adjustments.

TAKEOVERS BY BANKS

A residual phenomenon of the thrift bailout in the early 1990s was the great extent to which the commercial banking and thrift industries were merging through the acquisition of thrifts by banks. The FDIC Improvement Act of 1991 made thrift acquisition easier for banks, and banks were enjoying record high stock prices in the early 1990s. Banks tend to have a stronger balance sheet than thrifts, and bankers also already have the skills needed to manage a thrift.

WORK FORCE

In mid-1996, an estimated 254,308 people were employed in savings institutions in the United States. The Bureau of Labor Statistics (BLS) provides breakdowns of occupations within banks, savings institutions, and credit unions. In 1990, 23.4 percent of employees were tellers, 6.1 percent clerical supervisors, 5.6 percent financial managers, and 5.5 percent loan officers and counselors. Clerical positions combined, including tellers, general office clerks, secretaries, and other kinds of clerks, made up 63.2 percent of the work force. The BLS forecast that by the year 2005 the percentage of clerical workers employed would decline considerably, while financial managers, loan officers, accountants, and other management would increase proportionally.

A smaller labor force would need to perform more tasks, so banks and thrifts were starting to train employees using computerized tutorials on the job, right at the thrift branch itself, rather than sending employees to a traditional training center. While the number of bank tellers in 1995 increased by 2,000 from 1994, the number of full-time employees decreased by 9,247. Overall, the number of tellers decreased 10 percent over the past ten years.

SIC 6020
Occupations Employed by SIC 602 - Commercial Banks, Savings Institutions, Credit Unions

Occupation	% of Total 1994	Change to 2005
Bank tellers	27.8	-29.8
Clerical supervisors & managers	6.5	12.9
Loan officers & counselors	6.4	8.8
Financial managers	6.2	16.3
New accounts clerks, banking	5.8	1.2
Loan & credit clerks	5.2	-9.0
General office clerks	3.9	-32.6
Bookkeeping, accounting, & auditing clerks	3.7	-24.1
Secretaries, ex legal & medical	3.6	-18.1
General managers & top executives	3.0	-4.0
Management support workers nec	2.6	1.2
Clerical support workers nec	1.4	-19.1
Accountants & auditors	1.4	-14.0
Securities & financial services sales workers	1.3	11.3
Adjustment clerks	1.3	5.3
Statement clerks	1.1	-39.6
Duplicating, mail, & office machine operators	1.0	-41.0

Source: Industry-Occupation Matrix, Bureau of Labor Statistics. These data relate to one or more 3-digit SIC industry groups rather than to a single 4-digit SIC. The change reported for each occupation to the year 2005 is a percent of growth or decline as estimated by the Bureau of Labor Statistics. The abbreviation nec stands for 'not elsewhere classified'.

RESEARCH AND TECHNOLOGY

As the banking industry became ever more complex in the mid-1990s, banks around the world began to adopt new technologies and automation. Much of the investment was for Automatic Teller Machines (ATMs), teller work stations, check processing equipment, and related software. In the early 1990s, over 72,500 ATMs and over 138 million ATM cards were in use. The banks' increasing sophistication about computer systems and services led to greater reliance on vendors of automated systems equipment. Customer-activated media becoming widespread during the 1990s included ATMs, voice/audio response systems, and ''smart cards.'' These cards accessed accounts like ATMs, contained a microchip with information about the customer's accounts, and could be used as a debit card.

The most profound change has been caused by the capability of processing automated transfers of money between banks, companies, and consumers. Electronic funds transfers, or EFTs, are computer-based payment systems which substitute electronic and digital transfers for movements of cash and paper checks. Direct deposit has also eliminated some of the paper transfers between institutions and individuals.

Technology played an increasing role in how thrifts did business also. Thrifts were becoming more sales oriented in the wake of the bailout crisis, moving away from higher-risk ventures and back to consumer-oriented banking; for this reason, a prime application of technology was in customer relations. A variety of media was being used by thrifts to improve their services, both salesperson-activated and customer-activated.

As the amount of free time available to Americans declined, thrifts responded to the demand for faster service through electronic banking, phone banking, and direct deposit. In addition to a hope of improved service, thrifts looked ahead to cutting costs by using smaller, better-trained staffs supported by high-tech automation.

These new technologies have made a number of significant changes to the American market place, including: changes in the methods of personal finance and in the process of purchasing consumer goods and services; changes in the structure of financial and retail organizations and their methods of operation; changes in the flow of funds in the marketplace; increased potential for the invasion of personal privacy and new avenues for the occurrence of fraud and theft; and changes in the regulatory and competitive balance among financial institutions.

AMERICA AND THE WORLD

Most of the world's most important banks are based in countries other than the United States. Citibank, which was the U.S. largest bank in 1995, ranked 28th in assets compared to banks in the rest of the world. Japan, Germany, France, England, and Switzerland all have internationally significant banks. The world's largest banks maintain an extensive domestic and international banking presence and provide a wide range of financial services, limited by the regulations existing in their parent country.

Japan was home to eight of the top ten largest banks in the world in terms of assets at the end of 1995. All together, Japanese banks accounted for more than $8.2 trillion in assets at the end of 1995, or 34.2 percent of all the world's banking assets. As a group, German banks held more than $3.3 trillion in assets, or nearly 14 percent of the world's total. French banks maintained extensive foreign networks, which included operations in Europe, the Americas, Asia and the Pacific, the Middle East, and Africa. French banks as a group held assets of just over $2 trillion at the end of 1995, or about 8.4 percent of the world's total banking assets. In addition, British banks held 5.9 percent of the world's banking assets.

Most industrial countries have financial institutions to provide mortgages and house personal savings similar to the thrift institution in the United States. Because the thrift institution is segmented locally, with no institutions owning branches outside of the state where headquartered until 1992, most business done by thrifts is local. Since thrifts serve a domestic market, serving the local needs of individual savers and borrowers, thrifts do not have the international business as many commercial banks and brokerage houses do.

Globally, there has been a move towards less regulation of the financial services sector, including commercial banks. Specifically, banks worldwide are being allowed to offer a broader range of financial services, contrary to past practices. The European Economic Community's financial liberalization program has been a catalyst, encouraging the liberalization of American and Japanese policies to keep pace with their European competitors.

ASSOCIATIONS AND SOCIETIES

AMERICAN BANKERS ASSOCIATION
1120 Connecticut Ave. NW
Washington, DC 20036
Phone: (202) 663-5000
Fax: (202) 663-7533

AMERICA'S COMMUNITY BANKERS
900 9th St. NW, Ste. 400
Washington, DC 20006
Phone: (202) 857-3100
Fax: (202) 296-8716

BANKER'S ROUND TABLE
805 15th St. NW, Ste. 600
Washington, DC 20005
Phone: (202) 289-4322
Fax: (202) 628-1623

BRETTON WOODS COMMITTEE
1990 M St., Ste. 450
Washington, DC 20036
Phone: (202) 331-1616
Fax: (202) 785-9423
Members are corporate executives, government officials, college administrators, bankers, and other "National Leaders." Seeks to inform and educate the public as to the activities of the International Monetary Fund, the World Bank, and other multinational development banking organizations. Promotes U.S. participation in multinational banking.

CONSUMER BANKERS ASSOCIATION
1000 Wilson Blvd., Ste. 3012
Arlington, VA 22209-3908
Phone: (703) 276-1750
Fax: (703) 528-1290

INDEPENDENT BANKERS ASSOCIATION OF AMERICA
1 Thomas Cir. NW, Ste. 950
Washington, DC 20005
Phone: (800) 422-8439 or (202) 659-8111
Has a Federal Legislation Committee and a Regulation Review Committee.

MORTGAGE BANKERS ASSOCIATION OF AMERICA
c/o Janice Stango
1125 15th St. NW
Washington, DC 20005
Phone: (202) 861-6500
Fax: (202) 785-2967

PERIODICALS AND NEWSLETTERS

ABA BANKERS NEWS
American Bankers Association
Member Communications
1120 Connecticut Ave. NW
Washington, DC 20036-3971
Phone: (800) 872-7747 or (202) 663-5000
Fax: (202) 296-9258
Weekly. Members, $48.00 per year; non-members, $96.00 per year. Formerly Banker News Weekly. Incorporating Agricultural Banker.

ABA BANKING JOURNAL
American Bankers Association, Member Communications
Simmons-Boardman Books, Inc.
345 Hudson St., 17 Fl.
New York, NY 10014-4502

Phone: (212) 620-7200
Fax: (212) 633-1165
Monthly. $25.00 per year.

AMERICAN BANKER
American Banker-Bond Buyer
Newsletter Division
1 State St.
New York, NY 10004-1549
Phone: (800) 872-7747 or (212) 803-8200
Fax: (212) 943-2984
Daily. $712.00 per year.

AMERICA'S COMMUNITY BANKER
America's Community Bankers
900 19th St. NW, Ste. 400
Washington, DC 20006
Phone: (202) 857-3100
Fax: (202) 296-8716
Monthly. Members, $44.00 per year; non-members, $56.00 per year. Covers community banking operations and management. Formerly Savings and Community Banker.

BANK MARKETING
Bank Marketing Association
1120 Connecticut Ave. NW
Washington, DC 20036
Phone: (202) 663-5268
Fax: (202) 828-4540
Monthly. Members, $60.00 per year; non-members, $90.00 per year.

BANK RATE MONITOR: THE WEEKLY FINANCIAL RATE REPORTER
Advertising News Service, Inc.
PO Box 088888
North Palm Beach, FL 33408-8888
Phone: (800) 327-7717 or (407) 627-7330
Fax: (407) 627-7335
Weekly. $395.00 per year. Newsletter. Provides detailed information on interest rates currently paid by U.S. banks and savings institutions.

BANKERS' MAGAZINE
Warren, Gorham and Lamont, Inc.
1 Penn Plz., 42 Fl.
New York, NY 10119-4098
Phone: (800) 950-1210 or (800) 950-1213
Fax: (212) 971-5113
Bimonthly. $134.98. per year. Enables bankers to obtain a more generalized view of the industry. Contains articles for bankers, by bankers and top consultants in the field.

JOURNAL OF MONEY, CREDIT AND BANKING
Stephen G. Cecchetti and Paul D. Evans, editors
Ohio State University Press
1070 Carmack Rd.
Columbus, OH 43210
Phone: (614) 292-6930
Quarterly. Individuals $45.00 per year; institutions, $100.00 per year. Reports major findings in the study of financial markets, monetary and fiscal policy credit markets, money and banking, portfolio management, and related subjects.

JOURNAL OF RETAIL BANKING

Leonard L. Berry, editor
American Banker-Bond Buyer
1 State St., 31 Fl.
New York, NY 10004-1549
Phone: (800) 872-7747 or (212) 803-8200
Fax: (212) 946-6256
Quarterly. $97.00 per year.

OPERATIONS MANAGEMENT REPORT

Siefer Consultants, Inc.
PO Box 1384
Storm Lake, IA 50588
Phone: (800) 747-7342 or (712) 732-7340
Fax: (712) 732-7906
Monthly. $319.00 per year. Newsletter. Covers operations management for banks and other financial institutions.

PERSPECTIVE

America's Community Bankers
900 19th St. NW, Ste. 400
Washington, DC 20006
Phone: (202) 857-3100
Fax: (202) 296-8716
Weekly. $395.00 per year. Newsletter about regulatory and legislative events affecting community banks.

RTC REPORT (RESOLUTION TRUST CORPORATION)

Land Development Law Reporter
1401 16th St. NW
Washington, DC 20036
Phone: (202) 232-2144
Fax: (202) 232-4757
Weekly. $425.00 per year. Newsletter on activities of the Resolution Trust Corporation, as it attempts to dispose of real estate, mortgage packages, and other assets of failed or restructured savings institutions. Each issue lists major assets for sale and names and telephone numbers of contacts.

SAFE MONEY REPORT

Weiss Research, Inc.
2200 North Florida Mango Rd.
West Palm Beach, FL 33409
Phone: (800) 289-9222 or (407) 684-8100
Fax: (407) 684-9039
Monthly. $145.00 per year. Newsletter. Provides financial advice and current safety ratings of various banks, savings and loan companies, insurance companies, and securities dealers.

DATABASES

AMERICAN BANKER FULL TEXT

American Banker-Bond Buyer
Database Services
1 State St.
New York, NY 10004
Phone: (800) 872-7747 or (212) 803-8200
Fax: (212) 943-2222
Provides complete text online of the daily American Banker. *Inquire as to online cost and availability.*

BANKING INFORMATION SOURCE

UMI 620 S. 3rd St.
Louisville, KY 40202-2475
Phone: (800) 626-2823 or (502) 583-4111
Fax: (502) 589-5572
Provides indexing and abstracting of periodical and other literature from 1982 to date, with weekly updates. Covers the financial services industry: banks, savings institutions, investment houses, credit unions, insurance companies, and real estate organizations. Emphasis is on marketing and management. Inquire as to online cost and availability. (Formerly FINIS: Financial Industry Information Service.*)*

BANXQUOTE ONLINE

Masterfund, Inc.
100 Passaic Ave., Ste. 1
Fairfield, NJ 07004-3508
Phone: (201) 467-2400
Fax: (201) 575-9399
Covers federally insured banks and savings institutions in the United States. Provides daily updates online to interest rates being offered by each institution on certificates of deposit (including jumbo CDs) and money market accounts. Inquire as to online cost and availability.

CITIBASE (CITICORP ECONOMIC DATABASE)

FAME Software Corp.
77 Water St., 9 Fl.
New York, NY 10005
Phone: (212) 898-7800
Fax: (212) 742-8956
Presents over 6,000 statistical series relating to business, industry, finance, and economics. Includes series from Survey of Current Business *and many other sources. Time period is 1947 to date, with daily updates. Inquire as to online cost and availability.*

DRI FINANCIAL AND CREDIT STATISTICS

DRI/McGraw-Hill Data Products Division
24 Hartwell Ave.
Lexington, MA 02173
Phone: (800) 541-9914 or (617) 863-5100
Contains U.S. and international statistical data relating to money markets, interest rates, foreign exchange, banking, and stock and bond indexes. Time period is 1973 to date, with continuous updating. Inquire as to online cost and availability.

LEXIS FEDERAL BANKING LIBRARY

LEXIS-NEXIS
PO Box 933
Dayton, OH 45401
Phone: (800) 227-4908 or (513) 865-6800
Fax: (513) 865-6909
Provides legal decisions and regulatory material relating to the banking industry, as well as full text of banking journals. Time period varies. Inquire as to online cost and availability.

STATISTICS SOURCES

ALL OPERATING SAVINGS AND LOAN ASSOCIATIONS;
SELECTED BALANCE SHEET DATA AND FLOW OF
SAVINGS AND MORTGAGE LENDING ACTIVITY
Federal Home Loan Bank Board
320 First St.
Washington, DC 20552
Phone: (202) 377-6000
Monthly.

ASSET AND LIABILITY TRENDS: ALL OPERATING
SAVINGS AND LOAN ASSOCIATIONS BY TYPE OF
ASSOCIATION AND AREA
Federal Home Loan Bank Board
320 First St.
Washington, DC 20552
Phone: (202) 377-6000
Annual.

BANK OPERATING STATISTICS
Federal Deposit Insurance Corp.
550 17th St. NW
Washington, DC 20429
Phone: (202) 393-8400
Annual. Price on application. Based on Reports of Condition and Reports of Income.

BANK PROFITABILITY: STATISTICAL SUPPLEMENT -
FINANCIAL STATEMENTS OF BANKS
Organization for Economic Cooperation and Development
Available from OECD Publications and Information Center
2001 L St. NW, Ste. 700
Washington, DC 20036
Phone: (202) 785-6323
Fax: (202) 785-0350
Annual. $37.00. Presents data for 10 years on bank profitability in the 24 OECD member countries.

ECONOMIC INDICATORS
Council of Economic Advisors
Executive Office of the President
Available from U.S. Government Printing Office
Washington, DC 20402
Phone: (202) 512-1800
Fax: (202) 512-2250
Monthly. $33.00 per year.

FEDERAL RESERVE BULLETIN
U.S. Federal Reserve System
Board of Governors
Publications Services, Rm. MS-138
Washington, DC 20551
Phone: (202) 452-3000
Fax: (202) 728-5886
Monthly. $25.00 per year. Provides statistics on banking and the economy, including interest rates, money supply, and the Federal Reserve Board indexes of industrial production.

FINANCE, INSURANCE, AND REAL ESTATE USA:
INDUSTRY ANALYSES, STATISTICS, AND LEADING
COMPANIES
Arsen J. Darnay, editor
Gale Research Inc.

835 Penobscot Bldg.
Detroit, MI 48226-4094
Phone: (800) 877-GALE or (313) 961-2242
Fax: (313) 961-6083
1994. $195.00. Contains industry statistical data and a listing of leading companies for each of 50 Standard Industrial Classification (SIC) 4-digit codes covering finance, insurance, and real estate. Includes banks, mortgage banks, securities dealers, commodity brokers, real estate companies, and related firms. Several indexes are provided.

SAVINGS INSTITUTIONS SOURCE BOOK
United States League of Savings Institutions
111 E Wacker Dr.
Chicago, IL 60601
Phone: (312) 644-3100
Annual. $2.50.

SURVEY OF CURRENT BUSINESS
Available from U.S. Government Printing Office
Washington, DC 20402
Phone: (202) 512-1800
Fax: (202) 512-2250
Monthly. $41.00 per year. Issued by Bureau of Economic Analysis, U.S. Department of Commerce. Presents a wide variety of business and economic data.

GENERAL WORKS

BANKERS' ALMANAC
Reed Information Services, Ltd.
East Grinstead House, Windsor Court, East Grinstead
West Sussex, England RH19 1XA
Phone: 0134 232 6972
Fax: 0134 233 5612
Semiannual. $456.00. Four volumes. Formerly Bankers' Almanac and Yearbook.

THE BANKERS: THE NEXT GENERATION
Martin Mayer NAL-Dutton/Penguin USA
375 Hudson St.
New York, NY 10014-3657
Phone: (800) 526-0275 or (212) 366-2000
Fax: (212) 366-2666
1997. $29.95. A popularly written discussion of the future of banks, bankers, and banking.

THE GREATEST EVER BANK ROBBERY: THE
COLLAPSE OF THE SAVINGS AND LOAN INDUSTRY
Martin Mayer Macmillan Publishing Co., Inc.
200 Old Tappan Rd.
Old Tappan, NJ 07675
Phone: (800) 223-2336
Fax: (800) 445-6991
1990. $12.95.

INSIDE JOB: THE LOOTING OF AMERICA'S SAVINGS AND LOANS
Stephen Pizzo and others
McGraw-Hill, Inc.
1221 Avenue of the Americas
New York, NY 10020
Phone: (800) 722-4726 or (212) 512-2000
Fax: (212) 512-2821
1989. $19.95. Written by investigative journalists.

MICHIE ON BANKS ON BANKING
Michie Editorial Staff, editors
Michie Butterworth
PO Box 7587
Charlottesville, VA 22906
Phone: (800) 643-1279 or (800) 972-7600
Fax: (804) 972-7666
1994. $440.00. 13 volumes.

MONEY, BANKING, AND THE ECONOMY
Thomas Mayer and others
W. W. Norton & Co., Inc.
500 5th Ave.
New York, NY 10110
Phone: (800) 223-4830 or (800) 223-2584
Fax: (800) 458-6515
1995. Sixth edition. Price on application.

PRINCIPLES OF MONEY, BANKING AND FINANCIAL MARKETS BASIC
Lawrence S. Ritter and William L. Silber
HarperCollins Publishers, Inc.

10 E. 53rd St.
New York, NY 10022-5299
Phone: (800) 331-3761 or (212) 207-7000
Fax: (212) 207-7145
1993. $64.50. Eighth edition.

FURTHER READING

America's Community Bankers 1996 Annual Report and Related Statistics. Washington, 1996.

American Banker, 5 August 1996.

Hansell, Saul. "Bank Is Set to Buy a Brokerage Firm." *The New York Times,* 7 April 1997.

"More of Largest U.S. Banks Post Income Rise in Quarter." *The New York Times,* 17 April 1997.

"Statistical Reports." *American Banker.* 5 August 1996.

"Strong Quarterly Earnings Reported by Several Banks." *The New York Times,* 15 April 1997.

"The 1997 Fortune 500." *Fortune Magazine,* 28 April 1997.

Quarterly Banking Profile. Washington: Federal Deposit Insurance Corporation, 1997. ◄►

WINE INDUSTRY

The first commercial wine venture in the United States was in Pennsylvania in 1793. However, the majority of modern American wineries have been located in California, with Washington and New York coming in a distant second and third, respectively. California has accounted for over 90 percent of all U.S. wine production and over 70 percent of all wine sold in the United States. According to the Wine Institute, ''If viewed as a nation, California would rank sixth in worldwide wine production, following Spain but bigger than Germany.'' The dominant wine producer in California continues to be the Gallo family, controlling nearly 40 percent of the wine market.

According to a five-year study of wine consumption patterns in the United States, wine is drunk in moderation and usually with a meal. The report found that 49 percent of wine drinkers are between the ages of 45 and 64, and 82 percent of wine consumption takes place with a meal, typically dinner. Table wine has been the most popular kind of wine sold in the United States. Varietals, table wines made predominately of one kind of grape, have continued to grow in popularity, following the trend that consumers are drinking less, but better wine.

Wine sales in the United States have been on the rise since 1994, while per capita consumption rates have remained steady at 1.8 gallons. Consumer tastes have progressed to upscale wines, which has boosted the sales of varietals. As consumer demand for wine strengthens, the availability of grapes has weakened, driving up the price of grapes to an all-time high in 1995.

Fueling this increase in wine consumption has been the improved U.S. economy and the publicity of reports touting the benefits of moderate wine consumption. In 1996, the U.S. government for the first time acknowledged moderate wine consumption to be a part of a heart-healthy diet. This statement of public policy should only further benefit the growth of wine sales in the United States in the years to come.

Imported wine also has seen tremendous growth in the United States, and many California wine companies have established relationships with producers in Chile and Argentina to sell their wine. For example, the Canandaigua Wine Company, the second-largest wine seller in the United States, has established a relationship with Vino Santa Carolina Chilean wines to become that company's sole agent and exclusive importer for the United States.

BEVERAGES, ALCOHOLIC

SICs 2084, 2085

After *several successful growing seasons, wine makers have experienced a shortage of supply to due extremely popular demand for wine. As a result, producers have been importing vast amounts of grapes, varietals, and wine from other countries in order to complement their domestic output. These developments—coupled with the wine industry's success with new varietals and an increasing perception that wine offers some health benefits—bode well for wine sales in the coming years. For its part, the stagnating spirits industry has been pursuing such desperate measures as broadcast advertising to boost sales that have sagged for several years.*

Top 10 LEADING DOMESTIC DRY TABLE WINES

Ranked by: Sales volume, in thousands of dollars.

1. E & J Gallo Reserve Cellars, with $123,357 thousand
2. Gallo Livingston Cellars, $112,606
3. Carlo Rossi, $84,712
4. Franzia, $80,620
5. Sutter Home, $78,440
6. Almadea, $65,784
7. Glen Ellen Reserve, $64,835
8. Beringer, $58,661
9. August Sebastiani, $54,122
10. Woodbridge, $53,408

Source: *Beverage & Food Dynamics,* January/February, 1996, p. 12.

DISTILLED SPIRITS INDUSTRY

American consumption of distilled spirits rose slightly in 1996, breaking a dramatic 15-year decline. Nearly 135 million cases of liquor were sold in 1996, with Absolut's Vodka leading the way with 3.3 million cases. In second place was Jose Cuervo tequila with 2.5 million cases.

As American consumers continued to drink less frequently but better quality products, the premium category of distilled spirits grew. The resurgence of classic cocktails such as Martinis and Manhattans also helped the sale of premium dark spirits, although white spirits such as vodka and gin remained more popular.

Despite this small jump in sales, the liquor industry, which consisted of large, multinational corporations, was trying to counter the 23 percent decline in U.S. consumption rates since 1981. Citing the need to compete with marketers of beer and wine, the liquor industry made a controversial decision to lift a 48-year-old voluntary ban on television advertising.

Response to this decision was swift and came from a variety of sources, including President Clinton and various public interest organizations. Congress began to hold hearings regarding all advertising for alcoholic beverages on radio and television. The outcome of these hearings also would affect the ever-popular and growing presence of liquor companies on the World Wide Web.

On a brighter note, American liquor marketers continued to make inroads with product exportation. Claiming a banner year in 1995, U.S. exports of distilled spirits totaled 22 percent of industry sales. Volumes of whiskey, rum, and neutral grain spirits all increased in 1995.

All the major liquor companies had their eye on the international arena, especially the Asian market. Japan was already at the top of the U.S. export list, and has been a favorite home for American whiskey. Latin America also has been noted for its tremendous growth opportunity, especially for premium-priced products.

INDUSTRY OUTLOOK

WINE INDUSTRY

Following a 6.5 percent loss in 1993, wine sales in the United States have been rising, while per capita consumption remains steady at 1.8 gallons. According to the San Francisco-based Wine Institute, consumer demand for premium varietal wines spurred a 5 percent increase in California table wine sales in 1994—the strongest performance in more than a decade.

While most of the largest wine producers reported record sales, and consumer tastes moved upscale to more expensive wines, 1994 was noted as the best year for the wine industry since the late 1980s. "The end of the drought, the waning of phylloxera root louse problems and increased consumer demand all have wine makers singing a new tune," reported Clifford Carlsen of *The San Francisco Business Times.*

Total U.S. production again rose in 1995, up 10.3 percent at 437 million gallons. According to wine industry analyst Jon Frederickson of Gomberg, Fredrickson and Associates of San Francisco, California wine sales increased 8 percent in 1995 to a record $4.4 billion. Increased consumer demand and a relatively strong supply of fruit contributed to the industry's continued strong growth.

Following record wine sales and all-time high prices for grapes in 1995, the industry experienced another banner year in 1996. In fact, many North Coast wineries, with sales increases of 30 to 40 percent, didn't have enough wine to meet the staggering demand. "The only regret anyone has at the moment is that there isn't enough wine to sell, which is a good position to be in given some of the times in the past," said Patrick Campbell, owner of the Laurel Glen Winery in Glen Ellen.

HEALTH BENEFITS OF WINE

The improved economy and continuing news reports about the health benefits of moderate wine consumption has fueled the continued growth of the industry. Wine sales have been on the rise since the 1991 broadcast of a "60 Minutes" report linking moderate wine consumption with a reduced risk of heart attack. Called the French Paradox, two scientists found that

U.S. WINE, BRANDY, AND SPIRITS IMPORTS

(Billion dollars)

Source: U.S. Bureau of the Census

despite similar fat intake, France's heart attack rate was one-third of the United States. A key factor they attributed to this was the French custom of drinking wine with meals. Red wine sales have increased more than 75 percent since that 1991 report.

Wine sales should continue to increase, as the federal government took an unprecedented step in advocating moderate consumption. When the U.S. government issued new dietary guidelines in 1996, it acknowledged for the first time the benefits of moderate wine consumption. Previously, the government had warned that even small amounts of alcohol had "no net health benefit."

"Writing that language into the dietary guidelines was an extraordinary statement of public policy change

in the United States. It's a foundation we can build on into the next century," said John De Luca, president of the Wine Institute, the trade association for wine industry. He added that the revised guidelines culminated five years of work to redefine the image of wine, "putting it back on the dining room table where it's been for 2,000 years."

Leading the pack in wine sales have been the varietals, especially the fighting one. Relatively new to the industry, a "fighting" varietal has been defined as a value-priced, cork-finished 750 ml varietal wine. The leader in fighting varietals has been Glen Ellen, followed by Fetzer's Bel Arbors, Sebastiani's Country Wines and Swan Cellar label, Beringer's Napa Valley, and Robert Mondavi's Woodbridge. Tim Wallace, a Glen Ellen executive, told *Beverage Dynamics* that "fighting varietals are the foundation for the American wine industry in the future." And in 1996, the fighting varietal category has remained the largest single segment among growth markets.

Additional growth has come from consumers trading up from generic table wines into the fighting varietal category, or those moving from fighting varietals into the premiums.

SPARKLING WINE AND CHAMPAGNE

On the other hand, champagne sales continued to drop despite increases of specific brands. From a peak of 18.2 million 9-liter cases of sparkling wine and champagne in the United States in 1986, consumption fell to

SIC 2085 - Distilled & Blended Liquors
General Statistics

| Year | Companies | Establishments | | Employment | | | Compensation | | Production ($ million) | | | |
		Total	with 20 or more employees	Total (000)	Production Workers (000)	Hours (Mil)	Payroll ($ mil)	Wages ($/hr)	Cost of Materials	Value Added by Manufacture	Value of Shipments	Capital Invest.
1982	71	104	75	12.2	8.9	18.0	263.8	10.15	1,700.5	1,460.1	3,126.1	90.0
1983		98	71	11.3	8.2	16.9	261.1	10.91	1,839.3	1,534.7	3,396.7	87.2
1984		92	67	11.3	7.8	16.0	268.1	11.56	1,744.9	1,685.2	3,404.9	48.1
1985		85	64	10.5	7.4	15.1	267.6	12.03	1,846.1	1,690.9	3,494.8	37.3
1986		81	64	9.9	6.8	13.8	261.4	12.54	1,730.2	1,845.3	3,504.3	41.4
1987	47	71	56	8.8	6.3	12.4	240.2	13.05	1,499.9	2,054.8	3,441.2	43.9
1988		74	57	8.3	5.9	11.5	237.1	13.55	1,413.1	2,038.8	3,468.8	33.4
1989		63	50	7.1	5.3	10.8	225.8	13.74	1,423.9	2,163.9	3,601.9	37.6
1990		62	49	6.9	5.2	11.0	235.4	13.78	1,587.0	1,888.3	3,473.5	36.4
1991		64	45	7.4	5.2	10.6	236.7	14.23	1,545.2	2,147.4	3,656.0	59.1
1992	43	65	48	7.1	5.1	10.5	243.9	15.05	1,446.9	1,945.6	3,394.1	56.3
1993		62	47	7.0	5.1	10.4	245.1	15.49	1,472.1	2,112.9	3,568.8	42.1
1994		51P	40P	6.6	4.7	10.1	240.1	15.43	1,649.9	2,208.5	3,723.3P	39.7
1995		47P	37P	5.4P	3.9P	8.1P	229.8P	16.21P	1,580.2P	2,115.2P	3,723.3P	33.1P
1996		43P	34P	4.9P	3.6P	7.5P	227.2P	16.64P	1,594.1P	2,133.8P	3,756.1P	30.6P
1997		40P	32P	4.4P	3.2P	6.8P	224.5P	17.07P	1,608.0P	2,152.5P	3,788.9P	28.2P
1998		36P	29P	3.9P	2.9P	6.1P	221.9P	17.50P	1,622.0P	2,171.1P	3,821.7P	25.7P

Sources: 1982, 1987, 1992 Economic Census; Annual Survey of Manufactures, 83-86, 88-91, 93-94. Establishment counts for non-Census years are from County Business Patterns; establishment values for 83-84 are extrapolations. 'P's show projections by the editors. Industries reclassified in 87 will not have data for prior years.

12.3 million 9-liter cases in 1995. Causes for the decline are high prices for champagne, high taxes, high cost of shipping, and lack of consistent, high-profile marketing programs.

The good news is that quality of champagne, both domestic and imported has been rising. ''Champagne producers have begun to make a lighter, more elegant non-vintage brut, one that better suits the American palate.'' Dramatic improvements in taste and technique all have been pioneered in California's best sparkling wine regions—Carneros, Mendocino County, and the central coast. In return, these domestic producers have seen consumers move to brands that offer high quality at affordable prices.

DISTILLED SPIRITS INDUSTRY

For the first time in 15 years, American consumption of distilled spirits increased in 1996—albeit only a 0.3 percent rise. This small but significant jump bolstered the hopes of liquor industry leaders who long anticipated consumption rates to turn around.

Approximately 135 million cases of liquor goods were consumed in 1996, according to *Impact,* an industry trade journal. The biggest sellers were Seagram's Absolut Vodka (3.3 million cases, up 5.2 percent from 1995) and Grand Met's Jose Cuervo tequila (2.5 million cases, up 6 percent).

As with previous years, the recovery appears to be gaining at a much faster pace with white goods rather than dark. Vodka topped US distilled liquor sales in 1994, with more than 31 million cases sold. Canadian whiskey led sales of dark spirits with slightly more than 16 million cases.

The sales breakdown of other distilled spirits in 1994 were rum, 10.6 million cases; gin, 11.6 million cases; tequila, 4.5 million cases; cordials, 14.9 million cases; bourbon (including blended and straight), 13 million cases; blended whiskey, 7.2 million cases; scotch, 8.9 million cases; and Irish whiskey, 242,000 cases.

With 25 percent of the distilled market, vodka continue to surpass all other types of distilled spirits. In the past, vodka was popular because American consumers wanted lighter, less flavorful beverages. But as classic cocktails were revived in the 1990s, many were resurrected with a vodka base. Moreover, premium vodkas such as Ketel One, Absolut, and Skyy, were growing in popularity, as well as infused vodkas such as Absolut Citron, Absolut Kurrant, Finlandia Cranberry, Finlandia Pineapple, and Tanqueray Sterling Citrus.

Following in the footsteps of infused vodka, rum flavored with spices or citrus was also gaining popularity with American consumers. Captain Morgan Original Spiced Rum from Seagram captured the number two spot in the rum category with sales of 1 million cases in 1995, and Bacardi Limon claimed sales of more than 300,000 cases in its first nine months on the market.

Gin also posted a slight gain, but due more to the resurgence of gin cocktails rather than the introduction of new products. Marck Schuermann, director of public issues for DISCUS, cites what he calls ''anecdotal evidence,'' with the return of classic cocktails and martini bars.

The popularity of classic cocktails such as Manhattans and Rob Roys may also explain why dark spirits have shown increases, especially in the premium category. According to *Impact,* the top 25 premium and super-premium brands are expected to be up 4.9 percent to 28.8 million cases in 1996.

ADVERTISING CONTROVERSY

This good news for the liquor industry still can't match the 23 percent decline in distilled spirits consumption in the United States since 1981. Citing falling sales and the need to compete with wine and beer marketers, in November 1996 the board of the Distilled Spirits Council of the United States unanimously voted to lift a 48-year-old voluntary ban on television advertising.

Seagram Americas became the first spirits marketer to break the ban in June 1996 with its ad for Crown Royal Canadian whiskey on KRIS-TV in Corpus Christi, Texas. ABC, CBS, NBC, and Fox so far have refused to take liquor ads. But more than 1,000 television and cable providers may follow the lead of Black Entertainment Television and accept advertisements from distilled spirits marketers.

The issue of liquor advertising opened a floodgate of controversy, including admonishments from President Clinton, Mothers Against Drunk Drivers, and Reed Hundt, chairman of the Federal Trade Commission. All of these parties said the ban should remain to protect children. George Hacker of the advocacy group, Center for Science in the Public Interest, said the repeal of the broadcast ad ban ''marks the beginning of an open liquor-marketing season on America's children and teens.''

The Federal Communications Commission (FCC) began a formal inquiry into the placement and content of Seagram's ads, while the Federal Trade Commission followed with its own investigation. Congress also had taken up this issue with the Senate Commerce Committee telecommunications subcommittee hearings in

March 1997. Witnesses include the FTC Chairman Robert Pitofsky, FCC Chairman Reed Hundt, industry critics including former Senator George McGovern, the official spokesperson of the National Council on Alcoholism and Drug Dependence, and representatives of the beer, liquor, broadcast, and cable industries.

The outcome of these hearings would not only affect liquor advertising on broadcast and cable television, but also distilled spirits marketers presence on the Internet. All liquor companies—beer, wine and distilled spirits—turned to the Internet to disseminate product information. However, some organizations, such as the Center of Media Education, were claiming that beer and liquor companies were using the World Wide Web to attract underage drinkers. Some companies included a warning on their web sites that visitors must be at least 21 years old. These include Heublein Inc.'s web sites for Smirnoff vodka and Cuervo Gold tequila, and Joseph E. Seagram & Son's site for Captain Morgan's rum.

ORGANIZATION AND STRUCTURE

All wine makers and the distilled spirits industry have to sell their products through wholesalers and retailers to accommodate various federal, state, and local regulations regarding the sale of alcoholic beverages. The Federal Alcohol Administration Act (FAA) was established after the 13-year Prohibition Era ended in 1933. The Bureau of Alcohol, Tobacco and Firearms (ATF) is responsible for administering and enforcing the FAA, including qualifying wine makers and distilled spirits producers, collecting producer and wholesaler occupational taxes, and regulating trade practices, advertising, and labeling. Beyond the uniformity of the FAA, regulations vary greatly among the 50 states.

States can sell wine and distilled spirits in one of two ways, either in a controlled environment or using an open, licensed method. "Open" states have licensed retailers and wholesalers that handle the distribution and sale of alcoholic beverages. Thirty-two states and the District of Columbia are "open" states. The other 18 states operate under the control method, in which each state government buys and sells alcoholic beverages at the wholesale and retail levels. In addition to federal regulations, some states have set up their own independent agencies that are responsible for the administration, licensing, and enforcement of state laws and the collection of state revenues. Some state legislatures even have created their own Alcoholic Beverage Control (ABC) agencies with rule-making power, and 32 states allow their citizens to vote for or against the sale of liquor on a city or county-wide basis.

WORK FORCE

The *Ward's Business Directory of U.S. Private and Public Companies 1997* lists 144 companies that have produced wine and brandy in the United States. Most of these companies are privately held, with a handful of public companies such as Heublein, Hiram Walker, and the Seagram Company. In particular, the wine making industry employed over 17,000 workers. The majority of wineries have been family-owned, located predominately in California, and have created a tremendous impact on that state's economy. Los Angeles-based Recon Research Corporation reported that the California wine industry has contributed nearly $1.5 billion annually to the Sonoma County economy, employing more than 3,600 people and creating secondary industrial employment of an additional 2,500 jobs.

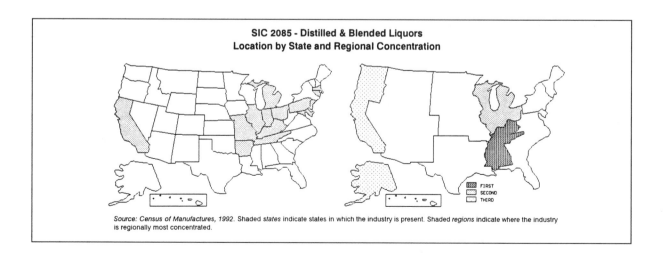

SIC 2085 - Distilled & Blended Liquors
Location by State and Regional Concentration

FIRST
SECOND
THIRD

Source: *Census of Manufactures, 1992.* Shaded *states* indicate states in which the industry is present. Shaded *regions* indicate where the industry is regionally most concentrated.

AMERICA AND THE WORLD

The impending shortage of California wine combined with growing consumer demand should open the door for wines coming into the United States from Italy, France, Chile, Argentina, and other wine-producing countries. Overseas planting of premium varietals have been growing at a fast pace and will be a significant new source of wine for U.S. consumers. In fact, California wineries already were buying unprecedented amounts of overseas wine to meet consumer demand for low-priced everyday wine and to expand their existing line of products in the mid-1990s. For example, in 1996 Robert Mondavi began importing a Chilean line of wines, the Caletara brand, priced in the $6 to $9 range. A second brand, Edwardo Chadwick was introduced in the $12 to $15 range, followed by a brand in an even higher price range. In 1995, the winery also launched a line of Italian varietals.

Wines from Chile continue to make inroads into the American market. According to *Beverage Dynamics,* wines from Chile have sold well in the United States since 1986. Chilean wines exports grew from $10.4 million in 1985 to $181.7 million in 1995. The United States alone imported about $40 million worth of Chilean wine in 1995. Again, U.S. companies were seizing the opportunity to push Chilean wines. The Brown-Forman Beverage Company began working with a line of Chilean wine with the brand name, Carmen, in 1993. In the mid-1990s, the nation's second-largest wine marketer, Canandaigua, became sole agent and exclusive importer for Vino Santa Carolina Chilean wines.

Another emerging wine growing country has been Australia. Demand for Australian wine skyrocketed as American consumers enjoy the Australian style of wine. Its worldwide trademark of generous flavors, soft tannins, and accessible fruit made this wine easier to like when young, a perfect style of wine for Americans. In 1990, the Australians shipped only 578,000 cases of wine to the United States. In comparison, case shipments to the United States by the end of 1996 were projected to reach 2 million. Moreover, the Australian Wine Bureau reports that more than 4 million cases of Australian wine would be shipped to the United States by 2001, and by 2026, shipments should total more than 10 million cases with an estimated value of $440 million.

U.S. exports of distilled spirits reached a record high in 1995, according to DICUS. Since 1991, U.S. distilled spirits have doubled both in value and volume. In 1991, U.S. distilled spirits exports were less than 10 percent of total industry sales; in 1995, they totaled 22 percent of industry sales. Volume exports of U.S. whiskey, rum, and neutral grain spirits categories all increased in 1995, while U.S. whiskey, brandy, gin, cordials, and neutral grain spirits increased in value.

"International expansion represents a great opportunity for distillers. Leading spirit brands already enjoy worldwide cachet, especially within the whiskey and cognac categories," reported Jim Barrett in the *Value Line Investment Survey.* Export opportunities can be found in the fast-growing markets of the Asia Pacific region, Latin America, and the former Soviet Bloc. "Not only are these expanding markets, but the growth is generally occurring among higher-margin, deluxe brands. What's more, trade barriers have recently been lifted in a number of countries, such as India and Taiwan," added Barrett.

The Asia Pacific area has included some of the largest whiskey markets in world, with Japan at the top of the U.S. export list. The rapid ascent of a middle class in these countries bodes well for the future of beverage alcohol marketers. "Export is the hot spot," Barry M. Berish, president of Jim Beam Brands Co., noted in *Business Week.*

U.S. whiskey exports led the product categories with a 15.5 percent increase in value to $278 million and a 9.8 percent increase in volume. Japan, Germany, and Australia were significant growth markets for exporting U.S. whiskey in 1995. Japan accounts for 26 percent of the total value of U.S. exports with an 11 percent increase in sales over 1994. Germany accounts for 17.6 percent with an 18 percent increase compared to 1994. Australia accounts for 12.8 percent, with a 21 percent increase in 1995 sales.

Beverage alcohol marketers also were beginning to focus on growth in other countries. After successful penetration of the Japanese market, whiskey advertising could be found in Britain and other affluent markets. Latin America, for example, has become the second greatest growth opportunity, particularly for premium-priced scotch marketers like Seagram. Sales of scotch grew over 50 percent in 1991 in Venezuela, with much of the growth occurring among higher-priced brands, such as Chivas Regal Scotch. Scotch whisky has remained the most popular distilled spirit in the world and has been sold in 190 countries.

ASSOCIATIONS AND SOCIETIES

AMERICAN SOCIETY FOR ENOLOGY AND VITICULTURE
PO Box 1855
Davis, CA 95617
Phone: (916) 753-3142
Fax: (916) 753-3318

AMERICAN WINE SOCIETY
3006 Latta Rd.
Rochester, NY 14612
Phone: (716) 225-7613
Fax: (716) 225-7613

DISTILLED SPIRITS COUNCIL OF THE UNITED STATES
1250 Eye St. NW, Ste. 900
Washington, DC 20005
Phone: (202) 628-3544
Fax: (202) 682-8888

SOCIETY OF WINE EDUCATORS
132 Shaker Rd., Ste. 14
East Longmeadow, MA 01028
Phone: (413) 567-8272
Fax: (413) 567-2051

WINE AND SPIRITS GUILD OF AMERICA
c/o Max B. Green
1766 Dupont Ave. S.
Minneapolis, MN 55403
Phone: (612) 377-6459
Fax: (612) 377-6211

WINE AND SPIRITS WHOLESALERS OF AMERICA
1023 15th St. NW, 4 Fl.
Washington, DC 20005
Phone: (202) 371-9792
Fax: (202) 789-2405

WINE INSTITUTE
c/o Librarian
425 Market St., Ste. 1000
San Francisco, CA 94105
Phone: (415) 512-0151
Fax: (415) 442-0742

PERIODICALS AND NEWSLETTERS

AMERICAN JOURNAL OF ENOLOGY AND VITICULTURE
American Society for Enology and Viticulture
PO Box 1855
Davis, CA 95617
Phone: (916) 753-3142
Fax: (916) 753-3318
Quarterly. $95.00 per year.

BUREAU OF ALCOHOL, TOBACCO, AND FIREARMS QUARTERLY BULLETIN
Bureau of Alcohol, Tobacco, and Firearms
U.S. Department of the Treasury
Available from U.S. Government Printing Office
Washington, DC 20402
Phone: (202) 512-1800
Fax: (202) 512-2250
Quarterly. $14.00 per year. Laws and regulations.

IMPACT: U.S. NEWS AND RESEARCH FOR THE WINE, SPIRITS, AND BEER INDUSTRIES
M. Shanken Communications, Inc.
387 Park Ave. S
New York, NY 10016
Phone: (212) 684-4224
Fax: (212) 684-5424
Biweekly. $375.00 per year. Newsletter covering the marketing, economic, and financial aspects of alcoholic beverages.

KANE'S BEVERAGE WEEK: THE NEWSLETTER OF BEVERAGE MARKETING
Whitaker Newsletters, Inc.
313 South Ave.
Fanwood, NJ 07023
Phone: (908) 889-6336
Fax: (908) 889-6339
Weekly. $380.00 per year. Newsletter. Covers news relating to the alcoholic beverage industries, including social, health, and legal issues.

WINE ENTHUSIAST
8 Saw Mill River Rd.
Hawthorne, NY 10578
Phone: (914) 345-8463
Fax: (914) 345-3028
Six times a year. $14.95 per year. Covers domestic and world wine. Formerly Wine Times.

THE WINE SPECTATOR
M. Shanken Communications, Inc.
c/o Lynn Rittenband
387 Park Ave. S
New York, NY 10016
Phone: (800) 752-7799 or (212) 684-4224
Fax: (212) 684-5424
Semimonthly. $40.00 per year. Wine ratings.

WINES AND VINES: THE AUTHORITATIVE VOICE OF THE GRAPE AND WINE INDUSTRY
Hiaring Co.
1800 Lincoln Ave.
San Rafael, CA 94901-1298
Phone: (415) 453-9700
Fax: (415) 453-2517
Monthly. $32.50 per year.

DATABASES

***CITIBASE* (CITICORP ECONOMIC DATABASE)**
FAME Software Corp.
77 Water St., 9 Fl.
New York, NY 10005
Phone: (212) 898-7800
Fax: (212) 742-8956
Presents over 6,000 statistical series relating to business, industry, finance, and economics. Includes series from Survey of Current Business *and many other sources. Time period is 1947 to date, with daily updates. Inquire as to online cost and availability.*

VITIS: Viticulture and Enology Abstracts
[ONLINE]
International Food Information Service GmbH
Melibocusstr. 52, Postfach 710-444
Frankfurt 71, Germany D-6000
Phone: 4969- 669007-0
Fax: 4969- 669007-10
Covers the worldwide technical literature of grapes and wine from 1969 to present, with quarterly updates. Inquire as to online cost and availability

STATISTICS SOURCES

Business Statistics
Available from U.S. Government Printing Office
Washington, DC 20402
Phone: (202) 512-1800
Fax: (202) 512-2250
Biennial. $20.00. Issued by Bureau of Economic Analysis, U.S. Department of Commerce. Shows annual data for 29 years and monthly data for a recent four-year period. Statistics correspond to the Survey of Current Business.

Impact Beverage Trends in America
M. Shanken Communications, Inc.
387 Park Ave. S
New York, NY 10016
Phone: (212) 684-4224
Fax: (212) 684-5424
Annual. $695.00. Detailed compilations of data for various segments of the liquor, beer, and soft drink industries.

Jobson's Liquor Handbook: Statistics, Trends and Analysis for the Distilled Spirits Industry
Jobson Publishing Corp.
100 Avenue of the Americas
New York, NY 10013-1678
Phone: (212) 274-7000
Fax: (212) 431-0500
Annual. $265.00. Formerly Liquor Handbook.

Monthly Statistical Release: Distilled Spirits
U.S. Bureau of Alcohol, Tobacco, and Firearms
Treasury Dept.
Washington, DC 20226
Phone: (202) 927-8500
Monthly.

Survey of Current Business
Available from U.S. Government Printing Office
Washington, DC 20402
Phone: (202) 512-1800
Fax: (202) 512-2250
Monthly. $41.00 per year. Issued by Bureau of Economic Analysis, U.S. Department of Commerce. Presents a wide variety of business and economic data.

Wines and Vines Annual Statistical Issue
Hiaring Co.
1800 Lincoln Ave.

San Rafael, CA 94901-1298
Phone: (415) 453-9700
Fax: (415) 453-2517
Annual. $5.00.

GENERAL WORKS

The U.S. Distilled Spirits: Impact Databank Market Review and Forecast
M. Shanken Communications, Inc.
387 Park Ave. S
New York, NY 10016
Phone: (212) 684-4224
Fax: (212) 684-5424
Annual. $745.00. Includes industry commentary and statistics.

The U.S. Wine Market: Impact Databank Review and Forecast
M. Shanken Communications, Inc.
387 Park Ave. S
New York, NY 10016
Phone: (212) 684-4224
Fax: (212) 684-5424
Annual. $745.00. Includes industry commentary and statistics.

FURTHER READING

Berger, Dan. "Australian Wines." *Beverage & Food Dynamics,* January/February 1997.

———. "Robust Year of Sales Gives Wine Makers a Healthy Glow." *San Francisco Business Times,* 15 November 1996.

Holmgren, Elizabeth. "60 Minutes Revisits the French Paradox with More Good News!" Wine Trader: Health and Social Issues Report, 1996. Available from http://www. Wines.com/winetrader/196his.html.

"Knowing and Understanding Distilled Spirits." BeverageNet Home Page, 1996. Available from http://www.aip.com.

Shore, Teri. "More Import Perspectives. Foreign Supplies Could Help California Wines." *Wine Business Monthly,* February 1996.

"Spirits Not So Down, Consumption Continues to Sink, but Shows Signs of Leveling Off." *Beverage Industry,* August 1996.

"Ten Events That Made News (Spirits TV advertising)." *Advertising Age,* 23 December 1996.

Ward's Business Directory of U.S. Private and Public Companies. Detroit: Gale Research Inc., 1997.

"Wine Drinker Profiled." *Beverage Dynamics,* March 1992.

Beer has been a part of the American lifestyle since the discovery of America and the creation of the United States. Records show that beer was brewed in colonial America and was made by American Indians. Through the years, beer has served cultural, spiritual, and even medicinal purposes. With nearly 80 million American beer drinkers, beer has become one of the most popular beverages, second only to water and tea.

Each year, the U.S. malt beverage industry produces and sells more than 2.5 billion cases of beer, or about 190.2 million barrels. A barrel of beer is equal to two kegs or 31 gallons, which is roughly 13.8 24-unit cases of 12-ounce cans or bottles. The wholesale value of malt beverage shipments averages approximately $15 billion annually. According to the Beer Institute, the trade association for the malt beverage industry, the United States is the world's largest producer of beer, brewing more than 20 percent of the world's volume.

Domestic sales for beer rose a small but significant 1 percent in 1996, breaking a ten-year stalemate in consumption rates. This growth can be attributed to the strength of microbrews, which continue to post double-digit growth, and imported beer, which saw record figures in 1995.

Three major companies hold nearly 78 percent of the market share in the United States. These breweries are Anheuser-Busch (A-B), located in St. Louis, Missouri; Miller Brewing Company in Milwaukee, Wisconsin; and Coors Brewing Company in Golden, Colorado.

The two top-selling brands, Budweiser and Bud Light, both belonged to Anheuser-Busch, along with 45 percent of the market share and 75 percent of the industry profits. In second place was Miller with the third-best selling product, Miller Light. Ranked third was Coors Brewing Company with the fourth most-popular beer, Coors Light.

Although light beer continues to dominate the market with a 37 percent consumption rate, microbrews and specialty beer also continue to grow in popularity. Since the industry-leader Boston Beer Company was founded in 1984, the microbrew business has grown into a $1-billion industry. And the market segment is projected to grow from now through 2000, capturing 6 percent of the total domestic beer market.

Another good sign for the U.S. beer industry is its strong showing overseas. Various markets are starting to become accessible, especially the most eagerly sought Asian market. Japan continues to be the largest market for U.S. beer, but export rates also have climbed in Hong Kong, Brazil, Taiwan, Canada, and Russia.

BEVERAGES, MALT

SIC 2082

After *years of flat sales, the beer brewing industry has experienced modest overall growth in the mid-1990s. This growth was due to the phenomenal popularity of the relatively small microbrew and import market segment. Growth in this market sector has soared an average of 40 percent over the past decade, and industry insiders predict that by 2000 it will capture 6 percent of the beer market from current levels of 1.5 percent. Despite these promising developments, the Bureau of Labor Statistics estimates that virtually all occupations within the beer industry would decline in the percentage of total employed by the year 2000.*

Top 10 MOST POPULAR DOMESTIC BEER BRANDS

Ranked by: Sales in 1994, in millions of 2.25-gallon cases.

1. Budweiser, with 571.3 million cases
2. Bud Light, 218.3
3. Miller Lite, 213.9
4. Coors Light, 179.0
5. Busch, 114.5
6. Natural Light, 99.4
7. Miller Genuine Draft, 95.0
8. Milwaukee's Best, 81.0
9. Miller High Life, 74.7
10. Old Milwaukee, 63.5

Source: *Adams/Jobson's Liquor Handbook* (annual), Adams/Jobson Publishing, 1995, p. 309.

INDUSTRY OUTLOOK

Total sales volume for the domestic beer market rose 1 percent in 1996, a small but symbolic gesture breaking a decade-long stagnation in consumption rates. Although incremental, this industry growth can be attributed to the continued rise in microbrews, which has been posting double-digit growth since 1995, and to imported beers. Both segments are significant but small; microbrews make up only 2 percent of the market and imports account for just 5 percent.

''I think that the issue that the major brewers have to deal with is that the combination of microbrews and imports are skimming the cream off the top,'' says Emanuel Goldman, a leading drink analyst for Paine Webber. ''It's an industry that is basically not growing. The beer per cap is undergoing a very gradual decline, and so what you have is what has existed for some time in the distilled spirits business, people drinking less but drinking better,'' said Goldman.

The three big leaders in the beer industry continue to be Anheuser-Busch, Miller, and Coors. With the two top-selling brands, Budweiser and Bud Light, A-B dominates the domestic beer market. In 1996, A-B increased its market share from 44 percent to 45.2 percent, according to a report published in *Beer Marketer's Insights*. A-B shipped more than twice as much beer than second-place Miller, who had 21.8 percent of the market and the third best-selling product, Miller Light. Coors Brewing Company, with its fourth-place Coors Light, dropped market share from 10.1 percent in 1995 to 9.9 percent in 1996.

A-B sells 45 percent of U.S. beer volume, but controls over 75 percent of the industry's profits. The rest of the industry battles for the remaining 25 percent of the profit pool. As a result, companies have begun to consolidate with others to save in operational expenditures. So, in 1995 fourth-place Stroh Brewery Company acquired G. Heileman, makers of Colt 45, Old Style, and Henry Weinhard, among other labels.

''Stroh and Heilman are partners now under a common umbrella . . . because of the necessity of it. Coors will have to find a partner with which to consolidate to achieve long-term profitability. And although it's part of a very large and wealthy company, Miller's share of industry profits is declining even while its share of market has been relatively stable,'' said Martin Romm, a leading industry analyst for First Boston.

Causes for this stagnant market have and continue to be attributed to the effects of the federal excise tax hike in 1991, unfavorable demographics (not enough 21-year-olds), and continuing health concerns regarding alcohol consumption. A bit of good news for the beer industry is that the mini baby-boom generation is about to come of age, so the flat market of 21-year-olds should be growing soon.

Attempting to boost incremental sales and expand the beer market, companies have been continuing to introduce new products—often creating entirely new segments such as light beer, nonalcoholic beer, ice beer, bottled draft beer, and clear malt liquor drinks such as Zima.

Light beer has maintained the largest share of beer consumption at 37.25 percent—more than 70 million barrels in 1996, according to figures from R.S. Weinberg & Associates. Nonalcoholic beer also has helped the beer business to grow. Although small compared to total beer consumption, volume of nonalcoholic beer has more than doubled since its 1989 level and remained steady since 1991. O'Doul's by Anheuser-Busch accounts for half of the non-alcoholic market share.

The one market segment that everyone has been turning to is the craft beer or microbrews. Sales in this segment have been growing at an average of 40 percent a year for the last ten years. According to the Institute for Brewing Studies, specialty brewing in the United States grew from a $600-million industry in 1992 to $1-billion industry in 1994.

In an industry of mature brands, companies were looking at the future of microbrews. Even the big names were offering craft brews. In 1994, A-B, the largest brewer in the United States, bought a stake in Seattle's Redhook Ale Brewery, while Coors Brewing Company landed Killian's Irish Red.

The undisputed leader of the microbrew segment has been the Boston Beer Company (BBC) and its product Samuel Adams. The tenth largest beer producer in the country, BBC manufactured 700 barrels in 1994, only about three one-thousandths of the beer sold in the United States. However small, its volume still is greater than the total of the next six microbrewers combined.

When the BBC was founded in 1984, fewer than 40 micro-breweries existed. Since then, an estimated 500 small breweries and brew pubs have opened, with an additional 50 added each year from 1985 on.

"The microbrewery segment is expected to grow to a six percent domestic market share by 2000 from 2.5 percent now, but not every brewer in business today will be around then," says Mike Gerend, president of Wisconsin Brewing Co. Many companies have tried to cash in on the microbrewing craze but Gerend thinks a true microbrew will be most successful in its hometown market and will survive on consumer loyalty.

ORGANIZATION AND STRUCTURE

The industry has consistently been dominated by three major U.S. breweries, yet, regardless of size, all breweries have to sell their products through wholesalers and retailers. This distribution channel is the result of accommodating the variety of federal, state, and local regulations regarding the sale of alcoholic beverages.

FEDERAL AND STATE REGULATION

The Federal Alcohol Administration Act (FAA) was put into place at the end of Prohibition in 1933. Since that time, the Bureau of Alcohol, Tobacco and Firearms (ATF) has been responsible for administering and enforcing the FAA, including qualifying brewers, collecting brewer and wholesaler occupational taxes, and regulating trade practices, advertising, and labeling.

Beyond the uniformity of the FAA, regulations varied greatly among the 50 states, as the Beer Institute reported in their testimony to the U.S. Senate regarding the Malt Beverage Interbrand Competition Act. Probably the most dramatic example of regulatory diversity has been the way that states have allowed beer to be sold. States sell beer in one of two ways, either in a controlled environment or using an open, licensed method. "Open" states license retailers and wholesalers to handle the distribution and sale of alcoholic beverages. Thirty-two states and the District of Columbia are considered "open" states. The other 18 states operate under the control method, in which each state government buys and sells alcoholic beverages at the wholesale and retail levels.

In addition to federal regulations, some states have set up independent agencies that have been responsible for the administration, licensing, and enforcement of state laws and the collection of state revenues. Additionally, some state legislatures created their own Alcoholic Beverage Control (ABC) agencies with rule-making power, and 32 states have allowed citizens to vote for or against the sale of liquor in various cities or counties.

WORK FORCE

The U.S. beer industry consists of 54 leading breweries that employ approximately 97,000 people in all areas of the industry (including non-manufacturing areas). According to the Beer Institute, "Brewery workers' wages are among the highest of more than 350 industries annually surveyed by the U.S. Department of Labor. These men and women take home approximately

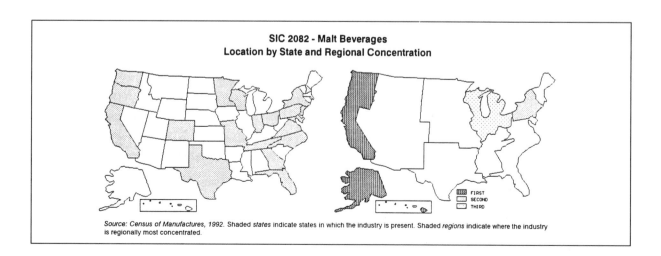

SIC 2082 - Malt Beverages
Location by State and Regional Concentration

FIRST
SECOND
THIRD

Source: Census of Manufactures, 1992. Shaded states indicate states in which the industry is present. Shaded regions indicate where the industry is regionally most concentrated.

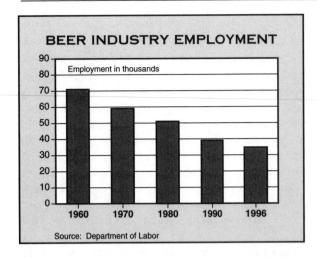

BEER INDUSTRY EMPLOYMENT

Employment in thousands

Source: Department of Labor

industry would decline in the percentage of total employed by the year 2000. Those jobs that include "hands-on" involvement, such as freight, stock and material movers, hand packers, and testers, were predicted to decline by at least 25 percent.

AMERICA AND THE WORLD

EXPORTS

Faced with consumption rates at a stand still at home, U.S. companies turned to the international arena to grow their markets. A-B was considering opportunities from Latin America to Europe and the Far East. Competitors feared that the company would eventually work with French company Kronenbourg (part of the Danone group), which would give A-B a strong distribution network in Europe.

U.S. companies were looking for markets with financial strength and disposable income, such as Latin America and the Asian marketplace. In fact, it seemed that beer companies throughout the world were rushing into the exploding markets of Thailand, Vietnam, and most importantly China.

"The marketplace around the world has opened up in the very recent past. So, in part, our abilities to go abroad have been enable by the world freeing up in terms of access," said Michael Marranzino, chief international officer at Coors Brewing Company and reported in *Beverage Industry.*

$2.2 billion a year in salaries and wages with additional millions paid in the form of fringe benefits and retirement programs." Bureau of Labor Statistics data indicates, however, that the number of employees directly involved in the industry has dropped over the past several decades, from more than 71,000 workers in 1960 to a little over 40,000 employees at the end of the 1980s.

The top five states that are home to the largest number of brewery employees are New York, Wisconsin, Pennsylvania, California, and Washington. The largest numbers of employees worked as packaging and filling machine operators, driver-sales workers, salespeople, truck drivers, tractor operators, supervisors, and laborers. Estimates by the Bureau of Labor Statistics showed that virtually all occupations within the beer

SIC 2082 - Malt Beverages
General Statistics

| Year | Com-panies | Establishments | | Employment | | | Compensation | | Production ($ million) | | | | |
		Total	with 20 or more employees	Total (000)	Production Workers (000)	Hours (Mil)	Payroll ($ mil)	Wages ($/hr)	Cost of Materials	Value Added by Manufacture	Value of Shipments	Capital Invest.
1982	67	109	74	43.0	29.5	57.5	1,307.9	15.37	6,669.7	4,534.8	11,183.2	665.0
1983		109	72	40.7	28.5	55.1	1,302.6	16.19	6,443.2	5,324.6	11,797.5	599.8
1984		109	70	38.8	27.4	51.8	1,313.6	17.99	6,485.0	5,393.7	11,868.2	594.1
1985		110	67	40.3	27.0	52.6	1,357.8	18.10	6,529.1	5,681.1	12,215.8	372.2
1986		119	66	34.0	24.8	50.5	1,255.1	17.64	6,502.5	6,184.5	12,677.9	578.3
1987	91	134	64	31.9	22.7	44.7	1,355.4	20.76	6,311.8	7,284.8	13,618.6	473.6
1988		139	68	32.4	23.2	42.7	1,316.6	21.20	6,414.0	7,450.8	13,870.7	570.3
1989		150	71	32.0	23.3	43.8	1,364.6	21.26	6,555.0	7,783.3	14,321.2	601.8
1990		154	81	34.0	23.5	44.3	1,425.1	21.34	6,988.5	8,192.8	15,186.2	542.8
1991		177	85	32.4	23.5	43.1	1,445.8	22.30	6,885.8	9,036.7	15,924.9	649.0
1992	160	194	75	34.5	25.1	45.9	1,566.7	22.89	7,179.8	10,189.3	17,340.2	565.0
1993		215	91	35.3	25.3	46.5	1,596.3	22.71	7,125.3	9,543.2	16,656.3	479.3
1994		205P	83P	33.5	23.6	46.6	1,565.9	23.01	6,941.8	9,847.2	16,794.8	563.5
1995		215P	84P	30.8P	22.4P	41.4P	1,576.5P	24.62P	7,370.1P	10,454.8P	17,831.1P	541.1P
1996		224P	86P	30.1P	22.0P	40.4P	1,602.0P	25.27P	7,589.7P	10,766.3P	18,362.4P	538.7P
1997		234P	87P	29.4P	21.6P	39.5P	1,627.5P	25.92P	7,809.4P	11,077.9P	18,893.7P	536.3P
1998		243P	89P	28.7P	21.2P	38.5P	1,653.0P	26.57P	8,029.0P	11,389.4P	19,425.0P	533.9P

Sources: 1982, 1987, 1992 *Economic Census; Annual Survey of Manufactures,* 83-86, 88-91, 93-94. Establishment counts for non-Census years are from *County Business Patterns;* establishment values for 83-84 are extrapolations. 'P's show projections by the editors. Industries reclassified in 87 will not have data for prior years.

According to the U.S. Department of Commerce, Japan was the largest market for U.S. beer in the mid-1990s, although sales were actually down 16.6 percent in the country in 1995. Sales came in 62 percent higher than in 1994 in Hong Kong, 214.5 percent higher in Brazil, 108.6 percent higher in Taiwan, 33.6 percent higher in Canada, and 78.9 percent higher in Russia.

IMPORTS

The total U.S. imported beer market hit an all-time high in 1995, with volume topping out at an estimated 343.5 million gallons, as reported by *Beverage Marketing*. This growth represented a 5.5 percent jump in volume from 1994 and was almost a 40 percent improvement of U.S. imported beers as compared to ten years ago.

"Thirty years ago the imported beer market in the U.S. basically did not exist," says Michael Bellas, president of *Beverage Marketing*. "In 1965, only 8.8 million cases [19.8 million gallons] of beer was imported into the United States. Since that time, the imported beer market has sustained compound annual volume growth of 10 percent. In 10 of the last 20 years, import growth rates have been in the double-digits."

The surge in imports to the United States was attributed to the American consumer's desire for high quality, full-bodied brews; lower total alcohol consumption; and becoming accustomed to higher prices for both domestic craft brews and imported brands. Among the world's best-selling beers, only Heineken, the Danish Carlsberg, and Guinness may be regarded as truly international. The Dutch sell 90 percent of the their beer outside the Netherlands.

North America and the Caribbean countries (Mexico, Canada, Jamaica) led exports in 1995, with 165.8 million gallons of beer shipped to the United States, up from 160 million gallons in 1994. The Europeans exported a record 161.8 million gallons of beer to the United States, up almost 8 percent from 1994. The Asian/Pacific region exported 7.4 million gallons to the United States—virtually the same figure as in 1994.

ASSOCIATIONS AND SOCIETIES

AMERICAN SOCIETY OF BREWING CHEMISTS
3340 Pilot Knob Rd.
Saint Paul, MN 55121-2097
Phone: (612) 454-7250
Fax: (612) 454-0766

BEER INSTITUTE
1225 Eye St. NW, Ste. 825
Washington, DC 20005
Phone: (202) 737-2337
Fax: (202) 737-7004

BREWERS' ASSOCIATION OF AMERICA
PO Box 876
Belmar, NJ 07719-0876
Phone: (908) 280-9153
Fax: (908) 681-1891

MASTER BREWERS ASSOCIATION OF THE AMERICAS
2421 N. Mayfair Rd., No. 310
Wauwatosa, WI 53226-1407
Phone: (608) 231-3446
Fax: (608) 231-2470

NATIONAL BEER WHOLESALERS' ASSOCIATION
1100 S. Washington
Alexandria, VA 22041
Phone: (703) 683-4300
Fax: (703) 683-8965

PERIODICALS AND NEWSLETTERS

AMERICAN SOCIETY OF BREWING CHEMISTS JOURNAL
American Society of Brewing Chemists Journal
3340 Pilot Knob Rd.
Saint Paul, MN 55121-2097
Phone: (612) 454-7250
Fax: (612) 454-0766
Quarterly. Free to members; non-members, $115.00 per year.

ASBC NEWSLETTER
American Society of Brewing Chemists
3340 Pilot Knob Rd.
Saint Paul, MN 55121-2097
Phone: (612) 454-7250
Fax: (612) 454-0766
Quarterly. $25.00 per year.

BEER MARKETER'S INSIGHTS
Beer Marketer's Insights, Inc.
51 Virginia Ave. W
West Nyack, NY 10994
Phone: (914) 358-7751
23 times a year. $310.00 per year. Newsletter for brewers and wholesalers.

BREWERS DIGEST
Dori Whitney, editor
Siebel Publishing Co., Inc.
4049 W. Peterson Ave.
Chicago, IL 60646
Phone: (312) 463-3401
Monthly. $25.00 per year. Covers all aspects of brewing.

IMPACT: U.S. NEWS AND RESEARCH FOR THE WINE, SPIRITS, AND BEER INDUSTRIES
M. Shanken Communications, Inc.
387 Park Ave. S
New York, NY 10016
Phone: (212) 684-4224
Fax: (212) 684-5424
Biweekly. $375.00 per year. Newsletter covering the marketing, economic, and financial aspects of alcoholic beverages.

*KANE'S BEVERAGE WEEK: THE NEWSLETTER OF
BEVERAGE MARKETING*
Whitaker Newsletters, Inc.
313 South Ave.
Fanwood, NJ 07023
Phone: (908) 889-6336
Fax: (908) 889-6339
*Weekly. $380.00 per year. Newsletter. Covers news relating to
the alcoholic beverage industries, including social, health, and
legal issues.*

MBAA TECHNICAL QUARTERLY
Master Brewers Association of the Americas
2421 N. Mayfair Rd., Ste. 310
Madison, WI 53226-1407
Phone: (414) 774-8558
*Quarterly. $60.00 per year. Includes membership. Text in En-
glish and Spanish.*

DATABASES

CITIBASE (CITICORP ECONOMIC DATABASE)
FAME Software Corp.
77 Water St., 9 Fl.
New York, NY 10005
Phone: (212) 898-7800
Fax: (212) 742-8956
*Presents over 6,000 statistical series relating to business, indus-
try, finance, and economics. Includes series from* Survey of
Current Business *and many other sources. Time period is 1947
to date, with daily updates. Inquire as to online cost and avail-
ability.*

STATISTICS SOURCES

BEER STATISTICS NEWS
Beer Marketer's Insights, Inc.
51 Virginia Ave. W
West Nyack, NY 10994
Phone: (914) 358-7751
*24 times a year. $265.00 per year. Market share and shipments
by region and brewer.*

IMPACT BEVERAGE TRENDS IN AMERICA
M. Shanken Communications, Inc.
387 Park Ave. S
New York, NY 10016
Phone: (212) 684-4224
Fax: (212) 684-5424
*Annual. $695.00. Detailed compilations of data for various seg-
ments of the liquor, beer, and soft drink industries.*

JOURNAL OF COMMERCE AND COMMERCIAL
Journal of Commerce Inc.
2 World Trade Center, 27 Fl.
New York, NY 10048-0203
Phone: (212) 837-7000
Fax: (212) 837-7035
Daily, except Saturday and Sunday. $349.00 per year.

MONTHLY STATISTICAL RELEASE: BEER
U.S. Bureau of Alcohol, Tobacco, and Firearms
Treasury Dept.
Washington, DC 20226
Phone: (202) 927-8500
Monthly.

SURVEY OF CURRENT BUSINESS
Available from U.S. Government Printing Office
Washington, DC 20402
Phone: (202) 512-1800
Fax: (202) 512-2250
*Monthly. $41.00 per year. Issued by Bureau of Economic Analy-
sis, U.S. Department of Commerce. Presents a wide variety of
business and economic data.*

GENERAL WORKS

BREWERS ALMANAC
Beer Institute
1225 Eye St. NW, Ste. 825
Washington, DC 20005
Phone: (202) 737-2337
Fax: (202) 737-7004
Annual. $150.00.

*THE U.S. BEER MARKET: IMPACT DATABANK REVIEW
AND FORECAST*
M. Shanken Communications, Inc.
387 Park Ave. S
New York, NY 10016
Phone: (212) 684-4224
Fax: (212) 684-5424
Annual. $745.00. Includes industry commentary and statistics.

MODERN BREWERY AGE BLUE BOOK
Business Journals, Inc.
50 Day St.
East Norwalk, CT 06856
Phone: (203) 853-6015
Fax: (203) 852-8175
Annual. $175.00. Supplement to Modern Brewery Age.

MALTING AND BREWING SCIENCE
J.S. Hough and others
Routledge, Chapman and Hall, Inc.
29 W. 35th St.
New York, NY 10001-2291
Phone: (212) 244-3336
Fax: (800) 248-4724
1982. $150.00 Second edition. Two volumes.

*NATIONAL LICENSED BEVERAGE
ASSOCIATION-MEMBERS DIRECTORY*
National Licensed Beverage Association
4214 King St. W
Alexandria, VA 22302-1507
Phone: (800) 441-9893 or (703) 671-7575
Fax: (703) 845-0310
Annual. $30.00.

FURTHER READING

''Economic Impact of the Beer Industry.'' Washington: Beer Institute.

Holleran, Joan. ''Craft brews, a beer rabbit?'' *Beverage Industry,* January 1997.

''It's a Small World for US Brewers.'' *Beverage Industry,* May 1996.

Mullins, Robert. ''Microbrewers See Slower Growth, Shake-out.'' *The Business Journal-Milwaukee,* 4 January 1997.

Sfiligoj, Eric. ''The Europeans strike back.'' *Beverage World,* February 1996.

Smit, Barbara. ''Global Beer War Set to Explode.'' *The European,* 25 July 1996. ➤

16

BOOK PUBLISHING AND PRINTING

SIC 2731

An area representing enormous growth potential for the publishing industry through the end of the twentieth century is the Internet. Used by hundreds of publishing companies and distributors to advertise products and to display catalogs online, the Internet offers publishers a new way to reach customers all over the world. Book publishers are also finding themselves in a position of having to adapt quickly to new media and technologies that profoundly affect the function and layout of the traditional book. Industry analysts predict that publishers will invest heavily in CD-ROM and Internet technology well into the next millennium.

INDUSTRY SNAPSHOT

The book publishing industry experienced extraordinary growth over the past three decades, with annual book sales of $1.68 billion in 1963 rising to $17.17 billion by 1993. A study conducted by the NPD Group, Inc. revealed that approximately 1.5 billion books were bought by American consumers in 1995, with 500 million of these being juvenile titles. Areas of strongest sales growth included children's books, professional/technical books, and religious books—particularly sacred texts. As reported by Jim Milliot of *Publisher's Weekly,* consumers spent close to $24 billion on books in 1994 alone. That figure approached $25 billion in 1995. In a 1996 report, the American Booksellers Association indicated book purchasing rose by over 30 percent between 1991 and 1994. The leading metropolitan areas for book sales included Los Angeles, New York, Chicago, Boston, and Washington D.C.

Top 10 TOP CORPORATIONS IN THE PUBLISHING/PRINTING INDUSTRY

Ranked by: Revenue in 1995, in millions of dollars.

1. R. R. Donnelley & Sons, with $6,512 million
2. Gannett, $4,007
3. Times Mirror Co., $3,491
4. Reader's Digest Association, $3,069
5. McGraw-Hill, $2,935
6. Tribune Co., $2,864
7. Knight-Ridder, $2,752
8. New York Times Co., $2,409
9. Dow Jones, $2,284
10. American Greetings Corp., $1,878

Source: *Fortune,* Fortune 500 Largest U.S. Corporations (annual), April 29, 1996, p. F-59.

Part of the increase in the early 1990s was attributed to the proliferation of large retail bookstore chains. ''Superstores'' offering comfortable browsing areas, coffee bars, and special events such as book-signings, author readings, and children's story hours, provided an enjoyable atmosphere for consumers while expanding the overall market for books. In the mid-1990s, the two biggest players in this arena were Borders Group, Inc. and Barnes & Noble, Inc. Another factor that influenced growth was the move by many publishers toward the creation of ''books'' in electronic formats. Electronic publishing exposed book publishers to unprecedented competition from software and communications companies, which resulted in significant new pressure on the bottom line.

INDUSTRY OUTLOOK

The book publishing industry faced transformation entering the mid-1990s. Many observers noted that the industry, once characterized as gentlemanly and literary, had quickly become more cutthroat and businesslike. *National Review* cited as evidence the trend for large publishing houses to replace long-time chief executives, best known for their "literary sensibilities," with industry outsiders steeped in "modern management techniques." As a result, many employees within the publishing industry shifted focus from building relationships with authors and carefully tailoring manuscripts to cutting costs and analyzing profit and loss statements. Former Pantheon managing director Andre Schiffrin noted in *The Nation* an increasing trend among modern day publishing houses to set higher and higher profit targets, which often ranged from 12 to 15 percent in 1996; this figure contrasted starkly with the typical 1920s publishing company's average profit of 4 percent. Rising overheads also contributed to the financial strain placed on publishers in the mid-1990s, making many companies even more vulnerable.

Another factor affecting the book publishing industry was the proliferation of large, influential retail bookstore chains. While these chains expanded the overall market for books, they also had the power to limit pricing and affect the selection of books that publishers could offer profitably. Some analysts also worried that chains would disrupt the business of independent booksellers, who were often closely linked to tastes within their communities and provided a market for more eclectic books. *The Nation* noted in 1996 that, "In a series of lawsuits brought by the American Booksellers Association, the independents have charged that the large publishers favor the chains through unfair practices." The argument was that the big publishers allegedly paid generously to have bestsellers prominently displayed and advertised within the stores while the smaller publishers did not have the means to compete in such a system.

The two biggest retail book selling chains, Borders Group Inc. and Barnes & Noble Inc., expanded aggressively throughout the United States, opening outlets reaching from New York's World Trade Center to the west coast. In 1995, Borders boasted sales of $1.75 billion while Barnes & Noble posted a total revenue figure of $1.97 billion. In 1996, the potential for such giants to continue expansion efforts was unhindered,

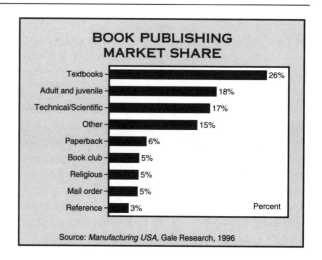

BOOK PUBLISHING MARKET SHARE

Textbooks – 26%
Adult and juvenile – 18%
Technical/Scientific – 17%
Other – 15%
Paperback – 6%
Book club – 5%
Religious – 5%
Mail order – 5%
Reference – 3%

Percent

Source: *Manufacturing USA*, Gale Research, 1996

with over 140 U.S. metropolitan markets still without one of these "superstores." *The Wall Street Journal* offered analyst Amy Ryan's assertion that the expansion could go on "through the year 2000 and . . . the U.S. can support 1,500 such outlets."

Book publishers also faced a challenge to continued profitability due to the 1980s legacy of offering huge cash advances to prominent authors. Large advances were criticized within the industry for preventing publishers from nurturing talented, yet less well-known authors. However, other industry observers argued that the proceeds from one best-seller could often support a number of "more literary" releases. Overall, many publishers expressed the intention to limit future advances. Book publishers also faced keen competition for the leisure time of traditional customers from cable television, VCRs, video games, multimedia products, and the Internet. Many publishers also faced shrinking profit margins in key areas. For example, author royalties generally accounted for 10 to 15 percent of the cover price of trade books, which left publishers with an average margin of 9.5 percent. For textbooks and professional books, however—which were less expensive to produce and usually sold in larger quantities—houses obtained an average margin of 20 percent. Many book publishers responded to these challenges by cutting costs, streamlining operations, adopting new technologies, and investigating the marketing potential of electronic products such as CD-ROMs and on-line information delivery.

As the U.S. economy began to recover in the mid-1990s, the outlook for the book publishing industry also began to improve. Shifting demographics pointed toward higher enrollment levels in schools and colleges, while the Clinton administration appeared likely to increase funding for libraries and the arts. Many publishers expected growth among medical and health care-related titles to correspond with concerns of the aging U.S.

population, as well as growth in professional and technical titles to support rapid changes in office technology. In 1995, the latter expectation was born out and evidenced in part by an 82 percent increase in revenues from the sale of computer books for that year alone.

Also in 1995, the market for juvenile trade books had begun to rebound. Sales in that category reached $1.35 billion and *Book Industry Trends 1996* projected that domestic consumer expenditures on children's books would nearly double to $2.67 billion by the year 2000. According to the American Association of Publishers, 500 million children's books were purchased domestically in 1995, as the juvenile publishing segment posted a gain of 4 percent over the previous year.

ORGANIZATION AND STRUCTURE

Over 20,000 companies participated in the book publishing industry in the early to mid-1990s. However, the industry was dominated by several giant publishing houses. According to *Trade Book Publishers, 1996: Analysis by Category,* the top 12 trade book publishers accounted for nearly 85 percent of the overall U.S. book publishing market. These large publishers consolidated many of the smaller imprints in the early 1990s in order to cut costs and reposition themselves for the onset of electronic publishing. However, this concentration of power among relatively few publishers led to criticism regarding the quality and diversity of materials published. Industry observers saw an increasing role for small presses to publish works of literary quality that did not necessarily have enormous sales potential.

Products within the book publishing industry could be divided into six major categories: adult trade; juvenile trade; mass market; professional, technical, and reference; university press; and religious books. Trade books, representing the largest share of the book market, encompassed all general-interest publications, such as adult and juvenile fiction, nonfiction, advice, and how-to books. In 1995, the adult trade category alone posted net sales of over $4.3 billion according to *Book Industry Trends 1996*. In the mass market paperback category, net sales approached $1.35 billion for 1995; net sales for professional titles reached almost $3.87 billion. The expansion of large chain bookstores and the population growth among school-age children and high-income adults were among the factors that contributed to the growth of these sales.

The book publishing process was fairly similar across these product categories. Most books originated as a concept or idea, which was either submitted by an outside author or generated internally by the publisher. The concept was usually refined using market analysis, and the final decision to proceed resulted from a comparison of the product's expected costs and potential revenues. Next came the actual compilation of the book's content, followed by editorial work to ensure its quality and tailor it specifically to a target market. Meanwhile, the marketing and art departments designed the finished product, including type style, page size and layout, presentation of graphics, and appearance of the cover. Then the book was typeset (set in final, camera-ready form for printing), either by an outside vendor or with an in-house desktop publishing system. Finally, the book was transformed into plates, printed, and bound, usually by an outside vendor or affiliated company rather than the publishing house.

Book publishers sold products to the following primary markets: chain and independent retail bookstores; college bookstores; elementary and high schools; libraries, universities, and other institutions. Among these markets, large chain bookstores proliferated and gained

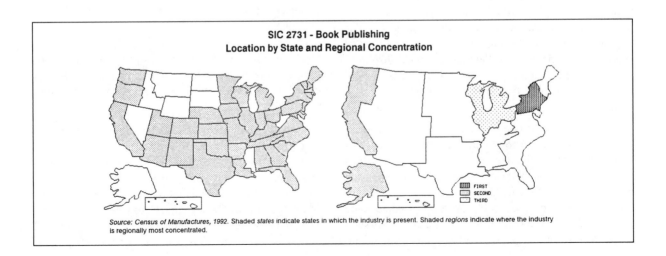

SIC 2731 - Book Publishing
Location by State and Regional Concentration

FIRST
SECOND
THIRD

Source: Census of Manufactures, 1992. Shaded states indicate states in which the industry is present. Shaded regions indicate where the industry is regionally most concentrated.

importance in the early 1990s, making book-buying into a form of entertainment and siphoning sales away from mail order and book clubs. In addition, the library market, though small, was considered crucial in that it guaranteed publishers a minimum number of sales and, traditionally, required comparatively little in terms of marketing attention. On-line bookselling, the newest and fastest growing retail format, provided consumers with relatively quick access to over 1 million titles purchasable via the Internet.

WORK FORCE

In an assessment for *Black Enterprise,* Lolis Eric Elie called book publishing ''an industry that rewards creativity, treasures personal taste, and provides opportunities to combine work with a socially responsible endeavor.'' In addition to editorial work, publishing offered career potential for individuals with backgrounds in business, marketing, sales, graphic design, and computer applications. Traditionally, however, ''low entry-level salaries, long hours, and slow advancement have deterred those who tried their hand in the field,'' Elie continued.

Some industry observers predicted that technology would redefine the roles of everyone in the publishing industry in the late 1990s. As Susan Trowbridge, vice president of publishing technology at Addison-Wesley, explained in *Publishers Weekly,* ''the new technological capabilities are causing us to re-examine the roles and procedures of all the publishing participants, from author to editor to designer to manufacturer.'' Trowbridge foresaw desktop publishing technology moving upstream into editorial functions as well as downstream to manufacturers; a more coordinated focus on the development of multimedia products, involving teamwork between editorial, marketing, and technical experts; and increased automation of administrative processes, such as scheduling and cost-tracking. Employees in all sectors of the publishing industry increasingly required knowledge of computers in order to be successful in their careers.

RESEARCH AND TECHNOLOGY

The traditional, printed book might never disappear completely, but new technology revolutionized production, distribution, and nearly every other aspect of operations in the publishing industry in the 1990s. As *Publishers Weekly* predicted, ''The definition of 'publisher' will change. It won't just refer to a person who makes books, but a person who holds information or intellectual property, and disseminates that information in any way he or she can benefit from it.'' Most publishers began to store information in digital form on computer systems so that it could be readily translated into a variety of electronic product formats.

SIC 2731 - Book Publishing
General Statistics

| Year | Companies | Establishments | | Employment | | | Compensation | | Production ($ million) | | | |
		Total	with 20 or more employees	Total (000)	Production Workers (000)	Hours (Mil)	Payroll ($ mil)	Wages ($/hr)	Cost of Materials	Value Added by Manufacture	Value of Shipments	Capital Invest.
1982	2,007	2,130	420	67.1	15.2	30.8	1,327.3	7.70	2,420.0	5,291.5	7,740.0	174.1
1983		2,094	427	69.3	17.1	33.0	1,474.9	8.42	2,683.2	5,823.8	8,427.4	163.6
1984		2,058	434	69.4	14.9	27.2	1,600.3	9.86	2,890.1	6,722.9	9,459.2	199.4
1985		2,023	440	70.9	15.6	28.6	1,672.1	9.78	3,021.1	7,395.8	10,196.2	232.1
1986		2,013	449	71.6	14.4	25.6	1,775.6	10.13	3,099.8	7,755.9	10,731.5	202.8
1987	2,180	2,298	424	70.1	15.9	28.7	1,859.8	10.67	3,663.2	9,110.7	12,619.5	239.7
1988		2,180	428	70.2	16.5	30.4	2,009.8	10.76	3,988.1	9,851.9	13,570.7	302.4
1989		2,164	463	73.6	17.1	30.2	2,132.3	11.56	4,365.5	9,915.5	14,074.2	319.1
1990		2,144	448	74.4	17.3	31.2	2,299.9	11.68	4,465.5	10,919.5	15,317.9	329.1
1991		2,284	451	77.3	17.1	30.0	2,514.1	12.72	5,001.4	11,683.3	16,596.1	330.5
1992	2,504	2,644	500	79.6	18.6	35.5	2,675.7	12.49	5,337.7	11,494.4	16,731.1	326.7
1993		2,699	473	83.2	18.2	34.5	2,799.2	12.90	5,806.8	12,742.9	18,615.9	282.0
1994		2,540P	479P	87.1	18.7	34.8	2,935.6	13.27	5,826.7	13,681.0	19,418.9	283.0
1995		2,588P	484P	84.1P	18.7P	33.9P	3,022.0P	13.96P	6,081.0P	14,278.1P	20,266.5P	352.0P
1996		2,636P	489P	85.5P	19.0P	34.4P	3,156.2P	14.40P	6,377.7P	14,974.6P	21,255.1P	365.0P
1997		2,684P	494P	86.9P	19.3P	34.8P	3,290.4P	14.83P	6,674.3P	15,671.1P	22,243.7P	378.1P
1998		2,732P	499P	88.3P	19.6P	35.3P	3,424.6P	15.27P	6,970.9P	16,367.6P	23,232.3P	391.2P

Sources: 1982, 1987, 1992 *Economic Census; Annual Survey of Manufactures,* 83-86, 88-91, 93-94. Establishment counts for non-Census years are from *County Business Patterns;* establishment values for 83-84 are extrapolations. 'P's show projections by the editors. Industries reclassified in 87 will not have data for prior years.

SIC 2731
Occupations Employed by SIC 273 - Books

Occupation	% of Total 1994	Change to 2005
Writers & editors, incl technical writers	7.7	14.5
Sales & related workers nec	5.8	14.5
Bindery machine operators & set-up operators	5.3	14.5
Secretaries, ex legal & medical	3.2	4.3
Machine feeders & offbearers	3.1	3.1
General office clerks	3.1	-2.3
General managers & top executives	3.0	8.7
Offset lithographic press operators	2.7	37.5
Professional workers nec	2.5	37.5
Adjustment clerks	2.4	37.5
Hand packers & packagers	2.3	-1.8
Helpers, laborers, & material movers nec	2.2	14.5
Strippers, printing	2.1	2.1
Clerical supervisors & managers	2.0	17.2
Clerical support workers nec	2.0	-8.4
Freight, stock, & material movers, hand	2.0	-8.4
Bookkeeping, accounting, & auditing clerks	2.0	-14.1
Blue collar worker supervisors	2.0	5.5
Marketing, advertising, & PR managers	1.9	14.5
Printing press machine setters, operators	1.9	14.5
Order clerks, materials, merchandise, & service	1.8	12.1
Traffic, shipping, & receiving clerks	1.7	10.2
Assemblers, fabricators, & hand workers nec	1.6	14.6
Managers & administrators nec	1.5	14.5
Proofreaders & copy markers	1.4	-25.5
Artists & commercial artists	1.4	16.4
Printing, binding, & related workers nec	1.2	14.5
Systems analysts	1.2	83.2
Production, planning, & expediting clerks	1.1	37.4
Computer programmers	1.1	-7.2
Management support workers nec	1.0	14.6

Source: Industry-Occupation Matrix, Bureau of Labor Statistics. These data relate to one or more 3-digit SIC industry groups rather than to a single 4-digit SIC. The change reported for each occupation to the year 2005 is a percent of growth or decline as estimated by the Bureau of Labor Statistics. The abbreviation nec stands for 'not elsewhere classified'.

The advent of new technology raised a number of interesting issues within the publishing industry. Publishers faced unprecedented competition from software and communications companies entering the electronic publishing market. Second, authors and publishers disagree about who owns electronic publication rights, and significantly more complex contract negotiations have become the norm. Additionally, some confusion arose about which channels of distribution would be most appropriate for electronic products, since bookstores, software stores, on-line subscriptions, and direct mail all formed possible outlets. All of these issues had strong implications for the current organization and future staffing of book publishers. They had to become more flexible and technologically adept in order to compete.

Accessing information electronically offered a number of advantages for consumers. For example, CD-ROM products allowed easy sorting of information from a wide variety of databases and made it possible to combine text, graphics, sound, and animation. Some examples of innovative CD-ROM products included a dictionary that could pronounce words, an encyclopedia that could show video clips about entries, and a book that could help a child learn to read. Another common format for electronic information was on-line through computer subscription services and via the Internet. On-line materials were less expensive for publishers to distribute than paper, easier—in some cases—for users to search, and also provided quick publication for time-sensitive information such as medical advances.

By the mid-1990s, the Internet was being used as a means to sidestep the middleman in sales transactions. By 1996, the leading on-line book provider was Amazon.com, a company founded only two years earlier in a garage. Owned by Jeff Bezos, the firm employed 85 people, had estimated sales of $5 million, boasted a stock list of over one million titles, and was experiencing extraordinary sales growth. According to Steve Potash, as quoted in *Publishers Weekly*, "After software, books are the most popular type of product sold on the Internet. The most popular electronic-book categories on the Web are reference, professional and self-help." Though bookselling sites have burgeoned on the World Wide Web, insiders cautioned publishers and booksellers not to expect the Internet to take the place of bookstores but to view the new online marketplace as yet another avenue for reaching consumers.

Several industry analysts predicted that environmental issues would gain importance within the publishing industry. For example, some consumer groups demanded that books, especially paperbacks, be made recyclable. Publishers cooperated with printing and binding companies to make book-binding processes and cover materials more environmentally sound, and some products were developed that could be unbound easily. In 1995, the Environmental Protection Agency announced, as part of its 1994 Common Sense Initiative, an air toxics rule for the printing and publishing industry that would cut dangerous air emissions resulting from printing and package production processes. The proposal was expected to impact 127 existing printing and publishing facilities in the U.S. and any future facilities to be built.

AMERICA AND THE WORLD

The U.S. publishing industry was by far the world's leading exporter of books. Exports accounted for nearly 10 percent of U.S. publishers' shipments in 1993, or about $1.7 billion. According to the U.S. Department of Commerce, book exports reached $1.76 billion in 1995 (displaying a 4 percent increase over 1994) while unit sales increased to over 885 million. Half of U.S. exports were textbooks or professional and technical products.

The major markets for U.S. book exports were Canada, the United Kingdom, Japan, Australia, Germany, and Mexico. In 1995, the biggest increase was in exports to South Korea. The predominance of U.S. exports was explained in part by the increasing numbers of people worldwide who used the English language to conduct business. Total U.S. imports of books reached $1 billion in 1992, an increase of 13 percent over the previous year. By 1995, 530 million books worth $1.2 billion entered the U.S. with the largest increases coming from Canada, Mexico, China, and Italy according to *Publishers Weekly*. The United Kingdom, Hong Kong, Japan, Thailand, South Korea, and Canada were the sources for most imported books.

Industry analysts in the early 1990s expected international sales of U.S. books to continue to improve, particularly in emerging markets such as the former Soviet Union, Mexico and Latin America, and Asia. U.S. publishers faced some challenges in international sales, however, due to inconsistent application of copyright, or intellectual property right, laws overseas. Publishers of audio books and electronic products, in particular, were displeased with the lack of specific protection afforded by the General Agreement on Tariffs and Trade (GATT) when it concluded in late 1993.

ASSOCIATIONS AND SOCIETIES

ASSOCIATION OF AMERICAN PUBLISHERS
71 5th Ave.
New York, NY 10003-3004
Phone: (212) 255-0200
Fax: (212) 255-7007

BOOK INDUSTRY STUDY GROUP
160 5th Ave.
New York, NY 10010
Phone: (212) 929-1393
Fax: (212) 989-7542

BOOK MANUFACTURERS INSTITUTE
45 William St., Ste. 245
Wellesley, MA 02181-4007
Phone: (617) 239-0103
Fax: (617) 239-0106

PI BETA ALPHA
RR 2, PO Box 172
Bloomington, IL 61704
Phone: (309) 378-4007
Formerly Professional Bookmen of America.

WOMEN'S NATIONAL BOOK ASSOCIATION
160 5th Ave., Rm. 604
New York, NY 10010
Phone: (212) 675-7805
Fax: (212) 989-7542

PERIODICALS AND NEWSLETTERS

BOOK MARKETING UPDATE
Open Horizons Publishing
PO Box 205
Fairfield, IA 52556-0205
Phone: (515) 472-6130
Fax: (515) 472-1560
Monthly. $60.00 per year. Newsletter for book publishers.

BOOK PUBLISHING REPORT
SIMBA Information, Inc.
PO Box 4234
Stamford, CT 06907-0234
Phone: (800) 307-2529 or (203) 358-4344
Fax: (203) 358-5824
Weekly. $479.00 per year. Newsletter. Covers book publishing mergers, marketing, finance, personnel, and trends in general. Formerly BP Report on the Business of Book Publishing.

COMPUTER PUBLISHING AND ADVERTISING REPORT: THE BIWEEKLY NEWSLETTER FOR PUBLISHING AND ADVERTISING EXECUTIVES IN THE COMPUTER FIELD
SIMBA Information, Inc.
PO Box 4234
Stamford, CT 06907-0234
Phone: (800) 307-2529 or (203) 358-4344
Fax: (203) 358-5824
Biweekly. $525.00 per year. Newsletter. Covers computer publishing and computer-related advertising in periodicals and other media. Provides data on computer book sales and advertising in computer magazines.

PUBLISHERS WEEKLY: THE INTERNATIONAL NEWS MAGAZINE OF BOOK PUBLISHING
Cahners Publishing Co.
249 W. 17th St.
New York, NY 10011
Phone: (800) 662-7776 or (212) 645-0067
Fax: (212) 242-7216
51 times a year. $129.00 per year. The international news magazine of book publishing.

PUBLISHING MARKETS
Cahners Publishing Co.
275 Washington St.
Newton, MA 05158
Phone: (617) 964-3030

DATABASES

BAKER & TAYLOR
Baker & Taylor Information and Entertainment Services
Posts a newsletter and other information targeted towards academic booksellers, including lists of best-selling and upcoming books. Time span: October, 1995, to date. When established: 1995. Updating frequency: Monthly. Fees: Free.

- URL: http://www.baker-taylor.com/Academia/Academia.html

LISA Online: Library and Information Science Abstracts
Bowker-Saur, Reed Reference Publishing
121 Chanlon Rd.
New Providence, NJ 07974
Phone: (800) 521-8110 or (908) 464-6800
Fax: (908) 665-6688
Provides abstracting and indexing of the world's library and information science literature from 1969 to the present. Covers a wide variety of topics in over 550 journals from 60 countries, with monthly updates. Inquire as to online cost and availability.

WILSONLINE: Wilson Publishers Directory
H. W. Wilson Co.
950 University Ave.
Bronx, NY 10452
Phone: (800) 367-6770 or (718) 588-8400
Fax: (718) 590-1617
Provides names and addresses of more than 34,000 English-language book publishers and distributors appearing in Cumulative Book Index *and other H. W. Wilson databases. Updated three times a week. Inquire as to online cost and availability.*

STATISTICS SOURCES

Book Industry Trends
Book Industry Study Group, Inc.
160 5th Ave.
New York, NY 10010
Phone: (212) 929-1393
Fax: (212) 989-7542
Annual. $450.00.

U.S. Industrial Outlook: Forecasts for Selected Manufacturing and Service Industries
Available from U.S. Government Printing Office
Washington, DC 20402
Phone: (202) 512-1800
Fax: (202) 512-2250
Annual. $37.00. (Replaced in 1995 by U.S. Global Trade Outlook.*) Issued by the International Trade Administration, U.S. Department of Commerce. Provides basic data, outlook for the current year, and "Long-Term Prospects" (five-year projections) for a wide variety of products and services. Includes high technology industries. Available on the world wide web at gopher://gopher.umsl.edu:70/11/library/govdocs/usio94*

GENERAL WORKS

American Book-Trade Directory
R.R. Bowker
121 Chanlon Rd.
New Providence, NJ 07974
Phone: (800) 521- 8110 or (908) 464-6800
Fax: (908) 665-6688

Annual. $215.00. More than 24,500 book stores and other book outlets in the U.S. and Canada; 1,400 U.S. and Canadian book wholesalers and paperback distributors.

Book Publishing Career Directory
Gale Research
835 Penobscot Bldg.
Detroit, MI 48226-4094
Phone: (800) 877-GALE or (313) 961-2242
Fax: (313) 961-6083
1992. $29.95, hardcover; $17.95, softcover. Fifth edition. Includes information on careers in various kinds of publishing, including university, independent, trade, religious, book club, and electronic. Provides advice from "insiders," resume suggestions, a directory of companies that may offer entry-level positions, and a directory of career information sources.

Bowker Annual Library and Book Trade Almanac
R.R. Bowker
121 Chanlon Rd.
New Providence, NJ 07974
Phone: (800) 521-8110 or (908) 464-6800
Fax: (908) 665-6688
Annual. $159.95. Lists of accredited library schools; scholarships for education in library science; library organizations; major libraries; publishing and book sellers organizations. Includes statistics and news of the book business.

Literary Market Place: The Directory of the American Book Publishing Industry
R.R. Bowker
121 Chanlon Rd.
New Providence, NJ 07974
Phone: (800) 521- 8110 or (908) 464-6800
Fax: (908) 665-6688
Annual. $158.00. Over 15,000 firms or organizations offering services related to the publishing industry.

Publishers Directory: A Guide to New and Established Private and Special-Interest, Avant-Garde and Alternative, Organizational Association, Government and Institution Presses
Gale Research
835 Penobscot Bldg.
Detroit, MI 48226-4094
Phone: (800) 877-GALE or (313) 961-2242
Fax: (313) 961-6083
Annual. $255.00.

Publishers, Distributors, and Wholesalers of the United States
R.R. Bowker
121 Chanlon Rd.
New Providence, NJ 07974
Phone: (800) 521- 8110 or (908) 464-6800
Fax: (908) 665-6688
Annual. $152.00. Lists 64,500 publishers, distributors, and wholesalers.

FURTHER READING

Book Industry Trends 1996. New York: Book Industry Study Group, Inc., 1996.

''Computer Books Fastest Growing Sector—Study.'' *Media Daily,* 18 July 1996.

''The Market for Children's Books Is Still Large, But It Is Changing Significantly,'' *YouthMarkets Alert,* 1 June 1996.

Moran, Susan. ''Amazon.com Forges New Sales Channel.'' *Webweek,* 19 August 1996.

''Multimedia Future Uncertain for Many Book Publishers.'' *Multimedia Business Report,* 7 June 1996

Mutter, John. ''The Bookstore of the 21st Century.'' *Publishers Weekly,* 22 July 1996.

Schiffrin, Andre. ''The Corporatization of Publishing.'' *The Nation,* 3 June 1996.

''Slow Growth in Consumer Book Purchases Last Year, New Study Shows.'' *American Association of Publishers Monthly Report,* September 1996. Available from http://www.publishers.org/news/releases/9610.html.

CABLE AND OTHER PAY TELEVISION SERVICES

SIC 4841

Cable companies that lead the way in developing new technology and offering a vast array of programming capabilities are expected to emerge as the leaders in this market. Companies that invest in fiber-optics cabling to improve transmission quality should have an advantage in the bidding process used to award franchise rights for geographic areas. Expansion of channel capacity will allow cable providers to grow revenue by offering additional programming and pay-per-view channels. This expansion is crucial for cable companies to compete with direct satellite service providers. Recent advances in technology are not only making direct satellite services more affordable for consumers, but insiders predict that they will soon correct the problem of their inability to provide local broadcast feeds to subscribers. Such advances will surely draw viewers away from cable companies who cannot offer the same breadth and quality of programming.

The cable television industry was developed in the United States in the late 1940s to serve small communities unable to receive conventional television signals due to difficult terrain or physical distance from television stations. Cable also provided improved television reception to remote areas. The original systems were centered around a collective antenna for regions with poor or nonexistent reception. Cable systems located their antennas in areas where reception was good, captured broadcast signals, and then relayed them by cable to subscribers for a fee. In 1950 cable systems operated in only 70 communities and served 14,000 subscribers.

By 1995 there were approximately 11,800 cable systems with 62 million subscribers (65.3 percent of all television households) in the United States. The average cable system provided 30 or more channels, as well as other services such as custom programming and pay-per-view options. The average monthly fee for a cable subscription was $23.00.

Top 10 TOP CABLE MULTIPLE SYSTEM OPERATORS

Ranked by: Number of subscribers in 1995, in millions.

1. Tele-Communications Inc., with 14.0 million subscribers
2. Time Warner Cable Group, 11.0
3. Cox Cable, 3.2
4. Continental Cablevision, 3.1
5. Comcast, 3.0
6. Cablevision Systems Corp., 2.6
7. Adelphia Communications, 1.6
7. Century Communications, 1.6
9. Jones Intercable/Spacelink, 1.3
10. Falcon Cable TV, 1.1

Source: *Mediaweek*, July 31, 1995, p. 9.

Traditional underground cable lines are just one of several methods used to transmit video signals from the broadcaster to the home. Pay television companies must decide which transmission method or combination of methods is the most effective in serving their customers Overall, there are four basic ways to broadcast a video signal:

- Terrestrial—a transmission tower on the ground sends a picture directly to a television aerial. This mechanism is easy to install but reception is often poor and only a few channels can be carried. This method is traditionally used to broadcast network channels.

- Coaxial or Fiber-Optic Cable—these TV signals travel through an underground cable. The cable is time-consuming and expensive to install and is used primarily in densely populated urban areas.

- Microwave—a multichannel, multipoint distribution system (MMDS) carries signals from a television studio to a microwave transmitter, which then relays them to rooftop receivers on apartment blocks. These receivers are relatively small dishes that are easy to install and maintain. Microwave transmission is a low cost alternative to cabling and is feasible in areas where there are large distances between transmitting stations and subscribers (e.g. South America).

- Satellite—a broadcaster uplinks a signal to a transponder on a satellite, which re-transmits either to home dishes or to a satellite master dish (SMATV) located on the roof of a high-rise block. Satellite transmission is common in remote rural areas where cable installation can be problematic. Subscribers pay hook-up and access fees to the satellite owners.

During the late 1990s, however, satellite television services made their presence felt in the pay television industry by providing an alternative to increasingly expensive cable service. Providers dramatically reduced set-up costs—which was initially a major drawback for consumers—by cutting satellite dish prices to $200; what is more, after the initial purchase and installation fees, satellite dish providers gave viewers many more channels for a monthly fee that rivaled cable rates. The biggest drawback to satellite television was its inability to carry local broadcast channels. The *Los Angeles Times* predicted that 20 percent of U.S. households would use satellite services by the year 2000, when the service claimed only 4 percent in 1996. Telephone companies also hoped to enter the pay television business, but such services were still only available in isolated test markets.

INDUSTRY OUTLOOK

The cable television industry has proved to be very resilient. It has successfully responded to recession, regulation and deregulation, and the entry of meaningful video service competitors such as telephone companies, direct broadcast satellite systems (DBS), and computer firms. The future appears to hold more of the same. Although the demand for basic cable service will proba-

bly increase only modestly in the future, the industry is expected to undergo a second phase of significant growth due to emerging technologies and system upgrades which make it possible for cable firms to expand channel capacity and services dramatically. At the same time, satellite television providers made impressive progress in building their subscriber base, and several new players began providing satellite services.

INVESTMENT IN TECHNOLOGY

Investment in fiber-optic technology and digital compression is allowing cable providers to expand channel capacity, offer interactive services, and carry voice, data, and video signals simultaneously on a single line. Each of these areas represents a significant opportunity to increase revenue. Both technologies, however, require an enormous investment for cable companies. Installation of fiber-optic cable and the introduction of digital boxes in cable homes will be a gradual process.

Fiber-optic cabling improves signal quality and range. Companies that invest in fiber-optics to improve transmission quality should have an advantage in the bidding process used to award franchise rights for geographic areas. The greater the number of franchise rights, the greater the number of subscribers, and the greater the amount of total revenue accruing to a company. Four of the largest players in the industry (Tele-Communications, Inc. (TCI), Time Warner, Continental Cablevision Inc., and Cablevision Systems Corp.) have invested heavily in this strategy. TCI invested $2 billion in the mid-1990s, a clear indication that the industry views investment in fiber-optics as a critical component in ensuring long-term financial success.

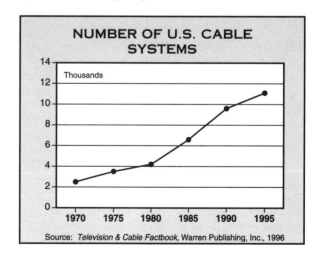

NUMBER OF U.S. CABLE SYSTEMS

Thousands

Source: *Television & Cable Factbook*, Warren Publishing, Inc., 1996

RESPONSE TO REGULATION

Because regulations change so frequently, the ability to influence and leverage new regulations becomes a crucial success factor. If a company can dictate how a regulation is written or interpreted in order to exploit an internal core competency, then they will be best positioned to profit from the change. Conversely, cable companies can be negatively impacted by regulations that restrict their ability to expand service areas, affect rate structures, and introduce new products.

During the late 1990s, cable operators and telephone companies entering the television business were not only adjusting to the new federal government guidelines, but they also faced the demands of local governments who were trying to maintain local control of rates and public rights-of-way. An April 1996 ruling eliminated rate regulation in areas where a cable company had non-DBS competition. Local governments complained that better proof of the new competition's effectiveness was needed in each case before rate deregulation was allowed. Squabbles of use of public rights-of-way also cropped up, as in the case where the city of Troy, Michigan, required TCI to obtain a telecommunications franchise when it wanted to create a new system. Such arguments prompted cable and telephone companies to join in asking to rein in local regulators.

PROGRAMMING CAPABILITIES

A *MediaWeek* poll revealed that 65 percent of cable TV subscribers would cancel their subscriptions if broadcast signals were dropped. The poll suggests that network-affiliated TV stations have considerable leverage in their retransmission consent fee negotiations with cable providers. Ironically, the networks are waiving retransmission consent fees in exchange for getting the cable operators to air network-owned cable programs. The potential for revenue growth in the current cable industry is primarily through controlling programming. Offering more options to the customer results in increased advertising income and subscription revenue. This increased cash flow assists in the development of new and improved services, further driving the company's revenue growth.

ECONOMIES OF SCALE

Size is necessary to achieve economies of scale and to provide cash flow for investments into research and development, development of new programming and markets, and acquisitions. Large companies can gain economies of scale in purchasing equipment, satellite time, and programming. In addition, by being large enough to be able to purchase its own satellite, a cable company gains significant control over costs and programming. Through ownership of large libraries of information (music, video, etc.), the cable company not only controls costs, but also drives other competitors

through access to that programming. Finally, programming consists mainly of large fixed costs; with a large cable company, this fixed cost is spread over a larger base, resulting in increased profits. This is particularly important for development of fiber-optics.

INCREASED COMPETITION

Customer dissatisfaction and rising cable costs have served to feed the growing satellite television industry with new viewers. A 1996 *Broadcasting & Cable* survey indicated that cable subscribers in New York, Los Angeles, and Chicago were increasingly dissatisfied with cable services. Almost a third of respondents said that they were "neutral or dissatisfied" with the cable product. The survey also indicated that satellite service was the most easily identified alternative to cable. Thus, when TCI raised its rates by 21 percent during the summer of 1996, it lost some 70,000 subscribers. In Denver, it was estimated that 1,500 former TCI customers turned to satellite service.

Phone companies have been investing in and upgrading phone lines to fiber-optics for some time—with the intention of transmitting video signals. Companies such as TCI, U.S. West, Bell South, Time Warner, Microsoft, IBM, Sony Corp., Intel, and Silicon Graphics are trying to position themselves as major providers of service and support in this emerging market sector. Even utilities are laying fiber-optic cable when they install new lines in order to position themselves as water, gas, electric, voice, data, and video providers.

FEDERAL REGULATION

The domestic cable industry is highly regulated by the U.S. government. Regulations affect cable system ownership, rate structures, channel limits, types of programming, and permission to access programming. This involvement is based on two factors: first, because of the high fixed investment in installation, the industry lends itself to being a natural monopoly with limited competition; and second, the sensitive nature and importance to national security of communications technology.

In 1986 the FCC decided to allow cable companies to freely set monthly service rates and rate increases in any market that already provided at least three over-the-air broadcast signals to nonsubscribers. Prior to 1986, cable companies were limited to a mandated five percent cap on annual rate increases. Re-regulation was proposed in 1992 because various groups claimed that the cable industry abused its privilege to set monthly rates by gouging consumers. Congress, under pressure from consumer groups, haggled with President George Bush, who was against re-regulation. After a failed attempt by the FCC to control the situation by redefining some rules, Congress overrode the president's veto and passed the controversial Cable Television Consumer Protection and Competition Act of 1992. This bill reversed cable companies' freedom to set rates. However, local governments were given the power to regulate rates for basic cable programming in their areas.

The act also contained programming regulations. Programming could no longer be denied to competitors and it must be offered at "fair terms." The bill required cable companies to pay royalties to over-the-air broadcasters. Networks have complained for years that cable companies were in essence charging subscribers for network developed programming that was free to them and pocketing a subscriber fee. One other provision of this bill limited the size of multiple system operators and the number of channels a system could devote to programming in which it had an interest.

A regulation implemented in June 1992 allowed the television networks to buy local cable TV systems. However, a TV network's cable holdings could not exceed 10 percent of the nation's homes that are passed by cable wire or 50 percent of the households in a single market. In addition, a 1984 ruling stated that a company cannot own a TV station and a cable system in the same market. The intended effect of these rulings was to speed up the unraveling of traditional network and affiliate relationships. The resulting alliances between cable and over-the-air industries would impact the competitive environment among entertainment providers.

The Telecommunications Act of 1996 also did much to deregulate cable television, with the hope of further stimulating competition in the television industry. The act served to revise 62 years of telecommunications law and eliminated some features of the 1992 Cable Act that were seen as punitive by the industry. Most notably, fees for upper service tiers would be deregulated on March 31, 1999 in large cable systems, while such services were deregulated immediately in smaller franchises. The bill also eliminated the 1984 restriction that prevented individual companies from offering cable and phone services to the same market.

Government regulations have a significant impact on the ways in which cable companies compete. In the mature cable TV market, revenue growth comes primarily from rate increases. Government regulations will impact existing companies by limiting revenue growth from this source. In the long run, the industry is expected to benefit from being pushed to develop other revenue resources, such as cable modems and telecommunication services. The regulatory environment is constantly changing—and there are gains that will accrue to the companies best able to influence and adjust to new regulatory initiatives.

RESEARCH AND TECHNOLOGY

Although there have been a number of advances in cable technology, the most promising is digital compression. Compression technologies enable broadcasters to squeeze several channels of video programming onto a single existing channel in much the same way as compression software conserves storage space on a computer. Compression converts the analog signals, currently used in broadcasting, to digital signals. This allows ten channels to be transmitted along the same bandwidth of coaxial cable that would normally be capable of handling a single uncompressed signal. Compression would allow cable companies to offer more than 500 channels, ten times the number available today.

Even with the advent of compression technology, coaxial cable does have its limitations. Coaxial cable uses radio waves to transmit video images. Its drawbacks include a limitation on the number of signals that can be transmitted simultaneously and the distance that such signals can travel before they begin to degrade. Its advantage is that it is already installed in millions of homes across the country. Fiber-optic cable, on the other hand, uses light to transmit video images. It is superior to coaxial cable in terms of bandwidth or signal capacity, transmission speed, signal distance, and clarity. However, fiber-optic cable has a daunting limitation—it is prohibitively expensive.

Fiber-optics technology has allowed companies to develop "video-on-demand," an interactive service that may be the wave of the future. It allows customers to order the transmission of movies and special events by using a hybrid television/computer terminal and enables them to view these programs at their leisure. These systems are expected to be able to handle high-definition television and provide links to computers, facsimile machines, and personal communications networks. The one drawback to the video-on-demand concept is that the subscriber cannot pause, rewind, or otherwise fiddle with the program, capabilities taken for granted when using a VCR.

The development of cable modems has allowed cable companies to enter the Internet access business. At a time when established providers such as CompuServe and America Online are struggling to deal with quickly expanding numbers of Internet users, cable operators hope to use the superior speed of cable modems to lure away their customers. Cable modems take advantage of the industry's use of coaxial cable, which can provide transmission speeds up to 400 times faster than traditional phone lines. However, the equipment cost for such service—between $300 and $750 per modem in 1996—was an early stumbling block. At that time, in a Time

Warner test market in Elmira, New York, monthly fees were about $40.00. Three other of the largest cable companies were also making investments connected with cable modem technology. TCI , Comcast , and Cox Communications invested in @Home Network , an on-line information and entertainment service. TCI's initial foray into Internet services in the San Francisco area was expected to charge $40.00 per month for unlimited access, including a modem leasing fee.

.

AMERICA AND THE WORLD

The cable industry is highly regulated, not only in the United States, but also overseas. As a result, high entry barriers exist causing companies to compete on a national basis. Because the U.S. market is saturated, American companies are looking to expand overseas in an effort to sustain growth. Asia, Latin America, and Europe have been identified as areas with high potential. The strategies companies are pursuing to break into overseas markets include joint ventures and alliances. The major obstacles companies must overcome to become global are government regulation and lack of infrastructure. In Asia, for example, most governments still maintain tight control over the industry, which limits a foreign national company's ability to compete.

The cable industry will never be more than a multidomestic industry so long as regulation denies ownership of all or a majority share of a local cable company by a foreign organization. The opportunities for growth in the emerging markets will be enjoyed by local companies, but the opportunities for cross-border operations still exist. A lack of technology and programming expertise provides opportunities for U.S. companies to partner with the regional operators to gain footholds in overseas markets, preempting European and Asian providers. However, as these new markets develop, they will develop the programming to cater to local preferences and culture. To stay competitive, U.S. companies will have to adapt and develop programs for these new markets, instead of just offering dubbed-over U.S. programming.

ASSOCIATIONS AND SOCIETIES

CABLE TELECOMMUNICATIONS ASSOCIATION
3950 Chain Bridge Rd.
Fairfax, VA 22030-1005
Phone: (703) 691-8875
Fax: (703) 691-8911
Concerned with promoting the legal and regulatory interests of cable television station owners and operators.

CABLE TELEVISION ADMINISTRATION AND MARKETING SOCIETY
201 N. Union, Ste. 440
Alexandria, VA 23314
Phone: (703) 549-4200
Fax: (703) 684-1167

CABLETELEVISION ADVERTISING BUREAU
757 3rd Ave.
New York, NY 10017
Phone: (212) 751-7770
Fax: (212) 832-3268

NATIONAL CABLE TELEVISION ASSOCIATION
1724 Massachusetts Ave. NW
Washington, DC 20036
Phone: (202) 775-3550
Fax: (202) 775-3695

NATIONAL CABLE TELEVISION INSTITUTE
801 W. Mineral Ave.
Littleton, CO 80120-4501
Phone: (303) 797-9393
Fax: (303) 797-9394

SOCIETY OF CABLE TELEVISION ENGINEERS
669 Exton Commons
Exton, PA 19341
Phone: (215) 363-6888
Fax: (215) 363-5898

PERIODICALS AND NEWSLETTERS

BROADCASTING & CABLE
Cahners Publishing Co.
Entertainment Division
1750 DeSales St. NW
Washington, DC 20036
Phone: (800) 554-5729 or (202) 659-2340
Fax: (202) 429-0651
Weekly. $99.00 per year. Formerly Broadcasting.

CABLE TV PROGRAMMING: NEWSLETTER ON PROGRAMS FOR PAY CABLE TV AND ANALYSIS OF BASIC CABLE NETWORKS
Paul Kagan Associates, Inc.
126 Clock Tower Pl.
Carmel, CA 93923
Phone: (408) 624-1536
Fax: (408) 625-3225
Monthly. $625.00 per year.

CABLE TV TECHNOLOGY: NEWSLETTER ON TECHNICAL ADVANCES, CONSTRUCTION OF NEW SYSTEMS AND REBUILD OF EXISTING SYSTEMS
Paul Kagan Associates, Inc.
126 Clock Tower Pl.
Carmel, CA 93923
Phone: (408) 624-1536
Fax: (408) 625-3225
Monthly. $625.00 per year. Newsletter. Contains news of cable TV technical advances.

CABLEVISION: THE ANALYSIS AND FEATURES
BI-WEEKLY OF THE CABLE TELEVISION INDUSTRY
Capital Cities-ABC, Inc.
825 7th Ave.
New York, NY 10019
Phone: (212) 887-0400
Fax: (212) 887-8585
Biweekly. $55.00 per year.

MULTICHANNEL NEWS
Chilton Co.
825 7th Ave.
New York, NY 10019
Phone: (212) 887-8400
Fax: (212) 887-8384
Weekly. $78.00 per year. Covers the business, programming, marketing, and technology concerns of cable television operators and their suppliers.

TELEVISION DIGEST WITH CONSUMER ELECTRONICS
Warren Publishing, Inc.
2115 Ward Ct. NW
Washington, DC 20037
Phone: (202) 872-9200
Fax: (202) 293-3435
Weekly. $848.00 per year. Newsletter featuring new consumer entertainment products utilizing electronics. Also covers the television broadcasting and cable TV industries, with corporate and industry news.

ONLINE DATABASES

ABI/INFORM
UMI/Data Courier
620 S. 3rd St.
Louisville, KY 40202
Phone: (800) 626-2823 or (502) 583-4111
Fax: (502) 589-5572
Provides online indexing to business-related material occurring in over 800 periodicals from 1971 to the present. Inquire as to online cost and availability.

GALE DATABASE OF PUBLICATIONS AND BROADCAST MEDIA
Gale Research
835 Penobscot Bldg.
Detroit, MI 48226-4094
Phone: (800) 877-GALE or (313) 961-2242
Fax: (313) 961-6083
An online directory containing detailed information on over 67,000 periodicals, newspapers, broadcast stations, cable systems, directories, and newsletters. Corresponds to the following print sources: Gale Directory of Publications and Broadcast Media; Directories in Print; City and State Directories in Print; Newsletters in Print. Semiannual updates. Inquire as to online cost and availability.

PROMT: PREDICASTS OVERVIEW OF MARKETS AND TECHNOLOGY
Information Access Co.
362 Lakeside Dr.
Foster City, CA 94404

Phone: (800) 321-6388 or (415) 378-5000
Fax: (415) 358-4759
Companies, products, applied technologies and markets. U.S. and international literature coverage, 1972 to date. Daily updates. Inquire as to online cost and availability. Provides abstracts from more than 1,200 publications.

TV LINK: FILM & TELEVISION WEBSITE ARCHIVE
Neoglyphics Media Corp.
1735 N. Paulina St., Ste. 200
Chicago, IL 60622
Phone: (773) 395-6200
Links to the world wide web sites of more than 100 TV shows, motion picture studios, professional and commercial organizations, broadcast schedules, TV networks and broadcasters, newsgroups, film festivals, and related sites around the world. This site is a resource for both industry professionals and audiences.

STATISTICS SOURCES

CABLE TELEVISION REVENUES
U.S. Federal Communications Commission
Washington, DC 20554
Phone: (202) 418-0200
Annual.

CABLE TV FACTS
Cabletelevision Advertising Bureau
757 3rd Ave.
New York, NY 10017
Phone: (212) 751-7770
Fax: (212) 832-3268
Annual. $10.00. Provides statistics on cable TV and cable TV advertising in the United States.

TELEVISION AND CABLE FACTBOOK
Warren Publishing, Inc.
2115 Ward Ct. NW
Washington, DC 20037
Phone: (202) 872-9200
Fax: (202) 293-3435
Annual. $425.00. Three volumes. Commercial and noncommercial television stations and networks.

GENERAL WORKS

ALL ABOUT CABLE
New York Law Publishing Co.
111 8th Ave.
New York, NY 10011
Phone: (800) 888-8300 or (212) 741-8300
$80.00. Periodic updates.

BROADCASTING & CABLE YEARBOOK
R.R. Bowker
121 Chanlon Rd.
New Providence, NJ 07974
Phone: (800) 521-8110 or (908) 464-6800
Fax: (908) 665-6688

Annual. *$159.95. Two volumes. Published in conjunction with* Broadcasting

CABLE AND STATION COVERAGE ATLAS

Warren Publishing, Inc.
1836 Jefferson Pl. NW
Washington, DC 20037
Phone: (202) 872-9200
Fax: (202) 293-3435
Annual. $360.00.

CABLE TV FINANCIAL DATABOOK

Paul Kagan Associates, Inc.
126 Clock Tower Pl.
Carmel, CA 93923
Phone: (408) 624-1536
Fax: (408) 625-3225
Annual. $195.00. Sourcebook for key financial data on cable television. Includes analysis of operating results of private and public cable television companies, historical data, and projections.

FURTHER READING

Cleland, Kim. "System Operators Tout Speed to Web Crawlers." *Advertising Age,* 25 March 1996.

Halonen, Doug. "Baby Bells' Video Fever Cools Down." *Electronic Media,* 16 December 1996.

Hofmeister, Sallie. "Satellites Face Woes as They Tug at Cable." *Los Angeles Times,* 12 November 1996.

Lieberman, David. "Upgrade Costs Frighten Some Firms Off Fast Track." *USA Today,* 5 February 1997.

Standard & Poor's Industry Surveys. New York: Standard & Poor's, 1996.

Time Warner Inc. "Broadband Wagon." New York, 1997. Available from http://pathfinder.com/ @@XULgUApHy90qbf/corp/officialword/ar/arcable.html.

Mail-order selling, or direct marketing, generated $594.4 billion in consumer sales and $498.1 billion in business-to-business sales in 1995. The period of greatest growth occurred during the 1980s, when mail-order selling activity leapt more than 300 percent. From 1990 to 1996, mail order sales grew at a rate of over 9.9 percent per year, about 1.7 times the average growth of general merchandise, apparel, and furniture store sales. Catalog selling and home shopping via television or computer generated $46 billion in 1995, with online sales reaching $500 million. However, as of 1995, non-store sales accounted for only about 2 percent of all retail sales in the United States.

The catalog industry was maturing and price competition was posing a formidable challenge for industry competitors, and many catalog and mail-order retailers were still enjoying positive growth rates going into the mid-1990s, although slight declines were seen from 1993 to 1995. In an effort to boost earnings, companies were increasing their use of market segmentation techniques and were applying computerized database marketing tactics. Mail-order selling was also gaining popularity in other parts of the globe, providing overseas opportunities for many U.S. firms.

CATALOG AND MAIL-ORDER HOUSES

SIC 5961

Buoyed *by consumer trends toward convenience shopping and by new media such as the Internet, catalog and mail-order firms have largely recovered from the stagnation of the early 1990s and are expected to enjoy robust sales growth into the twenty-first century. Employment is also forecast to continue to grow, but the nature of mail-order employment will continue to change as direct sellers adopt new technologies to better automate their businesses and to keep up with consumer preferences. While many mail-order houses are increasingly looking to international markets for growth, international postage rates and other barriers have dampened the cost-effectiveness of cross-border marketing by traditional mail in some of these markets.*

TOP U.S. MAIL ORDER BUSINESSES

Ranked by: Mail order sales, in millions of dollars.

1. United Services Automobile Association, with $4,640.0 million
2. J. C. Penney, $3,512.0
3. Tele-Communications Inc., $3,393.7
4. Gateway 2000, $2,701.2
5. Dell Computer Corp., $2,585.0
6. AARP/Prudential, 2,500.0
7. GEICO Corp., $2,476.3
8. Time Warner Cable Group, $2,329.3
9. AT & T, $2,000.0
10. DEC Direct, $1,800.0

Source: *Direct Marketing,* October, 1995, p. 56.

Perhaps the most revolutionary development in the industry, however, was in the realm of "home shopping," the increasingly popular practice in which consumers phone in orders for merchandise seen on cable shopping channels such as the Quality Value Convenience Channel (QVC) and the Home Shopping Network, Inc., which reach approximately 60 million

---

viewers—about two-thirds of all households with televisions. In 1993 *Business Week* noted that home shopping was "already a $2 billion-plus industry and growing fast about 20 percent a year." As cable systems upgrade to offer hundreds of channels, and, eventually, digital and interactive technologies, home shopping expects to expand in even greater ways. The goal of home shopping is creating video mall, where shoppers will browse through channels as through individual stores, ask for information and advice, order, and pay all in the comforts of home. This vision had not yet been realized by the late 1990s, but was being developed and tested by many cable and marketing companies.

By 1995, one of the fastest growing areas, accounting for $500 million in sales, was "cyberspace," or online computer selling. One of the first companies to test online selling was 1-800-Flowers, which generated $15 million, or 10 percent of their total business, from Internet sales in 1995.

INDUSTRY OUTLOOK

In response to the relatively inclement business environment of the early 1990s, catalog and mail-order houses scrambled to increase sales and profit margins. Companies emphasized customer satisfaction by gathering data on preferences and wants, and then carefully tailoring their products and promotions accordingly. Companies also eliminated large, general audience catalogs, and relied instead on specialty niche promotions.

Part of the customer satisfaction strategy included the integration of advanced database management techniques. By gathering and storing consumer information on a computer database, retailers were able to determine what, when, and how to market to each of their customers. For many companies, database marketing became an exact science that allowed them to maximize the efficiency of every advertising dollar. Indeed, many companies offered products to potentially new customers at a loss so that they could gather information on the consumer and generate profits from follow-up sales.

Firms also beefed up their inventory control systems in the early 1990s. Just-in-time management techniques, whereby warehousers kept minimum stock on hand and relied on prompt delivery by suppliers, became standard for most successful large mail-order houses. Value pricing, too, became an important strategy for many firms. By improving the quality of their merchandise, increasing service, and reducing prices, many successful competitors were able to overcome reduced margins by increasing market share and sales volume, and taking advantage of follow-up sales opportunities.

Some mail-order firms adjusted by changing their image, laying off employees, or advertising through new marketing channels, such as television home-shopping networks. L.L. Bean, for instance, successfully adapted to a reduced demand for its upscale baby-boom apparel lines by reemphasizing its traditional outdoor equipment and its clothes.

HOT SEGMENTS

Despite reduced overall mail-order growth and profitability, the industry continued to enjoy greater growth than most other retail channels throughout the 1990s, in part because of demographic shifts in the customer base. Furthermore, many product divisions continued to show solid revenue gains. Library and school supplies, drugs and vitamins, children's products, physical fitness equipment, and some electronics showed stronger than average rises in mail-order activity.

The electronic retailing segment of the industry has grown rapidly as consumers became more computer savvy. Dell Computer Corporation and Gateway 2000, Inc. consistently rank in the top ten catalog and mail order houses, with sales of $7.7 billion and $5 billion respectively in 1996.

ORGANIZATION AND STRUCTURE

The catalog and mail-order house industry encompasses companies that sell products through all "nonstore" retail channels, including radio, television, and computers. Although larger retailers, such as J.C. Penney, typically maintained an inventory warehouse, most industry participants kept little, if any, inventory on hand. When a customer ordered a product, the retailer contacted a wholesale company that shipped the product to the retailer or directly to the customer.

Because they refrained from traditional retail purchasing, manufacturing, and inventory management activities, many nonstore retailers were essentially marketing companies. Some catalog companies, for instance, simply assembled a group of complimentary products manufactured by other companies and tried to market those items in a catalog to customers that would be most interested in them. Similarly, many direct mail and broadcast media retailers essentially acted as middlemen, selling products that were manufactured and stored by wholesalers.

Three categories of nonstore retailing include business, consumer, and charitable sales. Throughout the 1990s, consumer sales accounted for approximately 50 percent of industry revenues, while business and charitable sales each garnered about 25 percent of the market. About 60 percent of consumer nonstore sales were products, while the remaining 40 percent were services. Of nonstore consumer product sales, about 80 percent were derived from specialty items that were not commonly available in stores. The remaining 20 percent came from sales of general merchandise. Of nonstore sales of consumer services, about 40 percent of revenues were garnered from financial services.

ADVANTAGES OF NONSTORE RETAILING

Nonstore retail companies benefited from numerous advantages associated with mail and broadcast media marketing. In the case of catalog and direct-mail marketing, retailers enjoyed more efficient access to markets than did stores. Using tailored customer lists, companies could carefully advertise to select segments of the market. A company that sold products through a toy catalog, for instance, might choose to send its catalog only to households with children aged three to seven years. That same company might also offer a winter toy catalog, which it would send only to households in specific northern states.

Besides avoiding the fixed costs associated with operating a retail store, securing the advantages associated with segmented marketing, and often reducing their inventory costs, nonstore retailers enjoyed access to national markets at a minimal cost. This allowed companies to market seasonal items or highly specialized products aimed at distinct market segments. In contrast, a retail store might find it unprofitable to keep an inventory of such specialty items because the local market would not generate sufficient demand. This benefit was especially pronounced in the case of business-to-business direct mail and catalogs, which provided an important sales channel for products which could not be profitably offered in stores or sold face to face.

Catalog and mail retailers also enjoyed greater control over the marketing message than did stores. Catalogs and direct-mail pieces, for instance, allowed consumers to digest large amounts of information about a product in the privacy of their own home. Mail-order companies were also able to tailor the same product's advertising differently for various market niches.

One tremendous advantage that companies in this industry enjoyed, however—whether they secure sales via catalogs, direct mail, or television home shopping—is the elimination or severe curtailment of two expenses that have a tremendous impact on the bottom line of traditional retailers: rent and sales work force. And another advantage was that even small to mid-size companies can use mail order to grow their business and/or

give their current business a larger presence in the market without expanding overhead costs.

The primary disadvantage of mail and broadcast retailing is in high advertising costs. The cost of producing and delivering catalogs, fulfilling orders, and servicing customers often left retailers with slim profit margins, or losses, if the response to a promotion was poor. The cost of mailing a simple letter and brochure typically ranged from 40 to 65 cents per piece, and the retailer often expected only .5 percent to 3 percent of the recipients to actually purchase a product. In fact, a 2 percent response rate is considered highly successful in the mail-order business. Although response to a catalog was often higher, usually between 3 percent and 6 percent, production costs often exceeded $3 per catalog.

WORK FORCE

Employment in the catalog and mail-order house industry was expected to grow faster than employment in most other U.S. retail sectors in the 1990s and early 2000s. Advances in automation and information systems, however, could curtail job growth as companies eliminate labor-intensive positions. Despite expected growth, the catalog and mail-order industry offered relatively meager employment opportunities in relation to businesses with similar sales volumes. The greatest job growth was expected to occur among computer programmers and information systems professionals, who were needed to integrate and streamline customer, inventory, and financial information. Jobs in sales, photography, layout, and design were likely to increase between 50 percent and 65 percent. Labor and blue-collar positions were forecast to expand as well—by about 50 percent. Positions in management, finance, and information systems should also realize growth rates of 50 percent to 60 percent by 2005.

In 1995, U.S. employment figures showed that more than 19.1 million jobs were related to the direct marketing industry, including 10.8 million in consumer direct marketing and 8.3 million in business-to-business direct marketing. In the consumer division, that represented a 3.4 percent growth rate from 1990 to 1995, and 3.0 percent growth rate from 1995 to 2000. In business-to-business direct marketing, those employment figures represented a 4.3 percent growth rate form 1990 to 1995, and a 4.9 percent growth rate from 1995 to 2000.

RESEARCH AND TECHNOLOGY

The most successful catalog and mail-order house companies increasingly moved their computer systems toward client/server architecture with relational databases and distributed processing. Information databases would eventually allow companies to produce highly specific catalogs and marketing materials tailored to smaller groups, or even individuals. A company might be able to print a set of catalogs, for instance, each of which contained a different product mix and marketing message. Just-in-time inventory practices would assume a primary role in helping companies to maintain profit margins through lower fixed costs and better customer service.

New advertising media will complement traditional broadcast, print, and telephone channels. The burgeoning multimedia environment will eventually integrate video, telecommunications, optical disk technology, and personal computers. Advertisers will be forced to adjust their marketing techniques as consumers gain more control in choosing which ads and media they internalize. Advancements in recycled paper, printing technology, and ink would likely help the industry move toward reduced waste and lower production costs. At the same time, the proliferation of specialty cable television channels that reach more homogenous niche markets was expected to increase the efficiency of broadcast advertising.

AMERICA AND THE WORLD

The U.S. catalog and mail-order industry was the largest and most advanced in the world. There are two basic reasons for this industry's continual growth: a large population and a relatively high income level. Although other countries may be more densely populated, they do not have a large enough number of people who have the extra income to buy mail-order products.

Mail-order retailers in the United States benefited from several other advantages not present in most other countries. Most importantly, U.S. retailers enjoyed access to the largest industrialized, relatively homogenous market in the world. As a result, multiple economies of scale existed for domestic merchandisers. An entire U.S. mailing list industry has emerged, for example, allowing retailers to efficiently attack specific market niches.

Another very important advantage for the U.S. mail-order industry was low postal rates. U.S. bulk and first-class postal rates were the lowest in the world. Postal rates in much of Europe, for instance, were twice as high as U.S. rates, making it difficult for companies to

successfully promote products through the mail. Higher shipping charges further diluted profit potential in overseas markets.

In addition to these factors, most foreign mail-order markets were characterized by: relatively limited media availability; much tighter government regulation of advertising content and product approval requirements; a lack of public understanding and acceptance of mail order; language and cultural barriers; low credit card penetration; and a lack of toll-free numbers. Furthermore, in some European countries many types of mail promotion were banned for environmental and social reasons. The European mail-order industry also suffered from a lack of uniform postal and business standards.

According to the Direct Marketing Association, in 1994, 22.2 percent of U.S. consumer marketers were selling outside the United States, as well as 43.5 percent of business marketers. The top five most profitable non-U.S. markets for U.S. marketers in 1994 were (in order): Canada, United Kingdom, Australia/New Zealand, Japan, and Germany.

Direct marketing in the United Kingdom experienced phenomenal growth from the early 1980s through the mid-1990s, more than doubling between 1983 and 1992. In 1995, the direct mail industry was generating over 12 billion British pounds in yearly income in the UK, and provided approximately 25,000 jobs.

China has proven to be an extremely difficult market, with its volatile political situation and vast cultural differences. However, some American magazines were being successfully marketed in Chinese language version, and in the mid-1990s, McCall's pattern books were successfully marketed because they are easily manufactured and have very little text.

One of the fastest-growing nonstore retail markets in the world during the 1980s and early 1990s was Japan. Revenues in that country jumped from about $5 billion in 1981 to over $12 billion by 1990, and over $15 billion by 1993. Much of the growth was a result of increasing numbers of women in the work force. Women, in fact, accounted for about 90 percent of all mail-order sales in Japan. The integration of technology by mail-order houses also contributed to the jump in sales.

The most popular purchases by the Japanese were women's clothing, underwear, and men's clothing. Another concept unique to Japan was the U.S. Commerce Department's American Catalog House, where U.S. catalogs were displayed for the public to peruse. Catalogs could then be purchased by consumers for a nominal fee, or orders could be faxed to U.S. companies on the spot.

Foreign sales by domestic catalog and mail-order houses has traditionally been limited by language and cost barriers. Despite the inefficiency of nonstore retailing in many overseas markets, however, several U.S. and foreign firms have successfully penetrated other markets. Cross-border sales between the United States and the European Union (EU), particularly, steadily increased throughout the 1990s, spurred in part by increasingly uniform EU markets.

The most exportable mail-order products in the 1990s, in order of revenue size, were information, education, and collectible products. In addition, several U.S. firms had successfully marketed specialty American products in some Asian countries. Some of the most successful offshore U.S. mail-order enterprises included Hanna Anderson, Austad's, Eddie Bauer, L.L. Bean, Black Box, Inmac, Myron Manufacturing, and Recreational Equipment Incorporated (REI).

Spearheaded by Barry Diller, the QVC/Home Shopping Network made electronic home shopping a global phenomenon. In the mid-1990s, the company began broadcasting in Japan and Canada, as well as Britain, Ireland, and parts of Europe in an alliance with British Sky Broadcasting, and plans to expand broadcasting to several other European and Latin American countries.

ASSOCIATIONS AND SOCIETIES

ASSOCIATION OF DIRECTORY PUBLISHERS
105 Summer St.
Wrentham, MA 02093
Phone: (508) 883-3688
Fax: (508) 883-3717

NATIONAL ASSOCIATION OF CATALOG SHOWROOM MERCHANDISERS
PO Box 736
East Northport, NY 11731
Phone: (800) 334-4711 or (516) 754-6041
Fax: (516) 754-4364

NATIONAL CATALOG MANAGERS ASSOCIATION
c/o Anthony G. Adkins
735 Tollgate Rd.
Elgin, IL 60123-9332
Phone: (800) 323-8024 or (708) 742-0700
Fax: (708) 742-5064

PERIODICALS AND NEWSLETTERS

CATALOG AGE
Cowles Business Media, Inc.
PO Box 4949
Stamford, CT 06907-0949
Phone: (800) 795-5445 or (203) 358-9900
Fax: (203) 357-9014

Monthly. Free to qualified personnel; others, $65.00 per year. Edited for catalog marketing and management personnel.

CSM
CSM Marketing, Inc.
195 Smithtown Blvd.
Nesconset, NY 11767-1849
Monthly. $30.00 per year. Formerly Catalog Showroom Merchandiser.

DM NEWS: THE NEWSPAPER OF DIRECT MARKETING
DM News 19
W. 21st St.
New York, NY 10010
Phone: (212) 741-2095
Fax: (212) 633-9367
47 times a year. Free to qualified personnel; others, $75.00 per year. Includes special feature issues on catalog marketing, telephone marketing, database marketing, and fundraising. Available on the world wide web at http://www.dmnews.com

SIMBA REPORT ON DIRECTORY PUBLISHING
SIMBA Information, Inc.
PO Box 4234
Stamford, CT 06907-0234
Phone: (800) 307-2529 or (203) 358-4344
Fax: (203) 358-5824
Monthly. $115.00 per year. Newsletter. Covers developments and trends in the directory publishing industry, including publisher profiles, start-ups, corporate acquisitions, and business opportunities. Formerly Morgan Report on Directory Publishing.

YELLOW PAGES AND DIRECTORY REPORT: THE NEWSLETTER FOR THE DIRECTORY PUBLISHING INDUSTRY
Simba Information, Inc.
PO Box 7430
Wilton, CT 06897-7430
Phone: (203) 834-0033
Fax: (203) 834-1771
Semimonthly. $499.00 per year. Newsletter. Covers the yellow pages publishing industry, including electronic directory publishing, directory advertising, and special interest directories.

YELLOW PAGES AND DIRECTORY REPORT: THE NEWSLETTER FOR THE DIRECTORY PUBLISHING INDUSTRY
SIMBA Information, Inc.
PO Box 4234
Stamford, CT 06907-0234
Phone: (800) 307-2529 or (203) 358-4344
Fax: (203) 358-5824
Semimonthly. $549.00 per year. Newsletter. Covers the yellow pages publishing industry, including electronic directory publishing, directory advertising, and special interest directories.

DATABASES

BOOKS IN PRINT ONLINE

Bowker Electronic Publishing
121 Chanlon Rd.
New Providence, NJ 07974
Phone: (800) 323-3288 or (908) 464-6800
Fax: (908) 665-3528
The online version of Books in Print, Forthcoming Books, Paperbound Books in Print, *and other Bowker bibliographic publications: lists the books of over 30,000 U.S. publishers. Includes books recently declared out-of-print. Updated monthly. Inquire as to online cost and availability.*

GALE DATABASE OF PUBLICATIONS AND BROADCAST MEDIA

Gale Research Inc.
835 Penobscot Bldg.
Detroit, MI 48226-4094
Phone: (800) 877-GALE or (313) 961-2242
Fax: (313) 961-6083
An online directory containing detailed information on over 67,000 periodicals, newspapers, broadcast stations, cable systems, directories, and newsletters. Corresponds to the following print sources: Gale Directory of Publications and Broadcast Media; Directories in Print; City and State Directories in Print; Newsletters in Print. *Semiannual updates. Inquire as to online cost and availability.*

SWITCHBOARD

Database America Banyan Systems Inc.
A nationwide directory of residences and businesses. Compiled from published telephone books. Time span: Current information. When established: 1996. Updating frequency: As needed. Fees: Free.

- URL: http://www.switchboard.com

FURTHER READING

Geller, Lois K. *Response! The Complete Guide to Profitable Direct Marketing.* New York: The Free Press, 1996.

Niemira, Michael. ''Are Nonstore Sales a Threat to Traditional Store Business?,'' *Chain Store Age,* September 1996.

Ray, Debra and George Reis. ''Catalog Sales Projected to Reach $74.6 Billion by Year End.'' *Direct Marketing,* August 1996.

INDUSTRY SNAPSHOT

Consumer awareness of health and nutrition played a major part in shaping the industry during the mid- to late 1990s. Many national cereal manufacturers were also playing the acquisitions and mergers game to enter popular breakfast foods markets; for example, Kellogg Company purchased Lender's Bagels from Kraft Foods to enter the very popular and trendy bagel market. Bagels were the fastest growing segment of the cereal foods market in the mid- to late 1990s.

CEREAL BREAKFAST FOODS

SIC 2043

In the mid-1990s, breakfast cereal makers underwent major repositioning, rethinking their product development procedures. Burdened with high development costs and new product failure rates, manufacturers were scaling back product introductions. Even though co-branding products slowed the development process, co-branded products were being introduced by many national manufacturers.

 Top 7 COMPANIES SELLING THE MOST READY-TO-EAT CEREALS

Ranked by: Market share from 1995 to 1996, in percent.

1. The M. W. Kellogg Co., with 36.3%
2. General Mills, 26.4%
3. Post/Nabisco, 16.1%
4. Quaker Oats, 7.6%
5. Private label, 6.5%
6. Ralcorp, 4.2%
7. Others, total 2.9%

Source: *Prepared Foods*, May, 1996, p. 174.

INDUSTRY OUTLOOK

Sales of cereals rose from 2.3 percent in 1988 to 3.1 percent in 1993. The primary reason for this according to *ID: The Voice of Foodservice Distribution* was the growing awareness of consumers on the nutritional aspects of foods they ate. One of the hottest growth segments in the early 1990s was the ready-to-eat cereals, which were available as rolled, puffed, and extruded in a variety of flavors.

Hot cereals, which included oat, corn, wheat, and rice, continued to dominate sales during the cooler seasons, while the sales of cold cereals remained consistent through the year. Cold weather increased sales of hot cereals with a total of 75 percent of hot cereal sales being made between October and February. Between September 1993 to September 1994 hot cereal sales was at $367.6 million, an increase of 6.9 percent over hot cereal sales between September 1992 and September 1993, according to *Supermarket News*. The entire breakfast cereal industry generated $8.1 billion in 1994, up from $7.7 billion in 1993.

The breakfast cereal industry's product development activity in 1995 seemed to have been affected by criticisms from consumer advocates, politicians and food editors, according to *Prepared Foods.* Critics lambasted cereal producers over alleged high cereal prices and profits, which as a result inhibited product introductions. According to *Prepared Foods,* only 128 new labels were launched in 1995 with very few of them coming from the Big Five cereal companies.

A price war erupted in the U.S. breakfast cereal market in 1996 following a long period of high cereal prices. According to *The Financial Times,* analysts said that producers had been greedy and continued to raise prices in the belief that their brands were so strong that consumers would pay inflated prices. The exorbitant prices of national brand name cereals forced consumers to seek lower price brand name cereals.

As a result, according to *Supermarket Business,* private cereal brand name products took 9 percent of the market away from the top national brand manufacturers during the period ending April 21, 1996. To compensate for the lost sales large brand manufacturers decided to reduce prices of cereals. According to *Supermarket Business,* analysts predicted that such a price reduction would hurt sales in the short-run but would eventually help improve the companies' long-term profits.

AMERICA AND THE WORLD

Kellogg was the first American company to enter the foreign market for ready-to-eat cereals. In 1914 the company began distribution in Ontario, Canada, and ten years later the company began operations in Australia. Kellogg opened its first plant in England in 1938 and began operations on the European continent in the

1950s. By the early 1990s Kellogg distributed its products to 150 nations and in some of these markets held a market share as large as 80 percent.

English-speaking nations represented the largest cereal markets. Consumption in non-English markets was estimated at only one-fourth the amount consumed by English speakers. For example, during the early 1990s per capita consumption of ready-to-eat cereal in England was 13.3 pounds per person, but in France it was only 1.8 pounds. On the European continent, consumption averaged 3 pounds per year. Shifting attention away from traditional breakfasts and focusing interest on low-cholesterol, convenient snack alternatives, cereal makers viewed low per capita consumption areas as potential growth fields. In Spain sales were growing at a rate of 20 percent per year; in Portugal they were growing at an annual rate of 50 percent. Some industry forecasters estimated that by the year 2000 the European cereal market would experience more than a four-fold increase and reach $6.5 billion.

In 1991, Kellogg announced a joint venture plan to build a cereal plant in Eastern Europe to supply the Baltic states and parts of the former Soviet Union. The plant, located in Riga, Latvia, was expected to be ready for production in 1994. Kellogg also announced plans to build plants in India and China. Ground-breaking for the production facility in Bombay, India, was accomplished in October 1992 and the plant was also expected to begin production in 1994. The company's Chinese facility, to be located in the Guangdong Province, was scheduled for completion in 1995.

General Mills was also active in expanding its overseas operations. In Europe, General Mills and Nestle formed a joint venture called Cereal Partners Worldwide (CPW). In 1992, CPW claimed a 15 percent share of the United Kingdom market and planned an aggressive ex-

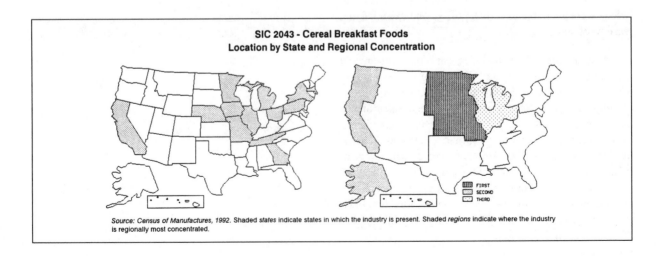

SIC 2043 - Cereal Breakfast Foods
Location by State and Regional Concentration

FIRST
SECOND
THIRD

Source: Census of Manufactures, 1992. Shaded states indicate states in which the industry is present. Shaded regions indicate where the industry is regionally most concentrated.

pansion campaign on the European continent. CPW also planned to enter the Mexican market and expand into Malaysia, Thailand, Philippines, Singapore, Indonesia, and Brunei.

ASSOCIATIONS AND SOCIETIES

AMERICAN ASSOCIATION OF CEREAL CHEMISTS
3340 Pilot Knb Rd.
St. Paul, MN 55121-2097
Phone: (612) 454-7250
Professional society of scientists and other individuals in the cereal processing industry.

GENERAL WORKS

BREAKFAST CEREALS AND HOW THEY ARE MADE
American Association of Cereal Chemists
3340 Pilot Knob Rd.
St. Paul, MN 55121
Phone: (612) 454-7250

1990.

CEREAL CHEMISTRY
American Assn. of Cereal Chemists
3340 Pilot Knob Rd.
St. Paul, MN 55121-2097
Phone: (612) 454-7250

FURTHER READING

Friedman, Martin. "Breakfast Cereals-Asleep at the Table?" *Prepared Foods,* 15 April 1996.

Kelley, B.G. "Breakfast Foods." *Supermarket Business,* September 1996.

"Kellogg Will Buy Lenders Bagels from Kraft." *The New York Times,* 19 November 1996.

Thompson, Stephanie. "Kelloggs Lenders Buy: The Right Category?" *Brandweek,* 2 December 1996.

Tomkins, Richard. "Crunch Time for US Cereal Makers." *The Financial Times,* 27 June 1996.

SIC 2043 - Cereal Breakfast Foods
General Statistics

| Year | Companies | Establishments | | Employment | | | Compensation | | Production ($ million) | | | |
		Total	with 20 or more employees	Total (000)	Production Workers (000)	Hours (Mil)	Payroll ($ mil)	Wages ($/hr)	Cost of Materials	Value Added by Manufacture	Value of Shipments	Capital Invest.
1982	32	52	37	15.6	12.8	25.5	424.4	12.91	1,475.0	2,622.8	4,131.9	165.4
1983		52	37	16.3	13.3	26.7	483.0	14.09	1,502.0	3,069.3	4,571.9	176.7
1984		52	37	16.2	13.2	26.8	525.9	15.49	1,636.2	3,478.6	5,107.2	189.3
1985		52	38	16.3	13.3	27.3	563.1	16.38	1,721.2	3,994.7	5,718.1	228.3
1986		49	33	16.4	13.3	27.8	585.1	16.72	1,681.4	4,513.1	6,167.6	270.1
1987	33	53	34	16.0	13.1	28.4	598.9	16.85	1,669.8	4,904.5	6,565.7	333.4
1988		56	35	16.4	13.7	30.4	654.6	17.29	1,823.3	5,463.8	7,274.4	394.5
1989		55	35	16.0	13.2	30.2	665.1	17.62	2,150.4	5,754.1	7,912.3	483.1
1990		57	36	15.7	13.1	29.0	384.0	18.84	2,371.4	6,325.3	8,704.6	396.8
1991		62	40	15.7	12.7	27.1	707.1	20.62	2,371.5	6,580.7	8,954.4	297.9
1992	42	65	42	16.1	13.1	29.7	745.3	20.12	2,470.9	7,338.1	9,798.6	396.6
1993		65	40	17.6	14.4	31.6	761.8	19.26	2,835.0	7,762.6	10,615.0	396.4
1994		64P	39P	17.1	14.1	31.1	765.2	19.61	2,770.1	8,720.8	11,506.5	339.1
1995		66P	40P	16.7P	13.7P	31.4P	774.6P	21.30P	2,809.4P	8,844.6P	11,669.8P	450.7P
1996		67P	40P	16.8P	13.8P	31.8P	798.8P	21.87P	2,954.1P	9,300.0P	12,270.7P	470.3P
1997		68P	40P	16.9P	13.9P	32.2P	823.1P	22.43P	3,098.7P	9,755.4P	12,871.5P	490.0P
1998		70P	41P	16.9P	13.9P	32.6P	847.3P	22.99P	3,243.4P	10,210.8P	13,472.4P	509.7P

Sources: 1982, 1987, 1992 *Economic Census; Annual Survey of Manufactures,* 83-86, 88-91, 93-94. Establishment counts for non-Census years are from *County Business Patterns;* establishment values for 83-84 are extrapolations. 'P's show projections by the editors. Industries reclassified in 87 will not have data for prior years.

CHEMICALS, AGRICULTURAL

SIC 2870.

Cyclical markets and the rising cost of environmental regulation compliance have left the U.S. agricultural chemical industry with less-than-fertile growth prospects in the late 1990s. Some sectors are still highly lucrative, however, and foreign markets, which are typically less regulated, are still considered attractive. This $23 billion industry has worked to counter its reputation as a source of compounds that are toxic to humans and the broader environment alike.

Fertilizers, pesticides, and herbicides are highly scrutinized by such federal agencies as the Environmental Protection Agency (EPA) to ensure they do not threaten human health and environmental quality. There have been numerous attempts on the national and local level to alternately regulate and deregulate the environmental impact of this industry. Recently, the trend has been toward heightened regulation.

Top 9 TOP INSECTICIDE PRODUCERS

Ranked by: Sales, in millions of dollars

1. Bayer, $1,065
2. AgrEvo, $699
3. Rhone-Poulenc, $670
4. Dow Elanco, $520
5. Zeneca, $510
6. FMC, $500
7. DuPont, $230
8. Ciba, $180
9. BASF, $80

Source: *Chemicalweek*, August 7, 1996, p. 29, from Lehman Brothers.

Added to these woes are the limited outlook for agricultural chemicals in U.S. markets, which are considered mature, and the cyclical downturns in crop prices and production that can diminish chemical sales for a given growing season. Manufacturers have responded by pursuing research into products that are more environmentally palatable and by seeking out new markets for their goods to reduce dependence on the traditional agricultural customer base.

INDUSTRY OUTLOOK

Agricultural chemical production falls in four main categories: nitrogen-based fertilizer manufacturing, phosphate-based fertilizer manufacturing, mixed fertilizer production, and pesticide production. In practice, many of the same firms produce in multiple categories.

NITROGENOUS FERTILIZERS

The main source of nitrogen for fertilizer production is atmospheric nitrogen, of which there is abundant supply; it has been estimated that there are about 35,000 tons of nitrogen over every acre of land. In order for plants to utilize this element, however, it must first be combined with either oxygen or hydrogen in a process called "fixation."

The primary ingredient of most nitrogenous fertilizers is anhydrous ammonia, which the fertilizer industry typically forms by fixing atmospheric nitrogen with the hydrogen found in natural gas—methane. The resultant compound is a gas that is 82.25 percent nitrogen. This gas is stored in containers that are pressurized and usually refrigerated, and it may be directly applied as a fertilizer beneath the soil surface with the use of injection equipment. Anhydrous ammonia is the least expensive and one of the more common nitrogenous fertilizers used for direct application in the United States.

Anhydrous ammonia may be reacted with nitric acid to produce ammonium nitrate. While it is an excellent fertilizer, ammonium nitrate is also highly combustible. Once the world's leading directly-applied nitrogenous fertilizer, it appeared to be giving way to urea. Produced by reacting anhydrous ammonia with carbon dioxide, urea has a higher nitrogen content and is easier and safer to store and handle than ammonium nitrate. In 1996, the total production of ammonium nitrate was at 8.3 million short tons while urea was at 8.1 million short tons. The value of urea production was considerably less than ammonium nitrate, however. The total value of nitrogenous fertilizers was more than $4 billion entering the late 1990s.

PHOSPHATIC FERTILIZERS

These fertilizers are produced from phosphate rock, which was the only commercially important source of fertilizer phosphorus in the 1990s. Chief sources of the world supply of phosphate rock are the United States—principally Florida and North Carolina—the Kola Peninsula in Russia, and Morocco. After mining, the phosphate rock must be refined and concentrated for use as fertilizer.

About 45 percent of the phosphatic fertilizer produced in the United States is used on its domestic corn crop, so corn acreage is one determinant of domestic demand; other determinants are grain prices, the ability of U.S. farmers to compete globally, and the weather. Short term fluctuations in the domestic market are thus difficult to predict, but prices were expected to rebound by the mid- to late-1990s. The export market also held some promise for the long term, given the U.S. industry's cost advantage over many foreign producers with respect to phosphate rock and sulphur, two key raw materials.

In 1994-95, phosphate fertilizer production experienced a 3.2 percent growth rate. Exports grew 10.9 percent, and consumption was up 2.2 percent. Phosphatic fertilizer shipments were valued at $5.2 billion in 1995.

MIXED FERTILIZERS

There are three major types of mixed fertilizers: homogeneous mixtures, bulk blends, and fluids. A key

SIC 2874 - Phosphatic Fertilizers
General Statistics

| Year | Com-panies | Establishments | | Employment | | | Compensation | | Production ($ million) | | | |
		Total	with 20 or more employees	Total (000)	Production Workers (000)	Hours (Mil)	Payroll ($ mil)	Wages ($/hr)	Cost of Materials	Value Added by Manufacture	Value of Shipments	Capital Invest.
1982	69	110	76	14.3	9.7	20.0	328.2	10.34	3,055.8	760.5	3,921.9	229.6
1983		109	73	12.9	9.1	19.0	308.0	10.85	2,981.4	965.5	3,969.4	99.2
1984		108	70	13.0	8.9	18.8	337.2	11.54	3,576.6	1,065.0	4,541.1	139.8
1985		108	68	13.0	8.7	18.0	350.5	12.12	3,392.1	771.4	4,184.2	178.7
1986		97	63	11.3	7.3	15.1	321.9	12.66	2,709.6	612.4	3,396.4	218.2
1987	55	77	42	9.4	6.2	13.2	286.2	12.94	2,612.4	1,167.2	3,819.3	63.6
1988		75	40	10.4	7.1	15.8	324.7	13.10	2,882.2	1,619.5	4,474.2	133.7
1989		77	38	11.2	7.4	16.1	348.5	13.55	3,035.7	1,167.0	4,187.3	132.2
1990		75	37	11.0	7.5	17.0	364.0	13.70	3,462.4	1,151.1	4,636.2	137.5
1991		71	38	10.3	7.3	16.4	368.4	14.65	3,619.4	1,372.6	4,983.9	197.1
1992	54	75	41	9.5	6.7	15.8	342.1	13.82	3,076.4	1,245.5	4,332.8	307.7
1993		84	41	9.4	6.6	14.5	332.6	14.70	2,625.9	975.4	3,648.0	149.9
1994		64P	27P	8.5	6.2	13.7	339.0	16.69	3,006.8	1,632.0	4,596.5	159.3
1995		61P	23P	8.3P	5.9P	13.7P	350.4P	16.08P	2,924.5P	1,587.3P	4,470.6P	183.0P
1996		57P	19P	7.9P	5.6P	13.3P	352.6P	16.50P	2,949.1P	1,600.7P	4,508.3P	185.6P
1997		53P	15P	7.5P	5.4P	12.9P	354.9P	16.92P	2,973.7P	1,614.1P	4,546.0P	188.1P
1998		49P	11P	7.1P	5.1P	12.5P	357.1P	17.34P	2,998.4P	1,627.4P	4,583.6P	190.7P

Sources: 1982, 1987, 1992 Economic Census; Annual Survey of Manufactures, 83-86, 88-91, 93-94. Establishment counts for non-Census years are from County Business Patterns; establishment values for 83-84 are extrapolations. 'P's show projections by the editors. Industries reclassified in 87 will not have data for prior years.

process performed by producers of homogeneous mixtures, as well as by producers of fertilizer materials, is granulation. Before the granulation process, nongranulated dry fertilizer powders had a tendency to form hardened cakes, which made the product difficult to handle. The hardened cakes were not always broken up easily, and explosives were sometimes used to break up these cakes on heaps of stored fertilizer. Another problem with fertilizer mixes before the granulation process was the propensity for the component fertilizer materials to segregate, according to particle sizes, during transport and handling. Granulation addresses the problem of caking and segregation by forming the constituent parts of the fertilizer mix into larger granules which are relatively equal in size and which each have the same nutrient analysis. The manufacture of this type of mixed fertilizer is a complex process requiring sophisticated equipment.

Bulk blending plants, by contrast, do not perform granulation or any chemical processes and their basic equipment needs are rudimentary (i.e., bins, front-end loaders, mixers, and scales). They keep an assortment of fertilizer materials on site, from which they select desired proportions for mixing together, often to suit the specific nutrient needs of the customer. The mix may be bagged, or it may be taken directly to the customer's field and applied.

Fluid mixed fertilizers have the smallest share of the mixed fertilizer market. They are generally made by either the hot-mix or cold-mix process. Hot-mix plants combine ammonia with phosphoric acid, a reaction which releases considerable heat. The cold-mix process usually does not involve heat-producing chemical reactions, and the equipment needs for cold-mix plants are simpler than those for hot-mix plants.

The commercial usage of multi-nutrient fertilizers is somewhat controversial. Some governments have argued against the practice on the grounds that optimal results are obtained when farmers tailor their fertilizer usage to their specific crop/soil combination, and that this is best done with the use of single-nutrient fertilizers applied in the proper proportions. Research results have supported that argument, and advances in soil nutrient analysis technique have made it easier to determine which specific nutrient a particular plot of land may need. The result of the arguments has been a trend away from the use of mixed fertilizers. Data for fertilizer consumption in the United States, covering the period between 1955 and 1980, indicates that beginning in 1955 the use of mixtures was roughly twice that of direct application fertilizer materials. Over the subsequent years the use of single-nutrient fertilizers grew, both in absolute terms and relative to mixtures, and in the early 1970s surpassed the use of mixtures. However, the manufacture of mixed fertilizers remains a major agricultural chemical segment.

In 1995, this segment's shipments were an estimated $2.2 billion, and they were expected to increase to $2.3 billion in 1998.

SIC 2873 - Nitrogenous Fertilizers
General Statistics

| Year | Companies | Establishments | | Employment | | | Compensation | | Production ($ million) | | | |
		Total	with 20 or more employees	Total (000)	Production Workers (000)	Hours (Mil)	Payroll ($ mil)	Wages ($/hr)	Cost of Materials	Value Added by Manufacture	Value of Shipments	Capital Invest.
1982	109	143	75	10.4	6.3	13.5	268.1	11.58	2,395.3	981.0	3,391.1	145.3
1983		137	73	8.7	5.1	10.8	231.0	12.18	2,006.8	913.2	2,950.2	55.3
1984		131	71	8.5	5.2	10.8	244.0	12.67	2,346.3	1,307.1	3,574.8	77.9
1985		124	70	8.7	5.4	11.0	259.5	13.62	2,393.9	1,086.3	3,469.6	112.5
1986		128	72	6.6	4.0	8.8	202.4	12.97	1,433.6	626.6	2,177.6	84.9
1987	117	164	72	7.4	4.5	9.6	222.8	13.04	1,503.5	874.7	2,447.2	36.9
1988		159	81	7.2	4.4	9.6	222.0	12.96	1,626.4	1,173.2	2,761.1	48.1
1989		157	80	6.8	4.4	9.7	231.6	14.03	1,724.4	1,156.8	2,866.0	122.7
1990		151	81	7.2	4.8	10.4	253.6	13.80	1,905.3	1,213.3	3,113.4	99.4
1991		155	85	7.3	4.7	10.3	260.2	14.77	1,982.1	1,290.5	3,238.1	220.1
1992	103	152	77	7.0	4.7	10.1	257.6	15.65	1,871.7	1,262.5	3,174.6	208.8
1993		166	82	7.0	4.7	10.3	270.4	16.11	2,118.8	1,341.6	3,467.1	186.0
1994		165P	83P	8.0	5.4	11.8	308.1	16.69	2,251.2	1,965.6	4,246.1	174.6
1995		168P	84P	6.5P	4.5P	10.0P	271.8P	16.48P	1,824.3P	1,592.9P	3,440.9P	189.8P
1996		170P	85P	6.3P	4.5P	9.9P	275.1P	16.86P	1,846.8P	1,612.5P	3,483.3P	199.7P
1997		173P	87P	6.1P	4.4P	9.8P	278.5P	17.23P	1,869.2P	1,632.1P	3,525.6P	209.5P
1998		176P	88P	6.0P	4.3P	9.7P	281.8P	17.61P	1,891.7P	1,651.7P	3,568.0P	219.3P

Sources: 1982, 1987, 1992 Economic Census; Annual Survey of Manufactures, 83-86, 88-91, 93-94. Establishment counts for non-Census years are from County Business Patterns; establishment values for 83-84 are extrapolations. 'P's show projections by the editors. Industries reclassified in 87 will not have data for prior years.

PESTICIDES AND MISCELLANEOUS CHEMICALS

During the 1980s, the pesticide segment faced increased economic pressures due to governmental regulations aimed at addressing environmental and food safety issues. The regulation led to a dramatic increase in research and development costs, as companies were forced to conduct exhaustive toxicology tests for pesticide effects on the environment, fish, and wildlife, as well as on human life. Faced with increased costs and a mature domestic market for their product, the industry rationalized and consolidated.

An important trend in this segment has been toward innovative use of adjuvants, which include a wide range of inert additives designed to make pesticides more effective. Examples are attractants, defoaming agents, extenders (which prolong the active life of the pesticide by screening out ultraviolet light), stickers (which prevent pesticides from washing off the treated crop in the rain), and surfactants. The market for these products is much smaller than the market for pesticides, but may benefit from the same regulations that plague the pesticide industry because adjuvants serve to lower pesticide dosage requirements and do not need to be registered with the EPA.

Pesticides are typically manufactured in a concentrated form, and need to be mixed with adjuvants before they are of practical use to the consumer. This mixing process is called "formulation," and some establishments, which do not manufacture the concentrated form, may formulate the pesticide for the end user who may be a commercial farmer or just a homeowner with a lawn or garden. Manufacturers of the principal adjuvant ingredients supply their product to adjuvant formulators/distributors who prepare the product and market it for sale to pesticide manufacturers.

About 85 percent of domestic pesticide sales are to the agriculture industry, with the remainder going to residential users. Herbicides account for more than half of U.S. pesticide consumption, while insecticides carry approximately one-quarter of the market, and the remainer is filled out by fungicides and miscellaneous chemicals. The largest crops for pesticide application include corn, soybeans, and cotton.

ORGANIZATION AND STRUCTURE

Federal legislation has held the industry accountable for the safety of its chemical products. In general, the political climate in the 1990s did not favor the domestic pesticide industry. The Clinton administration announced a program to reduce the use of agricultural

pesticides in the United States, and appeared to support the proposed Circle of Poison Prevention Act, which would prohibit U.S. manufacturers from exporting those pesticides that are banned in this country. The "circle of poison" refers to the U.S. export of pesticides, which are banned domestically, and the subsequent use of those pesticides on crops in foreign countries, which are then imported back into the United States. The pesticide industry argued that the proposed bill will inappropriately apply U.S. risk/benefit criteria to countries where the benefits may outweigh the risks, thereby depriving those countries of needed improvements to their food supply; will fail to distinguish between pesticides, which have been refused registration by the EPA for public health reasons from those pesticides, which the manufacturers have decided not to register in the United States due to a poor domestic demand; and will simply allow competitors from other countries to gain global market share by selling identical pesticides to the same countries. The combination of industry-adverse regulation in the United States and the proposed export restraint on pesticides is the impetus for the trend among pesticide manufacturers to send research and development and production operations overseas.

On August 3, 1996, President Clinton signed the Food Safety Protection Act, fundamentally improving the way pesticides are regulated in food. Under the new law, all exposures to pesticides must be shown to be safe for infants and children, with a clear consideration of the sensitivity of the young to these chemicals. In addition, when determining a safe level for a pesticide in food, the EPA must explicitly account for all infant and child exposures to other pesticides and toxic chemicals that share a common toxic mechanism.

Under prior law, farmer profits could justify risks that would otherwise be deemed unacceptable, and no explicit protection of infants and children was required. This framework was largely repealed and replaced by a uniform standard of safety with very narrow exceptions. And, when exceptions to the new health standard are granted for a specific pesticide, the public is informed through the markets of all foods treated with that pesticide.

WORK FORCE

Employment levels in the agricultural chemical industry increased slightly in the early 1990s but then declined through the mid-1990s, a trend projected by the Bureau of Labor Statistics to continue through 2000. In 1996, according to U.S. Department of Labor figures, total employment was at 52,000 persons, of whom ap-

SIC 2873
Occupations Employed by SIC 287 - Agricultural Chemicals

Occupation	% of Total 1994	Change to 2005
Chemical plant & system operators	9.4	-5.2
Blue collar worker supervisors	6.8	-24.7
Industrial machinery mechanics	5.3	-13.1
Chemical equipment controllers, operators	5.2	-36.8
Sales & related workers nec	4.4	-21.0
Crushing & mixing machine operators	3.4	-21.0
Packaging & filling machine operators	3.4	-21.0
Truck drivers light & heavy	3.4	-18.5
Helpers, laborers, & material movers nec	3.2	-21.0
Science & mathematics technicians	2.9	-21.0
Maintenance repairers, general utility	2.8	-28.9
General managers & top executives	2.8	-25.1
Industrial truck & tractor operators	2.6	-21.0
Secretaries, ex legal & medical	2.2	-28.1
Material moving equipment operators nec	2.1	-21.0
Freight, stock, & material movers, hand	2.0	-36.8
Bookkeeping, accounting, & auditing clerks	1.9	-40.8
Chemists	1.7	-21.0
General office clerks	1.7	-32.6
Hand packers & packagers	1.6	-32.2
Industrial production managers	1.3	-21.1
Electricians	1.3	-25.8
Chemical engineers	1.3	-21.0
Marketing, advertising, & PR managers	1.2	-21.0
Clerical supervisors & managers	1.1	-19.1
Machine feeders & offbearers	1.1	-28.8
Managers & administrators nec	1.0	-21.1

Source: Industry-Occupation Matrix, Bureau of Labor Statistics. These data relate to one or more 3-digit SIC industry groups rather than to a single 4-digit SIC. The change reported for each occupation to the year 2005 is a percent of growth or decline as estimated by the Bureau of Labor Statistics. The abbreviation nec stands for 'not elsewhere classified'.

proximately 60 percent were production workers. Occupations in the industry include chemical equipment controllers, chemical plant and system operators, maintenance repairers, truck drivers, secretaries, mechanics, chemists, electricians, warehouse workers, shipping clerks, and office workers. Average pay in the industry is consistently higher than that for manufacturing industries in general.

RESEARCH AND TECHNOLOGY

Research and development costs have risen to high levels and are expected to continue to rise as regulatory requirements for more environmentally safe chemicals increase. The 1990s ushered in a trend among agrochemical manufacturers to develop low-dosage pesticides as a means of reducing the amount of chemical residue left on crops. Monsanto Company, for example, has a policy that any new pesticides that it develops must be designed for low-dosage application, must have low toxicity, and must have low impact on the environment.

Another area which holds promise for the industry is biotechnology. Biotechnology involves the genetic engineering of plants to make them resistant to diseases, insects, drought, pollution, and herbicides, in addition to the use of bacteria and viruses to create biological insecticides. One especially promising group of viruses for use as "bioinsecticides" is the baculoviruses. These viruses are naturally occurring and only attack specific insects; they pose no threat to humans, wildlife, or non-targeted insects.

AMERICA AND THE WORLD

The United States is a leading international producer of agricultural chemicals. It is the world's largest manufacturer of pesticides, followed by Germany and Japan, and has enjoyed a favorable pesticide trade balance with the rest of the world into the 1990s, even though the ratio of exports to imports fell from 2.3 to 1.9 during the first three years of the 1990s. The largest market for U.S. exports of pesticides is Japan, which accounted for about 10 percent in 1996.

ASSOCIATIONS AND SOCIETIES

AMERICAN CROP PROTECTION
1156 15th St. NW, Ste. 400
Washington, DC 20005
Phone: (202) 296-1585
Fax: (202) 463-0474

AOAC INTERNATIONAL
2200 Wilson Blvd., Ste. 400
Arlington, VA 22201
Phone: (703) 522-3032
Fax: (703) 522-5468

ASSOCIATION OF OFFICIAL ANALYTICAL CHEMISTS
2200 Wilson Blvd., Ste. 400
Arlington, VA 22209-3301
Phone: (703) 522-3032
Fax: (703) 522-5468

THE FERTILIZER INSTITUTE
501 2nd Ave. NE
Washington, DC 20002
Phone: (202) 675-8250
Fax: (202) 544-8123

NATIONAL FERTILIZER SOLUTIONS ASSOCIATION
339 Consort Dr.
Manchester, MO 63011
Phone: (314) 256-4900
Fax: (314) 256-4901

PERIODICALS AND NEWSLETTERS

AOAC INTERNATIONAL JOURNAL
Association of Official Analytical Chemists
2200 Wilson Blvd., Ste. 400
Arlington, VA 22201-3301
Phone: (703) 522-3032
Fax: (703) 522-5468
Bimonthly. Free to members; non-members and institutions, $160.00 per year. Formerly Association of Official Analytical Chemist Journal.

FARM CHEMICALS
Meister Publishing Co.
37733 Euclid Ave.
Willoughby, OH 44094
Phone: (800) 527-7740 or (216) 942-2000
Fax: (216) 975-3447
Monthly. $20.00 per year.

FERTILIZER PROGRESS
501 2nd St. NE
Washington, DC 20002
Phone: (202) 675-8250
Bimonthly. $25.00 per year.

SOIL SCIENCE
Williams and Wilkins Co.
428 E. Preston St.
Baltimore, MD 21202
Phone: (800) 638-0672 or (800) 638-6423
Fax: (410) 528-4312
Monthly. Individuals, $84.00 per year; institutions, $149.00 per year.

WACA NEWS
Western Agricultural Chemicals Association
3835 N. Freeway Blvd., Ste. 140
Sacramento, CA 95834
Phone: (916) 446-9222
Fax: (916) 565-0113
Quarterly. Free.

DATABASES

AGRICOLA
U.S. National Agricultural Library
Beltsville, MD 20705
Phone: (301) 504-6813
Fax: (301) 504-7473
Covers worldwide agricultural literature. Over 2.8 million citations, 1970 to present, with monthly updates. Inquire as to online cost and availability.

CA SEARCH
Chemical Abstracts Service
2540 Olentangy River Rd.
Columbus, OH 43210
Phone: (614) 447-3731
Fax: (614) 447-3751
Guide to chemical literature, 1967 to present. Inquire as to online cost and availability.

DERWENT CROP PROTECTION FILE
Derwent, Inc.
1313 Dolley Madison Blvd., Ste. 401
McLean, VA 22101
Phone: (800) 451-3451 or (703) 790-0400
Fax: (703) 790-1426
Provides citations to the international journal literature of agricultural chemicals and pesticides from 1968 to date, with updating eight times per year. Formerly PESTDOC. *Inquire as to online cost and availability.*

DRI CHEMICAL FORECAST
DRI/McGraw-Hill, Data Products Division
24 Hartwell Ave.
Lexington, MA 02173
Phone: (800) 541-9914 or (617) 863-5100
Supply-demand and price forecasts are given quarterly and annually for over 120 U.S. chemical products. Quarterly forecasts generally extend three years, while annual forecasts cover five to ten years. Inquire as to online cost and availability.

STATISTICS SOURCES

ANNUAL SURVEY OF MANUFACTURES
Bureau of the Census, U.S. Department of Commerce
Available from U.S. Government Printing Office
Washington, DC 20402
Phone: (202) 512-1800
Fax: (202) 512-2250

FAO FERTILIZER YEARBOOK
United Nations Food and Agriculture Organization
Available from UNIPUB
4611-F Assembly Dr.
Lanham, MD 20706-4391
Phone: (800) 274-4888 or (301) 459-2255
Fax: (301) 459-0056
Annual. $40.00. Formerly Annual Fertilizer Review.

FERTILIZER FACTS AND FIGURES
Fertilizer Institute
501 2nd Ave. NE
Washington, DC 20002
Phone: (202) 675-8250
Fax: (202) 544-8123
Annual.

U.S. INDUSTRIAL OUTLOOK: FORECASTS FOR SELECTED MANUFACTURING AND SERVICE INDUSTRIES
Available from U.S. Government Printing Office
Washington, DC 20402
Phone: (202) 512-1800
Fax: (202) 512-2250
Annual. $37.00. (Replaced in 1995 by U.S. Global Trade Outlook.*) Issued by the International Trade Administration, U.S. Department of Commerce. Provides basic data, outlook for the current year, and "Long-Term Prospects" (five-year projections) for a wide variety of products and services. Includes high technology industries. Available on the world wide web at gopher://gopher.umsl.edu:70/11/library/govdocs/usio94*

GENERAL WORKS

CROP PROTECTION CHEMICALS REFERENCE

John Wiley & Sons, Inc.
605 3rd Ave.
New York, NY 10158-0012
Phone: (800) 225-5945 or (212) 850-6000
Fax: (212) 850-6088
1993. Ninth edition. Price on application. Contains the complete text of product labels. Indexed by manufacturer, product category, crop use, chemical name, and brand name.

DIRECTORY OF FERTILIZER PLANTS IN THE UNITED STATES

Association of American Plant Food Control Officials, Inc.
Division of Regulatory
University of Kentucky
Lexington, KY 40546
Phone: (606) 257-2668
Quadrennial. $25.00. Lists over 13,000 fertilizer manufacturers and retail outlets.

FARM CHEMICALS HANDBOOK

Meister Publishing Co.
37733 Euclid Ave.
Willoughby, OH 44094
Phone: (800) 527-7740 or (216) 942-2000
Fax: (216) 975-3447
Annual. $69.00. Manufacturers and suppliers of fertilizers, pesticides, and related equipment used in agribusiness.

OFFICIAL METHODS OF ANALYSIS OF AOAC

Association of Official Analytical Chemists
2200 Wilson Blvd., Ste. 400

Arlington, VA 22201
Phone: (703) 522-3032
Fax: (703) 522-5468
Quinquennial. $215.00. 15th edition.

FURTHER READING

Darnay, Arsen J., ed. *Manufacturing USA*. 5th ed. Detroit: Gale Research, 1996.

EPA Homepage. Available from http://www.epa.gov.

''Global Pesticide Market Grows in 1996.'' Available from http://www.corpwatch.orgtrac/corner/worldnews/other/other26.html.

Lazich, Robert S., ed. *Market Share Reporter*. Detroit: Gale Research, 1997.

''Nitrogenous Fertilizers.'' *Fertilizer Statistics-Summary Table 1994-1995.* Available from http://www.fao.org/WAICENT/faoinfo/economic/ferstat/nitr_gr.htm.

U.S. Bureau of the Census. *Statistical Abstract of the United States*. Washington: GPO, 1996.

———. ''Value of Product Shipments.'' *1995 Annual Survey of Manufactures*. Washington: GPO, 1997.

U.S. Department of Labor. *Employment, Hours, and Earnings, United States, 1988-96*. Washington: GPO, August 1996.

The inorganic chemicals industry makes up the bulk of basic chemical production. Inorganic chemicals are those derived from inanimate earth materials such as minerals and the atmosphere. They are differentiated from organic chemicals, which are derived from plant and animal sources. Organic chemicals are based on carbon; inorganic chemicals are based on all other naturally occurring and synthetically produced elements. The major chemicals within this classification are known as "basic" chemicals. They are also sometimes referred to as "heavy," "bulk," or "commodity" chemicals. Manufacturers typically produce them from ores or brines, or as co-products or by-products of other processes. They serve industrial users who put them to work in the creation of other products. Some common applications include their uses as processing aids and chemical catalysts. Inorganic chemicals are also used as ingredients in non-chemical products. The primary markets for chemical products are paper, housing, automobiles, water treatment, fertilizer, petroleum refining, steel production, manufacturing, and soap and detergent production.

CHEMICALS, INDUSTRIAL INORGANIC

SIC 2810

Although several market disruptions and new environmental regulations stymied the industrial organic chemical industry in the mid-1990s, analysts forecast modest growth for this sector through the end of the decade. Overall growth in the alkalies and chlorine sector is expect to reach 2 to 3 percent, although the slowest expansion will come from the chlorine segment. In the industrial gases sector, nitrogen sales are up with more growth predicted in the coming years. Furthermore, in the inorganic pigments market, sales of titanium dioxide—which had slowed in the mid-1990s—were expected to increase 2 percent annually to 2000.

ALKALIES AND CHLORINE

Sulfuric acid is by far the largest volume inorganic chemical. It is used primarily as a chemical reagent in a variety of industrial processes with a largest end use in fertilizer production. About three-fourths of domestic sulfuric acid is used for phosphate fertilizer. Hydrogen peroxide is a rapidly growing sector of the inorganic chemicals industry. Pulp and paper manufacturing account for more than half the demand for hydrogen peroxide, as it becomes a more viable option than chlorine for the chemical bleaching of paper. It is also used to de-ink paper before the recycling process. Other uses for hydrogen peroxide are in water and waste treatment and for bleaching textiles. The two primary commodities offered by the alkalies and chlorine industry are chlorine and sodium hydroxide (caustic soda). Together they represent about 82 percent of all shipments. The third largest commodity, soda ash, which is an alkali product used in glass making, water treatment, pulp bleaching, and detergent manufacturing, accounts for only 14 percent of shipments. Other remaining products account for 4 percent.

According to U.S. Department of Commerce statistics, shipments within the alkalies and chlorine industry totaled $3.3 billion in 1995. In current dollars, the industry more than doubled since 1987 when it shipped $1.5 billion worth of products. Growth patterns of the various industry segments varied. Although overall growth within the chlorine and alkalies industry was expected to increase at a rate of 2 percent to 3 percent through the mid-1990s, some industry forecasters predicted the slowest growth would occur within the chlorine segment.

Top 10 LARGEST INDUSTRIAL CHEMICAL/ SYNTHETIC MATERIAL COMPANIES

Ranked by: Sales in 1995, in millions of dollars.

1. Dow Chemical, with $20,200 million
2. Monsanto, $8,962
3. Union Carbide, $5,888
4. Eastman Chemical Co., $5,040
5. Lyondell Petrochemical, $4,936
6. ARCO Chemical, $4,282
7. Rohm & Haas, $3,884
8. Air Products & Chemicals, $3,865
9. Olin, $3,150
10. Praxair Inc., $3,146

Source: *ChemicalWeek,* ChemicalWeek 300 (annual), May 8, 1996, p. 53.

INDUSTRIAL GASES

In the United States, industrial gases touch virtually every facet of twentieth-century life. The three major atmospheric gases, oxygen, nitrogen, and argon, are used in steel production. Oxygen enhances kiln firing to reduce brick making costs. Liquid oxygen and liquid hydrogen fuel rockets. Nitrogen is used in brewing beer, recycling tires, and applying metallic finishes on toys. Liquid nitrogen and liquid carbon dioxide are used to make plastic fittings for moldings, enhance oil recovery from wells, and enable solvent recycling. Argon contributes to stainless steel manufacturing and serves as a component in fluorescent tube lighting.

The industrial gas industry differs from many other types of manufacturing because its raw materials are primarily extracted from the atmosphere. The two principal gases produced by the industry are nitrogen and oxygen. Dry air is composed of 78.1 percent nitrogen, 20.9 percent oxygen, and just under 1 percent argon. All other atmospheric gases, often called rare gases, make up the remaining one-tenth of a percent. Additional industrial gases such as hydrogen, acetylene, and carbon dioxide are obtained as co-products or by-products from other operations. Production costs within the industry are divided fairly evenly among labor, energy, and distribution.

According to the U.S. Census Bureau, the industrial gases industry shipped products valued at $3.6 billion in 1995. Although industry sales declined in the late 1980s, growth was achieved during the early and mid-1990s. In 1996, U.S. oxygen production was estimated at 668 billion cubic feet; nitrogen production at 1.03 trillion cubic feet; hydrogen production at 271 billion cubic feet; and argon production was approximately 18 billion cubic feet. The United States likewise produced more than 5 million short tons of liquid carbon dioxide and 235,000 short tons of solid carbon dioxide.

INORGANIC PIGMENTS

Inorganic pigments are classified as single-metal oxides, mixed-metal oxides, and earth colors. Single-metal oxides include pigments made from titanium, zinc, cobalt, and chromium. Mixed-metal oxides include pigments such as cobalt aluminate blue, which is used in ceramic glazes, and nickel antimony titanate, manganese antimony titanate, and chromium antimony titanate, which are used for outdoor coatings and plastic siding. Earth colors, including siennas, ochers, and umbers, are generally made from iron oxides and lead chromates. A method of high-temperature firing called calcination is used to produce pigments with improved heat resistance.

Pigment manufacturers supply inorganic colors in a variety of forms such as powders, pastes, granules, slurries, and suspensions. Pigment users include manufacturers of paints and stains, printing inks, plastics, synthetic textiles, paper, cosmetics, contact lenses, soaps and detergents, wax, modeling clay, chalks, crayons, artists' colors, concrete and masonry products, and ceramics.

Within the inorganic pigments classification, the largest selling individual pigment is titanium dioxide (TiO_2), a white pigment with opacifying characteristics. Titanium dioxide is by far the most widely used white pigment in the world. It is a solid that melts at over 1800 degrees Celsius. It has a higher refractive index than everything except diamonds. It is polymorphous and exists in three crystal structures: rutile, anatase, and brookite. To utilize titanium dioxide's special properties, it must be developed to an ideal particle size. Most often, the particle size is one half the wavelength of visible light or about 0.3 microns.

INDUSTRY OUTLOOK

The outlook for inorganic chemicals in 1996 was mixed. The hydrogen peroxide commodity was sold out and prices were expected to remain the same until more product became available. Chlorine and sodium chlorate were expected to drop slightly from their strong 1995 levels, and sodium bicarbonate sales would reflect growth in gross domestic product.

ALKALIES AND CHLORINE

The demand for hydrogen peroxide was 1 billion pounds in 1994, 1.1 billion pounds in 1995, and was expected to be 1.55 billion pounds in 1999. The expected growth rate of 8 to 10 percent would fall short in 1996, when the pulp market crashed. As the pulp market used 60 percent of all hydrogen peroxide in North America, the pulp and paper industries dictated, to a large degree, the livelihood of hydrogen peroxide. The market had been going so well up until then, that hydrogen peroxide makers were not incredibly hurt by the sudden decrease in activity, and some manufactures were even relieved for the opportunity for maintenance.

Gains in the fertilizer market caused the demand for sulfur to increase 5 percent from 1993 to 1994. Another healthy gain occurred in 1995 due to increased fertilizer consumption. Sulfur sales were expected to remain closely tied to U.S. and world fertilizer demand.

Sulfuric acid recovered well in 1995 from reduced levels of 1993 and 1994. In March of 1994, the industry hit bottom with prices falling to $8 and $9 per ton. By 1995 sulfuric acid was up to $35 per ton. This was beginning to approach the $50-per-ton record high of the late 1980s.

The better market of the mid-1990s was due to an increase in demand for phosphate fertilizers and more use by the copper industry. As copper prices doubled in the first two months of 1995, more sulfuric acid was suddenly needed as copper miners tried to extract as much copper as quickly as possible. Another contributing factor was that imports of sulfuric acid from non-Canadian sources were almost nonexistent in 1995. The import rate had dropped from 684,000 metric tons in 1993 to 333,000 metric tons in 1994. Shipping prices from Germany, for example, were more expensive per ton than the sulfuric acid was worth.

Figures released by the U.S. Bureau of Census for the chlor-alkali industry in 1995 showed domestic total production at $3.3 billion in shipments, with contributions to this total from chlorine (compressed or liquefied) at $849.7 million, sodium hydroxide or caustic soda at $2.06 billion, and other alkalies at $382.3 million.

Prices for chlorine increased by $25 to $40 per ton at the end of 1996 and again in early 1997, by Dow, Occidental, and Vulcan. Increases were due to several factors: 1) previous expansions in downstream production of chlorine derivatives not having been matched by corresponding expansions in chlor-alkali plants, demand thus exceeding supply; 2) failures at two Dow chlor-alkali rectifiers (Freeport, Texas), with resultant production delays due to repairs; 3) a 30 day loss of production at LaRoche Industries' Gramercy, Louisiana plant, due to a fire that caused a daily 50 percent reduction in the normal 300 tons per day output; and 4) the seasonal spring increase in homebuilding, with its attendant increase in demand for PVC products.

SIC 2812 - Alkalies and Chlorine
General Statistics

Year	Com-panies	Establishments Total	Establishments with 20 or more employees	Employment Total (000)	Employment Production Workers (000)	Employment Hours (Mil)	Compensation Payroll ($ mil)	Compensation Wages ($/hr)	Production ($ million) Cost of Materials	Production ($ million) Value Added by Manufacture	Production ($ million) Value of Shipments	Production ($ million) Capital Invest.
1982	35	51	34	7.6	5.0	9.8	215.7	13.77	856.3	728.8	1,570.5	134.4
1983		50	33	7.3	4.8	9.8	217.9	13.96	898.6	765.0	1,666.8	200.3
1984		49	32	7.4	5.1	10.6	239.7	15.26	984.0	869.6	1,872.4	149.5
1985		48	32	8.2	5.6	11.2	263.2	15.00	978.4	1,073.7	2,042.4	175.2
1986		51	33	6.7	4.5	9.0	218.3	15.24	957.9	1,028.0	2,010.9	122.1
1987	27	45	31	5.0	3.5	7.3	165.3	15.07	809.0	732.1	1,547.9	68.4
1988		50	32	6.5	4.4	9.4	237.5	16.90	1,159.9	1,324.1	2,469.3	104.2
1989		47	33	5.2	4.6	10.0	248.7	16.67	1,309.9	1,383.6	2,699.0	155.6
1990		46	32	5.0	4.7	10.1	263.3	17.40	1,265.8	1,449.9	2,709.8	127.0
1991		52	35	7.5	5.2	11.0	303.5	18.15	1,347.6	1,394.1	2,728.9	144.6
1992	34	51	33	8.0	5.4	11.3	353.3	20.53	1,393.4	1,408.1	2,786.9	176.2
1993		51	33	7.7	5.3	11.1	351.6	20.95	1,425.2	1,093.6	2,480.9	181.5
1994		50P	33P	6.2	4.2	8.9	287.2	21.70	1,121.8	1,015.6	2,171.1	126.5
1995		50P	33P	6.4P	4.8P	10.3P	329.9P	21.55P	1,459.7P	1,321.6P	2,825.2P	142.4P
1996		50P	33P	6.4P	4.8P	10.3P	340.0P	22.20P	1,505.0P	1,362.5P	2,912.7P	142.2P
1997		50P	33P	6.3P	4.8P	10.4P	350.2P	22.85P	1,550.3P	1,403.5P	3,000.3P	142.0P
1998		50P	33P	6.3P	4.7P	10.4P	360.3P	23.51P	1,595.5P	1,444.5P	3,087.9P	141.9P

Sources: 1982, 1987, 1992 *Economic Census*; *Annual Survey of Manufactures*, 83-86, 88-91, 93-94. Establishment counts for non-Census years are from *County Business Patterns*; establishment values for 83-84 are extrapolations. 'P's show projections by the editors. Industries reclassified in 87 will not have data for prior years.

During the first quarter of 1997, caustic soda prices continued to decrease with prices reported in February at about $95 per ton on the Gulf. Although caustic soda prices dropped $100 per ton in the year from early 1996 to early 1997, it was believed by April 1997 that prices had bottomed out. Severe flooding in the Midwest, limited transport on the Mississippi River due to elevated levels, the Dow and LaRoche production problems, and other unforeseen difficulties during the first quarter helped to stabilize prices in part by their effects on caustic soda inventories.

INDUSTRIAL GASES

Although demand for nitrogen in 1960 had been practically nonexistent, by the early 1990s nitrogen sales surpassed the sales of all other industrial gases. Nitrogen and oxygen sales combined accounted for approximately two-thirds of the industry's sales in 1995. Carbon dioxide, hydrogen, and argon sales ranked a distant third, fourth, and fifth, respectively.

Because nitrogen does not readily react with other materials, several industries use it as a "blanketing agent," which is a compound able to prevent unwanted reactions. For example, when nitrogen is used as a blanketing agent with embers, it prevents them from igniting. Nitrogen is therefore used to ensure product quality and improve plant safety. Oil producers use nitrogen to stimulate and pressurize wells. The gas also finds use in steel processing, food production, cooling, refrigeration and freezing systems, solvent recovery, chemical and glass production, and in the electronics and aerospace industries. Nitrogen production rebounded in 1996 after a decline in 1995.

Measured in terms of sales volume, the second most significant industrial gas in the 1990s was oxygen, which is used to intensify or control combustion in a variety of industries. Its other uses include speeding fermentation, providing life support, and controlling odors. Chemical manufacturers, brick makers, and metal fabricators all rely on oxygen. Innovative uses include processes aimed at restoring or maintaining environmental integrity. Oxygen is used in hazardous waste cleanup efforts, waste water treatment facilities, and coal gasification systems (a process designed to reduce the hazardous emissions associated with burning coal). One of the fastest growing areas of oxygen use in the 1990s, however, was as a replacement for chlorine in bleaching, especially by pulp and paper manufacturers because the oxygen process pollutes less.

INORGANIC PIGMENTS

As the inorganic pigments industry entered the 1990s, the largest single product manufactured was titanium dioxide. Titanium dioxide production relied on two different raw materials containing titanium: ilmenite and natural rutile. Both minerals were primarily mined in Australia and South Africa. Ilmenite contained less titanium than rutile, but it was more plentiful and less expensive.

The industry implemented several price increases in 1995, and 1996 saw a downturn in the market for titanium dioxide. The worldwide price index dropped several cents per pound. Pigments in general showed a moderate growth, indicating a mature market.

Demand for titanium dioxide is expected to grow from 2 to 4 percent annually to the year 2000. The U.S. market is slightly lower, with an expected growth rate of 1.8 percent per year. In 1996 the North American market for titanium dioxide was about 1.239 million metric tons per year and was expected to reach 1.538 metric tons by the year 2000. In 1996, the average selling price for titanium dioxide was $1,940 per metric ton, and the global average price was $1,947 per metric ton or roughly $1 per pound.

ENVIRONMENTAL ISSUES

In 1994 the Environmental Protection Agency announced that chemical companies in the United States would have to cut their manufacturing plants' toxic air pollution by almost 90 percent from 1990 levels. The rule, noted the *Detroit Free Press,* "requires the companies . . . to install equipment to better prevent evaporation and leaks of 112 toxic chemicals. . . . About 370 chemical plants in 38 states will be forced to cut toxic air pollution by a total of 506,000 tons, an EPA statement said." While the new rules, instituted as a part of the 1990 Clean Air Act, would involve significant expenditures on capital improvements for the affected companies, regulators noted that chemical companies have already taken significant steps to address the new requirements in anticipation of the announcement.

Environmental issues continued to affect the worldwide chlorine industry in 1997, matters that were clearly reflected in the peroxide market, which is linked to the pulp and paper market. Due to excessive pulp inventories in 1996, pulp prices declined. Prior to the crash, peroxide growth was forecast at 10-12 percent annually through 2000, but afterward, at only 5-8 percent.

The initial impetus for increased hydrogen peroxide demand in the pulp and paper industry was conversion of pulp mills from elemental chlorine use due to new EPA regulations, to either chlorine dioxide (which may be generated, in turn, from sodium chlorate) or hydrogen peroxide.

By the beginning of 1997, most U.S. pulp plants had stopped using elemental chlorine for bleaching and substituted chlorine dioxide to eliminate dioxin production. During the same period, a bill was introduced in Congress to force U.S. pulp plants to use totally chlorine free (TCF) bleaching processes, a move favored by many environmentalists as a means to reduce dioxin pollution. The EPA was therefore debating between two possible rules—to either allow chlorine-based plants to substitute chlorine dioxide or to require partial substitution of chlorine dioxide with oxygen. The Chlorine Chemistry Council and paper workers' unions supported the shift to chlorine dioxide, arguing that partial substitution of oxygen would be very costly (perhaps $1 billion) and potentially eliminate thousands of jobs.

The trend away from chlorine use was highly beneficial for the peroxide market, and by 1996 the six producers in North America (DuPont, Solvay, Degussa, Chemprox, FMC, and Eka Nobel) were gearing up for plant expansions to increase North American capacity to roughly 2 billion pounds by 1998, an increase of more than 800 million pounds over previous levels.

Questions about environmental degradation and the toxicity of heavy metals challenged the inorganic pigment industry throughout the 1980s and early 1990s. Heavy metals such as lead, cadmium, chromium, and mercury were associated with ailments including cancer and liver disease. Both the Congress and the EPA considered legislative and regulatory initiatives to control, limit, and in some cases ban, the use of several of the industry's essential raw materials. Some manufacturers responded by backing away from heavy-metal pigments. Others defended their formulations and offered evidence that if raw materials were banned, certain colors would become unavailable.

In addition to struggling with direct toxicity problems, pigment manufacturers faced charges claiming that their disposal of heavy-metals used in pigments were threatening the nation's water supplies. Products undergoing incineration or degradation in landfill sites created a potential hazard as heavy metals were released into the environment. As a result of this growing environmental concern, the Conference of North East Governors (representing nine northern states) and the legislatures in several other states began working toward bans on heavy metals in packaging materials. During the early 1990s, industry watchers expected the number of environmental regulations regarding the use of heavy metals in pigments to increase.

WORK FORCE

According to government statistics for 1992, the inorganic chemicals industry employed 88,000 workers. By 1995, the number of employees dropped to 73,700. Four states accounted for more than half the employment within the industry: South Carolina, Tennessee, Washington, and Ohio. Of the almost 700 companies classified in the industry, about 50 percent employed fewer than 20 people.

SIC 2813 - Industrial Gases
General Statistics

Year	Companies	Establishments		Employment			Compensation		Production ($ million)			
		Total	with 20 or more employees	Total (000)	Production Workers (000)	Hours (Mil)	Payroll ($ mil)	Wages ($/hr)	Cost of Materials	Value Added by Manufacture	Value of Shipments	Capital Invest.
1982	107	563	105	7.3	4.3	9.9	174.0	10.18	967.2	1,055.3	2,019.3	223.7
1983		561	116	7.2	3.9	8.8	168.1	10.25	959.9	1,169.6	2,111.9	107.5
1984		559	127	7.9	4.4	9.7	197.2	10.73	1,073.0	1,290.3	2,363.5	263.9
1985		557	139	8.5	4.5	10.5	223.3	10.95	949.1	1,466.7	2,416.0	212.5
1986		566	145	8.6	4.0	8.8	248.4	12.73	1,002.6	1,386.7	2,401.9	122.1
1987	103	594	135	8.1	4.0	8.5	241.4	13.56	1,052.9	1,572.5	2,617.8	104.3
1988		573	126	8.1	4.4	9.4	245.3	13.51	1,134.4	1,589.1	2,721.2	73.0
1989		576	143	9.9	4.7	10.0	261.4	14.00	1,087.2	1,686.2	2,731.5	121.0
1990		587	149	9.9	4.8	9.7	282.8	14.56	1,154.2	1,919.2	3,058.1	177.8
1991		650	144	9.2	4.9	10.4	300.2	14.33	1,148.9	2,047.0	3,193.9	289.7
1992	112	592	122	7.7	4.2	9.1	261.8	14.65	1,012.2	2,076.2	3,095.7	146.3
1993		616	129	7.8	4.1	8.9	275.2	15.02	1,092.7	2,353.2	3,435.7	163.7
1994		621P	142P	8.0	4.2	9.2	289.3	15.72	1,013.2	2,388.9	3,415.7	174.5
1995		626P	144P	8.8P	4.5P	9.3P	313.2P	16.44P	1,059.3P	2,497.6P	3,571.2P	162.9P
1996		632P	146P	8.9P	4.5P	9.3P	323.1P	16.92P	1,094.7P	2,581.0P	3,690.3P	162.2P
1997		638P	147P	9.0P	4.5P	9.3P	333.0P	17.39P	1,130.0P	2,664.3P	3,809.5P	161.5P
1998		644P	149P	9.0P	4.5P	9.3P	342.9P	17.87P	1,165.4P	2,747.6P	3,928.6P	160.8P

Sources: 1982, 1987, 1992 *Economic Census; Annual Survey of Manufactures,* 83-86, 88-91, 93-94. Establishment counts for non-Census years are from *County Business Patterns;* establishment values for 83-84 are extrapolations. 'P's show projections by the editors. Industries reclassified in 87 will not have data for prior years.

One of the major issues confronting the industry's labor force was worker health and safety. The chemical industry has had a long history of exposing its workers to hazardous situations. For example, in the latter half of the 1800s, the Leblanc method of reacting sulfuric acid on salt to produce alkali created hydrochloric acid gas as a by-product. The hydrochloric acid gas rotted workers' teeth, led to chronic bronchitis, and caused skin ailments. Moreover, industrial accidents involving chemicals often resulted in greater harm to workers and the environment than accidents in other industries.

SIC 2861
Occupations Employed by SIC 286 - Industrial Organic Chemicals

Occupation	% of Total 1994	Change to 2005
Chemical equipment controllers, operators	10.6	-5.2
Chemical plant & system operators	8.9	-5.2
Blue collar worker supervisors	7.4	-5.7
Science & mathematics technicians	7.0	-5.2
Maintenance repairers, general utility	4.3	-14.7
Chemists	3.8	-5.2
Chemical engineers	3.7	13.8
Secretaries, ex legal & medical	2.7	-13.7
Industrial machinery mechanics	2.3	4.3
Sales & related workers nec	1.9	-5.2
Helpers, laborers, & material movers nec	1.8	-5.2
General office clerks	1.8	-19.2
Precision instrument repairers	1.7	28.0
Crushing & mixing machine operators	1.7	-5.2
Engineering technicians & technologists nec	1.6	-5.2
General managers & top executives	1.3	-10.0
Industrial production managers	1.3	-5.2
Mechanical engineers	1.2	4.3
Electricians	1.2	-11.0
Engineering, mathematical, & science managers	1.1	7.7
Electrical & electronic technicians,technologists	1.1	-5.2
Managers & administrators nec	1.1	-5.2
Freight, stock, & material movers, hand	1.1	-24.2
Bookkeeping, accounting, & auditing clerks	1.0	-28.9
Plumbers, pipefitters, & steamfitters	1.0	-5.1

Source: Industry-Occupation Matrix, Bureau of Labor Statistics. These data relate to one or more 3-digit SIC industry groups rather than to a single 4-digit SIC. The change reported for each occupation to the year 2005 is a percent of growth or decline as estimated by the Bureau of Labor Statistics. The abbreviation nec stands for 'not elsewhere classified'.

To address the needs of workers, Congress passed the Occupational Safety and Health Act of 1970. The Act created the Occupational Safety and Health Administration (OSHA) within the U.S. Department of Labor. OSHA's responsibilities include establishing safe standards for chemical exposure and keeping workers informed of potential risks. Chemical companies also began to address safety needs with greater vigor and introduced increasing numbers of voluntary measures to help ensure employee and public safety.

RESEARCH AND TECHNOLOGY

As the chemicals industry evolved during the twentieth century, the cost of investigating and developing new products was very high. Many new compounds studied by researchers were rejected because they failed to meet expectations, were too expensive to produce, or posed safety problems. Another related problem was rapid obsolescence of products and related manufacturing methods. Because technologies changed so quickly, new products were sometimes outdated before their developing companies could recapture costs associated with research and development. Additionally, as technologies changed, many manufacturing methods also became obsolete.

By the 1990s, many products within this industrial classification were considered basic commodities. As a result, research activities to develop new products were conducted with less vigor than in other segments of the chemical industry. Instead of focusing on new product development, most research focused on ways to reduce production costs by reducing labor costs, cutting energy needs, improving process efficiencies, and finding new applications for existing products. Researchers also investigated ways to meet environmental mandates by curtailing emissions, putting waste products to work, recapturing materials, and rendering hazardous substances inert.

In the alkalies and chlorine sector, a new use for sulfuric acid, called the Santa Cruz In Situ Mining Research Project, was experimented with in 1996. This project demonstrated the environmental, technical, and economic feasibility of in situ, or "in place" mining. The goal was to reach copper that was buried too deeply and was of too low a grade to be mined by conventional methods. A dilute solution of sulfuric acid was injected nearly 1,600 feet below the earth's surface into undisturbed granite bedrock containing soluble copper oxide minerals. The solution was then recovered through wells and pumped to the surface where it was processed and re-injected to the mining zone in a closed loop.

Pollution abatement was one of the most rapidly developing areas of study within the industrial gases industry. Researchers were examining methods of improving waste water treatment by oxygen injection. Recovery systems using nitrogen to condense and recapture solvents and chemical vapors helped manufacturers come into compliance with the Clean Air Act Amendments of 1990. An innovative technology based on carbon dioxide offered promise for reducing the environmental impact of solvent use within the paint and coatings industry. Additionally, carbon dioxide-based refrigeration systems were introduced to replace systems that relied on chlorofluorocarbons (CFCs).

Research into new or refined uses for industrial gases also continued. Liquid nitrogen was being considered as a possible aid in reducing problems associated with cracking in structural concrete. Xenon provided sun-like brightness to meet the special lighting needs of airports, stadiums, the motion picture industry, and copying machine manufacturers. Other rare gases were also being developed for use in diagnostic technologies and pharmaceutical applications.

Much of the developing technology within the inorganic pigments industry attempted to lessen the risks such pigments presented to humans and the environment. One innovation, called silica encapsulation, involved encasing pigment particles or crystals within a shell of silica (a glass like substance). Researchers claimed that encapsulated lead chromate pigments were protected from chemical, photochemical, and thermal degradation. The encapsulation process also reduced their toxicity by making them less able to be absorbed by the body. Researchers also claimed that silica encapsulation improved the brightness and intensity of the pigments, making them better suited for use in high-temperature applications such as plastic manufacturing.

Other researchers were examining methods of producing low dust, low soluble cadmium pigments. One newly developed product line contained less than one part per million of soluble cadmium, falling under the threshold defined by the EPA to identify a hazardous waste material. Low dust products also helped industry manufacturers to meet the standards set by the Occupational Safety and Health Administration.

AMERICA AND THE WORLD

Chlorine production in the United States accounts for almost 30 percent of the world's capacity, but there is little international movement of chlorine because of difficulties related to its transportation and storage. Producers generally prefer to erect production facilities in regions where demand exists.

Analysts predicted that worldwide chlorine demand would grow at a rate of less than 1 percent per year, but they forecasted wide regional fluctuations. Japan, Europe, and Canada were expected to experience declining demand for chlorine. High demand growth rates, however, were predicted for the Middle East, where annual increases of about 9 percent were expected. Other regions with potentially rapid growth rates were the Asian Pacific, Latin America, and Africa.

The global market for industrial gases was estimated at $20 billion in the early 1990s. Because of problems related to the transportation and storage of gas products, most production occurred close to its point of use. There was, therefore, very little international trade in industrial gases. Instead of transporting products, large international corporations functioned by operating production facilities in many countries.

The types and volumes of gases provided in an area depended on the development of the region's economy. Regions with emerging economies typically required high volumes of oxygen, whereas countries with economies based on high-technology and service, needed greater amounts of nitrogen. According to the BOC Group, the ratio of nitrogen sales to oxygen sales could be used as a measurement of a nation's industrial development.

Industry estimates suggested that titanium dioxide accounted for about 30 percent of global pigment sales,

SIC 2819 - Industrial Inorganic Chemicals, nec
Industry Data by State

| State | Establish-ments | Shipments | | | Employment | | | | Cost as % of Shipments | Investment per Employee ($) |
		Total ($ mil)	% of U.S.	Per Establ.	Total Number	% of U.S.	Per Establ.	Wages ($/hour)		
Tennessee	20	1,909.2	10.5	95.5	10,600	13.4	530	15.53	23.5	-
Texas	53	1,348.5	7.4	25.4	4,100	5.2	77	17.90	62.6	20,732
New Jersey	34	1,033.8	5.7	30.4	2,400	3.0	71	15.11	59.2	8,833
California	64	958.7	5.3	15.0	2,700	3.4	42	15.09	40.8	12,593
Ohio	38	957.8	5.3	25.2	3,400	4.3	89	16.91	52.0	4,176
Louisiana	27	924.9	5.1	34.3	2,200	2.8	81	16.44	56.2	59,000
Kentucky	10	756.1	4.2	75.6	2,900	3.7	290	16.89	46.5	1,414
Illinois	32	631.6	3.5	19.7	2,100	2.7	66	15.03	47.5	18,048
North Carolina	18	542.8	3.0	30.2	2,400	3.0	133	18.44	34.0	18,667
Alabama	20	502.2	2.8	25.1	1,700	2.1	85	16.35	54.1	16,059

*Source: 1992 Economic Census. The states are in descending order of shipments or establishments (if shipment data are missing for the majority). The symbol (D) appears when data are withheld to prevent disclosure of competitive information. States marked with (D) are sorted by number of establishments. A dash (-) indicates that the data element cannot be calculated; * indicates the midpoint of a range.*

and demand for the white pigment was expected to grow at approximately 3 percent per year. Forecasters expected new global production capacity, estimated to add 850,000 tons between 1990 and 1995, to result in a slight over-supply and keep prices down.

Western Europe, however, was expected to see reduced production. Approximately 73 percent of the region's existing capacity was based on the sulfate process, which was subject to increasing criticism from environmental groups. A European Union directive to stop ocean dumping of wastes, slated to take effect at the end of 1993, was expected to increase operating expenses by about 15 percent and force older plants out of the global market.

ASSOCIATIONS AND SOCIETIES

AMERICAN CHEMICAL SOCIETY
1155 16th St. NW
Washington, DC 20036
Phone: (800) 227-5558 or (202) 872-4600

ASSOCIATION OF CONSULTING CHEMISTS AND CHEMICAL ENGINEERS
295 Madison Ave., 27 Fl.
New York, NY 10017
Phone: (212) 983-3160
Fax: (212) 983-3161

CHEMICAL MANAGEMENT AND RESOURCES ASSOCIATION
60 Bay St., Ste. 702
Staten Island, NY 10305
Phone: (718) 876-8800
Members are individuals engaged in chemical market research.

CHEMICAL MANUFACTURERS ASSOCIATION
2501 M St. NW
Washington, DC 20037
Phone: (202) 887-1100
Fax: (202) 887-1237

NATIONAL ASSOCIATION OF CHEMICAL DISTRIBUTORS
1101 17th St. NW, Ste. 1200
Washington, DC 20036
Phone: (202) 296-9200
Fax: (202) 296-0023

PERIODICALS AND NEWSLETTERS

AMERICAN OIL CHEMISTS' SOCIETY JOURNAL
PO Box 3489
Champaign, IL 61821-0489
Phone: (217) 359-2344
Fax: (217) 351-8091

Monthly. $185.00 per year. Includes INFORM: International News on Fats, Oils and Related Materials.

CHEMICAL PROCESSING
Putman Publishing Co.
301 E. Erie St.
Chicago, IL 60611
Phone: (312) 644-2020
Fax: (312) 644-1131
12 times a year. Free to qualified personnel; others, $45.00 per year.

CHEMICAL WEEK
Chemical Week Associates
888 7th Ave., 26 Fl.
New York, NY 10106-2698
Phone: (212) 621-4900
Fax: (212) 621-4949
Weekly. $99.00 per year. Includes annual Buyers' Guide.

CPI PURCHASING: THE MAGAZINE ABOUT BUYING FOR THE CHEMICAL AND PROCESS INDUSTRIES
Cahners Publishing Co., Inc.
275 Washington St.
Newton, MA 02158-1630
Phone: (800) 662-7776 or (617) 964-3030
Fax: (617) 558-4327
Monthly. $74.95 per year.

JOURNAL OF CHEMICAL INFORMATION AND COMPUTER SCIENCES
American Chemical Society
1155 16th St. NW
Washington, DC 20036
Phone: (800) 227-5558 or (202) 872-4600
Fax: (202) 872-6067
Bimonthly. Members, $20.00 per year; non-members, $180.00 per year

DATABASES

CA SEARCH
Chemical Abstracts Service
2540 Olentangy River Rd.
Columbus, OH 43210
Phone: (614) 447-3731
Fax: (614) 447-3751
Guide to chemical literature, 1967 to present. Inquire as to online cost and availability.

CHEM-BANK
Silver Platter Information, Inc.
100 River Ridge Rd.
Norwood, MA 02062
Phone: (800) 343-0064 or (617) 769-2599
Fax: (617) 769-8763
Quarterly. $1,350.00 per year. Provides CD-ROM information on hazardous substances, including 96,000 chemicals in the Registry of Toxic Effects of Chemical Substances *and 60,000 materials covered by the* Toxic Substances Control Act Initial Inventory.

CITIBASE (CITICORP ECONOMIC DATABASE)

FAME Software Corp.
77 Water St., 9 Fl.
New York, NY 10005
Phone: (212) 898-7800
Fax: (212) 742-8956
Presents over 6,000 statistical series relating to business, industry, finance, and economics. Includes series from Survey of Current Business *and many other sources. Time period is 1947 to date, with daily updates. Inquire as to online cost and availability.*

DRI CHEMICAL FORECAST

DRI/McGraw-Hill, Data Products Division
24 Hartwell Ave.
Lexington, MA 02173
Phone: (800) 541-9914 or (617) 863-5100
Supply-demand and price forecasts are given quarterly and annually for over 120 U.S. chemical products. Quarterly forecasts generally extend 3 years, while annual forecasts cover 5 to 10 years. Inquire as to online cost and availability.

U.S. FORECASTS

Information Access Co.
362 Lakeside Dr.
Foster City, CA 94404
Phone: (800) 321-6388 or (415) 358-4643
Fax: (415) 358-4759
Provides numeric abstracts of a wide range of published forecasts relating to specific U.S. products, markets, and industries. Time period is 1971 to date. Inquire as to online cost and availability.

STATISTICS SOURCES

ANNUAL REVIEW OF THE CHEMICAL INDUSTRY

United Nations
2 United Nations Plz., Rm. DC2-853
New York, NY 10017
Phone: (800) 253-9646 or (212) 963-8302
Fax: (212) 963-3489
Annual. $42.00.

UNITED STATES CENSUS OF MANUFACTURES

U.S. Bureau of the Census
Washington, DC 20233-0800
Phone: (301) 457-4100
Fax: (301) 457-3842
Quinquennial. Results presented in reports, tape, CD-ROM, and diskette files.

GENERAL WORKS

CHEMICAL REGULATION REPORTER: A WEEKLY REVIEW OF AFFECTING CHEMICAL USERS AND MANUFACTURERS

Bureau of National Affairs, Inc.
1250 23rd St. NW
Washington, DC 20037
Phone: (800) 372-1033 or (202) 452-4200
Fax: (202) 822-8092
Weekly. $1,500.00 per year. Six Volumes. Looseleaf.

CHEMICAL SUBSTANCES CONTROL

Bureau of National Affairs, Inc.
1250 23rd St. NW
Washington, DC 20037
Phone: (800) 372-1033 or (202) 452-4200
Fax: (202) 822-8092
Biweekly. $610.00 per year. Looseleaf. Covers legal aspects of chemical substance management.

CHEMICAL WEEK-BUYER'S GUIDE

Chemical Week Associates
888 7th Ave., 26 Fl.
New York, NY 10106-2698
Phone: (212) 621-4900
Fax: (212) 621-4949 or (212) 621-4950
Annual. $99.00. Included in subscription to Chemical Week.

CPI PURCHASING CHEMICALS YELLOW PAGES

Cahners Publishing Co.
275 Washington St.
Newton, MA 02158
Phone: (617) 558-4642
Fax: (617) 558-4506
Annual. $40.00. Formerly Chemicals Directory.

FURTHER READING

Air Products and Chemicals, Inc. *1996 Annual Report.* Allentown, PA, 1996.

Brand, Tony. "Bleaches Brighten Abroad." Special Report, *Chemical Market Reporter,* 27 January 1997.

Chapman, Peter. "Chemical Outlook '96: Inorganic Chemicals." *Chemical Marketing Reporter* 249, no. 3 (15 January 1996): 14.

"Inorganic Chemicals." *Standard And Poor's Industry Surveys.* New York: Standard and Poor's Corporation, 1997.

"Inorganic Pigments." *Standard & Poor's Industry Surveys.* New York: Standard & Poor's Corporation, 1997.

"Peroxide Producers Jolted by Pulp Crash." *Chemical Marketing Reporter* 249, no. 8 (19 February 1996): 3, 23.

"Production By the U.S. Chemical Industry: Production Growth Sputtered in Most Sectors." *Chemical and Engineering News* 74, no. 26 (24 June 1996) 40-46.

Scott, Alex. "Chlor-Alkali Standards Proposed." *Chemical Week,* 12 March 1997.

U.S. Bureau of the Census. *1995 Annual Survey of Manufacturers.* Washington: GPO, 1997.

U.S. Bureau of the Census. "Industrial Gases." *Current Industrial Reports.* Washington: GPO, 1997.

Ward's Business Directory of U.S. Public and Private Companies. Detroit: Gale, 1997. ━━►

U.S. manufacturers produced $11 billion worth of industrial chemicals in 1993, or about 25 percent of global output. The 180 U.S. companies employed 23,000 workers and exported almost $1.4 billion worth of products per year in the early 1990s. Industry output provided an important supply of base manufacturing material for pharmaceutical, dye, fuel, and agricultural sectors.

Industry sales surged throughout the 1980s, as revenue jumped from about $7 billion to over $11 billion by the end of the decade. Prices declined in the early 1990s because of large capacity additions that came into effect. During the early 1990s, temporary price upswings caused by the war in the Persian Gulf were the only relief periods for the industry. Sales improved again by 1994, and into 1995, as prices and margins began to rise. This period was the industry's best financial performance since the late 1980s. By mid-1995, prices fell again. In 1996, varying levels of growth were observed in all major segments of the industry. One reason for the instability of the industry was the inability to predict the supply and demand for organic materials.

CHEMICALS, INDUSTRIAL ORGANIC

SIC 2860

Having endured a period of economic turbulence in the early to mid-1990s, the industrial organic chemicals industry was looking to maintain and sustain modest growth in most sectors through the turn of the twenty-first century. Overall employment levels will continue to drop, following a trend predicted by the U.S. Bureau of labor Statistics of as much as 25 to 35 percent from 1990 to 2005.

Top 10 MOST PRODUCED CHEMICALS

Ranked by: Production in 1995, in billions of pounds.

1. Sulfuric acid, with 95.36 billion pounds
2. Nitrogen, 68.04
3. Oxygen, 53.48
4. Ethylene, 46.97
5. Lime, 41.23
6. Ammonia, 35.60
7. Phosphoric acid, 26.19
7. Sodium hydroxide, 26.19
9. Propylene, 25.69
10. Chlorine, 25.09

Source: *Chemical & Engineering News*, April 8, 1996, p. 17.

For example, benzene, styrene, and mixed xylenes saturated the market from July through December of 1996, while cyclohexane and phenol were not being produced quick enough to meet demands. Demand for some organic products, such as toluene fluctuated from year to year making it difficult to gauge production.

INDUSTRY OUTLOOK

After steady growth through 1989, industrial organic chemical manufacturers suffered serious setbacks in the early 1990s. A U.S. and global economic recession slowed profit growth, as the value of petrochemical and related products sales dropped 1.5 percent in 1990 to $54.1 billion. Sales rose just 1 percent in both 1991 and 1992 (using inflation adjusted dollars), and overall organic chemical output rose only slightly between 1990 and 1992. Moreover, this tepid growth, was offset by stagnant prices and declining profits. From its peak of nearly 10 percent in 1988, chemical industry profit margins sank to about 5 percent in 1992.

Compounding industry woes in the early 1990s was excess production capacity, the result of expansion in the previous half decade. Oversupply was still depressing organic prices into the mid-1990s, thus eliminating profit growth. Despite ongoing successful efforts to increase productivity and improve products, U.S. competitors were unable to overcome the effects of the latest downturn. Even a slow but steady increase in organic exports did little to alleviate the impact of sluggish domestic markets. After all, U.S. imports rose at a rate about 15 times greater than U.S. exports in 1992, augmenting downward price pressures.

In an effort to buoy earnings, domestic competitors continued restructuring in the 1990s. Companies were cutting costs out of every phase of the production process, often leading to massive lay-offs. DuPont, for example, announced a work force reduction of as many as 4,500 employees in late 1993, adding to about 5,500 lay-offs made by that company since 1991. Likewise, Dow Chemical eliminated 4,700 jobs in 1993, and Air Products reduced its work force by 1,300. Many companies were also restructuring by selling unprofitable operations and focusing on their core competencies.

While revenues improved and prices gained slightly in 1993, overcapacity and weak markets persisted into 1994. Industry shipments grew between 1 and 2 percent in 1993, and were expected to increase similarly in the near term. This growth was expected to eventually reduce overcapacity, however, allowing manufacturers to raise prices slightly. The effects of a reduction in oversupply may be offset by the diminished stature of U.S. producers in the global marketplace. U.S. firms will increasingly be forced to shift production from high-volume commodity-like organics to low-volume specialty and high-tech compounds that demand higher prices.

PERFORMANCE OF KEY SEGMENTS

Shipment growth rates of ethylene were expected to be at 3 to 4 percent through the year 2000. Ethylene output was 47 billion pounds in 1995, an increase of 5.3 percent from the 44.6 billion pounds of 1994. Production was up 6 percent in 1994, even though there were supply problems. In 1995, the industry operated at 94.5 percent capacity, versus 93.1 percent in 1994. In 1992, domestic competitors made about 41 billion pounds of ethylene valued at over $8 billion—more than 15 percent of industry revenues. As ethylene demand continues to grow, the industry must increase capacity. At the expected growth rate of 3 to 4 percent, the industry will need to add a new facility each year to prevent a material shortage. However, no new major plants are expected to be built until 1998. Exxon Corp. plans to open an ethylene plant in Texas in 1998 to produce about 1.5 billion pounds of ethylene per year.

A joint venture involving Lyondell Petrochemical, Union Carbide Corp., and Quantum Chemical is also expected to open a new Texas operation in 1998. This plant will also produce about 1.5 billion pounds of ethylene per year. These three companies combined produce and use about 25 percent of the U.S. capacity of ethylene, and they intend to use the new plant for their own needs.

Production of propylene rose 7.3 percent in 1995, and at year's end, inventories of propylene were twice those of 1994. Selling prices dropped from the mid-1995 high of 23.75 cents to 16.25 cents per pound. Long-term propylene demand is expected to rise at about 3.5 percent per year through the year 2000. Though the United States produces more than 3 billion pounds of butadiene per year, it has historically imported most of its butadiene from Europe. Butadiene production rose about 7 percent in 1994 and 9 percent in 1995. At the end of 1995, the industry inventory was at a relatively high level of 271 million pounds—12 percent higher than 1994. Therefore, lower prices were expected in 1996.

The price of methanol almost tripled in 1994 reaching $1.55 per gallon, but by the end of 1994, it was back down to 42 cents. Methanol production in 1995 was slightly higher than the previous year with the largest producers being Methanex Corp., Terra Industries, Borden Chemical and Plastics, Lyondell Petrochemical, Quantum Chemical, Hoechst-Celanese, Georgia Gulf, and Ashland Petroleum.

MTBE production topped 10.5 billion pounds in the early 1990s as prices were driven up by the Clean Air Act Amendments of 1990 which required the use of gasolines containing oxygenates such as MTBE. Beginning in 1992, the sale of oxygenated fuels was required during the winter months in 37 U.S. metropolitan areas that did not meet the federal air standards for carbon monoxide. In January 1995, year-round use began in nine regions as dictated by the Clean Air Act. The demand of MTBE was not as high as expected in 1995, though, as some states were able to get out of the program. Also, higher methane costs made it less desirable than other octane enhancers. Prices were expected to return to pre-1994 levels to finish the 1990s. Major producers of methanol included Beaumont Methanol, Borden, Lyondell Petrochemical, Quantum Chemical, and Georgia Gulf.

From 1982 to 1997, global demand for benzene doubled, and steady growth was predicted to continue at about 5 percent through the year 2000. Demand in 1996 was more than 27.0 million metric tons and was expected to increase to about 28.5 metric tons in 1997. The top U.S. benzene producers, including Amoco, Dow, Exxon, and Shell, controlled roughly half, or one billion gallons, of the total 2.4 billion gallons of U.S. benzene production.

Demand for cyclohexane was expected to grow from its 1.0 million metric tons in 1996 to approximately 1.1 million tons in 1997. No new cyclohexane plants were expected to come into operation until 1999, when Chevron planned to open a 75 million-gallon Saudi facility. The market will have little impetus to change until this Facility is built. The end of 1996 saw toluene at its highest price levels since early 1995. This increase was because toluene was the aromatic of choice for blenders who were adding octane to their gasolines.

1996 saw an increase in crude prices and a drop in chemical prices. Many producers had to operate reformers at minimum levels, which significantly cut the production of mixed xylenes. After reducing inventories and production levels, the supplies of mixed xylenes were decreased allowing prices to rise again. Worldwide demand of styrene was approximately 17 million metric tons in 1996. With annual growth at 4.5 percent, demand should approach 18 million metric tons in 1997. That same year, the U.S. demand for phenol was more than 4.1 billion pounds. By the year 2000, if growth remained at 3 percent, it was expected to be over 4.7 billion pounds.

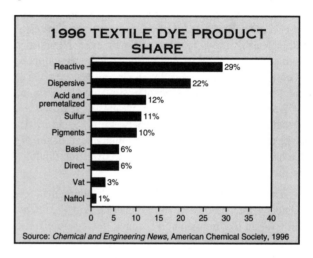

Source: *Chemical and Engineering News*, American Chemical Society, 1996

Demand for synthetic organic pigments and dyes will increase, but U.S. production will likely remain

SIC 2865 - Cyclic Crudes and Intermediates
General Statistics

Year	Com-panies	Establishments		Employment			Compensation		Production ($ million)			
		Total	with 20 or more employees	Total (000)	Production Workers (000)	Hours (Mil)	Payroll ($ mil)	Wages ($/hr)	Cost of Materials	Value Added by Manufacture	Value of Shipments	Capital Invest.
1982	143	189	134	27.3	16.0	32.3	731.0	12.30	5,007.8	2,031.5	7,138.2	454.7
1983		187	132	26.4	15.6	31.2	749.5	13.12	5,036.9	2,333.8	7,398.0	532.4
1984		185	130	23.3	14.0	28.5	699.1	13.83	5,172.1	2,679.7	7,762.0	261.9
1985		182	128	23.4	13.7	27.5	728.9	14.31	5,328.9	2,824.2	8,209.8	383.4
1986		183	123	22.0	12.7	26.3	735.1	15.04	4,242.3	2,687.9	7,013.4	332.6
1987	131	186	121	22.8	13.4	27.6	786.6	15.76	5,502.7	3,414.2	8,859.4	378.8
1988		186	123	23.9	13.9	29.5	877.8	16.01	6,121.7	4,252.5	10,301.9	428.3
1989		181	126	23.3	13.9	29.5	873.6	16.34	7,020.7	3,794.2	10,812.0	584.9
1990		185	130	23.4	13.9	29.6	910.9	16.84	7,027.7	3,980.1	10,892.6	954.9
1991		190	132	23.5	14.1	30.9	962.0	16.96	6,796.4	3,830.3	10,651.8	713.9
1992	150	206	143	22.2	13.2	29.1	934.6	17.10	6,311.4	3,333.0	9,572.8	540.7
1993		213	137	23.3	13.4	28.9	1,028.1	18.27	6,457.2	3,710.6	10,177.0	669.5
1994		200P	134P	22.7	13.1	28.9	1,017.6	18.17	6,954.1	4,205.8	11,151.5	564.6
1995		202P	134P	22.0P	12.9P	28.8P	1,048.5P	19.01P	7,246.6P	4,382.7P	11,620.6P	711.7P
1996		204P	135P	21.7P	12.7P	28.7P	1,077.1P	19.48P	7,459.9P	4,511.7P	11,962.7P	738.6P
1997		205P	135P	21.5P	12.6P	28.7P	1,105.6P	19.96P	7,673.3P	4,640.7P	12,304.7P	765.5P
1998		207P	136P	21.2P	12.4P	28.6P	1,134.1P	20.43P	7,886.6P	4,769.7P	12,646.8P	792.5P

Sources: 1982, 1987, 1992 *Economic Census*; *Annual Survey of Manufactures*, 83-86, 88-91, 93-94. Establishment counts for non-Census years are from *County Business Patterns*; establishment values for 83-84 are extrapolations. 'P's show projections by the editors. Industries reclassified in 87 will not have data for prior years.

stagnant, or decline, as exports flood the market. Pharmaceutical intermediates and fuel additives will offer some of the greatest profit potential, as will environmentally safe compounds. In order to remain competitive in the global markets of the 1990s, U.S. producers have been forced to focus their efforts on the development of high-tech, high-margin specialty intermediates and dyes. Consumers of large-volume, low-tech, commodity-like aromatics, intermediates, and dyes will continue to seek low-cost producers in emerging nations.

REGULATORY ISSUES

While increasing federal and state regulations posed an ongoing challenge to chemical industry participants, positive signs indicated that the industry was successfully clearing these hurdles and was even benefiting from some laws. The overall chemical industry reduced its emissions of TRI wastes by 34 percent between 1988 and 1991 and expected to display similar reductions in 1992 and 1993. Water and air emissions were down by 19 and 29 percent, respectively, between 1988 and 1991, while underground injections had fallen a significant 34 percent. During the same period, moreover, total industry production climbed 11 percent.

Despite industry gains, chemical pollutants remained a major concern for regulators, and President Bill Clinton's administration planned to step-up efforts to reduce toxic emissions. Some regulations, though, were expected to boost industry profits. The Clean Air Act Amendments of 1990, for example, required automobile carbon-monoxide emissions to fall below certain levels by 1995. As a result, the demand for organic gasoline additives that allow such reductions was forecast to balloon.

Besides environmental restrictions, manufacturers were also burdened with increased costs related to new safety initiatives. The EPA's proposed risk management rule, for example, was pending in 1994. This law was designed to prevent, detect, and respond to the release of extremely hazardous substances from chemical plants that affected neighboring communities. Companies would be required to develop emergency response plans and implement new prevention programs under the proposal.

A similar Occupational Health and Safety Administration (OSHA) law, passed by Congress in 1992, was aimed at preventing accidents in the work place. OSHA estimated that its new law would cost about $863 million per year between 1992 and 1997. The EPA rule, according to government estimates, would cost $503 million in the first year but would save $890 million in environmental damage and response costs. Organic chemical producers also anticipated expenses starting in 1994 as a result of a CMA initiative. The CMA's Responsible Care Program would require its members to file safety incident reports for manufacturing mishaps.

Information submitted to the EPA in 1996 showed that emissions of toxic chemicals had decreased more than 60 percent between 1988 and 1994. Member companies of the Chemical Manufacturing Association (CMA) cut releases to the water, air, and land by more than 400 million pounds.

The Toxic Release Inventory of 1994 showed that 49 percent of the chemicals on the inventory were recycled or recovered for energy, 44 percent were treated, and 7 percent were released to the environment. Due to the industry's pollution prevention efforts, air releases were cut from 546 million pounds in 1988 to 230 million pounds in 1994—a 58 percent reduction. Surface water discharges were reduced to 7 million pounds in 1994—an 87 percent improvement over the 53 million pounds released in 1988. Land disposal declined 43 percent, from 77 million pounds to 28 million pounds.

The EPA considered underground injection wells "safer than virtually all other waste disposal practices." To dispose of highly diluted wastes, they were injected into EPA-permitted wells, drilled deep into special geologic formations that contained, and in some cases neutralized the waste. This remained the largest waste disposal system reported to the TRI, and CMA companies cut the annual amount of waste disposed this way by nearly 1 billion pounds since 1988—a 76 percent reduction. CMA members reduced the emissions and off-site transfers of 17 high priority chemicals in 1994, ahead of the deadline set by the EPA for 1995.

In 1994, the EPA added 286 chemicals to its inventory list, nearly doubling its size. The CMA contended that some of these were innocuous, and the EPA stood the risk of confusing the public with what was truly hazardous and what was not.

ORGANIZATION AND STRUCTURE

The chemical industry is divided into organic and inorganic substances. Inorganic chemicals—which are derived from the inanimate material of the earth's crust—include compounds such as sulfuric acid, sulfur, phosphoric acid, and hydrogen peroxide. Organic chemicals are so named because in the industry's early days they were obtained from living organisms. Today they are derived from substances that contain carbon—such as petroleum, coal, and natural gas. Petroleum-based chemicals, or petrochemicals, account for about 80 percent of industry output by weight and 50 percent of production by value.

Organic chemicals, particularly petrochemicals, play an indispensable role in modern society. They are essential ingredients to plastics, synthetic fibers, rubber, fertilizers, and chemical intermediates, which are converted into a plethora of consumer and industrial products. They are the primary building blocks of important materials supporting health, food, transportation, and communication industries. Organic substances have also made possible many important specialty items—such as protective clothing and materials used for space exploration.

Organics constituted about 66 percent, or $54 billion, of the $81 billion chemical industry in 1992. Inorganic and agricultural chemicals made up the remainder of production. Likewise, the chemical industry represented about 46 percent of the overall chemicals and related products industry. Other segments of the general industry include synthetic materials—such as plastic and fibers—and chemical products—like paint, drugs, and soap.

Because organic chemicals are used to make so many products within the overall chemical and related products divisions, the industry eludes clear definition. Most industrial organic chemicals, in fact, are consumed by chemical-related businesses. The remaining organic output was used by numerous manufacturing sectors. Steel and aluminum mills, paper mills, semiconductor manufacturers, drug companies, carpet mills, and battery

producers were relatively large customers. Other chemical uses included the production of items such as pipe, photographic equipment, electrical insulation, and food containers.

WORK FORCE

Approximately 100,000 workers served the industrial organic chemical industry in 1992. This represented a decline of about 10 percent since the early 1980s. Production workers accounted for about 76,000 of this group. Their numbers declined 6 percent in 1992 and averaged an annual reduction rate of 1 percent between 1982 and 1992. Largely to blame for cutbacks in both white and blue collar jobs were productivity increases achieved by manufacturers. Efficiency gains in the overall chemical industry averaged about 4 percent per year between 1983 and 1992, which was more than enough to offset gains from increased output. Furthermore, productivity jumped an impressive 6.4 percent in 1992, compared to average gains of just 2.9 percent in all other U.S. manufacturing businesses.

Employment growth in the organic chemical industry is expected to remain weak, and future employment prospects are bleak. Although output was rising going into 1994 and some firms were adding production workers, major producers continued to announce lay-offs, particularly of white collar management employees. Blue collar workers that will suffer most from long term

SIC 2869 - Industrial Organic Chemicals, nec
General Statistics

Year	Companies	Establishments		Employment			Compensation		Production ($ million)			
		Total	with 20 or more employees	Total (000)	Production Workers (000)	Hours (Mil)	Payroll ($ mil)	Wages ($/hr)	Cost of Materials	Value Added by Manufacture	Value of Shipments	Capital Invest.
1982	488	688	376	111.8	65.0	131.1	3,191.3	13.08	19,989.0	10,093.5	30,394.4	2,580.5
1983		670	379	106.7	62.9	128.1	3,237.1	13.87	21,210.5	12,017.4	33,262.0	1,821.6
1984		652	382	103.4	60.7	124.3	3,395.6	14.73	23,112.9	13,054.8	35,777.0	1,617.7
1985		635	384	96.5	56.3	115.6	3,293.3	15.31	20,948.8	11,875.9	33,061.7	1,613.5
1986		619	383	86.7	51.3	106.6	3,097.2	15.88	17,778.7	11,822.2	29,759.7	1,491.0
1987*	491	699	431	100.3	57.9	122.4	3,696.4	16.03	24,226.0	17,902.1	42,189.1	1,986.9
1988		685	432	97.1	56.9	122.3	3,717.2	16.62	27,102.2	22,448.1	49,103.6	2,753.6
1989		651	419	100.0	58.3	125.1	3,944.8	17.17	29,433.1	25,299.1	54,512.4	3,484.2
1990		648	424	103.2	58.8	126.2	4,216.3	17.93	30,091.0	24,492.4	54,160.0	4,156.2
1991		661	421	101.0	58.4	125.0	4,403.0	18.61	30,671.3	22,248.0	53,069.3	4,537.6
1992	489	705	428	100.1	57.4	126.3	4,504.8	19.07	31,860.6	22,511.7	54,254.2	4,216.6
1993		695	429	97.5	57.5	127.0	4,503.0	19.01	30,666.7	22,674.8	53,364.2	3,358.3
1994		683P	425P	89.3	52.6	116.2	4,501.0	20.74	33,449.2	24,328.6	57,670.5	2,958.9
1995		684P	424P	94.4P	55.2P	122.9P	4,798.0P	20.90P	34,299.9P	24,947.4P	59,137.2P	4,096.2P
1996		686P	424P	93.5P	54.8P	122.7P	4,934.1P	21.51P	35,182.4P	25,589.2P	60,658.8P	4,243.8P
1997		687P	423P	92.6P	54.3P	122.5P	5,070.1P	22.12P	36,064.9P	26,231.1P	62,180.3P	4,391.5P
1998		689P	423P	91.7P	53.9P	122.3P	5,206.2P	22.73P	36,947.4P	26,872.9P	63,701.8P	4,539.2P

Sources: 1982, 1987, 1992 Economic Census; Annual Survey of Manufactures, 83-86, 88-91, 93-94. Establishment counts are from County Business Patterns for non-Census years; establishment counts for 83-84 are extrapolations. * indicates that industry content changed in 87; earlier years use 77 SICs. 'P's mark projections.

trends, however. Positions for chemical equipment controllers, which account for a full 9 percent of the organic chemical industry work force, will fall by 25 percent between 1990 and 2005, according to the Bureau of Labor statistics. In fact, jobs for most production workers—such as technicians, supervisors, and machine operators—are expected to plummet by 5 to 35 percent by 2005.

SIC 2812
Occupations Employed by SIC 281 - Industrial Inorganic Chemicals

Occupation	% of Total 1994	Change to 2005
Chemical equipment controllers, operators	7.8	-15.9
Blue collar worker supervisors	5.4	-5.3
Management support workers nec	5.3	-6.6
Chemical plant & system operators	4.7	-6.6
Science & mathematics technicians	3.8	-6.6
Secretaries, ex legal & medical	3.3	-15.0
Chemical engineers	3.3	2.8
Maintenance repairers, general utility	3.0	-15.9
Industrial machinery mechanics	3.0	2.7
Truck drivers light & heavy	2.8	-3.7
Engineers nec	2.3	40.1
Sales & related workers nec	2.3	-6.6
General office clerks	2.0	-20.3
Chemists	2.0	-6.6
General managers & top executives	1.9	-11.4
Inspectors, testers, & graders, precision	1.9	-6.6
Managers & administrators nec	1.8	-6.6
Industrial production managers	1.7	-6.6
Engineering, mathematical, & science managers	1.7	6.1
Packaging & filling machine operators	1.6	-6.6
Crushing & mixing machine operators	1.5	-6.6
Mechanical engineers	1.3	2.8
Helpers, laborers, & material movers nec	1.3	-6.6
Electricians	1.2	-12.3
Machine operators nec	1.1	-17.7
Plant & system operators nec	1.1	-17.5
Precision instrument repairers	1.0	-6.6
Accountants & auditors	1.0	-6.6

Source: Industry-Occupation Matrix, Bureau of Labor Statistics. These data relate to one or more 3-digit SIC industry groups rather than to a single 4-digit SIC. The change reported for each occupation to the year 2005 is a percent of growth or decline as estimated by the Bureau of Labor Statistics. The abbreviation nec stands for 'not elsewhere classified'.

Jobs for white collar workers and support staff will also fall. The demand for administrators and managers will decline 14 percent between 1990 and 2005, and clerical jobs will plunge almost 25 percent. General management and top executive positions will drop by 18 percent. Even chemists will see opportunities erode by about 6 percent. On the bright side, some engineering jobs will rise 3 percent. Sales and marketing positions, moreover, will jump 5 percent. The need for systems analysts and computer scientists in this industry are expected to increase by 22 percent by 2005.

AMERICA AND THE WORLD

The U.S. industrial organic chemical industry is a large part of a global industry and was shipping over $11 billion worth of output overseas during the mid-1990s. American manufacturers produced more than 25 percent of global organic output in the early 1990s and accounted for one-quarter of all U.S. chemical exports. Chemical exports, in turn, represented 10 percent of total U.S. merchandise exports. The U.S. organics industry remains the largest and most technologically advanced in the world. Its supremacy has waned considerably since the 1950s, however, when U.S. organic producers supplied more than 50 percent of global output.

The largest foreign buyer of U.S. petrochemicals in 1991 was Canada, consuming 11.3 percent of exported shipments. Japan, the second largest importer, purchased 9.6 percent of all petrochemical exports, while China represented 8.7 percent of the foreign market. Taiwan and Belgium each bought about 7 percent of U.S. exports. East Asia was the largest region of U.S. organic consumption, constituting 25 percent of overseas orders. The European Community represented a combined 23 percent of foreign demand.

Despite the strength of the U.S. organic industry, foreign competition continued to erode its comparative might. Although American companies managed to boost organic exports again in 1992 by about 1 percent, imports advanced 15 percent, and the industry's trade surplus slipped to about $1.6 billion; three years earlier the surplus had exceeded $2.3 billion. Indeed, as the percentage of U.S. chemical exports represented by organics declined from 30 percent in the mid-1980s, the proportion of U.S. imports made up of organics climbed to 33 percent.

Economic stagnation in key export markets—such as Japan and the European Community helped importers increase their share of the U.S. market in the early 1990s. However, long-term structural changes in global chemical markets were also at work. Importantly, producers in emerging economies were increasingly challenging U.S. suppliers for both domestic and export sales. In fact, overall chemical exports by developing nations rocketed nearly 400 percent during the 1980s—from $10.5 billion in 1980 to $38.8 billion in 1991. East Asian countries, particularly, were increasing production. Of 28 new ethylene producers preparing to begin operation in the mid-1990s, for instance, 18 were in the Far East, and only one was in Japan. Likewise, 46 percent of new global styrene capacity scheduled to be added by 1995 was in the Far East. New competitors in South America, Africa, and the Middle East also threatened to depress both global and domestic prices and reduce U.S. market share.

The largest importer of petrochemicals to the United States in 1991 was Canada, supplying nearly 15 percent of imports. Germany and Japan supplied 14.3 and 12.7 percent, respectively, of all cross-border purchases by Americans. The United Kingdom held about 9 percent of the U.S. import market, and France captured 6.3 percent. The European Community supplied 43 percent of U.S. petrochemical imports. Although Mexico supplied only a small share of imports in the early 1990s, that country's import activity was expected to rise substantially throughout the decade in the wake of the North American Free Trade Agreement (NAFTA) passed in 1993. NAFTA eliminated tariffs on cross-border chemical sales.

In the long term, growing foreign organic chemical production will result in fierce competition and reduced opportunities for U.S. manufacturers. The United States, Europe, and Japan will remain the key producers, but much of the market for high-volume, commodity-like organics will be surrendered to emerging powers. To sustain profitability, U.S. competitors will be forced to boost their production of high tech compounds that will outperform existing chemicals and open new markets.

ASSOCIATIONS AND SOCIETIES

AMERICAN CHEMICAL SOCIETY
1155 16th St. NW
Washington, DC 20036
Phone: (800) 227-5558 or (202) 872-4600

ASSOCIATION OF CONSULTING CHEMISTS AND CHEMICAL ENGINEERS
295 Madison Ave., 27 Fl.
New York, NY 10017
Phone: (212) 983-3160
Fax: (212) 983-3161

CHEMICAL MANAGEMENT AND RESOURCES ASSOCIATION
60 Bay St., Ste. 702
Staten Island, NY 10305
Phone: (718) 876-8800
Members are individuals engaged in chemical market research.

CHEMICAL MANUFACTURERS ASSOCIATION
2501 M St. NW
Washington, DC 20037
Phone: (202) 887-1100
Fax: (202) 887-1237

NATIONAL ASSOCIATION OF CHEMICAL DISTRIBUTORS
1101 17th St. NW, Ste. 1200
Washington, DC 20036
Phone: (202) 296-9200
Fax: (202) 296-0023

PERIODICALS AND NEWSLETTERS

AMERICAN OIL CHEMISTS' SOCIETY JOURNAL
PO Box 3489
Champaign, IL 61821-0489
Phone: (217) 359-2344
Fax: (217) 351-8091
Monthly. $185.00 per year. Includes INFORM: International News on Fats, Oils and Related Materials.

CHEMICAL PROCESSING
Putman Publishing Co.
301 E. Erie St.
Chicago, IL 60611
Phone: (312) 644-2020
Fax: (312) 644-1131
12 times a year. Free to qualified personnel; others, $45.00 per year.

CHEMICAL WEEK
Chemical Week Associates
888 7th Ave., 26 Fl.
New York, NY 10106-2698
Phone: (212) 621-4900
Fax: (212) 621-4949
Weekly. $99.00 per year. Includes annual Buyers' Guide.

CPI PURCHASING: THE MAGAZINE ABOUT BUYING FOR THE CHEMICAL AND PROCESS INDUSTRIES
Cahners Publishing Co., Inc.
275 Washington St.
Newton, MA 02158-1630
Phone: (800) 662-7776 or (617) 964-3030
Fax: (617) 558-4327
Monthly. $74.95 per year.

JOURNAL OF CHEMICAL INFORMATION AND COMPUTER SCIENCES
American Chemical Society
1155 16th St. NW
Washington, DC 20036
Phone: (800) 227-5558 or (202) 872-4600
Fax: (202) 872-6067
Bimonthly. Members, $20.00 per year; non-members, $180.00 per year

DATABASES

CA SEARCH
Chemical Abstracts Service
2540 Olentangy River Rd.
Columbus, OH 43210
Phone: (614) 447-3731
Fax: (614) 447-3751
Guide to chemical literature, 1967 to present. Inquire as to online cost and availability.

CHEM-BANK
Silver Platter Information, Inc.
100 River Ridge Rd.
Norwood, MA 02062
Phone: (800) 343-0064 or (617) 769-2599
Fax: (617) 769-8763
Quarterly. $1,350.00 per year. Provides CD-ROM information on hazardous substances, including 96,000 chemicals in the Registry of Toxic Effects of Chemical Substances *and 60,000 materials covered by the* Toxic Substances Control Act Initial Inventory.

CITIBASE (CITICORP ECONOMIC DATABASE)
FAME Software Corp.
77 Water St., 9 Fl.
New York, NY 10005
Phone: (212) 898-7800
Fax: (212) 742-8956
Presents over 6,000 statistical series relating to business, industry, finance, and economics. Includes series from Survey of Current Business *and many other sources. Time period is 1947 to date, with daily updates. Inquire as to online cost and availability.*

DRI CHEMICAL FORECAST
DRI/McGraw-Hill, Data Products Division
24 Hartwell Ave.
Lexington, MA 02173
Phone: (800) 541-9914 or (617) 863-5100
Supply-demand and price forecasts are given quarterly and annually for over 120 U.S. chemical products. Quarterly forecasts generally extend 3 years, while annual forecasts cover 5 to 10 years. Inquire as to online cost and availability.

U.S. FORECASTS
Information Access Co.
362 Lakeside Dr.
Foster City, CA 94404
Phone: (800) 321-6388 or (415) 358-4643
Fax: (415) 358-4759
Provides numeric abstracts of a wide range of published forecasts relating to specific U.S. products, markets, and industries. Time period is 1971 to date. Inquire as to online cost and availability.

STATISTICS SOURCES

ANNUAL REVIEW OF THE CHEMICAL INDUSTRY
United Nations
2 United Nations Plz., Rm. DC2-853
New York, NY 10017

Phone: (800) 253-9646 or (212) 963-8302
Fax: (212) 963-3489
Annual. $42.00.

SYNTHETIC ORGANIC CHEMICALS: UNITED STATES PRODUCTION AND SALES
International Trade Commission
Available from U.S. Government Printing Office
Washington, DC 20402
Phone: (202) 512-1800
Fax: (202) 512-2250
Annual. $26.00.

UNITED STATES CENSUS OF MANUFACTURES
U.S. Bureau of the Census
Washington, DC 20233-0800
Phone: (301) 457-4100
Fax: (301) 457-3842
Quinquennial. Results presented in reports, tape, CD-ROM, and diskette files.

GENERAL WORKS

CHEMICAL REGULATION REPORTER: A WEEKLY REVIEW OF AFFECTING CHEMICAL USERS AND MANUFACTURERS
Bureau of National Affairs, Inc.
1250 23rd St. NW
Washington, DC 20037
Phone: (800) 372-1033 or (202) 452-4200
Fax: (202) 822-8092
Weekly. $1,500.00 per year. Six Volumes. Looseleaf.

CHEMICAL SUBSTANCES CONTROL
Bureau of National Affairs, Inc.
1250 23rd St. NW
Washington, DC 20037
Phone: (800) 372-1033 or (202) 452-4200
Fax: (202) 822-8092
Biweekly. $610.00 per year. Looseleaf. Covers legal aspects of chemical substance management.

CHEMICAL WEEK-BUYER'S GUIDE
Chemical Week Associates
888 7th Ave., 26 Fl.
New York, NY 10106-2698
Phone: (212) 621-4900
Fax: (212) 621-4949 or (212) 621-4950
Annual. $99.00. Included in subscription to Chemical Week.

CPI PURCHASING CHEMICALS YELLOW PAGES
Cahners Publishing Co.
275 Washington St.
Newton, MA 02158
Phone: (617) 558-4642
Fax: (617) 558-4506
Annual. $40.00. Formerly Chemicals Directory.

FURTHER READING

Hess, Glenn. "Toxic Emissions Decline." *Chemical Marketing Reporter,* 7 October 1996.

"Organic Chemicals." Available from http://www.bayer.de/bayer/english/2xxxarb/2200/2210/2210.htm.

Standard & Poor's Industry Surveys, New York: Standard & Poor's Corporation, 8 February 1996.

"Industrial Organic Chemicals: Growth Projected for Organics." *Standard and Poor's Industry Surveys.* New York: Standard and Poor's Corporation, 1997. ◄►

23

COAL MINING

SIC 1200

The *coal industry in the mid-1990s was characterized by price erosion, strict environmental controls, labor unrest, increasing foreign competition, stagnant growth in demand, and increasing energy taxes. To combat these negative influences, producers were striving to raise productivity, increase surface mining, consolidate, and take advantage of new environmental technologies. Industry participants had already experienced significant achievements in these areas by 1997.*

Coal generates more than 50 percent of U.S. electric power and accounts for about 25 percent of total U.S. energy consumption. It also represents a major export product. In 1995, American producers exported approximately 89 million short tons of coal. The coal industry shipped about $20 billion worth of coal per year in the early 1990s, while employing over 100,000 workers. An additional 100,000 to 150,000 U.S. workers held jobs that were dependent on the industry's output, such as coal transportation.

Top 10 TOP U.S. COAL PRODUCERS

Ranked by: Millions of short tons produced.

1. Peabody Holding Company, Inc., 69.7
2. Cyprus AMAX Minerals, 65.3
3. Consol Energy Inc., 50.7
4. Zeiglar Coal Holding Co., 37.5
5. ARCO Coal Co., 37.4
6. Kennecott Energy Co., 36.7
7. Exxon Coal USA Inc., 28.1
8. Texas Utilities Co., 27.6
9. Montana Power Co., 26.4
10. North American Coal Corp., 26.3

Source: *Coal Data: A Reference,* February 1995, p. 20, from Energy Information Administration and *Coal Industry Annual, 1993.*

The U.S. bituminous coal industry is the second largest in the world, accounting for about 27 percent of global production in the mid-1990s. In addition, approximately 25 percent of total world coal reserves are located on U.S. lands, providing enough coal to meet an estimated 450 years of domestic demand. Bituminous and lignite surface mining represents about 60 percent of total industry output.

Underground coal mining has been practiced in the United States since the 1800s and was the dominant mining technique for most of the twentieth century. By the early 1990s, underground U.S. mines were producing about 400 million tons of coal per year. In addition, underground operations were responsible for exporting over 60 million tons of product—more than 50 percent of all U.S. coal exports. Despite its large size and its importance to energy and industrial markets, the U.S. underground coal mining industry is in some fundamental ways a troubled one. These difficulties first manifested themselves in the late 1960s and have continued unabated throughout the early 1990s. A primary threat to industry participants has been the rapid proliferation of relatively efficient surface mines. Other detriments, though, include increasing environmental constraints, labor problems, stagnant demand growth, and foreign competition.

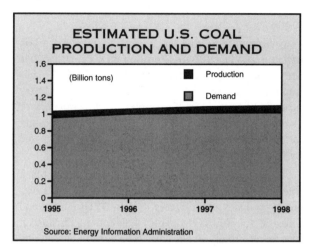

ESTIMATED U.S. COAL PRODUCTION AND DEMAND

Source: Energy Information Administration

Anthracite is a hard coal containing a high percentage of fixed carbon and a low percentage of volatile matter, such as sulfur and ash, containing over 90 percent of fixed carbon, less than 5 percent of volatile matter (gases), and a very small percentage of moisture (usually less than 5 percent). With these desirable qualities, anthracite coal is ranked higher than other, more commonly used coals like bituminous and lignite because it has over twice the energy content of these other coals. Thus, it provides a longer burning potential and is, accordingly, a higher energy fuel.

In 1995, 134 mines were engaged in the extraction of Pennsylvania anthracite, employing 1,069 miners. Production for the year was 4.6 million short tons, less than 0.5 percent of total U.S. coal production. Most of the original markets for anthracite were relinquished long ago to natural gas, fuel oil, and other coals such as bituminous and lignite coal. In the mid-1990s, anthracite maintained a small share of a niche market, consisting primarily of coal-fired home-heating units. In fact, anthracite mining has been declining steadily for many years, from peak production in 1918 when anthracite mines produced 99,612 thousand short tons.

According to the most recent data from the *Census of Mineral Industries,* the coal mining services industry employed a work force of 4,600 production workers in 1992, 15 percent above the figure for 1987. Total value of shipments and receipts was $538.4 million. These workers added value through their services to the coal mining process of $378.3 million. Although this figure was higher than in 1987, it was still below the peak reached in 1982 at $418.1 million. Although coal mining services as an industry has grown in absolute terms

(relative to total coal production), its share of total coal production in terms of dollar value was less than 2 percent.

INDUSTRY OUTLOOK

The U.S. coal industry was still strong in the mid-1990s, second only to China in terms of coal production, but growth was sluggish and prices continued to fall. Electric utilities remained by far the largest consumers of coal, and demand from this sector was expected to remain steady well into the future. The industry was marked by consolidation as smaller, less efficient mines closed and some large non-mining corporations who had acquired coal mines during the seventies sold withdrew. Large mining companies expanded by acquiring these existing operations more often than by opening new mines. Production shifted west where economies of scale could be brought to bear on operating costs, and where large deposits of the low-sulfur coals desired by the utilities were located. Surface mines in the western states accounted for 69.7 percent of production; in fact, the nine largest mines in the United States were in low-sulfur beds in Wyoming and represented 18.8 percent of coal production.

Given these conditions, in which narrow profit margins forced coal operators to seek every possible means of lowering operating costs, expanding opportunities existed for mining service companies, which were able to accomplish some aspects of the mining process at a lower cost. Companies in this industry segment provided much needed flexibility to mine operators.

Overall coal production realized very modest gains from 1991 to 1995, averaging 0.9 percent annual growth. There was no increase from 1994 to 1995, though figures for 1996 indicated growth of over 2 percent. Surface mining, however, grew steadily. While coal production east of the Mississippi, where most underground mines were located, fell 3.9 percent from 1994 to 1995 to 544 million short tons, coal production in the western states, where surface mines predominate, increased by 4.6 percent to a record 489 million short tons. Prices continued to decline, though, at the same time that production costs were rising. One bright spot in the mid-1990s was a 24 percent increase in exports, the first annual increase since 1991.

Underground mining companies in the early 1990s were still grappling with many of the problems that arose in the previous two decades. Although the westward shift away from eastern underground mines had subsided by the mid-1980s, stagnant demand for underground coal was hurting producers. Closure of some small inefficient mines along with increased use of new production methods such as longwall systems resulted in higher productivity, which increased 5.9 percent across the underground mining industry from 1991 to 1995, but industry unemployment was rampant, as many miners were left without jobs in the wake of rising automation and productivity. The number of miners employed at underground mines fell an average of 7.2 percent during this same period. Furthermore, increased foreign competition and domestic over-production was keeping a lid on coal prices, which steadily declined, dropping an average of 5.6 percent each year from 1986 to 1995.

The anthracite coal mining industry remained in a basically stagnant condition in 1995. Since 1991 the number of operating mines had fallen by 24 percent and the number of miners by about 8 percent. Productivity per miner increased during this same period, but was still well below that of bituminous miners. Productivity at Pennsylvania bituminous underground mines in 1995 was 3.56 short tons per hour per miner, while at anthracite mines it was 0.86 tons. For surface mines, the disparity was not as great at 2.95 tons compared to 2.30, but was still significant. There were 2.4 times as many bituminous mines as anthracite in Pennsylvania in 1995, but they produced more than 12 times as much coal. Reflecting the disparity in productivity was the price of the product. Expressed in 1992 dollars, the price for anthracite averaged $37.01 per ton, while the average price for all U.S. coal was $17.52. The outlook for real growth in the industry was grim. With the market for anthracite flat, there was little incentive for mining companies to open new mines or install production enhancing technology such as longwall systems.

ORGANIZATION AND STRUCTURE

The coal mining industry is made up of four types of mining: surface, underground, anthracite, and mining service companies. In addition, Four grades of coal mined in the coal industry include lignite, subbituminous, bituminous, and anthracite. Each grade differs in moisture content, volatile matter, and fixed carbon content. Anthracite, the highest grade material, accounts for less than 0.5 percent of total output.

Bituminous coal, or soft coal, is the most common type of coal produced in the United States. It represents over 70 percent of total industry output and accounts for approximately 50 percent of total U.S. reserves. The mineral is composed of 80 to 90 percent carbon and about 10 to 20 percent moisture. A ton of bituminous coal typically generates 19 to 30 million BTUs and ignites at between 700 and 900 degrees Fahrenheit. Bituminous coal possesses a relatively low sulfur content, which causes it to burn more cleanly than some lower grades. Because of its properties, bituminous coal is the principal steam coal used for generating electricity. It is also the primary coking coal used in the steel-making process.

Subbituminous coal has a 75 to 85 percent carbon content. It produces 16 to 24 million BTUs per ton and is used primarily to generate electricity. In 1995, subbituminous coal represented 31.7 percent of industry output. Although its sulfur content is low relative to lignite, a high moisture content, along with other negative properties, makes it less desirable than higher coal grades for most applications.

Lignite, the lowest ranked coal, is a brownish-black mineral containing a moisture content of 30 to 40 percent. It produces about 9 to 17 million BTUs per ton and ignites at roughly 600 degrees Fahrenheit. Because it deteriorates rapidly in air, has a high sulfur content, and is liable to combust spontaneously, lignite is used mainly to generate electricity in power plants that are close to mines. In 1995, lignite accounted for 8.3 percent of industry production. Lignite is also subject to high royalties charged by the federal government.

According to the Energy Information Administration, 2,104 mines operated in 25 states in 1995. Surface mining was the exclusive mining technique used in 9 of those states. Mines range in size from small facilities that generate several thousand tons of coal per year to mammoth surface operations that extract 10 to 20 million tons per year. The surface mining industry produced over 636 million tons of coal in 1995. Another 396 million tons were extracted by the underground mining industry.

Because surface mining is less expensive and more productive than traditional underground mining, new surface extraction technology has allowed this method to dominate U.S. coal production. The amount of coal produced per worker hour at a surface mine, for instance, topped 6 tons in 1990 and reached 8.48 tons in 1995. In contrast, the tonnage produced per worker hour at underground mines averaged about 3.39 tons in 1995. Moreover, producers are able to remove an estimated 90 percent of the coal at surface mines, while underground mines permit only a 50 to 80 percent extraction rate, depending on the mining method used.

Both surface and underground methods were used in the extraction of anthracite. In 1995, 270,000 short tons were produced by underground mines and 4.1 million tons by surface mines. Surface mining is usually practiced on relatively flat ground; the coal is recovered from a depth of less than 200 feet. To reach coal deposits, miners must first remove the overburden, or strata, that covers the coal bed. Between 1 and 30 cubic yards of strata must be excavated for each ton of coal recovered. Dragline excavators, power shovels, bulldozers, front-end loaders, scrapers, and other heavy pieces of equipment are used to move the strata and extract the coal.

The increase of mining services as an industry in its own right largely reflected cost-cutting measures on the part of the coal mining industry. They often cut costs by increasing use of nonunion workers to perform many of the tasks previously performed by union workers. Contract mining services also grew due to the fact that many larger coal interests simply diversified their operations or got out of certain aspects of coal mining.

Top U.S. Coal Producers

Production is shown in millions of short tons.

	Prod.	Share
Peabody Holding Co. Inc.	69.7	7.4%
Cyprus Minerals Co.	65.3	6.9
Consol Energy Inc.	50.7	5.4
Zeigler Coal Holding Co.	37.5	4.0
ARCO Coal Co.	37.4	4.0
Kennecott Energy Co.	36.7	3.9
Exxon Coal USA Inc.	28.1	3.0
Texas Utilities Co.	27.6	2.9
Montana Power Co.	26.4	2.8
North American Coal Corp. . . .	26.3	2.8

Source: *Coal Data: A Reference*, February 1995, p. 20, from Energy Information Administration and *Coal Industry Annual, 1993*.

With specific services contracted out, firms can avoid a large commitment of capital investment and small entrepreneurs have seen a profitable opening. Thus, faced with erratic demand conditions, the industry has seen an increase in flexible conditions of production, including just-in-time production methods, which create smooth production, reduce turnover times, and thereby reduce downtime. Flexible work rules involving eradication of union work rules—or at the very least, union cooperation—have contributed to mine efficiency. In any case, with various degrees of contract services, the number of large independent operators continues to decline according to some industry observers, with efficiency forcing the competition process.

In 1992, approximately 358 establishments (and 320 companies) provided services to the coal industry on a contract basis. These companies provided services ranging from removal of overburden, stripping the mine face, auguring or culm bank mining, drilling services, mine tunneling, and shaft sinking. Most of these establishments and multi-establishment firms were small; only 65 had more than 19 employees, and of these only 4 had 100 or more. Average value added per production worker for coal mining services was $82,200 in 1992, up from $69,900 in 1987, a figure that was significantly below the average of $134,724 for the bituminous coal and lignite mining industry but slightly above the average of $68,375 for anthracite mining, which became a relatively dead industry.

The most significant revenue source in the coal mining services industry was strip mining, which totaled $95.8 million in industry shipments in 1992. Stripping overburden followed with $52.9 million. Sinking mine shafts and driving mine tunnels generated revenue of $38.5 million, and drilling and blasting generated $25.2 million. Other coal mining services not specifically classified produced $101.5 million in industry revenue, and another $198.9 million was estimated from incomplete data, including data for smaller enterprises.

WORK FORCE

The number of workers employed by U.S. coal producers continued declining in 1995 to about 90,000 (excluding management and office workers). Although surface mining operations are less susceptible to labor cutbacks than underground mining facilities, surface mines are considerably less labor intensive and provide fewer job opportunities per ton of coal produced than do underground mines. Labor positions in the surface mining industry are concentrated in the maintenance and operation of heavy machinery. In addition, surface mining companies have a higher proportion of management and clerical workers than the overall coal industry.

Employment opportunities in the surface mining industry have been limited. Labor unions have pushed hard to get companies that have opened new surface mining operations to employ workers that were displaced from underground mining jobs. This factor, in addition to constantly rising automation and productivity, make coal industry employment highly competitive. Even new positions in management remained limited in the early 1990s—a result of generally tepid industry growth.

Unions were increasingly concerned about job security in the early 1990s. Coal companies argued that rising costs were pinching profit margins. Union leaders pointed out that coal production had increased 200 percent over the past two decades, while costs had been reduced by 50 percent, largely through payroll savings. Labor negotiators also charged mine companies with shifting production to non-union facilities. By the end of 1993, however, the United Mine Workers Union had agreed to terms with both the Bituminous Coal Operators Association and the Independent Coal Bargaining Alliance, the multiemployer bargaining groups of the industry, and had signed five-year contracts. This was only accomplished, however, after bitter strike actions and negotiations with the association.

Job opportunities are expected to continue to degenerate in the underground coal mining industry. Labor positions that do become available are expected to go to unemployed union members per new labor agreements. The average number of miners at underground mines in 1995 was 57,879, down 6 percent from 1994, and down 26 percent from 1991 levels.

RESEARCH AND TECHNOLOGY

To maintain economic viability and their position in the global export market, the U.S. coal mining industry continued to rely on technological advances to overcome imposing barriers that faced them. Of great importance were projects to improve the cleanliness and efficiency of coal-fired electric power plants. The U.S. Department of Energy was developing five categories of research. Low-emission boiler systems incorporated advanced combustion and innovative flue gas cleaning systems in the initial design for new power plants. Pressurized fluidized bed combustion captured sulfur pollutants inside the boiler instead of in the stack, and allowed combustion at temperatures below the point at which most nitrogen pollutants form. The integrated gasification combined cycle (IGCC) employed coal gasification rather than traditional combustion and combined a steam turbine driven by exhaust heat with the gas turbine driven by the coal gas. Indirectly fired cycles employed a design that heated a working fluid such as air to turn the turbine rather than the hot gases of combustion. Finally, integrated gasification-fuel cell combinations would link a coal gasifier with a fuel cell. By 1995, pressurized fluidized bed combustion systems and IGCC systems were in commercial use.

AMERICA AND THE WORLD

Of the estimated 490 billion tons of coal reserves in the United States, only about 150 billion tons are accessible through surface mining. Nevertheless, this reserve ensures a dominant U.S. position in the future global coal mining industry. In addition to healthy reserves, U.S. coal companies have achieved the highest productivity of any coal-producing nation. While the United States places second to Australia as the largest coal exporter, America remained the largest total coal producer until the early 1990s when China assumed the lead.

In 1995 the United States exported 88.5 million tons of coal—an increase of 17.2 million tons. The primary reason for the increase was the substantial growth in the demand for U.S. steam coal. Exports to Europe more than doubled compared to 1994. At the same time, the United States imported less than 1 percent of its coal needs. Japan remained the single largest consumer of U.S. coal in 1995, absorbing 11.7 million tons. Canada was the second largest customer at 9.4 million tons.

ASSOCIATIONS AND SOCIETIES

NATIONAL INDEPENDENT COAL OPERATORS ASSOCIATION
PO Box 354
Richlands, VA 24641
Phone: (703) 963-9011

NATIONAL COAL ASSOCIATION
1130 17th St. NW
Washington, DC 20036
Phone: (202) 463-2625
Fax: (202) 463-6152

ROCKY MOUNTAIN COAL MINING INSTITUTE
3000 Youngfield, Ste. 324
Lakewood, CO 80215-6545
Phone: (303) 238-9099
Fax: (303) 238-0509

PERIODICALS AND NEWSLETTERS

BLACK DIAMOND
Black Diamond Co., Inc.
159 Pierce Rd.
Highland Park, IL 60035-5326
Phone: (708) 922-8031
Monthly. $36.00 per year.

COAL
Intertec Publishing Corp.
29 N. Wacker Dr.
Chicago, IL 60606
Phone: (800) 621-9907 or (800) 543-7771
Fax: (312) 726-2574
Monthly. $36.00 per year. Formed by the merger of Coal Age *and* Coal Mining.

COAL AND SYNFUELS TECHNOLOGY

Pasha Publications, Inc.
1616 N. Fort Myer Dr., Ste. 1000
Arlington, VA 22209-3107
Phone: (703) 528-1244
Fax: (703) 528-1253
Weekly. $790.00 per year. Newsletter. Formerly Synfuels Week.

COAL MINING NEWSLETTER

National Safety Council Periodicals
Dept. 1121
Spring Lake Dr.
Itasca, IL 60143
Phone: (800) 621-7619 or (708) 775-2281
Fax: (708) 285-9114
Bimonthly. Members, $15.00 per year; non-members, $19.00 per year.

COAL OUTLOOK

Pasha Publications, Inc.
1616 N. Fort Myer Dr., Ste. 1000
Arlington, VA 22209-3107
Phone: (703) 528-1244
Fax: (703) 528-1253
Weekly. $775.00 per year.

COAL WEEK

McGraw-Hill
1221 Avenue of the Americas
New York, NY 10020
Phone: (800) 722-4726 or (212) 512-2000
Fax: (212) 512-2821
Weekly. $950.00 per year. Newsletter. Edited as "a weekly intelligence report for executives in the coal industry and peripheral operations." Covers prices, markets, politics, and coal economics. (Energy and Business Newsletters.)

NATIONAL INDEPENDENT COAL LEADER: DEDICATED TO SAFETY IN THE MINING INDUSTRY

National Independent Coal Operators Association
1514 Front St.
Richlands, VA 24641
Phone: (703) 963-9011
Monthly. $6.00 per year.

DATABASES

CITIBASE (CITICORP ECONOMIC DATABASE)

FAME Software Corp.
77 Water St., 9 Fl.
New York, NY 10005
Phone: (212) 898-7800
Fax: (212) 742-8956
Presents over 6,000 statistical series relating to business, industry, finance, and economics. Includes series from Survey of Current Business *and many other sources. Time period is 1947 to date, with daily updates. Inquire as to online cost and availability.*

ENERGY SCIENCE AND TECHNOLOGY

U.S. Dept. of Energy, Office of Scientific and Technical Information
PO Box 62

Oak Ridge, TN 37831
Phone: (615) 576-9362
Fax: (615) 576-2865
Contains abstracts and citations to literature in all fields of energy from 1974 to date, with biweekly updates. Formerly DOE Energy Data Base. *Inquire as to online cost and availability.*

ENERGYLINE

Congressional Information Service, Inc.
4520 East-West Hwy., Ste. 800
Bethesda, MD 20814-3389
Phone: (800) 638-8380 or (301) 654-1550
Fax: (301) 654-4033
Provides online citations and abstracts to the literature of all forms of energy: petroleum, natural gas, coal, nuclear power, solar energy, etc. Time period is 1971 to date. Monthly updates. Inquire as to online cost and availability.

STATISTICS SOURCES

ANNUAL ENERGY REVIEW

Available from U.S. Government Printing Office
Washington, DC 20402
Phone: (202) 512-1800
Fax: (202) 512-2250
Annual. Issued by the Energy Information Administration, Office of Energy Markets and End Use, U.S. Department of Energy. Presents long-term historical as well as recent data on production, consumption, stocks, imports, exports, and prices of the principal energy commodities in the United States.

COAL DATA

National Coal Association
1130 17th St. NW
Washington, DC 20036
Phone: (202) 463-2640
Fax: (202) 463-6152
Annual. Individuals, $75.00; non-profit institutions, $50.00. Data on 50 largest bituminous coal mines.

COAL TRANSPORTATION STATISTICS

National Coal Association
1130 17th St. NW
Washington, DC 20036
Phone: (202) 463-2640
Fax: (202) 463-6152
Annual. Non-profit organizations, $25.00; others, $35.00. Formerly Coal Traffic Annual.

MONTHLY ENERGY REVIEW

Available from U.S. Government Printing Office
Washington, DC 20402
Phone: (202) 512-1800
Fax: (202) 512-2250
Monthly. $87.00 per year. Issued by the Energy Information Administration, Office of Energy Markets and End Use, U.S. Departmennt of Energy. Contains current and historical statistics on U.S. production, storage, imports, and consumption of petroleum, natural gas, and coal.

QUARTERLY COAL REPORT
Energy Information Administration, U.S. Department of Energy
Available from U.S. Government Printing Office
Washington, DC 20402
Phone: (202) 512-1800
Fax: (202) 512-2250
Quarterly. $28.00 per year. Annual summary.

WEEKLY COAL PRODUCTION
Energy Information Administration, U.S. Department of Energy
Available from U.S. Government Printing Office
Washington, DC 20402
Phone: (202) 512-1800
Fax: (202) 512-2250
Weekly. $85.00 per year. Gives data on U.S. production of bituminous, lignite and anthracite coals.

GENERAL WORKS

COAL FACTS
National Coal Association
1130 17th St. NW
Washington, DC 20036
Phone: (202) 463-2631
Fax: (202) 463-6152
Annual. $15.00.

COAL INFORMATION
Organization for Economic Cooperation and Development
OECD
Publications and Information Center
2001 L St., Ste. 700
Washington, DC 20036
Phone: (202) 785-6323
Fax: (202) 785-0350
Annual. $120.00. A yearly report on world coal market trends and prospects.

COAL LAW AND REGULATION
Matthew Bender and Co. Inc.
11 Penn Plz.
New York, NY 10017
Phone: (800) 223-1940 or (212) 967-7707
Five looseleaf volumes. Periodic supplementation.

COAL AND MODERN COAL PROCESSING: AN INTRODUCTION
G.J. Pitt and G.R. Millward, editors
Academic Press, Inc.
525 B St., Ste. 1900
San Diego, CA 92101-4495
Phone: (800) 321-5068 or (619) 231-0926
Fax: (800) 336-7377 or (619) 699-6715
1979. $61.00.

COAL LIQUEFACTION FUNDAMENTALS
Darrell Duayne Whitehurst, editor
American Chemical Society
1155 16th St. NW
Washington, DC 20036
Phone: (800) 227-5558 or (202) 872-4600
Fax: (202) 872-6067
1980. $49.95.

KEYSTONE COAL INDUSTRY MANUAL
Maclean Hunter Publishing Co.
29 N. Wacker Dr.
Chicago, IL 60606
Phone: (800) 621-9907 or (312) 726-2802
Fax: (312) 726-2574
Annual. $190.00.

FURTHER READING

Chambers, Ann. "Coal to Dominate Generation to 2015." *Power Engineering,* July 1996.

Massey, David. "Coal: An Industry in Transition." *Electric Perspectives,* 1 January 1995.

National Mining Association. "Salient Statistics of the Mining Industry." Available from http://www.nma.org/salient.html.

U.S. Department of Energy. Energy Information Administration. *Coal Annual 1995.* Washington: GPO, 1996.

U.S. Department of the Interior. Office of Surface Mining. *1996 Annual Report.* Washington: GPO, 1997.

U.S. Department of Labor. Mining Safety and Health Administration. "Mine Accident, Injury, Illness, Employment, and Coal Production Statistics, 1996." Available from http://www.msha.gov/ALLCOAL.HTM.

24

COMPUTER PERIPHERAL EQUIPMENT

SIC 3577

As *demand for computers increased through the mid-1990s, the computer peripheral industry was expected to maintain steady growth through the end of the decade. The industry's unit sales are expected to rise from 250,000 units in 1996 to over 1.6 million units by the year 2000. Regardless of this industry's positive sales, approximately 20,000 jobs would be eliminated by 1998.*

INDUSTRY SNAPSHOT

Peripheral equipment accounted for a major share of U.S. computer industry revenues. In the early 1990s, for instance, computer peripherals from all industries represented about $65 billion, or 20 percent, of the global computer equipment and services market. By the mid-1990s, the number of establishments in the industry totaled 800—by the year 1998, this number was expected to reach 937. *Manufacturing USA* reported that an estimated 46,700 people were employed by these establishments in 1997.

MOST PROFITABLE COMPUTER PERIPHERALS COMPANIES

Ranked by: Profits per employee in 1995, in thousands of dollars.

1. Cisco Systems, with $194.1 thousand
2. Micron Technology, $150.5
3. EMC, $94.7
4. Intel Corp., $88.1
5. Linear Technology, $83.3
6. Applied Materials, $65.7
7. LSI Logic, $61.5
8. 3Com Corp., $54.4
9. Bay Networks, $52.7
10. Atmel, $46.5

Source: *Forbes*, Forbes 500s (annual), April 22, 1996, p. 280.

Peripheral manufacturers benefited from new markets created by technological advancements in the computer industry. Faster, less-expensive personal computers (PCs) with greater memory capacity boosted peripheral sales, as did the increasing interest in multimedia equipment, which incorporated the capabilities of computers, telephones, video display terminals, and fax machines. In addition, as the popularity of the Internet grew rapidly in the mid- to late 1990s, companies that manufactured routers, switches, and other networking equipment reaped the benefits. Throughout the 1990s, industry competitors hastened to bring out new technology to take advantage of computer advancements and broaden the scope of the peripheral market.

INDUSTRY OUTLOOK

In the early 1990s, the peripherals industry exceeded growth in other computer equipment industry segments, largely due to the severe price slashing by PC vendors effected during this time. As PC manufacturers' revenues fell in the early 1990s, the number of shipped units increased substantially, prompting a greater demand for all types of add-on peripherals.

Annual sales of scanners and other electronic imaging peripherals multiplied at a rate of nearly 20 percent in 1992 to about $2 billion. Furthermore, this segment of the peripherals industry enjoyed relatively high profit margins, and analysts predicted that annual scanner sales would increase 100 percent by the end of 1997. Falling prices, more powerful software and technology, the proliferation of color scanners, and advances in computer memory storage techniques were the dominant factors driving market growth in this segment, while flatbed scanners would continue accounting for the majority of product sales.

Printer shipments were expected to jump from over 10 million units in 1995 to about 24 million by 1998, worth nearly $19 billion. By 1998, laser printers would likely hold a 50 percent share of the printer market, while ink-jets would represent over 30 percent.

Cathyode ray tube (CRT) displays utilized technology that had been changed only slightly during the 1990s—resulting in a price-intensive commodity environment for CRT vendors. Liquid crystal displays (LCDs), in contrast, still offered solid growth and profit opportunities. Sales and prices of color LCDs were particularly competitive. From $917 million in 1992, color LCD sales reached nearly $3 billion in 1996. Advances in LCD technology were expected to keep profit margins relatively high through the rest of the decade.

Sales of multimedia peripherals, such as computer sound-systems, were expected to post strong gains throughout the 1990s. Creative Technology Ltd., which led the industry with two-thirds of the market in 1993 sales of add-on sound boards and chips that could digitally recreate human speech, offered evidence of this sector's viability. It was also quick to develop computer add-ons called circuit cards that could give PCs the ability to show full-motion video.

With the increasing popularity of the Internet and World Wide Web, the need for multimedia video and sound systems became more in demand through the 1990s. By 1994, 75 percent of consumer PCs included audio capability.

ORGANIZATION AND STRUCTURE

Facilitating communication with a computer's processor, peripheral equipment is used with supercomputers, mainframes, minicomputers, workstations, and personal computers. The three largest categories of peripherals are graphic displays, printers, and scanners. In addition to the major peripheral categories, numerous miscellaneous products include: computer input devices, computer sound systems, magnetic ink recognition devices, graphic and technical plotters, graphics production equipment, and various multimedia devices.

GRAPHIC DISPLAYS

The most popular types of graphic displays are traditional cathode ray tube (CRT) monitors and flat panel liquid crystal displays (LCDs). Although some displays are built into computer terminals, most are offered as peripheral devices that may be added to a personal computer or network terminal. A video card interfaces between the monitor and the CPU, allowing compatibility for specific monitors and computer systems.

CRTs provide either monochrome or color graphics and deliver varying degrees of flexibility, performance, resolution quality, and size. Low resolution monitors, for instance, contained 640 x 480 pixels per inch, while higher resolution CRTs could deliver 1,280 x 1,024; 1,600 x 1,200; or more pixels per inch. Most CRTs measured between 10 and 17 inches diagonally. CRT prices ranged from $50 for monochrome displays to several thousand dollars for large, high-definition color monitors. In 1995, over 2 million CRTs were shipped by U.S. manufacturers.

Among the fastest growing and most dynamic segments of the graphic display market was the LCD. In 1995, manufacturers shipped more than 140,000 units—an almost 20,000-unit increase over 1994. Because LCDs were flat, they were the display of choice for the rapidly growing notebook computer industry. Although far fewer LCDs than CRTs were purchased in the early 1990s, LCDs provided manufacturers with much larger profit margins than older, commodity-like CRTs. Global LCD sales grew to over $3.1 billion in 1992. Monochrome displays accounted for more than 70 percent of LCD revenues in the early 1990s. The remaining 30 percent of sales represented a variety of color LCDs. However, as technology improved, the color LCD market rapidly surpassed monochrome as consumers demanded color displays into the late 1990s. About 75 percent of all color LCDs sold were passive-matrix displays, also called super-twisted nematic (STN). Active-matrix displays, also called thin-film transistors

(TFTs), made up the remaining 25 percent of color LCDs. TFTs provided the highest graphic quality in this segment and mimicked large semiconductors in which many transistors functioned as a cohesive unit. High-tech TFTs sold for an average price of $1,200 in 1992—about twice as much as passive-matrix LCDs. Most LCD screen sizes ranged from 8.5 to 10.4 inches.

INPUT DEVICES

Before the introduction and rapid growth of multimedia computer systems, the input device segment faced near extinction. Input devices include computer keyboards, mice, joysticks, and virtual reality headsets. In 1993, the market had revenues of $600 million and grew to over $1 billion in 1995. Manufacturers of keyboards alone shipped over 80 million units in 1995. The nearly universal adoption in the early 1990s of graphical operating systems such as Microsoft Windows in the consumer software market pushed sales of mice up rapidly. By 1997, most new consumer computer systems sold also included a mouse.

PRINTERS

The three principal printer types are dot-matrix, ink-jet, and laser. Dot-matrix printers were one of the first responses to demands by computer users for an output device that offered more flexibility than impact character printers. Dot-matrix devices dominated the printer market and continued to account for over 50 percent of unit sales in the early 1990s but offered relatively poor resolution. By the mid-1990s, the dot-matrix printer was largely being replaced since it offered smaller profit margins and did not appeal to consumers as much as newer technology. Dot-matrix prices typically ranged from $75 to $200.

Ink-jet printers, which averaged between $200 and $700 in price, featured much higher resolution and flexibility than dot-matrix technology. Ink-jets commonly offered resolution of 300 to 600 dots per inch (dpi) and provided several fonts and graphic capabilities. According to the market research firm International Data Corp., color ink-jet printers were expected to continue to grow to 97 percent of the ink-jet market by 1998. Ink-jets were expected to grow to 30 percent of the U.S. printer market by 1998. More than 4.3 million ink-jet printers valued at more than $960 million were shipped by U.S. firms in 1995.

Laser printers ranged in price from about $700 for low-end personal devices to between $1,500 and $3,000 for heavy-duty business printers in 1993. Laser printers typically offered 300 to 1,200 dpi resolution in 1997. However, laser printers were typically faster, more flexible, and usually had a greater paper handling capacity than ink-jets. In 1995, manufacturers shipped over 3.5 million laser printers worth $3.5 billion. Laser printers were forecast to achieve 50 percent of the printer market by 1998.

SCANNERS

Peripheral scanners are used to translate optical images to electronic signals. Able to recognize characters, line art, gray-scale, and color images, scanners use photosensitive arrays that reflect light to digitize printed information. The three types of scanners common in the 1990s were handheld, desktop, and drum. Drum scanners are not considered peripheral equipment, however, because they were a high-end tool used primarily in the printing industry.

Desktop, or flatbed, scanners were the most common device. Using optical character recognition (OCR) technology, these scanners were most often used to translate printed pages into a document that could be viewed, searched, and manipulated using a word processor. As the technology grew, desktop scanners were also frequently used to input and manipulate photographs and other graphic images. Typical flatbed scanners had a resolution of 300 to 1,200 dpi. In 1995, manufacturers shipped approximately 540,000 flatbed scanners worth $350 million. Handheld scanners were priced much lower than flatbeds and were regarded as more useful for scanning small graphics. They also delivered lower resolution and limited OCR compatibility. In 1992, approximately $1 billion worth of scanners were sold worldwide. As the storage devices increased in type and capacity, scanners became more prevalent for storing images and text by the late 1990s.

WORK FORCE

Like most other computer-related segments, the peripheral industry was expected to realize a significant reduction in its work force during the 1990s. This downsizing was expected to occur even among the industry's more successful companies, due to increased productivity gains and mergers effected to benefit from economies of scale. Nearly 20,000 jobs were expected to be eliminated between 1994 and 1998.

RESEARCH AND TECHNOLOGY

U.S. firms were on the leading edge of almost every peripheral technology in the industry in the mid-1990s. At least two efforts were underway during this time to advance the role of U.S. firms in the production of the rapidly growing color LCD market. One was a joint venture between Motorola Inc. and In Focus Systems—Motif. Motif sought to develop high-quality LCDs that could be manufactured inexpensively. The other effort was initiated by the Defense Advanced Research Projects Agency (DARPA). DARPA planned to provide $15 million in seed money for a consortium of large and small companies that would assemble the framework necessary to effectively compete in the color LCD market.

Scanner and printer manufacturers were striving toward similar technological and productivity goals. The demand for higher resolution, faster input and output, lower production costs, and greater flexibility were driving investment and development in both printer categories. In 1997, manufacturers were already delivering low-end laser printers capable of printing 600 dpi or greater.

Advances in the input devices market focused on ease and multifunctions. In 1995, Other 90% Technologies of California was working on a mouse that controls action by reading the electromagnetic signals within the user s skin. Arizona-based SC&T had keyboards with built-in radios and telephones in development.

In the future, the computer peripheral industry will likely become increasingly integrated with complementary industries, as data processing, interface, storage, fiber optics, wireless, and digital broadband switching technologies converge into a massive multimedia industry. Scanners, printers, and displays would also likely be used in conjunction with other communications and information equipment.

ASSOCIATIONS AND SOCIETIES

CDLA, THE COMPUTER LEASING AND REMARKETING ASSOCIATION
1212 Potomac St. NW
Washington, DC 20007
Phone: (202) 333-0102
Fax: (202) 333-0180

COMPUTING TECHNOLOGY INDUSTRY ASSOCIATION
450 E. 22nd St., Ste. 230
Lombard, IL 60148
Phone: (708) 268-1818
Fax: (708) 268-1384
Members are resellers of various kinds of microcomputers and computer equipment. Formerly known as Association of Better Computer Dealers and then ABCD: The Microcomputer Industry Association.

CORPORATION FOR OPEN SYSTEMS INTERNATIONAL
8260 Willow Oaks Corporation Dr., Ste. 700
Fairfax, VA 22031
Phone: (703) 205-2700
Fax: (703) 846-8590
Promotes worldwide standardization of computer systems.

INTERACTIVE MULTIMEDIA ASSOCIATION
48 Maryland Ave., Ste. 202
Annapolis, MD 21401-8011
Phone: (410) 626-1380
Fax: (410) 263-0590
Members are companies, organizations, and institutions that produce interactive multimedia hardware and software.

PERIODICALS AND NEWSLETTERS

EDP WEEKLY: THE LEADING WEEKLY COMPUTER NEWS SUMMARY
Computer Age and E D P News Services
3918 Prosperity Ave., Ste. 310
Fairfax, VA 22031-3300
Phone: (703) 573-8400
Fax: (703) 573-8594
Weekly. $495.00 per year. Newsletter. Summarizes news from all areas of the computer and microcomputer industries.

INTERACTIVE HOME
Jupiter Communications Co.
627 Broadway, 2 Fl.
New York, NY 10012
Phone: (800) 488-4345 or (212) 780-6060
Fax: (212) 780-6075
Monthly. $475.00 per year. Newsletter on devices to bring the Internet into the average American home. Covers TV set-top boxes, game devices, telephones with display screens, handheld computer communication devices, the usual PCs, etc.

MULTIMEDIA NEWS
Interactive Multimedia Association
48 Maryland Ave., Ste. 202
Annapolis, MD 21401-8011
Phone: (410) 626-1380
Fax: (410) 263-0590
Bimonthly. Membership newsletter.

PC LETTER: THE INSIDER'S GUIDE TO THE PERSONAL COMPUTER INDUSTRY
Stewart Alsop, editor
155 Bovet Rd., Ste. 800
San Mateo, CA 94402-3115
Phone: (800) 432-2478 or (415) 592-8880
Fax: (415) 312-0547
22 times a year. $495.00 per year. Newsletter. Includes reviews of new PC hardware and software.

DATABASES

MICROCOMPUTER ABSTRACTS [ONLINE]
Information Today, Inc.
143 Old Marlton Pke.
Medford, NJ 08055-8750
Phone: (609) 654-6266
Fax: (609) 654-4309
Contains abstracts covering a wide variety of personal and business microcomputer literature appearing in more than 90 journals and popular magazines. Time period is 1981 to date, with monthly updates. Formerly Microcomputer Index. *Inquire as to online cost and availability.*

PREDICASTS FORECASTS: U.S.
Information Access Co.
362 Lakeside Dr.
Foster City, CA 94404
Phone: (800) 321-6388 or (415) 378-5000
Fax: (415) 358-4759
Provides numeric abstracts of a wide range of published forecasts relating to specific U.S. products, markets, and industries. Monthly updates. Time period is 1971 to date. Inquire as to online cost and availability.

PROMT: PREDICASTS OVERVIEW OF MARKETS AND TECHNOLOGY
Information Access Co.
362 Lakeside Dr.
Foster City, CA 94404
Phone: (800) 321-6388 or (415) 378-5000
Fax: (415) 358-4759
Companies, products, applied technologies and markets. U.S. and international literature coverage, 1972 to date. Daily updates. Inquire as to online cost and availability. Provides abstracts from more than 1,200 publications.

WILSONLINE: APPLIED SCIENCE AND TECHNOLOGY ABSTRACTS
H. W. Wilson Co.
950 University Ave.
Bronx, NY 10452
Phone: (800) 367-6770 or (718) 588-8400
Fax: (718) 590-1617
Provides online indexing and abstracting of 400 major scientific, technical, industrial, and engineering periodicals. Time period is 1983 to date for indexing and 1993 to date for abstracting, with updating twice a week. Inquire as to online cost and availability.

STATISTICS SOURCES

COMPUTERS AND OFFICE AND ACCOUNTING MACHINES
U.S. Bureau of the Census
Washington, DC 20233-0800
Phone: (301) 457-4100
Fax: (301) 457-3842
Annual. Provides data on shipments: value, quantity, imports, and exports. (Current Industrial Reports, MA-35R.)

PREDICASTS FORECASTS
Information Access Co.
362 Lakeside Dr.
Foster City, CA 94404
Phone: (800) 321-6388 or (415) 358-4643
Fax: (415) 358-4759
Quarterly, with annual cumulation. $950.00 per year. Provides short-range and long-range forecasts of U.S. industry, product, service, economic, demographic, and financial data. Arranged according to Standard Industrial Classification (SIC) numbers, with projected annual growth rate given for each of the 50,000 series. Sources are over 500 publications issued by various organizations.

GENERAL WORKS

COMPUTER BUYER'S GUIDE AND HANDBOOK
Bedford Communications, Inc.
150 5th Ave.
New York, Ny 10011
Phone: (800) 877-5487 or (212) 807-8220
Subscription at $36.00 per year includes six issues of the bimonthly Computer Buyer's Guide and Handbook *and six issues of the bimonthly* Laptop Buyer's Guide and Handbook. *Includes equipment reviews, articles, comparison charts, and "Street Price Guide" (discounted prices with names, addresses, and telephone numbers of dealers).*

COMPUTER PARTS AND SUPPLIES
American Business Directories, Inc.
5711 S. 86th Cir.
Omaha, NE 68127
Phone: (402) 593-4600
Fax: (402) 331-1505
Annual. $395.00. Lists 8,857 dealers. Compiled from U.S. Yellow Pages.

DATA SOURCES
Ziff-Davis Publishing Co.
1 Park Ave.
New York, NY 10016
Phone: (800) 289-9929 or (212) 503-5861
Fax: (212) 502-5800
Semiannual. $495.00 per year. Three volumes, covering (1) hardware, (2) software, and (3) data communications. Lists about 10,000 suppliers, with information on all types of software and all sizes of computers and related equipment.

DIRECTORY OF VALUE ADDED RESELLERS
Chain Store Guide Information Services
3922 Coconut Palm Dr.
Tampa, Fl 33619
Phone: (800) 925-2288 or (813) 664-6700
Fax: (813) 664-6810
Annual. $280.00. Provides information on computer companies that modify, enhance, or customize hardware or software. Includes system houses, systems integrators, turnkey systems specialists, original equipment manufacturers, and value added retailers.

FURTHER READING

Howard, Bill. "A Scanner on Every Desk." *PC Magazine,* 9 April 1996.

Niemond, George A. "Computer and Peripherals Industry." *The Value Line Investment Survey,* 24 January 1997.

Ransdell, Eric. "The Mouse that Really Roared." *U.S. News & World Report,* 20 May 1996.

Ryan, Ken. "Printer Power." *HFN, The Weekly Newspaper for the Home Furnishing Network,* 29 April 1996.

U.S. Bureau of the Census. "Computer and Office Accounting Machines." *Current Industrial Reports.* Washington: GPO, 1996. Available from http://www.census.gov/industry/ma35r95.txt. ━━●

25

INDUSTRY SNAPSHOT

Valued at more than $37 billion in 1995, custom programming revenues increased by roughly 75 percent in the first half of the 1990s. The industry typically serves mid- to large-sized businesses needing specialized computer applications that are not available on the mass market or requiring customization of existing applications. Custom programming services are provided both by software programming vendors and by in-house programmers of computer technology firms. Computer programming services vary widely and change fairly rapidly as new technologies emerge.

The industry's growth slowed somewhat in the early 1990s due to greater availability of powerful prepackaged software programs for business applications that were compatible with standardized computer architecture, particularly IBM-compatible PCS. Previously these applications might have required proprietary programming on a mainframe computer or on other less standard computer hardware. Nonetheless prospects for custom programming services remained strong in the late 1990s as many businesses still relied upon original and expanded proprietary software compatible with numerous computer platforms and operating systems.

INDUSTRY OUTLOOK

Despite a slight slowdown in the growth rate of computer programming services in the mid-1990s, the industry appeared to be quite healthy. As companies emerged from a recession in the early 1990s, many found that an antidote to their smaller size was spending more on computer professional services. With increased use of information services such as electronic mail and networked computers, programming services enjoyed strong demand.

Computer-assisted software engineering tools, prepackaged software, and graphic user interfaces (GUIs), however, made it more difficult for computer programming services companies to maintain their high rate of growth in the 1990s. Some of the companies kept their edge by moving from programming software to software modifications and enhancements. Others marketed their services to companies that needed assistance integrating new software purchases. These systems integrators, chosen over custom programmers at times, were called on to integrate prepackaged software and hardware into a cohesive system.

Information systems, known as IS in the field, came into prominence in the late 1980s and early 1990s. Almost every business in the United States, from the

COMPUTER PROGRAMMING SERVICES

SIC 7371

With computer technology touching virtually every facet of modern society, the demand for computer programming services will only increase in the coming years. As a result, the projected need for computer services from 1990 to 2005 was much greater than for other jobs in the information technology industry. Burgeoning computer and Internet technologies will contribute to the sustained growth of the programming sector.

**SIC 7371 - Computer Programming Services
General Statistics**

	Establish-ments	Employment (000)	Payroll ($ mil.)	Revenues ($ mil.)
1987	14,687	184.2	6,286.6	14,170.2*
1988	13,182	202.5	7,781.4	-*
1989	12,057	208.4	8,086.3	-*
1990	12,443	217.2	8,906.8	22,213.0
1991	13,225	220.5	9,483.8	20,852.0
1992	23,265	242.7	10,890.2	23,236.0
1993	23,225	262.1	12,067.5	26,084.0
1994	22,719P	266.3P	12,637.2P	26,595.5P
1995	24,396P	277.9P	13,528.6P	27,995.2P
1996	26,072P	289.5P	14,419.9P	29,394.9P

Sources: Data for 1982, 1987, and 1992 are from *Census of Service Industries*, Bureau of the Census, U.S. Department of Commerce. Revenue data are from the *Service Annual Survey* or from the Census. Revenue data from the Census are labelled with *. Data for 1988-1991 and 1993, when shown, are derived from *County Business Patterns* for those years from the Bureau of the Census. A P indicates projections made by the editor.

smallest to the largest, was using computers in their day-to-day business and planning. Computer programming services became a necessity rather than a luxury.

Many companies funded in-house IS departments that handled everything from programming to technical support for internal users. Some companies that were able to do their own programming still hired computer service firms in the 1990s. As technology advanced, service firms helped companies maximize the benefits of their expensive computer systems. End users needed assistance with maintenance as well as with programming, installation, and integration. Computer service companies were called on to help users decide what software to buy, to help users create custom specifications, and to modify prepackaged software.

By the mid-1990s, much of the work performed by U.S. custom programmers was for foreign clients. Companies in Europe and eastern Asia were turning increasingly to U.S.-based computer professional services companies to create software or computer systems to help them compete in the global economy. Many computer programming companies sought out corporations that had just been privatized, such as those in the former Soviet Union. These corporations needed, in many instances, to create computer systems from the ground up, providing long-term work for U.S. programmers.

At the same time, many U.S. companies were "outsourcing," or sending their programming projects to outside companies. Many made use of foreign programmers who billed at a rate far below that of U.S. programmers. In the mid-1990s, contract programmers charged between $50 and $150 per hour depending on the seniority of the programmer. Contract programmers from other countries charged about $20 per hour.

Corporate executives needed speed and accuracy from their programmers. Some employers experienced legal problems with these independent, part-time contractors, who received no health or insurance benefits. The employer in these cases did not have rights to the programmer's creative output.

ORGANIZATION AND STRUCTURE

Computer programming services, along with systems integration services, and consulting and training, composed computer professional services. Combined, these services were offered by more than 4,000 companies and many more sole proprietorships in the United States in the mid-1990s. Many companies from other fields also were joining the industry by developing their own computer services departments. These companies usually found they could earn substantial profits in the field. Some telecommunications giants joined the industry through acquisitions, and some accounting firms and computer manufacturers also expanded their computer professional services segments.

Both the National Association of Computer Consultant Businesses (NACCB) and Independent Computer Consultants Association (ICCA) had members involved in contract programming. These trade associations represented their members in different ways. NACCB, headquartered in Washington, D.C., lobbied government officials on behalf of member businesses. ICCA ran its non-profit association out of St. Louis and offered certification exams. Successful completion of a computerized test allowed a member to be designated a Certified Computing Professional.

WORK FORCE

The industry employed about 271,400 programmers, support personnel, and managers in 1996, an 11.4 percent increase from 1995, and strong demand for programmers in this and related industries was expected to continue into the twenty-first century. The average hourly wage for non-supervisory workers in the industry was $21.57, which was well above the average wage for most industries in the United States. Computer services companies are considered better than average places to work in terms of working conditions and fringe benefits. Professionals employed by computer programming firms received on-going education and training in new technologies. More programmers were needed in software maintenance than in software development, and these maintenance programmers were required to be familiar with many types of hardware and software. They were required to learn client-server technology and to be flexible enough to work as development programmers. Those programmers with broad training and in-depth knowledge of several fields had the greatest potential for success. The projected need for computer services from 1990 to 2005 was much better than for other jobs in the information technology industry.

According to the Bureau of Labor Statistics, job categories for computer services workers were predominately white-collar positions. Unlike workers in telecommunications equipment, who were more likely to find jobs as precision workers, computer services workers were more likely to work as professionals, technicians, or managers.

RESEARCH AND TECHNOLOGY

With such technology as client-server systems and networks gaining popularity, programmers needed traditional skills as well as knowledge of the latest technologies. Some industry firms instituted team programming in which experienced programmers created application models, and newer programmers created standards and worked with clients to define objectives.

While computer-aided software engineering, or CASE, made it easier for in-house computer programmers to work without the help of outside firms, those

firms looked for other ways to make use of their expertise. Programmers and programming companies marketed their skills in various programming languages. They also developed expertise in "middleware", which helped their clients communicate through their applications.

SIC 7371
Occupations Employed by SIC 7371 - Computer and Data Processing Services

Occupation	% of Total 1994	Change to 2005
Computer programmers	16.0	52.5
Systems analysts	9.2	194.7
Computer engineers	6.4	165.1
Sales & related workers nec	6.0	86.0
General managers & top executives	4.8	49.4
Data entry keyers, ex composing	4.2	-24.5
Secretaries, ex legal & medical	3.0	11.5
Computer operators, ex peripheral equipment	2.9	-58.7
Engineering, mathematical, & science managers	2.7	49.0
Data processing equipment repairers	2.3	57.4
Professional workers nec	2.3	136.1
Computer scientists nec	2.1	186.4
General office clerks	2.0	34.3
Marketing, advertising, & PR managers	2.0	73.2
Bookkeeping, accounting, & auditing clerks	2.0	18.1
Clerical supervisors & managers	1.9	17.1
Management support workers nec	1.8	57.4
Electrical & electronics engineers	1.6	67.6
Writers & editors, incl technical writers	1.5	88.9
Financial managers	1.3	57.4
Receptionists & information clerks	1.3	57.4
Electrical & electronic technicians, technologists	1.3	57.4
Managers & administrators nec	1.2	57.3
Clerical support workers nec	1.1	25.9
Adjustment clerks	1.1	88.9
Accountants & auditors	1.0	57.4

Source: *Industry-Occupation Matrix*, Bureau of Labor Statistics. These data relate to one or more 3-digit SIC industry groups rather than to a single 4-digit SIC. The change reported for each occupation to the year 2005 is a percent of growth or decline as estimated by the Bureau of Labor Statistics. The abbreviation nec stands for 'not elsewhere classified'.

SIC 7371 - Computer Programming Services
Industry Data by State

State	Establishments			Employment			Payroll			Revenues - 1992 ($ mil.)			% change 87-92	
	1987	1992	% of US 92	1987	1992	% of US 92	1987 ($ mil.)	1992 ($ mil.)	$ Per Empl. 92	Total ($ mil.)	Per Estab.	$ Per Empl. 92	Revenues	Payroll
California	2,601	3,433	52.7	35,192	35,543	56.2	1,311.6	1,746.6	49,142	3,986.1	1.2	112,148	26.5	33.2
Virginia	606	948	14.6	20,029	26,532	41.9	655.5	1,150.9	43,380	2,500.6	2.6	94,247	72.7	75.6
New Jersey	1,016	1,596	24.5	13,990	16,122	25.5	558.6	874.8	54,263	1,840.8	1.2	114,181	49.4	56.6
New York	1,340	1,895	29.1	11,908	16,434	26.0	457.4	720.5	43,840	1,488.9	0.8	90,600	38.1	57.5
Texas	909	1,456	22.4	10,041	14,952	23.6	343.3	696.0	46,547	1,451.5	1.0	97,079	80.8	102.7
Maryland	454	737	11.3	11,041	15,021	23.7	336.4	651.3	43,356	1,315.2	1.8	87,554	104.9	93.6
Massachusetts	611	839	12.9	7,994	10,702	16.9	298.7	526.4	49,187	1,241.5	1.5	116,008	90.2	76.2
Colorado	311	558	8.6	4,573	7,868	12.4	156.5	362.8	46,116	901.0	1.6	114,519	151.4	131.9
Illinois	685	1,289	19.8	7,073	9,772	15.4	239.2	454.7	46,530	894.8	0.7	91,570	70.6	90.1
Florida	649	1,242	19.1	6,571	8,967	14.2	218.1	386.7	43,120	872.0	0.7	97,242	69.2	77.3

Source: *Census of Service Industries*, 1987 and 1992, Bureau of the Census, U.S. Department of Commerce. Data are sorted by 1992 revenues and, if revenues are unavailable, by establishments in 1992. (D) indicates that data are withheld by the source to avoid disclosure of competitive information. A dash (-) indicates that data are not available. Percentage changes between 1987 and 1992 are calculated using numbers that have *not* been rounded; hence they may not be reproducible from the values shown.

AMERICA AND THE WORLD

The United States was a leader in computer programming as well as in other computer professional services. Some U.S. firms hired foreign programmers for skills that were far less expensive than the hourly fees charged by American programmers. British programmers, for example, had a good grasp of UNIX, which was widely installed in the United Kingdom, and programmers from the former Soviet Union were often fluent in five or more programming languages. Most companies paid foreign programmers less and passed their savings on to their customers.

Computer professional services such as programming were encouraged by the passage of the North American Free Trade Agreement and the expansion of the General Agreement on Tariffs and Trade. The U.S.-Canada Free Trade Agreement of 1989 led some U.S. computer services companies to expand into other markets by buying Canadian firms. Some U.S. companies also had subsidiaries in South America and Europe.

Custom programming was being exported by U.S. firms at an increased rate in the early 1990s. The Commerce Department described the industry as having outstanding prospects for exporting success. According to the Bureau of Economic Analysis, exports of U.S. computer services totaled $3.4 billion in 1994, while imports were only $500 million. Most of these sales were realized through affiliate organizations overseas and, according to U.S. Department of Commerce statistics, computer service exports topped $12.9 billion in 1993. In the period from 1989 to 1993, these sales increased by a yearly average of 23%. ''Europe accounted for about 74 percent of these exports, followed by Asia with 19 percent,'' write Julie Thorne and Richard Brown in *Industry, Trade, and Technology Review.* ''Industry representatives note that the Asian market for computer services is relatively young, and growth rates are expected to be much higher in Asia than in Europe over the next few years.''

The European Community encouraged mergers and acquisitions among Western Europe's computer professional services firms. This had the potential to intensify competition for U.S. companies. At the same time, several foreign companies thrived by offering lower-cost programming to U.S. companies, and a few Japanese, Canadian, and British computer services firms bought U.S.-based computer services firms in the early 1990s.

The General Agreement on Trade in Services, or GATS, one of the primary arrangements establishing the World Trade Organization, has the capacity to revolutionize the computer services industry. The GATS agreement, which went into effect on January 1, 1995, helps reduce trade barriers between countries and opens U.S. and foreign markets to global competition.

ASSOCIATIONS AND SOCIETIES

DATAQUEST, INC.
1290 Ridder Park Dr.
San Jose, CA 95131
Phone: (408) 437-8000

NATIONAL ASSOCIATION OF PROFESSIONAL WORD PROCESSING TECHNICIANS
PO Box 1444
Philadelphia, PA 19105
Phone: (215) 698-8525

OFFICE AUTOMATION SOCIETY INTERNATIONAL
6348 Munhall Ct.
PO Box 374
McLean, VA 22101
Phone: (703) 821-6650

PERIODICALS AND NEWSLETTERS

DATAMATION
275 Washington St.
Newton, MA 02158
Phone: (617) 964-3030

DISTRIBUTED COMPUTING
Patricia Seybold Group
148 State St., 7th Fl.
Boston, MA 02109
Phone: (617) 742-5200
Fax: (617) 742-1028
Monthly. $495.00 per year. Newsletter. Formerly Patricia Seybold's Network Monitoring.

OFFICE AUTOMATION REPORT
Automated Offices, Ltd.
1123 Broadway
New York, NY 10010
Phone: (212) 924-8989
Monthly. $45.00 per year. Newsletter. News and analysis for managers involved in integrating office systems.

TYPE WORLD: THE NEWSPAPER FOR PAGE PROCESSING, ELECTRONIC PUBLISHING, TYPESETTING AND GRAPHIC COMMUNICATIONS
Pennwell Publishing Co.
1 Technology Pk.
Westford, MA 01886
Phone: (508) 392-2157
Fax: (508) 692-7806
18 times a year. $30.00 per year.

GENERAL WORKS

DATA SOURCES
Ziff-Davis Publishing Co.
1 Park Ave.
New York, NY 10016
Phone: (800) 289-9929 or (212) 503-5861
Fax: (212) 502-5800
Semiannual. $495.00 per year. Three volumes, covering (1) hardware, (2) software, and (3) data communications. Lists about 10,000 suppliers, with information on all types of software and all sizes of computers and related equipment.

DATAPRO DIRECTORY OF MICROCOMPUTER SOFTWARE
Datapro Information Services Group
600 Delran Pky.
Delran, NJ 08075
Phone: (800) 328-2776 or (609) 764-0100
Fax: (609) 764-2580
Two looseleaf volumes. Monthly updates. $779.00 per year. Detailed information about personal computer software and software companies.

DATAPRO REPORTS ON OFFICE AUTOMATION
Datapro Information Services Group
600 Delran Pkwy.
Delran, NJ 08075
Phone: (800) 328-2776 or (609) 764-0100
Fax: (609) 764-2580
Three looseleaf volumes. Monthly updates. $1,075.00 per year. Covers word processing, typewriters, dictation machines, copiers, printing systems, office furniture, addressing/mailing equipment, office telecommunications, facsimile equipment, microforms, calculators, audio-visual equipment, and filing systems.

ELECTRONIC OFFICE: MANAGEMENT AND TECHNOLOGY
Faulkner Information Services, Inc.
114 Cooper Ctr.
7905 Browning Rd.
Pennsauken, NJ 08109
Phone: (800) 843-0460 or (609) 662-2070
Fax: (609) 662-3380
Two looseleaf volumes, with monthly supplements. $990.00 per year. Contains product reports and other information relating to automated office and integrated services.

SECRETARIAL/WORD PROCESSING SERVICE
Entrepreneur, Inc.
2392 Morse Ave.
Irvine, CA 92714
Phone: (800) 421-2300 or (714) 261-2325
Fax: (714) 851-9088
Looseleaf. $59.50. A practical guide to starting a secretarial and word processing business. Covers profit potential, start-up costs, market size evaluation, owner's time required, site selection, pricing, accounting, advertising, promotion, etc.

FURTHER READING

Goff, Leslie. "A Vanishing Breed?" *Computerworld,* 11 April 1994, 119.

Halper, Mark. "Outsourcers Sharpen Re-engineering Skills." *Computerworld,* 11 April 1994, 30.

Thorne, Julie, and Richard Brown. "Computer Services: Examination of Commitments Scheduled under the General Agreement on Trade in Services." *Industry, Trade, and Technology Review,* July 1996.

COMPUTERS, ELECTRONIC

SIC 3571

With predictions that computer industry spending will total $860 billion dollars in 1997, an increase of 11 percent over 1996, the industry is still going strong. Still, that figure represents a growth slowdown from average industry growth in the early 1990s, and further deceleration is expected. The industry is unlikely to increase its 33 percent consumer market penetration without price decreases, and analysts predict future revenue will be closely tied to replacement sales. The response to growth slowdowns from PC manufacturers has been the release of sub-$1000 PCs, the targeting of a $500 price point for NCs, essentially trimmed-down PCs dependent upon a server connection for processing power and storage, and the marketing of incremental improvements to existing products to promote system "upgrades." Analysts are skeptical about whether increased market penetration from these tactics will be significant.

Top 10 COMPUTER AND OFFICE EQUIPMENT CORPORATIONS WITH THE HIGHEST REVENUES

Ranked by: Revenue in 1995, in millions of dollars.

1. IBM, with $71,940 million
2. Hewlett-Packard, $31,519
3. Compaq Computer Corp., $14,755
4. Digital Equipment, $13,813
5. Apple Computer Inc., $11,062
6. Sun Microsystems, $5,902
7. Dell Computer Corp., $5,296
8. Seagate Technology, $4,540
9. Pitney Bowes, $3,861
10. Gateway 2000, $3,676

Source: *Fortune,* Fortune 500 Largest U.S. Corporations (annual), April 29, 1996, p. F-47.

Following a period of rampant expansion in the 1970s and 1980s, the industry's growth slowed down in the early 1990s, but then picked up pace again by the mid-1990s. Total U.S. manufacturers' shipments for computers in 1995 were valued at $50.3 billion, an increase of 31.5 percent over the previous year's total of $38.26 billion. The number of computer units shipped in 1995 totaled 20.5 million, up 22.9 percent from 16.7 million in 1994. There were 205 manufacturers of electronic computers in the United States in 1995. The general outlook for the industry remained very positive heading into the late 1990s.

INDUSTRY OUTLOOK

Despite the slowing growth of the industry in the early 1990s and an apparent saturation of the market, developments within the computer industry have the potential to bring about a return to fast-paced growth in the late 1990s.

The biggest trend in the computer market since the end of the 1980s has been the adoption of networks of

PCs, particularly in the client-server configuration. At the high end, such networks have come to replace mid-range systems, and at the low end, such as in small offices, they offer sharing of data between previously unlinked PCs. Where in the past an organization would have a single mid-range computer shared by many simultaneous users through terminals, now each user had his own full-featured computer at his desktop, the client computer, while still being able to share central data located on a server computer. As more businesses found it advantageous to migrate to client-server systems, sales for new PCs and LAN servers grew enormously.

The continued growth in sales of PCs to expand and upgrade LAN users is no longer assured, however. In the mid-1990s an entirely new computer category emerged, called the network computer. The network computer (or NC, as opposed to PC) is an inexpensive, low-powered unit that utilizes the processing power and memory of the server computer to which it is connected over a network. Network computers may or may not have a hard drive to run software applications locally. Those that do not execute software that is on a server accessed through the Internet or a local network. Dubbed NC-S (network computer-server), models available in early 1997 included HDS Network Systems Inc.'s @workStation, Wyse Technology Inc.'s Winterm, and Network Computers Devices Inc.'s Explora. By contrast, NC-C (network computer-client) computers execute computers on the local desktop, and available models include IBM's Network Station, Sun Microsystems Inc.'s JavaStation, and devices from Acorn Computer Group Ltd. with technology licensed from Oracle Corp.'s Network Computing subsidiary. Whether they will succeed in competing with full-featured PCs is still uncertain.

Another major development contributing to the acceleration in computer sales in the mid-1990s was the incredible growth in popularity of the Internet and online services. On the one hand, the presence of the Internet and commercial online services spurred on further growth of the home computer market, as people who did not yet have computers finally decided to buy them for the purpose of getting on-line. At the same time, more and more businesses and organizations were putting their information on the Internet, a trend that fueled the sales of servers for use as Internet host computers. The popularity of the Internet among companies led to the emergence of internal corporate intranets, which was yet another use for more, new LAN servers. The Internet was also the impetus for development of the network computer. The idea was that there were potential users of the Internet who did not want to pay the higher price of a full-featured computer. For the home user, the NC does

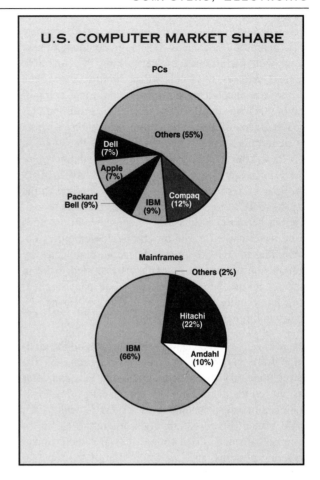

U.S. COMPUTER MARKET SHARE

PCs

Others (55%)
Dell (7%)
Apple (7%)
Packard Bell (9%)
IBM (9%)
Compaq (12%)

Mainframes

Others (2%)
Hitachi (22%)
IBM (66%)
Amdahl (10%)

not even have its own monitor, but uses a television screen instead.

Also encouraging the growth in computer sales is the advancement in multimedia technology. Multimedia refers to the incorporation of detailed graphics, sound, animation, or video into a computer program. In order to fully support such complex software, computers with ever faster processing speeds are required. The processing demands for multimedia encouraged purchases of faster, more powerful computers by existing computer owners wanting to "upgrade." It is predicted that 44.1 percent of PCs sold to home users in 1997 will be to homes that already own PCs.

Finally, the ever-present trend of lower costs in computer components, and the resulting lower prices that can be asked for the end products, continues to fuel sales. Consumers and businesses are not hesitant to replace only slightly outdated computers, since newer models offer greater capabilities at the same or even lower prices than the older models.

INDUSTRY SEGMENT STATUS

After a period of stagnation in the early 1990s, the mainframe market picked up again by 1994. Client/

server architecture, which at first seemed to compete with mainframes, actually began to be implemented along with mainframes, by networking PCs to mainframe computers. In 1993 less than 3 million networked PCs were connected to mainframe or mid-range computers, but this was expected to increase to 29 million PCs by 1997, according to WorkGroup Technologies. Costs for mainframes have also been falling with the adoption of a new kind of chip called CMOS (complementary metal-oxide semiconductor). It costs $18,000/MIPS (millions of instructions per second) as opposed to the $23,000/MIPS cost of the bipolar chips that it is replacing. Furthermore, CMOS-based computers do not need to be water-cooled as the bipolar-based computers do. According to a 1995 survey of leading companies by Softlab, the mainframe computer is expected to be in mainstream use past the year 2000. For many applications that require large volumes of data processing, the mainframe remains the best solution.

Mid-range computers have also withstood the challenge from networked PCs and workstations, as the server function that both mid-range and PCs can offer has blurred the distinction between the categories. Positioning mid-range computers as servers to which PCs could be networked has involved migrating to "open systems" of standardized connectivity architectures and operating systems, such as Unix. One of the top two mid-range manufacturers, DEC, migrated from proprietary operating system software to Unix and the "open-systems" that it offers. At the start of 1995, Unix owned a 44 percent share of the market share in the enterprise resource planning arena, while IBM's proprietary OS/400 had fallen to 40 percent. Nevertheless, IBM has stayed on top by moving to superior computing technology. In 1995, IBM migrated its AS/400 mid-range series from 48-bit CISC architecture to 64-bit RISC architecture, and had enormous sales of 70,000

units in 1996. By 1997, HP still had not migrated its HP 3000 to 64-bit processing.

The distinction between high-end PCs and workstations has become blurred, and thus the status of the workstation market segment depends on how it is defined. Sales of traditional workstations, which are based on RISC processors and run the Unix operating system, slowed toward the second half of the 1990s. Meanwhile, Intel processor-based personal workstations running Windows NT were poised for enormous growth. International Data Corp. predicted that the traditional workstation market would grow at only about 5 percent per year during the second half of the 1990s, while the personal workstation market would sustain the 40 percent-range growth it experienced in 1996.

The PC segment of the industry is the largest and most closely watched, but after more than a decade of shifting technologies, competitors, and marketing strategies, the industry segment achieved relative maturity and stability by the mid-1990s. After a period of price reductions, the marketing strategy shifted to keep prices around $2,000 for a fully configured system, but to add more and more features.

In the mid-1990s notebook computer sales were on the rise. One reason for the increasing popularity of notebook computers was that their screens, whose images were previously of poor quality, increased in size and clarity due to the drop in price in technology that allowed manufacturers to use higher-end, 12.1-inch TFT (thin film transistor) displays.

ORGANIZATION AND STRUCTURE

The computer industry is segmented by product category. Different kinds of computers have differing com-

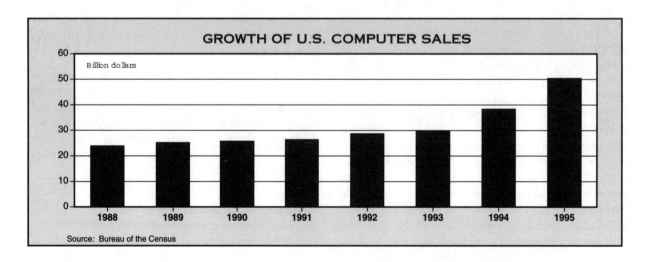

GROWTH OF U.S. COMPUTER SALES

Billion dollars

1988	
1989	
1990	
1991	
1992	
1993	
1994	
1995	

Source: Bureau of the Census

ponents, performance, and price levels, and, to a certain extent, service different functions and markets.

At the most fundamental level, electronic computers can be categorized as either analog or digital. Analog computers are electromechanical devices whose operation is based on continuously variable quantities such as lengths, weights, or voltages. Digital computers, by contrast, operate by processing discrete quantities of digits or characters. Digital computers offer greater flexibility in programming. Thus, almost all computers today are digital. Analog computers are designed only for very specific functions. Digital computers, on the other hand, usually serve general functions. It is the configuration of added software and peripheral hardware devices, however, that makes a digital computer suited for specific functions. In 1995, general purpose digital computer shipments accounted for $49.5 billion out of the computer industry total of $50.3 billion, and 20.38 units shipped out of a total of 20.52 million units.

General purpose digital computers are traditionally categorized by computer size and processing power. These main categories are supercomputers, mainframes, mid-range systems, and microcomputers.

SUPERCOMPUTERS

Supercomputers are high-speed number crunchers that allow scientists, engineers, and government researchers to process and manipulate massive amounts of data very quickly. Their performance is typically measured in terms of billions of floating point operations per second, or gigaflops, as opposed to millions of instructions per second (MIPS) assigned to most other types of computers. The fastest supercomputer, delivered in December 1996, reached processing speeds of 1.06 teraflops, or trillions of floating point operations-per-second. These technological taskmasters are used to complete complex feats, such as forecasting weather, designing ships and automobiles, conducting nuclear research, and carrying out advanced simulations.

An important distinction exists between traditional high-powered "vector," and low-powered "parallel" supercomputers. The newer parallel devices join as many as tens of thousands of cheap microprocessors to accomplish what vector systems achieve with a handful of more expensive processors. Though usually less expensive, systems that use Massively Parallel Processing (MPP) technology can perform many tasks faster than traditional vector systems.

MAINFRAME COMPUTERS

Mainframe computers generally offer less raw computational power than supercomputers, and are most often used to handle large volumes of general purpose

business or institutional applications. Users access the mainframe through satellite terminals that are connected to the system. Some mainframes also offer add-on features that make them competitive with low-end supercomputers. Systems range between $500,000 and $30 million. In 1996, mainframe processing speeds ranged from approximately 50 MIPS to over 360 MIPS.

MID-RANGE COMPUTERS

Mid-range computers, also called minicomputers serve anywhere from a few to several hundred users, either locally or at remote locations. Small to medium-sized businesses, company departments, and manufacturing facilities commonly use mid-range systems for communications processing, automation, reporting, and networking. Mid-range systems often employ vendor-developed proprietary applications, which are tailored to the organization's needs. Newer "open systems," though, allow the use of standardized operating systems and applications. Mid-range computers can range in price from $10,000 to approximately $1 million.

MICROCOMPUTERS

Microcomputers, or personal computers (PCs), unlike the systems mentioned above that serve users at satellite terminals, are single-user self-contained units. They offer the least raw computing power of any segment of the industry, but provide the greatest amount of flexibility, diversity, and portability. Although PCs are well-suited for home and personal use, about two-thirds of all units sold in the early 1990s were used for business and professional purposes. Prices ranged from $250 for low-powered clones to more than $25,000 for fully configured systems with advanced graphic and communications capabilities. This segment includes laptop and notebook computers.

Workstations are a special class of high-powered microcomputers. Because of technological advances in the 1980s, many workstations are capable of performing intensive research, engineering, and graphics tasks that allow them to compete with low-end supercomputers and mainframes. High-performance microprocessors allow many workstations to employ high-resolution or 3-D graphic interfaces, sophisticated multi-task software, and advanced communication capabilities. Workstation prices can range from $3,000 to over $100,000. The traditional definition of workstations are microcomputers based on RISC (reduced instruction set computing) microprocessor design, but the distinction between workstations and other personal computers is becoming increasingly blurred.

LOCAL AREA NETWORK SERVERS

A new category of computers that has emerged is based on function, rather than structure. These are Local Area Network (LAN) servers, which are the newest, fastest growing category of computers. Servers are similar to mid-range or mainframe computers in function, by serving multiple users with shared data, yet are similar to personal computers in structure, by being based on microprocessors. In fact, the lowest-end servers are merely high-end personal computers or workstations configured with the necessary software and telecommunications hardware. High-end servers contain multiple microprocessors, and have begun to cut into the market traditionally served by mid-range or mainframe computers.

Top Computer Firms - 1994

IBM
Hewlett-Packard
   Digital Equipment
Compaq
Apple
   AT&T G.I.S.
   Unisys
   Olivetti

Firms are ranked by revenues in billions of dollars. Shares of the group are shown in percent.

	Rev. ($ mil.)	% of Group
IBM	$ 64.1	44.5%
Hewlett-Packard	25.0	17.3
Digital Equipment	13.5	9.4
Compaq	10.9	7.6
Apple	9.2	6.4
AT&T G.I.S.	8.5	5.9
Unisys	7.4	5.1
Olivetti	5.6	3.9

Source: *New York Times*, September 21, 1995, p. C5, from *Hoover's Guide to Computer Companies*.

Personal computers make up the largest segment of the computer industry. Total PC and workstation shipments in 1995 were $36.23 billion in value and 15.7 million units. Despite the disappointments, the notebook market—which has been fueling the PC industry's overall unit sales growth—still grew 21.3 percent to 8.9 million units shipped worldwide in 1995, according to International Data Corp. Although sales were greater than sales in any other industry segment, low producer concentration and a commodity-like environment resulted in the PC segment having the lowest profit margins in the computer industry. For instance, while margins on PCs were typically between 5 and 30 percent, mainframe producers often earned a mark-up of 50 to 70 percent.

WORK FORCE

The computer industry employs large numbers of electrical engineers, programmers, assemblers, and technicians. In fact, these occupations represent about 30 percent of the industry total. Companies also hire large numbers of people for miscellaneous management, sales, and clerical positions. Coming into the mid-1990s, employment in the entire computer industry, of which electronic computer manufacturers represented about 50 percent, totaled about 220,000. Employment was significantly down from the industry peak in the mid-1980s, when electronic computer manufacturers employed over 150,000 workers.

Despite the continued growth in industry sales, employment in the industry has been declining since its peak in 1984. Between 1984 and 1995, the computer manufacturing industry lost 32 percent of its workforce, an average annual rate of 3 percent. The computer industry is one of the more highly automated manufacturing industries, and many manual assembly jobs have been eliminated. By 1996 only 35 percent of all jobs in the industry were directly involved in production, compared with 65 percent in 1960 and compared with 70 percent in the manufacturing sector as a whole in 1996. Companies that had traditionally been computer manufacturers shifted part of their activities to software and service, as these areas became more profitable. Many computer manufacturers transferred some of their production facilities overseas to take advantage of lower labor costs. In addition, more foreign-owned computer companies are supplying the U.S. market with either computers or parts through imports. Companies are expected to continue to introduce labor-saving automation and to outsource manufacturing activities to low-cost foreign producers. Furthermore, corporate alliances should moderate the demand for research and development professionals.

While the demand for programmers in the industry was expected to rise slightly, the demand for other occupations will likely fall, according to the Bureau of Labor Statistics. The demand for engineers, for instance, will slip about 3.5 percent by 2005. Likewise, technician and engineering management jobs will fall by 2 to 5 percent. Manufacturing jobs, especially, will disappear. The demand for electrical and electronic assemblers, for example, will likely plummet 55 percent by 2005. Analysts project that assemblers and fabricator positions will decline by about 37 percent, while the demand for production planning professionals will fall over 20 percent.

Management executive positions are expected to decrease as well—by an estimated 22 percent. Even the number of lower level management jobs is expected to fall by about 20 percent by 2005. The one bright spot in the job picture is an expected 47 percent increase in the demand for systems analysts and computer scientists. This group currently accounts for only about 2.4 percent of employment in the computer and office equipment industries.

Professionals with bachelor's degrees in computer engineering (BSCE) were in high demand in the mid-1990s. Computer and business-equipment manufacturers planned to hire almost 66 percent more graduates in 1997 than in 1996. Graduates with BSCE degrees could expect starting salaries on average of $37,301 in 1997, up 5.9 percent over 1996. Many of these new employees were not directly involved in computer manufacturing, but rather in services. Most of the biggest computing companies—IBM, Unisys, and DEC—have extensive and growing service and consulting divisions that hire hundreds of new graduates every year.

RESEARCH AND TECHNOLOGY

The computer industry has historically benefited from considerable government funds in research and development. This was especially the case during the Cold War. More recently, government funding of research in high technology industries has declined, and according to a study by the Institute for the Future, the industry's own investments in research have not been as great to make up the difference. Furthermore, in the early and mid-1990s computer companies were decreasing the percentage of their revenues that they invested in R&D. Computer companies still invest considerable resources in new product research and development, but this is mostly for the short term. Long-term basic research in entirely new technologies is not funded as well as it was in the past. Shorter product life cycles and a commoditization of the computer industry have contributed to this trend.

Nevertheless, the computer industry remains very technology-driven. Many of the technological innovations that impact the computer industry are being developed in other, related industries, however. These include faster and more powerful microprocessors developed by the semiconductor industry, the capacity for more memory storage developed by the computer storage device industry, the support of more detailed graphic and video developed by manufacturers of computer monitors and displays, faster communications capabilities between computers developed by the telecommunications equipment industry, and more robust operating systems and sophisticated applications developed by the computer

software industry. A trend toward smaller, faster, cheaper machines with greater memory will continue.

One continuing trend that is common among all these aspects of computers and related devices is miniaturization. Beginning with the invention of the microprocessor chip in 1971, and followed by the ability to store more data on smaller data storage media, the development of flat-panel displays, and computer system designs that better conserve space, computers have been getting smaller while retaining or increasing their processing power. *PC Magazine* predicts that the majority of computers by 2000 will be laptop-size.

Which standards to support for the new computer peripheral technologies is a major issue in the area of new technologies. For example, in the area of 56K bit/sec modems, AST Computer, Inc., Compaq Computer Corp., Hewlett-Packard Co., and Toshiba Corp. said they would support K56Flex, the protocol proposed in November 1996 by Rockwell and Lucent. However, Hitachi Ltd. and Dell Computer Corp. announced support for the competing U.S. Robotics x2 technology standard.

Another trend in computers is the integration of communications and processing equipment technologies that allow computers to act as telephones, answering machines, video-conferencing devices, and, television sets. Still cameras, video cameras, and video players may also be attached. Eventually the distinction between television sets and computers will be blurred. Not only is broadcast receiver hardware available as an add-on component for computers, but NCs and high-definition television sets whose screens can display the same high resolution of computers, will turn television sets into computers.

AMERICA AND THE WORLD

U.S. computer companies continued to dominate the world equipment industry in the 1990s, though they have been gradually losing market share since the mid-1980s. In 1996 exports were estimated to have accounted for 45 percent of all U.S. computer equipment shipments, which also included peripherals and parts. This rate of exports remained constant throughout the first half of the 1990s. The United States maintains a positive trade balance in computers, although the trade gap is narrowing. In computer parts and peripherals, however, the United States has had a growing trade deficit since 1991.

U.S. exports of computers were increasing only gradually in the 1990s and not as quickly as the industry was growing overall. According to U.S. Department of

Commerce statistics, exports of computer systems increased from $8.1 billion in 1990 to $9.48 billion in 1996, an increase of less than 3 percent annually. Exports actually declined by 8.2 percent in 1996 from $10.33 billion in 1995. Exports of peripherals and parts, meanwhile, have been increasing more rapidly.

Europe continued to be the largest foreign market for the U.S. computer industry in the late 1990s. Europe accounted for $14.4 billion or 38 percent of all U.S. computer, computer peripheral, and computer part exports in 1996. Asia was second, with $11.7 billion or 31 percent of U.S. computer equipment exports that year. Latin America was the fastest growing market, with computer equipment exports to the region increasing 32 percent from 1995 to 1996. Canada, Japan, and the United Kingdom are the top three export destinations for U.S. computer equipment.

Imports of computers to the United States, according to the U.S. Department of Commerce, increased from $2.7 billion in 1990 to $6.37 billion in 1996, an average rate of 15 percent per year. Imports jumped 26 percent in 1996 from the previous year. Imports of peripherals and computer parts have been increasing at an even faster rate. Asia is the largest exporter of computer equipment to the United States, accounting for $48.4 billion or 81 percent of all computer, computer peripheral, and computer part imports in 1996. The leading exporters are Japan and Singapore.

In terms of overall market growth for PCs, the western European PC market grew by 7.1 percent in 1996 to 15.9 million units, according to preliminary results from International Data Corp. PC shipments in Latin America grew by over 30 percent in 1996 to reach 3.1 million units, due to strong PC growth in Mexico, Colombia, Argentina, and Brazil according to Dataquest. Brazil was the leading Latin American market with 1.3 million units shipped in 1996. Mexico, on the other hand, was the fastest-growing country with a 73 percent increase of shipments over 1995. In both western European and Latin American markets, U.S. manufacturers account for the majority of the shipments.

The U.S. computer industry faces its most serious competition abroad from Japanese computer makers. Although the United States still maintains a technological advantage in large-scale systems and workstations, some Japanese competitors have made significant strides in those segments. Although Japanese companies have been trying to infiltrate the supercomputer market, over 90 percent of which is controlled by U.S. companies, their systems have offered limited performance and have lagged behind in MPP technology. Acquisition of U.S. and European firms, in addition to their own research and development, will likely make Japanese manufac-

turers contenders for supercomputer market share in the future. The Japanese domestic market for all computer categories, meanwhile, is the only one not dominated by the United States, partly due to Japanese protectionism. A U.S.-Japanese trade agreement that went into effect in 1993 belatedly helped open the Japanese public sector to U.S. firms.

The global market for U.S. computers is expected to offer even more opportunities as emerging economies demand more high-tech equipment and tariffs on the imports of computers are reduced. The International Trade Agreement approved in December 1996 by 28 countries was expected to eventually free U.S. computer manufacturers of having to pay customs tariffs in stages by January 1, 2000.

ASSOCIATIONS AND SOCIETIES

ASSOCIATION OF COMPUTER USERS
PO Box 2189
Berkeley, CA 94702-0189
Phone: (800) 327-9893 or (510) 549-4331
Fax: (510) 549-4331
Members are users of small computers for business applications.

ASSOCIATION FOR COMPUTING MACHINERY
1515 Broadway
New York, NY 10036-5701
Phone: (212) 869-7440
Fax: (212) 944-1318
Includes many Special Interest Groups.

COMPUTER AND AUTOMATED SYSTEMS ASSOCIATION OF SOCIETY OF MANUFACTURING ENGINEERS
PO Box 930
Dearborn, MI 48121-0930
Phone: (313) 271-1500
Fax: (313) 271-2861
Sponsored by the Society of Manufacturing Engineers.

INFORMATION TECHNOLOGY ASSOCIATION OF AMERICA
1616 N. Fort Myer Dr., Ste. 1300
Arlington, VA 22209
Phone: (703) 522-5055
Fax: (703) 525-2279
Members are computer software and services companies. Maintains an Information Systems Integration Services Section. Formerly ADAPSO: The Computer Software and Services Industry Association.

PERIODICALS AND NEWSLETTERS

ASSOCIATION FOR COMPUTING MACHINERY JOURNAL
Association for Computing Machinery
1515 Broadway, 17 Fl.
New York, NY 10036-5701
Phone: (212) 869-7440
Fax: (212) 944-1318
Quarterly. Free to members; non-member, $100.00 per year.

COMPUTER
IEEE Computer Society Press
10662 Los Vaqueros Cir.
Los Alamitos, CA 90720-1264
Phone: (800) 272-6657 or (714) 821-8380
Fax: (714) 821-4641
Monthly. Free to members; non-members, $. Edited for computer technology professionals.

COMPUTER LETTER: BUSINESS ISSUES IN TECHNOLOGY
Technologic Partners, Inc.
419 Park Ave. S, Ste. 500
New York, NY 10016-8410
Phone: (212) 696-9330
Fax: (212) 696-9793
40 times a year. $495.00 per year. Computer industry newsletter with emphasis on information for investors. Formerly Technologic Partners' Computer Letters.

COMPUTER RESELLER NEWS: THE NEWSPAPER FOR MICROCOMPUTER RESELLING
CMP Publications, Inc.
600 Community Dr.
Manhasset, NY 11030
Phone: (516) 562-5000
Fax: (516) 365-4601
Weekly. $189.00 per year. Includes bimonthly supplement. Incorporates Computer Reseller Sources *and* Macintosh News. *Formerly* Computer Retailer News.

COMPUTER SHOPPER: THE COMPUTER MAGAZINE FOR DIRECT BUYERS
Coastal Associates Publishing, L.P.
Computer Publications Div.
1 Park Ave.
New York, NY 10016
Phone: (800) 999-7467
Fax: (212) 503-3999
Monthly. $39.50 per year. Nationwide marketplace for computer equipment.

IBM JOURNAL OF RESEARCH AND DEVELOPMENT
IBM Corp.
500 Columbus Ave.
Thornwood, NY 10594
Phone: (914) 742-5850
Bimonthly. $74.50 per year.

INTERNET COMPUTING
IEEE Computer Society
10662 Los Vacqueros Cir.
Los Alamitos, CA 90720-1264
Phone: (714) 821-8380
Fax: (714) 821-4010

Bimonthly. Price on application. Covers technology, standards, research, and engineering for the Internet and the World Wide Web. Affiliated with the Institute of Electrical and Electronics Engineers.

MACWORLD
MacWorld Communications
501 2nd St., Ste. 600
San Francisco, CA 94107
Phone: (415) 243-0505
Monthly. $30.00 per year. For Macintosh personal computer users.

DATABASES

COMPUTER AND MATHEMATICS SEARCH
Institute for Scientific Information
3501 Market St.
Philadelphia, PA 19104
Phone: (800) 336-4474 or (800) 523-1850
Fax: (215) 386-2911
Provides online citations to the worldwide literature of computer science and mathematics. Time period is 1980 to date, with weekly updates. Inquire as to online cost and availability.

COMPUTER DATABASE
Information Access Co.
362 Lakeside Dr.
Foster City, CA 94404
Phone: (800) 227-8431 or (415) 378-5000
Fax: (415) 378-5369
Provides online citations with abstracts to material appearing in about 150 trade journals and newsletters in the subject areas of computers, telecommunications, and electronics. Time period is 1983 to date, with weekly updates. Inquire as to online cost and availability.

CSA ENGINEERING
Cambridge Scientific Abstracts
7200 Wisconsin Ave., Ste. 601
Bethesda, MD 20814
Phone: (800) 843-7751 or (301) 961-6750
Fax: (301) 961-6720
Provides the online version of Computer and Information Systems Abstracts, Electronics and Communications Abstracts, Health and Safety Science Abstracts ISMEC: Mechanical Engineering Abstracts (Information Service in Mechanical Engineering) *and* Solid State and Superconductivity Abstracts. *Time period is 1981 to date, with monthly updates. Inquire as to online cost and availability.*

INTERNET COMPUTER INDEX
Proper Publishing
A directory that provides links to hundreds of worldwide databases, special interest groups, files, and other information on PC, Macintosh, and Unix computers. Fees: Free. Gopher: ici.proper.com URL: http://ici.proper.com E-mail: infoatsproper.com

PATHFINDER
Association for Computing Machinery
Contains topical listings of information sources related to various areas of computing. Includes periodicals, special interest

---

groups, ACM books, and other resources. Time span: Current information. Updating frequency: As needed. Fees: Free. URL: http://auth.pathfinder.com/auth/createacct.cgi

WILSONLINE: APPLIED SCIENCE AND TECHNOLOGY ABSTRACTS

H. W. Wilson Co.
950 University Ave.
Bronx, NY 10452
Phone: (800) 367-6770 or (718) 588-8400
Fax: (718) 590-1617
Provides online indexing and abstracting of 400 major scientific, technical, industrial, and engineering periodicals. Time period is 1983 to date for indexing and 1993 to date for abstracting, with updating twice a week. Inquire as to online cost and availability.

STATISTICS SOURCES

COMPUTERS AND OFFICE AND ACCOUNTING MACHINES

U.S. Bureau of the Census
Washington, DC 20233-0800
Phone: (301) 457-4100
Fax: (301) 457-3842
Annual. Provides data on shipments: value, quantity, imports, and exports. (Current Industrial Reports, MA-35R.)

GENERAL WORKS

ADVANCES IN COMPUTERS

Academic Press, Inc.
525 B St., Ste. 1900
San Diego, CA 92101
Phone: (800) 321-5068 or (619) 231-0926
Fax: (800) 336-7377 or (619) 699-6715
Irregular. Price on application.

COMPUTER INDUSTRY ALMANAC

Karen Juliussen and Egil Juliussen
Available from Hoover's, Inc.
1033 La Posada Dr., Ste. 250
Austin, TX 78752
Phone: (800) 486-8666 or (512) 374-4500
Fax: (512) 374-4501
Annual. $62.95. Published by Computer Industry Almanac, Inc. Analyzes recent trends in various segments of the computer industry, with forecasts, employment data and industry salary information. Includes directories of computer companies, industry organizations, and publications.

BEING DIGITAL

Nicholas Negroponte
Alfred A. Knopf, Inc.
201 E. 50th St.
New York, NY 10022
Phone: (800) 733-3000 or (212) 751-2600
Fax: (212) 572-2593

1995. $23.00. A kind of history of multimedia, with visions of future technology and public participation. Predicts how computers will affect society in years to come.

COMPUTERS

Timothy Trainor and Diane Krasnewich
McGraw-Hill, Inc.
1221 Avenue of the Americas
New York, NY 10020
Phone: (800) 722-4726 or (212) 512-2000
Fax: (212) 512-2821
1994. Price on application. Fourth edition.

COMPUTERS AND INFORMATION PROCESSING

William M. Fuori and Louis V. Gioia
Prentice Hall
Rte. 9W
Englewood Cliffs, NJ 07632
Phone: (800) 922-0579 or (201) 592-2000
Fax: (201) 592-0696
1994. Price on application. Fourth edition.

INTRODUCING COMPUTERS: CONCEPTS, SYSTEMS, AND APPLICATIONS

Robert H. Blissmer
John Wiley & Sons, Inc.
605 3rd Ave.
New York, NY 10158-0012
Phone: (800) 225-5945 or (212) 850-6000
Fax: (212) 850-6088
Annual. $14.50. Revised yearly to keep pace with technological change.

MANAGEMENT INFORMATION SYSTEMS: A STUDY OF COMPUTER-BASED INFORMATION SYSTEMS

Raymond McLeod
Macmillan Publishing Co.
866 3rd Ave., 21 Fl.
New York, NY 10022
Phone: (800) 257-5755 or (212) 702-2000
Fax: (212) 713-8143
1995. Price on application. Sixth edition.

FURTHER READING

Bellinger, Robert. "More Jobs, Better Offers for '97 Computer Grads." Electronic Engineering Times, 25 November 1996.

"Computers - Major." Moody's Industry Review, 4 October 1996.

Damore, Kelley, and Deborah Gage. "Servers." Computer Reseller News, 3 June 1996.

Darnay, Arsen J., ed. Manufacturing USA. 5th ed. Detroit: Gale Research, 1996.

"Strong Industry Demand Fuels Transpacific Flow of Computer Parts, Finished Goods to Pacific Rim." Traffic World, 3 June 1996.

Thibodeau, Patrick. "Trade Pact Could Boost Computer Sales." Computerworld, 16 December 1996.

Upbin, Bruce. "Annual Report on American Industry: Computers & Communications." *Forbes,* 13 January 1997.

U.S. Department of Commerce. Office of Computers and Business Equipment. "Computer Industry Trends and Trade Data." 21 January 1996. Available from http://www.ita.doc.gov/industry/computers/data4.txt.

"Western European PC Market Grows 7.1 Percent Year on Year, According to IDC." *PR Newswire,* 4 February 1997.

CONCRETE, GYPSUM, AND PLASTER PRODUCTS

SIC 3270

When *spending on infrastructure and construction increases for all facets of the construction industry there are corollary increases in product shipments. In the mid-1990s, increased public works projects, financed through increased sales of tax-exempt bonds in the United States, were expected to increase 5 to 8 percent with a slight downturn expected in 1996. In addition to a healthy bond market, healthier state and local government budgets, which have been fraught with deficits since the 1980s, were expected to improve and stimulate public works spending.*

In 1996 the concrete block and brick industry had approximately 17,900 employees, an increase of 12 percent above the 16,000 workers reported in the industry in 1993. Establishments in the industry shipped products with a total value of $2.6 billion in 1996. An estimated $1.5 million of those receipts were solely for concrete block and brick products. The 17,900 employees in the industry in 1996 earned a total of $519.7 million. Of that, 10,000 were production workers.

Concrete is a leading material resource for building construction and for various products because of its strength, ability to be molded into any shape, resistance to fire and weather, and because of the availability of materials from which it is made. Concrete's limited strength under tensile stress was substantially overcome by reinforcement with steel and other materials in various ways. Concrete businesses in the early 1990s furnished much of the basic resources for the construction industries, as well as for utilitarian and artistic products like railroad ties and birdbaths. A few of the larger construction contractors manufactured their own concrete materials and products, while others relied on concrete producers for their products.

The products included in the concrete products, except block and brick industry are made of concrete, formed and hardened at the cement facility, and shipped in finished form to customers or users. Many of the items are prefabricated parts to be assembled into buildings, bridges, or parking structures. Pipe is another major segment of the industry. Other products include a variety of utilitarian and decorative items, such as burial vaults, septic tanks, monuments, and bird baths. In contrast to products that are poured on-site, the products of this industry are made in a controlled environment, away from a construction job site. Such controlled production conditions enable concrete products to be made more structurally sound and in accordance with construction specifications.

The ready-mixed concrete industry includes businesses that make concrete and deliver it to contractors or other customers for constructing buildings, bridges, roads, sidewalks, or other facilities. The concrete production process involves the use of large scale equipment and machinery located reasonably near to where the concrete is to be used, so that the concrete can be delivered while it is still soft enough to be shaped.

The ready-mixed concrete industry is heavily dependent on its primary customers, which are constructors of homes, industrial and office buildings, highways, and bridges. Consequently, the industry's market generally shadows the cyclical markets served by construction industries. For example, in the early 1990s the market for public works construction was strong while the other building markets were weak. Construction in public works projects in the United States alone—infrastructure construction ranging from construction of public buildings, highways, and conduits for utilities—was expected to continue through the decade, then predicted to level off at about $120 billion through 1998. Concrete industries were developing new technologies in the 1980s and 1990s to make concrete building parts stronger and more attractive, which helped the industry to reinforce its market in the construction industries.

Lime, or quick-lime, is calcium oxide derived from naturally occurring calcium carbonate. Its total production in the United States ranked fifth among all chemicals. Lime is produced at 109 plants in 33 states as well as in Puerto Rico, with the greatest number of plants operating in Colorado, Montana, and Wyoming. The total value of the product in 1994 was more than $1 million.

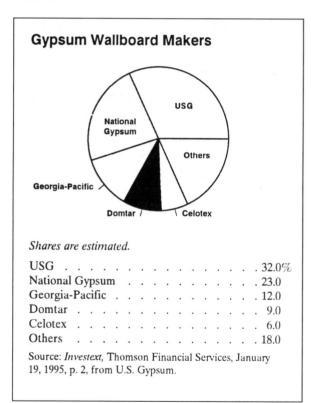

Gypsum Wallboard Makers

Shares are estimated.

USG	32.0%
National Gypsum	23.0
Georgia-Pacific	12.0
Domtar	9.0
Celotex	6.0
Others	18.0

Source: *Investext,* Thomson Financial Services, January 19, 1995, p. 2, from U.S. Gypsum.

Companies predominately employed in manufacturing plaster, plasterboard, and other gypsum products constitute the gypsum products industry. The manufacturers in this industry produce products such as acoustical plaster, wallboard, cement, insulating plaster, orthopedic plaster (for casts), plaster of paris, and gypsum rock, lath, and tile. Gypsum, or hydrated calcium sulfate, has been an important construction material for centu-

ries. It is mined from hardened ocean and saline-lake brine deposits. Natural supplies of the material are abundant, particularly in the United States, Canada, France, Italy, and Britain. The largest U.S. lime producing states are Oklahoma, Iowa, Texas, Michigan, Nevada, California, and Indiana. These states contributed 75 percent of the total domestic production of lime, producing more than a million tons each in 1994.

INDUSTRY OUTLOOK

United States total cement consumption grew by 19.2 percent between 1991 and 1994; March 1995 cement prices were 5.3 percent higher than the previous year. Also, production in 1995 was reported to be reaching capacity, save in New England and California, where the industry was feeling the impact of slower economic recovery.

Many of the larger ready-mixed concrete companies benefitted from centralized purchasing, marketing, and engineering operations. Many were involved in manufacturing fields related to concrete production, such as making concrete pipe, railroad ties, and construction structural elements. Because of the benefits of size, it was expected that the trend toward larger companies in the industry would continue.

While some core lime markets remained stagnant into the mid-1990s, other segments were expected to buoy production volume and industry earnings throughout the next decades. Flue gas desulfurization in 1996 accounted for 15 percent of all lime sales and, as the market segment with the fastest growth, was poised to continue with utility deregulation. As environmental restrictions increase, so too will lime uses related to treating wastes. In 1995 alone, two Midwestern utilities that invested in new lime scrubbers increased the market by a single-year record amount.

After being hammered by brutal markets, gypsum producers experienced a slight reprieve in 1993 as industry revenues rose a tepid 4 percent. Gypsum demand was forecast to rise about 3 percent per year through the mid-1990s. Prices were also expected to recover, albeit very slowly. New manufacturing technologies, mostly aimed at reducing energy consumption, were expected to raise productivity and boost profit margins. Demand increased in 1994 because of increased domestic construction. Sales increased 12 percent, while value rose 48 percent to $2.6 billion.

ORGANIZATION AND STRUCTURE

The great majority of customers for concrete products are building contractors and construction firms. This required industry firms to deal with architects and engineers as well as management. Many of the industry's sales comprised standard or off-the-shelf items that were produced, warehoused, and sold to multiple customers. Other items were tailor-made to the specific design of particular buildings, bridges, parking structures, or other facilities. Where products made of plastic or lumber were possible alternatives, precast concrete products are sometimes preferred and selected for environmental reasons.

Companies in the industry tended to grow by acquisitions and mergers. The greater size enabled the companies to spread their marketing, research, and engineering costs over a larger number of activities. Industry firms also joined to form several trade groups, which generally conducted research into materials and methods to improve the products, performed promotion of the product specialty, and represented the industry in governmental matters. These associations included the American Concrete Institute, the American Concrete Pressure Pipe Association the Concrete Reinforcing Steel Institute, the Post-Tensioning Institute, the Portland Cement Association, the American Segmental Bridge Institute, and the Precast/Prestressed Concrete Institute.

Industry firms continually conduct research to improve the qualities of concrete products. Areas of focus include workability, strength, durability, weight, and insulating ability. Minimum quality standards for products were established by the American Society for Testing and Materials (ASTM), and are continuously modified as technology develops and changes.

Many ready-mixed concrete companies are relatively small, having customers in one community or a limited region, primarily because soft concrete cannot be delivered beyond about 20 miles from where it is made. Yet to produce the concrete economically requires considerable expenditures for plant and trucking facilities. Most concrete plants were fixed, but some were portable and could be moved close to major construction sites. Most of the ready-mixed concrete producers are also involved in related concrete businesses, such as the mining of sand and gravel, the production of crushed stone, cement manufacture, or the manufacture of concrete blocks, pipe, building structural elements, and other concrete products. Many larger companies have grown by expanding their territories as well as by purchasing smaller local firms.

Blast furnace operators and steel manufacturers consume the largest amounts of lime products to melt and process steel. Steel production usage, the traditional driving force in this industry, consumed about 31 percent of industry output in 1994. Total use in chemical and industrial applications represented 64 percent of the lime market. Chemical firms, for example, use lime-related products in the production of plastic resins. Environmental uses, such as water, sewage, and smokestack emissions treatment, accounted for 26 percent of lime usage in 1994, and construction industries con-

SIC 3271 - Concrete Block & Brick
General Statistics

Year	Companies	Establishments		Employment			Compensation		Production ($ million)			
		Total	with 20 or more employees	Total (000)	Production Workers (000)	Hours (Mil)	Payroll ($ mil)	Wages ($/hr)	Cost of Materials	Value Added by Manufacture	Value of Shipments	Capital Invest.
1982	1,039	1,155	251	15.5	9.1	17.8	261.9	7.51	718.4	577.8	1,301.8	37.6
1983		1,114	265	15.9	9.5	17.9	282.4	7.92	858.5	731.1	1,581.9	107.9
1984		1,073	279	16.2	9.7	18.9	297.2	7.87	894.5	746.1	1,632.2	56.4
1985		1,031	292	16.0	9.5	18.8	311.0	8.41	936.9	771.9	1,689.7	72.5
1986		1,000	313	16.1	9.4	20.0	337.1	8.65	1,080.1	922.0	1,989.4	70.6
1987	976	1,129	339	18.6	10.8	23.5	411.8	9.20	1,185.6	1,071.7	2,245.8	72.0
1988		1,043	322	18.3	10.4	22.9	433.2	9.71	1,207.3	1,125.3	2,338.8	39.5
1989		998	316	18.0	10.4	22.2	432.0	9.51	1,194.5	1,087.9	2,282.1	75.1
1990		977	309	17.8	10.5	22.0	438.9	9.73	1,162.5	1,134.3	2,304.0	65.9
1991		948	265	17.8	9.9	22.4	461.8	10.07	1,072.6	1,064.2	2,143.8	48.8
1992	887	1,071	290	16.4	9.2	20.3	429.9	10.27	1,025.1	1,030.8	2,051.1	57.3
1993		963	276	16.0	9.1	19.7	411.3	10.47	1,104.5	1,019.4	2,125.2	50.5
1994		957P	304P	17.6	10.0	21.8	471.5	10.93	1,225.0	1,137.4	2,350.2	74.9
1995		944P	306P	17.8P	10.0P	22.6P	502.7P	11.19P	1,298.7P	1,205.8P	2,491.6P	58.5P
1996		931P	307P	17.9P	10.0P	22.9P	519.7P	11.46P	1,335.1P	1,239.6P	2,561.5P	57.7P
1997		918P	309P	18.0P	10.0P	23.2P	536.8P	11.74P	1,371.5P	1,273.4P	2,631.3P	57.0P
1998		905P	311P	18.2P	10.0P	23.5P	553.9P	12.01P	1,407.9P	1,307.2P	2,701.1P	56.2P

Sources: 1982, 1987, 1992 *Economic Census*; *Annual Survey of Manufactures*, 83-86, 88-91, 93-94. Establishment counts for non-Census years are from *County Business Patterns*; establishment values for 83-84 are extrapolations. 'P's show projections by the editors. Industries reclassified in 87 will not have data for prior years.

sumed about 8 percent, with refractory dolomite usage consuming 2 percent of United States total lime production.

Lime is considered a commodity, and industry profit margins are typically low. However, new applications for lime allowed the industry to realize steady demand growth throughout the mid-1900s and even through the 1980s. Between 1982 and 1988, for instance, sales of lime expanded 35 percent, from $543 million to about $830 million. Growth faltered in the late 1980s and early 1990s, and lime production dipped to about 17.5 million tons and $720 million in 1991. World production has been tapering off each year since 1990. U.S. lime producers were poised for recovery in 1993 and 1994; production in those years was 16.8 million metric tons at a value of $965 million, according to the Bureau of Mines, and 17.4 million metric tons worth just over $1 billion.

Gypsum is used as a fertilizer, a filler in paper and textiles, and a retarding agent in cement. About 80 percent of total gypsum output, however, is used to make plaster that is formed into building products. When combined with water and additives, plaster becomes a white cementing material that sets and hardens by chemical reaction. It is an excellent construction material for interior walls because it is inexpensive, easy to install, fire retardant, and acts as a noise insulator.

The United States remains the largest consumer of wallboard, accounting for more than half of world sales in 1994. About 75 percent of the gypsum used in the United States is used in wallboard. About 40 percent of wallboard products are used in new residential construction. Another 35 percent of industry output is used for remodeling and repair, and 10 percent goes into new commercial construction. The remaining 15 percent of the market consists of numerous miscellaneous applications, such as mobile home walls.

Because the industry is dependent on new residential construction, sales are closely linked to U.S. housing starts. Strong housing markets during the post-World War II U.S. economic expansion pushed industry sales close to $2 billion in the late 1970s. But a housing slump in the early 1980s kept revenues to $2.3 billion in 1982. A recovery in housing starts boosted gypsum industry sales to a peak of nearly $2.7 billion in 1987. A U.S. economic recession and depressed housing markets in the late 1980s and early 1990s, however, pummeled industry participants. Receipts plunged below $2 billion annually in the early 1990s, and wallboard prices crashed from $127 per thousand square feet in 1985 to $67 in 1992. In 1994, plant production was increased slightly; prices between December 1993 and 1994 rose 13 percent, with an average price of $149 per thousand square feet.

WORK FORCE

The concrete products industry employed 61,000 people in 1991 and earned a total of $1.4 billion, for an average of $23,062 per employee. Almost 74 percent of the industry employees were hourly workers, who earned an average of $9.56 per hour. The industry's white collar jobs encompassed accounting, engineering, estimating, marketing, and management.

Most of the employees in the ready-mixed concrete industry were production workers. Larger companies and many smaller companies used computers not only for accounting but for controlling the processes of concrete mixing and other production operations. The larger companies in particular employed skilled engineers to help refine mixing and production processes.

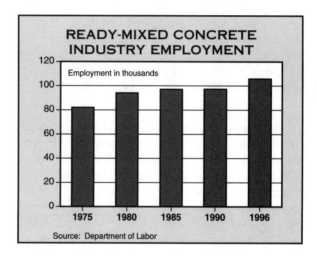

READY-MIXED CONCRETE INDUSTRY EMPLOYMENT

Employment in thousands

Source: Department of Labor

A recovering economy and new lime applications will help boost industry employment between 1990 and 2005, according to the U.S. Bureau of Labor statistics. Lime manufacturers employed about 4,500 workers in the early 1990s, down from more than 5,500 in the early 1980s. Despite continued productivity gains, however, jobs in most occupations should rise by 5 to 20 percent by 2005. Truck drivers, which make up about 30 percent of the entire work force, will see their opportunities jump by 13 percent. Industrial production management jobs will grow approximately 23 percent. Sales and marketing positions will likely increase 27 percent.

RESEARCH AND TECHNOLOGY

Industry firms conducted continuous research throughout the twentieth century to enhance the qualities of concrete products and construction operations and to improve the methods for producing and delivering concrete. Additional advancements were made by businessmen and managers, as with the adaptation of trucks for deliveries and mixing in the early part of the century.

Continual and sometimes dramatic changes in science and engineering produced positive changes in the industry. Industrialization of the precast concrete products industry began in earnest in the 1960s and 1970s as an increasing number of improvements in the strength and other qualities of concrete were made by scientific, engineering, and chemical research and analyses. Technicians in these specialties combined steel with concrete to enable its use in large bridge and skyscraper structural elements, as well as applied computers and automation to control and mix raw material ingredients accurately. Many studies and tests were conducted to determine the effects of different material ingredients, and varying proportions of those ingredients, in producing desired new concrete qualities. These scientific activities were performed by both individual companies—each hoping to improve its own competitive position—and industry supported trade associations and institutes.

In the mid-1990s, there was some controversy in the United States regarding the manufacture of concrete-related products using cement made in hazardous waste burning kilns. It was thought that perhaps the toxic chemicals not destroyed in the process could leach through the pipe or other products and into the environment; however, there has been little research that would either support or refute these claims. The concern spawned legislation at the local government level banning the use of or sale of "toxic cement," including the use of concrete pipe manufactured with cement made from hazardous waste fueled kilns in public water supplies. The use of used tires as a kiln fuel was also challenged by environmental regulations. Proponents, however, argued that using spent tires was an effective form of recycling. Both practices have met with numerous legal challenges.

For years concrete producers and industry groups endeavored to improve concrete's strength, durability, uniformity, appearance, drying time, and weight. By the early 1990s, concrete's compression strength had been increased to withstand 20,000 pounds per square inch (psi), while in laboratory experiments strengths of 100,000 psi were reached. In the 1960s, 5,800 psi was considered high-strength concrete.

The American Society of Civil Engineers established the Civil Engineering Research Council (CERC)

SIC 3271 Occupations Employed by SIC 327 - Concrete, Gypsum, and Plaster Products		
Occupation	% of Total 1994	Change to 2005
Truck drivers light & heavy	31.4	-10.5
Helpers, laborers, & material movers nec	4.6	-13.2
General managers & top executives	4.3	-17.6
Blue collar worker supervisors	4.2	-19.9
Sales & related workers nec	3.2	-13.2
Bookkeeping, accounting, & auditing clerks	2.5	-34.9
Industrial truck & tractor operators	2.5	-13.2
Bus & truck mechanics & diesel engine specialists	2.4	-13.2
Dispatchers, ex police, fire, & ambulance	2.4	-13.2
Extruding & forming machine workers	2.3	21.6
Assemblers, fabricators, & hand workers nec	2.2	-13.2
Precision workers nec	2.2	4.2
Concrete & terrazzo finishers	2.2	-13.2
Crushing & mixing machine operators	2.1	-13.2
General office clerks	1.8	-26.0
Helpers, construction trades	1.8	-13.2
Industrial machinery mechanics	1.7	-4.5
Industrial production managers	1.5	-13.1
Secretaries, ex legal & medical	1.4	-20.9
Maintenance repairers, general utility	1.4	-21.9
Welders & cutters	1.3	-13.1
Freight, stock, & material movers, hand	1.2	-30.5
Machine feeders & offbearers	1.1	-21.9

Source: *Industry-Occupation Matrix*, Bureau of Labor Statistics. These data relate to one or more 3-digit SIC industry groups rather than to a single 4-digit SIC. The change reported for each occupation to the year 2005 is a percent of growth or decline as estimated by the Bureau of Labor Statistics. The abbreviation nec stands for 'not elsewhere classified'.

to spearhead a program of construction product improvements the society considered to be essential to meet infrastructure needs for the twenty-first century. The CERC developed plans to work with government, industry, and trade groups in designing and perfecting higher strength concrete.

Ready-mixed concrete companies as well as trade groups were continuously seeking more efficient manufacturing and processing approaches. Examples included enabling longer delivery span, reducing truck and equipment maintenance costs, facilitating filling of bags, and automated setting of concrete curbs.

AMERICA AND THE WORLD

The principal international relationships of the ready-mixed concrete industry have been that some of the raw materials have been received from overseas, growing operations in the United States have been foreign owned, and some American companies have had facilities that produced concrete in other countries. Concrete transactions between countries were somewhat limited by the fact that ready-mixed concrete production and sales were local operations. Also, hardened concrete products, like pipe and concrete block, were prohibitively expensive to ship overseas because of their weight. However, there have been significant cases of international ownership of ready-mixed and other concrete operations.

In the 1980s, cement from foreign sources filled more 15 percent of U.S. needs, but not without conflict. A battle between cement producers in the United States and Mexico started in the late 1980s and escalated through the next decade. Mexico's Cemex—the largest producer in that country as well as the globe's fourth largest firm in the industry—was accused of dumping product in the United States. The U.S. Department of Commerce started tacking on anti-dumping duties in 1990, which were raised again in May of 1995 from 43 percent to 62 percent. *The Economist* reported that 19 U.S. manufacturers grumbled because the duty was considered too low. The United States imported 11.3 million tons of concrete in 1994, 60 percent more than was imported in 1993 and the most since 1990, according to *The Economist.*

ASSOCIATIONS AND SOCIETIES

AMERICAN CONCRETE INSTITUTE
PO Box 19150
Detroit, MI 48219
Phone: (313) 532-2600
Fax: (313) 538-0655

NATIONAL CONCRETE MASONRY ASSOCIATION
2302 Horse Pen Rd.
Herndon, VA 22071-3406
Phone: (703) 713-1900
Fax: (703) 713-1910

NATIONAL READY MIXED CONCRETE ASSOCIATION
900 Spring St.
Silver Spring, MD 20910
Phone: (301) 587-1400
Fax: (301) 585-4219

PERIODICALS AND NEWSLETTERS

ABERDEEN'S CONCRETE JOURNAL: THE CONCRETE PRODUCER'S FAVORITE MAGAZINE
Aberdeen Group
426 S. Westgate St.
Addison, IL 60101
Phone: (800) 837-0870 or (630) 543-0870
Fax: (630) 543-3112
Monthly. $33.00 per year. Covers the production and marketing of various concrete products, including precast and prestressed concrete.

ABERDEEN'S CONCRETE REPAIR DIGEST: THE MAGAZINE FOR THE CONCRETE REPAIR SPECIALIST
Aberdeen Group
426 S. Westgate St.
Addison, IL 60101
Phone: (800) 837-0870 or (630) 543-0870
Fax: (630) 543-3112
Bimonthly. $21.00 per year. Edited for specialists in the repair, maintenance, and restoration of concrete construction. Covers technology, marketing, and management.

ACI STRUCTURAL JOURNAL
American Concrete Institute
PO Box 19150, Redford Sta.
Detroit, MI 48219
Phone: (313) 532-2600
Fax: (313) 538-0655
Bimonthly. Free to members; non-members, $101.00 per year.

CONCRETE PRODUCTS
Intertec Publishing Corp.
29 N. Wacker Dr.
Chicago, IL 60606
Phone: (800) 621-9907 or (800) 543-7771
Fax: (312) 726-2574
Monthly. $36.00 per year.

GENERAL WORKS

ACI DIRECTORY
American Concrete Institute
22400 W. 7 Mile Rd.
Detroit, MI 48219
Phone: (313) 532-2600
Fax: (313) 538-0655
Biennial. Members, $16.95; non-members, $56.50.

CONCRETE PRODUCER NEWS-BUYER'S GUIDE
Edgell Communications, Inc.
7500 Old Oak Blvd.
Cleveland, OH 44130
Phone: (800) 225-4569 or (216) 826-2839
Annual. $28.00.

CONCRETE TECHNOLOGY
Adam Neville and others
John Wiley & Sons, Inc.
605 3rd Ave.
New York, NY 10158-0012
Phone: (212) 850-6000
Fax: (212) 850-6088
1987 $67.95.

DESIGN OF CONCRETE STRUCTURES
Arthur H. Nilson
McGraw-Hill, Inc.
1221 Avenue of the Americas
New York, NY 10020
Phone: (800) 722-4726 or (212) 512-2000
Fax: (212) 512-2821
1991. $44.76. 11th edition.

FURTHER READING

Chapman, Peter. "Lime Growth Doesn't Meet Expectations." *Chemical Marketing Reporter,* 1 January 1996, 5.

"Lime Demand Eases, But Market Remains Strong." *Industrial Specialties News,* 6 May 1996.

Sawinski, Diane, and Wendy Mason, eds. *Encyclopedia of Global Industries.* Detroit: Gale Research, 1996.

U.S. Department of the Interior. Bureau of Mines. *Minerals Yearbook: Metals and Minerals, Vol. I.* Washington:GPO, n.d.

The construction business has become increasingly international in scope during the past 15 years. Multinational companies are expanding markets and looking to build new production facilities. The top 225 international contractors have revenues from construction outside their home country, showing an increase from $92.2 billion in 1994 to $105 billion in 1995.

In 1996, home builders enjoyed a boom year as housing starts rose about 8 percent, to 1.5 million units, the highest level since 1987. Contractors were benefitting from a rise in housing starts—following a major industry slowdown during the late 1980s. This sustained surge in housing starts, which began in 1992 and continued through early 1996, was made possible by an improved national economic picture and low interest rates.

Top 10 LARGEST HOUSING CONSTRUCTION COMPANIES

Ranked by: Gross revenue in 1995, in millions of dollars.

1. Centex Corp., with $3,074 million
2. Pulte Home Corp., $1,936
3. Ryland Group, $1,590
4. Kaufman & Broad Home Corp., $1,397
5. U.S. Home Corp., $1,108
6. Lincoln Property Co., $1,082
7. NVR, $910
7. Del Webb Corp., $910
9. Lennar Corp., $870
10. MDC Holdings Inc., $866

Source: *Builder*, May, 1996, p. 186+.

Although low interest rates buoyed industry earnings, the home ownership rate among younger Americans has steadily declined since the 1970s. Furthermore, high construction costs, new regulations, changing demographics, and income disparity, are all drags on the industry in America. On the bright side, the manufactured housing and remodeling sectors posted strong earnings growth.

The recovery of the U.S. manufacturing sector is expected to result in strong demand for industrial construction during the rest of this decade. Although the long-term outlook for industrial construction is subject to many factors, industry analysts expect it to be the strongest construction sector to the end of the decade. Echoing this optimism is the wave of speculative industrial manufacturing sites that began in the mid-1990s.

CONSTRUC-TION, BUILDING

SIC 1500.

Growth in the construction industry is expected to be mixed in the latter part of the 1990s. Forecasts called for a 3 percent increase in 1997 in institutional construction, followed by a 2.8 percent increase in 1998. This trend, along with rising office rents, was expected to benefit the construction industry. Nonresidential construction spending is expected to grow 3.1 percent in 1997, reaching $204 billion. Analysts predict a single-digit vacancy rate in office space by the end of 1998—the lowest level since 1982.

INDUSTRY OUTLOOK

After a five-year decline in housing starts—one of the longest in U.S. history—the single-family home construction industry experienced a relatively weak recovery in 1992. Starts surged about 20 percent to 1.06 million. Analysts had expected a much greater recovery because fixed mortgage rates had dropped to a 20-year low in 1992 of less than 8 percent. Because homebuilding has traditionally led the United States economy out of recessions and has served as a leading economic indicator for other industries, both contractors and consumers were disappointed.

The value of new residential construction in 1996 was expected to reach $126.8 billion up 15 percent for 1995. Housing is thought to be near its peak and the market is expected to slip 1 percent in 1997. Construction starts are expected to increase for nonresidential markets with an increase in contracts for industrial, education, medical, government, and apartment buildings. Construction starts are expected to increase and industry analysts predict an 11 percent for apartments.

Private nonresidential construction in the United States has fluctuated according to the success of key sectors such as office buildings and institutions. An industry high mark of nearly $200 billion in 1990 was the last good turn for several years until the industry saw massive growth in 1995 and construction spending jumped to nearly $170 billion. In contrast to office construction, the retail construction market has remained strong since the 1980s. Construction spending in this area jumped to $32 billion in 1996, a 5.1 increase from 1995. However, analysts believe that the market is now overbuilt, as evidenced by a decline in retail sales. The expected growth rate for the retail construction market in 1997 was 5.7 percent, but only 1.6 percent for 1998.

The volatile hotel/motel sector suffered tremendous losses in the early 1990s. In 1991, construction spending dropped 35 percent; it fell another 47 percent in 1992. However, the industry had exceptional growth in the mid-1990s. In 1995, construction spending rose dramatically to $6.4 billion, an increase of 55.9 percent. Spending for the first nine months of 1996 was more than $8 billion—annual growth was 48 percent. 1997 was projected to bring a decline of 12.4 percent in hotel/motel construction; however in 1998, the industry will grow again by 3.1 percent. These high levels were attributed mainly to increased casino construction and tourism.

Construction of educational facilities has increased during the 1990s. Higher school enrollments led to growth in school construction and building improvements. Spending in this area was expected to grow 4.4 percent in 1997, reaching a total of $34.2 billion. Forecasts for 1998 showed another increase of 3.1 percent. Other sectors in this industry were also expected to grow. Construction spending on hospitals and other health care facilities was more than $11 billion during the first nine months of 1996, a 1.5 percent increase over the same period in 1995. This figure was expected to rise 4.4 percent in 1997 to $16.6 billion. Spending was expected to grow an additional 3.3 percent in 1998. Construction of other types of institutions—public administrative buildings, courthouses, jails, and religious and recreational buildings—will not fare as well, however. These areas were expected to grow just 1.4 percent, reaching a level of $41.9 billion in 1997. The primary reason for this slow growth is a lack of public funding for new projects.

The nonresidential repair and renovation market, in general, was seen as having a more secure future than that of new construction. The commercial building boom of the 1980s produced, among other results, record vacancy rates for warehouses, and this over-supply was expected to diminish the market for new warehouse construction for some time. Similarly, remodeling and repair markets in the housing industry offered stronger growth opportunities for contractors than the new home market. In fact, by the year 2000 professionally installed remodeling will be nearly as big a business as new residential construction. It is expected that aging baby boomers will help these segments to sustain about 7 percent annual growth throughout the 1990s.

FINANCIAL MARKET INFLUENCE

In 1993, the average interest rates on 30-year fixed rate mortgages fell to 7.20 percent, the lowest since 1968. Accordingly, housing starts began to recover, and reached 1.4 million units by 1994. Low mortgage rates effectively sliced the cost of home ownership by about 20 percent, and rebounding regional economies that had finally shaken off the 1990-1991 recession increased consumer confidence.

Also impacting the industry in the early 1990s were the increasingly stringent loan requirements set up by banks in the wake of the savings and loan crisis. To counter banks taking a risk position in these projects, developers and their subsequent construction firms were increasingly being asked to take an equity position or become a part owner in projects they design or build.

In the 1980s and early 1990s, several factors compelled the building industry to seek new means for acquiring financing for land purchases: the federal Tax Reform Act of 1986, the revision of commercial banks' loan underwriting standards, and the decline of the U.S. savings and loan industry. One such approach was the formation of ''land bank partnerships'' in which investors pooled their resources to purchase land and used provisions in the tax code to avoid the costs associated with carrying the debt from the purchase of land on their balance sheets.

INDUSTRY CHALLENGES

One of the largest hurdles faced by prospective operative builders was arranging financing through banks, which are much more inclined to lend money to established builders. In some markets construction financing was provided to builders by their suppliers (such as lumber companies) which could monitor the builder's financing needs and construction progress by observing how much materials they had ordered or used. Other sources of residential building loans include pension funds and insurance companies. Because construction costs can vary significantly over a two-month period, some builders planned to construct only the number of homes projected by their monthly research, then concentrated on selling the homes before beginning actual construction.

Single-family homebuilders ranked costly government regulation second only to the slow economy as the greatest challenge facing the industry. Indeed, costs associated with new impact fees, building codes, environmental rules, safety laws, and other regulations seemed to be spiraling out of control in some areas. Local fees required to build a home in San Francisco, one of the most heavily regulated areas, exceeded $30,000 in the mid-1990s. Examples of government laws that must also be complied with include laws relating to the inspection and approval of works, the acceptance of plans, the use of certain materials, the conditions under which labor may be employed, and health and safety regulations, etc. Moreover, equipment that comes on site has to be certified safe for use under the conditions of use.

Since construction contractors operate under a significant amount of federal, state, and local regulation, they often utilize members of the legal profession. The attorney a contractor selects must be experienced and have complete knowledge of contract law with particular reference to laws that affect contracts between general contractors, owners, and subcontractors. The various arenas of law that impact general contractors that may require legal representation include: negotiations, preparing and reviewing contracts, labor law, lien laws, bankruptcy laws, litigation, corporate structure, and general counsel. Attorney services are needed for almost every step of the construction process.

Many of the construction industry's biggest customers had largely completed the process of transformation required by tighter environmental standards, and ecological concerns had less welcome consequences as well. As Tim Grogan noted in *Engineering News-Record*, "forecasts . . . are at the mercy of the fickle lumber market. It is experiencing a severe supply shortage triggered by the long-running dispute between the timber industry and environmentalists over the harvesting of old-growth forests in the [Pacific] Northwest." In addition, pollution created insurance problems for U.S. contractors when general carriers started to drop this area of liability from their standard coverage.

ORGANIZATION AND STRUCTURE

The single-family housing construction industry is unique for an industry of its size because it is highly fragmented and dispersed. The typical home is built by a contractor that produces fewer than 25 houses each year. In 1995, the market shares of the top five single-family home builders in 44 major metropolitan areas ranged from 5.9 percent to 58.6 percent. Altogether, the top five

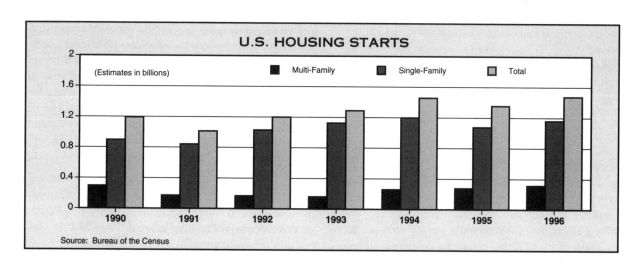

U.S. HOUSING STARTS

(Estimates in billions) ■ Multi-Family ■ Single-Family ☐ Total

Source: Bureau of the Census

builders in these markets accounted for 21.8 percent of all single-family permits issued in those markets. For 1995, *Ward's Business Directory* listed 642 companies with revenues of $19.97 billion and 37,600 employees engaged in single-family housing construction.

The lack of concentration in the industry reflects the labor intensity and logistical complexity characteristic of on-site homebuilding. Regional and state building codes, trade unions, demographics, and environmental regulations combine to make the competitive structure of each local market unique. Many workers from various trades must be coordinated to complete a home. Moreover, many construction materials are less expensive when purchased regionally. Finally, the localized nature of housing markets prohibits many national economies of scale.

In addition to new home construction, single-family home contractors also are engaged in maintenance-and-repair and home improvement work. Maintenance and repair included painting, mudjacking, replacement of appliances, and similar work. Improvements consisted of additions and alterations to existing structures involving major interior and exterior changes. Replacement of major items such as furnaces and water heaters are also considered home improvements. In 1997, Americans were expected to spend a record $119 billion on home improvements. As baby boomers reach middle age, Americans are staying in their homes longer than they did previously. The median number of years Americans remain in one home is now 13 versus 10 a decade ago. Nearly two-thirds of the dollars Americans spend on home improvements are targeted for optional upgrades, such as kitchens, bathrooms, and family rooms, rather than for repair work. In 1989, the split was approximately 50-50.

The residential building industry during the 1990s was highly competitive, with only a few firms competing at the national level. Builders compete on the basis of location, reputation, quality of construction, price, design quality, and amenities, among other factors. Builders with strong administrative and paperwork processing operations, superior on-site management, and sound construction systems were generally the most competitive.

In 1993, *Builder* magazine listed the following factors as the problems most often cited by home builders as "critical" to the success of their operations: worker's compensation claims; increasing lumber prices; Occupational Health and Safety Administration inspections; stormwater management and permit regulations; environmental regulations concerning protection of wetlands; government environmental impact fees; endangered species regulations; economic confidence levels; government procedures for development approval; and mandated health insurance legislation. Other problems affecting some home-builders include poor design and shoddy workmanship, such as the use of moist lumber, poor soil testing, or inadequate concrete mixes.

WORK FORCE

About 5 percent of the U.S. labor force is employed by one branch or another of the construction industry. Despite its size, this work force was by no means monolithic. Employment in construction was seasonal, leading to pronounced swings in the number of workers employed over the course of a year. Moreover, the skilled members of the work force engaged in a wide variety of different crafts or specialties. As a result, no single voice could adequately represent the various needs and interests of all of these workers, which somehow had to be accommodated to general concerns. Such considerations were particularly important for reasons cited by Daniel Quinn Mills in *The Construction Industry:* "employers and unions are placed in a much more intimate relationship than in many other industries. Contractors and unions must negotiate not only wages and working conditions but also hiring and training practices as well. In an unstable industry, the need to develop and retain a skilled labor force requires that employers and unions agree on practices to preserve the job opportunities of craftsmen." Further adding to the lack of uniformity in the work force were the tendencies for skilled workers to identify with their specialties rather than with a particular employer and for all employees to change employers often, to switch frequently from site to site, to work beside teams hired by other employers, and to engage to an unusual extent in self-supervision.

The construction industry is a labor intensive industry and has always been so. There are approximately 4.6 million employees currently in the construction industry. This is about 10 percent less than the 1990 level. Additionally, there are about 1.4 million individuals who are self-employed as proprietors and working partners. In spite of the fact that construction wages have not increased significantly, construction still remains one of the highest paying industries, as measured by hourly and weekly earnings. Average hourly earnings for employees in the construction industry have ranged from $13 to $14 in recent years.

There was a labor shortage of qualified and available construction workers in the mid-1990s. It is expected that there will be a larger group of 16-to 19-year-olds entering the work force in the next few years.

RESEARCH AND TECHNOLOGY

Industry advances in productivity and technology since World War II created vast improvements in the quality, integrity, and comfort of housing. The percentage of new homes with more than 2,400 square feet, for example, increased from 11 percent in 1977 to 28 percent by 1995. During the same period, the percentage of new houses with a garage for two or more cars jumped from 60 percent to 76 percent. Likewise, 87 percent of all new homes had two or more bathrooms in 1995, compared to 70 percent in 1977.

Builders have also been able to improve housing through the use of cheaper and stronger materials, such as plastics and alloys. Bathtubs and sinks made of cultured marble generated huge savings for buyers. Integrated energy and communications systems have allowed significant gains in energy efficiency. Between 1980 and 1987, new systems and insulation helped to decrease average household energy consumption from about 140 million BTUs to less than 120. Other amenities, such as electric garage openers and security systems, have added to home quality as well.

Going into the 1990s, the construction industry will increasingly rely on new construction techniques, better materials, and energy saving advances to increase productivity and boost profit margins in a mature industry. Improvements in the quality of prefabricated housing will allow builders to deliver larger, higher quality homes at lower prices. Advances in manufactured, or mobile, home quality will propel this segment past a 20 percent share of all new housing starts by the year 2000.

ASSOCIATIONS AND SOCIETIES

AMERICAN BUILDING CONTRACTORS ASSOCIATION
12123-A Woodruff Ave.
Downey, CA 90241
Phone: (310) 803-5520

AMERICAN SUBCONTRACTORS ASSOCIATION
1004 Duke St.
Alexandria, VA 22314
Phone: (703) 684-3450
Fax: (703) 836-3482

ASSOCIATED BUILDERS AND CONTRACTORS
1300 N. 17th St.
Rosslyn, VA 22209
Phone: (703) 812-2000

ASSOCIATED EQUIPMENT DISTRIBUTORS
615 W. 22nd St.
Oak Brook, IL 60521
Phone: (800) 388-0650 or (708) 574-0650
Fax: (708) 574-0132

ASSOCIATED GENERAL CONTRACTORS OF AMERICA
1957 E St. NW
Washington, DC 20006
Phone: (202) 393-2040
Fax: (202) 347-4004

BUILDING AND CONSTRUCTION TRADES DEPARTMENT - AFL-CIO
815 16th St. NW, Ste. 603
Washington, DC 20006
Phone: (202) 347-1461
Fax: (202) 628-0724

BUILDING OFFICIALS AND CODE ADMINISTRATORS INTERNATIONAL
4051 W. Flossmoor Rd.
Country Club Hills, IL 60477-5795
Phone: (708) 799-2300
Fax: (708) 799-4981

CONSTRUCTION INDUSTRY MANUFACTURERS ASSOCIATION
111 E. Wisconsin Dr., Ste. 940
Milwaukee, WI 53202
Phone: (414) 272-0943

NATIONAL ASSOCIATION OF HOME BUILDERS OF THE UNITED STATES
1201 15th St. NW
Washington, DC 20005
Phone: (202) 822-0200
Fax: (202) 822-0559

NATIONAL BUILDING MATERIAL DISTRIBUTORS ASSOCIATION
401 N. Michigan Ave.
Chicago, IL 60611
Phone: (312) 321-6845
Fax: (312) 644-0310

NATIONAL CONSTRUCTORS ASSOCIATION
1730 M St. NW, Ste. 503
Washington, DC 20036
Phone: (202) 466-8880
Fax: (202) 466-7512

PERIODICALS AND NEWSLETTERS

BUILDER
Hanley-Wood Inc.
655 15th St. NW, Ste. 475
Washington, DC 20005
Phone: (202) 737-0717
Fax: (202) 737-2439
Monthly. $25.00 per year.

BUILDING MATERIAL RETAILER
National and Building Material Dealers Association
40 Ivy St. SE
Washington, DC 20003
Phone: (800) 328-9125 or (202) 547-2230

Monthly. $25.00 per year. Includes special feature issues on hand and power tools, lumber, roofing, kitchens, flooring, windows and doors, and insulation.

CONSTRUCTION LAW ADVISER: MONTHLY PRACTICAL ADVICE FOR LAWYERS AND CONSTRUCTION PROFESSIONALS

Clark Boardman
Callaghan 155 Pfingsten Rd.
Deerfield, IL 60015
Phone: (800) 323-1336 or (708) 948-7000
Fax: (708) 948-9340
Monthly. $295.00 per year. Newsletter.

CONSTRUCTION SPECIFIER: FOR COMMERCIAL AND INDUSTRIAL CONSTRUCTION

Construction Specifications Institute
601 Madison St.
Alexandria, VA 22314
Phone: (800) 689-2900 or (703) 684-0300
Fax: (703) 684-0465
Monthly. Free to members; non-members, $36.00 per year; universities, $30.00 per year. Technical aspects of the construction industry.

GOVERNMENT CONTRACTOR

Federal Publications, Inc.
1120 20th St. NW, Ste. 500 S
Washington, DC 20036
Phone: (202) 337-7000
Fax: (202) 659-2233
Biweekly. $896.00 per year.

PROFESSIONAL BUILDER AND REMODELER

Cahners Publishing Co.
PO Box 5080
Des Plaines, IL 60017-5080
Phone: (800) 662-7776 or (708) 635-8800
Fax: (708) 635-9950
Monthly. $139.95 per year. Provides price and market forecasts on industrial products, components and materials. Office products, business systems and transportation. Formerly Professional Builder.

PROSALES: FOR DEALERS AND DISTRIBUTORS SERVING THE PROFESSIONAL CONTRACTOR

Hanley-Wood Inc.
655 15th St. NW, Ste. 475
Washington, DC 20005
Phone: (202) 737-0717
Fax: (202) 737-2439
Eight times a year. Includes special feature issues on selling, credit, financing, and the marketing of power tools.

THE SUBCONTRACTOR

American Subcontractors Association
1004 Duke St.
Alexandria, VA 22314-3588
Phone: (703) 684-3450
Monthly. $40.00 per year.

DATABASES

AMERICAN STATISTICS INDEX: A COMPREHENSIVE GUIDE AND INDEX TO THE STATISTICAL PUBLICATIONS OF THE UNITED STATES GOVERNMENT [ONLINE]

Congressional Information Service, Inc.
4520 East-West Hwy.
Bethesda, MD 20814-3389
Phone: (800) 638-8380 or (301) 654-1550
Fax: (301) 657-3203
Indexes and abstracts, 1973 to date. Inquire as to online cost and availability.

ARCHITECTURE, ENGINEERING AND CONSTRUCTION INFOCENTER

AEC Infocenter
Covers the architecture, engineering, construction, and home-building industries. Includes a building-product library, which lists products used in various construction formats. Fees: Free.

- URL: http://www.aecinfo.com

STATISTICS SOURCES

CONSTRUCTION REVIEW

Industry and Trade Administration, U.S. Dept. of Commerce
Available from U.S. Government Printing Office
Washington, DC 20402
Phone: (202) 512-1800
Fax: (202) 512-2250
Quarterly. $18.00 per year. Provides virtually all of the government's current statistics pertaining to construction.

HOUSING STARTS

Bureau of the Census
U.S. Department of Commerce
Washington, DC 20233
Phone: (301) 763-5731
Construction Reports, Series C20.

UNITED STATES CENSUS OF CONSTRUCTION INDUSTRIES

U.S. Bureau of the Census
Washington, DC 20233-0800
Phone: (202) 512-1800
Fax: (202) 512-2250
Quinquennial. Results presented in reports, tape, and CD-ROM files.

VALUE OF NEW CONSTRUCTION PUT IN PLACE

U.S. Bureau of the Census
Available from U.S. Government Printing Office
Washington, DC 20402
Phone: (202) 512-1800
Fax: (202) 512-2250
Monthly. $27.00 per year.

GENERAL WORKS

BUILDER AND CONTRACTOR-ASSOCIATED BUILDERS AND CONTRACTORS MEMBERSHIP DIRECTORY
Associated Builders and Contractors
729 15th St. NW
Washington, DC 20005
Phone: (202) 637-8800
Fax: (202) 347-1121
Annual. $150.00. Formerly Associated Builders and Contractors-National Membership Directory

CONSTRUCTION CONTRACTING
Richard H. Clough and Glenn A. Sears
John Wiley and Sons, Inc.
605 3rd Ave.
New York, NY 10158-0012
Phone: (800) 225-5945 or (212) 850-6000
Fax: (212) 850-6088
1994. $69.95. Sixth edition.

CONSTRUCTION CONTRACTS AND SPECIFICATIONS
Glenn M. Hardie
Prentice-Hall
200 Old Tappan Rd.
Old Tappan, NJ 07675
Phone: (800) 922-0579
Fax: (800) 445-6991
1981. $49.00.

FUNDAMENTALS OF CONSTRUCTION ESTIMATING AND COST ACCOUNTING, WITH COMPUTER APPLICATIONS
Keith Collier
Prentice-Hall
200 Old Tappan Rd.
Old Tappan, NJ 07675
Phone: (800) 922-0579
Fax: (800) 445-6991
1987. $82.00. Second edition.

FURTHER READING

Belsky, Gary. "Your Best Housing Deals," *Money,* April 1997.

Grogan, Tim. "Forecast '97." *ENR Journal,* January 1997.

———. "Nonresidential Construction: Keep Them Wagons Rollin'." *Building Construction & Design* 38 (1997), no. 1.

Lowder, Darin. "Construction Labor: Where Are the Workers?" *Housing Economics,* November 1996.

Lubove, Seth. "Construction." *Forbes,* 13 January 1997.

"Operative Builders." *Census of Construction Industries, 1992. Industry Series,* Washington: U.S. Department of Commerce, 1995.

CONSTRUCTION, HEAVY

SIC 1600

Due to a strong and gradually expanding economy in the mid-1990s, the heavy construction industry has enjoyed a long period of prosperity. The constant-dollar value of new construction in 1996 increased slightly from 1995. The construction contract awards growth rate was 6 percent in 1996, but was expected to slip to 3.5 percent in 1997. However, this downturn will not last long as more and more states implement programs to repair deteriorating highways, bridges, and tunnels.

HIGHWAY CONSTRUCTION

According to President Bill Clinton's statement of 12 March 1997, concerning the National Economic Crossroads Transportation Efficiency Act (NEXTEA), there were approximately 12 million people employed in transportation and transportation-related industries. One million of those jobs had been created since 1994. This represented just over 10 percent of the total civilian workforce. The NEXTEA program proposed for about $175 billion to be spent between 1998 and 2003 for the improvement of bridges, highways and transit systems. NEXTEA authorized an 11 percent increase over the Intermodal Surface Transportation Efficiency Act (ISTEA) of 1991. It concentrated on improving border crossings and developing major trade corridors within the United States. According to President Clinton, this bill would create tens of thousands of jobs. From another angle, an analysis by the American Road and Transportation Builders Association (ARTBA) found that Clinton's 1998-2002 transportation budget would "throw 106,000 transportation construction industry employees out of work over the next five years."

Most of the funding for federally-subsidized highway and airport projects comes from excise taxes on fuel, airplane fares, trucks, and related products. Americans also spend more than $1 billion annually on tolls.

Top 10 TOP CONTRACTORS, 1995

Ranked by: 1995 revenues, in millions of dollars.

1. Fluor Daniel Inc., $7,501
2. Bechtel Group Inc., $7,407
3. Jacobs Engineering Group Inc., $3,610
4. Trafalgar House Engineering & Const., $3,387
5. Centex Construction Group, $2,968
6. Brown & Root Inc., $2,742
7. The Turner Corp., $2,727
8. Raytheon Engineers & Constructors Intl., $2,467
9. Kiewit Construction Group Inc., $2,212
10. Foster Wheeler Corp., $2,132

Source: *ENR*, May 20, 1996, p.48.

The Clinton Administration's proposed budget for fiscal 1995 included significant investments in the country's infrastructure, which was widely regarded as badly in need of repair. The budget stipulated $20 billion for highways, $1 billion for air travel, $3.8 billion for mass transit, and $500 million for railroads.

BRIDGE AND TUNNEL CONSTRUCTION

Roughly 25 percent of the money spent on highway construction in the United States is used for bridge, tunnel, and elevated highway construction, with the remainder spent on "flatwork" such as highways and interstates. The vast majority of the construction work performed by industry firms in 1992 (72 percent) was for bridge and elevated highway construction, while tunnel construction composed only about 12 percent of industry construction. The remaining 17 percent of the industry's construction work encompassed highway, street, and related facilities construction; sewage treatment and water treatment plant construction; and sewer, water main, and related facilities construction. In 1992, 884 industry establishments specialized in bridge and elevated highway construction, while only 122 firms specialized in tunnel construction.

In the early 1990s, approximately 1,041 establishments employing 43,701 workers generated $7.2 billion in business. The average salary per industry employee was $34,000 and $31,000 for construction workers. Establishments employing 20 or more employees represented 47 percent of all industry firms but accounted for fully 90 percent of all business performed. U.S. participation in international bridge, tunnel, and elevated highway projects diminished in the 1990s, and by some estimates the U.S. construction industry had fallen far behind the pace of change in infrastructure construction technology and building methods. In the mid-1990s the tardiness of the American transportation infrastructure construction industry in modernizing its building methods and technologies was causing it to lose global market share to Japanese and European firms. With the passage of the National Highway System Designation Act of 1995, billions of new federal dollars for highway repair and construction work were expected to provide the U.S. bridge, tunnel, and elevated highway industry with important new sources of revenue into the next century.

INDUSTRY OUTLOOK

HIGHWAY CONSTRUCTION

Although spending on operations and maintenance has remained relatively stable since completion of the interstate system, there has been a steady trend toward disinvestment on the part of the federal government. Although capital investment has been declining, highway use in this country has increased dramatically, according to the report. In 1962, the United States spent $42 for every 1,000 vehicle miles traveled (VMT) on highway infrastructure. This level of investment has been declining steadily. In 1982, the rate was at $12 per 1,000 VMT. This figure rose slightly since that time and leveled off at around $16 per 1,000 VMT in the mid-1990s.

Many analysts feel that growing concern about the state of the nation's infrastructure, including its highway system, could result in a period of robust growth for members of the highway construction industry during the 1990s. At the very least, highway construction expenditures will need to keep pace with the demands for road maintenance and repair throughout the nation. This commitment is needed to insure the transportation infrastructure, an essential component of the American economy, retains its structural integrity and efficiency.

Top Heavy Contractors

Firms are ranked by 1995 revenues in millions of dollars. Data include transportation, sewer, water, and hazardous waste construction.

Kiewit Construction Group Inc.	$ 1,553.8
Bechtel Group Inc.	1,527.1
Granite Construction Co.	895.0
Jacobs Engineering Group Inc.	688.6
Morrison Knudsen Corp.	663.9
OHM Corp.	507.7
Spectrum Construction Group	500.5
The Parsons Corp.	455.6
ICF Kaiser International Inc.	359.4
Tutor-Saliba Corp.	357.7
Fluor Daniel Inc.	348.8
Raytheon Engineers & Constructors Intl.	330.1
Modern Continental Const. Co.	293.9
Perini Corp.	291.2
J.A. Jones Inc.	281.1

Source: *ENR*, May 20, 1996, p. 82.

Several states have committed themselves to substantial road building programs, despite the fact that total state government spending on road construction has increased only slightly faster than the inflation rate. Voters in California approved a relatively large gasoline tax to fund billions of dollars in road improvements. The California legislature, in the meantime, approved the implementation of four toll roads. The state suffered a tremendous blow in January 1994, however, when a massive earthquake crippled the highway system of Los Angeles, its most populous city. Repairs to the area's highways and bridges are expected to cost billions of dollars and will take years to complete.

BRIDGE AND TUNNEL CONSTRUCTION

According to a U.S. Department of Transportation report on the status of the nation's highways, bridges, and transit systems, $49.9 billion was required to maintain the condition and performance of the nation's highways and bridges in 1994. In 1991 it was estimated that approximately 72 percent of existing U.S. bridges were built before 1935 and estimates of the nation's roughly 575,000 bridges that were structurally or functionally deficient in the early 1990s ranged from 14 to 40 percent, with those in New York in most need of repair. In addition, the Federal Highway Administration estimated that another 21 percent of U.S. bridges were not only deficient but obsolete, leaving a grand total of 225,000 to 231,000 below-par bridges nationwide. Roughly 42 percent of the backlog for bridge rehabilitation in the early 1990s involved pavement costs, and the remaining 58 percent was for constructing additional capacity. By 1996 the estimated cost of upgrading the backlog of deficient U.S. bridges had risen to about $72 billion. By 1998 the value of new construction for highways, including elevated highways and bridges, was expected to increase to almost $39 billion.

UTILITY CONSTRUCTION

Gas pipeline companies reported an industry gas-plant investment of more than $59.8 billion in 1995, compared with $57 billion in 1994, $55.6 billion in 1993, and $55.5 billion in 1992. Despite nearly stagnant operating revenues, natural gas and petroleum liquids pipeline companies increased their net incomes slightly in 1995 by continuing with efficiency efforts that were begun in 1994. The total number of miles operated by these companies increased only 1 percent, or 5,000 miles, from 1994 to 1995, according to the U.S. Federal Energy Regulatory Commission (FERC).

The utility construction industry is exceptionally sensitive to fluctuations in tax legislation and the investment community, and has experienced a decline over the past several years, with only sluggish growth anticipated in the near future. The pipeline construction industry, however, has benefitted from declining spot market prices and increased consumer demand for natural gas. As a result, there has been a dramatic increase in building activity for that sector. The water and sewer construction segments are responsive to legislative actions and government spending. Decreased federal outlays, and financially strapped state and local governments have created slow-growth conditions for this segment of the industry. However, legislative mandates that foster modernization and replacement of older aqueduct systems are expected to create long-term growth.

WORK FORCE

Although employment in the entire construction industry plummeted from over 5 million to less than 4.5 million during the recession of the late 1980s and early 1990s, the miscellaneous heavy construction industry fared better than most other segments of the construction market. In fact, certain areas of this industry were realizing significant employment growth in the 1990s. Most growth was expected to occur in sectors that benefitted from increased federal spending or from federal mandates requiring businesses and localities to invest in construction.

Significant growth was expected to occur in miscellaneous activities related to environmental construction such as wastewater treatment, retrofits of energy producing facilities that were polluting the atmosphere, and land reclamation. Greatest growth, however, was likely to occur in international markets, which were seven times larger than the U.S. market and were growing at a relatively rapid pace.

Job positions in the miscellaneous heavy construction industry were similar to those available in related heavy construction industries. Jobs in construction management, skilled trade work, physical labor, equipment operation, and sales were representative of the overall construction industry. Growth was most likely to occur in positions that required technical knowledge, as more firms were relying on advanced technology to reduce costs and become more competitive in the crowded market.

A multitude of niche opportunities existed in miscellaneous projects, as well. For instance, high-paying jobs in weapons disarmament and battlefield reclamation were on the rise as foreign governments increasingly sought U.S. expertise in removing and detonating live explosives that remained after armed conflicts. Another growing field was removal of underground storage tanks, many of which were leaking hazardous residues and were contaminating surrounding soil and water tables.

The U.S. Department of Commerce estimates that road building generates more than 1.5 million American jobs. The federal-aid highway construction program alone generates nearly 750,000 jobs.

RESEARCH AND TECHNOLOGY

HIGHWAY CONSTRUCTION

Addressing the subject of technology and highway construction and administration, Thomas D. Larson,

U.S. Federal Highway Administrator, said " . . . the research and technology component of a potential future highway program will provide the expanded level of funding necessary to support a long-term aggressive commitment to improving highway productivity through the development, demonstration, and deployment of available and evolving technology for both operations and construction."

Proposed legislation envisions a program that would be established on a multilayer basis with the following major components: 1) attention to long-range fundamental and applied research and development activities for pavement and structure materials and construction methods, safety and traffic research, and improved techniques and technologies for environmental management; 2) a focus on intelligent vehicle/highway systems programs in four key areas—advanced traffic management systems, advanced driver information systems, automated vehicle control systems, and advanced commercial vehicle operations; and 3) a program for motor carrier research activities, including vehicle characteristics, human factors studies, regulatory and program analysis, and other motor carrier-related research.

A new technology in highway construction in 1996 was the use of rubberized asphalt. Roads made with recycled tire chips showed less frost heave than conventional roads. Tire chips also proved much better than soil as an insulator, limiting the depth of frost and therefore the damage of winter. Using rubber in retaining walls reduced the pressure on those walls, allowing them to be lighter, thinner and less expensive.

Studies by the Federal Highway Administration (FHWA) and university research programs in 1995 aimed to use robotics in highway construction. These included the development of an Automatic Pavement Crack-Sealing Machine and a Pothole-Repairing Machine. Another area of research was directed at improving work zone safety and minimizing traffic congestion with the use of robotic aids.

BRIDGE AND TUNNEL CONSTRUCTION

Between 1988 and mid-1993, the FHWA 's Strategic Highway Research Program developed 130 products aimed at improving highway construction and operation methods, including new pavement engineering techniques and concrete and asphalt with enhanced performance characteristics. By 1996, more than 100 case studies reporting the program's development of successfully implemented technologies had been documented. These included a new road-surfacing material known as Superpave, spray-injection technologies for filling potholes, bridge management software, and concrete anticorrosion technologies. Similarly, the FHWA's

Geotechnical Research program developed improvements for bridge foundations, retaining walls, and embankments and maintained experimentation sites for assessing new methods for quantifying the properties and behavior of soils to predict their suitability for highway and bridge construction.

Among the many advances in bridge, tunnel, and elevated highway construction equipment in the 1980s and 1990s was the increased use of highway and bridge surface groovers and grinders using diamond-tipped saw blades to cut grooves into pavement for vehicle traction and water drainage. Also utilized more frequently was an underground excavating machine for cutting two-lane road arch tunnels through hard granite. The machine formerly had been used only in underground mining, offering an alternative to drilling and breaking rock by hydraulic wedge or nonexplosive demolition.

The introduction of engineering/design and project management software had a profound effect on the way bridge, tunnel, and elevated highway construction firms conducted their business. Among the advantages such packages offered was the capability to produce clean and accurate technical drawings by users without drafting skills, correct and replot drawings in a fraction of the time required by manual methods, quickly optimize designs to explore alternative approaches to a project, and better understand a project's total design features through three-dimensional visualization and imaging features.

AMERICA AND THE WORLD

The U.S. highway and road system has not kept pace with those of other countries. Highway capital investment relative to the economies in Japan, Korea, and Germany, for instance, has been significantly higher over recent years than similar investment in America. In 1988, for example, Japan spent over 1.8 percent of its Gross National Product (GNP) on highway infrastructure. That is almost triple the amount that the United States invested in highways, 0.7 percent of its GNP.

Comparing capital spending per vehicle miles traveled (VMT), it is obvious Japan is substantially outspending other nations in highway development and maintenance. In 1988, Japan invested $150 for every 1,000 WMT—nine times the U.S. investment. In the same year, Korea spent $95 per 1,000 VMT and Germany expended $30 per 1,000 VMT. The U.S. spent only $16 per 1,000 VMT.

Despite lagging investment, America's road building technology remains strong. In fact, although the

United States comes up short in terms of highway infrastructure investment, it continues to export highway technology to other nations through the Department of Transportation's Federal Highway Administration (FHWA).

ASSOCIATIONS AND SOCIETIES

ASSOCIATED EQUIPMENT DISTRIBUTORS
615 W. 22nd St.
Oak Brook, IL 60521
Phone: (800) 388-0650 or (708) 574-0650
Fax: (708) 574-0132

CONSTRUCTION INDUSTRY MANUFACTURERS ASSOCIATION
111 E. Wisconsin Dr., Ste. 940
Milwaukee, WI 53202
Phone: (414) 272-0943

PERIODICALS AND NEWSLETTERS

CONSTRUCTION EQUIPMENT DISTRIBUTION
Associated Equipment Distributors
615 W. 22nd St.
Oak Brook, IL 60521
Phone: (708) 574-0650
Fax: (708) 574-0132
Monthly. Members, $20.00 per year; non-members, $40.00 per year.

EQUIPMENT TODAY
Johnson Hill Press, Inc.
PO Box 803
Fort Atkinson, WI 53538-0803
Phone: (800) 547-7377 or (414) 563-6388
Fax: (414) 563-1699
Monthly. $50.00 per year. Formerly Equipment Guide News.

STATISTICS SOURCES

U.S. INDUSTRIAL OUTLOOK: FORECASTS FOR SELECTED MANUFACTURING AND SERVICE INDUSTRIES
Available from U.S. Government Printing Office
Washington, DC 20402

Phone: (202) 512-1800
Fax: (202) 512-2250
Annual. $37.00. (Replaced in 1995 by U.S. Global Trade Outlook.*) Issued by the International Trade Administration, U.S. Department of Commerce. Provides basic data, outlook for the current year, and "Long-Term Prospects" (five-year projections) for a wide variety of products and services. Includes high technology industries. Available on the world wide web at gopher://gopher.umsl.edu:70/11/library/govdocs/usio94*

GENERAL WORKS

CONSTRUCTION CONTRACTING
Richard H. Clough and Glenn A. Sears
John Wiley and Sons, Inc.
605 3rd Ave.
New York, NY 10158-0012
Phone: (800) 225-5945 or (212) 850-6000
Fax: (212) 850-6088
1994. $69.95. Sixth edition.

FURTHER READING

Flynn, Larry. "Bridge Trends Buoy Industry." *Roads and Bridges,* 1 November 1996.

"Highway Information Update." 22 May 1996. Available from http://cti1.volpe.dot.gov/ohim/vol1no1.html.

Moody, Gerald R. "The U.S. International Construction Industry." Office of Business and Industrial Analysis, U.S. Department of Commerce, January 1996, Available from http://netsite.esa.doc.gov/obia.

"President Clinton Unveils Reauthorization Proposal for Transportation for the Twenty-First Century." U.S. Department of Transportation, 12 March 1997. Available from http://www.dot.gov/affairs/dot3097.htm.

"Proposed Clinton Budget Plan Would Slash Highway and Airport Programs." American Road and Transportation Builders Association, 7 February 1997. Available from http://www.artba-hq.org/docs/newsrel/1997/97-02-07.htm.

Sheriff, Margie. "Innovations in Technology." *Roads and Bridges,* 1 March 1996, 18.

U.S. Transportation Construction Industry Profile. Washington: American Road & Transportation Builders Association.

Ward's Business Directory of U.S. Private and Public Companies. Detroit: Gale Research, 1997. ━━

30

COTTON BROADWOVEN FABRIC MILLS

SIC 2211

New housing starts, which showed strength in the mid-1990s, are the chief factor outside of trade matters affecting manufacturers of broadwoven cotton fabrics for home furnishings. While housing starts are projected to come down to 1.38 million units after climbing to 1.46 million in 1996, the high level of turnover in vintage homes is also a positive factor for sales of textile home furnishings and other interior furnishings due to remodeling and redecoration. Employment and income are on the rise and wholesale textile and apparel prices are projected to rise 0.5 percent after gaining 1.3 percent in 1996.

INDUSTRY SNAPSHOT

Manufacturing of cotton broadwovens—like most segments of textiles—is a mature industry. Since the mid-1980s, major U.S. firms in the industry have pursued growth largely through mergers, acquisitions, and foreign markets; they maximized profits typically through cost cutting and sourcing low-cost labor from foreign countries. The industry faces formidable competition on price from imported textiles, particularly those from Asian nations and Mexico. Nonetheless, the value of U.S. industry shipments rose modestly throughout the first half of the 1990s and totaled more than $6.5 billion by 1995. Real growth after inflation, however, was only at about 7 percent for the six-year period.

Top 10 LEADING TEXTILE MILLS, 1995

Ranked by: Sales, in millions of dollars.

1. Spring Industries, $2,233
2. Burlington Industries, $2,207
3. Westpoint Stevens, $1,649
4. Unifi, $1,596
5. Wellman, $1,109
6. Cone Mills, $910
7. Guilford Mills, $774
8. Dixie Yarns, $670
9. Galey & Lord, $460
10. Dan River, $384

Source: *DNR*, March 19,1996, p. 12, from Morgan Stanley & Co.

INDUSTRY OUTLOOK

Cotton remains a viable material for the textile market despite predictions in the 1960s and 1970s that manmade products would completely replace natural fiber. Cotton's inherent qualities, such as absorbency and breathability, and new fabric finishes have kept the fiber's market share strong. In 1995, U.S. manufacturers produced some 4.5 billion square yards of broadwoven cotton fabrics, according to the U.S. Department of Commerce. That same year, Cotton Incorporated reported that among the different fibers used in apparel and home fabrics, cotton use was larger than for any other single fiber. Cotton's competitiveness can be partially attributed to improvements such as the all-cotton, wrinkle resistant fabrics that are particularly popular for making men's pants, softer finishes, and flame-retardant treatments. Researchers are also developing antibacterial finishes and temperature responsive treatments for cottons.

ORGANIZATION AND STRUCTURE

Fabric weavers are generally vertically integrated companies that produce their own yarn. The primary reason for integrated weaving plants is that despite fashion changes that occur in the woven segment, yarn counts—the size of the yarn—as well as fabric constructions remain fairly stable. Fabric knitters, on the other hand, are faced with constant changes in yarn size and construction. Therefore, most knitters find it more economical to purchase yarn from sales yarn companies.

The general state of the economy, coupled with the level of consumer confidence, has a great impact on operations engaged in the manufacture of broadwoven cotton fabrics for apparel products. This has obviously been the case over the last several years, with companies producing fabrics for apparel enjoying success or decline in direct relationship to the state of the economy.

Several factors affect the demand for broadwoven cotton fabrics for industrial use. These include the success of the automotive industry, the activity in new highways, bridges, etc., and the nature of the agriculture industry. A significant section of the agriculture industry—cotton farming—also has a tremendous influence on the annual success of producers of broadwoven cotton fabrics for any application. The price of raw materials are often affected by weather and other natural factors. Shortages in U.S. cotton production plagued the industry in 1995, when prices shot above $1.00 per pound—costs that have not been seen since the American Civil War. At the same time, foreign crops were reduced by the boll worm in China and by the leaf curl virus in Pakistan. In 1996-97 cotton acreage in the United States was expected to fall by 10 percent because of the higher returns then available in the soybean, corn, and wheat markets.

RESEARCH AND TECHNOLOGY

Manufacturers of broadwoven cotton fabrics are replacing shuttle looms with shuttleless weaving machines as rapidly as economically feasible. In 1993, approximately half of the approximate 100,000 weaving machines in the United States were shuttleless, which offer geometrically higher weaving speeds than those of shuttle systems. Use of electronics in the broadwoven manufacturing process has permitted even higher increases in speeds. Speeds on any filling insertion system vary depending on type and width of fabric being woven.

When first developed, each shuttleless filling insertion system was designed specifically for a somewhat narrow fabric application range. As systems have been improved, modified, and computerized, the application ranges have broadened considerably. Projectile, flexible rapier, and rigid rapier systems are more versatile and can handle heavier, more complicated styles such as plaid upholstery. However, modifications to air-jet systems have broadened the application range to include more than just simple, lightweight styles such as printcloth and sheeting. Burlington Industries and Swift Textiles now both produce heavyweight denim on air-jet machines, and a few companies have begun experimenting with heavyweight upholstery fabrics on air jets as well. Electronic technology has contributed greatly to the operation of shuttleless weaving machines, paving the way for installation of automation features on shuttleless weaving machines such as automatic filling break repair, automatic cloth removal at specified lengths and automatic filling supply cone replenishment.

The biggest contribution made by electronic technology to broadwoven cotton manufacturing is in monitoring and control of the operation. Microprocessor-driven systems monitor and provide real-time data on efficiency, production, and quality. The data can be provided for any time period the manufacturer wishes to designate. This data can also be supplied for an individual machine or several machines grouped by style, job assignment, etc. Such information permits the evaluation of styles, fabrics, etc. and gives the broadwoven fabrics manufacturer the ability to select those materials most suited for the production machinery available.

As electronic systems become more advanced, they not only permit monitoring of the operation, but control of many of the functions as well. Modern systems can detect many mechanical and electrical problems. Depending on the sophistication of the system and the severity of the problem, the system can correct the problem, signal technicians as to the nature of the problem, or stop the machine until the problem is corrected. Totally automated systems (known as "lights out" operations) have been created for spinning machines, while complete automation of the weaving process is still far from being cost effective.

Computerization of the textile industry has been a critical part of the quick response (QR) programs that are being adopted by companies in an attempt to shorten the time between the placement of retail orders and the delivery of textile goods to their stores. The companies coordinating such programs communicate using bar codes and electronic data interchange. With the ability to pinpoint production times and quantities, mills can direct production according to individual orders. The mills, as well as apparel manufacturers and retailers, benefit from the resulting reduction in inventory costs. QR programs also reduce forced mark-downs and stockouts on the retail level.

AMERICA AND THE WORLD

A number of factors influence the success of companies engaged in the manufacturing of broadwoven cotton fabrics, but none has the impact equal that of international trade. For a number of years, imports—particularly in the apparel fabrics sector—have steadily risen, severely affecting operation of U.S. manufacturers of broadwoven cotton fabrics. Manufacturers of broadwoven cotton fabrics are impacted by imported garments—which are usually cut and sewn from fabrics manufactured in the same country as the garments—as well as fabrics.

The summer of 1993 was a watershed in the history of textile and apparel imports. The months of June, July, August, and September represented the four largest importing months in history in this area for America. Each month set a new all-time record for that particular period. Total imports during the trimester were 5.85 billion square meters, more than was imported during the entire year of 1982. The trade deficit is of increasing concern to the textile industry, as companies look for growth in international sales. U.S. textile exports experienced steady growth during the 1980s and the first half of the 1990s. In 1995, however, the United States still imported twice the dollar amount of cotton broadwovens it exported.

The North American Free Trade Agreement (NAFTA) of 1993 was expected to benefit U.S. manufacturers of broadwoven cotton fabrics in the long run, according to the American Textile Manufacturers Institute (ATMI). The General Agreement on Tariffs and Trade (GATT), however, could be detrimental to the long-range success of U.S. broadwoven cotton manufacturers, according to ATMI.

NAFTA, which became official January 1, 1994, effectively eliminates trade barriers between Canada, Mexico, and the United States. Gradual elimination of tariffs on U.S. textile exports to Mexico is seen as a major motivator for sales. Some U.S. companies are, in fact, spending millions of dollars to increase capacity as a result of the passage of NAFTA. The agreement was to eliminate tariffs on 89 percent of U.S.-made fabric exports to Mexico over a five-year period beginning January 1, 1994. Mexico eliminated tariffs on U.S. products such as denim, twills, cotton terry towels, curtains, and drapes immediately in 1994.

By early 1997, U.S. Department of Commerce data indicated that increased trade with Mexico and Canada had begun to reduce the dominance of Asian countries in textile imports to the United States. Mexican textile/apparel imports had increased 40 percent in the first three quarters of 1995, while Canadian shipments to the United States increased by 18 percent. At the same time, Chinese imports dropped by 23 percent and shipments from Hong Kong, Korea, and Thailand fell by 10 to 12 percent. U.S. textile mills benefited from this scenario because U.S. yarns and fabrics are used in 80 percent of Mexican apparel, while China uses very little of these products. Caribbean nations, which have made a special trade pact with the United States, are also enjoying increased textile and apparel imports, and should further stimulate U.S. mill performance. While the signing of NAFTA raised the hopes of manufacturers of broadwoven cotton fabrics, signing of GATT had just the opposite effect. This agreement phased out tariffs on textiles set by the MultiFiber Arrangement (MFA) by 2005.

SIC 2211 - Broadwoven Fabric Mills, Cotton
Industry Data by State

| State | Establish-ments | Shipments | | | Employment | | | | Cost as % of Shipments | Investment per Employee ($) |
		Total ($ mil)	% of U.S.	Per Establ.	Total Number	% of U.S.	Per Establ.	Wages ($/hour)		
North Carolina	39	1,978.4	34.0	50.7	18,600	33.3	477	8.88	64.6	2,661
Georgia	31	1,375.0	23.6	44.4	14,000	25.0	452	8.63	52.1	3,150
South Carolina	41	1,313.0	22.6	32.0	11,900	21.3	290	8.95	57.4	2,496
Alabama	7	434.7	7.5	62.1	4,100	7.3	586	9.43	46.1	5,293
Texas	19	198.5	3.4	10.4	2,100	3.8	111	9.10	46.8	-
Pennsylvania	13	30.1	0.5	2.3	400	0.7	31	9.57	49.8	-
California	35	16.3	0.3	0.5	200	0.4	6	6.50	49.1	1,500
New Jersey	17	15.4	0.3	0.9	200	0.4	12	10.33	52.6	2,000
New York	25	13.4	0.2	0.5	200	0.4	8	7.67	58.2	500
Tennessee	7	(D)	-	-	1,750 *	3.1	250	-	-	-

Source: 1992 Economic Census. The states are in descending order of shipments or establishments (if shipment data are missing for the majority). The symbol (D) appears when data are withheld to prevent disclosure of competitive information. States marked with (D) are sorted by number of establishments. A dash (-) indicates that the data element cannot be calculated; * indicates the midpoint of a range.

ASSOCIATIONS AND SOCIETIES

AMERICAN COTTON SHIPPERS ASSOCIATION
PO Box 3366
Memphis, TN 38173
Phone: (901) 525-2272
Fax: (901) 527-8303

AMERICAN ASSOCIATION FOR TEXTILE TECHNOLOGY
PO Box 99
Gastonia, NC 28053
Phone: (704) 824-3522
Fax: (704) 824-0630

AMERICAN ASSOCIATION OF TEXTILE CHEMISTS AND COLORISTS
PO Box 12215
Research
Triangle Park, NC 27709-2215
Phone: (919) 549-8141
Fax: (919) 549-8933

AMERICAN TEXTILE MANUFACTURERS INSTITUTE
1801 K St., Ste. 900
Washington, DC 20006
Phone: (202) 862-0500
Fax: (202) 862-0570

COTTON COUNCIL INTERNATIONAL
1521 New Hampshire Ave.
Washington, DC 20036
Phone: (202) 745-7805
Fax: (202) 483-4040

COTTON INCORPORATED
1370 Avenue of the Americas
New York, NY 10019
Phone: (212) 586-1070
Fax: (212) 265-5386

NATIONAL COTTON COUNCIL OF AMERICA
PO Box 12285
Memphis, TN 38182-0285
Phone: (901) 274-9030
Fax: (901) 725-0510

TEXTILE DISTRIBUTORS ASSOCIATION
45 W. 36th St., 3 Fl.
New York, NY 10018
Phone: (212) 563-0400

TEXTILE INSTITUTE
10 Blackfriars St.
Manchester M3 5DR, England
Phone: 161-8 34-8457
Fax: 161-8 35-3087
Members from more than 100 countries are involved with textile industry management, marketing, science, and technology.

PERIODICALS AND NEWSLETTERS

BARRON'S: NATIONAL BUSINESS AND FINANCIAL WEEKLY
Dow Jones and Co., Inc.
200 Liberty St.
New York, NY 10281
Phone: (800) 416-3546 or (212) 416-2700
Fax: (212) 416-2829
Weekly. $129.00 per year.

COTTON DIGEST INTERNATIONAL
Cotton Digest Co.
PO Box 820768
Houston, TX 77282-0768
Phone: (713) 977-1644
Fax: (713) 467-6935
Monthly. $40.00 per year. Formerly Cotton Digest.

DNR
Fairchild Fashion and Merchandising Group
7 W. 34th St.
New York, NY 10001
Phone: (800) 247-6622 or (212) 630-3990
Fax: (212) 630-3862
Daily. $62.00 per year. Formerly Daily News Record.

LDB INTERIOR TEXTILES
Columbia Communications, Inc.
370 Lexington Ave.
New York, NY 10017
Phone: (212) 532-9290
Fax: (212) 779-8345
Monthly. $35.00 per year. Formerly Interior Textiles.

TEXTILE HORIZONS: PROVIDING ESSENTIAL READING FOR ALL PRESENT AND FUTURE DECISION MAKERS IN TEXTILES AND FASHION WORLDWIDE
Textile Institute
Benjamin Dent and Co. Ltd.
23 Bloomsbury Sq.
London, England WC1A 2PJ
Phone: 0171 637 2211
Fax: 0171 637 2248
Monthly. $130.00 per year.

TEXTILE RESEARCH JOURNAL
Textile Research Institute
PO Box 625
Princeton, NJ 08543
Phone: (609) 924-3150
Fax: (609) 683-7836
Monthly. $195.00 per year.

TEXTILE WORLD
Maclean Hunter Publishing Co.
Textile Publications
4170 Ashford-Dunwoody Rd., Ste. 420
Atlanta, GA 30319
Phone: (404) 847-2770
Fax: (404) 252-6150
Monthly. Free to qualified personnel; others, $42.00 per year.

DATABASES

CITIBASE (CITICORP ECONOMIC DATABASE)
FAME Software Corp.
77 Water St., 9 Fl.
New York, NY 10005
Phone: (212) 898-7800
Fax: (212) 742-8956
Presents over 6,000 statistical series relating to business, industry, finance, and economics. Includes series from Survey of Current Business *and many other sources. Time period is 1947 to date, with daily updates. Inquire as to online cost and availability.*

TEXTILE TECHNOLOGY DIGEST [ONLINE]
Institute of Textile Technology
Textile Information Center
2551 Ivy Rd.
Charlottesville, VA 22903-4614
Phone: (804) 296-5511
Fax: (804) 977-5400
Contains indexing and abstracting of more than 800 worldwide journals and monographs in various areas of textile technology, production, and management. Time period is 1978 to date, with monthly updating. Inquire as to online cost and availability.

TITUS
Institut Textile de France
280 av. Aristide-Briand-BP141 92223
Bagneuv Cedex, France
Phone: 01-46 641540
Citations and abstracts of the worldwide literature on textiles, 1968 to present. Inquire as to online cost and availability.

WORLD TEXTILES
Elsevier Science, Inc.
655 Avenue of the Americas
New York, NY 10010
Phone: (800) 457-3633 or (212) 989-5800
Fax: (212) 633-3680
Provides abstracting from 1983 and indexing from 1970 of worldwide textile literature (periodicals, books, pamphlets, and reports). Includes U.S., European, and British patent information. Updating is monthly. Inquire as to online cost and availability.

STATISTICS SOURCES

BROADWOVEN FABRICS (GRAY)
U.S. Bureau of the Census
Washington, DC 20233-0800
Phone: (301) 457-4100
Fax: (301) 457-3842
Quarterly. Provides statistical data on production, value, shipments, and consumption. Includes woolen and worsted fabrics, tire fabrics, cotton broadwoven fabrics, etc. (Current Industrial Reports, MQ-22T.)

BUSINESS STATISTICS
Available from U.S. Government Printing Office
Washington, DC 20402
Phone: (202) 512-1800
Fax: (202) 512-2250
Biennial. $20.00. Issued by Bureau of Economic Analysis, U.S. Department of Commerce. Shows annual data for 29 years and monthly data for a recent four-year period. Statistics correspond to the Survey of Current Business.

CONSUMPTION ON THE WOOLEN SYSTEM AND WORSTED COMBING
U.S. Bureau of the Census
Washington, DC 20233-0800
Phone: (301) 457-4100
Fax: (301) 457-3842
Quarterly and annual. Provides data on consumption of fibers in woolen and worsted spinning mills, by class of fibers and end use. (Current Industrial Reports, MQ-22D.)

FAIRCHILD'S TEXTILE AND APPAREL FINANCIAL DIRECTORY
Fairchild Books, Fairchild Publications, Inc.
Seven W 34th St.
New York, NY 10001
Phone: (800) 247-6622 or (212) 630-3880
Annual. $85.00. Provides statistical and analytical marketing data, including industry concentration, materials consumed, import/export sales, value of shipments, retail sales by outlet type, advertising expenditures, consumer buying habits, and industry trends.

SURVEY OF CURRENT BUSINESS
Available from U.S. Government Printing Office
Washington, DC 20402
Phone: (202) 512-1800
Fax: (202) 512-2250
Monthly. $41.00 per year. Issued by Bureau of Economic Analysis, U.S. Department of Commerce. Presents a wide variety of business and economic data.

GENERAL WORKS

DAVISON'S TEXTILE BLUEBOOK
Davison Publishing Co.
PO Box 477
Ridgewood, NJ 07451
Phone: (201) 445-3135
Fax: (201) 445-4397
Annual. $121.00. Over 8,400 companies in the textile industry in the United States, Canada, and Mexico, including about 4,400 textile plants.

FABRIC SCIENCE
Fairchild Books
7 W. 34th St.
New York, NY 10001
Phone: (800) 247-6622 or (212) 630-3885
Looseleaf. $22.50, including swatch kit.

HISTORY OF TEXTILES
Kay Wilson
Westview Press
5500 Central Ave.
Boulder, CO 80301-2847
Phone: (800) 456-1995 or (303) 444-3541
Fax: (303) 449-3356
1981. $27.95.

FURTHER READING

Soras, Dr. Constantine G. "A Better Year For Textiles." *America's Textiles International,* January 1997. Available from http://www.billian.com/textiles/january1997/abetter.html.

Cotton Incorporated. "Cotton Perspective." April 1996.

Lee, Jill. "Textile Advances Enhance Cotton Markets." *Agricultural Research,* May 1996.

Rozelle, Walter N. "Parras Cone: A Product of A NAFTA Partnership." *Textile World,* February 1996.

———. "Business Outlook." *Textile World,* January 1997.

U.S. Bureau of the Census. "Broadwoven Fabrics." *Current Industrial Reports,* 10 June 1996. Available from http://www.census.gov.

31

INDUSTRY SNAPSHOT

Traditionally, companies providing data processing services have used their own extensive computer facilities and proprietary software. This practice enables them to divide the cost among many users, which makes the services more affordable for each company. Trends are developing, however, that include placing the contractor's hardware in the client's site or utilizing existing client hardware. This practice reduces the vendor's costs, as well as their revenues, while placing an increased burden on the client. The contractors generally welcome the chance to exclude hardware costs and to make their clients responsible for computer maintenance and upkeep. By doing this, the vendors can focus on software.

Poor economic conditions slowed the growth of some types of processing, such as credit cards and payroll, while other segments, such as medical claims and utilities, continued to grow at a steady rate. Outsourcing of computer services allowed companies to control costs, consolidate efforts, and efficiently utilize resources. The outsourcing segment of this industry totaled $9 billion in 1992.

The outsourcing trend resulted in contract awards of more than $100 million with durations of five to ten years. Some companies abandoned their in-house computer staffs in an effort to conserve financial and human resources, but many outsourced only a portion of their tasks to contractors. Some companies opted to outsource a portion of their activities, which reduced the need for expanded hardware and computer operators.

The major growth area in the industry was electronic data interchange (EDI), or the exchange of documents such as invoices and purchase orders. This area was expanded to include payments as well as invoices, and it was growing among suppliers and purchasers. EDI reduced collection costs, time, and errors. EDI expenditures were estimated at $1 billion in the early 1990s.

DATA PREPARATION AND PROCESSING

SIC 7374

The data preparation and processing services industry had estimated revenues of $45.7 billion in the early 1990s. Revenues were expected to continue growing through 1997. Trends toward outsourcing data processing services continued to grow as corporations and the government hired independent contractors to perform specific tasks.

INDUSTRY OUTLOOK

In the late 1990s, this industry was growing rapidly along with the rest of the high-technology industry. Overall data processing providers enjoyed healthy growth in the mid- to late 1990s, with the commercial demand for their services growing substantively. Activity was strongest in the communications and financial services sectors where the demand for integrated information technology expertise opened up new opportunities for resourceful companies.

Stock prices of bank technology companies increased dramatically with most firms posting double digit gains in the mid-1990s. However, small bank data processing companies were struggling in the mid-1990s due to consolidation in the banking industry and the increasing use of personal computer based technology. Data processing firms were forced to employ a variety of strategies to stay competitive—including offering more services, improving client relations, and adding more customers like credit unions and thrifts.

**SIC 7374 - Data Processing Services
General Statistics**

	Establish-ments	Employment (000)	Payroll ($ mil.)	Revenues ($ mil.)
1983	-	-	-	12,556.0
1984	-	-	-	14,120.0
1985	-	-	-	15,158.0
1986	-	-	-	16,414.0
1987	7,332	202.7	4,580.0	17,022.0
1988	6,811	217.9	5,445.6	18,868.0
1989	6,776	222.7	5,817.9	19,959.0
1990	6,773	228.9	6,442.7	20,731.0
1991	6,821	225.2	6,682.2	18,951.0
1992	7,286	230.3	6,795.9	20,575.0
1993	7,093	235.7	7,567.5	22,758.0
1994	7,024P	241.4P	7,979.9P	23,361.8P
1995	7,034P	245.9P	8,427.3P	24,268.9P
1996	7,044P	250.4P	8,874.7P	25,176.0P

Sources: Data for 1982, 1987, and 1992 are from *Census of Service Industries*, Bureau of the Census, U.S. Department of Commerce. Revenue data are from the *Service Annual Survey* or from the Census. Revenue data from the Census are labelled with *. Data for 1988-1991 and 1993, when shown, are derived from *County Business Patterns* for those years from the Bureau of the Census. A P indicates projections made by the editor.

While the fast paced high-technology industry was booming with many new inventions and enhancements, so was the data preparation and processing industry. The computer animation sector of this industry, especially, had tremendous success with the phenomenal success of the first full length computer animated movie, "Toy Story," marketed and financed by Disney and produced by Pixar. The market for computer generated animated motion pictures was expected to grow following the success of "Toy Story." Besides Pixar, many other companies like Pacific Data Images were also involved in making computer animated films during the mid- to late 1990s.

ORGANIZATION AND STRUCTURE

In 1989, firms providing data processing services totaled 6,811, and employment totaled 217,900. In 1996, the number of firms had increased to over 7,000, and employment was estimated at 250,400. The industry ranged from small family-type operations to large multinational companies. The top ten companies accounted for approximately 50 percent of the industry's revenue. An analysis of the 50 leading companies in *Services Industries USA* noted that while some of the data processing service companies were public corporations, many were subsidiaries, joint ventures, divisions, or affiliates of larger corporations. The industry was concentrated in California, Texas, New York, Florida, New Jersey, Pennsylvania, Illinois, Massachusetts, Maryland, Michigan, and Ohio; more than 200 data processing service establishments operated in these states.

WORK FORCE

Some industry segments, such as data entry and keypunch services, did not require a college or university education, but instead could be filled by high school or technical school graduates. Most segments preferred workers with a college education, despite the training they provided—in-house education at specific companies enabled workers to learn their duties. An interest and background in computer science was typically desirable for this industry.

RESEARCH AND TECHNOLOGY

The future of the industry depends upon overcoming barriers, including "unfair competition, industry regulation, taxation, high telecommunication costs, and inefficient telecommunication infrastructure," according to the *U.S. Industrial Outlook*. Electronic data interchange services and outsourcing will remain the brightest spots in the data preparation and processing industry.

Focusing on vertical markets and responding to customers' perceived needs will be essential in the future. The hardware industry continues to evolve rapidly, and data services firms will be able to produce information for their customers at a lower cost than if the companies brought the systems in-house. As outsourcing continues to become a major market segment, some of the smaller corporations providing this service will be usurped by the major players, such as Electronic Data Systems and International Business Machines. Fewer corporations will find investing in the large-scale systems necessary for complete data processing outsourcing to be fiscally viable, and the larger outsourcing firms will prosper. Companies will be inclined to take advantage of fixed costs for data processing procedures, instead of the variable costs associated with maintaining a system in-house. The economy will encourage other companies to pursue outside data processing and computer services, and this industry will continue to grow.

SIC 7374
Occupations Employed by SIC 7374 - Computer and Data Processing Services

Occupation	% of Total 1994	Change to 2005
Computer programmers	16.0	52.5
Systems analysts	9.2	194.7
Computer engineers	6.4	165.1
Sales & related workers nec	6.0	86.0
General managers & top executives	4.8	49.4
Data entry keyers, ex composing	4.2	-24.5
Secretaries, ex legal & medical	3.0	11.5
Computer operators, ex peripheral equipment	2.9	-58.7
Engineering, mathematical, & science managers	2.7	49.0
Data processing equipment repairers	2.3	57.4
Professional workers nec	2.3	136.1
Computer scientists nec	2.1	186.4
General office clerks	2.0	34.3
Marketing, advertising, & PR managers	2.0	73.2
Bookkeeping, accounting, & auditing clerks	2.0	18.1
Clerical supervisors & managers	1.9	17.1
Management support workers nec	1.8	57.4
Electrical & electronics engineers	1.6	67.6
Writers & editors, incl technical writers	1.5	88.9
Financial managers	1.3	57.4
Receptionists & information clerks	1.3	57.4
Electrical & electronic technicians,technologists	1.3	57.4
Managers & administrators nec	1.2	57.3
Clerical support workers nec	1.1	25.9
Adjustment clerks	1.1	88.9
Accountants & auditors	1.0	57.4

Source: *Industry-Occupation Matrix*, Bureau of Labor Statistics. These data relate to one or more 3-digit SIC industry groups rather than to a single 4-digit SIC. The change reported for each occupation to the year 2005 is a percent of growth or decline as estimated by the Bureau of Labor Statistics. The abbreviation nec stands for 'not elsewhere classified'.

Prosperous firms will be those that continue to expand the front-office, or customer-related, services that they offer to their clients. Computers will become more prevalent for electronic funds transfer, inventory control, and customer information systems. Front-office needs will continue to be time-sensitive, and data processing service providers will need to focus on innovations that allow corporations to supplement personnel with computer services.

AMERICA AND THE WORLD

The U.S. data processing services industry was the world's largest in the early 1990s, as noted in the *U.S. Industrial Outlook* handbook. Most American companies operated internationally and strove to function within vertical markets to tailor their services as business conditions changed.

The data processing industry received approximately 20 percent of its income from foreign sources. The percentage should continue to increase as electronic data interchange activity grows throughout multinational corporations. The United States faced less competition from Japanese companies in data processing services than in the hardware industry.

The industry operated with a favorable trade balance and will focus on foreign markets as U.S. companies operate internationally. Many U.S. companies were expanding overseas and seizing the opportunity to upgrade underdeveloped information industries, especially in Europe and Asia. Few foreign firms operated in the United States, but the number was growing.

North American expenditures on information services stood at $104 billion, or 52 percent of the world's total of $201 billion. European expenditures totaled $61 billion, and the Asian/Pacific expenses were $32 billion. In 1995, the expenditures were an estimated $193 billion by the United States, $143 billion by Europe, and $76 billion by Asia and the Pacific. The United States is projected to grow 13 percent, while the other two markets will each increase 19 percent. Foreign markets should continue to be plentiful as developing nations privatize their industry and modernize their businesses.

ASSOCIATIONS AND SOCIETIES

ASSOCIATION OF DATA COMMUNICATIONS USERS
PO Box 385728
Bloomington, MN 55438
Phone: (612) 881-6803
Fax: (612) 881-6709

COMPUTER AND COMMUNICATIONS INDUSTRY ASSOCIATION
666 11th St. NW, Ste. 600
Washington, DC 20001
Phone: (202) 783-0070
Fax: (202) 783-0534

DATA INTERCHANGE STANDARDS ASSOCIATION
1800 Diagonal Rd., Ste. 355
Alexandria, VA 22314
Phone: (703) 548-7005

ELECTRONIC DATA INTERCHANGE ASSOCIATION
225 Reinekers Ln., Ste. 550
Alexandria, VA 22314
Phone: (703) 838-8042

IEEE COMPUTER SOCIETY
1730 Massachusetts Ave. NW
Washington, DC 20036
Phone: (202) 371-0101
Fax: (202) 728-9614
A society of the Institute of Electrical and Electronics Engineers. Said to be the world's largest organization of computer professionals. Some of the specific committees are: Computer Communications; Computer Graphics; Computers in Education; Design Automation; Office Automation; Personal Computing; Robotics; Security and Privacy; Software Engineering.

INDEPENDENT DATA COMMUNICATIONS MANUFACTURERS ASSN.
1201 Pennsylvania Ave. NW
Washington, DC 20004
Phone: (202) 626-6600

INFORMATION INDUSTRY ASSOCIATION
555 New Jersey Ave. NW, Ste. 800
Washington, DC 20001
Phone: (202) 639-8262
Fax: (202) 638-4403

THE INFORMATION TECHNOLOGY ASSOCIATION OF AMERICA
1616 N. Fort Myer Dr., Ste. 1300
Arlington, VA 22209
Phone: (703) 522-5055

SPECIAL INTEREST GROUP ON DATA COMMUNICATION
Assn. for Computing Machinery
1515 Broadway
New York, NY 10036
Phone: (212) 869-7440
Fax: (212) 869-0481

SPECIAL INTEREST GROUP ON OFFICE INFORMATION SYSTEMS
Assn. for Computing Machinery
1515 Broadway
New York, NY 10036
Phone: (212) 869-7440
Fax: (212) 869-0481
Concerned with office automation and computer communications.

PERIODICALS AND NEWSLETTERS

ASSOCIATION OF DATA COMMUNICATIONS USERS NEWSLETTER
PO Box 385728
Bloomington, MN 55420
Phone: (612) 881-6803
Fax: (612) 881-6709
Monthly. Membership.

COMMUNICATIONS NEWS
American Society of Assn. Executives
Communications Section
1575 I St. NW
Washington, DC 20005

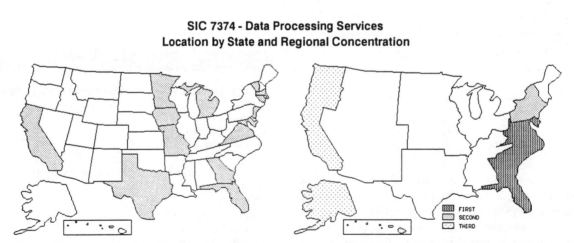

SIC 7374 - Data Processing Services
Location by State and Regional Concentration

FIRST
SECOND
THIRD

Source: Census of Service Industries, 1992, Bureau of the Census, U.S. Department of Commerce. Shaded states indicate states which have proportionately greater representation in the industry than would be indicated by the state's population; the ratio is based on revenues or establishments in 1992. Shaded regions indicate where the industry is regionally most concentrated.

Phone: (202) 626-2723
Fax: (202) 408-9635
Monthly. Membership.

COMMUNICATIONSWEEK

CMP Publications, Inc.
600 Community Dr.
Manhasset, NY 11030
Phone: (516) 562-5000
Fax: (516) 365-4601
Biweekly. $95.00 per year.

COMPUTER COMMUNICATIONS REVIEW

Special Interest Group on Data Communication
Assn. for Computing Machinery
1515 Broadway
New York, NY 10036
Phone: (212) 869-7440
Fax: (212) 869-0481
Quarterly. $37.00 per year.

COMPUTER INDUSTRY REPORT

International Data Corp.
41 West St.
Boston, MA 02111
Phone: (617) 423-9030
Fax: (617) 423-0712
Semimonthly. $495.00 per year. Newsletter. Annual supplement. Also known as "The Gray Sheet." Formerly EDP Industry Report.

COMPUTERWORLD: NEWSWEEKLY FOR INFORMATION SYSTEMS MANAGEMENT

Computerworld, Inc.
375 Cochituate Rd.
Framingham, MA 01701-9171
Phone: (508) 879-0700 Weekly. $48.00 per year.

DATA CHANNELS

Phillips Publishing, Inc.
7811 Montrose Rd.
Potomac, MD 20854
Phone: (800) 722-9000 or (301) 340-2100
Fax: (312) 424-4297
Biweekly. $597.00 per year. Newsletter.

DATA COMMUNICATIONS

McGraw-Hill, Inc.
1221 Avenue of the Americas
New York, NY 10020
Phone: (800) 722-4726 or (212) 512-2000
Fax: (212) 512-2821
Monthly. $95.00 per year.

DATAMATION

Cahners Publishing Co.
275 Washington St.
Newton, MA 02158
Phone: (617) 558-4281

EDI NEWS: THE EXECUTIVE CLEARINGHOUSE ON ELECTRONIC DATA INTERCHANGE

Phillips Publishing, Inc.
7811 Montrose Rd.
Potomac, MD 20854
Phone: (800) 722-9000 or (301) 340-2100
Fax: (301) 309-3847
Monthly. $397.00 per year. Newsletter.

EDI WORLD

2021 Coolidge St.
Hollywood, FL 33020
Phone: (305) 925-5900

INFORMATION TODAY: THE NEWSPAPER FOR USERS AND PRODUCERS OF ELECTRONIC INFORMATION SERVICES

Learned Information, Inc.
l43 Old Marlton Pke.
Medford, NJ 08055-8750
Phone: (609) 654-6266
Fax: (609) 654-4309
Eleven times a year. $39.95 per year.

JOURNAL OF DATA AND COMPUTER COMMUNICATIONS

Auerbach Publishers
1 Penn Plz.
New York, NY 10119
Phone: (800) 950-1218 or (212) 971-5000
Fax: (212) 971-5081
Quarterly. $110.00 per year.

NETWORK COMPUTING: COMPUTING IN A NETWORK ENVIRONMENT

CMP Publications, Inc.
600 Community Dr.
Manhasset, NY 11030
Phone: (516) 562-5000
Fax: (516) 365-4601
Monthly. $49.00 per year.

NETWORK WORLD: THE NEWSWEEKLY OF USER NETWORKING STRATEGIES

Network World, Inc.
161 Worcester Rd., 5th Fl.
Framingham, MA 01701
Phone: (508) 875-6400
Fax: (508) 879-3167
Weekly. Free to qualified personnel.

NETWORKING MANAGEMENT: FOR MIS, VOICE, DATA, VIDEO PROFESSIONALS

PennWell Publishing Co.
Advanced Technology Group
1 Technology Park Dr.
Westford, MA 01886-0989
Phone: (508) 692-0700
Fax: (508) 692-7831
Monthly. $42.00 per year.

TELEMATICS AND INFORMATICS
Pergamon Press, Inc.
Journals Div.
660 White Plains Rd.
Tarrytown, NY 10591-5153
Phone: (800) 257-5755 or (914) 524-9200
Fax: (914) 333-2444
Quarterly. $430.00 per year.

DATABASES

COMPUTER DATABASE
Information Access Co.
362 Lakeside Dr.
Foster City, CA 94404
Phone: (800) 227-8431 or (415) 378-5000
Fax: (415) 378-5369
Provides online citations with abstracts to material appearing in about 150 trade journals and newsletters in the subject areas of computers, telecommunications, and electronics. Time period is 1983 to date, with weekly updates.

MICROCOMPUTER INDEX (ONLINE)
Learned Information, Inc.
143 Old Marlton Pke.
Medford, NJ 08055-8750
Phone: (609) 654-6266
Fax: (609) 654-4309
Indexes and abstracts specialized microcomputer and personal computing periodicals, 1981 to present.

GENERAL WORKS

BULLETIN BOARD SYSTEMS FOR BUSINESS
Lamont Wood and Dana Blankenhorn
John Wiley & Sons, Inc.
605 3rd Ave.
New York, NY 10158-0012
Phone: (800) 225-5945 or (212) 850-6000
Fax: (212) 850-6088
1992. $34.95.

COMPUTER COMMUNICATIONS: A BUSINESS PERSPECTIVE
McGraw-Hill, Inc.
1221 Avenue of the Americas
New York, NY 10020
Phone: (800) 722-4726 or (212) 512-2000
Fax: (212) 512-2821
1993. $34.00.

COMPUTER COMMUNICATIONS: PRINCIPLES AND BUSINESS APPLICATIONS
McGraw-Hill, Inc.
1221 Avenue of the Americas
New York, NY 10020
Phone: (800) 722-4726 or (212) 512-2000
Fax: (212) 512-2821
1993. $18.95.

COMPUTER PHONE BOOK UPDATE
Computer Phone Book Update
175 5th Ave., Ste. 3371
New York, NY 10010
Monthly. $20.00 per year. Computer bulletin board systems.

COMPUTER REVIEW
594 Marrett Rd.
Lexington, MA 02173
Phone: (617) 861-0515
Semiannual. $345.00 per year. Reviews of specifications of top 10,000 computer products. Covers large companies to plug-in boards.

CYBERIA: LIFE IN THE TRENCHES OF HYPERSPACE
HarperCollins Publishers, Inc.
10 E. 53rd St.
New York, NY 10022-5299
Phone: (800)328-3443 or (212) 207-7000
Fax: (212) 207-7065
1994. $22.00.

DATA COMMUNICATIONS-BUYERS' GUIDE
McGraw-Hill, Inc.
1221 Avenue of the Americas
New York, NY 10020
Phone: (800) 722-4726 or (212) 512-2000
Fax: (212) 512-2821
Semiannual. $75.00.

DATA NETWORKING
Datapro Information Services Group
600 Delran Pkwy.
Delran, NJ 08075
Phone: (800) 328-2776
Four looseleaf volumes. Monthly updates. $1,255.00 per year. Includes information about software, hardware, and networks. Formerly Datapro Reports on Data Communications.

DATA SOURCES
Ziff-Davis Publishing Co.
1 Park Ave.
New York, NY 10016
Phone: (800) 289-9929 or (212) 503-5861
Fax: (212) 502-5800
Semiannual. $495.00 per year. Three volumes, covering (1) hardware, (2) software, and (3) data communications. Lists about 10,000 suppliers, with information on all types of software and all sizes of computers and related equipment.

DATAPRO DIRECTORY OF MICROCOMPUTER SOFTWARE
Datapro Information Services Group
600 Delran Pkwy.
Delran, NJ 08075
Phone: (800) 328-2776 or (609) 764-0100
Fax: (609) 764-2580
Two looseleaf volumes. Monthly updates. $779.00 per year. Detailed information about personal computer software and software companies.

DATAPRO MANAGEMENT OF DATA COMMUNICATIONS
Datapro Information Services Group
600 Delran Pkwy.
Delran, NJ 08075

Phone: (800) 328-2776 or (609) 764-0100
Fax: (609) 764-2580
Two looseleaf volumes. Monthly supplementation. $799.00 per year. Covers planning, implementation, and maintenance.

DATAPRO REPORTS ON PC AND LAN COMMUNICATIONS

Datapro Information Services Group
600 Delran Pkwy.
Delran, NJ 08075
Phone: (800) 328-2776 or (609)764-0100
Fax: (609) 764-2580
Three looseleaf volumes. Monthly updates. $945.00 per year. A compilation of information about personal computer software, hardware, and networks, including PC-to-mainframe links. Formerly Datapro Reports on PC Communications.

FAULKNER'S ENTERPRISE NETWORKING

Faulkner Information Services, Inc.
114 Cooper Ctr.
7950 Browning Rd.
Pennsauken, NJ 08109-4319
Phone: (800) 843-0460 or (609) 622-2070
Fax: (609) 662-3380
Three looseleaf volumes, with monthly supplements. $1507.00 per year. Contains product reports and management articles

relating to computer communications and networking. Available on CD-ROM. Quarterly updates. Formerly Data Communications Reports.

INFORMATION SOURCES: THE ANNUAL DIRECTORY OF THE INFORMATION INDUSTRY ASSOCIATION

Information Industry Assn.
555 New Jersey Ave., Ste. 800
Washington, DC 20001
Phone: (202) 639-8262
Fax: (202) 638-4403
Annual. $128.00.

FURTHER READING

Parkes, Christopher. "Computers Making Cool Movies." *The Financial Times,* 11 November 1996.

Posch, Robert. "Database Marketing Has a Good Year." *Direct Marketing,* February 1996.

"Services." *Computer Industry Report,* 17 March 1995.

DEFENSE AND ARMAMENTS

SIC 3480

Although *industry analysts foresee modest economic growth for the U.S. small arms and ammunition industry, employment levels are expected to decline due to increased investment in automation technology and a larger commitment to overseas manufacturing. According to the Bureau of Labor statistics this industry employed nearly 50,000 workers in 1996. This figure represented a significant decrease since the 1980s and was expected to further decline entering the twenty-first century. Emerging international markets are expected to provide small arms and ammunition producers with new export opportunities, which will help stabilize the industry as a whole.*

With the emergence of strong sport, defense, and construction markets in the mid-1990s, the U.S. small arms ammunition industry had become a $920 million business, employing about 7,500 workers. Although the ammunition industry's shipments totalled approximately $2 billion, ammunition producers operated in relative obscurity. These companies employed approximately 11,500 people and shipped $1.386 billion worth of small arms. Most major manufacturers enjoyed steady growth and a strengthening market from 1987 into early to mid-1990s.

In recent years, ammunition makers were engaged in fierce competition to maintain their share of a mature industry characterized by homogenous products. To boost sales and differentiate their products, manufacturers were offering specialized merchandise that appealed to niche market segments. They were also striving to increase productivity through automation. For its own part, the small arms industry has been cyclical and subject to many external pressures, including the general state of the economy, worldwide military conflicts, and public and political vagaries concerning private ownership of firearms. By the mid-1990s, public debate concerning the "right" of citizens to own firearms, especially handguns and assault rifles reached new heights of acrimony.

Top 10 WORLD'S LEADING DEFENSE FIRMS

Ranked by: Defense Revenues in 1994, in millions of U.S. dollars.

1. Lockheed Martin (U.S.), with $14,400.0 million
2. McDonnell Douglas Corp. (U.S.), $9,229.0
3. British Aerospace (U.K.), $7,265.8
4. Hughes Electronics Corp. (U.S.), $6,300.0
5. Northrop Corp. (U.S.), $5,410.0
6. Loral (U.S.), $5,209.8
7. Boeing (U.S.), $4,752.0
8. Thomson Group (France), $4,420.9
9. General Electric PLC (U.K.), $4,320.5
10. United Technologies (U.S.), $3,800.0

Source; *Defense News,* Top 100 Firms (annual), July 31, 1995, p. 8.

The ammunition industry is about 70 percent as large as the entire firearms industry that it complements. The comparably high-profile firearm industry receives large amounts of press and is often the target of state and federal regulatory initiatives. Ammunition makers, however, operate in relative obscurity, with little publicity, regulation, or outside analysis of the industry. One reason that the industry has such a low profile is that most of its products are homogenous, resulting in a commodity-like business environment that is not dynamic. In addition, the largest producers in the industry are owned by massive conglomerates that view ammunition operations as relatively small sideline businesses.

INDUSTRY OUTLOOK

To boost profits in the 1990s, small ammunition producers were slowly raising productivity, selling through new marketing channels, and offering new niche products. Manufacturers invested an average of $25 million per year into production facilities in the 1980s, a very low investment compared to most other industries. Despite that low figure, industry employment fell from about 7.4 million to 6.3 million workers during the decade, at the same time that overall production increased. Winchester, for instance, installed computer-controlled cartridge loading machines that allowed the company to produce 9 mm cartridges and other popular ammunition at a rate of up to 450 units per minute. Despite industry efforts at low-cost, high-volume production in some areas, most manufacturers still used some very old production techniques. Even at Winchester many low-volume products in 1993 were still loaded at rates of 40 to 60 per minute using machines the company acquired in 1931. Lead shot, moreover, was produced using a two-century old process.

Besides moderate productivity gains, producers were benefitting from new marketing channels. Sporting goods stores and gun shops continued to account for a declining share of total ammunition sales, as they had since the 1980s. Instead, discount stores such as Wal-Mart and Kmart, accounted for 30 percent to 50 percent of commercial sales by 1992. In addition, mail order catalog sales were becoming an increasingly important channel of distribution. One of the largest ammunition catalogers, AcuSport Corp. of Ohio, increased mail order sales from $30 million in 1988 to over $75 million by 1992.

Many producers were also developing new bullet types to appeal to niche market segments. These unique items offered higher profit margins than popular commodity ammunition. Police and handgun owners, for instance, had proved a viable market for sales of specialty bullets. The Black Talon, for example, was a bullet designed to enter a person's body, spread out, and extend tiny razors that stopped the bullet inside the body. Other ammunition was designed to explode on impact and release tiny pellets into its target, or pierce metal plate or protective gear.

As the mid-1990s approached, an area of potential growth for industry competitors was the export market. Productivity gains realized in the 1980s allowed U.S. producers to stem an influx of cheap import ammunition from Brazil and the Far East during that decade. As their production costs became more globally competitive, some manufacturers began eyeing burgeoning foreign ammunition markets. Exports already accounted for more than 10 percent of total U.S. production in the early 1990s. Foreign producers had captured less than 20 percent of the U.S. ammunition market by 1992, and import growth seemed to have stabilized.

REGULATORY EFFORTS

Largely in reaction to soaring crime rates in major cities, various federal and state initiatives sought to tether the industry in the early 1990s. However, the small arms ammunition industry remained loosely regulated. Congress, with the support of the National Rifle Association (NRA), did succeed in banning certain types of "cop-killer" bullets, designed to penetrate bullet-proof vests. That ban represented the only piece of legislation ever passed to limit the direct sale of small arms ammunition.

Senator Daniel Patrick Moynihan (New York) proposed legislation in the early 1990s to ban the sale of 9 mm, .25 caliber, and .32 caliber ammunition, which together accounted for 50 percent of the bullets fired at police officers. He also tried to pass legislation making many pistol cartridges prohibitively expensive. Moynihan was unsuccessful in both attempts. Critics argued that such laws could not be enforced and would have a negligible effect on crime.

In 1994, President Bill Clinton signed the Brady Bill, which called for a waiting period for handgun purchases and required local police authorities to conduct an investigation before issuing a permit to purchase a handgun. However, because of a general fear of crime, and social and civil unrest, the sale of handguns and those military style assault rifles that were still legal skyrocketed along with ammunition for these arms. Many such firearms and ammunition were in short supply causing a booming business among gun stores, distributors, importers, and manufacturers. As a result, in 1995 the National Alliance of Stocking Gun Dealers predicted an annual growth rate of nearly 6 percent.

ORGANIZATION AND STRUCTURE

Ammunition producers manufacture both cartridges and shells. The two types of cartridges used in rifles and pistols are rimfire and centerfire. Rimfire cartridges are comprised of a soft lead bullet, a case most often made of brass and the smokeless propellant (powder). The priming compound is spun into the rim of the case. When the firearm's firing pin strikes and indents the rim of the cartridge, the priming mixture ignites and in turn ignites the propellant, hence the name "rimfire." Centerfire cartridges differ in that a separate primer is seated in the base or head of the cartridge. When struck by the firing pin the primer ignites the propellant via the flash hole in the base of the cartridge, hence the name "centerfire." Cartridges developing relatively low pressure (such as the common .22 caliber cartridges for both rifles and pistols) lend themselves to the rimfire configuration because the brass head of the cartridge can be thin enough to allow ignition of the propellant.

Prior to the Civil War, both large and small bore rifle and pistol cartridges were rimfire because they developed relatively low internal pressures when ignited. In the post-Civil War period, however, more powerful cartridges began to be developed. These cartridges reached subsequently higher pressures and thus required case heads too thick to be indented by a firing pin. The centerfire ignition system solved this problem and is used in the same configuration in the 1990s for high pressure cartridges. Shotgun shells are also centerfire, but are made up of a paper or plastic cylinder with a brass base or head. The shell is filled with powder followed by a cupped plastic wad filled with birdshot or much larger buckshot. Birdshot may be lead or steel while buckshot is lead. Federal law mandates that all duck and goose hunting be done with steel shot. It has been found that wildfowl accidentally ingesting spent lead shot while feeding are subject to lead poisoning. Shotgun shells may also be loaded with a single heavy slug which in various configurations is made of lead or a lead alloy. Slugs are used in law enforcement and for hunting big game such as deer. In addition to cartridges and shells, the small arms ammunition industry also includes the manufacture of BBs and pellets, which are most commonly fired from spring- or pneumatic-powered pistols and rifles.

Rimfire cartridges were typically .22 caliber and used in rifles and pistols designated "small-bore" and accounted for about 8 percent of industry sales in 1992. Centerfire pistol cartridges, including those cartridges such as the .44 Magnum, which could be interchanged between pistols and rifles, represented about 14 percent of revenues. Centerfire rifle ammunition made up an

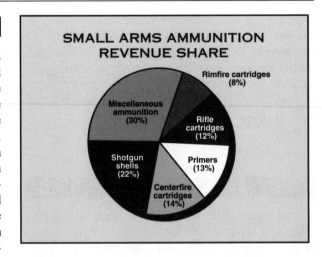

SMALL ARMS AMMUNITION REVENUE SHARE

Rimfire cartridges (8%)
Miscellaneous ammunition (30%)
Rifle cartridges (12%)
Shotgun shells (22%)
Primers (13%)
Centerfire cartridges (14%)

additional 12 percent of sales, while shotgun shells accounted for about 22 percent of industry shipments. Primers and other ammunition components sold separately garnered about a 13 percent share of the market, and miscellaneous ammunition products accounted for the remaining 30 percent of industry revenues. A significant portion of miscellaneous ammunition was ramset shells, used in the construction industry to drive nails into concrete.

Small arms ammunition is produced primarily for three types of firearms: handguns, including both semiautomatics and revolvers; shotguns; and rifles. In addition to these categories, smaller markets exist for fully automatic rifles as well as for BB and pellet guns. When using a single-action or double-action revolver the rounds of ammunition are loaded into the firearm's cylinder. The hammer of a single-action revolver (most "cowboy" pistols are single-action) must be pulled back or cocked by the shooter's thumb. This causes the cylinder to rotate aligning the cartridge with the barrel. When the trigger is pulled the hammer falls crushing the primer and igniting the cartridge. A double-action revolver (the modern police revolver is typical) may be fired single-action or by pulling on the trigger with the hammer in the down position. The latter move will cause the cylinder to rotate while simultaneously cocking the hammer. When the trigger reaches the end of its pull, the hammer falls causing the newly aligned cartridge to fire.

Semiautomatic pistols and some semiautomatic rifles hold rounds of ammunition in a spring-loaded clip. In early semiautomatics, the force of recoil ejected the fired case and loaded a fresh cartridge into the barrel. Semiautomatics in the 1990s, however, bleed off gas from a fired cartridge. This gas works against a piston which ejects the fired case and loads a fresh round in the barrel. Both methods also recock the weapon, but before it can fire again the trigger must be first disengaged and then pulled again. Fully automatic weapons, such as machine guns and military assault rifles, continue to fire and reload rounds as long as the shooter does not release the trigger. Federal law prohibits most citizens from owning or having in their possession fully automatic weapons.

Ammunition sold to the general public represented about 40 percent of industry sales in the 1980s. Sales to the federal government for military and other uses accounted for about 20 percent of sales, a figure that fell to about 15 percent in the early 1990s. Exports consumed approximately 10 percent of sales. Cement and hydraulic industries made up about 6 percent of market share, while state and local governments and police accounted for about 5 percent. Various industrial and construction industries accounted for the remaining 20 percent of sales. Hunters purchase 80 percent of the ammunition sold to the general public, or about 30 percent of total industry output. In addition to the use of rifles and shotguns for sport purposes, about 60 percent of hunters also own handguns, making people in that group significant consumers of pistol ammunition.

in the United States. Also to blame was the high cost of product liability insurance in the United States, which some manufacturers considered a greater long-term threat to the industry than efforts to ban or restrict firearms. Nearly all major gun manufacturers were hit with multi-million dollar lawsuits in the 1980s.

Foreign gunmakers also established manufacturing facilities in the United States in the 1980s to avoid restrictions on imports, including Italy's Pietro Beretta Fabbrica Amri and Belgium's Fabrique Nationale. In 1985, Beretta USA signed a contract to provide 9 mm handguns to the U.S. military, ending Colt's 100-year dominance of military sidearms. Three years later, Fabrique Nationale wrested the Army contract for the M-16 automatic rifle away from Colt. The losses were a major reason that Colt Industries eventually sold its firearms division to a group of private investors. Two other famous names in American gunmaking, Winchester and Smith & Wesson, were also sold in the 1980s to avoid bankruptcy.

WORK FORCE

Employment in the small arms ammunition industry was expected to decrease between 1990 and 2005, according to the U.S. Bureau of Labor Statistics. In 1992, there were 20,000 people employed in the small arms and small arms ammunition industry. This figure was expected to decline to between 14,000 and 15,000 by 2005. Productivity gains, movement of production facilities to countries with cheaper labor, and stagnant domestic market growth were expected to contribute to this trend. Jobs for assemblers and fabricators, which represented a leading 14 percent of industry positions, were forecast to fall by more than 50 percent. Other manufacturing positions, which accounted for the bulk of industry employment, were expected to decline by 25 percent to 50 percent. General management and executive positions were also expected to drop by more than 40 percent. Workers already employed in the industry, however, continued to enjoy higher wages than workers in most other U.S. manufacturing industries in the 1990s.

AMERICA AND THE WORLD

Less costly foreign imports also affected the U.S. small arms and ammunition industry, reducing the profit margin on the sale of guns. Foreign imports were less costly because of high U.S. wages and the fact that many gun factories were among the oldest industrial facilities

ASSOCIATIONS AND SOCIETIES

AMERICAN DEFENSE PREPAREDNESS ASSOCIATION
2101 Wilson Blvd., Ste. 400
Arlington, VA 22201-3061
Phone: (703) 522-1820
Fax: (703) 522-1885
Concerned with industrial preparedness for national defense.

NATIONAL DEFENSE TRANSPORTATION ASSOCIATION
50 S. Pickett St., Ste. 220
Alexandria, VA 22304-3008
Phone: (703) 751-5011
Fax: (703) 823-8761

NATIONAL RIFLE ASSOCIATION OF AMERICA
1600 Rhode Island Ave. NW
Washington, DC 20036
Phone: (800) 368-5714 or (202) 868-6000

PERIODICALS AND NEWSLETTERS

AIR FORCE JOURNAL OF LOGISTICS
Available from U.S. Government Printing Office
Washington, DC 20402
Phone: (202) 512-1800
Fax: (202) 512-2250
Quarterly. $9.00 per year. Issued by the Air Force Logistics Management Center, Air Force Department, Defense Department. Presents research and information of interest to professional Air Force logisticians.

AMERICAN FIREARMS INDUSTRY
National Assn. of Federally Licensed Firearms Dealers
2455 E. Sunrise Blvd., 9th Fl.
Fort Lauderdale, FL 33304-3118
Phone: (305) 561-3505
Fax: (305) 561-4129
Monthly. $25.00 per year.

AMERICAN RIFLEMAN
National Rifle Assn. of America
NRA Publications
470 Spring Park Pl., Ste. 1000
Herndon, VA 22070
Phone: (703) 481-3340
Fax: (703) 481-3376
Monthly.

ARMED FORCES JOURNAL INTERNATIONAL
Armed Forces Journal International, Inc.
2000 L St. NW, Ste. 520
Washington, DC 20036
Phone: (202) 296-0450
Fax: (202) 296-5727
Monthly. $35.00 per year. A defense magazine for career military officers and industry executives. Covers defense events, plans, policies, budgets, and innovations.

BUREAU OF ALCOHOL, TOBACCO, AND FIREARMS QUARTERLY BULLETIN
Bureau of Alcohol, Tobacco, and Firearms
U.S. Department of the Treasury
Available from U.S. Government Printing Office
Washington, DC 20402
Phone: (202) 783-3238
Quarterly. $19.00 per year. Laws and regulations.

DEFENSE
Available from U.S. Government Printing Office
Washington, DC 20402
Phone: (202) 512-1800
Fax: (202) 512-2250
Bimonthly. $10.00 per year. Issued by the American Forces Information Service, U.S. Department of Defense. Contains information on defense expenditures, policies, and weapons programs.

DEFENSE & ECONOMY WORLD REPORT
Government Business Worldwide Reports
PO Box 5997
Washington, DC 20016
Phone: (202) 244-7050
Fax: (202) 244-5410
Biweekly. $350.00 per year. Definitive information on the international defense industry and its government customers.

DEFENSE INDUSTRY REPORT
Phillips Publishing, Inc.
7811 Montrose Rd.
Potomac, MD 20854
Phone: (800) 722-9000 or (301) 340-2100
Fax: (301) 424-4297
Biweekly. $795.00 per year. Newsletter.

DEFENSE MARKETING INTERNATIONAL
Phillips Business Information, Inc.
1201 Seven Locks Rd., Ste. 300

Potomac, MD 20854
Phone: (800) 777-5006 or (301) 340-2100
Fax: (301) 424-4297
Biweekly. $645.00 per year. Newsletter. Covers international defense technology industries.

DEFENSE MONITOR
Center for Defense Information
1500 Massachusetts Ave. NW
Washington, DC 20005
Fax: (212) 862-0708
Ten times a year. $25.00 per year.

GUNS AND AMMO
Petersen Publishing Co.
8490 Sunset Blvd.
Los Angeles, CA 90069
Phone: (213) 854-2222
Monthly. $21.94 per year.

GUNS: FINEST IN THE FIREARMS FIELD
Publishers' Development Corp.
591 Camino de la Reina, Ste. 200
San Diego, CA 92108
Phone: (800) 537-3006 or (619) 297-5350
Fax: (619) 297-5353
Monthly. $19.95 per year.

NATIONAL DEFENSE
American Defense Preparedness Association
2101 Wilson Blvd., Ste. 400
Arlington, VA 22201-3061
Phone: (703) 522-1820
Fax: (703) 522-1885
10 times a year. Free to members; non-members, $30.00 per year.

ONLINE DATABASES

AEROSPACE/DEFENSE MARKETS AND TECHNOLOGY
Information Access Co.
362 Lakeside Dr.
Foster City, CA 94404
Phone: (800) 321-6388 or (415) 358-4643
Fax: (415) 358-4759
Abstracts of commercial aerospace/defense related literature, 1982 to date. Also includes information about major defense contracts awarded by the U.S. Department of Defense. International coverage. Inquire as to online cost and availability.

CITIBASE (CITICORP ECONOMIC DATABASE)
FAME Software Corp.
77 Water St., 9 Fl.
New York, NY 10005
Phone: (212) 898-7800
Fax: (212) 742-8956
Presents over 6,000 statistical series relating to business, industry, finance, and economics. Includes series from Survey of Current Business and many other sources. Time period is 1947 to date, with daily updates. Inquire as to online cost and availability.

JANE'S ELECTRONIC INFORMATION SYSTEM
BTG, Inc.
The complete texts of Jane's Information Group's renowned defense and aerospace publications, some with images. Time span: Current information. When established: 1994. Fees: Free. URL: http://www.btg.com/janes/welcome.html

STATISTICS SOURCES

BUSINESS STATISTICS
Available from U.S. Government Printing Office
Washington, DC 20402
Phone: (202) 512-1800
Fax: (202) 512-2250
Biennial. $20.00. Issued by Bureau of Economic Analysis, U.S. Department of Commerce. Shows annual data for 29 years and monthly data for a recent four-year period. Statistics correspond to the Survey of Current Business.

CIVILIAN MANPOWER STATISTICS
Available from U.S. Government Printing Office
Washington, DC 20402
Phone: (202) 512-1800
Fax: (202) 512-2250
Quarterly. $12.00 per year. Issued by U.S. Department of Defense. Provides data on civilian employment in U.S. defense industries.

SURVEY OF CURRENT BUSINESS
Available from U.S. Government Printing Office
Washington, DC 20402
Phone: (202) 512-1800
Fax: (202) 512-2250
Monthly. $41.00 per year. Issued by Bureau of Economic Analysis, U.S. Department of Commerce. Presents a wide variety of business and economic data.

WORLD FACTBOOK
Available from National Technical Information Service
5285 Port Royal Rd.
Springfield, VA 22161
Phone: (800) 553-6847 or (703) 487-4600
Fax: (703) 321-8547
Annual. $33.50. Prepared by the Central Intelligence Agency. For all countries of the world, provides current economic, demographic, geographic, communications, government, de-
fense force, and illicit drug trade information (where applicable).

GENERAL WORKS

BRASSEY'S DEFENSE YEARBOOK
Brassey's, Inc.
Marketing Dept.
1313 Dolly Madison Blvd., Ste. 401
Mc Lean, VA 22102-3101
Phone: (703) 442-4535
Fax: (703) 442-9848
Annual. $58.00. Formerly RUSI and Brassey's Defence Yearbook.

UNITED NATIONS DISARMAMENT YEARBOOK
United Nations Publications
2 United Nations Plz., Rm. DC2-853
New York, NY 10017
Phone: (800) 253-9646 or (212) 963-8302
Fax: (212) 963-3489
Annual. $45.00. Text in English, French, Spanish, and Russian.

FURTHER READING

Darnay, Arsen J., ed. *Manufacturing USA*. 5th ed. Detroit: Gale Research, 1996.

Hausman, Robert M. ''U.S. Repeating Arms Co.'' *Shooting Industry*, March 1996.

Knox, Neal. ''Knox's Notebook.'' *American Rifleman*, August 1996.

Robinson, Jerome B. ''The Next Generation of Shooters.''*Field & Stream*, May 1996.

Thurman, Russ. ''Firearms Business Analysis.'' *Shooting Industry*, June 1996.

———. ''Local Gun Sales Healthy.'' *Shooting Industry*, May 1996.

Tomkins, Richard. ''The Four-Gun Family in Their Sights.''*Financial Times*, 2 March 1996.

EDUCATIONAL SERVICES

SIC 8200

Between 1996 and 2006, enrollment in the public school sector—by far the largest segment of the U.S. school system—was projected to grow by 2 percent at the elementary level and by 15 percent at the secondary level. Such an expansion will without a doubt strain various educational issues, including funding, class size, and curriculum. Colleges and universities will continue to see operating costs soar in all areas— scholarships, administration, student services, faculty, research, and maintenance. As a result, tuition, room, and board costs to attend college will grow, typically higher than the rate of overall inflation.

During the 1994-95 school year, a total of 86,221 U.S. public schools served 44.1 million students. This represented an increase of 1.4 percent over the number of students reported for the previous school year. According to the National Center for Education Statistics (NCES), enrollment in public elementary and secondary schools rose 16 percent between 1985 and 1996. The fastest growth occurred in the elementary grades where enrollment rose from 27 million to a record high of 32.8 million in 1996, an increase of 21 percent. Secondary enrollments at first declined eight percent from 1985 to 1990 but then increased by 15 percent to reach 13 million in 1996. In 1993-94, 12 percent of all students were served in programs for the disabled compared to 10 percent in 1980-81. Much of this rise may be attributed to the increasing proportion of children identified as learning disabled which rose from four percent of enrollment in 1980-81 to six percent of enrollment in 1993-94.

The most recent statistics from the NCES reported that there were a total of 4.97 million students enrolled in 26,093 private elementary and secondary schools. Catholic schools accounted for 51 percent of these students while other religious schools accounted for 34 percent and nonsectarian schools claimed a 15 percent share. The proportion of students in private schools has changed little over the last ten years. The percentage of private elementary and secondary students decreased slightly from 12 percent in 1985 to 11 percent in 1996.

The expenditures of public and private schools in the elementary and secondary grades were expected to total $318 billion for the 1995-96 school year. Of this figure, $288 billion was spent by the public school system. Local authorities provided 45.3 percent of school revenues, state governments provided 47.7 percent, and the federal government supplied seven percent. Average per pupil expenditures amounted to $5,653. After being adjusted for inflation, this represented an increase in spending of 33 percent over the decade.

There are currently about 3,530 colleges and universities in the United States. The government projects that in 1998 a total of 11.8 million students will be enrolled at public colleges, universities, and professional schools, and another 3.3 million will be enrolled at private institutions. According to a survey conducted by Peterson's, during the 1995-96 school year approximately 2,200 four-year colleges and universities in the United States enrolled more than 8 million students and nearly 6 million students were enrolled at 1,500 two-year institutions. More than half of all U.S. undergraduates are enrolled at four-year institutions and the majority of students enrolled at four-year institutes are undergraduates (as opposed to graduate and doctoral students). According to *The College Handbook,* of the more than 500 universities in the United States, about 320 offer doctoral degrees.

BEST RANKED NATIONAL UNIVERSITIES

Ranked by: Composite score in 6 academic areas: reputation, student selectivity, faculty strength, resources, graduation rate, and alumni satisfaction. Overall score is based on the school's percentile when measured in the 6 categories.

1. Harvard University (MA), with a score of 100.0
2. Princeton University (NJ), 98.8
2. Yale University (CT), 98.8
4. Stanford University (CA), 98.1
5. Massachusetts Institute of Technology, 98.0
6. Duke University (NC), 96.8
7. California Institute of Technology, 95.5
7. Dartmouth College (NH), 95.5
9. Brown University (RI), 95.3
10. Johns Hopkins University (MD), 94.6

Source: *U.S. News & World Report,* America's Best Colleges (annual), September 18, 1995, p. 126.

Federal studies show that U.S. colleges and universities spent more than $171 billion in expenditures in 1992. Further studies conducted by Peterson's reveals that most (27.8 percent) colleges and universities are controlled by the state, followed by 25.7 percent under independent religious control and independent non-profit control (19.4 percent); less than 1 percent are federally-controlled. The majority of college campuses are located in small towns, closely followed by urban settings and suburban areas, with the fewest located in rural areas.

Private four-year colleges and universities demand the highest annual tuition, followed by independent two-year institutes; public four-year institutions come next, and two-year public schools charge the lowest tuition. The average tuition and fees for the 1995-96 academic year ranged from $1,643 at two-year public colleges to $10,612 at four-year private institutions, according to Peterson's Annual Survey of Undergraduate Institutions.

More than 1,500 institutions in the United States offered courses at the junior, community, or technical college level to more than 6 million students in 1996. This type of institution is often referred to as a two-year college, though this designation only pertains to establishments that provide students with an Associate's de-

gree. Students at these institutions pay relatively low tuition compared to fees charged by colleges and universities. Federal, state, and local appropriations and grants support public community colleges, which account for the majority of these schools, while private community colleges receive funds from a variety of sources.

INDUSTRY OUTLOOK

ELEMENTARY AND HIGH SCHOOLS

As the education establishment entered the 1990s, efforts aimed at improving learning opportunities for all America's children intensified. The number of high school graduates in 1994-95 totaled about 2.6 million. Between 1980 and 1994, the number of GED (General Educational Development) credentials issued rose from 488,000 to 498,000. Americans 25 years old and older holding high school diplomas or GED credentials increased from 69 percent to 89 percent. At the same time, overall drop out rates fell from 14.1 percent to 12 percent, although they varied by ethnicity. The drop out rate for non-Hispanic whites was 8.6 percent, down from 11.4 percent in 1980; for blacks it was 12.1 percent, down from 19.1 percent; and, for Hispanics, the drop out rate fell from 35.2 percent to 30 percent.

Between 1984-85 and 1994-95, SAT (Scholastic Aptitude Test) math scores improved seven points but verbal scores fell three points. Combined scores showed substantial increases for black students (up 22 points) and Asian American students (up 34 points) while white students' scores increased by only seven points. Although considerable differences still exist among students from different racial/ethnic groups, these differences narrowed between 1984-85 and 1994-95. Despite the gains posted by black students, blacks' average scores remained 202 points under average scores for white students, and although non-Hispanic whites outperformed their Asian-American counterparts by 30 points on verbal scores, math scores for Asian-American students topped scores received by whites by 40 points.

Despite improvements made by blacks and other minorities, minority students continued to score below white students in many standardized tests and educational assessments. The most recent (1994) National Assessment of Educational Progress (NEAP) results in reading suggest that minority groups may be beginning to lose some of the earlier gains they had made relative to whites. The problem was heightened by the fact that minority students were statistically in the majority at 22 of the nation's largest 25 school districts. According to statements made by the U.S. Department of Education, school reforms made under the Elementary and Secondary Education Act "seldom triggered the kinds of transforming that our schools need—particularly in economically disadvantaged communities."

Many schools' problems were associated with economically disadvantaged students. According to statistics, tenth grade students from districts with high rates of poverty were found to have drop out rates twice as high as those from schools in districts with little poverty. In 1993, the U.S. Department of Education reported that more than 50 percent of the students in schools containing the nation's highest concentrations of poverty were judged to be low achievers. In schools with the least poverty, only about eight percent of the students were judged to be low achievers. Because of the ramifications of poverty on education, 30 states were involved in lawsuits over disparities in education spending created by differences in local property taxes. In two states, Alabama and Massachusetts, the courts ruled that disparities in school funding violated the states' constitutions.

In 1996, the U.S. Department of Education estimated that more than half a million students were home schooled, which accounted for about one percent of the total school age population, a 30 percent jump from the 1991 figure. Sixty one percent of parents polled ranked dissatisfaction with public school environment and instruction as a primary motivation for home schooling, topping religion which was listed by 21 percent. Lack of discipline moved ahead of lack of financial support and use of drugs as the item most frequently cited by the public as a major problem facing the public schools in 1995.

Some people turned to private schools for alternatives to public education. According to the National Center for Education Statistics, however, private school enrollment did not increase significantly. Between 1981 and 1991, 11 to 12 percent of elementary and secondary school students were served by private schools. One factor keeping private school enrollment down was the high cost of tuition. Tuition charged by private schools varied according to the type of school. In general, schools with religious orientations had lower tuition than nonsectarian schools. For students at Catholic elementary schools, the mean tuition paid during 1993-94 was $1,628 per student; at other religious elementary schools it was $2,606; and at nonsectarian elementary schools it was $4,693. In all schools, tuition was higher at the secondary level. Catholic high school tuition averaged $3,643; other religious high schools averaged $5,261; and nonsectarian high schools averaged $9,525.

The Catholic school system represented the nation's largest nonpublic educational system. It had originally been established to educate the children of Catholic immigrants. Declines in attendance, attributed to demographic shifts, led to declining enrollment during the 1970s, 1980s, and early 1990s. By the 1995-96 school year, the number of Catholic schools had fallen to 8,243 with a student population of 2.5 million, the smallest number reported since the 1920s. To combat the declines, schools began promoting themselves and reemphasizing the value of a Catholic education because of its traditional, rigorous academic curriculum.

COLLEGES AND UNIVERSITIES

A consensus is emerging in the 1990s that the colleges and universities are going to have to change the way they do business in some fundamental ways in order to survive. As *Business Week* noted in 1993, "Long the crown jewel in America's educational system and the envy of the world, academe has failed to rein in its soaring costs . . . like many U.S. companies, colleges have no alternative but to boost productivity and streamline operations. Higher education is a huge, sprawling enterprise with sclerotic bureaucracies and too many marginal operations." As a result of these ominous developments, *Business Week* notes that "a growing number of universities are embracing the restructuring mantra and hacking away at administrative and faculty bloat. They are trying to move away from an overemphasis on research and toward teaching."

The higher education industry is also an increasingly competitive one. While student enrollment has increased to more than 14 million annually, the number of institutions, public and private, battling for those students has also increased. More than 3,500 institutions of higher education are currently operating in the United States.

Many colleges and universities, however, are financially troubled. Operating costs continue to soar in all areas—scholarships, administration, student services, faculty, research, and maintenance. As a result, tuition, room, and board costs to attend college grow, typically higher than the rate of overall inflation.

Paul B. Firstenberg, writing in *Management Review,* writes that "For two decades, most private universities have faced these financial pressures, but not many have adapted in the fundamental ways that may be necessary for survival. They've cut expenses at the margin, boosted tuition, redoubled fund-raising efforts, and kept their fingers crossed. That strategy has led to a 300 percent tuition increase at private institutions between 1970 and 1987, 70 percent higher than the increases at public institutions."

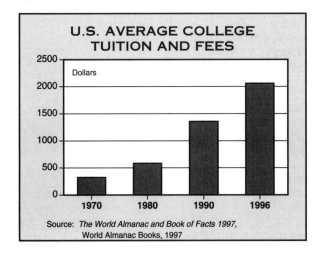

U.S. AVERAGE COLLEGE TUITION AND FEES

Source: *The World Almanac and Book of Facts 1997*, World Almanac Books, 1997

COMMUNITY COLLEGES

Community colleges have recently reevaluated their curricula. In the early 1990s, it was determined that fewer students were earning Associate degrees and less than a quarter were transferring to four-year colleges. The pattern that many students seemed to be following was horizontal rather than vertical. This behavior was attributed to student scheduling conflicts and career considerations, rather than a lack of ambition or inability to pursue a goal. Community colleges have tried to address these problems by providing alternative means of participating in class—often through the use of modern technology. For instance, community college libraries are being transformed into "resource centers."

In regard to growth in the community college industry, at least one expert, Arthur M. Cohen, long-time director of the Educational Resources Information Center (ERIC) Clearinghouse for Junior Colleges, believes that community colleges have reached a saturation point in the United States. Because these institutions are within easy access to virtually every community, no further dramatic growth is expected. According to Cohen, "Few new institutions will open in the years ahead because a community college is now within commuting distance of most of the nation's population. There will be very little contraction in enrollment. . . . Funding for various programs will continue to be provided. . . . The colleges are here to stay in their current form."

WORK FORCE

In 1996, the U.S. educational system was served by 1.9 million elementary school teachers and 1.2 million secondary school teachers. This total of 3.1 million teachers represented an increase of 18 percent over figures for 1986. Of the nation's elementary and secondary teachers, 2.7 million taught in public schools and 0.4 million taught in private schools.

Although teachers' salaries had lost purchasing power to inflation during the 1970s, the 1980s brought increases which recouped earlier losses. According to statistics released by the U.S. Department of Education, after making adjustments for inflation, teachers' salaries increased six percent between 1985-86 and 1995-96. During the 1995-96 school year, public school teacher salaries averaged $37,846. Virtually all of the increase occurred during the 1980s. Since 1990-91, the average salary for teachers actually fell after adjusting for inflation. In general, private school teacher salaries were much lower. One report revealed that the average salary for a teacher in a private school during 1994 was $21,968.

Faculty members, by far the largest and most visible component of the work force in colleges and universities, assume a number of diverse roles in higher education. Duties typically include teaching, appointment and promotion of colleagues, conferring tenure, curriculum planning, and student admission evaluations. Faculty usually operate within specific academic or administrative departments and are represented in faculties, senates, committees, and, in some cases, bargaining or arbitration units.

The average academic year salary for a full-ranking professor at a public university in 1996 was $59,800; at an independent college, the average salary was $71,200. This does not include fringe benefits, which can range between $10,000 and $12,000. Salaries are dependent upon expertise and standing. Professors in the sciences tend to earn more than those in the humanities.

AMERICA AND THE WORLD

Critics of the American educational system claimed that although per pupil spending in the United States was higher than in many other industrialized nations, American students were often outperformed by their peers around the world. Schools in the United States, however, were structured differently from many schools overseas and offered wider educational opportunities to a more diverse student population. In the United States, elementary schools had been structured to prepare students for secondary school, and secondary schools were structured to prepare students for higher education. In many other places, the progression of educational opportunity was less unified. Primary schools provided a basic education for the masses. Separate preparatory schools trained children of the higher social classes for a secondary or higher education. Once committed to either a primary school or a preparatory school, very few students could move to the other system.

Higher education in the United States continues to enjoy a great deal of prestige around the world. In 1990-91, the number of foreign students enrolled in U.S. colleges and universities reached an all-time high of 407,529. This was the first time in history that enrollment of foreign students exceeded 400,000. Foreign students continue to value an American business education above all other forms of learning available in this country. Until recently, engineering was the most popular subject amongst foreigners. This discipline, though, has fallen behind programs such as the Masters of Business Administration. Other popular areas of study for foreign students include mathematics, computer sciences, and physical life sciences.

The foreign student population in American universities and colleges is largely composed of students from China, Japan (the two leading senders of foreign students), Korea, and Taiwan. There has also been a relatively recent increase in the number of students coming from Europe, Latin America, Africa, and the Middle East. In the early 1990s, approximately 45 percent of graduate students in American colleges and universities were foreign students. Observers feel that this trend will continue and that foreign students will continue to represent a significant percentage of the population of colleges and universities.

ASSOCIATIONS AND SOCIETIES

ACADEMY FOR EDUCATIONAL DEVELOPMENT
1255 23rd St. NW
Washington, DC 20037
Phone: (202) 862-1900
Fax: (202) 862-1947

AMERICAN ASSOCIATION FOR ADULT AND CONTINUING EDUCATION
2101 Wilson Blvd., Ste. 925
Arlington, VA 22201
Phone: (703) 522-2234
Fax: (703) 522-2250

AMERICAN ASSOCIATION OF SCHOOL ADMINISTRATORS
1801 N Moore St.
Arlington, VA 22209
Phone: (703) 528-0700 or (703) 528-2146
Fax: (703) 841-1543

AMERICAN COUNCIL ON EDUCATION
1 Dupont Cir. NW, Ste. 800
Washington, DC 20036
Phone: (202) 939-9300
Fax: (202) 833-4760

AMERICAN VOCATIONAL ASSOCIATION
1410 King St.
Alexandria, VA 22314
Phone: (800) 892-2274 or (703) 683-3111
Fax: (703) 683-7424

AMERICAN VOCATIONAL EDUCATIONAL RESEARCH ASSOCIATION
c/o Curt Finch
Virginia Tech Division of Vocational and Technical Education
Blacksburg, VA 24601-0254
Phone: (703) 231-8175
Fax: (703) 231-8175

ASSOCIATION FOR CONTINUING HIGHER EDUCATION
Indiana University Purdue University at Indianapolis
620 Union Dr., Rm. 143 N
Indianapolis, IN 46202
Phone: (317) 274-2637
Fax: (317) 274-4016

CENTER ON EDUCATION AND TRAINING FOR EMPLOYMENT
Ohio State University
1900 Kenny Rd.
Columbus, OH 43210
Phone: (800) 848-4815 or (614) 292-4353
Fax: (614) 292-1260

COUNCIL FOR THE ADVANCEMENT AND SUPPORT OF EDUCATION
1 Dupont Cir. NW, Ste. 400
Washington, DC 20036
Phone: (202) 328-5900
Fax: (202) 387-4973

COUNCIL OF GRADUATE SCHOOLS
1 Dupont Cir. NW, Ste. 430
Washington, DC 20036
Phone: (202) 223-3791

NATIONAL ASSOCIATION OF INDEPENDENT SCHOOLS
1620 L St. NW
Washington, DC 20036-5605
Phone: (202) 973-9700
Fax: (202) 973-9790

NATIONAL EDUCATION ASSOCIATION
1201 16th St. NW
Washington, DC 20036
Phone: (202) 833-4000
Fax: (202) 822-7974

NATIONAL UNIVERSITY CONTINUING EDUCATION ASSOCIATION
1 Dupont Cir. NW, Ste. 615
Washington, DC 20036
Phone: (202) 659-3130
Fax: (202) 785-0374

NATIONAL SCHOOL BOARDS ASSOCIATION
1680 Duke St.
Alexandria, VA 22314
Phone: (703) 838-6722
Fax: (703) 683-7590

PERIODICALS AND NEWSLETTERS

AMERICAN SCHOOL AND UNIVERSITY: FACILITIES, PURCHASING, AND BUSINESS ADMINISTRATION
Intertec Publishing Group
9800 Metcalf Overland
Park, KS 66212-2215
Phone: (800) 543-7771 or (913) 341-1300
Fax: (913) 967-1901
Monthly. $65.00 per year.

AMERICAN SCHOOL BOARD JOURNAL
National School Boards Association
1680 Duke St.
Alexandria, VA 22314
Phone: (703) 838-6722
Fax: (703) 549-6719
Monthly. $48.00 per year. How to advice for community leaders who want to improve their schools.

CHANGE: THE MAGAZINE OF HIGHER LEARNING
Heldre Publications
1319 18th St. NW
Washington, DC 20036-1802
Phone: (202) 296-6267
Fax: (202) 296-5149
Bimonthly. Individuals, $31.00 per year; institutions, $60.00 per year.

COLLEGE AND UNIVERSITY
American Assn. of Collegiate Registrars and Admissions Officers
1 Dupont Cir. NW, Ste. 330
Washington, DC 20036
Phone: (202) 293-9161
Fax: (202) 872-8857
Quarterly. Free to members; non-members, $30.00 per year. Addresses issues in higher education; looks at new procedures, policies, technology; reviews new publications.

EDUCATIONAL ADMINISTRATION QUARTERLY
Sage Publications, Inc.
2455 Teller Rd.
Thousand Oaks, CA 91320
Phone: (805) 499-0721
Fax: (805) 499-0871
Quarterly. $130.00 per year. (Corwin Press.)

EDUCATIONAL MARKETER
SIMBA Information, Inc.
PO Box 4234
Stamford, CT 06907-0234
Phone: (800) 307-2529 or (203) 358-4344
Fax: (203) 358-5824
Weekly. $349.00 per year. Newsletter. Edited for suppliers of educational materials to schools and colleges at all levels. Covers print and electronic publishing, software, audiovisual items, and multimedia. Includes corporate news and educational statistics.

EDUCATIONAL RECORD: THE MAGAZINE OF HIGHER EDUCATION
American Council on Education
1 Dupont Cir. NW
Washington, DC 20036
Phone: (202) 939-9300
Quarterly. $25.00 per year.

INDEPENDENT SCHOOL
National Association of Independent Schools
1620 L St. NW
Washington, DC 20036-5605
Three times a year. $17.50 per year. An open forum for exchange of information about elementary and secondary education in general, and independent education in particular.

JOURNAL OF HIGHER EDUCATION
Ohio State University Press
1070 Carmack Rd.
Columbus, OH 43210
Phone: (614) 292-6930
Bimonthly. Individuals, $30.00 per year; institutions, $55.00 per year. Issues important to faculty administrators and program managers in higher education.

SCHOOL BUSINESS AFFAIRS
Association of School Business Officials
11401 N Shore Dr.
Reston, VA 22090-4232
Phone: (703) 478-0405
Fax: (703) 478-0205
Monthly. Free to members; non-members, $68.00 per year.

SCHOOL PLANNING AND MANAGEMENT
Peter Li Inc.
330 Progress Rd.
Dayton, OH 45449
Phone: (800) 321-7003 or (513) 847-5900
Fax: (513) 847-5910
Monthly. $30.00 per year. Formerly School and College.

DATABASES

ERIC
Educational Resources Information Center ERIC Processing and Reference Facility
1301 Piccard Dr., Ste. 300
Rockville, MD 20850
Phone: (301) 258-5500
Fax: (301) 948-3695
Broad range of educational literature, 1966 to present. Inquire as to online cost and availability.

WILSONLINE: EDUCATION INDEX
H. W. Wilson Co.
950 University Ave.
Bronx, NY 10452
Phone: (800) 367-6770 or (718) 558-8400
Fax: (718) 590-1617

Indexes a wide variety of periodicals related to schools, colleges, and education, 1984 to date. Weekly updates. Inquire as to online cost and availability.

STATISTICS SOURCES

DIGEST OF EDUCATION STATISTICS
Available from U.S. Government Printing Office
Washington, DC 20402
Phone: (202) 512-1800
Fax: (202) 512-2250
Annual. $35.00. Covers all areas of education from kindergarten through graduate school. Includes data from both government and private sources. Compiled by National Center for Education Statistics, U.S. Department of Education.

SCHOOL ENROLLMENT, SOCIAL AND ECONOMIC CHARACTERISTICS OF STUDENTS
Available from U.S. Government Printing Office
Washington, DC 20402
Phone: (202) 512-1800
Fax: (202) 512-2250
Annual. $11.00. Issued by the U.S. Bureau of the Census. Presents detailed tabulations of data on school enrollment of the civilian noninstitutional population three years old and over. Covers nursery school, kindergarten, elementary school, high school, college, and graduate school. Information is provided on age, race, sex, family income, marital status, employment, and other characteristics.

STATISTICAL ABSTRACT OF THE UNITED STATES
Available from U.S. Government Printing Office
Washington, DC 20402
Phone: (202) 512-1800
Fax: (202) 512-2250
Annual. $38.00. Issued by the U.S. Bureau of the Census.

GENERAL WORKS

EDUCATIONAL MEDIA AND TECHNOLOGY YEARBOOK
Libraries Unlimited, Inc.
PO Box 6633

Littleton, CO 80155-6633
Phone: (800) 237-6124 or (303) 770-1220
Fax: (303) 220-8843
Annual. $60.00.

NATIONAL SOCIETY FOR THE STUDY OF EDUCATION YEARBOOK
National Society for the Study of Education University of Chicago Press
5801 S. Ellis Ave., 4 Fl.
Chicago, IL 60637
Phone: (800) 621-2736 or (312) 702-7000
Fax: (312) 702-9756
Annual. Price varies. Two volumes per year.

FURTHER READING

Chandler, Susan. "Poisoned Ivy?" *Business Week,* 10 June 1996, 40.

The College Handbook, 1997. New York: College Entrance Examination Board, 1996.

Hawkins, Dana. "Clashes Grow as Homeschoolers Seek Access to Public Schools." *U.S. News & World Report,* 12 February 1996.

Larson, Erik. "Why Colleges Cost Too Much." *Time,* 17 March 1997, 46.

National Center for Educational Statistics. *Digest of Education Statistics: 1996.* Washington, DC: U.S. Department of Education, 1996.

National Education Association. *Estimate of School Statistics.* Washington, DC: National Education Association, 1996. Available at http://www.nea.org/info/society.html#estimate.

Peterson's Annual Survey Of Undergraduate Institutions. Peterson's. Available from http://www.peterson's.com/.

Peterson's Guide to Two-Year Colleges, 1997. Princeton, NJ: Peterson's, 1996. ◄━━

ELECTRIC SERVICE SECTOR

The electric service industry is less than 150 years old, but it runs America. In the span of a century, electricity replaced gas as a preferred means of lighting and succeeded steam engines in many growing industries. Electric service utilities are the nation's largest business, gauged according to capital investment and market value. Electricity is so widely available in modern American society that service disruptions are newsworthy. Throughout the twentieth century, its use has consistently increased. Although industry forecasters disagree about how rapidly demand will continue to grow, they generally agree that demand for electricity will continue to increase into the foreseeable future.

Electricity is measured in watts. A watt is a basic unit of electrical power equal to about 1/746th of one horsepower. A kilowatt is equal to 1,000 watts; a megawatt is equal to one-million watts; a gigawatt is equal to one billion watts. Electricity is sold in kilowatt-hours (kWh). One kWh equals the amount of electrical energy needed to keep ten 100-watt bulbs burning for one hour. Not all the electricity generated is available to be sold. Some is used by the power plant and some is dissipated during transmission and distribution. Furthermore, because electricity cannot be stored, it must be used or lost.

In 1995, U.S. electric utilities generated a total of 2,944 billion kilowatt-hours. More than half the electricity, 1,652 billion kWh, was derived from coal-powered generation. The second largest producer was nuclear generation. The nation's 109 nuclear plants provided 673 billion kWh. Other significant sources were hydroelectricity (293 billion kWh), natural gas (307 billion kWh), and petroleum (60 billion kWh). Geothermal, wind, solar and other nontraditional sources combined to provide approximately 6.4 billion kWh.

NATURAL GAS SECTOR

Traditionally, the natural gas industry has consisted of three primary activities: exploring for and producing natural gas; transporting the gas from production centers to market regions; and distributing gas to end users. Throughout the development of the industry, some companies have been involved in all three areas, while others have focused their efforts on only one or two.

The natural gas transmission segment of the industry includes gathering lines, storage facilities, and pipeline systems. Gathering lines transport gas from producing wells to facilities, where impurities are removed, and to processing plants that separate methane from other types of natural gas. Methane can then be injected into storage or sent into a transmission pipeline.

ELECTRIC AND GAS SERVICES

SIC 4910, 4920, 4930

The electric and gas services industry has enjoyed tremendous financial success by providing consumers with an essential commodity. Unfortunately, demand for electricity and natural gas has been so great in recent years that the government at both the federal and state levels has approved or given serious consideration to several initiatives that would produce a viable energy conservation agenda for the future. Offsetting fears that such legislation could jeopardize the economic well being of the industry is a trend toward greater deregulation, which would allow power companies to penetrate previously closed markets.

LARGEST CORPORATIONS IN THE ELECTRIC AND GAS UTILITIES INDUSTRY

Ranked by: Revenue in 1995, in millions of dollars.

1. Pacific Gas & Electric Co., with $9,622 million
2. Southern, $9,180
3. Edison International, $8,405
4. Unicom Corp., $6,910
5. Consolidated Edison Co. of New York Inc., $6,402
6. Entergy Corp., $6,274
7. Public Service Enterprise Group, $6,164
8. American Electric Power, $5,670
9. Texas Utilities Co., $5,639
10. FPL Group Inc., $5,592

Source: *Fortune,* Fortune 500 Largest U.S. Corporations (annual), April 29, 1996, p. F-48+.

Within the United States, gas flows primarily in a northeasterly direction from four major producing areas centered in Texas, Oklahoma, Louisiana, and the Gulf of Mexico, toward the eastern states and the Midwest. A smaller, but increasing, amount of gas is transported from Texas and Canada into California.

Most of the natural gas used in the United States is transported through interconnected webs of underground pipelines. Individual pipes vary in size from about five feet in diameter to less than an inch. The largest pipes collect gas in producing areas; the smallest pipes deliver gas to individual households.

By the early 1990s, more than 250,000 miles of pipeline transported domestic natural gas to 47 of the contiguous states. Vermont imported its gas from Canada. Major pipeline construction projects completed during 1992 were expected to increase the capacity and efficiency of the natural gas transmission network. Additional pipeline construction was expected to continue throughout the decade.

INDUSTRY OUTLOOK

CONSERVATION EFFORTS

Electric utilities implemented a number of methods to reduce sulfur emissions from burning coal. Some began using a process in which the coal was crushed and treated to reduce its sulfur content. Others switched from high-sulfur content coal to low-sulfur coal. Still other utilities invested in a process called "flue gas desulfuri-

zation" (commonly referred to as "scrubbing") to remove sulfur from the gases created by combustion.

Burning coal also produces nitrogen oxides and carbon dioxide. Nitrogen oxides are primarily found in dust, dirt, soot, smoke and droplets in the air. Carbon dioxide is cited as a contributing factor to global warming. Although there is no agreement in the scientific community on whether human activity is influencing global temperatures, utility experts acknowledged the issue was politically real and anticipated forthcoming regulations on carbon dioxide emissions.

Industry analysts offered differing projections about the U.S. electric power producers' ability to meet anticipated increases in demand for electricity. Some forecasters anticipated decreases in demand as conservation efforts increased. Many utilities invested in programs called "demand-side management" to encourage customers to use less electricity. Conservation efforts were often seen as less expensive alternates to the construction of additional generating plants. The Energy Information Association, an agency of the Department of Energy, projected demand increases between 1990 and 2010 in the range of 1.3 to 1.9 percent per year.

The North American Electric Reliability Council estimated that national reserve capacities, a measure of unused generating ability, would drop below 20 percent by the end of the century and that in some areas reserve capacity would fall more. Some industry analysts calculated that high demand increases would accompany a recovering economy. They predicted reserves would be insufficient to meet the nation's needs in the twenty-first century.

DEREGULATION

By the mid-1990s, the electric services industry had entered a period of radical change. Technological advances and an increasing demand for customer choice had prompted public utilities commissions in over 20 states, as well as the FERC, to propose deregulation of electricity generation, slowly exposing existing monopolies to competition, and giving consumers the opportunity to buy power from any broker or supplier—not just their local monopoly. The reaction of the industry— even established utilities whose monopolies could be affected—was generally positive. Kenneth Lay, chairman and CEO of Enron Corporation, one of the world's largest producers of electric power, believed that opportunities for well-positioned energy companies had never been better, arguing that companies able to capitalize on prevailing trends in the industry—privatization in developing countries, deregulation in developed countries, and the shift to cleaner technology and fuels—could look forward to a prosperous future.

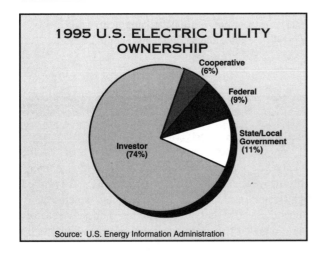

1995 U.S. ELECTRIC UTILITY OWNERSHIP

Cooperative (6%)

Federal (9%)

State/Local Government (11%)

Investor (74%)

Source: U.S. Energy Information Administration

One likely result of deregulation, according to most analysts, would be increasing consolidation and the emergence of a few dominant power companies. As in other deregulated industries, there was even the possibility that competition would ultimately push market consolidation to the point where most of the world's energy demands were met by a handful of mammoth utility and energy-services companies.

On April 24th 1996, the FERC officially opened the electric services business to competition with two separate rulings—Order No. 888 and Order No. 889. The first, Order No. 888, required that public utilities offer to sell electric power to other providers or utilities at the same rates they charged themselves. At the same time, the utility providing transmission service (the "wheeling utility") would be compensated for the use of its lines. Order No. 889 required electric utilities to establish electronic systems to share information about available transmission capacity.

The largest integrated natural gas company in the world and the largest non-regulated wholesaler of electricity in the United States, Enron was at the forefront of the drive towards deregulation. Also pushing deregulation was one of the nation's largest utilities, Illinois Power. In April 1996, the company became the first utility to allow its largest customers to pick the supplier of their choice. Other major utilities such as California's Pacific Gas and Electric and the Southeast's Southern Company were also moved quickly to implement radical restructuring and remove regulatory roadblocks to competition.

By 1997, competition in the industry had accelerated dramatically, spurred by the rise of a growing number of independent power producers, brokers, and energy marketers. In the third quarter of 1996 alone, these tough new competitors sold enough electricity to power 31 million homes—in an industry that had not even existed a few years earlier. Independent producers and

marketers came in all sizes, from small brokers such as California-based New Energy Ventures to Houston-based giant, Enron.

HIGH DEMAND FOR NATURAL GAS

Through a 1.3 million-mile network of underground pipes, natural gas was distributed to approximately 175 million American consumers in the mid-1990s. Gas service is provided in all 50 states by 1,200 gas distribution companies, pulling from about 288,000 natural gas wells. Domestic demand for natural gas hit its peak in 1972 when consumption was 22 trillion cubic feet. In succeeding years, questions about gas availability and climbing prices led to shrinking demand. Consumption fell to 16 trillion cubic feet in 1986 before beginning to grow again. By the early 1990s, natural gas was making a sustained comeback. Natural gas gained popularity as a favored fuel because of its environmental advantages and its availability as a domestic resource. In 1996, American users consumed more than 1,039 trillion cubic feet of natural gas. The largest portion went to residential users, who accounted for about 50 percent. U.S. industry used about 41 percent. A small amount, equal to approximately 0.0004 trillion cubic feet, was used to fuel natural gas vehicles.

Natural gas provided about 25 percent of domestic energy use in 1996. Nearly every segment using this gas, including the new housing market, existing residential homes, and the transportation sector, was expecting significant increases in the use of the fuel.

Under a plan proposed by the U.S. Department of Energy covering the years 1993 to 1998, the United States would increase reliance on natural gas in an effort to reduce dependence on foreign oil and foster American energy security, economic growth, and environmental quality. The Department of Energy plan called upon federal regulators to consider ways to improve the country's ability to utilize its domestic resources efficiently. One area under study was the impact of seasonal demand fluctuations on the efficient use of pipelines and storage facilities.

In addition to its environmental benefits, gas was also judged to be a cost-effective source for power generation. A study done by ICF Resources compared the costs of electricity produced by a natural gas combined cycle plant, a coal-fired plant, and a nuclear power plant. A gas-combined cycle generating plant produces electricity with a combination of gas turbines and steam turbines. The steam turbines operate by using waste heat from the combustion process required to spin the gas turbines.

The study, after considering construction, operating, maintenance, and fuel costs, found that although fuel costs for gas were higher than for coal or nuclear plants, construction, operation, and maintenance costs for gas combined cycle plants were lower. The report concluded that construction costs for a gas-combined cycle plant averaged $683 per kilowatt of capacity; a coal-fired plant averaged $1,820 per kilowatt of capacity; and a nuclear facility cost approximately $1,980 per kilowatt of capacity. The total cost of the electricity generated was estimated to be 6.3 cents per kilowatt-hour in a gas combined cycle plant, 9.7 for a coal-fired plant, and 9.1 for a nuclear plant.

WORK FORCE·

The slack economy of the early 1990s affected the availability of jobs within the electric services industry. Utilities saw their sales flatten and costs increase. As profits declined many companies continued or instituted reductions in their work forces. For example, the Southern Company had 2,000 fewer employees at the end of 1991 than it did in 1985. Georgia Power, a subsidiary of the Southern Company, announced plans to eliminate 900 positions by 1995. And, Philadelphia Electric announced a 20 percent planned work force reduction in its nuclear power program. Between 1990 and 1995, the total number of employees in the industry fell 11 percent, from 454,400 in 1990 to 404,000 in 1995. Hourly wages for production workers in the industry increased from $15.80 in 1990 to $18.54 in 1995.

Despite reductions in numbers of workers, the electric services industry continues to be a major employer, providing jobs for more than 400,000 people in the United States. The utility industry employs people in four major areas: generation, transmission, distribution, and administration. Because the industry relied on emerging technology, it needed engineers and scientists as well as clerks and technicians.

RESEARCH AND TECHNOLOGY

ELECTRIC SERVICE SECTOR

As the electric service industry prepared for the twenty-first century, researchers were studying many potential technological innovations. Advanced light-water reactors (ALR) were being developed by General Electric and Westinghouse. The new reactors were intended to reduce construction time and costs by using standardized designs. Another improvement over older, conventional reactors was the use of passive safety systems, which depended on natural physical laws (such as gravity) rather than human intervention to respond to problems.

In response to the challenges of the Clean Air Act Amendments of 1990, methods to burn coal with fewer emissions are being explored. One promising innovation was the development of an integrated gasification combined-cycle (IGCC) power plant. The IGCC generator was designed to use partially oxidized coal as a fuel, a process that virtually eliminated air pollutants. The first commercial IGCC unit began operating at Tampa Electric Company (Florida) in September 1996.

Environmental concerns also encouraged interest in renewable energy sources. By 1995, the only renewable energy source being used for substantial amounts of electricity was water, used in hydroelectric generation. In the mid-1990s, the combined output from all other renewable sources, such as hydroelectric, wind, geothermal, and biofuels (which included wood, waste, and alcohol fuels) totaled only about .08 percent of the electricity generated in the United States.

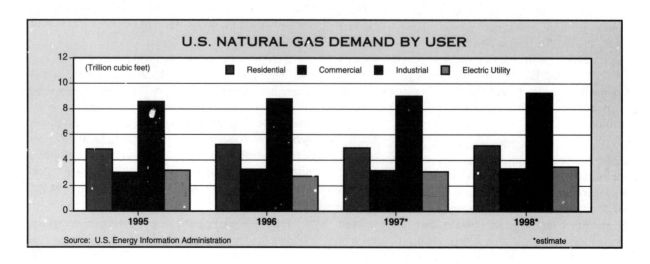

U.S. NATURAL GAS DEMAND BY USER

(Trillion cubic feet) Residential Commercial Industrial Electric Utility

1995   1996   1997*   1998*

Source: U.S. Energy Information Administration   *estimate

One hopeful experiment with solar generation was conducted in a California desert. Approximately 900 mirrors were set to focus light from the sun and generate 10 megawatts of power. If the project met expectations, Southern California Edison planned to consider building 200 megawatt plants using the technology. In another solar project, Southern California Edison and Texas Instruments were testing a new type of solar cell using tiny silicon balls. The material, called "Spheral Solar" held promise for application in remote sunny areas, especially in Third World nations.

Developments in wind generation technology also looked encouraging. During the early 1980s wind generators produced power at an average cost of 30 cents per kilowatt-hour. By the early 1990s costs had dropped to 11 cents per kWh. Researchers hoped that improved technology would produce wind-generated power at a cost of six cents per kWh by 2010. Site selection for wind generation was critical because even small differences in average wind speed had substantial effects on the amount of electricity generated.

Another source of renewable energy under exploration was geothermal power. Most of the geothermal production in the United States was from a single plant operated by the Pacific Gas and Electric Company in California. Investigators were researching methods to extract heat from hot dry rock, which is found everywhere on earth at sufficient depths. One study underway in New Mexico during 1992 offered promising results. Scientists drilled a hole 12,000 feet deep and pumped water into it. They were able to extract 100 gallons of water per minute at temperatures high enough to generate electricity.

Not all the research underway during the early 1990s involved power generation. Many utilities were investigating robot technology for use in operations, maintenance, transmission, and distribution. Interest in robotics intensified when utilities realized that robots could be used in potentially hazardous situations. The use of robots helped reduce human exposure to radiation following the Three Mile Island accident. Robots could also work on lines carrying live current or inside vessels with toxic substances. A robot able to perform maintenance tasks on live wires was commercially introduced in 1992. Another robot, able to inspect high-voltage lines and towers, was under development. A pipe-crawling robot, developed by Public Service Electric & Gas's Energy Technology Development Center, was able to inspect pipes where human access was impossible and perform some types of repairs.

In 1996, the world's first utility-scale molten carbonate fuel cell (MCFC) power plant began operation in Santa Clara, California. Generating two megawatt of power from natural gas without combustion and with very low emissions, the plant was part of a demonstration program closely monitored by more than 30 utilities who had signed tentative commitments to purchase commercial MCFC units.

NATURAL GAS SERVICE SECTOR

Research efforts undertaken by transmission and distribution companies focused primarily in two areas: expanding natural gas markets and improving natural gas conveyance. One of the most popular technologies under investigation was the evolution of natural gas fueled vehicles (NGVs). In 1996, about 40,000 NGVs were in operation in the United States. Although the amount used for NGVs accounted for only a small fraction of U.S. natural gas consumption, it represented a 26 percent increase over 1990. Four states—Arizona, Indiana, Ohio, and Washington—made up approximately 60 percent of the nation's demand for natural gas for vehicle use. Moreover, advanced NGVs have been proven to reduce carbon monoxide and nitrogen oxide emissions by as much as 90 percent and 85 percent, respectively.

Interest in NGV technology was expanding, especially in areas affected by urban pollution, because NGVs burn much cleaner than traditional gasoline-fueled vehicles. By the early 1990s, all three major American automobile manufacturers were building vehicles capable of running on natural gas. In 1992, General Motors Corporation manufactured more than 2,300 GMC Sierra pickup trucks that ran exclusively on natural gas. Gas utilities and transmission companies in many parts of the country were investigating methods of financing, constructing, and operating natural gas fueling stations for both public and private fleet use.

Another emerging technology involved gas-powered cooling for refrigeration and air conditioning. Although large air conditioning systems had already been developed for use in industrial and commercial applications, air conditioning units small enough for private home use were commercially available by the mid-1990s. In addition to expanding markets for natural gas, gas cooling technologies were expected to help reduce summer peaks in demand for electricity.

In the arena of natural gas conveyance, one area under investigation was pipeline maintenance. According to estimates of the U.S. Department of Transportation, approximately 800,000 to 900,000 leaks in gas mains and service lines occur every year. In addition to presenting a potential disaster, lost gas represents lost earnings. In order to make gas line repairs, utilities must find the precise location of defective pipe segments, remove soil or pavement at the site, repair or replace the pipe, and then restore the site.

A pipe repair technique being jointly developed by Consolidated Natural Gas Company, East Ohio Gas Company, and PLS International (a company specializing in robotics technology) was called the PLS 3000. The PLS 3000 system used a sealed probe to examine low-pressure gas lines while they were still in use. The probe was expected to help identify specific problems such as water infiltration, pipeline distortions, cracks, or other problems in the pipes and pinpoint their locations. Although early models proved expensive, initial users judged the PLS 3000 cost effective in urban areas where excavation costs were substantial.

AMERICA AND THE WORLD

In the mid-1990s, the United States led the world in net generation of electricity, with 3,459 billion kWh produced. Japan was second, with 904 billion kWh. Other leaders include China (859 billion kWh), Russia (833 billion kWh), Canada (537 billion kWh), Germany (495 billion kWh), and France (451 billion kWh).

Fossil-fuel fired generation accounted for 63 percent of the worldwide production of electricity in 1990. Hydroelectric power produced 24 percent and nuclear sources provided 12 percent. Analysts expected coal-fired generation to continue to provide a significant portion of the world's electricity. The International Energy Agency projected that worldwide power generation would remain the predominant market for hard coal. Such predictions raised concern about the environmental quality in developing nations. To help address this concern, the Energy Policy Act of 1992 included the authorization of a program through which clean coal technology could be exported to other nations.

Nuclear power was also a method through which some countries were addressing pollution concerns. In 1995, Lithuania produced a greater percentage of its domestic electricity (85 percent) through nuclear generation than any other nation. The United States produced the world's largest amount of electricity from nuclear power (673 billion kWh), yet nuclear generation accounted for only about 22 percent of its total production. Behind the United States, other top nuclear countries included France (358 billion kWh), Japan (286 billion kWh), and Germany (154 billion kWh).

Imports and exports both played an important role in U.S. natural gas markets. During the early years of the 1990s imports from Canada and exports to Mexico were at their highest levels in history. The United States also imported liquefied natural gas from Algeria. The liquified natural gas, transported by special tanker ships and kept in liquid form through refrigeration and pressure, entered U.S. pipeline systems after being regasified at special facilities in Louisiana. Canadian gas, however, accounted for the bulk of U.S. imports. In the early 1990s, imports from Canada equaled 96 percent of total natural gas imports and were up 18 percent over the previous year. Canadian supplies had the greatest impact in the northeastern and Californian markets.

In terms of natural gas production, the United States ranked second in the world, averaging about 17 trillion cubic feet per year. The world's top producer, the former Soviet Union, produced about 26 trillion cubic feet per year. Canada ranked third, producing about three and a half trillion cubic feet annually. The world's fourth largest producer, The Netherlands, supplied about three trillion cubic feet per year. The Netherlands obtained gas from both onshore and offshore facilities, exporting it through pipelines to Germany, Belgium, France, and Italy.

ASSOCIATIONS AND SOCIETIES

AMERICAN GAS ASSOCIATION
1515 Wilson Blvd.
Arlington, VA 22209
Phone: (703) 841-8400
Fax: (703) 841-8406

AMERICAN PUBLIC GAS ASSOCIATION
11094-D Lee Hwy., Ste. 102
Fairfax, VA 22030
Phone: (703) 352-3890
Fax: (703) 352-1271

AMERICAN PUBLIC POWER ASSOCIATION
2301 M St. NW
Washington, DC 20037
Phone: (202) 467-2900
Fax: (202) 467-2910

ASSOCIATION OF EDISON ILLUMINATING COMPANIES
600 N. 18th St.
Birmingham, AL 35291-0992
Phone: (205) 250-2530
Fax: (205) 250-2540

EDISON ELECTRIC INSTITUTE
701 Pennsylvania Ave. NW
Washington, DC 20004-2696
Phone: (202) 508-5000
Fax: (202) 508-5786

INSTITUTE OF GAS TECHNOLOGY
1700 S. Mount Prospect Rd.
Des Plaines, IL 60018-1804

Phone: (708) 768-0500
Fax: (708) 768-0516

INTERSTATE NATURAL GAS ASSOCIATION OF AMERICA
555 13th St. NW, Ste. 300W
Washington, DC 20004
Phone: (202) 626-3200
Fax: (202) 626-3250

NATIONAL PROPANE GAS ASSOCIATION
1600 Eisenhower Ln., Ste. 100
Lisle, IL 60532
Phone: (708) 515-0600
Fax: (708) 515-8774

PERIODICALS AND NEWSLETTERS

AMERICAN GAS
1515 Wilson Blvd.
Arlington, VA 22209
Phone: (703) 841-8400
Fax: (703) 841-8406
11 times a year. $39.00 per year. Formerly American Gas Association Monthly.

AMERICAN PUBLIC GAS ASSOCIATION NEWSLETTER
American Public Gas Association
11094-D Lee Hwy., Ste. 102
Fairfax, VA 22030
Phone: (703) 352-3890
Fax: (703) 352-1271
Biweekly. Membership.

ELECTRIC UTILITY WEEK: THE ELECTRIC UTILITY INDUSTRY NEWSLETTER
McGraw-Hill, Inc.
1221 Avenue of the Americas
New York, NY 10020
Phone: (800) 722-4726 or (212) 512-2000
Fax: (212) 512-2821
Weekly. $1,175.00 per year. Newsletter.

ELECTRICAL WORLD
McGraw-Hill, Inc.
1221 Avenue of the Americas
New York, NY 10020
Phone: (800) 722-4726 or (212) 512-3288
Fax: (212) 512-2821
Monthly. $55.00 per year.

EPRI JOURNAL
Electric Power Research Institute
PO Box 10412
Palo Alto, CA 94303-0813
Phone: (415) 855-2730
Eight times a year. Controlled circulation.

GAS INDUSTRIES MAGAZINE
Gas Industries and Appliance News, Inc.
PO Box 558
Park Ridge, IL 60068
Phone: (312) 693-3682
Fax: (312) 696-3445
Monthly. $20.00 per year.

OIL AND GAS JOURNAL
PennWell Publishing Co.
PO Box 1260
Tulsa, OK 74102
Phone: (918) 835-3161
Fax: (918) 831-9497
Weekly. Qualified personnel, $52.00 per year; others, $95.00 per year.

OIL AND GAS TAX QUARTERLY
Matthew Bender & Co., Inc.
11 Penn Plz.
New York, NY 10001-2006
Phone: (800) 223-1940 or (212) 967-7707
Quarterly. $150.00 per year.

PUBLIC POWER
American Public Power Association
2301 M St. NW
Washington, DC 20037-1484
Phone: (202) 467-2948
Fax: (202) 467-2910
Bimonthly. $35.00 per year.

PUBLIC POWER WEEKLY NEWSLETTER
American Public Power Association
2301 M St. NW
Washington, DC 20037-1484
Phone: (202) 467-2947
Fax: (202) 467-2910
Weekly. $250.00 per year. Newsletter.

UTILITY AUTOMATION
PennWell Publishing Co.
1241 S. Sheridan Rd.
Tulsa, OK 74112
Phone: (800) 784-0745 or (918) 831-9590
Fax: (918) 831-9599
Bimonthly. $35.00 per year. Covers new information technologies for electric utilities, including automated meter reading, distribution management systems, and customer information systems.

DATABASES

APIBIZ **(PETROLEUM-ENERGY NEWS)**
American Petroleum Institute
Central Abstracting and Information Services
275 7th Ave.
New York, NY 10001
Phone: (212) 366-4040
Fax: (212) 366-4298
Indexing of newsletters and business journals in the petroleum and energy areas, 1975 to present. Inquire as to online cost and availability.

CITIBASE (CITICORP ECONOMIC DATABASE)

FAME Software Corp.
77 Water St., 9 Fl.
New York, NY 10005
Phone: (212) 898-7800
Fax: (212) 742-8956

Presents over 6,000 statistical series relating to business, industry, finance, and economics. Includes series from Survey of Current Business and many other sources. Time period is 1947 to date, with daily updates. Inquire as to online cost and availability.

ELECTRIC IDEAS CLEARINGHOUSE BULLETIN BOARD SYSTEM

Washington State Energy Office
Provides up-to-date information for energy professionals and students; includes a technical assistance hotline, an electronic bulletin board, job listings, and online publications, among other things. Established: 1990. Updating frequency: Weekly. Fees: Free. URL: http://www.eicbbs.wseo.wa.gov/ Modem: (800)762-3319 (Pacific); (206)956-2212 (other areas).

ENERGY SCIENCE AND TECHNOLOGY

U.S. Dept. of Energy
Office of Scientific and Technical Information
PO Box 62
Oak Ridge, TN 37831
Phone: (615) 576-9362
Fax: (615) 576-2865

Contains abstracts and citations to literature in all fields of energy from 1974 to date, with biweekly updates. Formerly DOE Energy Data Base. Inquire as to online cost and availability.

F & S INDEX

Information Access Co.
362 Lakeside Dr.
Foster City, CA 94404
Phone: (800) 321-6388 or (415-358-4643)
Fax: (415) 358-4759

Contains about four million citations to worldwide business, financial, and industrial or consumer product literature appearing from 1972 to date. Weekly updates. Inquire as to online cost and availability.

STATISTICS SOURCES

ANNUAL ENERGY REVIEW

Available from U.S. Government Printing Office
Washington, DC 20402
Phone: (202) 512-1800
Fax: (202) 512-2250

Annual. Issued by the Energy Information Administration, Office of Energy Markets and End Use, U.S. Department of Energy. Presents long-term historical as well as recent data on production, consumption, stocks, imports, exports, and prices of the principal energy commodities in the U.S.

EEI STATISTICAL RELEASES: ELECTRIC OUTPUT

Edison Electric Institute
701 Pennsylvania Ave. NW
Washington, DC 20004-2696
Phone: (202) 508-5000
Fax: (202) 508-5759
Weekly. $65.00.

ELECTRIC POWER MONTHLY

Available from U.S. Government Printing Office
Washington, DC 20402
Phone: (202) 512-1800
Fax: (202) 512-2250

Monthly. $87.00 per year. Issued by the Office of Coal and Electric Power Statistics, Energy Information Administration, U.S. Department of Energy. Contains statistical data relating to electric utility operation, capability, fuel use, and prices.

FINANCIAL STATISTICS OF MAJOR PUBLICLY OWNED ELECTRIC UTILITIES IN THE U.S.

U.S. Energy Information Administration
U.S. Department of Energy
Available from U.S. Government Printing Office
Washington, DC 20402
Phone: (202) 512-1800
Fax: (202) 512-2250
Annual. $35.00.

GAS DATA BOOK

American Gas Association
1515 Wilson Blvd.
Arlington, VA 22209
Phone: (703) 841-8400
Fax: (703) 841-8406
Annual.

GAS FACTS: A STATISTICAL RECORD OF THE GAS UTILITY INDUSTRY

American Gas Association
1515 Wilson Blvd.
Arlington, VA 22209
Phone: (703) 841-8490
Fax: (703) 841-8406
Annual. Members, $28.00; non-members, $55.00.

INVENTORY OF POWER PLANTS IN THE UNITED STATES

Energy Information Administration
U.S. Department of Energy
Available from U.S. Government Printing Office
Washington, DC 20402
Phone: (202) 512-1800
Fax: (202) 512-2250
Annual. $25.00.

POCKETBOOK OF ELECTRIC UTILITY INDUSTRY STATISTICS

Edison Electric Institute
701 Pennsylvania Ave. NW
Washington, DC 20004
Phone: (202) 508-5000
Fax: (202) 508-5759
Annual.

STATISTICAL YEAR BOOK OF THE ELECTRIC UTILITY INDUSTRY

Edison Electric Institute
701 Pennsylvania Ave. NW
Washington, DC 20004
Phone: (202) 508-5000
Fax: (202) 508-5759
Annual. $45.00.

GENERAL WORKS

ANNUAL INSTITUTE ON OIL AND GAS LAW AND TAXATION

Matthew Bender & Co., Inc.
11 Penn Plz.
New York, NY 10001-2006
Phone: (800) 223-1940 or (212) 967-7707
Annual. $90.00. Answers to current legal and tax problems, including cases and regulations implementing tax reduction and tax form.

PUBLIC POWER DIRECTORY

American Public Power Association
2301 M St. NW
Washington, DC 20037-1484
Phone: (202) 467-2900
Fax: (202) 467-2910
Annual. $90.00. List of more than 2,000 local publicly owned electric utilities in the United States and its possessions.

QUESTIONS AND ANSWERS ABOUT THE ELECTRIC UTILITY INDUSTRY

Edison Electric Institute
701 Pennsylvania Ave. NW
Washington, DC 20004
Phone: (202) 508-5000
Fax: (202) 508-5759
Annual.

YEAR-END SUMMARY OF THE ELECTRIC POWER SITUATION IN THE UNITED STATES

Edison Electric Institute
701 Pennsylvania Ave. NW
Washington, DC 20004

Phone: (202) 508-5000
Fax: (202) 508-5759
Annual. $7.00.

WALTER SKINNER'S OIL AND GAS INTERNATIONAL YEAR BOOK

Financial Times of London
14 E. 60th St.
New York, NY 10022
Phone: (212) 752-4500
Price on application.

FURTHER READING

''Competition in the Electric Power Industry.'' *The Electric Power Industry Today.* Edison Electric Institute, February 1997.

''Gas Industry Online.'' American Gas Association, 1997. Available from http://www.aga.com.

''Electric Utilities.'' *Standard and Poor's Industry Surveys.* New York: MacGraw Hill, September, 1997.

''Energy Secretary O'Leary to Dedicate Tampa Electric's Polk Power Plant.'' TECO Energy, 1997. Available from http://www.teco.net/teco/TENRDdctPlk.html?Polk#first_hit.

''Generation.'' Electric Power Research Institute, 1997.

Mack, Toni. ''Electric Utilities.'' *Forbes,* January 13, 1997.

''Natural Gas Week.'' National Gas Supply Association, 1997. Available from http://www.gri.org. ◄━━

ELECTRIC LIGHTING AND WIRING EQUIPMENT

SIC 3640

Going into the mid-1990s, U.S. bulb producers were battling a sluggish domestic economy. Sales were down, and many market segments had matured. Some manufacturers, however, were boosting profits with high-tech lamps and bulbs that could burn longer, brighter, and more efficiently. The implementation of laws prohibiting the continued manufacture of more than 45 electric lamps that didn't meet newly established energy standards will create additional changes in the market in the years to come.

The first practical light bulbs were invented in 1878. A bulb industry emerged early in the twentieth century as an infrastructure capable of carrying electricity to the general population evolved. By the early 1980s, about 70 U.S. firms were selling over $2 billion worth of bulbs and tubes each year. Erratic market growth during the 1980s pushed industry sales to approximately $2.8 billion per year by 1992. By 1995, sales had increased to $2.9 billion, with 26,200 individuals employed in the industry. Industry sales were estimated to reach $3.6 billion for 1997.

In the mid-1990s, the current-carrying wiring devices industry was divided into six major categories: switches, wire connectors, convenience and power outlets, lampholders, metal contacts, and other devices such as plug caps and connector bodies. Miscellaneous products encompass items such as trolley line materials, lightning protectors, and fluorescent starters. The value of all industry shipments in 1995 was about $4.8 billion.

Most noncurrent-carrying wiring products are consumed by the nonresidential construction sector. A leading 51 percent of industry output in the mid-1990s was attributed to electrical conduit and fittings, which includes conduit, connectors, junction boxes, and related products. Pole and transmission line hardware, which was purchased by cable television and utility companies, comprised about 17 percent of production. The remainder of the market was highly fragmented. Store and restaurant construction, for example, accounted for about 1 percent of sales, as did construction related to mobile homes. Other industry outputs included highway and street construction, sewer system development, industrial controls, and lawn and garden equipment. The total value of shipments in 1995 reached $4 billion, and the total value of exported shipments was about $1 billion.

About 50 percent of the residential electric lighting fixtures industry revenues in the mid-1990s were derived from stationary, or mounted, fixtures, such as ceiling and wall lamps. Portable lamps, like movable desk and floor lamps, accounted for about 36 percent of shipments. The remainder of revenues were garnered from the sale of lamp shades and various types of parts and accessories. The total value of shipments in 1995 was $2 billion, and about 4 percent of production was exported.

Healthy commercial development throughout most of the 1980s resulted in average annual revenue growth of nearly 8 percent for the commercial fixture industry. By 1990, sales topped $3 billion per year. Despite a severe downturn in commercial development in 1989 and the early 1990s, sales dipped only 1 percent in 1991

U.S. Lamp Shipments

Shipments are shown for 1992 and estimated for 1997 in millions of dollars.

	1992	1997	Share
Fluorescents	$ 965	$ 1,380	37.8%
Large incandescents	1,047	1,275	34.9
Miniature incandescents . .	483	530	14.5
HID and other electrical discharge	306	435	11.9
Photographic incandescents	52	35	1.0

Source: *Purchasing*, March 7, 1996, p. 70, from Freedonia Group.

before increasing an encouraging 4 percent in 1992. Healthy institutional demand and sales of fixtures for new energy-saving bulbs continued to buoy earnings in 1994-95, as industry revenues climbed to around $3.5 billion, up more than 16 percent from 1992. Industry projections show revenues surpassing $4 billion by 1998. About 80 percent of industry output in the mid-1990s was used for commercial and institutional purposes, and 15 percent was utilized in industrial applications. Approximately 4 percent of production was exported. The largest single market for commercial lighting devices was office buildings, which purchased about 9 percent of all fixtures produced by both residential and commercial fixture manufacturers. Hospitals and parking garages both consumed about 1 percent of production. The remainder of the market was highly fragmented.

Companies that manufacture vehicular lighting equipment generally do so for a wide range of vehicles, including automobiles, airplanes, trains, boats, bicycles, motorcycles, and amusement rides. Also, companies frequently work together on the same lighting project, often on a contractor-subcontractor basis. According to the *1995 Annual Survey of Manufactures* the vehicular lighting equipment industry shipped goods to the value of approximately $3.0 billion and employed approximately 17,400 people. This was an increase from the previous year's figure of $2.7 billion and 15,600 employees.

The two major groupings in the miscellaneous lighting equipment industry are outdoor lighting equipment, which constituted 57 percent of industry output in the mid-1990s, and electric and nonelectric equipment not elsewhere classified, which represented 37 percent of industry production. The majority of products in this category are hand portable lighting equipment, such as flashlights and lanterns. The remainder of the market is highly fragmented among various electric and nonelectric devices. Personal consumption expenditures repre-

sent about 16 percent of consumption, and 4 percent of the industry's output is exported. Institutional and commercial sectors account for the majority of sales.

INDUSTRY OUTLOOK

Going into the mid-1990s, U.S. electric lamp manufacturers were hoping to benefit from slowly strengthening commercial and residential construction industries. Nevertheless, demand from builders was expected to remain suppressed indefinitely. Instead, bulb makers were focusing on increasing profits through sales of advanced lamps that could reduce energy consumption, improve lighting, boost longevity, and minimize adverse environmental impacts. Compact fluorescent and halogen bulbs, particularly, offered solid growth potential. Sources estimate that for 1997, sales of fluorescent lamps will account for 37.8 percent of total industry sales, followed by large incandescents (34.9 percent), miniature incandescents (14.5 percent), electrical discharges (11.9 percent), and photo incandescents (1 percent).

The National Energy Security Act of 1992 effectively mandated the use of such advanced bulbs. The act sought to prevent the sale of inefficient fluorescent light bulbs beginning in 1994, and other energy-inefficient bulbs by 1995. It banned most standard four- and eight-foot fluorescent light tubes, some incandescent reflector lamps, and many types of flood lamps. Likewise, the Environmental Protection Agency's (EPA) "Green Lights" voluntary conservation program was designed to encourage corporations to install new lighting. Full national participation, according to the EPA, could reduce total U.S. electric consumption by 10 percent and slash lighting electricity requirements by 50 percent, resulting in an annual $18.6 billion savings. By January 1, 1996, consumers were having to pay approximately 4 to 6 percent more for their bulbs due to the implementation of the Act.

In the mid-1990s, wiring device manufacturers benefitted from steady residential construction markets, and an upsurge in home renovations. In addition, new government building regulations mandated the use of certain wiring products. The National Electrical Code (NEC) that was implemented in 1993, for example, required the installation of special ground-fault circuit interrupters (GFCIs) that detect ground faults and shut off power to protected circuits. The revised 1996 NEC code augmented GFCI requirements. The sale of these and other devices are expected to bolster industry growth, as total shipments are projected to reach nearly $6 billion by the end of the decade.

To compensate for slow domestic sales, some industry participants capitalized on expanding export demand, which rose as a result of a weak U.S. dollar. Exports gained 14 percent in 1991, reaching a record $1.4 billion, or nearly 30 percent of total shipments, but growth of exports was flat through 1995. In combination with slow export growth, imports increased significantly in the mid-1990s, adding to the deficit trend that began in the early 1990s. Major importers into the United States were Japan, Mexico, Taiwan, and Germany. Imports from Mexico were expected to continue growing in the mid-1990s, particularly in light of the North American Free Trade Agreement (NAFTA), which was initiated in 1994.

Many U.S. residential lighting fixture producers rejuvenated lagging margins with sales of the new energy-saving lighting equipment, while others sought profit growth through mergers and acquisitions. The number of companies dwindled from about 650 in the early 1980s to 498 in 1994, as companies combined forces to survive withering demand. Despite consolidation, the residential lighting fixture industry remained fragmented in the mid-1990s. The majority of the top 50 competitors had sales of less than $25 million in the mid-1990s and employed fewer than 400 workers.

ORGANIZATION AND STRUCTURE

The light bulb and electric lamp industry provides a practical means of converting electric energy into usable light. In the mid-1990s about 25 percent of all the electricity sold in the United States was used for lighting. Besides illuminating businesses, schools, and homes, light bulbs are used in a plethora of applications and products—including automobiles, flashlights, sports fields, medical equipment, airport runways, and emergency exit signs. The industry produces thousands of different bulbs, tubes, strobes, and flashes. But the three primary products sold by U.S. electric lamp manufacturers are incandescent, fluorescent, and electric-discharge lights and bulbs.

Approximately 35 percent of light bulb industry revenues in the mid-1990s were derived from sales to individual consumers. State and local governments, including schools, hotels, and hospitals account for small percentages of revenues. The remainder of the market was highly fragmented. Motor vehicle manufacturers and electric utilities consume small portions of total production units.

A severe depression in commercial development and stagnant institutional construction markets contributed to industry decline in the early 1990s. Sales slipped by about 2.5 percent in 1990 and continued to fade approximately 1.5 percent per year through 1993. Although sales reached nearly $4 billion in 1994, growth in 1995 was nearly flat, with revenues increasing only 2 percent. From the mid-1990s through the end of the decade, analysts expected only a slight reprieve from these lackluster markets, as sales were forecast to grow slowly at 2 to 3 percent through 1998.

SIC 3648 - Lighting Equipment, nec
General Statistics

Year	Com-panies	Establishments		Employment			Compensation		Production ($ million)			
		Total	with 20 or more employees	Total (000)	Production Workers (000)	Hours (Mil)	Payroll ($ mil)	Wages ($/hr)	Cost of Materials	Value Added by Manufacture	Value of Shipments	Capital Invest.
1982	222	233	113	12.2	8.5	16.1	207.9	7.53	454.4	566.4	1,028.0	28.0
1983		230	113	11.8	8.4	15.8	210.5	7.58	458.6	539.0	992.9	17.1
1984		227	113	13.9	9.8	18.9	251.3	7.61	614.1	693.7	1,303.5	33.9
1985		224	113	13.6	9.4	18.6	272.7	8.24	670.3	843.9	1,515.5	43.4
1986		226	111	13.2	9.1	17.5	270.6	8.58	681.2	922.9	1,607.3	32.5
1987	246	262	128	14.4	9.9	19.3	304.4	8.63	801.5	884.7	1,673.9	31.3
1988		251	127	15.1	10.1	19.9	344.8	9.39	917.2	952.3	1,863.1	32.1
1989		251	130	14.7	9.9	19.5	337.4	9.33	962.2	933.6	1,889.3	48.5
1990		248	130	16.4	9.7	19.2	347.6	9.26	958.2	883.6	1,849.5	46.8
1991		249	131	14.1	9.3	18.6	350.4	9.89	938.2	897.0	1,838.5	33.5
1992	272	293	132	14.5	9.3	18.7	394.3	10.21	1,018.0	1,073.8	2,083.5	50.9
1993		289	123	15.5	10.1	20.1	434.1	10.26	1,170.3	1,118.2	2,290.1	49.2
1994		283P	134P	14.9	9.5	17.9	425.4	11.80	1,235.8	1,470.3	2,672.7	52.9
1995		288P	136P	15.9P	10.0P	19.8P	450.7P	11.27P	1,180.1P	1,404.0P	2,552.3P	53.6P
1996		294P	138P	16.2P	10.1P	20.0P	469.5P	11.58P	1,233.8P	1,467.9P	2,668.4P	55.8P
1997		299P	140P	16.4P	10.1P	20.2P	488.2P	11.89P	1,287.5P	1,531.9P	2,784.6P	58.0P
1998		304P	142P	16.7P	10.2P	20.4P	507.0P	12.20P	1,341.3P	1,595.8P	2,900.8P	60.1P

Sources: 1982, 1987, 1992 Economic Census; Annual Survey of Manufactures, 83-86, 88-91, 93-94. Establishment counts for non-Census years are from County Business Patterns; establishment values for 83-84 are extrapolations. 'P's show projections by the editors. Industries reclassified in 87 will not have data for prior years.

WORK FORCE

Although sales and production volume increased for most industry participants during the 1980s, aggregate employment actually dropped about 12 percent to less than 20,000 in the early 1990s. Manufacturing productivity gains and management restructuring were the primary culprits of recessed employment figures. For 1995, the work force actually rose to 26,000—an increase of 23 percent over the early 1990s. This increase may be due in part to the implementation of the National Energy Policy Act of 1992 (EPACT), which called for compliance by 1995. Manufacturers had to cease production of certain energy-inefficient lamps and replace them with new products that met the new standards. Additionally, the increase in housing construction in the mid-1990s called for greater lamp production.

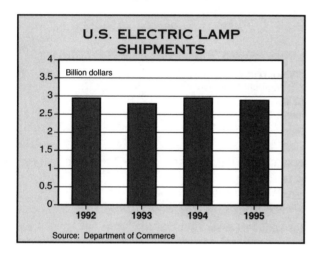

Source: Department of Commerce

Jobs for production workers, which accounted for a leading 53 percent of this industry's work force in 1995, will likely decline by 2005, according to the Bureau of Labor Statistics. Productivity gains, management restructuring, and the movement of some manufacturing activities to foreign countries were the primary reasons for work force reductions. Although many labor positions will be eliminated between 1996 and 2005, according to the Bureau of Labor Statistics, some jobs, such as those for sales and marketing professionals, are likely to increase.

RESEARCH AND TECHNOLOGY

As light bulb producers labored to develop new, high-tech lamps that could increase their market share and boost profit margins, a steady stream of technological advancements greeted consumers in the mid-1990s. Most bulbs offered superior lighting characteristics,

SIC 3641
Occupations Employed by SIC 364 - Electric Lighting and Wiring Equipment

Occupation	% of Total 1994	Change to 2005
Assemblers, fabricators, & hand workers nec	16.0	-7.4
Electrical & electronic assemblers	7.6	-16.7
Blue collar worker supervisors	3.7	-20.3
Inspectors, testers, & graders, precision	3.2	-35.2
Plastic molding machine workers	3.2	11.1
Machine operators nec	2.5	-34.7
Industrial machinery mechanics	2.5	25.0
Sales & related workers nec	2.1	-7.4
Electrical & electronic equipment assemblers	1.9	-7.4
General managers & top executives	1.9	-12.2
Machine feeders & offbearers	1.8	-16.7
Traffic, shipping, & receiving clerks	1.7	-10.9
Helpers, laborers, & material movers nec	1.6	-7.4
Tool & die makers	1.5	-25.2
Hand packers & packagers	1.5	-20.6
Sheet metal workers & duct installers	1.5	-7.4
Machinists	1.5	-30.5
Freight, stock, & material movers, hand	1.4	-25.9
Industrial truck & tractor operators	1.3	-7.4
Machine tool cutting & forming etc. nec	1.2	-25.9
Production, planning, & expediting clerks	1.2	-7.4
Secretaries, ex legal & medical	1.2	-15.7
Maintenance repairers, general utility	1.1	-16.6
Industrial production managers	1.0	-7.4
Coating, painting, & spraying machine workers	1.0	-7.4

Source: *Industry-Occupation Matrix*, Bureau of Labor Statistics. These data relate to one or more 3-digit SIC industry groups rather than to a single 4-digit SIC. The change reported for each occupation to the year 2005 is a percent of growth or decline as estimated by the Bureau of Labor Statistics. The abbreviation nec stands for 'not elsewhere classified'.

greater efficiency, and improved longevity. Other advances were making bulbs more environmentally safe for disposal; this is a particularly relevant development in the case of fluorescent bulbs, which contain mercury.

AMERICA AND THE WORLD

Besides domestic sales, many manufacturers were also striving to take advantage of growth opportunities overseas. Global electric lamp sales were estimated at about $9 billion in the mid-1990s and were expected to increase to about $11.5 billion by the turn of the century. U.S. producers met nearly 30 percent of worldwide demand in the mid-1990s and hoped to further boost their global market share. Although low-cost foreign manufacturers posed significant obstacles to exporters of traditional, commodity-like incandescent bulbs, U.S. manufacturers maintained a decided advantage in markets for high-tech lamps.

The United States was expected to import more automotive parts and accessories, including vehicular lighting equipment, than it exports through the middle of the 1990s. This trade imbalance is due chiefly to increased shipments from Japan. Overall, however, *U.S. Industrial Outlook* projects that U.S. parts exports should increase slowly. Other opportunities exist for U.S. manufacturers, however. Some U.S. companies are looking to Mexico for increased export business, mainly because of the North American Free Trade Agreement. Others are exploring joint ventures with foreign manufacturers and acquiring overseas manufacturing facilities. Foreign investment in the U.S. parts industry is also expected to grow slowly.

ASSOCIATIONS AND SOCIETIES

AMERICAN LIGHTING ASSOCIATION
PO Box 580160
Dallas, TX 75258
Phone: (214) 698-9898 or (214) 698-9901
Fax: (214) 698-9899

ELECTRICAL APPARATUS SERVICE ASSOCIATION
1331 Baur Blvd.
St. Louis, MO 63132
Phone: (314) 993-2220
Fax: (314) 993-1269

ELECTRICAL EQUIPMENT REPRESENTATIVES ASSOCIATION
406 W. 34th St., Ste. 628
Kansas City, MO 64111
Phone: (816) 753-0210
Fax: (816) 753-1954

ELECTRICAL GENERATING SYSTEMS ASSOCIATION
10251 W. Sample Rd., Ste. B
Coral Springs, FL 33065-3939
Phone: (305) 755-2677
Fax: (305) 755-2679

ILLUMINATING ENGINEERING SOCIETY OF NORTH AMERICA
120 Wall St., 17 Fl.
New York, NY 10005-4001
Phone: (212) 248-5000
Fax: (212) 248-5017
Members are lighting engineers, designers, architects, and manufacturers.

INDEPENDENT ELECTRICAL CONTRACTORS
507 Wythe St.
Alexandria, VA 22314
Phone: (703) 549-7351
Fax: (703) 549-7448

INSTITUTE OF ELECTRICAL AND ELECTRONICS ENGINEERS
345 E. 47th St.
New York, NY 10017
Phone: (212) 705-7900
Fax: (212) 705-4929

INTERNATIONAL ASSOCIATION OF ELECTRICAL INSPECTORS
901 Waterfall Way, No. 602
Richardson, TX 75080
Phone: (800) 786-4234 or (214) 235-1455
Fax: (214) 235-3855

INTERNATIONAL ASSOCIATION OF LIGHTING MANAGEMENT
34-C Washington Rd.,
Princeton Junction, NJ 08550-1028
Phone: (609) 799-5501
Fax: (609) 799-7032

JOINT ELECTRON DEVICE ENGINEERING COUNCIL
2001 Pennsylvania Ave. NW, Ste. 900
Washington, DC 20006
Phone: (202) 457-4971
Fax: (202) 457-4985

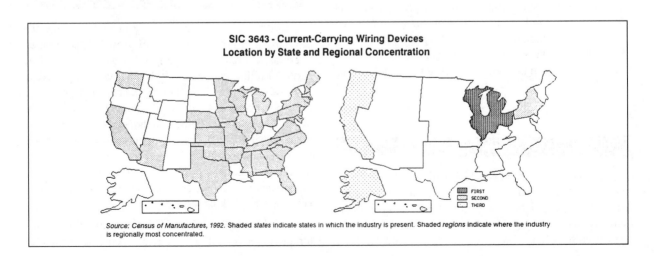

SIC 3643 - Current-Carrying Wiring Devices
Location by State and Regional Concentration

FIRST
SECOND
THIRD

Source: Census of Manufactures, 1992. Shaded *states* indicate states in which the industry is present. Shaded *regions* indicate where the industry is regionally most concentrated.

JOINT INDUSTRY BOARD OF THE ELECTRICAL INDUSTRY
158-11 Harry Van Arsdale, Jr. Ave.
Flushing, NY 11365
Phone: (718) 591-2000
Fax: (718) 380-7741
Concerned with labor-management relations of electrical contractors.

LIGHTING RESEARCH INSTITUTE
120 Wall St., 17 Fl.
New York, NY 10002-4001
Phone: (212) 248-5014
Fax: (212) 248-5019

NATIONAL APPLIANCE PARTS SUPPLIERS ASSOCIATION
14415 SE Mill Plain, Ste. 105B-205
Vancouver, WA 98684
Phone: (206) 834-3805
Fax: (206) 834-3507

NATIONAL ELECTRICAL CONTRACTORS ASSOCIATION
3 Bethesda Metro Center, Ste. 1100
Bethesda, MD 20814
Phone: (301) 657-3110
Fax: (301) 961-4500

NATIONAL ELECTRICAL MANUFACTURERS ASSOCIATION
2101 L St. NW, Ste. 300
Washington, DC 20037
Phone: (202) 457-8400
Fax: (202) 457-8411

POWER AND COMMUNICATION CONTRACTORS ASSOCIATION
6301 Stevenson Ave., Ste. 1
Alexandria, VA 22304
Phone: (703) 823-1555
Fax: (703) 823-5064

PERIODICALS AND NEWSLETTERS

APPLIANCE MANUFACTURER
Business News Publishing Co.
5900 Harper Rd., No. 105
Solon, OH 44139
Phone: (216) 349-3060
Fax: (216) 248-0187
Monthly. $55.00 per year.

CEE NEWS
Intertech Publishing Corp.
9800 Metcalf Ave.
Overland Park, KS 66212-2215
Phone: (800) 654-6776 or (913) 341-1300
Fax: (913) 967-1898
Monthly. Controlled circulation. Formerly Electrical Construction Technology.

ELECTRICAL CONSTRUCTION AND MAINTENANCE (EC&M)
Intertec Publishing Corp.
9800 Metcalf
Overland Park, KS 66212-2215
Phone: (800) 654-6776 or (913) 341-1300
Fax: (913) 967-1898
Monthly. Free to qualified personnel; others, $45.00 per year.

ELECTRICAL CONTRACTOR MAGAZINE
National Electrical Contractors Association
3 Bethesda Metro Center, Ste. 1100
Bethesda, MD 20814
Phone: (301) 657-3110
Fax: (301) 215-4500
Monthly. Price on application.

HOME LIGHTING AND ACCESSORIES
Doctorow Communications, Inc.
1033 Clifton Ave.
Clifton, NJ 07013
Phone: (201) 779-1600
Fax: (201) 779-3242
Monthly. $30.00 per year. Trade magazine of the residential lighting industry for retailers, distributors, designers, architects, specifiers, manufacturers and all lighting professionals.

IEEE INDUSTRY APPLICATIONS MAGAZINE
Institute of Electrical and Electronics Engineers
345 East 47th St.
New York, NY 10017-2394
Phone: (800) 678-4333 or (212) 705-7900
Fax: (212) 752-4929
Bimonthly. $120.00 per year. Covers new industrial applications of power conversion, drives, lighting, and control. Emphasis is on the petroleum, chemical, rubber, plastics, textile, and mining industries.

LD & A: (LIGHTING DESIGN AND APPLICATION)
Illuminating Engineering Society
120 Wall St., 17 Fl.
New York, NY 10005-4001
Phone: (212) 248-5000
Fax: (212) 248-5017
Monthly. $39.00 per year. Information on current events, products, projects and people in the lighting industry.

NATIONAL HOME CENTER NEWS: THE NEWSPAPER FOR RETAILERS SERVING HOMEOWNERS AND CONTRACTORS
Lebhar-Friedman, Inc.
425 Park Ave.
New York, NY 10022
Phone: (212) 756-5151
Fax: (212) 756-5139
Biweekly. $79.00 per year. Includes special feature issues on hardware and tools, building materials, millwork, electrical supplies, lighting, and kitchens.

STATISTICS SOURCES

ELECTRIC LAMPS
U.S. Bureau of the Census
Washington, DC 20233-0800
Phone: (301) 457-4100
Fax: (301) 457-3842
Quarterly and annual. Provides data on shipments: value, quantity, imports, and exports. (Current Industrial Reports, MQ-36B.)

PREDICASTS BASEBOOK
Information Access Co.
362 Lakeside Dr.
Foster City, CA 94404
Phone: (800) 321-6388 or (415) 358-4643
Fax: (415) 358-4759
Annual. $700. Provides industry, product, service, economic, demographic, and financial statistics for the United States. Arranged according to Standard Industrial Classification (SIC) numbers, with 14 years of data (where available) and annual growth rate given for each of the 35,000 series. Sources are over 350 statistical publications issued mainly by government agencies and trade associations.

U.S. INDUSTRIAL OUTLOOK: FORECASTS FOR SELECTED MANUFACTURING AND SERVICE INDUSTRIES
Available from U.S. Government Printing Office
Washington, DC 20402
Phone: (202) 512-1800
Fax: (202) 512-2250
Annual. $37.00. (Replaced in 1995 by U.S. Global Trade Outlook.) Issued by the International Trade Administration, U.S. Department of Commerce. Provides basic data, outlook for the current year, and "Long-Term Prospects" (five-year projections) for a wide variety of products and services. Includes high technology industries. Available on the world wide web at gopher://gopher.umsl.edu:70/11/library/govdocs/usio94.

GENERAL WORKS

EC&M ELECTRICAL PRODUCTS YEARBOOK (ELECTRICAL CONSTRUCTION AND MAINTENANCE)
Intertec Publishing Corp.
Electrical Publishing Group
9800 Metcalf Ave.
Overland Park, KS 66212-2215
Phone: (800) 654-6776 or (913) 967-1838
Fax: (913) 967-1898
Annual. Free to qualified personnel; others, $10.00.

FURTHER READING

Brooks, Andree. "Fire Hazards Seen in Some Torchere-Style Halogen Lamps." *The New York Times,* 16 January 1997, C2.

Darnay, Arsen J., ed. *Manufacturing USA.* 5th ed. Detroit: Gale Research, 1996.

Ramstad, Evan. "Prospects Dim for Hot, Costly Halogens." *Wall Street Journal,* 10 March 1997, B1+.

"Retailers Light the Way Through New Bulb Mandates." *Stores,* May 1996, 83-84.

U.S. Department of Commerce. Bureau of the Census. *Current Industrial Reports, Wiring Devices and Supplies, 1995.* Washington, 1996. Available from http://www.census.gov/industry/ma36k95.txt.

U.S. Department of Labor. Bureau of Labor Statistics. *Employment, Hours, and Earnings, United States, 1988-96.* Washington: GPO, 1997. ━━

ELEVATORS AND MOVING STAIRWAYS

SIC 3534

While *the future of the industry largely depends on the condition of the real estate and construction markets, it will also be influenced by elevator industry's ability to sell clients on new technological developments, particularly those implementing the use of sophisticated computerized control systems. Further, with the advent of various types of new computer technology, the future of the industry will largely be determined by the ability of elevator manufacturers to convince consumers that extensive modernization projects are necessary. Without the support of a strong U.S. economy in the future, it appears doubtful that such expenses would be justified by companies attempting to cut costs.*

INDUSTRY SNAPSHOT

The elevator and moving stairway industry manufactures a series of products designed for the vertical transportation of both materials and passengers. Machines manufactured for the exclusive purpose of moving materials, such as freight elevators and automobile lifts, comprise a small niche of the wide-ranging materials handling market. The majority of company revenues come from manufacturing passenger elevators and escalators, from producing parts required for elevator renovation and modernization, and from servicing elevators.

The livelihood of this industry is based mostly on the well-being of the construction industry, since new buildings need new elevators. The demand for elevators in 1995 and 1996 was fairly low in the United States and Europe, but operations in Southeast Asia have increased with most of the large elevator firms selling products there. The value of U.S. shipments was projected to rise each year from 1991 to 1996, with a value of $1.32 billion expected in 1996. The number of people employed in the business dropped consistently through the years, but hourly wages were slightly higher in this industry than the national manufacturing average.

INDUSTRY OUTLOOK

In 1996 the international elevator industry faced increased competition and slow growth in the construction industry. Large European companies were in financial straits. A Swiss engineering firm produced 1995 profits that were one-half of the preceding year's and a Finnish company closed several of its factories. The American firm, which controlled about one-fifth of the market, saw a 20 percent rise in operating profits in 1995; with $5.3 billion in sales, the company made $511 million in profits.

From 1990 to 1995, the demand for elevators and escalators fell from 90,000 units annually to 70,000 units. Large international firms and small local companies all suffered. They responded to the crunch by cutting costs, decreasing the number of employees, simplifying designs, and consolidating operations. In 1991 there were 175 companies operating in the elevator industry; in 1997, there were only 34—the top companies of which were subsidiaries of larger corporations.

Historically, the servicing of elevators has been the privilege of the manufacturer, but in recent years the service sector has become a fiercely competitive market of its own. Servicing contracts are considered lucrative due to the fact that an elevator will cost its owner as much in repairs as the initial cost during its first twenty years of operation. To ward off the competition, companies started installing elevators equipped with sophisticated electronics systems which allow engineers to monitor elevators from a remote location for imminent faults and problems. Remote monitoring technology enables engineers to identify problems and maintain elevators before breakdowns occur.

ORGANIZATION AND STRUCTURE

In 1991, 175 companies manufactured elevators and moving stairways, generating over $1.18 billion in shipments. Elevators and moving stairways accounted for approximately 75 percent of total shipments, while parts and attachments produced for separate sale resulted in another 18 percent. Electric and hydraulic passenger elevators—combining for roughly 45 percent of the industry's total shipments—were the largest product groups within the industry; automobile lifts—10 percent of the total figure—were the next largest group; followed by freight elevators, other types of non-farm elevators, and moving stairways and escalators—with each accounting for less than 6 percent of total shipments.

At that time, the industry as a whole spent over $712 million on raw materials, which translated to about $4 million per company—roughly 12 percent below the average for all construction and related machinery establishments. New capital expenditures, at $28.5 million for the industry as a whole, or roughly $163,000 per company, also fell well below the overall industry group average of $230,000. The projected cost of materials in 1996 was nearly $800 million, a figure that had steadily risen since 1987.

In an attempt to combat the unfavorable economic conditions of the early 1990s, the elevator industry attempted to fill the void in new elevator contracts by shifting its attention to the renovation and modernization of models installed 20 or more years ago. By replacing old control panels with new machinery and computer technology, the elevator industry hoped to survive the effects of the glutted real estate market. Elevator manufacturers also sought to take advantage of the new opportunities for renovation made available by the passage of legislation which required elevators be modified to provide greater handicapped accessibility in public and private buildings.

The introduction of sophisticated technology into the elevator service industry also fostered greater competition between major manufacturers and smaller independent firms who derived much of their business from the service market. In an effort to guarantee future service and renovation contracts on the elevators that they produced, many of the larger companies in the industry refused to release information about the design and electronic composition of their elevators. Although such proprietorship was frowned upon by governing organizations, the profit margin on new elevators—about 5 percent—encouraged companies to protect their large capital investments in this manner.

WORK FORCE

Elevator and moving stairway companies employed an average of 57 people, approximately three less than the average for all manufacturing industries. Of the 175 firms operating in 1991, 55 percent employed fewer than 20 workers. However, 69 percent of all employees in the industry were concentrated in establishments employing more than 100 people. While several of the industry's leading companies were subsidiaries of public companies, 31 of the 49 companies generating the highest revenues in the mid-1990s were privately owned.

Employees in the elevator and moving stairway industry made a projected $14.27 per hour in 1996, about 11 percent higher than the national average for manufacturing jobs. However, white-collar workers employed at an average annual salary of $36,968, earned wages roughly 6 percent below the average for related industrial machinery fields.

Elevator and moving stairway companies are located throughout the United States, with the greatest number of employees being found in the East. New York posted the greatest concentration of any state with 20 locations and 765 total employees. New York, combined with Pennsylvania and New Jersey, operated 24 percent of all companies and employed 18 percent of the industry's total workforce. Other major sectors of elevator and escalator producers could be found in Ohio, Illinois, Michigan, and California.

RESEARCH AND TECHNOLOGY

One of the most promising developments in domestic elevator technology came in Otis's introduction of a new type of computer software that used "fuzzy logic" to decide upon the best way to accommodate the various traffic needs of a modern office building. This type of artificial intelligence software distinguished itself from the standard computer logic governing conventional modern elevators by its ability to process uncertainties of information more efficiently. Rather than simply sending the closest elevator when a patron signaled, fuzzy logic took into account the number of people waiting for elevators throughout the building, hoping to avoid the common problem of sending an elevator to service one individual at the expense of several left waiting somewhere else. In 1996 Otis began showing the Odyssey, a multidirectional system of transistor elevator cabs, which could take a person from parking lot to penthouse, even in structures more than 1,000 meters high.

ASSOCIATIONS AND SOCIETIES

AMERICAN SOCIETY OF MECHANICAL ENGINEERS
345 E. 47th St.
New York, NY 10017
Phone: (800) 843-2763 or (212) 705-7722
Fax: (212) 705-7674

NATIONAL ASSOCIATION OF ELEVATOR CONTRACTORS
1298 Wellbrook Cir.
Conyers, GA 30207
Phone: (404) 760-9660
Fax: (404) 760-9714

NATIONAL ELEVATOR INDUSTRY, INC.
185 Bridge Plz. N
Fort Lee, NJ 07024
Phone: (201) 944-3211
Fax: (201) 944-5483

PERIODICALS AND NEWSLETTERS

ELEVATOR WORLD
Elevator World, Inc.
PO Box 6507
Mobile, AL 36660
Phone: (205) 479-4514
Fax: (205) 479-7043
Monthly. $52.00 per year.

NATIONAL ELEVATOR INDUSTRY, INC. NEWSLETTER
National Elevator Industry, Inc.
185 Bridge Plz. N
Fort Lee, NJ 07024
Phone: (201) 944-3211
Fax: (201) 944-5483
Quarterly. Price on application.

FURTHER READING

Darnay, Arsen J., ed. *Manufacturing USA.* Detroit: Gale Research, 1996.

Brown, Randy. ''Need a Lift?'' *Buildings,* December 1996.

''Schindler's Lift: Elevators.'' *The Economist,* 16 March 1996.

''World of Otis—Who Are We?'' Available from fttp://www.nao.otis.com/whoweare.htm.

ENGINEERING SERVICES

SIC 8711

The *American Society of Civil Engineers (ASCE) anticipated increased demand for civil engineers during the late 1990s. Two factors expected to drive demand were economic recovery within the United States and the North American Free Trade Agreement (NAFTA). NAFTA suspended residency requirements for obtaining Canadian and Mexican licenses, which was expected to create a new market for American engineers in Canada and Mexico. Also helping the domestic market, developing nations are expected to turn to U.S. firms for help in developing their infrastructure and industrial base. In already developed nations, the problem of deteriorating infrastructure and the need to provide more updated services, such as advanced motor vehicle traffic routing, are expected to provide opportunities for U.S. firms.*

INDUSTRY SNAPSHOT

Engineering covers a vast array of specialties touching virtually every aspect of life. The profession is categorized into disciplines representing designated areas of interest, though not all commentators define the disciplines in the same way. Some choose many narrow descriptions while others rely on fewer, more broadly drawn, classifications. By far, the most significant trend in the industry is computerization. Calculators and drafting boards have been replaced with computers equipped with CAD/CAM and 3-D software.

Top 10 MOST PRODUCTIVE DESIGN FIRMS IN ENGINEERING/CONSTRUCTION

Ranked by: Billings in 1995, in millions of dollars.

1. The Parsons Corp. (CA), with $927.7 million
2. Brown & Root Inc. (TX), $872.8
3. Raytheon Engineers & Constructors Inc. (MA), $846.0
4. Fluor Daniel Inc. (CA), $786.0
5. CH2M Hill Cos. Ltd. (CO), $721.3
6. Jacobs Engineering Group Inc. (CA), $698.0
7. Stone & Webster Engineering Corp. (MA), $654.5
8. Rust International Inc. (AL), $572.0
9. ABB Lummus Crest Inc. (NJ), $559.0
10. Parsons Brinckerhoff Inc. (NY), $521.3

Source: *ENR*, Top 500 Design Firms (annual), April 1, 1996, p. 52+.

There were an estimated 43,000 establishments involved in the engineering services industry in 1996—an increase of nearly 20 percent from just a decade before. Bringing total revenues of an estimated $78 billion, the industry employed approximately 755,000 individuals.

INDUSTRY OUTLOOK

In the mid-1990s, engineering and design firms were finally seeing the end of the recession that began in the early 1990s. A combination of factors such as the need for downsizing and limited resources in many industries increased the demand for engineering companies. Engineering companies were not only being sought after as consultants but as partners in day-to-day operations.

The top 500 design firms garnered a collective total of $29.4 billion in billings during 1995, up 5.2 percent over the $27.95 billion seen in 1994. According to *ENR*, analysts and industry executives attributed the improvement to the international market, where some $5.21 billion in billings were seen in 1995.

Numerous opportunities were opening up for U.S. environmental engineering firms, both in the United States and worldwide. Worldwide demand for design and construction of petrochemical plants and refineries resulted in a boom for engineering and construction firms. A survey conducted by *The Oil and Gas Journal* revealed that 59 percent of 291 sites were in the Asia/ Pacific region, with 60 sites in China.

As a result of the international demand, many construction design firms were expanding internationally, in spite of many economies and currencies being plagued with problems. Local construction firms were also bringing world class resources to clients by entering partnerships or by merging with global firms. In the domestic arena, deregulation of the utility industry, resulted in competitive pressure among engineering firms. The engineering firms were forced to take new risks to remain competitive and keep revenues flowing.

SIC 8711 - Engineering Services General Statistics

	Establish-ments	Employment (000)	Payroll ($ mil.)	Revenues ($ mil.)
1982	26,412	441.2	11,783.5	27,270.1*
1987	36,086	558.4	18,215.7	41,614.6*
1988	35,589	592.1	20,970.9	-*
1989	32,721	623.6	22,544.8	-*
1990	33,089	651.6	24,901.1	61,473.0
1991	33,974	652.1	25,485.3	59,732.0
1992	41,834	657.6	27,246.8	61,174.0
1993	41,529	655.7	27,425.8	61,277.0
1994	40,968P	711.2P	29,959.5P	61,127.5P
1995	42,063P	733.0P	31,510.1P	61,212.9P
1996	43,158P	754.9P	33,060.6P	61,298.3P

Sources: Data for 1982, 1987, and 1992 are from *Census of Service Industries*, Bureau of the Census, U.S. Department of Commerce. Revenue data are from the *Service Annual Survey* or from the Census. Revenue data from the Census are labelled with *. Data for 1988-1991 and 1993, when shown, are derived from *County Business Patterns* for those years from the Bureau of the Census. A P indicates projections made by the editor.

ORGANIZATION AND STRUCTURE

During the early 1990s, the largest engineering discipline, as measured by membership in engineering societies, was electrical and electronic engineering. The Institute of Electrical and Electronics Engineers, Inc. (IEEE), with 230,000 U.S. members and a presence in 150 countries, described itself as "the world's largest technical professional society."

Engineering establishments served two major classes of clients: government (representing 41.6 percent of fees charged) and; industrial, commercial, and other firms (representing 35.4 percent). Other classes of clients included architectural firms, construction companies, individuals, other engineering firms, and private institutions.

The types of projects undertaken by engineering establishments included industrial and processing plants and systems (19 percent); power generating and transmission facilities (18.9 percent); naval and aeronautical equipment (13.5 percent); water supply and sanitation facilities (8.1 percent); highways, roads, bridges, and streets (6.9 percent); commercial buildings (5.3 percent); and public and institutional facilities such as hospitals and educational facilities (3.3 percent).

WORK FORCE

The engineering services industry employed an estimated 755,000 people in 1996, an increase of nearly 200,000 workers since 1987. Their combined annual payroll totaled $33 billion. In addition to engineers, establishments providing engineering services employed a wide variety of professional and non-professional workers including laborers, technicians, financial and office staff members, and managers. The top two states in terms of number of employees and number of establishments were California and Texas.

To obtain a bachelor of science degree in engineering (B.S.E), most engineers attend a four-year college accredited by the Accreditation Board for Engineering and Technology (ABET). Demand for engineers was high during the late 1980s. According to one estimate, half of all job offerings available through college campus recruitment centers went to engineering students, even though engineering students represented only about 10 percent of the student body. They found jobs with a variety of establishments, including those providing contract engineering services. As a result, the number of engineers in the United States exceeded the number of people employed directly by the engineering services industry.

According to statistics and projections issued by the U.S. Bureau of Labor Statistics, most engineering disciplines will see growth by the end of the century. For example, the number of electrical engineers was expec-

SIC 8711
Occupations Employed by SIC 8711 - Engineering and Architectural Services

Occupation	% of Total 1994	Change to 2005
Drafters	12.1	10.2
Civil engineers, including traffic engineers	9.0	38.9
Architects, ex landscape & marine	7.0	18.9
Surveyors	6.8	-6.2
Engineering technicians & technologists nec	5.9	41.5
Secretaries, ex legal & medical	5.0	28.8
Electrical & electronics engineers	4.3	50.7
Engineering, mathematical, & science managers	4.2	87.5
General managers & top executives	3.6	34.3
Mechanical engineers	3.6	55.8
General office clerks	2.2	20.7
Engineers nec	2.2	27.4
Electrical & electronic technicians,technologists	2.0	41.5
Bookkeeping, accounting, & auditing clerks	2.0	6.1
Designers, ex interior designers	1.6	55.7
Construction & building inspectors	1.5	91.0
Computer engineers	1.5	109.6
Typists & word processors	1.3	-29.2
Financial managers	1.1	41.5
Computer programmers	1.0	14.6

Source: Industry-Occupation Matrix, Bureau of Labor Statistics. These data relate to one or more 3-digit SIC industry groups rather than to a single 4-digit SIC. The change reported for each occupation to the year 2005 is a percent of growth or decline as estimated by the Bureau of Labor Statistics. The abbreviation nec stands for 'not elsewhere classified'.

ted to rise from 439,000 in 1988 to 615,000 by the year 2000. The number of mechanical engineers was expected to increase from 225,000 to 247,000. The number of petroleum engineers, however, was forecast to remain level at approximately 20,000.

Salaries for engineers varied according to discipline and education. Nicholas Basta, author of *Opportunities in Engineering Careers,* reported that the 186,000 civil engineers working in 1988 earned approximately 10 to 20 percent less than other types of engineers. Information on salaries for civil engineers was compiled by the American Society of Civil Engineers (ASCE). In 1993, the organization reported that median average salaries for entry-level civil engineers varied from $28,000 to $35,900 depending on geographic region. Lowest salaries were recorded in New England and the highest in the far west.

RESEARCH AND TECHNOLOGY

The U.S. economy was built on technology and its continued health rests on technological advancement. The National Manufacturing Week trade show, held at McCormick Place in Chicago, offered engineers a chance to display new technology. Among the items featured in a booth sponsored by *Design News,* for example, were an ornithopter (a prototype airplane able to fly with sustained and controlled flapping wings), virtual reality technology, light weight insulators known as "aerogels," and an improved lunar work vehicle.

Other projects under development during the 1990s by U.S. engineering teams involved superconductors, robotics, fuel cells, particle beams, magnetic-levitation trains, radioactive waste storage, and advanced computer-integrated manufacturing. Chemical engineers continued investigating new materials for advanced information and communications, studying environmental issues, and contributing to public health technologies.

AMERICA AND THE WORLD

Demand for U.S. engineer services is closely tied to conditions in other countries. Increased competition from foreign nations pressured U.S. companies to expand productivity and reduce the cost of high-tech engineering services during the 1980s and 1990s. In 1970, the United States held a 51-percent share of the global high-technology engineering services market. By 1986, the U.S. market share had fallen to 42 percent. During the same time, Japanese presence increased from 16 percent to 32 percent. Competition was expected to remain high. In 1990, the National Science Board estimated that U.S. global competitors had science and engineering labor forces comparable to that of the United States and that the number of scientists and engineers in competing nations was rising faster than in the United States.

Although the United States historically has boasted a trade surplus in high-tech goods and services, 1986 marked the first year the United States experienced a deficit in high-tech trading. During that year, the United States exported only 15 percent of the high-tech goods it produced. In contrast, West Germany exported 61 percent of its production, the United Kingdom exported 54 percent, France exported 38 percent, and Japan exported 22 percent.

U.S. construction engineers were also facing increased competition in the global marketplace. According to figures compiled by the U.S. Department of Commerce, the annual worldwide construction market was estimated at $3 trillion. Japan represented the largest market segment in the 1990s. The Japanese market, however, was largely closed to U.S. firms. Overseas markets for U.S. construction engineers with growth potential were located in the Middle East (particularly Saudi Arabia and Kuwait), East Asia, Latin America, and Europe.

ASSOCIATIONS AND SOCIETIES

AMERICAN SOCIETY OF CIVIL ENGINEERS
c/o Kelly Cunningham
1015 15th St. NW, Ste. 600
Washington, DC 20005
Phone: (202) 789-2200

AMERICAN SOCIETY OF MECHANICAL ENGINEERS
345 E. 47th St.
New York, NY 10017
Phone: (800) 843-2763 or (212) 705-7722
Fax: (212) 705-7674

PERIODICALS AND NEWSLETTERS

AMERICAN SOCIETY OF CIVIL ENGINEERS.
PROCEEDINGS
American Society of Civil Engineers
345 E. 47th St.
New York, NY 10017-2398
Phone: (800) 548-2723 or (212) 705-7496
Fax: (212) 980-4681
Monthly. $2,289.00 per year. Consist of the Journals of the various Divisions of the Society.

ASCE NEWS
American Society of Civil Engineers
345 E. 47th St.
New York, NY 10017-2398
Phone: (800) 548-2723 or (212) 705-7496
Fax: (212) 980-4681
Monthly. $36.00 per year. Newsletter.

CIVIL ENGINEERING
American Society of Civil Engineers
345 E. 47th St.
New York, NY 10017-2398
Phone: (800) 548-2723 or (212) 705-7496
Fax: (212) 980-4681
Monthly. $85.00 per year.

CIVIL ENGINEERING MAGAZINE
American Society of Civil Engineers
345 E. 47th St.
New York, NY 10017-2398
Phone: (800) 548-2723 or (212) 705-7496
Fax: (212) 980-4681
Monthly. $81.00 per year.

ENR (ENGINEERING NEWS-RECORD)
The McGraw-Hill Cos.
1221 Avenue of the Americas
New York, NY 10020-1095
Phone: (800) 262-4729 or (800) 722-4726
Fax: (212) 512-2565
Weekly. $69.00 per year.

INTERNATIONAL JOURNAL OF MECHANICAL SCIENCES
Elsevier Science
660 White Plains Rd.
Tarrytown, NY 10591-5153
Phone: (914) 524-9200
Fax: (914) 333-2444
Monthly. $1,074.00 per year.

JOURNAL OF APPLIED MECHANICS
American Society of Mechanical Engineers
345 E. 47th St.
New York, NY 10017
Phone: (800) 843-2763 or (212) 705-7722
Fax: (212) 705-7674
Quarterly. Members, $29.00 per year; non-members, $120.00 per year.

JOURNAL OF HEAT TRANSFER
American Society of Mechanical Engineers
345 E. 47th St.
New York, NY 10017
Phone: (800) 843-2763 or (212) 705-7722
Fax: (212) 705-7674
Quarterly. Members, $29.00 per year; non-members, $155.00 per year.

SIC 8711 - Engineering Services
Industry Data by State

State	Establishments			Employment			Payroll			Revenues - 1992 ($ mil.)			% change 87-92	
	1987	1992	% of US 92	1987	1992	% of US 92	1987 ($ mil.)	1992 ($ mil.)	$ Per Empl. 92	Total ($ mil.)	Per Estab.	$ Per Empl. 92	Revenues	Payroll
California	5,920	6,524	51.7	80,762	93,075	55.4	2,925.8	4,064.4	43,668	10,208.3	1.6	109,678	42.5	38.9
Texas	2,800	3,116	24.7	40,622	53,205	31.7	1,286.5	2,367.3	44,494	6,270.4	2.0	117,854	82.6	84.0
Pennsylvania	1,516	1,797	14.3	36,870	38,666	23.0	1,238.7	1,498.8	38,763	4,586.4	2.6	118,615	34.0	21.0
New York	1,877	2,039	16.2	34,261	36,090	21.5	1,262.4	1,627.5	45,096	3,983.8	2.0	110,384	41.4	28.9
Massachusetts	1,189	1,248	9.9	32,659	28,454	16.9	1,195.9	1,370.1	48,152	3,418.1	2.7	120,128	17.3	14.6
Maryland	865	1,057	8.4	30,391	39,667	23.6	1,014.9	1,633.5	41,181	3,139.4	3.0	79,143	60.2	61.0
Virginia	1,144	1,431	11.3	34,067	34,418	20.5	1,052.3	1,351.3	39,263	3,054.4	2.1	88,746	44.5	28.4
Michigan	1,402	1,673	13.3	22,764	28,844	17.2	731.8	1,206.1	41,816	2,686.7	1.6	93,146	90.9	64.8
New Jersey	1,399	1,632	12.9	22,280	22,897	13.6	785.9	1,079.7	47,157	2,651.0	1.6	115,780	50.2	37.4
Florida	2,092	2,475	19.6	25,752	26,515	15.8	718.6	959.0	36,168	2,395.3	1.0	90,339	51.8	33.4

Source: Census of Service Industries, 1987 and 1992, Bureau of the Census, U.S. Department of Commerce. Data are sorted by 1992 revenues and, if revenues are unavailable, by establishments in 1992. (D) indicates that data are withheld by the source to avoid disclosure of competitive information. A dash (-) indicates that data are not available. Percentage changes between 1987 and 1992 are calculated using numbers that have not been rounded; hence they may not be reproducible from the values shown.

JOURNAL OF TURBOMACHINERY

American Society of Mechanical Engineers
345 E. 47th St.
New York, NY 10017
Phone: (800) 843-2763 or (212) 705-7722
Fax: (212) 705-7674
Quarterly. Members, $29.00 per year; non-members, $100.00 per year. Formerly Journal of Engineering for Gas Turbines and Power.

MECHANICAL ENGINEERING

American Society of Mechanical Engineers
345 E. 47th St.
New York, NY 10017
Phone: (800) 843-2763 or (212) 705-7722
Fax: (212) 705-7674
Monthly. Members, $17.00 per year; non-members, $45.00 per year.

DATABASES

CIVIL ENGINEERING DATABASE (CEDB)

American Society of Civil Engineers
345 E. 47th St.
New York, NY 10017-2398
Phone: (800) 548-2723 or (212) 705-7496
Fax: (212) 980-4681
Provides abstracts of the U.S. and international literature of civil engineering, 1975 to date. Inquire as to online cost and availability.

COMPENDEX PLUS

Engineering Information, Inc.
Castle Point on the Hudson
Hoboken, NJ 07030
Phone: (800) 221-1044 or (201) 216-8500
Fax: (201) 216-8532
Provides online indexing and abstracting of the world's engineering and technical information appearing in journals, reports, books, and proceedings. Time period is 1970 to date, with weekly updates. Inquire as to online cost and availability.

CSA ENGINEERING

Cambridge Scientific Abstracts
7200 Wisconsin Ave., Ste. 601
Bethesda, MD 20814
Phone: (800) 843-7751 or (301) 961-6750
Fax: (301) 961-6720
Provides the online version of Computer and Information Systems Abstracts, Electronics and Communications Abstracts, Health and Safety Science Abstracts, ISMEC: Mechanical Engineering Abstracts (Information Service in Mechanical Engineering) *and* Solid State and Superconductivity Abstracts. *Time period is 1981 to date, with monthly updates. Inquire as to online cost and availability.*

NTIS BIBLIOGRAPHIC DATA BASE

National Technical Information Service
5285 Port Royal Rd.
Springfield, VA 22161
Phone: (703) 487-4600
Fax: (703) 321-8547
Contains citations and abstracts to unrestricted reports of government-sponsored research, 1964 to date. Covers a wide range of technical, engineering, business, and social science topics. Monthly updates. Inquire as to online cost and availability.

WILSONLINE: APPLIED SCIENCE AND TECHNOLOGY ABSTRACTS

H. W. Wilson Co.
950 University Ave.
Bronx, NY 10452
Phone: (800) 367-6770 or (718) 588-8400
Fax: (718) 590-1617
Provides online indexing and abstracting of 400 major scientific, technical, industrial, and engineering periodicals. Time period is 1983 to date for indexing and 1993 to date for abstracting, with updating twice a week. Inquire as to online cost and availability.

GENERAL WORKS

AMERICAN SOCIETY OF CIVIL ENGINEERS: TRANSACTIONS

American Society of Civil Engineers
345 E. 47th St.
New York, NY 10017-2398
Phone: (800) 548-2723 or (212) 705-7496
Fax: (212) 980-4681
Annual. $124.00.

CIVIL ENGINEERING FOR THE PLANT ENGINEER

Max Schwartz Krieger Publishing Co.
PO Box 9542
Melbourne, FL 32902-9542
Phone: (407) 724-9542
Fax: (407) 951-3671
1984. $36.50. Second edition. Written for industrial and plant engineers

FURTHER READING

Rhodes, Anne K. "Engineering/Construction Firms Adjust to Downsized Process Sector." *The Oil and Gas Journal,* 27 March 1995.

"The Top 500 Design Firms." *ENR,* 1 April 1996.

Tulacz, Gary J. "Asia Continues to Power International Design Quest." *ENR,* 3 April 1995. ◀━

The United States has three major shorelines situated along the Atlantic Ocean, the Gulf of Mexico, and the Pacific Ocean. Together these shores, including those of Alaska and Hawaii, span more than 12,000 miles. As do many other nations, the United States holds economic jurisdiction over waters out to a distance of 200 nautical miles. This area is called the nation's Exclusive Economic Zone (EEZ). The U.S. EEZ contains more than 2.2 million square miles. These waters are estimated to contain about 20 percent of the harvestable seafood in the world.

The United States commercial fishing industry has been generally successful during the 1990s. In 1995 U.S. imports totaled $2.45 billion, a 24 percent increase from 1994's value of $1.97 billion. U.S. finfish exports increased by 13 percent during the same period. The 1995 value was $2.01 billion, up from $1.79 billion in 1994. Shellfish imports decreased by 2 percent in the mid-1990s. In 1995, the United States imported more than $3.65 billion of shellfish, down from $3.72 billion in 1994. U.S. exports followed a similar trend. The 1995 value of exported shellfish was $596 million, a 14 percent drop from 1994's total of $695 million.

FISHING, COMMERCIAL

SIC 0910

Industry analysts predict slow growth for the commercial fishing industry despite concerted efforts to raise the per capita consumption of fish from its current level of about 15 pounds to 20 pounds by the year 2000. The largest potential for growth in consumer shellfish demand in the 1990s was expected to be shrimp; however, insiders question whether fishermen can harvest increased amounts of shrimp without damaging the ability of populations to sustain themselves. It is more likely that growth in the industry will come from increases in exports and from the expansion of nonedible markets such as the production of livestock feed.

Top 5 TOP CITIES FOR SALT WATER FISHING

Ranked by: The percentage of the population that fishes.

1. Houston, 15.4%
2. Philadelphia, 11.3%
3. Los Angeles/Long Beach, 5.3%
4. Washington, D.C., 4.7%
5. Boston, 4.6%

Source: *Motor Boating and Sailing*, June 1996, p. 34, from National Sporting Goods Association.

Industry analysts do not expect consumer demand for fishery products to rise as sharply during the 1990s as they did during the 1980s. Annual per capita consumption of fishery products rose from 12.7 pounds in 1981 to a high of 16.2 pounds in 1987. Since 1987, consumption has fallen off and stabilized at approximately 15 pounds per person per year. Although the National Fisheries Institute has set a goal of increasing annual per capita consumption to 20 pounds by the year 2000, it is more likely that growth in the industry will come from increases in exports and from the expansion of noredible markets such as the production of livestock feed.

INDUSTRY OUTLOOK

The decade of the 1990s has been one mixed with promise and problems for the U.S. commercial fisheries. Consumer demand was expected to remain stable, total catches were on an upward trend, and increases in sales were expected to be limited only by the availability of preferred species. The problems centered on charges that fish populations were being seriously depleted because of the combined impacts of over-harvesting and environmental degradation.

Fishermen are often in agreement with conservationists and environmentalists in discussing ominous environmental trends in the areas of breeding ground pollution, shoreline development, and loss of wetlands. Approximately 75 percent of U.S.-produced seafood needs bays and estuaries for breeding grounds, but both types of marine environments have suffered from pollution. Several states have been particularly hard-hit. The state of Louisiana loses about 50 square miles of breeding ground every year. California has lost more than 90 percent of its original coastal wetlands.

Throughout the 1990s, catches of many important species were significantly down across the lower 48 states from their levels in the 1980s. In addition to habitat impairment, conservationists and environmentalists blamed these drops on over-fishing. Critics of the fishing industry claim that nearly half of the U.S. coastal finfish populations are being depleted because the size of current harvests outweigh the ability of the populations to reproduce themselves. Some scientists estimated that as many as 14 species face commercial extinction, a situation wherein too few fish of that species would remain to harvest them economically. The New England, Middle Atlantic, South Atlantic, and Gulf regions all saw total catches drop below their 1980 levels, although rising prices helped to stabilize the value of the harvest.

One important species of fish cited as an example is menhaden, an oily, bony fish that is related to herring and harvested in the Atlantic and Gulf of Mexico. Large scale harvesting of menhaden began in the nineteenth century following the discovery that its oil could be used as a substitute for whale oil. Twentieth century uses for menhaden included the production of fish oil, the production of fish meal, and as a bait fish.

Although the Gulf population has remained stable, the Atlantic menhaden population has seen wide fluctuations. The largest Atlantic landings took place in the mid-1950s. During the middle of the following decade, the larger, older fish disappeared and landings tumbled. During the 1970s the population appeared to make a tentative comeback, but in 1982 the Atlantic States Marine Fisheries Commission found it necessary to recommend protective regulations. In 1985 U.S. fishermen landed 2.7 billion pounds of menhaden, but Atlantic takings declined steadily. As a result, the last meal plant in Maine was shut down in September 1988. By 1990 total landings of menhaden had fallen to 1.96 billion pounds.

"Bycatch" has been another problem plaguing the fishing industry during the 1990s. "Bycatch" refers to unintentionally caught fish, birds, marine mammals, and turtles that are seriously injured or killed. In 1990 Alaskan trawlers fishing primarily for pollock reported throwing away 550 million pounds of other edible groundfish such as cod and halibut. The practice was condemned by critics as wasteful, and fishermen realized that public concern over real or even perceived threats to non-target species could have negative consequences. Indeed, concern about the number of dolphins killed as a result of bycatching prompted several well-publicized boycotts of leading tuna producers.

The fishing industry also faces other challenges associated with marine mammals. For example, in 1990 the population of northern sea lions along Alaska's Aleutian Chain and in the Gulf of Alaska was in a state of decline. Regulators considered restricting commercial fishing because fishermen were competing with the seals for fish.

In an effort to avoid further legislative involvement, fishermen organized the National Industry Bycatch Coalition in 1992 to discuss possible solutions. The Coalition's goals included the development of new technologies for cleaner fishing; promotion of education in how to use bycatch-reduction gear; support of management style changes to reduce throw-away rates; reduction of bycatch of threatened, endangered, and over-fished species to the absolute minimum; reduction of the rate of bycatch mortality; and the development of valuable uses for dead bycatch. The coalition also expressed a determination to work with conservation groups rather than adopt an adversarial stance.

ORGANIZATION AND STRUCTURE

Historically, independent fishermen caught fish and sold them to local packers or processors who re-sold them to retail markets. Although the U.S. fishing fleet still contains independent fishermen, large corporations are becoming increasingly involved in all aspects of seafood distribution.

The U.S. fisheries industry is managed by the National Marine Fisheries Service (NMFS). The NMFS is responsible for regulating commercial fishing, finding ways to control over-fishing of exploited species, collecting data, and publishing reports about commercial landings. The fishing industry, however, remains a lightly regulated one. Critics of the NMFS have sometimes accused the agency of concentrating efforts on helping fishermen maximize profits at the expense of protecting fish populations.

The NMFS, however, has instituted a number of regulatory measures designed to control and protect fish populations. One way in which the NMFS has regulated fishing is through the use of limited seasons for selected species. Because of intense pressure on selected populations, some seasons are short. Pacific halibut, for example, was once fished during a six-month season. By the early 1990s, the season was limited to two 24-hour periods. In September 1991 approximately 6,000 boats landed 23.7 million pounds of halibut in one day.

The NMFS also tested the use of quotas and limited entry into established fisheries as a means of regulating stressed fish populations. Such programs have included a moratorium on new entrants into the fishery, quotas based on catch histories of the vessel or fisherman, quotas based on a percentage of the total allowable catch, quotas on specific poundage, quotas based on vessel size or gear, and quotas that can be purchased or traded.

RESEARCH AND TECHNOLOGY

The two essential ingredients in the fishing industry are detecting fish (hunting) and catching fish (gathering). Until the modern era, fish detection was done primarily by the eye. The twentieth century introduced new methods of looking for fish. Aircraft scouting, satellite data, echo sounders, and other electronic equipment enabled fishermen to search more efficiently. Innovations were also made in catching fish. Nets made of new materials were rot resistant, less susceptible to abrasion, and more elastic. Larger purse-seines became possible when better methods of hauling them were developed. Trawling became more efficient and diverse when faster and lighter trawls were made.

Research continued during the 1990s on ways to improve on the various aspects of finfish harvesting. Areas under exploration included the introduction of electrical devices to herd fish into nets, the utilization of acoustical devices to hear noises characteristic of particular species, the development of more sophisticated methods of determining detailed water conditions, and determination of the applicability of luring fish with light, sound, chemicals, and electricity.

In addition to the technical aspects of finding and catching fish, researchers continue looking into ways to ameliorate the social, political, and economic problems of the industry. Promoters research fish species not previously used commercially and work on finding processing methods to make under-exploited stocks more acceptable to American consumers. New versions of bycatch-reduction gear are being developed and tested. Scientists continue in their endeavors to understand interspecies relationships in an effort to make fisheries management more successful.

Despite modern innovations, commercial fishing is still basically a hunting and gathering operation. As research efforts continue, modern technological advances aimed at improving fishermen's livelihood often seem to run at cross purposes with regulatory efforts to preserve fish stocks.

AMERICA AND THE WORLD

Overfishing remains a severe problem internationally, with stocks of food fish dropping severely in Southeastern Asian waters, the North Sea, and the Mediterranean Sea. The reduced fish stocks threaten not only American and European industries, but also the economies of some developing countries. Part of the problem lies in the fact that western-style management techniques out-compete traditional third-world country industries. Between 1950 and 1989, fishing catches worldwide increased from approximately 20 million tons to about 100 million tons, much of it from western commercial fleets. According to a report in *International Agricultural Development,* 7.5 million people in India rely directly on commercial or personal fishing for their livelihoods, while in the Philippines 38,000 fishermen are put out of work because of overfishing and competition each year. Exports of fish make up a significant proportion of the gross national product of Thailand. Western countries have taken some steps to address these concerns. The European Union, for example, adopted a strategy that called for a 20 percent cut in its fishing fleet between 1993 and 1996, but most fisheries management experts believe that this may not be enough.

ASSOCIATIONS AND SOCIETIES

AMERICAN FISHERIES SOCIETY
5410 Grosvenor Ln., Ste. 110 Bethesda, MD 20814
Phone: (301) 897-8616
Fax: (310) 897-8096

AMERICAN SEAFOOD DISTRIBUTORS ASSOCIATION
1525 Wilson Blvd., Ste. 500 Rosslyn, VA 22209
Phone: (703) 524-8800
Fax: (703) 524-4619

NATIONAL SHELLFISHERIES ASSOCIATION
c/o Dr. Thomas Soniat Department of Biological Sciences
University of New Orleans-Lakefront New Orleans, LA
70148
Phone: (504) 286-7042

UNITED STATES TUNA FOUNDATION
1101 17th St. NW, Ste. 609
Washington, DC 20036
Phone: (202) 857-0610
Fax: (202) 331-9686

DATABASES

**AQUATIC SCIENCES AND FISHERIES ABSTRACTS
SERIES (ONLINE)**
Cambridge Scientific Abstracts 7200 Wisconsin Ave., 6 Fl.
Bethesda, MD 20814
Phone: (800) 843-7751 (301) 961-6700
*Indexing and abstracting of the literature of marine life, 1975 to
present.*

NATIONAL MARINE FISHERIES SERVICE
*Contains information on this government body and its publica-
tions and audio/visual products. Fees: Free. URL: http://
kingfish.ssp.nmfs.gov/*

STATISTICS SOURCES

FAO FISHERY SERIES
United Nations Food and Agriculture Organization UNIPUB
4611-F Assembly Dr. Lanham, MD 20706-4391
Phone: (800) 274-4888 or (301) 459-2255
Fax: (301) 459-0056
*Irregular. Price varies. Text in English, French, and Spanish.
Incorporates Yearbook of Fishery Statistics.*

FISHERIES OF THE UNITED STATES
Available from U.S. Government Printing Office
Washington, DC 20402
Phone: (202) 512-1800
Fax: (202) 512-2250
*Annual. $8.00. Issued by the National Marine Fisheries Service,
National Oceanic and Atmospheric Administration, U.S. De-
partment of Commerce.*

IMPORTS AND EXPORTS OF FISHERY PRODUCTS
National Marine Fisheries Service U.S. Dept. of Commerce
Washington, DC 20235
Phone: (202) 482-4190
Annual.

FURTHER READING

''Fisheries: Overfishing Nets Disaster.'' *International Agricultural Development,*May/June, 1995.

National Marine Fisheries Service. Available at http://
kingfish.ssp.nmfs.gov/ ◆

In 1995, sales from flour and grain mill products totaled an estimated $6.6 billion, a substantial drop from sales of $7 billion in 1994. Nonetheless, the industry's sales and production were larger than those of the 1980s and the early 1990s. According to a U.S. Census of Manufacturers estimate, the industry had 354 active mills in 1996. In addition, states with the largest number of active mills included Kansas, New York, Minnesota, Ohio, California, and Missouri in 1996.

Although any grain (rice, oats, barley, corn, millet, sorghum, and wheat) can be ground into flour, most of the world's flour is produced from wheat. Using standard milling procedures, 100 pounds of wheat yields approximately 72 pounds of white flour. In addition to flour, the milling process produced millfeeds, which are made from pieces of bran and other portions of the wheat kernel. Millfeeds are used as ingredients in livestock food.

Flour can be packaged for sale to the household or bakery markets or used as an ingredient in bakery mixes, breads or doughs, or pastas. Different bread varieties are made with varying recipes, but on average 100 pounds of flour can make about 150 one-pound loaves of bread. The bread and cake industry consume approximately 70 percent of the flour milled in the United States. Other flour products include cookies, cereals, gravies, soups, whiskeys, and beers. Flour products are also used in non-food applications such as the manufacture of plywood adhesives, industrial starches, fertilizers, paving mixes, polishes, and cosmetics. Approximately 85 percent of the flour used by industrial users is milled from hard and durum wheat varieties.

Furthermore, mills use a process called fractionation to separate the flour according to the fineness of its particles. Course fractions are reground. Intermediate fractions are used in applications requiring low amounts of protein, and fine fraction flour is blended with other flours or used alone in applications where high protein content was necessary. White flour is often bleached with agents such as potassium bromide, iodate, acetone peroxide, azodicarbonamide, ascorbic acid, and chlorine dioxide. In addition to providing consistent coloring, bleaching improves the condition of the flour gluten which improves its baking quality.

White flour is made only with the endosperm portion of the wheat kernel. Farina is also made from the endosperm, but it is ground to produce a granular product. The term ''wheat germ'' refers to the part of the wheat kernel from which a seed sprouts. It contains oil which is sometimes extracted for separate processing. Wheat germ is also used in breakfast cereals, breads, and

FLOUR AND OTHER GRAIN MILL PRODUCTS

SICs 2041, 2045

Despite an increase in sales of flour and grain mill products since the early 1970s, the industry faces challenges about dissatisfaction with the quality of flour, the possibility of declining protein quality, and potentially inferior products produced by contemporary milling practices.

other bakery products. Whole wheat flour, also called graham flour, is made from the endosperm, bran, and germ combined. It has a higher protein content than regular white flour. Pastas such as spaghetti, macaroni, and noodles are made from durum wheat. A popular pasta ingredient, "semolina" is a granular grind of durum endosperm, comparable to farina.

INDUSTRY OUTLOOK

Although overall flour consumption declined somewhat during the early 1970s, annual per capita flour consumption increased by about 69 pounds between 1970 and 1994 to a total of 179.7 pounds. Industry analysts attributed gains to increased consumption of fiber, bran, and whole grain products along with growing consumption of such flour-based convenience foods as sandwiches and pizzas. Wheat flour consumption led at 144.5 pounds per person, followed by milled corn at 23.7 pounds, milled oats at 9.2 pounds, and milled rye at .6 pounds.

The diverse end uses of flours requires a wide variety of milled grain products produced from different types of wheat. During the latter part of the twentieth century, 14 different wheat species were grown. The three most frequently used varieties were common wheat (*Triticum aestivum*), club wheat (*Triticum compactum*), and durum wheat (*Triticum durum*). Together,

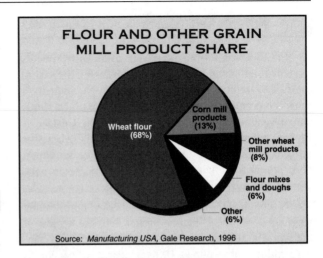

FLOUR AND OTHER GRAIN MILL PRODUCT SHARE

Wheat flour (68%)
Corn mill products (13%)
Other wheat mill products (8%)
Flour mixes and doughs (6%)
Other (6%)

Source: *Manufacturing USA*, Gale Research, 1996

these three account for 90 percent of the wheat grown in the United States.

Different wheats are classified as "hard," "soft," or "durum." Hard wheats are used to make flours for breads and rolls. Soft wheats are used primarily in cakes, cookies, crackers, and prepared mixes. Durum wheat is almost exclusively used to make pasta products. Although a single modern flour mill might offer more than one product, it typically grounds only one class of wheat. Approximately 70 percent of the U.S. milling capacity during the late 1980s was devoted to hard wheat. Soft wheat mills accounted for 20 percent, durum wheat accounted for 8 percent, and mills dedicated to whole wheat production represented 2 percent of the nation's milling capacity.

SIC 2041 - Flour & Other Grain Mill Products
General Statistics

| Year | Com-panies | Establishments | | Employment | | | Compensation | | Production ($ million) | | | |
		Total	with 20 or more employees	Total (000)	Production Workers (000)	Hours (Mil)	Payroll ($ mil)	Wages ($/hr)	Cost of Materials	Value Added by Manufacture	Value of Shipments	Capital Invest.
1982	251	360	174	15.1	11.4	24.2	323.0	9.64	3,825.5	1,094.3	4,932.8	90.6
1983		357	175	14.7	10.9	24.2	335.4	9.81	4,012.1	1,198.4	5,228.6	64.6
1984		354	176	13.9	10.3	22.3	335.5	10.51	4,108.5	1,208.0	5,305.7	68.7
1985		352	176	13.3	9.8	21.0	331.5	10.96	4,039.0	1,159.4	5,204.6	82.7
1986		357	177	13.5	9.9	21.4	348.7	11.28	3,642.5	1,345.9	5,003.1	62.8
1987	240	358	165	13.3	9.9	21.4	354.6	11.50	3,657.0	1,336.7	4,984.8	79.5
1988		353	170	12.8	9.6	21.3	351.0	11.71	3,781.4	1,439.4	5,205.0	130.3
1989		353	170	13.2	9.0	20.0	339.6	11.58	4,362.6	1,420.3	5,776.5	92.4
1990		348	169	12.8	9.1	19.9	351.0	12.08	4,348.0	1,251.3	5,624.7	114.2
1991		344	165	12.4	9.2	20.4	362.0	12.18	3,806.2	1,394.4	5,207.1	152.1
1992	230	365	172	13.1	9.5	21.5	408.9	12.87	4,675.3	1,624.5	6,294.4	253.5
1993		359	175	13.4	9.9	22.1	420.8	13.08	4,990.7	1,885.2	6,837.2	119.7
1994		354P	169P	12.7	9.2	21.3	397.0	12.68	5,186.8	1,908.0	7,089.1	95.9
1995		354P	168P	12.3P	8.8P	20.2P	406.3P	13.43P	4,850.5P	1,784.3P	6,629.4P	160.9P
1996		354P	168P	12.2P	8.7P	20.0P	413.1P	13.70P	4,958.9P	1,824.2P	6,777.7P	168.5P
1997		353P	167P	12.0P	8.6P	19.8P	420.0P	13.97P	5,067.4P	1,864.1P	6,925.9P	176.0P
1998		353P	167P	11.8P	8.4P	19.6P	426.8P	14.24P	5,175.8P	1,904.0P	7,074.1P	183.5P

Sources: 1982, 1987, 1992 *Economic Census; Annual Survey of Manufactures*, 83-86, 88-91, 93-94. Establishment counts for non-Census years are from *County Business Patterns*; establishment values for 83-84 are extrapolations. 'P's show projections by the editors. Industries reclassified in 87 will not have data for prior years.

As the grain mill products industry entered the 1990s, the number of mills declined, but the capacity per mill continued to increase. Between 1973 and 1990, the average mill increased in size by 70 percent, but the total number of mills in the United States fell by 25 percent. However, the number of mills remained steadier throughout the mid-1990s with only mild declines in the number of operations, and analysts predicted that it would remain steady throughout the end of the 1990s.

In the 1990s, more than half of the nation's milling capacity is concentrated in mills with individual daily capacities exceeding a million pounds. The trend toward corporate mills was driven by the goals of reducing labor and transportation costs and thereby increasing profits. The average daily wheat milling capacity, for example, was about 14 million pounds in 1996, up about 1 million pounds from 1994's daily capacity of 13 million.

One of the biggest challenges facing the grain mill industry is the charge that flour performance is diminishing. Industry researchers speculate that one cause of deteriorating quality is a national grain breeding program that had emphasized increasing yield per acre without paying sufficient attention to the quality of the end products produced with the grain. Other possible causes include: a drop in the amount of protein; a declining protein quality; an ever-increasing number of wheat varieties; the impact of agricultural practices such as irrigation and fertilizers; and milling practices which improve efficiency but potentially produced inferior results.

WORK FORCE

According to a U.S. Census of Manufacturers estimate, employment within the U.S. flour and grain mills

products industry totaled 12,300 in 1996. This figure represents a drop of about 1,000 employees since 1993. As of 1994, employees within this industry earned about $12 per hour. Out of the 354 active mills, 168 maintained a staff of 20 or more workers. Establishments in this industry maintained an average of 49 employees and each laborer cost the industry about $102,970. Mills also produced 279,017 shipments per employee.

Safety issues within the industry include dust control, noise abatement, and controlling hazards that presented risks for fire and explosions. Concentrations of grain dust above certain limits are susceptible to burning rapidly if ignited. Dust control is also necessary to limit possible worker exposure to microorganisms, pesticide residues, toxins, insect parts, and animal hairs. Some studies suggest that workers with high levels of exposure to grain dust might be susceptible to respiratory diseases such as chronic bronchitis. Noise in mills was primarily attributed to pneumatic blowers and vehicles.

To control potential work place hazards, modern mills reduce dust generation by minimizing grain handling, reducing the velocity of grain movement, and install enclosed conveyor systems. Protection from excessive noise is achieved by isolating work stations and limiting exposure.

ASSOCIATIONS AND SOCIETIES

AMERICAN CORN MILLERS' FEDERATION
600 Maryland Ave. SW, Ste. 305 W
Washington, DC 20024
Phone: (202) 554-1614

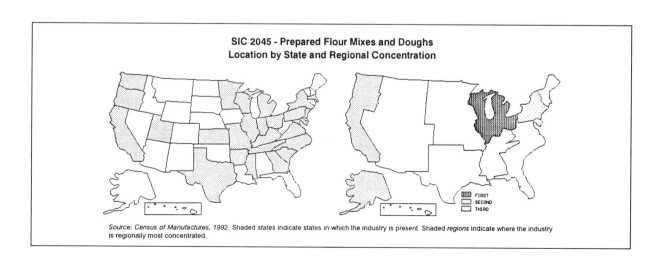

SIC 2045 - Prepared Flour Mixes and Doughs
Location by State and Regional Concentration

FIRST
SECOND
THIRD

Source: Census of Manufactures, 1992. Shaded states indicate states in which the industry is present. Shaded regions indicate where the industry is regionally most concentrated.

AMERICAN INSTITUTE OF BAKING
1213 Bakers Way
Manhattan, KS 66502
Phone: (913) 537-4750
Fax: (913) 537-1493

ASSOCIATION OF OPERATIVE MILLERS
5001 College Blvd., Ste. 104
Leawood, KS 66211
Phone: (913) 338-3377
Fax: (913) 338-3553

MILLERS' NATIONAL FEDERATION
600 Maryland Ave. SW, Ste. 305-W
Washington, DC 20024
Phone: (202) 484-2200

NATIONAL ASSOCIATION OF FLOUR DISTRIBUTORS
c/o The Compass Group
PO Box 84
Montville, NJ
Phone: (201) 316-6686

PERIODICALS AND NEWSLETTERS

MILLING AND BAKING NEWS
Sosland Publishing Co.
4800 Main, Ste. 100 Kansas City, KS 64112
Phone: (816) 756-1000
Weekly. $72.00 per year. News magazine for the breadstuffs industry.

DATABASES

CITIBASE (CITICORP ECONOMIC DATABASE)
FAME Software Corp.
77 Water St., 9 Fl.
New York, NY 10005
Phone: (212) 898-7800
Fax: (212) 742-8956

Presents over 6,000 statistical series relating to business, industry, finance, and economics. Includes series from Survey of Current Business and many other sources. Time period is 1947 to date, with daily updates. Inquire as to online cost and availability.

STATISTICS SOURCES

AGRICULTURAL STATISTICS
Available from U.S. Government Printing Office
Washington, DC 20402
Phone: (202) 512-1800
Fax: (202) 512-2250
Annual. $21.00. Produced by the National Agricultural Statistics Service, U.S. Department of Agriculture. Provides a wide variety of statistical data relating to agricultural production, supplies, consumption, prices/price-supports, foreign trade, costs, and returns, as well as farm labor, loans, income, and population. In many cases, historical data is shown annually for 10 years. In addition to farm data, includes detailed fishery statistics.

FLOUR MILLING PRODUCTS
U.S. Bureau of the Census
Washington, DC 20233-0800
Phone: (301) 457-4100
Fax: (301) 457-3842
Monthly and annual. Covers production, mill stocks, exports, and imports of wheat and rye flour. (Current Industrial Reports, M20A.)

FURTHER READING

Darnay, Arsen J., ed. *Manufacturing USA*. 5th ed. Detroit: Gale Research, 1996.

Grand Metropolitan Annual Report 1996. London: Grand Metropolitan, 1996.

U.S. Census Bureau. ''Current Industrial Reports. Washington: 2 April 1997. Available from: http://www.census.gov/ftp/pub/industry/m20a9702.txt. ◀▬

The number of companies in the United States involved in the production of nonrubber men's dress, street, and work footwear remained constant in the mid-1990s at around 200, but the impact of imports continued to pose a threat to the market share held by domestic companies. Footwear Industries of America (FIA) reported that imports captured over 75 percent of the domestic men's market that year, up from 73 percent in 1993, continuing a growth trend that began more than three decades ago.

The U.S. women's footwear industry is dominated by large companies that design and manufacture a wide variety of shoes each year. For many years, it has been heavily influenced by the continuing popularity of rubber-soled athletic shoes and other outdoor-oriented casual models that do not fall directly into this category. A steady market of consumers eager for new styles, along with the short life span of a pair of shoes, have produced lucrative profits for the nation's well-established footwear manufacturers. According to Footwear Industries of America, U.S. companies produced and shipped nearly 49.5 million pairs of women's shoes in 1995 with a total value of more than $1.1 billion.

FOOTWEAR, NONRUBBER

SIC 3140

The *U.S. nonrubber footwear industry will continue to face stiff competition from importers who benefit from traditionally low tariff rates. The majority of international competition for this market sector will come from such Far East countries as China, Taiwan, and Indonesia, but emerging markets in South America will also challenge domestic footwear sales. U.S. companies will strive to reduce costs to remain competitive by maintaining various manufacturing operations overseas where labor and production costs are lower, but greater care will be taken to monitor work conditions to avoid a backlash from the U.S. public and labor groups. Shoe exports by U.S. companies have risen dramatically in the 1990s—by nearly 50 percent—and insiders predict that this trend will continue into the next century.*

Top 10 **BEST-SELLING ATHLETIC FOOTWEAR BRANDS**

Ranked by: Total sales, in billions of dollars.

1. Nike (Nike), with $2.01 billion
2. Reebok/Avia (Reebok International), $1.52
3. Adidas (Adidas America), $.33
4. Keds (Keds), $.305
5. Converse (Converse), $.298
6. L.A. Gear (L.A. Gear), $.296
7. Fila (Fila USA), $.291
8. Asics (Asics Tiger), $.187
9. Etonic (Etonic), $.147
10. New Balance (New Balance Athletic Shoe), $.130

Source: *Brandweek,* Superbrands: America's Top 2,000 Brands, October 9, 1995, p. 128.

In relation to the overall footwear industry, women's models accounted for about 31 percent of all shoes produced by manufacturers in the United States and 32 percent of the total value of these shoes. Like the men's shoe industry, the import of foreign-made footwear has been the biggest problem for domestic women's shoe manufacturers as comparably stylish but

---

lower priced models made outside the United States continue to dominate the market. Approximately 10 times as many imports as domestically made women's shoes were sold in the United States in 1995, arriving from such countries as China, Brazil, and Indonesia. These imports carried lower price tags than similar American-made styles, primarily because of the lower labor and production costs. The house slippers industry is the smallest division within the nonrubber footwear industry. There were an estimated 19 establishments in 1996, the lowest in 15 years, down from 31 in 1992. In 1995 shipments of house slippers declined almost 50 percent from 1994 to a product value of $113 million.

INDUSTRY OUTLOOK

Nearly 56 million of the 159 million total pairs of nonrubber footwear produced by companies in the United States in 1995 were men's shoes, according to the FIA. The overall total marks a continuing decrease in American production that has been measured every year since 642 million pairs were manufactured domestically in 1968. During that period, imports and domestics also swapped relative positions, with the latter accounting for more than 78 percent of the market three decades ago and less than 12 percent of it in 1995. More than 170 million out of the 1.08 billion total imports that year were men's shoes, up from the 133 million out of nearly 975 million imported in 1992. China increased its leading share of the U.S. market from around one half to two-thirds of the total imported during that time, with Brazil second at nearly 9 percent, Indonesia third at 6.5 percent, Italy fourth at 4 percent and Thailand fifth at 2 percent. Approximately 20.5 million pairs of nonrubber footwear were exported by U.S. companies in 1995, of which 5.5 million were men's. Japan imported the most, with 12.5 percent of the total, followed by Canada with 11.6 percent; Mexico, the leading importer of American-made shoes in 1992 with 13.6 percent of the market, dropped to third place with 6 percent in 1995.

The domestic women's footwear industry has continued to undergo a slow but consistent decline as imports hold steady, per-capita consumption in the United States drops, and Americans find they can wear the same shoes for many different occasions. The total value of shipments for America's women's shoe manufacturers reached a peak of $1.4 billion in 1988, and began dropping from 2 to 9 percent in each subsequent year until reaching $1.17 billion in 1995. Over the same period, U.S. production fell nearly 35 percent. With U.S. per-capita shoe consumption falling from more than five pairs in the 1960s to 4.2 pairs in the 1990s, industry

analysts have predicted the decline will continue. However, the growing popularity of casual shoes—boosted by the ongoing prominence of athletic styles and their increasing acceptance in the workplace and various social settings—has led to some optimism. Imported women's footwear, which reached nearly 497 million pairs in 1995, dwarfed the 49.4 million pairs manufactured domestically that year; at the same time, U.S. women's shoe exports increased slightly to total 3.7 million pairs.

Fourteen U.S. shoe factories closed and two opened in 1995, according to the FIA, leaving about 200 manufacturers operating 341 plants in 31 states, as production continued shifting overseas to take advantage of lower labor costs. One exception to the trend was men's work shoes, where domestic production hit nearly 14.9 million in 1995—representing a 34 percent increase from 1993. Another submarket that remained strong was made up of the firms that produced top-quality leather dress shoes or filled unique export markets, such as bootmaker Tony Lama, Inc. in El Paso, Texas. In 1989, Tony Lama, Jr., then the company's chairperson, told *Nation's Business,* "They don't make original cowboy boots everywhere in the world. [Foreign customers] don't mind spending money on a fine pair of cowboy boots, but its important that they be made in America." *Footwear* + reported in 1997 that exports of Western boots continued to grow, particularly to Germany, France, Norway, Sweden, and Denmark.

ORGANIZATION AND STRUCTURE

Unveiling a wide assortment of new shoe styles each season is how industry leaders regularly improve their product lines and increase their market shares. A shoe company's in-house design staff, which closely monitors European and American fashion trends and then develops appropriate new versions of their firm's basic products, is a key aspect of these manufacturing operations—and one of the most expensive parts of the entire process. Consequently, more and more companies have attempted to reduce overall costs by relocating many preliminary manufacturing tasks to foreign factories where labor expenses are lower; however, shoes are returned often to the United States for a number of final production steps. The finished footwear is then distributed to stores around the nation by marketing teams that negotiate with retail outlets and department stores in an effort to place as much of their company's products on display shelves as possible. Competition is fierce and dramatic shifts within the industry based on the smallest stylistic or structural innovation are commonplace. To keep up with these changes, much of the industry's design, marketing, and management personnel meet at annual trade gatherings like the Fashion Footwear Association of New York show, the National Shoe Fair, and Shoes in New York.

WORK FORCE

The U.S. nonrubber footwear industry employed 53,800 people in 1995, the FIA reported, 43,900 of whom were production workers. The total represented a 7.1 percent decline from the year before and a 77 percent decrease since 1968, when employment was 233,400. The domestic industry's direct manufacturing payroll was $1.1 billion in 1995, with production employees earning an average of $7.67 per hour—up from $7.01 in 1992. A comparison of Indonesia's basic hourly wage of about 30 cents (in U.S. dollars), cited in a 1996 *Business Week* story, as well as the 50 cents per hour paid in China, graphically shows why production has largely shifted to those countries in recent years. Even the average salary in Taiwan, reportedly the highest among major foreign competitors, was less than half the U.S. figure.

Footwear manufacturers based in the United States have increasingly moved their production operations overseas to boost their profits and, according to Footwear Industries of America, shoe imports have accordingly risen by 516 percent between 1968 and 1995.

About 89 percent of all non-rubber footwear designed for U.S. consumption is now produced in some 100 foreign countries primarily noted for having relatively few government rules on working conditions, health and safety matters, and the right to unionize. China, Brazil, and Indonesia alone accounted for nearly 84 percent of all non-rubber footwear imports in 1995, while several aggressive newcomers were attempting to move into the U.S. marketplace. Among them was Colombia, where hourly wages were just $3-$4 an hour. Only six million pairs of shoes were produced for export in the mid-1990s; local officials predicted, however, that this total would be increased to 15-20 million pairs by the turn of the century.

The continuing decline in domestically produced footwear in recent years resulted in the closure of 1,200 U.S. shoe factories between 1968 and 1995, and a loss of nearly 180,000 direct manufacturing jobs during that time. According to the FIA, though, about 53,800 people remained employed domestically that year by nearly 200 manufacturers operating 341 plants in 31 states.

RESEARCH AND TECHNOLOGY

Like other industries, the production and sale of U.S. footwear has been greatly changed by computer technology. Companies have invested large sums of money to integrate the latest electronic equipment into all facets of their operations. In the research and devel-

SIC 3143 - Men's Footwear, Except Athletic
General Statistics

| Year | Companies | Establishments | | Employment | | | Compensation | | Production ($ million) | | | |
		Total	with 20 or more employees	Total (000)	Production Workers (000)	Hours (Mil)	Payroll ($ mil)	Wages ($/hr)	Cost of Materials	Value Added by Manufacture	Value of Shipments	Capital Invest.
1982	129	203	159	46.5	40.7	69.6	503.1	5.49	1,141.3	1,101.1	2,261.4	28.3
1983		190	147	43.0	38.0	67.1	494.1	5.68	1,120.5	1,138.7	2,264.0	18.8
1984		177	135	40.1	35.3	61.5	472.7	5.99	1,104.0	1,118.9	2,230.6	28.0
1985		165	124	34.9	30.8	53.8	435.9	6.26	1,031.8	1,051.4	2,070.5	28.9
1986		147	110	31.8	28.0	49.3	416.6	6.41	968.8	913.1	1,891.4	16.2
1987	110	154	111	31.6	27.5	51.3	434.1	6.36	1,056.6	1,046.7	2,104.8	17.4
1988		154	115			49.0	438.0		1,095.8	1,093.6	2,168.0	17.4
1989		141	106	30.3	26.6	47.4	462.1	7.22	1,157.8	1,083.1	2,228.4	21.2
1990		129	96	28.4	24.6	44.0	444.9	7.11	1,080.3	1,058.6	2,148.8	22.8
1991		135	89	24.5	21.0	35.4	387.0	7.74	1,054.5	997.9	2,064.0	18.1
1992	108	140	88	24.2	20.0	36.6	398.9	7.72	1,135.6	1,087.7	2,209.5	32.8
1993		143	89	24.6	20.8	40.9	430.3	7.56	1,183.8	1,196.5	2,351.1	26.1
1994		120P	74P	24.0	20.5	39.7	421.6	7.80	1,177.5	1,353.3	2,461.0	43.3
1995		114P	68P			31.2P	396.7P		1,087.1P	1,249.4P	2,272.1P	29.6P
1996		109P	61P			28.6P	390.3P		1,092.8P	1,256.0P	2,284.0P	30.3P
1997		103P	55P			25.9P	383.9P		1,098.5P	1,262.5P	2,295.9P	31.0P
1998		98P	49P			23.3P	377.5P		1,104.2P	1,269.1P	2,307.8P	31.7P

Sources: 1982, 1987, 1992 Economic Census; Annual Survey of Manufactures, 83-86, 88-91, 93-94. Establishment counts for non-Census years are from County Business Patterns; establishment values for 83-84 are extrapolations. 'P's show projections by the editors. Industries reclassified in 87 will not have data for prior years.

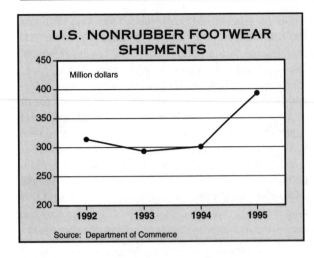

U.S. NONRUBBER FOOTWEAR SHIPMENTS

Million dollars

Source: Department of Commerce

opment segment, the use of computer-aided design (CAD) is now common, and many firms have integrated it with computer-aided manufacturing (CAM) processes. The combination allows shoes to be produced in America more quickly and accurately, which dramatically lowered production costs but also eliminated jobs. The women's footwear industry in particular has additionally brought robotics technology into the manufacturing process, utilizing robots to move shoes from one production module to the next. Computers are also used extensively in the industry's management sector, usually tracking production figures and coordinating them with distribution results and sales totals.

AMERICA AND THE WORLD

Considered one of the most open footwear markets in the world because it was one of the few industrialized nations that did not impose high import tariffs, the United States accounted for 29 percent of all world imports in 1995. The FIA reported that U.S. imports of nonrubber footwear grew by 516 percent between 1968, when President Lyndon Johnson cut tariffs in half, and 1995, when import penetration reached 88.6 percent. More than 2,000 footwear plants operated in the United States at the start of 1968, but only 341 were open at the end of 1995—an average of nearly 60 factory closings every year.

After 1968, several attempts were made to impose higher import tariffs, most notable of which was the Textile, Apparel, and Footwear Act of 1990 vetoed by President George Bush. Similar bills had been rejected by Congress in 1985 and 1988. Also during this time, the industry filed complaints about unfair trade practices with the International Trade Commission (ITC), but in 1984 the ITC ruled that the U.S. footwear industry was

not being harmed by imports. The Senate Finance Committee initiated a case with the ITC the following year, which resulted in a recommendation for five years of global quotas, but the plan was tabled in the early 1990s.

After the Textile, Apparel, and Footwear Act was vetoed in 1990, the FIA—which had lobbied for import protection—effectively gave up the fight. Fawn Evenson, then executive director of the FIA, told *The Journal of Commerce and Commercial* in 1992, "We literally spent millions of dollars on trade cases. We almost went broke trying to protect jobs."

In 1990, the FIA voted to expand its membership to include importers and tacitly supported the North American Free Trade Agreement (NAFTA) by focusing its efforts on ensuring that Mexico would not become a transit point for duty free shoes from other countries, most of which imposed tariffs of 25 percent or more on U.S. exports or locked out U.S. companies entirely. Evenson explained, "We are importers. We've stopped quota battles. We're going to spend a lot more time on market access and on exports. We're now going to devote our efforts to companies that are surviving."

One consequence of the increasing drive to manufacture U.S. footwear abroad was the widespread exposure in 1996 of the so-called "sweatshop" conditions under which many of these items were produced. Nike Inc., which made 70 million pairs of shoes in Indonesia alone that year, bore much of the criticism when publications like *Business Week* reported on the difficult conditions in many of its Asian factories. Under pressure from the public and U.S. labor groups, the Beaverton, Oregon-based firm vowed to correct the violations.

Manufacturers of women's footwear in the United States continue to face strong competition from cheaper imports. The amount of imported shoes on the American market has increased greatly in recent years, from 175 million pairs in 1968 to 374 million in 1978, and from 941 million pairs in 1986 to 1.08 billion in 1995. The majority of these shoes now come from the Far East, with imports from China growing by 39 percent each year since 1981 to top 716 million pairs in 1995. U.S. companies learned to reduce costs further by shipping cut footwear patterns to plants in Third World countries, where they were then either partially or completely assembled. The firms did this because it was cheaper for the footwear to be only partially assembled abroad, since American companies pay a lower duty (typically 5 percent) on unfinished goods being re-exported to the United States. The final, less labor-intensive manufacturing details—such as bottoming, finishing, and packing—are then completed at home.

On the other side of the international trade front, American companies shipped more than 20.5 million pairs of footwear abroad for sale in 1995—of which about 18 percent were women's models. The value of all U.S. shoe exports that year was $367 million, up more than 44 percent from the value in 1990. Japan received nearly 12.5 percent of this total, followed by Canada at 11.6 percent; Mexico, the biggest foreign market for American footwear only two years earlier, fell to just 6 percent. The United Kingdom, Hong Kong, France, Honduras, and Germany accounted for the rest of the exports.

Several consequences for the American women's footwear industry developed after the 1993 ratification of the North American Free Trade Agreement (NAFTA) by the United States, Canada, and Mexico. Under the agreement's guidelines, duties on shoes produced in Mexico were to be reduced over a 10-year period, which some thought could lead to an increase in imports. However, NAFTA's rules also addressed the origin of shoes produced in Mexico, setting limits on the amount of materials that could be produced in countries with burgeoning shoe industries in Central and South America. These content regulations should help insure that third-country manufacturers do not nominally assemble shoes in Mexico, then ship them to the United States and benefit from the reduced tariffs. These South and Central American countries, however, are also involved in negotiating similar trade agreements with the United States, which could result in lowered or nonexistent tariffs on U.S. imports in the late 1990s.

ASSOCIATIONS AND SOCIETIES

FOOTWEAR DISTRIBUTORS AND RETAILERS OF AMERICA
1319 F St. NW, 700
Washington, DC 20004
Phone: (202) 737-5660
Fax: (202) 638-2615

FOOTWEAR INDUSTRIES OF AMERICA
1420 K St. NW Ste. 600
Washington, DC 20005
Phone: (202) 789-1420
Fax: (202) 789-4058

NATIONAL SHOE RETAILERS ASSOCIATION
9861 Broken Land Pky, Ste. 255
Columbia, MD 21046-1151
Phone: (800) 673-8446 or (410) 381-8282
Fax: (410) 381-1167

PERIODICALS AND NEWSLETTERS

AMERICAN SHOEMAKING
James Sutton
Shoe Trades Publishing Co.
PO Box 198
Cambridge, MA 02140
Phone: (617) 648-8160
Fax: (617) 492-0126
Monthly. $49.00 per year.

SIC 3144 - Women's Footwear Except Athletic
General Statistics

Year	Com-panies	Establishments		Employment			Compensation		Production ($ million)			
		Total	with 20 or more employees	Total (000)	Production Workers (000)	Hours (Mil)	Payroll ($ mil)	Wages ($/hr)	Cost of Materials	Value Added by Manufacture	Value of Shipments	Capital Invest.
1982	209	293	226	48.4	43.4	77.1	483.1	5.10	821.9	1,107.0	1,933.2	20.2
1983		268	208	46.5	41.5	74.4	495.4	5.29	809.9	1,156.2	1,957.7	22.8
1984		243	190	40.7	36.1	63.7	431.2	5.32	737.1	987.1	1,728.1	23.2
1985		219	172	34.3	30.3	54.9	378.8	5.39	684.1	919.6	1,613.0	12.3
1986		192	148	30.2	26.3	46.5	341.9	5.80	597.8	812.3	1,425.9	13.8
1987	122	163	123	26.6	23.7	45.5	320.0	5.56	572.4	755.8	1,316.0	11.3
1988		156	113			44.7	320.2		655.4	716.2	1,373.5	12.4
1989		137	104	24.5	20.5	40.5	290.3	5.57	645.7	703.0	1,351.3	11.1
1990		128	99	22.2	19.1	35.8	292.8	5.96	727.9	682.7	1,393.2	13.4
1991		126	95	19.0	17.0	31.0	247.9	6.10	505.5	633.7	1,153.7	9.1
1992	99	127	77	15.0	13.2	23.7	219.5	7.01	479.6	636.9	1,095.1	10.5
1993		124	77	14.4	12.7	22.5	219.8	7.50	449.1	569.4	1,010.3	6.8
1994		77P	45P	14.4	12.8	22.5	211.8	7.31	403.4	550.2	949.9	7.6
1995		61P	31P			12.3P	158.9P		359.7P	490.7P	847.1P	5.1P
1996		45P	17P			7.7P	134.9P		325.7P	444.3P	767.0P	3.9P
1997		29P	3P			3.0P	110.9P		291.7P	397.9P	686.9P	2.7P
1998		13P					86.8P		257.7P	351.5P	606.8P	1.5P

Sources: 1982, 1987, 1992 *Economic Census*; *Annual Survey of Manufactures*, 83-86, 88-91, 93-94. Establishment counts for non-Census years are from *County Business Patterns*; establishment values for 83-84 are extrapolations. 'P's show projections by the editors. Industries reclassified in 87 will not have data for prior years.

FOOTWEAR NEWS
Fairchild Fashion and Merchandising Group
7 W 34th St.
New York, NY 10001
Phone: (800) 247-6622 or (212) 630-3880
Weekly. Retailers. $51.00 per year; others, $62.00 per year.

DATABASES

CITIBASE (CITICORP ECONOMIC DATABASE)
FAME Software Corp.
77 Water St., 9 Fl.
New York, NY 10005
Phone: (212) 898-7800
Fax: (212) 742-8956
Presents over 6,000 statistical series relating to business, industry, finance, and economics. Includes series from Survey of Current Business *and many other sources. Time period is 1947 to date, with daily updates. Inquire as to online cost and availability.*

STATISTICS SOURCES

BUSINESS STATISTICS
Available from U.S. Government Printing Office
Washington, DC 20402
Phone: (202) 512-1800
Fax: (202) 512-2250
Biennial. $20.00. Issued by Bureau of Economic Analysis, U.S. Department of Commerce. Shows annual data for 29 years and monthly data for a recent four-year period. Statistics correspond to the Survey of Current Business.

FOOTWEAR
U.S. Bureau of the Census
Washington, DC 20233-0800
Phone: (301) 457-4100
Fax: (301) 457-3842

Quarterly. Covers production and value of shipments of leather and rubber footwear. (Current Industrial Reports, MQ-31A.)

SURVEY OF CURRENT BUSINESS
Available from U.S. Government Printing Office
Washington, DC 20402
Phone: (202) 512-1800
Fax: (202) 512-2250
Monthly. $41.00 per year. Issued by Bureau of Economic Analysis, U.S. Department of Commerce. Presents a wide variety of business and economic data.

FURTHER READING

Bentz, Kristen. "True West." *Footwear +*, March 1997, 24.

Clifford, Mark. "Pangs of Conscience." *Business Week,* 29 July 1996, 46-47.

"Current Highlights of the Nonrubber Footwear Industry." Washington: Footwear Industries of America, 25 July 1996. Available from http://www.fia.org/

Lucas, Allison. "Heart and Sole." *Sales & Marketing Management,* May 1996, 30.

Peale, Cliff. "Luxottica Settles Terms of U.S. Shoe Sale." *Cincinnati Post,* 30 May 1996.

Strassel, Kimberly. "Nine West Plans U.S. Plant Closings, Paring 1,000 Jobs." *The Wall Street Journal,* 13 February 1997, C16.

Tedeschi, Mark. "Colombia Out To Lure Shoe Business." *Footwear News,* 4 March 1996, 2.

Waxler, Caroline. "Walking Wounded." *Forbes,* 20 May 1996, 280.

In the last decade, the forest industry has been forced to embrace numerous changes due to the social, economic, and political pressures that have markedly reduced the number of acres that can be harvested for timber. Many in the industry have looked first to public agencies and forest product corporations for employment, but even at the single largest employer, the U.S. Forest Service—a department of the U.S. Department of Agriculture—downsizing has become a regular phenomenon. Despite this trend, many owners of small forest tracts are hiring forestry consultants to help manage their land in an effort to capitalize on rising lumber and timber prices due to reductions in timber cutting on national forests. As profits from timber growing increase, forest product companies—especially the ones with large land holdings—are utilizing more of the services that this industry sector can offer.

As of 1996, over 737 million acres, approximately one-third of the total U.S. land area, was forested. In the Pacific Northwest states of Oregon, Washington, and California, over 10 million acres of old-growth forest—wilderness which has never been harvested—can be still found. The majority of this forest land was owned by non-federal public agencies, the forest industry, farmers and ranchers, and other private individuals.

Fire fighting and prevention, pest control, and forest management plans were implemented in the 1980s and 1990s, utilizing the philosophy of managing forests as complex ecosystems containing interdependent communities of plants, animals, and microbes. This new way of looking at forests was greatly influenced by the declining number of U.S. forest lands during the early 1970s. Reforestation and new forestry management efforts started, in part to prevent the decline of 1.5 million acres of forest land each year from 1970 to 1987. The reforestation forest management efforts began to pay off by the early 1990s; at that time, the rate of U.S. forest depletion had decreased to approximately a half a million acres per year. Despite this impressive success, government sources still project a decline of four percent of forest land to about 703 million acres by the year 2040.

Historically, the forest industry has been divided between federal and private sectors. Oftentimes, the two groups will engage in cooperative efforts to manage and harvest forest lands; frequently, the two sides will also be at odds with regard to these same issues. With the rise of industrial forestry in the late 1900s, budding forestry products companies developed individual management plans, fire and pest control systems, and business priorities. As early as 1904, the Weyerhaeuser Timber Co. reforested 1.3 million acres of timberland in Washington

FORESTRY

SIC 0800

Despite the projection that U.S. forest land will steadily decrease by four percent until 2040, the private and public sectors of the forest industry have been largely successful in collaborating to bring unbridled deforestation under control. The result has been higher timber prices—and hence higher profits—for private companies and satisfactory ecological and environmental gains for the government. Global initiatives to address deforestation, acid rain deposits, endangered species, and global warming will continue to have a pronounced impact on the forest industry into the next millenium.

Top 10 LEADERS IN THE FOREST PRODUCTS INDUSTRY

Ranked by: Revenue in 1995, in millions of dollars.

1. International Paper, with $19,797 million
2. Georgia-Pacific, $14,292
3. Kimberly-Clark, $13,789
4. Weyerhaeuser Co., $11,788
5. Stone Container, $7,351
6. Champion International, $6,972
7. James River, $6,800
8. Mead, $5,179
9. Boise Cascade, $5,058
10. Union Camp Corp., $4,212

Source: *Fortune*, Fortune 500 Largest U.S. Corporations (annual), April 29, 1996, p. F-52.

---

state, and following the 1903 and 1908 fires in the Northeast and the 1902 and 1910 fires in Idaho and the Northwest, private companies drafted the first fire protection organizations.

With the establishment of the U.S. Forest Service in 1905, the private sector for the first time faced the threat of federal regulation of private timber harvesting. Even though federal forests accounted for less than one-fifth of total U.S. forest land, government regulations influenced private industry in such areas as logging, road construction, reforestation mandates, taxation of private forests, and use of herbicides and pesticides. Entering the 1990s, private forest land owners and forest industry leaders took exception to many federal regulations, arguing that forest management plans for public forest lands were incompatible with the market-driven interests of private foresters.

INDUSTRY OUTLOOK

Starting in the mid-1980s, world attention focused on the interrelated problems of global deforestation—especially in tropical forests—and its possible contributions to such environmental problems as global warming. At the 1990 Economic Summit in Houston, Texas, President George Bush proposed a global forest convention to address problems of deforestation, biodiversity, and forest management. At the 1991 Economic Summit in London, these concerns were reiterated in anticipation of the Earth Summit meeting scheduled for June of 1992 in Brazil. Capitalizing on many of the issues raised in these conferences, Bill Clinton and his running mate, Al Gore, attracted considerable support from environmentalist groups in the 1992 presidential elections.

DEFORESTATION

By 1993 more than 100 acres of rain forest were being destroyed every hour of the day. The worst victims were the particularly fragile and ecologically rich rain forests in Brazil, Indonesia, and other locations. In the 1990s, attention was also focused on the former Soviet Union, where huge tracts of untapped timber were in danger of uncontrolled exploitation. International pressure to curb deforestation in these areas assumed many forms: diplomacy and negotiations around committee tables; export bans and taxes on tropical wood products in Indonesia, Malaysia, and the Philippines; and such creative alternatives as debt-for-nature swaps. Illustrating this last strategy, in 1987 Conservation International acquired $650,000 of Bolivia's debt in exchange for that government's establishment of a 1.5 million hectares forest reserve to be managed for sustainable development. These and other measures required substantial funding: the World Resources Institute (WRI) estimated a cost of approximately $8 billion to address deforestation between 1985 and 1990 alone.

International concern about deforestation stemmed from links between rates of forest destruction and global warming. Increased carbon dioxide in the earth's atmosphere was shown to trap the sun's heat. Since trees replace the carbon dioxide with oxygen, researchers maintained that fewer trees contributed to more carbon dioxide and faster global warming, with potentially devastating consequences to world ecosystems. In 1991 the Global Change Research Program was initiated by the U.S. Forest Service to increase understanding of climate changes.

Another condition affecting the forestry services industry was the ongoing battle between the use of public and private forest land for market-driven purposes or for more environmentally conscious purposes, whether or not they made money. At the center of this contentious issue stood the fate of old-growth forests in the Pacific Northwest. Actions to protect diverse ecosystems of the ancient forests raised concern over the impact on small, timber-dependent communities. The northern spotted owl, a regional inhabitant protected under the Endangered Species Act of 1990, became a focal point for the differences between environment and industry, and between public and private forest lands. Many critics of the established system proposed complete privatization of timberlands, arguing that the federally managed system of multiple use and sustained yield also lost tremendous amounts of public money. Additionally, a new challenge to the spotted-owl logging protections arose in March

---

1997 when a federal appeals court allowed for new timber industry challenges to Northwest logging reductions that were ordered by President Clinton in 1993. Clinton's Northwest Forest Plan dropped logging levels on national forests in Oregon, Washington, and Northern California to approximately one-fourth the annual averages of the 1980s. The logging industry alleged the administration violated many procedural requirements that prevented government officials who drafted the plan from obtaining critical information that formulated the logging strategy.

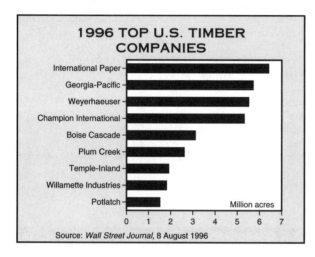

1996 TOP U.S. TIMBER COMPANIES

Source: *Wall Street Journal*, 8 August 1996

NEW FORESTRY INITIATIVES

During into the 1990s, the forest industry saw the enactment of numerous forest-related initiatives. 1991 marked the first year of the America the Beautiful program, in which the U.S. Forest Service worked with state foresters to plant a goal of 970 million trees in rural areas and 30 million trees in urban areas. In March of 1991, the National Tree Trust, a private nonprofit group designed to raise funds for tree planting, opened offices in Washington, D.C. In October of 1993, President Clinton announced the recognition of National Forest Products Week, a period during which Americans were invited to participate in ceremonies and activities calling attention to the need for healthy and productive forests. And following a program calling for ''New Perspectives,'' or ''New Forestry,'' from the 1990s on, the U.S. Forest Service proposed new ways of incorporating the concept of biodiversity into national forestry management.

WORK FORCE

The range in starting salaries for professional foresters is relatively small among public agencies. In the U.S. Forest Service, the minimum pay in 1996 was $18,340, and a person who performed above average in college could earn an annual salary of at least $22,717. Starting salaries for forestry technicians were $2,000 to $4,000 a year less than those for professional foresters. Top salaries of over $50,000 for professionals were common in public agencies, and more successful employees were earning over $60,000 per year.

RESEARCH AND TECHNOLOGY

In the early 1990s, the advent of the technology called GPS, global positioning systems, revolutionized the way foresters do their work. It is comprised of advanced software, computers, and satellites that can locate a point anywhere in the world. Hand-held GPS receiver systems are now available at affordable prices that give an instantaneous readout of the receiver's longitude, latitude, and elevation. Forestry applications include: improved mapping of roads and walking trails; exact acreage measurements for harvesting, planting, or burn sites; better night walking; increased accuracy in finding archaeological sites or specific wildlife habitats; and exceptional tracking of every vehicle in a forest fleet.

AMERICA AND THE WORLD

The issues of deforestation, acid deposition, climate change, and endangered species were problems that crossed national boundaries. During the 1980s and 1990s, natural resource issues helped create an international forestry emphasis. Many U.S. companies and organizations specializing in forestry services increasingly contributed to reforestation efforts in forests from the Amazon to Malaysia. The authorization of the 1990 Farm Bill communicated to the world that the U.S. Forest Service supported forestry services work on an international basis. It coordinated efforts with the Department of State and other organizations to curb deforestation issues at a global level. The Foreign Operations Appropriations Act of 1990 authorized increased funds for international forestry services performed by various agencies including the U.S. Agency for International Development (AID).

Indeed, by the 1990s the forest industry had become international in scope. One example of such internationalism was the decision of the U.S company Applied Energy Services (AES) to reforest 52 million trees in Guatemala in order to offset carbon dioxide emissions from its coal-fired power plant in Connecticut. AES's planting project began in June of 1989, with a projected time frame of ten years and a cost of $15.7 million. In addition, the U.S. Forest Service worked with over 100 organizations and numerous countries on its Tropical Forestry Program. Latin America, the Caribbean, and South Pacific gained the most attention in that area. The U.S. Forest Service also cooperated with foreign countries—including Spain, Israel, and Brazil—in managing fires and forest insect and disease problems.

ASSOCIATIONS AND SOCIETIES

AMERICAN FOREST AND PAPER ASSOCIATION
1111 19th St. NW, Ste. 800
Washington, DC 20036
Phone: (202) 463-2700
Fax: (202) 463-2785

AMERICAN WOOD PRESERVERS INSTITUTE
1945 Old Gallows Rd., Ste. 150
Vienna, VA 22182
Phone: (703) 893-4005
Fax: (703) 893-8492

FOREST PRODUCTS SOCIETY
2801 Marshall Ct.
Madison, WI 53705
Phone: (608) 231-1361
Fax: (608) 231-2152

NATIONAL HARDWOOD LUMBER ASSOCIATION
PO Box 34518
Memphis, TN 38184-0518
Phone: (901) 377-1818
Fax: (901) 382-6419
Members are hardwood lumber and veneer manufacturers and distributors. Users of hardwood products are also members.

WOOD PRODUCTS MANUFACTURERS ASSOCIATION
175 State Rd.
E Westminster, MA 01473-1208
Phone: (508) 874-5445
Fax: (508) 874-9946

PERIODICALS AND NEWSLETTERS

FOREST INDUSTRIES
Miller Freeman, Inc.
600 Harrison St.
San Francisco, CA 94107
Phone: (415) 905-2200
Monthly. $65.00 per Year.

FOREST PRODUCTS JOURNAL
Forest Products Research Society
2801 Marshall Ct.
Madison, WI 53705
Phone: (608) 231-1361
Fax: (608) 231-2152
10 times a year. $135.00 per year.

IN FOCUS
National Forest Products Association
1250 Connecticut Ave. NW, Ste. 200
Washington, DC 20036
Phone: (202) 463-2700
Biweekly. Free to members; non-members, $120.00.

JOURNAL OF SUSTAINABLE FORESTRY
Haworth Press, Inc.
10 Alice St.
Binghamton, NY 13904-1580
Phone: (800) 342-9678 or (607) 722-5857
Fax: (607) 722-1424
Quarterly. $90.00 per year. Two volumes. An academic and practical journal. Topics include forest management, forest economics, and wood science.

WOOD TECHNOLOGY: LOGGING, PULPWOOD, FORESTRY, LUMBER, PANELS
Miller Freeman, Inc.
600 Harrison St.
San Francisco, CA 94107
Phone: (800) 444-4881 or (800) 227-4675
Fax: (913) 841-2624
Monthly. Free to qualified personnel; others, $75.00 per year. Formerly Forest Industries.

DATABASES

AGRICULTURE VIRTUAL LIBRARY
North Carolina State University, National Integrated Pest Management Network
Contains documents, collections, directories, and information about organizations related to agronomy, animal husbandry, fisheries, forestry, horticulture, industrial applications, range management, veterinary medicine, and wildlife management. Includes mirror sites for European users. Time span: Current information. Updating frequency: As needed. Fees: Free. URL: http://ipm_www.ncsu.edu/cernag/cern.html

CAB ABSTRACTS
CAB International North America
845 North Park Ave.
Tucson, AZ 85719
Phone: (800) 528-4841 or (602) 621-7897
Fax: (602) 621-3816
Contains 46 specialized abstract collections covering over 10,000 journals and monographs in the areas of agriculture, horticulture, forest products, farm products, nutrition, dairy science, poultry, grains, animal health, entomology, etc. Time period is 1972 to date, with monthly updates. Inquire as to online cost and availability. CAB Abstracts on CD-ROM also available, with annual updating.

PAPERCHEM DATABASE
Information Services Div.
Institute of Paper Science and Technology
500 10th St. NW
Atlanta, GA 30318
Phone: (404) 853-9500
Fax: (404) 853-9510

*Worldwide coverage of the scientific and technical paper indus-
try chemical literature, including patents, 1967 to present.
Monthly updates. Inquire as to online cost and availability.*

STATISTICS SOURCES

AGRICULTURAL STATISTICS
Available from U.S. Government Printing Office
Washington, DC 20402
Phone: (202) 512-1800
Fax: (202) 512-2250
*Annual. $21.00. Produced by the National Agricultural Statis-
tics Service, U.S. Department of Agriculture. Provides a wide
variety of statistical data relating to agricultural production,
supplies, consumption, prices/price-supports, foreign trade,
costs, and returns, as well as farm labor, loans, income, and
population. In many cases, historical data is shown annually for
10 years. In addition to farm data, includes detailed fishery
statistics.*

LUMBER PRODUCTION AND MILL STOCKS
U.S. Bureau of the Census
Washington, DC 20233-0800
Phone: (301) 457-4100
Fax: (301) 457-3842
Annual. (Current Industrial Reports MA-24T).

TIMBER BULLETIN
Economic Commission for Europe
United Nations Publications
2 United Nations Plz., Rm. DC2-853
New York, NY 10017
Phone: (800) 253-9646 or (212) 963-8302
Fax: (212) 963-3489
*Seven times a year. $95.00 per year. Contains international
statistics on forest products, including price, production, and
foreign trade data.*

UNITED STATES TIMBER PRODUCTION, TRADE, CONSUMPTION, AND PRICE STATISTICS
Forest Service
U.S. Dept. of Agriculture
Washington, DC 20250
Phone: (202) 720-3760
Annual.

YEARBOOK OF FOREST PRODUCTS
Food and Agriculture Organization of the United Nations
Available from UNIPUB
4611-F Assembly Dr.
Lanham, MD 20706-4391
Phone: (800) 274-4888 or (301) 459-2255
Fax: (301) 459-0056
Annual. $50.00. Test in English, French and Spanish.

GENERAL WORKS

DECISION-MAKING IN FOREST MANAGEMENT
M. R. Williams
John Wiley and Sons, Inc.

605 3rd Ave.
New York, NY 10158-0012
Phone: (800) 526-5368 or (212) 850-6000
Fax: (212) 850-6088
*1988. $105.00. Second edition. (Forestry Research Press
Series).*

DIRECTORY OF THE FOREST PRODUCTS INDUSTRY
Miller Freeman, Inc.
600 Harrison St.
San Francisco, CA 94107
Phone: (415) 905-2200
*Biennial. $197.00. Lists sawmills, panelmills, logging opera-
tions, plywood products, wood products, distributors, etc. Geo-
graphic arrangement, with an index to specialties.*

FOREST PRODUCTS AND WOOD SCIENCE: AN INTRODUCTION
John G. Haygreen and Jim L. Bowyer
Iowa State University Press
2121 S. State Ave.
Ames, IA 50014-8300
Phone: (800) 862-6657 or (515) 292-0140
Fax: (515) 292-0140
1989. $45.95. Second revised edition.

INTRODUCTION TO FOREST SCIENCE
Raymond A. Young
John Wiley and Sons, Inc.
605 3rd Ave.
New York, NY 10158-0012
Phone: (800) 225-5945 or (212) 850-6000
Fax: (212) 850-6088
1990. Second edition. Price on application.

WOOD TECHNOLOGY-EQUIPMENT CATALOG AND BUYERS' GUIDE
Miller Freeman, Inc.
600 Harrison St.
San Francisco, CA 94107
Phone: (800) 444-4881 or (800) 227-4675
Fax: (913) 841-2624
*Annual. $55.00. Formerly Forest Industries-Equipment Catalog
and Buyer's Guide.*

FURTHER READING

"Another Green World." *The Economist,* June 1995, p. 74.

National Aerial Firefighting Safety and Efficiency Project
(NAFSEP). Available at http://maps.arc.nasa.gov/

"Quick Facts About Our Industry," Boise Cascade & American
Forest and Paper Association, April 1997. Available at http://
www.bc.com/indust.html

Steen, Harold K. *The U.S. Forest Service.* Seattle, WA: University of Washington Press, 1976.

*World Resources, 1992-93; A Report by The World Resources
Institute.* New York: Oxford University Press, 1992.

FURNITURE, HOUSEHOLD

SIC 2510

The *household furniture industry was expected to expand modestly throughout the remainder of the 1990s. Strong sales of upscale furniture to bay-boomer consumers coupled with high demand for ready-to-assemble (RTA) furniture has created a climate of stability in the industry. Positive growth in the new house and remodeling sectors further ensures the continued success of the household furniture market.*

The $22.2 billion household furniture manufacturing industry is comprised of such segments as wood furniture, upholstered furniture, metal furniture, mattresses, foundations, and convertible beds, and wood cases for audio and visual equipment. The market for wood household furniture—the leading industry segment—has been estimated to be worth over $10.4 billion in 1996. Most furniture sold in this category (30 percent) was for the bedroom; with living rooms, dens, and libraries (20 percent) and kitchens and dining rooms (20 percent) accounting for large shares of the market as well.

 FURNITURE MANUFACTURERS WITH THE GREATEST REVENUES

Ranked by: Revenue in 1995, in millions of dollars.

1. Masco Home Furnishings, with $2,014.0 million
2. Furniture Brands International, $1,073.9
3. La-Z-Boy Chair, $914.9
4. Klaussner Furniture Industries Inc., $655.0
5. LADD, $614.5
6. Thomasville, $550.2
7. Bassett Furniture, $490.8
8. Ethan Allen, $482.4
9. Sauder Woodworking, $465.0
10. Ashley, $370.0

Source: *Furniture/Today*, Top 25 Furniture Manufacturers (annual), May 13, 1996, p. 24.

Ready-to-assemble (RTA) furniture was extremely popular in the 1990s, partly due to an improvement in the quality of the material. Typical products offered wood veneer finishes and details like rounded corners and beveled glass doors. A piece of RTA furniture can be assembled quickly, usually in less than an hour. O'Sullivan Industries has even utilized Velcro fasteners instead of screws to help speed up assembly. An average price of $225 for a ready-to-assemble desk was 65 percent less than a factory-finished product. The low cost of RTA furniture and the ease of stocking it has made it popular among large mass merchandisers and warehouse-type stores, which had themselves become more popular among consumers.

The upholstered furniture industry is defined primarily by the materials with which the products are constructed, rather than the end product itself. All products feature wood frames and fabric or leather upholstery. Establishments within this industry produce a wide range of upholstered furniture for the home, including such upholstered living room furniture as chairs, rockers, couches, sofas, and recliners. Products manufactured in this industry include other household furniture as well as juvenile furniture.

Establishments in this upholstered furniture industry produce goods that are sold to distributors or directly to retailers. Manufacturers produce goods for sale at a variety of price points and under a variety of brand names. *Standard and Poor's Industry Survey* estimated that approximately 44 percent of upholstered furniture is sold through furniture stores, 10 percent through department stores, and 44 percent through mass merchandisers. According to *1995 Annual Survey of Manufactures*, establishments in this industry shipped an estimated $7.45 billion worth of products in 1994. This amount equaled approximately 30 percent of the total sales recorded by the household furniture manufacturing industry as a whole.

The metal furniture industry, which enjoyed its heyday in the early to mid twentieth century, has recently enjoyed a modest comeback. Many consumers have purchased metal furniture items as part of a kind of retro-fashion movement designed to capture the nostalgia of the 1950s. Moreover, throughout the 1990s metal furniture was still prevalent in schools and hospitals. In addition, the popularity of daybeds and futons in the mid 1990s has lead to a slight resurgence in the metal furniture industry. Metal chairs and tables are still being produced in the United States today. The newer, 1990s forms of furniture are geared towards works of art rather than functional pieces of furniture.

The industry sector that manufactures mattresses, foundations, and convertible beds sold approximately $3.5 billion dollars worth of products in 1995, an increase of about 8 percent over 1993 figures, according to the *1995 Annual Survey of Manufactures*. These manufacturers create products to be sold under different brand names at a variety of price points. A high quality mattress can cost the retail consumer as much as $899 or more. Establishments in this industry distribute their goods to specialty stores that deal only in mattresses and foundations. According to the 1994 edition of *Standard and Poor's Industry Surveys,* 45 percent of bedding is sold through such stores, followed by discount stores and department stores, which sell 13 and 12 percent of manufacturer's goods, respectively.

Another segment of the larger household furniture industry is comprised of companies principally employed in manufacturing wood cases for audio and visual equipment. This industry produces such products as wooden speaker boxes, stereo cabinets, sewing machine cases, and television cabinets. About 60 percent of industry output in the early 1990s consisted of TV cabinets, or cases for combinations of TV, stereo, or radio. Stereo and radio cabinets constituted 20 percent of the market. Wooden sewing machine cases accounted for only 3 percent of industry sales, and miscellaneous items comprised the remainder of revenues. Radio and television manufacturers consumed nearly 85 percent of industry production in the early 1990s. Personal consumption expenditures represented less than 8 percent of sales.

INDUSTRY OUTLOOK

Furniture manufacturers benefited from an expanding market in the early 1990s, leading to approximately 5 to 6 percent growth between 1992 and 1993 alone. The industry is influenced by the rate of new home construction and the number of existing homes being remodeled. *Standard and Poor's* estimated that the upholstered wood household furniture industry alone will continue to

SIC 2512 - Upholstered Household Furniture Industry Data by State

State	Establish- ments	Shipments			Employment				Cost as % of Shipments	Investment per Employee ($)
		Total ($ mil)	% of U.S.	Per Establ.	Total Number	% of U.S.	Per Establ.	Wages ($/hour)		
North Carolina	288	1,929.9	31.0	6.7	24,200	30.6	84	9.39	52.9	851
Mississippi	135	1,537.1	24.7	11.4	18,200	23.0	135	8.63	56.2	1,132
California	195	626.5	10.1	3.2	7,700	9.7	39	8.73	50.6	506
Tennessee	58	584.6	9.4	10.1	8,700	11.0	150	7.84	45.8	1,034
Indiana	22	148.5	2.4	6.8	1,600	2.0	73	9.20	58.6	-
Iowa	6	145.1	2.3	24.2	1,700	2.1	283	9.89	53.2	-
Missouri	8	137.8	2.2	17.2	1,600	2.0	200	9.42	43.7	-
Pennsylvania	36	125.4	2.0	3.5	1,400	1.8	39	7.63	50.4	643
Texas	44	115.9	1.9	2.6	1,600	2.0	36	6.93	44.4	688
Virginia	15	94.3	1.5	6.3	1,300	1.6	87	7.81	59.7	-

Source: 1992 *Economic Census.* The states are in descending order of shipments or establishments (if shipment data are missing for the majority). The symbol (D) appears when data are withheld to prevent disclosure of competitive information. States marked with (D) are sorted by number of establishments. A dash (-) indicates that the data element cannot be calculated; * indicates the midpoint of a range.

SIC 2511 Occupations Employed by SIC 251 - Household Furniture		
Occupation	% of Total 1994	Change to 2005
Assemblers, fabricators, & hand workers nec	13.5	-6.7
Upholsterers	7.7	12.4
Sewing machine operators, non-garment	7.1	26.0
Woodworking machine workers	5.6	-25.3
Cabinetmakers & bench carpenters	4.8	58.6
Wood machinists	4.5	30.6
Blue collar worker supervisors	3.9	-13.5
Furniture finishers	3.7	21.8
Head sawyers & sawing machine workers	3.0	-39.3
Helpers, laborers, & material movers nec	2.9	-6.7
Freight, stock, & material movers, hand	2.5	-25.3
Coating, painting, & spraying machine workers	2.0	16.6
Hand packers & packagers	1.9	-20.0
Truck drivers light & heavy	1.9	-3.8
General managers & top executives	1.7	-11.5
Machine feeders & offbearers	1.7	-16.0
Traffic, shipping, & receiving clerks	1.7	-10.2
Cutters & trimmers, hand	1.6	-6.7
Sales & related workers nec	1.5	-6.7
Inspectors, testers, & graders, precision	1.5	-6.7
Grinders & polishers, hand	1.2	-25.4
General office clerks	1.1	-20.4
Precision woodworkers nec	1.0	2.7

Source: Industry-Occupation Matrix, Bureau of Labor Statistics. These data relate to one or more 3-digit SIC industry groups rather than to a single 4-digit SIC. The change reported for each occupation to the year 2005 is a percent of growth or decline as estimated by the Bureau of Labor Statistics. The abbreviation nec stands for 'not elsewhere classified'.

expand through the mid-1990s due to changing demographics. Baby Boomers are "getting older and richer and will soon want nicer things to suit their more upscale lifestyles."

In addition to a broadening market, new retailing techniques are affecting the furniture industry. *Standard and Poor's* noted a growing tendency among manufacturers to enter into agreement with a retailer to open a gallery devoted to the manufacturer's goods, a concept that has been "very successful in attracting customers and generating sales." The arrangement is mutually advantageous because the retailer has proprietary rights on the goods while the manufacturer gets a dedicated retail outlet for its merchandise.

The only serious threat to the household furniture industry during the 1990s has been the prospect of dealing with some government regulation. The Environmental Protection Agency attempted to reduce volatile organic compound (VOC) emissions from chemicals used in furniture finishes. However, the furniture industry was able to postpone some environmental legislation.

WORK FORCE

The wood household furniture industry employed over 125,000 people in the United States in the

mid-1990s. Next to the wood furniture sector, the upholstered furniture industry is an important source of jobs. According to the *1995 Annual Survey of Manufactures,* the industry employs approximately 89,700 people and maintains a payroll of approximately \$1.91 billion. The employment figures were up from the *1992 Census of Manufactures,* which reported employment of only 79,200 people, and from the previous 1987 data, which reported employment of 82,100. The household furniture industry is generally populated by smaller manufacturing facilities. Of the approximately 840 establishments in operation, about 500 had less than 20 employees.

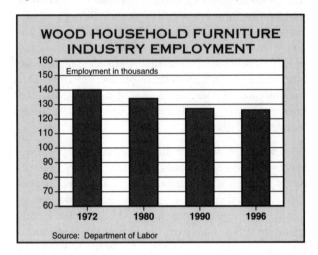

WOOD HOUSEHOLD FURNITURE INDUSTRY EMPLOYMENT

Employment in thousands

Source: Department of Labor

AMERICA AND THE WORLD

Most exports of American wood household furniture went to Canada (39 percent), Mexico (12 percent), and Saudi Arabia (9 percent). Imports came from Taiwan (29 percent), Canada (14 percent), and Mexico (7 percent). International trade liberalization agreements such as the General Agreement on Tarrifs and Trade (GATT) and the North American Free Trade Agreement (NAFTA) were likely to increase U.S. exports of wood household furniture, though developing nations were poised to pursue aggressive forest management and export policies.

ASSOCIATIONS AND SOCIETIES

AMERICAN FURNITURE MANUFACTURERS ASSOCIATION
PO Box HP-7
High Point, NC 27261
Phone: (919) 884-5000
Fax: (919) 884-5303

NATIONAL HOME FURNISHINGS ASSOCIATION
PO Box 2396
High Point, NC 27261
Phone: (800) 888-9590 or (919) 883-1650
Fax: (919) 883-1195

NATIONAL MOVING AND STORAGE ASSOCIATION
11150 Main St., Ste. 402
Fairfax, VA 22030-5066
Phone: (800) 538-6672 or (703) 761-8813
Fax: (703) 934-9712

UNITED FURNITURE WORKERS OF AMERICA INSURANCE AND PENSION FUND
1910 Airlane Rd.
Nashville, TN 37224
Phone: (615) 889-8860

PERIODICALS AND NEWSLETTERS

FDM: FURNITURE DESIGN AND MANUFACTURING
Cahners Publishing Co.
PO Box 5080
Des Plaines, IL 60017-5080
Phone: (800) 662-7776 or (708) 635-8800
Fax: (708) 390-2618
Monthly. $55.00 per year. Edited for furniture executives, production managers, and designers. Covers the manufacturing of household, office, and institutional furniture, store fixtures, and kitchen and bathroom cabinets.

FURNITURE/TODAY: THE WEEKLY BUSINESS NEWSPAPER OF THE FURNITURE INDUSTRY
Cahners Business Newspapers
7025 Albert Pick Rd.
Greensboro, NC 27409
Phone: (910) 605-0121
Fax: (910) 605-1143
Weekly. $79.95 per year.

FURNITURE WORLD
Towse Publishing Co.
530 5th Ave.
Pelham, NY 10803-1206
Phone: (914) 738-6744
Fax: (914) 738-6820
Monthly. $16.00 per year. Formerly Furniture World and Furniture Buyer and Decorator.

HFD (HOME FURNISHING DAILY)
Fairchild Fashion and Merchandising Group
7 W. 34th St.
New York, NY 10001
Phone: (800) 247-6622 or (212) 630-3880
Weekly. $44.95 per year.

DATABASES

CITIBASE (CITICORP ECONOMIC DATABASE)
FAME Software Corp.
77 Water St., 9 Fl.
New York, NY 10005
Phone: (212) 898-7800
Fax: (212) 742-8956
Presents over 6,000 statistical series relating to business, industry, finance, and economics. Includes series from Survey of Current Business *and many other sources. Time period is 1947 to date, with daily updates. Inquire as to online cost and availability.*

STATISTICS SOURCES

BUSINESS STATISTICS
Available from U.S. Government Printing Office
Washington, DC 20402
Phone: (202) 512-1800
Fax: (202) 512-2250
Biennial. $20.00. Issued by Bureau of Economic Analysis, U.S. Department of Commerce. Shows annual data for 29 years and monthly data for a recent four-year period. Statistics correspond to the Survey of Current Business.

FAIRCHILD FACT FILE: HOUSEHOLD FURNITURE AND BEDDING
Fairchild Publications
7 W. 34th St.
New York, NY 10001
Phone: (800) 247-6622 or (212) 630-3880
Fax: (212) 630-3868
Biennial. $25.00. Provides statistical and analytical marketing data, including industry concentration, materials consumed, import/export sales, value of shipments, retail sales by outlet type, advertising expenditures, consumer buying habits, and industry trends.

SURVEY OF CURRENT BUSINESS
Available from U.S. Government Printing Office
Washington, DC 20402
Phone: (202) 512-1800
Fax: (202) 512-2250
Monthly. $41.00 per year. Issued by Bureau of Economic Analysis, U.S. Department of Commerce. Presents a wide variety of business and economic data.

GENERAL WORKS

DIRECTORY OF HOME FURNISHINGS RETAILERS
Chain Store Guide Information Services
3922 Coconut Palm Rd.
Tampa, Fl 33619
Phone: (800) 925-2288 or (813) 664-6700
Fax: (813) 664-6810
Annual. $269.00. Includes furniture retailers and wholesalers.

FURNITURE DESIGN AND MANUFACTURING: SOURCE OF SUPPLY DIRECTORY ISSUE
Delta Communications, Inc.
455 N. Cityfront Plaza Dr., 24 Fl.
Phone: (312) 222-2000
Fax: (312) 222-2026
Annual. $25.00. Product-classified list of over 1,800 suppliers to the furniture and cabinet industries.

FURTHER READING

Adams, Larry. "Soft Landing Means Economy to Grow, But Slow." *Wood and Wood Products,* January 1996.

American Furniture Manufacturers Association. High Point, NC.

Darnay, Arsen J., ed. *Manufacturing USA.* Detroit: Gale Research, 1996.

Drill, Larry. "Stop the Ax." *Modern Paint and Coatings,* August 1996.

U.S. Bureau of the Census. *1995 Census of Manufactures.* Washington: GPO, 1997.

U.S. Bureau of the Census. *Annual Survey of Manufactures.* Washington: GPO, 1997.

Ward's Business Directory of U.S. Private and Public Companies. Detroit: Gale Research 1997.

The glass products industry remained contradictory in the 1990s, with some segments of the industry (such as purchased glass products) experiencing significant growth, and others (glass containers) continuing to decline. In the mid-1990s, there were 1,537 establishments in the purchased glass products industry, an increase of approximately 8 percent since 1989. In 1995, the industry shipped $7.9 billion worth of products, a 29 percent increase over 1990. The pressed and blown glass industry had 500 establishments in 1996, producing shipments valued at $5 billion in 1996. However, shipments were down for the glass containers segment of the industry, from $4.9 billion in 1990 to $4.3 billion in 1995, a decrease of 12 percent. Despite aggressive industry promotions to increase the use of glass containers, the market did not pick up.

GLASS PRODUCTS

SICs 3220, 3230

By 1998, the value of purchased glass shipments is expected to rise to $9.5 billion, up 20 percent from 1995. The value of pressed and blown glass shipments is also expected to increase to $5.23 billion in 1998, up 4 percent from 1996. Overall projections for employment in the glass industry were not bright going into the twenty-first century. All positions except extruding and forming machine workers, which were expected to increase about 22 percent, were expected to decrease in numbers by 33 to 51 percent by the year 2005.

 **LEADING CHEMICAL PROCESSING COMPANIES MANUFACTURING GLASS AND GLASS PRODUCTS**

Ranked by: Sales in 1995, in millions of dollars.

1. Corning, with $5,346.1 million
2. Owens-Illinois, $3,763.2
3. Owens-Corning, $3,612
4. Ball Corp., $2,591.7
5. USG Corp., $2,444
6. Schuller, $1,391.5
7. Texas Industries, $830.5
8. Lancaster Colony Corp., $795.1
9. Southdown, $596.1
10. Global Industrial Technology, $594.3

Source: *ChemicalWeek*, ChemicalWeek 300 (annual), May 8, 1996, p. 56.

The pressed and blown glass industry in the mid-1990s experienced low margins, high competition, and high technology. While glass tableware and cooking dishes did not share the high-tech image of fiber optic cables and devices, research and development continued for better materials for these purposes. Likewise, new marketing approaches, such as creative packaging and merchandizing, were constantly investigated.

In 1996, production of glass containers amounted to 253.8 million gross; shipments amounted to 257.3 million gross. At best, the glass container industry can be described as flat. Continued overcapacity and the threat of conversion to alternative packaging stands to keep price increases in the 3.0 to 3.5 percent range. Since the 1980s, the glass container market has suffered a steady loss of market share to alternate plastic and can packaging. Analysts point to the beer industry as a major factor causing the decline of the glass container industry. More than 85 percent of the decline was due to brewers switching to aluminum cans, and the lingering residual of this change still poses an imminently significant threat. Statistics may well support this threat. Although shipment and production of beer bottles remain high, at about 88 million, analysts feared a decline as higher price tags forced consumers to switch to lower-price canned beer.

ENVIRONMENTAL ISSUES

Flexibility may determine the glass container's response to its environmental challenges. Glass is 100 percent recyclable. A used glass container can be melted and repeatedly made into a new glass container. Furthermore, glass recycling creates no additional waste or by-products. Yet glass recycling ranks lower than that of plastic. The Glass Packaging Institute (GPI), the glass container industry's trade group, questions the EPA's statistics quoting the recycling rate for glass at 10 to 12 percent, plastic at 20 percent, and aluminum cans at 55 percent. Still, glass retains a positive recyclability per-

ception. In contrast, recyclability of plastic beverage containers is accepted by only 20.7 percent of consumers.

Recent testimony before a Congressional subcommittee by the Glass Packaging Institute cited three major problems for the glass industry's recycling program: (1) because plants are located primarily on the East and West coasts and the Southeast, transporting recycled glass from community collection facilities to these plants proves expensive; (2) recycling of increasing amounts of imported green containers exceeds the domestic demand for these containers; and (3) because of loose quality control at local collection sites, mixing recyclable and nonrecyclable glass damages the manufacturing process. The most viable recycling solution, according to some experts, comes from less packaging. In the last ten years, 16-ounce glass bottles have been reduced by 30 percent, thus lowering the amounts of materials and waste.

Another industry drawback related to recycling and cited by the GPI relates to forced deposit laws requiring a consumer to pay a deposit and then return the containers to the store for a refund. The industry perceives such legislation as devastating to the market share of environmentally friendly glass containers and argues that it sways consumers to use plastic. GPI believes the most effective way to reduce solid waste is not forced deposit laws, but comprehensive curbside recycling. The practice of bottle refilling as an alternative to recycling may experience a comeback.

SIC 3221 - Glass Containers
General Statistics

| Year | Com-panies | Establishments | | Employment | | | Compensation | | Production ($ million) | | | | |
		Total	with 20 or more employees	Total (000)	Production Workers (000)	Hours (Mil)	Payroll ($ mil)	Wages ($/hr)	Cost of Materials	Value Added by Manufacture	Value of Shipments	Capital Invest.
1982	41	128	113	59.0	51.7	101.0	1,306.4	10.81	2,521.8	2,739.1	5,216.8	297.4
1983		124	109	55.0	48.1	94.3	1,295.0	11.52	2,402.9	2,492.5	4,860.2	187.0
1984		120	105	48.5	42.3	79.8	1,191.7	12.39	2,187.2	2,246.2	4,478.5	185.3
1985		117	102	44.1	38.5	76.9	1,144.4	12.53	2,143.2	2,406.4	4,600.3	182.9
1986		107	93	42.8	37.8	75.8	1,083.4	12.10	1,997.3	2,649.5	4,627.4	211.4
1987	35	106	93	41.1	36.0	70.8	1,065.2	12.60	2,037.9	2,766.2	4,777.9	226.6
1988		104	94	39.7	34.5	71.0	1,083.5	12.68	2,090.8	2,697.3	4,704.4	239.8
1989		102	92	39.5	34.5	65.0	1,073.3	13.63	2,256.9	2,599.4	4,812.2	214.4
1990		99	88	37.6	32.1	62.2	1,076.1	14.38	2,287.2	2,751.4	4,946.1	258.0
1991		99	84	34.5	30.1	59.7	1,068.9	14.84	2,213.7	2,635.4	4,888.3	285.6
1992	16	76	76	32.3	28.1	57.3	1,052.4	15.28	1,903.7	3,038.4	4,859.6	233.0
1993		78	74	30.6	26.4	53.0	999.1	15.87	1,879.9	2,750.3	4,824.8	218.4
1994		77P	72P	28.8	25.0	49.9	962.8	16.00	1,778.0	2,903.3	4,681.3	238.2
1995		73P	69P	25.3P	21.8P	44.1P	941.3P	16.39P	1,814.7P	2,963.2P	4,777.9P	243.8P
1996		68P	65P	23.1P	19.8P	40.3P	917.5P	16.82P	1,814.0P	2,962.1P	4,776.1P	245.9P
1997		64P	62P	20.8P	17.8P	36.5P	893.7P	17.24P	1,813.3P	2,961.0P	4,774.3P	248.0P
1998		60P	59P	18.6P	15.8P	32.7P	869.9P	17.66P	1,812.6P	2,959.8P	4,772.5P	250.0P

Sources: 1982, 1987, 1992 *Economic Census*; *Annual Survey of Manufactures*, 83-86, 88-91, 93-94. Establishment counts for non-Census years are from *County Business Patterns*; establishment values for 83-84 are extrapolations. 'P's show projections by the editors. Industries reclassified in 87 will not have data for prior years.

The Glass Packaging Institute noted that the 1990s began with five major bottling companies switching from plastic to glass containers, citing as reasons consumer preference, environmental climate, and packaging costs. According to investment analysts, however, falling resin prices could be an omen signaling a return to plastic. Until the glass container industry develops a more cost-competitive, lighter weight, or break-resistant package, analysts foresee fewer gains derived from the anticipated growth of the soft drink market.

Another challenge facing the glass container industry involves raw materials leftover from the manufacturing process. According to an industry spokesperson, only 85-90 percent of the melted raw materials are converted to a marketable product. The remaining 10-15 percent of raw material becomes cullet or discarded waste, mostly broken glass. Industry leaders are attempting to devise satisfactory uses for this cullet.

ORGANIZATION AND STRUCTURE

Firms in the purchased glass products industry are distinguished from other glass manufacturing firms—known as primary glass manufacturers—in that products are not made directly from raw glass materials but from secondary glass purchased from other companies.

Companies within the industry manufacture everyday home glass products, such as mirrors, beverage glasses, lighting fixture glass, window glass, and automobile glass. Industry products are also used in an extensive number of industrial, technical, and other non-household applications such as safety and bullet-proof glass, industrial safety glasses and welding lenses, cathode ray tube screens, and high-tolerance specialty glass products such as elapsed-time indicators and gravity-sensing electrolytic transducers.

Another industry segment, pressed and blown glass, experienced a resurgence of interest in the United States, and small craft shops could be found across the country where artisans sold their wares, displayed their techniques, and often taught classes. However, these shops were generally neither involved nor interested in producing the mass quantities of machine-made glassware supplied by such large corporations as the Corning conglomerate.

Product share within the industry was split between six types of goods. Textile glass fiber accounted for 30.82 percent of the overall market; machine-made table, kitchen, art, and novelty glassware claimed 19.13 percent; machine-made lighting and electronic glassware took another 28.27 percent; all other machine-made glassware accounted for 15.79 percent; handmade pressed and blown glassware claimed 2.89 percent; and pressed and blown glass not specified by kind comprised 3.10 percent. Materials consumed in the greatest amounts by the industry included plastic film and sheets, unsupported glass, all types of glass sand, and paperboard boxes.

The glass container industry manufactures two basic types of containers: narrow neck and wide mouth containers. The industry further classifies containers by their end use, creating categories of glass designated for food, beverages, beer, liquor, wine; chemical, household, and industrial uses; toiletries and cosmetics; and other uses including medicinal and health supplies. Wide mouth and narrow neck bottles are used interchangeably, depending on the product, but tradition or utility occasionally dictates specific bottle types. For example, milk is normally packaged in wide mouth containers, both wide mouth and narrow neck bottles are used for cosmetics, while narrow neck bottles are more practical for perfumes.

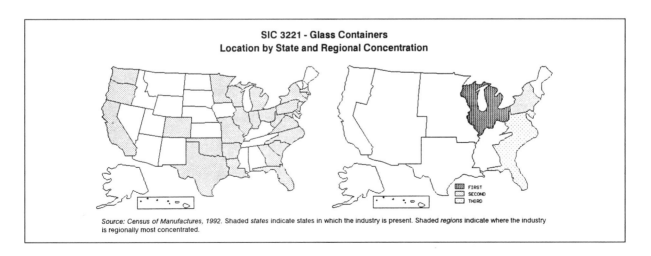

SIC 3221 - Glass Containers
Location by State and Regional Concentration

FIRST
SECOND
THIRD

Source: Census of Manufactures, 1992. Shaded states indicate states in which the industry is present. Shaded regions indicate where the industry is regionally most concentrated.

WORK FORCE

Employment has increased steadily in the purchased glass industry, from 50,000 in the mid-1980s to an estimated 62,000 by 1996. Production workers comprised 76 percent (47,800) of all employees in the industry, an increase of 5 percent since 1990. Production workers' average hourly earnings were $10.92 in 1995, up 12 percent since 1990. Employment in the pressed and blown glass industry in 1996 was estimated at 33,200—with 27,600 working in production. The average hourly wage had increased to $15.18. The glass containers industry employed a total of 25,500 in 1995, down 32 percent since 1990. Production workers' average weekly hours were 44.2 in 1995, down from 42.1 in 1990. Production workers' average hourly earnings were $14.51 in 1995, up from $13.16 in 1990.

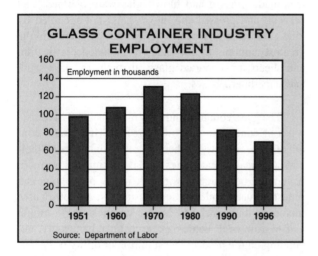

GLASS CONTAINER INDUSTRY EMPLOYMENT

Employment in thousands

Source: Department of Labor

Noting significant improvements in labor productivity per unit, an Owens-Illinois spokesperson commented that producing a quality product still requires an excessive amount of work. Labor constitutes 35 percent of the cost of glass, but only 9 percent and 13 percent for cans and plastic, respectively. Although use of sophisticated control systems in the future will require more operator interpretation rather than intervention, production workers must be better trained and more knowledgeable than most manufacturing employees.

RESEARCH AND TECHNOLOGY

To date, a few technologies have demonstrated capacity for breaking up oil and grease found in glass container plant wastewater. One technology consists of carbon absorption, a process in which wastewater passes through a bed of activated carbon that absorbs the oil and grease. This process is more applicable to small flows with relatively low oil and grease loadings. The process of chemical coagulation followed by dissolved air flotation (DAF) is another process where chemical emulsion breakers and other processes are added to wastewater to break emulsion. DAF has been successfully used and research studies continue to study various emulsion breaking chemistries.

Since 1975, compliance with national standards has enabled glass container manufacturers to make significant improvements in control of oil and grease in wastewater. In the 1990s, companies placed greater emphasis on research and development to upgrade wastewater treatment technologies to comply with stringent state and local effluent standards.

In the future, the recyclable features of glass products could play a major role in safe disposal of hazardous waste, according to the editor of *Glass Industry*. The Department of Energy opened a new $1.3-billion Defense Waste Processing Facility in South Carolina designed to test the feasibility of encasing radioactive materials in glass. This process, known as vitrification, entails encasing hazardous waste in "logs" of strong glass, wrapped in steel. Steel cylinders measuring 10 feet high and 2 feet around each hold 165 gallons of waste.

SIC 3221
Occupations Employed by SIC 322 - Glass and Glassware, Pressed Or Blown

Occupation	% of Total 1994	Change to 2005
Inspectors, testers, & graders, precision	13.6	-39.1
Hand packers & packagers	7.9	-47.8
Helpers, laborers, & material movers nec	7.4	-39.1
Extruding & forming machine workers	7.1	-33.0
Extruding & forming machine workers	5.9	21.9
Industrial machinery mechanics	4.9	-33.0
Blue collar worker supervisors	4.9	-41.9
Industrial truck & tractor operators	3.9	-39.1
Assemblers, fabricators, & hand workers nec	3.3	-39.1
Packaging & filling machine operators	3.2	-39.1
Machine feeders & offbearers	3.2	-45.2
Maintenance repairers, general utility	2.4	-45.1
Furnace, kiln, or kettle operators	2.1	-63.5
Precision workers nec	2.0	-45.2
Freight, stock, & material movers, hand	1.9	-51.2
Crushing & mixing machine operators	1.5	-39.1
Machine forming operators, metal & plastic	1.5	-39.1
Machinists	1.2	-39.1
Grinders & polishers, hand	1.1	-39.1
Electricians	1.1	-42.8
Industrial production managers	1.1	-39.1
Engineering technicians & technologists nec	1.0	-39.1

Source: *Industry-Occupation Matrix*, Bureau of Labor Statistics. These data relate to one or more 3-digit SIC industry groups rather than to a single 4-digit SIC. The change reported for each occupation to the year 2005 is a percent of growth or decline as estimated by the Bureau of Labor Statistics. The abbreviation nec stands for 'not elsewhere classified'.

Parallelling this project was an experiment during the 1990s at the California-based Lawrence Livermore National Laboratory on radioactivity released from glass. A computer model was designed to predict the release of radioactivity, if any, from a nuclear waste repository incorporating glass. To ensure adequate leakage prevention of harmful radioactive material from glass, scientists performed a variety of laboratory experiments and computer simulations of potential environmental scenarios that might be affected by radioactive leaks.

Large and small glass container manufacturers have spent millions for high-tech equipment and computerized operations. Part of the $40 million Anchor Glass expended in the 1990s was for the installation of sophisticated quality control equipment on all the company's production lines. Wheaton Glass completed a $10-million investment in manufacturing operations of containers for the parenteral drug and the cosmetics industries. Over a period of three years, Kerr invested in excess of $22 million for improvements such as computerized furnace control systems, high-productivity forming machines, and quality control equipment.

ASSOCIATIONS AND SOCIETIES

ASSOCIATED GLASS AND POTTERY MANUFACTURERS
c/o Kingwood Ceramics, Inc.
373 Maple Dr.
Greensburg, PA 15601
Phone: (412) 834-8822

ALUMINUM, BRICK AND GLASS WORKERS INTERNATIONAL UNION
3362 Hollenberg Dr.
Bridgeton, MO 63044
Phone: (314) 739-6142
Fax: (314) 739-1216

GLASS ASSOCIATION OF NORTH AMERICA
White Lakes Professional Bldg.
3310 SW Harrison St.
Topeka, KS 66611-2279
Phone: (913) 266-7013
Fax: (913) 266-0272

NATIONAL GLASS ASSOCIATION
8200 Greensboro Dr., 3 Fl.
Mc Lean, VA 22102-3881
Phone: (703) 442-4890
Fax: (703) 442-0603

SEALED INSULATING GLASS MANUFACTURERS ASSOCIATION
401 N. Michigan Ave.
Chicago, IL 60611
Phone: (312) 644-6610
Fax: (312) 321-6869

PERIODICALS AND NEWSLETTERS

AMERICAN GLASS REVIEW
Doctorow Communications, Inc.
1033 Clifton Ave.
Clifton, NJ 07013
Phone: (201) 779-1600
Fax: (201) 779-3242
Monthly. $25.00 per year. Covers the manufacture, distribution and processing of flat glass, industrial glass, scientific and optical glass, etc. Includes American Glass Review Glass Factory Directory.

GLASS DIGEST: MANAGEMENT MAGAZINE SERVING THE FLAT GLASS, ARCHITECTURAL METAL AND ALLIED PRODUCTS INDUSTRY
Ashlee Publishing Co., Inc.
310 Madison Ave., Ste. 1926
New York, NY 10017-6098
Phone: (212) 682-7681
Fax: (212) 697-8331
Monthly. $30.00 per year.

GLASS MAGAZINE
National Glass Association
8200 Greensboro Dr., Ste. 302
Mc Lean, VA 22102
Phone: (703) 442-4890
Fax: (703) 442-0630
Monthly. $34.95 per year.

U.S. GLASS, METAL, AND GLAZING
Key Communications, Inc.
PO Box 569
Garrisonville, VA 22463
Phone: (540) 720-5584
Fax: (540) 720-5687
Monthly. $35.00 per year. Edited for glass fabricators, glaziers, distributors, and retailers. Special feature issues are devoted to architectural glass, mirror glass, windows, storefronts, hardware, machinery, sealants, and adhesives. Regular topics include automobile glass and fenestration (window design and placement).

DATABASES

***CITIBASE* (CITICORP ECONOMIC DATABASE)**
FAME Software Corp.
77 Water St., 9 Fl.
New York, NY 10005
Phone: (212) 898-7800
Fax: (212) 742-8956
Presents over 6,000 statistical series relating to business, industry, finance, and economics. Includes series from Survey of Current Business *and many other sources. Time period is 1947 to date, with daily updates. Inquire as to online cost and availability.*

STATISTICS SOURCES

BUSINESS STATISTICS
Available from U.S. Government Printing Office
Washington, DC 20402
Phone: (202) 512-1800
Fax: (202) 512-2250
Biennial. $20.00. Issued by Bureau of Economic Analysis, U.S. Department of Commerce. Shows annual data for 29 years and monthly data for a recent four-year period. Statistics correspond to the Survey of Current Business.

SURVEY OF CURRENT BUSINESS
Available from U.S. Government Printing Office
Washington, DC 20402
Phone: (202) 512-1800
Fax: (202) 512-2250
Monthly. $41.00 per year. Issued by Bureau of Economic Analysis, U.S. Department of Commerce. Presents a wide variety of business and economic data.

GENERAL WORKS

THE CONSTITUTION OF GLASSES: A DYNAMIC INTERPRETATION
W.A. Weyl and E.C. Marboe
Books on Demand
300 N. Zeeb Rd.

Ann Arbor, MI 48106-1346
Phone: (800) 521-0600 or (313) 761-4700
Fax: (313) 665-5022
Vol. 1, $111.80; Vol. 2, part 1, $121.20; Vol. 2, part 2, $160.00. Three volumes.

GLASS SCIENCE
Robert H. Doremus
John Wiley and Sons, Inc.
605 3rd Ave.
New York, NY 10158-0012
Phone: (800) 526-5368 or (212) 850-6000
Fax: (212) 850-6088
1994. $74.95. Second edition.

FURTHER READING

Darnay, Arsen J. *Manufacturing USA.* 5th ed. Detroit: Gale Research, 1996.

"Hoover's Online." Austin, TX: Hoover's, Inc., 1997. Available from http://www.hoovers.com.

U.S. Bureau of the Census. *1995 Annual Survey of Manufactures.* Washington: GPO, 1997.

Department of Commerce. "Glass Containers: Summary for 1996." *Current Industrial Reports.* Washington: GPO, 1996.

INDUSTRY SNAPSHOT

There were approximately 18,000 hardware stores in the United States in 1996. There were also roughly 10,000 home centers, which combine goods related to hardware retailing with those associated with building materials retailing. Most hardware stores were independently owned. The average hardware store had sales of more than $1 million annually in the 1990s. The average home center was considerably larger, with sales of about $4 million. Warehouse home centers were even larger and averaged between $12 million and $15 million in annual sales. As a whole, hardware retailing was worth approximately $15.2 billion in 1996, according to the U.S. Census Bureau, a 21 percent increase over 1990 in current dollars and an 83 percent current dollar increase over 1980.

HARDWARE AND HAND TOOLS

SICs 3420, 5251

Industry experts project that the hardware and hand tools industry will continue to benefit from consumers in the home improvement market until at least 2015. However, independent and small hardware stores will face stiff competition from an increasing number of hardware warehouse stores like Home Depot and superstores such as Walmart and Kmart.

Top 10 BEST HARDWARE BRANDS ACCORDING TO DISCOUNTERS

Ranked by: Percent of discounters naming brand as best in 1995.

1. Black & Decker, with 63%
2. Stanley, 47%
3. General Electric, 18%
4. Popular Mechanics, 12%
5. Rubbermaid, 5%
5. Skil, 5%
5. Shop Vac, 5%
5. Glidden, 5%
5. BenchTop, 5%
10. Bull Dog, 3%

Source: *Discount Store News,* Top Brands Survey (annual), October 16, 1995, p. 82.

The retail hardware industry manufactures a diverse range of products, including saw blades and handsaws, hand edge tools, brackets, clamps, couplings, door locks, fireplace equipment, handcuffs, nut crackers, and piano hardware. In 1995 industry shipments reached $10.6 billion, according to the *1995 Census of Manufactures*—an increase of 26 percent over the 1987 figures, but an increase of only about 1 percent over the 1994 figures. Employment in the industry decreased during the 1994-95 period, going down from 79,000 to 77,800 employees. Payrolls, however, increased during the same period, rising from $2.26 billion to $2.28 billion, an increase of 0.8 percent.

INDUSTRY OUTLOOK

Throughout the 1990s, the retail hardware industry maintained a strong market performance. A survey by *Do-It-Yourself Retailing Magazine* in 1992 found that 80 percent of all households were involved in some type of home improvement activity. In addition, the survey found that home improvement activity should remain strong at least until 2015, when the last of the baby boom generation grows beyond the prime do-it-yourself age. In the early 1990s, there were more than 80 million Americans in the 25- to 45-year-old age group, which is considered the prime group for home improvement projects, compared to about 60 million in 1980, which suggested a strong future for the industry.

However, there were concerns that the industry had peaked in terms of real growth in the 1980s. Retail sales for all hardware outlets were generally flat from 1989 to 1992. This led to concerns that the industry faced a future of segmentation and consolidation, led by the chain stores at the expense of the independents. Optimists, however, pointed to the fact that independent hardware retailers still accounted for about half of the industry's total sales in 1992. Convenience, including proximity, rather than price, was the deciding purchasing factor for the majority of hardware buyers.

Most retail hardware stores were still family-owned businesses in the 1990s, many with histories extending back four or five generations. In the majority of these stores, sons and daughters worked along side their parents. However, only about half of the owners responding to a survey by *Hardware Age Magazine* in 1990 expected the stores to pass on to the next generation. Those who expected someday to sell their stores to outsiders cited hard work, long hours, an uncertain future, and a lower-class image for hardware store owners as contributing factors to the decreasing appeal of hardware store ownership. Cotter & Company even established an intergenerational transition program for store owners.

Hardware stores sold outside the family were often purchased by long-time employees. Many hardware stores established employee stock ownership programs that made it easier for employees to take over ownership someday. The industry also reported renewed interest in store ownership from former business executives who left their jobs either voluntarily or involuntarily during corporate downsizing. About 85 percent of the store owners in the *Hardware Age* survey believed it was likely their stores would still be operating in 2000.

Store owners also were more likely to cite competition from discount retailers such as Kmart and Wal-Mart as the most serious threat to their businesses, rather than from other hardware stores or home centers. Financially,

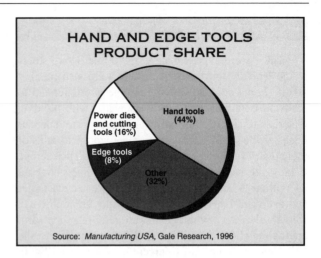

HAND AND EDGE TOOLS PRODUCT SHARE

Power dies and cutting tools (16%)
Hand tools (44%)
Edge tools (8%)
Other (32%)

Source: *Manufacturing USA*, Gale Research, 1996

the strongest independent hardware stores appeared to be those who had staked out a variety of niche markets, such as kitchen remodeling centers and lawn and garden centers. Some wholesale cooperatives, such as Our Own Hardware and ServiStar, were helping members establish tool rental departments. But, *Hardware Age* found that store owners were reluctant to make radical changes in their businesses and did not plan to change their product mix. They were, however, interested in bypassing traditional distribution channels to buy direct from the manufacturers. This sentiment angered wholesalers who believed they had been successful in strengthening relationships with store owners. A major change in the distribution system could alter significantly the retail hardware industry in the future.

Although none of the other warehouse hardware companies had come close to duplicating the success of Home Depot, warehouse stores were likely to continue expanding in the 1990s. Lowe's, which began experimenting with larger stores in 1984, made a corporate decision in 1988 to hold the line at about 60,000 square feet. In the early 1990s, however, the company reconsidered larger stores and built a substantial number—more than half of its entire store count—by the mid-1990s. Another leading company with major expansion plans in the early 1990s was the Hechinger Co., which operated a chain of traditional hardware stores. In 1988, Hechinger purchased Home Quarters Warehouse Inc., and in 1991, the company opened its first warehouse-size Home Project Center.

ORGANIZATION AND STRUCTURE

Most of the 18,000 U.S. retail hardware stores were independent businesses. However, almost all of them were affiliated with a nationwide wholesaler offering retail store advertising and identification programs, and private label brands. This created the appearance for consumers of a more structured industry. Many of these wholesalers were actually cooperatives owned by the independent hardware store owners, forming a distribution system that originated in the early twentieth century. Dealer-owned wholesalers sold only to member stores, but member stores could buy merchandise from other wholesalers or directly from manufacturers.

The largest dealer-owned cooperative was Chicago-based Cotter & Company, with more than 7,500 members. Cotter operations, worth $2.5 billion in 1996, manufacture and distribute products to member-owner stores under the retail trade names of True Value Hardware and V & S Variety Stores. Ace Hardware Corporation, based in Oak Brook, Illinois, was the second largest cooperative with more than 5,000 members. Other dealer-owned wholesalers and their store identification programs included: ServiStar Corp., based in Butler, Pennsylvania; Hardware Wholesalers, Inc., Fort Wayne, Indiana, (Do-It Centers); Our Own Hardware Co., Burnsville, Minnesota (How-To Centers), and United Hardware Distributing Co. (Hardware Hank Stores). ServiStar also owned Coast to Coast Stores, Inc., a Minneapolis-based distributor providing a national identification program for its franchise stores.

Most retail hardware stores had less than 20,000 square feet of floor space. Larger formats were categorized by the National Retail Hardware Association as home centers. Home centers averaged more than 30,000 square feet and usually combined lumber with a greater selection of hardware products to create a one-stop shopping environment for home repair and improvement projects. Home centers usually bought directly from the manufacturers and often sold to commercial accounts as well as individual consumers.

The home center segment also included large warehouse-style hardware stores that averaged nearly 100,000 square feet and earned between $12 million and $15 million in annual sales. Warehouse stores began to appear in the late 1970s and had a notable impact on the retail hardware industry. In the early 1990s, industry analysts predicted the warehouse format to revolutionize the industry; while they attracted a great deal of attention and a significant customer base, warehouse chains such as Home Depot accounted for only about 12 percent of industry sales in the mid- to late 1990s.

Because of their size, warehouse stores were able to negotiate greater discounts from their wholesalers, or more often, directly from the manufacturers. Warehouse stores also based their retail business on garnering a high volume of sales, rather than by pursuing high profit

margins. This forced smaller, independent hardware stores and chains, which traditionally had operated on high margins, to lower their prices, become more efficient, redesign their stores, improve customer service, and often to bypass their wholesalers and deal directly with manufacturers to get the best price. Many hardware stores were unable to adjust to this new operating style and went out of business. Wholesalers, too, were affected; one industry estimate noted that the number of middle-man distributors declined 50 percent during the 1980s.

Lawn Care Equipment Engines

This table shows the leading producer of 2-20 horsepower lawn and garden equipment engines.

Briggs & Stratton	65.0%
Others	35.0

Source: *Financial World*, October 30, 1995, p. 35, from Smith Barney.

WORK FORCE

The industry employed approximately 150,000 people in the mid-1990s. The average hardware store employed 12 full or part-time employees. Entry-level workers were usually paid at or near the minimum wage. This was not likely to change, although store owners were finding it increasingly difficult to hire competent help.

The growth of home centers also was affecting the ability of hardware store owners to hire good employees. Home centers often hired away experienced employees at higher wages. They also offered employee training programs and more opportunity for advancement. Home Depot was a leader in hiring employees with a construction or building industry background to improve service. A lower margin of profit made it more difficult for hardware store owners to attract and retain good employees with higher wages. The problem was especially critical in small towns. The wholesale cooperatives were attempting to help their members by instituting employee training programs.

ASSOCIATIONS AND SOCIETIES

AMERICAN HARDWARE MANUFACTURERS ASSOCIATION
810 N. Plaza Dr.
Schaumburg, IL 60173
Phone: (708) 605-1025
Fax: (708) 605-1093

BUILDERS' HARDWARE MANUFACTURERS ASSOCIATION
355 Lexington Ave., 17 Fl.
New York, NY 10017
Phone: (212) 661-4261
Fax: (212) 370-9047

DOOR AND HARDWARE INSTITUTE
14170 Newbrook Dr.
Chantilly, VA 22021-2223
Phone: (703) 222-2010
Fax: (703) 222-2410

INTERNATIONAL HARDWARE DISTRIBUTORS ASSOCIATION
401 N. Michigan Ave., Ste. 2200
Chicago, IL 60611
Phone: (312) 644-6610
Fax: (312) 321-6869

NATIONAL RETAIL HARDWARE ASSOCIATION
5822 W. 74th St.,
Indianapolis, IN 46278
Phone: (800) 772-4424 or (312) 290-0338
Fax: (317) 328-4354

NATIONAL TOOLING AND MACHINING ASSOCIATION
9300 Livingston Rd.
Fort Washington, MD 20744
Phone: (800) 248-6862 or (301) 248-6200
Fax: (301) 248-7104

PERIODICALS AND NEWSLETTERS

AMERICAN TOOL, DIE AND STAMPING NEWS
Eagle Publications
42400 9 Mile, Ste. B
Novi, MI 48050
Phone: (800) 783-3491 or (810) 347-3490
Fax: (313) 347-3492
Bimonthly. Controlled circulation.

BLUEPRINT
Door and Hardware Institute
14170 Newbrook Dr.
Chantilly, VA 22021
Phone: (703) 222-2010
Fax: (703) 222-2410
Six times a year. Membership.

CUTTING TOOL ENGINEERING
CTE Publications, Inc.
400 Skokie Blvd., Ste. 395
Northbrook, IL 60062-7903

Phone: (708) 441-7520
Fax: (708) 441-8740
Nine times a year. $30.00 per year.

DO-IT-YOURSELF RETAILING: HARDWARE, HOME CENTERS, LUMBERYARDS
National Retail Hardware Association
5822 W. 74th St.
Indianapolis, IN 46278
Phone: (317) 297-1190
Fax: (317) 328-4354
Monthly. $15.00 per year. Formerly Hardware Retailing.

DOORS AND HARDWARE
Door and Hardware Institute
14170 Newbrook Dr.
Chantilly, VA 22021-2223
Phone: (703) 222-2010
Fax: (703) 222-2410
Monthly. $45.00 per year.

HARDWARE AGE
Chilton Co.
201 King of Prussia Rd.
Radnor, PA 19089-0230
Phone: (800) 695-1214 or (610) 964-4000
Fax: (610) 964-4284
Monthly. $75.00 per year.

TOOLING AND PRODUCTION: THE MAGAZINE OF METALWORKING MANUFACTURING
Huebcore Communications, Inc.
29100 Aurora Rd., Ste. 200
Solon, OH 44139
Phone: (216) 248-1125
Fax: (216) 248-0187
Monthly. $90.00 per year.

DATABASES

THOMAS REGISTER ONLINE
Thomas Publishing Co., Inc.
5 Penn Plz.
New York, NY 10001
Phone: (212) 695-0500
Fax: (212) 290-7362
Provides concise information on approximately 155,000 U.S. companies, mainly manufacturers, with over 50,000 product classifications. Indexes over 115,000 trade names. Information is updated semiannually. Inquire as to online cost and availability.

STATISTICS SOURCES

MONTHLY RETAIL TRADE: SALES AND INVENTORIES
Available from U.S. Government Printing Office
Washington, DC 20402
Phone: (202) 512-1800
Fax: (202) 512-2250
Monthly, with annual summary. $57.00 per year. Issued by Bureau of the Census, U.S. Department of Commerce. Includes Advance Monthly Retail Sales.

FURTHER READING

Darnay, Arsen J., and Gary Alampi, eds. *Wholesale and Retail Trade USA*. Detroit: Gale Research, 1995.

U.S. Bureau of the Census. Current Business Reports. *Combined Annual and Revised Monthly Retail Trade.* Washington: GPO, 1997.

U.S. Bureau of the Census. ''Estimated Monthly Retail Sales.'' Washington, 1997.

HOSPITALS

SIC 8060

Although *hospital costs are still increasing through the late 1990s, hospital staffs are expected to expand at the slowest pace of all industries in the health care sector through the year 2005. This slow pace is due to consolidations and cost-cutting efforts seen throughout the industry. Governmental legislation is expected to play a large role in the industry, as establishments were trying to increase revenue while corresponding with regulations.*

The three types of hospitals are general medical and surgical, psychiatric, and specialty. General medical and surgical is the largest U.S. segment with about 6,400 hospitals in the mid-1990s. Made up of both non-profit and profit-making establishments, they employed slightly more than 5 million workers and took in about $410 billion in annual gross revenues. This accounted for nearly one-half of the nation's total annual health care employment and health care expenditures, placing hospitals, especially general medical and surgical, at the center of the health care industry.

In the mid-1990s, approximately 700 U.S. psychiatric hospitals were in operation with about 121,000 beds, according to the American Hospital Association. Also during this time, individual psychiatric hospital admissions rose by 27 percent. The third segment, specialty hospitals, provided hospital services for patients who have usually already seen a physician at a general hospital or medical office. The American Hospital Association reported roughly 220 specialty hospitals in the United States.

In recent years, hospitals in America have been increasingly under pressure by government and businesses to provide higher quality service at lower costs while increasing access and preserving patient choice. A move to emphasize outpatient over inpatient care, and efforts to use health maintenance organizations (HMOs) and other cost-cutting measures implemented by employers, has dramatically altered the business over the past several decades. One result is a trend toward more academic medical centers, more ambulatory surgery, and fewer community hospitals, which have declined in total number by 17 percent since 1981. As pressure to enact such changes continued, hospitals were approaching the end of the twentieth century with persistent uncertainty about the direction and shape of their industry's future.

Many hospitals have reduced their inpatient services while increasing their outpatient services and facilities. However, the average occupancy rate at psychiatric hospitals has been 80 percent, compared to 60 percent in general hospitals and even lower rates in some specialty hospitals. Hospitals that do not rely heavily on Medicare payments have been generally more profitable than other types of hospitals. Occupancy rates in psychiatric hospitals fell from 85.2 percent in 1980 down to only 80.3 in the mid-1990s. This trend was due, in part, to the number of closings and reorganizations of state psychiatric hospitals. During the first half of the 1990s, more state hospitals were closed than the total number during the 1970s and 1980s combined.

Top 10 LARGEST HEALTHCARE SYSTEMS

Ranked by: Net patient revenues in 1995, in millions of dollars.

1. Columbia/HCA Healthcare Corp., with $17,155.6 million
2. Kaiser Permanente, $12,290.2
3. Tenet Healthcare Corp., $5,152.7
4. Daughters of Charity National Health Systems, $3,807.5
5. New York City Health & Hospitals Corp., $3,772.6
6. Beverly Enterprises, $3,170.6
7. Catholic Healthcare West, $2,314.7
8. OrNda HealthCorp, $1,820.0
9. Mercy Health Services, $1,796.1
10. Catholic Health Network, $1,582.4

Source: *Modern Healthcare,* Modern Healthcare Multi-Unit Providers Survey (annual), May 20, 1996, p. 62.

Entering the 1990s, establishments in the larger health care industry were faced with cost-cutting measures imposed by economic factors and anticipated government reforms targeted at health care. Some specialty hospitals, such as those treating tuberculosis and cancer, have grown in response to increases in the number of people with these ailments. On the other hand, maternity hospitals, for example, have decreased in number as technology and social changes have increased the number of general hospitals with birthing facilities.

INDUSTRY OUTLOOK

As a result of overexpansion of facilities in the 1970s and the economic recession at the beginning of the 1990s, hospitals have been struggling without easy access to capital and charitable funding. Between 1985 and 1995, according to *Modern Healthcare,* approximately 600 acute care hospitals closed and eliminated about 180,000 beds. Even so, some believed that with the ongoing fiscal belt-tightening as many as 447,000 unnecessary beds still remained—enough to fill almost 2,500 hospitals.

In order to deal with the various financial problems they faced, some companies in this industry have been increasing their psychiatric units and rehabilitation clinics, both of which are high-profit facilities. Nearly all hospitals have been expanding their outpatient services, which generally bring in lower profits than inpatient units but yield continuous revenues, and many are automating routine administrative tasks.

According to *Hospitals,* this industry also entered the 1990s suffering from a public image problem that could affect the non-profit status of most hospitals in America. This had resulted from public criticisms of hospital pricing practices, the growing number of malpractice cases, and the way in which hospitals have taken on a more business-like approach to managing their establishments. The decision by 447 formerly single-unit community hospitals to merge with larger corporations in 1995—along with the conversion that year of 58 non-profit hospitals to for-profit status—did not help the industry's overall public image.

The business-like approach that generally marks the entire industry has been characterized by "quality management." Instead of leaving the quality of care in the hands of individual practitioners, hospitals have started instituting measures to prevent faulty processes from occurring. Quality management was originally adopted by hospitals to improve food service and lower the length of patient stays; however, in the 1990s, this approach was also used for clinical decisions and processes.

The industry's shift towards more outpatient care has affected hospital management. Although hospitals account for outpatient care separately from inpatient treatment, management of the two types of services has traditionally been under one supervisor. However, in the 1990s, hospitals started moving towards specialized management, which would unite the various types of outpatient services while keeping them separate from inpatient care.

Health care costs were increasing in the mid-1990s. For example, annual psychiatric care expenses reached $12.3 billion, an increase from 1980's total of $5.8 billion. Also, psychiatric hospitals increased their room rates by 20 percent during that time. In addition, psychiatric hospitals were growing due to increases in patient insurance for mental health care. Due to the indeterminate and complex nature of many mental health treatments, most mental health costs were not reimbursed by insurance companies. Consequently, people in need of psychiatric treatment often avoided it for financial reasons. By the end of the twentieth century, more psychiatric services were expected to be covered. Also, analysts expected the industry to expand in the 1990s as insurance companies and government sources began increasing their psychiatric coverage to patients. Moreover, awareness of mental disorders and the growing field of geriatric psychology was predicted to expand the size and range of services carried out by these establishments.

ORGANIZATION AND STRUCTURE

Hospitals are generally categorized as non-profit or profit-making, while many hospitals can also be state and local government establishments. The United States had 3,139 non-profit, 719 profit-making, and 1,678 government general medical and surgical hospitals in 1996. About 82 percent, providing 3.6 beds for every 1,000 U.S. residents, were further described as "community hospitals," meaning they were facilities and services open to the public, which therefore excluded federal, long-term hospitals, psychiatric and special hospitals, and hospitals of institutions such as prisons. During the 1990s, community hospitals have increasingly become part of multihospital systems, where one owner or an ownership group owns more than one hospital. The Public Citizen Health Research Group found that 1 in 12 community hospitals across the United States was involved in merger activity in 1995 alone. The leading example that year was the $5.6 billion acquisition of Healthtrust by Columbia/HCA Healthcare Corp., itself the product of a 1994 merger between Columbia Healthcare Corp. and Hospital Corp. of America.

In the mid-1990s, 266 psychiatric hospitals were government controlled, 358 were proprietary controlled, and 113 were non-profit controlled. More than one-half of the facilities had 75 beds or more, and only 24 had less than 25 beds. The U.S. government owned the vast majority of tuberculosis and chronic disease hospitals; alcohol and drug abuse rehabilitation hospitals and cancer hospitals tended to be privately owned.

Hospitals receive their revenues from different sources according to the services they provide to patients. The largest source of income to community hospitals in the 1990s came from Medicare and Medicaid programs, but tightening restrictions and the ongoing possibility of additional cutbacks have increasingly im-

pacted these two income sources since the 1980s. The remainder of all hospital revenues came primarily from third-party payers like private health insurance plans and, to a much smaller extent, directly from patients.

Hospital expenses are strongly affected by legislation, costs of medical technology, and trends in medical practice. As they continually rose throughout the 1990s, on-site administrative, food service, maintenance, and laundry support often were streamlined—or contracted out—in response. To counteract rising costs, many hospitals also attempted to expand their revenues by increasing their role in community health maintenance efforts beyond traditional emergency, obstetrics, and inpatient care to include disease prevention and patient education programs such as weight reduction, drug rehabilitation, prenatal care, and pediatric wellness.

Internally, hospitals are structured around an administrative staff that oversees nursing and administrative functions and separately operated medical staff and ancillary services—such as a pharmacy and the services of various therapists.

WORK FORCE

In 1995, general medical and surgical hospitals employed slightly more than 5 million workers. Nearly 3.7 million had been employed in 1993, which itself represented a 2.4 percent increase from 1990. This total was comprised of salaried staff—including administrators, clerical workers, laboratory technicians, physical therapists, dietitians, and allied health personnel who are independent clinical workers assisting physicians and medical specialists—as well as physicians and nurses. According to the Bureau of Labor Statistics' *Occupational Outlook Handbook*, general medical and surgical

SIC 8062 - General Medical & Surgical Hospitals
Industry Data by State

State	Establishments 1987	1992	% of US 92	Employment 1987	1992	% of US 92	Payroll 1987 ($ mil.)	1992 ($ mil.)	$ Per Empl. 92	Revenues - 1992 ($ mil.) Total ($ mil.)	Per Estab.	$ Per Empl. 92	% change 87-92 Revenues	Payroll
California	506	473	42.5	384,625	413,841	44.6	9,215.5	13,202.3	31,902	31,775.9	67.2	76,783	53.7	43.3
New York	276	257	23.1	332,761	384,068	41.4	7,640.0	12,472.8	32,475	24,466.7	95.2	63,704	65.4	63.3
Texas	488	434	39.0	215,044	251,028	27.1	4,115.2	6,731.8	26,817	17,204.3	39.6	68,535	74.5	63.6
Pennsylvania	230	229	20.6	216,577	253,828	27.4	4,460.7	6,873.9	27,081	15,485.2	67.6	61,006	57.6	54.1
Florida	238	234	21.0	178,740	214,295	23.1	3,615.5	5,932.2	27,682	15,043.7	64.3	70,201	69.5	64.1
Illinois	240	215	19.3	207,401	225,283	24.3	4,210.1	5,890.5	26,147	13,662.3	63.5	60,645	49.6	39.9
Ohio	198	193	17.3	193,843	210,784	22.7	3,995.9	5,431.3	25,767	12,689.0	65.7	60,199	49.3	35.9
Michigan	191	179	16.1	149,642	170,870	18.4	3,254.9	4,633.6	27,118	10,395.1	58.1	60,837	51.1	42.4
New Jersey	101	101	9.1	115,563	136,496	14.7	2,347.3	4,113.6	30,138	8,835.0	87.5	64,727	83.8	75.3
Massachusetts	108	95	8.5	120,634	125,266	13.5	2,403.9	3,545.1	28,301	7,779.7	81.9	62,105	57.9	47.5

Source: Census of Service Industries, 1987 and 1992, Bureau of the Census, U.S. Department of Commerce. Data are sorted by 1992 revenues and, if revenues are unavailable, by establishments in 1992. (D) indicates that data are withheld by the source to avoid disclosure of competitive information. A dash (-) indicates that data are not available. Percentage changes between 1987 and 1992 are calculated using numbers that have *not* been rounded; hence they may not be reproducible from the values shown.

hospitals employed about 1.3 million registered nurses (RNs) and 281,000 licensed practical nurses (LPNs) in 1994. Nearly 135,000 physicians worked in general hospitals that year.

The overall job outlook for people working in hospitals is not as good as it was at the start of the 1990s when community and non-community hospitals were experiencing severe worker shortages. But, since the 1970s, there has been a shortage of nurses. Job prospects for them are expected to remain favorable through 2005, although it is anticipated that hospital employment will grow slowly and more nurses will go to work in home health, long-term, and ambulatory care facilities.

The increase in hospital paperwork generated by private insurance companies and government insurance programs has created growth for specialized occupations, such as medical record technicians. These workers are responsible for patient records and for providing statistical reports to insurers and hospital administrators.

In 1994, approximately 135,000 physicians, both M.D.s and D.O.s, were based in hospitals. That year, salaries—which varied greatly according to number of years in practice, geographic region, and other factors—averaged $189,300 annually for allopathic physicians. Salaries for specialists were generally much higher; radiologists, for example, earned $240,000 and obstetricians/gynecologists earned $200,000. Due to the better salaries offered in specialties, the number of general practitioners has been decreasing.

In the mid-1990s, approximately 270,000 people were employed in specialty hospitals in the United

States. Based on the figures available, the distribution of this work force can be summed up in four categories: physicians and dentists, registered nurses (RNs), licensed practical nurses (LPNs) and other salaried employees—such as administrators, laboratory technicians and occupational and physical therapists.

	SIC 8062 Occupations Employed by SIC 8062 - Hospitals, Public and Private		
Occupation		% of Total 1994	Change to 2005
Registered nurses		24.8	12.5
Nursing aides, orderlies, & attendants		6.3	12.5
Licensed practical nurses		5.4	1.2
Janitors & cleaners, incl maids		3.6	1.2
General office clerks		3.2	-4.1
Clinical lab technologists & technicians		3.1	-4.0
Managers & administrators nec		2.8	12.4
Health professionals & paraprofessionals nec		2.1	35.0
Physicians		2.0	12.5
Secretaries, ex legal & medical		2.0	2.4
Radiologic technologists & technicians		2.0	23.7
Health service workers nec		1.6	43.4
Respiratory therapists		1.4	35.0
Social workers		1.4	18.9
Food preparation workers		1.3	-13.7
Psychiatric technicians		1.2	-0.4
Psychiatric aides		1.2	5.1
Interviewing clerks, ex personnel & social welfare		1.1	12.5
Medical secretaries		1.1	12.5
Food counter, fountain, & related workers		1.0	-26.9

Source: *Industry-Occupation Matrix*, Bureau of Labor Statistics. These data relate to one or more 3-digit SIC industry groups rather than to a single 4-digit SIC. The change reported for each occupation to the year 2005 is a percent of growth or decline as estimated by the Bureau of Labor Statistics. The abbreviation nec stands for 'not elsewhere classified'.

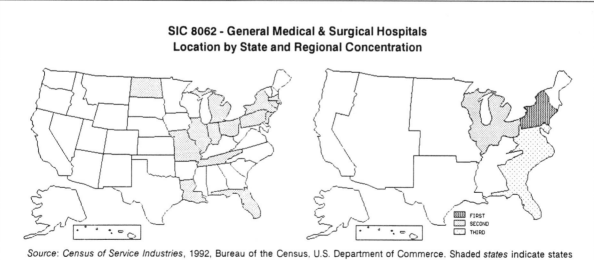

SIC 8062 - General Medical & Surgical Hospitals
Location by State and Regional Concentration

FIRST
SECOND
THIRD

Source: *Census of Service Industries*, 1992, Bureau of the Census, U.S. Department of Commerce. Shaded *states* indicate states which have proportionately greater representation in the industry than would be indicated by the state's population; the ratio is based on revenues or establishments in 1992. Shaded *regions* indicate where the industry is regionally most concentrated.

GROWTH OF U.S. HOSPITAL EMPLOYMENT

Employment in millions

Source: *National Employment, Hours, and Earnings,*
U.S. Bureau of Labor Statistics, 1997

Within these four categories, the number of workers at the major types of specialty hospitals differed significantly. In the early 1990s, tuberculosis hospitals, for which payroll accounted for roughly 63 percent of their expenses, had 30 physicians and dentists, 144 registered nurses, 105 licensed practical nurses, and 4,727 other salaried personnel. At the same time, chronic disease hospitals payroll costs accounted for nearly 74 percent of their expenses. These institutions employed 364 physicians and dentists, 1,745 registered nurses, 949 licensed practical nurses, and over 15,000 other salaried personnel.

RESEARCH AND TECHNOLOGY

Since the 1970s, technological advances have largely contributed to the number of outpatient surgeries available in hospitals. Less invasive procedures have been made possible by radiology and new surgical instruments and techniques.

In inpatient treatment, the last half of the twentieth century has witnessed tremendous advances in transplant surgery. In 1990, over 10 percent of community hospitals performed organ transplants. With over 20,000 patients on waiting lists for transplants, continued research and technological developments were expected to address the increasing needs.

AIDS treatment and research was another area in which growth was expected to continue. Services for AIDS patients are likely to change with advances in drug treatments, such as AZT and Pentamidine. Moreover, research continues in specialized physical and respiratory therapy for AIDS sufferers.

Larger hospitals—rather than smaller hospitals—have traditionally had an easier time investing in sophisticated medical technologies and gathering the expertise necessary to utilize them. This was cited by many ob-

servers as an additional reason that smaller hospitals were having financial difficulties in the mid-1990s or allowing themselves to be acquired by larger competitors.

Specialty hospitals rely strongly on developments in research and technology. Research in biotechnology is expected to have a tremendous impact on cancer treatments provided by cancer hospitals and general hospitals. Radiation and chemotherapy, which have been the main forms of cancer treatment since the 1970s, may be replaced by biotech drugs. The Pharmaceutical Manufacturers Association cites numerous cancer-treating biotechnology drugs under development, while *Hospitals* noted that such research advances could mean that "biotech will shift the site for treatment from inside to outside—from external, systemic treatments like radiation and chemotherapy, to targeted, tumor-specific drugs that strengthen and then deploy the body's immune system to destroy cancer cells." This basic change in cancer treatment is expected to have a profound effect on cancer hospitals as it is likely to shift the emphasis from long-term inpatient facilities—needed for many radiation and chemotherapy treatment programs—to short-term inpatient and outpatient care. The trend toward outpatient cancer care had already started though, independent of biotech research, as a result of cost-cutting by many hospitals.

Another significant development in cancer treatment that will also expand the use of outpatient services has been in bone marrow transplants. Traditionally, bone marrow transplants have required long hospital stays ranging from a few weeks to a month and, from the hospitals' viewpoint, extensive staffing for the follow-up care and related administrative duties. In the early 1990s, advances in the use of laser technology and other less-invasive procedures allowed many types of bone marrow transplants to be performed on an outpatient basis.

Research in the 1990s has led to the development of a number of prosthetic and other devices related to orthopedics. Orthopedics will also be affected by developments in biotechnology and biomaterials, as well as research and development with carbon composite prostheses and thermoplastic prostheses.

Technological advances in computer systems have also assisted many specialty hospitals by providing networks of information, which can be linked among hospitals throughout the country. Throughout the 1990s, these hospitals increasingly shared information on treatments through the use of treatment registries available on computer networks.

AMERICA AND THE WORLD

As part of the larger health care industry, hospitals are expected to experience considerable growth in overseas markets as countries in western Europe expand their privatized services and countries in eastern Europe seek to fill shortages in general medical services. Only since the late 1970s have American hospitals sought business overseas, and at first they opened only a few hospitals in Canada, Great Britain, and Spain.

Business America reported that American health care providers were increasingly looking toward countries in Europe and Asia, as well as in the Middle East, for expansion opportunities in 1996. U.S. enterprises also had established more than 12 arrangements with local providers in the former Soviet Union and eastern Europe.

ASSOCIATIONS AND SOCIETIES

AMERICAN ACADEMY OF MEDICAL ADMINISTRATORS
30555 Southfield Rd., Ste. 150
Southfield, MI 48076-7747
Phone: (810) 540-4310
Fax: (810) 645-0590
Members are executives and middle managers in health care administration.

AMERICAN ASSOCIATION OF HEALTHCARE CONSULTANTS
11208 Waples Mill Rd., Ste. 109
Fairfax, VA 22230
Phone: (703) 691-2242
Members are professional consultants who specialize in the health care industry.

AMERICAN BOARD OF MEDICAL SPECIALTIES
1007 Church St., Ste. 404
Evanston, IL 30201-5913
Phone: (708) 491-9091
Fax: (708) 328-3596
Functions as the parent organization for U.S. medical specialty boards.

AMERICAN COLLEGE OF HEALTH CARE ADMINISTRATORS
325 S. Patrick St.
Alexandria, VA 22314
Phone: (703) 549-5822
Fax: (703) 739-7901

AMERICAN COLLEGE OF HEALTHCARE EXECUTIVES
1 N. Franklin, Ste. 1700
Chicago, IL 60611
Phone: (312) 943-2800
Fax: (312) 424-0023

AMERICAN HEALTH CARE ASSOCIATION
1201 L St. NW
Washington, DC 20005
Phone: (202) 842-4444
Fax: (202) 842-3860
Formerly American Nursing Home Association.

AMERICAN HOSPITAL ASSOCIATION
1 N. Franklin, Ste. 27
Chicago, IL 60606
Phone: (312) 422-3000
Fax: (312) 422-4796

AMERICAN MANAGED CARE AND REVIEW ASSOCIATION
1200 19th St. NW, No. 200
Washington, DC 20036-2437
Phone: (202) 728-0506
Fax: (202) 728-0609
Members are alternate health care organizations, including HMOs.

AMERICAN MEDICAL ASSOCIATION
515 N. State St.
Chicago, IL 60610
Phone: (312) 464-5000
Fax: (312) 464-4184
Concerned with retirement planning and other financial planning for physicians 55 years of age or older.

AMERICAN NURSES' ASSOCIATION
600 Maryland Ave. SW, Ste. 100W
Washington, DC 20024-2571
Phone: (202) 651-7000
Fax: (202) 651-7001

HEALTHCARE FINANCIAL MANAGEMENT ASSOCIATION
2 Westbrook Corporate Center, Ste. 700
Westchester, IL 60154
Phone: (708) 531-9600
Fax: (708) 531-0032

HEALTHCARE FINANCING STUDY GROUP
1919 Pennsylvania Ave. NW, Ste. 800
Washington, DC 20006
Phone: (202) 887-1400
Fax: (202) 466-2198
Concerned with the provision of capital financing for health care institutions.

MEDICAL GROUP MANAGEMENT ASSOCIATION
104 Inverness Terrace E
Englewood, CA 80112
Phone: (303) 799-1111
Fax: (303) 643-4427
Members are medical group managers.

NATIONAL ASSOCIATION FOR MEDICAL EQUIPMENT SERVICES
625 Slaters Ln., Ste. 200
Alexandria, VA 22314-1171
Phone: (703) 836-6263
Fax: (703) 836-6730

Members are durable medical equipment and oxygen suppliers, mainly for home health care. Has Legislative Affairs Committee that is concerned with Medicare/Medicaid benefits.

NATIONAL COMMITTEE FOR QUALITY HEALTH CARE

1500 K St. NW, Ste. 360
Washington, DC 20005
Phone: (202) 347-5731
Fax: (202) 347-5836
Promotes efficient expenditures in the health care field. Members include hospitals, health maintenance organizations, and nursing homes.

PERIODICALS AND NEWSLETTERS

AHA NEWS

American Hospital Publishing, Inc.
737 North Michigan Ave., Ste. 700
Chicago, IL 60611-2615
Phone: (800) 621-6902 or (312) 440-6800
Fax: (312) 440-1158
Weekly. $100.00 per year. Newsletter edited for hospital and health care industry administrators. Covers health care news events and legislative activity. (An American Hospital Association publication.)

AMERICAN JOURNAL OF NURSING

American Journal of Nursing Co.
555 W. 57th St.
New York, NY 10019
Phone: (212) 582-8820
Fax: (212) 586-5462
Monthly. Individuals, $35.00 per year; institutions, $45.00 per year. For registered nurses. Emphasis on the latest technological advances affecting nursing care.

AMERICAN MEDICAL NEWS

American Medical Association
515 N. State St.
Chicago, IL 60610
Phone: (800) 621-8335 or (312) 464-0183
Fax: (312) 464-5834
Weekly. $100.00 per year. Economic and legal news for the medical profession.

THE BLUE SHEET: HEALTH POLICY AND BIOMEDICAL RESEARCH

F-D-C Reports, Inc.
5550 Friendship Blvd., Ste. 1
Chevy Chase, MD 20815-7278
Phone: (800) 332-2181 or (301) 657-9830
Fax: (301) 664-7248
Weekly. $480.00 per year. Newsletter. Health policy topics include Medicare, the education and supply of health professionals, and public health. Biomedical topics are related to research, regulations, and the role of the National Science Foundation.

CHANGING MEDICAL MARKETS: THE INTERNATIONAL MONTHLY NEWSLETTER FOR EXECUTIVES IN THE HEALTHCARE AND BIOTECHNOLOGY INDUSTRIES

Theta Corp.
Theta Bldg.
Middlefield, CT 06455
Phone: (203) 349-1054
Fax: (2030 349-1227
Monthly. $195.00 per year.

FAULKNER AND GRAY'S MEDICINE AND HEALTH

Faulkner & Gray
Healthcare Information Center
1133 15th St. NW, Ste. 450
Washington, DC 20005
Phone: (202) 828-4150
Fax: (202) 828-2352
Weekly. $495.00 per year. Newsletter on socioeconomic developments relating to the health care industry. Formerly McGraw-Hill's Washington Report on Medicine and Health.

HEALTH ALLIANCE ALERT

Faulkner & Gray
Healthcare Information Center
1133 15th St. NW, Ste. 450
Washington, DC 20005
Phone: (202) 828-4150
Fax: (202) 828-2352
Weekly. $450.00 per year. Newsletter. Formerly Health Business.

HEALTH CARE COMPETITION WEEK

Capitol Publications, Inc.
1101 King St., Ste. 444
Alexandria, VA 22314
Phone: (703) 683-4100
Fax: (703) 739-6517
Weekly. $438.00 per year. Newsletter.

HEALTH CARE CONSTRUCTION REPORT

Available from FIND/SVP, Inc.
625 Avenue of the Americas
New York, NY 10011
Phone: (800) 346-3787 or (212) 645-4500
Fax: (212) 645-7681
Monthly. $250.00 per year. Newsletter containing information on specific hospital and other health care facility construction projects. Includes name of project manager, size, cost, scheduled dates of construction, etc.

HEALTH CARE FINANCING REVIEW

Available from U.S. Government Printing Office
Washington, DC 20402
Phone: (202) 512-1800
Fax: (202) 512-2250
Quarterly. $29.00 per year. Issued by the Health Care Financing Administration, U.S. Department of Health and Human Services. Presents articles by professionals in the areas of health care costs and financing.

HEALTH CARE STRATEGIC MANAGEMENT: THE NEWSLETTER FOR HOSPITAL STRATEGIES

Business Word, Inc.
5350 S. Roslyn St., Ste. 400
Englewood, CO 80111-2145

Phone: (303) 290-8500
Fax: (303) 290-9025
Monthly. $187.00 per year. Planning, marketing and resource allocation.

HEALTH FACILITIES MANAGEMENT

American Hospital Publishing, Inc.
737 N. Michigan Ave., Ste. 700
Chicago, IL 60611-2615
Phone: (800) 621-6902 or (312) 440-6800
Fax: (312) 440-1158
Monthly. $30.00 per year. Covers building maintenance and engineering for hospitals and nursing homes. (An American Hospital Association publication.)

HEALTH INDUSTRY TODAY: THE MARKET LETTER FOR HEALTH CARE INDUSTRY VENDORS

Business Word, Inc.
5350 S. Roslyn St., Ste. 400
Englewood, CO 80111-2145
Phone: (303) 290-8500
Fax: (303) 290-9025
Monthly. $277.00 per year.

HEALTH NEWS DAILY

FDC Reports, Inc.
5550 Friendship Blvd., Ste. 1
Chevy Chase, MD 20815-7278
Phone: (301) 657-9830
Fax: (301) 656-3094
Daily. $1,250.00 per year. Newsletter providing broad coverage of the healthc are business, including government policy, regulation, research, finance, and insurance. Contains news of pharmaceuticals, medical devices, biotechnology, and healthcare delivery in general.

HEALTHCARE EXECUTIVE

American College of Healthcare Executives
840 N. Lake Shore Dr.
Chicago, IL 60611
Phone: (312) 943-0544
Fax: (312) 943-3791
Bimonthly. $45.00 per year. Focuses on critical management issues.

HEALTHCARE FINANCIAL MANAGEMENT

Healthcare Financial Management Association
2 Westbrook Corporate Center, Ste. 700
Westchester, IL 60154
Phone: (800) 252-4362 or (708) 531-9600
Fax: (708) 531-0032
Monthly. $70.00 per year.

HEALTHCARE INFORMATION MANAGEMENT

Healthcare Information and Management Systems Society
840 N. Lake Shore Dr.
Chicago, IL 60611-2431
Phone: (312) 280-6680
Fax: (312) 280-4152
Quarterly. Membership. Formerly Health Care Systems.

HEALTHCARE MARKETING REPORT

HMR Publication Group
PO Box 76002
Atlanta, GA 30358-1002
Phone: (404) 457-6105
Fax: (404) 457-0049
Monthly. $135.00 per year.

HOSPITAL AND HEALTH SERVICES ADMINISTRATION

Health Administration Press
1021 E. Huron St.
Ann Arbor, MI 48104-9990
Phone: (708) 450-9952
Fax: (708) 450-1618
Quarterly. $55.00 per year. Information on the latest trends, developments and innovations in the industry.

HOSPITALS AND HEALTH NETWORKS

American Hospital Publishing, Inc.
737 N. Michigan Ave., Ste. 700,
Chicago, IL 60611-2615
Phone: (800) 621-6902 or (312) 440-6800
Fax: (312) 440-1158
Semimonthly. $60.00 per year. Covers the general management of hospitals, nursing homes, and managed care organizations. Formerly Hospitals. (An American Hospital Association publication.)

JAMA: THE JOURNAL OF THE AMERICAN MEDICAL ASSOCIATION

American Medical Association
515 N. State St.
Chicago, IL 60610
Phone: (800) 621-8335 or (312) 464-0183
Fax: (312) 464-5834
Weekly. $115.00 per year.

MEDICAL GROUP MANAGEMENT JOURNAL

Medical Group Management Association
104 Inverness Ter. E
Englewood, CO 80112-5306
Phone: (303) 759-1111
Fax: (303) 799-1683
Bimonthly. $46.50 per year.

MEDICAL REFERENCE SERVICES QUARTERLY

Haworth Press, Inc.
10 Alice St.
Binghamton, NY 13904-1580
Phone: (800) 342-9678 or (607) 722-5857
Fax: (607) 722-1424
Quarterly. $105.00 per year. An academic and practical journal for medical reference librarians.

MEDICAL TRIBUNE: WORLD NEWS OF MEDICINE AND ITS PRACTICE

Medical Tribune, Inc.
100 Avenue of the Americas, 9 Fl.
New York, NY 10013-1606
Phone: (212) 674-8500
Fax: (212) 529-8490
26 times a year. Free to qualified personnel; others, $75.00 per year.

MEDICAL UTILIZATION MANAGEMENT
Faulkner & Gray
Healthcare Information Center
1133 15th St. NW Ste. 450
Washington, DC 20005
Phone: (202) 828-4150
Fax: (202) 828-2352
Semimonthly. $395.00 per year. Newsletter. Formerly Medical
Utilization Review.

MEDICAL WORLD NEWS: THE NEWSMAGAZINE OF MEDICINE
Medical Tribune, Inc.
100 Avenue of the Americas
New York, NY 10013-1606
Phone: (212) 674-8500
Fax: (212) 529-8490
Semimonthly. Free to qualified personnel; others, $75.00 per year.

MODERN HEALTHCARE: THE NEWSMAGAZINE FOR ADMINISTRATORS AND MANAGERS IN HOSPITALS AND OTHER HEALTHCARE INSTITUTIONS
Crain Communications, Inc.
740 N. Rush St.
Chicago, IL 60611-2590
Phone: (800) 678-9595 or (312) 649-5341
Fax: (312) 280-3189
Weekly. $110.00 per year.

MODERN MEDICINE
Advanstar Communications, Inc.,
7500 Old Oak Blvd.
Cleveland, OH 44130
Phone: (800) 346-0085 or (216) 243-8100
Fax: (216) 891-2726
Monthly. $50.00 per year.

NEW ENGLAND JOURNAL OF MEDICINE
Massachusetts Medical Society
1440 Main St.
Waltham, MA 02254
Phone: (800) 843-6356 or (617) 893-3800
Fax: (617) 893-8103
*Weekly. $96.00 per year. The official journal of the Massachu-
setts Medical Society.*

WASHINGTON HEALTH RECORD
Faulkner & Gray
Healthcare Information Center
1133 15th St. NW, Ste. 450
Washington, DC 20005
Phone: (202) 828-4150
Fax: (202) 828-2352
Weekly. $195.00 per year. Newsletter on federal health regulations.

DATABASES

BIOBUSINESS
BIOSIS
2100 Arch St.
Philadelphia, PA 19103
Phone: (800) 523-4806 or (215) 587-4800
Fax: (215) 587-2016

*Provides abstracts of international periodical literature relating
to business applications of biological and medical research,
1985 to date. Inquire as to online cost and availability.*

EMBASE
Elsevier Science, Inc.
655 Avenue of the Americas
PO Box 945
New York, NY 10010
Phone: (212) 989-5800
Fax: (212) 633-3975
*Worldwide medical literature, 1974 to present. Weekly updates.
Inquire as to online cost and availability.*

F-D-C REPORTS
FDC Reports, Inc.
5550 Friendship Blvd., Ste. 1
Chevy Chase, MD 20815
Phone: (301) 657-9830
Fax: (301) 656-3094
*An online version of "The Gray Sheet" (medical devices), "The
Pink Sheet" (pharmaceuticals), and "The Rose Sheet" (cosmet-
ics). Contains full-text information on legal, technical, corpo-
rate, financial, and marketing developments from 1987 to date,
with weekly updates. Inquire as to online cost and availability.*

HEALTH PLANNING AND ADMINISTRATION
Medlars Management Section
National Library of Medicine
8600 Rockville Pke.
Bethesda, MD 20209
Phone: (800) 638-8480 or (301) 496-6193
*Provides indexing and abstracting of non-clinical literature
relating to health care delivery, 1975 to date. Monthly updates.
Inquire as to online cost and availability.*

MEDLINE
Medlars Management Section
National Library of Medicine
8600 Rockville Pke.
Bethesda, MD 20894
Phone: (800) 638-8480 or (301) 496-6193
*Provides indexing and abstracting of worldwide medical litera-
ture, 1966 to date. Inquire as to online cost and availability.*

MEDSEARCH AMERICA, INC.
*Delivers nationwide access to healthcare recruiting. Employers
can post job postings or ads with private e-mail box responses;
search resumes; and offer outplacement services, custom search
and pre-screening services, company profiles and recruitment
information, and direct dial-up accounts. Job seekers can post
and code resumes, and search healthcare job listings, healthcare
career advice columns, career resources information, member
employer profiles and services, and a schedule of healthcare
events. Time span: Current information. Updating frequency: As
needed. Fees: Free. Gopher: gopher.medsearch.com URL: gopher://gopher.medsearch.com/*

STATISTICS SOURCES

ECONOMIC TRENDS
American Hospital Association
1 N. Franklin St.
Chicago, IL 60606

Phone: (312) 422-3000
Fax: (312) 422-4651
Quarterly. $135.00 per year. Provides statistics and analysis relating to hospital utilization, finances, and staffing.

HEALTH AND ENVIRONMENT IN AMERICA'S TOP-RATED CITIES: A STATISTICAL PROFILE

Andrew Garoogian, editor
Universal Reference Publications
1355 W. Palmetto Park Rd., Ste. 315
Boca Raton, FL 33486-9927
Phone: (800) 377-7551 or (561) 997-7557
Fax: (561) 997-6756
Biennial. $75.00. Covers 75 U.S. cities. Includes statistical and other data on a wide variety of topics, such as air quality, water quality, recycling, hospitals, physicians, health care costs, death rates, infant mortality, accidents, and suicides.

HEALTH CARE COSTS

DRI/McGraw-Hill
24 Hartwell Ave.
Lexington, MA 02173
Phone: (617) 863-5100
Fax: (617) 860-6332
Quarterly. $605.00 per year. Cost indexes for hospitals, nursing homes, and home healthcare agencies.

HOSPITAL STATISTICS

American Hospital Association
1 N. Franklin St.
Chicago, IL 60606
Phone: (312) 422-3000
Fax: (312) 422-4651
Annual. $195.00. Provides detailed statistical data on the nation's hospitals, including revenues, expenses, utilization, and personnel.

INTERSTUDY COMPETITIVE EDGE

InterStudy
2001 Killebrew Dr., Ste. 122
Bloomington, MN 55425
Phone: (612) 474-1176
Fax: (612) 474-1613
Semiannual. $630.00 per year. Provides data on the managed health care industry.

INTERSTUDY QUALITY EDGE

InterStudy
2001 Killebrew Dr., Ste. 122
Bloomington, MN 55425
Phone: (612) 474-1176
Fax: (612) 474-1613
Annual. $380.00. Provides data relative to the quality of care (outcomes) provided by managed health care organizations.

UNIVERSAL HEALTHCARE ALMANAC: A COMPLETE GUIDE FOR THE HEALTHCARE PROFESSIONAL - FACTS, FIGURES, ANALYSIS

Silver & Cherner
10221 N. 32nd St., Ste. J-1
Phoenix, AZ 85028-3849
Phone: (602) 996-2220
Looseleaf, with quarterly updates. $160.00 for first year, then $125.00 per year. Includes a wide variety of health care statistics: national expenditures, hospital data, health insurance, health

professionals, vital statistics, demographics, etc. Years of coverage vary, with long range forecasts provided in some cases.

GENERAL WORKS

ADVANCES IN HEALTH ECONOMICS AND HEALTH SERVICES RESEARCH

Richard N. Scheffler and Lewis Rossiter, editors
JAI Press, Inc.
PO Box 1678
Greenwich, CT 06836-1678
Phone: (203) 661-7602
Fax: (203) 661-0792
Annual. $63.50.

ANNUAL REVIEW OF MEDICINE: SELECTED TOPICS IN THE CLINICAL SCIENCES

Annual Reviews, Inc.
PO Box 10139
Palo Alto, CA 94303-0139
Phone: (800) 523-8635 or (415) 493-4400
Fax: (415) 855-9815
Annual. $47.00.

ANNUAL REVIEW OF PUBLIC HEALTH

Annual Reviews, Inc.
PO Box 10139
Palo Alto, CA 94303-0139
Phone: (800) 523-8635 or (415) 493-4400
Fax: (415) 855-9815
Annual. $52.00.

MANAGEMENT OF HEALTHCARE ORGANIZATIONS

Kerry D. Carson and others
South-Western Publishing Co.
5101 Madison Rd.
Cincinnati, OH 45227
Phone: (800) 543-0487 or (513) 271-8811
Fax: (513) 527-6956
1995. $55.95.

MARKETING HEALTH CARE INTO THE TWENTY-FIRST CENTURY: THE CHANGING DYNAMIC

Alan K. Vitberg
Haworth Press, Inc.
10 Alice St.
Binghamton, NY 13904-1580
Phone: (800) 429-6784 or (607) 722-5857
Fax: (800) 895-0582 or (607) 722-1424
1996. $29.95.

MEDICAL CARE, MEDICAL COSTS: THE SEARCH FOR A HEALTH INSURANCE POLICY

Rashi Fein
Harvard University Press 79
Garden St.
Cambridge, MA 02138
Phone: (617) 495-2600
Fax: (617) 495-8924
1989. $15.50.

REFORM OF HEALTH CARE SYSTEMS: A REVIEW OF SEVENTEEN OECD COUNTRIES
Organization for Economic Cooperation and Development
OECD Publications and Information Center,
2001 L St. NW, Ste. 700,
Washington, DC 20036-4910
Phone: (800) 456-6323 or (202) 785-6323
Fax: (202) 785-0350
1994. $86.00. An extensive review of attempts by major countries to control health care costs.

FURTHER READING

Darnay, Arsen J., ed. *Service Industries USA.* 3rd ed. Detroit: Gale Research, 1996.

''Health Care Industry Study Report.'' National Defense University's Industrial College of the Armed Forces, 1996. Available from http://198.80.36.91/ndu/icaf/ishea.html.

National Association of State Mental Health Program Directors. ''State Mental Health Agency Profile: System Highlights.'' November 1996. Available from http://www.nasmhpd.org/nri/SHSP_RPT.HTM.

Occupational Outlook Handbook. Bureau of Labor Statistics, 1996. Availablefrom http://stats.bls.gov/oco/.

Plock, Ernest. ''The Global Healthcare Services Market is Growing Fast As Foreign Consumers Look for Better Medical Care.'' *Business America,* July 1996, 18.

''Time 25.'' *Time,* 17 June 1996.

U.S. Bureau of the Census. *Statistical Abstract of the United States: 1996.* Washington: GPO, 1996.

U.S. Department of Labor. *Occupational Outlook Handbook.* 1996-97 ed. Washington: GPO, 1996.

The hotel and motel industry has played a vital role in the development of trade, commerce, and travel in the United States. In supplying everything from a inexpensive night's accommodation on the road to meeting and convention spaces and coordination for large corporate events, the hotel and motel industry has become a significant segment of the domestic economy. In fact, the industry's revenues total about $74 billion annually.

In the United States, there are approximately 3.34 million rooms at approximately 45,000 properties, or about one hotel room for every 80 U.S. citizens. Roughly one-third of these are at suburban locations, and another third are on highways. The rest are located in cities (16 percent), resort sites (12 percent), and alongside airport strips (7 percent). The room supply is rising most significantly in suburban areas, and new construction is focused primarily on limited-service facilities—an increasingly popular option for cost-conscious travelers not inclined to frequent more elaborate full-service properties.

HOTELS AND MOTELS

SIC 7011

The American Hotel & Motel Association expects that more than 1 billion people will be traveling worldwide by 2006, with international tourism dollars totaling more than $7.1 trillion. The United States will continue to be the primary destination for tourists, attracting upwards of 49.8 million people by 1999. Employment in the industry will also continue to rise, reaching 1.89 million people in 2005, according to the U.S. Department of Labor.

TOP HOTEL COMPANIES BY SYSTEMWIDE REVENUES

Ranked by: Systemwide revenue in 1995, in thousands of dollars.

1. Holiday Inn Worldwide, with $5,800,000 thousand
2. Marriott, $5,327,000
3. Best Western, $4,900,000
4. ITT Sheraton Corp., $4,100,000
5. HFS, $4,000,000
6. Carlson Hospitality Group, $2,900,000
7. Hilton International, $2,862,800
8. Forte Hotels Inc., $2,700,000
8. Hyatt Hotels Corp., $2,700,000
10. Choice, $2,200,000

Source: *Business Travel News*, Business Travel Survey (annual), May 27, 1996, p. 64.

Tracking the industry by region shows huge variabilities depending on location. Among major cities, for instance, average room rates in 1995 fell between $134 for New York to around $58 for Norfolk, Virginia. Occupancy levels range dramatically as well, depending on location and regional economic factors. The southern California market, as a whole has been depressed, while Florida continues to experience gains in room sales; indeed, Orlando has become the largest hotel market in the U.S., with about 85,000 rooms. Los Angeles, Las

---

Vegas, Chicago, Washington, D.C., and New York each boast between 65,000 and 80,000 rooms.

In recent years, modest gains in occupancy and the average room rate have resulted in higher operating margins in all types of hotels. The industry's performance in 1992 to 1995 represented four consecutive years of improving profitability. Over that time frame, little new inventory was added in most markets. In contrast, in the late 1980s and early 1990s, many hotels were distressed. In 1995, the industry's pre-tax profits exceeded $6 billion. This compares favorably with a $5.7 billion loss experienced by the industry in 1990.

Today, demand is strong in most parts of the country. Construction has increased at the low and middle ends of the market, largely in franchised properties of large hotel chains. However, the full service side of the market is seeing little new construction.

INDUSTRY OUTLOOK

During the 1990s, the industry finally absorbed the capacity created by the phenomenal building activity of the 1980s. Lodging industry profits have improved dramatically in recent years, helped by stronger consumer demands and the absence of significant new capacity.

A number of noticeable trends occurred during the mid-1990s. These include more construction, further automation of labor-intensive functions, additional emphasis on business related amenities, involvement by hotel companies in time-sharing projects, and the growing popularity of extended-stay hotels. Construction has increased as companies increasingly look to develop new chains by building new facilities. The automation of labor intensive functions, such as hotel check-in and check-out should assist in reducing long-term operating costs and increasing customer satisfaction. Business related amenities, such as voice mail and fax services, appeal especially to business travelers. Involvement by hotel companies in time-sharing projects is a means for companies to leverage their expertise in real estate and financing. Extended-stay facilities offer such amenities as separate living room areas and kitchen facilities.

While the industry has recovered, there are concerns related to the proliferation of brand names. An advantage associated with being part of a chain is the familiarity that the name can bring to customers. However, with more brands in the marketplace, there are both more choices for travelers and a greater likelihood of images and names blurring with one another.

SIC 7011 - Hotels, Motels General Statistics

	Establish-ments	Employment (000)	Payroll ($ mil.)	Revenues ($ mil.)
1982	37,639	1,076.2	9,067.2	32,221.2*
1983	-	-	-	36,350.0
1984	-	-	-	39,916.0
1985	-	-	-	43,472.0
1986	-	-	-	45,779.0
1987	40,424	1,380.2	14,134.7	51,633.0
1988	38,799	1,333.4	15,220.2	56,065.0
1989	39,510	1,409.3	16,697.4	58,138.0
1990	39,247	1,463.1	18,252.9	62,138.0
1991	40,892	1,440.8	18,553.9	58,289.0
1992	41,684	1,455.9	19,186.6	61,369.0
1993	42,597	1,477.0	20,732.8	64,312.0
1994	41,968P	1,561.5P	21,786.7P	69,367.1P
1995	42,310P	1,597.2P	22,853.2P	72,178.9P
1996	42,653P	1,633.0P	23,919.8P	74,990.7P

Sources: Data for 1982, 1987, and 1992 are from Census of Service Industries, Bureau of the Census, U.S. Department of Commerce. Revenue data are from the Service Annual Survey or from the Census. Revenue data from the Census are labelled with *. Data for 1988-1991 and 1993, when shown, are derived from County Business Patterns for those years from the Bureau of the Census. A P indicates projections made by the editor.

ORGANIZATION AND STRUCTURE

The strict divisions of the hotel and motel industry differ somewhat depending on which analyst is making them. Most analysts classify the industry into full- and limited-service enterprises. Full-service hotels still constitute the majority of all properties, although this number is dwindling. Typically, they are large properties—averaging about 280 rooms—that often generate about 30 percent of operating income from food, beverage, and other services such as restaurants, room service, and meeting spaces. Limited-service hotels, by contrast, are smaller establishments—averaging about 130 rooms—that do not offer food and beverage services or extra facilities. Thus, they rely on room sales for close to 95 percent of their revenue base.

The expenses each type of hotel must pay to operate various areas, such as room maintenance, food and beverages, and telephones, also differ enormously, and these can diminish profit margins considerably in years with low occupancy rates, especially given that hotels must keep room rates down in such years as well. Full-service hotels with significant departmental expenses have, in general, been hurt far more by the oversupply of the industry. Occupancy rates have not been markedly different from those of limited-service hotels, but room rates have been kept far too low to pay for the cost of servicing them.

All-suite hotels came to prominence in the late 1980s and, because their segment's demand growth remains healthy, continue to capture a lot of attention. Such hotels—most of which are branches of specific brand chains—usually offer consumers both a living and a bedroom area. While most all-suites offer both food and beverage services, this is not always the case. Indeed, limited-service all-suites often report substantially more attractive profit margins—again, as a result of much lower departmental expenses—and have subsequently attracted increasing interest. Occupancy rates for these hotels have been higher than those of full-service counterparts, relative to the rest of the industry, without a tremendous drop-off in room rates.

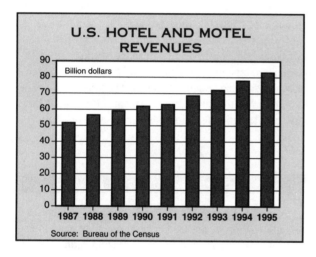

U.S. HOTEL AND MOTEL REVENUES

Billion dollars

Source: Bureau of the Census

Resorts, hotels with gambling facilities, and conference/convention center hotels represent three smaller but important industry categories. Like all-suites, demand growth and occupancy rates have generally been higher than the average and will probably remain so simply because they are so capital intensive to build and maintain. Casino hotels have grown in popularity due to the expansion of legalized gambling, and the convention center property-type has become a popular component of efforts to re-invigorate urban infrastructure.

The casino segment of the hotel industry currently remains clustered in Las Vegas and Atlantic City. In Las Vegas, several new spectacular destination resorts, such as the Luxor and New York, New York, were constructed in the mid-1990s. In contrast to convention center hotels and resort hotels, most hotels with gambling ventures tend to offer low room rates; the gambling activity of the hotel patrons is thus central to the establishment's success. In recent years, the gaming industry has attempted to market its resort hotels to entire families.

The resort phenomenon is also highly regional and, inasmuch as they have had to become more price competitive, resort hotels perhaps rely more on overall regional promotion than anything else. The South Atlantic (primarily Florida) has grown into the country's most lively resort region. Even after a number of years of steady growth, its occupancy rates are still the highest of any region in the country, regularly upwards of 75 percent. The second largest resort market in revenue, the Mountain and Pacific region, has steadily lost market share in recent years.

INDUSTRY STRATEGIES

There are essentially three forms of participation in the hotel and motel industry: straight ownership of properties, management agreements, and franchising or licensing a brand name. Most large hotel companies are active in all three categories, keeping themselves flexible to utilize varied strategies as the market dictates. Owning a hotel is a capital-intensive endeavor but imparts control and can be very lucrative in an expanding market when asset values show sizable appreciation. Managing other party's hotels has become a widespread activity of the major hotel companies as a way to continue expanding their operations in a depressed market. Some of the leading chains moved toward managing in the 1980s.

The trend away from straight ownership, and its inherent risks, has given franchising a greater appeal. Large franchise chains are first and foremost based on the benefits of name recognition, for which an operator either pays a straight fee or gives up a percentage of revenue—along with other advantages like access to reservations systems. The name represents a specific concept and standard, consistent at every location. This familiarity appeals to consumers. It also provides greater efficiency of a company's use of resources, especially as the chain grows. Through license or franchise agreements, hotel companies can generate revenues from limited capital investments and can market their product more pointedly. In an attempt to segment the market, some companies have successfully developed a variety of chains that are advertised aggressively and provide varying levels of service.

Ambitious to expand their lodging chains, many companies have turned to conversions of existing hotels rather than new construction in an already bloated market. The scope of industry conversions has more than doubled since 1988 with approximately half of these involved switching chain affiliations.

AFFILIATIONS AND PARTNERSHIPS

As the travel industry became increasingly sophisticated and global in nature, hotel operators have developed competitive advantages through agreements of various kinds with other industries that serve travelers. Frequent-flyer/guest/renter programs have been developed in cooperation with airline and car rental companies. These programs offer "points" for air travel, hotel visits, and car rentals, which can be redeemed for upgrades and awards through any of the three partners. These programs are geared towards fostering brand loyalty, both in the individual leisure traveler who receives regular statements and in the corporate traveler who, through side agreements with certain companies, often is given corporate rates or some other preferred-customer benefits.

Relationships with travel agencies and tour operators are also an integral element in the success of many hotels. Agencies, which book approximately 40 percent of the hotel rooms in the United States, have become a crucial sales mechanism for the industry, and many hotels have created centralized commission payment systems to make agents more confident about prompt and accurate payments of commissions—generally between 5 to 10 percent. Many hotels also feature toll-free travel agent help desks to answer questions about commissions and to help with reservation system problems. Agreements with tour operators to offer substantial room discounts on bulk bookings are ubiquitous in the hotel and motel industry as properties benefit not only from the added business but by the free publicity from appearances in tour operator brochures.

ASSOCIATIONS

The American Hotel and Motel Association (AHMA) is the major trade association of the industry. It conducts surveys and industry analysis and keeps its members up to date on industry trends through newsletters and educational conferences. The AHMA serves primarily, however, as a promotional mechanism to speak for the industry, both in lobby efforts aimed at national and regional governments through its affiliated state associations and in publicity campaigns. The AHMA works in partnership with 51 member state associations representing more than 10,000 member properties. AHMA member properties account for 75 percent of total revenues generated by the industry. The stated goal of the organization is to provide a favorable business environment in which the lodging industry can prosper.

WORK FORCE

The hotel and motel industry employs more than 1.5 million part- and full-time workers. Its work force is highly diverse. It often includes minimum-wage restaurant staff, room and building maintenance workers, middle-income administrative and marketing positions, and high-salary upper management personnel. The primary union in the industry is the Hotel Employees and Restaurant Employees International Union based in New York City.

AMERICA AND THE WORLD

Most of the major U.S. hotel companies have expanded into Europe and should continue to expand international operations with the increasing numbers of

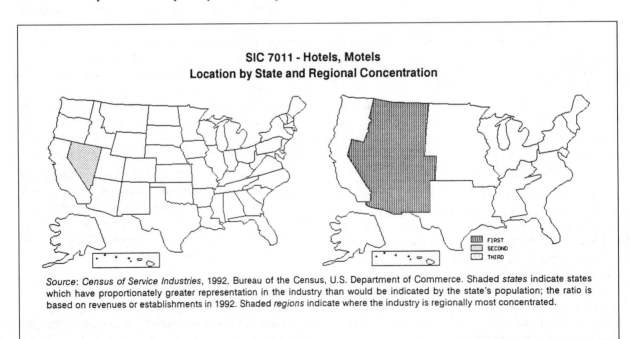

SIC 7011 - Hotels, Motels
Location by State and Regional Concentration

FIRST
SECOND
THIRD

Source: *Census of Service Industries*, 1992, Bureau of the Census, U.S. Department of Commerce. Shaded *states* indicate states which have proportionately greater representation in the industry than would be indicated by the state's population; the ratio is based on revenues or establishments in 1992. Shaded *regions* indicate where the industry is regionally most concentrated.

SIC 7011
Occupations Employed by SIC 7011 - Hotels and Other Lodging Places

Occupation	% of Total 1994	Change to 2005
Janitors & cleaners, incl maids	23.8	10.7
Waiters & waitresses	9.5	0.4
Hotel desk clerks	8.3	20.3
Food preparation workers	4.0	-3.7
Cooks, restaurant	3.9	13.0
Maintenance repairers, general utility	3.3	24.4
Dining room & cafeteria attendants & bar helpers	2.8	-18.4
Food counter, fountain, & related workers	2.7	18.6
Amusement & recreation attendants	2.6	57.2
Cashiers	2.5	38.4
Bartenders	2.4	0.5
Food service & lodging managers	2.4	13.0
Institutional cleaning supervisors	2.3	13.8
Service workers nec	2.2	38.4
Laundry & drycleaning machine operators	1.9	55.2
General managers & top executives	1.8	31.3
Guards	1.6	24.6
Baggage porters & bellhops	1.5	26.3
Bookkeeping, accounting, & auditing clerks	1.5	3.8
Gardeners & groundskeepers, ex farm	1.3	24.6
Clerical supervisors & managers	1.1	41.6
Hosts & hostesses, restaurant, lounge, coffee shop	1.1	0.5
Secretaries, ex legal & medical	1.0	26.0

Source: *Industry-Occupation Matrix*, Bureau of Labor Statistics. These data relate to one or more 3-digit SIC industry groups rather than to a single 4-digit SIC. The change reported for each occupation to the year 2005 is a percent of growth or decline as estimated by the Bureau of Labor Statistics. The abbreviation nec stands for 'not elsewhere classified'.

world travelers. Since more U.S. travelers are leaving the country for both business and leisure, many U.S. chains are expanding oversees. The opening of Eastern Europe, coupled with the movement to lift international trade barriers, has given further momentum to the enthusiasm for developing international operations. The *IHA White Paper on the Global Hospitality Industry* estimated that the hotel industry worldwide generated more than $247 billion in 1994. The industry employed more than 11.1 million people worldwide and represents about 5 percent of the world's total work force.

ASSOCIATIONS AND SOCIETIES

AMERICAN HOTEL AND MOTEL ASSOCIATION
1201 New York Ave. NW, Ste. 600
Washington, DC 20005-3931
Phone: (202) 289-3100
Fax: (202) 289-3199

HOSPITALITY SALES AND MARKETING ASSOCIATION INTERNATIONAL
1300 L St. NW, Ste. 800
Washington, DC 20005
Phone: (202) 789-0089
Fax: (202) 789-1725

PERIODICALS AND NEWSLETTERS

THE CORNELL HOTEL AND RESTAURANT ADMINISTRATION QUARTERLY
Elsevier Science Publishing Co.
Cornell University School of Hotel Administration
PO Box 882, Madison Square Sta.
New York, NY 10159
Phone: (212) 989-5800
Fax: (212) 633-3990
Quarterly. $112.00 per year.

HOTEL AND MOTEL MANAGEMENT
Advanstar Communications, Inc.
7500 Old Oak Blvd.
Cleveland, OH 44130
Phone: (800) 346-0085 or (216) 243-8100
Fax: (216) 891-2726
21 times a year. $35.00 per year.

JOURNAL OF HOSPITALITY AND LEISURE MARKETING: THE INTERNATIONAL FORUM FOR RESEARCH, THEORY AND PRACTICE
Haworth Press, Inc.
10 Alice St.
Binghamton, NY 13904-1580
Phone: (800) 342-9678 or (607) 722-5857
Fax: (607) 722-1424
Quarterly. $75.00 per year. An academic and practical journal covering various aspects of hotel, restaurant, and recreational marketing.

JOURNAL OF INTERNATIONAL HOSPITALITY, LEISURE, AND TOURISM MANAGEMENT: A MULTINATIONAL AND CROSS-CULTURAL JOURNAL OF APPLIED RESEARCH
Haworth Press, Inc.
10 Alice St.
Binghamton, NY 13904-1580
Phone: (800) 429-6784 or (607) 722-5857
Fax: (800) 895-0582 or (607) 722-1424
Quarterly. $85.00 per year. An academic journal with articles relating to lodging, food service, travel, tourism, and the hospitality/leisure industries in general. (International Business Press.)

DATABASES

CITIBASE (CITICORP ECONOMIC DATABASE)
FAME Software Corp.
77 Water St., 9 Fl.
New York, NY 10005
Phone: (212) 898-7800
Fax: (212) 742-8956
Presents over 6,000 statistical series relating to business, industry, finance, and economics. Includes series from Survey of Current Business and many other sources. Time period is 1947 to date, with daily updates. Inquire as to online cost and availability.

STATISTICS SOURCES

BUSINESS STATISTICS
Available from U.S. Government Printing Office
Washington, DC 20402
Phone: (202) 512-1800
Fax: (202) 512-2250
Biennial. $20.00. Issued by Bureau of Economic Analysis, U.S. Department of Commerce. Shows annual data for 29 years and monthly data for a recent four-year period. Statistics correspond to the Survey of Current Business.

OUTLOOK FOR TRAVEL AND TOURISM
U.S. Travel Data Center
1100 New York Ave. NW, Ste. 450-W
Washington, DC 20005-3934
Phone: (202) 408-1832
Fax: (202) 408-1255
Annual. $130.00. Contains forecasts of the performance of the U.S. travel industry, including air travel, business travel, recreation (attractions), and accommodations.

SURVEY OF CURRENT BUSINESS
Available from U.S. Government Printing Office
Washington, DC 20402
Phone: (202) 512-1800
Fax: (202) 512-2250
Monthly. $41.00 per year. Issued by Bureau of Economic Analysis, U.S. Department of Commerce. Presents a wide variety of business and economic data.

TRENDS IN THE HOTEL INDUSTRY: USA EDITION
Pannell Kerr Forster
425 California St., Ste. 1650
San Francisco, CA 94104
Phone: (415) 421-5378
Fax: (415) 956-7708
Annual. $150.00. Includes financial data. (International edition also available.)

GENERAL WORKS

THE LODGING AND FOOD SERVICE INDUSTRY
Gerald W. Lattin and others
Educational Institute of the American Hotel & Motel Association
PO Box 1240
East Lansing, MI 48826
Phone: (800) 752-4567 or (517) 353-3500

1993. $53.95. Third edition. General survey of the hospitality industry.

MANAGEMENT OF HOTEL AND MOTEL SECURITY
Harvey Burstein
Marcel Dekker, Inc.
270 Madison Ave.
New York, NY 10016
Phone: (800) 228-1160 or (212) 696-9000
Fax: (212) 685-4540
1980. $85.00. (Occupational Safety and Health Series).

MARKETING MANAGEMENT FOR THE HOSPITALITY INDUSTRY: A STRATEGIC APPROACH
Allen Z. Reich
John Wiley and Sons, Inc.
605 3rd Ave.
New York, NY 10158-0012
Phone: (800) 225-5945 or (212) 850-6000
Fax: (212) 850-6088
1995. Price on application.

PURCHASING, SELECTION AND PROCUREMENT FOR THE HOSPITALITY INDUSTRY
John M. Stefanelli
John Wiley and Sons, Inc.
605 3rd Ave.
New York, NY 10158-0012
Phone: (800) 526-5368 or (212) 850-6000
Fax: (212) 850-6088
1992. Third edition. Price on application.

FURTHER READING

American Hotel & Motel Association. *Lodging.* Available from http://www.ahma.com/lodpro.html.

"Hotels Increase in Value." *Hotel & Motel Management.* 19 February 1996.

Lloyd-Jones, Anne R., and Stephen Rushmore. "Recent Trends in Hotel Management Contracts." *Real Estate Finance Journal,* Summer 1996. ◄━━

More than 1000 companies provided accident and health insurance in the United States in 1995, writing $100.27 billion in premiums. Of those, the top 300 companies accounted for $98.23 billion, or 98 percent of the industry's total net premiums written in 1995. The top five companies in terms of accident and health premiums written in 1995 accounted for 21 percent of the industry's total, or $21.21 billion.

Accident and health insurers have been plagued with ten consecutive years of industry-wide underwriting losses, from 1985 through 1995. Underwriting losses occur when benefits paid out exceed premiums written in any given year. Consequently, accident and health insurers have relied on investment income as well as cost reductions to offset these losses in order to achieve profitability.

INSURANCE, ACCIDENT AND HEALTH

SIC 6321

Faced with spiraling health care costs, competition from managed health care plans, and possible governmental intervention, accident and health insurers are experiencing intense pressure to become more competitive. In order to succeed, insurers will need to increase cost-efficiency, develop and maintain stable investment portfolios, and develop new products or services that provide alternatives to traditional insurance coverage.

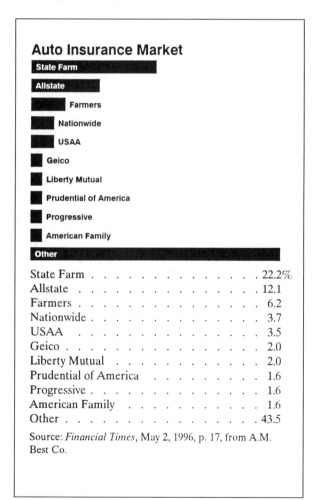

Auto Insurance Market

State Farm	22.2%
Allstate	12.1
Farmers	6.2
Nationwide	3.7
USAA	3.5
Geico	2.0
Liberty Mutual	2.0
Prudential of America	1.6
Progressive	1.6
American Family	1.6
Other	43.5

Source: *Financial Times*, May 2, 1996, p. 17, from A.M. Best Co.

In the mid-1990s, commercial carriers as well as Blue Cross & Blue Shield plans faced earnings pressure due to higher medical claims and higher expenses. The increasing growth of managed care companies forced many carriers to suppress necessary rate increases in the face of intense price competition. While the outlook remained stable to positive for commercial carriers that made strong local market adjustments, small- and medium-sized indemnity carriers faced a less promising outlook. Fewer competitors were expected to exist in the future, as companies would exit markets and product offerings and others would be absorbed in mergers and acquisitions.

INDUSTRY OUTLOOK

The accident and health insurance segment recorded a record underwriting loss of $4.6 billion in 1995, more than doubling the segment's 1994 underwriting loss of $2.03 billion. The last year that accident and health insurance reported an underwriting gain was 1985. As in recent years past, intense competition, richer benefits, and inadequate premium rates contributed to the weak financial performance of most health insurance organizations. Most Blue Cross & Blue Shield plans were less profitable in 1996 than in 1995, with narrower profit margins resulting from increased pricing pressure from other managed care organizations.

Accident and health insurers remain under growing pressure to maintain profitability. Higher medical claims and higher expenses increased earnings pressure in 1996. Intense price competition dramatically affected the medical loss ratios of accident and health insurers. With HMOs and other managed care organizations aggressively increasing their enrollment, some well-known commercial carriers left the health insurance business in 1996. Those leaving the field included Massachusetts Mutual Life Insurance Co. and John Hancock Mutual Life Insurance Co. Uncertainties about health care reform, changing demographics, and potential tax reforms on nonqualified products were expected to continue to pressure accident and health insurers.

INVESTMENT INCOME

With a pool of large reserves to invest, insurance companies can offset some of their underwriting losses with investment income. Managers of insurance company investment portfolios were rewarded with a fairly stable year in 1996, after 1995 when interest rates rose dramatically. In November of 1996 the Dow Jones Industrial Average broke 6500 for the first time. In the bond market, life and health insurers increased their holdings of below-investment grade bonds to 6.1 percent of their fixed income portfolio, still well below the levels maintained during the late 1980s and early 1990s. Insur-

ance investment in mortgage-backed securities continued to decline in 1996 as a percentage of fixed income portfolios, dropping to 26 percent after being reduced to 30 percent in 1995 and 33 percent in 1994.

SPIRALING HEALTH CARE COSTS

Rising health care costs made underwriting profits difficult to obtain for insurers. As costs escalate, so do claims by policy holders. Insurers have been unable to raise premium rates at the same rate as health care inflation rates. Some critics maintain that the current insurance system is partly to blame for escalating health care costs because it provides little incentive for providers to control costs. In fact, some observers believe that the current system provides an incentive for providers to perform superfluous tests, procedures, and services. Many other factors, though, have contributed to the rise in costs. They include: the burgeoning elderly population that requires additional health care, increased reliance on expensive medical equipment and technology, the shift of some costs from the government to private insurers, the costs of long-term illnesses such as AIDS and cancer, and an overall greater demand for health care services. Moreover, the meteoric rise in the cost of medical malpractice insurance has also taken its toll.

Medical savings accounts (MSAs), given improved tax status as part of the Health Insurance Reform Act of 1996 (also known as the Kassebaum-Kennedy bill), promised to offer employers a chance to reduce their health-care costs. As envisioned, MSAs would combine a high-deductible catastrophic health insurance plan with an employer-paid account that employees could use to pay their regular medical expenses. Commercial carriers were prepared to join the MSA market should they prove to be popular.

INDUSTRY REFORM

Accident/health insurers are under increasing pressure from both state and federal governing bodies that seek to regulate the industry. After President Clinton's national health-care reforms failed in 1994, state initiatives dominated the reform agenda in 1994 and 1995 and continued into 1996. The political realities of election year 1996 again forced Congress to address the issue of health-care reform at the national level. The result was the passage of the Kassebaum-Kennedy health insurance reform package.

Key elements of the Kassebaum-Kennedy bill of 1996 included portability, guaranteed coverages, group purchasing for small groups, and medical savings accounts (MSAs). While the impact of this legislation has yet to be determined on accident and health insurers, some companies left states that had enacted similar reforms concerning community rating, guaranteed issue, and similar measures.

FUTURE EXPECTATIONS

No line of insurance faces a more uncertain future than accident/health, especially regarding health care reform, changing demographics, and potential tax reforms. Managed care alternatives experienced explosive growth in 1995 and 1996, and were expected to continue gaining market share at the expense of commercial carriers. Additional competition may come from banks, mutual funds, and other financial institutions that may start offering plans that compete directly for traditional health insurance dollars.

Despite these threats, several long-term considerations offered promise for a stronger accident and health insurance industry. Demographic influences, such as income growth, wealth accumulation, population and work force changes, and increased home ownership could all serve to increase the demand for certain types of insurance products. The aging of the baby boom population should also increase demand for health care insurance products. To succeed in the 1990s, competitive accident/health insurers need to become more cost-efficient, develop stable investment portfolios, and develop new products or services that provide alternatives to traditional insurance coverage.

ORGANIZATION AND STRUCTURE

Accident and health insurance is provided on an indemnity basis by commercial carriers and Blue Cross & Blue Shield plans. Under indemnity insurance, the insurer pays the insured directly for any hospital or physician costs for which the insured is covered. Other providers of accident/health insurance include specialty health insurers, self-funded employer plans, and government plans. The accident and health line consists of the following categories: group, credit, collectively renewable, noncancelable, guaranteed renewable, nonrenewable, and other individual health and accident lines.

Group accident and health was the largest category of accident/health in 1995, accounting for $58.69 billion in net premiums written. Group insurance insures a pool of enrollees and offers benefits derived from economies of scale. Group insurance benefits include lower premiums and deductibles, more comprehensive coverage, and fewer restrictions. In the past, many insurers emphasized group insurance because it typically provided higher profit margins. In 1995 group plans accounted for 58.5 percent of all accident and health insurance premiums written. Group plans are most commonly offered through employers or industry associations.

Accident/health insurance companies may also provide service plans in connection with health care providers. Insurance companies arrange to pay health care providers for any service for which an enrollee has coverage. Under the service plan, the insurance company effectively agrees to provide the insured with health care services, rather than reimbursement dollars. Service plans offer the advantages of reduced paperwork and reduced financial liability for the insured.

In addition to voluntary insurance, a second type of private health insurance is managed health care. Managed care plans, or prepaid health plans, have increased in popularity during the 1980s and the 1990s. By the mid-1990s, managed care plans had proven their ability to control medical costs more effectively than traditional fee-for-service insurance plans. Under a managed care plan, a person can enroll in an organization that charges a monthly fee. In return for this monthly fee, the enrollee

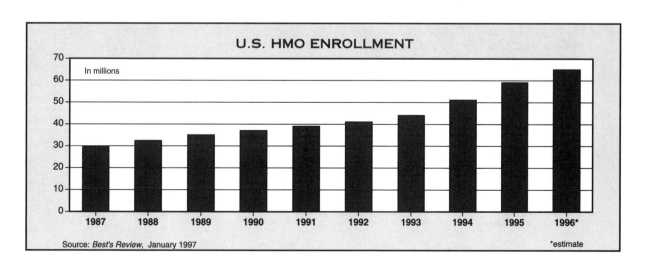

U.S. HMO ENROLLMENT

In millions

Source: *Best's Review*, January 1997   *estimate

receives access to health care services from the organization. Organizations that offer such prepaid plans include Health Maintenance Organizations (HMOs), Preferred Provider Organizations (PPOs), and Exclusive Provider Organizations.

Legislation also has an impact on the insurance industry. Accident/health insurers in the United States are subject to regulation at both the state and federal levels. Many of the regulations are designed to require that insurers maintain sufficient reserves to cover future liabilities. Other regulations require that companies not discriminate against certain customers or raise premium rates above certain levels that are deemed competitive by the governing body. Additional legislation that has had a significant impact on the industry relates to Medicare and Medicaid, which ensure coverage for elderly and poor citizens.

WORK FORCE

Employment in the accident/health insurance industry is representative of employment in the overall insurance industry, which also encompasses life and property/casualty insurance. In fact, most people employed in accident/health insurance work for multi-line insurers.

Employers in the insurance industry consist mainly of either insurance carriers or insurance agents and brokers. In 1995 there were approximately 306,100 home office personnel employed in health insurance out of an insur-

ance industry total of 1.54 million. That same year there were approximately 696,800 agents, brokers, and service personnel employed in the insurance industry, with many of these agents and brokers selling multiple lines of insurance, including accident/health. Government sources estimated there were 418,000 insurance agents and brokers employed in 1994, with approximately 30 percent of all agents and brokers being self-employed.

Jobs in the accident/health industry include administrative support, sales, executive, and managerial positions. Over half of all employment in the insurance industry is in the area of administrative support, which includes secretaries, word processors, and bookkeepers. Other occupations in this category include insurance policy processing clerks, claims clerks, and claims examiners and investigators.

Twenty percent of insurance employees have executive, administrative, or managerial jobs. Many of these workers are underwriters that evaluate applications to determine the risk involved in issuing a policy. Underwriters gather information on applications, review associated risks, and apply underwriting standards to reach a decision about whether or not to cover applicants for insurance. Typical career progression is from underwriter to senior underwriter to underwriting manager. Because many underwriting managers progress into general management, this occupation is popular for those seeking access to upper level management opportunities.

Other administrators and managers are employed as accountants, investment managers, or policy managers.

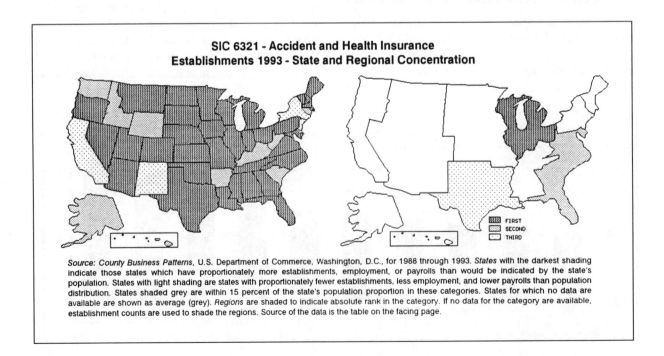

SIC 6321 - Accident and Health Insurance Establishments 1993 - State and Regional Concentration

FIRST
SECOND
THIRD

Source: County Business Patterns, U.S. Department of Commerce, Washington, D.C., for 1988 through 1993. *States* with the darkest shading indicate those states which have proportionately more establishments, employment, or payrolls than would be indicated by the state's population. States with light shading are states with proportionately fewer establishments, less employment, and lower payrolls than population distribution. States shaded grey are within 15 percent of the state's population proportion in these categories. States for which no data are available are shown as average (grey). *Regions* are shaded to indicate absolute rank in the category. If no data for the category are available, establishment counts are used to shade the regions. Source of the data is the table on the facing page.

SIC 6321
Occupations Employed by SIC 632 - Medical Service and Health Insurance

Occupation	% of Total 1994	Change to 2005
Insurance adjusters, examiners, & investigators	7.9	16.2
Insurance claims clerks	7.5	10.6
General office clerks	5.6	-5.6
Adjustment clerks	5.6	49.4
Insurance policy processing clerks	4.9	10.6
Clerical supervisors & managers	4.9	13.2
Secretaries, ex legal & medical	4.3	0.7
Claims examiners, insurance	4.0	10.6
Insurance sales workers	3.8	-4.3
Clerical support workers nec	3.3	-11.5
Data entry keyers, ex composing	3.0	-18.3
Computer programmers	2.9	-10.4
Management support workers nec	2.9	32.8
General managers & top executives	2.8	5.0
Systems analysts	2.8	77.0
Managers & administrators nec	2.1	10.6
Accountants & auditors	2.0	10.6
Registered nurses	2.0	64.7
Bookkeeping, accounting, & auditing clerks	1.9	-17.0
Sales & related workers nec	1.6	10.6
Receptionists & information clerks	1.5	10.6
Mail clerks, ex machine operators, postal service	1.2	-20.3
Health professionals & paraprofessionals nec	1.2	10.6
Computer operators, ex peripheral equipment	1.2	-37.1
File clerks	1.2	-44.7
Correspondence clerks	1.2	-22.5
Operations research analysts	1.1	44.0
Underwriters	1.1	37.2

Source: Industry-Occupation Matrix, Bureau of Labor Statistics. These data relate to one or more 3-digit SIC industry groups rather than to a single 4-digit SIC. The change reported for each occupation to the year 2005 is a percent of growth or decline as estimated by the Bureau of Labor Statistics. The abbreviation nec stands for 'not elsewhere classified'.

Statistically, one of the most lucrative and rewarding opportunities in this category is that of actuary. Actuaries use mathematical models and statistical techniques to analyze risk and to create and price accident/health products. Candidates for managerial positions usually have a college degree as well as knowledge of finance, economics, or accounting.

RESEARCH AND TECHNOLOGY

As markets became more competitive and profit margins continued to narrow during the 1990s, successful insurers were those that best utilized the efficiencies that automation and innovation could provide. A 1996 study of 25 top life/health insurers revealed that key success factors included efficiency in information technology, policy holder service, and underwriting.

With narrower margins and intense price competition, cost reduction continued to play an important role in achieving profitability for accident/health insurers.

Besides reorganization and downsizing, the most effective way to achieve these ends was through computer automation. By implementing information technologies already proven effective in manufacturing industries, insurers hoped to significantly improve customer service, reduce errors, improve new product delivery time, and reduce human intervention.

By integrating all their company information into one system, insurers were able to synthesize efforts in product development, marketing, sales, and customer service. In addition, many companies were putting new litigation management systems to work for them that allowed law departments to accelerate access to legal research data, internal company information, and client data. This information is used to protect company interests and combat fraud.

Examples of new technology that accident/health insurers were integrating into the industry in the 1990s included open-systems architecture computer systems, network computing, computer-aided software-engineering tools, multi-media training tools, and information management and delivery systems that use satellites. Industry regulators were also using this new technology to identify potentially insolvent insurers.

Another facet of research and technology, and one that has hindered the accident/health insurance industry, relates to the technological innovation that characterizes the health care industry. Although new medical technology has saved lives and improved the quality of health care in the United States, it has also created a financial burden for health insurers and has increased the likelihood of federal intervention that may negatively impact the industry.

On the other hand, the industry is seeing an increased emphasis on medical technology that serves to create more efficient procedures and services. These advances could help pave the way toward reduced costs as well as improved service in the future.

AMERICA AND THE WORLD

The United States' accident and health insurance industry is the largest and most advanced in the world. Although it was originally modeled after the British health insurance system, the industry in America differs from that of many other industrialized nations because it is one of the most privatized in the world. While most other nations, such as Canada and Britain, have already addressed rising costs and inaccessibility of health care with nationalized plans, the United States has maintained a relatively competitive and private system, with the notable exceptions of Medicare and Medicaid.

U.S. life insurers have established international operations largely through acquisitions and joint ventures. New opportunities were expected to open up in Europe toward the end of the 1990s, as European countries began to dismantle their welfare states and privatize such areas as pension coverage, health, and unemployment insurance.

ASSOCIATIONS AND SOCIETIES

ALLIANCE OF AMERICAN INSURERS
1501 Woodfield Rd., Ste. 400-W
Schaumburg, IL 60173-4980
Phone: (708) 330-8500
Fax: (708) 330-8602

AMERICAN INSURANCE ASSOCIATION
1130 Connecticut Ave. NW, Ste. 1000
Washington, DC 20036
Phone: (202) 828-7100 or (202) 828-7183
Fax: (202) 293-1219

AMERICAN INSURERS HIGHWAY SAFETY ALLIANCE
1501 Woodfield Rd., Ste. 400W
Schaumburg, IL 60173-4980
Phone: (708) 330-8500
Fax: (708) 330-8602

BLUE CROSS AND BLUE SHIELD ASSOCIATION
676 N. Saint Clair St.
Chicago, IL 60611
Phone: (312) 440-6000

DISABILITY INSURANCE TRAINING COUNCIL
1000 Connecticut Ave. NW, Ste. 810
Washington, DC 20036
Phone: (202) 223-5533
Fax: (202) 785-2274
Functions as an educational entity of the National Association of Health Underwriters. Maintains the Disability Training Insurance Council and provides seminars for insurance professionals on disability income insurance.

HEALTH INSURANCE ASSOCIATION OF AMERICA
1025 Connecticut Ave. NW, Ste. 1200
Washington, DC 20036
Phone: (202) 233-7780

INSURANCE INFORMATION INSTITUTE
110 William St.
New York, NY 10038
Phone: (212) 669-9200
Fax: (212) 732-1916

INSURANCE SERVICES OFFICE
7 World Trade Center
New York, NY 10048
Phone: (212) 898-6000

NATIONAL ASSOCIATION OF HEALTH UNDERWRITERS
1000 Connecticut Ave. NW, Ste. 1111
Washington, DC 20036
Phone: (202) 223-5533

NATIONAL ASSOCIATION OF INSURANCE BROKERS
1401 New York Ave. NW, Ste. 720
Washington, DC 20005
Phone: (202) 628-6700
Fax: (202) 628-6707

PERIODICALS AND NEWSLETTERS

AUTOMOBILE INSURANCE LOSSES, COLLISION, COMPREHENSIVE AND INJURY COVERAGES, VARIATIONS BY MAKE AND SERIES
Highway Loss Data Institute
c/o Stephen L. Oesch
1005 N. Glebe Rd., Ste. 800
Arlington, VA 22201
Phone: (703) 247-1600
Fax: (703) 247-1678
Semiannual. Free.

BEST'S REVIEW: LIFE-HEALTH INSURANCE EDITION
A. M. Best Co.
Oldwick, NJ 08858
Phone: (201) 439-2200
Monthly. $16.00 per year. Editorial coverage of significant trends and happenings.

BUSINESS AND HEALTH
Medical Economics Co., Inc.
680 Kinderkamock Rd.
Oradell, NJ 07649
Phone: (201) 262-3030
Fax: (201) 262-5461
Monthly. $85.00 per year. Edited for purchasers of employee health care services and employee health insurance.

HEALTH INSURANCE UNDERWRITER
National Association of Health Underwriters
100 Connecticut Ave. NW, Ste. 1111
Washington, DC 20006
Phone: (202) 223-5533
11 times a year. Members, $18.00 per year; non-members, $40.00 per year.

JOURNAL OF RISK AND INSURANCE
American Risk and Insurance Association
c/o Dr. Patricia Cheshier
California State University
School of Business
6000 J St.
Sacramento, CA 95819-6088
Quarterly. $90.00 per year.

DATABASES

ABI/INFORM
UMI/Data Courier
620 S. 3rd St.
Louisville, KY 40202
Phone: (800) 626-2823 or (502) 583-4111
Fax: (502) 589-5572
Provides online indexing to business-related material occurring in over 800 periodicals from 1971 to the present. Inquire as to online cost and availability.

BESTLINK
A. M. Best Co. Ambest Rd.
Oldwick, NJ 08858
Phone: (908) 439-2200
Fax: (908) 439-3296
Financial data on about 4,400 insurance companies. Updated quarterly. Inquire as to online cost and availability.

INSURANCE NEWS NETWORK
Insurance News Network
Contains information for consumers on home, auto, and life insurance, and special sections on some states. Includes information on viatical settlements that explains about receiving life insurance benefits while still alive. Fees: Free.

- URL: http://www.insure.com

INSURANCE PERIODICALS INDEX [ONLINE]
NILS Publishing Co.
21625 Prairie St.
Chatsworth, CA 91311
Phone: (800) 423-5910 or (818) 998-8830
Fax: (818) 718-8482
Compiled by the Insurance and Employee Benefits Div., Special Libraries Association. Corresponds to the printed Insurance Periodicals Index, *but with abstracts and biweekly updates. Time period is 1984 to date. Inquire as to online cost and availability.*

STATISTICS SOURCES

ACCIDENT FACTS
National Safety Council Statistics
Dept. 1121 Spring Lake Dr.
Itasca, IL 60143
Phone: (800) 621-7619 or (708) 285-1121
Fax: (708) 285-9114
Annual. $18.95.

HEALTH INSURANCE COMPANY FINANCIAL DATA
The National Underwriter Co.
505 Gest St.
Cincinnati, OH 45203
Phone: (513) 721-2140
Annual.

HEALTH INSURANCE STATISTICS
U.S. Social Security Administration
Available from U.S. Government Printing Office
Washington, DC 20402
Phone: (202) 783-3238

NATIONAL UNDERWRITER PROFILES
National Underwriter Co.
505 Gest St.
Cincinnati, OH 45203
Phone: (800) 543-0874 or (513) 721-2140
Fax: (513) 721-0126
Annual. $36.50. In three editions: Life Insurers, Health Insurers, and Property-Casualty Insurers financial and operating results summarized for 1,500 fire, casualty, and surety companies. Formerly Argus F. C. and S. Chart.

PROPERTY-CASUALTY INSURANCE FACTS
Insurance Information Institute
110 William St.
New York, NY 10038
Phone: (212) 669-9200
Annual. $22.50. Formerly Insurance Facts.

GENERAL WORKS

ACCIDENT FACTS
National Safety Council
444 N. Michigan Ave.
Chicago, IL 60611
Phone: (800) 621-7619 or (312) 527-4800
Annual. $15.00.

AFFORDABLE EMPLOYEE HEALTH CARE: OPTIONS FOR A MODEL BENEFITS PLAN
AMACOM
American Management Association
135 W. 50th St.
New York, NY 10020
Phone: (212) 586-8100
Fax: (212) 903-8168
1991. $69.95. A management view of health insurance for employees.

GUIDE TO LIABILITY INSURANCE
The Rough Notes Co., Inc.
1200 N. Meridian St.
Indianapolis, IN 46206
Phone: (800) 428-4384 or (317) 634-1541
Fax: (317) 634-1041
$29.50. A study guide and reference book for understanding ISO's New Commercial General Liability policy and to resolve numerous questions and problems.

INSURANCE ALMANAC: WHO, WHAT, WHEN AND WHERE IN INSURANCE
Donald E. Wolff, editor
Underwriter Printing and Publishing Co.
50 E. Palisade Ave.
Englewood, NJ 07631
Phone: (800) 526-4700 or (201) 569-8808
Fax: (201) 569-8817
Annual. $115.00. Lists insurance agencies and brokerage firms; U.S. and Canadian insurance companies, adjusters, appraisers, auditors, investigators, insurance officials, and insurance organizations.

MODERN ACCIDENT INVESTIGATION AND ANALYSIS:
AN EXECUTIVE GUIDE TO ACCIDENT INVESTIGATION
Ted S. Ferry
John Wiley and Sons, Inc.
605 3rd Ave.
New York, NY 10158-0012
Phone: (800) 526-5368 or (212) 850-6000
Fax: (212) 850-6088
1988. $89.95. Second edition.

FURTHER READING

Bond, Michael T. et al. "Medical Savings Accounts: the Newest Medical Cost Reduction Tool for Employers." *Business Horizons,* July-August 1996, 59.

Lenckus, Dave. "Efficiency a Common Trait of Top Life/Health Companies." *Business Insurance,* 26 August 1996, 11.

Natarajan, Kartik. "European Health Insurance Market Emerges," *National Underwriter Life & Health-Financial Services Edition,* 28 October 1996, 2.

Nowacki, Manfred J. et al. "Prognosis: Guarded." *Best's Review, Life/Health Edition,* January 1997.

Occupational Outlook Handbook, 1996-97 Edition. Washington, DC: U.S. Department of Labor, 1996.

Upton, Thomas S. and Michael L. Albanese. "Sharpening the Focus on Investment Management." *Best's Review: Life/ Health Edition,* January 1997. ◄►

The insurance industry in America, particularly the life insurance industry, is considered a fundamental pillar of the economy. With sales, assets, and investments in the multi-billion dollar range, the industry is a cornerstone of free market enterprise in the United States and around the world. With premium receipts in 1995 of $339.2 billion ($98.9 billion for life insurance, $159.96 billion for annuities, and $80.35 billion for health insurance), life insurance companies represent one of the highest revenue-generating industries in the nation. Not uniform by any means, the industry is marked by a number of corporations selling the same product in a variety of ways, and earning varying amounts of money selling the same product.

INSURANCE, LIFE

SIC 6311

With *billions of dollars in investments and assets totaling trillions of dollars the insurance industry has a financial network that can accommadate the diverse financial needs of its clients, particularly in an increasingly competitive global investment market. In recent years, insurance companies have increased their domestic stock holdings, taking advantage of the strength of their investment portfolios and a favorable economic climate. In addition to strong domestic markets, international acquisitions have placed insurance companies in the position to withstand competition from the growing number of alternative distribution channels. Considering their existing base in the financial services industry and the health of domestic and international markets, insurance companies should continue to dominate their well financed industry.*

Top 10 **MOST ADMIRED LIFE INSURANCE CORPORATIONS**

Ranked by: Scores (1-10) derived from a survey of senior executives, outside directors, and security analysts in 1995.

1. American International Group, with a score of 7.15
2. State Farm Group, 6.63
3. New York Life, 6.37
4. Teachers Insurance & Annuity, 6.33
5. Travelers Inc., 6.03
6. Nationwide Insurance Enterprise, 5.81
7. Metropolitan Life Insurance Co., 5.72
8. CIGNA, 5.35
9. Aetna Life & Casualty, 5.17
10. Prudential Insurance Co. of America, 5.09

Source: *Fortune,* America's Most Admired Corporations (annual), March 4, 1996, p. F-1.

Continuing its record-setting trend, life insurance in force reached a record high in 1995 of $12.6 trillion, an increase of 7.7 percent over 1994. Life insurance remained by far the largest segment of all insurance sold. Purchases of individual and group life insurance in 1995 were $1.6 trillion. Traditional whole life and combination insurance accounted for 55 percent of policies sold, a decrease from 58 percent in 1993. Universal and variable life insurance accounted for 21 percent of new sales. Approximately 78 percent of all U.S. households owned some form of life insurance in 1994, and the average amount per insured household was $159,100.

The average size of life insurance policies sold also continued to increase. In 1995, the average new individual policy was $82,310, compared to $79,710 in 1994 and $75,350 in 1990. Approximately half of all new policies purchased in 1994 were for people between the ages of 25 and 44, with 38 percent of those insured buying term policies and 22 percent buying universal or variable life policies.

Total premium receipts for 1995 totaled $339.2 billion for life insurance companies. This represented an increase of 3.9 percent over 1994. Receipts came from three sources: $98.9 billion from life insurance, $159.9 billion from annuities, and $80.4 billion from health insurance. Benefit payments reached a record $165.7 billion from life insurance policies and annuities during 1995, an increase of 11.4 percent over 1994. Of that total, more than $85.8 billion was paid to life insurance policyholders, $46.4 billion to annuitants, and $33.5 billion to beneficiaries.

Assets of U.S. life insurance companies reached a record high of $2.1 trillion in December 1995. This represented an increase of 10.4 percent, or $201 billion, over 1994. Assets of U.S. life insurance companies were invested in corporate bonds, government securities, stocks, mortgages, real estate, policy loans, and other assets. Taking advantage of a strong bull market in stocks, U.S. life insurance companies increased their holdings in stock by 32 percent over 1994.

Managers of insurance company investment portfolios were rewarded with a fairly stable year in 1996, after 1995 when interest rates rose dramatically. In November 1996 the Dow Jones Industrial Average broke 6500 for the first time. In the bond market, life and health insurers increased their holdings of below-investment grade bonds to 6.1 percent of their fixed income portfolio, still well below the levels maintained during the late 1980s and early 1990s. Insurance investment in mortgage-backed securities continued to decline in 1996 as a percentage of fixed income portfolios, reaching 26 percent after being reduced to 30 percent in 1995 and 33 percent in 1994. Overall, the financial stability of the industry continued to improve.

Looking ahead to the year 2000, life insurance companies are facing an increasingly competitive marketplace. Based on a recent U.S. Supreme Court ruling, national banks would be able to sell insurance from branches or operations located in small towns. That ruling opened up a new distribution channel for life insurance through face-to-face sales at local banks. While most life insurance continues to be sold by agents on a face-to-face basis, other alternative distribution channels such as direct response and worksite marketing are gaining in popularity. Regulators in the United States appear ready to allow new combinations of banks, insurers, and investment firms, making it more likely that life insur-

SIC 6310 - Life Insurance Establishments, Employment, and Payroll

	Establishments	Mid-March Employment	1st Q. Wages (annualiz. $ mil.)	Payroll per Empl. 1st Q. (annualiz.)	Annual Payroll ($ mil.)
1988	14,445	538,287	14,285.8	26,539	13,733.0
1989	14,330	568,796	15,864.8	27,892	14,828.2
%	-0.8	5.7	11.1	5.1	8.0
1990	14,057	571,775	16,703.5	29,213	16,272.5
%	-1.9	0.5	5.3	4.7	9.7
1991	14,461	616,584	18,702.3	30,332	17,993.8
%	2.9	7.8	12.0	3.8	10.6
1992	14,531	625,841	20,415.7	32,621	19,507.9
%	0.5	1.5	9.2	7.5	8.4
1993	12,691	618,304	20,282.2	32,803	19,716.8
%	-12.7	-1.2	-0.7	0.6	1.1
% 88-93	-12.1	14.9	42.0	23.6	43.6

Source: County Business Patterns, U.S. Department of Commerce, Washington, D.C., for 1988 through 1993. Payroll per employee is calculated using mid-March employment and 1st Quarter wages, annualized. Annual payroll, also shown, may not equal the annualized 1st Quarter wages. Rows headed by a percent sign (%) indicate change from the previous year. na stands for not available. The symbol (D) indicates that data are withheld by the source to avoid disclosure of competitive information. A dash (-) indicates that data are not available or cannot be calculated.

ance will become part of the broader financial services industry, and not remain a stand-alone industry. In the global marketplace, life insurers are likely to find themselves competing with vast, well-capitalized, and technologically advanced international organizations.

ORGANIZATION AND STRUCTURE

Although insurance companies may operate according to similar principles, the life insurance industry is hardly homogeneous. Companies do not charge the same amount for premiums, do not charge for expenses the same way, do not pay the same amount of commission to sales agents, do not provide the same kind or amount of training, do not sell the same products, and are not equally solvent. The one commonality throughout the industry is that licensed life insurance salespeople act as agents for their companies. These agents write several different kinds of life products, or policies, that the company offers.

Nearly all life insurance is issued by either mutual or stock life insurance companies. Mutuals have no stockholders, only policy holders, and the policyholders elect the board of directors who run the company. In this way, mutual policyholders participate in the fiscal management of the company and share in decisions regarding mortality expense, overhead costs, and investment rate of return. With $5.2 billion worth of life insurance in force, mutuals accounted for 35.7 percent of all the life insurance in force with U.S. life companies in 1995. Stock companies, on the other hand, are owned by their stockholders. They provided $9.4 billion worth of life insurance, or 64.3 percent of the total. Other sources of life insurance include fraternal societies and the federal government. Taking all of these sources into account, there was $12.9 trillion of life insurance in force at the end of 1995, or an average of $131,600 per American household.

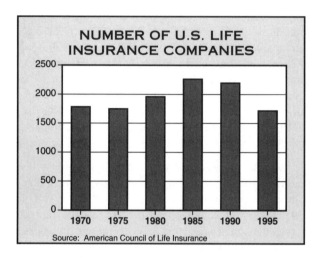

NUMBER OF U.S. LIFE INSURANCE COMPANIES

Source: American Council of Life Insurance

There are four major categories of life insurance: ordinary, group, industrial, and credit. Ordinary life insurance accounted for approximately 60 percent of all life insurance in force at the end of 1995. More than doubling from 1985 to 1995, there was $7.5 trillion of ordinary life insurance in force in the United States at the end of 1995, with whole life insurance accounting for more than half of that total. Most of the rest of the ordinary life insurance in force was accounted for by some type of term life insurance. From 1985 to 1995 the amount of group life insurance increased from $2.6 trillion to $4.8 trillion, with term life accounting for nearly all group life insurance in force. Industrial life insurance decreased over the decade from $28.2 billion in 1985 to $20.0 billion in 1995. The amount of credit life insurance, which is designed to pay the balance of loans in case the borrower should die, increased from $199.5 billion in 1993 to $231.3 billion in 1995.

Half of all full-time workers in commerce and industry in the United States are enrolled in retirement plans other than Social Security. Private pension plans are established by private agencies such as commercial, industrial, labor and service organizations, and nonprofit organizations. Individual Retirement Accounts (IRAs) or Keogh Plans are set up by individuals. Pension plans can be administered by the holder of the plan, placed

with banks or trust companies, or insured with life insurance companies. At the end of 1995, life insurance companies covered plans with 65.4 million persons and provided retirement income to 6.4 million people. More than 24 million people were covered by government-administered plans at the end of 1995. The federal Old-Age and Survivors Insurance (OASI) system, part of the Social Security program, remained the most comprehensive government retirement program offered, covering 173 million people eligible for Social Security benefits at the end of 1995.

WORK FORCE

There were approximately 1,700 U.S. life insurance companies in operation in 1995. The number has decreased steadily since 1988, when there were 2,343 companies. Overall, the U.S. insurance business employed some 2.24 million people in all of its branches in 1995. Of that total, there were approximately 1.54 million home office insurance personnel, 575,100 of whom were in life insurance. There were approximately 696,800 insurance agents, brokers, and service personnel employed in 1995. While the number of home office personnel engaged in life insurance declined from 581,100 in 1994 to 575,100 in 1995, the number of insurance agents, brokers, and service personnel steadily increased from 663,300 in 1990 to 696,800 in 1995. Approximately 30 percent of all insurance agents were self-employed.

Agents usually receive some sort of financial assistance from the companies they are affiliated with while they build a client base. They are also usually placed on a stipend or retainer, which is often replaced by straight retainer to cover monthly expenses. Life insurance companies often assist agents with basic expenses such as office furniture and supplies, though most agents cover their own travel, telephone, entertainment, and other expenses. Agents may receive commissions in two ways: a first-year commission for making the sale (usually 55 percent of the total first-year premium), or a series of smaller commissions paid when the insured pays his or her annual premium (usually 5 percent of the yearly payments for 9 years). Most companies will not pay renewal commissions to agents who resign.

Incomes of insurance agents vary greatly. Income depends very much on the agents own skill and knowledge of the industry, as well as the strength of the industry and market. Each year, about 20,000 agents qualify for the "Million Dollar Round Table" by selling policies with a face value of more than $1 million. Agents in their first 5 to 10 years on the job earned an average of $42,000 in the

SIC 6310
Occupations Employed by SIC 631 - Life Insurance

Occupation	% of Total 1994	Change to 2005
Insurance sales workers	19.2	-4.9
General office clerks	6.6	-41.4
Insurance policy processing clerks	5.7	4.9
Insurance claims clerks	4.4	15.3
Management support workers nec	4.2	31.9
Clerical supervisors & managers	3.9	12.4
Secretaries, ex legal & medical	3.8	0.1
Insurance adjusters, examiners, & investigators	3.6	15.4
Computer programmers	2.9	-11.0
Systems analysts	2.7	75.8
General managers & top executives	2.7	4.3
Underwriters	2.6	15.3
Managers & administrators nec	2.3	9.8
Clerical support workers nec	2.3	-12.1
Marketing & sales worker supervisors	2.3	9.9
Bookkeeping, accounting, & auditing clerks	2.1	-17.6
Adjustment clerks	1.8	25.8
Accountants & auditors	1.7	26.4
Professional workers nec	1.5	64.9
Claims examiners, insurance	1.5	9.9
Sales & related workers nec	1.2	9.9
Typists & word processors	1.0	-45.0

Source: *Industry-Occupation Matrix*, Bureau of Labor Statistics. These data relate to one or more 3-digit SIC industry groups rather than to a single 4-digit SIC. The change reported for each occupation to the year 2005 is a percent of growth or decline as estimated by the Bureau of Labor Statistics. The abbreviation nec stands for 'not elsewhere classified'.

early 1990s. Those with 10 or more years selling life insurance averaged $65,000 a year. The median annual earnings of salaried insurance sales workers was $31,620 in 1994, with a middle range of $22,050 to $46,380. The top 10 percent earned over $69,990, while the lowest 10 percent earned $15,500 or less.

Widely varying economic conditions, personal income levels, living and health standards, and other circumstances make it difficult to make direct comparisons of national levels of life insurance ownership between countries. One statistical measure that reduces the influence of these diverse factors is the ratio of life insurance in force to national income. This ratio has generally shown improvement in most countries since 1984. In the United States, for example, that ratio was 191 percent in 1994, indicating that the amount of life insurance in force in the United States equaled 191 percent of U.S. national income. In 1994, Japan led all nations, followed by Korea (349 percent), South Africa (250 percent), Canada (245 percent), Ireland (233 percent), and the Netherlands (220 percent). Other countries whose life insurance in force exceeded their national income included Australia, France, Sweden, Norway, Denmark, and Germany.

Looking ahead to the year 2000, U.S. life insurers face the prospect of having increasingly larger global competitors operating in their own market. At the end of 1995, there were only three U.S. life insurers ranked among the top ten insurers globally based on assets. Prudential ranked fifth in the world, followed by Teachers Insurance Annuity Association (TIAA/CREF) at eighth, and Metropolitan Life at tenth. Three of the top four largest insurers were based in Japan. Since 1950, when 74 percent of all insurance premiums originated in North America, the percentage of total premiums shifted

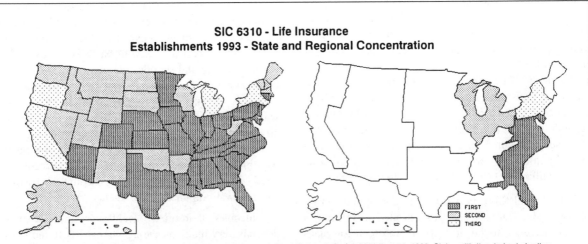

SIC 6310 - Life Insurance
Establishments 1993 - State and Regional Concentration

FIRST
SECOND
THIRD

Source: *County Business Patterns*, U.S. Department of Commerce, Washington, D.C., for 1988 through 1993. *States* with the darkest shading indicate those states which have proportionately more establishments, employment, or payrolls than would be indicated by the state's population. States with light shading are states with proportionately fewer establishments, less employment, and lower payrolls than population distribution. States shaded grey are within 15 percent of the state's population proportion in these categories. States for which no data are available are shown as average (grey). *Regions* are shaded to indicate absolute rank in the category. If no data for the category are available, establishment counts are used to shade the regions. Source of the data is the table on the facing page.

away from the United States. By 1994, only 32 percent of all insurance premiums originated in North America, and 68 percent came from the rest of the world.

U.S. life insurers have established international operations largely through acquisitions and joint ventures. New opportunities were expected to open up in Europe toward the end of the 1990s, as European countries began to dismantle their welfare states and privatize such areas as pension coverage, health, and unemployment insurance. Latin America was a hot market for U.S. life insurers in the mid-1990s, as companies were attracted by stabilizing economies, growing middle classes, and the privatization of some state-run pension programs. Aetna Inc., for example, was expected to invest as much as $390 million for a 49 percent stake in a joint venture with Brazil's largest insurer, Sul America Seguros. Other life insurers with expanded operations in Latin America included Metropolitan Life, ITT Hartford Group, New York Life, and Principal Financial Group.

ASSOCIATIONS AND SOCIETIES

ALLIANCE OF AMERICAN INSURERS
1501 Woodfield Rd., Ste. 400-W
Schaumburg, IL 60173-4980
Phone: (708) 330-8500
Fax: (708) 330-8602

AMERICAN COUNCIL OF LIFE INSURANCE
1001 Pennsylvania Ave. NW
Washington, DC 20004-2599
Phone: (800) 942-4242 or (202) 624-2000
Fax: (202) 624-2319

AMERICAN INSURANCE ASSOCIATION
1130 Connecticut Ave. NW, Ste. 1000
Washington, DC 20036
Phone: (202) 828-7100 or (202) 828-7183
Fax: (202) 293-1219

AMERICAN SOCIETY OF CLU AND CHFC
270 S. Bryn Mawr Ave.
Bryn Mawr, PA 19010
Phone: (610) 526-2500
Fax: (610) 527-4010

ASSOCIATION OF LIFE INSURANCE COUNSEL
c/o Frank D. Casciano
520 Broad St.
Newark, NJ 07102-3184
Phone: (201) 481-4526
Fax: (201) 268-4335
Members are attorneys for life insurance companies.

CASUALTY ACTUARIAL SOCIETY
1100 N. Glebe Rd., Ste. 600
Arlington, VA 22201
Phone: (703) 276-3100
Fax: (703) 276-3108

CONFERENCE OF CASUALTY INSURANCE COMPANIES
3601 Vincennes Rd.
Indianapolis, IN 46268
Phone: (317) 872-4061
Fax: (317) 879-8408

COUNCIL OF INSURANCE AGENTS AND BROKERS
316 Pennsylvania Ave. SE, Ste. 400
Washington, DC 20003
Phone: (202) 547-6616
Fax: (202) 546-0597

CPCU SOCIETY
PO Box 3009
Malvern, PA 19355
Phone: (215) 251-2728
Fax: (215) 251-2761

LIMRA INTERNATIONAL
PO Box 208
Hartford, CT 06141
Phone: (800) 235-4672 or (203) 688-3358
Fax: (203) 298-9555

NATIONAL ASSOCIATION OF CASUALTY AND SURETY EXECUTIVES
1130 Connecticut Ave. NW, Ste. 1000
Washington, DC 20036
Phone: (202) 828-7104
Fax: (202) 293-1219

NATIONAL ASSOCIATION OF LIFE UNDERWRITERS
1922 F St. NW
Washington, DC 20006-4387
Phone: (202) 331-6000
Fax: (202) 331-2179

PERIODICALS AND NEWSLETTERS

ANNUITY AND LIFE INSURANCE SHOPPER
United States Annuities
98 Hoffman Rd.
Englishtown, NJ 07726-8021
Phone: (800) 872-6684 or (908) 521-5110
Fax: (908) 521-5113
Quarterly. $45.00 per year. Provides information on rates and performance for fixed annuities, variable annuities, and term life policies issued by more than 250 insurance companies.

BEST'S REVIEW. PROPERTY-CASUALTY INSURANCE
A.M. Best Co.
Ambest Rd.
Oldwick, NJ 08858
Phone: (908) 439-2200
Fax: (908) 439-3296
Monthly. $21.00 per year. Editorial coverage of significant industry trends, developments, and important events.

BROKER WORLD
Insurance Publications, Inc.
10709 Barkley, Ste. 3
Overland Park, KS 66211
Phone: (800) 762-3387 or (913) 383-9191
Fax: (913) 383-1247
Monthly. $9.00 per year. Edited for independent insurance agents and brokers. Special feature issue topics include annuities, disability insurance, estate planning, and life insurance.

BUSINESS INSURANCE: NEWS MAGAZINE FOR CORPORATE RISK, EMPLOYEE BENEFIT AND FINANCIAL EXECUTIVES
Crain Communications, Inc.
740 N. Rush St.
Chicago, IL 60611-2590
Phone: (800) 678-9595 or (312) 649-5200
Fax: (312) 649-5360
Weekly. $80.00 per year. Covers a wide variety of business insurance topics, including risk management, employee benefits, workers compensation, marine insurance, and casualty insurance.

FIRE, CASUALTY AND SURETY BULLETIN
National Underwriter Co.
505 Gest St.
Cincinnati, OH 45203
Phone: (800) 543-0874 or (513) 721-2140
Fax: (513) 721-0126
Monthly. $267.50 per year. Five base volumes. Monthly updates.

THE INSURANCE FORUM: FOR THE UNFETTERED EXCHANGE OF IDEAS ABOUT INSURANCE
Joseph M. Belth, editor
Insurance Forum, Inc.
PO Box 245
Ellettsville, IN 47429
Phone: (812) 876-6502
Monthly. $60.00 per year. Newsletter. Provides analysis of the insurance business, including occasional special issues showing the ratings of about 1,600 life-health insurance companies, as determined by four major rating services: Duff & Phelps Credit Rating Co., Moody's Investors Service, Standard & Poor's Corp., and Weiss Research, Inc.

INSURANCE JOURNAL
Wells Publishing Co.
9191 Towne Centre Dr., No. 550
San Diego, CA 92122-1231
Phone: (619) 455-7717
Fax: (619) 546-1462
Biweekly. Controlled circulation. Provides updated news and information to independent insurance agents and brokers.

JOURNAL OF THE AMERICAN SOCIETY OF CLU
American Society of CLU and ChFC
270 S. Bryn Mawr Ave.
Bryn Mawr, PA 19010-2195
Phone: (610) 526-2500
Fax: (610) 527-4010
Bimonthly. $32.00 per year. Provides information on life insurance and financial planning, including estate planning, retirement, tax planning, trusts, business insurance, long-term care insurance, disability insurance, and employee benefits. (CLU is

Chartered Life Underwriter and ChFC is Chartered Financial Consultant.)

JOURNAL OF RISK AND INSURANCE
American Risk and Insurance Association
c/o Dr. Patricia Cheshier
California State University School of Business
6000 J St.
Sacramento, CA 95819-6088
Quarterly. $90.00 per year.

LIFE ASSOCIATION NEWS
National Association of Life Underwriters
1922 F St. NW
Washington, DC 20006-4387
Phone: (800) 247-4074 or (202) 331-6070
Fax: (202) 835-9068
Monthly. $6.00 per year. Edited for individual life and health insurance agents. Among the topics included are disability insurance and long-term care insurance.

LIFE INSURANCE PLANNING
Maxwell MacMillan Professional and Business Reference Publishing.
910 Sylvan Ave.
Englewood Cliffs, NJ 07632-3310
Phone: (201) 592-2000
Fax: (201) 816-3569
Looseleaf service $261.00 per year. Monthly supplementation.

LIFE INSURANCE SELLING
Commerce Publishing Co.
408 Olive St.
St. Louis, MO 63102
Phone: (314) 421-5445
Fax: (314) 421-1070
Monthly. $12.00 per year. Includes special issues on health insurance, disability insurance, annuities, and long-term care insurance.

NATIONAL UNDERWRITER, PROPERTY AND CASUALTY EDITION
National Underwriter Co.
505 Gest St.
Cincinnati, OH 45203
Phone: (800) 543-0874 or (513) 721-2140
Fax: (513) 721-0126
Weekly. $80.00 per year.

RISK MANAGEMENT
Risk Management Society Publishing, Inc.
205 E. 42nd St.
New York, NY 10017
Phone: (212) 986-9364
Fax: (212) 986-9716
Monthly. $48.00 per year.

DATABASES

BESTLINK
A. M. Best Co.
Ambest Rd.
Oldwick, NJ 08858

Phone: (908) 439-2200
Fax: (908) 439-3296
Financial data on about 4,400 insurance companies. Updated quarterly. Inquire as to online cost and availability.

INSURANCE NEWS NETWORK

Insurance News Network
Contains information for consumers on home, auto, and life insurance, and special sections on some states. Includes information on viatical settlements that explains about receiving life insurance benefits while still alive. Fees: Free.

- URL: http://www.insure.com

INSURANCE PERIODICALS INDEX [ONLINE]

NILS Publishing Co.
21625 Prairie St.
Chatsworth, CA 91311
Phone: (800) 423-5910 or (818) 998-8830
Fax: (818) 718-8482
Compiled by the Insurance and Employee Benefits Div., Special Libraries Association. Corresponds to the printed Insurance Periodicals Index, *but with abstracts and biweekly updates. Time period is 1984 to date. Inquire as to online cost and availability.*

STATISTICS SOURCES

BEST'S AGGREGATES AND AVERAGES: PROPERTY-CASUALTY

A. M. Best Co.
Ambest Rd.
Oldwick, NJ 08858
Phone: (908) 439-2200
Fax: (908) 439-3296
Annual. $285.00. Statistical summary of composite property casualty business. 400 pages of historical data, underwriting expenses and underwriting experience by line.

FINANCE, INSURANCE, AND REAL ESTATE USA: INDUSTRY ANALYSES, STATISTICS, AND LEADING COMPANIES

Arsen J. Darnay, editor
Gale Research
835 Penobscot Bldg.
Detroit, MI 48226-4094
Phone: (800) 877-GALE or (313) 961-2242
Fax: (313) 961-6083
1994. $195.00. Contains industry statistical data and a listing of leading companies for each of 50 Standard Industrial Classification (SIC) 4-digit codes covering finance, insurance, and real estate. Includes banks, mortgage banks, securities dealers, commodity brokers, real estate companies, and related firms. Several indexes are provided.

INSURANCE STATISTICS YEARBOOK

Organization for Economic Cooperation and Development
OECD Publications and Information Center
2001 L St. NW, Ste. 700
Washington, DC 20036-4910
Phone: (800) 456-6323 or (202) 785-6323
Fax: (202) 785-0350
Annual. $55.00. Presents detailed statistics on insurance premiums collected in OECD countries, by type of insurance.

LIFE INSURANCE FACT BOOK

American Council of Life Insurance
1001 Pennsylvania Ave. NW
Washington, DC 20004-2599
Phone: (202) 624-2000
Bennial. Free.

MORNINGSTAR VARIABLE ANNUITY/LIFE PERFORMANCE REPORT

Morningstar, Inc.
225 W. Wacker Dr.
Chicago, IL 60606
Phone: (800) 876-5005 or (312) 696-6000
Fax: (312) 696-6001
Monthly. $125.00 per year. Provides detailed statistics and ratings for more than 2,000 variable annuities and variable-life products.

PROPERTY-CASUALTY INSURANCE FACTS

Insurance Information Institute
110 William St.
New York, NY 10038
Phone: (212) 669-9200
Annual. $22.50. Formerly Insurance Facts.

GENERAL WORKS

CASUALTY ACTUARIAL SOCIETY YEARBOOK

Casualty Actuarial Society
1100 N. Glebe Rd., No. 600
Arlington, VA 22201-4714
Phone: (703) 276-3100
Fax: (703) 276-3108
Annual. $40.00. Approximately 2,292 actuaries working in insurance other than life insurance.

INSURANCE LAW REVIEW

Clark Boardman Callaghan
155 Pfingsten Rd.
Deerfield, IL 60015
Phone: (800) 323-1336 or (708) 948-7000
Fax: (708) 948-9340
Annual. $95.00. Provides yearly review of legal topics within the casualty insurance area, including professional liability, product liability, and environmental issues.

LIFE INSURANCE IN ESTATE PLANNING

James C. Munch, Jr.
Little, Brown and Co.
Time and Life Bldg.
1271 Avenue of the Americas
New York, NY 10020
Phone: (800) 343-9204 or (800) 759-0190
Fax: (800) 890-0875 or (212) 522-2067
1981. $80.00. Includes current supplement.

THE LIFETIME BOOK OF MONEY MANAGEMENT
Grace W. Weinstein
Gale Research
835 Penobscot Bldg.
Detroit, MI 48226-4094
Phone: (800) 877-GALE or (313) 961-2242
Fax: (313) 961-6083
1993. $40.00, hardcover. $15.95, softcover. Third edition. Gives popularly-written advice on investments, life and health insurance, owning a home, credit, retirement, estate planning, and other personal finance topics.

YOUR LIFE INSURANCE OPTIONS
Alan Lavine
John Wiley and Sons, Inc.
605 3rd Ave.
New York, NY 10158-0012
Phone: (800) 225-5945 or (212) 850-6000
Fax: (212) 850-6088
1993. $45.00. Tells how to buy life insurance, including the selection of a company and agent. Describes term life, whole life, variable life, universal life, and annuities. Includes a glossary of insurance terms and jargon.

FURTHER READING

1996 Life Insurance Fact Book. Washington, DC: American Council of Life Insurance, 1996.

Albanese, Michael L., and Cynthia J. Crosson. "Gap Widens Between Haves and Have-Nots." *Best's Review: Life/Health Edition,* January 1997.

Mayewski, Larry G. et al. "The New Value Proposition." *Best's Review: Life/Health Edition,* January 1997.

Scism, Leslie. "Aetna Joins the Crowd of U.S. Insurers Making Investments in Latin America." *Wall Street Journal,* 4 February 1997.

Upton, Thomas S., and Michael L. Albanese. "Sharpening the Focus on Investment Management." *Best's Review: Life/Health Edition,* January 1997.

U.S. Department of Labor. *Occupational Outlook Handbook, 1996-97 Edition.* Washington: GPO, 1996.

IRON AND STEEL FOUNDRIES

SIC 3320

The *foundry industry ranks among the top ten manufacturing segments in the United States, despite the fact that it has been battered by technological developments and competitive forces during the last two decades. An integral part of most major market segments in the United States, the fortunes of this industry—perhaps more than most others—rely on the stability and growth of the domestic economy. Given the sustained growth of the American economy throughout the late 1990s, most industry analysts have predicted modest growth in this sector as well.*

INDUSTRY SNAPSHOT

The steel and iron manufacturing industry has historically been driven by the rapid growth of industrialization both domestically and abroad. However, in recent decades the iron foundries have faltered under the intense pressure of foreign competition and a proliferation of inexpensive materials better suited to manufacturers' needs than steel. In 1995 more than 3,100 U.S. metal foundries made over 100,000 distinct products and produced more than 14.4 billion metric tons of product. At the same time, total industry shipments were at only 33 percent of the tonnage shipped in 1978. Throughout the 1980s, iron shipments steadily decreased, causing many manufacturers to go out of business. However, due to technological advancements and capacity gains through consolidations, output per remaining producer rose. The current growth in iron shipments is largely due to its increasing recognition as being economical and structurally sound; in some cases, it can replace steel forgings and welds.

High interest rates during the 1980s raised the industry's cost of capital, which is the price to finance and replace existing operations. This trend practically shut off any new capital expenditures on plant and equipment in the United States. The high dollar, high interest rates, and high cost of capital made it expensive to reinvest in the business of producing iron castings. Even now, with a weakened dollar and improved quality of American iron castings in the 1990s, imports are still likely to remain high. The offshore competitors that gained strong inroads to the American market are not likely to give up the market share easily.

INDUSTRY OUTLOOK

Steel and iron foundries rely on the health of many crucial segments of the U.S. economy to spur growth within their own market sector. The automotive, railroad, construction, agricultural implement, and hardware industries are the leading consumers for iron castings. With the increase in new housing during the late 1990s, there will also be a corresponding increase in demand for iron needed for boiler and radiator castings, valves and fittings, and pumps and compressors. This industry is also being aided by an increased volume in exports of heavy equipment—such as diesel engines, farm, and construction equipment. At the same time, many iron products are being replaced by plastic components in this industry; this substitution is also occurring in the refrigerant and air conditioning markets.

The automobile market, which places orders for forged gears and shafts in power transmissions, is expected to contribute to the growth of the iron industry into the twenty-first century. This development has arisen despite the fact that automakers had traditionally used more nonferrous and aluminum parts in an effort to make automobiles lighter and more fuel efficient. Specialty industrial machinery—such as that used for paper, printing, and plastic manufacturing and for farm and construction equipment—will also maintain a strong demand for iron. The recent development of austempered ductile iron (ADI) has allowed this metal to challenge forgings and cast steels in operations requiring strength and durability.

Investment casting has rebounded strongly from the recession of the early 1990s, and the demand for this material throughout the last half of the decade is strong in the commercial investment casting applications. The United States had more than 300 members in the investment casting industry at the end of 1996. These foundries shipped 15.7 million tons of casting valued at $29.3 billion—40,000 tons of which were steel investment casting shipments. Investment casting, independent of the metal poured, totaled 143,000 tons in 1996, and analysts expect this number to increase steadily, reaching 195,000 tons by 2006. Approximately 49,000 tons of commercial valves were expected to be shipped in 1997; the total shipments for that year were forecast at 147,000 tons.

Steel investment castings require high quality steel due to the intricate nature of parts cast using this process. Because extreme precision is required in producing these castings, any inclusions in the metal will ruin a part. The primary quality issue facing the steel industry in the 1990s was the cleanliness of steel. Clean steel is important to the industry because steel that is free of tramp elements, slag, and dross creates better quality parts. By the 1990s, significant progress had been made in clean steel production. However, future studies were expected to establish a method of quantifying the cleanliness of steel and find the relationship between cleanliness, mechanical properties, and design performance.

Current challenges facing the iron foundry industry include the demand for cheaper, lighter, and stronger components; changing markets; and foreign competition. In an effort to maximize their bottom line, many domestic end-use manufacturers are substituting plastics, ceramics, composites, lighter alloys, and nonferrous castings for iron in appliances, aerospace equipment, builder's hardware, and automotive components to help them compete in a global economy and to meet government regulations. In addition, changing markets always pose a serious threat to the steel and iron industry. The

forecast for a continued expansion of the economy to the end of the century leads to an optimistic outlook for the casting industry. Steady demand for American-made cars, trucks, farm equipment, machine tools, freight cars, and oil field machinery should maintain the need for iron castings. Finally, foreign competition continues to establish a solid presence in domestic markets. Approximately 28 percent of all plumbing fittings used in the United States in 1995 were imported. Thailand has been particularly responsible for the decline in American foundry's market shares in plumbing and electrical fitting castings. Recently, tariffs have been levied on these products in an effort to increase their sales price in the United States.

ORGANIZATION AND STRUCTURE

Historically, the automotive and aerospace industries were the largest customers of iron foundries. Companies in these industries found that outsourcing the casting business was a cheaper alternative than under-utilizing plant and labor capacities. Iron, on the other hand, has experienced some growth in the automotive industry as the mechanical properties of the metal make it an attractive alternative to heavier cast components. Subsequently, other segments of the industry are growing in response to changing market demands. For example, the automotive industry has switched most engine components to aluminum in response to consumer demands for lighter, more fuel efficient cars.

The foundry industry has also increased its worldwide marketability by certification through the International Organization for Standardization. This series of certifications, referred to as ISO 9000, offered a distinct competitive advantage for those who qualified and passed the certification audit. Although the audit was intensive, the result was the receipt of an internationally recognized benchmark standard which signified the recipient was paying attention to details and distinguishing itself as a manufacturer of quality castings, engineered with integrity.

WORK FORCE

In general, most labor-oriented occupations in the steel and iron foundries expected continued work force reductions through the 1990s. In 1996, the foundry industry employed approximately 217,000 people. However, the number of workers in this industry is expected to decline steadily until it reaches the end of a slump in 1998. The decline is primarily due to the shift by the automotive industry to nonferrous or aluminum components. The trend in this industry is for labor productivity to increase from a yearly total of 130,800 tons of casting shipments per worker to 133,000 tons of shipments by the year 2000. The occupations facing the most substantial reductions—30 percent and more, included worker supervisors, plastic and metal machine workers, plastic and metal grinding machine operators, maintenance, electricians, and machine tool cutting operators. Other occupations facing reductions—20 to 30 percent—included fabricators, assemblers, hand workers, general laborers, precision workers, molding machine operators, inspectors, welders, truck and tractor operators, and mechanists. The only occupations expecting to gain employment levels were hand grinders and polishers.

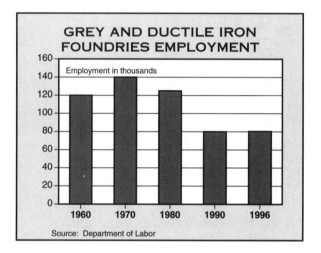

GREY AND DUCTILE IRON FOUNDRIES EMPLOYMENT

Employment in thousands

Source: Department of Labor

RESEARCH AND TECHNOLOGY

Conditions in the iron foundry industry—and in particular, iron production—have improved during the 1990s. Contractors were looking for less expensive alternatives to forged steel components in lower stress applications where the mechanical properties of iron would suffice. Iron's low production price tag was enticing to both manufacturers and consumers and served as one of the primary incentives for its use. Computer technology displaced the standard "pour and pray" method of metal casting and helped engineers optimize casting designs. The competitive edge this technology offered was substantial, especially considering the accuracy it lent to the price quoting process.

A major technological advancement in the foundry industry entered the market in the early 1990s. This advancement was known as either Rapid Prototyping or Functional Prototyping. Rapid prototyping is a computerized system that uses stereo lithography and selective laser sintering to create a three-dimensional shape that has been drawn on a computer aided drafting station. A computer takes the three dimensional model and mathematically slices it into layers of specific thickness. Each layer is transmitted digitally from the design unit to the production unit where the material of choice is used to build the shape layer by layer. Using this new technology, a designer could take a customer's idea, design it, and, in several hours or days, depending on the size of the part, have a prototype available for the customer to evaluate. The new technology dramatically reduced both the time and expense of producing intricate designs.

Steel investment foundries are not necessarily in a class of their own. Many foundries practice investment casting regardless of the metal type, and many steel foundries may practice several casting processes beside investment. Relatively few steel foundries, with respect to the entire steel foundry industry, exclusively used the investment casting process. One particular advantage of the investment casting process is that, compared to other casting processes, it is not harmful to the environment. The sand used can be further recycled; and since the process involves no chemical binders, there is no danger of producing hazardous fumes. With less waste and fewer pollutants produced, this process was not severely affected by increasing environmental legislation.

For future survival, the American iron industry must keep up with the technological changes in the industry. Technologies delivered high-quality parts, and the increased technological support that must accompany such inventory practices put pressure on many small domestic iron foundries to meet these changes in the marketplace. Those foundries that cannot make these transitions will not likely survive. New investments in operations to improve melting, alloying, metal flow, die and mold filling temperature control, and lubrication will all help in this regard. Today's global marketplace also demands stronger quality control, price restrictions, and tighter specifications. The days of testing sand moisture by hand are over, for today computer controls are what drive the most exacting tolerances. Partnership arrangements between foundries and their customers and suppliers will help to promote future growth. Pricing, quality assurance, service, and the consolidation of suppliers creating efficient production practices to keep costs low, and response time to customers high, will help protect domestic iron operations from further market declines.

AMERICA AND THE WORLD

The foundry industry faced tremendous challenges in the global marketplace in the 1990s. During the

1980s, foreign competitors who offered timely delivery of better quality castings at lower prices emerged. During the recession of the late 1980s and early 1990s, consumers turned to overseas suppliers, leaving the domestic producers behind. Consequently, U.S. foundries were operating at no more than 50 percent capacity by the mid-1980s. During the five-year period from 1991 to 1995, there was a shift in metal cast production from the Pacific Rim to North America. The United States and Canada increased 63 percent and 56 percent respectively, while Japan dropped 12 percent. The 1995 ranking of the five largest and iron producers was: the United States, 20 percent; China, 16 percent; the Commonwealth of Independent States (CIS), 15 percent; Japan, 10 percent and Germany, 6 percent. With the demise of communism in the former U.S.S.R., much of their production capacity remains underutilized. For example, Ukraine produced 6 million tons of casting in 1985 and reported a little less than 1 million tons in 1995.

The financial impact of environmental and safety regulations continued to beleaguer foundries throughout the 1990s. For example, Mexico was being pressured by the United States to install air pollution control devices in the early 1990s. However, Mexican laws included a loophole which did not require the devices to operate. In Korea, foundry workers were not provided with safety equipment—such as eye protection, hard hats, respiratory devices, or ear plugs. Additionally, workman's compensation and minimum wage were much higher in the United States. The benefits that American workers enjoyed, and often took for granted, added significantly to the costs of U.S. companies. In financial terms, foreign competitors legally had an edge toward profit during the 1990s. In 1994, the ratification of the North American Free Trade Agreement or NAFTA economically linked the United States, Canada, and Mexico. The agreement created one of the largest free trade zones in the world. International trade, especially the enforcement of export and import regulations, drastically changed.

Many steel foundries have found that they must export their products in order to prosper and grow. At the same time questions arise as to how labor costs, environmental regulations, and product dumping issues across the steel industry would be resolved. The North American Steel Council (NASC) was founded to address NAFTA related disagreements. The council consists of approximately twelve CEOs from steel companies in Mexico, Canada, and the United States belonging to the American Iron and Steel Institute (AISI) . The NASC is responsible for addressing trade issues associated with the steel industry and develop mutually acceptable solutions where possible. Despite these efforts, anti-dumping

and countervailing laws were still in place in the member countries because NAFTA free-trade codes were worthless without unified support in the United States, Mexico, and Canada.

ASSOCIATIONS AND SOCIETIES

AMERICAN FOUNDRYMEN'S SOCIETY
505 State St.
Des Plaines, IL 60016-8399
Phone: (800) 537-4237 or (708) 824-0181
Fax: (708) 824-7848

AMERICAN IRON AND STEEL INSTITUTE
1101 17th St. NW
Washington, DC 20036-4700
Phone: (202) 452-7100
Fax: (212) 463-6573

ASSOCIATION OF IRON AND STEEL ENGINEERS
3 Gateway Center, Ste. 2350
Pittsburgh, PA 15222
Phone: (412) 281-6323
Fax: (412) 281-4657

ASSOCIATION OF STEEL DISTRIBUTORS
401 N. Michigan Ave.
Chicago, IL 60601-4267
Phone: (312) 644-6610
Fax: (312) 321-6897

CASTING INDUSTRY SUPPLIERS ASSOCIATION
PO Box 280
Greendale, WI 53129
Phone: (414) 423-8655

INSTITUTE OF SCRAP RECYCLING INDUSTRIES
1325 G St. NW, Ste. 1000
Washington, DC 20005
Phone: (202) 737-1770
Fax: (202) 626-0900

IRON AND STEEL SOCIETY
410 Commonwealth Dr.
Warrendale, PA 15086-7512
Phone: (412) 776-1535
Fax: (412) 776-0430

NON-FERROUS FOUNDERS SOCIETY
455 State St., Ste. 100
Des Plaines, IL 60016
Phone: (708) 299-0950
Fax: (708) 299-3598
Members are manufacturers of brass, bronze, aluminum and other nonferrous cas tings.

STEEL FOUNDERS' SOCIETY OF AMERICA
Cast Metals Federation Bldg.
455 State St.
Des Plaines, IL 60016
Phone: (708) 299-9160
Fax: (708) 299-3105

STEEL SERVICE CENTER INSTITUTE
1600 Terminal Tower
Cleveland, OH 44113
Phone: (216) 694-3630

PERIODICALS AND NEWSLETTERS

ADVANCED MATERIALS AND PROCESSES
ASM International, Periodical Publication
Materials Park, OH 44073-0002
Phone: (216) 338-5151
Fax: (216) 338-4634
Monthly. $120.00 per year. Incorporating Metal Progress.*Technical information and reports on new developments in the technology of engineered materials and manufacturing processes.*

FOUNDRY MANAGEMENT AND TECHNOLOGY
Penton Publishing, Inc.
1100 Superior Ave.
Cleveland, OH 44114-2543
Phone: (800) 321-7003 or (216) 696-7000
Fax: (216) 696-8765
Monthly. Free to qualified personnel; others, $45.00 per year. Coverage includes nonferrous casting technology and production.

IRON AND STEEL ENGINEER
Association of Iron and Steel Engineers
3 Gateway Center, Ste. 2350
Pittsburgh, PA 15222
Phone: (412) 281-6323
Fax: (412) 281-4657
Monthly. $50.00 per year.

MODERN CASTING
American Foundrymen's Society
505 State St.
Des Plaines, IL 60016-8399
Phone: (800) 537-4237 or (708) 824-0181
Fax: (708) 824-7848
Monthly. $45.00 per year.

NEW STEEL: MINI AND INTEGRATED MILL MANAGEMENT AND TECHNOLOGIES
Chilton Co.
191 S. Gary Ave.
Carol Stream, IL 60188
Phone: (708) 665-1000
Fax: (708) 462-2862
Monthly. $35.00 per year. Covers the primary metals industry, both ferrous and nonferrous. Includes technical, marketing, and product development articles. Formerly Iron Age.

STEEL TIMES INTERNATIONAL
Argus Business Media Ltd. Fuels and Metals Journals
Queensway House, Two Queensway
Redhill, Surrey, England RH1 1QS
Phone: 01737 768611
Fax: 01737 761685
Six times a year. $183.60 per year.

33 METALPRODUCING: FOR PRIMARY PRODUCERS OF STEEL, ALUMINUM, AND COPPER-B ASE ALLOYS
Penton Publishing
1100 Superior Ave.
Cleveland, OH 44114-2543
Phone: (800) 321-7003 or (216) 696-7000
Fax: (216) 696-7648
Monthly. $50.00 per year. Covers metal production technology and methods and industry news. Includes a bimonthly Nonferrous Supplement.

DATABASES

CITIBASE (CITICORP ECONOMIC DATABASE)
FAME Software Corp.
77 Water St., 9 Fl.
New York, NY 10005
Phone: (212) 898-7800
Fax: (212) 742-8956
Presents over 6,000 statistical series relating to business, industry, finance, and economics. Includes series from Survey of Current Business *and many other sources. Time period is 1947 to date, with daily updates. Inquire as to online cost and availability.*

MATERIALS BUSINESS FILE
ASM International Materials Information
9639 Kinsman Rd.
Materials Park, OH 44073
Phone: (216) 338-5151
Fax: (216) 338-4634
Provides online abstracts and citations to worldwide materials literature, covering the business and industrial aspects of metals, plastics, ceramics, and composites. Corresponds to Steels Alert, Nonferrous Metals Alert, *and* Polymers/Ceramics/Composites Alert. *Time period is 1985 to date, with monthly updates. Inquire as to online cost and availability.*

METADEX (METALS ABSTRACTS/ALLOYS INDEX)
ASM International
Materials Information
Materials Park, OH 44073
Phone: (800) 336-5152 or (216) 338-5151
Fax: (216) 338-4634
Worldwide literature on the science and practice of metallurgy, 1966 to present. Detailed alloys indexing, 1974 to present. Monthly updates. Inquire as to online cost and availability.

PROMT: PREDICASTS OVERVIEW OF MARKETS AND TECHNOLOGY
Information Access Co.
362 Lakeside Dr.
Foster City, CA 94404
Phone: (800) 321-6388 or (415) 378-5000
Fax: (415) 358-4759
Companies, products, applied technologies and markets. U.S. and international literature coverage, 1972 to date. Daily updates. Inquire as to online cost and availability. Provides abstracts from more than 1,200 publications.

STATISTICS SOURCES

AMERICAN IRON AND STEEL ANNUAL STATISTICAL REPORT
American Iron and Steel Institute
1101 17th St. NW
Washington, DC 20036-4700
Phone: (202) 452-7100
Fax: (202) 463-6573
Bimonthly. $25.00 per year.

BUSINESS STATISTICS
Available from U.S. Government Printing Office
Washington, DC 20402
Phone: (202) 512-1800
Fax: (202) 512-2250
Biennial. $20.00. Issued by Bureau of Economic Analysis, U.S. Department of Commerce. Shows annual data for 29 years and monthly data for a recent four-year period. Statistics correspond to the Survey of Current Business.

NONFERROUS CASTINGS
U.S. Bureau of the Census
Washington, DC 20233-0800
Phone: (301) 457-4100
Fax: (301) 457-3842
Annual. (Current Industrial Reports MA-33E.)

OECD IRON AND STEEL INDUSTRY
Organization for Economic Cooperation and Development
Available from OECD Publications and Information Center
2001 L St. NW, Ste. 700
Washington, DC 20036-4910
Phone: (202) 785-6323
Fax: (202) 785-0350
Annual. Price varies. Data for orders, production, manpower, imports, exports, consumption, prices and investment in the iron and steel industry in OECD member countries.

OECD STEEL MARKET AND OUTLOOK
Organization for Economic Cooperation and Development
OECD Publications and Information Center
2001 L St. NW, Ste. 700
Washington, DC 20036-4910

Phone: (202) 785-6323
Fax: (202) 785-0350
Annual. Price varies.

STATISTICS OF WORLD TRADE IN STEEL
United Nations Economic Commission for Europe
Available from United Nations Publications
2 United Nations Plz., Rm. DC2-853
New York, NY 10017
Phone: (800) 253-9646 or (212) 963-8302
Fax: (212) 963-3489
Annual. $25.00.

STEEL MILL PRODUCTS
U.S. Bureau of the Census
Washington, DC 20233-0800
Phone: (301) 457-4100
Fax: (301) 457-3842
Annual. (Current Industrial Reports MA-33B).

SURVEY OF CURRENT BUSINESS
Available from U.S. Government Printing Office
Washington, DC 20402
Phone: (202) 512-1800
Fax: (202) 512-2250
Monthly. $41.00 per year. Issued by Bureau of Economic Analysis, U.S. Department of Commerce. Presents a wide variety of business and economic data.

FURTHER READING

Annual Survey of Manufacturers. Washington: U.S. Bureau of Census, 1996.

Darnay, Arsen J., ed. *Manufacturing USA: Industry Analyses, Statistics, and Leading Companies.*5th ed. Detroit: Gale Research, Inc., 1996.

Delch, D. K. ''Free Trade: Patient Needs Resuscitation.'' *American Metal Market,* 25 Nov. 1996, p 14.

Horton, Robert. ''Brisk Demand Fuels Investment Casting Technology Innovations.'' *Modern Casting,* December 1996, p 45.

Despite predictions for an optimistic future for the jewelry industry, such was not the case in the early 1990s. The industry took a downturn after 1993, and jewelry sales continued to languish into 1995. One sign of recovery was seen when the Jewelry Manufacturers Association reported an increas in attendance at their 1995 exhibition by overseas companies, including buyers from South America, Japan, Ireland, the Czech Republic, and Romania.

Legislation regarding environmental issues had an adverse effect on the jewelry industry. Clean air and water laws enacted in the 1990s presented challenges to manufacturers, particularly those firms involved in electroplating, causing the cost of the process to increase significantly. Such establishments were generally required to have wastewater treatment facilities that removed harmful chemicals and metals from discharge water, and some manufacturers were also required to install air scrubbers to clean exhaust.

JEWELRY

SICs 3911, 3961

Expectations of an improved economy, the hope that customers would begin indulging in long-deferred purchases, and a resurgence in the wearing of fashion jewelry accessories all led industry experts to project an optimistic future for the industry. Overall, the jewelry industry will continue to increase gradually through the remainder of the 1990s. By 1998, production values for precious metal jewelry were expected to reach $4.997 billion, and those for costume jewelry were expected to reach $1.672 billion.

INDUSTRY OUTLOOK

There were almost 900 firms actively manufacturing costume jewelry in the United States in the late 1990s, and the combined value of goods produced by these companies totaled $1.604 billion in 1996. Nearly 10 percent of the industry's total production was exported to other countries, including Canada and Mexico. In 1990 the U.S. Department of Commerce identified 2,147 manufacturers of precious metal in the United States. In 1993, the estimated value of precious metal jewelry shipments was $4.4 billion, an increase of 7 percent from the 1991 figures. Nonetheless, some retailers experienced sales decreases because of lowered consumer confidence and decreased discretionary income.

Costume jewelry sales in the early 1990s were noteworthy, as consumers hit hard by the recession of the late 1980s became less likely to purchase fine jewelry. Indeed, some of the largest U.S. fine jewelry firms suffered severe financial setbacks in the early 1990s, a fate that did not befall costume jewelry companies at that time. A newly popular niche in the market was the "fakes" category that marketed relatively inexpensive pieces that look amazingly similar to the genuine article. Industry analysts noted that the economic downturn of the mid- to late 1990s, while affecting consumer spending, had relatively little effect on the overall health of the industry.

Beginning in 1995, the costume jewelry industry began to experience an economic uplift. According to Amanda Meadus and Wendy Hessen of *WWD*, "designer-manufacturers" were in the best position for a comeback. The largest of those companies were Carolee Designs and Erwin Pearl, each of whose sales volumes was estimated to be $50 million. As of August of 1995, retailers and vendors were reporting a definite upturn in costume jewelry sales. According to Wendy Hessen of *WWD*, "manufacturers were reporting relatively steady reorders, and stores reported stronger-then-anticipated sales."

The government continued to play an important role in the industry. Costume jewelry manufacturers found it necessary to upgrade facilities in order to comply with environmental legislation. While such measures meant increased costs, the industry remained healthy and expected to benefit from free trade agreements signed by the government during the mid-1990s.

ORGANIZATION AND STRUCTURE

The precious metal jewelry industry encompasses retailers, wholesalers, manufacturers, and suppliers, including lapidaries, refiners, stone dealers, findings manufacturers (manufacturers of the small parts used in making jewelry, such as clasps and other items), and subcontractors who provide services such as polishing and electroplating. Manufacturing firms in the precious metal jewelry industry tend to be small establishments and are concentrated in the New York City area. The industry's major expenses are the costs of raw materials and highly skilled workers.

Two major issues of concern to the precious metal jewelry industry are the 10 percent luxury tax imposed on jewelry sales exceeding $10,000 and environmental regulations related to manufacturing processes. Regulations concerning the removal of toxic levels of metals used in electroplating have added financial burdens to many manufacturers and subcontractors. Beginning in May 1993, products that were made with ozone-depleting chemicals were required to carry identifying labels.

American costume jewelry companies manufacture products using various methods, primarily using base metals, including tin and lead, to fashion such findings as clasps and pin-backs, the basic components of a finished piece. One manufacturing process used is stamping, a labor-intensive method that produces a finer, more polished piece of metal. The more typical method in the shaping of metal for costume jewelry however, is casting, which involves pouring molten metal into a mold. This process lends itself more readily to mass-production of the jewelry. Manufacturers also utilize relatively recent methods of centrifugal casting and injection molding of plastic. The findings produced from these processes are then used to fabricate finished pieces or sold to individual costume jewelry houses. Another integral function is electroplating, the electrolytic process of coating base metals with a small amount of a precious metal to give the jewelry its gold or silver appearance.

Most large costume jewelry companies sell their wares through department stores, an innovative marketing strategy that evolved in the 1950s. Earrings are one of the biggest sellers, followed in volume by necklaces and pins. One-third of all costume jewelry purchased in the United States is purchased as a gift—Christmas, Mother's Day, and Valentine's Day are the peak selling seasons. Two-thirds is purchased for individual use. Costume jewelry is also a popular product on the novel home-shopping networks found on cable channels, with celebrities such as Kenneth Jay Lane and Joan Rivers appearing on-camera to sell their wares.

WORK FORCE

Employment figures for the costume jewelry industry rose from a five-year low of 166,000 by the close of 1992 to 180,000 by 1996. However, average hourly wages for production workers in the field increased to a high of $8.00 per hour. Also of benefit to industry employees, the increase in public awareness of such repetitive-injury afflictions as carpal-tunnel syndrome resulted in improved working conditions. The precious metals industry employed approximately 35,300 people in 1993, a figure that was below the 37,500 workers in the industry reported in 1987. By 1996 the employment rate was slightly higher at about 35,700. Four states—California, New York, Rhode Island, and Massachusetts—accounted for about 56 percent of all employment in the industry, and firms shipped 63 percent of goods.

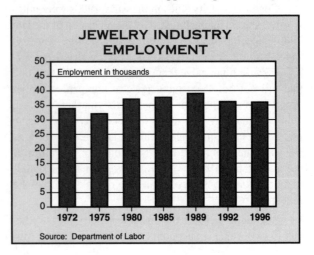

JEWELRY INDUSTRY EMPLOYMENT

Employment in thousands

Source: Department of Labor

AMERICA AND THE WORLD

Despite the falling value of the U.S. dollar abroad, the United States maintained an unfavorable trade balance in 1992. Italy, one of the United States' major competitors, supplied 40 percent of all precious metal jewelry imports in 1992. Thailand, Israel, and Hong Kong were also key suppliers. Thailand and Israel both benefitted from the Generalized System of Preferences (GSP), a program that permits developing countries to export some products to the United States duty-free.

The main markets for U.S. exports of precious metal jewelry were Switzerland, Japan, and Thailand. Exports to Mexico are expected to increase after ratification of the North American Free Trade Agreement, which enables American goods to enter Mexico duty-free. Most Mexican goods already enter the United States duty-free under the GSP; tariffs between Canada and the United States were already being eliminated under the U.S.-Canada Free Trade Agreement. Some industry experts also hoped that the establishment of product standards for the European Community would benefit the United States. In 1995 the value of exports was $402.9 million.

ASSOCIATIONS AND SOCIETIES

GEMOLOGICAL INSTITUTE OF AMERICA
1660 Stewart St.
Santa Monica, CA 90404
Phone: (800) 421-7250 or (310) 829-2991
Fax: (310) 828-0247

JEWELERS BOARD OF TRADE
PO Box 6928
Providence, RI 02940

JEWELERS OF AMERICA
1185 6th Ave., 30 Fl.
New York, NY 10036
Phone: (800) 223-0673 or (212) 768-8777
Fax: (212) 768-8087

JEWELERS SECURITY ALLIANCE OF THE U.S.
6 E. 45th St.
New York, NY 10017
Phone: (800) 537-0067 or (212) 687-0328
Fax: (212) 808-9168

JEWELERS VIGILANCE COMMITTEE
401 E. 34th St., Ste. N13A
New York, NY 10016
Phone: (212) 532-1919

JEWELRY INFORMATION CENTER
8 W. 19th St., 4 Fl.
New York, NY 10011
Phone: (212) 727-0130
Fax: (212) 463-8054

JEWELRY MANUFACTURERS ASSOCIATION
1430 Broadway, Ste. 1603
New York, NY 10018
Phone: (212) 730-2900
Fax: (212) 221-3540

MANUFACTURING JEWELERS AND SILVERSMITHS OF AMERICA
100 India St.
Providence, RI 02903-4300
Phone: (800) 444-6572 or (401) 274-3840
Fax: (401) 274-0265

PERIODICALS AND NEWSLETTERS

AMERICAN JEWELRY MANUFACTURER
Chilton Book Co.
201 King of Prussia Rd.
Radnor, PA 19089-0230
Phone: (800) 695-1214 or (610) 964-4000
Fax: (610) 964-4745
Monthly. $36.00 per year.

JEWELERS' CIRCULAR-KEYSTONE
Chilton Co.
201 King of Prussia Rd.
Radnor, PA 19089-0230
Phone: (800) 695-1214 or (610) 964-4000
Fax: (215) 964-4273
Monthly. $95.00 per year.

MODERN JEWELER
Vance Publishing Corp.
10901 W. 84th Ter. 3 Pine Ridge Plz.
Lenexa, KS 66214
Phone: (913) 438-8700
Fax: (913) 438-0695
Monthly. $25.00 per year. Edited for retail jewelers. Covers the merchandising of jewelry, gems, and watches.

NATIONAL JEWELER
Miller Freeman, Inc.
1515 Broadway
New York, NY 10036
Phone: (800) 444-4881 or (800) 227-4675
Fax: (913) 841-2624
Bimonthly. $480.00 per year. For jewelry retailers.

DATABASES

PROMT: PREDICASTS OVERVIEW OF MARKETS AND TECHNOLOGY

Information Access Co.
362 Lakeside Dr.
Foster City, CA 94404
Phone: (800) 321-6388 or (415) 378-5000
Fax: (415) 358-4759
Companies, products, applied technologies and markets. U.S. and international literature coverage, 1972 to date. Daily updates. Inquire as to online cost and availability. Provides abstracts from more than 1,200 publications.

STATISTICS SOURCES

CURRENT BUSINESS REPORTS: MONTHLY WHOLESALE TRADE

U.S. Bureau of the Census
Available from U.S. Government Printing Office
Washington, DC 20402
Phone: (202) 512-1800
Fax: (202) 512-2250
$16.00 per year.

U.S. INDUSTRIAL OUTLOOK: FORECASTS FOR SELECTED MANUFACTURING AND SERVICE INDUSTRIES

Available from U.S. Government Printing Office
Washington, DC 20402
Phone: (202) 512-1800
Fax: (202) 512-2250
Annual. $37.00. (Replaced in 1995 by U.S. Global Trade Outlook.*) Issued by the International Trade Administration, U.S. Department of Commerce. Provides basic data, outlook for the current year, and "Long-Term Prospects" (five-year projections) for a wide variety of products and services. Includes high technology industries. Available on the world wide web at gopher://gopher.umsl.edu:70/11/library/govdocs/usio94*

FURTHER READING

Frankovich, George R. *The Jewelry Industry,* Providence, RI: Manufacturing Jewelers and Silversmiths of America.

Hessen, Wendy. "Fashion Jewelry: Outlook Positive." *WWD,* 28 August 1995. Available from http://sbweb2.med.iacnet.com.

Hughes Jr., Allan J. "Jewelry Industry Stages a Shining Show." Available from http://www.pbn.com/W031797/jewelry.htm.

INDUSTRY SNAPSHOT

The legal service industry is the largest professional service industry in the nation. The industry collects more than $115 billion in annual revenue—more than five times the annual revenue collected by advertising firms, almost three times the revenue collected by accounting and auditing firms, and approximately the same amount of revenue as that generated by the automobile industry. The legal services industry employs nearly one million people, with approximately 70 percent of the work force comprised of practicing attorneys. The legal services industry is a dynamic force in our society for preserving a harmonious society, maintaining social order, and resolving disputes.

LEGAL SERVICES

SIC 8111

The legal industry in the United States is facing a number of contemporary issues regarding internal firm structure, external competition, and diversified growth. While it continues to enjoy some of the highest revenues among the service industries, competition from paralegal (or ancillary) services is forcing the further contraction of the industry into larger firms, more and more patterned after traditional corporations. Diversification is another strategy for maintaining the profitability of the industry, as individuals and firms carve out niche markets.

Top 10 LARGEST LAW FIRMS

Ranked by: Total number of lawyers in 1995.

1. Baker & McKenzie, with 1,703 lawyers
2. Skadden, Arps, Slate, Meagher & Flom, 1,052
3. Jones, Day, Reavis & Pogue, 1,016
4. Morgan, Lewis & Bockius, 751
5. Mayer, Brown & Platt, 668
6. Sidley & Austin, 656
7. Gibson, Dunn & Crutcher, 646
8. Fulbright & Jaworski, 640
9. Weil, Gotshal & Manges, 603
10. Latham & Watkins, 598

Source: *Lawyers Almanac* (annual), Aspen Law & Business, 1996, p. A-1+.

INDUSTRY OUTLOOK

Fueled both by decreased economic vitality and increased competition between law firms, the traditional "partnership track" is changing within the industry. Previously, there was an unspoken promise among major law firms that a summer job between the second and third year of law school was a practical guarantee of a permanent position after graduation, with a relatively safe period of tenure as an associate for at least one year and up to five years. Those attorneys enduring the five years as an associate were usually offered a partnership position. However, the partnership path has become more arduous, with the apprenticeship period prior to "making partner" ten years or longer. Further, many candidates with partnership potential have simply been rejected. To keep revenues ahead of costs, law firms have had to increase the ratio of associates to partners from a one to one ratio to five partners for every six associates, according to an American Bar Association (ABA) report.

This change in the dynamics of legal career progression has led to two internal innovations within the industry. The first is an increased use of paralegals to do the work formerly assigned to associates. According to some estimates, the number of paralegal positions could increase by 100 percent over the next decade. The second strategy is to develop a new position, the ''career attorney.'' Law firms offer those individuals who have little or no chance of making partner a higher salary than other associates for staying with the firm.

Another structural innovation to maintain competitiveness is increased use of branch offices and acquisitions. By the early 1990s, 30 percent of the lawyers in the nation's 250 largest firms practiced in branch offices. The *ABA Journal* noted that ''branches have become a major weapon in many law firm's arsenal to fight for new business and increased market share.'' Many large U.S. law firms are looking overseas to international opportunities as well. As Ward Bower, a consultant with the Philadelphia office of Altman, Weil and Pensa, said in the *ABA Journal*, ''The costs of overseas expansion are very heavy, so the downside can be great, but so is the potential.''

Some within the industry feel a trend is emerging towards increased size and concentration among the largest firms. An ABA report from the early 1990s indicated that, by the year 2001, approximately 20 to 50 law firms will dominate the legal profession, while mid-sized firms will become increasingly specialized in an attempt to carve out niche markets. In addition, the report speculated that the largest law firms will double in size, employing 3,000 or more attorneys. Small firms will continue to handle issues such as landlord-tenant disputes, traffic violations, and a variety of criminal matters that have been the traditional province of the small firm. However, increased competition from legal chains such as Hyatt Legal Services, coupled with spiraling overhead costs, will force the small or solo practitioners to be better organized and more efficient.

The trend towards increased size in law firms has lead to an increasing need for professional management. The law firm is faced with dual pressures of the need for increased responsiveness to client needs and demands, counterbalanced by the need to generate revenue. Furthermore, increased size is creating an additional impediment to effective management; firms with 200 or more partners cannot run a firm as a democracy. The trend is towards creating a new position, an executive director, who will function as a chief operating officer. This individual will have minimal legal responsibility and perhaps will not even be lawyer. In fact, a recent ABA report indicates that, by the turn of the century, nonlawyers may be established as partners at law firms, even the most prestigious ones.

In addition to professional management, law firms are (and will continue) adopting other structures of more traditional business organizations. These include practice managers (similar to product managers) who augment service delivery and expedite performance appraisal in diverse sub-disciplines (e.g. tax, litigation, etc.) within the profession.

Lawyers are facing increased competitive pressure from paralegal firms offering low-cost legal services. Independent paralegals increased in number from approximately 200 individuals in 1985 to an estimated 6,000 in 1992, a trend which is expected to continue. These nonlawyer practitioners are offering legal services in such areas as will and living trust preparation and child-support arrangements, although ancillary services are permitted only when they are offered in-house and in conjunction with legal representation and supervised by lawyers. Concerns expressed by the ABA in conjunction with the ancillary businesses include the danger of loss of confidentiality and conflict of interest and the distraction of lawyers from their duties of law practice and their professional responsibilities. In contrast, members of the legal community indicate that full-service law firms al-

SIC 8111 - Legal Services
Industry Data by State

State	Establishments			Employment			Payroll			Revenues - 1992 ($ mil.)			% change 87-92	
	1987	1992	% of US 92	1987	1992	% of US 92	1987 ($ mil.)	1992 ($ mil.)	$ Per Empl. 92	Total ($ mil.)	Per Estab.	$ Per Empl. 92	Revenues	Payroll
California	19,307	20,756	47.1	111,948	132,588	47.5	4,254.6	6,494.5	48,983	16,311.5	0.8	123,024	56.5	52.6
New York	12,160	12,481	28.3	94,852	101,755	36.4	3,342.6	4,892.8	48,084	14,286.6	1.1	140,401	43.6	46.4
Texas	8,992	10,769	24.4	52,024	63,032	22.6	1,833.8	2,980.3	47,282	7,565.0	0.7	120,018	55.9	62.5
Illinois	6,483	6,845	15.5	41,802	47,082	16.9	1,485.2	2,205.4	46,841	5,784.6	0.8	122,863	53.4	48.5
Florida	8,965	10,871	24.7	49,793	56,524	20.2	1,822.0	2,647.8	46,845	5,394.0	0.5	95,429	45.9	45.3
D.C.	1,550	1,492	3.4	24,923	29,030	10.4	1,075.9	1,662.1	57,255	4,631.4	3.1	159,539	54.8	54.5
Pennsylvania	5,325	5,943	13.5	35,606	42,990	15.4	1,035.9	1,720.2	40,013	4,397.5	0.7	102,290	60.0	66.1
New Jersey	5,159	5,720	13.0	31,215	35,635	12.8	931.9	1,459.8	40,965	3,498.4	0.6	98,175	55.3	56.6
Massachusetts	4,042	4,462	10.1	25,765	27,606	9.9	773.7	1,171.7	42,442	3,267.7	0.7	118,371	52.9	51.4
Ohio	4,959	5,211	11.8	26,105	29,176	10.4	715.3	1,022.7	35,052	2,754.7	0.5	94,416	45.2	43.0

Source: Census of Service Industries, 1987 and 1992, Bureau of the Census, U.S. Department of Commerce. Data are sorted by 1992 revenues and, if revenues are unavailable, by establishments in 1992. (D) indicates that data are withheld by the source to avoid disclosure of competitive information. A dash (-) indicates that data are not available. Percentage changes between 1987 and 1992 are calculated using numbers that have *not* been rounded; hence they may not be reproducible from the values shown.

low attorneys the opportunity to better serve their clients. Proponents of ancillary businesses, though, indicate that professional diversification is already practiced by accounting firms that do tax law and banks that engage in estate planning. Diversification, supporters argue, allows law firms to remain competitive.

U.S. LEGAL SERVICES TOTAL REVENUES

Billion dollars

Source: Department of Commmerce

ORGANIZATION AND STRUCTURE

An attorney, also known as a lawyer, is an agent; a person appointed to act on behalf of another. The right to assume this agency relationship is granted by state statutes dictating admission to the state bar. Admission to the bar confers the authority or license to practice law. Requirements for admission usually includes three years of college, graduation from an ABA accredited law school, residency requirements, and successful completion of the bar examination. Some states such as California have varying practices regarding study requirements and allow apprenticeships in lieu of academic study. In addition, some states rely entirely upon their own bar examinations while others utilize a "multistate" examination. Attorneys admitted to the bar in one state may not practice in another without permission of the other state's authority. Practicing law without proper accreditation is a punishable and sometimes criminal offense. While there has never been a nationwide bar exam, 46 states require that the applicant pass the MBE (multistate bar exam) as part of the admission process.

Lawyers are admitted to the bar for life; however, misconduct can bring suspension or disbarment as well as other appropriate punishment. As a general axiom, any conduct that would have prevented admission to the bar will be sufficient to suspend or disbar an attorney. The general criterion is whether or not the attorney is deemed fit for the confidence and trust required in the attorney-client relationship.

The bar review industry is an extremely concentrated and competitive industry wherein five firms control 90 percent of the market. The five major players in the industry—Bar/Bri, PMBR, SMH, Barpassers, and Reed—aggressively pursue the limited market of 58,000 annual exam takers, which generate $50 million in revenues. Bar/Bri is the leader amongst such reviewers. Founded in 1967, over 600,000 students have taken the course.

LEGAL SERVICE PROVIDERS

The four broad categories of legal service providers in the United States, with a variety of subcategories and practitioners under each, are as follows:

According to the Sixth Amendment to the U.S. Constitution and affirmed by the landmark Supreme Court case *Gideon v. Wainwright*, all individuals are entitled to legal services regardless of ability to pay. Due to the high cost of legal counsel, public legal assistance programs have been established for people who cannot afford legal counsel.

In 1963, Clarence Earl Gideon, an uneducated gambler and petty thief, insisted on his right to legal counsel. The Supreme Court and Justice Hugo Black upheld this right, indicating: "Any person hauled into court who is too poor to hire a lawyer cannot be assured a fair trial unless counsel is provided for him . . . This seems to us to be an obvious truth." The courts have expanded the ruling in *Gideon* to apply to all criminal cases. This has led to the establishment of two types of public legal offices: public defenders and legal aid offices.

Public defenders represent criminal defendants. A criminal case is distinguished from a civil case by two primary elements. In a civil suit, someone has sustained a loss or harm as the result of some act (or failure to act) by another. The individual filing the act is seeking compensation (either monetary or performance) rather than seeking punishment, as in a criminal case. Secondly, a civil case is usually filed by an individual party against another; a criminal case is filed by the state against an individual. The current state of public defense has been enormously strained by caseloads that have overwhelmed defense attorneys, as well as a paucity of funds. By the mid-1990s, the bulk of criminal justice resources went to police protection, prisons, and prosecutors, leaving only 2.3 percent of the criminal defense budget for public-defender services. Legal aid offices represent the civil counterpart of public defenders. These organizations represent those who cannot afford legal counsel in civil matters such as tort litigation (i.e. law suits resulting from negligence, etc.). Eligibility guidelines for access to public legal services vary depending on location, family size, and household income.

Hundreds of attorneys work for the government at each of the three levels: local, state and federal. Tax dollars are used to fund these positions. Government attorneys are primarily engaged in legal problems concerning government service (e.g. Bureau of Consumer Protection, Human Relations Commission, or Department of Environmental Resources) or government-regulated industries (e.g. Public Utilities Commission).

Nonprofit organizations provide free representation to individual cases that relate to the organization's unique interests. Special interest organizations such as the Environmental Defense Fund, the National Association for the Advancement of Colored People (NAACP), and the American Civil Liberties Union (ACLU) are engaged in the provision of legal services.

In addition to career nonprofit lawyers, charitable legal services or pro bono work is becoming increasingly prevalent as a mandatory part of legal education. Several law schools have mandated public service requirements for graduating students in the 1990s. Tulane University School of Law requires that graduating students perform at least 20 hours of public service law. Beginning with the class of 1996, Columbia University School of Law required its students to complete 40 hours of pro bono work over a period of two years. At other schools, nonprofit work is voluntary—New York University's entering class pledged to perform 95 hours of community service work apiece during their three-year tenure. In addition, more than 50 law schools have initiated programs to ease the debt burden of graduates who go into nonprofit practice.

The most prevalent form of legal service provider is the private attorney. There are two basic types of private attorney: individual or sole practitioners, and group practitioners or law firms. Group practices fall into three primary categories: informal arrangements in which two or more lawyers share office space and support services; partnerships; and legal corporations. Partnerships and legal corporations are designated as law firms. An American Bar Association survey indicates that practices with five or less attorneys comprise 25 percent of the industry. Approximately 31 percent of lawyers engage in practice as partners or as associates of law firms with 20 or more practitioners. Law firms range in size from two practitioners to large, multi-divisional firms engaging more than 100 associates. An additional category of private lawyers are employed by large corporations as house counsel.

A recent survey of ABA membership indicated that 80 percent of attorneys work in private practice with law firms and another 10 percent work in corporate law departments. Thus, approximately 90 percent work in private practice. The remainder is divided between government, judiciary, and academia.

ECONOMIC STRUCTURE

Most of the $115 billion annually collected by lawyers and law firms is collected through direct billing of legal fees. There are four fee arrangements generally

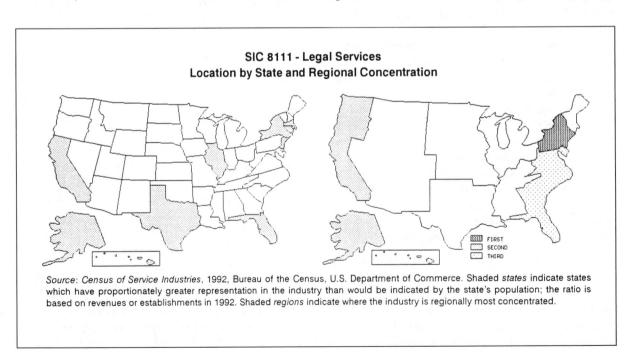

SIC 8111 - Legal Services
Location by State and Regional Concentration

FIRST
SECOND
THIRD

Source: Census of Service Industries, 1992, Bureau of the Census, U.S. Department of Commerce. Shaded *states* indicate states which have proportionately greater representation in the industry than would be indicated by the state's population; the ratio is based on revenues or establishments in 1992. Shaded *regions* indicate where the industry is regionally most concentrated.

utilized within the industry: contingent fees, hourly rates, retainers, and fixed fees.

Contingent fees are common for attorneys in civil practice. A large percentage of civil case fee arrangements are structured so that the attorney is only compensated if she is successful in obtaining a settlement on the client's behalf. The fee is usually a percentage of the amount of the settlement. Some contingent fees can range as high as 60 percent of an eventual settlement, with the industry standard hovering around 30 to 35 percent of the amount of the settlement. Contingent fee arrangements also require the client to cover the expenses accrued in filing a complaint, engaging in discovery and either negotiating a settlement or trying the case in court. These expenses are the responsibility of the client, whatever the outcome.

An hourly rate is assessed based on the amount of time an attorney invests in a case. However, trends within the industry towards increased client accountability have led to modifications in the traditional practice of "billable hours." Consulting firms that advise both law firms and clients about billing practices have become more common. These firms have assisted law firms in assessing their service provision costs and investments and allocating these costs to clients in the form of equitable fee-setting. Fee-consulting firms have also been able to save clients from 10 to 30 percent on their legal bills.

A retainer is an advance payment estimated to cover the cost of legal services. Retainers are based on an estimate of the time spent by the lawyer, the complexity of the legal issues in question, and the potential amount of money involved in the action.

Fixed fees are usually assessed for simple legal tasks, such as deed preparation, no contest divorce, consumer bankruptcy, etc. Fixed fees are those in which the client pays in advance a fixed amount for a certain legal service—for example, $50 for preparation of a deed—regardless of the length of time it takes the attorney to complete the task.

WORK FORCE

The total work force in the legal services industry was approximately 940,000 in 1994. The majority of the work force—over 700,000 employees—is composed of practicing attorneys. The remainder of the industry's workers are primarily support staff personnel such as paralegals and clerical support personnel.

Wages in the industry continue to rise at a rate above that set by most other industries. In the mid-1990s the average beginning lawyer earned $36,600 per year, and top graduates from top law schools started out at around $80,000 per year. Since 1990, the current economic climate has induced law firms to take a more conservative approach to hiring. Despite this "soft" market for recent law school graduates, average starting salaries have continued to accelerate. Graduates from prestigious law schools such as Yale University, Columbia University, New York University, and Georgetown University Law Center continue to receive average starting salaries in excess of $70,000. This demand for higher salaries is fueled in part by rising tuition costs at major law schools and heavy student loan burdens faced by recent graduates. Average associate salaries for young New York attorneys exceed $82,000.

SIC 8111
Occupations Employed by SIC 8111 - Legal Services

Occupation	% of Total 1994	Change to 2005
Lawyers	32.2	42.9
Legal secretaries	29.2	25.7
Paralegals	10.0	68.1
Receptionists & information clerks	4.1	57.1
Bookkeeping, accounting, & auditing clerks	4.1	17.8
General office clerks	2.9	34.0
Legal assistants, law clerks nec	2.6	25.7
Secretaries, ex legal & medical	2.1	3.3
Typists & word processors	2.0	-21.4
General managers & top executives	2.0	49.1
File clerks	2.0	48.0
Messengers	2.0	22.0

Source: *Industry-Occupation Matrix*, Bureau of Labor Statistics. These data relate to one or more 3-digit SIC industry groups rather than to a single 4-digit SIC. The change reported for each occupation to the year 2005 is a percent of growth or decline as estimated by the Bureau of Labor Statistics. The abbreviation nec stands for 'not elsewhere classified'.

There are several areas of the legal profession that are currently regarded as "hot" practice areas. These include bankruptcy and corporate reorganization, environmental law, alternative dispute resolution, and technology law. Environmental and technology practices are fueled by growing concerns and increasing legislation in regards to the environment and ubiquitous high-technology issues such as computer fraud and electronic funds transfer. In addition, firms operating in the increasingly competitive pharmaceutical and biotechnology businesses are seeking to protect their innovations through patents, accelerating the demand for patent attorneys and attorneys with technical training. Finally, the litigious nature of modern American society is expected to ensure a continued emphasis on legal mediation and arbitration.

In support services, paralegal work represents the area with the greatest employment potential. Law firms, rather than pay top salaries to law school graduates, are utilizing increasing numbers of paralegals to do routine work traditionally performed by new associates.

RESEARCH AND TECHNOLOGY

The practice of law has and will continue to become increasingly automated. Law office automation is becoming a necessity to improve office productivity and efficiency, to maintain cost controls and competitiveness, and to meet minimum standards of professional practice.

The evolution of the personal computer represents the primary focal point of automation in the legal industry. Currently, on-line databases made available through vendor services such as LEXIS-NEXIS or Westlaw allow the practitioner to expedite research. A report issued by the ABA Legal Technology Research Center in Chicago predicted that individual law firms will create their own in-house databases to draw on their past work and handle new matters more expeditiously. Furthermore, firms will create "expert" software that allows the entire firm to tap into a specialist's knowledge. For example, intricate areas such as tax and bankruptcy law will be embedded into substantive software.

ASSOCIATIONS AND SOCIETIES

AMERICAN BAR ASSOCIATION
750 N. Lake Shore Dr.
Chicago, IL 60611
Phone: (800) 621-6159 or (312) 988-5000
Fax: (312) 988-6281

AMERICAN COLLEGE OF TRIAL LAWYERS
8001 Irvine Center Dr., Ste. 960
Irvine, CA 92718
Phone: (714) 727-3194
Fax: (714) 727-3894

ASSOCIATION OF TRIAL LAWYERS OF AMERICA
1050 31st St. NW
Washington, DC 20007
Phone: (800) 424-2725 or (800) 344-3023
Fax: (202) 337-0977

DEFENSE RESEARCH AND TRIAL LAWYERS ASSOCIATION
750 N. Lake Shore Dr., Ste. 500
Chicago, IL 60611
Phone: (312) 944-0575
Members are attorneys, insurance companies, insurance adjusters, and others. Includes Product Liability and Professional Liability Committees.

NATIONAL LAWYERS GUILD
55 6th Ave.
New York, NY 10013
Phone: (212) 966-5000
Fax: (212) 966-9714

NATIONAL LEGAL AID AND DEFENDER ASSOCIATION
1625 K St. NW, 8 Fl.
Washington, DC 20006
Phone: (202) 452-0620
Fax: (202) 872-1031

TAX ANALYSTS
6830 N. Fairfax Dr.
Arlington, VA 22213
Phone: (800) 955-3444 or (703) 533-4400
Fax: (703) 533-4444
An advocacy group reviewing U.S. and foreign income tax developments. Includes a Tax Policy Advisory Board.

PERIODICALS AND NEWSLETTERS

THE AMERICAN LAWYER
American Lawyer Media L.P.
600 3rd Ave., 2 Fl.
New York, NY 10016
Phone: (212) 973-2800
Fax: (212) 972-6258
10 times a year. $565.00 per year. General information for American attorneys.

CHICAGO: THE LAWYER'S MAGAZINE
American Bar Association
750 N. Lake Shore Dr.
Chicago, IL 60611
Phone: (312) 988-5000
Fax: (312) 988-6014

LAW OFFICE ECONOMICS AND MANAGEMENT
Clark Boardman Callaghan
155 Pfingsten Rd.
Deerfield, IL 60015
Phone: (800) 323-1336
Fax: (708) 948-9340
Quarterly. $115.00 per year.

THE NATIONAL LAW JOURNAL: THE WEEKLY NEWSPAPER FOR THE PROFESSION
New York Law Publishing Co.
111 8th Ave.
New York, NY 10011
Phone: (800) 274-2893 or (212) 779-9200
Weekly. $124.00 per year. News and analysis of the latest developments in the law and the law profession.

OF COUNSEL: THE LEGAL PRACTICE REPORT
Aspen Law and Business
200 Orchard Ridge Dr.
Gaithersburg, MD 20878
Phone: (800) 638-8437 or (301) 417-9075
Fax: (301) 695-7931
Semimonthly. $325.00 per year. Newsletter on the management, marketing, personnel, and compensation of law firms.

THE PRACTICAL LAWYER
Committee on Continuing Professional Education
American Law Institute-American Bar Association
4025 Chestnut St.
Philadelphia, PA 19104-3099
Phone: (800) 253-6397 or (215) 243-1600
Fax: (215) 243-1664
Eight times a year. $35.00 per year.

THE PRACTICAL REAL ESTATE LAWYER
American Law Institute-American Bar Association Committee on Continuing Professional Education
4025 Chestnut St.
Philadelphia, PA 19104-3099
Phone: (800) 253-6397 or (215) 243-1600
Fax: (215) 243-1664
Bimonthly. $35.00 per year. Frequently includes legal forms for use in real estate practice.

TAXATION FOR LAWYERS
Warren, Gorham & Lamont, Inc.
1 Penn Plz., 42 Fl.
New York, NY 10119-4098
Phone: (800) 950-1210 or (800) 950-1213
Fax: (212) 971-5113
Bimonthly. $88.00 per year. Edited for attorneys who are not tax specialists. Emphasis is on tax planning, estates, trusts, partnerships, and taxation of real estate.

STATISTICS SOURCES

U.S. INDUSTRIAL OUTLOOK: FORECASTS FOR SELECTED MANUFACTURING AND SERVICE INDUSTRIES
Available from U.S. Government Printing Office
Washington, DC 20402
Phone: (202) 512-1800
Fax: (202) 512-2250

Annual. $37.00. (Replaced in 1995 by U.S. Global Trade Outlook.) Issued by the International Trade Administration, U.S. Department of Commerce. Provides basic data, outlook for the current year, annd "Long-Term Prospects" (five-year projections) for a wide variety of products and services. Includes high technology industries. Available on the world wide web at gopher://gopher.umsl.edu:70/11/library/govdocs/usio94

GENERAL WORKS

THE LAWYER'S ALMANAC; AN ENCYCLOPEDIA OF INFORMATION ABOUT LAW, LAWYERS, AND THE PROFESSION
Harcourt Brace and Co.
525 B St., Ste. 1900
San Diego, CA 92101-4495
Phone: (800) 831-7799 or (619) 699-6716
Fax: (619) 699-6596
1985. $60.00.

THE BETRAYED PROFESSION: LAWYERING AT THE END OF THE TWENTIETH CENTURY
Sol M. Linowitz and Martin Mayer
Charles Scribner's Sons
866 3rd Ave.
New York, NY 10022
Phone: (800) 257-5755 or (212) 702-2000
Fax: (212) 319-1216
1994. $25.00. A critical view of present-day lawyers and law firms.

FURTHER READING

*U.S. Occupational Outlook Handbook 1994-1995,*U.S. Bureau of Labor and Statistics, 1996. ◼

MACHINERY AND EQUIPMENT, GENERAL INDUSTRIAL

SIC 3560

The *general industrial industry began a slow recovery after the recession ended in the mid-1990s. In 1995, according to the 1995 Annual Survey of Manufactures, the industry employed 46,200 workers, a decrease of about 46 percent. However, this figure was 11.3 percent above the 41,500 workers in the industry reported in the 1992 census, and 13.8 percent above the 40,600 workers in the 1987 census. Industry productivity continued to rise as well, with $7.03 billion in value of goods reportedly shipped in 1995. This was 13.75 percent above the $6.18 billion worth of goods shipped in 1994 and 27.8 percent above the $5.5 billion shipped in 1992.*

The general industrial machinery and equipment industry is heavily dependent upon sales to other manufacturing businesses and to construction industries. In addition, about 30 percent of revenues are derived from exports. Intense capital investments during the U.S. industrial boom of the mid-1900s resulted in steady growth in demand for all types of industrial machinery.

Pumps are one of the most common machines used by industry today, second only to electric motors. As such the health of the pump manufacturing industry depends to a great extent on the general health of industrial America. Particularly important are the petrochemical and the pulp and paper industries, but steel making, electric power generation, oil and gas wells, fields and pipelines, sewage system construction, and general housing and commercial construction also depend on a variety of special purpose pumps.

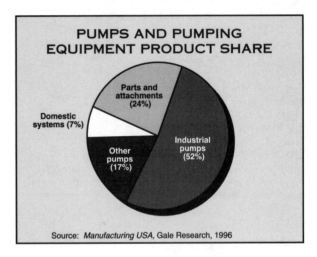

PUMPS AND PUMPING EQUIPMENT PRODUCT SHARE

Parts and attachments (24%)
Domestic systems (7%)
Other pumps (17%)
Industrial pumps (52%)

Source: *Manufacturing USA*, Gale Research, 1996

The ball and roller bearings industry is very large, but mature. It touches everything from space shuttles to household appliances, automobiles, dentist drills, roller skates, and computer disk drives. Because bearings are essential components of military and civilian machinery and equipment, the federal government has historically been a major customer of the industry. However, high labor and production costs have caused the bearing industry to lose business to foreign competitors who have been able to sell bearings of equal quality at lower prices. In the mid-1990s this industry was worth about $6 billion and employed more than 36,000 workers.

Compressors provide one of the most versatile forms of energy used in industry today. Compressed air as a power source ranks as the most commonly used, behind only electricity, gas, and water. In addition, compressors provide the motive force needed to economically transport gas and other materials in pipelines. Since compressors are required to operate in difficult environments and conditions, they wear quickly. As a result, the replacement parts portion of the industry composes a significant portion of shipments. In 1995, for example, the U.S. Bureau of the Census gave the value of air and gas compressor shipments at $2.7 billion, while additional parts and attachments shipments were valued at $663.1 million. Major markets for such products include the chemical industry, steel mills and blast furnaces, energy-related extraction industries, pipelines and well-drilling, and general construction.

The miscellaneous power transmission equipment segment of the machinery industry is comprised of companies that manufacture mechanical power transmission equipment and parts for industrial machinery. Products include ball joints, pulleys, bearings, drive chains, sprockets, shafts, couplings, and other parts. The industry provides basic mechanical power transmission components used in most industrial machinery. In 1995, industry shipments reached $2.13 million, according to the U.S. Department of Commerce. This is up from the 1992 value of $1.82 million. In 1995, firms in this industry averaged 142 employees per establishment, although the largest four establishments (by sales) each had 900 employees or more.

The market for miscellaneous transmission equipment is fragmented. Motor vehicle manufacturers were the largest buying sector, accounting for 10 percent of industry revenues in the early 1990s. The construction and farm machinery industries consumed 6 and 4 percent, respectively, of output. Motorcycle and bicycle makers purchased about 4 percent of production. Other significant markets for transmission equipment included shipbuilders, steel makers, the missile industry, and logging companies. About 8 percent of production is exported.

Between 1992 and 1995 the industrial process furnaces and ovens industry showed steady growth in both production and employment with shipments rising from $1.8 billion to $2.65 billion—an increase of 47 percent—and employment increasing from 17,000 to 18,700, an increase of 10 percent. The 1995 figures also represent a 4 percent increase over the 18,000 workers listed in the 1994 census, and an increase of about 20 percent over the $2.2 billion in shipments listed the same year.

INDUSTRY OUTLOOK

Rampant growth in U.S. capital spending slowed in the 1980s as foreign-manufactured goods reduced U.S. producers' share of capital goods markets. Machinery purchases by transportation industries were particularly slow. As a result, sales of miscellaneous machinery stagnated. Industry revenues lagged as a result of inflation and climbed at an average rate of about 2 percent per year during the 1980s to about $5.36 billion. Recessed commercial and residential construction markets added to industry woes in the late 1980s and early 1990s. Ailing manufacturers scrambled to sustain profitability by raising productivity, cutting their work force, and merging with or acquiring competitors.

Going into the mid-1990s, producers of miscellaneous machinery hoped to benefit from increased capital spending by the Clinton administration, an uptick in capital equipment replacements, and a devalued dollar, which was boosting exports. In addition, sales of machinery to some sectors showed signs of increasing. Construction equipment sales, for example, rose about 3 percent. However, spending on new manufacturing facilities and infrastructure was expected to remain flat at least through the mid-1990s.

Pumps and pumping equipment sales were estimated $6.5 billion in the mid-1990s up from $4.8 billion in 1990. The U.S. Census Bureau pegged industry revenues even higher, at $7.2 billion on unit sales of $20.2 million. Some analysts projected growth of more than 5 percent per year for the U.S. pump industry in the last five years of the twentieth century.

Because bearings are vital components of machinery, the market shows no signs of vanishing. While employment levels may drop as a reaction to increased automation of manufacturing processes, the shipment levels are not expected to drop. However, domestic manufacturers in the early 1990s were not investing the capital necessary to keep up with technical advances. New nondestructive quality control methods, such as using eddy currents to measure surface variance, monitoring interior surface integrity with x-rays, and verifying chemical composition through gas, are innovations that have improved the quality of bearings. As production and testing techniques improve, domestic manufacturers will be expected to implement this technology in order to compete. In 1995, the industry shipped more than 15 billion units valued at $5.8 billion, representing a 25 percent increase in current dollars since the early 1990s. Unit production was down, however, from 1994. Unmounted roller and ball bearings made up more than half of industry revenues. Growth has been relatively even across the different product segments of the industry. However, the buy-American push implemented by the U.S. Department of Defense and other manufacturers should allow bearing manufacturers to enjoy stability, and even expansion, through the year 2000.

The general industrial slowdown of the 1980s hit the compressor industry hard. Major clients like the nuclear power industry, oil well and pipeline industry, and the construction industry cut back on orders for new equipment and left existing components idle. A strong U.S. dollar made American products uncompetitive in foreign markets. By 1988, this started to change. A weakening dollar spurred exports and a general pickup in the manufacturing climate sparked new domestic orders in almost all sectors. The industry continued to modernize production by consolidating facilities and adopting sophisticated CAD/CAM systems and metalworking and casting technologies. New materials and designs were explored to extend the life of components in corrosive environments and to increase reliability. The steady growth experienced by the industry in the early 1990s was expected to continue. *Manufacturing USA* predicted that the value of air and gas compressor shipments would grow from the actual 1994 figure of $4.17 billion to $5.27 billion in 1998. At the same time it estimated that the number of production hours would increase from 27.4 million hours to 29.0 million hours, while the total number of establishments was expected to decrease from the 1993 count of 283 to 239 in 1998.

In 1995 the fans and blowers and air purification equipment industry generated more than $3.8 billion in sales, which represented a 22 percent preinflation increase over 1992. By product, centrifugal fans accounted for more than $1 billion alone, or nearly 28 percent of industry shipments; propeller and axial fans made up 20 percent of revenues; filtration equipment for incoming air made up 25 percent; filtration equipment for outgoing air made up 21 percent; and the remaining 6 percent was filled out by miscellaneous industrial and commercial fans and parts. The two smallest categories by sales also exhibited the highest growth in the 1990s, while sales of filtration equipment for incoming air have actually declined since the early 1990s. Other segments have shown average growth compared to the industry average. The industry was expected to benefit in the mid- and late 1990s from the Clean Air Act Amendments of 1990, because they imposed time limits on the reduction of specified hazardous industrial air pollutants. Compliance was expected to generate significant capital investment into this industry's products.

ORGANIZATION AND STRUCTURE

At nearly 50 percent of output, industrial pumps constituted the largest product class in the business. Replacement parts and accessories generated the next-largest share of sales, at about 25 percent, followed by domestic water systems and sump pump (12 percent), and oil and oil-field pumps (3 percent). Other miscellaneous pumps made up the remaining 10 percent.

The ball and roller bearing business is unusual because it is strictly a component manufacturing industry. The industry accommodates its markets by selling loose or packaged bearings; packaged bearings are installed in races that allow manufacturers to interchange complete bearing components. The industry has continued to evolve by developing new materials and lubricants and researching alternative uses for bearings. Bearings have been found to have almost limitless applications and are expected to be in demand as long as machines are manufactured.

Manufacturers of motor vehicles and related parts consume approximately 31 percent of the roller bearings and 38 percent of the ball bearings produced by the industry. General industry and machinery consume nearly 10 percent of the industry's roller bearings and just over 9 percent of its ball bearings. Construction and farm machinery together consume 17.2 percent of the industry's roller bearings and 16.1 percent of its ball bearings. The mining, oil drilling, and metalworking industries are also heavy consumers of antifriction bearings. Additionally, bearings of various types and sizes are widely used in refrigeration and heating equipment, motors and generators, aircraft and related parts, and railroad equipment.

WORK FORCE

As companies continue to automate production facilities and move manufacturing operations across U.S. borders, the U.S. Bureau of Labor Statistics suggests that general industrial machinery industry employment will continue to decline. Jobs for assemblers and fabricators, which make up over 10 percent of the work force, will likely decline 32 percent by 2005, as will positions for machinists. Management opportunities will also deteriorate significantly. Sales and marketing positions, on the other hand, may increase slightly.

Pump production made up about 29 percent of all labor in the industrial machinery group. Metal working craftsmen and machinists were three times more common in this industry than in manufacturing as a whole while laborers were half as common. Average hourly wages were estimated at $15.34 in 1996. The industry also employed a high proportion of non-production workers, perhaps indicative of its reliance on mechanical engineers.

RESEARCH AND TECHNOLOGY

The majority of industrial machinery is custom made to a client's specific requirements for use in complex applications where the failure of the machine could be disastrous. Consequently, manufacturing innovation stressed flexibility and reliability. Major innovations included the adoption of numerical and computer control manufacturing systems and the reliance on engineering expertise assisted by computer modeling software to custom design components for short run production. New corrosion resistant materials have been developed and refinements to old processes adopted. Specially designed metal-forming machines were created for the industry, including combination milling, radial drilling and facing machines, variable setting grinders that automatically form tapered shafts, and automatic tool changing devices controlled by NC tapes or computer software. Foundry operations for production of machine casings and core-making have advanced with rapid-cycle machinery, synchronous fabricating machinery, and a no-bake molding process using a resin binder and catalyst. Closer tolerances were achieved in components by replacing wooden molds and cores with ceramic.

The production of precision bearings is changing quickly, as technology allows greater and more accurate measurements to be taken. In 1989 it was announced that the Timken Company developed production equipment, gauges, and methods of manufacture to produce bearings called Precision Plus. The Precision Plus bearings boast a radial run-out of less than 40 millionths of an inch. Radial run-out is a measure of how closely the bearings will run in a perfect circle in a given bearing-ring path. Timken was able to create this new class of bearings through assessing grinding wheel variables such as type, speed of the wheel, feed rate into the wheel, coolant type, coolant temperature, and wheel dressing techniques. When bearings are produced to precision units of a millionth of an inch, shelf life becomes a factor. If bearings sit on a shelf for less than six months, the diameter can change several millionths of an inch. In high precision applications, this is unsatisfactory. Therefore, Timken developed a proprietary heat treatment process that prevents dimensional changes from occurring over time.

The Japanese are also aggressively researching alternative processing techniques and methods for improving corrosion resistance in aircraft quality bearings. New forms of failure analysis are also lending insights to the behavior of bearings under specific conditions. In both the United States and Japan, X-ray and gas chromatography are becoming more common nondestructive testing methods. High-temperature applications are also under aggressive study abroad at Japanese Universities and bearing manufacturers. Solid lubrication is an area where the United States leads the way in research, and the Japanese have shown keen interest in those findings.

One of the most innovative applications for bearings is in anti-lock braking (ABS) and traction control systems. ABS operates through electronically controlled bearings, which act as sensors. The sensors are able to relay information about wheel speeds to the car control system. The ABS computer receives information about the wheel speeds and decides if the regulation of brake fluid to one wheel will be necessary to prevent lock-up.

New and more stringent environmental regulations in the United States and around the world encouraged research into new air pollution abatement technology. This was especially true since some regulations called for pollution limitations in excess of what was technically possible at the time. However, the industry also found ways of applying old technologies in new ways. Some major areas of research included electrostatic precipitators with the addition of high-voltage direct-current pulses to capture fly-ash; filter bags treated with microporous films or membranes to keep dust cake out of the filter material; conditioning flue gas streams with sulfur trioxide or ammonia before filtering to improve the life of the filter; the development of sulfur trioxide generators to convert flue gases without the need of adding chemicals; new plastic materials to extend the concept of flue gas cooling with water beyond the wood products industry; and sorbent injection of such materials as carbon, char, and sodium sulfide to capture heavy metals like mercury.

AMERICA AND THE WORLD

Most industrial machinery is manufactured to international standards allowing American manufacturers to compete effectively in the international market. These same standards, however, also made the United States vulnerable to foreign competition, particularly on price and quality. During the early half of the 1980s, the strong American dollar made such competition particularly difficult, undermining an already weak industrial climate in American manufacturing. As a result, the U.S. merchandise trade deficit quadrupled between 1982 and 1984, reaching $145 billion. This effect showed up in the pump manufacturing industry, but was delayed. In 1985 the industry showed a trade surplus, but by 1987 it had become a $1.9 billion deficit. The drop of the value of the U.S. dollar, which began in March of 1985, provided new impetus for the pump industry. By 1987, the average export price expressed in foreign currency of pumps and other machinery had fallen 23.1 percent. By 1990, even though domestic prices increased an average of 5 percent each year, the foreign currency price of pumps and components dropped more than 11 percent. This made American operations more profitable, increased export volumes, and discouraged imports. It also encouraged foreign firms to establish manufacturing and assembly facilities in the United States.

In 1990, exports approached $1.1 billion while imports exceeded $.7 billion. By mid-decade, *Purchasing* magazine estimated foreign purchases at 45 percent of overall demand. This share was expected to decline as companies set up overseas manufacturing operations. Major markets for American products included Canada, Mexico, the United Kingdom, Saudi Arabia, West Germany, Venezuela, and Japan. The top importers included Japan, West Germany, Canada, and the United Kingdom. Emerging markets included Latin America, Africa, the Mideast, and Asia, especially China.

While the Japanese may appear to pose the most significant threat to U.S. bearing manufacturers, Singapore and Korea are mounting strong competitive campaigns against the Japanese. Also contending for world market share are the Europeans and some countries from the former Soviet Union. The North American Free Trade Agreement is expected to hurt the bearing industry as new plants are built in Mexico and lower manufacturing costs are realized. U.S. exports of bearings were valued at more than $900 million in 1995, while imports totaled more than $1.2 billion in the same year.

Globalization is particularly important in the air pollution abatement equipment (APC) sector. U.S. and European multinationals use direct investment, cross-border mergers, acquisitions, joint ventures, and foreign collaboration to gain entry to each other's markets and to other markets around the world. The main target markets for such equipment have been Asia, Eastern Europe, and Latin America, since the industry already faces significant competition from domestic producers in major trading partners like Japan, Germany, and France. Mexico is also a potentially significant market for U.S. fan and blower products. Many firms prefer to license to foreign manufacturers instead of competing directly, creating a brisk trade in environmental technology. Unlike the industry in general, this segment posted a trade surplus in the 1990s.

ASSOCIATIONS AND SOCIETIES

AMERICAN SUPPLY AND MACHINERY MANUFACTURERS ASSOCIATION
1300 Sumner Ave.
Cleveland, OH 44115-2851
Phone: (216) 241-7333
Fax: (216) 241-0105

INDUSTRIAL DISTRIBUTION ASSOCIATION
3 Corporate Sq., Ste. 201
Atlanta, GA 30329
Phone: (404) 325-2776
Fax: (404) 325-2784

PERIODICALS AND NEWSLETTERS

IEEE INDUSTRY APPLICATIONS MAGAZINE
Institute of Electrical and Electronics Engineers
345 E. 47th St.
New York, NY 10017-2394
Phone: (800) 678-4333 or (212) 705-7900
Fax: (212) 752-4929
Bimonthly. $120.00 per year. Covers new industrial applications of power conversion, drives, lighting, and control. Emphasis is on the petroleum, chemical, rubber, plastics, textile, and mining industries.

INDUSTRIAL DISTRIBUTION: FOR INDUSTRIAL DISTRIBUTORS AND THEIR SALES PERSONNEL
Cahners Publishing Co., Inc.
275 Washington St.
Newton, MA 02158-1630
Phone: (800) 662-7776 or (617) 964-3030
Fax: (617) 558-4327
16 times a year. $64.95 per year.

INDUSTRIAL EQUIPMENT NEWS
Thomas Publishing Co.
5 Penn Plz. 250 W. 34th St.
New York, NY 10001
Phone: (800) 222-7900 or (212) 695-0500
Fax: (212) 629-1585
Monthly. Free. What's new in equipment, parts and materials.

NEW EQUIPMENT DIGEST
Penton Publishing
1100 Superior Ave.
Cleveland, OH 44114-2543
Phone: (800) 321-7003 or (216) 696-7000
Fax: (216) 696-8765
Monthly. Free to qualified personnel; others, $50.00 per year.

DATABASES

PROMT: PREDICASTS OVERVIEW OF MARKETS AND TECHNOLOGY
Information Access Co.
362 Lakeside Dr.
Foster City, CA 94404
Phone: (800) 321-6388 or (415) 378-5000
Fax: (415) 358-4759
Companies, products, applied technologies and markets. U.S. and international literature coverage, 1972 to date. Daily updates. Inquire as to online cost and availability. Provides abstracts from more than 1,200 publications.

THOMAS REGISTER ONLINE
Thomas Publishing Co., Inc.
5 Penn Plz.
New York, NY 10001
Phone: (212) 695-0500
Fax: (212) 290-7362
Provides concise information on approximately 155,000 U.S. companies, mainly manufacturers, with over 50,000 product classifications. Indexes over 115,000 trade names. Information is updated semiannually. Inquire as to online cost and availability.

STATISTICS SOURCES

U.S. INDUSTRIAL OUTLOOK: FORECASTS FOR SELECTED MANUFACTURING AND SERVICE INDUSTRIES
Available from U.S. Government Printing Office
Washington, DC 20402
Phone: (202) 512-1800
Fax: (202) 512-2250
Annual. $37.00. (Replaced in 1995 by U.S. Global Trade Outlook.) Issued by the International Trade Administration, U.S.

Department of Commerce. Provides basic data, outlook for the current year, and "Long-Term Prospects" (five-year projections) for a wide variety of products and services. Includes high technology industries.

- Gopher://gopher.umsl.edu:70/11/library/govdocs/usio94

FURTHER READING

Darnay, Arsen J., ed. *Manufacturing USA.* Detroit: Gale Research, 1996.

Moody's Industrial Manual, New York: Investors Service, Inc., 1996.

———. *1995 Annual Survey of Manufactures.* Washington: GPO, 1997.

U.S. Department of Commerce. International Trade Administration. *U.S. Industrial Outlook 1994.* Washington: GPO, 1994. Available from http://sci.dixie.edu/businessinformation/industryoutlooks/industryoutlooks.html. ━●━

MACHINERY, REFRIGERATION AND SERVICE INDUSTRY

SIC 3580

Despite *continued productivity increases and the movement of some manufacturing facilities to foreign countries, employment prospects for the overall service machinery industry were positive. Opportunities for most occupations were expected to swell by 10 to 20 percent between 1990 and 2005, according to the U.S. Bureau of Labor Statistics.*

REFRIGERATION AND AIR CONDITIONING

High interest rates and a sluggish economy slowed new construction in the late 1980s and early 1990s. This slowdown in construction softened the demand for new heating, refrigeration, and air conditioning equipment, but spurred the repair and up-grade replacement segment of the industry. Much of the housing built in the 1950s, 1960s, and 1970s needed replacement equipment since the average domestic furnace or air conditioner had a useful life of only 20 years. Many American power utilities promoted energy conservation and higher efficiency upgrades. However, U.S. manufacturers shipped 5.7 million air conditioners in 1996, up 11 percent from 1995.

The Clean Air Act of 1990, which introduced extensive air-quality standards and the incremental reduction and eventual banning of chlorofluorocarbons (CFCs) by the year 2000, challenged the industry to improve its technology. This challenge caused uncertainty in the industry as new systems were developed, using chemicals that were not compatible with the old refrigerants. In the early 1990s, the fear of products becoming obsolete caused the industry to stagnate, while alternative refrigerants were researched.

Top 10 **TOP CENTRAL AIR CONDITIONER MAKERS, 1995**

Ranked by: Residential air conditioner market for 1995.

1. United Technologies, 20%
2. Goodman, 15%
3. Rheem, 14%
4. American Standard, 12%
5. Lennox, 10%
6. Inter-City, 9%
7. York, 7%
8. Nordyne, 5%
9. Coleman, 3%
10. Raytheon, 3%

Source: *Appliance Manufacturer*, April 1996, p. 30, from industry reports.

AUTOMATIC VENDING MACHINES

In 1995, manufacturers' shipments of coin-operated vending machines totaled $767.0 million, an increase of 10 percent from the 1994 figure of $698.2 million. Shipments of beverage vending machines increased 20 percent, while confections and foods decreased 11 percent, from $239.0 million to $211.6 million. Approximately 4.7 million vending machines are on location throughout the 50 states, providing a 24-hour point of sale. Two of the most common places that vending machines are found are in schools and in the workplace. Industry sales of food and refreshments alone are estimated to exceed $25 billion annually. Non-food sales, including cigarettes, are estimated to approximate another $4 billion.

COMMERCIAL LAUNDRY EQUIPMENT

The largest product group in the commercial laundry equipment industry is washers and extractors, which account for almost 40 percent of sales. Commercial dryers and presses make up about 16 and 11 percent, respectively, of output. Dry cleaning equipment accounts for an additional 11 percent of production, while parts, attachments, and miscellaneous equipment represent the remainder of sales.

Hotels, hospitals, and contract laundry services that serve commercial and institutional customers were the biggest consumers of commercial laundry equipment in the early 1990s. Dry cleaners represented about 17 percent of the market. Government institutions, including the armed services, prisons, schools, and hospitals bought about 11 percent of industry output, and 12 percent of production was exported.

MEASURING AND DISPENSING PUMPS

In the early 1990s, multi-pump units, which offer several grades of gasoline from the same pump, accounted for about 22 percent of measuring and dispensing pumps industry sales. More traditional single-pump units still held a 19 percent share of the market. Lubricating oil pumps represented about 4 percent of output, and grease guns made up 3 percent of sales. Approximately 30 percent of industry revenues were made from the sale of parts and attachments, such as vapor recovery systems and replacement hoses. Non-industrial gas, oil, and grease pumps were a corollary of the proliferation of cars and trucks during the early and mid-1900s. As American society became increasingly mobile, markets for service station pumps expanded rapidly. Indeed, by the late 1990s the service station pump industry was shipping more than $600 million worth of products per year and employing about 8,000 workers.

MISCELLANEOUS SERVICE INDUSTRY MACHINERY

The largest segment of the miscellaneous service machine industry is food service equipment, which accounted for about 26 percent of industry revenues in the mid-1990s. Commercial ranges, stoves, and broilers made up the bulk of that group. Industrial floor and carpet cleaning equipment represented 12 percent of the market, as did miscellaneous sewage treatment products. Parts for water heaters and softeners accounted for 8 percent of sales. Other major categories include commercial car and bus washing equipment, commercial dishwashers, sand blasting machines, and industrial vacuum systems. In 1995, imports were valued at $122.4 million, while exports were valued at $228.6 million.

INDUSTRY OUTLOOK

REFRIGERATION AND AIR CONDITIONING

The 1990s marked a decade of revolutionary change for the heating, refrigeration, and air conditioning (HVAC) industry. The Center for Disease Control and Prevention reported 1,604 cases of Legionnaires' disease in the United States for 1994, but epidemiologists believed the total to range between 10,000 and 100,000 cases. Office building operators across the country were reporting cases of "sick-building syndrome," in which workers developed debilitating symptoms from a build-up of pollution levels in sealed, air conditioned buildings. In 1993, Congress passed a new energy bill, which mandated higher efficiency standards for heating and air conditioning appliances and promised to make the requirements stricter in 1998. But the most devastating event to the HVAC industry was the discovery of a seven million square kilometer hole in the ozone layer above the south pole, and the scientific evidence that linked that phenomenon to the release of chlorofluorocarbons (CFCs) into the atmosphere. That revelation threatened the basic component of the HVAC industry.

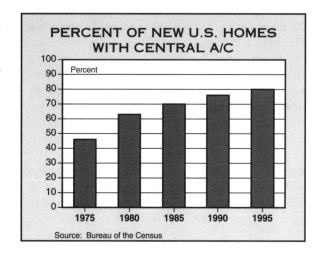

PERCENT OF NEW U.S. HOMES WITH CENTRAL A/C

Source: Bureau of the Census

According to the timetable set forth in 1990 under the Montreal Protocol, CFC production in developed nations was to be banned by the year 2000 but developing nations could continue to produce them until 2010. As a temporary replacement refrigerant, hydrochlorofluorocarbons (HCFCs) were scheduled for phase-out in 2030. This answered a concern by developing nations that the ban would work to the advantage of European and American firms who had the money to invest in alternative refrigerant technology. Manufacturers in those two regions produced two-thirds of the world's CFCs at that time.

Also in 1990, the refrigeration industry petitioned the Environmental Protection Agency (EPA) to develop and issue uniform national recycling standards and requirements in anticipation of the large quantities of old refrigerant that would need to be removed from refurbished machinery. In 1992, the Air Conditioning and refrigeration Institute (ARI) estimated the existing stock of refrigeration and air conditioning equipment in the United States exceeded $135 billion. In February 1992, President George Bush reset the Montreal Protocol timetable, moving its requirements ahead by four years and calling for other nations to follow suit. On January 1, 1996, the production of chlorofluorocarbons was banned in the United States and other developed countries. Hydrofluorocarbon blends were already being used as refrigerants since they were legal until 2010 and these could be used to service old HCFC equipment until 2020.

The problem for the industry revolved around finding a suitable replacement refrigerant that could be produced quickly enough to meet the phase-out schedule. To make the ban effective, that technology would have to be shared with developing nations in order to persuade them not to continue building their own CFC industry. Refrigerant engineers looked for chemical combinations that were not flammable, corrosive, or toxic and that would operate reasonably well in existing equipment. The lubricants in the old systems had to be compatible with the new gases and in some cases new lubricants had to be found. In addition, the new designs had to meet the higher energy efficiency standards of 1993. Most of the new chemicals worked reasonably well but not as efficiently as CFCs, therefore, equipment redesigns were necessary to meet the efficiency ratings. The research and new technology added to the cost of the machinery at a time when sales of refrigeration equipment were at best stagnant. Another round of higher energy requirements were slated to go into effect in 1998, but the industry could not build towards that higher target because the standard was still being developed.

AUTOMATIC VENDING MACHINES

Several significant changes were taking place in the vending industry in the 1990s. Some resulted from new technology, while others stemmed more directly from general societal changes. New machines developed during this time were capable of vending food of much higher quality than was previously possible. This ability was having a particularly noticeable effect in the work place, as corporate downsizing necessitated the replacement of many company cafeterias with vending areas. With a new emphasis on hot, nutritious foods, the major manufacturers began producing machines that sold items such as french fries, fresh pizza, and a much broader line of microwaveable frozen foods.

The sharp decline in cigarette smoking the United States throughout the 1990s has had a dramatic impact on the vending industry. Once a huge seller as one the four C's of vending, cigarettes only generated a small portion of the vending operator's revenue compared to the considerable percentage of revenue cigarettes generated in the 1960s (at 45.5 percent). Dick Bakala, owner of Dick's Vending Service, notes that while cigarettes used to make up 20 percent of his business, they now make up only 2 percent.

MEASURING AND DISPENSING PUMPS

Going into the mid-1990s, pump manufacturers scrambled to revive profits by introducing new gas pump systems, focusing on the multi-pump market, and incorporating computer technology into their machines. New pumps with point-of-sale credit card devices, for example, allowed customers to fill a vehicle with gas and pay without leaving their car, thus reducing labor costs. Likewise, to help service stations comply with Federal "Stage II" vapor recovery guidelines, producers of vapor recovery pumps and attachments were introducing a variety of new systems and designs.

ORGANIZATION AND STRUCTURE

REFRIGERATION AND AIR CONDITIONING

The number of firms in the HVAC industry rose slowly in the 1980s from 730 companies operating 865 establishments in 1982 to 769 companies operating 891 establishments in 1994. The state of Ohio with 44 establishments produced 11.3 percent of the total U.S. shipments and 10.1 percent of the total number of workers employed in the heating and air conditioning industry. The largest number of establishments, 118, were located in Texas and accounted for 8.9 percent of the shipments in the United States and 9.7 percent of the total work force.

AUTOMATIC VENDING MACHINES

The U.S. Department of Commerce reported that 47 companies were engaged in manufacturing coin-operated vending machines in 1994. Of these, 14 manufactured beverage machines, 18 manufactured machines that sold food and confections, and 32 manufactured other types of vending machines, including those selling cigarettes, water, and postage stamps. Canned and bottled soft drink machines made up by far the largest share of beverage machines manufactured in 1995, totaling 298,491 units. Among confection and food vending machines, those that sold bulk confections and charms predominated, totaling 128,097 (shipped in 1995) while bagged snacks and confections made up another significant share at 86,539.

The National Automatic Merchandising Association (NAMA) has been the most important trade organization in the vending industry in the 1990s. NAMA represents companies involved in every facet of vending, from machine manufacturers to suppliers of vended products. Founded in 1936, NAMA compiles a broad range of statistics and produces several periodicals, including a regular industry newsletter, a review of pertinent state legislation, and a labor issues bulletin. Headquartered in Chicago, the organization has 2,400 members, 35 state groups, and had an annual budget of about $2.5 million in 1996. The National Bulk Vendors Association (NBVA) concentrates specifically on the manufacture and operation of bulk vending equipment. The NBVA was founded in 1949 and is also based in Chicago.

MEASURING AND DISPENSING PUMPS

A U.S. economic recession in the late 1980s and early 1990s suppressed pump sales to about $1.03 billion per year in the early 1990s. As sales faltered, industry employment plummeted from a high of 9,400 in 1987 to about 8,000 by 1990. Figures for 1992 showed that employment levels were at 6,500 workers, 31 percent below 1987 levels, while the value of goods shipped slipped to $896.3 million. In 1993, however, the economy began to improve, and the industry responded. In 1995, according to the *1995 Annual Census of Manufactures,* the industry reported 7,300 employees and shipment of goods worth $1.48 billion—an increase of 12.3 percent and 6.0 percent respectively.

MISCELLANEOUS SERVICE INDUSTRY MACHINERY

General industry expansion between 1950 and 1980 resulted in aggregate shipments of more than $2.5 billion by the early 1980s. Steady growth of service industries during the 1980s, particularly food services, resulted in rapid growth. Sales went from about $2.6 billion in 1983

to $3.4 billion by 1986, and to $4.9 billion by 1990. As revenues grew at an average annual pace of almost 9 percent per year, industry employment jumped from 31,000 in the early 1980s to about 39,000 by the early 1990s. Employment levels reached 40,900 by 1994 and were expected to increase further to an estimated 44,200 by 1998.

WORK FORCE

Traditionally, the heating, refrigeration and air-conditioning manufacturing industry has been highly labor intensive. In 1994, the average number of production workers at an establishment in the industry was 107, compared to the average number of 34 workers in all other manufacturing. Much of the assembly work was done by hand fitting many small parts and cutting metal shapes with the use of templates. By the mid-1980s, the industry was shifting towards more automated production with the use of numerical control machining tools and welding robots. Eventually computerized control led to fully automated plants. Consequently, even though shipments increased between 1982 and 1995 from $12.4 billion to $26.2 billion, production worker employment experienced changes depending on market conditions. In 1982, 85,000 workers were employed in this industry raising to 103,200 in 1995.

Although sales and unit shipments in the commercial laundry equipment industry grew by more than 50 percent during the 1980s, industry employment rose less than 10 percent, to about 5,200. Industry consolidation, company restructuring, manufacturing productivity gains, and the movement of production facilities to Mexico all contributed to stagnant job growth. By the mid-1990s, however, jobs continued to increase slowly but steadily. The 1992 census of manufactures reported 4,700 workers employed in the industry, only 2 percent over the figure of 4,600 reported in the 1987 census. By 1994, however, that figure had risen to 4,800, and in 1995 it increased to 4,900. Although the growth level was still only 2 percent, the growth was happening over a much shorter period of time. The growth of jobs in the industry in 1995 was the same as that in the period 1992-94, and was the same as the period 1987-92.

RESEARCH AND TECHNOLOGY

REFRIGERATION AND AIR CONDITIONING

The challenges of the 1990s caused the industry to begin considering alternative technologies. Concerns over indoor air quality made it clear that heating, ventilation, humidification, and air cleaning could not be considered as separate fields of endeavor, but instead all must be integrated into the design of new buildings to become part of the essential operational architecture of an organic system.

The use of microelectronics for computer modeling and for control systems revolutionized the HVAC industry, by allowing more sophisticated designs and more accurate control to deliver energy savings and increased health and comfort levels. In 1993, 20,000 French families lived in fully automated houses, a concept catching on in America. The system controls lighting, heating, security, and entertainment devices. New HVAC systems were making the home more independent and self-sufficient. Another new technology, called cogeneration devices, uses basic refrigeration technology to cool or heat the structure, produce hot water, and generate sufficient electricity to run the house. Simpler systems sacrificed the cooling function by eliminating the refrigerant circuit. In both cases, a natural gas engine drives the generator to produce the electricity. The heat from the exhaust gas is reclaimed by water in the system's heating circuit. The full heat-pump system, which also gathers heat from outside the house, uses only half the gas needed by a conventional furnace, or two-thirds used in a high-efficiency condensing furnace.

AUTOMATIC VENDING MACHINES

Flexibility and security are two areas in which engineers in the vending industry were making great strides in the 1990s. The Merlin 2000 series, developed by a company called InterBev in 1989, provided a good example of the flexibility built into the new generation of vending machines. The Merlin 2000 machines could sell both sodas and juice from a single machine, with an improved mechanism for adjusting prices from one selection to the next.

Furthermore, electronic bill and coin changing mechanisms made fraud more difficult. A common form of vandalism, injecting salt water into the coin mechanisms, and putting the machine in "jackpot" mode by shorting out the electronic parts was circumvented by improved shielding of electronic components. Programmable security code devices were also installed on many new machines to prevent unauthorized individuals from tampering with pricing and removing money or merchandise. The most exciting of new vending technology has been the computerized capabilities of the machines to record their own vending statistics.

AMERICA AND THE WORLD

The 1994 worldwide air conditioning and refrigeration industry enjoyed a $40 to $45 billion market, with the majority being supplied by the United States and Japan. In 1995, U.S. exports were valued at $4.4 billion, an increase of 9 percent from 1994 levels. Mexico and Canada were the top two markets for export, and Asia was expected to offer the greatest opportunities for future growth. The United States represented 88.7 percent of the imports into Canada and 75 percent of the Mexican air conditioning equipment market. In 1992, France imported 52 percent of their refrigeration equipment from the United States whereas Japan dominated the import markets in Spain with 44 percent, Italy with 30 percent, and Singapore with 44 percent. China, with its 350 factories, was expected to have market growth of 30 percent annually.

ASSOCIATIONS AND SOCIETIES

AMERICAN SUPPLY AND MACHINERY MANUFACTURERS ASSOCIATION
1300 Sumner Ave.
Cleveland, OH 44115-2851
Phone: (216) 241-7333
Fax: (216) 241-0105

MACHINERY DEALERS NATIONAL ASSOCIATION
1110 Spring St.
Silver Spring, MD 20910
Phone: (301) 585-9494
Fax: (301) 585-7830

MANUFACTURERS ALLIANCE FOR PRODUCTIVITY AND INNOVATION
1525 Wilson Blvd., Ste. 900
Arlington, VA 22209
Phone: (703) 841-9000
Fax: (202) 331-7160

PERIODICALS AND NEWSLETTERS

AMERICAN MACHINIST
Penton Publishing, Inc.
1100 Superior Ave.
Cleveland, OH 44114-2543
Phone: (800) 321-7003 or (216) 696-7000
Fax: (216) 696-0177
Monthly. $65.00 per year.

DATABASES

CITIBASE (CITICORP ECONOMIC DATABASE)
FAME Software Corp.
77 Water St., 9 Fl.
New York, NY 10005
Phone: (212) 898-7800
Fax: (212) 742-8956
Presents over 6,000 statistical series relating to business, industry, finance, and economics. Includes series from **Survey of Current Business** *and many other sources. Time period is 1947 to date, with daily updates. Inquire as to online cost and availability.*

THOMAS REGISTER ONLINE
Thomas Publishing Co., Inc.
5 Penn Plz.
New York, NY 10001
Phone: (212) 695-0500
Fax: (212) 290-7362
Provides concise information on approximately 155,000 U.S. companies, mainly manufacturers, with over 50,000 product classifications. Indexes over 115,000 trade names. Information is updated semiannually. Inquire as to online cost and availability.

WILSONLINE: APPLIED SCIENCE AND TECHNOLOGY ABSTRACTS
H. W. Wilson Co.
950 University Ave.
Bronx, NY 10452
Phone: (800) 367-6770 or (718) 588-8400
Fax: (718) 590-1617
Provides online indexing and abstracting of 400 major scientific, technical, industrial, and engineering periodicals. Time period is 1983 to date for indexing and 1993 to date for abstracting, with updating twice a week. Inquire as to online cost and availability.

STATISTICS SOURCES

BUSINESS STATISTICS
Available from U.S. Government Printing Office
Washington, DC 20402
Phone: (202) 512-1800
Fax: (202) 512-2250
Biennial. $20.00. Issued by Bureau of Economic Analysis, U.S. Department of Commerce. Shows annual data for 29 years and monthly data for a recent four-year period. Statistics correspond to the Survey of Current Business.

ENCYCLOPEDIA OF AMERICAN INDUSTRIES
Gale Research
835 Penobscot Bldg.
Detroit, MI 48226-4094
Phone: (800) 877-GALE or (313) 961-2242
Fax: (800) 414-5043
1994. $500.00. Two volumes ($250.00 each). Volume one is Manufacturing Industries *and volume two is* Service *and* Non-Manufacturing Industries. *Provides the history, development, and recent status of approximately 1,000 industries. Includes statistical graphs, with industry and general indexes.*

SURVEY OF CURRENT BUSINESS
Available from U.S. Government Printing Office
Washington, DC 20402
Phone: (202) 512-1800
Fax: (202) 512-2250
Monthly. $41.00 per year. Issued by Bureau of Economic Analysis, U.S. Department of Commerce. Presents a wide variety of business and economic data.

UNITED STATES CENSUS OF MANUFACTURES
U.S. Bureau of the Census
Washington, DC 20233-0800
Phone: (301) 457-4100
Fax: (301) 457-3842
Quinquennial. Results presented in reports, tape, CD-ROM, and diskette files.

FURTHER READING

''About Vending.'' Chicago: National Automatic Merchandising Association, 1996. Available from http://www.vending.org/about.htm.

''Automatic Merchandiser.'' Fort Atkinson, WI: Johnson Jill Press, 1997. Available from http://www.amonline.com-Automatic Merchandiser.

Darnay, Arsen J., ed. *Manufacturing USA.* 5th ed. Detroit: Gale Research, 1996.

U.S. Bureau of the Census. *1995 Annual Survey of Manufactures.* Washington: GPO, 1997.

MACHINERY, SPECIAL INDUSTRY

SIC 3550

While a recession in the late 1980s and early 1990s depressed many domestic industrial machinery segments, semiconductor machine sales continued to grow. Renewed U.S. competitiveness in high-tech equipment manufacturing allowed domestic competitors to thwart their Japanese rivals. In addition, increased semiconductor demand from industries such as telecommunications augmented growth. Output was expected to expand throughout the mid- to late 1990s, though the cyclical nature of the industry was expected to drive output down in 1997.

The special industry machinery industry is comprised of companies that manufacture a wide variety of miscellaneous machines used to produce goods in other industries. Numerous product offerings range from broom making contraptions to zipper makers, although semiconductor manufacturing equipment account for the largest portion of the classification's output.

Despite being affected by business cycles in the microchip making industry, the long-term prospects for semiconductor equipment manufacturing appeared strong. In the mid- to late 1990s, there were several powerful trends behind the growing demand for silicon wafer fabrication systems. A global increase in PC sales drove increased demand for semiconductors of all kinds, plus new chips being produced required more memory. The rapid growth of telecommunications and the use of electronics in automobiles also increased semiconductor sales.

Top 4 TOP U.S. SEMICONDUCTOR EQUIPMENT MAKERS, 1995

Ranked by: Sales, in millions of dollars.

1. Applied Manufacturers, $3,500
2. Lam Research $1,030
3. Teradyne, $675
4. Vanan, $606

Source: *Electronic News*, March 4, 1996, p. 24, from VLSI Research Inc.

Between 1990 and 1994, the textile machinery industry experienced an increase in its shipment value from $1.505 billion to $1.908 billion. However, the number of employees and establishments engaged in the industry dropped slightly from 17,400 to 16,700 during that period. Between 1987 and 1990, textile manufacturers' capacity utilization dropped sharply from approximately 92 percent to below 82 percent, directly depressing the machinery industry. However, a strong resurgence was seen between 1990 and 1992, as capacity utilization increased from below 82 percent to nearly 90 percent. Inventories also grew significantly between 1985 and 1993, rising from a value of nearly $4.5 billion to $6.0 billion. During the mid-1990s, most companies in the machinery industry became much more competitive in the global marketplace by achieving significant cost reductions. These reductions were made by upgrading plants and equipment, reducing employment, increasing inventory turnover, and selling marginal businesses.

The United States is the world's leading producer of paper-making machinery. There were approximately 450 companies involved in making machinery for the printing trades industry in the mid-1990s. In 1995, these manufacturers shipped slightly more than $3 billion worth of equipment, an increase of 36 percent since 1992. The U.S. Department of Commerce estimated that shipments peaked at $2.8 billion in 1990, after five years of steady growth, but subsequently declined by 7 percent during the global recession of the early 1990s. Shipments returned to $2.8 billion by 1994, and were expected to reach $3.4 billion by 1998.

In the early 1990s, 516 establishments were engaged in the U.S. food processing machinery industry, employing nearly 18,000 people, and shipping nearly $2.2 billion of equipment that year. Approximately $741 million of manufactured machinery was exported to over 150 foreign markets in 1993. Domestically, nearly 20,000 food processing plants shipped $321 billion of processed food in 1988, and $345 billion in 1989. In 1996, the food industry marked sales of over $165 billion and employed over 1.6 million workers. U.S. citizens spent 16.7 percent of their disposable personal income on food in 1995, up from 9.1 percent in 1980. The machinery industry as a whole is stable, and growing in certain segments. The presence of foreign-made machinery, however, has been increasing since the early 1990s.

INDUSTRY OUTLOOK

Strategies adopted by U.S. semiconductor manufacturers in the 1980s began to pay off in the early 1990s. Aided by a weak dollar and a recession in Japan, U.S. producers boosted revenues to $5.8 billion in 1991. Although sales dropped 3 percent in 1992, shipments climbed an impressive 18 percent in 1993 to about $6 billion. Assisted by a technological lead in growing product segments and newfound productivity, U.S. manufacturers were able to recover a 4 percent share of the global market from Japan. In 1993 they held 51 percent, compared to 41 percent controlled by Japan.

Also boosting U.S. semiconductor equipment competitiveness was the development of Sematech, a joint private sector/government funded research and development consortium. Sematech was formed in 1987 to combat increasingly competitive Japanese semiconductor producers. In addition, industry participants on both sides of the Pacific benefitted from technology exchanges and partnerships with foreign and domestic competitors. Indeed, U.S. firms learned from the Japanese that traditional methods of developing and producing manufacturing technology in isolation from competitors were no longer feasible. While government funding for Sematech was reduced sharply in the mid-1990s, the organization restructured, increased dues, and remained a viable organization.

U.S. Semiconductor Equipment Makers

Applied Manufacturers

Lam Research

Teradyne

Vanan

Companies are ranked by 1995 sales in millions of dollars.

Applied Manufacturers . . . . $ 3,500
Lam Research 1,030
Teradyne 675
Vanan 606

Source: *Electronic News*, March 4, 1996, p. 24, from VLSI Research Inc.

However, in 1996 this strong growth rate slowed to 12 percent and semiconductor manufacturing equipment suppliers cut back on production and laid off workers. Conditions were expected to worsen in 1997. Elizabeth Schumann, senior market analyst for Semiconductor Equipment and Materials International in Mountain View, California, predicted that the industry's revenue would decrease 15 to 20 percent in 1997. However, growth rates of 15 percent or more were expected to return in 1998 and 1999.

According to *Manufacturing USA*, shipments in the textile machinery industry reached $1.9 billion in 1994 and are expected to climb to $2.1 billion by 1998. Due to higher sales volumes and increased efficiencies from capital investment in machinery, profits in the textiles industry exploded in the early 1990s. Record profits of $1.9 billion were reported in 1992, rising from $882 million in 1991 and $433 million in 1990. However, industry profits had dropped to $832 million by the end of 1996, despite predictions that the industry's explosive growth would continue.

ORGANIZATION AND STRUCTURE

The special industry machinery industry encompassed a plethora of devices as of the mid-1990s, including: tire retreading machinery, stone tumblers, tile making equipment, automotive frame straighteners, lumber drying kilns, cork cutters, brick makers, shoe repair equipment, leather-working devices, and plastic molding machines.

Semiconductor manufacturing equipment was the leading segment in this industry, and saw spectacular growth in the 1990s. For example, in 1987, shipments from this segment were valued at just $1.01 billion, but by 1992 had more than doubled to $2.27 billion, or 21.6 percent of the total industry's output, according to the U.S. Department of Commerce. By 1995, that total had ballooned even more, reaching $6.8 billion, or 38 percent of the industry's output.

The next largest industry category in 1995 was plastics working machinery and equipment, at $2.3 billion (13 percent), followed by chemical manufacturing machinery and equipment, at $1.06 billion (5.9 percent); printed circuit board manufacturing machinery, at $856 million (4.8 percent); automotive maintenance equipment, at $630 million (3.5 percent); foundry machinery and equipment, at $531 million (3 percent) and rubber working machinery and equipment, at $371 million (2.1 percent). Over 28 percent of this industry shipments in 1995, valued at $5.1 billion, were classified in an "all other" category. This category included petroleum refining machinery, glass making machinery, and footwear manufacturing machinery, among many other categories.

The textile machinery industry encompasses all machinery used from the start of the yarn-making process through weaving the cloth, final treatments, and dyeing. Most fabrics produced by weaving or knitting must

Plastics Machinery Demand

Demand is expected to increase from $2.1 billion in 1994 to $3.15 billion in 2000.

	1994	2000
Injection molding	61.6%	58.2%
Extrusion	11.5	10.9
Blow molding	12.5	15.6
Thermoforming	4.1	3.7
Other	10.3	11.6

Source: *Plastics News*, January 1, 1996, p. 9, from Freedonia Group Inc.

undergo a number of further processing treatments before they are ready for sale. In the finishing operations, the fabric is subjected to mechanical and chemical treatment, whereby its appearance and quality are improved and its commercial value is enhanced. Each ofthese processes requires different machinery, thus the scope of textile machinery is very broad.

Revenues derived from the sale of parts and accessories account for approximately 36 percent of yearly industry sales. Fiber-to-fabric textile machinery holds 9 percent of the product share. Fabric machinery for weaving, knitting, embroidering, braiding, tufting, and lace making comprises 6 percent of the industry. Finishing machinery claims a 5 percent product share. Machines used for bleaching, mercerizing, and dyeing claim 5.5 percent product share. Machinery for drying stocks, yarns, cloth, carpet, and other non-woven materials represents 4.2 percent of the product share. Non-specific machinery and machinery not-elsewhere classified represents the remaining 34.3 percent of the products manufactured by the industry.

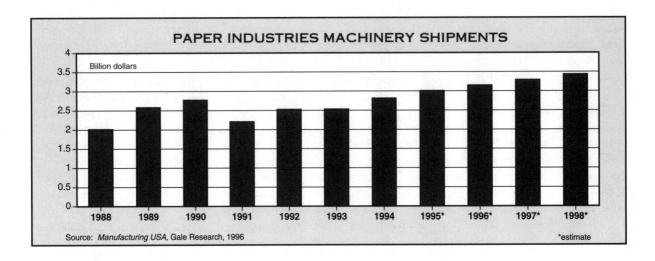

PAPER INDUSTRIES MACHINERY SHIPMENTS

Billion dollars

Source: *Manufacturing USA*, Gale Research, 1996

*estimate

WORK FORCE

Total employment was expected to remain stable throughout the 1990s. For example, total employment was 85,400 in 1990, and was expected to be 85,300 in 1995 and 85,800 in 1998. Industry wages were about 20 percent above the U.S. manufacturing industry average as of the mid-1990s.

The employment level in the textile machinery industry fluctuated from 17,500 employees in 1983 to 15,600 in 1987 and back up to 17,400 in 1990. The number of industry employees declined to 16,700 employees in 1994 and was expected to decrease by 10 percent to 15,000 employees in 1998. In 1994, the average hourly wage of industry employees was $11.92, up from 1988's average of $9.86 per hour, which was slightly below the average wage of $10.66 earned by employees of all other manufacturing industries. Wages are expected to reach $13.29 by 1998 as the employment level continues to decrease.

The industry is expected to make significant reductions in several occupations by 2005. The occupations anticipating cuts in excess of 10 percent include secretaries; drafters; engineering, mathematical, and science managers; bookkeeping, accounting, and auditing clerks; welding machine setters and operators; machine tool cutting operators (excluding those in North Carolina); general office clerks; and stock clerks. However, job opportunities for machine builders and North Carolina machine tool operators are expected to increase by at least 10 percent. Industrial machinery mechanics positions should increase by about 8 percent.

Employment in the printing machinery industry in 1995 was about the same as in 1990, which was 22,000. Within that time period there were significant fluctuations, the greatest between 1990 and 1991, when the figure decreased by 23 percent from 24,000 to about 19,000. In 1995, slightly more than 50 percent of all employees in the industry were production workers, about the same as in 1990. Production workers' average hourly earnings have increased from about $14.00 in 1990 to $15.00 in 1995.

Productivity in the food products machinery industry, as measured by output per production worker, increased somewhat between 1989 and 1994. The average value added per production worker rose from $112,901 in 1989 to $131,725 in 1994. Productivity has grown annually since 1981, largely owing to the increased automation of plants and equipment. The industry has been quick to adopt new technology, especially computer technology, to improve efficiency and create new product lines, and the capital to labor ratio has risen significantly since 1989.

While the industry's stock of machinery and equipment has grown in the late 1980s and early 1990s, the number of production worker man-hours has decreased steadily. Increased competition from imports has been a motivating force, as has consumer demand for a broader range of food products. Industry shipments increased by about 18 percent, from $2.63 million in 1992 to $2.84 million in 1996. The average hourly wage for an employee in this industry was $13.39 in 1995.

RESEARCH AND TECHNOLOGY

Semiconductor equipment manufacturers were heavily dependent upon research and technology to sustain competitiveness. They invested heavily in productivity, quality, customer service programs, and new plants and equipment during the 1980s and early to mid-1990s. Most importantly, though, research and development outlays allowed them to sharpen their competitive edge in the development of high-tech, value-added machinery. They especially advanced in the fast-growing market for chemical and physical vapor deposition equipment, which was expected to lead industry growth throughout the mid-1990s. They also stretched their lead in automatic test equipment technology.

In the latter half of the 1990s, development efforts were expected to emphasize, among other technologies, machinery for advanced multichip modules, which mounted multiple integrated circuits on one unit. Equipment for manufacturing liquid crystal displays (LCDs) should also be a priority. LCDs were used for flat-panel displays on portable computers, and were manufactured using a process similar to that used to make chips.

While American semiconductor manufacturing equipment companies were planning to continue investing in vital R & D projects, so were their Japanese rivals. Japan's government and semiconductor manufacturers planned to spend between $500 million and $1 billion from 1996 to 2001 on consortiums and cooperative research programs. This investment was seen as an attempt to counter the influence of Sematech, develop advanced technology, and improve the competitiveness of Japan's semiconductor industry in the growing South Korean and American markets.

AMERICA AND THE WORLD

In 1995, about a third of all special industry machinery shipments were exported. These shipments were valued at $5.3 billion, a 57 percent increase over 1994.

At the same time, imports were valued at $3.4 billion, a 30 percent increase over 1994.

U.S. semiconductor machinery producers were very active in the export market in the 1990s and increased their share of the global market from 35 percent in 1991 to 42 percent in 1992 and 51 percent in 1993. Japan supplied 41 percent of worldwide equipment demand in 1993, while Europe controlled about 8 percent of the market. Those percentages remained essentially the same in the mid-1990s. According to the Semiconductor Equipment & Materials Institute (SEMI), the trade association for equipment makers, U.S. equipment makers held a 50 percent share of total world sales in 1995, followed by Japanese suppliers with a 44 percent share, and European companies with 6 percent.

With the exception of lithography equipment, U.S. producers held a technological and market lead in front-end machinery. They also led in the production of testing equipment, though Japan was stronger in assembly and material handling markets. Going into the mid-1990s, the United States was positioned to take advantage of the fastest growing and most technologically advanced equipment segments. However, Japan was expected to again emerge as the world's largest semiconductor equipment consumer following its recession.

In the long run, partnerships between Japanese and U.S. equipment firms were expected to blur national distinctions. Demand for semiconductor manufacturing equipment in emerging markets should provide strong growth for producers in both countries. Purchases of equipment in China, for example, swelled 140 percent in 1993. U.S. overseas sales appeared likely to grow faster between 1994 and 1998 than in the previous five years.

Ratification of the North American Free Trade Agreement (NAFTA) opened new markets, expanded sales, and increased production for the textile industry. Canada and Mexico are the two largest export markets for U.S. textile and apparel products. These markets, which currently support more than 80,000 export-related jobs in the United States, are growing rapidly. U.S. exports to Canada have grown an average of 19 percent per year since 1986, reaching $2.5 billion in 1994 and resulting in a trade surplus in the sector of $892 million. U.S. exports to Mexico have increased by 25 percent on average each year since 1986, reaching $2.3 billion in 1994. U.S. imports from Mexico exceeded sector exports by $7 million in 1994, largely reflecting the increased use of offshore production, where cut fabric parts are exported to Mexico for assembly into apparel, and then re-exported to the United States. NAFTA contains a ''rule of origin'' clause that will gradually enable Canada, Mexico, and the United States to waive duties and quotas on products made from raw materials that

were produced in one of the three nations. Tariffs will be phased out in a maximum of ten years for products manufactured in North America that meet NAFTA rules of origin. In time, this will give U.S., Mexican, and Canadian manufacturers a competitive advantage over textile producers in other countries.

The dramatic political and economic changes in Europe and the former Soviet Union have also created new markets for textile machinery. However, while many machinery suppliers exist within Europe, their technology is inferior to that of the West and Japan. Consequently, textile producers in these European countries may look to U.S. manufacturers for assistance in modernizing their facilities.

With nearly half of its production exported, the U.S. textile machinery industry markets its equipment aggressively in many foreign markets. The major markets are China, Canada, Japan, Mexico, Germany, Thailand, and Italy. Shipments by the U.S. textile machinery industry are expected to grow at an annual real rate of about 3 percent through 1998. Growth will be spurred by the industry's ability to market its products competitively in expanding foreign markets.

Historically, the United States has been a net exporter of paper industries machinery, with Canada, the United Kingdom, Mexico, and Australia being its most important foreign markets. However, imports began growing in relation to exports during the 1970s, and in 1979 the balance tipped in favor of imports. Before the rise of imports, nearly 90 percent of all new paper-making machines installed in the United States came from U.S.-based manufacturers. By the early 1980s, however, 50 percent of the new machines came from foreign manufacturers.

Much of the imported machinery came from Germany, the leading exporter of paper industries machinery in the world. Finland, Sweden, Switzerland, and Japan have also sold significant amounts of paper-making machinery in the U.S. market. There was a brief recovery in 1982, when exports exceeded imports by about $110 million. However, the downward trend returned in 1983, and by 1987 the industry's trade deficit had grown to almost $300 million. Exports began to improve in the late 1980s and early 1990s, with imports accounting for 25.8 percent of total shipments and exports comprising 19.7 percent. The Department of Commerce estimated that the U.S. industry would again be a net exporter by 1993.

In 1995, 34 percent of the food product machinery manufactured in the United States was exported, with a value of $7.91 million. Maintenance parts for machinery constituted nearly 20 percent of exports. The United States' greatest export customers for food processing machinery in 1993 were Canada and Mexico, which grossed sales at approximately $253 million. Other major export markets were the United Kingdom, Central America, Chile, and Colombia.

In contrast, U.S. importing activity has grown steadily. The United States was the largest importer of food products machinery, spending $481 million. The Germans and Italians had been dominant suppliers throughout the 1990s, while additional machinery was imported from the Netherlands, Canada, Switzerland, Denmark, and France. Food-product machinery imported in 1995 amounted to $612 million, a 23 percent increase over the 1994 figure.

ASSOCIATIONS AND SOCIETIES

AMERICAN SUPPLY AND MACHINERY MANUFACTURERS ASSOCIATION
1300 Sumner Ave.
Cleveland, OH 44115-2851
Phone: (216) 241-7333
Fax: (216) 241-0105

MACHINERY DEALERS NATIONAL ASSOCIATION
1110 Spring St.
Silver Spring, MD 20910
Phone: (301) 585-9494
Fax: (301) 585-7830

MANUFACTURERS ALLIANCE FOR PRODUCTIVITY AND INNOVATION
1525 Wilson Blvd., Ste. 900
Arlington, VA 22209
Phone: (703) 841-9000
Fax: (202) 331-7160

PERIODICALS AND NEWSLETTERS

AMERICAN MACHINIST
Penton Publishing, Inc.
1100 Superior Ave.
Cleveland, OH 44114-2543
Phone: (800) 321-7003 or (216) 696-7000
Fax: (216) 696-0177
Monthly. $65.00 per year.

DATABASES

CITIBASE (CITICORP ECONOMIC DATABASE)
FAME Software Corp.
77 Water St., 9 Fl.
New York, NY 10005
Phone: (212) 898-7800
Fax: (212) 742-8956

Presents over 6,000 statistical series relating to business, industry, finance, and economics. Includes series from Survey of Current Business *and many other sources. Time period is 1947 to date, with daily updates. Inquire as to online cost and availability.*

THOMAS REGISTER ONLINE
Thomas Publishing Co., Inc.
5 Penn Plz.
New York, NY 10001
Phone: (212) 695-0500
Fax: (212) 290-7362
Provides concise information on approximately 155,000 U.S. companies, mainly manufacturers, with over 50,000 product classifications. Indexes over 115,000 trade names. Information is updated semiannually. Inquire as to online cost and availability.

WILSONLINE: APPLIED SCIENCE AND TECHNOLOGY ABSTRACTS
H. W. Wilson Co.
950 University Ave.
Bronx, NY 10452
Phone: (800) 367-6770 or (718) 588-8400
Fax: (718) 590-1617
Provides online indexing and abstracting of 400 major scientific, technical, industrial, and engineering periodicals. Time period is 1983 to date for indexing and 1993 to date for abstracting, with updating twice a week. Inquire as to online cost and availability.

STATISTICS SOURCES

BUSINESS STATISTICS
Available from U.S. Government Printing Office
Washington, DC 20402
Phone: (202) 512-1800
Fax: (202) 512-2250
Biennial. $20.00. Issued by Bureau of Economic Analysis, U.S. Department of Commerce. Shows annual data for 29 years and monthly data for a recent four-year period. Statistics correspond to the Survey of Current Business.

ENCYCLOPEDIA OF AMERICAN INDUSTRIES
Gale Research
835 Penobscot Bldg.
Detroit, MI 48226-4094
Phone: (800) 877-GALE or (313) 961-2242
Fax: (800) 414-5043
1994. $500.00. Two volumes ($250.00 each). Volume one is Manufacturing Industries *and volume two is* Service and Non-Manufacturing Industries. *Provides the history, development, and recent status of approximately 1,000 industries. Includes statistical graphs, with industry and general indexes.*

SURVEY OF CURRENT BUSINESS
Available from U.S. Government Printing Office
Washington, DC 20402
Phone: (202) 512-1800
Fax: (202) 512-2250
Monthly. $41.00 per year. Issued by Bureau of Economic Analysis, U.S. Department of Commerce. Presents a wide variety of business and economic data.

UNITED STATES CENSUS OF MANUFACTURES
U.S. Bureau of the Census
Washington, DC 20233-0800
Phone: (301) 457-4100
Fax: (301) 457-3842
Quinquennial. Results presented in reports, tape, CD-ROM, and diskette files.

FURTHER READING

Barrett, Larry. "Reversal of Fortunes Not Likely Anytime Soon for Chip Makers." *The Business Journal,* 30 December 1996, 16.

Darnay, Arsen J., ed. *Manufacturing USA.* 5th ed. Detroit: Gale Research, 1996.

Dun's Business Rankings, 1996. Bethlehem, PA: Dun & Brandstreet, Inc., 1996.

"The Industry." American Textile Machinery Association, 1997. Available from http://www.webmasters.net/atma/.

Pollack, Andrew. "Japan Aims to Regain Semiconductor Leadership." *New York Times,* 18 November 1996, C1.

Semiconductor Capital Equipment Industry Report. New York: PaineWebber Inc., 21 January 1997.

Standard & Poor's Industry Surveys. New York: Standard & Poor's Corporation, 1997.

U.S. Department of Labor. Bureau of Labor Statistics. *Employment, Hours, and Earnings.* Washington: GPO, 1996.

Management consulting, also known as business consulting, is a large, diverse industry that consists of firms providing advisory services, and often implementation assistance, in numerous specialty areas for a variety of organizations, including businesses, governments, and nonprofit agencies. Specialties include information technology consulting, strategic planning, employee benefits, sales training, environmental consulting, business re-engineering, litigation support, executive searches, human resources consulting, real estate consulting, and many other specialized practice areas.

MANAGEMENT CONSULTING SERVICES

SIC 8742

 Top 9 LEADING TYPES OF BUSINESS CONSULTING FIRMS

Ranked by: Type of consultation, in percent.

1. Information systems, with 69%
2. Training, 63%
3. Strategic planning, 38%
3. Technology implementation, 38%
5. Compensation, 35%
6. Change management, 33%
7. Process reengineering, 31%
8. Sales & marketing, 28%
9. Downsizing, 12%

Source: *Management Review*, October, 1995, p. 41.

With an annual growth rate of 15 percent, and yearly sales of close to $25 billion worldwide, management consulting represents a vital industry in the United States and abroad. While consulting firms operate in a variety of established categories, the demand for different areas of specialization, including environmental and health care consulting, is on the rise. By the beginning of the next century, the industry will see an increased use of technology, and firms will seek to employ people with related expertise. In the past decade, hiring practices have become more competitive as more highly educated graduates enter the market; at the same time, the need for less skilled workers, including typists and secretaries, has declined. Firms are likely to continue to diversify their employment hierarchies as the industry continues to expand overseas.

Consulting organizations range in size from the single-person agency to multinational corporations employing thousands of people. Because of the diversity in types of consulting firms and the relatively small size of many of those firms, exact sales figures for the industry vary according to the type of organization defined as a consulting firm. What is clear, however, is that management consulting services represent a substantial industry, with U.S. sales of nearly $14 billion. According to the *Directory of Management Consultants 1993,* the industry has been growing at a rate of approximately 15 percent per year. It is estimated that more than 100,000 management consultants were practicing in the United States in the early 1990s—most of those being employed by the larger consulting firms. Worldwide, management consulting firms generate approximately $25 billion in revenues. Indeed, many firms that were founded in the United States now derive a substantial portion of their revenues from international operations.

INDUSTRY OUTLOOK

INDUSTRY TRENDS

There are several trends in American business that are redefining what clients want from consulting firms, and therefore, what consulting firms are offering to their clients. According to the *U.S. Industrial Outlook 1994,* "Demand for professional services will slowly increase through the 1990s. A major force behind this growth will be the increased use of computers, integrated systems and other high technology equipment."

In the business environment of the 1990s, management level employees are increasingly well educated. Advanced degrees have become more common in business, especially in large organizations that have traditionally called upon management consultants for an intellectual edge. Since many clients now have management personnel who attended graduate business school, management consulting organizations no longer have a monopoly on this type of experience. This has made the industry more competitive, and has made clients more demanding of their consultants.

**SIC 8742 - Management Consulting Services
General Statistics**

	Establish-ments	Employment (000)	Payroll ($ mil.)	Revenues ($ mil.)
1987	28,809	189.5	5,708.5	13,267.6*
1988	25,988	218.1	7,403.2	-*
1989	22,695	216.9	7,693.5	-*
1990	24,512	226.0	8,639.0	28,137.0
1991	27,162	243.8	9,558.9	26,136.0
1992	34,104	215.4	9,750.4	32,794.0
1993	35,829	252.9	11,120.3	34,727.0
1994	34,408P	253.5P	11,809.9P	37,055.5P
1995	35,900P	261.0P	12,624.0P	39,698.3P
1996	37,391P	268.6P	13,438.1P	42,341.1P

Sources: Data for 1982, 1987, and 1992 are from *Census of Service Industries*, Bureau of the Census, U.S. Department of Commerce. Revenue data are from the *Service Annual Survey* or from the Census. Revenue data from the Census are labelled with *. Data for 1988-1991 and 1993, when shown, are derived from *County Business Patterns* for those years from the Bureau of the Census. A P indicates projections made by the editor.

At the same time, clients increasingly insist that their high-priced advisors actually create change instead of simply producing valuable but ineffectual reports. This has led to an implementation orientation that per-vades the industry. Client engagements of the 1990s often include an implementation phase in which the consulting firm works with the client to bring the recommendations to reality.

In order to minimize costs and reduce staff, many firms are turning to outside consultants, an alternative that has been greatly beneficial. The Internet has also been an instrument of change in the consulting industry.

INDUSTRY ASSOCIATIONS AND ACCREDITATION

There is no central licensing agency for management consultants. Nor are there any industry guidelines or regulations as standards for operating practices. The only form of acknowledgment for consulting expertise is the Certified Management Consultant designation, which is granted by the trade association, the Institute of Management Consultants.

Another primary industry association is ACME (formerly Association of Consulting Management Engineers). Both ACME and the Institute of Management Consultants operate as divisions of the Council of Consulting Organizations (CCO). Other industry associations include the Society of Professional Management Consultants, the Association of Management Consulting Firms, the Association of Management Consultants, and the Association of Internal Management Consultants.

INDUSTRY GROWTH

Most consulting firms predict positive growth trends in the foreseeable future for themselves. Although some of the current growth has occurred domestically, much of this trend can be attributed to international expansion. As clients become more cost-conscious, there arises both a challenge and an opportunity for management consulting firms to grow their businesses in the future.

In particular, several specialty areas of management consulting can be expected to grow over the next several years. First is the area of health care consulting. As businesses attempt to maintain quality health care plans for their employees while maintaining or reducing costs, opportunities are increasing for consultants to provide advice in this area. Similarly, as health care providers and service providers are held under increasing scrutiny by the public and the government, experts are in a good position to provide advice on matters such as cost-containment and operations efficiency.

Another growth area is that of environmental consulting. With the Clinton Administration's concern for environmental matters, and the increasing attention the issues have received by the press and the public in recent years, this broad practice area is primed for growth. Business re-engineering is also an area of growth.

ORGANIZATION AND STRUCTURE

INDIVIDUAL FIRMS

The most common organizational structure for a management consulting firm is that of a corporation. A typical consulting firm might employ research associates at the lower tier, with consultants and senior consultants at the next level; managing consultants follow in the hierarchy. At this level, individuals typically have greater degrees of client interaction, as well as responsibility for the success of consulting projects. Partners are situated at the top of a typical firm's hierarchy. In addition to running the operations of the organization, partners are generally responsible for bringing new business into the company.

Management consulting firms usually operate in project teams. Depending upon the firm and the assignment, consultants on project teams often spend more time at the site of the client's offices than they do at their own. There, they gather data and interact extensively with personnel from the client organization, make recommendations, and often work on implementing solutions. Frequently, client personnel will work as part of the consulting team for the duration of the project to ensure that the organization has input into the process. Client participation increases the likelihood that the solutions will be implemented effectively.

Management consulting firms generally operate on a project fee or hourly fee basis. Fees in the consulting industry tend to run very high, due to the significance of the problems that consultants help their clients to overcome.

INDUSTRY STRUCTURE

Management consulting firms vary in their areas of expertise; some organizations are devoted to specific practice areas, while others offer a broad range of services to varied clientele. For example, a consulting firm might specialize in providing clients with compensation and benefits packages, to the exclusion of all other services. Yet other firms might provide a broad range of advisory services—combining such varied forms of advice as consulting the chief executive officer on general business strategy and consulting a management information systems (MIS) executive on a new computer network. A major segment of the consulting market is occupied by consulting organizations that are part of Certified Public Accountant (CPA) firms. Such firms attempt to serve their tax and audit clients with management consulting services as well. Another type of consulting function is one that exists within a nonconsulting organization. Such internal consultants provide specialized services for their corporation; for example, an internal human resources consulting department within a Fortune 500 corporation might serve the varied divisions of the organization as if they were external clients.

In addition to providing expertise or advice, many management consultants also serve as process consultants. This approach recognizes that the client firm already possesses knowledge of its own industry and internal corporate environment that exceeds the knowledge available to the consultant. Therefore, the role of the management consultant consists of facilitating the process of extracting solutions from within the client organization and providing insight with an objective point of view.

Many sole proprietorships and small firms perform advisory services for a variety of industries, and in a multitude of specialty areas, throughout the world. Ac-

SIC 8742 - Management Consulting Services
Industry Data by State

State	Establishments			Employment			Payroll			Revenues - 1992 ($ mil.)			% change 87-92	
	1987	1992	% of US 92	1987	1992	% of US 92	1987 ($ mil.)	1992 ($ mil.)	$ Per Empl. 92	Total ($ mil.)	Per Estab.	$ Per Empl. 92	Revenues	Payroll
California	4,653	4,482	45.3	31,315	27,201	47.1	905.4	1,347.5	49,538	3,163.0	0.7	116,282	49.5	48.8
New York	2,731	2,802	28.3	18,669	19,051	33.0	660.9	1,178.9	61,883	2,761.5	1.0	144,952	81.6	78.4
Illinois	1,600	2,013	20.4	11,559	14,386	24.9	390.7	748.7	52,042	1,718.8	0.9	119,475	76.4	91.6
Massachusetts	1,097	1,325	13.4	9,988	11,797	20.4	410.5	730.0	61,876	1,590.4	1.2	134,811	73.2	77.8
New Jersey	1,417	1,660	16.8	8,103	13,044	22.6	280.7	516.4	39,585	1,290.1	0.8	98,903	90.4	83.9
Texas	1,713	1,946	19.7	10,010	14,461	25.0	299.3	544.0	37,615	1,268.8	0.7	87,741	75.4	81.7
Virginia	1,007	1,335	13.5	9,038	12,980	22.5	267.0	547.0	42,145	1,176.0	0.9	90,600	90.2	104.9
Florida	1,649	2,262	22.9	8,351	9,719	16.8	194.4	396.6	40,810	934.6	0.4	96,158	84.4	104.0
Georgia	682	1,002	10.1	4,875	6,843	11.8	162.2	334.5	48,877	865.4	0.9	126,458	142.5	106.2
Connecticut	734	833	8.4	4,992	5,530	9.6	206.8	342.1	61,871	862.1	1.0	155,893	66.2	65.4

Source: Census of Service Industries, 1987 and 1992, Bureau of the Census, U.S. Department of Commerce. Data are sorted by 1992 revenues and, if revenues are unavailable, by establishments in 1992. (D) indicates that data are withheld by the source to avoid disclosure of competitive information. A dash (-) indicates that data are not available. Percentage changes between 1987 and 1992 are calculated using numbers that have *not* been rounded; hence they may not be reproducible from the values shown.

cording to *Management Consulting 1993* writer David J. Collis, "Half of all consulting firms generate less than $500,000 in annual billings, and one-third employ fewer than four people." However, approximately 75 percent of total consulting revenues generated in the United States can be attributed to the 50 largest management consulting firms. It is these firms that do most of the consulting work and that employ the vast majority of professional management consultants.

Because the management consulting industry is un-regulated, any individual or company that offers advice in exchange for compensation may be classified as a consultant. For this reason, the definition of a management consulting firm often varies, depending upon the source of information. Nonetheless, an understanding of the industry can be ascertained by separating consulting firms into distinct categories and contrasting the categories. The following breakdown describes the most common and most widely recognized types of consulting organizations, first by organizational structure, and then by consulting specialty (also known as "practice area" within the industry).

LARGE CONSULTING FIRMS

This classification includes the largest players in the management consulting industry, whose primary service is providing expertise and consultation to management. The broad heading of large consulting firms encompasses the larger of the generalist consulting firms and

strategy consulting firms, which appear in the "Consulting Firms by Specialty" section below.

CPA FIRM CONSULTING DIVISIONS

Six big accounting firms control many of the largest management consulting firms in the world. In the United States, these firms generate more than $3 billion in revenue. Consulting divisions of Certified Public Accounting (CPA) firms, particularly the big six firms, are especially strong in the Information Technology/Management Information Systems (MIS) area of consulting. These firms typically offer strategic or generalist management consulting services as well. Examples of CPA firms with consulting practices include Andersen Consulting (division of Arthur Andersen), Deloitte & Touche Management Consulting (division of Deloitte & Touche), and Ernst & Young.

SMALL FIRMS/BOUTIQUES

Small firms or boutiques often provide specialized services or offer expertise that focuses on one industry or a single business practice area. These firms tend to be small, lesser known niche players that do not regularly compete directly with the larger consulting organizations. Many of these firms operate in a single, geographic region and some have only one client.

SOLE PRACTITIONERS

This group encompasses many outplaced or retired executives and part-time consultants who offer expertise

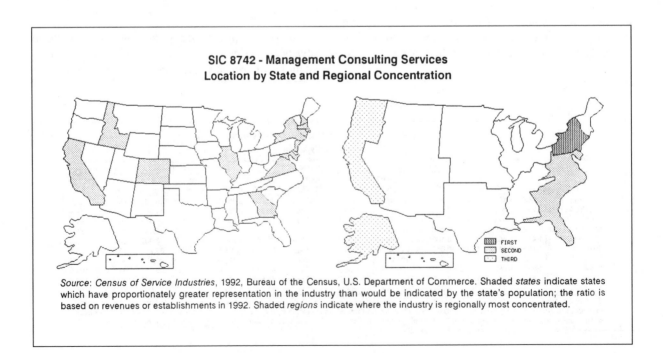

**SIC 8742 - Management Consulting Services
Location by State and Regional Concentration**

FIRST
SECOND
THIRD

Source: Census of Service Industries, 1992, Bureau of the Census, U.S. Department of Commerce. Shaded *states* indicate states which have proportionately greater representation in the industry than would be indicated by the state's population; the ratio is based on revenues or establishments in 1992. Shaded *regions* indicate where the industry is regionally most concentrated.

in areas where they have a great deal of experience. Sole practitioners are often engaged by smaller firms, and even their previous employers. This classification of the consulting industry also includes university professors who provide consulting in their areas of teaching expertise.

INTERNAL CONSULTING ORGANIZATIONS

Large corporations may have recurring project work for which the expertise of external management consultants would be required on an ongoing basis. Many such firms have developed internal consulting staffs in order to deal with this demand in a more cost-effective manner. Such internal organizations may be generalist or may specialize in corporate strategy, human resources issues, information technology, or other areas that are critical to the company's operation.

INFORMATION TECHNOLOGY (IT)/ MANAGEMENT INFORMATION SYSTEMS (MIS)

According to *Management Consulting 1993,* the information technology segment is the largest segment of the consulting industry. The big six CPA firms all provide expertise in this area, and draw substantial revenue from it as well. Firms that specialize in information technology tackle business problems by applying technology to provide solutions. One of the firms that is best known in IT/MIS consulting is Andersen Consulting.

COMPENSATION/BENEFITS CONSULTING

Compensation/benefits consulting firms represent the second largest independent segment of the industry in the United States. These firms offer services related to human resource management with specific expertise in practices such as developing corporate grading and compensation schemes, titling plans, and benefits packages. Examples of firms that practice primarily in the compensation/benefits consulting practice area include the Hay Group and Hewitt Associates.

GENERALIST CONSULTING

Generalist management consulting firms typically provide advice on strategy to their clients, but may also have internal expertise in specific industries, such as banking or health care; or in particular practice areas, such as new product development or operations. Generalist consulting firms often provide consulting in IT/MIS and compensation/benefits as well. Examples of generalist firms include McKinsey & Company, Inc., Booz, Allen & Hamilton, Inc., and Arthur D. Little, Inc.

STRATEGY CONSULTING

Strategy consulting firms specialize in providing advice on corporate strategy to senior executives. Strategy firms compete with generalist firms for strategic engagements, but do not provide the same nonstrategy services. However, as they expanded their lines of business, the larger strategy firms have become more difficult to distinguish from the generalist firms. Examples of firms that have traditionally been regarded as strategy firms include the Boston Consulting Group and Bain & Company.

SPECIALTY CONSULTING PRACTICE AREAS

This segment is by far the most difficult to define, for it encompasses so many different possible practice areas. Specialty consulting firms are often boutiques or small- to medium-size organizations that service a niche in the consulting market.

MARKETING CONSULTING FIRMS

These firms provide marketing research, product test markets, target market selection, and other services directly related to the marketing of client products or services. Perhaps the best known marketing consulting firm is Yankelovich, Skelly and White/Clancy Shulman Inc.

BUSINESS REENGINEERING/ ORGANIZATIONAL EFFECTIVENESS

Originated by the Index Group (Now CSC/Index, Inc.), this specialty in management consulting refers to the radical redesigning and rebuilding of the processes and functions of a business to re-create the company as a highly effective, cohesive whole that performs optimally. Increasingly, other consulting firms are developing this line of business as well, most notably Andersen Consulting.

ENVIRONMENTAL CONSULTING FIRMS

With increased public attention on the environment, and increased governmental concern over hazardous waste, environmental consulting firms have seen increased demand for their services in recent years.

HEALTH CARE CONSULTING

There are two primary specialties that fall under the heading of health care consulting. The first practice area is providing general advisory services such as strategy consultation or cost-containment studies for health service agencies (e.g., Health Maintenance Organizations, etc.) and hospitals. The second practice area is in helping corporations to select employee health benefit plans that minimize costs and provide the best health care coverage for the organization.

As health care costs continue to rise in the United States and concern for health coverage increases, this consulting specialty has experienced growth as well. In addition to specialty firms, which provide health care consulting, many of the larger consulting organizations also service this industry.

NEW BUSINESS DEVELOPMENT PRACTICES

Changes in the economy can affect firms in different ways. For instance, if the economy slows and businesses become more concerned with the bottom line, they may put off decisions such as automating. This negatively impacts the information technology segment of management consulting. At the same time, however, executives of corporations in hard times might be more prone to call upon a consulting firm that can help them to find ways to increase their revenues, contain their costs, or reduce their head count.

For consulting firms, approximately 20 percent of their costs derive from new business development. Costs for marketing activities include the production and distribution of promotional materials, salaries of partners who are responsible for client development and new business, and association memberships. The area in which firms may expend the greatest amount of resources, however, is in the competitive bidding process, also known in the industry as the "bake-off."

A bake-off occurs when a client with a problem approaches several consulting firms. Each firm spends time and money becoming acquainted with the client's organization, attempting to develop internal champions for their firm. The bake-off often involves several personnel from each consulting firm dedicating their time, without pay, at the site of the potential client in order to gather a better understanding of the problem. At the end of the competitive bidding process, the client chooses one of the firms, or none, and the remainder have invested resources without remuneration.

Because of the expense involved in acquiring new clients, consulting firms try to become the "house consultants" for their existing clients. In doing so, the firm may become so trusted by the client that it can bypass the competitive bake-off and be engaged directly by client management. This is an enviable position for a consulting firm, as it can minimize business development costs and ensure a more steady flow of income.

WORK FORCE

For the most part, large management consulting firms hire people with MBAs from top business schools as entry level consultants. For higher level positions, specialists may be recruited directly from the competition or from the industry. The latter is particularly true if an individual can offer industry expertise that would assist the consulting firm in expanding or servings its existing client base. Depending upon the industry and the needs of the particular firm, individuals with more advanced degrees or degrees in technical specialties (such as economics or computer science) may be selected as well. Some consulting firms will take academically strong candidates from top undergraduate schools as lower entry level consultants or analysts/researchers.

Overall, consultants in medium-to-large generalist or strategy firms are analytically oriented, well-educated individuals. In the past, management consultants in the United States were typically white males. Like other industries, consulting firms have been diversifying, especially as these firms increase their exposure in foreign markets.

The industry also comprises small firms, boutiques, and sole proprietorships that are composed of technical specialists such as information technologists or marketing consultants. These individuals may be displaced corporate professionals or individuals who have left larger consulting firms to start their own practices. It is also common for sole practitioners to perform consulting work on the side, in addition to their full-time positions with other companies.

Another segment of the consulting industry is comprised of university professors who consult to complementtheir full-time teaching positions. These professors typically hold advanced degrees and are specialists in a particular field of research. This segment of the consulting population is self-regulating via the Academy of Management, Division of Managerial Consultation, which provides a code of ethics for its 800 members. The fastest growing segment of this market is systems analysis and administrative services managers; typists, word processors, secretaries, and bookkeeping/accounting clerks will see the least amount of growth in the early years of the next century.

COMPENSATION

New management consultants in the top consulting firms are generally well paid relative to other industries. In addition to attractive salaries, many consulting firms offer signing bonuses as an incentive for top candidates to join their firms. Because of their high fees, premier consulting firms can afford to pay top salaries and retain the best people.

Although smaller firms vary in the compensation they provide, the typical management consultant is compensated as well as the top executives with whom he or

SIC 8742
Occupations Employed by SIC 8742 - Management and Public Relations

Occupation	% of Total 1994	Change to 2005
General managers & top executives	6.3	43.9
Secretaries, ex legal & medical	5.6	38.1
Sales & related workers nec	5.0	51.7
General office clerks	4.0	29.4
Management support workers nec	2.9	51.7
Financial managers	2.8	51.7
Bookkeeping, accounting, & auditing clerks	2.6	13.8
Professional workers nec	2.6	82.0
Managers & administrators nec	2.4	51.6
Marketing, advertising, & PR managers	2.3	29.5
Administrative services managers	2.3	97.2
Management analysts	2.2	51.1
Clerical supervisors & managers	2.0	55.2
Janitors & cleaners, incl maids	2.0	21.4
Public relations specialists & publicity writers	1.8	17.0
Accountants & auditors	1.8	89.6
Computer programmers	1.8	22.9
Receptionists & information clerks	1.8	51.7
Food preparation & service workers nec	1.7	36.8
Systems analysts	1.4	142.7
Health professionals & paraprofessionals nec	1.4	51.7
Clerical support workers nec	1.4	21.4
Engineering, mathematical, & science managers	1.3	72.3
Service workers nec	1.3	51.7
Engineers nec	1.3	82.0
Computer engineers	1.2	124.7
Maintenance repairers, general utility	1.1	36.5
Engineering technicians & technologists nec	1.1	51.7
Typists & word processors	1.1	-24.1
Helpers, laborers, & material movers nec	1.0	51.7

Source: *Industry-Occupation Matrix*, Bureau of Labor Statistics. These data relate to one or more 3-digit SIC industry groups rather than to a single 4-digit SIC. The change reported for each occupation to the year 2005 is a percent of growth or decline as estimated by the Bureau of Labor Statistics. The abbreviation nec stands for 'not elsewhere classified'.

she consults. Partners of consulting firms are even better compensated, as they share in the often substantial profits of the entire firm. In exchange for their significant compensation, however, consultants sacrifice by working extremely long hours and traveling extensively. It is common for consultants to spend more of their working hours at the client's site than at their own firm. Consultants also end up spending a great deal of time at airports and on the road.

RESEARCH AND TECHNOLOGY

The application of technology is a significant tool of the consulting industry. Many of the largest firms in the industry generate their revenue by applying technology solutions to business problems. An example of this is redesigning a distribution operation and inventory tracking system to automate the entire process with robotics, computers, scanners, and advanced software to control the system. Still other firms specialize in training corporate personnel to use technology.

Because of the high level of specialized knowledge that many management consulting firms possess, technical expertise may be the very reason for which a firm is engaged by a client. An example of such a rigorous application of technology and research is the type evidenced by Arthur D. Little, Inc. This historic consulting firm maintains research laboratories in the United States and in Europe. Arthur D. Little laboratories have produced advanced detection equipment for the U.S. Air Force and protective clothing for use by individuals who will be exposed to hazardous materials. Firms with technical expertise may be called in to assist in complex engineering or production problems that require the expertise of skilled scientists.

AMERICA AND THE WORLD

Many of the largest consulting firms in the United States are growing at a faster rate internationally than domestically. McKinsey and Company, Inc., an American firm whose name has become synonymous with management consulting, now generates approximately 60 percent of its revenue from international operations in such cities as Zurich, Milan, and Osaka.

ASSOCIATIONS AND SOCIETIES

ACME: THE ASSOCIATION OF MANAGEMENT CONSULTING FIRMS
521 5th Ave. 35th Fl.
New York, NY 10175-3598
Phone: (212) 697-9693
Fax: (212) 949-6571
Members are management consultants. One of the two divisions of the Council of Consulting Organizations.

INSTITUTE OF MANAGEMENT CONSULTANTS
521 5th Ave., 35 Fl.
New York, NY 10175-3598
Phone: (212) 697-8262
Fax: (212) 949-6571
Provides professional services and certification to management consultants. One of the two divisions of the Council of Consulting Organizations.

PERIODICALS AND NEWSLETTERS

CONSULTANTS NEWS
Kennedy Publications
Templeton Rd.
Fitzwilliam, NH 03447
Phone: (603) 585-6544
Fax: (603) 585-9555

Monthly. $158.00 per year. Newsletter. News and ideas for management consultants.

DATABASES

ABI/INFORM
UMI/Data Courier
620 S. 3rd St.
Louisville, KY 40202
Phone: (800) 626-2823 or (502) 583-4111
Fax: (502) 589-5572
Provides online indexing to business-related material occurring in over 800 periodicals from 1971 to the present. Inquire as to online cost and availability.

CONSULTANTS AND CONSULTING ORGANIZATIONS DIRECTORY: CCOD [ONLINE]
Gale Research
835 Penobscot Bldg.
Detroit, MI 48226-4094
Phone: (800) 877-GALE or (313) 961-2242
Fax: (313) 961-6815
Provides information on over 24,000 consulting organizations and individual consultants in all fields. Semiannual updates. Inquire as to online cost and availability.

WILSONLINE: WILSON BUSINESS ABSTRACTS
H. W. Wilson Co.
950 University Ave.
Bronx, NY 10452
Phone: (800) 367-6770 or (718) 588-8400
Fax: (718) 590-1617
Indexes and abstracts 350 major business periodicals, plus the Wall Street Journal *and the business section of the* New York Times. *Indexing is from 1982, abstracting from 1990, with the two newspapers included from 1993. Updated daily. Inquire as to online cost and availability. (Business Periodicals Index without abstracts is also available online.)*

STATISTICS SOURCES

AN ANALYSIS OF THE MANAGEMENT CONSULTING BUSINESS IN THE U.S. TODAY
Kennedy Publications
Templeton Rd.

Fitzwilliam, NH 03447
Phone: (800) 531-0007 or (603) 585-6544
Fax: (603) 585-9555
Annual. $35.00. Includes ranking of leading management consulting firms and estimates of market share and total revenue.

U.S. INDUSTRIAL OUTLOOK: FORECASTS FOR SELECTED MANUFACTURING AND SERVICE INDUSTRIES
Available from U.S. Government Printing Office
Washington, DC 20402
Phone: (202) 512-1800
Fax: (202) 512-2250
Annual. $37.00. (Replaced in 1995 by U.S. Global Trade Outlook.*) Issued by the International Trade Administration, U.S. Department of Commerce. Provides basic data, outlook for the current year, and "Long-Term Prospects" (five-year projections) for a wide variety of products and services. Includes high technology industries. Available on the world wide web at gopher://gopher.umsl.edu:70/11/library/govdocs/usio94*

GENERAL WORKS

THE WITCH DOCTORS: MAKING SENSE OF THE MANAGEMENT GURUS
John Micklethwait and Adrian Wooldridge
Random House, Inc.
201 E. 50th St.
New York, NY 10022
Phone: (800) 726-0600 or (212) 751-2600
Fax: (212) 572-8700
1996. $24.50. A critical, iconoclastic, and practical view of consultants, business school professors, and modern management theory, written by two members of the editorial staff of The Economist.

FURTHER READING

The Directory of Management Consultants 1993. Fitzwilliam, NH: Kennedy Publications, 1993.

Wheeler, Chris, ed. *Management Consulting 1993: Harvard Business School Career Guide.* Cambridge, MA: Harvard Business School Press, 1993.

Companies in this drug industry segment furnish the active ingredients used by pharmaceutical firms to manufacture their finished products, called pharmaceutical preparations. Active ingredients are the portion of a finished drug that creates the desired effect, therapeutic or preventive, for humans and animals. Extracts of crude drugs (not yet processed) derived from plant or animal sources are important examples of the components produced by this industry sector. By the 1960s, synthesized chemicals—either a manufactured copy of an organic or inorganic substance, or a new chemical entity (NCE)—had become common active ingredients in pharmaceuticals, from vitamin pills to hormones. Meanwhile, the biotechnology revolution, beginning in earnest in the 1980s, resulted in ways of inserting genetic material into small microorganisms. This made them miniature factories for the production of active drug ingredients like insulin, and in the process creating patentable new molecular entities (NME's).

MEDICINALS AND BOTANICALS

SIC 2833

Consolidations of pharmaceutical firms face acceleration in the late 1990s as a result of tough open-market competition due to time-consuming clinical trials and FDA approval and the financial burden they create. These consolidations spell rough times for independent generic producers caught between fluctuations in the supply of ingredients worldwide and the larger firms that control the current capacity on the ingredients in drugs coming off-patent.

Top Vitamin and Tonic Brands

Vitamin and tonic brand shares shown reflect sales of $1.259 billion in 1994 and $1.371 billion in 1995.

	1994	1995
Nature Made	10.3%	11.1%
Centrum	10.4	9.5
Your Life	7.6	7.4
Nature's Bounty	4.1	3.7
One-A-Day	3.2	3.1
Flintstones	2.4	2.2
Theragran	3.0	2.1
Private label	34.0	33.4
Other	25.0	27.5

Source: *Advertising Age*, January 1, 1996, p. 20, from Towne-Oller & Associates.

In the 1990s, technological advances and shrinking resources created a new interest in natural products and plant-derived drugs, although by the middle of the decade, there seemed to be mixed reactions from experts. One executive noted that the trend would not continue if significant drug discoveries did not occur in the latter half of the decade.

INDUSTRY OUTLOOK

In the late 1980s and early 1990s, pharmaceutical firms began to reverse their trend toward the in-house production of active ingredients in favor of a more complex combination of captive production and long-term contracts with outside custom suppliers. Among the factors fueling this trend were the early 1990s economic recession and excess world chemical capacity, the increasing costs in both time and money to negotiate regulatory hazards, the complexity of new drug compounds, and the desire to avoid tying up too much capital in supply factories. Pharmaceutical firms in the 1980s had found themselves spending 7 to 10 years of their 17-year patent period on new drugs going through clinical trials and awaiting subsequent FDA approval. By looking more to outside fine chemical suppliers, drug companies could, as the *Chemical Marketing Reporter* put it, be "spared the cost of planting steel in the ground to produce a substance that may still require government approvals and has yet to prove commercially viable." For those companies lucky enough to sign on with a major pharmaceutical manufacturer on a long-term supply contract, they could be assured of a 7 to 10 year market for their products. But, for the others, the competition in the open market promised to get tougher, suggesting consolidations might accelerate in the latter half of the 1990s.

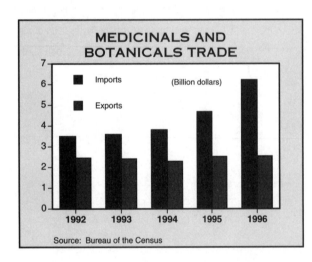

MEDICINALS AND BOTANICALS TRADE

Imports

Exports

(Billion dollars)

1992 1993 1994 1995 1996

Source: Bureau of the Census

Meanwhile, the highly politicized drive for healthcare reform in the late 1980s and early 1990s created downward pressure on the prices the big pharmaceutical firms could charge for their prescription drugs, even for new "breakthrough" treatment therapies that cost considerable amounts of money to develop. The immediate winners in this contest over drug prices seemed to be the smaller independent generics companies. Generics,

markedly cheaper therapeutic and chemical equivalents of prescription patented medicines, went into production once the patent protection on a prescription drug expired. Generics companies could manage cheap prices because they only had to copy—not research and develop—the drugs they produced.

Because of this, however, the active ingredients in generics accounted for almost half of their sale price—a ratio three to four times greater than prescription versions of the same drug. This made the generic companies susceptible to changes in the supply of active ingredients worldwide. When, as *Drug Topics* reported, the European Economic Community temporarily "outlawed the exportation of bulk/fine chemicals," generics companies were faced with a cut-off of 85 percent of their supply. At the same time, the prescription pharmaceutical firms controlled the current capacity on the active ingredients in their drugs coming off-patent. Combined with a wave of takeovers or start-ups of generics firms by large pharmaceutical producers, the cut-off in supplies threatened to squeeze independent generic producers out, and effectively extend prescription patents and higher drug prices much longer than healthcare reform advocates desired.

Makers of Herbal Supplements

Producers of herbal supplements are ranked by share of the market for the 12 months ended May 1995.

Sunsource Health Products	25.5%
Pharmavite	20.4
Leiner	7.1
Lichtwer Pharma	6.4
Nature's Bounty	4.2
Bayer	2.4
Kyolic	1.4
Other	32.6

Source: *Nonfoods Merchandising*, October 1995, p. 50, from Towne-Oller & Associates.

ORGANIZATION AND STRUCTURE

There were an estimated 234 establishments in the medicinals and botanicals industry in 1997. A large amount of these were divisions or subsidiaries of other firms. Parent firms that have developed in-house active ingredient suppliers are said to be "back-integrated," and their chemical products are referred to as "captive," dedicated to the parent firm, whereas chemicals produced by firms independent of the final purchaser are called "merchant."

Many "fine" chemical companies producing for the merchant market are contracted to large pharmaceutical companies to supply custom, or specialty chemicals, while others produce and sell them on the open market. The latter often manufacture well-known bulk pharmaceutical compounds, like those used in the production of aspirin. Custom and specialty chemicals are produced in smaller quantities than bulks and frequently combine several different chemical compounds called intermediates which are more expensive. Traditionally, "fine" chemicals were those that free had less impurities than industrial chemicals not intended for human consumption.

Both the back-integrated firms and the independent fine chemical companies are involved in the complex process of producing extracts of natural substances, synthetic inorganic and organic chemicals, or combinations of any or all of these, that go into most modern medicines. The specific formulas for these substances can be found in academic monographs, or in the official U.S. Pharmacopeia (USP) and the National Formulary (NF). If they have not yet been manufactured on an industrial scale or are entirely new compounds (NCE's or NME's), the pharmaceutical firm creates a document as a reference for its own in-house producers or as a guide to firms contracted to supply active ingredients. These references provide manufacturers with the acceptable legal standards of purity and potency for their products. A new manufacturing process, as well as an NCE or NME, is patentable in the United States.

Active ingredients from natural sources start as crude drugs. According to the standard text on drug extraction from natural sources, *Pharmacognosy,* crude drugs from vegetative or animal (even insect) origins are "natural substances that have undergone only the processes of collection and drying." Natural substances are those "found in nature . . . that have not had changes made in their molecular structure." The sources of these substances, medicinal plants or the animals from which glands and organs are needed, can either be raised commercially or collected in the wild. But environmental concerns tended to support the former in the 1980s and 1990s. Especially with plants, it is of vital importance that the correct species is identified before collection. Once a crude drug has been collected and the needed portions separated and cleaned, it must be safely stored or immediately processed, according to how quickly the active ingredient might spoil on lose its potency. Plants are often stored over long periods to help decompose unwanted plant components while leaving the desired portions intact. Animal glands and organs, however, are generally processed quickly to avoid deterioration.

If the crude drug is a plant, the active constituent (the ingredient desired for the final drug product) must be extracted. The first step in this procedure is grinding and mincing the appropriate plant parts, such as the leaves or the seeds. Production facilities in this industry house hammer mills, knife mills, and teeth mills designed to reduce leaves, stems, seeds, or roots to a manageable powder composed of evenly sized granules. Some plant products, such as herbal remedies, can be

SIC 2833 - Medicinals and Botanicals
General Statistics

| Year | Companies | Establishments | | Employment | | | Compensation | | Production ($ million) | | | |
		Total	with 20 or more employees	Total (000)	Production Workers (000)	Hours (Mil)	Payroll ($ mil)	Wages ($/hr)	Cost of Materials	Value Added by Manufacture	Value of Shipments	Capital Invest.
1982	209	228	94	17.8	10.2	20.9	463.2	10.95	1,335.2	2,054.7	3,397.9	283.6
1983		227	98	17.7	9.8	19.0	472.0	12.14	1,287.2	2,057.5	3,370.6	273.9
1984		226	102	17.3	9.5	18.0	497.5	12.50	1,446.8	1,992.4	3,410.3	260.8
1985		224	105	15.7	8.6	17.5	497.5	13.61	1,298.4	1,970.8	3,282.9	170.0
1986		223	107	15.8	8.3	16.6	497.6	14.15	1,285.0	1,854.9	3,153.1	147.2
1987	208	225	84	11.6	6.1	12.0	376.5	15.32	1,613.4	1,780.7	3,350.2	114.5
1988		223	93	11.3	6.2	11.7	381.4	16.09	2,052.9	2,086.2	4,150.4	150.5
1989		221	92	11.7	6.6	13.3	420.3	16.29	2,596.0	2,225.7	4,752.5	219.3
1990		226	93	12.7	6.5	13.1	423.4	17.35	2,579.2	2,392.2	4,919.4	194.5
1991		226	103	12.5	7.2	14.3	540.2	20.06	3,200.0	3,166.4	6,308.2	487.3
1992	208	225	74	13.0	7.4	15.1	587.1	18.91	3,245.9	3,365.7	6,438.5	550.5
1993		248	88	13.0	7.7	16.3	610.8	19.62	2,757.8	3,191.2	5,925.8	482.4
1994		231P	86P	13.9	7.8	15.6	613.7	19.71	2,953.0	3,163.7	6,189.3	504.7
1995		232P	85P	11.1P	6.3P	12.9P	567.0P	21.37P	3,173.7P	3,400.1P	6,651.8P	475.3P
1996		233P	83P	10.6P	6.1P	12.5P	577.8P	22.16P	3,319.5P	3,556.4P	6,957.5P	501.0P
1997		234P	82P	10.2P	5.8P	12.1P	588.7P	22.94P	3,465.4P	3,712.7P	7,263.3P	526.7P
1998		234P	81P	9.8P	5.6P	11.7P	599.6P	23.72P	3,611.3P	3,869.0P	7,569.1P	552.4P

Sources: 1982, 1987, 1992 *Economic Census*; *Annual Survey of Manufactures*, 83-86, 88-91, 93-94. Establishment counts for non-Census years are from *County Business Patterns*; establishment values for 83-84 are extrapolations. 'P's show projections by the editors. Industries reclassified in 87 will not have data for prior years.

sent at this point to be packaged for sale or combined into other preparations. For most plant-derived drugs, the powdered plant must be submitted to a series of solvent baths (a process called maceration), such as alcohol or ether, or a series of distillation procedures (in the case of volatile oils), that separate the desired ingredient from the crude material. Animal glands or organs are also minced, then mixed with a solvent that aids extraction and often preserves the substance. After centrifugation, the animal extract is filtered to separate remaining impurities. Antibiotic molds, on the other hand, are actually grown in large fermentation tanks. The molds release their medicinal yield into a fermenting medium or solution. These fluid mixtures of either mold, plant, or animal materials are submitted to "precipitation," which involves the application of either heat or freezing cold, or the addition of salts or some other compound that separates or isolates the target active ingredient from the fluid. Isolates are then sent to the customer in either powdered or fluid form to be assembled into a marketable drug.

Manufacturers of active ingredients ship their finished products in "batches" to the preparation firm awaiting them. The chemical composition of these shipments must match a parent batch (to ensure purity and strength), and must meet with the approval of the U.S. Food and Drug Administration (FDA) as well as the client company. Firms that desire a regular supply of high-quality materials will often inspect manufacturing plants before assigning a production contract for active ingredients. The FDA, besides comparing active ingredients to the gold standard, is responsible for assuring that every step in the process of pharmaceutical raw material production meets specific production standards.

AMERICA AND THE WORLD

Despite the twentieth century revolution in chemical pharmaceuticals, it was reported in *The Medicinal Plant Industry* that "50 percent to 80 percent of the developing world depends on traditional therapies for their health care," namely plant-derived remedies. In China and Southeast Asia, indigenous industries process and package plant-based remedies based on ancient recipes. Some processors utilize the same machinery and manufacturing expertise as American companies, while others are extremely small and use traditional methods. This system of traditional active ingredient production for drugs, except to the extent that Western-style medicines were adopted or locally produced for export to the West,

SIC 2833
Occupations Employed by SIC 283 - Drugs

Occupation	% of Total 1994	Change to 2005
Packaging & filling machine operators	7.8	11.2
Science & mathematics technicians	5.7	36.0
Biological scientists	5.5	49.6
Secretaries, ex legal & medical	5.3	12.5
Chemists	4.9	23.6
Sales & related workers nec	4.4	23.6
Chemical equipment controllers, operators	3.1	11.2
Inspectors, testers, & graders, precision	2.7	23.6
Engineering, mathematical, & science managers	2.2	40.4
Management support workers nec	2.0	23.6
Industrial machinery mechanics	1.8	36.0
Managers & administrators nec	1.8	23.5
General managers & top executives	1.8	17.3
Crushing & mixing machine operators	1.7	23.6
Marketing, advertising, & PR managers	1.7	23.6
Medical scientists	1.7	48.3
Hand packers & packagers	1.7	5.9
Systems analysts	1.6	97.7
Assemblers, fabricators, & hand workers nec	1.5	23.6
Freight, stock, & material movers, hand	1.5	-1.1
Janitors & cleaners, incl maids	1.5	-1.1
Industrial production managers	1.5	23.6
Machine operators nec	1.4	8.9
General office clerks	1.2	5.4
Traffic, shipping, & receiving clerks	1.2	18.9
Professional workers nec	1.2	48.3
Helpers, laborers, & material movers nec	1.1	23.6
Marketing & sales worker supervisors	1.1	23.6
Extruding & forming machine workers	1.1	36.0
Bookkeeping, accounting, & auditing clerks	1.0	-7.3

Source: *Industry-Occupation Matrix*, Bureau of Labor Statistics. These data relate to one or more 3-digit SIC industry groups rather than to a single 4-digit SIC. The change reported for each occupation to the year 2005 is a percent of growth or decline as estimated by the Bureau of Labor Statistics. The abbreviation nec stands for 'not elsewhere classified'.

remained relatively untouched by American corporate influences.

Suppliers of fine chemicals for American pharmaceuticals, however, have never been limited to the country's borders. European chemical companies, except for temporary alterations during various wars, have always had—and continued to have in the late twentieth century—a large presence in the American market. The *Chemical Marketing Reporter* noted in the early 1990s that the U.S. share of the fine chemicals market only totaled about 30 percent, while European companies controlled more than 50 percent. American producers, however, more than held their own in domestic markets. In the 1990s, industry leadership remained in European and American hands, which, with the addition of Japan, were estimated to control almost 90 percent of the market. A growing threat to this Western fine chemical hegemony were Asian and Indian producers, who do not have the strict Western environmental codes applied to U.S. producers. Asian producers showed themselves particularly competitive in the bulk pharmaceutical and intermediates classes.

ASSOCIATIONS AND SOCIETIES

COUNCIL ON FAMILY HEALTH
225 Park Ave. S, 17th Fl.
New York, NY 10003
Phone: (212) 598-3617
Members are drug manufacturers. Concerned with proper use of medications.

DRUG, CHEMICAL AND ALLIED TRADES ASSOCIATION
2 Roosevelt Blvd., Ste. 301
Syosset, NY 11719
Phone: (516) 496-3317
Fax: (516) 496-2231

DRUG INFORMATION ASSOCIATION
PO Box 113
Maple Glen, PA 19002
Phone: (215) 628-2288
Concerned with the technology of drug information processing.

NATIONAL ASSOCIATION OF PHARMACEUTICAL MANUFACTURERS
747 3rd Ave.
New York, NY 10017
Phone: (212) 838-3720
Fax: (212) 753-6832

NATIONAL PHARMACEUTICAL COUNCIL
1894 Preston White Dr.
Reston, VA 22091
Phone: (703) 620-6390
Members are drug manufacturers producing prescription medication.

PERIODICALS AND NEWSLETTERS

DRUG DEVELOPMENT RESEARCH
Wiley-Liss, Inc.
41 E. 11th St.
New York, NY 10003
Phone: 9800) 225-5945 or (212) 475-7700
Fax: (212) 850-6088
Monthly. $597.00 per year.

DRUG TOPICS
Medical Economics Publishing
5 Paragon Dr.
Montvale, NJ 07645
Phone: (800) 223-0581 or (201) 358-7200
Biweekly. $58.00 per year.

PHARMACEUTICAL ENGINEERING
International Society for Pharmaceutical Engineering, Inc.
3816 W. Linebaugh Ave., Ste. 412
Tampa, FL 33624
Phone: (813) 960-2105
Bimonthly. $30.00 per year. Feature articles provide practical application and specification information on the design, construction, supervision and maintenance of process equipment, plant systems, instrumentation and pharmaceutical facilities.

PHARMACEUTICAL PROCESSING
Gordon Publications
301 Gibraltor Dr.
Morris Plains, NJ 07950
Phone: (201) 292-5100. 12 times a year. Free to qualified personnel; others, $20.00 per year.

PHARMACEUTICAL TECHNOLOGY
Aster Publishing Corp.
859 Williamette St.
Eugene, OR 97440
Phone: (503) 343-1200
Fax: (503) 343-3641
Monthly. $54.00 per year. Practical hands on information about the manufacture of pharmaceutical products, focusing on applied technology.

STATISTICS SOURCES

ANNUAL SURVEY OF MANUFACTURES
U.S. Bureau of the Census
Available from U.S. Government Printing Office
Washington, DC 20402
Phone: (202) 783-3238
Annual.

CENSUS OF MANUFACTURES
U.S. Bureau of the Census
Available from U.S. Government Printing Office
Washington, DC 20402
Phone: (202) 783-3238
Quinquennial. Issued in parts that have varying prices.

GENERAL WORKS

AMERICAN DRUG INDEX
Facts and Comparisons
111 W. Port Plz., Ste. 423
St. Louis, MO 63146
Phone: (800) 223-0554 or (314) 878-2515
Annual. $34.50. Lists over 20,000 drug entries in dictionary style.

DRUG AND COSMETIC CATALOG
Edgell Communications, Inc.
1575 Eye St. NW
Washington, DC 20005
Phone: (800) 225-4569 or (216) 826-2839
Fax: (216) 891-2726
Annual. $20.00.

DRUG PRODUCT LIABILITY
Matthew Bender & Co., Inc.
11 Penn Plz.
New York, NY 10001
Phone: (800) 223-1940 or (212) 967-7707
Three looseleaf volumes. Periodic supplementation. Price on application. All aspects of drugs: manufacturing, marketing, distribution, quality control, multiple prescription problems, drug identification, FDA coverage, etc.

FOOD AND DRUG ADMINISTRATION
Shepard's McGraw-Hill, Inc.
PO Box 35300
Colorado Springs, CO 80935
Phone: (800) 525-2474 or (303) 577-7707
Two looseleaf volumes. Annual supplementation. Price on application. Discussion of regulations and procedures.

NATIONAL DRUG CODE DIRECTORY
U.S. Food and Drug Administration
Available from U.S. Government Printing Office
Washington, DC 20402
Phone: (202) 783-3238
Looseleaf. $76.00. Quarterly supplements. Lists manufacturers of commercially available human prescription drugs. Includes numbers (codes) for individual drugs and companies.

PHARMACEUTICAL MARKETERS DIRECTORY
CPS Communications, Inc.
7200 W. Camino Real, Ste. 215
Boca Raton, FL 33433
Phone: (407) 368-9301
Fax: (407) 368-7870
Annual. $140.00. Covers the entire healthcare field. Lists over 1,400 healthcare manufacturers, more than 300 ad agencies, *thousands of media and service suppliers and over 15,000 industry personnel.*

UNITED STATES PHARMACOPEIA AND NATIONAL FORMULARY
United States Pharmacopeial Convention
PO Box 2248
Rockville, MD 29852
Phone: (800) 227-8772 or (301) 881-0660
1990. $250.00. USP, 22st edition, NF, 17th edition.

FURTHER READING

"About Roche." F. Hoffmann-LaRoche Ltd., 1997. Available from: http://www.roche.com.

"Hoover's Company Capsules." Hoover's, Inc., 1997. Available from: http://www.hoovers.com.

Ward's Business Directory of U.S. Private and Public Companies, Detroit: Gale Research 1997.

Industry shipment levels remained fairly constant between the early 1980s and the mid-1990s. In the early 1980s, the value of shipments was $8.84 billion. By 1995 this value reached a high point of $10.82 billion. The lowest level during this period was in 1983 when the value of shipments was $7.95 billion. Employment levels showed a steady decrease since the early 1980s when 103,500 people were employed by this industry, 75,400 of whom were employed as production workers. In the early 1990s the total employment level dropped to a low of 70,700, then increased slightly to 71,300 in the mid-1990s. In 1995, this number increased again to 73,700. Production worker employment levels were at their lowest level of 50,800 in the early 1990s.

The fabricated structural metal industry's products were divided into four categories. Fabricated structural metal for buildings accounted for 52.9 percent of industry shipments; structural metal for bridges accounted for 6.2 percent; other fabricated structural metal accounted for 25.1 percent; and fabricated structural metal, not specified by kind, accounted for 15.8 percent.

METAL, FABRICATED STRUCTURAL

SIC 3441

Owing its consistent economic performance to increased productivity, corporate reorganization, and capital investments in new technologies, the fabricated structural metal market will maintain its present course. That course includes anticipated increases in several industry occupations, including machinists and truck drivers.

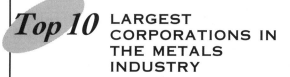

Top 10 LARGEST CORPORATIONS IN THE METALS INDUSTRY

Ranked by: Revenue in 1995, in millions of dollars.

1. Alcoa, with $12,655 million
2. Reynolds Metals, $7,252
3. Bethlehem Steel, $4,868
4. Inland Steel Industries, $4,781
5. LTV, $4,283
6. Phelps Dodge, $4,185
7. Nucor, $3,462
8. Alumax, $2,926
9. Maxxam, $2,565
10. AK Steel Holding, $2,257

Source: *Fortune,* Fortune 500 Largest U.S. Corporations (annual), April 29, 1996, p. F-57.

Average hourly wages in this industry were slightly lower than the average recorded by all manufacturing industries. In the early 1980s, average pay was $8.56 per hour; this steadily increased to $10.80 per hour by the early 1990s. In early 1996, the average pay for this industry was $11.42 per hour, which again was slightly less than the national standard for all manufacturing industries.

INDUSTRY OUTLOOK

Foreign competition forced the fabricated structural metal industry to focus on quality and the reduction of costs. During the 1980s, fabricated iron and steel products became so expensive (because of labor and other overhead costs), that many purchasers began buying products from foreign manufacturers. Increasing government regulations concerning environmental and safety issues also helped to increase production costs in the United States. Without similar government restrictions and regulations, developing countries stood as serious, competitive threats to U.S. manufacturers.

Although foreign competition adversely affected businesses in the 1980s, and a recession toward the end of the decade hindered capital investment, several signs indicated that the United States was effecting a turnaround. The productivity of American workers was increasing, and corporate reorganization of most companies helped to reduce costs. Capital investments in new equipment and advancing technology bolstered quality levels, while keeping costs in check. Diversification was a strategy employed by major structural metal producers looking for new opportunities in related markets.

ORGANIZATION AND STRUCTURE

Only Wyoming, Alaska, and Hawaii did not contain any fabricated structural metal manufacturing establishments. California's 251 establishments led the nation in value of shipments in the late 1980s, reaching $809.5 million. This accounted for 9.3 percent of total U.S. shipments that year. By the early 1990s, California shared that top spot with Texas, each state representing 8 percent of total U.S. shipments. Texas' 194 establishments made it the nation's top producing state with shipment value of $712.4 million. Following closely behind, California's 240 establishments made shipments valued at $710 million. The 6,300 employees in Texas earned an average of $9.08 an hour, while California's 5,500 workers were paid an average of $12.65 per hour. Employees in Connecticut earned the highest average pay in the industry at $14.17 per hour.

WORK FORCE

Several occupations were expected to increase their representation in the industry by the end of the 1990s. The number of combination machine tool operators was expected to grow by just more than 8 percent, cost estimators were expected to increase 12.6 percent, industrial production managers were expected to increase 15.5 percent, machinists were expected to increase 6.6 percent, light and heavy truck drivers were expected to increase 7.3 percent, and sales workers were expected to experience the highest hiring gain in the industry, increasing their numbers 18 percent.

FABRICATED STRUCTURAL METAL INDUSTRY EMPLOYMENT

Employment in thousands

Source: Department of Labor

RESEARCH AND TECHNOLOGY

Steel mills and iron casters have been around for centuries, but the principal technology has changed little. However, innovations in casting technology boosted the productivity of structural metal manufacturers. One manufacturer of casting equipment and systems experienced growth as a result of capital investments in continuous casters and a dual-stream ladle sequencing system, projects indicative of a trend in the structural metal industry to modernize facilities.

ASSOCIATIONS AND SOCIETIES

ALLIANCE OF METALWORKING INDUSTRIES
27027 Chardon Rd.
Richmond Heights, OH 44143
Phone: (216) 585-8800
Fax: (216) 585-3126

ALUMINUM ASSOCIATION
900 19th St. NW, Ste. 300
Washington, DC 20006
Phone: (202) 862-5104
Fax: (202) 862-5164

ALUMINUM RECYCLING ASSOCIATION
1000 16th St. NW, Ste. 400
Washington, DC 20036
Phone: (202) 785-0951
Fax: (202) 785-0210

AMERICAN ARCHITECTURAL MANUFACTURERS ASSOCIATION
1540 E. Dundee Rd., Ste. 310
Palatine, IL 60067
Phone: (708) 202-1350
Fax: (708) 202-1480
Members are manufacturers of a wide variety of architectural products. Includes a Residential/Commercial Window and Door Committee.

FABRICATORS AND MANUFACTURERS ASSOCIATION INTERNATIONAL
833 Featherstone Rd.
Rockford, IL 61107-6302
Phone: (815) 399-8700
Fax: (815) 399-7279
Members are individuals concerned with metal forming, cutting, and fabricating. Includes a Sheet Metal Division and the Tube and Pipe Fabricators Association.

NATIONAL ASSOCIATION OF ALUMINUM DISTRIBUTORS
1900 Arch St.
Philadelphia, PA 19103-1498
Phone: (215) 564-3484
Fax: (215) 963-9785

NON-FERROUS FOUNDERS SOCIETY
455 State St., Ste. 100
Des Plaines, IL 60016
Phone: (708) 299-0950
Fax: (708) 299-3598
Members are manufacturers of brass, bronze, aluminum and other nonferrous castings.

NON-FERROUS METALS PRODUCERS COMMITTEE
c/o Kenneth Button
Economic Consulting Service
1225 19th St. NW, Ste. 210
Washington, DC 20036
Phone: (202) 466-7720
Fax: (202) 466-2710
Members are copper, lead, and zinc producers. Promotes the copper, lead, and zinc mining and metal industries.

PERIODICALS AND NEWSLETTERS

AMERICAN METAL MARKET
Capital Cities - ABC Inc.
825 7th Ave.
New York, NY 10019
Phone: (212) 887-8560
Fax: (212) 887-8493
Daily. $560.00 per year. Provides daily news and pricing on the metals industry.

THE FABRICATOR
Fabricators and Manufacturers Association International
833 Featherstone Rd.
Rockford, IL 61107-6302
Phone: (815) 399-8700
Fax: (815) 399-7279

10 times a year. Free to qualified personnel; others, $30.00 per year. Covers the manufacture of sheet, coil, tube, pipe, and structural metal shapes.

LIGHT METAL AGE
Fellom Publishing Co.
170 S. Spruce Ave., Ste. 120S
San Francisco, CA 94080
Phone: (415) 588-8832
Fax: (415) 588-0901
Bimonthly. $35.00 per year. Edited for production and engineering executives of the aluminum industry and other nonferrous light metal industries.

METAL CENTER NEWS
Chilton Publications
191 S. Gary Ave.
Carol Stream, IL 60188
Phone: (708) 665-1000
Fax: (708) 462-2298
Monthly. $35.00 per year.

METALWORKING DIGEST
Gordon Publications, Inc.
PO Box 650
Morris Plains, NJ 07950-0650
Phone: (201) 361-9060
Fax: (201) 539-4376
Monthly. $48.00. Includes Metalworking Digest Literature Review.

METLFAX MAGAZINE
Huebcore Communications, Inc.
29100 Aurora Rd., Ste. 200
Solon, OH 44139
Phone: (216) 248-1125
Fax: (216) 686-0214
Monthly. $45.00 per year.

NEW STEEL: MINI AND INTEGRATED MILL MANAGEMENT AND TECHNOLOGIES
Chilton Co.
191 S. Gary Ave.
Carol Stream, IL 60188
Phone: (708) 665-1000
Fax: (708) 462-2862
Monthly. $35.00 per year. Covers the primary metals industry, both ferrous and nonferrous. Includes technical, marketing, and product development articles. Formerly Iron Age.

33 METALPRODUCING: FOR PRIMARY PRODUCERS OF STEEL, ALUMINUM, AND COPPER-BASE ALLOYS
Penton Publishing
1100 Superior Ave.
Cleveland, OH 44114-2543
Phone: (800) 321-7003 or (216) 696-7000
Fax: (216) 696-7648
Monthly. $50.00 per year. Covers metal production technology and methods and industry news. Includes a bimonthly Nonferrous Supplement.

DATABASES

F & S INDEX
Information Access Co.
362 Lakeside Dr.
Foster City, CA 94404
Phone: (800) 321-6388 or (415) 358-4643
Fax: (415) 358-4759
Contains about four million citations to worldwide business, financial, and industrial or consumer product literature appearing from 1972 to date. Weekly updates. Inquire as to online cost and availability.

MATERIALS BUSINESS FILE
ASM International
Materials Information
9639 Kinsman Rd.
Materials Park, OH 44073
Phone: (216) 338-5151
Fax: (216) 338-4634
Provides online abstracts and citations to worldwide materials literature, covering the business and industrial aspects of metals, plastics, ceramics, and composites. Corresponds to Steels Alert, Nonferrous Metals Alert, *and* Polymers/Ceramics/Composites Alert. *Time period is 1985 to date, with monthly updates. Inquire as to online cost and availability.*

METADEX (METALS ABSTRACTS/ALLOYS INDEX)
ASM International
Materials Information
Materials Park, OH 44073
Phone: (800) 336-5152 or (216) 338-5151
Fax: (216) 338-4634
Worldwide literature on the science and practice of metallurgy, 1966 to present. Detailed alloys indexing, 1974 to present. Monthly updates. Inquire as to online cost and availability.

STATISTICS SOURCES

ALUMINUM INDUSTRY
U.S. Bureau of Mines
Washington, DC 20241
Phone: (202) 501-9646
Monthly.

ALUMINUM STANDARDS AND DATA
Aluminum Association Inc.
900 19th St. NW, Ste. 300
Washington, DC 20006
Phone: (202) 862-5100

Fax: (202) 862-5164
Biennial. $25.00.

ALUMINUM STATISTICAL REVIEW
Aluminum Association Inc.
900 19th St. NW, Ste. 300
Washington, DC 20006
Phone: (202) 862-5100
Fax: (202) 862-5164
Annual. $50.00.

METAL STATISTICS
Capital Cities - ABC, Inc.
825 7th Ave.
New York, NY 10019
Phone: (212) 887-8532
Fax: (212) 887-8358
Annual. $95.00. Alphabetical list of metals, manufacturers, and suppliers. Price production comparisons, metals profiles, pricing tables.

NON-FERROUS METAL DATA
American Bureau of Metal Statistics
400 Plaza Dr.
Secaucus, NJ 07094
Phone: (201) 863-6900
Fax: (201) 863-6050
Annual. $350.00. Provides data on production, consumption, exports, imports, inventories, etc.

GENERAL WORKS

COMMODITY YEAR BOOK
Knight-Ridder Financial Publishing
30 S. Wacker Dr., Ste. 1820
Chicago, IL 60606
Phone: (800) 621-5271 or (312) 454-9116
Fax: (312) 454-0239
Annual. $70.00.

FURTHER READING

Bethlehem Steel Corporation website found at http://www.bethsteel.com/bspc-facilities.html.

Petry, Corinna. "Nucor's Cash Headed Into Modernization." *American Metal Market,* 30 December 1996.

Teaff, Rick. "Steel Chiefs Dash for Cash." *American Metal Market,* 30 May 1996. ◣

METAL MINING

SIC 1000

INDUSTRY SNAPSHOT

The metal mining industry is organized along the complex lines of worldwide consumption and supply, with different countries consuming different metals—in varying quantities—according to the demands of their industrial bases and capital goods markets. The London Metal Exchange (LME) serves as a primary barometer of price fluctuation in metals trading, reflecting the ever shifting balance between world demand and supply of those commodities.

Top 4 TOP U.S. COPPER PRODUCERS

Ranked by: Production in thousands of metric tons.

1. Phelps Dodge, 480.2 thousand
2. Kennecott, 335.5
3. Cyprus AMAX, 293.9
4. Magma Copper, 270.2

Source: *New York Times*, June 15, 1996, p. 16, from Copper Development Association and American Bureau of Metal Statistics.

The U.S. metal mining industry includes establishments that engage in mining a wide range of substances, including iron, copper, gold, silver, lead, zinc, ferro-alloy, and uranium ores. The health of the companies involved in metal mining is depending to a large degree on the worldwide status of the ore in which they specialize. Iron and vanadium ore mining outfits, for instance, are buoyed by the sustained growth of U.S. steel mills.

Due in part to Asia's economic growth, world iron ore production is expected to increase to 1.240 million metric tons (Mmt) from 1996 to 2006. Exports of zinc concentrates and imports of zinc metal were also expected to remain high in the United States through 2005 due to lack of capacity in refinery production. Even silver market fundamentals continued to improve, with constrained supply and increasing demand, though prices declined through the early 1990s. The overriding trend in modern metal mining has been toward the development of improved equipment to ensure better working conditions, the potential exploitation of lower-grade ores, and the design and construction of bigger and deeper mines.

INDUSTRY OUTLOOK

Most metal mining services companies are small operations engaged in the physical tasks involved in mining, as well as planning, development, and exploration. In this age of outsourcing, the metal mining services industry should be growing, but the decline in overall mining is limiting its growth. Where companies involved in metal mining services did not themselves develop new technologies, they made use of a plethora of advances made by other mining companies and associations.

IRON

The U.S. iron ore industry is totally dependent on the domestic steel industry, most notably the large integrated steelworks along the Great Lakes. These integrated manufacturers use blast furnaces to turn iron ore, coke, and limestone into pig iron and then into steel. The U.S. steel industry accounts for 98 percent of domestic iron ore consumption. During the 1990s, the steel industry was going through changes that adversely affected the iron ore industry. Some older facilities were expected to be closed by force due to more stringent environmental regulations. High labor and fuel costs, declining ore grades, and the inland location of the country's mines makes it difficult for the United States to compete in the world iron ore market. In 1996, shipments and production experienced a small decline.

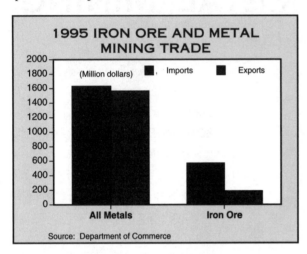

1995 IRON ORE AND METAL MINING TRADE

Source: Department of Commerce

Shipments in 1995 were 61.1 million metric tons (Mmt) and in 1996 were 60 Mmt. Domestic iron ore mine production showed a modest 1.2 percent drop in 1996, falling from 62 Mmt (million metric tons) in 1995 to 60 Mmt. In January 1997, U.S. mine production dropped 9.3 percent from the previous month according to the U.S. Geological Survey. U.S. steel consumption also dropped, to 80 million tons in 1996, from a high of 88 million tons in 1991. Big steel's restructuring has been dramatic over the last decade: capacity was cut in half to 50 million tons a year and employment was chopped from 179,000 to 92,000, a 51 percent decrease.

COPPER

Because the copper market is extremely sensitive to economic performance, prices are critically affected by world supply-and-demand developments. A projected modest recovery in industrialized nations during the mid-1990s, continued consumption increases by developing countries, and a slight decrease in world copper production should keep copper prices firm in the short term. In 1996, production of copper continued to increase to a record-high level. U.S. sales in the copper ore industry reached $10.5 billion in 1996. That same year, the U.S. economy consumed 2.62 million metric tons of copper, representing 23 percent of the world's copper

consumption. Imports and the secondary scrap market closed the deficit.

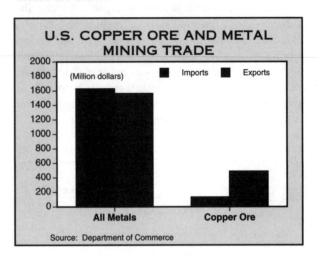

U.S. COPPER ORE AND METAL MINING TRADE

Source: Department of Commerce

LEAD AND ZINC

World demand for lead increased by approximately 10 percent in 1995, due largely to continuing demand for lead-acid storage batteries. Worldwide zinc consumption increased by 5.7 percent that same year, and domestic consumption of zinc increased 8 percent in 1996. Lead production in the United States also increased, from 394,000 metric tons in 1995 to 430,000 metric tons in 1996, an 8 percent rise. Zinc prices experienced a steady upturn in 1997, following a drop during 1996.

The U.S. Bureau of Mines projected annual lead demand to fall at a rate of 0.5 percent to 1.5 percent per year in the 1990s. Prime use of the lead battery (which traditionally made up 80 percent of total lead demand in the United States and 60 percent of world demand) is gradually being squeezed out by new technology. The outlook for zinc is more optimistic, but overall high capital costs are expected to put downward pressure on primary lead and zinc production.

In 1996, approximately 36 establishments were responsible for a total product estimated at $1.2 billion. Zinc production measured at roughly 620,000 metric tons and lead production was 430,000 metric tons in 1996. The industry's structure has gradually become more concentrated—the number of establishments fell from 88 in 1977 to 36 firms in 1996. The principal economic sectors or industries responsible for the purchase of lead and zinc were mostly manufacturers of lead and zinc intermediate products for industrial use.

GOLD

Mined on every continent except Antarctica, gold is used for a variety of applications. As a precious metal, gold is traditionally used as a backing for paper currency systems and as a hedge against inflation. In the mid-1990s, U.S. gold mine production was valued at approximately $4 billion. Of that, jewelry and other art-related pursuits accounted for 70 percent of U.S. gold consumption, industrial uses for 23 percent, and dental use, 7 percent, according to statistics from the U.S. Bureau of Mines.

Gold Production by State

Data are in kilograms for 1995.

	Kg.	Share
Nevada	221,000	70.8%
California	20,300	6.5
Montana	13,800	4.4
Idaho	2,940	0.9
Arizona	2,810	0.9
Other	51,500	16.5

Source: *American Metal Market*, July 25, 1996, p. 4, from United States Bureau of Mines.

SILVER

Silver entered the 1990s with a downward trend in price, suggesting a dreary outlook for many primary producers. The average Comex silver price of $5.32 for 1996 represented a fall of 24 percent from $7.01 in 1987. The sustained effects of a worldwide recession fueled a continuing stream of deflationary news that precipitated lower silver prices by reducing investors' interest in silver's traditional role as a hedge against inflation. With market prices often dipping below bare-minimum production costs, many primary producers were forced to close or cut back operations.

The early 1990s also saw dramatic reductions in secondary silver supply. Compared with the early 1980s, silver supply from scrap during the 1990s fell to approximately half its former level, due to lower prices, the prevalence of lower-content scrap, and restrictive sales policies on official reserves. Other secondary sources also declined. Most notably, the U.S. Defense Department's National Stockpile inventory of surplus silver was reduced from nearly 4,300 tons in 1982 to less than 1,500 tons in 1996. Several regulations were enacted in the early 1990s to control the rate and nature of the National Defense Stockpile: a 1992 law restricted the disposal of silver from the stockpile to coinage programs or government contractors for use in government projects.

FERROALLOYS

The early 1990s saw a deterioration of the domestic ferroalloy industry performance, reflecting a fall in Western world steel production, a sustained flood of exports from the CIS and China, and a backlash from oversupply dating back to the late 1980s. World crude steel output for the first ten months of 1996 was down by 1.4 percent. Prices and the purchase of ferroalloys should reflect that trend.

Several economic factors placed continued strain on steel—repercussions from the oversupply and price boom of the late 1980s, a flood of exports from Commonwealth of Independent States (CIS) and China, and the lingering effects of worldwide economic recession in the early 1990s. A glut of low-priced imports forced many ferroalloy companies, including world giants, to drastically reduce production and contend with losses and severely reduced profits. Moving into 1993, established market economy countries (EMEC) did not compensate for these factors with sufficient reduction of output, resulting in growing inventories and uncomfortably low commodity prices.

URANIUM AND VANADIUM

Uranium is a one-market commodity, solely dependent on nuclear powered electricity generation for its survival. As a result of the fall in this market, uranium inventories held by the United States continued to fall in 1992. That same year, production of uranium ore from underground mines fell to virtually zero, with any production of uranium coming from byproducts. According to the Energy Information Administration, at the end of 1995, only six mines were active, reflecting a declining trend that has continued from the late 1970s and early 1980s. Of these six mines, two were byproduct recovery plants. Vanadium is also primarily depending on a single market—the steel industry—on which it depends for almost 90 percent of its market demand.

MISCELLANEOUS METAL ORES

Approximately 48 establishments in the United States were engaged in the production of miscellaneous metal ores (not elsewhere classified) in 1995. These establishments had a total sales of $677 million in 1996, although the actual mining of these ores has been in decline over the past two decades, falling by 10.7 percent through the mid-1990s. Unfortunately, most of the ores classified in this category have decreased their share of the world market. Aluminum, which experienced a boom in world demand in the 1980s dropped from a 30 percent share in 1980 to 17 percent in 1995. In many of the other metal categories, U.S. consumption is almost entirely import-dependent—platinum at 90 percent; bauxite at 98 percent; and tin at 77 percent.

ENVIRONMENTAL ISSUES

The gold ore industry responded on numerous fronts to the environmental concerns of the 1980s and 1990s. Such issues as waste water, waste disposal, and land reclamation placed additional planning and economic pressures on mining companies, prompting many to seek development in other countries with less stringent regulations. Three environmental acts carried particular weight: The Resource Conservation and Recovery Act (RCRA) regulates both hazardous and nonhazardous solid waste; the Clean Water Act (CWA) regulates surface water discharges; and The Clean Air Act (CAA) regulates air emissions. These acts required mine owners to comply with terms of the National Pollutant Discharge Elimination System, which called for the monitoring and testing of storm water runoff. The American Mining Congress challenged the rule but was overridden in a 1992 court decision. In addition, in the mid-1990s, both the House and the Senate passed bills that would eliminate the ability of mining companies to take title to valuable federal lands containing gold, silver, and other "hard rock" minerals for only a few dollars an acre.

WORK FORCE

Anemic economic performance, increased use of labor-saving equipment, and downturns in minerals- and metals-consuming sectors accounted for job losses in the mining industry in the early 1990s. Metals and industrial minerals mining showed an employment decrease of more than 4 percent in the early 1990s. As a separate category, metals mining experienced smaller declines, with total employment falling 3 percent to 54,400.

With mining of ores at a virtual standstill, and output coming mainly from byproduct operations, employment for all occupations including mining, exploration, milling, and processing are all projected by the Energy Information Administration to decline, alongside the decline of the industry in general.

Many metal mine workers were union members of the United Steelworkers of America (USWA). Up until 1983, union contracts often included generous increases in wages and benefits. But the 1982 recession, subsequent large layoffs, and the need to reduce operating costs brought about new working relationships between the unions and company management. Reductions in real wages, more flexible work rules, and management/labor cooperation are more the norm today.

While more than half of the 4,200 jobs held by mining engineers in the early 1990s were in the mining industry, a large percentage transferred each year to other occupations, such as engineering consulting, government agencies, and manufacturing. Nevertheless, increasingly stringent environmental standards, as well as moves to increase production capacity and productivity while reducing operating costs, promised new challenges and some new opportunities for mining engineers in the metal mining services industry.

RESEARCH AND TECHNOLOGY

Technological advances in various areas of metal mining have proliferated in recent years. Affecting the iron ore industry, many of the integrated steelworks are now using fluxed pellets, which are created by adding fluxstone, limestone, and/or dolomite to the iron ore during the balling stage. An easier more reducible type of iron ore pellet is thus created. In 1990, U.S. production of fluxed pellets made up 39 percent of total iron ore pellet production.

The most recent advance in copper mining technology is the solvent extraction-electrowinning (SX-EW) method of production. The process is significantly less expensive than traditional methods because it involves fewer steps. It also reduces air pollution control costs because it avoids the smelting process. However, only oxide and secondary sulfide ores can use the SX-EW process. These ores are located close to the surface where they have been exposed to oxygen. It is estimated that only 15 percent of world copper reserves and 13 percent of U. S. copper reserves can be processed via the SX-EW method.

Companies and specialty metal mining services drew on new computer technology to assist in all phases of industry activity. In 1990, for example, Australia's Mount Isa mine used an Integrated Mine Planning system (IMPS)—a computer-aided drafting (CAD) system for geological interpretation and modeling. The system enabled engineers to integrate information from various departments (geology, mine design, and survey) and evaluate complex criteria—such as test clearances, drivers' lines of sight, and mobile equipment specs and compatibility—all at once. Other mining companies began using a new system designed to rapidly determine ore contacts and grades in underground metal mining. By measuring differences in the physical characteristics of relatively small mineral samples culled from drill holes, the system vastly reduced the amount of expensive core drilling sampling and assaying required for mine planning.

AMERICA AND THE WORLD

In 1996 world iron ore production was at 1,000 Mmt, setting a new record for world production. China's 40 percent rise in steel demand helped push output higher. China is the world's largest producer of iron ore, with output of 250 Mmt in 1996, and surpassed the former USSR as the world's largest producer in 1992. The former USSR's production was 78 Mmt in 1996, 44.5 percent lower than 1992's production of 175.2 Mmt.

The United States is the world's second-leading copper producer, producing 1.9 million metric tons of copper in 1996, second only to Chile. Chile produced 3 billion metric tons of copper in 1996. Other major producers include: Russia, Canada, Zambia, Peru, Australia, and Zaire. Private companies characterize the U.S. copper industry, while many countries operate government-owned copper mining operations. Also, political expedience often dictates that production and employment levels remain high despite operating losses. On the world market, these factors often give government-operated companies an advantage over U.S. producers. Nevertheless, U.S. producers remained strong competitors because of their successful drive to reduce production costs.

World mine production of gold in 1994 declined—production was 66 million troy ounces in 1993. World leaders include South Africa, the United States, and Australia. Other major producers include Brazil, Canada, Russia, and China. World bullion reserves for 1994 were estimated by the Bureau of Mines at 34,500 tons.

ASSOCIATIONS AND SOCIETIES

AMERICAN BUREAU OF METAL STATISTICS
PO Box Box 1405
Secaucus, NJ 07094-0905
Phone: (201) 863-6900
Fax: (201) 863-6050

AMERICAN MINING CONGRESS
1920 N St. NW, Ste. 300
Washington, DC 20036-1612
Phone: (202) 861-2800
Fax: (202) 861-7535

ASM INTERNATIONAL
9639 Kinsman Rd.
Materials Park, OH 44073-0002
Phone: (800) 336-5152 or (216) 338-5151
Fax: (216) 338-4634
Members are materials engineers, metallurgists, industry executives, educators, and others concerned with a wide range of materials and metals. Divisions include Aerospace, Composites,

Electronic Materials and Processing, Energy, Highway/ Off-Highway Vehicle, Joining, Materials Testing and Quality Control, Society of Carbide and Tool Engineers, and Surface Engineering. Formerly American Society for Metals.

INTERNATIONAL LEAD ZINC RESEARCH ORGANIZATION
2525 Meridian Pky. Research
Triangle Park, NC 27709
Phone: (919) 361-4647
Fax: (919) 361-1957

LEAD INDUSTRIES ASSOCIATION
292 Madison Ave.
New York, NY 10017
Phone: (212) 578-4750
Fax: (212) 648-7714

MINERALS, METALS, AND MATERIALS SOCIETY
420 Commonwealth Dr.
Warrendale, PA 15086
Phone: (412) 776-9000
Fax: (412) 776-3770
Members are metallurgists, metallurgical engineers, and materials scientists. Divisions include Light Metals and Electronic, Magnetic, and Photonic Materials. Formerly the Metallurgical Society.

MINING AND METALLURGICAL SOCIETY OF AMERICA
9 Escalle Ln.
Larkspur, CA 94939
Phone: (415) 924-7441
Fax: (415) 924-7463

NON-FERROUS METALS PRODUCERS COMMITTEE
c/o Kenneth Button
Economic Consulting Service
1225 19th St. NW, Ste. 210
Washington, DC 20036
Phone: (202) 466-7720
Fax: (202) 466-2710
Members are copper, lead, and zinc producers. Promotes the copper, lead, and zinc mining and metal industries.

SOCIETY OF MINING, METALLURGY, AND EXPLORATION
PO Box 625005
Littleton, CO 80162-5002
Phone: (303) 973-9550
Fax: (303) 973-3845

PERIODICALS AND NEWSLETTERS

ADVANCED MATERIALS AND PROCESSES
ASM International
Periodical Publication
Materials Park, OH 44073-0002
Phone: (216) 338-5151
Fax: (216) 338-4634
Monthly. $120.00 per year. Incorporating Metal Progress. *Technical information and reports on new developments in the technology of engineered materials and manufacturing processes.*

AMERICAN METAL MARKET
Capital Cities - ABC Inc.
825 7th Ave.
New York, NY 10019
Phone: (212) 887-8560
Fax: (212) 887-8493
Daily. $560.00 per year. Provides daily news and pricing on the metals industry.

COLORADO SCHOOL OF MINES QUARTERLY
Colorado School of Mines Press
1500 Illinois
Golden, CO 80401-1887
Phone: (303) 273-3000
Fax: (303) 273-3310
Quarterly. $50.00 per year.

EARTH AND MINERAL SCIENCES
College of Earth and Mineral Sciences
Pennsylvania State University
116 Deike Bldg.
University Park, PA 16802
Phone: (814) 863-4667
Three times a year. Free. Current research in material science, mineral engineering, geosciences, meteorology, geography and mineral economics.

ENGINEERING AND MINING JOURNAL (E&MJ)
Intertec Publishing Corp.
29 N Wacker Dr.
Chicago, IL 60606
Phone: (800) 621-9907 or (800) 543-7771
Fax: (312) 726-2574
Monthly. $60.00 per year.

JOM: JOURNAL OF METALS
Minerals, Metals, and Materials Society
420 Commonwealth Dr.
Warrendale, PA 15086
Phone: (412) 776-9080
Fax: (412) 776-3770
Monthly. $121.00 per year to individuals; $90.00 per year to institutions. A scholarly journal covering all phases of metals and metallurgy.

METAL CENTER NEWS
Chilton Publications
191 S. Gary Ave.
Carol Stream, IL 60188
Phone: (708) 665-1000
Fax: (708) 462-2298
Monthly. $35.00 per year.

METALLURGIA, THE JOURNAL OF METALS TECHNOLOGY, METAL FORMING AND THERMAL PROCESSING
Argus Business Media Ltd.
Fuels and Metals Journals
Queensway House, Two Queensway
Redhill, Surrey, England RH1 1QS
Phone: 01737 768611
Fax: 01737 761685
Monthly. $200.80 per year.

METALLURGICAL TRANSACTIONS A: PHYSICAL METALLURGY AND MATERIALS SCIENCE
ASM International
9639 Kinsman Rd.
Materials Park, OH 44073-0002
Phone: (800) 336-5152 or (216) 338-5151
Fax: (216) 338-4634
Monthly. $520.00 per year.

METALLURGICAL TRANSACTIONS B: PROCESS METALLURGY
ASM International
9639 Kinsman Rd.
Materials Park, OH 44073-0002
Phone: (800) 336-5152 or (216) 338-5151
Fax: (216) 338-4634
Bimonthly. $375.00 per year.

MINES MAGAZINE
Colorado School of Mines Alumni Association, Inc.
PO Box 1410
Golden, CO 80402
Phone: (303) 273-3291
Fax: (303) 273-3165
Seven times a year. $30.00 per year.

MINING RECORD
Howell Publishing Co.
PO Box 37510
Denver, CO 80237
Phone: (303) 770-6791
Fax: (303) 770-6796
Weekly. $39.00 per year.

MODERN METALS
Trend Publishing
625 N. Michigan Ave., Ste. 2500
Chicago, IL 60611
Phone: (312) 654-2300
Fax: (312) 654-2323
Monthly. $80.00 per year. Covers management and production for plants that fabricate and finish metals of various kinds.

THE NORTHERN MINER: DEVOTED TO THE MINERAL RESOURCES INDUSTRY OF CANADA
Southam Magazine Group
1450 Don Mills Rd.
Don Mills, ON, Canada M3B 2X7
Phone: (800) 387-0273 or (416) 445-6641
Fax: (416) 442-2272
Weekly. $70.00 per year.

DATABASES

GEOARCHIVE
Geosystems
PO Box 40 Didcot
Oxon, England Ox11 9BX
Phone: 1123- 581-3913

Citations to literature on geoscience and water. 1974 to present. Inquire as to online cost and availability.

GEOREF

American Geological Institute
4220 King St.
Alexandria, VA 22302-1507
Phone: (703) 379-2480
Fax: (703) 379-7563
Bibliography and index of geology and geosciences literature, 1785 to present. Inquire as to online cost and availability.

IMMAGE: INFORMATION ON MINING, METALLURGY, AND GEOLOGICAL EXPLORATION

Institution of Mining and Metallurgy
Library and Information Services
44 Portland Pl.
London W1N 4BR, England
Phone: 171 5 80 3802
Fax: 171 4 36 5388
Corresponds to the printed IMM Abstracts and Index. *Provides online citations to the worldwide literature of mining, metallurgy, and industrial nonferrous metals. (Does not include coal mining.) Time period is 1979 to date, with bimonthly updates. Inquire as to online cost and availability.*

MATERIALS BUSINESS FILE

Materials Information, ASM International
9639 Kinsman Rd.
Materials Park, OH 44073
Phone: (216) 338-5151
Fax: (216) 338-4634
Provides online abstracts and citations to worldwide materials literature, covering the business and industrial aspects of metals, plastics, ceramics, and composites. Corresponds to Steels Alert, Nonferrous Metals Alert, *and* Polymers/Ceramics/Composites Alert. *Time period is 1985 to date, with monthly updates. Inquire as to online cost and availability.*

METADEX (METALS ABSTRACTS/ALLOYS INDEX)

ASM International
Materials Information
Materials Park, OH 44073
Phone: (800) 336-5152 or (216) 338-5151
Fax: (216) 338-4634
Worldwide literature on the science and practice of metallurgy, 1966 to present. Detailed alloys indexing, 1974 to present. Monthly updates. Inquire as to online cost and availability.

MINTEC

Energy, Mines, and Resources, CANMET, Library & Documentation Services Div.
555 Booth St.
Ottawa, ON, Canada K1A 0G1
Phone: (613) 943-8773
Fax: (613) 952-2587
40,000 citations with abstracts to the worldwide literature on mining technology and related topics. 1968 to present. Inquire as to online cost and availability.

STATISTICS SOURCES

JOURNAL OF COMMERCE AND COMMERCIAL

Journal of Commerce Inc.
2 World Trade Center, 27 Fl.
New York, NY 10048-0203
Phone: (212) 837-7000
Fax: (212) 837-7035
Daily, except Saturday and Sunday. $349.00 per year.

LEAD AND ZINC STATISTICS

International Lead and Zinc Study Group
Metro House, 58 Saint James St.
London, England SW1A 1LD
Phone: 0171 499 9373
Fax: 0171 493 3725
Monthly. $220.00 per year.

LEAD INDUSTRY: MINERAL INDUSTRY SURVEYS

U.S. Bureau of Mines
Washington, DC 20241
Phone: (202) 501-9649
Monthly.

METAL STATISTICS

Capital Cities - ABC, Inc.
825 7th Ave.
New York, NY 10019
Phone: (212) 887-8532
Fax: (212) 887-8358
Annual. $95.00. Alphabetical list of metals, manufacturers, suppliers. Price production comparisons, metals profiles, pricing tables.

MINERALS YEARBOOK

Bureau of Mines, U.S. Department of the Interior
Available from U.S. Government Printing Office
Washington, DC 20402
Phone: (202) 512-1800
Fax: (202) 512-2250
Annual. Three volumes.

MINING MACHINERY AND EQUIPMENT

U.S. Bureau of the Census
Washington, DC 20233-0800
Phone: (301) 457-4100
Fax: (301) 457-3842
Annual. (Current Industrial Reports MA35F.)

UNITED STATES CENSUS OF MINERAL INDUSTRIES

Bureau of the Census, U.S. Department of Commerce
Available from U.S. Government Printing Office
Washington, DC 20402
Phone: (202) 512-1800
Fax: (202) 512-2250
Quinquennial.

U.S. INDUSTRIAL OUTLOOK: FORECASTS FOR SELECTED MANUFACTURING AND SERVICE INDUSTRIES

Available from U.S. Government Printing Office
Washington, DC 20402
Phone: (202) 512-1800
Fax: (202) 512-2250

Annual. $37.00. (Replaced in 1995 by U.S. Global Trade Outlook.) Issued by the International Trade Administration, U.S. Department of Commerce. Provides basic data, outlook for the current year, and "Long-Term Prospects" (five-year projections) for a wide variety of products and services. Includes high technology industries.

- Gopher://gopher.umsl.edu:70/11/library/govdocs/usio94

WORLD METAL STATISTICS
World Bureau of Metal Statistics
27a High St.
Ware, Herts, England SG12 9BA
Phone: 0192 046 1274
Fax: 0192 046 4258
Monthly. $1,850.00 per year.

FURTHER READING

Mineral Industry Surveys, U.S. Department of the Interior, U.S. Geological Survey, 14 March 1997.

Smith, Gerald R. "Lead." *Mineral Commodity Summaries.* U.S. Geological Survey, February 1997.

U.S. Department of Commerce. *1992 Census of Mineral Industries,* Washington: GPO, 1996.

U.S. Department of Energy, Energy Information Administration, Office of Coal, Nuclear, Electric and Alternate Fuels. *Domestic Uranium Mining and Milling Industry 1995: Viability Assessment,* Washington: U.S. Government Printing Office, December 1995.

U.S. Department of the Interior. *Minerals Yearbook: Metals and Minerals,* Vol.I. Washington: GPO, nd.

The U.S. motion picture and video production industry serves as a major supplier of entertainment and information to the world by producing videos, television programs, and movies which can be seen in more than 100 countries. Feature films alone garnered about $5.5 billion dollars in worldwide revenues for U.S. companies in 1995. Domestic audiences paid a total of $35 billion to enjoy all forms of filmed entertainment (movies, cable, and video) in 1992.

Despite these hefty profits, some segments of the industry felt the effects of the recession in the early 1990s. Fewer people went to the movies in 1992 than during any single year in the 1980s. Following the recession, box-office revenues climbed again, but competition from cable and video continued to erode the theatrical audience. By mid-decade, video sales accounted for the largest single source of revenue and had become a mainstay for the industry, accounting for an estimated 35 to 40 percent of total worldwide sales by the U.S. film industry. Growth in this sector was expected to continue through the remainder of the decade. In spite of low demand for rental videos, direct-to-consumer sales were growing steadily, assuring a lucrative market for years to come.

Several media conglomerates dominated the industry through the mid-1990s. In 1995, five companies had a combined U.S. box office market share of over 80 percent: Walt Disney Co., Warner Bros., Sony Corp., Universal Studios, and Paramount Pictures Corp. Disney, the leader for the second year in a row, captured a 19 percent share of the domestic market, followed by Warner Bros. with 16.3 percent, and Sony (Tri-Star and Columbia Pictures) with 12.8 percent.

World markets for films and television programs have long been critically important to U.S. producers and distributors. Over the last thirty years, foreign markets have generally accounted for about one-half of major U.S. producers' total sales in these industries. The success of American films and television productions in world markets is indicated both by industry trade balances and by comparisons with other film and television exporting nations. The United States has historically exported more than three times the total television programming exports of the next three leading exporting nations combined. In 1993, foreign sales of English-language films, video products, and free and pay television totaled $1.264 billion for the fiscal year ending June 30, according to the American Film Marketing Association. Theatrical revenue increased by three percent due to improved sales in Europe and the Far East. Europe continues to be the United States' largest grossing region

MOTION PICTURES

SIC 7800

Major film studios will continue the industry trend of releasing blockbuster, or "big-event," films to theater audiences in an effort to offset escalating production and marketing costs. Independent filmmakers—having enjoyed spectacular success and recognition at the 1997 Oscar awards—will exploit new opportunities to distribute their films as long as they maintain the focus of public attention. Videotape rental—a particularly lucrative market for film producers—will grow modestly throughout the rest of the 1990s; interestingly, videotape sales are expected to surpass rentals for the first time in 1998. Industry insiders predict that new distribution markets such as "pay-per-view" will add a new level of competition to the videotape rental industry as the technology is perfected and made available to more consumers.

for American distributors, contributing 60 percent of all revenues in 1993. Despite this success, foreign earnings for the U.S. film and television industries are reduced substantially by a variety of barriers to trade in foreign markets.

Although videos have surpassed theaters as the biggest contributor to film industry revenue, the United States' 29,700 movie screens create the initial market for a film's future formats. In fact, motion picture theaters remained a significant contributor to the film industry with over $7 billion in revenues in the early 1990s. These theater receipts contributed about one-third of total worldwide movie revenues. The industry, along with the rest of the U.S. economy, endured a recession in 1990 and 1991, but box office receipts rose from $4.8 billion in 1991 to a record $5.8 billion in 1996, driven by over $1.25 billion in ticket sales. By contrast, consumers in the United States spent $7.5 billion in 1995 to rent videotapes to view at home, according to a report by Paul Kagan Associates published in *Billboard*.

Top 10 TOP VIDEO STORE CHAINS

Ranked by: Revenue, in millions of dollars.

1. Blockbuster Video, with $2,639 million
2. West Coast Video, $195
3. Hollywood Video, $165
4. Movie Gallery, $125
5. Tower Records/Video, $84.5
6. Video Update Inc., $82.5
7. Moovies Inc., $49
8. Video Connection, $43.6
9. Palmer Video, $31
10. Home Vision Entertainment, $25.5

Source: *Video Store*, Video Store 100 (annual), December, 1995, p. 7.

The video rental industry has continued to grow steadily in the 1990s. However, competition is expected to increase from the "pay-per-view" market, which allows viewers to order movies and other programs from a growing "database" of shows. Indeed, rapidly changing technology makes the video rental business a volatile one that is continuously evolving. Video rental outlets are moving in several directions. For example, chains such as Blockbuster Entertainment Corp. are buying into other entertainment-related areas, such as music sales and film production, and entering into joint ventures that will improve the technology they can offer. Smaller, independent video outlets may stress their inventories of harder-to-find films and attentive customer service.

INDUSTRY OUTLOOK

In the early 1990s, the motion picture industry suffered from the effects of the recession. While movies brought in a record $5 billion at U.S. theaters in 1989, box office receipts declined in the following two years, totaling approximately $4.8 billion in 1991. Box office receipts rose to about $4.9 billion in 1992, but increased ticket prices accounted for much of this rise. Admissions actually declined from 1.1 billion in 1990 to about 977 million in 1992, sinking below the lowest levels of the 1980s. Decreasing attendance seemed to translate into a decreased volume of production. In the first half of 1992 production started on 173 films, down from the 224 films that were started in the first six months of 1991.

By 1995, box office sales were back up over the $5 billion mark, but profits continued to erode in spite of increasing sales to the video an TV markets. Much of the decline could be attributed to the rapidly inflating costs of production and the industry's increasing reliance on "blockbuster" films as a primary source of revenue. After the release in the early 1990s of such films as *Jurassic Park* and *Terminator 2,* Hollywood movies became special-effects extravaganzas, with each new film upping the ante in an attempt to dazzle an ever-more jaded audience. While some of these films were hugely profitable, they seldom brought in enough to cover less successful films. Not surprisingly, profit margins shrank, pressuring film producers to focus even more on producing sure-fire hits. So-called "big-event" films became the mainstay of Hollywood.

Hollywood inflation was also fueled by the studios' need to grab attention in a crowded marketplace. Marketing costs rose dramatically through the early part of the decade, jumping 20 percent between 1995 and 1996 alone. Talent fees also rose rapidly through this period, with actors such as Tom Cruise, Tom Hanks, Jim Carrey, and Arnold Schwartzenegger routinely demanding and getting anywhere from $10 to $20 million per picture. With costs leaping out of control, even major studios found it increasingly difficult to come up with the funds necessary to produce a "big-event" film. One solution was collaboration. In 1996, for example, Tri-Star teamed up with Disney to produce *Starship Troopers,* a big-budget science fiction film. Even without any major stars, this film was still expected to cost more than $100 million.

In an effort to draw larger audiences to "big-event" movies, the U.S. theater industry expanded dramatically in the early 1990s. The number of screens increased from about 24,000 in 1991 to nearly 30,000 by the end of 1996, up 7 percent (about 1,900) in the latter year alone. By the end of the year, there was one screen per 9,000 people.

The boom was driven in part by an increase in the number of movie releases from Hollywood, which was generating upwards of 300 feature films each year. The advent of the ''megaplex'' (16-plus screen complex) increased the number of screens exponentially with each new construction project. Mid-decade, this trend showed signs of migrating to international markets.

The nature of motion picture distribution was dramatically altered by the rise of home video in the 1980s and 1990s. Distributors increasingly relied on small-screen revenues to recoup their costs. With box office receipts shared between distributors and theater operators, the home video market came to be an important part of the distribution system. In 1995, movie distributors earned about $2.7 billion in rentals from U.S. and Canadian theaters and a similar amount overseas. On the other hand, video sales and licensing films for television broadcast brought in more than $10 billion. Overall, 25 to 30 percent of distributors' total revenues are derived from domestic theater rentals, with another 15 to 20 percent coming from foreign theaters. Worldwide videocassette sales account for 35 to 40 percent, and television provides the rest. Nevertheless, while home video has become the leading source of profit for distributors and offers many movies a new lease on life-films that would otherwise go straight into the company vaults are now routinely released on video without a theatrical run-box-office performance remains critical to a film's future success in the home video and television markets.

Entering the mid-1990s, consumer demand for video rentals began to stabilize somewhat as sales of VCRs began to slow down, a clear indication that the market is a saturated one. New VCR owners tend to be the most frequent renters of videos. As the novelty of VCR owning wears off, so does the number of rentals per household. In addition, an increasing segment of consumer video spending was going toward purchases

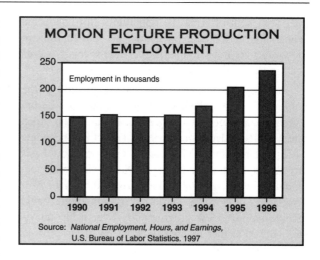

rather than rentals. According to Adams Media Research, in 1996, 54.9 percent of revenues from the home video market came from rentals, and 45.1 percent from sales. These shares are predicted to change to 50.3 percent for rentals and 49.7 percent for sales by 1998. One reason for the trend towards purchase over rental is the decreasing cost of buying a feature film on videocassette. In 1995, according to *Billboard,* the Disney-owned Buena Vista Home Video began pricing quality features at $9.99. Other film producers, such as MCA/Universal, are also making certain titles available for purchase at a low-cost and increasing numbers of households are building up film libraries.

Stores specializing in video rentals are not profiting in sales from home videos. According to *Fortune,* in 1996, the leading U.S. video rental outlet, Blockbuster, captured only 6 percent of the video sales market, while the discount store Wal-Mart, had a 25 percent share. However, a spokesman for Walt Disney's Buena Vista Home Video division told *Forbes* magazine that his company saw the purchase and rental markets as sepa-

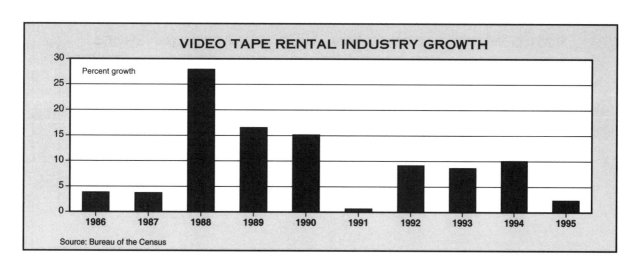

rate, with both offering the opportunity for handsome profits. Furthermore, mass merchants tend to remove videos that are not selling briskly, while specialty stores keep more in stock for both purchases and rentals.

Systems which can deliver movies directly to the home such as pay-per-view and direct-broadcast satellite television, are seen as the greatest threat to the video rental business. However, analysts expect pay-per-view to cost far more than video rental on a per-show basis through at least most of the 1990s, which will help maintain the video rental business. According to the *New York Times* in 1995, 21.3 million U.S. households could receive pay-per-view programming over cable television. By 2000 that number is expected to jump to 47 million households. The video industry has dismissed direct delivery systems as a major threat, citing surveys which show that consumers enjoy browsing through video stores and prefer spending ''pocket money'' on video rentals rather than receiving a monthly bill.

ORGANIZATION AND STRUCTURE

Production companies can be classified according to three major size categories: the ''majors,'' the ''mini-majors,'' and the ''independents.'' The majors include large conglomerates such as Warner Bros., Disney, Sony (owner of Columbia Pictures and Tri-Star), and Viacom (owner of Paramount). In the case of the majors, a single corporate structure often controls both the production and distribution of films, as well as an array of related operations through which the corporation can market movie soundtracks, toys, and other promotional tie-ins. Warner Bros., whose merger with Time, Inc. in 1989 dramatically strengthened its distribution system, presented one of the most striking examples of coordinated production and distribution. Some major film corpora-

tions have also invested in movie theaters, despite the history of anti-trust actions against theater chains owned by studios. Time Warner and Paramount, for example, share Cinamerica, and Sony owns Loews Theatres. Slightly smaller companies, often called ''mini-majors'' (Orion Pictures Corporation, for example), may have weaker distribution powers and may specialize in a specific segment of the film market, such as art films or action films. Small independent filmmakers may have no distribution capability at all and must depend entirely on outside distribution companies.

Because success in the film production industry depends largely on a wide distribution network and access to the substantial capital required to produce a film, the major film companies have obvious advantages over smaller companies. In addition to their distribution arms, many of the major studios have been operating long enough to have built up sizable film libraries which provide revenue through video sales or through sale or rental to television stations. These well-established companies are likely to wield substantial financial leverage and control physical production facilities. In fact, small production companies and independent filmmakers often rent the production facilities of the larger companies.

During the studio era of the 1920s through the 1940s, the major studios considered their stable of stars, directors, and other talent under long-term contract as assets. Movie companies in the 1990s, however, were more likely to sign contracts with artists for a single project. Such one-shot contracts have given talent agents considerable power over the production process. Often agents will assemble a ''package'' including a script, a director, and a star and sell the whole project to a studio. By performing much of the pre-production work on a project themselves, agents give their clients greater control over the kinds of projects they undertake. This sort of arrangement limits the movie company's artistic in-

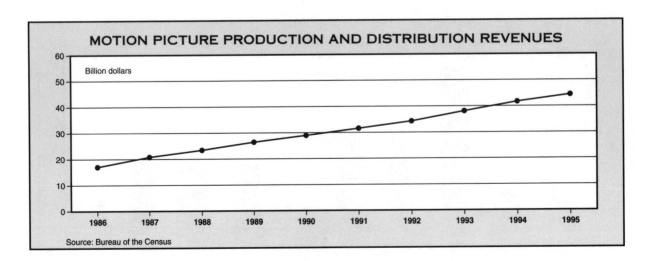

MOTION PICTURE PRODUCTION AND DISTRIBUTION REVENUES

Billion dollars

Source: Bureau of the Census

volvement to that of an investor who simply provides the money, facilities, and equipment required to complete the project.

The explosion of new television technologies since the late 1970s has had a significant impact on the financial structure of film production, and has helped to encourage independent production. Developments such as cable TV, videocassettes, and pay-TV services like Home Box Office (HBO) have stimulated demand for new films and created new options for film financing. These ancillary markets allow movie companies to sell distribution rights before production has even begun on a movie. HBO, for example, has helped to finance new movies in order to insure the steady supply of films necessary to fill its programming schedule. Video rentals have proven to be an even greater source of revenue for motion picture companies. While television accounted for about 15 percent of the money brought in by motion pictures in 1995, and theatrical releases accounted for 34 percent, videocassettes provided 48 percent of total revenues. By the time a feature film has been fully exploited, it will have been released in a theater, on home video and pay-per-view channels, on cable television, and on the major television networks.

Ancillary markets have been a boon to production companies of all sizes, but independent producers have had special cause to celebrate their rise. Lacking the financial leverage of the majors, small movie companies have often had to struggle to gather the capital required to make a film. The ability to sell ancillary rights to pay-cable and video companies has expanded the financial resources available to independents, resulting in a healthy growth of independent film production since the mid-1980s. By the mid-1990s, a growing network of satellite broadcasting systems, the arrival of an exciting new high-quality, low-cost consumer digital video system (DVD), and the latent potential of the Internet were creating an ever-widening range of distribution channels, all hungry for new content.

In addition to producing a steady supply of feature films, many movie studios also provide programming for television. Telefilm productions range from made-for-TV movies to half-hour situation comedies. Major movie studios accounted for approximately half of all prime-time programming for the networks during the early 1980s, with gaps filled by independent telefilm producers such as Mary Tyler Moore's MTM Enterprises . Prior to 1991 the Federal Communications Commission (FCC) actually restricted the amount of programming that networks could produce for themselves and prevented networks from owning a share in the syndication rights of the shows they exhibited. These restrictions were designed to prevent the networks from developing a monopoly over television programming and to maintain a competitive environment for the program production industry. In 1991 the FCC altered some of these restrictions, permitting networks to hold the syndication rights for 40 percent of the programming that they run during prime-time.

Total theater receipts are derived from three sources: admissions, concessions, and screen advertising. In 1996 admissions generated $5.8 billion in revenue for U.S. theaters. Concessions brought in over $1 billion more. Although a smaller percentage than ticket sales, concession income is a favorite of cinema operators because it commands a high profit margin that is not split with movie studios. In the early 1990s, concessions and screen advertising, a relatively recent phenomena, were considered potential avenues for growth. On-screen ads included live-action spots and slide-show-type reels that promote local businesses. The advertising concept was not particularly well-received by patrons and some distributors and by the late 1980s several studios rebelled against the practice. In fact, Walt Disney Co. and Warner Bros. banned on-screen advertising in theaters showing their films.

Once a feature film has completed its run in the theater, the film studio or production company, will sell videocassettes to rental outlets which then rents the videos to consumers. According to a 1996 Video Software Dealers Association (VSDA) "white paper," rental outlets typically pay between $50 to $80 per videocassette, which they then rent to customers for between $1 to $3 per night.

By 1995 there were some 27,000 establishments in the United States specializing in video rental, with consolidation and a transition to "superstores" (defined as offering at least 7,500 titles and 10,000 units) having brought the number down from 31,000 in 1990, according to the VSDA. Video specialty stores account for about 80 percent of total video rentals. The remaining 20 percent of rentals take place at other sites such as supermarkets, discount stores, and audio/video combination stores. In 1995, about 80 percent of video store revenues came from the rental of movies, about 10 percent from videocassette sales, and about 8 percent came from the rental of video games.

RESEARCH AND TECHNOLOGY

Just as home video and cable technologies have shaped the movie and video production industry by heightening the demand for programming, further advances in technology could stimulate production in the future. Pay-per-view, for example, has the potential to

SIC 7841 - Video Tape Rental
General Statistics

	Establish-ments	Employment (000)	Payroll ($ mil.)	Revenues ($ mil.)
1987	16,824	79.6	580.8	2,687.1*
1988	15,515	86.6	644.7	-*
1989	17,159	95.8	729.9	-*
1990	16,442	102.7	767.0	6,298.0
1991	17,459	108.9	816.4	5,581.0
1992	21,998	123.7	943.9	5,075.3*
1993	21,971	134.3	1,039.5	-*
1994	22,296P	140.4P	1,083.3P	-*
1995	23,322P	149.4P	1,156.9P	-*
1996	24,347P	158.4P	1,230.5P	-*

Sources: Data for 1982, 1987, and 1992 are from *Census of Service Industries*, Bureau of the Census, U.S. Department of Commerce. Revenue data are from the *Service Annual Survey* or from the Census. Revenue data from the Census are labelled with *. Data for 1988-1991 and 1993, when shown, are derived from *County Business Patterns* for those years from the Bureau of the Census. A P indicates projections made by the editor.

open up the market, but presents consumers with limited program choices and gives them less scheduling flexibility than a videocassette. Fiber optic cables and other techniques for compressing information could overcome these limitations by offering the viewer more program options and greater freedom of choice over when to watch them.

While improved pay-per-view technology would create new ways to deliver the same kinds of programs, other advances might create altogether new forms of filmed entertainment. By allowing viewers to play a movie on their computers, CD-ROMs make it possible for viewers to interact with a movie as they watch it. However, because of the limited storage capacity and low-grade picture quality of CD-ROMs, the format has been unable to climb out of its niche market status and is likely to soon be supplanted by DVD (an acronym variously said to stand for Digital Video Disc and Digital Versatile Disc). DVD is a CD-like system offering enormous storage capacity, picture quality superior to any conventional consumer video systems, and compatibility with both computer and television systems. Backed by all the major electronics manufacturers and supported by movie producers, DVD will no doubt establish itself as the leading consumer video standard by the end of the decade. Also in the works are such things as video-on-demand, whereby consumers could download a movie via the Internet or a similar delivery system. Such a

system could ultimately eliminate the need for storage media such as video discs or tapes altogether, as well as dramatically changing the nature of traditional broadcasting. Such interactive multimedia combinations of text and film have the potential to blur the line between the publishing industry and the entertainment industry, thereby opening up new aesthetic possibilities and new markets.

Advancements in technology in the multi-media marketplace are being incorporated into the motion picture industry and are changing the way traditional products are being developed, licensed, and distributed. Film is becoming a digital media and is acquiring many of the similarities found in software products such as video games. Conventional film companies are exploring the opportunities in interactive transmission and technology. Companies are digitizing their film libraries and exploring new ways to make this product available to distributors and consumers. Already, first run motion pictures are being shown outside the customary movie theater and are available in motorcoach bus tours. The transformation of the motion picture industry to a digital format and the increase in new technologies available to cable companies, the broadcast networks, and consumers will provide the public with an array of viewing possibilities.

AMERICA AND THE WORLD

The U.S. film industry continues to do good business in foreign markets despite trade barriers imposed by foreign governments. The European Community, for example, in the early 1990s required at least 50 percent of the television programs shown in member nations be of European origin "where practical," with the exception of some programming categories, such as news. France required that 60 percent of all its television programming originate in Europe and that at least 40 percent of the European programs originate in France. The U.S. government in large part objects to the trade barriers erected by the European Community against American movie and video programming. Another major market for American movies is Mexico. *Forbes* notes that more than 31 million theater tickets were sold in 1994 in Mexico City alone. Nearly 27 million of those tickets— 87 percent of the total—were for U.S. movies. This market is expected to continue to grow in the aftermath of the passage of the North American Free Trade Agreement (NAFTA). This legislation raised the ceiling on ticket prices and reduced the percentage of Mexican films each exhibitor is required to show from 50 percent to 30 percent, according to *Forbes*. The requirement will likely drop to 10 percent.

World markets for films and television programs have long been critically important to U.S. producers and distributors. During the past 30 years, foreign markets have generally accounted for about one-half of major U.S. producers' total sales in these industries. The success of American films and television productions in world markets is indicated both by industry trade balances and by comparisons with other film and television exporting nations. The United States has historically enjoyed tremendous advantages in these areas.

Nevertheless, motion picture and video tape distribution to other countries is hindered by several factors. Trade problems encountered in the media industries fall into two general classes: government-imposed non-tariff barriers and various forms of film and video piracy. These problems greatly reduce American industries' revenues in many markets. Non-tariff barriers include various quantitative restrictions, limitations on the repatriation of earnings, and discriminatory taxes. Perhaps even more important in terms of its effect on export earnings is video piracy. Producers' and distributors' losses due to piracy have increased enormously as a result of the growth of new copying and distribution technologies. The International Intellectual Property Alliance estimates that the American film industry lost between $15 and $17 billion in 1993 due to international piracy.

ASSOCIATIONS AND SOCIETIES

ACADEMY OF MOTION PICTURE ARTS AND SCIENCES
8949 Wilshire Blvd.
Beverly Hills, CA 90211
Phone: (310) 247-3000
Fax: (310) 247-9619

ALLIANCE OF MOTION PICTURE AND TELEVISION PRODUCERS
15503 Ventura Blvd.
Sherman Oaks, CA 91436-3140
Phone: (818) 995-3600
Fax: (818) 382-1793

AMERICAN SOCIETY OF T.V. CAMERAMEN AND INTERNATIONAL SOCIETY OF VIDEOGRAPHERS
4314 Hilary St.
Las Vegas, NV 89117
Phone: (702) 228-6704
A professional organization of video technicians.

ASSOCIATION OF CINEMA AND VIDEO LABORATORIES
c/o Frank Ricotta, Technicolor, Inc.
4050 Lankershin Blvd.
North Hollywood, CA 91608
Phone: (818) 769-8500
Fax: (818) 761-4835

DIRECTORS GUILD OF AMERICA
7920 Sunset Blvd.
Hollywood, CA 90046
Phone: (310) 289-2000
Fax: (310) 289-2029

HOME RECORDING RIGHTS COALITION
2300 N St. NW, Ste. 700
Washington, DC 20037
Phone: (800) 282-8273 or (202) 663-8957
Fax: (202) 663-8007
Opposes efforts to restrict or tax audiovideo recording by consumers.

ICIA EDUCATIONAL TECHNOLOGY DIVISION
3150 Spring St.
Fairfax, VA 22031-2399
Phone: (703) 273-7200
Fax: (703) 278-8082
Formerly National Audio-Visual Association

	Establishments			Employment			Payroll			Revenues - 1992 ($ mil.)			% change 87-92	
State	1987	1992	% of US 92	1987	1992	% of US 92	1987 ($ mil.)	1992 ($ mil.)	$ Per Empl. 92	Total ($ mil.)	Per Estab.	$ Per Empl. 92	Reve- nues	Pay- roll
California	1,890	2,484	46.8	9,566	13,138	46.2	72.6	111.0	8,446	643.9	0.3	49,011	82.6	52.8
Texas	924	1,398	26.3	4,452	8,831	31.1	34.8	69.6	7,886	397.6	0.3	45,021	135.4	100.1
New York	989	1,263	23.8	4,024	6,515	22.9	34.7	56.3	8,637	305.6	0.2	46,906	103.1	62.2
Florida	840	1,028	19.4	3,161	5,260	18.5	25.9	45.2	8,595	270.4	0.3	51,409	138.2	74.6
Illinois	740	1,057	19.9	3,751	6,315	22.2	28.6	47.1	7,455	259.9	0.2	41,160	103.3	64.5
Pennsylvania	637	891	16.8	3,359	5,281	18.6	24.9	40.0	7,566	214.6	0.2	40,637	71.2	60.3
Ohio	677	943	17.8	3,058	5,531	19.5	20.1	38.5	6,965	206.5	0.2	37,337	121.5	92.0
Michigan	679	787	14.8	3,023	4,899	17.2	19.6	35.2	7,186	191.4	0.2	39,071	108.8	79.8
New Jersey	485	583	11.0	1,917	3,064	10.8	15.4	27.4	8,947	148.7	0.3	48,538	95.8	77.8
Georgia	488	546	10.3	2,110	3,198	11.2	15.8	24.5	7,647	140.8	0.3	44,020	97.3	54.8

SIC 7841 - Video Tape Rental
Industry Data by State

Source: Census of Service Industries, 1987 and 1992, Bureau of the Census, U.S. Department of Commerce. Data are sorted by 1992 revenues and, if revenues are unavailable, by establishments in 1992. (D) indicates that data are withheld by the source to avoid disclosure of competitive information. A dash (-) indicates that data are not available. Percentage changes between 1987 and 1992 are calculated using numbers that have not been rounded; hence they may not be reproducible from the values shown.

INSTITUTE OF ELECTRICAL AND ELECTRONICS ENGINEERS; BROADCAST, CABLE AND CONSUMER ELECTRONICS SOCIETY
345 E 47th St.
New York, NY 10017
Phone: (212) 705-7900
Fax: (212) 705-4929

INTERACTIVE DIGITAL SOFTWARE ASSOCIATION
919 18th St. NW, Ste. 210
Washington, DC 20006
Phone: (202) 833-4372
Fax: (202) 833-4431
Members are interactive entertainment software publishers concerned with rating systems, software piracy, government relations, and other industry issues.

INTERNATIONAL COMMUNICATIONS INDUSTRIES ASSOCIATION
3150 Spring St.
Fairfax, VA 22031-2399
Phone: (800) 659-7469 or (703) 273-2700
Fax: (703) 278-8082
Members are manufacturers and suppliers of audio-visual, video, and computer graphics equipment and materials.

INTERNATIONAL TELEPRODUCTION SOCIETY
350 5th Ave., Ste. 2400
New York, NY 10118
Phone: (212) 629-3266
Fax: (212) 629-3265
Members are individuals interested in various aspects of prerecorded videotape production. Acts as a source of general information about videotape.

INTERNATIONAL TELEVISION ASSOCIATION
6311 N. O'Connor Rd., LB51,
Irving, TX 75039
Phone: (214) 869-1112
Fax: (214) 869-2980
Concerned with non-broadcast industrial television recording for business training and corporate communications. Maintains a world wide web site at http://www.itva.org.

ITA
505 8th Ave., 12A
New York, NY 10018
Phone: (212) 643-0620
Fax: (212) 643-0624
Members are manufacturers and distributors of audiotape, videotape, and associated equipment.

MOTION PICTURE ASSOCIATION OF AMERICA
1600 Eye St. NW
Washington, DC 20006
Phone: (202) 293-1966
Fax: (202) 452-9823

NATIONAL ASSOCIATION OF VIDEO DISTRIBUTORS
1255 23rd St. NW
Washington, DC 20037
Phone: (202) 872-8545
Fax: (202) 833-3636
Members are wholesalers of home video software, both tapes and discs.

PRODUCERS GUILD OF AMERICA
400 S Beverly Dr., Room 211
Beverly Hills, CA 90212
Phone: (310) 557-0807

PROFESSIONAL AUDIOVIDEO RETAILERS ASSOCIATION
10 E 22nd St.
Lombard, IL 60148
Phone: (708) 268-1500
Fax: (708) 953-8957
Members are retailers of high quality equipment.

PROFESSIONAL FILM AND VIDEO EQUIPMENT ASSOCIATION
PO Box 9436
Silver Spring, MD 20916-9436
Phone: (301) 460-8084
Fax: (301) 460-4337
Members are manufacturers and distributors of professional recording equipment.

SOCIETY OF MOTION PICTURE AND TELEVISION ENGINEERS
595 W Hartsdale Ave.
White Plains, NY 10607
Phone: (914) 761-1100
Fax: (914) 761-3115

VIDEO SOFTWARE DEALERS ASSOCIATION
16530 Ventura Blvd., Ste. 400
Encino, CA 91436
Phone: (818) 385-1500
Fax: (818) 385-0567
Members are retailers and wholesalers of videocassettes and videodiscs.

PERIODICALS AND NEWSLETTERS

BOXOFFICE
RLD Communications Inc.
1800 N. Highland Ave.
Hollywood, CA 90028
Phone: (213) 465-1186

DAILY VARIETY: NEWS OF THE ENTERTAINMENT INDUSTRY
Cahners Publishing Co.
Entertainment Division,
5700 Wilshire Blvd., Ste. 120
Los Angeles, CA 90036
Phone: (800) 552-3632 or (213) 857-6600
Fax: (213) 857-0494
Daily. $145.00 per year.

DV: DIGITAL VIDEO
Miller Freeman, Inc.
411 Borel Ave., Ste. 100
San Mateo, CA 94402
Phone: (888) 776-7002 or (415) 358-9500
Fax: (415) 358-8891

Monthly. $29.97 per year. Edited for producers and creators of digital media. Includes topics relating to video, audio, animation, multimedia, interactive design, and special effects. Covers both hardware and software, with product reviews. Formerly Digital Video Magazine.

ELECTRONIC MEDIA
Crain Communications, Inc.
740 N Rush St.
Chicago, IL 60611-2590
Phone: (800) 678-9595 or (312) 649-5341
Fax: (312) 649-5465
Weekly. $86.00 per year.

ENTERTAINMENT MARKETING LETTER
EPM Communications, Inc.
488 E 18th St.
Brooklyn, NY 11226
Phone: (718) 469-9330
Fax: (718) 469-7124
Monthly. $275.00 per year. Newsletter. Covers the marketing of various entertainment products. Includes television broadcasting, videocassettes, celebrity tours and tie-ins, radio broadcasting, and the music business.

THE FILM JOURNAL: TRADE PAPER FOR EXHIBITORS OF MOTION PICTURES
Pubsun Corp.
244 W 49th St., Ste. 200
New York, NY 10019
Phone: (212) 246-6460
Fax: (212) 265-6428
Monthly. $45.00 per year.

FILM QUARTERLY
University of California Press Journals Div.
Berkeley, CA 94720
Phone: (510) 642-7154
Fax: (510) 642-7127
Quarterly. Individuals, $23.00 per year; institutions, $49.00 per year.

THE HOLLYWOOD REPORTER
The Hollywood Reporter, Inc.
5055 Wilshire Blvd., 6 Fl.
Los Angeles, CA 90036
Phone: (213) 525-2000
Fax: (213) 525-2389
Daily. $149.00 per year. Covers the latest news in film, TV, cable, multimedia, music, and theatre. Includes box office grosses and entertainment industry financial data.

SMPTE JOURNAL
Society of Motion Picture and Television Engineers
595 W Hartsdale Ave.
White Plains, NY 10607-1824
Phone: (914) 761-1100
Fax: (914) 761-3115
Monthly. $90.00 per year.

TELEVISION DIGEST WITH CONSUMER ELECTRONICS
Warren Publishing, Inc.
2115 Ward Ct. NW
Washington, DC 20037
Phone: (202) 872-9200
Fax: (202) 293-3435

Weekly. $848.00 per year. Newsletter featuring new consumer entertainment products utilizing electronics. Also covers the television broadcasting and cable TV industries, with corporate and industry news.

TWICE: THIS WEEK IN CONSUMER ELECTRONICS
Cahners Publishing Co.
249 W 17th St.
New York, NY 10011
Phone: (800) 662-7776 or (212) 645-0067
Fax: (212) 337-7066
28 times a year. $85.00 per year. Free to qualified personnel. Contains marketing and manufacturing news relating to a wide variety of consumer electronic products, including video, audio, telephone, and home office equipment.

VIDEO BUSINESS
Capital Cities-ABC, Inc.
Diversified Publishing Group
825 7th Ave., 6 Fl.
New York, NY 10019
Phone: (212) 887-8400
Weekly. $70.00 per year.

VIDEO INVESTOR
Paul Kagan Associates, Inc.
126 Clock Tower Pl.
Carmel, CA 93923
Phone: (408) 624-1536
Fax: (408) 625-3225
Monthly. $575.00 per year. Newsletter on the pre-recorded videocassette industry. Includes statistics and forecasts. Formerly VCR Letter.

VIDEO MAGAZINE
Hachette-Filipacchi
1633 Broadway
New York, NY 10019
Phone: (800) 601-8345 or (212) 767-6000
Fax: (212) 767-5631
Monthly. $17.94 per year.

VIDEO RATING GUIDE FOR LIBRARIES
ABC-CLIO, Inc.
PO Box 1911
Santa Barbara, CA 93116-1911
Phone: (805) 968-1911
Fax: (805) 968-9685
Quarterly. $126.00 per year. Special-interest, information, and children's videos are reviewed and rated by librarians for library use.

VIDEO REVIEW
Media Works Group, Inc.
PO Box 2047
Larchmont, NY 10538-8247
Phone: (914) 576-8800
Fax: (914) 576-8841
Eight times a year. $15.97 per year. Covers audio and video hardware.

VIDEO STORE: TOMORROW'S RETAILING TODAY
Advanstar Communications, Inc.
7500 Old Oak Blvd.
Cleveland, OH 44130
Phone: (800) 346-0085 or (216) 243-8100
Fax: (216) 891-2726
Fifty times a year. $48.00 per year.

VIDEO SYSTEMS: THE MAGAZINE FOR VIDEO PROFESSIONALS
Intertec Publishing Corp.
9800 Metcalf Ave.
Overland Park, KS 66212-2215
Phone: (800) 654-6776 or (913) 341-1300
Fax: (913) 967-1898
Monthly. $45.00 per year.

VIDEO TECHNOLOGY NEWS
Phillips Business Information, Inc.
1201 7 Locks Rd., Ste. 300
Potomac, MD 20854
Phone: (800) 777-5006 or (301) 340-2100
Fax: (301) 424-4297
Biweekly. $595.00 per year. Newsletter. Covers the business and financial side of video technology developments.

VIDEO WEEK: DEVOTED TO THE BUSINESS OF PROGRAM SALES AND DISTRIBUTION FOR VIDEOCASSETTES, DISC, PAY TV AND ALLIED NEWS MEDIA
Warren Publishing, Inc.
2115 Ward Ct. NW
Washington, DC 20037
Phone: (202) 872-9200
Fax: (202) 293-3435
Weekly. $815.00 per year. Newsletter. Covers video industry news and corporate developments.

VIDEOGRAPHY
Miller Freeman PSN, Inc.
2 Park Ave., 18 Fl.
New York, NY 10016
Phone: (212) 213-3444
Fax: (212) 213-3484
Monthly. $30.00 per year.

DATABASES

MARKETING AND ADVERTISING REFERENCE SERVICE
Information Access Co.
362 Lakeside Dr.
Foster City, CA 94404
Phone: (800) 321-6388 or (415) 358-4643
Fax: (415) 358-4759
Provides abstracts of literature relating to consumer marketing and advertising, including all forms of advertising media. Time period is 1984 to date. Daily updates. Inquire as to online cost and availability.

PROMT: PREDICASTS OVERVIEW OF MARKETS AND TECHNOLOGY
Information Access Co.
362 Lakeside Dr.
Foster City, CA 94404
Phone: (800) 321-6388 or (415) 378-5000
Fax: (415) 358-4759
Companies, products, applied technologies and markets. U.S. and international literature coverage, 1972 to date. Daily updates. Inquire as to online cost and availability. Provides abstracts from more than 1,200 publications.

TV LINK: FILM & TELEVISION WEBSITE ARCHIVE
Neoglyphics Media Corp.
Links to the world wide web sites of more than 100 TV shows, motion picture studios, professional and commercial organizations, broadcast schedules, TV networks and broadcasters, newsgroups, film festivals, and related sites around the world. This site is a resource for both industry professionals and audiences.

VIDEOS FOR BUSINESS AND TRAINING
Gale Research
835 Penobscot Bldg.
Detroit, MI 48226-4094
Phone: (800) 877-GALE or (313) 961-2242
Fax: (313) 961-6815
Provides online descriptions of about 16,000 videocassette business training programs in over 200 professional and vocational categories. Annual updates. Inquire as to online cost and availability.

STATISTICS SOURCES

EARLY WARNING REPORT
Warren Publishing, Inc.
2115 Ward Ct. NW
Washington, DC 20037
Phone: (202) 872-9200
Fax: (202) 293-3435
Monthly. $1,075.00. Analyzes sales trends and inventory figures for the retail video industry.

LEISURE TIME BASIC ANALYSIS
Standard and Poor's
25 Broadway
New York, NY 10004
Phone: (212) 208-8702
March, 1990. Covering Motion pictures.

U.S. INDUSTRIAL OUTLOOK: FORECASTS FOR SELECTED MANUFACTURING AND SERVICE INDUSTRIES
Available from U.S. Government Printing Office
Washington, DC 20402
Phone: (202) 512-1800
Fax: (202) 512-2250
Annual. $37.00. (Replaced in 1995 by U.S. Global Trade Outlook.) Issued by the International Trade Administration, U.S. Department of Commerce. Provides basic data, outlook for the current year, and "Long-Term Prospects" (five-year projec-

tions) for a wide variety of products and services. Includes high technology industries.

- Gopher://gopher.umsl.edu:70/11/library/govdocs/ usio94

GENERAL WORKS

ANNUAL INDEX TO MOTION PICTURE CREDITS
Academy of Motion Picture Arts and Sciences
8949 Wilshire Blvd.
Beverly Hills, CA 90211-1972
Phone: (310) 274-3000
Fax: (310) 859-9351
Annual. $64.00.

BLU-BOOK DIRECTORY: HOLLYWOOD'S MOST COMPREHENSIVE ENTERTAINMENT DIRECTORY
The Hollywood Reporter, Inc.
6715 Sunset Blvd.
Hollywood, CA 90028
Phone: (213) 464-7411
Fax: (213) 469-8770
Annual. $57.00. Lists film and TV studios, actors and celebrities, investors, producers, production facilities, writers, business managers, support services, etc. Includes a listing of industry awards and award recipients.

CELEBRITY DIRECTORY: HOW TO REACH OVER 7,000 MOVIE-TV STARS AND OTHER FAMOUS CELEBRITIES
Axiom Information Resources
PO Box 8015
Ann Arbor, MI 48107
Phone: (313) 761-4842
Biennial. $34.95. Stars, agents, networks, studios, and other celebrities. Gives names and addresses.

MAGILL'S CINEMA ANNUAL
Gale Research
835 Penobscot Bldg.
Detroit, MI 48226-4094
Phone: (800) 877-GALE or (313) 961-2242
Fax: (800) 414-5043
Annual. $75.00. Provides reviews and facts for new films released each year in the United States. Typically covers about 500 movies, with nine indexes to title, director, screenwriter, actor, music, etc. Includes awards, obituaries, and "up-and-coming" performers of the year.

THE MOTION PICTURE GUIDE ANNUAL
R. R. Bowker
121 Chanlon Rd.
New Providence, NJ 07974
Phone: (800) 521-8110 or (908) 464-6800
Fax: (908) 665-6688
Annual. $164.95. Provides detailed information on every domestic and foreign film released theatrically in the U.S. during the year covered. (Annual volumes are available for older movies, beginning with the 1986 edition for films of 1985.)

FURTHER READING

Bielski, Lauren. "Coming Soon to a Theater Near You: HDTV Digital Movie Transmission." *Advanced Imaging,* April 1995, 30-31.

Darnay, Arsen J., ed. *Manufacturing USA: Industry Analyses, Statistics, and Leading Companies.* Detroit: Gale Research Inc., 1996.

"Filmed Entertainment." *Standard and Poor's Industry Surveys.* New York: McGraw Hill, January 1997.

Magiera, Marcy. "Public Chains Take Bigger Rental Share." *Video Business,* 29 March 1996, 1.

Masters, Kim. "Hollywood Fades to Red." *Time Magazine,* 1 July 1996.

Shapiro, Eben. "Viacom Resists Spinning Off Blockbuster and Weighs In-Store Servicing of PCs." *Wall Street Journal,* 3 October 1996, B5.

Video Software Dealers Association. *Home Video Industry White Paper on the Future of Home Video Entertainment,* Moorestown, N.J.: Video Software Dealers Association, 1996.

Ward's Business Directory. v.5, Detroit: Gale Research Inc., 1997.

MOTOR VEHICLES AND MOTOR VEHICLE EQUIPMENT

SIC 3710

After several years of remarkable profit gains, the motor vehicle industry is expected to become more stable. Flat automobile sales and increased competition from foreign automakers will create a climate of modest gains for the motor vehicle industry for the next several years. Due to concerted efforts on the part of the Clinton administration, the U.S. motor vehicle industry will see a marked increase in exports to countries that had previously maintained closed or restricted import markets. This new export opportunity will also influence growth in both the truck and bus body and parts and accessories sectors, although the parts and accessories sector can expect increased global competition and consolidation as companies maneuver for preferred supplier status with automakers.

The motor vehicle industry represents one of the largest segments within the U.S. economy and forms the core of the nation's industrial strength. In the mid-1990s, an estimated 121 million vehicles were on U.S. roads. The U.S. motor vehicle manufacturing industry consisted of three American, two German affiliated, and seven Japanese affiliated manufacturers of light vehicles (LV) plus five large and approximately 100 medium and smaller assemblers of commercial vehicles. Collectively, the industry produced nearly 12 million vehicles in 1995.

On an average, the industry generated one-sixth of all U.S. manufacturers' shipments of durable goods and consumed 30 percent of all iron, 15 percent of all steel, 25 percent of all aluminum, and 75 percent of all natural rubber purchased by U.S. industries. According to the U.S. Department of Commerce, on average, every dollar of manufacturing input in the United States allocated to producing motor vehicles added two and one-half dollars to the economy.

At the retail level in 1995, sales of motor vehicles exceeded $259 billion, or 3.6 percent of the nation's gross domestic product—the broadest measure of the nation's economic output. In 1992, sales totaled $205 billion, or 3.3 percent of the total Gross Domestic Product (GDP). In the second quarter of 1996, sales gained 3.5 percent over the same period in 1995, reaching an annualized total of $263 billion. The American Automobile Manufacturers Association (AAMA) estimated that in 1992, there were 589,000 establishments in the United States representing the motor vehicles industry and all related industries.

The truck and bus bodies industry had a boom in 1994 driven by the growing U.S. economy and an aging fleet. However, in 1996 the industry slumped. Truck sales tended to be volatile because they were subject to cyclical changes in the overall economy. The nation's industrial sector created the largest portion of freight tonnage, and changes in the volume of industrial freight shipments led to parallel shifts in total truck sales. Interest rates and fuel costs also impacted the industry.

Government forecasters and industry watchers predicted continued expansion of this motor vehicle segment during the mid-1990s. Although initial orders showed faster growth within the heavy duty truck segment, some analysts expected long term demand for medium duty trucks to outpace the heavier vehicles. Reasons cited included a growing number of service industries and "just-in-time" inventory practices. Service industries typically required smaller vehicles than manufacturing industries, and "just-in-time" inventory

LEADING CORPORATIONS IN THE MOTOR VEHICLES AND PARTS INDUSTRY

Ranked by: Revenue in 1995, in millions of dollars.

1. General Motors Corp., with $168,829 million
2. Ford Motor Co., $137,137
3. Chrysler Corp., $53,195
4. TRW, $10,172
5. Tenneco, $8,899
6. ITT Industries, $8,884
7. Johnson Controls, $8,330
8. Dana Corp., $7,795
9. Eaton Corp., $6,822
10. Navistar International, $6,342

Source: *Fortune,* Fortune 500 Largest U.S. Corporations (annual), April 29, 1996, p. F-57+.

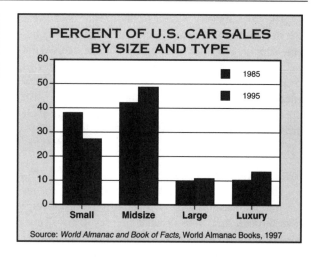

PERCENT OF U.S. CAR SALES BY SIZE AND TYPE

Source: *World Almanac and Book of Facts,* World Almanac Books, 1997

practices required smaller, more frequent deliveries, making the lighter trucks more economical.

A significant component of the motor vehicle industry, the parts and accessories market sector enjoys a crucial, symbiotic relationship with motor vehicle manufacturers. In fact, an estimated 15,000 parts and accessories are used in the production of motor vehicles. These parts represent the principle products of about 5,000 companies and a portion of the output of thousands of others. The annual U.S. production of motor vehicle parts and accessories is valued at over $90 billion. The Motor Equipment Manufacturers Association (MEMA) is the leading industry trade organization and compiles industry statistics.

INDUSTRY OUTLOOK

In 1994, for the first time since 1979, motor vehicle assembly in the United States exceeded that of Japan by 16 percent—a feat that was repeated in 1995 by 18 percent. The optimistic car and truck sales expected for 1995 however did not occur; the industry could not even beat the 15.2 million units sold in 1994. In the first half of 1996, vehicle exports increased by 3 percent, compared with the first half of 1995, reaching a total of almost $34 billion. In the first seven months of 1996, vehicle production was off a slight 2 percent. In 1994 the Big Three reported record earnings of $13.9 billion, followed by an additional $13 billion in 1995. Their profits in the second quarter of 1996, $4.8 billion, were 21 percent higher than in the second quarter of 1995.

Young buyers accounted for nearly 25 percent of car sales, and that figure was also declining. Auto manufacturers reexamined their marketing strategies and automobile designs to offer less expensive vehicles to the generation of buyers who were born in the 1960s and early 1970s. In keeping with the growing awareness of industrial recycling and economical production strategies, the auto industry increased its use of recycled materials.

TRUCK AND BUS BODIES

According to the American Automobile Manufacturers Association, all U.S. heavy truck makers set a monthly production record in June 1994—17,247 vehicles. The *Puget Sound Business Journal* pointed out that the key factor driving the industry upswing was the growing U.S. economy which directly affected the need for transportation equipment to move parts and finished products. The other factors for the demand were the age of the truck fleets, which were about eight years old in 1993, relatively low interest rates, and competition for trucking firms among customers. Another reason for the high demand was stated to be the federal government's deregulation of the trucking industry during the 1980s which heightened competition and forced weaker carriers out of business and caused most of the rest of the carriers to economize and delay truck purchases, says the *Oregonian.*

Analysts predicted that the Class 8 truck demand was expected to be robust through 1997. This projection proved to be wrong when the 1996 truck sales slumped 25 percent from 1995. According to *Forbes,* the business was in a serious recession; one of the key reasons was that freight sales were off, hence there was no rush to buy additional, or even replace, equipment. The other reason was that the average age of trucks—which was eight years—had been reduced to five because of the increased buying in the last few years, which meant that the truck fleet was fairly modern.

The truck makers were also under enormous pressure to improve productivity and efficiency and to become suppliers of high quality, low cost service. While trucking firms and carriers were struggling to attract drivers by providing creature comforts offered by new generation trucks, the truck manufacturers were also under pressure to provide amenities for drivers in their newer models to increase sales.

PARTS AND ACCESSORIES

The automobile industry continued to buy an increasing number of automotive parts from outside suppliers through the 1990s because it reduced costs, provided more flexibility, and allowed for a greater specialization of technology, according to an article in *Fortune* magazine. During the mid-1990s, the U.S. automotive parts industry comprised some 5,000 firms—including about 500 Japanese, European, and Canadian manufacturers—that supplied either the original equipment (OE) market, the replacement parts market, or both. According to the *U.S. Department of Commerce,* industry production hit an all-time high in 1994, reaching $134 billion. In 1995 output fell slightly to $131 billion, mirroring the slight decline in motor vehicle production. However, the motor vehicle parts industry represented a 25 percent growth since 1992.

The U.S. parts and accessories industry was dominated by 50 large manufacturers that accounted for the vast majority of sales. From 1992 to 1995, North American sales by these top 50 suppliers increased by almost 50 percent, growing from $68 billion to $101 billion, according to *U.S. Department of Commerce* reports. The United States was home to the world's sales leader, Delphi Automotive Systems, with 1995 global sales of over $26 billion—$10 billion more than its nearest foreign competitor.

WORK FORCE

During the early 1990s, approximately one of every seven jobs in the U.S. domestic economy related to the production, sale, operation, or maintenance of motor vehicles. As the *Detroit Free Press* noted in 1993, ''the U.S. auto industry was a major force in the creation of new jobs for many years, with employment peaking in 1978 at more than one million workers. But since then employment has slid and the industry is no longer a source of new jobs.'' The *Free Press* went on to point out that auto industry employment in 1992 was 812,200 jobs, of which a little over 413,000 were hourly positions. This was in part a result of increasing productivity per worker at the Big Three manufacturing plants—one of the primary reasons for the dramatic upswing in fortunes for GM, Ford, and Chrysler in the early 1990s. According to the U.S. Department of Commerce and the Federal Reserve Bank of Chicago, GM, Ford, and Chrysler have all, from 1980 to 1991, cut by at least one-third the number of worker hours required to assemble a vehicle.

According to the U.S. Department of Labor's Bureau of Labor Statistics, employment by producers of complete cars and trucks increased 4 percent in 1995, reaching a total of 355,000 workers. Auto workers were among the most productive and highest paid production workers in the country. In May 1996, their average weekly earnings totaled $980—85 percent greater than the $529 average earned by all U.S. manufacturing production workers. General Motors, Ford, and Chrysler provided three-fourths of the industry's total direct employment. Their payrolls listed a total of 721,000 employees in the United States in 1995, compared with 632,000 in 1992. By the year 2003, a University of Michigan study estimated that the Big Three would need to hire at least 168,000 employees for their U.S. operations.

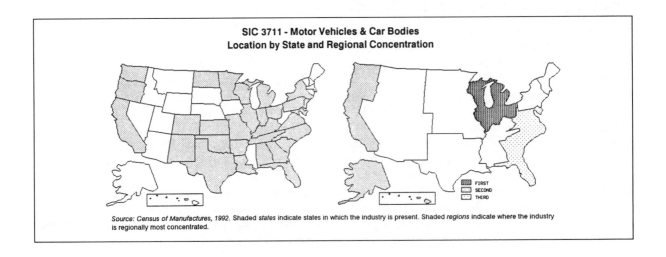

SIC 3711 - Motor Vehicles & Car Bodies
Location by State and Regional Concentration

FIRST
SECOND
THIRD

Source: Census of Manufactures, 1992. Shaded states indicate states in which the industry is present. Shaded regions indicate where the industry is regionally most concentrated.

SIC 3711
Occupations Employed by SIC 371 - Motor Vehicles and Equipment

Occupation	% of Total 1994	Change to 2005
Assemblers, fabricators, & hand workers nec	21.4	-12.2
Inspectors, testers, & graders, precision	3.4	-51.1
Engineers nec	3.4	5.4
Blue collar worker supervisors	3.4	-11.4
Machine operators nec	2.9	-30.3
Machine tool cutting operators, metal & plastic	2.6	-55.0
Welders & cutters	2.4	-29.8
Managers & administrators nec	2.1	-12.2
Engineering technicians & technologists nec	1.8	-12.2
Helpers, laborers, & material movers nec	1.8	-12.2
Metal & plastic machine workers nec	1.7	55.6
Welding machine setters, operators	1.7	-12.2
Tool & die makers	1.6	-8.8
Mechanics, installers, & repairers nec	1.6	-29.8
Machine tool cutting & forming etc. nec	1.6	5.4
Industrial truck & tractor operators	1.6	-29.8
Electricians	1.6	-17.6
Combination machine tool operators	1.5	40.5
Machine forming operators, metal & plastic	1.5	-56.1
Industrial machinery mechanics	1.4	-42.9
Sales & related workers nec	1.2	-12.2
Machine builders	1.1	31.7
Sheet metal workers & duct installers	1.0	-56.1

Source: *Industry-Occupation Matrix*, Bureau of Labor Statistics. These data relate to one or more 3-digit SIC industry groups rather than to a single 4-digit SIC. The change reported for each occupation to the year 2005 is a percent of growth or decline as estimated by the Bureau of Labor Statistics. The abbreviation nec stands for 'not elsewhere classified'.

The Bureau of Labor Statistics also revealed that at the end of 1995, the seven Japanese affiliates' total payroll was 40,700—an increase of 22 percent over 1992's level of 33,200. Expansion within their existing facilities, plus the addition of new factories, was expected to add several thousand more workers over the next several years to the employment roles of the Japanese affiliates. In 1998, for example, Toyota was expected to assemble a light truck in a $700 million plant in Indiana. The facility would have an annual capacity of 100,000 vehicles and was expected to hire 1,300 Americans. Other foreign car makers who were establishing new plants in the United States, like Benz's massive facility in Alabama, were expected to hire many Americans by the turn of the century.

RESEARCH AND TECHNOLOGY

Throughout the 1990s, private industrial research and government-funded research focused on improving fuel efficiency, developing alternative fuels, reducing vehicle emissions, developing environmentally friendly manufacturing processes, and recycling junked vehicles. Alternative fuels, such as ethanol and methanol mixtures, liquid natural gas (LNG), and liquid petroleum gas (LPG) were under investigation as clean burning energy sources. Researchers were also working on developing a viable electric car.

The U.S. Advanced Battery Consortium (USABC) was developed by the Big Three and the U.S. Department of Energy to work on new battery technology. Battery types other than conventional lead acid batteries included nickel cadmium, sodium sulfur, zinc air, nickel hydride, lithium polymer, and hydrogen fuel cells. Nickel cadmium batteries were preferred by Japanese manufacturers, although some critics claimed they were unsuited for mass production because cadmium was a scarce mineral and highly toxic.

Solar Car Corporation in Melbourne, Florida, was one of the country's pioneering organizations in the construction of hybrid solar/electric vehicles. Hybrid vehicles contained a small auxiliary engine powered by gasoline or other alternative fuel to assist in recharging batteries or extending a vehicle's range. Solar panels helped supplement the battery and extend its life from two to three years to five to six years. According to company statements, its electric vehicles were capable of attaining top speeds of 75 miles per hour and able to travel 50 to 80 miles before recharging.

Another type of alternate vehicle under development by the automotive industry was fueled by natural gas. According to the American Gas Association, an estimated 30,000 natural gas vehicles (NGVs) were operating in the United States in 1993. Some projections anticipated as many as 500,000 NGVs in the United States by the year 2000. In 1993 an estimated 700,000 were in use worldwide. Natural gas proponents cite several advantages the fuel holds over conventional gasoline—it costs 25 to 30 percent less than gasoline, produces 90 percent less carbon monoxide and 50 percent less hydrocarbons, and spurs increased engine efficiency. In addition, because of deep domestic reserves, natural gas holds the potential to help the United States reduce its dependence on imported oil.

In September 1993, the Partnership for a New Generation of Vehicles (PNGV) was established to develop technologies for a new generation of affordable, mid-size passenger vehicles that would travel the equivalent of 80 miles per gallon—three times greater than the average achieved in 1994—while at the same time producing much lower emissions. PNGV was coordinated by the U.S. Department of Commerce, from the government side, and on the industry side, it was coordinated by USCAR, the pre-competitive research venture established by

Chrysler, Ford, and General Motors. In addition, PNGV included research from over 350 automotive suppliers and universities. Research to develop new power plant, drive train, and chassis technologies were being studied, along with more economically efficient and environmentally safe ways of employing the manufacturing processes. According to the U.S. Department of Commerce, by the year 2000 each car company would have a PNGV concept car, followed by PNGV production prototypes in 2003.

The other alternate means of energy being researched was electricity. Besides the Big Three researching the electric car, many small private companies were also involved in the development of these cars. According to *Forbes* magazine, 10 percent of all new cars sold in California by the year 2003 must be zero emission vehicles, which means electric. Thus, in seven years Californians alone were supposed to be buying at least 200,000 electric cars annually.

Researchers within the automotive industry were also working on creating safer ways to manage traffic. To help further the advancement of traffic management, reduce traffic congestion, and lessen the number of accidents in congested urban regions, Congress appropriated $660 million to be spent during fiscal years 1992 through 1997 on a study of Intelligent Vehicle Highway Systems (IVHS). Potential IVHS technologies included radar, microwave, ultrasonics, and video. Its aim was to assist with driver tasks such as visibility and navigational assistance. Necessary ingredients included anti-lock brakes, better traction control, improved steering responses, refined suspension systems, and the ability to monitor tire pressure.

TRUCK AND BUS BODIES

During the early 1990s, truck and bus makers were facing many challenges to improve their environmental

and safety records. Research toward improving the industry's environmental impact focused on reducing vehicle emissions, improving fuel economy, and developing alternative fuels.

The Clean Air Act Amendments of 1990 imposed increasing reductions in vehicle emissions creating a need for expanded research in clean burning diesel technology. Efforts were also underway to make vehicles with increased fuel economy. Designers worked toward making lighter trucks with smaller dimensions, better aerodynamic styling, and improved engine performance. In a similar vein, some groups were advocating the development of alternate fuels. One of the most promising alternate fuels was natural gas. Many environmental groups favored natural gas over gasoline and diesel fuels because it emitted 90 percent less carbon monoxide and 50 percent less hydrocarbons.

Safety issues under investigation included searches for innovative designs offering improved driver visibility, better braking systems, and the development of collision avoidance technologies. Greyhound Lines, Inc. planned to provide radar collision avoidance on buses by the middle of the 1990s. The system under development used a light and buzzer to alert drivers when other vehicles got too close.

Other changes were also being studied. Manufacturers investigated possible alterations to improve driving and sleeping accommodations for truck operators. They were also developing advanced drive trains to permit the construction of trailers capable of carrying more cargo.

AMERICA AND THE WORLD

The United States motor vehicle market reached maturity over the course of the mid-1970s through the

SIC 3711 - Motor Vehicles & Car Bodies
Industry Data by State

| State | Establish-ments | Shipments | | | Employment | | | | Cost as % of Shipments | Investment per Employee ($) |
		Total ($ mil)	% of U.S.	Per Establ.	Total Number	% of U.S.	Per Establ.	Wages ($/hour)		
Michigan	49	42,091.3	27.5	859.0	76,900	33.7	1,569	22.73	69.5	6,164
Ohio	29	23,032.0	15.1	794.2	35,700	15.6	1,231	21.96	66.3	8,975
Missouri	14	16,070.7	10.5	1,147.9	15,200	6.7	1,086	23.19	71.3	-
Illinois	19	7,766.8	5.1	408.8	8,500	3.7	447	20.67	75.8	-
Indiana	34	4,983.1	3.3	146.6	5,800	2.5	171	22.10	64.0	3,966
California	57	2,980.1	1.9	52.3	8,000	3.5	140	20.39	78.4	-
Arkansas	6	39.6	0.0	6.6	100	0.0	17	11.00	71.7	-
Florida	22	(D)	-	-	375 *	0.2	17	-	-	-
Texas	20	(D)	-	-	3,750 *	1.6	188	-	-	-
Pennsylvania	16	(D)	-	-	1,750 *	0.8	109	-	-	-

*Source: 1992 Economic Census. The states are in descending order of shipments or establishments (if shipment data are missing for the majority). The symbol (D) appears when data are withheld to prevent disclosure of competitive information. States marked with (D) are sorted by number of establishments. A dash (-) indicates that the data element cannot be calculated; * indicates the midpoint of a range.*

mid-1990s, resulting in an annualized long term sales growth rate of just 1-2 percent per year. On the other hand, many foreign markets were expanding very rapidly. This simple supply and demand formula led the Clinton administration to make opening closed markets a high priority. Establishing the nation's first National Export Strategy to take advantage of the market opening initiatives enabled total U.S. motor vehicle exports to the world to grow impressively—rising from $18.8 billion in 1992 to $22.9 billion by the end of 1995, a 22 percent increase.

The Clinton administration's efforts to pry open the Japanese market produced a surge in exports to Japan, which increased by 250 percent between 1992 and 1995, reaching a total of $3.1 billion. Detroit auto makers were very pleased with the Clinton administration's deal with Japan. According to the *New York Times,* Chrysler's Chairman and CEO, Robert J. Eaton, said the Big Three would be able to compete in Japan and the Japanese would not be able to continue using high prices in Japan to subsidize lower car prices elsewhere.

At the end of 1994, U.S. motor vehicle exports to Mexico jumped 250 percent over the previous year, reaching $683 million—a direct result of the industry's renewed effort to export and the increased access to the Mexican market afforded by the 1994 implementation of the North American Free Trade Agreement (NAFTA). Mexico experienced a severe economic slump in 1995, and U.S. motor vehicle exports declined to $394 million for the year. However, they remained at a level 100 percent greater than in 1993—the year before the agreement became effective. Although additional efforts were necessary, initial efforts to open the Korean market were beginning to be successful U.S. shipments to Korea rose from 1992's $62 million to $88 million by the end of 1995, a 42 percent boost.

In the first half of 1996, total U.S. motor vehicle exports advanced by 3 percent over the same period in 1995, to a total of $12.7 billion. Exports to Japan jumped 23 percent, reaching $1.6 billion, while shipments to Mexico rose to $547 million, 175 percent greater than in the first half of 1995. Exports to Korea also increased, rising by 130 percent to a total of $106 million. According to the *U.S. Global Trade Outlook: 1995-2000,* East Asia and Latin America were likely to account for more than one-half of all the growth in the world motor vehicle market during the late 1990s. U.S. producers are expected to obtain export orders worth $6.5 billion in 2000.

TRUCK AND BUS BODIES

During the early 1990s, North America was the world's largest combined medium and heavy duty truck market. As a result, the region attracted interest from overseas establishments, and the U.S. market experienced an increasing presence of foreign owned participants. Three large foreign owned companies with domestic manufacturing facilities—Freightliner, Volvo GM, and Mack Trucks—increased their combined market share from about 20 percent in 1990 to about 22 percent in 1991. Japanese manufacturers—Isuzu Truck of America, Hino Diesel Trucks USA, Nissan Truck of

SIC 3711 - Motor Vehicles & Car Bodies
General Statistics

Year	Com-panies	Establishments		Employment			Compensation		Production ($ million)			
		Total	with 20 or more employees	Total (000)	Production Workers (000)	Hours (Mil)	Payroll ($ mil)	Wages ($/hr)	Cost of Materials	Value Added by Manufacture	Value of Shipments	Capital Invest.
1982	284	355	152	240.1	193.5	364.2	6,821.9	14.45	55,520.0	15,455.8	70,739.7	2,368.3
1983		349	157	260.7	216.5	446.2	8,266.6	14.75	73,818.2	22,608.0	95,930.8	1,106.4
1984		343	162	296.2	247.6	564.4	10,192.2	14.46	90,435.0	27,668.1	118,066.0	2,420.9
1985		338	166	295.8	249.7	522.4	10,670.3	16.70	94,220.6	28,061.1	122,327.4	2,904.7
1986		348	167	280.5	233.8	479.5	10,261.7	17.22	93,965.0	31,846.0	125,869.6	3,912.8
1987	351	413	174	281.3	235.5	472.7	10,376.4	17.33	97,520.4	36,117.7	133,345.6	4,121.4
1988		391	183	250.3	213.6	448.2	10,121.2	18.68	102,364.8	39,762.2	142,059.6	1,136.6
1989		393	187	246.6	212.5	440.2	10,390.9	19.40	102,345.2	46,873.4	149,315.2	2,373.9
1990		406	183	239.8	200.0	399.7	10,060.0	20.31	101,130.8	39,504.4	140,417.0	3,004.4
1991		408	171	218.1	178.5	367.8	9,802.5	21.32	88,403.2	45,146.9	133,861.2	3,261.9
1992	400	456	161	228.4	193.3	397.3	10,438.8	21.66	107,636.6	45,262.2	152,948.5	2,989.5
1993		466	160	224.2	191.0	409.6	11,154.2	22.61	120,458.8	47,272.0	167,825.8	4,033.9
1994		459P	176P	234.0	202.5	447.5	12,437.7	23.35	144,809.9	52,917.7	197,553.7	4,245.7
1995		470P	178P	221.3P	190.0P	404.3P	11,850.6P	24.16P	136,455.7P	49,864.9P	186,156.7P	3,901.7P
1996		481P	179P	216.6P	186.8P	398.8P	12,104.0P	24.95P	141,850.9P	51,836.4P	193,516.9P	4,042.8P
1997		492P	180P	212.0P	183.5P	393.2P	12,357.5P	25.74P	147,246.0P	53,807.9P	200,877.1P	4,183.9P
1998		502P	181P	207.4P	180.2P	387.7P	12,610.9P	26.52P	152,641.1P	55,779.5P	208,237.3P	4,325.1P

Sources: 1982, 1987, 1992 *Economic Census*; *Annual Survey of Manufactures*, 83-86, 88-91, 93-94. Establishment counts for non-Census years are from *County Business Patterns*; establishment values for 83-84 are extrapolations. 'P's show projections by the editors. Industries reclassified in 87 will not have data for prior years.

America, and Mitsubishi Fuso Truck of America—boosted their U.S. sales by 31 percent between 1991 and 1992.

Imported vehicles represented 11 percent of vehicles sold in the medium duty classes during 1991, up from 3.1 percent in 1986. Within the Class 8 segment, however, imports captured less than 1 percent of 1991's total sales. According to a Hino representative, differences between the heavy duty truck markets in the United States and Japan made the shipment of Class 8 trucks from Japanese manufacturers into the United States impractical. The U.S. market was unique because trucks were custom manufactured using a combination of in-house and outsourced components in accordance with a particular customer's specifications.

American exports of medium and heavy duty trucks totaled $1.1 billion in 1991—an increase over the $951 million recorded in 1990. The ability of U.S. companies to compete overseas was bolstered by a drop in the value of the dollar in relationship to the yen and European currencies. U.S. opportunities in the European Community, however, were limited by import duties ranging from 17 to 22 percent of the vehicles' landed value. Talks were underway to negotiate a more favorable tariff situation.

The biggest U.S. trading partner in heavy and medium duty trucks was Canada. Canada received 43 percent of U.S. exports and supplied 73 percent of U.S. imports. Some analysts expected Mexico to be the fastest growing market for U.S. medium and heavy duty trucks. Other growing overseas markets included South and Central America, Eastern Europe, and nations formed following the break up of the former Soviet Union.

U.S. exports to Mexico were expected to grow steadily over the turn of the century. The signing of the North American Free Trade Agreement (NAFTA) provided for Mexico's adoption of U.S. safety standards for trucking, and elimination of all restrictions on U.S. exports of medium and heavy duty trucks, buses, and special purpose motor vehicles to Mexico by January 1, 1999, among other provisions. In addition, analysts foresaw growing demand for U.S. built medium and heavy duty trucks, buses, and special purpose vehicles during the mid- to late 1990s as Mexico replaced its aging trucking fleet. New production of some of these vehicles in Mexico were also expected to utilize U.S. parts and components—another bonus for exports of U.S. OE and after market parts.

PARTS AND ACCESSORIES

U.S. parts manufacturers have been forced to match the growth in global operations of domestic auto makers to maintain their primary supply relationships. Additionally, international growth has been spurred by the desire to gain supply contracts with overseas vehicle manufacturers. Most leading domestic producers have established manufacturing facilities in the principle auto producing regions of the world—including Canada, Europe, and Mexico. In Europe alone, seven leading U.S. parts manufacturers have combined annual sales exceeding $1 billion. The global integration of the auto industry has led many suppliers to develop joint ventures with foreign parts producers. As the industry continues to globalize, increased U.S. supplier investments are expected in Mexico, Asia, and Europe.

The United States has posted a trade deficit in automotive parts since 1983, primarily due to a large deficit with Japan. Between 1989 and 1992, the parts trade deficit with Japan remained between $9 billion and $10 billion, accounting for one fifth of the overall trade deficit with Japan. Canada is the only major nation with which the United States has maintained a trade surplus, and Canada remains the leading trading partner of U.S.

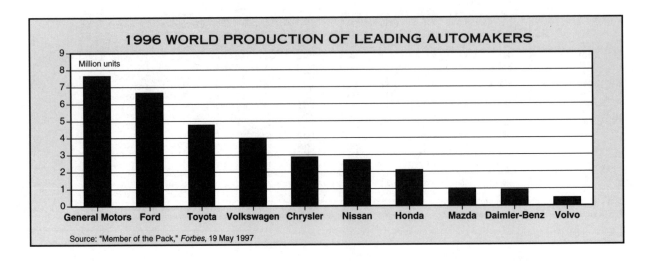

1996 WORLD PRODUCTION OF LEADING AUTOMAKERS

Million units

Source: "Member of the Pack," *Forbes*, 19 May 1997

firms. Between 1985 and 1991, Canada received over 60 percent of total U.S. parts exports and supplied one-third of total imports.

The number of foreign firms producing parts in the United States increased dramatically throughout the 1980s and early 1990s. In 1992, approximately 350 wholly owned foreign part plants, and over 120 joint ventures, operated in the United States. Japanese suppliers owned 167 U.S. parts plants and were part of 123 joint ventures. European firms, led by German manufacturers, owned 168 plants in the United States, and Canadian firms owned 17, with one joint venture. While fairly well established in Europe and Canada, U.S. penetration of the Japanese domestic market remained weak. In 1992 one wholly owned U.S. parts plant—and a few joint ventures—were operating in Japan.

Continued consolidation and increasing global competition are forecast for the automotive parts industry. The future prospects for large domestic producers are likely to depend on their ability to obtain contracts with Japanese transplant manufacturers as well as to retain contracts with the Big Three against competition from Japanese suppliers. For smaller second and third tier suppliers, the key is likely to be establishing strong relationships with primary suppliers.

Expanded efforts by the industry, backed by the Clinton Administration's work to increase U.S. access to the Japanese automotive parts market, resulted in a 58 percent increase in exports to Japan—growing from $1 billion in 1992 to $1.6 billion in 1995. Japanese car manufacturers purchased $19.9 billion worth of U.S. made automotive parts and materials in the 1994 fiscal year. Approximately 75 percent was spent to transplant Japanese manufacturing operations in the United States, while the remaining 25 percent was spent on exports to Japan. Exports to Mexico and Canada benefited from the passage of the North American Free Trade Agreement (NAFTA)—growing from $26 billion in 1993 to $29 billion in 1995.

During the first half of 1996, U.S. automotive parts exports to the world grew to $20.8 billion, up 3 percent from the previous period. Exports to Japan advanced 11 percent to $901 million. Exports to Canada and Mexico increased 6 percent to $15.1 billion as Mexico began to rebound from its 1995 slump.

ASSOCIATIONS AND SOCIETIES

AMERICAN AUTOMOBILE ASSOCIATION
1000 AAA Dr.
Heathrow, FL 32746-5063

Phone: (407) 444-7000
Fax: (407) 444-7380

AMERICAN AUTOMOBILE MANUFACTURERS ASSOCIATION
1401 H St. NW, Ste. 900
Washington, DC 20005
Phone: (202) 326-5500

AUTOMOTIVE AFFILIATED REPRESENTATIVES
401 N. Michigan Ave., Ste. 2100
Chicago, IL 60611
Phone: (312) 644-6610

AUTOMOTIVE PARTS & ACCESSORIES ASSOCIATION
4600 East-West Hwy., Ste. 300
Bethesda, MD 20814
Phone: (301) 654-6664

AUTOMOTIVE SERVICE INDUSTRY ASSOCIATION
25 NW Point Elk Grove
Village, IL 60007-1035
Phone: (708) 228-1310
Fax: (708) 228-1510
Members are distributors and manufacturers of automotive replacement parts.

AUTOMOTIVE TRADE ASSOCIATION EXECUTIVES
Executive Offices
8400 Westpark Dr.
McLean, VA 22102
Phone: (703) 821-7072

MOTOR AND EQUIPMENT MANUFACTURERS ASSOCIATION
PO Box 13966
Research Triangle Park, NC 27709-3966
Phone: (919) 549-4800
Fax: (919) 549-4824

MOTOR VEHICLE MANUFACTURERS ASSOCIATION OF THE UNITED STATES
7430 2nd Ave., Ste. 300
Detroit, MI 48202
Phone: (313) 872-4311
Fax: (313) 872-5400

NATIONAL AUTOMOBILE DEALERS ASSOCIATION
8400 Westpark Dr.
McLean, VA 22102
Phone: (703) 821-7050

NATIONAL AUTOMOTIVE PARTS ASSOCIATION
2999 Circle 75 Pky.
Atlanta, GA 30339
Phone: (404) 956-2200
Fax: (404) 956-2212

SOCIETY OF AUTOMOTIVE ENGINEERS INTERNATIONAL
400 Commonwealth Dr.
Warrendale, PA 15096-0001
Phone: (412) 776-4841
Fax: (412) 776-5760

PERIODICALS AND NEWSLETTERS

AUTO RETAIL REPORT
United Communications Group
11300 Rockville Pke., Ste. 1100
Rockville, MD 20852-3030
Phone: (301) 816-8950
Fax: (301) 816-8945
Biweekly. $427.00. per year. Incorporates Motor News Analysis.

AUTOCAR AND MOTOR
Haymarket Magazines, Ltd.
38-42 Hampton Rd.
Teddington, Middlesex, England TW11 OJE
Monthly. $150.00 per year. Incorporates Motor.

AUTOMOTIVE ENGINEERING MAGAZINE
Society of Automotive Engineers
400 Commonwealth Dr.
Warrendale, PA 15096
Phone: (412) 776-4841
Fax: (412) 776-4026
Monthly. $72.00 per year. Provides 86,000 automotive product planners and engineers with state-of-the-art technology that can be applied to the development of new and improved vehicles.

AUTOMOTIVE EXECUTIVE
National Automobile Dealers Assn.
8400 Westpark Dr.
McLean, VA 22102
Phone: (703) 821-7150
Fax: (703) 821-7234
Monthly. $24.00 per year.

AUTOMOTIVE INDUSTRIES
Chilton Co.
201 King of Prussia Rd.
Radnor, PA 19089-0230
Phone: (800) 695-1214 or (610) 964-4000
Fax: (610) 964-4745
Monthly. $55.00 per year.

AUTOMOTIVE INDUSTRIES INSIDER
Chilton Co.
201 King of Prussia Rd.
Radnor, PA 19089-0230
Phone: (800) 695-1214 or (610) 964-4000
Fax: (610) 964-4745
Biweekly. $395.00 per year. Newsletter with emphasis on new product data, technical developments, and automobile industry trends.

AUTOMOTIVE NEWS: ENGINEERING, FINANCIAL, MANUFACTURING, SALES, MARKETING, SERVICING
Crain Communications, Inc.
1400 Woodbridge Ave.
Detroit, MI 48207-3187
Phone: (313) 446-6000
Weekly. $78.00 per year. Business news coverage of the automobile industry at the retail, wholesale, and manufacturing levels. Includes statistics.

AUTOMOTIVE RECYCLING
Automotive and Recyclers Association
3975 Fair Ridge Dr., Ste. 20N
Fairfax, VA 22030-2906
Phone: (703) 385-1001
Bimonthly. $30.00 per year. Formerly Dismantlers Digest.

CHILTON'S AUTOMOTIVE MARKETING: A MONTHLY PUBLICATION FOR THE AUTOMOTIVE AFTERMARKET
Chilton Co.
201 King of Prussia Rd.
Radnor, PA 19089-0230
Phone: (800) 695-1214 or (610) 964-4000
Fax: (610) 964-4745
Monthly. $48.00 per year. Includes marketing of automobile batteries. Formerly Automotive Aftermarket News.

HEAVY DUTY TRUCKING
HIC Corporation
1800 E. Deere Ave.
Santa Ana, CA 92705
Phone: (714) 261-1636
Monthly.

ROAD AND TRACK
Hachette Magazines, Inc.
1499 Monrovia Ave.
Newport Beach, CA 92663
Phone: (800) 456-3084 or (714) 720-5300
Fax: (714) 631-2757
Monthly. $19.94 per year.

TRUCK SALES AND LEASING
1045 Taylor Ave., Ste.
214 Baltimore, MD 21204
Phone: (301) 828-1092
Monthly.

WARD'S AUTO WORLD
David C. Smith
Ward's Communications, Inc.
28 W. Adams St.
Detroit, MI 48226
Phone: (313) 962-4433
Fax: (313) 962-5593
Monthly. $47.00 per year. In-depth news and analysis of the automotive industry.

WARD'S AUTOMOTIVE REPORTS
Ward's Communications, Inc.
28 W. Adams St.
Detroit, MI 48226
Phone: (313) 962-4433
Fax: (313) 962-4532
Weekly. $950.00 per year. Vital statistical information on production, sales and inventory. Exclusive news of critical interest to the automotive industry. Ward's Automotive Yearbook *included with subscription.*

DATABASES

WARD'S AUTOINFOBANK
Ward's Communications, Inc.
3000 Town Center, Ste. 2750
Southfield, MI 48075
Phone: (810) 357-0800
Provides weekly, monthly, quarterly, and annual statistical data from 1965 to date for U.S. and imported cars and trucks. Covers production, shipments, sales, inventories, optional equipment, etc. Updating varies by series. Inquire as to online cost and availability.

STATISTICS SOURCES

AFTERMARKET FACT BOOK
Automotive Parts & Accessories Association
4600 East-West Hwy., Ste. 300
Bethesda, MD 20814-3415
Phone: (301) 654-6664
1993.

AMERICAN TRUCKING TRENDS
American Trucking Associations, Inc.
2200 Mill Rd.
Alexandria, VA 22314
Phone: (800) 225-8382 or (703) 838-1792
Fax: (703) 838-1992
Annual. $20.00

AUTOMOTIVE INDUSTRIES STATISTICAL ISSUE
Chilton Co.
201 King of Prussia Rd.
Radnor, PA 19089-0230
Phone: (800) 695-1214 or (61) 964-4000
Fax: (610) 964-4745
Annual. $7.50.

AUTOMOTIVE INDUSTRY DATA
AID Ltd.
City House
2-4 Dam St.
Lichfield, Staffs, England, WS13 GAA
Phone: (543) 44 257295
Twice monthly.

THE AUTOPARTS REPORT
International Trade Services
PO Box 5950
Betesda, MD 20814-5950
Phone: (301) 857-8454
Twice monthly.

MVMA MOTOR VEHICLE FACTS AND FIGURES
Motor Vehicle Manufacturers Assn. of the U.S., Inc.
7430 2nd Ave., Ste. 300
Detroit, MI 48202
Phone: (313) 872-4311
Annual. $7.50. Includes information on buses. Formed by the merger of Automobile Facts and Figures and Motor Truck Facts.

THE POWER REPORT ON AUTOMOTIVE MARKETING
J. D. Power and Associates
30401 Agoura Rd., Ste. 200
Agoura Hills, CA 91301
Phone: (818) 889-6330
Monthly.

GENERAL WORKS

AUTO MECHANICS FUNDAMENTALS
Martin W. Stockel
Goodheart-Willcox Co.
123 W. Taft Dr.
South Holland, IL 60473-2089
Phone: (800) 323-0440 or (708) 333-7200
Fax: (708) 333-9130
1990. $35.96.

THE CHANGING STRUCTURE OF THE U.S. AUTOMOTIVE PARTS INDUSTRY
Sean P. McAlinden and Brett C. Smith
Office for the Study of Automotive Transportation
Transportation Research Institute
University of Michigan
Ann Arbor, MI 48109
Phone: (313) 764-5592
February, 1993.

THE MACHINE THAT CHANGED THE WORLD
James P. Womack and others
Rawson Associates
866 3rd Ave.
New York, NY 10022
Phone: (800) 257-5755 or (212) 702-3436
Fax: (212) 605-3099
1990. $24.95. Based on a five-year study of the future of the automobile industry by the International Motor Vehicle Program at Massachusetts Institute of Technology.

SAE HANDBOOK
Society of Automotive Engineers
400 Commonwealth Dr.
Warrendale, PA 15096
Phone: (412) 776-4841
Fax: (412) 776-0790
Annual. $250.00. Four volumes. Contains standards, recommended practices and information reports on ground vehicle design, manufacturing, testing and performance.

WARD'S AUTOMOTIVE YEARBOOK
Ward's Communications, Inc.
28 W. Adams St.
Detroit, MI 48226
Phone: (313) 962-4433
Fax: (313) 962-4432
Annual. $220.00. Comprehensive statistical information on automotive production, sales, truck data and suppliers.

WORLD MOTOR VEHICLE DATA
Motor Vehicle Manufacturers Assn. of the U.S. Inc.
7430 2nd Ave., Ste. 300
Detroit, MI 48202
Phone: (313) 872-4311
Annual. $35.00.

FURTHER READING

Elridge, Earl. ''Korean Automakers Ready Bigger Plans for U.S. Sales.'' *The Detroit News,* 24 July 1996.

Hoffman, Gary. ''Suppliers Seek Bigger Chunk of Inside Jobs.'' *The Detroit News,* 19 July 1996.

''The New Car Market's Lost Generation: Auto Industry Struggles to Satisfy the Tastes of First-Time Buyers on a Budget.'' *New York Times,* 15 August 1996.

''The Next Supplier Evolution.'' *Automotive Industries,* 1 January 1996.

U.S. Department of Commerce. ''The Road Ahead.'' Office of Automotive Affairs. Washington: GPO, February 1997.

U.S. Department of Commerce. ''U.S. Automotive Industry Sector Report.'' Office of Automotive Affairs. Washington: GPO, 17 September 1996.

INDUSTRY SNAPSHOT

Approximately 250 companies in the United States were involved in manufacturing motors and generators in 1995. These companies recorded more than $10.4 billion in sales for products included in the SIC 3621 classification, which consisted of four primary product groups: fractional horsepower motors, integral horsepower motors and generators, prime mover generator sets, and parts and supplies for motors and generators. Other products manufactured by the industry included land transportation motors and fractional and integral motor generator sets. Of these products, fractional horsepower motors represented nearly 50 percent of the industry's shipments, followed by integral horsepower motors and generators, which accounted for 18.5 percent. Prime mover generator sets accounted for another 11.2 percent of the industry's shipments, while parts and supplies for motors and generators represented nearly 8 percent.

Motor and generator manufacturers are heavily dependent on the health of several industrial markets to sustain their growth. Fractional horsepower motors are used in various household appliances—including refrigerators, freezers, air conditioners, automatic dishwashers, and microwave ovens—as well as other products that require a small horsepower motor, such as computer disk drives. Consequently, fluctuations in the residential construction market and changes in consumer spending are mirrored by the fractional motor market.

Integral horsepower motors are best suited for industrial uses, where greater horsepower is required. Integral motors power vehicles used in large construction projects and provide the necessary power for many different types of manufacturing facilities. Any significant changes in nonresidential construction activity or capital expenditures in the industrial sector generally have parallel affects on integral motor production.

In addition to these market dependencies, motor and generator sales are affected by the vacillating costs of raw materials. Steel, an essential element in the production of motors, generators, and their related parts and supplies, is subject to pernicious price swings that could impinge on the industry's profit margin. Other materials, such as wire and brushes used in the manufacturing of motors and generators, also demonstrate a propensity for erratic jumps in price and have an appreciable affect on the motor and generator industry.

MOTORS AND GENERATORS

SIC 3621

The motor and generator industry was expected to expand at a compound annual rate of two percent through the late 1990s, suggesting the beginning of a recovery from the effects of the early 1990s recession. However, escalating energy costs, coupled with federal regulations requiring new energy efficiency standards, make the development of new technology and manufacturing processes intrinsic to any manufacturer's future profitability.

INDUSTRY OUTLOOK

During the recession of the early 1990s, lagging consumer spending and a decline in housing and indus-

SIC 3621
Occupations Employed by SIC 362 - Electrical Industrial Apparatus

Occupation	% of Total 1994	Change to 2005
Electrical & electronic assemblers	16.8	-28.3
Assemblers, fabricators, & hand workers nec	8.0	-20.3
Electrical & electronic equipment assemblers	4.3	-20.3
Inspectors, testers, & graders, precision	4.2	-44.2
Electrical & electronics engineers	3.3	-15.2
Blue collar worker supervisors	3.2	-33.5
Coil winders, tapers, & finishers	3.0	-36.3
Electrical & electronic technicians,technologists	2.3	-20.4
Machinists	2.2	-40.3
Sales & related workers nec	1.8	-20.3
Electromechanical equipment assemblers	1.5	-12.4
General managers & top executives	1.5	-24.4
Secretaries, ex legal & medical	1.4	-27.5
Drafters	1.3	-38.0
Stock clerks	1.3	-35.3
Machine assemblers	1.3	-28.3
Machine tool cutting & forming etc. nec	1.2	-36.3
Lathe & turning machine tool operators	1.2	-48.2
Traffic, shipping, & receiving clerks	1.1	-23.4
Industrial production managers	1.1	-20.3
Engineering, mathematical, & science managers	1.1	-9.5
Industrial machinery mechanics	1.1	7.5
Production, planning, & expediting clerks	1.0	-20.3

Source: Industry-Occupation Matrix, Bureau of Labor Statistics. These data relate to one or more 3-digit SIC industry groups rather than to a single 4-digit SIC. The change reported for each occupation to the year 2005 is a percent of growth or decline as estimated by the Bureau of Labor Statistics. The abbreviation nec stands for 'not elsewhere classified'.

trial construction compounded the existing difficulties associated with foreign competition, excess industry capacity, and cascading prices. The restoration of these integral markets was anticipated to improve the industry's condition as it moved into the twenty-first century, as was the development of new technology and manufacturing processes during the 1980s. Included in this improvement was the development of a highly efficient fractional motor in 1985 that enabled appliances to operate more quietly and at lower cost.

However, the industry needed further advances in the 1990s to ensure its viability. In the early 1990s, General Electric (GE) unveiled a variable-speed motor for air conditioning and heating equipment that operated 20 percent more efficiently than other motors used at the time. Manufacturers able to produce equally innovative and energy efficient products would most likely figure prominently in the industry's future.

ORGANIZATION AND STRUCTURE

The motor and generator industry is predominantly populated by medium- and large-sized companies, or those employing more than 20 people. The 75 largest establishments employ an average of 6,742 people. While this figure includes employees engaged in manufacturing or managing the production of some other types of goods, it is indicative of the relatively large size of facilities involved in the industry. On average, a motor and generator establishment employs 163 people, or more than three times the number of people employed in a typical manufacturing facility for all other U.S. industries.

Geographically, motor and generator production occurred throughout much of the nation, according to early 1990s *Census of Manufacturers* studies, but was particu-

SIC 3621 - Motors & Generators
General Statistics

Year	Companies	Establishments		Employment			Compensation		Production ($ million)			
		Total	with 20 or more employees	Total (000)	Production Workers (000)	Hours (Mil)	Payroll ($ mil)	Wages ($/hr)	Cost of Materials	Value Added by Manufacture	Value of Shipments	Capital Invest.
1982	348	471	324	84.1	61.0	114.3	1,545.7	8.61	2,525.9	3,434.3	6,058.1	275.4
1983		463	323	80.4	60.1	114.4	1,555.0	8.77	2,647.7	3,372.5	6,002.0	204.6
1984		455	322	84.2	63.3	124.5	1,743.5	9.22	2,915.7	3,929.3	6,760.5	244.9
1985		448	322	77.6	57.8	112.1	1,648.9	9.80	2,888.7	3,668.1	6,583.6	262.5
1986		432	305	75.6	55.5	108.1	1,681.7	10.01	2,921.1	3,623.4	6,608.1	232.7
1987	349	462	302	74.6	56.5	110.2	1,663.5	9.98	2,962.9	3,815.2	6,753.1	201.6
1988		475	312	75.7	58.0	115.0	1,785.8	10.36	3,504.1	4,182.5	7,601.4	205.2
1989		467	307	82.8	58.5	116.8	1,815.3	10.35	3,802.5	4,271.8	8,072.8	215.5
1990		466	312	78.5	55.1	108.5	1,751.1	10.62	3,634.5	4,005.3	7,672.2	238.8
1991		472	311	69.7	51.9	103.5	1,741.8	10.97	3,683.6	4,037.2	7,673.8	238.1
1992	370	470	274	67.9	52.0	104.1	1,764.6	11.23	3,812.9	4,244.3	8,039.7	242.0
1993		463	273	69.2	53.6	109.7	1,834.1	11.33	4,279.4	4,915.4	9,181.8	249.3
1994		469P	282P	74.0	58.1	118.6	1,914.2	10.90	4,705.5	4,777.2	9,429.3	290.5
1995		470P	278P	69.1P	52.7P	108.5P	1,890.4P	11.69P	4,622.4P	4,692.9P	9,262.9P	248.4P
1996		471P	274P	68.1P	52.1P	108.0P	1,913.8P	11.91P	4,753.9P	4,826.4P	9,526.4P	249.8P
1997		472P	270P	67.0P	51.5P	107.5P	1,937.2P	12.13P	4,885.5P	4,959.9P	9,789.9P	251.2P
1998		473P	266P	66.0P	50.9P	106.9P	1,960.6P	12.35P	5,017.0P	5,093.4P	10,053.4P	252.6P

Sources: 1982, 1987, 1992 Economic Census; Annual Survey of Manufactures, 83-86, 88-91, 93-94. Establishment counts for non-Census years are from County Business Patterns; establishment values for 83-84 are extrapolations. 'P's show projections by the editors. Industries reclassified in 87 will not have data for prior years.

larly concentrated in Wisconsin, Missouri, Arkansas and Ohio.

The costs involved in establishing and operating a motor and generator manufacturing facility are substantially higher than the average manufacturing facility. In the early 1990s, the average cost per establishment for raw manufacturing materials was $8.14 million in the motor and generator industry, compared to $4.54 million for the average of all manufacturing industries. The average investment for purchasing manufacturing machinery and paying for production retooling was $461,456 in the motor and generator industry, 55 percent higher than the average for other industries.

The relatively expensive nature of conducting business in the motor and generator industry tends to discourage the entry of small manufacturing companies. Since manufacturers frequently encounter expensive retooling costs—when a particular product becomes obsolete and is replaced by a new product, for example, or when a significant technological advancement dictates the implementation of a new production process—many companies manufacture a diverse line of products, some of which are excluded from the boundaries of the SIC 3621 classification. This diversity helps to insulate companies from potentially deleterious financial conditions affecting the motor and generator industry.

WORK FORCE

Total employment in the motor and generator industry decreased through much of the 1980s. This trend continued into the 1990s, as a nationwide recession weakened the motor and generator market. Beyond the negative effects of market fluctuations, manufacturing industries as a whole continued to streamline their operations by eliminating layers of managerial staff and al-

tering production processes to reduce the number of workers required to perform certain tasks. This general movement toward fewer employees per manufacturing facility made future reductions of the motor and generator industry employment base likely.

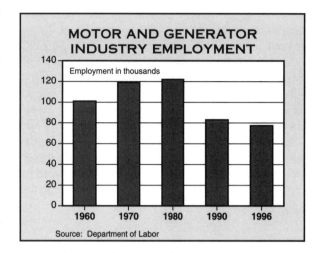

Of the 77,300 total people employed in the motor and generator industry, 61,800 were production workers. Managerial, administrative, and technical employees composed the remainder of the industry's work force. Generally, production workers were employed on a full-time basis and worked the same average number of hours per year as workers in other manufacturing industries and averaged $11.69 per hour.

AMERICA AND THE WORLD

The international market for motors and generators is intensely competitive, with Japan, Mexico, Canada, Germany, and the United Kingdom shipping just over $2 billion worth of products to the United States in 1991.

SIC 3621 - Motors & Generators
Industry Data by State

State	Establish-ments	Shipments			Employment				Cost as % of Shipments	Investment per Employee ($)
		Total ($ mil)	% of U.S.	Per Establ.	Total Number	% of U.S.	Per Establ.	Wages ($/hour)		
Wisconsin	32	776.7	9.7	24.3	6,200	9.1	194	10.63	52.2	4,323
Arkansas	12	683.8	8.5	57.0	5,600	8.2	467	10.37	44.5	3,857
Missouri	19	638.2	7.9	33.6	6,100	9.0	321	9.87	39.8	3,541
Ohio	34	608.0	7.6	17.9	5,400	8.0	159	11.17	41.4	3,463
Tennessee	16	591.5	7.4	37.0	5,200	7.7	325	9.88	51.6	3,423
Minnesota	15	534.2	6.6	35.6	3,000	4.4	200	18.39	44.1	4,333
Pennsylvania	27	378.0	4.7	14.0	3,500	5.2	130	11.88	38.3	3,600
Kentucky	8	357.4	4.4	44.7	2,500	3.7	313	9.21	54.3	6,200
Illinois	40	350.0	4.4	8.8	3,100	4.6	78	8.86	51.9	1,677
Mississippi	6	341.5	4.2	56.9	3,100	4.6	517	10.27	50.2	

Source: 1992 Economic Census. The states are in descending order of shipments or establishments (if shipment data are missing for the majority). The symbol (D) appears when data are withheld to prevent disclosure of competitive information. States marked with (D) are sorted by number of establishments. A dash (-) indicates that the data element cannot be calculated; * indicates the midpoint of a range.

Canada and Mexico combined for a 30.1 percent share of the U.S. import market, followed by the European Community with a 24 percent share, and Japan with a 22.4 percent share.

Exports from the United States totaled $2.016 billion in 1991, $15 million greater than the import total. The primary markets for motors and generators manufactured in the United States were Canada, Mexico, Nigeria, South Korea, and the Netherlands. Canada and Mexico accounted for the greatest share of U.S. exports at 31.4 percent, followed by East Asia at 19.9 percent, the European Community at 15.4 percent, and South America at 5.8 percent. The largest disparity between U.S. import and export totals in 1991 existed with Japan. For the year, Japan shipped $449 million worth of motor and generator products to the United States, compared to the $48 million worth of products the United States shipped to Japan.

ASSOCIATIONS AND SOCIETIES

ASSOCIATION OF DIESEL SPECIALISTS
9140 Ward Pky.
Kansas City, MO 64114
Phone: (816) 444-3500
Fax: (816) 444-0330

ENGINE MANUFACTURERS ASSOCIATION
401 N. Michigan Ave.
Chicago, IL 60611
Phone: (312) 644-6610
Fax: (312) 321-6869

PERIODICALS AND NEWSLETTERS

GAS TURBINE WORLD
Pequot Publishing, Inc.
PO Box 447

Southport, CT 06490
Phone: (203) 259-1812
Bimonthly. $60.00 per year.

STATISTICS SOURCES

MOTORS AND GENERATORS
Current Industrial Reports
U.S. Department of Commerce Bureau of the Census
Washington, DC 20233
Phone: (301) 763-4100

GENERAL WORKS

AUTOMOTIVE ENGINES: THEORY AND SERVICING
Herbert E. Ellinger and James D. Halderman
Prentice-Hall
200 Old Tappan Rd.
Old Tappan, NJ 07675
Phone: (800) 922-0579
Fax: (800) 445-6991
1990. $57.00. Second edition.

DIESEL PROGRESS: ENGINES AND DRIVES
Diesel and Gas Turbine Publications
13555 Bishop's Ct.
Brookfield, WI 53005
Phone: (414) 784-9177
Monthly. $60.00 per year. Formerly Diesel Progress North American.

FURTHER READING

Bureau of the Census. *Annual Survey of Manufacturers,* Washington: 1995.

Bureau of the Census. *Current Industrial Report,* Washington: 1996. ■

Since the 1960s, newspaper management has undergone a transformation from essentially family-run companies to the concerns of multimedia corporations. In 1963, the Times Mirror Company, owner of the Los Angeles Times, listed the firm on the New York Stock Exchange. Soon other newspapers went public. This led to the growth of newspaper chains and the proliferation of a profit-stressing corporate culture. Five companies were responsible for one-fourth of the newspapers read each day in the United States. As a result of this trend, newspapers became part of the entire communications system, rather than self-contained, strictly journalistic enterprises.

NEWSPAPER PUBLISHING AND PRINTING

SIC 2711

Engaged in a competition with electronic media for the attention of an increasingly dwindling readership, the U.S. newspaper industry has been compelled to expand not only its repertoire of marketing tactics, but also to attract the public with interesting, new features. Faced with decreasing ad revenue and surging production costs over the last decade, newspapers hoping to survive and flourish are now attempting to embrace the future via editions made available on the Internet and through online subscription databases.

Top 10 **TOP NEWSPAPER PUBLISHERS**

Ranked by: Revenue in 1994, in millions of dollars.

1. Gannett, with $3,002.0 million
2. Knight-Ridder, $2,194.5
3. Times Mirror Co., $2,063.0
4. New York Times Co., $1,968.3
5. Advance Publications, $1,926.0
6. Tribune Co., $1,292.4
7. Dow Jones, $1,114.0
8. Cox Enterprises, $891.0
9. Hearst Corp., $770.4
10. Thomson Corp., $731.0

Source: *Advertising Age,* August 14, 1995, p. 24.

The economic recession at the end of the 1980s brought heavy losses in advertising and circulation revenues. The effects were even felt by new publications. By 1991, papers with long histories, many of which had survived the Depression, were beginning to shut down as well. United Press International filed for bankruptcy for the second time in six years.

JOINT OPERATING AGREEMENTS

One solution to these dire conditions was the Joint Operating Agreement (JOA). Under the Newspaper Preservation Act of 1970, newspapers were largely exempt from antitrust suits. In a JOA, two or more newspapers are allowed to share the costs associated with operations, while maintaining separate editorial departments. However, the papers must prove that one would not survive if not for a JOA. One of the most substantial and controversial agreements, between Knight-Ridder's *Detroit Free Press* and Gannett's *Detroit News,* was finalized in November 1989 after a lengthy court battle.

ADVERTISING REVENUES AND CIRCULATION

For the first time since the Depression, in the early 1990s, there were back-to-back losses in annual advertising revenue as national, retail, and classified linage all shrunk. In response, advertising departments began to experiment with nontraditional solutions. Where they once aimed at reaching the greatest number of readers, they now refined their methods to reach geographically and demographically desirable readers via special sections, zoned editions, and electronically accessible news sites.

Ad revenues saw a decidedly positive turnaround begin in the mid-1990s, with revenues reaching $38 billion in 1996. The recovery was broad-based, spreading across all media and market categories. The largest increases were attributed to political elections and the 1996 Summer Olympics. Despite the upturn in ad revenues, circulation kept declining.

READERSHIP

A major concern of the newspaper industry has been its shrinking readership. The Newspaper Association of America's response to this trend has been to launch a multimedia campaign that is expected to draw in more advertisers and readers, including children; this broad-reaching promotion will cost $18 million. Through academic studies and marketing surveys, publishers attempted to discover who was reading the newspaper with regard to factors such as: age, gender, and financial status; frequency and duration of an average reading session; instances in which a newspaper was

shared by two or more people; and the sections of the paper read or ignored. In most cases these inquiries have yielded discouraging results. One such study revealed that between 1967 and 1989, the number of people aged 18 to 29 years who read a daily paper declined by 35 percent. This was attributed to parents passing on to their children their disinclination for newspaper reading, resulting in an ever-deepening alienation from the publications. The trend was linked to a pervasive apathy towards current events.

The inception of *USA Today* represented the industry's most revolutionary gesture towards appealing to a mass readership. Pioneered by Gannett's Allan Neuharth in 1982, USA Today incorporated such features as an easily read index on the front page, bold graphics featuring statistical information related to the day's events, and a large color weather map. By early 1996, *USA Today* had become the most widely circulated newspaper, with nearly two million readers, though it had yet to turn a profit.

ORGANIZATION AND STRUCTURE

FORMAT

A variety of publications could be called newspapers. The most common physical format is the gatefold, which is divided into individual sections. Pagination in a gatefold restarts in every section. The other major format, the tabloid, is read like a book or magazine. Tabloids usually have fewer articles than gatefolds, and are paginated without interruption from beginning to end. Traditionally, the content of tabloids has been considered less serious and less comprehensive than gatefolds.

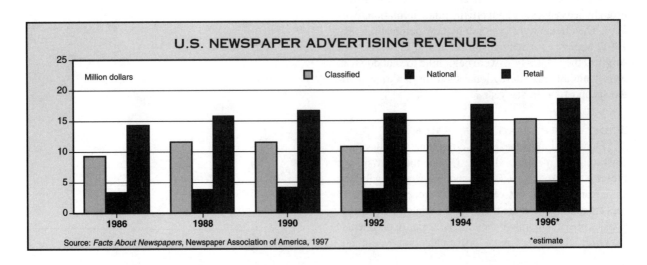

U.S. NEWSPAPER ADVERTISING REVENUES

Source: *Facts About Newspapers*, Newspaper Association of America, 1997

*estimate

FREQUENCY

Frequency of publication is another variable among newspapers. The papers with the greatest circulation are dailies; most of these issue a denser, more expensive Sunday edition. There are far more weeklies in operation, though their circulation is smaller. The two most common types of weeklies are the community newspaper and the alternative newspaper.

ADVERTISING

Most newspapers rely on circulation and advertising to finance their operations. Measured in linage, advertising amounts to about 80 percent of an average newspaper's income. Placement of advertisements is a significant factor; the section and page of an ad, as well as its size, will determine its price. Department stores traditionally have been a major source of advertising dollars, filling pages with pictures of their merchandise. Classified advertising is also a reliable and profitable endeavor for newspapers, adding up to 37 percent of total advertising income. This type of advertising is sold by the word.

SALES

Newspapers are sold in vending machines and privately owned newsstands, or by subscriptions which allow customers to pay a reduced rate per issue and have the paper delivered to their home or business. Newspapers profit from subscribers because they mean guaranteed, consistent sales. In determining a price for newspapers, publishers have to weigh the potential earnings from sales against what readers are willing to pay.

PRODUCTION COSTS

Averaging 50-60 percent of total costs, personnel represents the largest expenditure for newspapers. Departments include management, editorial, advertising, circulation, and production. Within the editorial department, the staff is divided according to paper sections, which may include: local and national news, sports, entertainment and the arts, business, opinion, and others, depending on the paper's size and focus.

Newsprint is the second-highest expenditure, averaging one-quarter of total costs. The United States consumes more than one-third of the world's newsprint, most of that going for the nation's newspapers. A dip in newsprint costs can save a newspaper during hard times, and since a failed newspaper means loss of business for the newsprint manufacturer, most offer substantial discounts from list prices. However, publishers such as the New York Times Company and the Tribune Company also own paper mills, and consequently suffer when newsprint sells at a low price. Equipment such as printing presses and cameras represents the third-largest expense for newspapers.

WORK FORCE

The newspaper industry employed 4.4 million people in 1996, including more than 2 million women. Production workers accounted for 34 percent of total employees, earning an average hourly wage of $12.39.

SIC 2711 - Newspapers
General Statistics

Year	Com-panies	Establishments		Employment			Compensation		Production ($ million)			
		Total	with 20 or more employees	Total (000)	Production Workers (000)	Hours (Mil)	Payroll ($ mil)	Wages ($/hr)	Cost of Materials	Value Added by Manufacture	Value of Shipments	Capital Invest.
1982	7,520	8,846	2,555	401.5	147.2	259.3	6,554.7	9.20	6,006.4	15,275.3	21,276.3	1,029.2
1983				404.1	150.0	263.6	7,059.1	9.86	5,991.5	17,298.2	23,259.4	991.3
1984				398.6	148.5	264.9	7,366.7	10.24	6,429.3	18,871.7	25,302.2	1,086.6
1985				411.0	151.3	265.9	7,904.7	10.64	6,584.6	20,426.3	27,014.7	1,429.7
1986				420.0	151.9	270.0	8,380.5	10.79	7,024.5	22,168.6	29,205.9	1,296.0
1987	7,465	9,091	2,617	434.4	148.4	262.6	9,025.0	11.38	7,533.4	24,310.7	31,850.1	1,522.7
1988				432.4	146.4	262.5	9,348.9	11.42	8,038.3	24,891.9	32,926.8	1,631.3
1989		8,605	2,832	430.9	147.4	253.8	9,842.3	11.82	8,218.4	25,929.7	34,145.8	1,984.5
1990				443.4	149.2	253.2	10,407.1	12.37	8,087.2	26,559.6	34,641.7	1,885.9
1991				428.4	145.1	251.6	10,308.7	12.27	7,606.2	26,092.7	33,702.1	1,537.8
1992	6,762	8,679	2,629	417.0	135.3	235.8	10,506.4	12.89	6,874.0	27,247.0	34,124.3	1,667.4
1993				410.3	131.9	223.8	10,395.5	12.90	6,906.6	27,744.7	34,651.0	1,262.4
1994				410.1	133.7	219.7	10,584.8	13.40	7,018.4	28,817.7	35,837.0	1,329.7
1995				428.3P	135.5P	228.3P	11,572.0P	13.76P	7,598.0P	31,197.7P	38,796.7P	1,721.4P
1996				429.7P	134.1P	224.8P	11,931.9P	14.09P	7,827.1P	32,138.1P	39,966.2P	1,762.3P
1997				431.1P	132.8P	221.3P	12,291.8P	14.42P	8,056.1P	33,078.5P	41,135.6P	1,803.2P
1998				432.5P	131.4P	217.8P	12,651.8P	14.74P	8,285.1P	34,018.9P	42,305.1P	1,844.2P

Sources: 1982, 1987, 1992 *Economic Census*; *Annual Survey of Manufactures*, 83-86, 88-91, 93-94. Establishment counts for non-Census years are from *County Business Patterns*; establishment values for 83-84 are extrapolations. 'P's show projections by the editors. Industries reclassified in 87 will not have data for prior years.

In light of the changes in newspaper management and production during the late 1980s and early 1990s, those working in the industry were obligated to learn new skills and take on new duties. Foremost among these were tasks related to the computer revolution, as word processing programs and developments in page design proliferated in newsrooms. Some of the procedures that were previously the domain of production departments—such as typesetting—were either made obsolete or were dramatically altered with technological developments. In addition, some departmental differences began to disappear, meaning that former specialized positions now required proficiency in many areas, as well as a general knowledge of all newspaper operations.

RESEARCH AND TECHNOLOGY

In the early 1990s, some newspapers began the move toward becoming electronic information providers. They made their databases available to subscribers, creating special editions and enhancing their classified ads. The five newspapers with the highest circulation—the *Wall Street Journal*, *USA Today*, the *New York Times*, the *Los Angeles Times*, and the *Washington Post*—all have online versions. By early 1997, 18 of Gannett's newspapers were online.

Despite being touted as the most important development in the industry since the invention of the printing press, online publications pose some challenges. Creating an online newspaper is both expensive and labor intensive. Since reading an on-screen publication is different than reading a newspaper, design and graphics are even more important and content must be adjusted accordingly. If an online newspaper has no subscription fee, advertisers are relied upon to absorb the costs. If those advertisers support an online version, they may pull their dollars from the print version. Finally, it is not clear if there are enough potential readers. In 1997, 15 to 20 percent of U.S. households had computers with modems; at what rate this market will grow is uncertain.

A 1996 survey by American Opinion Research indicated that while 45 percent of newspaper editors felt that the online services would hurt them in the long term, 44 percent said they believed online services would prove beneficial to the industry.

ASSOCIATIONS AND SOCIETIES

AMERICAN SOCIETY OF NEWSPAPER EDITORS
PO Box 4090
Reston, VA 22090-1700
Phone: (703) 648-1444
Fax: (703) 476-6125

AUDIT BUREAU OF CIRCULATIONS (ABC)
900 N. Meacham Rd.
Schaumburg, IL 60173-4968
Phone: (708) 605-0909
Fax: (708) 605-0483
Verifies newspaper and periodical circulation statements. Includes a Business Publications Industry Committee and a Magazine Directors Advisory Committee.

FULFILLMENT MANAGEMENT ASSOCIATION (FMA)
60 E. 42nd St., Ste. 1146
New York, NY 10165
Phone: (212) 661-1410
Fax: (212) 661-1412
Members includes publishing circulation executives. Includes a Training and Education Committee and a Career Guidance Committee.

SIC 2711 - Newspapers
Industry Data by State

| State | Establish-ments | Shipments | | | Employment | | | | Cost as % of Shipments | Investment per Employee ($) |
		Total ($ mil)	% of U.S.	Per Establ.	Total Number	% of U.S.	Per Establ.	Wages ($/hour)		
California	692	4,443.4	13.0	6.4	52,300	12.5	76	12.93	20.0	2,843
New York	504	3,341.4	9.8	6.6	31,600	7.6	63	18.34	21.0	5,927
Florida	329	2,189.3	6.4	6.7	22,800	5.5	69	12.51	19.7	2,162
Texas	634	1,938.4	5.7	3.1	20,800	5.0	33	10.33	24.8	1,572
Illinois	430	1,788.3	5.2	4.2	19,700	4.7	46	13.25	19.3	3,386
Pennsylvania	306	1,677.1	4.9	5.5	21,900	5.3	72	14.85	20.4	12,484
Ohio	286	1,364.0	4.0	4.8	16,600	4.0	58	12.63	20.0	7,446
Massachusetts	188	1,191.2	3.5	6.3	14,800	3.5	79	14.82	17.7	2,203
New Jersey	186	1,134.6	3.3	6.1	11,900	2.9	64	17.18	23.1	5,689
Virginia	174	1,065.6	3.1	6.1	11,300	2.7	65	10.24	22.2	1,699

Source: 1992 Economic Census. The states are in descending order of shipments or establishments (if shipment data are missing for the majority). The symbol (D) appears when data are withheld to prevent disclosure of competitive information. States marked with (D) are sorted by number of establishments. A dash (-) indicates that the data element cannot be calculated; * indicates the midpoint of a range.

NATIONAL FEDERATION OF PRESS WOMEN
PO Box 99,
Blue Springs, MO 64013
Phone: (816) 229-1666

NATIONAL NEWSPAPER ASSOCIATION
1525 Wilson Blvd., Ste. 550
Arlington, VA 22209
Phone: (703) 907-7900
Fax: (703) 907-7901

NATIONAL PRESS CLUB
National Press Bldg.,
529 14th St. NW
Washington, DC 20045
Phone: (202) 662-7500
Fax: (202) 662-7512

THE NEWSPAPER GUILD
8611 2nd Ave.
Silver Spring, MO 20910
Phone: (301) 585-2990

PERIODICALS AND NEWSLETTERS

***EDITOR AND PUBLISHER - THE FOURTH ESTATE:
SPOT NEWS AND FEATURES ABOUT NEWSPAPERS,
ADVERTISERS AND AGENCIES***
Editor and Publisher Co., Inc.
11 W 19th St., 10 Fl.
New York, NY 10011
Phone: (212) 675-4380
Fax: (212) 691-6939
*Weekly. $55.00 per year. Trade journal of the newspaper
industry.*

NEWSINC
Simba Information, Inc.
P.O. 7430
Wilton, CT 06897-7430
Phone: (203) 834-0033
Fax: (203) 834-1771
*Biweekly. $395.00 per year. Newsletter. Reports on trends in
mass media, especially with regard to newspaper publishing.*

NEWSINC.: THE BUSINESS OF NEWSPAPERS
SIMBA Information, Inc.
PO Box 4234
Stamford, CT 06907-0234
Phone: (800) 307-2529 or (203) 358-4344
Fax: (203) 358-5824
*Biweekly. $425.00 per year. Newsletter. Reports on trends in
mass media, especially with regard to newspaper publishing.
Articles on cable TV and other competitive media are included.*

NEWSPAPER FINANCIAL EXECUTIVES JOURNAL
International Newspaper Financial Executives
1600 Sunrise Valley Dr.
Reston, VA 22091
Phone: (703) 648-1160
Fax: (703) 476-5961
*10 times a year. $100.00. Provides financially related
information to newspaper executives.*

PUBLISHERS' AUXILIARY
National Newspaper Association
1525 Wilson Blvd. 550
Arlington, VA 22209-2411
Phone: (202) 466-7200
Biweekly. $55.00 per year.

DATABASES

***GALE DATABASE OF PUBLICATIONS AND BROADCAST
MEDIA***
Gale Research
835 Penobscot Bldg.
Detroit, MI 48226-4094
Phone: (800) 877-GALE or (313) 961-2242
Fax: (313) 961-6083
*An online directory containing detailed information on over
67,000 periodicals, newspapers, broadcast stations, cable sys-
tems, directories, and newsletters. Corresponds to the following
print sources:* Gale Directory of Publications and Broadcast
Media; Directories in Print; City and State Directories in Print;
Newsletters in Print. *Semiannual updates. Inquire as to online
cost and availability.*

INFORMATION BANK ABSTRACTS
New York Times Co.
229 W 43rd St.
New York, NY 10036
Phone: (212) 556-3575
Fax: (212) 556-1629
*Provides indexing and abstracting of current affairs, primarily
from the final late edition of* The New York Times *and the
Eastern edition of* The Wall Street Journal. *Time period is 1969
to present, with daily updates. Inquire as to online cost and
availability.*

MANAGEMENT CONTENTS
Information Access Corp.
362 Lakeside Dr.
Foster City, CA 94404
Phone: (800) 227-8431 or (415) 378-5000
Fax: (415) 358-4759
*Covers a wide range of management, financial, marketing, per-
sonnel, and administrative topics. About 140 leading business
journals are indexed and abstracted from 1974 to date, with
monthly updating. Inquire as to online cost and availability.*

NATIONAL NEWSPAPER INDEX
Information Access Corp.
362 Lakeside Dr.
Foster City, CA 94404
Phone: (800) 227-8431 or (415) 378-5000
Fax: (415) 358-4759
*Citations to news items in five major newspapers, 1979 to
present. Inquire as to online cost and availability.*

NEWSPAPER AND PERIODICAL ABSTRACTS
UMI/Data Courier
620 S 3rd St.
Louisville, KY 40202
Phone: (800) 626-2823 or (502) 583-4111
Fax: (502) 589-5572

Provides online coverage (citations and abstracts) of more than 25 major newspapers and about 1,000 general interest and professional periodicals. Covers business, current affairs, health, fitness, education, technology, government, consumer affairs, social problems, and many other subject areas. Time period is 1986 to date, with daily updates. Inquire as to online cost and availability.

TRADE & INDUSTRY INDEX
Information Access Co.
362 Lakeside Dr.
Foster City, CA 94404
Phone: (800) 227-8431 or (415) 378-5000
Fax: (415) 358-4759
Provides indexing of business periodicals, January 1981 to date. Daily updates. (Full text articles from some periodicals are available online, 1983 to date, in the companion database, Trade & Industry ASAP.) Inquire as to online cost and availability.

STATISTICS SOURCES

CIRCULATION [YEAR]
SRDS
1700 Higgins Rd.
Des Plaines, IL 60018
Phone: (800) 851-7737 or (847) 375-5000
Fax: (847) 375-5001
Annual. $165.00. Contains detailed statistical analysis of newspaper circulation by metropolitan area or county and data on television viewing by area. Includes maps.

U.S. INDUSTRIAL OUTLOOK: FORECASTS FOR SELECTED MANUFACTURING AND SERVICE INDUSTRIES
Available from U.S. Government Printing Office
Washington, DC 20402
Phone: (202) 512-1800
Fax: (202) 512-2250
Annual. $37.00. (Replaced in 1995 by U.S. Global Trade Outlook.) Issued by the International Trade Administration, U.S. Department of Commerce. Provides basic data, outlook for the current year, and "Long-Term Prospects" (five-year projections) for a wide variety of products and services. Includes high technology industries.

- Gopher://gopher.umsl.edu:70/11/library/govdocs/usio94

GENERAL WORKS

EDITOR AND PUBLISHER INTERNATIONAL YEARBOOK
Editor and Publisher Co., Inc.
11 W 19th St., 10 Fl.

New York, NY 10011
Phone: (212) 675-4380
Fax: (212) 691-6939
Annual. $100.00.

NATIONAL DIRECTORY OF COMMUNITY NEWSPAPERS
American Newspaper Representatives, Inc.
1000 Shelard Pky., No. 360
Minneapolis, MN 55426
Phone: (800) 752-6237 or (612) 545-1116
Fax: (612) 545-1481

NEWSPAPER RATES AND DATA
Standard Rate & Data Service, Inc.
2000 Clearwater Dr.
Oak Brook, IL 60521
Phone: (800) 323-4601 or (708) 574-6000
Fax: (708) 574-6541
Monthly. $485.00 per year. Advertising rates and other information about daily and Sunday newspapers. A complete new directory is issued each month.

NEWSPAPERS ONLINE
Biblio Data
PO Box 61
Needham Heights, MA 02194
Phone: (617) 444-1154
Fax: (617) 449-4584
Annual. $85.00. Provides information on regional and national newspapers in North Americathat are available online in full text. Includes data relating to electronic availability and electronic file inclusions policy.

FURTHER READING

Editor & Publisher Interactive. New York: The Editor & Publisher Co., 1997. Available from http://mediainfo.elpress.com.

Foroohar, Kambiz. "Chip Off the Old Block." *Forbes,* June 17, 1996.

Lazich, Robert S., ed. *Market Share Reporter.* Detroit: Gale Research, 1997.

Welcome to the Newspaper Association of America. Vienna, VA: Newspaper Association of America, 1997. Available from http://www.naa.org.

Welcome to Hoover's Online. Austin, TX: Hoover's, Inc., 1997.

Ziegler, Bart. "Stop the Presses: Publishers Scramble into On-line Services, but Payoff is Unclear." *Wall Street Journal,* April 26, 1995. ◀━━

As technological advancements within the computer industry keep automating more and more tasks, the future of the miscellaneous office machines seems bleak. The need for equipment such as typewriters and dictaphones has diminished, since the computer can perform all of the tasks for which these speciality machines were designed. As computer pricing becomes more competitive, computers will continue to pull the consumer away from the speciality machine market.

INDUSTRY SNAPSHOT

In the early 1990s, sales of miscellaneous office machines declined due to increased use of computers, foreign competition, lackluster economic growth, increased productivity, reduced corporate spending, and U.S. demographic changes. The value of shipments for the industry reached approximately $3.65 billion in 1994, but dropped every year since. In 1996 industry shipments were estimated to reach $3.16 billion; and by 1998, were expected to drop to $2.95 billion. The number of establishments in the office machines industry has also continuously decreased throughout the 1990s.

Top 9 — TOP OFFICE EQUIPMENT SHIPMENTS, 1996

Ranked by: Shipments in thousands of units.

1. Calculators, 55,750
2. Disk drives, 37,500
3. Computers, 24,468
4. Computer Printers, 14,555
5. Modems, 7,200
6. Fax Machines, 4,900
7. Display Terminals, 3,480
8. Typewriters, 2,065
9. Copiers, 1,650

Source: *Appliance Manufacturer*, January 1996, p. 107, from Information Technology Industry Council.

Manufacturers responded to the more competitive environment of the 1990s by integrating the latest technology into new product offerings, infiltrating new channels of distribution, and targeting home offices. In 1995, the number of business start-ups hit a 12-year high of 810,000.

INDUSTRY OUTLOOK

At the same time that computers and cellular phones were making industry waves, the U.S. business machine market experienced an economic recession in the late 1980s, due to reduced expenditures by large businesses. Revenues from miscellaneous business machines fell to about $3.2 billion in 1987. Although sales picked up in 1988 and 1989, shipments only reached $3.5 to $4.0 billion per year before slumping again in the early 1990s.

In addition to alternative technologies and the economic recession, manufacturers were also facing a more competitive market in the 1980s and early 1990s. Many products, such as typewriters and facsimile machines, had become low-cost commodity items that offered slim profit margins. In response to price competition from both domestic and foreign manufacturers, many U.S. companies moved their production operations overseas or increased automation in domestic facilities. The number of establishments in the industry dropped 23 percent from 1990 to 1996. As a result, industry employment in the United States plummeted from about 45,000 in 1982 to an estimated 20,000 going into the latter part of the 1990s.

INDUSTRY RESPONSE

In response to inclement market conditions, manufacturers tried to remain competitive. Besides diverting investments into competing industries, such as computer-related office products, producers tailored product offerings to appeal to the growth market of the 1990s—small businesses.

In 1989, industry analysts predicted that 25 million home offices would exist by the mid-1990s. Instead, about 40 million home offices emerged, representing an increase in 1992 of 2.2 million. Because the average home office spent $40 to $50 per week on business supplies, manufacturers catered to this segment.

While producers once sold products primarily through dedicated office device resellers, many companies were using 50 or more different types of retailers to move their equipment in the 1990s. One of the fastest growing distribution channels during this time was the discount superstore and business center, such as Wal-Mart Stores Inc., Office Depot, and Kmart. In the mid-1990s, manufacturers distributed an estimated 7 to 10 percent of their shipments through these retail chains, and some industry participants suggested that this figure would eventually exceed 20 or 30 percent. By 1997, there were more than 1,600 superstores in the North American market, with a potential for more than 3,000 stores according to some industry analysts.

Manufacturers were also boosting sales by emphasizing distribution through equipment leasing companies. Many businesses favored the lease agreement in order to take advantage of changing technology and certain tax benefits. In addition, leasing allowed companies to reduce their capital equipment investment—an important point in the capital-starved environment of the 1990s.

Some manufacturers looked forward to increased sales in Mexico as a result of the North American Free Trade Agreement (NAFTA), which was expected to increase capital spending in that nation. Furthermore, some competitors hoped to shore up their bottom line by moving manufacturing facilities south, where they could take advantage of inexpensive labor and a loosely regulated manufacturing environment.

ORGANIZATION AND STRUCTURE

TYPEWRITERS

Typewriters and word processing machines accounted for the largest segment of the miscellaneous business machines industry in the 1990s, representing more than 40 percent of total shipments. While most of the units sold were electronic typewriters, some companies were still marketing electromechanical typewriters, which resemble traditional manual typewriters, but use electricity to reduce the effort required by the typist and to increase the quality of type.

Electronic typewriters take the electromechanical concept a step further by reducing the number of moving parts and featuring advanced capabilities. For instance, many electronic typewriters can recall a series of pressed keys and then delete those characters from a sheet of paper on command. Some units also allow the typist to store a word or phrase in the machine's memory, which automatically recalls and prints on command.

A third model of typewriter is the personal word processor (PWP). PWPs allow the typist to view text on a screen before it is actually transferred to paper, much like a personal computer (PC). Most PWPs are simply an electronic typewriter with a liquid crystal display and a central processing unit attached. Unlike PCs, PWPs usually offer access only to internally stored proprietary software programs. Many PWPs are also equipped with spreadsheet software, and some advanced units offered disk drives, DOS compatibility, and hand-held scanners.

Typewriters and PWPs are less expensive and typically regarded as easier to use than most PCs. Compact electronic typewriters typically sold for $250 to $700 in the mid-1990s, while the most advanced PWP models sold for $2,000 to $6,000.

OTHER PRODUCTS

Making up the remaining 50 to 60 percent of the miscellaneous office machines industry are a variety of specialty devices. Dictation machines, for instance, are used by professionals and executives, for whom certain jobs require the recording of their voices for later transcription. Depending on the features offered, dictaphones ranged in price from $150 to $2,500 in the mid-1990s.

Shredders, used to destroy internal printed documents, also account for a slim segment of the market. In the mid-1990s, personal shredders used by small companies and professional practices ranged widely in options and prices. Inexpensive shredders can be purchased for as little as $500, while larger shredders usually started at about $5,000, and industrial, full-featured shredders are available for as much as $100,000.

The facsimile (fax) machine is also an important and popular product in the industry. The fax scans a document and produces electrical signals that are sent to another fax machine, which converts the signals into a copy of the original document. In the mid-1990s, the average large company sent 260 faxes per day, while mid-sized firms sent about 40 faxes per day.

A fifth major segment of the industry consists of mailroom equipment. In fact, various mail machines accounted for about 25 percent of industry sales in the 1990s. Designed to meter, sort, and track mail, such machines are used by the postal service, as well as private organizations. While sorting machines could mean an initial cost of anywhere from $5,000 to $500,000, they greatly reduce the cost of sorting mail manually from $35 per thousand to less than $3 per thousand pieces of mail. The most advanced sorters utilize optical character recognition (OCR) to read addresses and U.S. Postal Service bar codes.

RESEARCH AND TECHNOLOGY

Manufacturers sought to retain market share and revenues by delivering new products and technology in the early 1990s. PWPs represented efforts by typewriter companies to combat the dominance of PCs. New typewriters by Lexmark International Inc., a division of IBM, sought to combine the best features of typewriters and computers.

Competitors were also improving fax machines, often combining the functions of copiers, electronic mail, scanners, and computers into a single unit. In the mid-1990s, Sharp Electronics Corp. introduced the first two-sided, or duplex, fax machine, which could scan, collate, and fax a set of two-sided documents. Major advances were also occurring in the large postal machine market. Datatech, for instance, offered a new machine designed to address business envelopes with Delivery Point Barcodes—a feature that helped reduce postal rates.

ASSOCIATIONS AND SOCIETIES

BUSINESS PRODUCTS INDUSTRY ASSOCIATION
301 N Fairfax St.
Arlington, VA 22314
Phone: (800) 542-6672 or (703) 549-9040
Fax: (703) 683-7552

BUSINESS TECHNOLOGY ASSOCIATION
12411 Wornall Rd.
Kansas City, MO 64145
Phone: (816) 941-3100
Fax: (816) 941-2829

COMPUTER AND BUSINESS EQUIPMENT MANUFACTURERS ASSOCIATION
1250 Eye St. NW, Ste. 200
Washington, DC 20005
Phone: (202) 737-8888
Fax: (202) 638-4922

PERIODICALS AND NEWSLETTERS

MANAGING OFFICE TECHNOLOGY
Penton Publishing
1100 Superior Ave.
Cleveland, OH 44114-2543
Phone: (800) 321-7003 or (216) 696-7000
Fax: (216) 696-7648
Monthly. Free to qualified personnel. $45.00 per year. Special feature issue topics include document imaging, document management, office supplies, and office equipment. Formerly Modern Office Technology.

OFFICE PRODUCTS DEALER BUYING GUIDE AND DIRECTORY
Hitchcock Publishing Co.
191 S. Gary Ave.
Carol Stream, IL 60188
Phone: (708) 665-1000
Fax: (708) 462-2225
Semimonthly. $25.00 per year. Formerly Office Products Dealer.

PRINTER IMPRESSIONS
Buyers Laboratory, Inc.
20 Railroad Ave.
Hackensack, NJ 07601-3309
Phone: (201) 488-0404
Fax: (201) 488-0461
Monthly. $345.00 per year. Newsletter on the typewriter and computer printer industry, including test reports on individual machines. Formerly Typeline.

UPDATE: THE EXECUTIVE'S PURCHASING ADVISOR
Buyers Laboratory, Inc.
20 Railroad Ave.
Hackensack, NJ 07601-3309
Phone: (201) 488-0404
Fax: (201) 488-0464
Semimonthly. $95.00 per year. Newsletter.

DATABASES

GUIDE TO COMPUTER VENDORS

Systems for Business Accounting

Links to more than 800 hardware and software vendors o the world wide web. Includes a directory of several thousand computer companies, and a list of online computer magazines. When established: 1995. Fees: Free.

- URL: http://www.ronin.com/SBA

PROMT: PREDICASTS OVERVIEW OF MARKETS AND TECHNOLOGY

Information Access Co.
362 Lakeside Dr.
Foster City, CA 94404
Phone: (800) 321-6388 or (415) 378-5000
Fax: (415) 358-4759

Companies, products, applied technologies and markets. U.S. and international literature coverage, 1972 to date. Daily updates. Inquire as to online cost and availability. Provides abstracts from more than 1,200 publications.

STATISTICS SOURCES

COMPUTERS AND OFFICE AND ACCOUNTING MACHINES

U.S. Bureau of the Census
Washington, DC 20233-0800
Phone: (301) 457-4100
Fax: (301) 457-3842

Annual. Provides data on shipments: value, quantity, imports, and exports. (Current Industrial Reports, MA-35R.)

FURTHER READING

Darnay, Arsen, ed. *Manufacturing USA.* 5th ed. Detroit: Gale Research, 1996. ◆

Companies performing oil and gas exploration services are most often divisions or subsidiaries of major oil companies, although the industry also boasts several significant independent contractors. Many of the industry's leaders are known as integrated companies, which cover the entire oil and gas industry, from exploration to refining to distribution. As such, the exploration branch of the industry is affected by trends in the field as a whole. Two hundred fewer wells were completed in 1995 than the previous year. In 1995 crude oil reserves decreased by 106 million barrels to 22,351 million barrels. Natural gas reserves showed an increase of 1,309 billion cubic feet (Bcf) to 165,146 Bcf.

OIL AND GAS FIELD SERVICES

SIC 1380

In 1996 the production of oil in the United States was 6.74 million barrels per day (b/d), with 1.4 million b/d from Alaska and the remainder from the lower 48 states. Alaska is seen as the only state with the possibility of harboring large untapped oil and gas reserves, but new exploration on federally owned lands in the region has been forbidden by Congress due to growing environmental concerns. The only real growth sector for the industry is offshore, primarily in the Gulf of Mexico. Despite these restrictions on exploration, the Department of Energy (DOE) has forecasted strong opportunities for the export of U.S. energy services and technology through 2010.

TOP OILFIELD SERVICE PROVIDERS, 1995

Ranked by: Revenues, in millions of dollars.

1. Schlumberger, with $7,339 million
2. Halliburton, $5,602
3. Dresser Industries, $5,392
4. Western Atlas, $2,191
5. BJ Services, $574
6. Tidewater, $561

Source: *Forbes,* January 1, 1996, from Value Line Data Base Service and OneSource Information Services.

In 1995 there were a total of 21,750 wells in the continental United States, a decrease of 8,600 from 1990; of these, 8,257 were completed for oil; 8,363 for gas; and 5,130 were dry holes. The major American companies focused their exploration efforts elsewhere in the world, especially in the Middle East and the Commonwealth of Independent States. Despite slow American growth, the oil industry drilled 48,287 wells in 1990 (46 percent oil, 25 percent gas, and 22 percent dry). Of those outside the United States, nearly 92 percent of the drill sites established were offshore, illustrating increased industry reliance on difficult to locate undersea reserves.

The well head price for crude oil has shown a sharp increase from the early 1990s. It averaged $16.54 in 1991, and hit a high of $23.02 in the fourth quarter of 1996. Crude prices have fallen slightly, and are expected

---

to average between $21.00 and $21.50 per barrel. The average decline of about $1.00 per barrel was seen in the first quarter of 1997, partially due to the influx of Iraqi oil. Iraq has been permitted to sell oil on the world market, about 600,000 barrels a day, for humanitarian reasons (supplying its people with food and medicine). Gasoline prices also are expected to rise to $1.32 per gallon in the first quarter of 1997, up 12 cents from last year.

During recent years, when both oil and gas prices were low, service companies had been in demand to aid in workovers of existing wells, rather than assist in the costly process of new well generation. Service companies with technologically advanced products and services have fared the best, offering well production service that is both affordable, yet profitable.

Consumption of natural gas has also increased, gaining 3.8 percent over 1992's rate to capture approximately 25 percent of the U.S. energy market in 1993. In 1996, 21.99 trillion cubic feet (tcf) of natural gas was consumed, and usage was expected to rise to 22.38 tcf in 1997 and 23.25 tcf in 1998. Natural gas is expected to maintain its popularity throughout the decade. This preference will be beneficial to service companies, since it should translate into an increase in drilling sites and, subsequently, site maintenance opportunities.

For the most part, in the first half of the 1990s, U.S. exploration has been centered in the Gulf of Mexico and has been aimed at replacing lost production from maturing sites. According to Hanifen Imhoff Inc., natural gas prices and deliverability have been the primary drivers of drilling activity in the United States, especially in the Gulf of Mexico. In 1992, for example, 52 percent of rigs in operation were looking for oil, 46 percent for natural gas, and 2 percent other. In 1995, these U.S. rigs delivered their most production at 52.4 Bcf per day, and including Canadian exports of 8.1 Bcf per day, the implied maximum deliverability for U.S. natural gas markets was 60.5 Bcf/day. According to Hanifen Imhoff, given 1995's average consumption of 59.4 Bcf/day, the yield on an industry operating at 98.2 percent capacity had an very narrow 1.1 Bcf/day cushion.

Environmental concerns have also increased the cost of local drilling, further spurring American exploration firms to turn their attention to drilling outside of the United States, where regulation is sometimes slack and the possibility of untapped reserves significant. While exploration services underwent shifts in fortune prior to the 1990s, those changes were most often due to economic or political factors (such as the OPEC oil embargo of the mid-1970s) rather than environmental ones. The Oil Pollution Liability and Compensation Act of 1990 and the Clean Air Act of 1990, however, had some direct

Oilfield Service Providers

The leading companies in oilfield services are ranked by 1995 revenues in millions of dollars.

Schlumberger	$ 7,339
Halliburton	5,602
Dresser Industries	5,392
Western Atlas	2,191
BJ Services	574
Tidewater	561

Source: *Forbes*, January 1, 1996, p. 124, from Value Line Data Base Service and OneSource Information Services.

effect on exploration practices (the latter, among other things, tightened emission standards for offshore drilling activity). But most effects on exploration remained indirect—most new regulation and fines applied to vehicles, oil refineries, ships, and pipeline operations—the costs of which would reach oil and gas companies in general and then trickle down to exploration expenditures. With government rewarding the use of diesel fuel alternatives, more energy is being put into natural gas exploration and production than into crude oil.

ORGANIZATION AND STRUCTURE

Companies classified in this industry provide services intended to increase or improve well production. Services are provided throughout the life of the well, including the initial drilling, the completion phase that sets production, and the maintenance or stimulation of existing wells. Drilling for natural gas is similar to drilling for oil, but gas must be liquefied before it can be shipped. Apart from the natural gas liquids (NGL) that occur naturally at a well, all gas obtained must be cooled and pressurized into liquid natural gas (LNG) for transportation. NGL is mainly ethane, propane, butane, and natural gasoline; the gas from LNG is mainly composed of propane, propylene, butanes, and butylenes.

Establishments engaged in this industry also often provide routine maintenance work on wells already in production. One of the most common well servicing operations is the artificial lift installation. When a well is first drilled, the fluid is expected to flow to the surface. In order to maintain maximum recovery from the well, however, most need some form of artificial lift to help raise the fluid to the surface. Types of artificial lifts include gas lifts, sucker rod pumps, hydraulic pumps, and submersible pumps. Maintenance service also includes replacing parts, repairing tubing leaks, working on malfunctioning downhole equipment, and providing well clean-out services.

Contract drilling firms, which are the companies that actually drill the oil or gas well, work with the well operators. Operators are the companies that decide what kind of well to drill and determine its specifications. Operators hold the lease rights and operate the lease, as well. According to the *Fundamentals of Petroleum,* almost 98 percent of all gas and oil wells in the United States have been drilled by contract drilling firms. The drilling contractor usually is assisted by other companies, or subcontractors, that furnish specialized well services, such as casing and cementing.

WORK FORCE

With oil and gas prices remaining low, the forecast for jobs in oil and gas exploration is not robust. While cutbacks on the corporate level and in the oilfields continued into 1994, exploration workers, especially those with technical backgrounds, are still needed. Due to American oil companies' increasing focus on foreign drilling, more exploration jobs are available overseas than in the United States. While positions are not as plentiful as they were ten years ago, companies continue to hire engineers and geoscientists, and there is a steadily growing need for workers skilled in information technology, and this need will continue through the end of the 1990s.

Oil and gas exploration teams require a variety of subject expertise. Geophysicists, who apply the principles of physics to the science of geology, and geologists, who study the formation of the earth, evaluate incoming data from seismic vessels and onshore data collection. They then use sophisticated computer systems to interpret the data and make recommendations for when and where to drill. Engineers are needed to design oil and gas rigs and to oversee their use on site. Oil rig workers, who may live for weeks at a time on offshore rigs, are needed to operate the equipment. The oil companies themselves employ executive and clerical staff on the corporate level, but in the wake of increased cutbacks in the 1990s, these jobs are increasingly difficult to obtain, and companies are relying more and more on contract or freelance work instead of large permanent staffs.

According to the U.S. Department of Labor, approximately 160,000 people were employed by the Oil and Gas Field Services in early 1996. This figure illustrates a decrease from the 168,000 employees reported by the Department of Labor in 1995, and a dramatic drop from 1990's total of 198,300 people.

RESEARCH AND TECHNOLOGY

As the large oil companies cut back on domestic exploration through the 1990s, it became even more important to make as certain as possible the profitability of those explorations that were undertaken. Advances in research and technology in the contract drilling industry will continue to be the most critical factor to keep companies competitive. Technology for assessing the shape of underground earth formations and oil and gas deposits was introduced as early as 1927 by Schlumberger Ltd., which maintained a hold on the industry through 1996, with nearly $9 billion in annual revenues. Schlumberger's Maxis service, which assesses the characteristics of earth around a well, was introduced in the early 1990s. At a time when profits were flat and downsizing common, Schlumberger doubled its jobs in 1992, testament to the industry's ever-increasing reliance on high technology.

But Maxis was only one of many high-technology innovations that reduced oil exploration costs and more than halved finding costs for natural gas in the late 1980s and early 1990s. Other innovations included horizontal drilling, three-dimensional (3-D) seismography, and improvements in drilling in light sands. The majority of innovation is in offshore drilling, which requires much technological innovation in both the exploration and drilling stages. The Machar project in the North Sea used both advanced technology and an innovative system to tap a difficult oil well. Discovered in 1972 and estimated to hold 55 million barrels of recoverable oil, the reservoir was too complex to evaluate with the technology of the day, and considered too marginal economically.

In 1994, British Petroleum enlisted what became the Turnkey Additional Production (TAP) alliance, which drew together contractors to supply the best possible solutions, one of them being Schlumberger Integrated Project Management (IPM), managing well engineering and well construction. All parties participated in risk and reward, so all focused on reducing risk, maximizing efficiency, and maximizing return. Decisions were made rapidly by those nearest the action, instead of relying on a chain of management. The results were quick and impressive; instead of the usual one to two years typical when using the conventional approach, appraisal oil flowed in just 19 weeks. At the end of the 25-month project, there had been no work loss due to accidents, no leaks or spills, and an overall efficiency 7 percent above plan.

Three-dimensional (3-D) seismography, although invented in the 1960s, only became viable in the 1980s with advances in the computer and acoustical industries.

Ships equipped with two cables each carrying two source arrays (or "seismic streamers") cruise areas of suspected undersea oil and gas deposits. The streamers give off electric or air detonations whose waves are reflected off underwater rock formations below the level of the sea floor. Data is then processed onshore and the undersea floor mapped; although ships cover much terrain, it can take as much as a year and a half to interpret the data gained from 100 square miles. Because of the presence of above ground structures, 3-D seismography is impractical on land. Instead, trucks called "thumpers" send sonic waves through the ground by hammering the earth at specific sites; the wave data is then collected and interpreted.

Data interpretation is highly technical and involved; it uses excessive amounts of computer storage space, plus specialized computer software that sorts and analyzes the reams of incoming data. Advances in proprietary hardware and software are speeding up the process. Other technological advancements already in use are rig computerization and automation for daily drilling operations, such as Microsoft's Project Manager software.

The most promising areas to slash costs are in wellbore stability, described in *Drilling Contractor* as "the root of stuck-pipe problems that causes sidetracking, reaming back to bottom, numerous short trips, and excessive time spent conditioning the hole." One technological advancement that would assist in producing a stable hole is the development of a drilling fluid that would be as productive as an oil-base mud, but without the environmental drawbacks. The industry also needs to develop better techniques for waste handling and disposal in order to comply with environmental regulations.

Horizontal drilling uses drill bits driven by motors actually in the bits, instead of above ground motors, and can be directed with the help of computers and detailed mapping. Drillers use horizontal drilling in aging fields where earlier attempts might have missed oil trapped in narrow, vertical rock formations. Texas has remained the dominant region for horizontal drilling, with 80.7 percent of all horizontal wells. Some companies have begun to use the technique to search for new discoveries in North Dakota, Wyoming, and Colorado, where rock layers are similar to the ones in Texas fields, according to the *New York Times*.

Horizontal drilling activity has declined since its peak in 1991, but the decline mirrors that of the overall domestic drilling activity. Independent operators have been the most inclined to employ horizontal drilling, according to an Independent Petroleum Association of America (IPAA) survey of its members. Over 40 percent of the operators surveyed expect to participate in a horizontal drilling venture by 1995.

AMERICA AND THE WORLD

The American oil and gas industry is inextricably linked to the world industry. Because decisions about exploration are linked to the proven reserves of oil and gas available, it is important to note that over 75 percent of proven oil reserves are controlled by the Organization of Petroleum Exporting Countries (OPEC), although the vast majority of oil is consumed by non-OPEC nations, giving OPEC a tremendous influence on the world oil and gas market. American oil exploration, and that of other non-OPEC countries, has slowed in contrast to OPEC exploration. With the end of the Gulf War, members of OPEC followed the lead of relatively moderate Saudi Arabia and stabilized their pricing while increasing both exploration and production.

Meanwhile, the major U.S.-based petroleum companies are becoming increasingly involved in foreign exploration. In the early 1990s, money allocated to foreign exploration and development topped 50 percent of all exploration spending, as compared to 27 percent in the mid-1980s. In 1996, Exxon Corporation spent twice as much on foreign exploration as for domestic. Mobil Corporation spent $830 million on domestic exploration and $1.8 billion on overseas. In addition to the decreasing domestic exploration, world political and economic developments of the 1990s have made it more feasible and profitable to increase American investment in foreign exploration. Along with maintaining an already strong presence in the Mexican and Latin American markets, U.S. companies have increased investments in other areas of the world.

The dissolution of the Soviet Union provided increased opportunities for investment in that area's oil reserves. The Commonwealth of Independent States (CIS) saw the rise of joint exploration and drilling ventures, especially in Russia, between U.S. and Russian companies. Another area of increasing American investment is Southeast Asia, where U.S. exploration spending grew the most from the mid-1980s to the mid-1990s. The economies of Asian countries have become increasingly industrialized in recent years, and many governments in Asia, including China and Vietnam, have actively courted foreign investment and participation in local drilling by outside companies.

Companies from the United States have played roles in the discovery and production of oil in major fields in Mexico, Venezuela, Saudi Arabia, Kuwait, and Libya. Overseas operations have been particularly interested in service companies because of their ability to provide well workover and stimulation services to existing wells. Many countries have numerous wells in existence, but due to a lack of technology, have not been able to maximize production.

Latin America and Africa also are growing markets. The natural gas resources in South America are largely underdeveloped, but the industry is expected to undergo increased development, incurring a need for skilled personnel to build and maintain rigs and pipelines. The oil wells of Columbia and Peru are expected to double their production by the end of the century. Several natural gas pipeline projects are also planned in South America, the two most ambitious being the Bolivia-Brazil pipeline and the Argentina-Chile pipeline. After the year 2000, the African nations of Chad, the Ivory Coast, and Somalia, among others, are expected to join the market as oil producers.

The Department of Energy (DOE) has forecasted strong opportunities for the export of U.S. energy services and technology through 2010. The international market for oil and gas exploration, excluding former Eastern bloc nations and China, has been predicted to increase to $1.3 trillion per year from 1991 through 2010, as reported in *Oil & Gas Journal*. The DOE has estimated that U.S. vendors can capture $955 billion or 74 percent of that market.

Although overseas work can prove to be lucrative, it is not without its problems, most of which are not related to the task of drilling. Instead, contractors will have to learn about customs, work habits, and social behaviors for each country. Also, each market is decisively different, so what is known about one market will not be easily transferred to the next. Moreover, some overseas markets have grown to expect contract drillers to provide integrated services, ''where the driller's participation in the planning and the management of the drilling programs are the norm rather than the exception,'' reported Luigs in *Oil & Gas Journal*.

SOCIETY OF PETROLEUM ENGINEERS
PO Box 833836
Richardson, TX 75083-3836
Phone: (214) 669-3377
Fax: (214) 669-0135

PERIODICALS AND NEWSLETTERS

DRILLING MAGAZINE
Associated Publishers, Inc.
4703 W. Lover
Dallas, TX 75209
Phone: (214) 358-3456
Monthly. $34.50 per year.

JPT JOURNAL OF PETROLEUM TECHNOLOGY
Society of Petroleum Engineers
PO Box 833836
Richardson, TX 75083
Phone: (214) 952-9393
Monthly. $30.00 per year. Covers oil and gas exploration, drilling and production, engineering management, reservoir engineering, geothermal energy sources and emerging technologies. Also includes society news, programs, events and activities.

OIL, GAS, AND PETROCHEM EQUIPMENT
Penn Well Publishing Co.
PO Box 1260
Tulsa, OK 74101
Phone: (918) 835-3161
Monthly. Free to qualified personnel, others, $32.00 per year.

WORLD OIL
Gulf Publishing Co.
PO Box 2608
Houston, TX 77252
Phone: (800) 231-6275 or (713) 529-4301
Monthly. $24.00 per year. Covers worldwide oil and gas exploration, drilling and production.

ASSOCIATIONS AND SOCIETIES

PETROLEUM EQUIPMENT INSTITUTE
PO Box 2380
Tulsa, OK 74101
Phone: (918) 494-9696

PETROLEUM EQUIPMENT SUPPLIES ASSOCIATION
9225 Katy Fwy., Ste. 310
Houston, TX 77024
Phone: (713) 932-0168

STATISTICS SOURCES

THE OIL AND GAS PRODUCING INDUSTRY IN YOUR STATE
Independent Petroleum Association of America
Petroleum Independent Publishers, Inc.
1101 16th St. NW
Washington, DC 20036
Phone: (202) 857-4722
Annual. $75.00.

GENERAL WORKS

COMPOSITE CATALOG OF OIL FIELD EQUIPMENT AND SERVICES
Gulf Publishing Co.
PO Box 2608
Houston, TX 77252
Phone: (800) 231-6275 or (713) 529-4301
Biennial. $1,500.00.

GEOPHYSICAL DIRECTORY
Geophysical Directory, Inc.
2200 Welch Ave.
Houston, TX 77019
Phone: (713) 529-8789
Annual. $40.00. Worldwide coverage of companies and personnel using and providing supplies and services in petroleum and mineral exploration.

OFFSHORE SERVICES AND EQUIPMENT DIRECTORY
Greene Dot, Inc.
PO Box 28663
San Diego, CA 92128
Phone: (619) 485-7237
Annual. $235.00.

OILFIELD EQUIPMENT
Available from Off-the-Shelf Publications, Inc.
2171 Jericho Tpke.
Commack, NY 11725
Phone: (516) 462-2410
Fax: (516) 462-1842
1990. $1,950.00. Published by Leading Edge Reports. Market data with forecasts to 1995 for rotary drilling equipment and production oil well equipment.

OILFIELD SUPPLY INDUSTRY DIRECTORY
Midwest Register, Inc.
601 S. Boulder, Ste. 1001
Tulsa, OK 74119
Phone: (918) 582-2000

Annual. $40.00. Formerly Directory of Oil Well Supply Companies.

WORLD MARKET FOR ENGINES FOR AUTOMOBILES AND INDUSTRIAL VEHICLES
Available from Off-the-Shelf Publications, Inc.
2171 Jericho Tpke.
Commack, NY 11725
Phone: (516) 462-2410
Fax: (516) 462-1842
1990. $2,300.00. Published in Italy by Databank SpA. Market data with forecasts for six countries: U.S., Italy, Japan, Germany, U.K., and France.

FURTHER READING

"Machar and Beyond: A New Path to Profitable Growth." New York: Schlumberger Ltd. Available from http://www.slb.com/ir/ar/ar96/feature/machar1.htm.

"Natural Gas and Offshore Drilling Stocks." Hanifen Imhoff Inc. Investment Bankers, 26 June 1996.

"Oil & Gas News." *Aral Energy News.* Available from http://www.aral.com/newog.htm.

Palmeri, Christopher. "Annual Report on American Industry: Energy" *Forbes,* 13 January 1997.

"Shell Oil Company Announces Highest Ever Annual Net Income." Shell Corp. Available from http://www.shellus.com/news/press012197.html.

"State of the U.S. Oil and Natural Gas Industry." Washington: Independent Petroleum Asssociation of America. Available from http://www.ipaa.org/departments/information_services/state_of_the_industry.htm.

U.S. Department of Energy. Energy Information Administration. "Outlook Assumptions." Available from http://www.eia.doe.gov/emeu/steo/pub/otlkasum.html.

INDUSTRY SNAPSHOT

Over 500 companies in the United States were involved in manufacturing ophthalmic goods in the mid-1990s. These companies expected about $3.39 billion in 1997 shipment values for products covered in this industry classification. This figure represented an aggregate value of shipments largely derived from the production of the four primary products in the ophthalmic goods industry: ophthalmic lenses and frames, sunglasses, industrial eyewear, and contact lenses. Contact lenses, by far the dominant ophthalmic goods product in the mid-1990s, accounted for over 31 percent of the total shipments delivered by the industry, with soft contact lenses representing 22 percent of the contact lens product share. Plastic ophthalmic focus lenses accounted for approximately 15 percent of the industry's shipments, while ophthalmic frames and industrial eyewear each accounted for six percent of the product share. Nonprescription sunglasses represented four percent of the total shipments delivered by the industry. Other products within the ophthalmic goods industry include underwater goggles, reading and simple magnifiers, and an ophthalmic lens coating.

 TOP SPORTS OPTICS PRODUCERS

Ranked by: Sales in 1995, in millions of dollars.

1. Oakley, with $173.0 million
2. Ray Ban, $37.5
3. Bolle, $30.0
4. Smith Optics, $30.0
5. Gargoyles, $5.0

Source: *Sportstyle*, May 1996, p. 48.

The ophthalmic goods industry entered the 1990s with a decade of solid growth behind them, except for a temporary downturn in the mid-1980s. The value of shipments manufactured by the industry rose from $1.28 billion in 1982 to $2.27 billion in 1990, an increase partly attributable to the increasing popularity of sunglasses and to technological innovations in the development of contact lenses.

INDUSTRY OUTLOOK·

Although the number of contact lens wearers in the United States tapered off at approximately 24 million in

OPHTHALMIC GOODS

SIC 3851

The emergence of mail-order and discount ophthalmic good suppliers has optometrists and manufacturers banding together to retain their share of the market. In addition, the possibility of nationwide health care reform has industry leaders concerned about what provisions for vision care will be allowed. Nevertheless, the industry has experienced continued growth, with employment numbers projected on an upward trend, from 28,000 people in 1994 to 31,000 by 1998. Shipment values for products in 1997 was some 3.39 billion, with increases in subsequent years projected.

the four or five years prior to 1992, the dynamics within this segment of the ophthalmic goods industry were rapidly changing in the early 1990s. Disposable soft contact lenses, first marketed by Johnson & Johnson in 1988, grabbed the attention of consumers during the product's first years of availability and were expected to woo many contact lens wearers away from conventional contact lenses in the future. Projected to represent half of the contact lens market by 1995, disposable lenses appear to be the product of the future in the ophthalmic goods industry. Consequently, the ability of contact lens manufacturers to respond to this development could determine their success in the future.

Severely affected by the global recession in the early 1990s, the sunglass market plummeted 36 percent from $1.76 billion in sales in 1991 to $961 million in 1992. Especially sensitive to the health of the national economy, the sunglass market also suffered from its robust growth during the 1980s, as the proliferation of sunglass manufacturers exacerbated the effect of the stagnant economy and saturated the market. The surfeit of manufacturers entering the U.S. market from both the domestic and international fronts does not bode well for the immediate future of sunglass sales, but the growing trend of purchasing sunglasses for protection from ultra-violet rays could expand the market somewhat.

Additionally, pending legislation regarding the restructuring of the nation's healthcare system will undoubtedly affect individuals' ophthalmology coverage, and will in turn have a significant impact on ophthalmic goods manufacturers. Doubts concerning what provisions will be included for the optical industry, which ranks below the medical and dental industries in terms of size and strength, characterized the industry's anxiety the last time national health care legislation was seriously considered in the early and mid-1970s. These same concerns were revisited as the industry entered the mid-1990s.

Another factor in the eye-care industry was the emerging struggle featuring optometrists and manufacturers who joined together against mail-order outlets and, to a lesser degree, other discount outlets, who have sought to gain a share of the market in recent years. Many manufacturers, including the giants of the industry, refuse to sell lenses to mail-order companies or discount outlets that don't have eye-care professionals on-site.

The Contact Lens Council reported that more than half of all Americans needed vision correction of some sort in 1997; this number continues to grow with the aging Baby Boomers. Around 26 million Americans are contact lens wearers. The products that became available in 1995 were daily disposable lenses, and the introduction of additional colored contact lenses (either for cosmetic or prescriptive purposes), which became increasingly popular among lens wearers. Rigid gas permeable (RGP) lenses are also available, that have low content silicone/high decay flourosilicone acrylates.

The eyeglass market began to shift from 1994-1997 towards larger chains like Wal-Mart and LensCrafters.

SIC 3851 - Ophthalmic Goods
General Statistics

Year	Companies	Establishments Total	Establishments with 20 or more employees	Employment Total (000)	Employment Production Workers (000)	Employment Hours (Mil)	Compensation Payroll ($ mil)	Compensation Wages ($/hr)	Production Cost of Materials	Production Value Added by Manufacture	Production Value of Shipments	Production Capital Invest.
1982	389	409	123	26.3	17.3	35.1	416.9	6.13	388.0	886.5	1,287.2	41.6
1983				24.1	15.5	31.1	396.3	6.49	388.4	930.0	1,332.4	29.2
1984				25.1	16.6	33.1	433.0	6.64	398.3	1,009.1	1,350.7	63.5
1985				24.9	15.5	31.2	434.0	6.73	412.4	995.6	1,418.2	78.6
1986				21.7	14.3	28.6	414.6	7.26	472.2	933.5	1,411.2	92.6
1987	480	495	149	24.2	15.8	31.1	477.9	7.55	546.0	1,152.9	1,689.4	76.7
1988				25.5	17.6	33.8	499.9	8.02	621.3	1,345.1	1,945.8	88.6
1989		517	161	25.0	17.8	36.2	500.8	8.36	664.1	1,542.6	2,193.5	146.0
1990				28.0	19.8	40.3	605.0	8.62	672.5	1,625.6	2,274.7	137.2
1991				26.2	17.2	34.8	626.9	9.64	666.4	1,645.2	2,313.0	120.0
1992	526	569	150	29.6	19.9	40.2	716.3	9.59	748.0	1,950.6	2,692.1	202.4
1993				32.0	21.6	41.7	796.7	9.86	838.2	2,173.4	2,983.9	192.4
1994				28.2	18.8	36.4	719.1	10.09	865.9	2,095.6	2,928.5	200.3
1995				29.5P	20.2P	39.8P	769.4P	10.56P	910.1P	2,202.6P	3,078.0P	213.3P
1996				30.0P	20.6P	40.5P	802.0P	10.92P	956.2P	2,314.2P	3,234.0P	227.6P
1997				30.5P	21.0P	41.2P	834.6P	11.27P	1,002.3P	2,425.8P	3,389.9P	241.9P
1998				31.0P	21.4P	42.0P	867.2P	11.63P	1,048.5P	2,537.4P	3,545.9P	256.2P

Sources: 1982, 1987, 1992 Economic Census; Annual Survey of Manufactures, 83-86, 88-91, 93-94. Establishment counts for non-Census years are from County Business Patterns; establishment values for 83-84 are extrapolations. 'P's show projections by the editors. Industries reclassified in 87 will not have data for prior years.

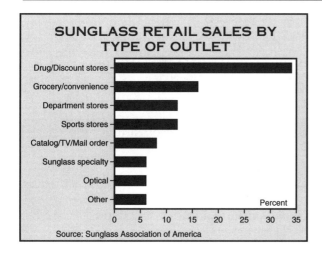

SUNGLASS RETAIL SALES BY TYPE OF OUTLET

Drug/Discount stores

Grocery/convenience

Department stores

Sports stores

Catalog/TV/Mail order

Sunglass specialty

Optical

Other

Percent

0 5 10 15 20 25 30 35

Source: Sunglass Association of America

The sunglass industry was estimated to be $2.5 billion, of which discount department stores were expected to be $183.3 million, although this was hard to estimate because of high theft rates. In addition to fashion being a reason for increased sunglasses sales, consumers were also more concerned about the protection of their eyes from ultraviolet rays on a year-round basis.

ORGANIZATION AND STRUCTURE

The ophthalmic goods industry was predominantly populated by relatively small manufacturing operations. Of the 517 establishments involved in producing ophthalmic goods in 1989, nearly 360, or 68 percent of all the facilities engaged in the industry, employed less than 20 people. Together, these 517 establishments represented all of the facilities operating in the industry that were operated by the approximately 500 companies engaged in manufacturing ophthalmic goods. Typically,

the larger companies do not solely manufacture ophthalmic goods, but rely on manufacturing a diverse line of products to generate sales. For example, the leading company in the industry, Bausch & Lomb Inc., garnered over 60 percent of its sales in 1991 from healthcare products.

A majority of the facilities engaged in manufacturing ophthalmic goods are located in the eastern United States, although California has the greatest number of establishments located in any one state. In terms of regional concentration, New York, New Jersey, and Pennsylvania, contain the most ophthalmic goods facilities, with 101 establishments. The Pacific region, including Alaska and Hawaii, ranked as the second most populated area of ophthalmic goods manufacturing facilities, solely by virtue of the 80 establishments located in California, the only state within the region to contain manufacturing facilities. Michigan, Illinois, and Ohio, home to 65 establishments, represent the nation's third largest regional concentration of ophthalmic facilities.

During the 1980s, the cost of conducting business in the ophthalmic goods industry rose sharply, far outpacing the increase in sales during the decade. In 1982, the industry recorded $1.28 billion in sales and spent $41 million on capital investment. By 1990, sales had climbed to $2.27 billion, but capital investment had more than tripled to $137 million. In 1998, capital investment was expected to reach $2.56 billion. Despite this exponential increase in capital outlays, the average investment of ophthalmic goods facilities was comparatively less expensive than the average investment of facilities in all other manufacturing industries. In 1989, $1,284,526 was the average cost for facilities operating in the ophthalmic goods industry, 72 percent below the $4,542,893 averaged by establishments in all other manufacturing industries. In 1992, the operating cost for the

SIC 3851 - Ophthalmic Goods
Industry Data by State

| State | Establish-ments | Shipments | | | Employment | | | | Cost as % of Shipments | Investment per Employee ($) |
		Total ($ mil)	% of U.S.	Per Establ.	Total Number	% of U.S.	Per Establ.	Wages ($/hour)		
Florida	35	518.1	19.2	14.8	4,500	15.2	129	10.16	25.0	-
California	80	392.8	14.6	4.9	3,800	12.8	48	10.81	22.6	3,211
New York	51	375.1	13.9	7.4	4,600	15.5	90	10.95	22.4	4,761
Texas	36	208.8	7.8	5.8	2,200	7.4	61	6.71	56.2	2,591
Massachusetts	33	171.7	6.4	5.2	2,200	7.4	67	9.48	31.1	-
Minnesota	14	96.3	3.6	6.9	1,300	4.4	93	8.50	39.7	-
New Jersey	25	56.0	2.1	2.2	700	2.4	28	6.50	37.3	2,000
Pennsylvania	25	54.7	2.0	2.2	600	2.0	24	8.20	37.8	3,833
Maryland	10	52.0	1.9	5.2	1,100	3.7	110	8.28	32.3	-
Virginia	11	51.0	1.9	4.6	1,000	3.4	91	8.20	52.5	2,500

Source: 1992 *Economic Census*. The states are in descending order of shipments or establishments (if shipment data are missing for the majority). The symbol (D) appears when data are withheld to prevent disclosure of competitive information. States marked with (D) are sorted by number of establishments. A dash (-) indicates that the data element cannot be calculated; * indicates the midpoint of a range.

industry was $1,314,587 while the average for all manufacturers was $4,239,462.

WORK FORCE

Employment within the industry shrank during the mid-1980s to a low of 21,700 but rebounded by the end of the decade to surpass levels established during the early 1980s. The ophthalmic goods industry employed 28,200 people in 1994, 18,800 of whom were production workers, with the remaining workers performing administrative, technical, or managerial duties. By 1998, the employment rate was expected to reach 31,000.

Typically, production workers in the ophthalmic goods industry are employed on a full-time basis, averaging 2 percent more hours per year than the average of production workers employed by other U.S. industries. However, they earn on average 20 percent less than other production workers. In 1989, the average hourly wage for production workers in the ophthalmic goods industry was $8.36, while the average wage in all other manufacturing industries was $10.49. The average annual salary of employees holding administrative, technical, or managerial positions in the industry was $31,416 in 1989. By 1994, the average wage was $10.09 per hour, and by 1998 this was expected to increase to $11.63.

ASSOCIATIONS AND SOCIETIES

AMERICAN ACADEMY OF OPTOMETRY
4330 East West Hwy., Ste. 1117
Bethesda, MD 20817-4408

Phone: (301) 718-6500
Fax: (301) 656-0989

AMERICAN BOARD OF OPHTHALMOLOGY
111 Presidential Blvd., Ste. 241
Bala Cynwyd, PA 19004
Phone: (215) 644-1175

AMERICAN BOARD OF OPTICIANRY
10341 Democracy Ln.
Fairfax, VA 22030
Phone: (703) 691-8356
Fax: (703) 691-3929

AMERICAN OPTOMETRIC ASSOCIATION
243 N Lindbergh Blvd.
St. Louis, MO 63141
Phone: (314) 991-4100
Fax: (314) 991-4101

AMERICAN OPTOMETRIC FOUNDATION
4330 East West Hwy., Ste. 1117
Bethesda, MD 20814-4480
Phone: (301) 718-6514
Fax: (301) 656-0989

AMERICAN SOCIETY FOR CONTEMPORARY OPHTHALMOLOGY
4711 W Golf Rd., Ste. 408
Skokie, IL 60076
Phone: (800) 621-4002 or (708) 568-1527

BETTER VISION INSTITUTE
1800 N Kent St., Ste. 904
Washington, DC 20009
Phone: (800) 424-8422 or (703) 243-1508
Fax: (703) 243-1537

NATIONAL ACADEMY OF OPTICIANRY
10111 Martin Luther King Jr. Hwy., Ste. 112
Bowie, MD 20720
Phone: (301) 577-4828
Fax: (301) 577-3880

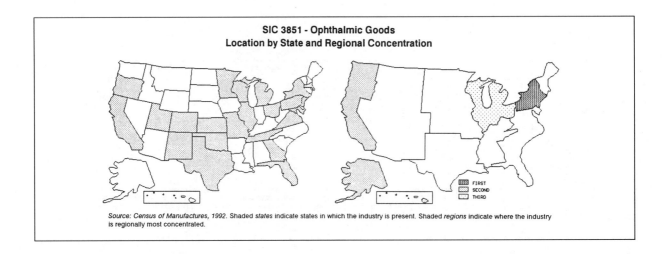

SIC 3851 - Ophthalmic Goods
Location by State and Regional Concentration

FIRST
SECOND
THIRD

Source: Census of Manufactures, 1992. Shaded *states* indicate states in which the industry is present. Shaded *regions* indicate where the industry is regionally most concentrated.

NATIONAL ASSOCIATION OF OPTOMETRISTS AND OPTICIANS
18903 S Miles Rd.
Cleveland, OH 44128
Phone: (216) 475-8925
Fax: (216) 475-8862

NATIONAL OPTOMETRIC ASSOCIATION
4426 Cambridge Ct.
Bloomington, IN 47401
Phone: (812) 855-4475
Fax: (812) 855-7045

OPHTHALMIC RESEARCH INSTITUTE
4330 East West Hwy., Ste. 1117
Bethesda, MD 20814-4408
Phone: (301) 718-6524
Fax: (301) 656-0989

OPTICAL INDUSTRY ASSOCIATION
6055 Arlington Blvd.
Falls Church, VA 22044
Phone: (703) 237-8433
Fax: (703) 237-0643

OPTICAL LABORATORIES ASSOCIATION
PO Box 2000
Merrifield, VA 22116-2000
Phone: (703) 359-2830
Fax: (703) 359-2834

OPTICAL SOCIETY OF AMERICA, MEDICAL OPTICS TECHNICAL GROUP
2010 Massachusetts Ave. NW
Washington, DC 20036
Phone: (202) 223-8130
Fax: (202) 223-1096

OPTICIANS ASSOCIATION OF AMERICA
10341 Democracy Ln.
Fairfax, VA 22030
Phone: (703) 691-8355
Fax: (703) 691-3929

PERIODICALS AND NEWSLETTERS

AMERICAN JOURNAL OF OPHTHALMOLOGY
Ophthalmic Publishing Co.
77 W Wacker Dr., Ste. 660
Chicago, IL 60601-1629
Phone: (312) 629-1690
Fax: (312) 629-1744
Monthly. Individuals, $66.00 per year; institutions, $99.00 per year.

AMERICAN OPTOMETRIC ASSOCIATION JOURNAL
John Potter, editor
American Optometric Association
243 N Lindbergh Blvd.
St. Louis, MO 63141
Phone: (314) 991-4100
Fax: (314) 991-4401
Monthly. Free to members; non-members, $50.00 per year.

AMERICAN OPTOMETRIC ASSOCIATION NEWS
American Optometric Association
243 N Lindbergh Blvd.
St. Louis, MO 63141
Phone: (314) 991-4100
Fax: (314) 991-4401
Semimonthly. $35.00 per year.

EYECARE BUSINESS: THE MAGAZINE FOR PROGRESSIVE DISPENSING
Cardinal Business Media, Inc.
1300 Virginia Dr., Ste. 400
Fort Washington, PA 19034
Phone: (215) 643-8000
Fax: (215) 643-8099
Monthly. $40.00 per year. Covers the business side of optometry and optical retailing. Each issue features "Frames and Fashion."

OPHTHALMOLOGY
Lippincott-Raven Publishers
227 South 6th St.
Philadelphia, PA 19106
Phone: (800) 777-2295 or (215) 238-4200
Monthly. Individuals, $135.00 per year; institutions, $205.00 per year.

OPHTHALMOLOGY TIMES
Advanstar Communications, Inc.
7500 Old Oak Blvd.
Cleveland, OH 44130
Phone: (800) 346-0085 or (216) 243-8100
Fax: (216) 891-2726
Semimonthly. $150.00 per year.

OPTOMETRIC MANAGEMENT: THE BUSINESS AND MARKETING MAGAZINE FOR OPTOMETRY
Cardinal Business Media, Inc.
1300 Virginia Dr., Ste. 400
Fort Washington, PA 19034
Phone: (215) 643-8000
Fax: (215) 643-8099
Monthly. $40.00 per year. Provides information and advice for optometrists on practice management and marketing.

DATABASES

EMBASE
Elsevier Science, Inc.
655 Avenue of the Americas
PO Box 945
New York, NY 10010
Phone: (212) 989-5800
Fax: (212) 633-3975
Worldwide medical literature, 1974 to present. Weekly updates. Inquire as to online cost and availability.

MEDLINE
Medlars Management Section
National Library of Medicine
8600 Rockville Pke.
Bethesda, MD 20894
Phone: (800) 638-8480 or (301) 496-6193

Provides indexing and abstracting of worldwide medical literature, 1966 to date. Inquire as to online cost and availability.

PREDICASTS FORECASTS: INTERNATIONAL
Information Access Co.
362 Lakeside Dr.
Foster City, CA 94404
Phone: (800) 321-6388 or (415) 378-5000
Fax: (415) 358-4759
Provides online short-range and long-range industry and product forecasts for all countries of the world except the U.S. Forecasts are abstracted from over 1,000 international sources. Time period is 1971 to date, with monthly updates. Inquire as to online cost and availability.

SCISEARCH
Institute for Scientific Information
3501 Market St.
Philadelphia, PA 19104
Phone: (800) 523-1850 or (215) 386-0100
Fax: (215) 386-2911
Broad, multidisciplinary index to the literature of science and technology, 1974 to present. Inquire as to online cost and availability. Coverage of literature is worldwide, with weekly updates.

STATISTICS SOURCES

ANNUAL SURVEY OF MANUFACTURES
Bureau of the Census, U.S. Department of Commerce
Available from U.S. Government Printing Office
Washington, DC 20402
Phone: (202) 512-1800
Fax: (202) 512-2250

U.S. INDUSTRIAL OUTLOOK: FORECASTS FOR SELECTED MANUFACTURING AND SERVICE INDUSTRIES
Available from U.S. Government Printing Office
Washington, DC 20402

Phone: (202) 512-1800
Fax: (202) 512-2250
Annual. $37.00. (Replaced in 1995 by U.S. Global Trade Outlook.) Issued by the International Trade Administration, U.S. Department of Commerce. Provides basic data, outlook for the current year, and "Long-Term Prospects" (five-year projections) for a wide variety of products and services. Includes high technology industries. Available on the world wide web at gopher://gopher.umsl.edu:70/11/library/govdocs/usio94.

WORLDCASTS: PRODUCT EDITION
Information Access Co.
362 Lakeside Dr.
Foster City, CA 94404
Phone: (800) 321-6388 or (415) 358-4643
Fax: (415) 358-4759
Quarterly. $925.00 per year. International business statistics and forecasts arranged by product. Each quarterly volume covers a particular group of products.

FURTHER READING

"Business is Bubbling." *Women's Wear Daily,* 20 May 1996, 171.

"Cytomegalovirus (Treatment) FDA Approves Eye Implant." *AIDS Weekly Plus,* 18 March 1996.

"Retailers Look on Bright Side with Sunglasses." *Drug Store News,* 18 November 1996, 18.

"Sport Optics." *Sportstyle,* May 1996, 18.

"Total Women's Accessories." *Accessories,* January 1997, 98.

"Vision Correction and Contact Lenses." *Contact Lens Council,* 1 July 1996. Available from http://www.iglobal.com/CLC/clc-01.html. ◀━

According to the U.S. Census Bureau's Current Industrial Reports, U.S. manufacturers shipped about 1.4 billion gallons of paint valued at $15.9 billion. About 700 firms produced paint in the United States in the mid-1990s, down from over 900 early in the decade. The paint and coatings business was considered a mature industry, with growth projected at about 1-2 percent annually.

Historically, paint remained a comparatively small, yet influential industry into the mid-1990s. Despite its relatively minor revenues, the industry's products affected virtually every aspect of modern life. From cars and homes, to containers for food and beverages, to appliances and furniture, paints and coatings protected, personalized, and beautified our surroundings. Some economists consider it a leading economic indicator.

PAINTS AND ALLIED PRODUCTS

SIC 2851

Increased automotive production and construction account for continued growth in paint manufacturing. Despite concerns about strict government regulations resulting in mergers and acquisitions and foreign ownership, technological advances—such as industrial coatings, including powder and radiation-cured types—forecasts estimate $18 billion on volume of 1.3 billion gallons by 2000.

 Top 8 LEADING PAINT, COATINGS, INKS AND PIGMENT COMPANIES

Ranked by: Sales in 1995, in millions of dollars.

1. Sherwin-Williams, with $3,273.8 million
2. RPM, $1,017.0
3. Valspar, $790.2
4. Benjamin Moore, $564.2
5. McWhorter Technologies, $311.4
6. Guardsman Products, $250.6
7. Standard Brands Paint, $112.2
8. Hitox Corp. of America, $11.0

Source: *ChemicalWeek*, ChemicalWeek 300 (annual), May 8, 1996, p. 56.

The paint industry has become essential to nine major manufacturing industries, including: automobiles, trucks and buses, metal cans, farm machinery and equipment, construction machinery and equipment, metal furniture and fixtures, wood furniture and fixtures, major appliances, and coil coating (high speed application of industrial coatings to continuous sheets, strips, and coils of aluminum or steel). Additionally, paint manufacturers influence the wider chemicals industry via their purchase of billions of dollars worth of raw materials. Paint and coatings were also an integral contributor to the new and resale housing industry.

The paint industry underwent significant changes in the early 1990s, including a gradual expansion of specialized end-user markets, progressively stricter environmental regulations, an increase in foreign corporate ownership, and an accelerating pace of consolidation. But in the mid-1990s, as raw material prices eased and demand in two key markets (automotive and housing) surged, paint manufacturers experienced an increase.

INDUSTRY OUTLOOK

In the 1990s, paint manufacturers' primary concerns centered on progressively stricter environmental regulations, increasing foreign ownership, greater likelihood of mergers and acquisitions, and accelerating technological advances.

Growth in manufacturing, especially autos and construction in the mid-1990s, fueled healthy expansion of the paint industry. Paced by double-digit volume gains in the water-based exterior coatings segment, dollar volume advanced 9 percent from 1993 to $15.9 billion in 1995. This trend accelerated into the first half of 1996, when volume increased 12.5 percent to 685 million gallons over the first half of 1995 and value jumped 16.4 percent to $8.3 billion in the period. The Freedonia Group forecast that domestic sales of paint and coatings would expand at an average annual rate of almost two percent, reaching $18 billion on volume of 1.3 billion gallons by the year 2000. Industrial coatings, especially powder and radiation-cured types, were expected to account for a significant portion of the growth.

ORGANIZATION AND STRUCTURE

The paint industry's first national professional organization, the National Paint, Oil, and Varnish Association, was founded in 1888 in Saratoga, New York. Industry associations proliferated in the early twentieth century until the Great Depression, when government officials and top paint company executives urged the creation of a single national organization. The National Paint, Varnish, and Lacquer Association was formed in 1933, and was later renamed the National Paint and Coatings Association (NPCA).

The NPCA's membership constituted over 75 percent of the entire paint industry in the 1990s. The organization existed to represent the industry to government regulators and the general public. Its public relations and educational programs focused primarily on the technical and aesthetic qualities of architectural paint. The group's annual "Clean-Up, Paint-Up, Fix-Up" campaign, which encouraged neighborhood pride through house painting, was first undertaken in 1912 and lasted through the early 1970s. In the 1990s, campaigns countered paint's persistently bad image as a noxious, but necessary, maintenance product. Following the lead of such successful "category marketers" as the cotton and milk industries, the NPCA promoted paint as a versatile decorating tool.

COMPETITIVE STRUCTURE

Numerous mergers, the high cost of regulation, and increasingly expensive, complex manufacturing pro-

SIC 2851 - Paints Varnishes Lacquers Enamels
General Statistics

| Year | Com-panies | Establishments | | Employment | | | Compensation | | Production ($ million) | | | | |
		Total	with 20 or more employees	Total (000)	Production Workers (000)	Hours (Mil)	Payroll ($ mil)	Wages ($/hr)	Cost of Materials	Value Added by Manufacture	Value of Shipments	Capital Invest.
1982	1,170	1,441	622	54.1	27.6	53.6	1,157.7	8.98	5,167.6	3,952.5	9,162.1	264.2
1983				53.6	27.5	54.1	1,207.7	9.32	5,577.3	4,706.3	10,194.6	280.1
1984				55.3	29.1	56.9	1,286.8	9.92	6,011.3	4,932.1	10,848.4	283.6
1985				55.5	29.0	56.9	1,359.5	10.48	6,396.8	5,169.3	11,562.4	336.3
1986				55.8	28.8	57.0	1,416.3	10.73	6,302.6	5,407.2	11,724.9	254.2
1987	1,123	1,426	626	55.2	28.3	56.3	1,491.3	11.16	6,508.9	6,220.5	12,702.4	275.1
1988				56.9	28.3	57.0	1,564.7	11.20	7,088.6	6,488.9	13,531.7	252.7
1989		1,409	641	55.0	27.7	55.8	1,607.5	11.69	7,291.5	6,453.0	13,656.3	240.8
1990				53.9	27.2	55.6	1,627.6	11.89	7,461.2	6,765.7	14,238.7	271.3
1991				51.1	25.2	52.1	1,568.2	12.09	7,434.7	6,784.1	14,254.9	255.7
1992	1,130	1,418	578	51.2	25.7	53.2	1,711.4	12.72	7,806.2	7,158.7	14,973.7	290.2
1993				50.3	25.9	53.4	1,697.7	13.00	8,293.3	7,722.7	16,030.3	256.3
1994				50.1	27.0	55.7	1,911.1	13.98	9,125.4	8,501.0	17,544.4	279.5
1995				50.8P	25.9P	54.3P	1,886.5P	13.91P	9,019.9P	8,402.7P	17,341.6P	263.0P
1996				50.4P	25.7P	54.2P	1,940.5P	14.28P	9,334.4P	8,695.7P	17,946.2P	261.6P
1997				50.0P	25.5P	54.0P	1,994.6P	14.65P	9,648.8P	8,988.6P	18,550.8P	260.3P
1998				49.6P	25.3P	53.9P	2,048.6P	15.02P	9,963.3P	9,281.6P	19,155.3P	259.0P

Sources: 1982, 1987, 1992 Economic Census; Annual Survey of Manufactures, 83-86, 88-91, 93-94. Establishment counts for non-Census years are from County Business Patterns; establishment values for 83-84 are extrapolations. 'P's show projections by the editors. Industries reclassified in 87 will not have data for prior years.

cesses began to have a cumulative effect on industry composition in the mid-1990s. Mergers and acquisitions reduced the number of companies in the industry from more than 900 to about 700 over the course of the early 1990s. By that time, the top three producers accounted for about 45 percent of U.S. shipments, up from less than 30 percent in 1990. The ten largest manufacturers comprised nearly two-thirds of the market. Industry observers expected consolidation to eliminate another 300 companies by the year 2000.

The geographic dispersal of paint manufacturers was historically dictated by the high transportation costs associated with paint distribution. The weight of prepared paint encouraged the development of a regionalized structure of small manufacturers by the end of the nineteenth century. Paint companies gravitated toward major population and industrial centers like Cleveland, New York, St. Louis, and Chicago. This arrangement dominated the industry until the 1940s and 1950s, when the leading paint manufacturers began to consolidate paint plants and develop wider distribution networks.

By the early 1960s, however, that trend reversed, and smaller branch plants were built to lower freight costs, avoid some state taxes, and facilitate more personalized service. In the late 1960s, about 66 percent of paint was consumed within 500 miles of its manufacture. Decentralization persisted through the 1990s, represented by the industry segment of tenacious small-to-medium-sized paint manufacturers who served limited regional markets.

MARKET SEGMENTS

Three basic segments existed within the industry: architectural coatings, Original Equipment Manufacturer (OEM) product coatings, and special purpose coatings.

Architectural coatings, known in the industry as trade sales paint and commonly referred to as house paint, comprised the largest segment, contributing 44 percent of annual gallonage and 38 percent of revenues in 1995. About 60 percent of the 617.5 million gallons of architectural coatings sold in 1995 were interior paints. Exterior paints contributed 36 percent (225.1 million gallons), and lacquers and all others accounted for the remainder of architectural paint shipped. Water-based, or latex, paints contributed for 76 percent of trade sales in 1996, up slightly from 73 percent in the early 1990s.

The bulk of architectural coatings were distributed through wholesale and retail outlets. Marketing these paints encompassed both formulation and aesthetic factors. Safety, durability, consistency, washability, and convenience were some common consumer concerns with regard to formulation. But color and appearance were also important, so paint manufacturers were often obliged to keep up with decorating trends.

Sales in this industry segment were keyed to weather (which could limit the application of exterior paints), new housing starts, sales of existing homes, and to a lesser degree, commercial and industrial construction. Architectural coatings were subject to competition from vinyl siding, wallpaper, wood paneling, and glass.

OEM paints constituted about 28 percent of industry gallonage in 1995. These products were often custom formulated in consultation with the end-user and applied during manufacturing. These coatings were used in such durable goods markets as automobiles, aircraft, appliances, furniture, metal containers, sheet and coil metals, and industrial equipment. Dollar shipments for this industry segment in 1995 were a record $5.3 billion, up more than 25 percent from the early 1990s. Strong automobile and consumer durables markets helped fuel volume growth as well, which rose from 339 million gallons in the early 1990s to 389.6 million gallons in 1995.

SIC 2851 - Paints Varnishes Lacquers Enamels
Industry Data by State

| State | Establish-ments | Shipments | | | Employment | | | | Cost as % of Shipments | Investment per Employee ($) |
		Total ($ mil)	% of U.S.	Per Establ.	Total Number	% of U.S.	Per Establ.	Wages ($/hour)		
Ohio	79	1,852.8	12.4	23.5	6,000	11.7	76	14.94	49.4	10,933
California	189	1,758.6	11.7	9.3	5,400	10.5	29	13.02	51.4	4,352
Illinois	125	1,675.5	11.2	13.4	5,500	10.7	44	12.73	52.2	-
Michigan	76	931.5	6.2	12.3	3,200	6.3	42	13.59	60.7	7,563
Texas	84	917.4	6.1	10.9	2,500	4.9	30	11.24	55.0	10,040
Pennsylvania	65	875.9	5.8	13.5	3,000	5.9	46	13.65	49.2	3,967
New Jersey	91	761.4	5.1	8.4	2,800	5.5	31	12.33	48.6	5,179
Georgia	45	637.3	4.3	14.2	1,500	2.9	33	11.41	58.4	3,667
Kentucky	26	588.1	3.9	22.6	1,200	2.3	46	10.94	36.4	4,417
Maryland	20	463.7	3.1	23.2	1,200	2.3	60	12.90	56.9	5,833

Source: 1992 *Economic Census*. The states are in descending order of shipments or establishments (if shipment data are missing for the majority). The symbol (D) appears when data are withheld to prevent disclosure of competitive information. States marked with (D) are sorted by number of establishments. A dash (-) indicates that the data element cannot be calculated; * indicates the midpoint of a range.

One major challenge facing OEM producers in the early 1990s was the increased use of plastics in automobiles and appliances, which created the need to match the paint finish of metal panels with plastic panels that were painted separately. Development of new applications technologies was another primary concern.

Special purpose or industrial coatings, which largely developed after World War II, accounted for less than one-fourth of industry volume in the mid-1990s. While similar to architectural coatings in that they could be classified as stock or shelf goods, special purpose coatings were formulated for specific applications or environmental conditions, and were often sold directly to the end user. Primary markets for these products included automotive and machinery refinishing, industrial maintenance (including factories, equipment, tanks, utilities, and railroads), bridges, traffic markings, metallic coatings, and marine coatings. Having declined both in terms of volume and revenues in the early 1990s, this industry segment rebounded to sales of $3.1 billion in volume of 194 million gallons by the mid-1990s.

WORK FORCE

The paint and coatings industry employed an estimated 50,500 Americans in 1996, down from about 61,800 in the early 1990s. Production workers comprised about 50 percent of that total. Another 25 percent of the industry's employees were managers and administrators, and 20 percent were professional chemists and sales representatives.

Production workers operated and fixed machinery, moved raw materials, and monitored the production process. High school graduates qualified for entry-level production jobs, and advancement into better-paying jobs requiring higher skills or more responsibility was possible through on-the-job experience or additional vocational training at a two-year technical college. Hourly earnings for paint production workers averaged nearly $13.50 in 1996, approximately 20 percent higher than the national average for manufacturing production jobs.

Most administrative and management positions required a bachelor's degree and experience in the industry. Support workers often held two-year technical degrees or some college, but these were not required.

Research and development specialists in the paint industry included chemists and chemical engineers. They typically conducted research and experimented with new products and processes. Advanced degrees were often essential for these positions. Some senior chemists were promoted to management positions.

Marketing and sales representatives promoted sales of their companies' products by developing new products, creating plans to market them, and advertising them to retail and industrial customers. These positions often required a degree in marketing, chemistry, or chemical engineering.

Employment in the paint and coatings industry was projected to continue its steady decline through the year 2005, with machine operators bearing the brunt of the cuts. Those positions were expected to decline by 29 percent. In line with the industry's strong emphasis on research and development, the number of chemists employed was expected to increase by over one-fourth by 2005. More efficient production processes, increased plant automation, growth of environmental awareness, health and safety concerns, and rising foreign competition were all expected to influence paint and coatings employment significantly and negatively.

RESEARCH AND TECHNOLOGY

As of the 1990s, paints and coatings incorporated a myriad of chemical compounds uniquely formulated to fulfill the varied requirements of hundreds of thousands of applications. The need for regulatory compliance helped make research and development a paramount concern as well as a major budget item, but the industry was not always so technically inclined.

From its inception in 1700 until the mid-1900s, paint formulation remained relatively unchanged. The switch from paste to ready-mixed paint in the 1860s and the mechanization of the manufacturing process in the mid-1880s were two significant innovations. But for the first half of the twentieth century, the manufacture of paint was a relatively simple process of mixing and grinding oils and pigments using "secret" recipes usually concocted by trial and error.

World War II inspired many innovations in paint formulation. One observer noted that there was more technological progress in the paint industry from 1947 to 1967 than in the previous 1,000 years. Product developments occurred so quickly that an estimated 90 percent of 1960's trade sales consisted of items that did not exist a decade before.

Most of the raw materials used in the contemporary paint industry were developed during the postwar era. They were derived from petroleum, then mixed in varying proportions with specific chemical agents to produce such distinct characteristics as durability, elasticity, and chemical and thermal resistance. By the mid-1960s, the major industrial paint manufacturers offered as many as 20,000 different products.

The 1980s and 1990s brought the industry's most significant and rapid changes. As one industry executive told *Industrial Paint & Powder* in the mid-1990s, "Technology has changed more in the last eight years than in the previous 80 years of our coatings business." These changes included the development of color paint and latex paint, which required no ventilation, was non-flammable and scrubbable, gave a good finish, was easy to remove from brushes, and dried in about 20 minutes. Driving much of the innovation, however, was government regulation.

Regulation of the industry accelerated dramatically during the environmentally conscious 1970s, when federal clean air regulations were adopted to encourage the production of less-polluting, less-toxic paints. By the beginning of the 1980s, nearly every aspect of the paint business was regulated. The Occupational Safety and Health Administration (OSHA) monitored the workplace. The Environmental Protection Agency (EPA) regulated the introduction, generation, transportation, treatment, and disposal of hazardous materials used in or produced by the coatings industry. The Consumer Product Safety Commission protected paint customers by controlling what could be bought and sold.

Although many in the paint industry resisted government efforts to monitor the business, state and federal regulation actually encouraged several technological advances. An early example of this phenomenon occurred just after the turn of the century, when legislation was enacted in North Dakota requiring formula labels on house paints. The idea gained popularity among consumers and congressmen throughout the country. But paint manufacturers feared revealing their "secret formulas," and warned that the new law would inhibit research on new formulations. In hindsight, the rules encouraged the use of quality ingredients and fostered more scientific formulations.

AMERICA AND THE WORLD

Due to prohibitive shipping expenses, overseas trade historically did not contribute significantly to the U.S. paint market. Nevertheless, the United States dominated what global paint trade did exist after World War I, when Germany relinquished its top position in chemicals. But after World War II, foreign countries grew increasingly self-sufficient.

The United States dominated the global paint industry in the mid-1900s, accounting for 40 percent of the $5.2 billion value and 50 percent of the supply. West Germany ranked a distant second with revenues of about $460 million, and Great Britain, France, and Italy followed suit.

In 1960, the industry's total export business constituted less than 2 percent of total production. During this decade tariffs, quotas, licensing and exchange restrictions, and special import fees hamstrung U.S. coatings manufacturers' world trade. Trade barriers encouraged some paint producers to enter into joint ventures with their foreign competitors so that they could market their products overseas.

Trade liberalization and reductions in transportation costs in the 1990s encouraged international trade. By mid-decade, foreign sales represented a small, but growing percentage of total domestic revenue, with exports doubling from the late 1980s to the mid-1990s. More than half of goods went to Canada and Mexico. While the U.S. paint industry maintained a positive balance of

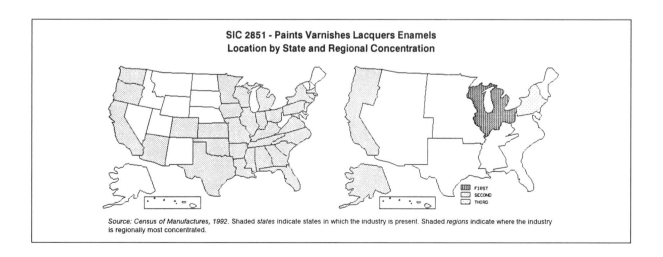

SIC 2851 - Paints Varnishes Lacquers Enamels
Location by State and Regional Concentration

FIRST
SECOND
THIRD

Source: Census of Manufactures, 1992. Shaded *states* indicate states in which the industry is present. Shaded *regions* indicate where the industry is regionally most concentrated.

trade in the early 1990s, Canada, Germany, Japan and Belgium had become the most significant importers.

Globalization of the paint industry occurred as U.S. companies followed their primary OEM customers from America to the Far East and other lower-cost areas. Economic liberalization drew many of the world's leading paint manufacturers to China, where joint ventures promised a piece of double-digit sales growth. At the same time, foreign producers sought growth through acquisition of U.S. paint companies. By 1995, ten multinational companies held an estimated 60 percent of total world production, compared with one-fifth in 1980.

ASSOCIATIONS AND SOCIETIES

FEDERATION OF SOCIETIES FOR COATINGS TECHNOLOGY
492 Norristown Rd.
Blue Bell, PA 19422
Phone: (215) 940-0777
Fax: (215) 940-0292

NATIONAL DECORATING PRODUCTS ASSOCIATION
1050 N Lindbergh Blvd.
Saint Louis, MO 63132-2994
Phone: (314) 991-3470
Fax: (314) 991-5039

NATIONAL PAINT AND COATINGS ASSOCIATION
1500 Rhode Island Ave. NW
Washington, DC 20005
Phone: (202) 462-6272

PAINTING AND DECORATING CONTRACTORS OF AMERICA
3913 Old Lee Hwy., Ste. 33B,
Fairfax, VA 22030
Phone: (800) 332-7322 or (703) 359-0826
Fax: (703) 359-2576

PERIODICALS AND NEWSLETTERS

AMERICAN PAINT AND COATINGS JOURNAL
American Paint Journal Co.
2911 Washington Ave.
Saint Louis, MO 63103
Phone: (314) 534-0301
Weekly. $25.00 per year.

AMERICAN PAINTING CONTRACTOR
American Paint Journal Co.
2911 Washington Ave.
Saint Louis, MO 63103
Phone: (314) 534-0301
Monthly. $25.00 per year.

DECORATING RETAILER
National Decorating Products Association
1050 N Lindbergh Blvd.
St. Louis, MO 63132
Phone: (800) 737-0107 or (314) 991-3470
Fax: (314) 991-5039
Monthly. $45.00 per year.

MODERN PAINT AND COATINGS
Argus, Inc.
6151 Powers Ferry Rd. NW
Atlanta, GA 30339-2941
Phone: (800) 443-4969 or (800) 955-2500
Fax: (404) 955-0400
Monthly. $49.00 per year.

PAINT AND COATINGS INDUSTRY
Business News Publishing Co.
755 W Big Beaver Rd., Ste. 1000
Troy, MI 48084
Phone: (800) 837-7370 or (313) 362-3700
Fax: (313) 362-0317
Nine times a year. $36.00 per year.

DATABASES

CITIBASE (CITICORP ECONOMIC DATABASE)
FAME Software Corp.
77 Water St., 9 Fl.
New York, NY 10005
Phone: (212) 898-7800
Fax: (212) 742-8956
Presents over 6,000 statistical series relating to business, industry, finance, and economics. Includes series from Survey of Current Business and many other sources. Time period is 1947 to date, with daily updates. Inquire as to online cost and availability.

WORLD SURFACE COATINGS ABSTRACTS [ONLINE]
Paint Research Association of Great Britain
Waldegrave Rd.
Teddington, Middlesex, England TW11 8LD
Phone: 181-9 77-4427
Fax: 181-9 43-4705
Indexing and abstracting of the literature of paint and surface coatings, 1976 to present. Monthly updates. Inquire as to online cost and availability.

STATISTICS SOURCES

CURRENT INDUSTRIAL REPORTS: PAINT
Bureau of the Census
U.S. Department of Commerce
Washington, DC 20233

PAINT AND ALLIED PRODUCTS ANNUAL SURVEY OF MANUFACTURERS
Bureau of the Census
U.S. Department of Commerce
Washington, DC 20233

PAINT, VARNISH, AND LACQUER
U.S. Bureau of the Census
Washington, DC 20233-0800
Phone: (301) 457-4100
Fax: (301) 457-3842
Quarterly and annual. Provides data on shipments: value, quantity, imports, and exports. Includes paint, varnish, lacquer, product finishes, and special purpose coatings. (Current Industrial Reports, MQ-28F.)

SURVEY OF CURRENT BUSINESS
Available from U.S. Government Printing Office
Washington, DC 20402
Phone: (202) 512-1800
Fax: (202) 512-2250
Monthly. $41.00 per year. Issued by Bureau of Economic Analysis, U.S. Department of Commerce. Presents a wide variety of business and economic data.

FURTHER READING

Bourguignon, Edward W. "Paint Industry Enjoys Strong First Half 1996." *American Paint & Coatings Journal,* 11 November 1996, 19.

Darnay, Arsen J., ed. *Manufacturing USA.* Detroit: Gale Research Inc., 1996.

Fattah, Hassan. "Paints and Coatings: Mergers Create an Altered Image." *Chemical Week,* 23 October 1996, 33-34.

Padow, Mark. "Not a Bad Year, Most Say, All Things Considered." *American Paint & Coatings Journal,* 16 December 1996, 17-18.

"Paints, Coatings Manufacturers Sales Highest in Decade." *American Paint & Coatings Journal,* 15 January 1996, 11.

"PPG Industries: Deemed to be One of the Biggest Makers of Automotive & Industrial Coatings in the World." *Paint and Coatings Industry,* July 1996, 49.

Standard & Poor's Industry Surveys. 8 February 1996, C51-C54.

Ward's Business Directory of U.S. Private and Public Companies. Detroit: Gale Research Inc., 1997.

PAPER MILLS

SIC 2621

Despite adjustments made to meet the demands of recycling mandates and environmental pressures, the paper mill industry continues to experience growth through the 1990s. Paper and paperboard companies plan to add capacity at a 1.5 percent annual rate through the end of the decade. On a tonnage basis, U.S. paper industry capacity was expected to expand from 99.1 million tons in 1996 to 103.7 million tons in 1999—a three-year increase of 4.6 million tons. The industry continues to make heavy capital expenditures. Investing in higher capacity, heavily automated machines will continue to decrease number of workers required, while increasing output. The industry is on target to reach a goal of recycling 50 percent of paper produced in the United States by the year 2000.

The United States produces more paper and paperboard than any country in the world. It has maintained this position by consistently producing about one-third of total world production, far more than any other country. While the paper industry remains prosperous and relatively unscathed by foreign competition, competition is rising across the globe as new regions—notably Asia and Latin America—develop strong paper industries.

Domestic U.S. paper and paperboard mills—of which there were 527 in 1995—produce about 90 percent of the paper consumed in the United States. In 1995, these mills used a total of 1,135 paper machines to produce all U.S.-made paper and paperboard, a reduction of 81 machines from 1993. The 1995 total included 751 machines producing paper and 384 machines producing paperboard. Taken as a whole, the U.S. pulp, paper, and converted paper products industry is the eighth largest U.S. manufacturing industry in dollar sales. While imports—mostly from Canada—account for about 10 to 12 percent of the paper consumed each year in the United States, domestic manufacturers dominate most segments of the industry.

Top 10 PAPER COMPANIES WITH THE HIGHEST SALES

Ranked by: Sales in 1994, in millions of dollars.

1. International Paper, with $14,966 million
2. Georgia-Pacific, $12,738
3. Weyerhaeuser Co., $10,398
4. Kimberly-Clark, $7,364
5. Stone Container, $5,749
6. James River, $5,417
7. Champion International, $5,318
8. Mead, $4,558
9. Boise Cascade, $4,140
10. Scott Paper Co., $3,581

Source: *Pulp & Paper North American Industry Fact Book*, Miller Freeman, 1996, p. 7.

While paper mills are separate from pulp mills in the Standard Industrial Classification System, the two are, in reality, directly connected. About 70 percent of all paper is produced at mills that are "integrated" with a pulp mill at the same site, both of which are typically owned by the same company. Almost all high volume "commodity" paper and paperboard grades—such as newsprint, uncoated free sheet, and linerboard—are produced in this fashion. Some smaller paper mills producing specialty grades may not be connected with a pulp mill.

They procure pulp from other mills owned by the same company or buy "market pulp" produced by other companies.

While growth in domestic markets has slowed in recent years, the U.S. paper industry still produces a vast amount of paper and paperboard. In 1995, total production reached 89.3 million tons of paper and paperboard, with 42.7 million tons being paper and 46.6 million tons being paperboard.

While papermaking is an energy intensive industry—being the third largest U.S. industrial consumer of energy—the pulp and paper industry itself produces well over half of the energy it uses through cogeneration and burning of waste fuels, such as bark and spent pulping chemicals.

INDUSTRY OUTLOOK

The paper industry of the 1990s is highly competitive, both in domestic and foreign markets. It has a modern, efficient manufacturing base, labor peace, and strong markets. However, the industry faces several major challenges, including environmental compliance, recycling, and alternative media.

ENVIRONMENTAL ISSUES

Environmental compliance has been a daunting—and expensive—challenge for the paper industry in the 1990s. There is sustained opposition from environmental groups and increased government regulation in nearly all steps of production. For example, the lumber industry in the Pacific Northwest has been drastically reduced in scale. Due to successful court challenges by environmental groups under the Endangered Species Act, tree harvests in the early to mid-1990s dropped to one sixth of harvesting levels in the mid-1980s. Despite the release of some lands for harvesting and permits for salvage logging issued in 1995, harvesting was still greatly reduced in the mid-1990s.

Pulp and paper mills in the Northwest dependent on the residue of lumber operations for raw material have had to look to new sources—even overseas—for sources of wood chips. Many northwestern U.S. mills have converted partially or completely to the use of recycled paper. Also, the pulping and bleaching of wood fiber was the focus of proposals for stringent and costly new federal regulation in the mid-1990s.

RECYCLING

While paper recycling was a major environmental challenge in the early 1990s, the industry's quick re-sponse to recycle more paper has convinced many of its critics—both in the public and government—that the industry was serious about recycling. The U.S. paper industry reached an overall recycling rate of 40 percent in 1993 and is on track to reach a goal of recycling 50 percent of all paper produced in the United States by the year 2000.

Recycling of certain grades, such as newsprint and old corrugated containers, has traditionally been high, while recycling rates for other grades, such as printing and writing papers, are growing rapidly. For example, over 59 percent of all newsprint used in the United States was recovered in 1994, up from just 29 percent in 1980. In linerboard, almost all capacity increases in the early 1990s came from new recycled linerboard mills, and by 1994 over 62 percent of old corrugated containers— known as OCC in the business—were being recovered, up from 47.9 percent in 1986.

Recycling of printing and writing paper, while lower than other grades, has also increased dramatically, thanks in part to aggressive state and federal legislation. In 1993, President Clinton signed an executive order mandating higher levels of recycled fiber in paper purchased by the federal government. In 1994, the recovery rate from printing and writing paper stood at 34.1 percent, up from just 22.9 percent in 1986.

The recycling process itself has some environmental liabilities. Most recycling mills generate a major waste stream and consume large amounts of purchased energy. With recycled newsprint, for example, only 85 percent of incoming newsprint is usable as fiber. The rest is unusable sludge that must be cleaned out of the process and then burned or placed in landfills. In some recycled grades, sludge can be up to 50 percent of the incoming waste paper. Considering that some mills make up to 2,500 tons per day of paper, sludge can become a major waste problem. Also, since recycling mills cannot burn bark or spent pulping chemicals to generate electricity on their own, they must purchase large amounts of power from local utilities.

In the mid-1990s, recycling began to change the geographic distribution of paper mills. So called "mini mills" begin to crop up near major U.S. cities. These mini mills remove ink and recycle old newsprint and other grades of wastepaper and make new newsprint and linerboard on relatively small paper machines. Since they are close to where much of the country's wastepaper is collected—major cities—they are able to greatly reduce shipping costs.

ALTERNATIVE MEDIA

A third major challenge to the paper industry comes from the electronic display and storage of information.

Despite early predictions that computers would soon replace paper in the "paperless office," computers encouraged users to print out even more paper than ever before, fueling a boom in printing and writing papers.

Today, computers are being used more often to replace paper for the storage and transfer of information previously accomplished only on paper. Even if a smaller percentage of this information is printed out, the use of paper should still grow. Several studies concluded that alternative media is not likely to affect consumption of paper until 2005, and that even then, only select grades are likely to be negatively affected by alternative media.

FINANCIAL CONDITIONS

In the early 1990s, the paper industry produced more paper than ever before but was unable to maintain effective pricing. Paper prices fell in 1991 and 1992, before beginning a sharp recovery in 1994 that lasted through most of 1995. In fact, in 1994 and 1995 average paper prices were up more than 50 percent, with prices of some grades increasing at even higher rates. These high prices led to record U.S. paper company profits in 1995. However, 1996 saw prices—and profits—plummeted once again, though not falling as low as they had in the early 1990s.

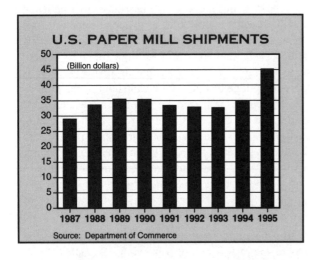

U.S. PAPER MILL SHIPMENTS
(Billion dollars)

Source: Department of Commerce

Operating rates are another key to profits in the paper industry. In general, operating rates—the percentage of time that mills are in operation—need to be at or over 90 percent for the mill to be profitable. This means most large mills operate 24 hours a day, 7 days a week. Operating rates dropped in 1990 and 1991, but rebounded to about 90 percent for paper producers and 95 percent for paperboard manufacturers in 1992. In 1993, the operating rate for all producers reached 93.7 percent and shot up to 96 percent in both 1994 and 1995. However, operating rates dropped dramatically in 1996

to about 89 percent as many producers took extensive downtime in an attempt to work off large inventories of pulp and paper products.

Another measure of paper industry economic health is capital expenditures for new plants and equipment. When paper companies are profitable, they tend to reinvest a large share of their profits into capital expenditures. Capital expenditures for the U.S. pulp and paper industry peaked in 1990, at about $18 billion, and stayed high in 1991 at about $17 billion. However, from 1992 to 1996, the rate of capital expenditures stayed within a range of $12 billion to $14 billion, and 1997 capital spending was expected to barely top $10 billion. Industry analysts suggest that this may reflect growing concern in the U.S. paper industry that domestic growth in paper consumption will remain low for some time.

ORGANIZATION AND STRUCTURE

The paper industry is the most capital intensive of all basic U.S. manufacturing industries, requiring nearly continuous major investments for plant and equipment. According to one ranking, the pulp and paper industry is twice as capital intensive as any other major U.S. industry. This has led major paper companies to invest in enormous, high speed machines that can use economies of scale to produce paper at the lowest possible cost.

After a burst of new mills and paper machines in the early 1990s, the mid-1990s saw relatively low growth in papermaking capacity. After increasing capacity at a 2.6 percent average annual rate from 1986 to 1995 and by 3.5 percent in 1996, paper and paperboard companies planned to add capacity at only a 1.5 percent rate during the period from 1997 to 1999. On a tonnage basis, U.S. paper industry capacity was expected to expand from 99.1 million tons in 1996 to 103.7 million tons in 1999— a three-year increase of 4.6 million tons.

In 1994, pulp and paper companies produced about 40 percent more tonnage with 4 percent fewer employees than in 1984. This was caused directly by paper companies' huge investment in higher capacity, heavily automated machines. For example, in 1995, the industry had the capacity to produce 95.7 million tons of paper and paperboard, up 5.6 percent more than 1993, while operating 6.7 percent fewer machines.

These large investments have created high fixed costs for paper companies. The expense of building and maintaining plants and equipment have become a much greater percentage of a paper company's total costs, while labor has become a lower percentage of costs. Because huge, automated mills need fewer people to run them, many in the industry assumed that paper companies could not adjust to lower demand by laying people off and taking capacity out for short periods. However, while that strategy appeared to be true during the paper industry's recession in the early 1990s, the industry used a completely different approach when prices began dropping during the last quarter of 1995. During that quarter and throughout 1996, many U.S. paper companies—particularly newsprint producers and linerboard producers—took extensive downtime to try to reduce both their own inventories and those of their customers.

WORK FORCE

Total employment in the pulp, paper and converting industries was about 619,000 in 1996, down slightly from 627,000 in 1992. This continues a long term trend of stable or slightly declining employment in the industry despite large capacity increases. Employee wage increases remained at or below the inflation rate in the early 1990s, averaging about 2.5 percent. These increases were far below the average 7.5 percent annual increases recorded during the period from 1975 to 1985.

Like other manufacturing industries, the paper industry employs many unionized workers. The heaviest concentrations of union employees are in older mills which were organized years ago. Almost all new pulp and paper mills are non-union operations, including mills constructed by companies with unionized mills in other locations. In general, the wages and benefits provided by non-union mills are comparable to unionized mills. There has been relative labor peace in the paper industry during the 1980s and 1990s. In exchange for salary increases, management was able to obtain work rule changes that allowed workers to perform more jobs

SIC 2621
Occupations Employed by SIC 262 - Pulp, Paper, and Paperboard Mills

Occupation	% of Total 1994	Change to 2005
Machine operators nec	11.9	13.8
Helpers, laborers, & material movers nec	7.6	-7.8
Blue collar worker supervisors	6.0	0.1
Paper goods machine setters & set-up operators	4.4	-26.2
Industrial machinery mechanics	3.8	1.4
Industrial truck & tractor operators	3.5	-7.8
Maintenance repairers, general utility	3.0	-7.8
Millwrights	2.9	-26.2
Crushing & mixing machine operators	2.7	-17.0
Cutting & slicing machine setters, operators	2.6	10.6
Inspectors, testers, & graders, precision	2.5	1.4
Electricians	2.2	-13.5
Extruding & forming machine workers	1.8	19.8
Machine feeders & offbearers	1.7	-17.0
Coating, painting, & spraying machine workers	1.4	-26.2
Secretaries, ex legal & medical	1.4	-16.1
Packaging & filling machine operators	1.4	-7.8
Plumbers, pipefitters, & steamfitters	1.3	-7.8
Freight, stock, & material movers, hand	1.2	-26.2
Chemical equipment controllers, operators	1.2	-26.2
Precision instrument repairers	1.1	19.9
Industrial production managers	1.1	-7.8
Boiler operators, low pressure	1.1	-7.8

Source: *Industry-Occupation Matrix*, Bureau of Labor Statistics. These data relate to one or more 3-digit SIC industry groups rather than to a single 4-digit SIC. The change reported for each occupation to the year 2005 is a percent of growth or decline as estimated by the Bureau of Labor Statistics. The abbreviation nec stands for 'not elsewhere classified'.

in the mill and eliminate pay differentials for Sunday and holiday pay.

RESEARCH AND TECHNOLOGY

Traditionally, papermaking research has focused on making faster, wider machines that experience fewer paper breaks. To support these goals, research is continuing in every area of the paper machine: the forming section, the press section, the drying section, and the

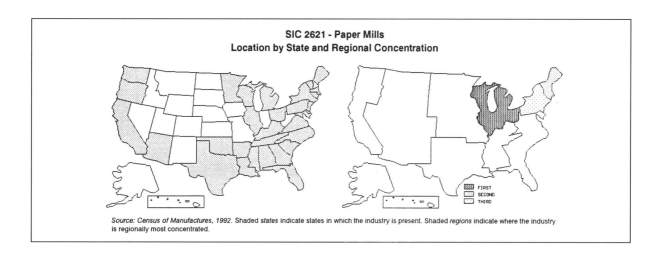

SIC 2621 - Paper Mills
Location by State and Regional Concentration

FIRST
SECOND
THIRD

Source: *Census of Manufactures, 1992*. Shaded *states* indicate states in which the industry is present. Shaded *regions* indicate where the industry is regionally most concentrated.

finishing and converting areas. Much of this research is being performed by supplier companies to the paper industry, which have traditionally assumed a much larger research role than the paper companies. However, paper companies—as well as suppliers—are expanding their support of cooperative research at the nation's pulp and paper schools, such as North Carolina State University, the University of Maine, and the University of Wisconsin-Stevens Point. They also support non-profit research groups such as the Institute of Paper Science and Technology, the Pulp and Paper Research Institute of Canada (PAPRICAN) and the Herty Foundation.

RECYCLED RESEARCH

Much of the research in the paper industry is focusing on how to effectively use more recycled fiber. This is particularly important as the paper industry works to meet its own challenge of recycling 50 percent of all paper produced by the year 2000 and government mandates such as President Clinton's 1993 executive order on recycled paper.

Much of this research will focus on improving the physical chemistry of the "flotation cells" of the deinking process. This technology uses air bubbles to literally "float" detached ink particles to the top of a mixture of ground up paper and water, where the inky froth is skimmed off. Improving the efficiency of this system would speed up production and lower costs.

Research will also focus on using new chemical processes to help produce recycled paper that matches virgin uncoated freesheet in quality. Uncoated freesheet, used in products such as copy paper, is one of the biggest grades of paper, and one of the most demanding in terms of quality.

One of the major initiatives involving the pulp and paper industry is Agenda 2020, a cooperative research project involving the U.S. Department of Energy, pulp and paper research institutions and leading paper companies. Agenda 2020 was prepared by the chief technology officers of major paper companies under the auspices of the American Forest and Paper Association, a trade association. The development of the document was spurred by the Department of Energy's "Industries of the Future" program, which seeks to fund research in specific industries—including pulp and paper—that will reduce energy intensiveness and improve environmental performance. The DOE prepared a draft document on the "Pulp Mill of the Future." That document was reviewed by the team of chief technology officers and modified to create Agenda 2020, which outlines six specific areas for R & D, including sustainable forest management; environmental; performance; energy performance; capital effectiveness; recycling and sensors and control.

In addition to research to complete Agenda 2020, there are hundreds of other ongoing research projects in the paper industry. The industry is seeking closer cooperation among all players—paper companies, suppliers, research institutions and government agencies, as it tries to improve on the complex art of making paper.

AMERICA AND THE WORLD

In 1995, the U.S. paper industry exported about 10.9 million tons of paper, paperboard, and converted products, over 11 percent of total industry production. During this same year, it imported 15.5 million tons of paper, paperboard, and converted products, mostly from Canada. Newsprint accounted for about half of these imports. (These figures do not include imports and exports

SIC 2621 - Paper Mills
Industry Data by State

| State | Establish-ments | Shipments | | | Employment | | | | Cost as % of Shipments | Investment per Employee ($) |
		Total ($ mil)	% of U.S.	Per Establ.	Total Number	% of U.S.	Per Establ.	Wages ($/hour)		
Wisconsin	35	4,446.7	13.6	127.0	19,200	14.7	549	17.30	54.9	21,755
Maine	13	2,934.5	9.0	225.7	12,500	9.6	962	18.03	60.9	19,864
Alabama	7	2,314.3	7.1	330.6	8,800	6.7	1,257	19.09	48.7	38,852
Washington	13	2,098.8	6.4	161.4	7,100	5.4	546	20.63	62.3	29,254
Louisiana	7	1,629.6	5.0	232.8	4,500	3.4	643	19.93	49.1	41,800
New York	32	1,567.1	4.8	49.0	7,400	5.7	231	15.69	56.9	13,162
Michigan	18	1,563.4	4.8	86.9	6,200	4.7	344	17.13	52.5	11,000
Pennsylvania	16	1,453.9	4.4	90.9	6,300	4.8	394	16.95	55.9	40,730
Ohio	11	1,364.4	4.2	124.0	6,000	4.6	545	17.54	49.9	16,850
Minnesota	7	1,340.4	4.1	191.5	5,400	4.1	771	19.98	56.6	21,741

Source: 1992 *Economic Census.* The states are in descending order of shipments or establishments (if shipment data are missing for the majority). The symbol (D) appears when data are withheld to prevent disclosure of competitive information. States marked with (D) are sorted by number of establishments. A dash (-) indicates that the data element cannot be calculated; * indicates the midpoint of a range.

of pulpwood chips and wood pulp, which are widely traded.)

Because of the large amount of market pulp and newsprint imported from Canada, the U.S. paper industry usually runs a trade deficit. For example, in 1995, the value of all U.S. paper, paperboard and converted product exports was $9.7 billion, while imports in these categories totaled $12.3 billion. This figure does not include about $1.56 billion for U.S. wastepaper exports in 1995, an area where the United States leads the world, with a large share of wastepaper exports going to the fiber-starved Asian countries. Japan and Korea are two of the leading Asian wastepaper importers.

Exports have played a key role in stabilizing the paper industry during the 1990s. As domestic sales of paper and allied products (including pulp) have only experienced slight growth from 1991 to 1996, at an average annual rate of 1.5 percent to 2 percent, exports increased 8.2 percent during the same period.

Overall, U.S. exports of paper and allied products—including wastepaper—were aided by the declining value of the U.S. dollar in the early 1990s and competitive pricing, though that advantage began to weaken in 1996 and early 1997 as the dollar continued to rise against most foreign currencies. Paperboard has long been a leading export product, and in 1995 the U.S. industry exported 6 million tons of paperboard. By contrast, a total of 3 million tons of paper was exported in 1995. Of the paper total, printing and writing paper accounted for 1.5 million tons.

While the U.S. paper industry exports products throughout the world, China has emerged as a major U.S. customer. In 1996, for example, China purchased $700 million worth of U.S. paper products, about 10 percent of all Chinese imports from the U.S.

NEWSPRINT GROWTH

Newsprint is one of the major areas where U.S. producers have become more competitive in the global economy. Canadian newsprint, which until the early 1980s held a dominant 60 percent share of total U.S. consumption, has fallen on hard times. In the late 1980s, Canadian newsprint became significantly less competitive with U.S. newsprint because of higher production costs, new state government requirements for recycled newsprint, and growing U.S. newsprint capacity. In 1993, Canadian newsprint accounted for only slightly more than 40 percent of U.S. newsprint consumption, compared with about 52 percent in 1991. Many Canadian newsprint mills are located in rural Quebec, far from recycled fiber sources, and are old and have high production costs. As a result, many market observers expect the Canadian market share to decrease. However,

some Canadian producers have made aggressive moves to obtain recycled fiber and build mills closer to urban areas in order to compete in the market for recycled newsprint.

The Japanese market remains a major challenge for U.S. producers. Despite major cost advantages, U.S. producers have a very small market share of the $70 billion Japanese paper and paperboard market, which is second only to the United States in size. This low market share has been attributed to structural impediments in the Japanese market and a general reluctance by Japanese customers to use imported products.

In 1992 the U.S. industry achieved a major breakthrough, after lengthy negotiations, a formal five-year agreement was concluded between the governments of the United States and Japan on measures designed to open Japan's paper market to foreign suppliers. The agreement requires the Japanese government to encourage Japanese paper distributors, converters, printers and other major consumers of paper products to use more imported paper and develop long-term buying relationships with foreign producers. Paper users in Japan are also expected to establish nondiscriminatory purchasing practices and develop purchasing guidelines that can be followed by both domestic and foreign suppliers of paper and paper products. Under the agreement, the two governments periodically review the implementation of the pact.

From 1992 to 1996, however, the U.S. share of the Japanese paper market increased by only 0.5 percent, from 3.6 percent to 4.1 percent. The United States contends that if all barriers were eliminated, Japanese imports of foreign paper products would increase four-fold. As a result of the lack of progress, in 1995 the U.S. Trade Representative placed the government of Japan on a Super 301 ''Watch List,'' which allows the U.S. government to monitor trade activities of a foreign country's markets in order to determine whether U.S. and other foreign suppliers are being discriminated against.

PROSPECTS

While the global economy slowed considerably in the early 1990s and went into recession in some areas, most U.S. producers remained very competitive worldwide. The U.S. industry still maintains substantial raw material and energy advantages over many of its foreign competitors. The United States also employs a large, well-trained work force that has access to modern process control technology and scheduling software. Given these advantages, the U.S. paper industry should have a long-term competitive edge over other paper producers in Japan, Europe, and Scandinavia. However, Asian and Latin American producers invested large amounts of capital in the 1990s to build modern, world-class pulp and paper facilities. These mills, which use very low cost fiber largely from hardwood and softwood plantations, have emerged as formidable global competitors.

ASSOCIATIONS AND SOCIETIES

NATIONAL PAPER TRADE ASSOCIATION
c/o John J. Buckley
111 Great Neck Rd.
Great Neck, NY 11021
Phone: (516) 829-3070
Fax: (516) 829-3074

PAPER INDUSTRY MANAGEMENT ASSOCIATION
1699 Wall St., Ste. 212
Mount Prospect, IL 60056-5782
Phone: (708) 956-0250
Fax: (708) 956-0520

TAPPI
Technology Park/Atlanta
PO Box 105113
Atlanta, GA 30348-5113
Phone: (800) 332-8686 or (404) 446-1400
Fax: (404) 446-6947

PERIODICALS AND NEWSLETTERS

AMERICAN PAPERMAKER
ASM Communications, Inc.
57 Executive Park S., Ste. 310
Atlanta, GA 30329
Phone: (404) 325-9153

PAPER AGE
Global Publications
77 Waldron Ave.
GlenRock, NJ 07452-2830
Phone: (201) 666-2262
Fax: (201) 666-9046
Monthly. $20.00 per year.

PULP AND PAPER
Miller Freeman, Inc.
600 Harrison St.
San Francisco, CA 94107
Phone: (800) 444-4881 or (800) 227-4675
Fax: (913) 841-2624
Monthly. Free to qualified personnel; others, $100.00 per year.

PULP AND PAPER WEEK
Miller Freeman, Inc.
600 Harrison St.
San Francisco, CA 94107
Phone: (800) 444-4881 or (800) 227-4675
Fax: (913) 841-2624
Weekly. $637.00 per year. Newsletter.

RECYCLED PAPER NEWS
CERMA, Inc.
5528 Hempstead Way
Springfield, VA 22151
Phone: (703) 750-1158

TAPPI JOURNAL
Technical Association of the Pulp and Paper Industry, Inc.
Technology Park-Atlanta
PO Box 105113
Atlanta, GA 30348
Phone: (404) 446-1400
Fax: (404) 446-6947
Monthly. Membership.

DATABASES

CITIBASE (**CITICORP ECONOMIC DATABASE**)
FAME Software Corp.
77 Water St., 9 Fl.
New York, NY 10005
Phone: (212) 898-7800
Fax: (212) 742-8956
Presents over 6,000 statistical series relating to business, industry, finance, and economics. Includes series from Survey of Current Business *and many other sources. Time period is 1947 to date, with daily updates. Inquire as to online cost and availability.*

PAPERCHEM DATABASE
Information Services Div.
Institute of Paper Science and Technology
500 10th St. NW
Atlanta, GA 30318
Phone: (404) 853-9500
Fax: (404) 853-9510
Worldwide coverage of the scientific and technical paper industry chemical literature, including patents, 1967 to present. Monthly updates. Inquire as to online cost and availability.

PIRA
Technical Centre for the Paper and Board, Printing and Packaging Industries
Randalls Rd.
Leatherhead, Surrey, England KT22 7RU
Phone: 1372- 376161
Fax: 1372- 360104
Citations and abstracts pertaining to bookbinding and other pulp, paper, and packaging industries, 1975 to present. Inquire as to online cost and availability.

PREDICASTS FORECASTS: U.S.
Information Access Co.
362 Lakeside Dr.
Foster City, CA 94404
Phone: (800) 321-6388 or (415) 378-5000
Fax: (415) 358-4759
Provides numeric abstracts of a wide range of published forecasts relating to specific U.S. products, markets, and industries. Monthly updates. Time period is 1971 to date. Inquire as to online cost and availability.

U.S. TIME SERIES

Information Access Co.
362 Lakeside Dr.
Foster City, CA 94404
Phone: (800) 321-6388 or (415) 358-4643
Fax: (415) 358-4759
Contains annual time series of historical data. Online version of Predicasts Basebook. *Broad coverage of data from private and government sources on U.S. economy, products and industries. Some time series start as early as 1957. Inquire as to online cost and availability.*

STATISTICS SOURCES

ENCYCLOPEDIA OF AMERICAN INDUSTRIES

Gale Research
835 Penobscot Bldg.
Detroit, MI 48226-4094
Phone: (800) 877-GALE or (313) 961-2242
Fax: (800) 414-5043
1994. $500.00. Two volumes ($250.00 each). Volume one is Manufacturing Industries *and volume two is* Service and Non-Manufacturing Industries. *Provides the history, development, and recent status of approximately 1,000 industries. Includes statistical graphs, with industry and general indexes.*

PREDICASTS BASEBOOK

Information Access Co.
362 Lakeside Dr.,
Foster City, CA 94404
Phone: (800) 321-6388 or (415) 358-4643
Fax: (415) 358-4759
Annual. $700. Provides industry, product, service, economic, demographic, and financial statistics for the United States. Arranged according to Standard Industrial Classification (SIC) numbers, with 14 years of data (where available) and annual growth rate given for each of the 35,000 series. Sources are over 350 statistical publications issued mainly by government agencies and trade associations.

THE PULP AND PAPER INDUSTRY IN THE OECD MEMBER COUNTRIES

Organization for Economic Cooperation and Development
Available from OECD Publications and Information Center
2001 L St. NW, Ste. 700
Washington, DC 20036-4910
Phone: (202) 785-6323
Fax: (202) 785-0350
Annual. Presents annual data on production, consumption, capacity, utilization, and foreign trade. Covers 33 pulp and paper products in the 24 OECD countries.

STATISTICS OF PAPER, PAPERBOARD AND WOOD PULP

Forest and Paper Association
1111 19th St. NW
Washington, DC 20036
Phone: (202) 463-2700
Fax: (202) 463-2785
Annual. $365.00. Formerly Statistics of Paper and Paperboard.

SURVEY OF CURRENT BUSINESS

Available from U.S. Government Printing Office
Washington, DC 20402
Phone: (202) 512-1800
Fax: (202) 512-2250
Monthly. $41.00 per year. Issued by Bureau of Economic Analysis, U.S. Department of Commerce. Presents a wide variety of business and economic data.

FURTHER READING

Paper, Paperboard, Pulp Capacity and Fiber Consumption. Washington: American Forest & Paper Association, 1996.

Stanley, Gary. "Paperboard, Imports, and Exports to Fuel 1997 Growth." *TAPPI Journal,* January 1997, 56. ◀▬

PAPERBOARD MILLS

SIC 2631

The increase in international and domestic trade in recent years has bolstered U.S. paperboard production to new levels. Significant increases in U.S. exports of paperboard are indicative of a strong international market, as most paperboard is used for shipping, and strong international trade has facilitated the need for improved production methods to meet the growing demands. New technological developments in recycling and production will allow for more efficient and cost effective production of materials to meet the growing demands of the industry.

U.S. paperboard mill production reached 46.6 million tons in 1995, a slight increase over the previous year, when production was 45.7 million tons. At this rate, paperboard outpaced production of paper in the United States in 1995, which checked in at 42.6 million tons.

The capacity of U.S. mills to produce paperboard is projected to grow from 52.9 million tons in 1997 to 54.3 million tons in 1999, a total increase of just 2.6 percent. Of this increase, 39 percent will come from the construction of new machines and 61 percent from improvements to existing machines.

Top 11 TOP U.S. CONTAINERBOARD MAKERS, 1995

Ranked by: Estimated capacity of 32.99 tons.

1. Stone Container, 13.1%
2. Georgia-Pacific, 7.8%
3. Temple-Inland, 7.8%
4. Weyerhaeuser, 7.2%
5. International Paper, 7.0%
6. Packaging Corporation of America, 6.2%
7. Jefferson Smurfit, 5.9%
8. Union Camp, 5.6%
9. Willamette Industries, 4.7%
10. Gaylord Container, 3.6%
11. Other, 29.6%

Source: *Investext*, Thomson Financial Services, October 17, 1995, p. 6.

The most extensive use of paperboard is to make shipping containers, cartons, and packaging. The vast majority of paperboard consumed in the United States is manufactured by U.S. paperboard producers. In addition to dominating the domestic market, U.S. paperboard producers hold a strong position in the international market, with exports reaching 6 million tons in 1995, 12.9 percent of total U.S. paperboard production of 46.6 million tons.

INDUSTRY OUTLOOK

Like other sectors of the U.S. pulp and paper industry, the 1990s have been volatile for U.S. paperboard mills. The industry saw depressed conditions in the early 1990s; booming demand and huge prices increases in 1994 and 1995; and falling prices in 1996. For example, year-end transaction prices for 42-pound kraft linerboard were $315 per ton in 1993 before shooting up to $430 per ton in 1994 and $480 per ton in 1995. However, this huge runup was followed by a huge drop in 1996, to $360 per ton. One of the reasons prices for linerboard and other paperboard grades fell hard in 1996 was that capacity increases far outpaced demand for the product, which was in some cases falling as customers worked off large amounts of inventory they had purchased in anticipation of future price increases. Some recovery was expected in 1997, with prices expected to reach $410 per ton.

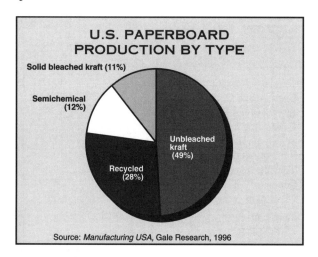

U.S. PAPERBOARD PRODUCTION BY TYPE

Solid bleached kraft (11%)

Semichemical (12%)

Unbleached kraft (49%)

Recycled (28%)

Source: *Manufacturing USA*, Gale Research, 1996

Predictably, the U.S. paperboard industry—after expanding capacity dramatically in 1996—planned only modest capacity increases for the rest of the decade. The total capacity of U.S. mills to make paperboard increased 2.5 million tons in 1996, a 5.1 percent increase over the previous year. Within the overall paperboard category, containerboard grades had a very large (6.1 percent) capacity increase in 1996, up by 2.1 million tons, and boxboard capacity was up by 419,000 tons, or 4.1 percent in 1996. However, from 1997 to 1999, growth in U.S. paperboard production was expected to drop down to just 1.7 percent on an annual basis, with containerboard holding to 1.7 percent annual increases. Boxboard capacity growth was expected to be somewhat higher during the period, at 2.3 percent, but the "all other" paperboard category was expected to barely grow at all, with just a 0.8 percent rate of annual increase. A 1.7 percent average annual growth in U.S. paperboard capacity from 1997 to 1999 was expected to increase capacity from 51.6 million tons to 54.3 million tons during the period.

While capacity, demand, and prices are the key elements determining the current status of the U.S. paperboard industry, other factors have also come into play. U.S. linerboard is recognized worldwide as being the highest quality and best performing linerboard for most packaging applications. One of the major changes in linerboard occurred in the early 1990s when "Rule 41, Item 22" of the freight classifications was changed to emphasize "ring crush," which measures resistance to compression, instead of bursting strength. This change allowed U.S. manufacturers to begin making more "high performance" linerboard, which is lighter in weight than traditional liner but still useful for shipping. As a result, U.S. producers have developed a number of high performance bleached and unbleached linerboard grades.

ORGANIZATION AND STRUCTURE

More paper and paperboard is used to make packaging than in any other single application. While most paperboard is still made from virgin fibers (trees), paperboard mills have traditionally used a large percentage of recycled fiber because of favorable economics. The use of recycled fiber in paperboard production is growing quickly, especially in products in which the reclaimed pulp does not need to be cleaned.

In the late 1980s and early 1990s, box shipments grew faster than the general economy. Through the rest of the 1990s, growth in box shipments is expected to track more closely with growth in the general economy. Since the majority of paperboard capacity is used to make materials for corrugated boxes, the background and development of paperboard mills tends to mirror growth in the use of these boxes.

As new methods helped improve the strength and durability of corrugated containers, their use in the general economy increased dramatically. Paperboard machines produced 15,545 tons per day. During the postwar years, the growth of corrugated containers more than kept pace with the general economy, which itself was growing rapidly. Paperboard accounted for slightly more than half of the overall production of paper and paperboard in the United States in 1995.

RESEARCH AND TECHNOLOGY

There is some interest in using new concepts such as stratification in making paperboard, which involves using a special headbox that can produce three or more layers simultaneously from different fiber sources. In this way, a layer of recycled fiber or some other lesser quality fiber source could be sandwiched between layers of better quality fiber. With newer model headboxes, these layers can be extremely thin.

Like other grades, much of the effort in research and technology in paperboard is to create machines that will produce a wider web of paperboard at higher speeds. In this way, paperboard mills can run their mills more productively. Also, as in other grades, mill processes are becoming more automated and less subject to product variation. This, and continual improvements in paperboard quality, are the main reasons that U.S. paperboard mills can continue to lead the world both in price and product quality.

AMERICA AND THE WORLD

Paperboard—particularly linerboard—is one of the strongest export products for the U.S. pulp and paper industry. U.S. linerboard mills, mostly in the southern United States, have traditionally been among the world's lowest-cost producers. In 1995, U.S. mills produced 6.04 million tons of paperboard for export with a value of $3.45 billion. Those exports represented 13 percent of total U.S. paperboard production.

Paperboard is a leading export product, accounting for just under 60 percent of all paper, paperboard, and converted product exports in 1995. By contrast, the United States imported a relatively small volume of paperboard in 1995, just 1.4 million tons, with a value of $810 million.

Mottled White Paperboard Makers

Jefferson Smurfit

Chesapeake Corp.

International Paper

Green Bay Packaging

St. Joe Paper

Stone Container

Temple-Inland

Simpson

Champion International

Market shares are shown based on an estimated capacity of 1.77 million tons in 1995.

Jefferson Smurfit	17.8%
Chesapeake Corp.	17.5
International Paper	12.9
Green Bay Packaging	12.7
St. Joe Paper	11.0
Stone Container	10.1
Temple-Inland	9.8
Simpson	4.5
Champion International	3.7

Source: *Investext,* Thomson Financial Services, October 17, 1995, p. 6.

SIC 2631 - Paperboard Mills
General Statistics

Year	Com-panies	Establishments		Employment			Compensation		Production ($ million)			
		Total	with 20 or more employees	Total (000)	Production Workers (000)	Hours (Mil)	Payroll ($ mil)	Wages ($/hr)	Cost of Materials	Value Added by Manufacture	Value of Shipments	Capital Invest.
1982	106	222	212	55.6	43.0	88.5	1,501.5	12.63	5,842.3	3,739.8	9,531.1	1,286.7
1983				53.6	41.4	87.0	1,558.7	13.50	6,098.4	3,985.7	10,099.9	527.3
1984				55.7	42.5	90.0	1,677.6	14.14	6,708.7	5,238.5	11,880.6	680.2
1985				53.9	41.1	86.5	1,668.4	14.35	6,171.7	4,299.6	10,494.0	1,043.4
1986				51.0	39.2	85.3	1,713.9	15.02	6,133.3	4,947.2	11,160.3	999.6
1987	91	205	200	52.3	40.1	88.5	1,858.8	15.56	6,839.7	6,914.3	13,729.7	772.6
1988				53.6	41.1	90.8	1,964.4	15.97	7,340.6	8,778.5	16,094.2	1,517.5
1989		221	202	52.1	40.3	89.2	1,958.3	16.26	7,563.6	8,798.6	16,319.3	1,653.3
1990				53.1	40.7	90.5	2,048.7	16.44	7,804.8	8,123.0	15,919.3	2,976.6
1991				50.6	39.0	86.5	2,027.4	16.90	7,781.1	7,257.2	15,013.1	2,152.3
1992	89	204	200	51.5	39.4	88.4	2,136.4	17.36	8,013.4	8,195.3	16,140.0	2,040.7
1993				53.3	40.5	90.0	2,244.2	17.69	8,657.0	7,525.7	16,164.8	1,643.3
1994				54.9	41.4	94.5	2,392.3	17.99	9,771.9	8,893.5	18,749.0	1,432.1
1995				52.1P	39.6P	91.0P	2,382.9P	18.65P	9,841.1P	8,956.5P	18,881.7P	2,211.8P
1996				51.9P	39.4P	91.3P	2,451.3P	19.07P	10,208.6P	9,290.9P	19,586.9P	2,322.0P
1997				51.8P	39.3P	91.7P	2,519.7P	19.49P	10,576.1P	9,625.4P	20,292.0P	2,432.2P
1998				51.6P	39.1P	92.0P	2,588.2P	19.92P	10,943.6P	9,959.9P	20,997.1P	2,542.4P

Sources: 1982, 1987, 1992 Economic Census; Annual Survey of Manufactures, 83-86, 88-91, 93-94. Establishment counts for non-Census years are from County Business Patterns; establishment values for 83-84 are extrapolations. 'P's show projections by the editors. Industries reclassified in 87 will not have data for prior years.

ASSOCIATIONS AND SOCIETIES

AMERICAN PAPER INSTITUTE
260 Madison Ave.
New York, NY 10016
Phone: (212) 340-0600

NATIONAL PAPER TRADE ASSOCIATION
c/o John J. Buckley
1111 Great Neck Rd.
Great Neck, NY 11021
Phone: (516) 829-3070

PAPER INDUSTRY MANAGEMENT ASSOCIATION
2400 E. Oakton St.
Arlington Heights, IL 60005
Phone: (312) 956-0250

PAPERBOARD PACKAGING COUNCIL
888 17th St. NW, Ste. 900
Washington, DC 20006
Phone: (202) 289-4100
Fax: (202) 289-4243

PERIODICALS AND NEWSLETTERS

OFFICIAL BOARD MARKETS
Magazines for Industry, Inc.
233 N. Michigan Ave.
Chicago, IL 60601
Phone: (312) 938-2300

PAPERBOARD PACKAGING
Advanstar Communications, Inc.
7500 Old Oak Blvd.
Cleveland, OH 44130
Phone: (800) 346-0085 or (216) 243-8100
Fax: (216) 891-2726
Monthly. $30.00 per year.

DATABASES

CITIBASE (CITICORP ECONOMIC DATABASE)
FAME Software Corp.
77 Water St., 9 Fl.
New York, NY 10005
Phone: (212) 898-7800
Fax: (212) 742-8956
Presents over 6,000 statistical series relating to business, industry, finance, and economics. Includes series from Survey of Current Business *and many other sources. Time period is 1947 to date, with daily updates. Inquire as to online cost and availability.*

PIRA
Technical Centre for the Paper and Board, Printing and Packaging Industries
Randalls Rd.
Leatherhead, Surrey, England KT22 7RU
Phone: 1372-376161
Fax: 1372-360104

Citations and abstracts pertaining to bookbinding and other pulp, paper, and packaging industries, 1975 to present. Inquire as to online cost and availability.

STATISTICS SOURCES

BUSINESS STATISTICS
Available from U.S. Government Printing Office
Washington, DC 20402
Phone: (202) 512-1800
Fax: (202) 512-2250
Biennial. $20.00. Issued by Bureau of Economic Analysis, U.S. Department of Commerce. Shows annual data for 29 years and monthly data for a recent four-year period. Statistics correspond to the Survey of Current Business.

PAPERBOARD PACKAGING: ECONOMIC REVIEW ISSUE
Advanstar Communications, Inc.
7500 Old Oak Blvd.
Cleveland, OH 44130
Phone: (800) 346-0085 or (216) 243-8100
Fax: (216) 891-2726
Annual.

STATISTICS OF PAPER, PAPERBOARD AND WOOD PULP
Forest and Paper Association
1111 19th St. NW
Washington, DC 20036
Phone: (202) 463-2700
Fax: (202) 463-2785
Annual. $365.00. Formerly Statistics of Paper and Paperboard.

SURVEY OF CURRENT BUSINESS
Available from U.S. Government Printing Office
Washington, DC 20402
Phone: (202) 512-1800
Fax: (202) 512-2250
Monthly. $41.00 per year. Issued by Bureau of Economic Analysis, U.S. Department of Commerce. Presents a wide variety of business and economic data.

WALDEN'S FIBER AND BOARD REPORT
Walden-Mott Corp.
475 Kinderkamack Rd.
Oradell, NJ 07649
Phone: (202) 261-2630

FURTHER READING

"Linerboard: Weaker Market Outlook Caused by Surge of New Capacity." *Pulp & Paper,* January 1996.

Paper, Paperboard, Pulp Capacity and Fiber Consumption. Washington: American Forest & Paper Association, 1996.

"Recycled Paperboard: Market Pricing Reacts to Weaker Demand and Lower Wastepaper Costs." *Pulp & Paper,* June 1996.

"U.S. Mills Looking for a Turnaround in 1997." *PIMA's North American Papermaker,* January 1997.

U.S. Trade and Industrial Outlook, 1997-1998. New York: McGraw-Hill, 1997.

PERFUMES, COSMETICS, AND TOILETRIES

SIC 2844

There *were approximately 770 establishments in the toilet preparations industry in 1996, employing an estimated 60,000 workers. The total value of industry shipments was an estimated $22.8 billion in 1997. Despite these strong numbers, concerns in the industry over animal rights and environmental issues, and any subsequent government legislation, figure prominently in its successful future.*

The nation's economic condition during the 1980s and early 1990s brought about changes in the industry's distribution patterns. Traditionally, retail products had been classified as upscale, mid-level, or low-scale, depending on where they were sold and their pricing structure. Upscale product lines were typically sold in major department stores or specialty boutiques; mid-level product lines were sold in department stores at lower prices; and low-scale product lines were sold in drug stores or through catalogs. Industry analysts reported that customers were turning away from upscale products and switching to lower priced brands which were increasingly being sold in mass market outlets. Department stores had sold almost 20 percent of upscale cosmetics in the mid-1980s, but by the early 1990s the figure had dropped to 12 percent, according to a study conducted by Business Trend Analysts reported in *Drug and Cosmetic Industry.*

 MOST PREFERRED WOMEN'S FRAGRANCES

Ranked by: Sales in 1995, in millions of dollars.

1. Vanilla Fields, with $35.5 million
2. Jovan, $33.3
3. Vanderbilt, $26.0
4. Lady Stetson, $23.0
5. Exclamation, $22.4

Source: *Brandweek*, Superbrands: America's Top 2,000 Brands, October 9, 1995, p. 124.

INDUSTRY OUTLOOK

As the perfume, cosmetic, and toiletry preparations industry entered the 1990s, it faced many challenges, including regulatory changes, product safety concerns, calls for scientific data to document product claims, increasing environmentalism, and pressure from the growing animal rights movement. Congress began investigating possible revisions to the traditional "drug" and "cosmetic" definitions established under the Food, Drug and Cosmetic Act. A report titled *Classification and Regulation of Cosmetics and Drugs: A Legal Overview and Alternatives for Legislative Change* included provisions for a third category of "cosmeceuticals" to include products like sunscreens that fell in the gap between "drugs" and "cosmetics." Some industry analysts welcomed legislative changes to clarify product distinctions but doubted whether manufacturers would accept proposals that would require safety and efficacy testing to substantiate label claims.

The FDA continued compiling complaints from customers about neurological reactions to perfumes including symptoms such as burning of the eyes, nose and throat, flushing, dizziness, nausea, difficulty in breathing, memory loss, and drowsiness. Some hospitals banned the use of perfumes by operating room nurses. A group calling itself the National Foundation of the Chemically Hypersensitive wanted to ban the use of fragrances in public meeting places.

Some spokesmen within the fragrance and cosmetic industry claimed that because no one had ever been killed or seriously injured as a result of fragrance use, the FDA's resources would be better spent on bigger health problems. They advocated individual avoidance of offending ingredients as a solution to skin irritations and allergic responses. Although the industry's safety record prior to the 1990s had been good, some seasoned industry watchers expressed concern about continued safety as many small, new companies emerged.

Growing concern about environmental issues also impacted the industry. Several surveys demonstrated increased awareness of pollution and related issues. In the mid-1970s, 64 percent of one survey's respondents favored banning products that polluted the environment; by the late 1980s, 73 percent supported such a ban. In another survey, 82 percent of respondents claimed to have changed purchasing decisions as a result of environmental concerns; 77 percent said that the environmental reputation of a company was important to them when making brand decisions; and 56 percent had refused to buy a product during the previous year because of environmental concerns. In the early 1990s, a New York survey group estimated that 18.8 million

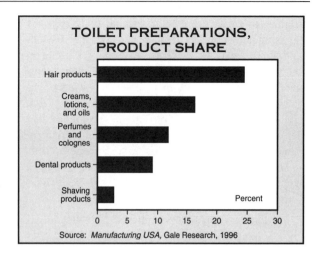

TOILET PREPARATIONS, PRODUCT SHARE

Source: *Manufacturing USA*, Gale Research, 1996

U.S. households were environmentally interested shoppers. These consumers, called "Green consumers," accounted for about 20 percent of the U.S. population and their number was expected to increase. In a report on Green consumers, the survey group cited three main concerns: animal rights and species preservation, availability of clean air and water, and waste management.

One of the most controversial environmental matters facing the fragrance industry was pressure to reduce its use of volatile organic chemicals (VOCs). The most popularly used VOC was ethyl alcohol, which functioned as a solvent. The industry claimed that water was not a good substitute for ethyl alcohol because many fragrance ingredients were not water soluble. Ingredients designed to help materials dissolve in water affected product texture and also presented possible safety concerns. Propellants and many other ingredients used within the industry were also VOCs.

VOCs were blamed for contributing to ground-level ozone. In California, VOC emissions from colognes,

SIC 2844 - Toilet Preparations
Industry Data by State

State	Establish-ments	Shipments			Employment				Cost as % of Shipments	Investment per Employee ($)
		Total ($ mil)	% of U.S.	Per Establ.	Total Number	% of U.S.	Per Establ.	Wages ($/hour)		
New Jersey	103	3,456.1	18.4	33.6	10,900	18.1	106	11.91	29.4	11,917
New York	92	2,126.3	11.3	23.1	8,600	14.3	93	8.44	21.5	2,733
Illinois	39	1,744.7	9.3	44.7	4,500	7.5	115	11.62	33.3	7,867
California	141	1,583.4	8.4	11.2	8,000	13.3	57	8.82	38.0	5,625
North Carolina	10	1,129.0	6.0	112.9	3,100	5.2	310	10.60	24.5	-
Connecticut	21	1,105.1	5.9	52.6	2,600	4.3	124	12.67	25.0	3,192
Texas	58	748.0	4.0	12.9	2,000	3.3	34	10.13	21.8	6,350
Ohio	24	705.8	3.8	29.4	1,900	3.2	79	12.52	32.8	6,526
Virginia	7	604.5	3.2	86.4	1,300	2.2	186	12.63	28.2	-
Minnesota	13	511.4	2.7	39.3	1,900	3.2	146	12.95	40.3	8,316

Source: 1992 *Economic Census*. The states are in descending order of shipments or establishments (if shipment data are missing for the majority). The symbol (D) appears when data are withheld to prevent disclosure of competitive information. States marked with (D) are sorted by number of establishments. A dash (-) indicates that the data element cannot be calculated; * indicates the midpoint of a range.

perfumes, toilet water, aftershaves, and body splashes were estimated at almost 1,700 pounds per day. Consequently in the early 1990s, California proposed limits on VOC usage in fragrances. New York and other states were expected to follow. In California, the proposed regulations scheduled to take effect on January 1, 1995, limited VOCs to 70 percent of perfumes, colognes, and toilet waters; 60 percent of aftershaves; and 50 percent of other fragrances. Industry negotiators and the California Air Resources Board agreed to exempt colognes, perfumes and toilet waters that were on the market before the regulations took effect.

In addition to planned compliance with VOC regulations, many fragrance and cosmetic companies brought "green" products to the market place. As some companies eliminated, reduced, or refabricated outer packaging to emphasize their concern about waste disposal problems, others, particularly fragrance manufacturers, expressed concern about the trend because packaging contributed to their image.

Critics claimed that many of the environmental efforts advertised by cosmetic and fragrance manufacturers were exaggerated, false, or meaningless. For example, "biodegradable" packages were incapable of degrading under conditions present in most landfills. Some products were labeled "ozone friendly" because they did not contain chlorofluorocarbons (CFCs), but CFCs had been banned since the late 1970s. "Recyclable" notations on plastic containers were meaningless when recycling plants for particular plastics (like polystyrene) were not available.

Along with increased environmental awareness came concern for healthy products. Items seen as safe for the environment were perceived as healthy for users. This philosophy drove a trend toward increased use of natural products containing ingredients such as proteins and vitamins. It also brought expanded use of botanical ingredients such as aloe, cucumber, and berry extracts. In perfumes, the trend led to the increasing popularity of discreet scents, floral freshness, and sea smells. In makeup, consumers began turning to functional products. Cosmetics were expected to do more than add color and cover skin imperfections. Buyers wanted products to contain ingredients such as sunscreens and emollients to nourish and protect their skin. The focus on natural products also led to more realistic product claims.

The emphasis on natural ingredients, however, extended only to plant sources. Animal products were shunned and animal-testing fell into disfavor. Many companies promoted cosmetic lines that were developed without animal testing. The Cosmetic, Toiletries, and Fragrance Association (CTFA)—founded in 1894 to represent manufacturers, distributors, and industry suppliers in an effort "to provide an environment free of unnecessary government regulation"—remained firm in its support of some animal testing, however. According to the CTFA, even products that claimed to use non-animal test methods relied on models that were acquired as a result of animal testing. The organization believed that human health and safety were more important than animal rights. The CTFA reported that 74 percent of Californians polled opposed legislation that would prohibit animal testing to insure product safety.

The most widely used animal test, and perhaps the most controversial, was the Draize Eye Irritancy Test. The Draize test involved putting drops in the eyes of albino rabbits so investigators could note redness, swelling, cloudiness, and opacity. Also of importance was the eye's ability to recover from any injuries sustained.

In addition to the social and political concerns surrounding animal testing, environmentalism, and product safety, the industry was also impacted by the nation's economic situation. The perfume, cosmetic, and personal care products industry had established a "recession proof" image when sales of inexpensive cosmetics had outsold mid-priced food items and clothing during the depression of the 1930s. Cosmetics also did well during the recessions of the 1960s and 1980s. The recession of the early 1990s, however, brought new challenges. Counterfeit products were offered at low prices. Customers resisted high prices and demanded value. The numbers of distribution channels for upscale lines decreased as traditional department stores closed. Costs associated with product promotion increased and marketers turned more often to expensive strategies such as giving free complementary products.

In an effort to move away from traditional department store cosmetic counters, upscale manufacturers turned to self-serve packaging and sold greater volumes to discounters. This enabled retailers to place items on sale. Depressed pricing, however, sometimes diminished a product's image. Bridge brands increasingly aimed at a niche between the upscale and mass markets. Mass marketers focused on increasing volumes to generate more profit.

ORGANIZATION AND STRUCTURE

The federal agency most often involved in regulatory encounters with the industry was the Food and Drug Administration (FDA). The FDA has required that color additives be tested and approved prior to use. It banned or restricted the use of some specific ingredients including mercury compounds, chloroform, and methylene chloride. Other regulations dictated that cosmetics contain no poisonous or harmful substances, no filthy, putrid, or decomposed substances, and that they must be manufactured and held under sanitary conditions. The FDA also instituted labeling requirements which compelled manufacturers to list cosmetic ingredients in descending order according to the quantity used, with some flexibility allowed for the protection of trade secrets. The FDA also had the authority to take legal action against cosmetic companies if problems developed with the safety of products already on the market. In order to do so, the agency was required to prove in court that the product was harmful or misbranded.

The FDA, however, did not require the same type of pre-market approval for cosmetics as was required for drugs. According to a report published in *FDA Consumer*, cosmetics were legally defined as "articles other than soap which are applied to the human body for cleansing, beautifying, promoting attractiveness, or altering the appearance." The FDA recognized 13 categories of cosmetics: skin care products, fragrances, manicure products, eye makeup, makeup other than eye makeup, hair coloring preparations, shampoos and other hair products, deodorants, shaving products, baby products, bath oils and bubble baths, mouthwashes, and sunscreens.

The distinction between cosmetics and drugs was sometimes vague. According to FDA guidelines, products claiming to offer medical benefits or physiological effects were over-the-counter (OTC) drugs. Examples of items with controversial classifications included antiperspirants, which were classified as OTC drugs in the late

1970s, sunscreen products that listed a Sun Protection Factor (SPF) number, hair care products claiming to protect or restore hair, and shampoos professing to cure or remove dandruff. If the FDA deemed a cosmetic product to be an OTC drug, it was regulated as a new drug. The manufacturer was then required to demonstrate product safety and efficacy in order to gain FDA approval.

The cosmetic industry, under the sponsorship of CTFA, developed the Cosmetic Ingredient Review (CIR) in the mid-1970s in order to gather information about ingredient safety and make the information available to manufacturers. Reviews were conducted by a panel of scientific and medical experts. One report claimed that by 1988, 85 percent of the 700 most frequently used cosmetic ingredients had been reviewed, were under review, or were being regulated or studied by other procedures such as the FDA's process of reviewing over-the-counter drugs. Another report claimed that a review performed by the National Institute of Occupational Safety and Health found that 884 of the 2,983 chemicals used as ingredients in cosmetics were toxic substances. The CTFA refuted the claim and maintained that scientific and medical studies demonstrated the safety of ingredients used within the industry.

The fragrance segment of the industry organized the Research Institute for Fragrance Materials (RIFM) in the mid-1960s to independently test and certify the safety of natural and chemical aromatics. During its first 25 years of operation, the RIFM tested approximately 1,400 different materials. The studies resulted in recommenda-

SIC 2844 - Toilet Preparations
General Statistics

Year	Companies	Establishments		Employment			Compensation		Production ($ million)			
		Total	with 20 or more employees	Total (000)	Production Workers (000)	Hours (Mil)	Payroll ($ mil)	Wages ($/hr)	Cost of Materials	Value Added by Manufacture	Value of Shipments	Capital Invest.
1982	596	639	257	60.4	35.8	68.6	1,102.1	7.59	3,026.3	7,124.4	10,183.2	220.7
1983		641	257	60.9	36.3	69.9	1,142.5	7.68	3,338.8	7,603.0	10,925.1	254.4
1984		643	257	60.9	35.9	67.6	1,208.4	8.38	3,450.2	8,310.0	11,664.9	231.3
1985		645	258	59.8	34.7	66.0	1,250.4	8.83	3,527.1	8,975.6	12,426.9	291.0
1986		654	266	58.8	33.8	66.0	1,388.1	9.32	3,647.0	9,725.1	13,332.9	276.9
1987	649	694	272	57.9	35.1	69.9	1,352.8	9.22	3,881.6	10,801.1	14,592.9	225.5
1988		687	277	64.9	40.5	78.1	1,551.3	9.08	4,445.1	12,053.2	16,293.6	292.6
1989		676	282	63.6	39.4	75.4	1,615.5	9.69	4,758.2	11,979.2	16,641.9	313.7
1990		682	284	63.6	38.1	74.3	1,620.6	10.14	4,904.6	12,104.2	17,048.4	280.4
1991		674	271	57.4	35.6	69.8	1,616.3	10.81	5,046.3	12,047.4	17,085.4	299.5
1992	707	756	305	60.1	37.2	75.6	1,783.3	10.82	5,611.3	13,167.2	18,753.5	507.3
1993		778	299	61.7	38.6	79.7	1,857.8	10.59	6,152.6	13,588.8	19,706.4	472.6
1994		750P	300P	57.6	35.3	72.8	1,796.6	10.93	6,482.1	13,327.2	19,736.0	490.6
1995		760P	305P	60.3P	37.8P	77.2P	1,940.0P	11.48P	6,945.4P	14,279.8P	21,146.7P	471.1P
1996		771P	309P	60.2P	37.9P	78.0P	2,005.2P	11.77P	7,221.6P	14,847.6P	21,987.6P	492.7P
1997		781P	313P	60.2P	38.1P	78.7P	2,070.4P	12.06P	7,497.8P	15,415.4P	22,828.4P	514.3P
1998		792P	317P	60.2P	38.2P	79.5P	2,135.6P	12.35P	7,773.9P	15,983.2P	23,669.3P	535.9P

Sources: 1982, 1987, 1992 *Economic Census; Annual Survey of Manufactures*, 83-86, 88-91, 93-94. Establishment counts for non-Census years are from *County Business Patterns*; establishment values for 83-84 are extrapolations. 'P's show projections by the editors. Industries reclassified in 87 will not have data for prior years.

tions to restrict or prohibit about 100 of the ingredients reviewed.

In an effort to further cooperation between cosmetic and fragrance manufacturers and the FDA, the regulatory agency instituted a voluntary registration program in which manufacturers participated in monitoring adverse reactions to products. The program provided for information exchanges among participants and with the government. By the early 1990s, more than 165 companies had registered and the FDA planned to expand the program to include a larger percentage of eligible participants and to provide more useful services.

SIC 2844
Occupations Employed by SIC 284 - Soap, Cleaners, and Toilet Goods

Occupation	% of Total 1994	Change to 2005
Packaging & filling machine operators	8.5	-30.1
Hand packers & packagers	6.3	-20.1
Assemblers, fabricators, & hand workers nec	5.7	16.5
Sales & related workers nec	4.9	16.5
Freight, stock, & material movers, hand	3.6	-6.8
Secretaries, ex legal & medical	3.5	6.0
Chemical equipment controllers, operators	3.0	4.8
Industrial machinery mechanics	2.7	28.1
Machine operators nec	2.6	2.6
Industrial truck & tractor operators	2.6	16.5
Chemists	2.5	28.1
Crushing & mixing machine operators	2.5	16.4
General managers & top executives	2.5	10.5
Traffic, shipping, & receiving clerks	2.2	12.1
Marketing, advertising, & PR managers	2.0	16.5
Science & mathematics technicians	1.8	16.5
Bookkeeping, accounting, & auditing clerks	1.8	-12.6
Maintenance repairers, general utility	1.7	4.8
Inspectors, testers, & graders, precision	1.6	16.5
General office clerks	1.6	-0.7
Order clerks, materials, merchandise, & service	1.5	13.9
Machine feeders & offbearers	1.5	4.8
Clerical supervisors & managers	1.5	19.1
Professional workers nec	1.4	39.7
Industrial production managers	1.4	16.4
Stock clerks	1.4	-5.3
Managers & administrators nec	1.3	16.4
Adjustment clerks	1.2	39.8
Accountants & auditors	1.2	16.5
Management support workers nec	1.1	16.4
Engineering, mathematical, & science managers	1.1	32.2
Truck drivers light & heavy	1.0	20.1

Source: Industry-Occupation Matrix, Bureau of Labor Statistics. These data relate to one or more 3-digit SIC industry groups rather than to a single 4-digit SIC. The change reported for each occupation to the year 2005 is a percent of growth or decline as estimated by the Bureau of Labor Statistics. The abbreviation nec stands for 'not elsewhere classified'.

WORK FORCE

Although industry shipment figures demonstrated overall growth during the 1980s and the early 1990s, employment figures fell. In the late 1980s, the toilet preparation industry employed 72,200. In the early 1990s, several manufacturers closed plants or an-

nounced future plant closings. In 1995, the industry employed 68,400.

Mergers, corporate acquisitions, and takeovers restructured the industry as major participants changed owners. Consolidation and cost cutting measures eliminated less profitable products and resulted in the loss of many blue and white collar jobs. A few companies were expanding employment opportunities but not at a pace sufficient to counteract the shrinking work forces at other organizations.

RESEARCH AND TECHNOLOGY

During the 1990s, research and technological improvements within the industry focused on reformulating products to move away from synthetic chemicals and to rely on natural products. Within the class of natural products, the primary emphasis was on vegetable and plant materials. Chemists also sought to meet customer demands for mildness and reduced toxicity. Within the growing sun-care segment of the industry, scientists researched products with improved protection, especially against year-round ultraviolet rays. Color market formulators worked to develop new silicon-based products which promised better color retention and improved waterproofing capabilities.

AMERICA AND THE WORLD

In the early 1990s, the United States was a net exporter of perfumes, cosmetics, and toilet preparations. Canada, the United Kingdom, Japan, and Mexico were major purchasers of U.S. goods. About 55 percent of the nation's imports were received from France. Other countries supplying products to the U.S. market included the United Kingdom, Japan, and Mexico. The worldwide fragrance market was estimated at $10 billion. Within this segment, U.S. demand represented the largest national market in the world, only slightly smaller than the entire European market. Demand in Japan was estimated to be about one third the size of the U.S. market.

As the industry moved increasingly toward globalization, new markets were developing in Latin America, Eastern Europe, and the Pacific Rim. While American increased their penetration in overseas markets, foreign companies increased their involvement in American markets. Globalization brought efforts to adopt common terminology, particularly in describing ingredients. The CTFA expected wider use of the CTFA Ingredient Dictionary.

ASSOCIATIONS AND SOCIETIES

AMERICAN ASSOCIATION OF COSMETOLOGY SCHOOLS
901 N. Washington St., Ste. 206
Alexandria, VA 22314-1535
Phone: (703) 845-1333
Fax: (703) 845-1336

AMERICAN SOCIETY OF PERFUMERS
PO Box 1551
West Caldwell, NJ 07004
Phone: (201) 808-6911
Members are professional perfumers.

COSMETIC, TOILETRY AND FRAGRANCE ASSOCIATION
1101 17th St. NW, Ste. 300
Washington, DC 20036
Phone: (202) 331-1770
Fax: (202) 331-1969

FRAGRANCE FOUNDATION
145 E. 32nd St., 14 Fl.
New York, NY 10016
Phone: (212) 725-2755
Fax: (212) 779-9058

NATIONAL COSMETOLOGY ASSOCIATION
3510 Olive St.
St. Louis, MO 63103
Phone: (800) 527-1683 or (314) 534-7980
Fax: (314) 534-8618

NATIONAL INTERSTATE COUNCIL OF STATE BOARDS OF COSMETOLOGY
Capitol Sta., PO Box 11390
Columbia, SC 29211
Phone: (803) 799-9800
Fax: (803) 376-2277

SOCIETY OF COSMETIC CHEMISTS
120 Wall St., Ste. 240
New York, NY 10005
Phone: (212) 668-1500

PERIODICALS AND NEWSLETTERS

CTFA NEWSLETTER
Cosmetic, Toiletry, and Fragrance Association
1101 17th St. NW
Washington, DC 20036
Phone: (202) 331-1770
Fax: (202) 331-1969
Bimonthly.

DRUG AND COSMETIC INDUSTRY
Advanstar Communications, Inc.
7500 Old Oak Blvd.
Cleveland, OH 44130

Phone: (800) 346-0085 or (216) 243-8100
Fax: (216) 891-2726
Monthly. $40.00 per year.

HOUSEHOLD AND PERSONAL PRODUCTS INDUSTRY: THE MAGAZINE FOR THE DETERGENT, SOAP, COSMETICS AND TOILETRY, WAX, POLISH AND AEROSOL INDUSTRIES
Rodman Publishing Corp.
PO Box 555
Ramsey, NJ 07446
Phone: (201) 825-2552
Fax: (201) 825-0553
Monthly. $48.00 per year. Covers marketing, packaging, production, technical innovations, private label developments, and aerosol packaging for soap, detergents, cosmetics, insecticides, and a variety of other household products.

PERFUMER AND FLAVORIST
Allured Publishing Corp.
362 S. Schmale Rd.
Carol Stream, IL 60188
Phone: (708) 653-2155
Fax: (708) 653-2192
Bimonthly. $110.00 per year. Provides information on the art and technology of flavors and fragrances, including essential oils, aroma chemicals, and spices.

THE ROSE SHEET: TOILETRIES, FRAGRANCES, AND SKIN CARE
FDC Reports, Inc.
5550 Friendship Blvd., Ste. 1
Chevy Chase, MD 20815-7278
Phone: (800) 332-2181 or (301) 657-9830
Fax: (301) 664-7248
Weekly. $500.00 per year. Newsletter. Provides news of the cosmetics industry, including regulations, new products, testing, corporate mergers, and product promotions.

SOAP/COSMETICS/CHEMICAL SPECIALTIES
PTN Publishing Corp.
445 Broad Hollow Rd.
Melville, NY 11747-4722
Phone: (516) 845-2700
Fax: (516) 845-7109
Monthly. $60.00 per year.

DATABASES

F-D-C REPORTS
FDC Reports, Inc.
5550 Friendship Blvd., Ste. 1
Chevy Chase, MD 20815
Phone: (301) 657-9830
Fax: (301) 656-3094
An online version of "The Gray Sheet" (medical devices), "The Pink Sheet" (pharmaceuticals), and "The Rose Sheet" (cosmetics). Contains full-text information on legal, technical, corporate, financial, and marketing developments from 1987 to date, with weekly updates. Inquire as to online cost and availability.

NIELSEN SCANTRACK U.S.

Nielsen Marketing Research
Nielsen Plz.
Northbrook, IL 60062
Phone: (312) 498-6300
Fax: (708) 205-4026
Includes the Nielsen Food Index and the Nielsen Health and Beauty Aid Index, with monthly updates and about 10 years of historical data. Provides detailed information on consumer sales, market share, distribution, inventories, and prices. Food, drug store products, alcoholic beverages, and other products are covered. Inquire as to online cost and availability.

PROMT: PREDICASTS OVERVIEW OF MARKETS AND TECHNOLOGY

Information Access Co.
362 Lakeside Dr.
Foster City, CA 94404
Phone: (800) 321-6388 or (415) 378-5000
Fax: (415) 358-4759
Companies, products, applied technologies and markets. U.S. and international literature coverage, 1972 to date. Daily updates. Inquire as to online cost and availability. Provides abstracts from more than 1,200 publications.

STATISTICS SOURCES

U.S. INDUSTRIAL OUTLOOK: FORECASTS FOR SELECTED MANUFACTURING AND SERVICE INDUSTRIES

Available from U.S. Government Printing Office
Washington, DC 20402
Phone: (202) 512-1800
Fax: (202) 512-2250
Annual. $37.00. (Replaced in 1995 by U.S. Global Trade Outlook.) Issued by the International Trade Administration, U.S. Department of Commerce. Provides basic data, outlook for the current year, and "Long-Term Prospects" (five-year projections) for a wide variety of products and services. Includes high technology industries. Available on the world wide web at gopher://gopher.umsl.edu:70/11/library/govdocs/usio94

FAIRCHILD FACT FILE: TOILETRIES, COSMETICS, FRAGRANCES, AND BEAUTY AIDS

Fairchild Publications
7 W. 34th St.
New York, NY 10001
Phone: (800) 247-6622 or (212) 630-3880
Fax: (212) 630-3868
Biennial. $25.00. Provides statistical and analytical marketing data, including industry concentration, materials consumed, import/export sales, value of shipments, retail sales by outlet type, advertising expenditures, consumer buying habits, and industry trends.

GENERAL WORKS

TOILETRIES, COSMETICS AND FRAGRANCES

Fairchild Books
7 W. 34th St.
New York, NY 10003
Phone: (800) 247-6622 or (212) 630-8885
1990. $37.50. Sixth edition.

FURTHER READING

Darnay, Arsen, ed.*Manufacturing USA,*5th ed. Detroit; Gale Research, 1996.

"Overseas Consumers Flock to U.S. Household and Personal Care Brands." *STREETnet,* 26 July 1996. Available from http://www.streetnet.com. *Streetnet;* 30 July 1996. Available from http://www.streetnet.com.

"Rapid International Growth." *STREETnet,* September 1996. "Pretty and Practical." *STREETnet,* 30 July 1996. Available from http://www.streetnet.com.

The first American magazines appeared in 1741, but like many of their successors, were doomed to swift failure. This inauspicious start notwithstanding, the periodicals industry burgeoned steadily over the following 250 years, employing an estimated 131,000 Americans by 1996, distributing upward of 11,000 publications, and generating annual revenues of more than $24.786 billion. Indispensable to Americans as a source of entertainment and information, magazine publishing also provides an essential advertising medium for other industries.

In the first half of the twentieth century the magazine publishing industry progressed steadily, without meteoric rises until the early 1980s. Then new production technology, positive demographic trends, and an accelerated need for information all came together to spur a doubling in revenues over the span of the decade. Unfortunately this growth spurt did not last: a widespread recession started in the late 1980s, just when periodical markets were starting on a disturbing tendency towards maturity and saturation. In response, major advertisers hastened to slash their budgets, bringing diminished revenues and dwindling profits to the publishing industry in general.

PERIODICAL PUBLISHING AND PRINTING

SIC 2721

The *periodicals industry rebounded from the economic depression of the late 1980s by changing the scope of many publications to cater to new niche markets and to target specific audiences with advertising. Many well-established magazines began on-line services, and a new market opened to exclusively electronic magazines. But the recovery from the low point of the early 1990s is expected to slow as markets mature; periodical manufacturers will concentrate on growing revenues and profit margins associated with circulation sales, and will continue efforts already begun to seek additional revenue from back-end sales to their subscriber databases.*

 **TOP MAGAZINES BY GROSS REVENUE**

Ranked by: Total revenue in 1995.

1. *TV Guide*, with $1,068,832
2. *People*, $801,153
3. *Sports Illustrated*, $697,381
4. *Time*, $672,626
5. *Reader's Digest*, $529,742
6. *Parade*, $515,591
7. *Newsweek*, $480,535
8. *Better Homes & Gardens*, $406,573
9. *PC Magazine*, $391,341
10. *Good Housekeeping*, $339,000

Source: *Advertising Age,* Ad Age 300 (annual), June 17, 1996, p. S-2.

The challenges produced by these two important problems found magazine publishers scrambling both to reduce costs and retain their share of U.S. advertising expenditures. To keep advertisers interested, many companies introduced niche periodicals. New magazines like Milwaukee-based *Reunions Magazine* and *Chicagoland Gardening* catered to smaller audiences, but offered their advertisers useful, tightly focused audiences. This eased the advertising situation somewhat, but also split the magazine market into highly-fragmented target areas.

INDUSTRY OUTLOOK

In response to the depressed market of the early 1990s, publishers subtly reduced the number of annual issues, cut postage costs by using four-digit zip code suffixes, used lighter-weight paper, and trucked products to regional distribution centers. The largest gains, though, were accomplished through layoffs, salary freezes, and benefit cutbacks. In the face of slow overall growth, publishers were also jockeying to take advantage of a few healthy industry niches. Regional magazines, for example, realized an increase in successful titles of 38 percent in the early 1990s. The number of not-for-profit periodicals, which make up about 18 percent of total consumer magazine circulation, jumped as well, by 22 percent. Rapid sales growth also occurred in travel, golf, camping, and pet publications. Erotic and pornographic titles continued to maintain strong sales through the decade; other growing niches related to crafts and games, fishing and hunting, comics, military, and computers.

The most rapid declines in the middle of the decade were taking place in periodicals related to airline flight, television and radio, all of which had previously offered solid gains. Boating, dancing, gardening, and dressmaking segment revenues were declining more slowly, as were magazines about horses and boating. Declining numbers of titles in the early 1990s were occurring in subjects related to health, men, motorcycles, and lifestyle.

As the 1990s progressed, however, certain categories regained in popularity, and new ones arose to plump revenues still further. Gardening, for example, became such a popular pastime across the country that periodicals like *Martha Stewart Living*, which also incorporates home decorating and other domestic arts, found an ever-broader market niche. Others, like *Modern Dad*, (circulation 100,000) are more tightly focused, catering for more specialized consumers.

Although U.S. media advertising expenditures grew by 5.4 percent between 1986 and 1996 (in inflation adjusted dollars), total periodical industry receipts were expected to rise by only 1 to 2 percent above inflation in the late 1990s. As a result, publishers will concentrate on growing revenues and profit margins associated with circulation sales. As markets mature, moreover, periodical manufacturers will increasingly seek additional revenues from back-end sales to their subscriber database. Many publishers had already initiated aggressive campaigns to sell products and materials that complement their publications. In an effort to pursue ever-greater advertising revenues, magazines will also begin offering different ads and editorial sections for the same publication, so that different customer segments will receive issues tailored to their demographic profile.

In the late 1990s, magazines are increasingly turning to online services, which offer benefits such as decreased dependence on advertisers. Many well-known magazines have offered electronic versions on consumer online services such as America Online and CompuServe. With the popularity of the World Wide Web, publishers have also begun hosting their own sites that often include back issues and other special features. There have also been numerous Internet-only publications, sometimes called e-zines, that offer similar content and format as their print-based competitors.

Environmental considerations will receive growing industry attention entering the twenty-first century. In the early 1990s, government and special interests were

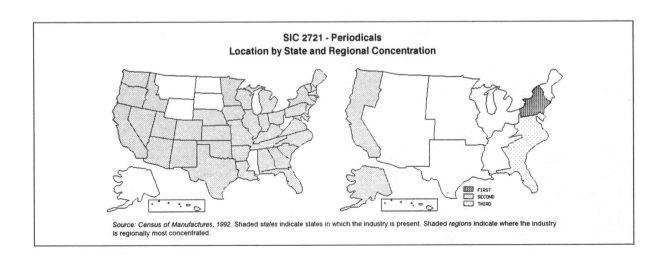

SIC 2721 - Periodicals
Location by State and Regional Concentration

FIRST
SECOND
THIRD

Source: Census of Manufactures, 1992. Shaded states indicate states in which the industry is present. Shaded regions indicate where the industry is regionally most concentrated.

already prodding publishers to reduce their use of hazardous inks and to utilize more recycled materials in their production processes. As Congress threatened to legislate the mandatory use of recycled paper, the number of publishers using at least some recycled materials increased to more than one-third by the middle of the decade.

ORGANIZATION AND STRUCTURE

Periodical publishers earn money either by selling advertising space in their pages to companies wanting display areas for their products, or by charging readers for subscriptions or individual issues. Thus the periodical's content is essentially a tool which can be fine-tuned in order to boost sales and ad revenues. Many publishers also generate income thorough database marketing techniques, such as selling subscriber lists or marketing "back-end" products and services to their customers.

Periodicals sales and ad revenues each account for about 50 percent of the average publisher's receipts. Although 80 percent of all periodicals are purchased through mail-order subscriptions, 30 percent of sales dollar volume is garnered through newsstand sales. As is the case with most items, the prices of magazines have risen during the 1990s. In 1992 the average annual subscription price of a U.S. periodical was about $27, while the typical newsstand price per individual issue was about $2.85. By the end of 1996, however, newsstand prices averaged $2.93, and subscription rates had risen to an average $29.42.

MARKETS

In 1988, according to McCann-Erickson, magazines received a 5.1 percent share of the print-media advertising market. By the end of 1996, their share had risen to 5.3 percent. This prompted publishers to find innovative ways to attract more advertising dollars. Some, like top-ranked *TV Guide*, cut their rate bases to advertisers, making up the difference in revenues by boosting the newsstand price of the magazine. Others started custom publishing magazines tailored to the needs of specific clients. In November 1996, *Business Week* noted two interesting examples. One, a richly illustrated Conde Nast publication, advertised only the expensive watches specified in its title, *Patek Phillipe*; the other, from Hachette Filipacci Magazines, was *Mercedes Momentum*, launched in 1995 specifically to attract more female purchasers to the Mercedes Benz automobile.

A second way to multiply advertising dollars is by paying close attention to previously skirted markets. Notable in this regard is Essence Communications, publishers of the highly successful *Essence*, a magazine for African-American women. Sparked by its own considerable experience, the company backed *Latina*, a bilingual Spanish-English magazine which made its debut in May 1996. Another trend in the advertising revenue field (introduced by Hachette Filipacci CEO David Pecker) is the practice of combining ads for two ostensibly unrelated products which are aimed at the same consumer.

SIC 2721 - Periodicals
General Statistics

| Year | Companies | Establishments | | Employment | | | Compensation | | Production ($ million) | | | |
		Total	with 20 or more employees	Total (000)	Production Workers (000)	Hours (Mil)	Payroll ($ mil)	Wages ($/hr)	Cost of Materials	Value Added by Manufacture	Value of Shipments	Capital Invest.
1982	3,144	3,328	690	94.0	17.4	31.9	1,986.1	7.62	4,568.1	6,910.9	11,478.0	194.8
1983				93.4	17.3	31.9	2,073.7	8.03	4,603.6	7,868.9	12,436.7	251.7
1984				93.5	16.2	28.8	2,231.7	8.71	5,117.6	8,943.9	14,052.6	267.4
1985				95.8	16.2	28.4	2,554.5	9.59	5,579.8	9,678.1	15,246.4	339.7
1986				98.1	14.2	24.9	2,710.9	11.60	5,558.1	10,196.0	15,719.4	274.1
1987	3,757	4,020	876	110.0	18.3	32.4	2,982.7	11.06	5,872.7	11,452.1	17,329.2	246.4
1988				111.4	19.1	33.8	3,152.1	11.99	6,201.9	12,439.6	18,611.8	246.1
1989		4,101	872	115.9	20.7	32.6	3,422.8	12.45	6,581.0	13,248.4	19,787.2	272.2
1990				115.2	21.6	35.4	3,658.5	13.09	6,579.6	13,847.7	20,396.7	274.8
1991				110.6	20.7	35.4	3,661.0	13.21	6,459.0	13,794.4	20,345.1	223.0
1992	4,390	4,699	991	116.2	20.1	39.0	4,074.5	13.40	6,200.9	15,833.0	22,033.9	234.4
1993				117.1	19.7	37.4	4,305.3	12.51	6,391.2	16,271.9	22,652.5	289.5
1994				116.4	18.3	34.5	4,273.9	12.97	5,903.1	15,821.4	21,723.3	306.6
1995				123.2P	20.9P	37.7P	4,618.7P	14.65P	6,638.9P	17,793.6P	24,431.2P	278.7P
1996				125.6P	21.2P	38.3P	4,827.0P	15.14P	6,895.1P	18,480.2P	25,373.9P	280.9P
1997				127.9P	21.6P	39.0P	5,035.3P	15.62P	7,151.3P	19,166.8P	26,316.7P	283.2P
1998				130.3P	21.9P	39.7P	5,243.6P	16.11P	7,407.5P	19,853.5P	27,259.5P	285.4P

Sources: 1982, 1987, 1992 *Economic Census*; *Annual Survey of Manufactures*, 83-86, 88-91, 93-94. Establishment counts for non-Census years are from *County Business Patterns*; establishment values for 83-84 are extrapolations. 'P's show projections by the editors. Industries reclassified in 87 will not have data for prior years.

Other strategies have included "licensing" the name of a magazine to a different product, as *Playboy* has done with recreational clubs.

COMPETITION

Approximately 11,000 American magazines are published each year, yet there are a few publishing companies which dominate the industry. In 1995, according to *Standard & Poor's Industry Survey* for 1996, the 10 largest consumer magazines generated 23 percent, or $4.8 billion of the total $24.7 billion in magazine revenues. Leading the pack in 1995 was *TV Guide*, ($1.1 billion) followed by *People*, *Sports Illustrated*, and *Time*.

Because competition for ad and circulation dollars is intense, the turnover rate of publications is enormous—particularly for start-up periodicals. In 1995 alone, 838 magazines debuted, but indications are that 50 percent of them are doomed to failure. Low barriers to entry (in comparison to most other industries) contribute to the high failure rate, because anyone with several thousand dollars and an idea can start a new periodical. Poor business planning and inadequate market research, however, usually accompany such endeavors.

The periodicals industry continued to expand steadily during the 1980s, a general increase in the demand for all types of current information and escalating advertising expenditures helping to boost circulation. Other stimulants came from burgeoning electronics technology, spurring a $275 million market niche for computer and office equipment magazines which had not existed at the beginning of the decade. Other industries which significantly increased their magazine ad expenditures included apparel and travel.

WORK FORCE

The periodical industry employed roughly 131,000 workers in 1996, according to the Magazine Publishers of America. Workers in the industry are relatively well paid and work fewer hours than the average manufacturing industry employee. The average production worker earned $13.42 per hour in 1995, compared to the manufacturing average of $12.37. Furthermore, the average work week in this industry was only 37.1 hours in 1995, compared with 41.6 hours for all other manufacturing sectors.

The industry is a major employer of writers, editors, and technical writers, which together constitute 13 percent of its work force. Many employees begin as copywriters, copyeditors, or production editors, and work

their way up to various editorial management positions. Senior editors, for example, traditionally write copy and may also manage other editorial employees or freelancers. But a salary survey presented in August 1996 by *Folio* pointed to an increased workload for senior editors, as a result of the corporate downsizing that has taken place during the 1990s. By 1996, salaries had risen considerably. The average senior editor on a business publication could now expect to earn $49,900 per year, and consumer magazines offered an average annual salary of $63,300.

Managing editors coordinate the editorial, art, and production departments of a publication and oversee proofreading and copywriting functions. Salaries for this job averaged $48,500 by 1996. Editors, who are responsible for directing the content of a publication, averaged $65,100 by 1996. Editorial managers, who may be called publishers, are responsible for setting editorial policy and managing operations. By 1996, the average for this position was $73,400. Base salaries as well as bonuses for all positions vary primarily according to the circulation volume of each periodical, by the frequency of its appearance, and by the number of pages in each issue.

Periodical producers also employ a large number of ad salespeople, who make up 12 percent of industry employment. Those employed in this field earned anywhere from $45,000 to $150,000 in 1996.

Although overall compensation slumped in the early 1990s, the long-term employment outlook for the periodicals industry was very positive going into the mid-1990s. Jobs for writers and editors were expected to increase by over 50 percent between 1990 and 2005, according to the Bureau of Labor Statistics. Sales and related positions, moreover, were expected to grow by over 65 percent. Indeed, almost every occupation in the industry was forecast to jump by over 30 percent. Jobs for executives, for example, should rise 28 percent, and administration and support staff will likely grow by over 30 percent. Opportunities for computer programmers should bound nearly 80 percent by 2005.

RESEARCH AND TECHNOLOGY

The growth in revenues by the middle of the decade resulted from a combination of higher rates and greater volume. To retain this increased share, publishers in the mid-1990s offered increased incentives and multi-media packages. Many also redesigned their publications and tried to eliminate marginal readership that diluted advertisement impact.

In 1993 a data-gathering service was started called Periodical Retail Information Management (PRIM) was introduced. The system was designed to provide timely and accurate data to retailers, wholesalers, and publishers. The system was expected to eventually assist with the distribution of more than 3,000 titles to more than 189,000 retailers each month, and would keep close track of title data related to each retailer's sales, including promotion and discount information.

In the long term, periodical publishers will start to view their role as providers of information services, rather than just product publishers. This will occur as electronic and digital publishing proliferates, and as publishers seek to enhance revenue streams through advanced media options. Many publishers were already experimenting with multimedia markets in the early 1990s, and several had been offering their periodicals on CD-ROM or online since the 1980s. Some analysts believe that electronic publishing, in some form, would dominate the industry by the 2010s, with paper publishing used only as a side or specialty media. Indeed, as the number of American households with a modem-equipped personal computer rose from 13 percent in 1993 to an estimated 25 percent by 1995, publishers were increasingly striving to take advantage of this media.

Evidencing the trend toward electronic media was a partnership formed in 1993 by Jeffrey Dearth, president of the *New Republic,* and Rob Raisch, president and founder of The Internet Co. Their online partnership, The Electronic Newsstand Inc., was designed to give print publishers a "point of presence" on the Internet. More than 50 magazines were represented on The Electronic Newsstand by 1994, including such titles as *Arthritis Today* and *New Yorker.* By the end of 1996, this number had soared dramatically, *Publisher's Weekly* counting a whopping 800 magazines on line. In November of 1996, *Folio* reported that on-line publishers had joined with members of other businesses to form a trade association called the Internet Advertising Bureau. Adweek Magazines, Hearst,

and Time Inc. New Media were among 70 others who paid their first annual $70,000 fee, in order to join discussions of such topics as advertising to children and agency and marketer relations.

SIC 2721
Occupations Employed by SIC 272 - Periodicals

Occupation	% of Total 1994	Change to 2005
Writers & editors, incl technical writers	15.0	28.7
Sales & related workers nec	10.8	28.7
Secretaries, ex legal & medical	5.1	17.2
General managers & top executives	5.0	22.1
Artists & commercial artists	3.7	60.4
Marketing, advertising, & PR managers	3.3	28.7
General office clerks	3.3	9.7
Bookkeeping, accounting, & auditing clerks	2.9	-3.5
Clerical supervisors & managers	2.4	31.6
Proofreaders & copy markers	2.3	-16.3
Managers & administrators nec	2.2	28.6
Machine feeders & offbearers	1.8	15.8
Reporters & correspondents	1.7	3.0
Marketing & sales worker supervisors	1.7	28.7
Typists & word processors	1.6	-35.7
Management support workers nec	1.5	28.6
Professional workers nec	1.4	54.4
Order clerks, materials, merchandise, & service	1.3	26.0
Advertising clerks	1.3	41.6
Computer programmers	1.2	4.2
Data entry keyers, ex composing	1.2	-5.0
Clerical support workers nec	1.2	2.9
Production, planning, & expediting clerks	1.1	28.6
Offset lithographic press operators	1.1	3.0
Adjustment clerks	1.1	54.4
Mail clerks, ex machine operators, postal service	1.1	-7.3

Source: *Industry-Occupation Matrix*, Bureau of Labor Statistics. These data relate to one or more 3-digit SIC industry groups rather than to a single 4-digit SIC. The change reported for each occupation to the year 2005 is a percent of growth or decline as estimated by the Bureau of Labor Statistics. The abbreviation nec stands for 'not elsewhere classified'.

AMERICA AND THE WORLD

In an effort to boost earnings in slow domestic markets, many periodical publishers in the early 1990s were seeking growth overseas. Although total industry exports amounted to only 3.5 percent of receipts in 1993, cross-border were expected to increase at a rate of 5 to 10 percent annually through the turn of the century. Furthermore, U.S. publishers had a stranglehold on domestic markets, as imports amounted to less than $170 million in the mid-1990s and the industry's trade surplus topped $600 million.

Canada consumed about 78 percent of all periodical exports in the early 1990s, but other countries were exhibiting solid market growth. The United Kingdom, for example, purchased 6 percent of periodical exports, and Mexico and the Netherlands each purchased 3 to 4 percent. Consumer and farm magazines were the greatest sellers. Helping to increase foreign sales in the early 1990s were U.S. joint ventures with overseas publishers that were directing local marketing and publishing efforts. For example, IDG, a global computer-related publisher, entered a joint venture in China to publish *Electronics International*, while 1996 brought a joint venture between *Newsweek* and a Russian banking, real estate, and communications conglomerate called Most, to produce *Itogi*, a news magazine aimed at the emerging highly-educated middle class in Russia. Top magazine circulations in Russia may run as high as 2 million, *FIPP Magazine World* claimed in January 1997.

While the majority of magazine exports have traditionally gone to English speaking foreigners, U.S. publishers began significant efforts during the 1980s and early 1990s to establish foreign editions of their publications, including *Fortune* and *Scientific American*. Some of these international efforts were defeated by the global recession of the early 1990s.

Despite some overseas success, the export potential for U.S. periodicals remained limited by multiple factors into the late-1990s. Most importantly, postal rates in most European and Asian countries are much higher than U.S. rates. This severely restricts subscription sales. U.S. publishers also often incur great difficulty obtaining effective mailing lists which they can use to market their publications. The U.S. list industry is highly advanced by comparison. Furthermore, some important markets like Germany have strict environmental and privacy regulations that limit periodical sales through the mail.

U.S. exporters will likely experience little relief from foreign regulations in the near future. Pending revisions to the European Union law on privacy and data protection, in fact, threaten to make it very costly for U.S. publishers to acquire customer lists. Nevertheless, Europe—with Asia and Latin America—will remain the focus of joint ventures and licensing arrangements aimed at boosting overseas sales. The North American Free Trade Agreement (NAFTA), signed in 1994, was expected to have a negligible impact on industry participants.

ASSOCIATIONS AND SOCIETIES

AMERICAN BUSINESS PRESS (ABP)
675 3rd Ave., Ste. 415
New York, NY 10017
Phone: (212) 661-6360
Fax: (212) 370-0736

Members are publishers of business and technical periodicals with audited circulation. Includes a Publishing Management Committee.

AMERICAN SOCIETY OF MAGAZINE EDITORS
919 3rd Ave.
New York, NY 10022
Phone: (212) 872-3700
Fax: (212) 888-4217

AUDIT BUREAU OF CIRCULATIONS (ABC)
900 N. Meacham Rd.
Schaumburg, IL 60173-4968
Phone: (708) 605-0909
Fax: (708) 605-0483
Verifies newspaper and periodical circulation statements. Includes a Business Publications Industry Committee and a Magazine Directors Advisory Committee.

BPA INTERNATIONAL
270 Madison Ave.
New York, NY 10016-0699
Phone: (212) 779-3200
Fax: (212) 779-3615
Verifies business and consumer periodical circulation statements. Includes a Circulation Managers Committee. Formerly Business Publications Audit of Circulation.

CIRCULATION COUNCIL OF DMA
11 W. 42nd St.
New York, NY 10036
Phone: (212) 768-7277
Fax: (212) 768-4546
A division of the Direct Marketing Association. Members include publishers and circulation directors.

COUNCIL FOR PERIODICAL DISTRIBUTORS ASSOCIATION
60 E 42nd St.
New York, NY 10165
Phone: (212) 818-0234
Fax: (212) 983-4699

FULFILLMENT MANAGEMENT ASSOCIATION (FMA)
60 E. 42nd St., Ste. 1146
New York, NY 10165
Phone: (212) 661-1410
Fax: (212) 661-1412
Members includes publishing circulation executives. Includes a Training and Education Committee and a Career Guidance Committee.

MAGAZINE PUBLISHERS OF AMERICA (MPA)
919 3rd Ave., 22 Fl.
New York, NY 10022
Phone: (212) 872-3700
Fax: (212) 888-4217
Members are publishers of consumer and other periodicals. Includes a Circulation Marketing Department.

PERIODICALS AND NEWSLETTERS

CIRCULATION MANAGEMENT
Ganesa Corp.
611 Broadway, Ste. 401
New York, NY 10012-2608
Phone: (212) 989-2133
Fax: (212) 620-0396
Monthly. Free to qualified personnel; others, $32.00 per year. Edited for circulation professionals in the magazine and newsletter publishing industry. Covers marketing, planning, promotion, management, budgeting, and related topics.

EBSCO BULLETIN OF SERIALS CHANGES
EBSCO Industries, Inc.
Title Information Dept.
Birmingham, AL 35201-1943
Phone: (800) 826-3024 or (205) 991-6600
Fax: (205) 995-1518
Bimonthly. $20.00 per year. New titles, discontinuations, title changes, mergers, etc.

FOLIO: THE MAGAZINE FOR MAGAZINE MANAGEMENT
Cowles Business Media
PO Box 4949
Stamford, CT 06907-0949
Phone: (800) 795-5445 or (203) 358-9900
Fax: (203) 357-9014
Semimonthly. $96.00 per year.

MAGAZINE AND BOOKSELLER: MASS MARKET RETAILERS AND PUBLISHERS' GUIDE
North American Publishing Co.
322 8th Ave., 3 Fl.
New York, NY 10001
Phone: (212) 620-7330
Fax: (212) 620-7335
Eight times a year. $49.00 per year.

SERIALS REVIEW
Jai Press
PO Box 1678
Greenwich, CT 06836-1678
Phone: (203) 661-7602
Fax: (203) 661-0792
Quarterly. Individuals, $70.00 per year; institutions, $110.00 per year.

DATABASES

GALE DATABASE OF PUBLICATIONS AND BROADCAST MEDIA
Gale Research
835 Penobscot Bldg.
Detroit, MI 48226-4094
Phone: (800) 877-GALE or (313) 961-2242
Fax: (313) 961-6083
An online directory containing detailed information on over 67,000 periodicals, newspapers, broadcast stations, cable systems, directories, and newsletters. Corresponds to the following print sources: Gale Directory of Publications and Broadcast Media; Directories in Print; City and State Directories in Print; Newsletters in Print. *Semiannual updates. Inquire as to online cost and availability.*

LC MARC: SERIALS
U.S. Library of Congress
Cataloging Distribution Service
Washington, DC 20541-5017
Phone: (202) 707-6100
Fax: (202) 707-1334
Provides online bibliographic records for about 700,000 periodicals cataloged by the Library of Congress since 1973. Updating is monthly. Inquire as to online cost and availability. (MARC is Machine Readable Cataloging.)

MAGAZINE INDEX
Information Access Corp.
362 Lakeside Dr.
Foster City, CA 94404
Phone: (800) 227-8431 or (415) 378-5000
Fax: (415) 358-4759
General magazine indexing (popular literature), 1973 to present. Inquire as to online cost and availability.

MANAGEMENT CONTENTS
Information Access Co.
362 Lakeside Dr.
Foster City, CA 94404
Phone: (800) 227-8431 or (415) 378-5000
Fax: (415) 358-4759
Covers a wide range of management, financial, marketing, personnel, and administrative topics. About 140 leading business journals are indexed and abstracted from 1974 to date, with monthly updating. Inquire as to online cost and availability.

NEWSPAPER AND PERIODICAL ABSTRACTS
UMI/Data Courier
620 South 3rd St.
Louisville, KY 40202
Phone: (800) 626-2823 or (502) 583-4111
Fax: (502) 589-5572
Provides online coverage (citations and abstracts) of more than 25 major newspapers and about 1,000 general interest and professional periodicals. Covers business, current affairs, health, fitness, education, technology, government, consumer affairs, social problems, and many other subject areas. Time period is 1986 to date, with daily updates. Inquire as to online cost and availability.

TRADE & INDUSTRY INDEX
Information Access Co.
362 Lakeside Dr.
Foster City, CA 94404
Phone: (800) 227-8431 or (415) 378-5000
Fax: (415) 358-4759
Provides indexing of business periodicals, January 1981 to date. Daily updates. (Full text articles from some periodicals are available online, 1983 to date, in the companion database, Trade & Industry ASAP.) Inquire as to online cost and availability.

ULRICH'S INTERNATIONAL PERIODICALS DIRECTORY ONLINE

Bowker Electronic Publishing
121 Chanlon Rd.
New Providence, NJ 07974
Phone: (800) 521-8110 or (908) 464-6800
Fax: (908) 665-3528

Includes over 150,000 periodicals currently published world-wide and publications discontinued since 1974. Corresponds to **Ulrich's International Periodcals Directory, Irregular Serials and Annuals, Bowker International Serials Database Update,** *and* **Sources of Serials.** *Inquire as to online cost and availability.*

STATISTICS SOURCES

CONSUMER MAGAZINE AND AGRI-MEDIA RATES AND DATA

Standard Rate and Data Service
3004 Glenview Rd.
Wilmette, IL 60091
Phone: (708) 256-6067

U.S. INDUSTRIAL OUTLOOK: FORECASTS FOR SELECTED MANUFACTURING AND SERVICE INDUSTRIES

Available from U.S. Government Printing Office
Washington, DC 20402
Phone: (202) 512-1800
Fax: (202) 512-2250

Annual. $37.00. (Replaced in 1995 by U.S. Global Trade Outlook.) *Issued by the International Trade Administration, U.S. Department of Commerce. Provides basic data, outlook for the current year, and "Long-Term Prospects" (five-year projections) for a wide variety of products and services. Includes high technology industries. Available on the world wide web at gopher://gopher.umsl.edu:70/11/library/govdocs/usio94*

GENERAL WORKS

BACON'S MAGAZINES DIRECTORIES

Bacon's Publishing Co.
332 S. Michigan Ave., Ste. 900
Chicago, IL 60604
Phone: (800) 261-0561 or (312) 922-2400
Fax: (312) 922-3127

Annual. $250.00 per year. Interedition update. Two voumes: Magazines *and* News. *Formerly* Bacon's Publicity Checker.

BUSINESS JOURNALS OF THE UNITED STATES: HISTORICAL GUIDES TO THE WORLD'S PERIODICALS AND NEWSPAPERS

William Fisher, editor
Greenwood Publishing Group, Inc.

88 Post Rd. W
Westport, CT 06881
Phone: (800) 225-5800 or (203) 226-3571
Fax: (203) 222-1502

1991. $69.50. Contains historical and descriptive essays covering over 100 leading business publications.

DIRECTORY OF BUSINESS INFORMATION RESOURCES: ASSOCIATIONS, NEWSLETTERS, MAGAZINES, TRADE SHOWS

Grey House Publishing, Inc.
Pocket Knife Sq.
Lakeville, CT 06039
Phone: (800) 562-2139 or (203) 435-0868
Fax: (800) 248-0115

Annual. $110.00. Provides concise information on associations, newsletters, magazines, and trade shows for each of 90 major industry groups. An "Entry & Company Index" serves as a guide to titles, publishers, and organizations.

STANDARD PERIODICAL DIRECTORY

Available from Gale Research
835 Penobscot Bldg.
Detroit, MI 48226-4094
Phone: (800) 877-GALE or (313) 961-2242
Fax: (313) 961-6083

Annual. $495.00. Published by Oxbridge Communications.

FURTHER READING

"Circ City: Here We Come!" *Folio,* 1 July 1996.

"The Latina Link in Two Languages." *Folio,* 1 September 1996.

Levine, Joshua. "Go Break a Leg." *Forbes,* 3 June 1996.

"Newsmagazines Take Hold in Russia." *Folio,* 1 November 1996.

Pogrebin, Robin. "Magazines Multiplying As Their Focuses Narrow." *New York Times,* 2 January 1997.

"Production Salaries Post Moderate Gains." *Folio,* 1 June 1966.

"Read All About It." *Business Week,* 18 November 1996.

Silber, Tony. "Outpacing Inflation And Then Some." *Folio,* 1 August 1996.

Standard & Poor's Industry Surveys, New York: Standard & Poor's Corporation, 1996.

"Trade Group Forms for Online Publishers." *Folio,* 1 November 1996.

The early 1990s were a time of struggle for U.S. crude petroleum and natural gas companies. Low oil and gas prices combined with slow economic growth, drilling bans, and lawsuits, all limited exploration. Oil production continued its long decline. However, the mid-1990s showed a large increase in revenues, and while domestic production has stagnated, production overseas is growing. In 1996, the crude petroleum and natural gas industry in the United States was a $425 billion business with 12,860 establishments employing 160,000 people. Crude prices are expected to decline an average of about $1 per barrel in 1997.

PETROLEUM AND NATURAL GAS

SIC 1311

Top 10 LEADING PETROLEUM AND NATURAL GAS PROCESSING COMPANIES

Ranked by: Total sales in 1995, in millions of dollars.

1. Exxon, with $107,893.0 million
2. Mobil Corp., $64,767.0
3. Texaco Inc., $35,551.0
4. Chevron Corp., $31,322.0
5. Amoco Corp., $27,066.0
6. Shell Oil Co., $24,298.0
7. ARCO, $15,819.0
8. Phillips Petroleum Co., $13,368.0
9. Ashland Oil Inc., $11,251.0
10. Costal Corp., $10,447.7

Source: *ChemicalWeek*, ChemicalWeek 300 (annual), May 8, 1996, p. 57.

__Natural__ gas production is expected to show a sharp increase through 2015, the result of rising prices, abundant reserves, and improved recovery technology. In 1998 production is projected to increase to 19.75 trillion cubic feet (tcf), up from 19.22 tcf projected in 1997. Natural gas consumption for 1998 is estimated at 23.25 tcf. Long-term oil prices are expected to rise as reservoirs are depleted and the need for additional exploration increases, possibly necessitating more workers. Job opportunities remain fair to poor, due to industry restructuring and consistently low prices for crude petroleum.

Since its peak in 1970 at 11.3 million barrels per day, crude oil production in the United States has been declining. In 1973, 9.2 million barrels per day was recovered; by 1995 the United States produced 6.5 million barrels of crude oil, and that figure was expected to decrease to 6.4 million barrels in 1996. Estimates predict an additional 3.6 percent decline in 1997. Prudhoe Bay, Alaska, has the largest oil field in the United States, yet production there is also expected to decline by about 15 percent in 1997.

U.S. oil companies earned solid profits in 1996. This achievement was due partly to the rising prices of crude oil and natural gas, and also to strong margins in refining and marketing operations. After Russia, the United States is the world's second largest producer of natural gas. In 1996, the United States produced 18.9 trillion cubic feet (tcf), consumed 21.7 tcf, and imported 2.8 tcf of natural gas.

INDUSTRY OUTLOOK

The U.S. crude petroleum and natural gas industry entered a period of decline after 1986 when production hit 8.35 million barrels per day. Three major factors figured in the decline: a shift away from petroleum as an energy source, low crude oil prices, and increasingly stringent environmental regulations—including drilling bans in some of the most promising areas of development. The number of rotary rigs drilling in the United States in 1995 was 723, a decrease of 52 rigs from 1994. This is the second lowest count since World War II, and a drastic decrease from the nearly 4,000 which were in operation in 1981. But in the first nine months of 1996, the number rose to 761, with 39 percent drilling for oil, 60 percent for gas, and 1 percent miscellaneous. As a result, the major thrust of drilling and exploration moved outside of the United States. Low crude oil prices also curbed the development of other sources of hydrocarbon liquids, such as oil shale, tar sands, and coal liquefaction.

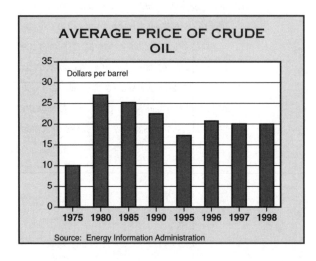

AVERAGE PRICE OF CRUDE OIL

Dollars per barrel

Source: Energy Information Administration

Despite the fact that oil supplied a smaller percentage of the total U.S. energy demand, that demand had increased significantly. As a result, the absolute amount of oil used by the United States continued growing (at a time when worldwide use had remained stable). By 1992 nearly 2 million miles of gas pipelines linked wells with consumers. Dependence on foreign oil imports reached a record-high 48.2 percent of domestic demand in 1993, up from 31.5 percent in 1985. In 1992 the amount of natural gas consumed rose 4.1 percent to 19.83 trillion cubic feet. The figure rose to 21.99 tcf in 1996.

ORGANIZATION AND STRUCTURE

ECONOMIC STRUCTURE

In 1996 the crude oil and natural gas industry earned more than $425 billion in revenue. The industry was affected by two fundamental economic factors—the international price of oil and the availability of capital. While decreasing overall domestic production, American companies have been increasing activities overseas. Mobil Corporation had an income of $686 million for domestic exploration and production—their international income was twice that amount. In 1995, Unocal spent 70 percent of capital, more than $1 billion, in the United States. In 1997, the company plans to spend about $900 million overseas, with only $440 million being spent on domestic projects.

While major oil companies usually funded drilling programs out of their own resources, independents relied heavily on outside investors. Favorable tax treatment for investors in oil and gas limited partnerships helped fuel an unprecedented boom of exploration and drilling in the late 1970s and early 1980s.

The companies in the crude petroleum and natural gas industry range from enormous conglomerates employing 100,000 people and generating revenues of more than $100 billion, to companies reporting less than $1 million in revenues with few employees. Despite the fact that some firms are very large, 53 percent have fewer than five employees and report revenues of $50 million or less. The average number of employees per establishment is 12; the average sales per establishment is $39.6 million. The industry reported 161,338 employees in 1996.

REGULATORY CLIMATE

Historically, the federal government has both helped and hindered the industry. The 1990 Omnibus Budget Reconciliation Act encouraged production by granting a tax credit for projects using enhanced recovery. It expanded the use of deductions for intangible drilling costs and the percentage depletion allowances, and provided a special deduction for independent oil and gas producers to apply against the alternative minimum tax. However, the decision to cancel the 1990 sale of leases for exploration on the Outer Continental Shelf off California, the Gulf Coast of Florida, and the Northeast hindered the discovery of new oil. The Oil Pollution and Liability Act of 1990 prohibited oil and gas exploration off the coast of North Carolina. That same law also hampered production by imposing federal liabilities on vessels and facilities for oil spills. In addition, the Act allowed states to impose their own forms of liability independently. As a result, drillers paid higher insurance rates for their offshore activities.

WORK FORCE

In 1996, the crude petroleum and natural gas industry employed more than 160,000 people. Wages in the industry ranked above average. Annual salaries for those who work in the United States were: landsman (land lease agent)—$35,300 to $51,200; petroleum engineer—$38,286 to $105,700; roustabout—$25,980 to $28,000; surveyor—$24,500 to $50,200. While most professionals are not unionized, other employees were often represented. Two prominent unions in the industry are the Associated Petroleum Employees Union and the Oil, Chemical and Atomic Workers International Union.

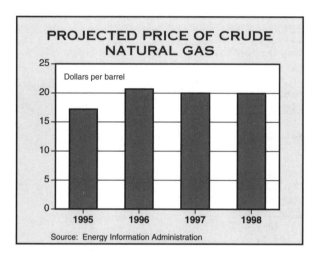

PROJECTED PRICE OF CRUDE
NATURAL GAS

Dollars per barrel

Source: Energy Information Administration

RESEARCH AND TECHNOLOGY

Directional drilling and enhanced oil recovery have been two of the latest areas of research and development. Directional drilling rapidly gained importance by allowing several wells to be drilled into different areas from a single derrick. The technique proved especially valuable offshore, where the cost of establishing a platform ran into the hundreds of millions of dollars. Onshore, directional drilling also limited environmental damage by reducing the number of rig locations needed.

Another advantage to directional drilling was the ability to drill a well horizontally across the top of a formation to maximize oil or gas recovery. Directional drilling is done with steerable drill bits which allow drillers to change the direction of the hole from the surface at any depth specified. A turbine motor, powered by the pressurized drilling mud circulating through the well, provides a high-speed twist to the drill bit.

OIL SHALE, TAR SANDS

In the early 1990s the attempt to produce liquids from oil shale involved several steps. The shale was mined, crushed, and heated in a retort to produce shale oil. Major problems with the technique included how to dispose of spent shale. In an oddity of nature, when oil is recovered from shale, the shale expands. Research in oil shale technology, like that for tar sands technology, had all but completely shelved because of low oil prices.

COAL LIQUEFACTION

Coal liquefaction, also called mild gasification, began to emerge from the purely experimental stage in the early 1990s. While promising technologies had been discovered, they required crude oil prices in the $38-per-barrel range to be feasible. The price of crude has ranged between $12.50 per barrel (1986) to about $20 per barrel in the early 1990s. Commercialization may depend on making commercial quantities of high-value chemical coproducts. The solid product of mild gasification can be made into formcoke and used in blast furnaces. Because the product would come from new plants meeting the most stringent environmental standards instead of traditional coke ovens, the environment would benefit as well.

Also in the early 1990s, a Wyoming project that received federal funding under the U.S. Department of Energy Clean Coal Technology Program was to produce two products, one solid, the other liquid. The solid product was a low-sulphur, high-energy, coal-like fuel able to be burned in powerplants and meet strict emissions standards. The liquid fuel could be used directly as a boiler fuel or as a refinery feedstock to produce gasoline and diesel. When fully operational, the plant was expected to produce 180,000 tons of high-energy solid fuel and 150,000 barrels of liquid each year using 1,000 tons of sub-bituminous coal per day. In all, 32 coal gasification and liquefaction projects were in various stages of development across the United States. But as crude oil prices increase, the economic benefits of coal liquefaction are beginning to attract attention. In its gaseous form, coal can be cleaned of more than 95 percent of its sulfur pollutants and virtually all of its ash impurities. The project began in 1992 and will run until 2000. By 2010, technology improvements will be able to lower the cost to 75 percent of what it is today.

AMERICA AND THE WORLD

The United States has been a leader in international oil exploration and production. U.S. companies have played roles in the discovery and production of oil in major fields in Mexico, Venezuela, Saudi Arabia, Kuwait, and Libya. While exploration and oil drilling have decreased in the continental United States and Alaska, all of the major American oil companies have increased their presence overseas. It is important to note that more than 75 percent of proven oil reserves are controlled by OPEC, although the vast majority of oil is consumed by non-OPEC nations—therefore giving OPEC a tremendous influence on the world oil and gas market.

American oil exploration, and that of other non-OPEC countries, has slowed in contrast to OPEC exploration. Meanwhile, the major U.S.-based petroleum companies are becoming increasingly involved in foreign exploration. In the early 1990s, money allocated to foreign exploration and development topped 50 percent of all exploration spending, as compared to 27 percent in the mid-1980s. World political and economic developments of the 1990s have made it more feasible and profitable to increase American investment in foreign exploration. U.S. companies have increased their investment in many areas of the world, particularly in Latin America. The natural gas industry in Central and South America has great potential. With the exception of Argentina and Venezuela, the industry is underdeveloped, with reserves equivalent to those found in North America. Columbia and Peru are expected to double their oil production by the end of the 1990s.

The dissolution of the Soviet Union provided increased opportunities for investment in that area's oil reserves. The CIS (Commonwealth of Independent States) has seen the rise of joint exploration and drilling ventures, especially in Russia, between U.S. and Russian companies. While recent instability in the former Soviet Union has slowed the natural gas industry, this is seen as a short term problem.

Another area of increasing American investment is Southeast Asia, where U.S. exploration spending grew the most from the mid-1980s to the mid-1990s. The economies of Asian countries have become increasingly industrialized in recent years, and many governments in Asia, including China and Vietnam, have actively courted foreign investment and participation in local drilling by outside companies. Deepwater fields offshore in the Philippines show great promise as well.

After decades of being a net exporter of petroleum, the United States crossed the line into international interdependency sometime in 1970, when production hit its peak and the last of the oil surplus that had guaranteed energy independence had been pumped into the pipeline. Other countries, particularly South Africa and Canada, are leaders in developing technology for the use of coal as a source of petroleum and gas. South Africa has the largest commercial coal gasification plant and the only commercial coal liquefaction plant in the world. But while oil production decreases, natural gas production in America is increasing and is expected to remain on an upward swing until 2015. As the largest supplier of natural gas after Russia, American companies are putting more effort into drilling for gas domestically rather than petroleum.

ASSOCIATIONS AND SOCIETIES

AMERICAN GAS ASSOCIATION
1515 Wilson Blvd.
Arlington, VA 22209
Phone: (703) 841-8400
Fax: (703) 841-8406

AMERICAN PETROLEUM INSTITUTE
1220 L St. NW
Washington, DC 20005
Phone: (202) 682-8000
Fax: (202) 682-8232

INDEPENDENT PETROLEUM ASSOCIATION OF AMERICA
1101 16th St. NW
Washington, DC 20036
Phone: (202) 857-4799 or (202) 857-4722

INSTITUTE OF GAS TECHNOLOGY
1700 S Mount Prospect Rd.
Des Plaines, IL 60018-1804
Phone: (708) 768-0500
Fax: (708) 768-0516

INTERSTATE NATURAL GAS ASSOCIATION OF AMERICA
555 13th St. NW, Ste. 300W
Washington, DC 20004
Phone: (202) 626-3200
Fax: (202) 626-3250

NATIONAL PETROLEUM COUNCIL
1625 K St. NW, Ste. 600
Washington, DC 20006
Phone: (202) 393-6100
Fax: (202) 331-8539

NATURAL GAS SUPPLY ASSOCIATION
1129 20th St. NW, Ste. 300
Washington, DC 20036
Phone: (202) 331-8900
Fax: (202) 452-6558

PERIODICALS AND NEWSLETTERS

AGA AMERICAN GAS
American Gas Association
1515 Wilson Blvd.
Arlington, VA 22209
Phone: (703) 841-8400
Fax: (703) 841-8406

11 times a year. $39.00 per year. Formerly American Gas Association Monthly.

AMERICAN PETROLEUM INSTITUTE. DIVISION OF STATISTICS. WEEKLY STATISTICAL BULLETIN
American Petroleum Institute
Publications Dept.
1220 L St. NW
Washington, DC 20005
Phone: (202) 682-8000
Weekly. Members, $80.00 per year; non-members, $110.00 per year.

ENERGY MANAGEMENT REPORT
Advanstar Communications, Inc.
7500 Old Oak Blvd.
Cleveland, OH 44130
Phone: (800) 346-0085 or (216) 243-8100
Fax: (216) 891-2726
Semimonthly. $108.00 per year.

GAS DIGEST: THE MAGAZINE OF GAS OPERATIONS
Tri-Plek Productions
11246 S Post Oak Rd., Ste. 204
Houston, TX 77035-5741
Phone: (713) 723-7456
Monthly. Qualified personnel, $12.00 per year; others, $20.00 per year. Articles and data relating to operations and management phases of natural gas operations.

GAS INDUSTRIES MAGAZINE
Gas Industries and Appliance News, Inc.
PO Box 558
Park Ridge, IL 60068
Phone: (312) 693-3682
Fax: (312) 696-3445
Monthly. $20.00 per year.

INTERNATIONAL OIL NEWS
William F. Bland Co.
PO Box 16666
Chapel Hill, NC 27516-6666
Phone: (919) 490-0700
Fax: (919) 490-3002
Weekly. $517.00 per year. Reports news of prime interest to top executives in the international oil industry.

LUNDBERG LETTER
Lundberg Survey, Inc.
PO Box 3996
North Hollywood, CA 91609-0996
Phone: (818) 768-5111
Fax: (818) 768-1883
Twice weekly. $399.00 per year. Petroleum newsletter.

NATIONAL PETROLEUM NEWS (NPN)
Hunter Publishing Ltd. Partnership
25 NW Blvd., Ste. 800
Elk Grove Village, IL 60007
Phone: (708) 427-9512
Fax: (708) 427-2041

NATURAL GAS
Executive Enterprises Publications Co., Inc.
22 W 21st St.
New York, NY 10010-6904

Phone: (800) 332-1105 or (212) 645-7880
Fax: (212) 645-1160
Monthly. $295.00 per year. Newsletter. Covers business, economic, regulatory, and high-technology news relating to the natural gas industry.

OIL DAILY: DAILY NEWSPAPER OF THE PETROLEUM INDUSTRY
Oil Daily Co.
1401 New York Ave. NW, Ste. 500
Washington, DC 20005
Phone: (202) 662-0700
Fax: (202) 783-8320
Daily. $897.00 per year. Newspaper for the petroleum industry.

OIL AND GAS ALERT
Research Institute of America, Inc.
90 5th Ave.
New York, NY 10011
Phone: (800) 431-2057 or (212) 645-4800
Fax: (212) 337-4279
Monthly. $150.00 per year. Newsletter.

OIL AND GAS JOURNAL
PennWell Publishing Co.
PO Box 1260
Tulsa, OK 74102
Phone: (918) 835-3161
Fax: (918) 831-9497
Weekly. Qualified personnel, $52.00 per year; others, $95.00 per year.

PETROLEUM NEWSLETTER
National Safety Council Periodicals
Dept. 1121 Spring Lake Dr.
Itasca, IL 60143
Phone: (800) 621-7619 or (708) 775-2281
Fax: (708) 285-9114
Bimonthly. Members, $15.00 per year; non-members, $19.00 per year.

DATABASES

APIBIZ (PETROLEUM-ENERGY NEWS)
American Petroleum Institute
Central Abstracting and Information Services
275 7th Ave.
New York, NY 10001
Phone: (212) 366-4040
Fax: (212) 366-4298
Indexing of newsletters and business journals in the petroleum and energy are as, 1975 to present. Inquire as to online cost and availability.

APILIT
American Petroleum Institute
Central Abstracting and Information Services
275 7th Ave.
New York, NY 10001
Phone: (212) 366-4040
Fax: (212) 366-4298

Worldwide technical literature on petroleum refining and petrochemical industry, 1964 to present. Inquire as to online cost and availability.

APIPAT

American Petroleum Institute
Central Abstracting and Information Services
275 7th Ave.
New York, NY 10001
Phone: (212) 366-4040
Fax: (212) 955-8312
Worldwide patent citations on petroleum refining and petrochemical industry, 1964 to present. Inquire as to online cost and availability.

CITIBASE (CITICORP ECONOMIC DATABASE)

FAME Software Corp.
77 Water St., 9 Fl.
New York, NY 10005
Phone: (212) 898-7800
Fax: (212) 742-8956
Presents over 6,000 statistical series relating to business, industry, finance, and economics. Includes series from Survey of Current Business and many other sources. Time period is 1947 to date, with daily updates. Inquire as to online cost and availability.

ENERGY SCIENCE AND TECHNOLOGY

U.S. Dept. of Energy
Office of Scientific and Technical Information
PO Box 62
Oak Ridge, TN 37831
Phone: (615) 576-9362
Fax: (615) 576-2865
Contains abstracts and citations to literature in all fields of energy from 1974 to date, with biweekly updates. Formerly DOE Energy Data Base. Inquire as to online cost and availability.

ENERGYLINE

Congressional Information Service, Inc.
4520 East-West Hwy., Ste. 800
Bethesda, MD 20814-3389
Phone: (800) 638-8380 or (301) 654-1550
Fax: (301) 654-4033
Provides online citations and abstracts to the literature of all forms of energy: petroleum, natural gas, coal, nuclear power, solar energy, etc. Time period is 1971 to date. Monthly updates. Inquire as to online cost and availability.

PLATT'S OIL PRICES

McGraw-Hill, Inc.
1221 Avenue of the Americas
New York, NY 10020
Phone: (800) 722-4726 or (212) 512-4686
Fax: (212) 512-4256
Various time series detailing domestic and foreign oil prices; daily updating. Time period 1970 to date. Inquire as to online cost and availability.

PREDICASTS FORECASTS: U.S.

Information Access Co.
362 Lakeside Dr.
Foster City, CA 94404
Phone: (800) 321-6388 or (415) 378-5000
Fax: (415) 358-4759

Provides numeric abstracts of a wide range of published forecasts relating to specific U.S. products, markets, and industries. Monthly updates. Time period is 1971 to date. Inquire as to online cost and availability.

TULSA (PETROLEUM ABSTRACTS)

Information Services
600 S. College
Harwell 101
Tulsa, OK 74104
Phone: (800) 247-8678 or (918) 631-2297
Fax: (918) 599-9361
Worldwide literature in the petroleum and natural gas areas, 1965 to present. Inquire as to online cost and availability. Includes petroleum exploration patents. Updated weekly. Over 600,000 entries.

STATISTICS SOURCES

ANNUAL ENERGY REVIEW

Available from U.S. Government Printing Office
Washington, DC 20402
Phone: (202) 512-1800
Fax: (202) 512-2250
Annual. Issued by the Energy Information Administration, Office of Energy Markets and End Use, U.S. Department of Energy. Presents long-term historical as well as recent data on production, consumption, stocks, imports, exports, and prices of the principal energy commodities in the U.S.

BASIC PETROLEUM DATA BOOK

American Petroleum Institute
Publications Section
1220 L St. NW
Washington, DC 20005
Phone: (202) 682-8000
Three times a year. Members, $120.00 per year; non-members, $150.00 per year.

BUSINESS STATISTICS

Available from U.S. Government Printing Office
Washington, DC 20402
Phone: (202) 512-1800
Fax: (202) 512-2250
Biennial. $20.00. Issued by Bureau of Economic Analysis, U.S. Department of Commerce. Shows annual data for 29 years and monthly data for a recent four-year period. Statistics correspond to the Survey of Current Business.

GAS FACTS: A STATISTICAL RECORD OF THE GAS UTILITY INDUSTRY

American Gas Association
1515 Wilson Blvd.,
Arlington, VA 22209
Phone: (703) 841-8490
Fax: (703) 841-8406
Annual. Members, $28.00; non-members, $55.00.

INTERNATIONAL ENERGY ANNUAL

Available from U.S. Government Printing Office
Washington, DC 20402
Phone: (202) 512-1800
Fax: (202) 512-2250

Annual. $15.00. Issued by the Energy Information Administration, U.S. Department of Energy. Provides production, consumption, import, and export data for primary energy commodities in more than 200 countries and areas. In addition to petroleum products and alcohol, renewable energy sources are covered (hydroelectric, geothermal, solar, and wind).

MONTHLY ENERGY REVIEW

Available from U.S. Government Printing Office
Washington, DC 20402
Phone: (202) 512-1800
Fax: (202) 512-2250
Monthly. $87.00 per year. Issued by the Energy Information Administration, Office of Energy Markets and End Use, U.S. Department of Energy. Contains current and historical statistics on U.S. production, storage, imports, and consumption of petroleum, natural gas, and coal.

NATURAL GAS MONTHLY

Energy Information Administration
U.S. Government Printing Office
Washington, DC 20402
Phone: (202) 512-1800
Fax: (202) 512-2250
Monthly. $77.00 per year. Annual cumulation. State and national data on production, storage, imports, exports and consumption of natural gas.

THE OIL AND GAS PRODUCING INDUSTRY IN YOUR STATE

Independent Petroleum Association of America
Petroleum Independent Publishers, Inc.
1101 16th St. NW
Washington, DC 20036
Phone: (202) 857-4722 *Annual. $75.00.*

PETROLEUM SUPPLY ANNUAL

Available from U.S. Government Printing Office
Washington, DC 20402
Phone: (202) 512-1800
Fax: (202) 512-2250
Annual. $42.00. Two volumes. Produced by the Energy Information Administration, U.S. Department of Energy. Contains worldwide data on the petroleum industry and petroleum products.

PETROLEUM SUPPLY MONTHLY

Available from U.S. Government Printing Office
Washington, DC 20402
Phone: (202) 512-1800
Fax: (202) 512-2250
Monthly. $83.00 per year. Produced by the Energy Information Administration, U.S. Department of Energy. Provides worldwide statistics on a wide variety of petroleum products. Covers production, supplies, exports and imports, transportation, refinery operations, and other aspects of the petroleum industry.

WEEKLY PETROLEUM STATUS REPORT

Energy Information Administration
Available from U.S. Government Printing Office
Washington, DC 20402
Phone: (202) 512-1800
Fax: (202) 512-2250
Weekly. $65.00 per year. Current statistics in the context of both historical information and selected prices and forecasts.

GENERAL WORKS

FEDERAL REGULATION OF ENERGY

Shepard's/McGraw-Hill, Inc.
PO Box 35300
Colorado Springs, CO 80935-3530
Phone: (800) 525-2474 or (303) 577-7707
Fax: (800) 525-0053
Looseleaf service. $95.00 per year. Annual supplementation. Includes sections on federal regulation of petroleum, natural gas, nuclear energy, coal, and electricity.

NATIONAL PETROLEUM NEWS-MARKET FACTS

Hunter Publishing Co. Inc.
950 Lee St.
Des Plaines, IL 60016
Phone: (708) 427-9512
Fax: (708) 296-8821
Annual. $60.00. Includes refiners and marketers of petroleum products. Formerly National Petroleum News-Fact Book.

PETROLEUM ENGINEER INTERNATIONAL DRILLING AND PRODUCTION YEARBOOK ISSUE

Hart Publications, Inc.
4545 Post Oak Pl., Ste. 210
Houston, TX 77027
Phone: (713) 993-9320
Fax: (713) 840-8585
Annual. $10.00.

SUMMERS ON OIL AND GAS

West Publishing Co.
College and School Div.
PO Box 64526
St. Paul, MN 55164-0526
Phone: (612) 228-2778
Periodic supplementation. Legal aspects of the petroleum industry.

FURTHER READING

Energy Information Administration. "Outlook Assumptions." Available from http://www.eia.doe.gov/emeu/steo/pub/otlkasum.html.

"Oil & Gas News." *Aral Energy News.* Available from http://www.aral.com/newog.htm.

"Sierra Pacific Power Company's Pinon Pine Project - A Preview of the Future." Project Facts, Department of Energy, Office of Fossil Energy. Available from http://www.metc.doe.gov/projfact/power/igcc/siercct.html.

"State of the U.S. Oil and Natural Gas Industry." Independent Petroleum Association of America. Available from http://www.ipaa.org/departments/information_services/state_of_the_industry.htm.

Yergin, Daniel. *The Prize, The Epic Quest for Oil, Money and Power,* New York: Simon & Schuster, 1991. ●

PETROLEUM REFINING

SIC 2911

Patience, thrift, and ingenuity will be paramount to survival in the refining industry. Downward trends seen in the 1980s and early 1990s is projected to continue. Demand for petroleum products is forecast to grow at only half the rate of the U.S. economy. New regulations will limit the use of products which once had diverse applications, restricting them by season, geographical area, applications, and production costs. Federal standards requirements are likely to continue to proliferate, absorbing time and capital and man for research and experimentation. A restructuring of the industry in response to these trends, and continuing in the established patterns of consolidation and downsizing, will likely occur and continue beyond the 1990s into the next century.

In the mid to late 1990s, the petroleum refining industry was engrossed in implementing day-to-day micro management strategies to remain profitable in the face of long-term environmental restrictions and short-term market volatility. Consistently flat market demand for gasoline combined with growing capitalization costs and the high number of companies competing in the industry required refiners to establish market niches and to expand their downstream operations to remain profitable.

Mergers and acquisitions were also a strong trend of this period. According to *Journal of Commerce and Commercial,* experts agreed that the trend towards mergers and acquisitions, especially in the heating oil industry, was not likely to slow down soon. The eroding share of oil in the home heating market continued to drive increased merger activity. Consolidations in the petroleum refining industry is primarily driven by the fact that the industry has arrived at a mature market state with little opportunity for growth except through mergers and acquisitions.

 LARGEST CORPORATIONS IN THE PETROLEUM REFINING INDUSTRY

Ranked by: Revenue in 1996, in millions of dollars.

1. Exxon, with $116,728 million
2. Mobil Corp., $71,129
3. Texaco Inc., $44,561
4. Chevron Corp., $37,580
5. Amoco Corp., $32,150
6. Atlantic Richfield Co., $18,592
7. Phillips Petroleum Co., $15,803
8. USX, $13,564
9. Coastal, $12,166
10. Ashland Oil Inc., $12,145

Source: *Fortune,* Fortune 500 Largest U.S. Corporations (annual), April 29, 1996, p. F-58.

Aroma chemicals, flavors, and fragrances—derivatives of petroleum refining—showed some of the only strong signs of growth in the industry through the mid 1990s. Consumption of flavors and fragrances products was estimated at more than $9.5 billion worldwide in 1995, and $1.2 billion for aroma chemicals. As many as 800 companies participated in the development of this business. The average growth rate for the industry was 5.7 percent between 1990 and 1995. Annual growth of 3.5-4 percent is projected through 1999, when consumption of flavors and fragrances products is expected to exceed $11 billion. The United States and Western Europe together account for 62 percent of flavors and fragrances consumption, and 70 percent of aroma chemicals consumption.

INDUSTRY OUTLOOK

Petroleum refining, like the rest of the oil industry, saw profits dwindle to a five-year low in 1992, while spending on refining simultaneously rose 8.3 percent in an effort to meet costs of upgrading and research into alternative processing. Moreover, the 1991 economic recession had prompted shutdowns totaling 114,850 b/cd capacity and had dampened domestic refined product consumption. Though most integrated firms diversified as protection against unpredictable commodity prices, diversification was not enough to keep commodities and refined products from falling through the mid-1990s. *Forbes* observed in 1994 that the price of oil at that time was near 20-year lows because world oil consumption actually fell by a minuscule amount in 1993 while "while oil supply exceeded world demand by about half a million barrels a day, swelling inventories."

Due to intense gasoline price competition, profit margins at service stations dwindled. Furthermore, surplus production capacity dropped the price of petrochemicals, and the weak economy sabotaged demand. Widespread domestic downsizing, along with massive staff reductions and much asset stripping, resulted in low morale in the industry. Added pressures from excess fuel oil stocks and costs of regulatory compliance kept refined product margins and refiner profitability low. Surplus oxygenates and gasoline dragged gasoline prices down despite a 2.5 cents per gallon rise in crude oil prices.

1996 sales by integrated international refineries went from a five-year average decline of 4.8 percent to a 12 month decline of 6 percent, with total shipment valued at $110 billion, the lowest figure in 15 years. The list of petroleum product casualties in the domestic arena was extensive. The meager increase in demand for motor gasoline in the early 1990s was projected to increase only slightly through the middle of the decade; record import levels would be necessary even to accommodate this demand as refinery capacity dropped. Jet fuel demand was down at mid-decade, demand for residual fuel oil hit its lowest point in decades, and distillate fuel oil

demand grew only modestly. The sole increase reported in the industry was in minor petroleum products.

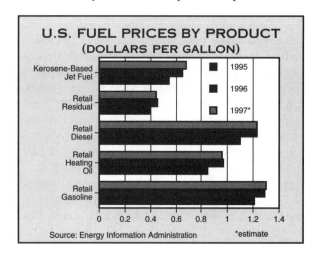

U.S. FUEL PRICES BY PRODUCT
(DOLLARS PER GALLON)

Source: Energy Information Administration   *estimate

Refiners entered the 1990s burdened by unpredictable supply and demand factors and the potential business consequences of the burgeoning environmental movement. Such issues as recycling, the hole in the ozone layer, and water pollution became an increasingly more important part of America's legislative agenda. Consequently, the business strategy of refiners shifted to finding cleaner-burning, more efficient fuels for smaller cars, as well as finding more environmentally friendly ways in which those fuels could be created.

The downward trends in the industry are projected to continue: petroleum refining and marketing companies did not do very well financially at the end of 1996. High crude oil prices resulted in low profits for downstream oil companies in North America, the Far East and Europe. Gulf Coast reformulated gasoline prices were expected to have been the worst, according to *The Oil Daily*.

ENVIRONMENTAL FACTORS

One legislative package designed to address environmental pollution has had a significant impact on the industry. 1990's Clean Air Act requires that America's 39 smoggiest cities substitute oxygenated gasoline for winter use beginning in November 1992. By 1995, the country's nine smoggiest cities—Baltimore, Chicago, Hartford, Houston, Los Angeles, Milwaukee, New York, Philadelphia, and San Diego—were to have implemented its Phase I specifications. Phase I stipulated that oxygenates (MTBE) be substituted for aromatics (which do not burn completely) in octane enhancers, essentially prescribing complete reformulation of automotive gasoline.

This new gasoline must have a minimum oxygen content of 2 percent by weight, a maximum of 1 percent benzene by volume, a maximum aromatics content of 25 percent, and no heavy metals. It must not cause an increase in nitrogen oxide emissions and must create less tailpipe emissions of volatile organic compounds and toxic air pollutants (relative to a baseline of 1990 summertime gasoline). The cost to refiners of implementing substitutions and reformulations prescribed in Phase I was estimated to run $3 billion to $5 billion. Furthermore, the California Air Resources Board (CARB) instituted standards exceeding those of the Clean Air Act, requiring them to be met by 1996. Some analysts predicted the CARB standards would eventually replace Clean Air standards nationwide. Costs of compliance prompted a spate of refinery closures in the early 1990s. Intense streamlining was required of major companies, particularly Chevron. Chevron drastically scaled back operations at its Port Arthur, Texas, refinery (140,000 b/cd lost) and cut its Richmond, California, refinery capacity by 40,000 b/cd.

Estimates for upcoming compliance costs for U.S. refiners fall within the $20 billion range, as four more major amendments of the Clean Air Act come into play. In October 1993 ultra low-sulfur diesel fuel (.05 percent by weight) was to be required nationally. January 1995 marked the deadline for nationwide Stage I gasoline reformulation, and Stage II should have been met by January 1997, requiring adherence to a "complex" model as opposed to Stage I's "simple" model. January 2000 will see an additional ten percent reduction in organic compounds and air toxics from the 1990 baseline fuel, with no increase in nitrogen oxides.

ORGANIZATION AND STRUCTURE

DOWNSTREAM

"Upstream" processes are first used to locate and remove oil from the earth; "downstream" processes are those used to turn crude oil into refined petroleum products. Downstream operations include pipelining crude oil to refining sites, refining crude into various products, and pipelining or otherwise transporting products to wholesalers, distributors, or retailers.

Because many downstream companies are subsidiaries of conglomerates that also maintain upstream subsidiaries, the sale of raw materials to refiners is often essentially a transfer of products between different operating units of the same corporation. Petroleum refiners, therefore, often depend on the upstream arms of their parent corporations for supplies of crude, and, in turn, supply wholesalers (who then sell to independent retailers) and retailers (company-owned gasoline stations, for example) who are also part of the same corporation. All major oil operating in this system are known as "integrated oil companies" non-integrated companies are often referred to as "independents."

This tendency toward massive, integrated supply systems affects the oil industry and refiners in that any shift in condition at any point in the crude-to-product chain is felt equally at all levels; economic trickle-down, as it exists in other industries, offers no stabilization.

Product yields per barrel have shifted with demand. In the early 1980s, 10.4 percent of a barrel went toward

---

SIC 2911 - Petroleum Refining
General Statistics

Year	Companies	Establishments		Employment			Compensation		Production ($ million)			
		Total	with 20 or more employees	Total (000)	Production Workers (000)	Hours (Mil)	Payroll ($ mil)	Wages ($/hr)	Cost of Materials	Value Added by Manufacture	Value of Shipments	Capital Invest.
1982	283	434	313	108.7	71.3	148.4	3,410.3	13.92	178,947.0	19,204.3	199,722.8	6,412.3
1983				103.5	66.7	141.3	3,440.4	15.20	163,416.7	17,880.8	182,591.8	4,319.1
1984				94.6	61.3	131.9	3,326.3	15.40	164,812.7	12,743.3	177,692.3	3,494.4
1985				85.7	56.1	119.9	3,073.0	16.05	153,095.1	13,659.5	167,501.8	3,037.5
1986				84.2	55.2	112.8	3,131.1	17.44	95,995.2	13,761.7	113,286.4	2,273.0
1987	201	309	221	74.6	50.0	103.3	2,845.5	17.39	104,826.4	14,223.3	118,186.2	2,035.0
1988				73.2	49.5	102.9	2,928.9	17.80	97,320.7	20,687.6	118,829.5	2,326.7
1989		326	219	72.4	47.9	104.6	2,984.1	17.77	110,521.6	21,580.0	131,192.3	2,986.9
1990				71.9	47.3	105.8	3,195.6	18.56	138,537.0	22,822.0	159,411.1	3,818.7
1991				73.9	47.6	106.5	3,448.4	19.46	123,916.8	19,795.7	145,391.5	5,600.8
1992	132	232	197	74.8	47.9	109.3	3,636.3	19.74	116,908.0	19,100.6	136,239.0	6,139.7
1993				73.1	47.3	106.5	3,735.3	21.04	110,279.0	18,710.3	129,961.1	5,985.8
1994				71.7	46.3	107.1	3,796.0	21.64	105,722.7	23,231.6	128,235.6	5,215.2
1995				61.9P	40.2P	93.7P	3,551.0P	21.87P	95,049.1P	20,886.2P	115,289.1P	5,029.1P
1996				59.1P	38.3P	90.6P	3,586.2P	22.45P	91,339.3P	20,071.0P	110,789.3P	5,158.0P
1997				56.2P	36.4P	87.5P	3,621.5P	23.03P	87,629.4P	19,255.8P	106,289.5P	5,286.9P
1998				53.4P	34.5P	84.4P	3,656.8P	23.61P	83,919.6P	18,440.6P	101,789.7P	5,415.8P

Sources: 1982, 1987, 1992 *Economic Census*; *Annual Survey of Manufactures*, 83-86, 88-91, 93-94. Establishment counts for non-Census years are from *County Business Patterns*; establishment values for 83-84 are extrapolations. 'P's show projections by the editors. Industries reclassified in 87 will not have data for prior years.

residual fuel oils; only 6.7 percent was used in such fuel oils in the mid-1990s. Moreover, while 7.6 percent of a 1980s barrel went for jet fuel, 10.3 percent of a 1990s barrel was used in jet fuel. This trend should continue, and may become more pronounced, as various emissions regulations are adopted. Federal requirements for low sulfur diesel fuel and reformulated gasoline should change the yield of a barrel of crude; at the same time, wastewater and toxic solids limitations will change the methods of obtaining yields.

FINANCIAL STRUCTURE

Once crude oil has been refined, its products may be sold as raw materials to other manufacturers, such as plastics or pharmaceutical companies. Other products may be in a final, packaged form and destined for retail sale in service stations or chemical companies.

Within an integrated oil company, a refinery's profits then are part of the total profits made on the front-end. Its ability to compete depends entirely on efficient production without excessive expenditures, so that retail prices can remain low. Like the supply-side interdependency of integrated oil companies, integrated profit margins are cumulative. They must absorb the costs of every aspect of the oil business, including geological research, refining procedures, and trucking the finished product, to show real net gain.

For refiners operating independently, turning a profit traditionally rested in purchasing crude at low enough rates to allow final product levels to match those of the integrated oils. Free from the overhead of exploration and test drilling, independents were able to compete effectively for years simply by taking advantage of plentiful, cheap supplies of crude. However, the increasingly stringent environmental requirements of the 1980s and 1990s put independents at a distinct disadvantage.

Even with low crude prices, facility upgrading cut deeply into revenues and forced profit margins to fall.

COMPETITIVE STRUCTURE

Integrated international oil companies, integrated domestic oil companies, and independent domestic refining/marketing companies comprise the petroleum refining industry in America. Like the oil business in general, refining was dominated in the early 1990s by integrated internationals, specifically a few large companies such as Exxon Corporation, Mobil Corporation, and Chevron Corporation—all of which ranked in the top ten of Fortune's 500 sales ranking.

Of the nonintegrated refining companies—independents that focused exclusively on refined goods production and marketing—Ashland Oil, Inc., Diamond Shamrock, Inc. (now Ultramar Diamond Shamrock), and Total Petroleum of North America stood out as major players. However, no independent companies competed on the same level as any integrated international in terms of net profits or refined goods sold.

Capacity also distinguished leading refiners as arms of integrated oils. Chevron and Exxon had over 1 million barrels per day capacity, with Amoco, Shell, Mobil, and BP America trailing closely. A further 26 companies had over 100,000 barrels per day capacity, and the smallest 44 had less than 100,000.

As the costs of upgrading refineries escalates, the difficulties of small refining operations will probably intensify. Only with mass infusion of capital can existing refineries remain viable through the end of the 1990s, and only large integrated oils have cashflow to divert. Even the majors struggled; Chevron, for example, put two of its refineries on the market in the mid-1990s and downsized several others. Analysts speculated that upgrading and compliance costs may continue to shift the

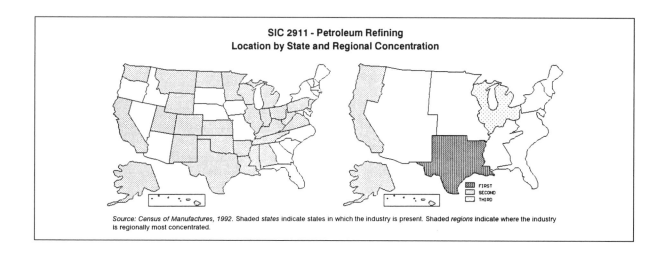

SIC 2911 - Petroleum Refining
Location by State and Regional Concentration

FIRST
SECOND
THIRD

Source: Census of Manufactures, 1992. Shaded states indicate states in which the industry is present. Shaded regions indicate where the industry is regionally most concentrated.

competitive structure of the American refined petroleum products market toward a monopoly by integrated internationals.

WORK FORCE

Refiners employed 103,800 people in the United States in 1995. Employees earned an average of $21.44 per hour doing a variety of tasks centering on keeping technical processes functioning smoothly. Within refineries, operators and craftsworkers monitored products via computers. They analyzed data and made adjustments to machinery to ensure optimum yields, repair faulty equipment, and make statistical reports on output. Mechanical engineers worked closely with operators, developing new machinery and making improvements whenever possible. These highly skilled technicians and scientists comprised the core of all refineries' staffs.

As refiners streamline staffs and close some operations altogether, employment prospects in petroleum refining during the 1990s were not encouraging. Large numbers of experienced workers may be laid off as domestic refining capacities shrink and majors shift operations overseas.

Labor negotiations through the mid-1990s had a major impact on industry employees. In 1993 the major oil refining outfits reached agreement with the Oil, Chemical and Atomic Workers on a new three-year contract that, according to the *Monthly Labor Review,* "struck a balance between the union's goal of improved wages and benefits, safety concerns, and a national health care program and the companies' desire to contain costs and retain operational flexibility." Labor goals in the petroleum refining industry have traditionally been articulated at the national level through the Oil, Chemical and Atomic workers, while the actual negotiations take place at the local level. As *Monthly Labor Review* observed, "the first [local] settlement serves as a pattern, with the terms of the new contract reached with the lead off oil company being matched by most other oil companies." This agreement set the tone for subsequent agreements for the 30,500 workers in the industry.

RESEARCH AND TECHNOLOGY

Although new advances in reformulating gasoline, substituting cleaner fuel bases, and eliminating production waste represent significant innovations in the industry, perhaps the most important revolution in petroleum refining technology involved the implementation of

SIC 2911
Occupations Employed by SIC 291 - Petroleum Refining

Occupation	% of Total 1994	Change to 2005
Gas & petroleum plant & system occupations	16.7	-6.1
Chemical equipment controllers, operators	6.1	-15.5
Chemical engineers	4.0	-6.1
Science & mathematics technicians	3.7	-6.1
Plumbers, pipefitters, & steamfitters	3.3	-6.1
Industrial machinery mechanics	3.1	3.3
Plant & system operators nec	2.7	24.4
Secretaries, ex legal & medical	2.3	-14.5
Management support workers nec	2.2	-6.1
Helpers, laborers, & material movers nec	2.1	-6.1
Precision instrument repairers	2.1	12.6
Chemical plant & system operators	2.0	-6.1
Material moving equipment operators nec	2.0	-6.1
Maintenance repairers, general utility	1.9	-15.5
Electricians	1.9	-11.9
Engineers nec	1.8	40.8
Chemists	1.7	-6.1
Engineering technicians & technologists nec	1.6	-6.1
Bookkeeping, accounting, & auditing clerks	1.6	-29.6
Accountants & auditors	1.6	-6.1
General office clerks	1.5	-20.0
Mechanical engineers	1.4	3.3
Truck drivers light & heavy	1.4	-3.2
General managers & top executives	1.2	-11.0
Managers & administrators nec	1.1	-6.1
Mechanics, installers, & repairers nec	1.1	-6.1
Engineering, mathematical, & science managers	1.1	6.6
Furnace, kiln, or kettle operators	1.0	12.6
Welders & cutters	1.0	-6.2
Crushing & mixing machine operators	1.0	-6.2

Source: *Industry-Occupation Matrix,* Bureau of Labor Statistics. These data relate to one or more 3-digit SIC industry groups rather than to a single 4-digit SIC. The change reported for each occupation to the year 2005 is a percent of growth or decline as estimated by the Bureau of Labor Statistics. The abbreviation nec stands for 'not elsewhere classified'.

computers. In the early 1990s, distilling and manufacturing industries relied on mainframes that could record, compile, and recall data on all elements, from viscosity to sulfur levels, in any given barrel of crude. Everything from measuring proportions of ingredients to monitoring chemical reactions could be performed with computers, and engineers relied as much on three-dimensional graphic and diagraming software as on actual valves and gages to determine improvements in processes.

With upstream technology breakthroughs such as 3-D seismography, horizontal and directional drilling, and enhanced oil recovery (EOR) helping to ensure that every drop of oil was pumped from the ground, the impetus to utilize every drop of oil at maximum efficiency had never been stronger. Computers allowed such efficiency not only by storing and retrieving data in a central, accessible medium, but also by cutting the time required for compilation and computation. Moreover, by implementing self-cleaning machines monitored by more sophisticated computers, petroleum refiners should be able to produce the low-toxicity fuels in demand, and eventually find new areas for growth.

AMERICA AND THE WORLD

America was a pioneer in petroleum refining, perfecting most technical procedures earlier than other nations, and developing synchronized upstream and downstream supply lines early. U.S. petroleum refiners are still regarded as the world leaders, with an average yield of 52 percent gasoline from every barrel of crude oil, as opposed to 25-30 percent for foreign equivalents. The main difference between American petroleum refiners and refiners elsewhere lies in the country's free market operations. In no other country has petroleum production and refining developed with such complete autonomy from government.

This autonomy has led to minor competitive disadvantages for Americans selling in nationalized markets in that, unlike foreign refinery products, no correlative subsidies or guarantees existed for American goods. However, global economic stagnation and widespread failure of centrally planned economies catalyzed a surge in privatization in markets during the early 1990s, as nationals went private in the petroleum industry worldwide, a trend anticipated to continue throughout the decade.

Many major national systems being privatized in the early 1990s were inspired by Mexico, whose president, Carlos Salinas de Gortari, used privatization as one method to turn around his country's flagging economy. The Mexican example was held by economists as a lesson in the ills of planned economies and the virtues of market controls, a lesson particularly applicable to republics of the former Soviet Union, struggling with the absolute collapse of their national systems.

In 1993, the Italian state petroleum holding company Ente Nazionale Idrocarburi began to unfold one of the largest privatization programs ever. Most key oil producing nations in Latin America, growing economies in the Asia-Pacific region, and much of western Europe were all in various stages of privatization in the early 1990s, depending on freer markets to sustain their national economies.

Members of the European Community faced challenges in both their individual privatization efforts and their collective energy legislative programs. For example, when EC efforts to reduce excess capacities required that Great Britain streamline some operations, the British public protested, claiming that mass unemployment in already-depressed areas would follow. Government systems were thereby forced to continue supporting unprofitable operations.

The situation in Great Britain highlighted the reason that nationalized petroleum may become an industry of the past: because of the decidedly global nature of petroleum markets, national systems might not be able to compete, once a majority of producer/refiners become private industries. As more organizations adopt efficient, profit-motivated structures, the standards for products worldwide may begin to resemble those in the United States in terms of stringent environmental standards. If so, the American market may become accessible to foreign competition.

There has already been a long history of joint venture and investment in the United States by refiners based overseas, and some of the integrated internationals which dominate in the United States are based in foreign countries, such as the Royal Dutch/Shell Group and British Petroleum.

The state energy companies of several OPEC countries, particularly Kuwait, Saudi Arabia, and Venezuela, invested heavily in U.S. downstream capacities in the early 1990s. Petreolos de Venezuela S.A. (PDVSA, the state petroleum company of Venezuela and Saudi Arabia) acquired the remaining 50 percent interest in Citgo Petroleum in 1991, becoming the full owner of this subsidiary. Star Enterprise, a 50/50 petroleum refining and marketing joint venture between Saudi Arabia's ARAMCO and Texaco, began operating in 1989. And Delta International, another state-owned Saudi company, began negotiating a joint venture with Fina Oil and Chemical, the U.S. subsidiary of Petrofina, a Belgian firm, for its U.S. refining and marketing operations. Furthermore, the as yet unprivatized Pemex Corporation of Mexico acquired a 50 percent interest in Shell Oil's Deer Park, Texas, refinery and began negotiations with other Gulf Coast refiners.

The increasingly complex subsidiary networks of integrated internationals should link many refineries in the United States in the next decade. As the global economy shrinks and ties between nations become stronger, the already cosmopolitan arena of petroleum refining will acknowledge increasingly fewer political borders. Consequently, American refiners may compete more directly with foreign firms for markets both at home and abroad.

ASSOCIATIONS AND SOCIETIES

AMERICAN INDEPENDENT REFINERS ASSOCIATION
1 Massachusetts Ave. NW, Ste. 300
Washington, DC 20001
Phone: (202) 682-1519
Fax: (202) 682-5909

AMERICAN PETROLEUM INSTITUTE
1220 L St. NW
Washington, DC 20005
Phone: (202) 682-8000
Fax: (202) 682-8232

INDEPENDENT PETROLEUM ASSOCIATION OF AMERICA
1101 16th St. NW
Washington, DC 20036
Phone: (202) 857-4799 or (202) 857-4722

NATIONAL PETROLEUM COUNCIL
1625 K St. NW, Ste. 600
Washington, DC 20006
Phone: (202) 393-6100
Fax: (202) 331-8539

NATIONAL PETROLEUM REFINERS ASSOCIATION
1899 L St. NW, Ste. 1000
Washington, DC 20036
Phone: (202) 457-0480
Fax: (202) 457-0486

PERIODICALS AND NEWSLETTERS

ENERGY MANAGEMENT REPORT
Advanstar Communications, Inc.
7500 Old Oak Blvd.
Cleveland, OH 44130
Phone: (800) 346-0085 or (216) 243-8100
Fax: (216) 891-2726
Semimonthly. $108.00 per year.

LUNDBERG LETTER
Lundberg Survey, Inc.
PO Box 3996
North Hollywood, CA 91609-0996
Phone: (818) 768-5111
Fax: (818) 768-1883
Twice weekly. $399.00 per year. Petroleum newsletter.

NATIONAL PETROLEUM NEWS (NPN)
Hunter Publishing Ltd. Partnership
25 NW Blvd., Ste. 800
Elk Grove Village, IL 60007
Phone: (708) 427-9512
Fax: (708) 427-2041
13 times a year. $60.00 per year.

OIL AND GAS JOURNAL
PennWell Publishing Co.
PO Box 1260
Tulsa, OK 74102
Phone: (918) 835-3161
Fax: (918) 831-9497
Weekly. Qualified personnel, $52.00 per year; others, $95.00 per year.

OIL DAILY: DAILY NEWSPAPER OF THE PETROLEUM INDUSTRY
Oil Daily Co.
1401 New York Ave. NW, Ste. 500
Washington, DC 20005
Phone: (202) 662-0700
Fax: (202) 783-8320
Daily. $897.00 per year. Newspaper for the petroleum industry.

DATABASES

APIBIZ (PETROLEUM-ENERGY NEWS)
American Petroleum Institute
Central Abstracting and Information Services
275 7th Ave.
New York, NY 10001
Phone: (212) 366-4040
Fax: (212) 366-4298
Indexing of newsletters and business journals in the petroleum and energy areas, 1975 to present. Inquire as to online cost and availability.

APILIT
American Petroleum Institute
Central Abstracting and Information Services
275 7th Ave.
New York, NY 10001
Phone: (212) 366-4040
Fax: (212) 366-4298
Worldwide technical literature on petroleum refining and petrochemical industry, 1964 to present. Inquire as to online cost and availability.

APIPAT
American Petroleum Institute
Central Abstracting and Information Services
275 7th Ave.
New York, NY 10001
Phone: (212) 366-4040
Fax: (212) 955-8312
Worldwide patent citations on petroleum refining and petrochemical industry, 1964 to present. Inquire as to online cost and availability.

ENERGY SCIENCE AND TECHNOLOGY
U.S. Dept. of Energy, Office of Scientific and Technical Information
PO Box 62
Oak Ridge, TN 37831
Phone: (615) 576-9362
Fax: (615) 576-2865
Contains abstracts and citations to literature in all fields of energy from 1974 to date, with biweekly updates. Formerly DOE Energy Data Base. Inquire as to online cost and availability.

ENERGYLINE
Congressional Information Service, Inc.
4520 East-West Hwy., Ste. 800
Bethesda, MD 20814-3389
Phone: (800) 638-8380 or (301) 654-1550
Fax: (301) 654-4033
Provides online citations and abstracts to the literature of all forms of energy: petroleum, natural gas, coal, nuclear power, solar energy, etc. Time period is 1971 to date. Monthly updates. Inquire as to online cost and availability.

PLATT'S OIL PRICES
McGraw-Hill, Inc.
1221 Avenue of the Americas
New York, NY 10020
Phone: (800) 722-4726 or (212) 512-4686
Fax: (212) 512-4256

Various time series detailing domestic and foreign oil prices; daily updating. Time period 1970 to date. Inquire as to online cost and availability.

STATISTICS SOURCES

ANNUAL ENERGY REVIEW
Available from U.S. Government Printing Office
Washington, DC 20402
Phone: (202) 512-1800
Fax: (202) 512-2250
Annual. Issued by the Energy Information Administration, Office of Energy Markets and End Use, U.S. Department of Energy. Presents long-term historical as well as recent data on production, consumption, stocks, imports, exports, and prices of the principal energy commodities in the U.S.

BASIC PETROLEUM DATA BOOK
American Petroleum Institute
Publications Section
1220 L St. NW
Washington, DC 20005
Phone: (202) 682-8000
Three times a year. Members, $120.00 per year; non-members, $150.00 per year.

ENCYCLOPEDIA OF AMERICAN INDUSTRIES
Gale Research
835 Penobscot Bldg.
Detroit, MI 48226-4094
Phone: (800) 877-GALE or (313) 961-2242
Fax: (800) 414-5043
1994. $500.00. Two volumes ($250.00 each). Volume one is Manufacturing Industries *and volume two is* Service and Non-Manufacturing Industries. *Provides the history, development, and recent status of approximately 1,000 industries. Includes statistical graphs, with industry and general indexes.*

MONTHLY ENERGY REVIEW
Available from U.S. Government Printing Office
Washington, DC 20402
Phone: (202) 512-1800
Fax: (202) 512-2250
Monthly. $87.00 per year. Issued by the Energy Information Administration, Office of Energy Markets and End Use, U.S. Department of Energy. Contains current and historical statistics on U.S. production, storage, imports, and consumption of petroleum, natural gas, and coal.

SHORT-TERM ENERGY OUTLOOK: QUARTERLY PROJECTIONS
Available from U.S. Government Printing Office
Washington, DC 20402
Phone: (202) 512-1800
Fax: (202) 512-2250
Quarterly. $16.00 per year. Issued by Energy Information Administration, U.S. Department of Energy. Contains forecasts of U.S. energy supply, demand, and prices.

WEEKLY PETROLEUM STATUS REPORT
Energy Information Administration
Available from U.S. Government Printing Office
Washington, DC 20402
Phone: (202) 512-1800
Fax: (202) 512-2250
Weekly. $65.00 per year. Current statistics in the context of both historical information and selected prices and forecasts.

GENERAL WORKS

ENERGY MANAGEMENT AND FEDERAL ENERGY GUIDELINES
Commerce Clearing House, Inc.
4025 W. Peterson Ave.
Chicago, IL 60646
Phone: (800) 248-3248 or (312) 583-8500
$1,300.00 per year. Seven looseleaf volumes. Periodic supplementation. Reports on petroleum allocation rules, conservation efforts, new technology, and other energy concerns.

FEDERAL REGULATION OF ENERGY
Shepard's/McGraw-Hill, Inc.
PO Box 35300
Colorado Springs, CO 80935-3530
Phone: (800) 525-2474 or (303) 577-7707
Fax: (800) 525-0053
Looseleaf service. $95.00 per year. Annual supplementation. Includes sections on federal regulation of petroleum, natural gas, nuclear energy, coal, and electricity.

NATIONAL PETROLEUM NEWS-MARKET FACTS
Hunter Publishing Co. Inc.
950 Lee St.
Des Plaines, IL 60016
Phone: (708) 427-9512
Fax: (708) 296-8821
Annual. $60.00. Includes refiners and marketers of petroleum products. Formerly National Petroleum News-Fact Book.

PETROLEUM ENGINEER INTERNATIONAL DRILLING AND PRODUCTION YEARBOOK ISSUE
Hart Publications, Inc.
4545 Post Oak Pl., Ste. 210
Houston, TX 77027
Phone: (713) 993-9320
Fax: (713) 840-8585
Annual. $10.00.

SUMMERS ON OIL AND GAS
West Publishing Co.
College and School Div.
PO Box 64526
St. Paul, MN 55164-0526
Phone: (612) 228-2778
Periodic supplementation. Legal aspects of the petroleum industry.

FURTHER READING

Basic Petroleum Data Book. Washington: American Petroleum Institute.

"Fuel Oil." *National Petroleum News,* August 1996, 88, no. 8. p. 56.

Kovski, Alan. "Refiners Endure Tough Quarter Burdened by High Crude Prices." *The Oil Daily,* 12 November 1996, 46, no. 215 7.

"OPEC's Joyride Was great While it Lasted." *Business Week,* 3 June 1996, p. 52.

Rosenberger, Gary. "Merger Trend Called Irreversible." *Journal of Commerce and Commercial,* 1 May 1996, 408, no. 28714, p. 7B.

U.S. Refiners Home in on Profits Amid Near Term Uncertainties. *The Oil and Gas Journal,* 1 July 1996, 94, no. 27, p. 27.

According to the U.S. Census Bureau's *Current Industrial Reports,* the pharmaceutical preparations industry shipped $49.5 billion worth of product in 1995. Those revenues do not rank the industry among the country's largest business categories, but average returns make this one of the world's most profitable enterprises. *Fortune* noted that "Drugmakers live in what seems like profit paradise; they are consistently among the highest-earning industries, and last year [1995] kept an average of 15 cents from every dollar of sales—tops among all industries on our global list."

Since World War II, which established the American drug industry on a permanent footing, pharmaceutical firms have expected a high level of profitability. The discovery and development of dozens of life-saving medications in company research labs created enormous demand for pharmaceuticals, while patent protection and sophisticated marketing structures maintained sales and profits. The high cost of drug development and marketing, though, tended to concentrate industry earnings in several large firms. Thus, as *Standard and Poor's* reported in 1996, despite hundreds of companies operating in the industry, the ten largest businesses accounted for over 50 percent of annual U.S. pharmaceutical sales in 1995. Even with strict regulatory oversight and periodic crises, like the Thalidomide scare of 1962, the American pharmaceutical industry, or at least its major players, managed to remain both profitable and largely beneficial to world health while avoiding the price controls commonplace in other industrialized nations.

Indeed, U.S. drugmakers faced the threat of increased regulation—including price controls—in the early 1990s. While it was defeated in 1994, the Clinton Administration's health care proposal did have an indirect affect on the industry, inspiring wholesale belt-tightening and a rash of mergers and acquisitions. Furthermore, the industry's earnings growth slowed from an annual average of 18 percent from 1987 to 1992 to 9 percent from 1991 to 1993. Downsizing helped boost the earnings growth rate to 12 percent by 1995.

Despite some victories, by the end of the 1980s the prospects for the preparations industry did not look bright. Decades of expensive applied research, a wide patent umbrella, strong overseas sales, and aggressive marketing had sustained high profit and growth in the American prescription pharmaceutical industry since World War II. The system produced important new therapies that prolonged lives, banished ancient diseases, and made the aches and pains of modern existence easier to bear for those who could afford to purchase these new medications. But the highly structured corporate re-

PHARMACEUTICAL PREPARATIONS

SIC 2834

While facing strict governmental regulation and consumer pressure in response to the spiraling cost of health care, the pharmaceutical preparations industry has remained strong. Industry leaders have moved to diversify, creating or acquiring generics, over-the-counter, and biotechnology divisions. New technological breakthroughs and the burgeoning cosmetic medications market, as well as an aging population with a high demand for pharmaceuticals, have contributed to the continuing success of the industry.

Top 10 LEADING PHARMACEUTICAL FIRMS

Ranked by: Sales in 1995, in millions of dollars.

1. Johnson & Johnson, with $18,842 million
2. Merck, $16,681.1
3. Bristol-Myers Squibb, $13,767
4. American Home Products, $13,376
5. Pfizer, $10,021.4
6. Abbott Laboratories, $10,012.1
7. Pharmacia & Upjohn, $7,094.6
8. Warner-Lambert Co., $7,039.8
9. Eli Lilly, $6,763.8
10. Rhone-Poulenc Rorer, $5,142.1

Source: *ChemicalWeek*, ChemicalWeek 300 (annual), May 8, 1996, p. 57.

search, manufacturing, and marketing systems of industry leaders also required that wonderful new medications carry what seemed to many improperly inflated price tags. Some analysts felt that price was determining costs rather than the other way around; critics claimed that the big brand pharmaceutical companies were charging unjustifiably high prices for drugs while spending more money on advertising, brand support, and lobbying efforts than they did for research and development. Meanwhile, the soaring costs of health care in general in the 1980s and early 1990s added fuel to demands for drug price control policies similar to those in Europe. Medications sold in Europe and America were reported to have price differentials exceeding 50 percent.

In 1991 legislation allowed state-funded Medicaid insurance programs to demand rebates from drug manufacturers for medications purchased by program recipients, resulting in downward price pressures. Standard and Poor's reported in its 1994 *Industry Surveys* that Medicaid accounted for about 15 percent of all U.S. pharmaceutical sales. Similar programs for the federal government's Medicare program were included in President Clinton's 1993 health care reform proposals. Downward pressures on drug prices also resulted from the advent in the 1980s and 1990s of private managed care organizations such as health maintenance organizations (HMOs). Standard and Poor's estimated that HMO enrollment alone may top 50 percent of the population by the year 2000. These organizations increasingly adopted restrictive drug formularies (lists of drugs that could or could not be purchased by an organization) that stressed economical medication in therapeutic groups, often demanding discounts from manufacturers and the use of cheaper brands or generics to treat illness. Both of these movements created what one industry analyst, Paul

Hanson, in an April 1994 *Chemical Week* article called a "strategic shift in power in pharmaceuticals from suppliers to consumers."

INDUSTRY OUTLOOK

Larger research budgets in the 1980s yielded a whole crop of profitable new drug therapies, including drugs for hypertension, ulcer relief, cholesterol treatment, and blood-clot dissolvers for heart-attack victims. Meanwhile, Ortho Pharmaceutical's (owned by Johnson & Johnson) anti-acne Retin-A, and Upjohn's baldness treatment Rogaine, created new markets for cosmetic drugs. Even standbys like aspirin enjoyed increased sales as a result of studies that showed its potential to avert some heart attacks. These positive trends are expected to continue through the end of the decade, especially with the breakthroughs in drug delivery systems and biotechnology.

Because of the increased pressure of the consumer market, and despite the failure of Clinton's health care reform plan, the over-the-counter (OTC) segment was expected to grow by more than 45 percent from $9.6 billion in 1995 to $14 billion by the year 2000. Many of the large branded firms, which continue to dominate the industry, bought or created generics divisions in the mid-1990s. The majors also moved to purchase smaller competitors or start their own innovative biotechnology companies.

ORGANIZATION AND STRUCTURE

Industry production and employment was concentrated in the northeast states of New Jersey, Pennsylvania, and New York. About 20 percent of all the country's drugs are shipped from New Jersey, home to industry leaders American Home Products Corp., Johnson & Johnson, and Merck and Company. Other states with high concentrations of drug companies were California, Illinois, Texas, Indiana, and Florida. Mergers and acquisitions continued to transform the competitive structure of the industry into the mid-1990s, as the leaders sought increased economies of scale.

Pharmaceutical preparations, or finished-form drugs, companies maintained their traditional leadership of the industry into the latter part of the century, constituting approximately 60 percent of pharmaceutical sales.

All companies in the pharmaceutical industry operate within a strict regulatory environment. Because it combines the manufacture of potentially harmful yet socially necessary products with the common business need for profit, the pharmaceutical industry has had a complex relationship with government regulators who were charged with protecting the public and encouraging business growth at the same time. Major incidents of adverse or fatal reactions from drugs, evidence of collusion or corruption within the industry, and the government's desire to move the industry in a particular direction had historically prompted new regulation. From the Food and Drug Administration (FDA) to the Federal Trade Commission (FTC), pharmaceutical companies and the federal government are linked at all stages, including development, production, and marketing.

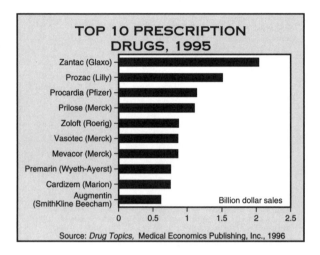

TOP 10 PRESCRIPTION DRUGS, 1995

Zantac (Glaxo)
Prozac (Lilly)
Procardia (Pfizer)
Prilose (Merck)
Zoloft (Roerig)
Vasotec (Merck)
Mevacor (Merck)
Premarin (Wyeth-Ayerst)
Cardizem (Marion)
Augmentin (SmithKline Beecham)

Billion dollar sales

0   0.5   1   1.5   2   2.5

Source: *Drug Topics,* Medical Economics Publishing, Inc., 1996

Division and segmentation also characterized the industry. Some segmentation resulted from federal regu-

lation, while the pressures of a highly competitive marketplace were responsible for the rest. One point of division for regulatory agencies was that between "ethical" drugs and over-the-counter (OTC) drugs. Ethical drugs require a prescription from a physician before being dispensed to the patient, while the consumer can purchase OTC medications (such as aspirins and antacids) without a doctor's prescription. Ethical drugs represented 60 percent of sales among preparations companies in 1995, while OTCs accounted for the remainder.

The ethical drug segment of the industry is further subdivided into "patented" and "generic" prescription drugs. Patented drugs are therapies developed by pharmaceutical companies whose formulas, production processes, and trade names (often called branded prescription drugs) enjoy 17-year protection under U.S. patent laws. Patented prescription drugs were the driving force behind pharmaceutical industry sales after World War II and continued market domination into the mid-1990s. Branded prescriptions also included almost all of the major breakthrough therapies developed in drug research labs since the 1940s, continuing the drug industry's unusual combination of health- and profit-driven research. Meanwhile, an alternative to some of the most popular OTC remedies are generics, markedly cheaper chemical and therapeutic equivalents of patented prescription drugs that go into production once brand name therapies have come "off-patent". Generics' share of the prescription drug market are expected to increase to over 66 percent by the turn of the century.

SIC 2834 - Pharmaceutical Preparations
General Statistics

Year	Com-panies	Establishments		Employment			Compensation		Production ($ million)			
		Total	with 20 or more employees	Total (000)	Production Workers (000)	Hours (Mil)	Payroll ($ mil)	Wages ($/hr)	Cost of Materials	Value Added by Manufacture	Value of Shipments	Capital Invest.
1982	584	683	332	124.4	62.2	120.0	3,052.5	9.69	5,529.8	13,484.0	18,997.6	861.2
1983		685	339	123.7	61.9	117.6	3,173.7	10.22	5,898.8	15,476.4	21,222.0	833.9
1984		687	346	123.8	59.7	111.0	3,367.1	10.96	6,169.9	16,922.6	22,887.6	1,060.0
1985		688	353	123.0	58.4	111.8	3,595.4	11.60	6,417.8	19,094.7	25,335.3	1,171.1
1986		678	354	124.2	58.7	113.5	3,780.3	12.00	7,661.4	20,597.9	28,179.3	1,057.8
1987	640	732	364	131.6	59.9	117.5	4,168.1	12.42	8,463.0	23,883.6	32,094.1	1,471.1
1988		718	376	133.4	60.8	119.0	4,458.3	12.93	9,755.5	26,327.4	35,825.4	1,724.9
1989		699	388	143.9	62.4	121.5	5,142.6	13.83	10,717.3	29,449.8	40,028.0	1,932.5
1990		680	392	144.0	61.5	121.5	5,530.9	14.71	11,763.7	32,744.7	44,182.3	1,808.7
1991		703	388	129.1	59.2	117.0	5,012.3	14.77	12,869.8	34,978.0	47,375.0	1,771.6
1992	585	691	365	122.8	62.5	126.9	4,949.4	14.71	13,542.5	37,229.3	50,417.9	2,450.0
1993		765	408	128.2	62.8	126.5	5,418.9	15.81	14,120.2	39,415.3	53,280.8	2,493.2
1994		725P	405P	134.2	68.6	133.3	5,753.8	16.04	14,497.3	42,614.8	56,960.5	2,713.7
1995		729P	411P	135.4P	63.9P	128.4P	6,049.8P	16.80P	15,249.6P	44,826.2P	59,916.4P	2,747.5P
1996		733P	417P	136.2P	64.3P	129.6P	6,283.3P	17.33P	16,094.6P	47,310.1P	63,236.5P	2,905.4P
1997		737P	423P	137.0P	64.6P	130.8P	6,516.8P	17.87P	16,939.6P	49,794.0P	66,556.5P	3,063.3P
1998		740P	429P	137.8P	65.0P	132.1P	6,750.2P	18.40P	17,784.6P	52,277.9P	69,876.6P	3,221.2P

Sources: 1982, 1987, 1992 *Economic Census; Annual Survey of Manufactures,* 83-86, 88-91, 93-94. Establishment counts for non-Census years are from *County Business Patterns;* establishment values for 83-84 are extrapolations. 'P's show projections by the editors. Industries reclassified in 87 will not have data for prior years.

In addition to drugs for human consumption, pharmaceutical companies produce drugs for the veterinary market. Accounting for a relatively small percentage of overall industry sales, many drug industry leaders either maintained specific animal health divisions or were involved in all areas of the animal health care industry. In 1995, Pfizer moved ahead of Merck and American Home Products in this segment with its acquisition of SmithKline Beecham's animal health operations.

Beginning in the early 1980s a new force entered the pharmaceutical arena—biotechnology. Though biotech companies managed to create and patent many exciting new treatments in the 1980s, they were generally inconsequential, lacked marketing structure, consumed vast amounts of research capital, and created little profit compared to those offered by the industry leaders. Nevertheless, biotechnology companies became the target of buyouts, mergers, and joint ventures in the 1980s and 1990s. In one such move, industry giant Roche purchased controlling interest in biotechnology pioneer Genentech in 1990.

WORK FORCE

Work in the preparations segment of the pharmaceutical industry is concentrated in the largest companies. About 43 percent of the estimated 141,400 people employed in the industry nationwide worked in production, while research, marketing, and administration accounted for the remainder. Merck and Squibb have been described as fulfilling places to work because of their aggressive research departments. Merck did, however, endure a 15-week strike by its unionized workers in 1985. Johnson & Johnson has also enjoyed a solid reputation as an employer, offering progressive child-care and maternity leave policies.

Even though the health care reform movement of the early 1990s failed, employees of the pharmaceutical industry faced large scale layoffs. The rise of managed care organizations (MCOs) and chain hospitals reduced the need for the large sales staffs major companies traditionally employed. Competitive pressures exacted a heavy toll on drug company employment in the mid-1990s, with an estimated 60,000 positions cut from 1993 to 1996. Most of the cuts were coming from marketing and promotion personnel rather than vital research and development employees. Industry observers noted that ongoing rationalizations of overcapacity would put thousands more out of work before the end of the decade.

SIC 2834 Occupations Employed by SIC 283 - Drugs		
Occupation	% of Total 1994	Change to 2005
Packaging & filling machine operators	7.8	11.2
Science & mathematics technicians	5.7	36.0
Biological scientists	5.5	49.6
Secretaries, ex legal & medical	5.3	12.5
Chemists	4.9	23.6
Sales & related workers nec	4.4	23.6
Chemical equipment controllers, operators	3.1	11.2
Inspectors, testers, & graders, precision	2.7	23.6
Engineering, mathematical, & science managers	2.2	40.4
Management support workers nec	2.0	23.6
Industrial machinery mechanics	1.8	36.0
Managers & administrators nec	1.8	23.5
General managers & top executives	1.8	17.3
Crushing & mixing machine operators	1.7	23.6
Marketing, advertising, & PR managers	1.7	23.6
Medical scientists	1.7	48.3
Hand packers & packagers	1.7	5.9
Systems analysts	1.6	97.7
Assemblers, fabricators, & hand workers nec	1.5	23.6
Freight, stock, & material movers, hand	1.5	-1.1
Janitors & cleaners, incl maids	1.5	-1.1
Industrial production managers	1.5	23.6
Machine operators nec	1.4	8.9
General office clerks	1.2	5.4
Traffic, shipping, & receiving clerks	1.2	18.9
Professional workers nec	1.2	48.3
Helpers, laborers, & material movers nec	1.1	23.6
Marketing & sales worker supervisors	1.1	23.6
Extruding & forming machine workers	1.1	36.0
Bookkeeping, accounting, & auditing clerks	1.0	-7.3

Source: *Industry-Occupation Matrix*, Bureau of Labor Statistics. These data relate to one or more 3-digit SIC industry groups rather than to a single 4-digit SIC. The change reported for each occupation to the year 2005 is a percent of growth or decline as estimated by the Bureau of Labor Statistics. The abbreviation nec stands for 'not elsewhere classified'.

RESEARCH AND TECHNOLOGY

Though the federal government and academic institutions pursue both basic and applied research that often directly affects drug development, approximately 90 percent of new drugs come from the drug industry. However, analysts emphasize the importance of researchers financed by the National Institutes of Health (NIH) in initiating ground-breaking drug developments, and the role of academic researchers (often with both NIH and drug company financing) in revolutionary cell-receptor research as well as initial chemical trials cannot be denied.

Research and development of drug therapies remained crucial to the industry. Standard and Poor's reported in its 1994 *Survey* that the drug industry's "ratio of research-to-sales ranks as the highest of all major domestic industrial groups," although competitive pressures did exert some downward force on this, the lifeblood of the business, through the mid-1990s.

For patented prescription producers, the actual research and development of new drugs, especially after the adoption of the 1962 FDA regulatory guidelines, had always been an intricate process, sometimes referred to as "playing chess with nature." Company researchers began by screening or developing any number of New Chemical Entities (NCE's) that showed promise in a therapeutic class, on a specific disease, or with a specific cell receptor. Once one of these showed therapeutic potential, the company proceeded to move the new compound through a series of preclinical trials with animals to determine its toxicity at various doses. After the initial testing, the research company generally patented its new chemical and announced to the FDA its intention to begin human trials. The potential drug then moved through three distinct phases of human clinical trials, often taking seven years. The process was designed to expose possible adverse reactions, determine safe and effective dosages for humans, and test treatment. Once an NCE successfully survived these trials, and 19 of 20 did not because of ineffectiveness or toxicity, the company submitted a completed New Drug Application (NDA) to the FDA seeking final market approval for the new therapy. Even after market approval, a fourth phase could result in a recall or new label warnings if the drug showed adverse reactions in the larger population.

By its own regulations, the FDA was supposed to complete an NDA review within six months. By the 1990s though, review time in the understaffed agency had risen to over two years. Thus, by the time a company's new drug reached market, almost ten of its 17 years of patent exclusivity had disappeared, a point drug companies used to justify high prices. To address this problem, and to raise more revenue in order to add review staff to the FDA, Congress passed the Prescription Drug User Fee Act in 1992 . This legislation generated over $325 million in five years and helped speed average NDAs by ten months. In fact, the FDA was expected to approve a record-breaking 30 new molecular entities in 1996.

Drug delivery systems and biotechnology were two particularly active areas of research and development in the mid-1990s. Seeking ways to improve the therapeutic and economic performance of their products, pharmaceutical companies began to expand beyond the traditional delivery systems to inhalation, transmucosal, transdermal, and implantation methods. Examples include: timed-release capsules, implantable pumps, computerized inhalers, and "lollipop" sedatives.

AMERICA AND THE WORLD

The U.S. Department of Commerce estimated that by the mid 1990s American pharmaceutical manufacturers produced nearly half of the major pharmaceuticals marketed worldwide, while the domestic market consumed approximately 65 percent of this output. Nevertheless, exports accounted for a significant portion of sales for several major American drug companies.

The formal economic integration of European Union (EU) countries did not immediately fulfill industry expectations. Before unification, American companies selling or producing in Europe navigated a mine field of conflicting national price controls (most European countries have national health care systems that control costs), quality standards, and approval requirements for each new drug introduction, while also worrying about adequate patent protection. Similar problems faced U.S. pharmaceutical companies in Japan, the country with the highest per capita consumption of pharmaceuticals in the world with over 20 percent of the global market.

The importance of international relationships illustrates the traditionally global character of the pharmaceutical industry. Like their European and Japanese counter-

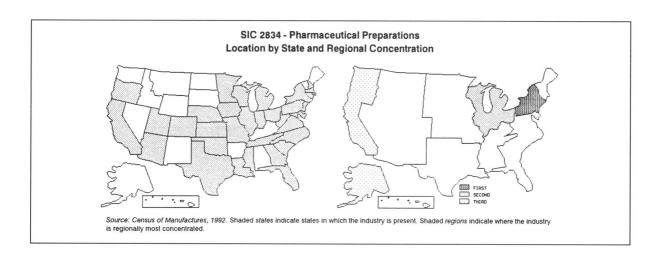

SIC 2834 - Pharmaceutical Preparations
Location by State and Regional Concentration

FIRST
SECOND
THIRD

Source: Census of Manufactures, 1992. Shaded *states* indicate states in which the industry is present. Shaded *regions* indicate where the industry is regionally most concentrated.

parts, American companies historically produced, manufactured, and marketed in each other's backyard. Rather than directly investing in full-scale overseas operations, many formed joint licensing agreements or joint ventures with home companies overseas to manufacture and market products in other countries. Many American pharmaceutical firms, however, continued to have overseas production and marketing networks under their own control. Giants such as Merck, American Home Products, and Eli Lilly operated worldwide, while many European firms maintained extensive U.S. operations.

ASSOCIATIONS AND SOCIETIES

AMERICAN PHARMACEUTICAL ASSOCIATION
2215 Constitution Ave. NW
Washington, DC 20037
Phone: (800) 237-2742 or (202) 628-4410
Fax: (202) 783-2351

GENERIC PHARMACEUTICAL INDUSTRY ASSOCIATION
1620 Eye St. NW, Ste. 800
Washington, DC 20006-4005
Phone: (202) 833-9070
Fax: (202) 833-9612
Members are manufacturers, wholesalers, and retailers of generic prescription drugs.

NATIONAL ASSOCIATION OF BOARDS OF PHARMACY
700 Busse Hwy.
Park Ridge, IL 60068
Phone: (708) 698-6227
Fax: (708) 698-0124

NATIONAL ASSOCIATION OF PHARMACEUTICAL MANUFACTURERS
320 Old Country Rd., Ste. 205
Garden City, NY 11530-1752
Phone: (516) 741-3699
Fax: (516) 741-3696

NATIONAL WHOLESALE DRUGGISTS' ASSOCIATION
1821 Michael Faraday Dr., Ste. 400
Reston, VA 22090-5348
Phone: (703) 787-0000
Fax: (703) 787-6930

NONPRESCRIPTION DRUG MANUFACTURERS ASSOCIATION
1150 Connecticut Ave. NW
Washington, DC 20036
Phone: (202) 429-9260
Fax: (202) 223-6835
Members are manufacturers and distributors of packaged, over-the-counter drugs.

PERIODICALS AND NEWSLETTERS

CLIN-ALERT
Information Today, Inc.
143 Old Marlton Pke.
Medford, NJ 08055-8750
Phone: (609) 654-6266
Fax: (609) 654-4309
Biweekly. $94.95 per year. Newsletter. Contains current abstracts of drug adverse reactions and interactions reported in over 600 medical journals. Includes quarterly cumulative indexes.

DRUG DEVELOPMENT RESEARCH
John Wiley and Sons, Inc.
Journal Div.
605 3rd Ave.
New York, NY 10158-0012
Phone: (800) 225-5945 or (212) 850-6000
Fax: (212) 850-6088
Monthly. $1,170.00 per year.

DRUG TOPICS
Medical Economics Publishing Co., Inc.
Five Paragon Dr.
Montvale, NJ 07645-1725
Phone: (800) 232-7379 or (201) 222-3045
Fax: (201) 573-1045
Semimonthly. $58.00 per year. Edited for retail pharmacists, hospital pharmacists, pharmacy chain store executives, wholesalers, buyers, and others concerned with drug dispensing and drug store management. Provides information on new products, including personal care items and cosmetics.

HEALTH NEWS DAILY
FDC Reports, Inc.
5550 Friendship Blvd., Ste. 1
Chevy Chase, MD 20815-7278
Phone: (301) 657-9830
Fax: (301) 656-3094
Daily. $1,250.00 per year. Newsletter providing broad coverage of the healthcare business, including government policy, regulation, research, finance, and insurance. Contains news of pharmaceuticals, medical devices, biotechnology, and healthcare delivery in general.

JOURNAL OF PHARMACEUTICAL MARKETING AND MANAGEMENT
Haworth Press, Inc.
10 Alice St.
Binghamton, NY 13904-1580
Phone: (800) 342-9678 or (607) 722-2493
Fax: (607) 722-1424
Quarterly. $150.00 per year.

PHARMACEUTICAL TECHNOLOGY
Advanstar Communications, Inc.
7500 Old Oak Blvd.
Cleveland, OH 44130
Phone: (800) 346-0085 or (216) 243-8100
Fax: (216) 891-2726
Monthly. $59.00 per year. Practical hands on information about the manufacture of pharmaceutical products, focusing on applied technology.

WHOLESALE DRUGS MAGAZINE
E L F Publications
333 W Hampden Ave., Ste. 1050
Englewood, CO 80110-2340
Phone: (303) 761-8818
Fax: (303) 761-2440
10 times a year. $15.00 per year.

DATABASES

DERWENT DRUG FILE
Derwent, Inc.
1313 Dolley Madison Blvd., Ste. 401
McLean, VA 22101
Phone: (800) 451-3451 or (703) 790-0400
Fax: (703) 790-1426
Provides indexing of the world's pharmaceutical journal literature since 1964, with monthly updates. Includes chemical substructures. Formerly RINGDOC. Inquire as to online cost and availability.

DRUG INFORMATION FULLTEXT
American Society of Hospital Pharmacists
7272 Wisconsin Ave.
Bethesda, MD 20814
Phone: (301) 657-4383
Fax: (301) 657-8278
Provides full text monographs from the American Hospital Formulary Service *and the* Handbook On Injectable Drugs. *Inquire as to online cost and availability.*

F-D-C REPORTS
FDC Reports, Inc.
5550 Friendship Blvd., Ste. 1
Chevy Chase, MD 20815
Phone: (301) 657-9830
Fax: (301) 656-3094
An online version of "The Gray Sheet" (medical devices), "The Pink Sheet" (pharmaceuticals), and "The Rose Sheet" (cosmetics). Contains full-text information on legal, technical, corporate, financial, and marketing developments from 1987 to date, with weekly updates. Inquire as to online cost and availability.

PNI (PHARMACEUTICAL NEWS INDEX)
UMI-Data Courier, Inc.
620 S 3rd St.
Louisville, KY 40202
Phone: (800) 626-2823 or (502) 583-4111
Fax: (502) 589-5572
Indexes major pharmaceutical industry newsletters, 1974 to present. Weekly updates. Inquire as to online cost and availability.

PREDICASTS FORECASTS: U.S.
Information Access Co.
362 Lakeside Dr.
Foster City, CA 94404
Phone: (800) 321-6388 or (415) 378-5000
Fax: (415) 358-4759
Provides numeric abstracts of a wide range of published forecasts relating to specific U.S. products, markets, and industries. Monthly updates. Time period is 1971 to date. Inquire as to online cost and availability.

STATISTICS SOURCES

ANNUAL SURVEY OF MANUFACTURES
Bureau of the Census, U.S. Department of Commerce
Available from U.S. Government Printing Office
Washington, DC 20402
Phone: (202) 512-1800
Fax: (202) 512-2250

NARCOTIC DRUGS: ESTIMATED WORLD REQUIREMENTS
International Narcotics Control Board
United Nations Publications
2 United Nations Plz., Rm. DC2-853
New York, NY 10017
Phone: (800) 253-9646 or (212) 963-8302
Fax: (212) 963-3489
Annual. Price varies. Includes production and utilization data relating to legal narcotics. Text in French, English and Spanish.

PHARMACEUTICAL MANUFACTURERS ASSOCIATION ANNUAL SURVEY REPORT
Pharmaceutical Manufacturers Association
110 15th St. NW
Washington, DC 20005
Phone: (202) 835-3400
Fax: (202) 835-3595
Annual. Free.

STANDARD & POOR'S INDUSTRY SURVEYS
Standard & Poor's Corp.
25 Broadway
New York, NY 10004
Phone: (800) 221-5277 or (212) 208-8000
Fax: (212) 412-0040
Weekly. $1,545.00 per year. Looseleaf service. Quarterly bound volumes, $875.00 per year. Discusses industry prospects and provides statistical tables.

STANDARD & POOR'S STATISTICAL SERVICE
Standard & Poor's Corp.
25 Broadway
New York, NY 10004
Phone: (800) 221-5277 or (212) 208-8000
Fax: (212) 412-0040
Monthly. $640.00 per year. Includes 10 Basic Statistics sections, Current Statistics Supplements and Annual Security Price Index Record.

GENERAL WORKS

APPROVED DRUG PRODUCTS
Health and Human Services
U.S. Government Printing Office
Washington, DC 20402
Phone: (202) 783-3238
Periodic supplementation. $95.00. Includes Therapeutic Equivalence Evaluations.

FOOD AND DRUG ADMINISTRATION
Shepard's McGraw-Hill, Inc.
PO Box 35300
Colorado Springs, CO 80935-3530
Phone: (800) 525-2474 or (303) 577-7707
Fax: (800) 525-0053
Two Looseleaf volumes. $180.00 per year. Annual supplementation. Discussion of regulations and procedures.

PHYSICIAN'S DESK REFERENCE
Medical Economics Publishing
5 Paragon Dr.
Montvale, NJ 07645
Phone: (800) 678-2681 or (201) 358-7500
Fax: (201) 573-0867
Annual. $58.90. Detailed descriptions of drug actions, side effects, dosage recommendations, etc.

PHYSICIAN'S DESK REFERENCE FOR NONPRESCRIPTION DRUGS
5 Paragon Dr.
Montvale, NJ 07645
Phone: (800) 678-2681 or (201) 358-7500
Fax: (201) 573-0867
Annual. $39.90. Detailed descriptions of over-the-counter drug actions, side effects, dosage recommendations, and so forth.

FURTHER READING

Darnay, Arsen J., ed. *Manufacturing USA.* 5th ed. Detroit: Gale Research, 1996.

Goldman, Jonathan. "Pharmaceuticals Are Looking Good." *Institutional Investor,* December 1996.

Hoover's Handbook of American Business. Austin, TX: Hoovers Inc., 1997.

Lerner, Matthew, and J. Robert Warren. "Delivering the Goods." *Chemical Marketing Reporter,* 5 August 1996.

"Mr. Nice Guy with a Mission." *Business Week Industrial Edition,* 25 November 1996, 132.

"Pharmaceutical Results Improve Helped By New Product Launches." *Chemical Market Reporter,* 27 January 1997, 15.

Schonfeld, Erick. "Yum! The New Treat In Biotech." *Fortune,* 14 October 1996, 293-294.

Standard & Poor's Industry Surveys. New York: Standard & Poor's Corporation, 29 August 1996.

Approximately 800 companies were involved in manufacturing photographic equipment and supplies in the United States in the mid-1990s. These companies together recorded an estimated $24.4 billion in shipments for products included in the classification. The aggregate value of shipments predominantly derived from the industry's six primary product groups: sensitized photographic film, paper, and plates; photocopy equipment; prepared photographic chemicals; still picture equipment; microfilming equipment; and motion picture equipment. Of the various products, still picture equipment had the highest share of the market in 1995 with 43.9 percent of sales, and sensitized photographic film accounted for 24.3 percent of sales, giving still photography equipment a commanding lead over other products within the industry. Photocopy equipment accounted for 23.2 percent of industry sales, and prepared photographic chemicals, microfilming equipment, and motion picture equipment together totaled 8.6 percent of industry sales.

PHOTOGRAPHIC EQUIPMENT AND SUPPLIES

SIC 3861

The Photographic Equipment and Supplies industry shows tremendous potential for growth, particularly as the market for digital imaging equipment develops. The early success of the Advanced Photo System piloted by the industry's leaders illustrates the renewed vitality of the photographic market. Diversification is a major trend among manufacturers; this trend should continue as new or improved technologies widen the market for photographic and digital imaging equipment.

U.S. Film Market Leaders

Kodak	70.0%
Fuji	10.0
Other	20.0

Source: *Asiaweek*, July 5, 1996, p. 64.

Growth in the photographic equipment and supplies industry was usually fueled by the introduction of new products utilizing innovative technology. Historically, the emergence of a new product into the market invigorated sales, which, in the case of still and motion camera equipment, also increased sales of film and related supplies. Since a majority of the products manufactured in the photographic equipment and supplies industry were considered leisure or non-essential goods, they were particularly sensitive to economic conditions and tended to suffer as a consequence of reduced consumer spending. However, its broad range of products insulated the industry from the effects of vacillating demand to some extent. For example, still picture film and photocopying equipment typically sold consistently despite economic downturns.

INDUSTRY OUTLOOK

The camcorder, introduced in 1983 and gaining steadily in popularity through the 1990s, provided a tremendous boost for photography sales. The camcorder's acceptance by the public helped to lay the foundation for consumer's interest in electronic imaging products. The advent of electronic imaging—a technology that utilized semiconductor sensors instead of film to record images and then displayed the images on television screens or computer monitors rather than paper—threatened to radically affect the sales of photographic equipment and supplies. Industry observers' and participants' reactions ranged from worry that the new format would entirely supplant conventional photographic equipment and supplies, to less severe predictions that electronic imaging would merely augment the existing market.

Initially, much of this debate was academic; electronic imaging products were prohibitively expensive and the quality of images were far inferior to those generated via film. However, as the technology improved and attracted the attention of an increasing number of consumers, concern increased as to which direction the photographic industry would follow. The digital field began to explode in the late 1990s. Digital point-and-shoot cameras were being developed with price tags ranging as low as $300 to $500. Only professional-style cameras had previously been available, and those came with price tags in the $20,000 range that kept everyone but commercial photographers and large studios out of the market. Even though the new hand-held digital cameras had relatively poor resolution, they were gaining quickly in popularity, with sales of digital equipment doubling annually. In 1995, 500,000 digital cameras were sold. That number jumped to 1.2 million in 1996, and was expected to continue doubling annually all the way through 2001, when sales were predicted to top a billion units.

The digital wave affected much more than just the photographic industry. With new digital imaging printers, copiers, cameras, software, and film, other industries were making the move into digital imaging. Throughout much of 1996 and 1997, the photocopier industry was also beginning to move heavily into digital equipment. Whether fully digitized, or using digital scanners with conventional toners, copiers were heading full force into the digital age. Most companies had brought digital lenses and optics into standard copiers, making them more efficient and higher quality, using less toner and appearing, sometimes, even sharper than the original document.

Xerox developed a high-end copier for sale in April 1997, mixing digital sensors with standard printing, that could print up to 135 copies per minute. The digital transition set up the photocopying industry for record sales figures in 1996. Canon, Inc. reported a record year for 1996 with a boost of 31 percent in their copier sales. Oce-Van der Grinten also reported record sales with a 57 percent jump. Xerox, after sitting on a second or third place ranking in sales, suddenly leapt to the top ranking of all companies within the field, and predicted a $200-million digital print boom in 1997.

ADVANCED PHOTO SYSTEMS

On April 22, 1996, five companies who had been working together on a new film format finally released the Advanced Photo System (APS). Kodak, Fuji, Canon, Nikon, and Minolta spent billions of dollars in research ($500 million by Kodak alone) in developing the new format. Working directly with consumers, these companies interviewed more than 22,000 people in 11 countries to develop a new format that would be easier to operate, create better pictures, and use some of the new digital technology alongside standard film formats. During the research, customers were given a camera-size wooden block, and told to place features where they thought they would be easiest and most efficient to operate, with fewer mistakes. Looking to make the new format augment rather than compete with the existing format, all five companies shared their research and development to avoid a conflict like the Beta-VHS competition in the 1980s which ultimately slowed the growth of the video industry.

The new format was to be a link between digital and standard film techniques. Silver-based emulsion technology was married with digital input and output devices to create the APS film and cameras. A new, highly durable, higher-resolution emulsion was developed with a magnetic covering for information storage. With this magnetic strip, in addition to technology being placed into the APS cameras, the film and camera can actually "speak" to each other. Standard cameras could previously only read film type and ISO off the film, and the film couldn't read anything from the camera. APS film and camera keep up a constant dialogue, sharing and storing information back and forth.

The new emulsion was developed due to the design of storing developed film in its original container. The new film had to have a stronger emulsion that could withstand the tight winding and unwinding involved in moving in and out of the canister. APS film was slightly smaller (24mm) but yielded a higher resolution print due to the new emulsion, which produced one half to one third the grain size of standard 35mm film. The emulsion, even with the added magnetic strip, was flatter, allowing for a greater length of film stored in a smaller area. It was also more durable, making it less susceptible to regular damage that comes over time.

Three formats were available to an APS camera user. With a switch of a button on the camera, a photographer could take 4x6 (standard 35mm dimensions), 4x7 (APS film dimension), or panoramic 4x10, previously available only on specific panoramic cameras. Once taken, the film stored information such as camera settings, format, time, date, exposure number, and even personal information provided by the photographer such as a title or names to be printed on the back of the print. Photofinishers, with new APS lab equipment, used the information to make the best possible print. For example, if the subject was washed out and the background was too dark, which happens in many night flash pictures, the printer could automatically read directly from the film the camera settings used in that particular picture, and adjust printing to bring down the subject and brighten the background. The photographer could also input that the settings chosen were intentional; the processor would read that information and print the picture as taken. The printer could also read the format chosen for the print and process it accordingly. The image taken was always uniform, with only the print being affected by the format choice, which allowed for different sized reprints to be made.

In a follow-up survey of APS customers, 90 percent felt the new system was better, and 70 percent believed they would take better pictures. The new system has been viewed as revolutionary by professional and amateur photographers alike, and Mitchell Gladstone, president of 30 Minute Photos, proclaimed the new format ''the industry's good luck charm.'' Companies saw amazing growth in 1996 as the new system began to take hold. During the month of December, when 30 percent of camera buying occurs, APS cameras were as high as 60 percent of non single lens reflex (SLR) cameras sold and 30 percent of all cameras sold. More than 5 percent of the more than two billion rolls of film sold in 1996 were APS, and it was still only eight months old. Kodak's goal was for APS to account for 20 percent of all film sales and 80 percent of all camera sales by the year 2000—APS was nearly there by 1997.

Although brand new, APS was greatly affecting manufacturers' sales, especially through the last quarter of 1996. Kodak saw its overall sales jump 5 percent despite the loss of Office Imaging, a division that manufactured and marketed photocopiers, which was sold during 1996. Not figuring the loss of revenue from that division into the overall sales, figures showed a 10 percent improvement. Fujifilm's sales also got a huge boost, jumping from $5.4 billion in 1995 to $10.2 billion in 1996. Their fourth quarter more than doubled between 1995 and 1996. Photofinishers, retailers, and manufacturers alike were expected to make vast improvements in sales through 1997 with the new format.

ORGANIZATION AND STRUCTURE

The photographic equipment and supplies industry is comprised mostly of small manufacturing operations. There were 832 facilities operating in the industry early

SIC 3861 - Photographic Equipment & Supplies
General Statistics

Year	Companies	Establishments		Employment			Compensation		Production ($ million)			
		Total	with 20 or more employees	Total (000)	Production Workers (000)	Hours (Mil)	Payroll ($ mil)	Wages ($/hr)	Cost of Materials	Value Added by Manufacture	Value of Shipments	Capital Invest.
1982	723	795	289	119.3	64.1	123.7	3,193.1	11.78	5,859.7	10,859.5	17,037.5	752.6
1983				110.2	57.6	112.7	3,117.6	12.41	5,887.0	11,654.7	17,366.3	587.3
1984				104.0	53.7	108.4	3,137.8	12.92	5,682.4	12,960.9	18,701.9	665.4
1985				98.5	50.2	100.4	3,128.8	13.72	5,890.1	12,257.4	18,114.4	834.2
1986				94.6	47.6	95.0	2,870.2	13.00	6,110.5	12,355.9	18,580.4	697.0
1987	719	787	279	88.0	44.8	92.1	2,878.3	13.29	6,233.5	12,908.0	19,240.5	681.0
1988				87.5	43.9	92.8	2,963.4	13.11	6,638.0	14,223.2	20,545.8	809.7
1989		806	309	87.0	43.9	96.9	3,134.3	13.41	6,935.4	15,804.2	22,737.8	1,008.2
1990				79.3	41.2	91.8	2,937.4	13.69	6,439.2	14,527.2	21,018.2	1,008.6
1991				78.0	40.0	87.5	3,044.1	14.73	6,686.4	14,603.3	21,397.8	1,089.2
1992	831	904	264	77.5	39.4	90.7	3,069.3	14.65	7,058.7	14,885.4	22,149.8	808.1
1993				75.7	38.0	86.6	2,881.0	14.64	6,750.5	15,916.8	22,367.8	775.4
1994				64.8	34.8	77.7	2,716.6	15.80	7,011.4	16,057.0	23,367.6	755.3
1995				62.7P	31.7P	76.7P	2,844.8P	15.42P	7,157.9P	16,392.6P	23,855.9P	930.3P
1996				58.9P	29.6P	73.9P	2,821.8P	15.68P	7,314.5P	16,751.2P	24,377.9P	948.1P
1997				55.0P	27.5P	71.0P	2,798.8P	15.94P	7,471.2P	17,109.9P	24,899.9P	965.9P
1998				51.2P	25.5P	68.2P	2,775.9P	16.19P	7,627.8P	17,468.6P	25,421.9P	983.7P

Sources: 1982, 1987, 1992 Economic Census; Annual Survey of Manufactures, 83-86, 88-91, 93-94. Establishment counts for non-Census years are from County Business Patterns; establishment values for 83-84 are extrapolations. 'P's show projections by the editors. Industries reclassified in 87 will not have data for prior years.

in the 1990s, with California, Illinois, Massachusetts, and New York holding the most facilities. In 1987 most of the facilities were concentrated in the mid-Atlantic states, while by the mid-1990s they were beginning to spread out across the country.

The operating costs associated with a photographic equipment and supplies facility, at $7.1 million per year, were much higher than the average manufacturing facility in the mid-1990s, with an average of only $1.7 million. This gap is likely to widen as electronic imaging products, which require more expensive equipment to manufacture than conventional photographic products, gain popularity and cause more manufacturers to convert their facilities.

WORK FORCE

Total employment in the photographic equipment and supplies industry declined during the 1980s, as corporate restructuring, consolidations, and layoffs established a decade-long trend of employment instability. From over 130,000 employees in 1980, employment dropped steadily through the mid-1990s. Of the more than 70,500 people employed in the photographic equipment and supplies industry in 1994, there was a fairly even split between production workers and salaried employees (or those performing managerial, administrative, or technical duties). A proportionately larger number of production jobs were lost during the decade of employment decline, which narrowed the discrepancy between production and salaried positions in the industry to nearly equal representation.

PHOTOGRAPHIC EQUIPMENT INDUSTRY EMPLOYMENT

Employment in thousands

Source: Department of Labor

Generally, production workers were employed on a full-time basis, with regular overtime. Production workers in the photographic equipment and supplies industry earned an average of $14.70 per hour in 1992. This hourly wage increased in 1994 to $15.11, about $.35 higher than the average hourly wage of the highest paid worker in the entire manufacturing field, which was $14.75.

AMERICA AND THE WORLD

Historically, foreign manufacturers of photographic equipment and supplies have enjoyed considerable success competing in the U.S. market. This tradition continued in the early 1990s, as a global recession exacerbated the competition for flagging consumer spending and retarded the sales of U.S. products overseas. Exports of domestic photographic products were flat in 1992 at an estimated $3.8 billion, after a 10 percent increase in 1991. In 1993, after slumping for so long, exports began to rise again to $4.6 billion in 1995, 12.2 percent growth between 1994 and 1995. The rise was partially attributable to Japan's own economic slump, which decreased the competition. During the first six months of 1996, exports increased 10 percent over the same period of 1995 to $2.3 billion. Sensitized film, paper, and plates accounted for 47 percent of the export total, and had the fastest growth rate at 17 percent. Photocopying equipment and photographic chemicals both increased about 8 percent. Still picture equipment increased by 2 percent. Motion picture equipment continued to decline, down 14 percent from 1995.

The European Union accounted for $1.4 billion of all domestic photographic sales overseas, the largest export market for U.S. manufacturers in 1995. North America, mainly Canada and Mexico, was the second largest market at $1.2 billion in sales, followed by the rest of the Americas with $715 million. Exports to Japan were rising again, back up to $522 million for 1995, and was getting nearer to the $533 million high of 1991.

Imports of photographic equipment and supplies to the United States increased in 1995 to $8.84 billion, the highest they had been in years. Through the first six months of 1996, however, it dipped again, dropping to an estimated $8.1 billion by the end of 1996. Imported motion picture equipment and copying equipment rose while everything else was decreasing. Motion picture equipment went up by over 33 percent, and copying equipment rose 2.6 percent. Imports of still picture equipment dropped 6.9 percent, sensitized film dropped 1.6 percent, and photo chemicals went down by 8.5 percent through the first half of 1996. Despite motion picture equipment's rise, the overall change in imports had decreased by a little more than 1 percent.

The majority of U.S. imports were manufactured in Japan, which has continually increased its international presence since supplanting West Germany in 1962 as the world's second-largest exporter. Japanese manufacturers attained their commanding position in the international photographic industry by producing inexpensive, reliable photographic equipment that employed the latest technological advancements. Japan used these two marketing and manufacturing strategies to increase its share of the international photographic market since the early 1960s, and gained a solid position as the United States' major competitor. In 1995, Japan accounted for $5.1 billion of the import total of $8.8 billion in the United States. The European Union followed with $1.5 billion, and North America accounted for $581 million.

As exports continued to grow and imports continued to shrink, the trade balance had been narrowing. The expected economic recovery of international markets, particularly in Europe, could ameliorate overseas sales, especially considering the low saturation level of photographic equipment in Eastern Europe and the European Community. However, the economic slump in Japan through the mid-1990s, the worst since the late 1970s, continued to affect the trade balance as exports to Japan were steadily dropping through 1994. Moreover, any reduction of the tariff and trade barriers among European Community countries could have a positive effect on U.S. export performance as well. Within North America, the North American Free Trade Agreement (NAFTA) had eased the traffic of photographic products among Mexico, Canada, and the United States, an arrangement that promised to benefit photographic equipment and supplies manufacturers in the United States. Photographic trade balance between the United States and NAFTA was $555 million in 1995, with imports totaling $581 million and exports bringing in $1.14 billion. The trade balance had been improving overall as consumers in the United States purchased fewer foreign-made still picture products. In 1993 the trade deficit had gone to $3.3 billion, $4.0 billion in 1994, and by 1995 there was a trade deficit of $4.3 billion. Through the first six months of 1996 the deficit was narrowing. For the first half of 1995, the trade deficit was $1.9 billion, which had declined to $1.7 billion for the same period of 1996.

ASSOCIATIONS AND SOCIETIES

PHOTOGRAPHIC MANUFACTURERS AND DISTRIBUTORS ASSOCIATION
1120 Avenue of the Americas, 4 Fl.
New York, NY 10026
Phone: (908) 679-3460
Fax: (908) 679-2294

PHOTOGRAPHIC SOCIETY OF AMERICA
3000 United Founders Blvd., Ste. 103
Oklahoma City, OK 73112
Phone: (405) 843-1437
Fax: (405) 843-1438

PROFESSIONAL PHOTOGRAPHERS OF AMERICA
57 Forsyth St. NW, Ste. 1600
Atlanta, GA 30303
Phone: (800) 742-7468 or (404) 522-8600

SOCIETY FOR IMAGING SCIENCE AND TECHNOLOGY
7003 Kilworth Ln.
Springfield, VA 22151
Phone: (703) 642-9090
Fax: (703) 642-9094

PERIODICALS AND NEWSLETTERS

JOURNAL OF IMAGING SCIENCE AND TECHNOLOGY
Harold Lockwood, editor
Society for Imaging Science and Technolgy
7003 Kilworth Ln.
Springfield, VA 22151
Phone: (703) 642-9090
Fax: (703) 642-9094

SIC 3085 - Plastics Bottles
Industry Data by State

State	Establish- ments	Shipments			Employment				Cost as % of Shipments	Investment per Employee ($)
		Total ($ mil)	% of U.S.	Per Establ.	Total Number	% of U.S.	Per Establ.	Wages ($/hour)		
Ohio	32	518.7	11.6	16.2	3,800	11.6	119	10.41	46.5	4,947
California	56	505.7	11.3	9.0	4,100	12.5	73	9.59	51.6	9,098
Illinois	33	439.3	9.9	13.3	2,900	8.9	88	10.94	47.0	9,138
New Jersey	26	365.3	8.2	14.1	2,900	8.9	112	11.66	52.4	6,241
Texas	27	296.6	6.7	11.0	2,000	6.1	74	9.56	60.9	9,900
Pennsylvania	28	213.0	4.8	7.6	1,900	5.8	68	9.77	50.2	4,684
Kentucky	11	157.8	3.5	14.3	1,100	3.4	100	9.47	48.6	12,273
Missouri	16	147.5	3.3	9.2	1,500	4.6	94	8.89	45.3	7,867
Florida	17	144.5	3.2	8.5	900	2.8	53	9.88	59.8	2,444
North Carolina	7	139.8	3.1	20.0	700	2.1	100	9.38	61.8	-

Source: 1992 *Economic Census*. The states are in descending order of shipments or establishments (if shipment data are missing for the majority). The symbol (D) appears when data are withheld to prevent disclosure of competitive information. States marked with (D) are sorted by number of establishments. A dash (-) indicates that the data element cannot be calculated; * indicates the midpoint of a range.

Bimonthly. $120.00 per year. Formerly Journal of Imaging Technology.

PHOTO BUSINESS
BPI Communications, Inc.
1515 Broadway, 39 Fl.
New York, NY 10036
Phone: (800) 344-7119 or (212) 536-5025
Fax: (212) 921-2486
Weekly. $45.00 per year. Formerly Photo Weekly.

PHOTO MARKETING
Photo Marketing Association International
3000 Picture Pl.
Jackson, MI 49201
Phone: (517) 788-8100
Fax: (517) 788-8371
Monthly. $30.00 per year.

PTN-MASTER BUYING GUIDE AND DIRECTORY (PHOTOGRAPHIC TRADE NEWS): MAIN ENTRANCE TO THE RETAIL PHOTOGRAPHIC MARKET
PTN Publishing Corp.
455 Broad Hollow Rd.
Melville, NY 11747-4722
Phone: (516) 845-2700
Fax: (516) 845-7109
Annual. $25.00 per year. Marketing magazine for the photo, video and photo finishing retailer. Formerly Photographic Trade News Master Buying Guide and Directory.

SHUTTERBUG
Patch Communications
5211 S Washington Ave.
Titusville, FL 32780
Phone: (407) 268-5010
Fax: (407) 267-7216
Monthly. $19.95 per year. Articles about new equipment, test reports on film accessories, how-to articles, etc.

DATABASES

F & S INDEX
Information Access Co.
362 Lakeside Dr.
Foster City, CA 94404
Phone: (800) 321-6388 or (415-358-4643
Fax: (415) 358-4759
Contains about four million citations to worldwide business, financial, and industrial or consumer product literature appearing from 1972 to date. Weekly updates. Inquire as to online cost and availability.

WILSONLINE: ART INDEX
H. W. Wilson Co.
950 University Ave.
Bronx, NY 10452

Phone: (800) 367-6770 or (718) 558-8400
Fax: (718) 590-1617
Indexes a wide variety of art-related periodicals, 1984 to date. Weekly updates. Inquire as to online cost and availability.

STATISTICS SOURCES

U.S. INDUSTRIAL OUTLOOK: FORECASTS FOR SELECTED MANUFACTURING AND SERVICE INDUSTRIES
Available from U.S. Government Printing Office
Washington, DC 20402
Phone: (202) 512-1800
Fax: (202) 512-2250
Annual. $37.00. (Replaced in 1995 by U.S. Global Trade Outlook.*) Issued by the International Trade Administration, U.S. Department of Commerce. Provides basic data, outlook for the current year, and "Long-Term Prospects" (five-year projections) for a wide variety of products and services. Includes high technology industries. Available on the world wide web at gopher://gopher.umsl.edu:70/11/library/govdocs/usio94.*

GENERAL WORKS

POPULAR PHOTOGRAPHY DIRECTORY AND BUYING GUIDE ISSUE
Hachette Magazine, Inc.
1633 Broadway
New York, NY 10009
Phone: (800) 876-9011 or (212) 767-6000
Fax: (212) 767-5615
Annual. $3.95.

FURTHER READING

"Infotrends Study Shows Digital Camera Market Is Doubling Annually." *Business Wire,* 10 February 1997. Available from http://www.businesswire.com.

Lazich, Robert S., ed. *Market Share Reporter.* Detroit: Gale Research, 1997.

"Small Copiers/Big Advantage." *PRNewswire,* 24 February 1997. Available from http://www.prnewswire.com.

U.S. Department of Commerce. *U.S. Trade Summary,* Washington: GPO, 1996.

White, Larry. "APS. . . It's Finally Here! The Advanced Photo System: Will It Change Photography Forever?" *Hyperzine,* 10 February 1997. Available from http://www.hyperzine.com.

Synthetic plastic was invented late in the eighteenth century, but did not reach widespread use in the United States until the 1900s. Swift advances in chemical and manufacturing technologies during the twentieth century, however, made plastic one of America's most important manufacturing materials. Massive demand for plastic had propelled the industry past $43.5 billion in annual sales by 1995. Plastic manufacturers employed over 69,000 workers in 1995 and exported more than $4 billion worth of material.

An economic recession in 1989, which lingered through 1993, stabilized the demand for plastics. Transportation, consumer and industrial, and packaging sectors all temporarily scaled back their consumption of resins. The construction industry, which had plunged into a virtual depression by 1990, proved a major detriment to sales growth for all types of plastics. Revenues slipped nearly $2 billion in 1990, to $31.3 billion. Correspondingly, employment shrank nearly three percent the following year, to about 61,000. Buoying earnings, however, was a 30 percent growth in 1991 exports—largely a result of a weak U.S. dollar.

Despite a lull in prices, profits, and revenues throughout the early 1990s, the industry showed signs of renewed growth. Prices and production picked up, and the U.S. economy as a whole began to improve. Although employment continued to decline, analysts remained optimistic, citing newly developed additives and compounds as boding well for the industry's continued success.

PLASTICS MATERIALS AND RESINS

SIC 2821

New additives and plastic blends have increased in demand, opening entirely new markets for resins and prompting other industries to substitute plastic for more expensive, less flexible organic products. Furthermore, as many segments of the industry matured and became more competitive, falling prices allowed plastics to penetrate a number of metal, glass, and wood markets. Reinforcing downward pricing pressures were massive industry investments in research, development, and more efficient production facilities, allowing producers to remain extremely competitive domestically.

 MOST HEAVILY CONSUMED COMMODITY THERMOPLASTICS WORLDWIDE

Ranked by: Resin type, 1994

1. Polyethylene
2. PVC
3. Polypropylene
4. Polystyrene
5. ABS/SAN

Source: *Chemical Industries Newsletter,* September/October, 1995, p. 9.

About 500 manufacturers competed in the plastics industry in the early 1990s, making it highly concentrated in comparison to most other U.S. manufacturing businesses. The average revenue per plastics establishment during this time was over $65 million—about eight times

---

greater than the average for all other U.S. industries. The top eight producers controlled 40 percent of the market in 1987, while the top 20 firms accounted for 66 percent of production. Like many other capital intensive and concentrated industries, high barriers to entry, such as large start-up costs and technical competency, discourage potential entrants from vying for market share.

The largest consumer of plastics in the early 1990s was the packaging industry, which created bags, bottles, food containers, and related items. That sector purchased about 30 percent of all plastics shipped. Building and construction supply manufacturers, which made plastic pipe, conduit, geotextiles, and other materials, represented about 20 percent of the plastics market. Exports accounted for an impressive 20 percent of industry output, while the remaining 30 percent of shipments were consumed by various commercial, institutional, and consumer markets. Electrical appliance and electronic component manufacturers, for instance, bought about five percent of all plastics in 1991.

In the mid-1990s, many producers began to realize the benefits of cost reduction efforts implemented over the past several years. Such efforts included reducing employment, restructuring management, and closing some production facilities. Growth in emerging foreign markets, as well as solid expansion of various niches of the resin market, also encouraged competitors. Continuing development of new compounds, spurred by ever-increasing expenditures on research and development, were boosting the industry's overall share of the U.S. economy.

INDUSTRY OUTLOOK

INDUSTRY SEGMENT PERFORMANCE

Thermoplastic resins, which led industry gains throughout the 1980s, continued to experience demand growth in the mid-1990s, particularly in the area of high-grade, low-volume resins that could serve niche markets. High-tech applications in the auto and aerospace industries for engineering and advanced resins, for example, were proliferating. Intermediate and commodity products were showing gains too. After posting an average annual production growth rate of 7 percent between 1982 and 1991, thermoplastics advanced six percent in 1992. Value of shipments totaled $37,710 in 1994, a 12.3 percent increase from 1993.

The important polyethylene segment, which accounted for over 40 percent (22 billion pounds) of total thermoplastic output, grew slightly less than 6 percent in the mid 1990s. Demand for high-density polyethylene, which made up 50 percent of that segment, increased at a rate of 7 percent in 1993. Prices in this category had stabilized by 1993. New technology promised several advances in polyethylene resins in the late 1990s. New compounds were being marketed in 1993, for instance, that allowed producers of shrink-wrap, carpet wrap, liner, and other film products to reduce the thickness of their material by 30 percent without compromising strength.

PVC resin production grew 7 percent in 1992 to about ten billion pounds—a disappointing figure compared to the 9 percent increases between 1982 and 1991.

SIC 2821 - Plastics Materials & Resins
General Statistics

Year	Companies	Establishments		Employment			Compensation		Production ($ million)			
		Total	with 20 or more employees	Total (000)	Production Workers (000)	Hours (Mil)	Payroll ($ mil)	Wages ($/hr)	Cost of Materials	Value Added by Manufacture	Value of Shipments	Capital Invest.
1982	264	441	310	54.7	32.8	67.4	1,435.3	11.73	10,812.0	4,785.6	15,813.7	899.2
1983		451	320	53.2	32.7	67.3	1,505.6	12.84	12,298.4	6,716.7	18,935.8	756.4
1984		461	330	54.2	33.2	69.8	1,650.9	13.33	13,298.9	7,653.9	20,776.3	925.3
1985		470	340	55.4	34.4	71.1	1,818.6	14.33	13,201.3	7,036.3	20,261.8	1,115.1
1986		477	350	54.7	34.1	72.2	1,893.6	15.06	13,233.7	8,149.4	21,483.7	1,264.2
1987	288	480	320	56.3	34.9	75.6	2,005.8	15.24	15,410.4	10,872.9	26,245.5	1,247.2
1988		487	331	58.3	36.0	79.8	2,169.9	15.37	19,333.8	13,196.7	32,109.9	1,605.8
1989		498	346	61.4	37.8	83.7	2,383.2	15.92	20,292.9	12,991.2	33,256.7	1,966.2
1990		510	343	61.8	37.9	82.5	2,485.7	16.88	19,390.9	12,195.3	31,325.8	2,436.6
1991		519	341	60.5	36.7	80.8	2,479.9	17.25	18,593.4	11,012.2	29,565.8	2,251.7
1992	240	449	340	60.4	35.9	78.5	2,671.6	18.71	18,839.8	12,494.7	31,303.9	1,707.3
1993		501	352	62.2	36.6	80.9	2,799.3	18.75	19,500.6	11,953.5	31,545.6	1,925.9
1994		509P	352P	69.2	40.6	90.0	3,150.0	19.37	21,937.8	15,116.8	36,964.6	2,554.9
1995		513P	354P	66.0P	39.3P	88.3P	3,126.3P	19.98P	22,503.2P	15,506.4P	37,917.3P	2,565.2P
1996		518P	357P	67.1P	39.8P	89.9P	3,260.3P	20.59P	23,438.0P	16,150.6P	39,492.4P	2,704.7P
1997		522P	360P	68.1P	40.3P	91.5P	3,394.3P	21.19P	24,372.8P	16,794.7P	41,067.6P	2,844.1P
1998		527P	362P	69.2P	40.9P	93.2P	3,528.3P	21.80P	25,307.6P	17,438.9P	42,642.7P	2,983.6P

Sources: 1982, 1987, 1992 *Economic Census*; *Annual Survey of Manufactures*, 83-86, 88-91, 93-94. Establishment counts for non-Census years are from *County Business Patterns*; establishment values for 83-84 are extrapolations. 'P's show projections by the editors. Industries reclassified in 87 will not have data for prior years.

Recessed growth was largely a result of environmental restrictions implemented by both domestic and international governments. Switzerland, for example, instituted a ban on PVC water bottles in 1992 while the Netherlands contemplated similar actions. In Austria, European producers were embroiled in a lawsuit against the environmental activist group Greenpeace, which ran an advertising campaign equating PVC with poison in 1991. By 1995 production increased to 12 billion pounds.

Polypropylene, the third major thermoplastic, grew an encouraging 9 percent in 1992 to 8.4 billion pounds produced, up from 1 percent annual growth between 1982 and 1991. Aided by new technological improvements and strong demand overseas, this resin was expected to realize solid gains. Nearly 11 billion pounds were produced in 1995. Prices have increased in 1996 in an effort to restore profits, and a 10 percent growth was predicted. High-tech resins used in car interiors and appliances were leading this segment.

Smaller thermoplastic segments posted the greatest advances in the mid-1990s. Production of styrene-butadiene, polyamides, and thermoplastic polyester grew about 15 percent. These three categories represented a combined output of about 5.7 billion pounds. Improved additives, particularly colorants, were boosting styrene-butadiene sales, though long-term growth of that resin was in question. While sales of polyester suffered due to environmental concerns, the material was becoming a viable substitute for telephone and light poles, steel and concrete, and other construction materials.

While thermosetting resins lagged behind thermostats during the 1980s, they were posting solid gains in the mid-1990s. Total thermoset output jumped 7 percent to 6.3 billion pounds in 1992, contrasting with average annual gains of just four percent between 1982 and 1991. By 1995 7.5 billion pounds were being produced. Phenolics, the largest thermoset segment, increased ten percent in 1992 to 2.9 billion pounds and continued to increase to 3.2 billion pounds in 1995. New applications for transportation and other high-volume markets, improved additives and compounds, and low prices all contributed to the surge.

In 1992 and 1993 many industries including the plastics materials and resins industry which were sailing in a mature economy started slowing down. To set the recovery in motion, the industry started contending with capacity constraints and longer lead times. Production for all plastics by US producers was up by about 3.4% over 1994.

In 1996 there were about 410 operating companies in the United States, whose primary products fell under the umbrella of plastics materials and resins. The plastics industry continued to be one of the strongest performers in the U.S. economy, growing by an annual average of 4.8% since the late 1960s.

Plastics were considered cost-efficient, durable and chemical resistant materials, that provided design flexibility in appliance manufacturing. Major appliance manufacturing companies utilized 55 percent of the annual plastic demand. The annual demand for plastics in the appliance manufacturing industry was predicted to be 4.6 percent, with the estimated totals for the year 2000 amounting to 2 billion pounds. The demand for plastics among small electric manufacturers also increased by 5 percent annually. Producers of automotive plastics had increased sales by 10-20 percent, in 1994, because of increased manufacturing of automobiles. In 1997, plastics manufacturers tried to displace the use of metals in the auto industry in underhood components. Plastics makers predicted that use of plastics such as nylon for underhood automobile parts would continue to replace metals.

ORGANIZATION AND STRUCTURE

Plastics provide an important alternative to natural materials for a plethora of applications. One of the most important distinguishing factors between plastic and other materials, is plastic's ability to "creep" under load, or gradually stretch or flow when subjected to stress. While metals and ceramics exhibit this property as well, they do so only at much higher temperatures. Plastics also resist erosion and do not require a coating to protect them against inorganic acids, bases, and water or salt solutions. Perhaps the greatest advantage that plastics offer, however, is their ability to be molded into any shape and to be processed to exhibit any of a massive number of physical characteristics.

Four major commercial divisions of plastic resins are manufactured. Commodity resins, which represent the bulk of industry production, are low-tech plastics available in standardized formulas from many companies throughout the world. Intermediate resins are generally considered more advanced and somewhat specialized in comparison to commodity resins. Similarly, engineering resins generally exhibit more advanced performance characteristics and are produced on a smaller scale than other types of resin. Finally, advanced resins are generally those most capable of withstanding impact and high heat, carrying loads, and resisting attacks by chemicals and solvents.

The two main classes of plastic are thermosets and thermoplastics. Thermoplastics accounted for about 83 percent of industry output. They solidify by cooling and may be remelted repeatedly to form new shapes. Examples of thermoplastic resins are polyethylene, polypropylene, and polystyrene. Polyethylene is the highest volume plastic, accounting for about 40 percent of thermoplastic production, and is used primarily to create packaging, though many consumer and institutional products are made as well. Major manufacturers of this resin include Quantum Chemical, Union Carbide, and Dow Chemical Co.

Polyvinyl chloride (PVC) makes up the second largest share of the thermoplastics segment. It is used primarily to make gutters, pipes, siding, windows, and other products used by construction and building industries. Polypropylene, another thermoplastic, is used mainly in the creation of fiber and filaments, as well as in the production of packaging and molded consumer products.

Polystyrene, a fourth major thermoplastic product, is used to make disposable packaging, furniture finishings, and miscellaneous consumer products. Other thermoplastics segments include polyamide resins, styrene-butadiene, and some polyesters.

Thermosets, the other division of the plastics industry, account for about seventeen percent of output. Unlike thermoplastics, thermosets harden by chemical reaction, and cannot be melted and shaped after they are created. Thermosets are also considered the more mature and less dynamic segment of the industry.

Typical thermosets include phenolics, urea-formaldehyde resins, epoxies, and polyester. Phenolics, which account for over 50 percent of all thermoset production, are used principally for construction products. Such materials include plywood adhesives, insulation, laminates, moldings, and abrasives. Urea, the second largest segment of the thermoset division, is also used as an adhesive for plywood and particle board. Other uses of this resin include protective coatings and textile and paper treating and coating.

Thermoset polyesters are used to create plastics that are reinforced with glass fiber and other materials. They are also used to make various construction supplies such as boat and marine equipment, transportation products, and electronics. Epoxy is primarily used as a protective coating for metal goods, but is also used in multiple construction applications.

WORK FORCE

In 1995, about 75,100 workers were employed in the plastics industry. This represented a slight decline since 1990, when employment hit a peak of 62,400. Despite solid increases in the bulk weight of resins produced, producers hesitated to hire more workers, echoing a trend that prevailed throughout the 1980s, during which the value of production rose over 100 percent while total employment grew only 13 percent. The reduced work force resulted from massive increases in productivity, attained through elimination of managers, automation of manufacturing facilities, and the displacement of support staff by computer and information systems. Furthermore, decreased employment figures reflected the fact that established workers were putting in more hours.

Despite stagnant job growth, the plastics industry offered opportunities for qualified individuals in the mid-1990s. Production workers, which made up about 60 percent of the industry work force, were among the highest paid industrial workers in the United States. The average 1995 production wage of $17.93 was 69 percent greater than the average for all other U.S. manufacturers.

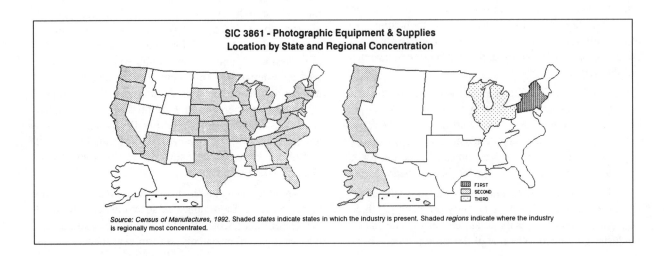

SIC 3861 - Photographic Equipment & Supplies
Location by State and Regional Concentration

FIRST
SECOND
THIRD

Source: *Census of Manufactures, 1992.* Shaded *states* indicate states in which the industry is present. Shaded *regions* indicate where the industry is regionally most concentrated.

Manufacturing positions were on the decline, however, and fell 5 percent in 1992 alone.

SIC 2821
Occupations Employed by SIC 282 - Plastics Materials and Synthetics

Occupation	% of Total 1994	Change to 2005
Chemical equipment controllers, operators	8.7	-16.4
Extruding & forming machine workers	7.9	46.3
Textile draw-out & winding machine operators	5.6	12.8
Blue collar worker supervisors	5.4	-19.5
Science & mathematics technicians	4.2	-16.4
Chemical plant & system operators	3.7	-16.4
Secretaries, ex legal & medical	2.9	-23.9
Industrial machinery mechanics	2.8	-8.1
Chemical engineers	2.7	-16.4
Inspectors, testers, & graders, precision	2.7	-16.4
Maintenance repairers, general utility	2.6	-24.8
Sales & related workers nec	2.4	-16.4
Textile machine setters & set-up operators	1.9	-58.2
Machine operators nec	1.8	-26.3
Helpers, laborers, & material movers nec	1.4	-16.4
Packaging & filling machine operators	1.4	-16.4
General office clerks	1.3	-28.7
Chemists	1.3	-16.4
General managers & top executives	1.2	-20.7
Electricians	1.2	-21.5
Management support workers nec	1.2	-16.4
Mechanical engineers	1.2	-8.0
Crushing & mixing machine operators	1.2	-16.4
Managers & administrators nec	1.1	-16.5
Industrial production managers	1.1	-16.4
Engineering technicians & technologists nec	1.0	-16.4

Source: *Industry-Occupation Matrix*, Bureau of Labor Statistics. These data relate to one or more 3-digit SIC industry groups rather than to a single 4-digit SIC. The change reported for each occupation to the year 2005 is a percent of growth or decline as estimated by the Bureau of Labor Statistics. The abbreviation nec stands for 'not elsewhere classified'.

The industry remained a major supplier of high-paying jobs for those specializing in science, particularly chemists. The average chemist's annual salary in 1994 was $45,400. Chemists with master's degrees averaged $53,500, while those holding doctorates earned an average of $66,000. Opportunities for such highly educated workers decreased only slightly in the early 1990s. Nevertheless, unemployment among chemists was at its highest level since 1983, and despite salary increases of more than four percent in 1992, unemployment grew to 7.2 percent.

Although industry output and profits were expected to rise steadily, jobs for production workers were likely to drop by 10 to 20 percent on average between 1990 and 2005, according to the Bureau of Labor Statistics. Experts estimated that opportunities for machine operators would realize the greatest decline—over 25 percent—and that mechanic and equipment controller jobs would fall 15 percent or more. Increases in work force were expected to affect positions related to sales, marketing, and advertising as well as engineering, mathematics, and science.

RESEARCH AND TECHNOLOGY

Research and development related to new products focused on the creation of specialty materials for niche markets, designing high-performance resins, and upgrading the properties of commodity thermoplastics. Thermoplastic research and development also concentrated on formulating resins that could compete with lower-priced materials. New additives and alloys played an important role in such advancements. However, emerging polymerization technology also offered strong growth potential for cutting-edge manufacturers. For instance, numerous and promising breakthroughs in bimodal resins, which typically combined two polymer types, were helping to enhance the balance of properties and processability of plastics.

Technological advancements occurring in other industries also promised to boost plastics sales. Resin processors, for instance, had developed new extrusion and molding devices, allowing manufacturers to maximize the benefits of new compounds and alloys. Such compounds held promise for makers of cars and appliance manufacturers, which sought stronger, lightweight materials. Similarly, processing techniques that complemented lighter, stronger, and thinner plastics promised to boost the use of plastics in all types of packaging applications.

New biodegradable plastics, including weak-link and bacterial polymers, also offered growth opportunities in the industry. Although the price of many biodegradable plastics in the mid 1990s was between 2 and 25 times greater than traditional resins, prices were expected to fall as the technology was refined. Biodegradable plastics were considered important for reducing the volume and longevity of waste in landfills; in the early 1990s, plastics accounted for about 10 percent of all solid waste.

One of the most interesting discoveries occurred in 1993, when Maurice Ward unveiled a new polymer that withstood heat, lasers, and flames with little or no damage, and let off virtually no toxic fumes in the process. "Starlite," as the new plastic was called, was intended to serve as a flame retardant material, though its uses could be widespread.

From 1996 to 1997, consumption of plastics in North American-built cars and light duty trucks was expected to decline nearly 2 pounds per vehicle as a result of materials conversions by the automakers; steel was expected to become the principal beneficiary of these conversions. For the first time small to medium size auto components made in plastics, suffered an average net decline per vehicle of 1.8 to 2 pounds. However interior applications for plastic trim and panel components was expected to expand somewhat in 1997 because of increasing vehicle dimensions and interior space.

AMERICA AND THE WORLD

The U.S. plastics industry, by far the largest and most advanced in the world, was heavily dependent on exports in the mid-1990s. Overseas sales accounted for about $8.5 billion, or over 20 percent of U.S. resin output in 1994. Plastics accounted for about 25 percent of total U.S. chemical exports, and U.S. resin producers accounted for an estimated 36 percent of total world production in 1992. Japan, the next largest producer, manufactured less than half that amount, at 16 percent of world output, and Germany placed third with a 9 percent share of the market.

European and Japanese suppliers suffered setbacks even worse than those faced by U.S. manufacturers in the late 1980s. Overcapacity and relatively low productivity plagued European community producers. Moreover, after realizing chemical industry profits of over $2 billion per year in both 1988 and 1989, Japanese plastics producers were hammered in the early 1990s by weak foreign and domestic demand. Net profits plunged to just over $1 billion per year in 1992 and 1993, as exports and revenues declined, and the country remained mired in a severe recession.

Although U.S. plastics exports doubled during the 1980s and continued to grow rapidly in the early 1990s, the United States was steadily losing its share of the global market. Expanded overseas production, particularly in the Far East, was displacing U.S. sales. Nevertheless, burgeoning foreign markets offered promising prospects for growth to savvy U.S. exporters. Furthermore, U.S. technology and productivity had succeeded in protecting domestic market share. The U.S. plastic industry maintained a combined trade surplus of about $5.2 billion in 1994. Plastic imports, moreover, accounted for only $1.8 billion of the domestic market.

The two largest buyers of U.S. plastics are Canada and Mexico. Together in 1996 they purchased $4.9 billion in exports. Belgium purchased 7.1 percent of overseas shipments, while Japan and the Netherlands each consumed about 6.9 percent of resin exports. Canada was also the largest exporter of chemicals to the United States, with 33 percent of all foreign sales. Japan held a 17 percent share of the U.S. import market, while Germany followed with 14 percent. The United Kingdom and France each represented about 5 percent of plastic imports.

Although U.S. exports were expected to rise two percent in 1993, observers had initially hoped for a much greater increase. Weak European and Asian markets were primarily to blame; many Asian consumers were beginning to rely on new domestic sources of resins and plastics, while the European community was simply mired in a recession. Latin American markets, in contrast, were proving surprisingly vital. Shipments to Mexico, for instance, nearly doubled between 1988 and 1992, explaining the industry's strong support for the North American Free Trade Agreement (NAFTA). Industry participants in 1993 were also strongly supportive of the pending General Agreement on Tariffs and Trade, an agreement that promised to significantly boost sales in Europe.

Unable to penetrate U.S. markets, foreign companies participated in U.S. plastics markets primarily through direct investment during the 1980s and early 1990s. Foreign chemical companies that invested in U.S. companies sought access to U.S. technology, markets, and research and development. Such investment was expected to continue throughout the 1990s, though on a smaller scale.

In 1996, makers of masterbatches or plastic concentrates with pigments and additives already mixed in were increasingly considering acquisitions as global competition gradually took over the industry. North America accounted for 35 percent of masterbatch sales, Europe accounted for 33 percent, and Asia for 27 percent. "Consolidation and globalization are the overriding themes in the 2.9 billion pound masterbatch business," said the *Chemical Marketing Reporter*. In 1996, five acrylic resins and plastics producers held 71 percent of the total capacity in North America, Western Europe, and Japan.

ASSOCIATIONS AND SOCIETIES

DECORATIVE LAMINATE PRODUCTS ASSOCIATION
13924 Braddock Rd.
Centreville, VA 22020
Phone: (800) 684-3572
Fax: (703) 222-6180

SOCIETY OF PLASTICS ENGINEERS
14 Fairfield Dr.
Brookfield, CT 06804-0403
Phone: (203) 775-0471
Fax: (203) 775-8490

SOCIETY OF THE PLASTICS INDUSTRY
1275 K St. NW, Ste. 400
Washington, DC 20005
Phone: (202) 371-5200
Fax: (202) 371-1022

PERIODICALS AND NEWSLETTERS

ADVANCES IN POLYMER TECHNOLOGY
John Wiley & Sons, Inc., Journals Div.
605 3rd Ave.
New York, NY 10158-0012
Phone: (800) 526-5368 or (212) 850-6000
Quarterly. $476.00 per year.

JOURNAL OF APPLIED POLYMER SCIENCE
John Wiley & Sons, Inc., Journals Div.
605 3rd Ave.
New York, NY 10158-0012
Phone: (800) 526-5368 or (212) 850-6645
Fax: (212) 850-6021
Weekly. $6,604.00 per year.

JOURNAL OF ELASTOMERS AND PLASTICS
Melvyn A. Kohudic, editor
Technomic Publishing Co.
851 New Holland Ave.
Lancaster, PA 17604
Phone: (800) 223-9936 or (717) 291-5609
Fax: (717) 295-4538
Quarterly. $215.00 per year.

PLASTICS ENGINEERING
Society of Plastics Engineers, Inc.
14 Fairfield Dr.
Brookfield, CT 06804-0403
Phone: (203) 775-0471
Fax: (203) 775-8490
Monthly. $50.00 per year.

PLASTICS MACHINERY AND EQUIPMENT: FOR THOSE WHO SELECT AND BUY PLASTICS PROCESSING MACHINERY AND EQUIPMENT
Advanstar Communications, Inc.
7500 Old Oak Blvd.
Cleveland, OH 44130
Phone: (800) 346-0085 or (216) 243-8100
Fax: (216) 891-2726
Monthly. Free to qualified personnel; others, $40.00 per year.

PLASTICS TECHNOLOGY: MACHINERY/MATERIALS SYSTEMS FOR MAXIMUM PRODUCTIVITY
Bill Communications, Inc.
355 Park Ave. S, 3 Fl.
New York, NY 10010-1789
Phone: (800) 253-6708 or (212) 592-6200
Fax: (212) 592-6209
13 times a year. $65.00 per year.

DATABASES

DRI CHEMICAL FORECAST
DRI/McGraw-Hill, Data Products Division
24 Hartwell Ave.
Lexington, MA 02173
Phone: (800) 541-9914 or (617) 863-5100
Supply-demand and price forecasts are given quarterly and annually for over 120 U.S. chemical products. Quarterly forecasts generally extend three years, while annual forecasts cover five to ten years. Inquire as to online cost and availability.

ENGINEERED MATERIALS ABSTRACTS [ONLINE]
Materials Information, ASM International
9639 Kinsman Rd.
Materials Park, OH 44073
Phone: (216) 338-5151
Fax: (216) 338-4634
Provides online citations to the technical and engineering literature of plastic, ceramic, and composite materials. Time period is 1986 to date, with monthly updates. Inquire as to online cost and availability.

MATERIALS BUSINESS FILE
Materials Information, ASM International
9639 Kinsman Rd.
Materials Park, OH 44073
Phone: (216) 338-5151
Fax: (216) 338-4634
Provides online abstracts and citations to worldwide materials literature, covering the business and industrial aspects of metals, plastics, ceramics, and composites. Corresponds to Steels Alert, Nonferrous Metals Alert, *and* Polymers/Ceramics/Composites Alert. *Time period is 1985 to date, with monthly updates. Inquire as to online cost and availability.*

WILSONLINE: APPLIED SCIENCE AND TECHNOLOGY ABSTRACTS
H. W. Wilson Co.
950 University Ave.
Bronx, NY 10452
Phone: (800) 367-6770 or (718) 588-8400
Fax: (718) 590-1617
Provides online indexing and abstracting of 400 major scientific, technical, industrial, and engineering periodicals. Time period is 1983 to date for indexing and 1993 to date for abstracting, with updating twice a week. Inquire as to online cost and availability.

STATISTICS SOURCES

ENCYCLOPEDIA OF AMERICAN INDUSTRIES
Gale Research
835 Penobscot Bldg.
Detroit, MI 48226-4094
Phone: (800) 877-GALE or (313) 961-2242
Fax: (800) 414-5043
1994. $500.00. Two volumes ($250.00 each). Volume one is Manufacturing Industries *and volume two is* Service and Non-Manufacturing Industries. *Provides the history, development, and recent status of approximately 1,000 industries. Includes statistical graphs, with industry and general indexes.*

FACTS AND FIGURES OF THE U.S. PLASTICS INDUSTRY
The Society of the Plastics Industry
1275 K St. NW
Washington, DC 20005
Phone: (202) 371-5200

THE RAUCH GUIDE TO THE U.S. PLASTICS INDUSTRY
Rauch Associates, Inc.
PO Box 6802
Bridgewater, NJ 08807
Phone: (908) 231-9548

GENERAL WORKS

MODERN PLASTICS ENCYCLOPEDIA
PO Box 602
Highstown, NJ 08520-9955
Phone: (800) 257-9402

PLASTICS TECHNOLOGY MANUFACTURING HANDBOOK AND BUYER'S GUIDE
Bill Communications, Inc.
355 Park Ave. S, 5 Fl.

New York, Ny 10010-1789
Phone: (800) 253-6708 or (212) 592-6200
Fax: (212) 592-6209
Annual. $41.95.

FURTHER READING

"4.6% Annual Growth Predicted." *Appliance Manufacturer,* August 1996.

Shearer, Brent. "Masterbatch Resin Business Turning Regional to Global." *Chemical Marketing Reporter,* 26 August 1996.

Phelan, Mark. "Plastics Suppliers Take the Battle Underhood." *Automotive Industries,* January 1997.

Wrigley, Al. "Steel Wins back AUto Parts from Plastics." *American Metal Market,* 9 September 1996.

"Global Forecast 1996." *Chemical Week,* 3 January 1996.

Chemical Economics Handbook, SRI Consulting, 1996.

Companies in the plastics products industry manufacture a multitude of items, ranging from clothespins and air mattresses to shoe soles and septic tanks. This industry accounted for approximately 60 percent of all plastics products sales in the early 1990s. Although the markets for miscellaneous plastics products are extremely fragmented, a few major categories stand out. For instance, miscellaneous plastic packaging, such as caps, food trays, and bubble wrap, constituted a leading 12 percent of shipments in the 1990s. Fabricated plastics used for vehicles, such as turn indicator housings, also made up 12 percent of the market. Plastics used to make electrical devices accounted for about 8 percent of industry sales, and plastic siding contributed 2 percent of revenues. Other major product groups included doors and window frames, dinnerware and kitchenware, and plastic furniture parts.

PLASTICS PRODUCTS

SIC 3080

The plastics industry's 470,000-member work force will benefit in the future from strong growth in demand for plastics products. However, productivity gains achieved through automation and the integration of more efficient processing techniques will contribute to a lag between shipment growth and new jobs. Opportunities for laborers will likely expand 30 to 40 percent between 1990 and 2005, according to the U.S. Bureau of Labor Statistics.

Top 10 TOP PLASTIC & FILM SHEET MAKERS, 1995

Ranked by: Sales in millions of dollars.

1. DuPont Co., $1,300
2. Mobile Chemical Co., $1,000
3. Bemis Co. Inc., $653
4. First Brands Corp., $619
5. American National Can Co., $500
6. Cryovac Division, $500
7. Printpack Inc., $465
8. Huntsman Packaging Corp., $437
9. ICI Americas Inc., $433
10. James River Corp. Packaging Business, $420

Source: *Plastics News*, September 18, 1995, p. 23.

U.S. sales of miscellaneous plastics products expanded rapidly during the 1980s, but increased competition, both at home and abroad, contributed to lagging price growth. Total U.S. plastics products shipments were $105 billion by 1995. About 53 percent—or $55.3 billion—of that total was comprised of miscellaneous goods from this industry. Despite a late 1980s and early 1990s U.S. recession, shipment growth persisted as new additives and processing techniques were introduced.

The value of shipments in the plastics film and sheet industry in 1996 was $12.9 billion, up from $12.6 billion in 1994. About 800 establishments operated in the industry, and 62 percent of these establishments had 20 or more employees. The average firm size as measured by the number of production workers per establishment was

34 percent larger than that for the manufacturing sector as a whole.

The value of shipments in the plastics profile shapes industry in 1995 was $4.2 billion, up from $3.9 billion in 1994, according to the *1995 Census of Manufactures*. The industry employed 27,600 production workers in 1995, up from the 27,000 employed in 1994 and above the previous peak of 21,300 in 1989. The top products by share in the industry are those made from vinyl (16 percent), polyethylene (16 percent), polypropylene (12 percent), polystyrene (10 percent), nylon (4 percent), acrylates (4 percent), and styrene copolymer (1 percent).

Establishments engaged in the manufacture of plastic plates, sheets, and related products shipped goods valued at $2.26 billion in 1993 (not adjusted for inflation). This figure remained in line with a generally flat trend in the industry in recent years. The total value of shipments increased by 5 percent from 1987 to 1990. The industry lagged behind the growth of plastics products in general, which experienced growth in shipments of over 17 percent during the same period. By 1996 the value of shipments increased to about $2.31 billion. Projections for 1998 did not reflect a substantial increase—$2.33 billion.

Establishments manufacturing plastics pipe produced a total of approximately $3.85 billion dollars worth of product in 1995. This figure marked a significant increase of approximately one-third in the total value of shipments from 1990. The industry lagged behind the growth of plastics products in general, which experienced growth in shipments of over 17 percent during the same period. In recent years, however, plastics pipe as a commodity has, in general, been able to maintain a large advantage over competitors in nonplastics piping. Although markets stagnated in the 1980s and early 1990s, plastics piping markets grew at a

rate four times faster than that of nonplastics markets. In addition, research and development spurred new products and cheaper methods of production. The continuing advancements in processing technology are opening new markets and applications throughout the world.

In 1995 U.S. producers shipped $6.3 billion worth of plastic bottles, a 70 percent increase over the 1990 level of $3.7 billion. Imports into the United States reached $162 million in 1995, while exports totaled $220 million. In the mid-1990s, there were 405 establishments in the industry, an increase of 42 percent since 1990, when there were 284 establishments.

Approximately 1,300 establishments were engaged in the manufacture of plastics foam products in 1996. In the mid-1990s, the industry manufactured products estimated at $10.1 million dollars. This figure remained in line with a generally upward production trend in the industry since 1987. Total value of shipments increased by over 31 percent from 1987 to 1993, higher than the increase in plastics products in general, which grew at a 17 percent rate over the same period. By 1996, the value of shipments was estimated to have increased another 15 percent to $11.8 billion.

There were 644 establishments in the custom compounding industry in the mid-1990s, an increase of 69 percent since 1990. Industry shipments totaled $6.0 billion in 1995, an increase of 87 percent over 1990, when shipments totaled $3.2 billion. There were 25,531 employees in the industry in the mid-1990s, an increase of 41 percent since 1990.

In the 1990s, plastics plumbing products included among other items bathtubs, sinks, and lavatories. The value of industry shipments increased from $709 million in 1987 to an estimated $1.46 billion in 1996. There were about 420 establishments in the industry. Approximately one-third of these establishments had 20 or more em-

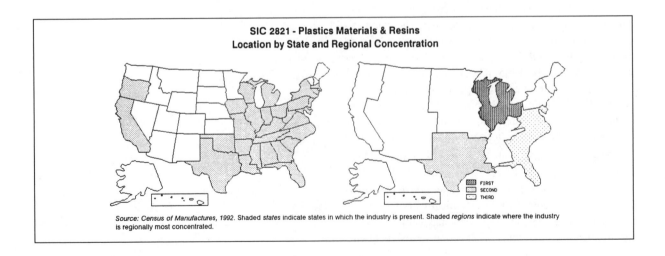

SIC 2821 - Plastics Materials & Resins
Location by State and Regional Concentration

FIRST
SECOND
THIRD

Source: Census of Manufactures, 1992. Shaded states indicate states in which the industry is present. Shaded regions indicate where the industry is regionally most concentrated.

ployees. Average firm size as measured by the number of production workers per establishment was 15 percent lower than that for the manufacturing sector as a whole.

INDUSTRY OUTLOOK

Overall, the plastics products market is expected to decline at a rate of 4 to 5 percent per year through the late-1990s, in real terms, according to U.S. industry projections. Plastics applications in building and construction—a category that includes not only piping, but also conduits and pipe fittings—comprise the second largest category of consumption at 21.1 percent; the largest category is packaging, which has 29.6 percent of total plastics markets. The underground piping market is the largest use segment of plastics pipe—water, drain, waste, vent, sewer and drain, gas, irrigation, conduit and pressure—and remains the largest market for plastics piping not only in the United States but in the world.

Significant recycling advances have been made in the industry but the portion of total plastics recycled remains low compared with total production or consumption. The industry is responding to public pressure to develop environmentally safer products and to advance recycling into all of its product areas. Efforts are underway between the industry and federal, state, and local governments to evaluate the merits of various policies.

While new technologies will further the trend toward the replacement of non-plastics materials with plastics, there is some concern over the feasibility of plastics recycling, which may lead some to shift back to older materials such as aluminum, copper, and other metals. From the production side, industry efforts to implement computer-aided design and manufacture (CAD/CAM) is expected to lead to drastic reductions in costs, reductions in turnover time, and decrease some of the environmental concerns by minimizing material waste.

Two dominant trends in the custom compounding industry in the early 1990s included increased competition and a growing demand for specialty and high-tech compounds. For example, fast growing product segments included electrically conductive plastic compounds, specialty color-concentrates, and liquid-crystal polymers. Although most custom compounding companies continued to realize revenue and profit gains in the early 1990s, greater competition was diminishing overall profit growth. Indeed, compounding firms in Taiwan, Singapore, Indonesia, and other low-cost manufacturing countries were vying for U.S. export market share.

Besides greater foreign competition, several major U.S. resin suppliers were entering the custom com-

pounding arena by providing small orders of highly tailored materials. To combat new competition and to reduce costs associated with research, development, and environmental regulations, many custom compounders were acquiring or merging with their competitors. In addition, some commodity resin producers were acquiring custom compounding firms as a means of diversifying their operations.

Industry conditions for plastics plumbing fixtures suggest future growth. The overall trend in shipments was strongly upward from 1987 to 1996, increasing by 49 percent in real terms over the period, with 1996 a peak year. Capital investments increased even more rapidly, with $15 million invested in 1987, $19 million in 1988, $69 million in 1989, $110 million in 1990, and $91 million in 1991. There was a sharp drop-off in 1992 to $31 million, after which investments started rising again to $31.2 million in 1993 and $57 million in 1994. The value of imports of plastics plumbing fixtures increased from $24 million in 1989 to an estimated $59 million in 1996, while the value of exports increased from $19 million to $40 million for these same years.

ORGANIZATION AND STRUCTURE

The plastics product industry is served by the Chemical Fabrics and Film Association, headquartered in Cleveland, Ohio. The association, formerly known as the Plastic Coatings and Film Association, was founded in 1927 and has 23 members. The association publishes industry standards and an annual directory and also organizes an annual convention. In addition, the plastics plumbing fixtures industry is served by the Plumbing Manufacturers Institute, headquartered in Glen Ellyn, Illinois. It was founded in 1956 and has 50 members. The Institute, which organizes semiannual conventions, has committees on codes, government affairs, standards, intra-industry, and statistics.

The major sources of input for the plastics industry were overwhelmingly from the manufacturing sector, which accounted for nearly 63 percent of sector input. The single major input was plastic materials and resins, which comprised 36.2 percent of inputs. Wholesale trade accounted for 8.5 percent of inputs, while imports—undifferentiated by industry sector—contributed 5.8 percent of sector input.

In 1996 approximately 328 establishments were engaged in the production of laminated plastic plate and sheet. That number was projected to increase by approximately 20 percent by 1998, while the number of production workers was projected to decrease by 10 percent. The existing 1996 establishments employed 14,600 workers, 10,800 of which were production workers. During 1994, the average value added per production worker was $105,925—a figure, which compared less than favorably with an overall average of $134,084 for all U.S. manufacturing industries.

In the mid-1990s, the principal sectors responsible for the purchase of miscellaneous plastics products were hospitals, which bought 5.6 percent of sector output, followed by electronic components with 5.2 percent, and personal consumption with 4.3 percent. Exports made up 4.0 percent of total product sales.

In 1995, approximately 275 establishments were engaged in the production of plastics pipe. Each establishment employed an average of approximately 61 employees, 46 of which were production workers. In 1994, the average value added per production worker was $119,330. This figure compared less than favorably with an overall average of $134,084 calculated for of all U.S. manufacturing industries.

In 1996, approximately 1,300 establishments were engaged in the production of plastic foam products. These businesses employed approximately 49 employees per establishment, of which 34 were production workers. The average value added per production worker was $72,991, a small figure compared to an average of $93,930 calculated for the average of all U.S. manufacturing industries.

WORK FORCE

Over the period covering 1991 to 1994, total employment in the plastics products industry overall rose by 13 percent. In 1995, the major occupational categories for the plastics products industry were: plastic molding machine operators, who made up 17.8 percent of total employment; assemblers and fabricators, who made up 8.6 percent; and packers and packagers, who comprised 4.8 percent. Approximately 20 percent of industry employees were engaged in some type of managerial or supervisory function or clerical, transportation, and accounting/financial tasks. The remaining employees were engaged in production activity. Production worker employment followed roughly the same trend, rising from 47,800 to 55,800 in 1996. The increase is expected to maintain moderate growth until at least 1998.

The industry job categories with the largest projected growth to 2005 were largely non-production jobs: sales and related workers, projected to grow by 69 percent; industrial production managers, 64.2 percent; industrial machinery mechanics, 50.9 percent; and tool & die makers, 44.9 percent. Categories uniformly forecast to grow by 35.8 percent were: blue collar worker supervisors; hand packers and packagers; inspectors, testers and graders; freight, stock, and material movers; and extruding and forming machine operators.

Concerning the industry's income distribution, while average hourly earnings of production workers in plastic products production rose from $3.27 in 1972 to $8.43 in 1987, the purchasing power of these wages actually declined by 10 percent. General payroll per employee, adjusted for inflation, fell from an average of $18,215 to $17,903. From 1987 to 1996, average hourly earnings rose by about 28 percent to $11.62. From 1972 to 1987, in terms of value added per production worker, wages per hour rose about two and one half times, while the value added per hour by these production workers rose by over three times, a shift in income distribution away from wages and toward profits.

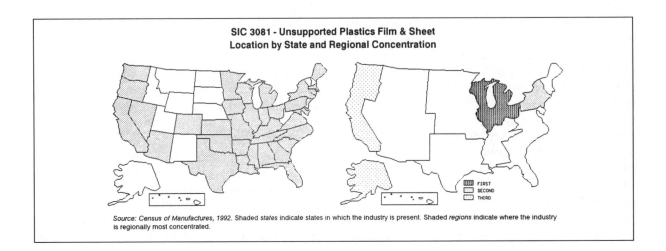

SIC 3081 - Unsupported Plastics Film & Sheet
Location by State and Regional Concentration

FIRST
SECOND
THIRD

Source: Census of Manufactures, 1992. Shaded *states* indicate states in which the industry is present. Shaded *regions* indicate where the industry is regionally most concentrated.

RESEARCH AND TECHNOLOGY

Going into the mid-1990s, major technological trends in the plastics products industry included recyclability and faster concept-to-production cycles. Indeed, many companies were ardently seeking flexible processing, extrusion, and molding techniques that would allow them to design and quickly manufacture new products. One of the most important recycling tactics was "design-for-recycling," whereby plastics products and devices are created in such a way that they can be efficiently ground, melted, and reused. For example, glue and adhesives that can contaminate reground materials were being eliminated from manufactured plastic goods.

Significant expenditures were also being directed toward the development of new environmentally safe compounds. Companies were striving to meet new chlorofluorocarbon (CFC) emission regulations by developing compounds that would not require hazardous manufacturing processes. Similarly, new additives and compounds were under development in the mid-1990s that would accelerate the natural breakdown of plastics products and reduce landfill waste. Although technologies like weak-link and bacterial polymers showed promise, extremely high production costs made them commercially impractical for most purposes in 1994.

AMERICA AND THE WORLD

One of the regions of greatest growth was China. Its plastics products shipments soared more than 200 percent during the 1980s, reaching approximately 4.1 billion tons by the early 1990s and reflecting average annual growth of about 12.5 percent. Chinese manufac-

turers suffered, however, from a lack of production equipment and access to processed raw materials. Although China's economic growth will stimulate increased imports, a low per capita plastic consumption will keep overall growth to 7 percent annually between 1997 and 2001. As capacity accelerates to meet demand during the 1990s, China will likely become a formidable competitor in export markets, particularly in fast growing East Asian countries. Asia, in general, is a strong growth area with predicted annual growth rates of 10 percent, especially in ethylene propylene, vinyl chloride, and acrylonitrile. Within the Asian market, the largest increases could occur among ASEAN (Association of Southeastern Asian Nations) members, as new complexes come online. The rapid increase of plastics consumption within the Asian market has stimulated U.S. producers to look at investing in local production plants.

Imports may also rise in the wake of the North American Free Trade Agreement (NAFTA), as U.S. manufacturers move production facilities south of the border to take advantage of inexpensive labor and reduced environmental restrictions. After Canada, Mexico was the second biggest importer of plastics goods into the United States during the mid-1990s. Mexican imports should rise rapidly over the next 5 to 10 years as Asian producers infiltrate the Mexican market to meet NAFTA requirements that 6 percent of a duty-free product's components be made in North America.

The General Agreement on Tariffs and Trade (GATT) treaty has limited international import duties on resins to 6.5 percent by the year 2000, down from an average of 12.5 percent. The impact of the new tariffs on the market structure is still uncertain, although most predictions lean toward further increases in international trade.

SIC 3086 - Plastics Foam Products
Industry Data by State

State	Establish-ments	Shipments			Employment				Cost as % of Shipments	Investment per Employee ($)
		Total ($ mil)	% of U.S.	Per Establ.	Total Number	% of U.S.	Per Establ.	Wages ($/hour)		
California	171	996.8	10.5	5.8	7,100	10.6	42	10.02	53.4	4,239
Texas	83	652.8	6.9	7.9	4,100	6.1	49	9.75	51.9	5,707
Pennsylvania	60	610.5	6.4	10.2	3,800	5.7	63	11.00	61.3	14,000
North Carolina	70	585.0	6.2	8.4	4,200	6.3	60	9.95	56.6	4,238
Illinois	47	525.2	5.5	11.2	3,000	4.5	64	11.78	52.9	3,867
Ohio	62	516.7	5.4	8.3	3,400	5.1	55	10.41	61.5	2,824
Indiana	41	477.3	5.0	11.6	3,500	5.2	85	9.90	56.2	3,086
Michigan	59	473.9	5.0	8.0	3,800	5.7	64	10.67	59.9	10,895
Tennessee	48	464.8	4.9	9.7	3,500	5.2	73	10.37	59.3	2,657
Georgia	39	449.2	4.7	11.5	3,200	4.8	82	10.12	50.8	8,250

Source: 1992 *Economic Census*. The states are in descending order of shipments or establishments (if shipment data are missing for the majority). The symbol (D) appears when data are withheld to prevent disclosure of competitive information. States marked with (D) are sorted by number of establishments. A dash (-) indicates that the data element cannot be calculated; * indicates the midpoint of a range.

ASSOCIATIONS AND SOCIETIES

DECORATIVE LAMINATE PRODUCTS ASSOCIATION
13924 Braddock Rd.
Centreville, VA 22020
Phone: (800) 684-3572
Fax: (703) 222-6180

SOCIETY OF PLASTICS ENGINEERS
14 Fairfield Dr.
Brookfield, CT 06804-0403
Phone: (203) 775-0471
Fax: (203) 775-8490

SOCIETY OF THE PLASTICS INDUSTRY
1275 K St. NW, Ste. 400
Washington, DC 20005
Phone: (202) 371-5200
Fax: (202) 371-1022

PERIODICALS AND NEWSLETTERS

ADVANCES IN POLYMER TECHNOLOGY
John Wiley & Sons, Inc., Journals Div.
605 3rd Ave.
New York, NY 10158-0012
Phone: (800) 526-5368 or (212) 850-6000
Quarterly. $476.00 per year.

JOURNAL OF APPLIED POLYMER SCIENCE
John Wiley & Sons, Inc., Journals Div.
605 3rd Ave.
New York, NY 10158-0012
Phone: (800) 526-5368 or (212) 850-6645
Fax: (212) 850-6021
Weekly. $6,604.00 per year.

JOURNAL OF ELASTOMERS AND PLASTICS
Melvyn A. Kohudic, editor
Technomic Publishing Co.
851 New Holland Ave.
Lancaster, PA 17604
Phone: (800) 223-9936 or (717) 291-5609
Fax: (717) 295-4538
Quarterly. $215.00 per year.

PLASTICS ENGINEERING
Society of Plastics Engineers, Inc.
14 Fairfield Dr.
Brookfield, CT 06804-0403
Phone: (203) 775-0471
Fax: (203) 775-8490
Monthly. $50.00 per year.

PLASTICS MACHINERY AND EQUIPMENT: FOR THOSE WHO SELECT AND BUY PLASTICS PROCESSING MACHINERY AND EQUIPMENT
Advanstar Communications, Inc.
7500 Old Oak Blvd.
Cleveland, OH 44130
Phone: (800) 346-0085 or (216) 243-8100
Fax: (216) 891-2726
Monthly. Free to qualified personnel; others, $40.00 per year.

PLASTICS TECHNOLOGY: MACHINERY/MATERIALS SYSTEMS FOR MAXIMUM PRODUCTIVITY
Bill Communications, Inc.
355 Park Ave. S, 3 Fl.
New York, NY 10010-1789
Phone: (800) 253-6708 or (212) 592-6200
Fax: (212) 592-6209
13 times a year. $65.00 per year.

DATABASES

DRI CHEMICAL FORECAST
DRI/McGraw-Hill, Data Products Division
24 Hartwell Ave.
Lexington, MA 02173
Phone: (800) 541-9914 or (617) 863-5100
Supply-demand and price forecasts are given quarterly and annually for over 120 U.S. chemical products. Quarterly forecasts generally extend three years, while annual forecasts cover five to ten years. Inquire as to online cost and availability.

ENGINEERED MATERIALS ABSTRACTS [ONLINE]
Materials Information, ASM International
9639 Kinsman Rd.
Materials Park, OH 44073
Phone: (216) 338-5151
Fax: (216) 338-4634
Provides online citations to the technical and engineering literature of plastic, ceramic, and composite materials. Time period is 1986 to date, with monthly updates. Inquire as to online cost and availability.

MATERIALS BUSINESS FILE
Materials Information, ASM International
9639 Kinsman Rd.
Materials Park, OH 44073
Phone: (216) 338-5151
Fax: (216) 338-4634
Provides online abstracts and citations to worldwide materials literature, covering the business and industrial aspects of metals, plastics, ceramics, and composites. Corresponds to Steels Alert, Nonferrous Metals Alert, *and* Polymers/Ceramics/Composites Alert. *Time period is 1985 to date, with monthly updates. Inquire as to online cost and availability.*

WILSONLINE: APPLIED SCIENCE AND TECHNOLOGY ABSTRACTS
H. W. Wilson Co.
950 University Ave.
Bronx, NY 10452
Phone: (800) 367-6770 or (718) 588-8400
Fax: (718) 590-1617
Provides online indexing and abstracting of 400 major scientific, technical, industrial, and engineering periodicals. Time period is 1983 to date for indexing and 1993 to date for abstracting, with updating twice a week. Inquire as to online cost and availability.

STATISTICS SOURCES

ENCYCLOPEDIA OF AMERICAN INDUSTRIES
Gale Research
835 Penobscot Bldg.

Detroit, MI 48226-4094
Phone: (800) 877-GALE or (313) 961-2242
Fax: (800) 414-5043
1994. $500.00. Two volumes ($250.00 each). Volume one is Manufacturing Industries *and volume two is* Service and Non-Manufacturing Industries. *Provides the history, development, and recent status of approximately 1,000 industries. Includes statistical graphs, with industry and general indexes.*

FACTS AND FIGURES OF THE U.S. PLASTICS INDUSTRY
The Society of the Plastics Industry
1275 K St. NW
Washington, DC 20005
Phone: (202) 371-5200

THE RAUCH GUIDE TO THE U.S. PLASTICS INDUSTRY
Rauch Associates, Inc.
PO Box 6802
Bridgewater, NJ 08807
Phone: (908) 231-9548

GENERAL WORKS

MODERN PLASTICS ENCYCLOPEDIA
PO Box 602
Highstown, NJ 08520-9955
Phone: (800) 257-9402

PLASTICS TECHNOLOGY MANUFACTURING HANDBOOK AND BUYER'S GUIDE
Bill Communications, Inc.
355 Park Ave. S, 5 Fl.
New York, Ny 10010-1789
Phone: (800) 253-6708 or (212) 592-6200
Fax: (212) 592-6209
Annual. $41.95.

FURTHER READING

Darnay, Arsen J., ed. *Manufacturing USA.* 5th ed. Detroit: Gale Research, 1996.

Encyclopedia of Associations. Detroit: Gale Research, 1997.

U.S. Bureau of the Census. *1994 County Business Patterns.* Washington: GPO, 1996.

———. *1995 Annual Survey of Manufactures.* Washington: GPO, 1997.

———. *1995 Census of Manufactures.* Washington: GPO, 1997.

POSTAL SERVICES

SIC 4311

With the stated goal of becoming a premier provider of 21st-century postal communications, the United States Postal Service continues to invest heavily in technology and equipment, including robotics and electronic postmarking, in an effort to streamline processes and increase efficiency rates. In addition, in June 1997 the Governors of the Postal Service announced plans to request a one-cent increase in stamp prices, and a two-cent price cut for some bill payments and transactions, to take effect no sooner than May 1998.

The United States Postal Service was one of the largest organizations in the world, with approximately 761,000 employees and an annual budget of $53 billion. It handled about 183 billion pieces of mail through an extremely complicated system of carefully coordinated activities. In addition to the national headquarters in Washington, D.C., the U.S. Postal Service consisted of regional and field division offices that together supervised approximately 40,000 post offices, branches, stations, and community post offices throughout the United States. If the Postal Service were a private company, it would have been the ninth largest in the country in 1996, with total revenues of more than $54 billion.

The U.S. Postal Service was created as an independent establishment out of the old Post Office Department by the Postal Reorganization Act of 1970, and commenced operations on July 1, 1971. The industry was highly labor intensive, with employee wages and benefits accounting for 85 percent of the system's total costs. To cope with its soaring costs, the organization increased postal rates consistently, from 6 cents at the onset of the Postal Reorganization Act to 32 cents in the 1990s for first-class letters. It also faced increasing competition from private mail and package delivery services, as well as from electronic information systems that reduced the need for postal services.

INDUSTRY OUTLOOK

The U.S. Postal Service played a significant role in the development of the United States. Not only did it foster unity among the diverse individuals scattered over the nation, but it also contributed largely to the development of U.S. business. In the early 1990s, however, the U.S. Postal Service received criticism from several sources. For example, customers complained about frequent rate increases, slow service, and lost mail. Proponents countered that the U.S. Postal Service actually improved the performance of the U.S. mail system in many dimensions, including finances, productivity, and service delivery.

In the final years of the twentieth century, the U.S. Postal Service was, as Postmaster General Marvin Runyon stated in the 1996 Annual Report, "A race for tomorrow against the toughest, most agile competition in its history." Runyon pledged to deliver new records for service and financial achievements while creating a new, wider range of communications products for its customers.

Investments of approximately $3.3 billion will be used for additional facilities, technology, and equipment. The funds will also help bring the Postal Service into the age of robotics, with 100 robotic mail transport systems pegged for testing in 1997 as the first step toward automating that function in mail processing plants. Additional plans included the introduction of such products as electronic postmarking and terminals designed to take credit and debit cards.

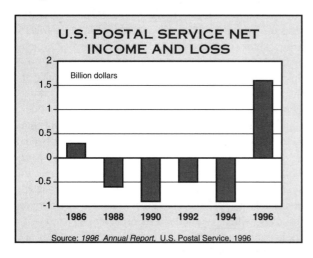

U.S. POSTAL SERVICE NET INCOME AND LOSS

Source: *1996 Annual Report*, U.S. Postal Service, 1996

ORGANIZATION AND STRUCTURE

The purpose of the U.S. Postal Service was to process and deliver mail to individuals and businesses within the United States. This mission also entailed handling mail efficiently and protecting it from loss or theft. The Postal Service handled about 183 billion pieces of mail in 1996 through its interrelated system of 40,000 post office branches.

ORGANIZATIONAL HIERARCHY

At the top of the Postal Service's organizational hierarchy is a team of 39 officers. In charge of these officers is the Postmaster General (PMG) and the Deputy Postmaster General, whose authority derived from the Postal Reorganization Act. The PMG is appointed by the nine governors of the Postal Service, who are, in turn, appointed by the President with the advice and permission of the Senate for overlapping nine-year terms. The governors and the PMG together appoint the deputy PMG, and these 11 people together form the board of governors. The remaining officers are appointed by the PMG, and the board of governors determine the nature and scope of activities of these officers. These officers consist of two associate postmasters general, five senior assistant postmasters general, nineteen assistant postmasters general, six other headquarters functional heads, and five regional postmasters general. In addition to

these officers, there are approximately 800 other persons in senior management positions in the country.

GEOGRAPHICAL DISTRIBUTION

The activities of the Postal Service are divided over five postal regions: central, eastern, northeastern, southern, and western. The reason for such field division is to reduce administrative layers and incorporate operating management expertise as near as possible to the locations where postal services are offered to the public. Each of the five regions have a number of "field divisions" that are regarded as the Postal Service's key organizational units, with all other local offices reporting to a division. Moreover, there are 74 field divisions located in key cities throughout the country, and there is a regional chief inspector at each of the five regions of the Postal Service. Any information and complaints with regard to postal violations are required to be presented to the closest postal inspector in authority. The five regional postmasters general are in charge of all the postal activities in a geographical region.

ECONOMIC STRUCTURE

The Postal Service is not considered a business, but rather a governmental institution designed to serve the American public. However, when Congress created the Postal Service as an "independent establishment" of the federal government, one of the main objectives was to assure financial stability and self-sufficiency for the organization. In the 1970s, this seemed a highly ambitious goal. At that time not only did the Postal Service suffer from long-standing operating problems and deficit-producing services, but it also faced a high inflation rate and rising cost of fuel. For example, inflation raised the Postal Service's aggregate costs for its employees' coverage under the Civil Service Retirement program from $445 million in fiscal 1972 to $1.72 billion in 1982. In addition, in the late 1970s the Postal Service paid $3.5 million annually to operate its innumerable vehicles. Despite these hurdles of the 1970s, the Postal Service managed to break even financially by the end of the 1980s. During the 1980s, revenues exceeded expenditures by about $500 million. By the 1990s, the annual budget of the Postal Service was approximately $31 billion.

WORK FORCE

As many as 761,000 people, or approximately 1 percent of the total U.S. labor force, worked for the U.S. Postal Service in 1996. These individuals worked in facilities with contingents varying in size from 1 to more than 40,000 employees. The largest category of postal employees consisted of clerks and mail handlers, which constituted 44 percent of the work force, or about 350,000 individuals. The next largest category included delivery carriers and vehicle drivers, constituting 237,000 employees, or 30 percent of the total work force. Nearly 8 percent of this figure, or 65,000 individuals, were full- and part-time rural delivery carriers who performed a variety of tasks. More than 50,000 people held supervisory and managerial positions, and over 29,000 attended to building and vehicle maintenance. There were 28,000 postmasters in total, and the rest of the work force filled a number of specialized jobs that ranged from security officer to the postmaster general.

The postal employees in the United States are unionized. The four major organizations that represent the postal work force in collective bargaining with management over wages and other terms and conditions of employment are: the National Association of Letter Carriers (NALC); the American Postal Workers Union (APWU); the National Rural Letter Carriers' Association (NRLCA); and the National Post Office Mail Handlers, Watchmen, Messengers, and Group Leaders Division of Laborers' International Union of North America (Mail Handlers). The APWU and the NALC, representing clerks and carriers respectively, were the two largest of these organizations.

During the early 1990s, the U.S. Postal Service suffered a series of highly publicized, unfortunate incidents involving disgruntled or former employees. At post offices in several cities, these employees brought a gun to work and shot fellow workers and managers. These incidents occurred far more frequently at post offices than in other businesses, raising concerns about the working environment. Some observers attributed the violence to the fact that relations between post office workers and management had grown increasingly tense, and claimed that some disturbed individuals were unable to handle the everyday stress of the job. Others blamed the strong employee unions for making it difficult for managers to discipline or terminate workers with behavioral or emotional problems. The Postal Service tried to address these concerns through reorganizations, offers of counseling, and training programs.

RESEARCH AND TECHNOLOGY

Advances in electronic technologies changed the way that people communicated with each other and threatened the very existence of the Postal Service. The improved capabilities of electronic communication technologies, such as microcomputers, facsimile systems, high-speed printers, broadband satellite connections, and video display instruments, made communication quicker and mail delivery less necessary. In particular, two technological advances presented alternative channels to mail delivery that were of concern to the Postal Service: electronic funds transfer and electronic mail.

ELECTRONIC FUNDS TRANSFER

Financial institutions in the early 1990s increasingly substituted paperless, computer-based systems of transfering funds (i.e., checks and cash) for conventional payment systems such as mail delivery. Electronic systems for funds transfer had two primary applications that directly affected the Postal Service's activities: direct electronic deposit of payments, often called "direct deposit," allowed people to bypass the mail system and electronically deposit their paychecks, retirement benefits, dividends, or Social Security benefits; and payment of bills through preauthorized debits allowed people to pay bills electronically at any convenient automated teller machine (ATM), without using the Postal Service. Moreover, with a personal microcomputer and a modem, people could contact their financial institution electronically from home or work, and pay bills on the spot without using the mail system.

ELECTRONIC MAIL

Significant advances in the area of telecommunications allowed people to send documents by facsimile (fax) machine. These machines operated similarly to a typical office copying machine, but had the additional ability to transmit a document electronically to another fax machine via telephone lines. Computer-based message systems, or electronic mail (e-mail), were another result of advances in computer technology. E-mail described the transfer and storage of documents via electronic means (usually a personal computer). The typical electronic mail procedure occurred when one party created a document on his or her computer and sent the document to another party's computer at a different location. The second party could access the document at his or her convenience by retrieving it via a computer display terminal or printer.

In the early 1990s, the U.S. Postal Service also made strides toward automating some of its operations, including mail sorting. For instance, businesses that sent many pieces of mail daily could obtain lower rates by adding bar codes to envelopes for easy sorting. Industry analysts claimed that the Postal Service stood to gain $40 to $80 million in annual cost savings for each 1 percent of the mail it processed automatically.

In the late 1990s, the U.S. Postal Service entered the "age of postal robotics" with plans to put 100 robotic mail tray transport systems into mail processing plants in

1997 to improve employee working conditions, cut costs, and increase reliability.

AMERICA AND THE WORLD

Despite growing concern, the U.S. Postal Service maintained the lowest postal rate among many industrialized nations. For example, U.S. first-class postage, which was increased to 32 cents in 1996, still compared favorably to the 1996 rates (converted to U.S. currency) charged in Sweden, at 48 cents; France, at 54 cents; Switzerland, at 64 cents; Germany, at 66 cents; and Japan, at 72 cents.

ASSOCIATIONS AND SOCIETIES

ADVERTISING MAIL MARKETING ASSOCIATION
1333 F St. NW, Ste. 710
Washington, DC 20004-1108
Phone: (202) 347-0055
Fax: (202) 347-0789

ASSOCIATION OF PAID CIRCULATION PUBLICATIONS
1211 Connecticut Ave. NW, Ste. 610
Washington, DC 20036
Phone: (202) 296-8487
Fax: 202)2 96-0343

PARCEL SHIPPERS ASSOCIATION
1211 Connecticut Ave. NW
Washington, DC 20036
Phone: (202) 296-3690
Fax: (202) 296-0343

PERIODICALS AND NEWSLETTERS

POSTAL BULLETIN
Available from U.S. Government Printing Office
Washington, DC 20402
Phone: (202) 512-1800
Fax: (202) 512-2250
Biweekly. $81.00 per year. Issued by the United States Postal Service. Contains orders, instructions, and information relating to U.S. mail service.

POSTAL LIFE: THE MAGAZINE FOR POSTAL EMPLOYEES
Available from U.S. Government Printing Office
Washington, DC 20402
Phone: (202) 783-3238
Fax: (202) 512-2233
Bimonthly. $14.00 per year. Issued by the Department of Public and Employee Communications, United States Postal Service. Contains articles on new methods, techniques, and programs of the United States Postal Service.

POSTAL WORLD
United Communications Group
11300 Rockville Pke., Ste. 1100
Rockville, MD 20852-3030
Phone: (301) 816-8950
Fax: (301) 816-8945
Biweekly. $349.00 per year. Newsletter for mail users.

STATISTICS SOURCES

ANNUAL REPORT OF POSTMASTER GENERAL
U.S. Postal Service
Washington, DC 20260
Phone: (202) 268-2000
Annual.

REVENUE AND COST ANALYSIS REPORT
U.S. Postal Service
Washington, DC 20260
Phone: (202) 268-2000
Annual.

GENERAL WORKS

DOMESTIC MAIL MANUAL
Available from U.S. Government Printing Office
Washington, DC 20402
Phone: (202) 783-3238
Semiannual. $56.00 per year. Issued by the U.S. Postal Service. Contains rates, regulations, classes of mail, special services, etc., for mail within the U.S.

INTERNATIONAL MAIL MANUAL
Available from U.S. Government Printing Office
Washington, DC 20402
Phone: (202) 783-3238
Semiannual. $17.00 per year. Issued by the U.S. Postal Service. Contains rates, regulations, classes of mail, special services, etc., for mail sent from the U.S. to foreign countries.

NATIONAL FIVE DIGIT ZIP CODE AND POST OFFICE DIRECTORY
National Address Information Center
United States Postal Service
6060 Primacy Pky., Ste. 101
Memphis, TN 38188-0001
Phone: (800) 238-3150 or (901) 268-3520
Fax: (901) 767-8853
Annual. $15.00.

FURTHER READING

Cebry, Michael E. ''Management Science in Automating Postal Operations: Facility and Equipment Planning in the United States Postal Service.'' *Interfaces,* January/February 1992.

''On the Money,'' *1996 Annual Report of the United States Postal Service.*

United States Postal Service Homepage. Available at http://www.usps.gov/ ◄►

PRINTING, COMMERCIAL

SIC 2750

Advances *in technology and a strong economy have helped to keep the commercial printing industry relatively stable throughout the present decade, and moderate increases in revenue and industry growth are predicted for the late 1990s. Processes are becoming increasingly computer-automated and quality is improving. Growth will be seen in general marketing and promotional products; one-stop print shops, particularly off-set lithography printers, will be particularly strong. The entire industry should see a 6 percent increase in sales through the end of the decade.*

Commercial printing brought in revenues totaling approximately $68 billion in 1996, and employed nearly 700,000 people. The industry has been relatively stable through the 1990s, with modest increases in revenue, even faced with increased environmental challenges. Employment in the industry has been decreasing slowly as more and more aspects of the printing process are automated and computer controlled.

Top 10 PRINTING COMPANIES WITH THE HIGHEST SALES

Ranked by: Sales in 1996, in millions of dollars.

1. R. R. Donnelley & Sons
    (Chicago, IL), with $6,599.0 million
2. Hallmark
    (Kansas City, MO), $3,600.0
3. Quebecor Printing Inc.
    (Quebec, Canada), $3,110.3
4. Moore Corp. Ltd.
    (Ontario, Canada), $2,517.7
5. American Greetings Corp.
    (Cleveland, OH), $2,172.3
6. Deluxe Corp.
    (St. Paul, MN), $1,895.7
7. World Color Press Inc.
    (New York, NY), $1,641.4
8. Banta Corp.
    (Menasha, WI), $1,083.8
9. Quad/Graphics
    (Pewaukee, WI), $1,002.1
10. Treasure Chest Advertising Co. Inc.
    (Glendora, CA), $900.0

Source: *American Printer,* American Printer's 100+ (annual), July, 1995, p. 28+.

Commercial printing involves several different processes, each of which has specific product applications. All the processes involve the transfer of an image from a matrix (a stone, a metal plate, or film) to a substrate (paper, plastic, metal, etc.) using a press. Lithography accounts for about half of all the printing done in the United States; it is used extensively in advertising materials and in printing labels, posters, calendars, and maps. Gravure printing is used particularly for jobs which require especially large runs, as gravure retains the crispness of the original image throughout the printing job. Although this process is expensive, the quality of the product is very high and it is used for many magazines and high end advertisements, as well as for mass-distributed catalogs and directories, and for some labels and wrappers. Flexography and screen printing are still other techniques used in commercial printing, primarily for packaging materials, signage, and bumper stickers.

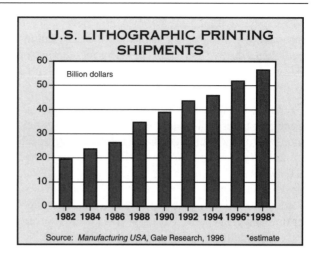

U.S. LITHOGRAPHIC PRINTING SHIPMENTS

Billion dollars

Source: *Manufacturing USA*, Gale Research, 1996   *estimate

INDUSTRY OUTLOOK

The mid-1990s was a trying time for many in the industry. Rising postage costs, rising paper costs, and threats of recession kept many companies lean. According to a July 1996 article in *American Printer,* a survey of the top fifth of domestic printing firms indicated more than half were involved in mergers or acquisitions. The larger the company, the more likely the chance of merger. In February 1997, *Publishing & Production Executive* suggested that the consolidation trend was fueled by the printing customer's demand for a one-stop shop. The huge capital investments required to stay competitive in the industry were also a factor. Aggressive competition among printers cut profit margins close.

But the market, while not exhibiting tremendous growth through the decade, remained strong and showed promise for the future. The "hot" markets for the turn of the century, said Ron Davis of the Printing Industries of America (PIA), would be "general marketing and promotional." The PIA predicted that the industry would do well into the late 1990s, seeing a growth in sales of approximately 6 percent.

The industry was revamped during the 1980s and 1990s, and traditional mechanical printers' skills were not sufficient in leading shops. From electronic prepress to digital presses, the new standard of commercial printing equipment was redefining the craft in terms of the electronic era. New technology was a two-edged sword. According to a 1996 study by the National Association of Printers and Lithographers, the cost of staying "state-of-the-art" with regard to new software and hardware was the leading threat to overall profitability for the industry. Interestingly, the same survey identified the key strength of the industry as having state-of-the-art equipment that could handle a broad range of work. The second most serious "threat to profitability" was closer kin to it the learning curve of keeping current with new technology and converting to new systems.

Because of advances in offset lithography, some predicted that letterpress and flexography would fall into disuse. Enhanced technologies emerged, however, and brought increased interest in flexo. A 1992 article in *Graphic Arts Monthly* claimed that nearly all telephone directories and full-color newspaper comics were being printed by flexography and that the volume of regular newspaper sections printed by flexography had doubled

within the previous few years. The report anticipated that the future availability of better paper grades and improved inks would also bring increased use among magazine printers. Many current letterpress operations looking to upgrade may look to flexo as well, since flexo is a less expensive printing process and is being technologically developed more quickly.

Gravure is also in possible danger due to the improvements in off-set lithography. Because this process is expensive, and because other forms of printing are turning out higher quality products, the future of gravure is not clear. The one area in which gravure excels is in decorative wall coverings and vinyl flooring; this field is undisputed by other printing processes.

Screen printers in the 1990s benefited from four-color-process work refinements, computerized design, increased press speeds, and environmentally responsive improvements. In anticipation of governmental regulations mandating cuts in solvent use, screen printers began turning to water-based inks cured with ultraviolet (UV) light. Traditional inks contained solvents to aid in drying; UV inks were dried with UV light.

In the mid-1990s, a new kind of printing technology emerged that allowed digital files to be uploaded into the memory of an elcographic press. No film and no plates were used; rather, the image in the memory was translated into a series of electrical pulses. A special ink—a waterbase with pigment polymers and salts to enhance conductivity—coagulated in response to the pulses, and was cold-offset onto the paper. This new process was first utilized in short-run, high-speed markets, and industry prognosticators expected it to grow quickly into the high-speed publishing arena.

On the horizon in the late 1990s, the dominance of 6-color presses was being challenged by 8-color sheet-fed "perfectors" that could print both sides of a sheet of paper during one pass through the press. At prices ranging from $2.7 to $4 million dollars, these behemoth machines were considered expensive, but incredibly productive and a sure contender for the wave of the future. By 1997, they were already widely adopted by printers in Europe.

All of the advances in printing technology are allowing the industry to address what the National Association of Printers & Lithographers identified as the seven key industry trends in a November 1996 report published in *GATF World,* the magazine of the Graphic Arts Technical Foundation. The trends, in order of importance, were: more color, graphics, and complex designs; shorter run-lengths; paper and material cost inflation; severe price competition among printers; much quicker turn-around times; black and white printing now going to copying machine technology; and clients insisting on higher quality.

WORK FORCE

In 1996, approximately 700,000 Americans were employed in the commercial printing industry. The workers within the industry face rapid changes as new production methods and materials are adopted. Some, critical of the innovations, have claimed that craftsmanship is being replaced with technology; others claim that technological improvements enhance traditional craftsmanship. Changes resulted in the elimination of some job classifications but created shortages of experienced labor in others. The prepress and postpress areas were expected to yield the greatest gains in employment opportunity, while traditional jobs such as those of ''strippers'' were being eliminated by computerized prepress.

According to U.S. government statistics, approximately 37,000 establishments were involved in commercial printing during the early 1990s. The National Association of Printers and Lithographers stated that ''Though commercial printing is a huge industry, it is an industry of numerous small businesses, embodying the U.S. entrepreneurial spirit.'' Forty-three percent of commercial printing establishments employed fewer than four employees; 66.2 percent employed fewer than ten; 85 percent fewer than 20; and 93.4 percent of the nation's commercial printers employed fewer than 50 employees.

In the mid-1990s, the median weekly wage for a press operator was $432, according to the U.S. Bureau of Labor Statistics. Employment in this sector was expected to grow slowly through 2005, because although demand for the printed product will increase, technology will enable one professional offset press operator to print

SIC 2752
Occupations Employed by SIC 275 - Commercial Printing and Business Forms

Occupation	% of Total 1994	Change to 2005
Offset lithographic press operators	9.2	3.9
Printing press machine setters, operators	8.1	3.9
Bindery machine operators & set-up operators	6.5	-10.1
Sales & related workers nec	5.9	29.9
General managers & top executives	4.4	23.2
Strippers, printing	3.4	15.8
Blue collar worker supervisors	3.2	17.8
Machine feeders & offbearers	3.0	16.9
Bookkeeping, accounting, & auditing clerks	2.1	-2.6
Hand packers & packagers	2.1	22.5
General office clerks	1.9	10.8
Printing, binding, & related workers nec	1.8	29.9
Traffic, shipping, & receiving clerks	1.7	25.0
Assemblers, fabricators, & hand workers nec	1.7	29.9
Job printers	1.6	-22.1
Artists & commercial artists	1.5	31.9
Typesetting & composing machine operators	1.5	-67.5
Platemakers	1.4	-9.1
Cost estimators	1.3	29.4
Order clerks, materials, merchandise, & service	1.3	27.1
Cutting & slicing machine setters, operators	1.3	16.9
Production, planning, & expediting clerks	1.3	37.2
Camera operators	1.3	3.9
Secretaries, ex legal & medical	1.3	18.2
Industrial production managers	1.3	-9.1
Screen printing machine setters & set-up operators	1.3	29.9
Helpers, laborers, & material movers nec	1.2	29.9
Truck drivers light & heavy	1.2	33.9
Electronic pagination systems workers	1.1	107.8
Paste-up workers	1.1	-15.6

Source: *Industry-Occupation Matrix,* Bureau of Labor Statistics. These data relate to one or more 3-digit SIC industry groups rather than to a single 4-digit SIC. The change reported for each occupation to the year 2005 is a percent of growth or decline as estimated by the Bureau of Labor Statistics. The abbreviation nec stands for 'not elsewhere classified'.

more quickly and more efficiently than several were able to do in the past.

RESEARCH AND TECHNOLOGY

Evolving technology played a vital role in the development of the commercial printing industry. Analysts estimated that printers invested more than $2 billion in new technology during the early 1990s to maintain their competitiveness. The development of high-quality copying machines drove printers to adopt presses capable of offering more benefits. Innovations brought improvements in color capacity, press speeds, and automation.

As press speeds approached 2,500 feet per minute, automated equipment became increasingly important because of human physical limitations. New methods of feeding paper into the press and taking printed matter away from the press were developed. Researchers designed computers to help achieve optimal results by automatically monitoring press temperatures, plate register (how images fit together), and web tension. One device that facilitated the development of higher speed presses was a densitometer. A densitometer was a device used to insure color integrity throughout an entire press run by automatically making adjustments to the ink fountains. Prior to the development of densitometers, ink fountain adjustments were made by an experienced pressman based on visual perception.

Other technological changes were aimed at improving the ability to quickly set up a press and to reduce paper waste. One area under study was the automatic setting of press variables from prepress operations. For example, if computerized color separations could be used to directly set press ink keys, exact color reproductions could be made without wasting time and paper in experimental attempts to duplicate the required visual results. Other evolving technologies included faster plate changes, reductions in the amount of blank space required to lock plates onto press cylinders, additional in-line finishing capabilities, optimized material handling at the end of the press run, and better photographic reproductions.

Another innovation developed during the early 1990s was a hybrid of web-fed technology and plateless printing, in which a special light-sensitive drum was used to print variable information for each impression made during a press run. This computer enhanced system enabled its operators to offer personalized, mass-printed output. One industry analyst predicted that as computer and printing technologies advanced, future recipients of documents would be unable to tell the difference between an item printed on a printing press and one individually generated with a computer.

The 1990s saw a great deal of research into improving the environmental impact of commercial printing because of U.S. Occupational Safety and Health Administration (OSHA) compliance issues, the Pollution Prevention Act of 1990, and the Clean Air Act Amendment. Traditional toluene-based inks, which were strictly regulated and rated by the U.S. Environmental Protection Agency as both VOCs (Volatile Organic Compound) and HAPs (Hazardous Air Pollutants), were slated to be phased out by water-based inks. However, the technology was still in a developmental stage. Promising developments included mixing acetone, a non-hazardous but flammable substance, with water to increase ink drying time, and multicolor pressruns that used a waterbased ink as only one of the colors. One study noted that, in a typical four-color (cyan, yellow, magenta, and black) printing run, if a water-based ink were used just for the yellow component, toluene emissions would be reduced 35%. Full color water-based printing was not a reality by the mid- to late 1990s.

Technology also provided competition for the commercial printing industry. Many short-run publications were complemented by material on CD-ROM or on a website. Referenced in the February 1997 *Publishing & Production Executive*, a study of 1,000 U.S. consumers commissioned by the Printing Industries of America (PIA) found that only 21 percent of those surveyed thought that electronic media would replace print. Many felt that electronic and print media would remain independent methods of information. The advance of electronic media into the short-run market, however, could

SIC 2752 - Commercial Printing, Lithographic
General Statistics

Year	Com-panies	Establishments		Employment			Compensation		Production ($ million)			
		Total	with 20 or more employees	Total (000)	Production Workers (000)	Hours (Mil)	Payroll ($ mil)	Wages ($/hr)	Cost of Materials	Value Added by Manufacture	Value of Shipments	Capital Invest.
1982	17,332	17,842	3,184	311.9	234.1	434.0	5,746.4	9.06	8,406.4	11,045.1	19,441.6	958.1
1983		17,879	3,299	315.1	236.9	440.1	6,052.1	9.39	9,025.3	11,741.8	20,754.0	962.7
1984		17,916	3,414	334.9	249.0	473.8	6,841.5	9.60	10,485.0	13,271.2	23,646.2	1,279.7
1985		17,952	3,529	335.4	248.2	472.7	7,097.5	10.04	11,079.8	13,949.0	25,024.8	1,410.7
1986		18,031	3,585	337.0	247.9	487.5	7,513.3	10.05	11,598.9	14,819.2	26,371.1	1,335.9
1987	24,328	24,980	4,099	403.0	292.9	580.5	9,132.1	10.14	14,581.7	18,162.1	32,698.2	1,537.3
1988		23,460	4,197	405.2	293.2	586.7	9,524.3	10.36	15,758.3	18,997.0	34,727.0	1,435.4
1989		22,623	4,207	414.7	306.3	615.5	10,149.0	10.57	16,727.9	20,416.1	37,128.0	1,627.6
1990		22,535	4,170	410.1	307.3	631.0	10,606.7	10.72	17,623.2	21,230.3	38,877.4	1,662.4
1991		23,622	4,025	400.1	290.8	594.8	10,386.6	11.04	16,788.0	20,952.4	37,718.9	1,370.0
1992	28,489	29,344	4,251	439.9	317.4	653.0	12,047.5	11.76	18,723.1	24,842.5	43,588.2	1,629.4
1993		27,996	4,265	437.6	319.1	654.7	12,298.9	11.94	19,304.5	25,406.9	44,704.2	1,682.2
1994		28,606P	4,532P	439.8	319.3	664.8	12,618.2	11.94	19,432.4	26,473.9	45,846.8	1,958.8
1995		29,620P	4,636P	466.2P	337.7P	709.3P	13,476.5P	12.18P	20,973.1P	28,572.9P	49,481.8P	1,897.0P
1996		30,634P	4,741P	478.0P	345.7P	730.5P	14,082.8P	12.42P	21,964.0P	29,922.9P	51,819.6P	1,960.9P
1997		31,648P	4,845P	489.9P	353.7P	751.7P	14,689.2P	12.66P	22,954.9P	31,272.8P	54,157.4P	2,024.7P
1998		32,662P	4,950P	501.7P	361.7P	772.9P	15,295.6P	12.90P	23,945.8P	32,622.7P	56,495.2P	2,088.6P

Sources: 1982, 1987, 1992 *Economic Census*; *Annual Survey of Manufactures*, 83-86, 88-91, 93-94. Establishment counts for non-Census years are from *County Business Patterns*; establishment values for 83-84 are extrapolations. 'P's show projections by the editors. Industries reclassified in 87 will not have data for prior years.

be a driver to encourage printers to expand into electronic publishing, or to take over increasingly large segments of what has been traditionally gravure's domain long, multicolor press runs.

Going into the late 1990s, industry leaders appeared in agreement that long-run magazine and catalog publishing was unthreatened by electronic publishing at least for the next decade. Many industry giants, like Quebecor and Quad/Graphics, welcomed digital publishing by advertising their services online and using webpages as marketing tools.

AMERICA AND THE WORLD

Some industry watchers note that U.S. printers and publishers were poised to succeed as agreements such as the North American Free Trade Agreement (NAFTA) and the Uruguay Round of the General Agreement on Tariffs and Trade (GATT) increased the viability of exporting U.S. printing abroad and increased U.S. copyright protection. Also, U.S. printers looked forward to reaping the advantage of having American English as the world's standard language of trade, science, and commerce.

ASSOCIATIONS AND SOCIETIES

ASSOCIATION FOR SUPPLIERS OF PRINTING AND PUBLISHING TECHNOLOGIES
1899 Preston White Dr.
Reston, VA 22091-4326
Phone: (703) 264-7200
Fax: (703) 620-0994

NATIONAL ASSOCIATION OF PRINTERS AND LITHOGRAPHERS
780 Palisade Ave.
Teaneck, NJ 07666
Phone: (800) 642-6275 or (201) 342-0700
Fax: (201) 692-0286

NATIONAL ASSOCIATION OF QUICK PRINTERS
401 N. Michigan Ave.
Chicago, IL 60611-4267
Phone: (312) 644-6610
Fax: (312) 245-1084

PRINTING INDUSTRIES OF AMERICA
100 Daingerfield Rd.
Alexandria, VA 22314
Phone: (800) 742-2666 or (703) 519-8100
Fax: (703) 548-3227

PERIODICALS AND NEWSLETTERS

AMERICAN PRINTER
Intertec Publishing Corp.
29 N. Wacker Dr.
Chicago, IL 60606
Phone: (800) 621-9907 or (800) 543-7771
Fax: (312) 726-2574
Monthly. $50.00 per year. Serves the printing and lithographic industries and allied manufacturing and service segments.

GRAPHIC ARTS MONTHLY
Cahners Publishing Co.
249 W. 17th St.
New York, NY 10011
Phone: (800) 662-7776 or (212) 463-6834
Fax: (212) 463-6530
Monthly. $85.00 per year.

IN-PLANT PRINTER INCLUDING CORPORATE IMAGING
Innis Publishing Co.
PO Box 368
Northbrook, IL 60062
Phone: (800) 247-3036 or (708) 564-5940
Fax: (708) 564-8381
Bimonthly. $45.00 per year. Formerly In-Plant Printer and Electronic Publisher.

PRINTING IMPRESSIONS
North American Publishing Co.
401 N. Broad St.
Philadelphia, PA 19108-9988
Phone: (800) 777-8074 or (215) 238-5300
Fax: (215) 238-5457
Bimonthly. Free to qualified personnel; others, $75.00 per year.

QUICK PRINTING: THE INFORMATION SOURCE FOR COMMERCIAL COPYSHOPS AND PRINTSHOPS
Coast Publishing, Inc.
1680 SW Bayshore Blvd.
Port St. Lucie, FL 34984
Phone: (407) 879-6666
Fax: (407) 879-7388
Monthly. $25.00 per year.

DATABASES

CITIBASE (CITICORP ECONOMIC DATABASE)
FAME Software Corp.
77 Water St., 9 Fl.
New York, NY 10005
Phone: (212) 898-7800
Fax: (212) 742-8956
Presents over 6,000 statistical series relating to business, industry, finance, and economics. Includes series from Survey of Current Business *and many other sources. Time period is 1947 to date, with daily updates. Inquire as to online cost and availability.*

STATISTICS SOURCES

BUSINESS STATISTICS
Available from U.S. Government Printing Office
Washington, DC 20402
Phone: (202) 512-1800
Fax: (202) 512-2250
Biennial. $20.00. Issued by Bureau of Economic Analysis, U.S. Department of Commerce. Shows annual data for 29 years and monthly data for a recent four-year period. Statistics correspond to the Survey of Current Business.

SURVEY OF CURRENT BUSINESS
Available from U.S. Government Printing Office
Washington, DC 20402
Phone: (202) 512-1800
Fax: (202) 512-2250
Monthly. $41.00 per year. Issued by Bureau of Economic Analysis, U.S. Department of Commerce. Presents a wide variety of business and economic data.

GENERAL WORKS

GRAPHIC ARTS MONTHLY-PRINTING INDUSTRY SOURCEBOOK
Cahners Magazines
249 W. 17th St.
New York, NY 10011
Phone: (212) 463-6828
Fax: (212) 242-6631

Annual. $50.00. About 1,900 manufacturers and distributors of graphic arts equipment, supplies, and services. Also includes list of corporate electronic publishers.

FURTHER READING

"Austrian Machine Corporation." Cranston, RI: Austrian Machine, Inc., 1997.

Castegnier, Pierre. "Elcography: a New Digital Printing Alternative." *GATF World,* January/February 1997.

"A Commitment to Gravure Excellence." *Gravure,* fall 1996.

Darnay, Arsen J., ed. *Manufacturing USA,* 5th ed. Detroit: Gale Research, 1996.

Dun's Business Rankings. Bethlehem, PA: Dun & Bradstreet, 1996.

Kendra, Erika. "1997 Technology Forecast—Flexography." *GATF World,* January/February 1997.

"Printer's Perspective: 1996 in Review." *Publishing & Production Executive,* February 1997.

"Printers' Profits Remain Healthy Despite Drop." *GATF World,* July/August 1996.

"Tracking the Trends: Merger Activity in Top Printing Firms." *American Printer,* July 1996.

U.S. Bureau of Labor Statistics.*Occupational Outlook Handbook.* Washington: GPO, 1996. Available from http://stats.bls.gov/oco/ocos231.htm.

PULP MILLS

SIC 2611

With concerted efforts to recycle papermaking products and replenish trees that are lost to the pulping process, the future of the pulp industry and the environment looks promising. If society can continue to reduce the amount of forestland used for tree harvesting, and the pulp industry can continue to network globally and develop more export markets, then the environment and the pulp industry will prosper.

The U.S. pulp industry is by far the world's largest. In 1995, the United States produced 90 million metric tons of wood pulp, representing 53.4 percent of the 168.3 million metric tons produced worldwide. The next largest producer, Canada, produced 27.5 million metric tons. Most of the pulp made in the United States is chemical pulp, which is produced by a chemical digesting process that converts wood chips into pulp by chemically liberating the cellulose fibers from the lignin that holds them together in the wood. Mechanical pulps are made with large "grinders," which physically shred the wood pulp into individual fibers. Some processes combine elements of mechanical and chemical pulping.

After the wood chips are digested or ground, they are called wood pulp. If the pulp will be used for white paper, it is bleached. At this point, the pulp is ready to be used in papermaking. Various grades of pulp can be made from softwood trees, such as southern pine; hardwood trees, such as oak; or from other sources that include recovered paper; rags; or agricultural products, such as cotton linters, kenaf, bagasse, or straw.

In the mid-1990s, there were approximately 189 U.S. wood pulp mills producing a variety of pulps, about 7 percent fewer than in the beginning of the century. Most of this pulp was used in integrated pulp and paper mills, which means that the pulp mill and the paper mill were owned by the same company and operated in many cases at the same location. There were numerous smaller paper mills, however, that were not connected with a pulp mill; they purchased "market pulp" on the open market from other pulp producers. Some companies produced only market pulp; other companies sold the excess pulp that could not be used by their paper machines.

INDUSTRY OUTLOOK

The U.S. pulp industry in the 1990s saw much price fluctuation. In the early to mid-1990s, the industry was affected by low pulp prices and high levels of spending required to meet environmental demands. By 1993, after factoring out inflation, the price of pulp was the lowest it had been in decades. However, in 1994, pulp prices began a meteoric rise, which saw prices double in less than two years. 1996 saw a steep fall in pulp prices. For the year, the average price for NBSK, a grade of pulp, was $591 per metric ton, falling from a high of $860 per metric ton in the first quarter of 1996, to a low of $500 per metric ton in the second quarter. Prices recovered to $600 per metric ton at the end of 1996.

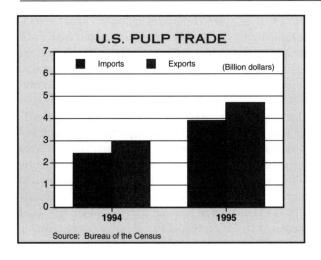

U.S. PULP TRADE

Imports   Exports   (Billion dollars)

Source: Bureau of the Census

WATER REGULATIONS

Environmental pressure on pulp mills continues in three areas: water regulations, recycling, and timber harvesting. The most recent wave of water regulations have been spurred by the desire to eliminate or reduce to nondetectable levels the toxic chemical dioxin, which was discovered in small amounts in pulp mill water-borne effluent in the mid-1980s. Despite the lack of hard evidence that dioxin in minute quantities poses a human health risk, the paper industry voluntarily spent more than $1 billion to reduce dioxin discharges by over 90 percent by the mid-1990s.

In 1993, the Environmental Protection Agency (EPA) proposed new regulations further restricting dioxin emissions by pulp mills, among other toxic chemicals. These regulations resulted from research the EPA had begun in the late 1980s, when it formed a "pulp and paper cluster group" to coordinate regulatory actions involving the industry.

The EPA's pulp and paper cluster group focused on two major rule making efforts. The first involved issuing revised effluent guidelines mandated by the Clean Water Act and required by a consent decree signed by the EPA after being sued by environmental groups over dioxin discharges from pulp mills. The second area involved defining maximum achievable control technology (MACT) emissions standards for pulp and paper mills, which was required under the Clean Air Act Amendments of 1990.

The Clean Air Act Amendments dramatically changed the allowable types and amounts of emissions. Based on emissions such as ozone, carbon monoxide, and particulates, regions of the United States can be classified as "nonattainment areas," and can be subject to severe restrictions.

While formulating new regulations, the EPA worked with the pulp industry through the "stakehold-

ers" process. This allowed the pulp industry to develop new testing and process treatment methods; introduce scientific data and research; and offer advice on the environmental, economic, and industrial impact of EPA's findings. Through this cooperation, standards regulating chemical oxygen demand (COD), biochemical oxygen demand (BOD), color, and adsorbable organic halides (AOX) were revamped and made less costly to the industry.

One controversy regarding pulp bleaching that arose in the early 1990s appeared to be resolved by the mid-1990s. Advocates of totally chlorine bleaching (TCF), in which no chlorine compounds are used to bleach pulp (including chlorine dioxide), argued that the process was environmentally superior to elemental chlorine free (ECF) bleaching, which uses chlorine dioxide. While this process has some following in Europe, only two pulp mills in the United States were producing TCF pulp in 1996.

RECYCLING

The second major environmental trend affecting the pulp industry is recycling. Public interest in paper recycling began to build in the late 1980s and peaked in the early 1990s. The push for recycling—primarily through federal and state legislation—continues and paper companies are now marketing a wide variety of new recycled grades.

Much of the impetus for recycling came from the government, and various local state and federal government rules still regulate the recycling process. Many of these laws specify precise levels of "postconsumer" content (paper that has been used and discarded by a consumer) and restrict the amount of "preconsumer" wastepaper that can be used.

Paper companies also face other recycling regulations, including: restrictions on products' use of "green labeling" claims; limits on permissible types of packaging; strict requirements on secondary fiber content; procurement preferences for certain kinds of recycled paper; and surcharges on paper products not meeting certain recycled standards.

Demand for recycled paper and recycling regulations are significant for pulp producers because they must manufacture the recycled pulp to be used in making the paper that meets the specifications. In the early to mid-1990s, the pulp and paper industry responded by building large numbers of recycled paper processing plants. However, while paper recycling is an important part of waste minimization, it should also be noted that recycling itself generates a considerable waste stream. In recycled newsprint pulp mills, for example, only 85 percent of incoming newsprint is usable as fiber. The rest is unusable sludge that must be cleaned out of the process and then burned or placed in landfills. In some recycled grades, sludge can be up to 50 percent of the incoming waste paper.

TIMBER HARVESTING

The third major environmental challenge facing pulp mills in the 1990s is timber harvesting, which is used to create lumber products as well as pulpwood. Access to pulpwood is vital for all virgin wood pulp mills, but that access has been severely restricted in some areas—most notably the Pacific Northwest. Court decisions in the early 1990s reduced harvesting drastically in many national forests and other federal areas in the Northwest. By 1996, small tracts of timber in the Northwest were being released for harvesting and special provisions allowed some "salvage" logging of timber damaged by fire and other natural phenomena. However, harvest rates still remained well below historic levels in the Pacific Northwest. The American Forest & Paper Association said that the unusually high number of U.S. forest fires in 1996 in that region was due to poor forest management of federal lands that left large amounts of underbrush, dead and dying trees, and unthinned strands of trees as highly flammable fuel. This situation led some pulp mills in the Northwest to close and others to seek raw materials from different sources, such as recycled paper and foreign wood chips. The long term effects are likely to permanently reduce tree harvesting and pulping in the Pacific Northwest, and pulp producers in foreign countries and the southern United States are likely to take up the lost volume.

Forest products companies and pulp and paper companies around the country still face pressure from environmental groups and government bodies to change their harvesting practices. Many groups want to eliminate clearcutting, which the industry argues is the most efficient harvesting method and is environmentally sustainable, provided that the clear cut is replanted. In the early to mid-1990s, the U.S. forest products industries—which include the pulp industry—planted more trees than they cut down. From the early 1980s to the early 1990s, forest growth exceeded the volume of trees cut or burned in forest fires. From the early 1970s to the early 1990s, the number of trees growing in the United States increased by 20 percent. Even in areas where the pulp and paper industry has access to virgin fiber, however, there is concern that in coming years there may be shortages of virgin fiber. That is one reason almost no new virgin pulp mills were being built in the United States during the mid-1990s. Pulp producers hope that by improving the growth rate of trees through genetic research, they will be able to increase the amount of wood grown on the same amount of land.

THE BUSINESS CYCLE

Aside from environmental challenges, in the early to mid-1990s, U.S. pulp mills experienced volatile swings between profits and losses. When demand began to increase again in early 1994, there was little excess capacity to supply the new demand. Pulp prices surged dramatically and quickly, reaching $910 per metric ton by the third quarter of 1995. Market pulp producers

SIC 2611 - Pulp Mills
General Statistics

Year	Companies	Establishments Total	Establishments with 20 or more employees	Employment Total (000)	Employment Production Workers (000)	Employment Hours (Mil)	Compensation Payroll ($ mil)	Compensation Wages ($/hr)	Production ($ million) Cost of Materials	Production ($ million) Value Added by Manufacture	Production ($ million) Value of Shipments	Production ($ million) Capital Invest.
1982	29	43	41	16.7	12.8	24.8	467.5	13.88	1,986.5	1,113.8	3,110.4	658.6
1983				16.9	12.9	25.9	508.7	14.55	2,003.8	1,239.4	3,261.4	915.7
1984				16.8	12.9	26.5	549.0	15.54	2,267.3	1,599.4	3,841.1	600.4
1985				16.3	12.4	25.5	555.4	16.20	2,095.0	1,133.1	3,228.0	745.0
1986				15.3	11.8	25.6	593.7	17.53	2,212.7	1,590.8	3,837.3	874.6
1987	26	39	38	14.2	11.0	23.9	535.1	16.60	2,019.4	2,281.4	4,313.7	231.2
1988				14.4	11.2	23.9	559.5	17.28	2,159.5	3,116.5	5,260.1	309.2
1989		46	38	15.2	11.7	25.4	602.6	17.43	2,547.5	3,938.6	6,416.1	696.8
1990				16.1	12.3	27.7	668.0	17.48	2,885.3	3,416.4	6,239.1	1,053.6
1991				16.8	12.8	27.6	697.3	18.36	2,889.6	2,446.2	5,329.4	990.9
1992	29	45	44	15.9	12.1	26.3	689.1	19.07	2,957.7	2,554.7	5,465.6	772.3
1993				14.2	10.8	23.1	627.1	19.49	2,487.8	1,711.1	4,282.1	426.0
1994				12.3	9.4	20.3	569.8	19.98	2,445.5	1,926.4	4,423.9	258.9
1995				14.0P	10.7P	24.0P	679.0P	20.36P	3,204.3P	2,524.1P	5,796.5P	556.5P
1996				13.7P	10.5P	23.8P	692.2P	20.82P	3,303.6P	2,602.3P	5,976.1P	542.2P
1997				13.5P	10.3P	23.6P	705.4P	21.27P	3,402.9P	2,680.5P	6,155.8P	527.9P
1998				13.3P	10.1P	23.5P	718.7P	21.72P	3,502.2P	2,758.8P	6,335.4P	513.7P

Sources: 1982, 1987, 1992 Economic Census; Annual Survey of Manufactures, 83-86, 88-91, 93-94. Establishment counts for non-Census years are from County Business Patterns; establishment values for 83-84 are extrapolations. 'P's show projections by the editors. Industries reclassified in 87 will not have data for prior years.

again enjoyed record profits, and speculation centered on pulp prices remaining high into the next century. However, much of the runup in pulp prices appeared to be caused by customers stocking up on inventory in anticipation of future price increases. When these customers stopped taking new shipments of pulp, prices dropped dramatically. Also, U.S. pulp producers were beginning, in the mid-1990s, to be affected by very large pulping capacity additions in Asia and South America. These trends appear to have made U.S. pulp producers very cautious about future capacity increases. Total U.S. wood pulp capacity—including market pulp and captive pulp—is slated to rise slightly from 62.4 million metric tons in 1995 to 64.1 million metric tons in 1999, an average annual growth rate of just 0.7 percent.

ORGANIZATION AND STRUCTURE

In most cases, pulp mills need to be located near their raw materials—trees or wastepaper—to minimize transportation costs. The United States has a very large growing stock of pulpwood in several areas: the Pacific Northwest, the upper Midwest, the Northeast, and the Southeast. This, combined with an efficient manufacturing base, makes the United States the low cost producer of many grades of pulp throughout the world. However, by the mid-1990s, this position was beginning to be challenged by a new generation of pulp mills, largely in South America and southeast Asia. These mills have access to fast-growing hardwood and softwood fiber, which dramatically reduces operating costs. This new capacity made the global pulp market very competitive, and increased the volatility of pulp prices.

While the pulping and papermaking processes are very energy intensive, the industry has become an efficient user of energy by burning its own waste byproducts, such as tree bark and spent chemicals from the pulping process. In the mid-1990s, the pulp and paper industry generated well over half of the energy needed to run its mills. From the early 1970s to the early 1990s, the industry reduced oil consumption by nearly 66 percent and natural gas consumption by 10 percent, while increasing production capacity by 60 percent.

Pulp mills and paper mills use a large amount of water from lakes, rivers, and in some cases oceans. They must reuse and/or clean all of this water before it is returned to the body of water from which it came. In the early years of the industry, pulp mills would discharge untreated waste (effluent) back into the receiving body of water. Beginning in the late 1960s, however, the industry began operating under strict regulations, which required primary, secondary, and in some cases tertiary

wastewater treatment. Mills also reuse a large portion of the water they used elsewhere in the pulping and papermaking process, and water that cannot be reused goes to large outdoor water treatment plants. The process of cleaning and reusing water is commonly called "closing the mill."

CAPTIVE PULP

The vast majority of pulp produced in the United States—about 85 percent in 1995—is considered "captive" because it is used in an integrated pulp and paper operation and is not sold on the open market. Market pulp sold on domestic and foreign markets accounted for the remaining 15 percent of total U.S. pulp production. While captive pulp accounts for the majority of pulp used in the United States, much more information and documentation is available for market pulp since it is bought and sold publicly.

While wood pulp production has been expanding in recent years, the percentage of virgin wood fiber used in paper and board production in the United States and other countries dropped from about 75 percent in 1970 to just 60 percent in 1997. This increased use of recovered paper has been driven partly by society's desire to reduce the amount of paper going to landfills, and partly by pulp producers realizing that virgin fiber will be increasingly hard to sustain in years to come.

North American paper producers have dramatically increased their use of recovered paper in recent years. The American Forest and Paper Association, the Washington, D.C.-based trade association that represents the paper industry, has a goal of recycling 50 percent of all paper produced by the year 2000. From 1997 to 1999, recovered paper consumption is expected to increase at an average rate of 2.9 percent, about twice the pace of paper and paperboard capacity growth during the same three-year period.

Virgin wood fiber also faces a challenge from the growing use of mineral coatings and inert fillers, mainly in printing and writing papers. Producers of these grades have completed a long-term shift from acid pulp to alkaline pulp. One reason for this shift is that paper produced from acid pulp becomes brittle and breaks up over time, while alkaline papers tend to last longer. The main reason, however, is that alkaline papermaking tends to be less expensive since it permits greater use of fillers, such as calcium carbonate, that replace a percentage of the wood fiber in the finished paper. In U.S. printing and writing papers, such as copy paper, the amount of filler can be 10 to 20 percent of the finished paper or higher. The cost of fillers is about one third that of wood pulp, so paper mills have a financial incentive to increase their use of fillers. Papermakers use filler not only to reduce the amount of wood fiber used, but also to increase the smoothness and opacity of their finished products.

While the percentage of wood pulp in finished paper products will continue to decline, the use of wood pulp will still grow—at least slightly—as the entire market for paper expands. Global production of wood pulp should grow about 2 percent per year for the next two decades worldwide. In the United States, wood pulp will probably grow more slowly since growth in recycled fiber will be strong. For example, U.S. wood pulp capacity is projected to rise just 0.5 percent per year between 1997 and 1999. However, foreign markets will likely absorb an increasing amount of U.S. market wood pulp.

CHEMICAL PULP

Within the overall market for wood pulp, the use of chemical pulp—mostly kraft pulp, which is produced using the sulfate process—is increasing. In 1995, chemical pulp accounted for 68.5 percent of all pulp produced throughout the world, up from 66 percent in 1970. This figure is expected to reach 70 percent in 1997. In the United States, chemical pulp accounts for an even higher percentage of wood pulp capacity—81.5 percent in 1995. Semichemical pulp accounted for about 6.2 percent and mechanical pulp for 9.9 percent in 1995, with other grades accounting for the remaining 2.4 percent.

As it has been for some time, kraft pulp was the primary product of the U.S. market wood pulp industry in the 1990s. In 1996, U.S. kraft market pulp mills had total capacity of 10.9 million tons. Market chemical pulp, with 1996 capacity of 9.69 million tons, accounted for 87 percent of that total, while market dissolving pulp, at 1.44 million tons, accounted for the remainder.

Overall, U.S. market wood pulp capacity was expected to remain flat through much of the 1990s. While some small fluctuations are expected, total market wood pulp capacity was expected to drop by 1 percent between 1995 and 1999, from 11.13 million tons to 11.01 million tons. The main reason for this decline is that major capacity increases are being concentrated in recovered paper market pulp, which is made from recycled paper. The capacity of U.S. recovered paper market pulp producers jumped from 959,000 tons in 1995 to 1.4 million tons in 1996, and is expected to reach 2.0 million tons by 1999.

The United States has almost 30 percent of the world's capacity to produce paper and paperboard and more than one-third of the world's capacity to produce wood pulp. As mentioned earlier, the majority of U.S. paper mills are integrated with captive pulp mills that do not sell pulp on the open market. Despite this fact, the United States is a major importer and exporter of market pulp. In the mid-1990s, the United States produced 9.0 million tons of market wood pulp, imported 3.75 million tons, and exported 5.79 million tons.

WORK FORCE

Total employment in the pulp, paper, and converting industries was about 619,000 in 1996. The level of employment declined during the early to mid-1990s despite large capacity increases. Employee wage increases remained at or below the inflation rate in the 1990s, averaging about 2.5 percent.

SIC 2611
Occupations Employed by SIC 261 - Pulp, Paper, and Paperboard Mills

Occupation	% of Total 1994	Change to 2005
Machine operators nec	11.9	13.8
Helpers, laborers, & material movers nec	7.6	-7.8
Blue collar worker supervisors	6.0	0.1
Paper goods machine setters & set-up operators	4.4	-26.2
Industrial machinery mechanics	3.8	1.4
Industrial truck & tractor operators	3.5	-7.8
Maintenance repairers, general utility	3.0	-7.8
Millwrights	2.9	-26.2
Crushing & mixing machine operators	2.7	-17.0
Cutting & slicing machine setters, operators	2.6	10.6
Inspectors, testers, & graders, precision	2.5	1.4
Electricians	2.2	-13.5
Extruding & forming machine workers	1.8	19.8
Machine feeders & offbearers	1.7	-17.0
Coating, painting, & spraying machine workers	1.4	-26.2
Secretaries, ex legal & medical	1.4	-16.1
Packaging & filling machine operators	1.4	-7.8
Plumbers, pipefitters, & steamfitters	1.3	-7.8
Freight, stock, & material movers, hand	1.2	-26.2
Chemical equipment controllers, operators	1.2	-26.2
Precision instrument repairers	1.1	19.9
Industrial production managers	1.1	-7.8
Boiler operators, low pressure	1.1	-7.8

Source: *Industry-Occupation Matrix*, Bureau of Labor Statistics. These data relate to one or more 3-digit SIC industry groups rather than to a single 4-digit SIC. The change reported for each occupation to the year 2005 is a percent of growth or decline as estimated by the Bureau of Labor Statistics. The abbreviation nec stands for 'not elsewhere classified'.

Like other manufacturing industries, the pulp and paper industry employs many unionized workers. However, the heaviest concentrations of union employees are in older mills, which were organized years ago. Almost all new pulp and paper mills are nonunion operations, including mills constructed by companies with unionized mills in other locations. In general, the wages and benefits provided by nonunion mills are comparable to unionized mills.

RESEARCH AND TECHNOLOGY

Pulping processes, both chemical and mechanical, are likely to see continued improvement in research and technology. Pulp mills will focus on higher energy recovery, which can then be used in other mill processes. This will be essential to the future profitability of many mills facing competition from mills with lower cost structures. Energy is already a major cost for the pulp and paper industry, which is one of the largest industrial users of electricity. Other areas of improvement include: the use of additives to speed up the chemical digesting process to increase fiber yields; new technical and environmental processes to reduce air and water pollution; and increased process control, monitoring, and automation. Similar measures to keep costs down and productivity high will be needed for the industry to remain competitive and expand its market share in world pulp consuming markets.

Widely regarded as impossible just a decade ago, the "closed mill" (which reuses or cleans all of its waste materials) appears to be feasible. The Institute of Paper Science and Technology has been directed by its member companies to increase its research efforts on how heat and contaminants build up in closed pulping and papermaking systems; where the optimum "purge" points are in the process; and how to deal with the increased metal corrosion in closed systems. Many industry experts consider the truly closed mill to be a decade or two away. However, others argue that this may not be practical, for it will be too costly to implement. They argue that the industry should focus on the "minimum impact mill," which while producing some effluent, does not harm the environment in any substantial way.

Another major research area affecting pulp mills is in high yield forestry. The industry needs to reduce the time it takes to produce a mature pulpwood tree from 28 years to about 7 or 8 years, so they can compete with pulpwood from countries such as Brazil, which can produce a mature pulpwood tree in seven years, and to reduce the amount of forestland used for harvesting trees. This will require major investment in plant biology and other high-tech genetic research. This area in particular will require more extensive networking between the pulp and paper companies, research institutions, and government agencies. One of the major research initiatives involving the pulp industry is Agenda 2020, a cooperative research project involving the U.S. Department of Energy (DOE), pulp and paper research institutions, and leading paper companies. Agenda 2020 was prepared by the chief technology officers of major paper companies under the auspices of the American Forest & Paper Association. It outlined six specific areas for research and development, including sustainable forest management; environmental performance; energy performance; capital effectiveness; recycling; and sensors and control.

AMERICA AND THE WORLD

Market pulp is a truly global commodity, with prices changing quickly in response to capacity changes, inventory levels, and purchase levels. While market pulp is produced in about 25 countries, more than two-thirds of world output comes from five northern countries: the United States, Canada, Sweden, Finland, and Norway. Global demand for woodpulp totaled nearly 160 million metric tons in 1995, about 5 million tons more than in 1994. Nonwood pulp demand was about 20 million metric tons in 1995. Of the total 180 million metric tons, about 30 million metric tons (17 percent) was shipped as market pulp.

Southern Hemisphere pulp producers expanded their operations extensively during the mid-1990s. New, technologically advanced market pulp mills were built in

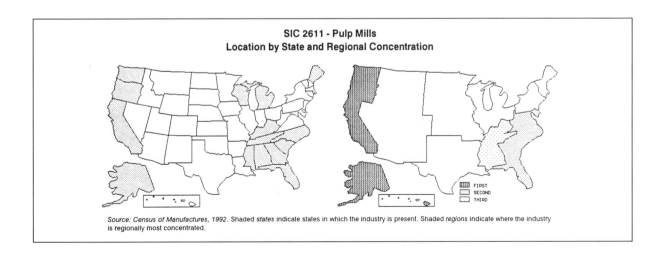

SIC 2611 - Pulp Mills
Location by State and Regional Concentration

FIRST
SECOND
THIRD

Source: Census of Manufactures, 1992. Shaded *states* indicate states in which the industry is present. Shaded *regions* indicate where the industry is regionally most concentrated.

China, Indonesia, Brazil, Chile, and Argentina. Some of these mills include North American pulp and paper companies as investors. One major advantage of mills in South America and southeast Asia is access to incredibly fast-growing pulpwood trees, which reach pulping maturity in about seven years or less, compared to 30 years. Other advantages of these new pulp mills include lower operating costs, lower labor costs, and less costly environmental regulation.

INCREASED FOREIGN DEMAND

In the early to mid-1990s, production in the U.S. wood pulp industry was relatively flat due to recessionary conditions in the early 1990s; flat or declining domestic markets; and growing use of secondary fiber. That situation was expected to continue from the mid- to late 1990s, with capacity expected to grow only 0.4 percent annually from 1995 to 1999. Market pulp shipments by U.S. producers increased from 8.4 million tons in 1994 to 9.0 million tons in 1995, but a decline in shipments of around 5 percent was estimated for 1996.

U.S. wood pulp exports are a relatively small but still significant portion of total U.S. wood pulp production. In 1995, the United States produced 65.8 million ton of wood pulp and exported 7.43 million tons (while importing 5.86 million tons). Chemical pulp was by far the leading grade of pulp exported by the United States in 1995, accounting for 7.25 million tons out of the total of 7.43 million tons. Groundwood and thermomechanical pulp accounted for the rest, with just 183,000 tons exported. Japan and South Korea have traditionally been the largest U.S. market pulp customers.

Despite producing and exporting large volumes of market pulp, the U.S. pulp and paper industry still imports a substantial amount. In 1995, the United States imported 5.97 million tons of wood pulp with a value of $3.7 billion. Canada has traditionally been the leading U.S. supplier, accounting for around 85 percent of the total in 1995.

REASONS TO IMPORT

While the U.S. has the capacity to supply all the pulp it needs for domestic paper production, it still imports pulp in order to exploit the different properties of foreign market pulp. The domestic market pulp industry is largely based on southern pine and hardwood, and many U.S. mills prefer the special properties of other grades, such as NBSK, produced in Canada, and eucalyptus pulp produced in countries such as Brazil. At the same time, a large number of foreign paper mills covet the southern pine and hardwood market pulp produced by U.S. pulp mills.

Despite sluggish growth and new foreign competition, the United States was expected to remain a strong global market pulp competitor throughout the 1990s. The combination of relatively low cost fiber resources, energy and water supplies, and improvement in product technology and operating conditions will likely allow the U.S. pulp industry to remain the leader among world producers. However, competition for sales in the United States and overseas will intensify as foreign pulp and paper producers in developing regions such as Latin America, Asia, and eastern Europe improve pulp quality and compete harder in major consuming markets in North America, Asia, and Europe. One major change in the global pulp market may be developing with the mid-1990s launch of various pulp futures markets, including the Helsinki Pulp Options Exchange and the OM Group's London Exchange. Futures markets may bring more price stability to the pulp market and even out some of the extreme price fluctuations that have plagued the global market pulp industry.

ASSOCIATIONS AND SOCIETIES

AMERICAN PULPWOOD ASSOCIATION
1025 Vermont Ave. NW, Ste. 1020
Washington, DC 20005
Phone: (202) 347-2900
Fax: (202) 783-2685

NATIONAL PAPER TRADE ASSOCIATION
c/o John J. Buckley, 111 Great Neck Rd.
Great Neck, NY 11021
Phone: (516) 829-3070
Fax: (516) 829-3074

PAPER INDUSTRY MANAGEMENT ASSOCIATION
1699 Wall St. Ste. 212
Mount Prospect, IL 60056-5782
Phone: (708) 956-0250
Fax: (708) 956-0520

TAPPI
Technology Park/Atlanta
PO Box 105113
Atlanta, GA 30348-5113
Phone: (800) 332-8686 or (404) 446-1400
Fax: (404) 446-6947

PERIODICALS AND NEWSLETTERS

AMERICAN PAPERMAKER
ASM Communications, Inc.
57 Executive Park S., Ste. 310
Atlanta, GA 30329
Phone: (404) 325-9153

PAPER AGE
Global Publications
77 Waldron Ave.
GlenRock, NJ 07452-2830
Phone: (201) 666-2262
Fax: (201) 666-9046
Monthly. $20.00 per year.

PULP AND PAPER
Miller Freeman, Inc.
600 Harrison St.
San Francisco, CA 94107
Phone: (800) 444-4881 or (800) 227-4675
Fax: (913) 841-2624
Monthly. Free to qualified personnel; others, $100.00 per year.

PULP AND PAPER WEEK
Miller Freeman, Inc.
600 Harrison St.
San Francisco, CA 94107
Phone: (800) 444-4881 or (800) 227-4675
Fax: (913) 841-2624
Weekly. $637.00 per year. Newsletter.

RECYCLED PAPER NEWS
CERMA, Inc.
5528 Hempstead Way
Springfield, VA 22151
Phone: (703) 750-1158

TAPPI JOURNAL
Technical Association of the Pulp and Paper Industry, Inc.
Technology Park-Atlanta
PO Box 105113
Atlanta, GA 30348
Phone: (404) 446-1400
Fax: (404) 446-6947
Monthly. Membership.

DATABASES

CITIBASE (CITICORP ECONOMIC DATABASE)
FAME Software Corp.
77 Water St., 9 Fl.
New York, NY 10005
Phone: (212) 898-7800
Fax: (212) 742-8956
Presents over 6,000 statistical series relating to business, industry, finance, and economics. Includes series from Survey of Current Business *and many other sources. Time period is 1947 to date, with daily updates. Inquire as to online cost and availability.*

PAPERCHEM DATABASE
Information Services Div.
Institute of Paper Science and Technology
500 10th St. NW
Atlanta, GA 30318
Phone: (404) 853-9500
Fax: (404) 853-9510
Worldwide coverage of the scientific and technical paper industry chemical literature, including patents, 1967 to present. Monthly updates. Inquire as to online cost and availability.

PIRA
Technical Centre for the Paper and Board, Printing and Packaging Industries
Randalls Rd.
Leatherhead, Surrey, England KT22 7RU
Phone: 1372- 376161
Fax: 1372- 360104
Citations and abstracts pertaining to bookbinding and other pulp, paper, and packaging industries, 1975 to present. Inquire as to online cost and availability.

PREDICASTS FORECASTS: U.S.
Information Access Co.
362 Lakeside Dr.
Foster City, CA 94404
Phone: (800) 321-6388 or (415) 378-5000
Fax: (415) 358-4759
Provides numeric abstracts of a wide range of published forecasts relating to specific U.S. products, markets, and industries. Monthly updates. Time period is 1971 to date. Inquire as to online cost and availability.

U.S. TIME SERIES
Information Access Co.
362 Lakeside Dr.
Foster City, CA 94404
Phone: (800) 321-6388 or (415) 358-4643
Fax: (415) 358-4759
Contains annual time series of historical data. Online version of Predicasts Basebook. *Broad coverage of data from private and government sources on U.S. economy, products and industries. Some time series start as early as 1957. Inquire as to online cost and availability.*

STATISTICS SOURCES

ENCYCLOPEDIA OF AMERICAN INDUSTRIES
Gale Research
835 Penobscot Bldg.
Detroit, MI 48226-4094
Phone: (800) 877-GALE or (313) 961-2242
Fax: (800) 414-5043
1994. $500.00. Two volumes ($250.00 each). Volume one is Manufacturing Industries *and volume two is* Service and Non-Manufacturing Industries. *Provides the history, development, and recent status of approximately 1,000 industries. Includes statistical graphs, with industry and general indexes.*

PREDICASTS BASEBOOK
Information Access Co.
362 Lakeside Dr.,
Foster City, CA 94404
Phone: (800) 321-6388 or (415) 358-4643
Fax: (415) 358-4759
Annual. $700. Provides industry, product, service, economic, demographic, and financial statistics for the United States. Arranged according to Standard Industrial Classification (SIC) numbers, with 14 years of data (where available) and annual growth rate given for each of the 35,000 series. Sources are over 350 statistical publications issued mainly by government agencies and trade associations.

THE PULP AND PAPER INDUSTRY IN THE OECD MEMBER COUNTRIES

Organization for Economic Cooperation and Development
Available from OECD Publications and Information Center
2001 L St. NW, Ste. 700
Washington, DC 20036-4910
Phone: (202) 785-6323
Fax: (202) 785-0350
Annual. Presents annual data on production, consumption, capacity, utilization, and foreign trade. Covers 33 pulp and paper products in the 24 OECD countries.

STATISTICS OF PAPER, PAPERBOARD AND WOOD PULP

Forest and Paper Association
1111 19th St. NW
Washington, DC 20036
Phone: (202) 463-2700
Fax: (202) 463-2785
Annual. $365.00. Formerly Statistics of Paper and Paperboard.

SURVEY OF CURRENT BUSINESS

Available from U.S. Government Printing Office
Washington, DC 20402

Phone: (202) 512-1800
Fax: (202) 512-2250
Monthly. $41.00 per year. Issued by Bureau of Economic Analysis, U.S. Department of Commerce. Presents a wide variety of business and economic data.

FURTHER READING

''Market Pulp: Is There a Cure for Volatility?'' *PIMA's International Papermaker,* February 1997.

''Market Pulp: Recent Collapse, Still Uncertain Demand Challenges Efforts to Return to Upcycle.'' *Pulp & Paper,* August 1996.

Paper, Paperboard, Pulp Capacity and Fiber Consumption. Washington: American Forest & Paper Association, 1996.

''U.S. Paper Industry Will See More Globalization, Slower Growth in 1997.'' *Pulp & Paper,* January 1997.

U.S. Trade and Industrial Outlook, 1997-1998. New York: McGraw-Hill, 1997.

As the television broadcasting industry prepared to enter the twenty-first century, it faced a staggering number of challenges brought on by new competition, regulatory changes, and technological developments. Broadcasters had to contend with their established rival, cable television, as well as with the new Fox, Paramount, and Warner Brothers ''netlets,'' and newcomers from the telephone, satellite broadcast, and computer industries. New federal rules regarding ownership, programming content, and digital transmission also served to reshape the competitive landscape. Among the long-established networks—ABC, CBS, and NBC—the struggle for the top ratings position was intensified as 2 of the 3 acquired new owners. In 1995, ABC was purchased by The Walt Disney Co. and CBS was purchased by Westinghouse.

In this frenetic atmosphere, the once-bleak outlook of the networks in the early 1990s improved considerably. Although they continued to see a drop in audience share from the previous decade, the networks still held a strong position in prime-time ratings and saw increased advertising revenues. Beginning in 1995, the major networks gained new syndication revenues resulting from a relaxation of federal regulations. They also began creating their own cable networks, such as ESPN2 and MSNBC, using their considerable production resources. Furthermore, viewing audiences made it clear that they do not want cable television service that does not include local broadcast network affiliates. Thus, the networks became increasingly concerned with production and programming, as they created a strong role for themselves in the growing system of television delivery and services. Writing for *Time,* Richard Zoglin commented, ''If the network business is thriving, it is as a radically different sort of business. The line between distributors (the networks) and suppliers (outside producers) is being blurred. The networks, given the chance to produce and own their own shows, are acting more like studios, while the studios, afraid of being squeezed out, are trying to become networks.''

Radio broadcasting, too, is thriving. In 1995, there were 12,001 radio stations in the United States. Of these, 4,906 were commercial AM stations, 5,285 were commercial FM stations, and 1,810 were noncommercial FM stations. The improving health of the industry is indicated by an 11 percent growth in advertising for 1994, for a total of $10.7 billion, the fastest growth spurt since the mid-1980s. As Standard & Poor's noted in their 1996 *Industry Surveys,* ''The success of radio, a technology born decades before the transistor may seem paradoxical in the age of computers. According to the [Radio Advertising Bureau], 99 of every 100 households has a radio

RADIO AND TELEVISION BROADCASTING STATIONS

SIC 4830

Though the early 1990s projected nothing but bleak returns within the television industry, the major studios established several major in-roads to increasing their profitability and stand poised to enjoy strong performance throughout the remaining 1990s. The radio industry's performance will be more consistent, maintaining its presence (99 of every 100 households has a radio) and financial health (11 percent advertising growth in the mid-1990s).

Top 10 **MOST POPULAR TV AND RADIO STATION GROUPS**

Ranked by: Radio division's estimated gross revenue for 1995.

1. Westinghouse/CBS, with $509,300,000
2. Infinity Broadcasting Corp., $361,000,000
3. Capital Cities/ABC/Disney, $273,300,000
4. Evergreen Media/Pyramid, $265,200,000
5. Chancellor Broadcasting/Shamrock, $185,200,000
6. Cox Broadcasting, $145,900,000
7. Clear Channel Communications, $136,600,000
8. Citicasters/OmniAmerica, $135,000,000
9. Jacor Communications, $130,000,000
10. American Radio Systems, $122,400,000

Source: *Broadcasting & Cable*, September 18, 1995, p. 37.

and the average number of radios per household is 5.6 . . . the typical listener tunes in for 3 hours and 20 minutes on average each day.''

INDUSTRY OUTLOOK

Myriad issues have continued to unfold across the broad range of communications and information industries. While cable companies were once the competitive focus of television broadcasters, they have faced a far greater number of challenges and demands. In addition to the expanding reach of the computer-based information superhighway and its attendant technological impact on other media, the networks and netlets face stiff competition from film studios, cable companies, telephone companies, computer companies, consumer-electronics companies, and publishers.

COMPETITION

In 1995, cable systems actually experienced a drop in subscribers and reached about 65 percent of television homes. Subscribers balked at price hikes that followed rate deregulation and some opted for satellite television services. The *Los Angeles Times* predicted that the number of television households with satellite service would jump from the 1996 rate of 4 percent to 20 percent in the year 2000. In order to give broadcasters the chance to compete against pay television services and the netlets, the Federal Communications Commission (FCC) agreed to gradually lift a ban on the syndication of network programming. Previously, networks were wholly dependent on advertisers for their revenue and only had access to the airwaves by permission of the government, while

cable companies could charge subscribers as well as advertisers. In 1993, the networks gained rights to profit from re-runs of prime-time shows. This triumph for the networks affected the outside producers that made and financed much of the prime-time programming. Permitted to undertake a greater proportion of in-house production of prime-time programming, the networks could now negotiate for more financially rewarding deals with outside producers. By 1995, all such restrictions on network ownership of programming and on their right to syndicate programs were lifted.

Moreover, industry analysts note several strengths that advertiser-supported broadcast television still has over its competitors in the pay television industry. As *Time* stated in 1993, ''Advertisers will still crave network television's unique ability to reach a critical mass of consumers at one swoop.'' The 1996 *Standard and Poor's Industry Surveys* confirmed that broadcast television advertising remained strong, with 9 percent growth expected in 1995, and predicted that prime-time ad sales would increase by 30 percent for the 1995/96 season. Standard & Poor's also noted that more advertisers are spending money on television programming, in the tradition of Procter & Gamble Co.'s backing of daytime soap operas *The Guiding Light, Another World,* and *As the World Turns.* For example, the Paramount Television Group made a deal with a consortium of advertisers called Television Production Partners in March 1995 to produce movies, specials, and limited series. The backers, including companies such as Reebok International Ltd., General Motors Corp., and AT&T, agreed to spend some $130 million on the projects.

NETWORKS WAR WITH NIELSEN

With an eye on advertising revenues, the networks found fault with Nielsen Media Research, the company that has long provided the broadcasters and advertisers with viewership ratings. Changes in Nielsen methodology coincided with a reported decline in NFL football ratings, which caused both NBC and Fox to question their validity. CBS also complained about the accuracy of ratings for the CBS Evening News. The networks were concerned that Nielsen's new methods of selecting participants and an increased sample size were skewing the resulting ratings. In December 1996, Fox, CBS, NBC, and ABC, joined ranks to criticize the research company by placing ads in media and advertising trade publications that denounced Nielsen's claims of reliability. As *Broadcasting and Cable* reported, the ads read ''Our confidence in Nielsen is DOWN'' and ''There is a growing disparity between local overnight ratings and national ratings.'' At the same time, the FCC was asked to investigate Nielsen's services.

THE PROGRAMMING CONTENT DEBATE

Another issue that the networks and the cable television industries faced was that of violent programming content. Under pressure from the federal government, CBS, ABC, NBC, and Fox all agreed to place parental advisory labels on violent programming—in order to avoid having a system imposed upon them. The group unveiled its age-based ratings system that is similar to that of the movie industry in December 1996, which labels programs (with the exception of news) with one of six categories ranging from children's programming to shows for mature audiences: TV-Y, TV-Y7, TV-G, TV-PG, TV-14, and TVM. Viewers see the appropriate icon in the upper left corner of the television screen at the beginning of the program and, if the program exceeds one hour in length, at the beginning of subsequent hours. At the same time, the federal government was proceeding with plans to give parents the ability to black out violent programming with a device called the V-chip. Mandated by the White House and Congress in 1996, television manufacturers were waiting for FCC specifications before adding the chip to new television models and designing V-chip converter boxes.

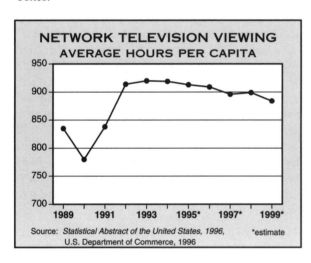

NETWORK TELEVISION VIEWING
AVERAGE HOURS PER CAPITA

Source: *Statistical Abstract of the United States, 1996,*
U.S. Department of Commerce, 1996   *estimate

DIGITAL TELEVISION

At the close of 1996, the industry moved one step closer to digital transmission of television signals, as the FCC selected a DTV standard. The "Grand Alliance Standard" was adopted, minus specifications regarding picture formats on which the broadcast, computer, and film industries could not agree. Video compression, sound delivery, and transmission of signals were part of the specifications. The commission still needed to determine how long broadcasters could use existing analog channels, how digital channels would be assigned, and if high-definition programming would be required.

In the radio industry, the most dramatic impact was felt after the Telecommunications Act of 1996 . The largest radio corporations, which had grown in profit and size during the 1980s by acquiring additional stations, were given the opportunity to expand even further, thanks to looser ownership guidelines. The resulting consolidation of station ownership among a relative handful of large companies was characterized as "The modern version of the Oklahoma land rush," by the *Pittsburgh Post Gazette.* Broadcast companies quickly sought to achieve a concentration of stations in single major markets. This boon to large companies meant the prospect of hard times for small owners and for radio station employees. The *Minneapolis Star and Tribune* reported an estimated 30 percent employment cut in the industry, on a national basis. Listeners, however, were expected to benefit, as "The remaining fewer owners will be freer to try new niches . . . . an owner of multiple stations will not want his or her own stations to compete with each other."

During the year following deregulation, the size of the growing companies was tested at the urging of advertising executives. Concerned that concentrated ownership would increase the cost of radioadvertising, the American Association of Advertising Agencies expressed concerns to FCC regulators. Subsequently, the U.S. Department of Justice began to look at the new, larger radio groups for antitrust offenses. For the first time, radio broadcasting companies were reaching proportions that required a merger review by the Federal Trade Commission. Local marketing agreements (LMAs), which allow a buyer to run a station prior to FCC licensing approval, were scrutinized. When Westinghouse Electric Company was in the process of buying Infinity Broadcasting in 1996—for $3.9 billion—it served as a test case on the issue. The Justice Department ruled that broadcasting companies would be limited to a 40 percent share of any given market. In this instance, Westinghouse was forced to divest itself of two radio stations in Boston and Philadelphia.

ORGANIZATION AND STRUCTURE

The networks include in their stables both network-owned stations, which are often flagship stations in major media markets, and affiliated stations, independently owned stations that have contractual agreements with a network to broadcast its line of programming. *Variety* noted in December of 1996 that the merger of Westinghouse with CBS "had no greater impact than on the station side, where both companies had established strong station businesses long before their teaming." At the same time, the acquisition of New World Communications by Fox Televisions Stations Group contributed to the radical changes that took place among station holdings. Fox vaulted from being a medium-sized group to the largest operation in 1996, with 22 stations (including channels in New York, Los Angeles, Chicago, and Philadelphia) and 35 percent penetration of U.S. television households. CBS followed with 14 network-owned stations (including stations in New York, Los Angeles, Chicago, and Philadelphia), reaching 32 percent of all American homes. NBC ranked third with 11 stations (including channels in New York, Chicago, Los Angeles, and Washington, D.C.) and 25 percent penetration. ABC, which had led the industry in 1992, ranked fourth with 10 network-owned stations (including stations in New York, Los Angeles, Chicago, and Philadelphia) and 24 percent penetrationin the late 1990s. Running a close fifth was Tribune Broadcasting with 10 stations and 22 percent penetration.

The shakeup in station ownership started in May 1994, when Fox lured 12 stations affiliated with the other networks, including several in major markets, to its side. This affiliation switch, the biggest in television history, signaled a significant change in the balance of power between the networks and individual television stations. Dennis FitzSimons, president of Tribune Television, noted in *Business Week* that the deal highlighted the importance of distribution of programming—something that has been ignored recently. Furthermore, it gives the control back to the stations. Fox's success in these matters subsequently inspired the creation of additional netlets, the United Paramount Network and the Warner Brothers (WB) Television Network. It is important to note, however, that these three entities do not fit the FCC definition of "network" and have been dubbed "netlets" by the industry.

The radio station industry is divided into two basic groups, commercial and noncommercial stations. Commercial stations earn their revenues from advertisers who pay for radio advertising time based on listener ratings. Noncommercial stations (also called "educational" or "public" stations) earn revenues from public subscriptions or, in the cases of colleges and religious stations, from the institutions they represent.

Network programs, mainly news, are transmitted to many more radio stations than are owned by the network. Similarly, outside programming, such as pop music's Top 40 countdowns, are produced within the entertainment industry and sold on tape to stations throughout the country.

Many of the large radio stations hire media research firms to better understand listener tastes. Small radio stations conduct these services exclusively in-house.

The differences between large and small stations are also revealed by their internal organization. Large stations have additional station management and employ promotion and public affairs directors.

RESEARCH AND TECHNOLOGY

Satellite transmission and Internet broadcasting—known as "netcasting"—promised to radically change the radio industry in the late 1990s. Broadcasters awaited the formulation of FCC guidelines that would give them the ability to market services akin to that of cable television. Subscription satellite radio would deliver improved sound over AM and FM bands through digital audio broadcasting (DAB), providing CD quality. The creation of such stations was seen as part of a trend that gave large broadcasters increased control of radio. Small stations—especially rural operations—were threatened by the prospect of satellite radio. AM and FM stations were expected to compete by providing digital broadcasting within their bands.

A less pressing but inevitable source of competition was developing on the Internet. Netcasting of radio programming hampered technological obstacles that reduced the quality of its sound, but showed a potential to provide listeners with unprecedented options. As Cameron Crotty noted in *Macworld,* "Even with audio that sounds like an AM radio submerged in olive oil and video that's limited to a few tiny frames per second, netcasting's essentially worldwide reach and on-demand content offer experiences that aren't available anywhere else." Fledgling netcasting sites on the World Wide Web included the Baltimore Orioles' baseball broadcasts, National Public Radio, and the ABC radio network.

AMERICA AND THE WORLD

Since radio frequencies operate at low- and medium-levels, there has not been an international market for radio stations in the strict sense. However, high-frequency bands are allocated for broadcast between nations through the U.S. Information Agency. Most of these stations are Voice of America (VOA), Radio Free Europe, and Radio Liberty, which broadcast mostly in foreign languages and are not regulated by the FCC.

For over 40 years, these services have been government owned, but in the early 1990s, a presidential task force suggested privatization on the premise that pro-Western ideals were not needed in the newly democratized eastern Europe. The VOA Europe responded by airing English-language popular music and selling advertising time. Such formats were expected to be successful, especially in eastern Europe, where there was a strong interest in American culture and in learning English; moreover, at this time many new radio stations in Eastern Europe were run on small budgets, where the use of prerecorded popular programs had a market. In 1996, Voice of America broadcasts expanded to Tuzla, Bosnia-Herzegovina, while U.S. troops participated in peacekeeping efforts in that country. That same year, the Asia Pacific Network was also created, having been mandated by the U.S. International Broadcasting Act of 1994 . The act prescribed a "new broadcasting service to the people of the People's Republic of China and other countries of Asia, which lack adequate sources of free information and ideas, [which] would enhance the promotion of information and ideas, while advancing the goals of United Sates foreign policy."

ASSOCIATIONS AND SOCIETIES

ACADEMY OF TELEVISION ARTS AND SCIENCES
5220 Lankershim Blvd.
North Hollywood, CA 91601
Phone: (818) 754-2800
Fax: (818) 761-2827

ALLIANCE OF MOTION PICTURE AND TELEVISION PRODUCERS
15503 Ventura Blvd.
Sherman Oaks, CA 91436-3140
Phone: (818) 995-3600
Fax: (818) 382-1793

AMERICAN SPORTSCASTERS ASSOCIATION
5 Beekman St., Ste. 814
New York, NY 10038
Phone: (212) 227-8080
Fax: (212) 571-0556
Members are radio and television sportscasters.

ASSOCIATION OF AMERICA'S PUBLIC TELEVISED STATIONS
1350 Connecticut Ave. NW, Ste. 200
Washington, DC 20036
Phone: (202) 887-1700
Fax: (202) 293-2422
The Association maintains a world wide web site at http:// www.universe.digex. net:80/~apts

BROADCAST EDUCATION ASSOCIATION
1771 N St. NW
Washington, DC 20036-2891
Phone: (202) 429-5355

NATIONAL ASSOCIATION OF BROADCASTERS
1771 N M St. NW
Washington, DC 20036
Phone: (202) 429-5300
Fax: (202) 429-5343

SOCIETY OF BROADCAST ENGINEERS
8445 Keystone Crossing, Ste. 140
Indianapolis, IN 46240
Phone: (317) 253-1640
Fax: (317) 253-0418

STATION REPRESENTATIVES ASSOCIATION
230 Park Ave.
New York, NY 10169
Phone: (212) 687-2484
Fax: (212) 972-4372
Members are sales representatives concerned with the sale of radio and television "spot" advertising.

PERIODICALS AND NEWSLETTERS

BROADCAST ENGINEERING: JOURNAL OF BROADCAST TECHNOLOGY
Intertec Publishing Corp.
9800 Metcalf Ave.
Overland Park, KS 66212-2215
Phone: (800) 654-6776 or (913) 341-1300
Fax: (913) 967-1898
Monthly. Free to qualified personnel; others, $50.00 per year. Technical magazine for the broadcast industry.

BROADCAST INVESTOR: NEWSLETTER ON RADIO-TV STATION FINANCE
Paul Kagan Associates, Inc.
126 Clock Tower Pl.
Carmel, CA 93923
Phone: (408) 624-1536
Fax: (408) 625-3225
Monthly. $695.00 per year. Newsletter for investors in publicly held radio and television broadcasting companies.

BROADCASTING & CABLE
Cahners Publishing Co.
Entertainment Division
1750 DeSales St. NW
Washington, DC 20036
Phone: (800) 554-5729 or (202) 659-2340
Fax: (202) 429-0651
Weekly. $99.00 per year. Formerly Broadcasting.

JOURNAL OF BROADCASTING AND ELECTRONIC MEDIA
Broadcast Education Association
1771 N St. NW
Washington, DC 20036-2891
Phone: (202) 429-5355
Quarterly. $75.00 per year. Scholarly articles about developments, trends and research.

RADIO WORLD
IMAS Publishing
5827 Columbia Pke., 3 Fl.
Falls Church, VA 22041
Phone: (703) 998-7600
Fax: (703) 998-2966
Biweekly. Price on application. Emphasis is on radio broadcast engineering and equipment.

TELEVISION BROADCAST
Miller Freeman PSN, Inc.
2 Park Ave., 18 Fl.
New York, NY 10016
Phone: (212) 213-3444
Fax: (212) 213-3484
Monthly. Free to qualified personnel; others, $38.00 per year.

TELEVISION DIGEST WITH CONSUMER ELECTRONICS
Warren Publishing, Inc.
2115 Ward Court NW
Washington, DC 20037
Phone: (202) 872-9200
Fax: (202) 293-3435
Weekly. $848.00 per year. Newsletter featuring new consumer entertainment products utilizing electronics. Also covers the television broadcasting and cable TV industries, with corporate and industry news.

TELEVISION QUARTERLY
National Academy of Television Arts and Sciences
c/o Ed Eberung
111 W 57th St., Ste. 1020
New York, NY 10019
Phone: (212) 586-8424
Fax: (212) 246-8129
Quarterly. $30.00 per year.

TUNED IN: RADIO WORLD'S MANAGEMENT MAGAZINE
IMAS Publishing
5827 Columbia Pke., 3 Fl.
Falls Church, VA 22041
Phone: (703) 998-7600
Fax: (703) 998-2966
Monthly. Price on application. Edited for radio broadcasting managers and producers, with an emphasis on marketing.

TV TECHNOLOGY
Industrial Marketing Advisory Services, Inc.
5827 Columbia Pke., Ste. 310
Falls Church, VA 22041
Phone: (703) 998-7600
Fax: (703) 998-2966
14 times a year. $18.00 per year.

DATABASES

GALE DATABASE OF PUBLICATIONS AND BROADCAST MEDIA
Gale Research
835 Penobscot Bldg.
Detroit, MI 48226-4094

Phone: (800) 877-GALE or (313) 961-2242
Fax: (313) 961-6083
An online directory containing detailed information on over 67,000 periodicals, newspapers, broadcast stations, cable systems, directories, and newsletters. Corresponds to the following print sources: Gale Directory of Publications and Broadcast Media; Directories in Print; City and State Directories in Print; Newsletters in Print. *Semiannual updates. Inquire as to online cost and availability.*

HOME PAGE OF THE CORPORATION FOR PUBLIC BROADCASTING
Center for Public Broadcasting
Information by and about the Corporation for Public Broadcasting, including its annual report, other publications, grants for local PBS stations, and job openings. Fees: Free. URL: http:// www.cpb.org.

PBS ONLINE
Public Broadcasting Service
Contains a wide variety of information and services for both the public broadcasting community and the consumer. URL: http:// www.pbs.org/.

TV LINK: FILM & TELEVISION WEBSITE ARCHIVE
Neoglyphics Media Corp.
Links to the world wide web sites of more than 100 TV shows, motion picture studios, professional and commercial organizations, broadcast schedules, TV networks and broadcasters, newsgroups, film festivals, and related sites around the world. This site is a resource for both industry professionals and audiences.

STATISTICAL SOURCES

CIRCULATION [YEAR]
SRDS
1700 Higgins Rd.
Des Plaines, IL 60018
Phone: (800) 851-7737 or (847) 375-5000
Fax: (847) 375-5001
Annual. $165.00. Contains detailed statistical analysis of newspaper circulation by metropolitan area or county and data on television viewing by area. Includes maps.

KAGAN MEDIA INDEX
Paul Kagan Associates, Inc.
126 Clock Tower Pl.
Carmel, CA 93923
Phone: (408) 624-1536
Fax: (408) 625-3225
Monthly. $475.00 per year. Provides electronic and entertainment media industry statistics. Includes television, radio, motion pictures, and home video.

STATISTICAL TRENDS IN BROADCASTING
John Blair and Co.
1290 Avenue of the Americas
New York, NY 10104
Phone: (212) 603-5000
Annual.

TELEVISION AND CABLE FACTBOOK

Warren Publishing, Inc.
2115 Ward Court NW
Washington, DC 20037
Phone: (202) 872-9200
Fax: (202) 293-3435
Annual. $425.00. Three volumes. Commercial and noncommercial television stations and networks.

T.V. BROADCAST DATA BASE

Federal Communications Commission
National Technical Information Service
5285 Port Royal Rd.
Springfield, VA 22161
Phone: (800) 553-6847 or (703) 487-4600
Fax: (703) 321-8547
Monthly. $360.00 per year.

UNITED STATES CENSUS OF SERVICE INDUSTRIES

U.S. Bureau of the Census
Washington, DC 20233-0800
Phone: (301) 457-4100
Fax: (301) 457-3842
Quinquennial. Various reports available.

Phone: (800) 877-GALE or (313) 961-2242
Fax: (313) 961-6083
Annual. $315.00. Three Volumes. A guide to publications and broadcasting stations in the U.S. and Canada, including newspapers, magazines, journals, radio stations, and cable systems. Geographic arrangement. Volume three consists of statistical tables, maps, subject indexes, and title index. Formerly Ayer Directory of Publications.

PERSPECTIVES ON RADIO AND TELEVISION: TELECOMMUNICATION IN THE UNITED STATES

F. Leslie Smith
HarperCollins College
10 E. 53rd St.
New York, NY 10022-5299
Phone: (800) 242-7737 or (212) 207-7000
1990. $43.25. Third edition.

RADIO PROGRAMMING PROFILE

B/F Communication Services, Inc.
66 Chesnut Ln.
Woodbury, NY 11797
Phone: (516) 364-2593
Three times a year. $295.00 per volume. Two volumes. Lists about 3,000 AM and Fm radio stations in top 200 markets.

GENERAL WORKS

BROADCASTING & CABLE YEARBOOK

R.R. Bowker
121 Chanlon Rd.
New Providence, NJ 07974
Phone: (800) 521-8110 or (908) 464-6800
Fax: (908) 665-6688
Annual. $159.95. Two volumes. Published in conjunction with Broadcasting *magazine. Provides information on U.S. and Canadian TV stations, radio stations, cable TV companies, and radio-TV services of various kinds.*

GALE DIRECTORY OF PUBLICATIONS AND BROADCAST MEDIA

Gale Research
835 Penobscot Bldg.
Detroit, MI 48226-4094

FURTHER READING

Herndon, John. ''Radio May Be the Next Domain for 'Superstation' Concept.'' *Austin American-Statesman,* 16 May 1996.

Hofmeister, Sallie. ''Westinghouse/CBS to Launch First Cable Channel.'' *Los Angeles Times,* 21 August 1996.

McClellan, Steve. ''Combined Nets Take Aim at Nielsen.'' *Broadcasting & Cable,* 30 December 1996.

McConnell, Chris. ''Advertisers Raise Red Flag Over Supergroups.'' *Broadcasting & Cable,* 19 July 1996.

Schneider, Michael. ''Nielsen, Networks Ratings War Mounts.'' *Electronic Media,* 16 December 1996.

Standard & Poor's Industry Surveys. Vol. 2. New York: Standard & Poor's, 1996.

81

RAILROAD TRANSPOR- TATION

SIC 4000

With *significant time and money being dedicated to technological advances, increasing efficiency and decreasing the work force, the top railroad companies will continue to dominate the industry. In the mid-1990s, the 11 largest companies accounted for 91 percent of freight revenue. But the increased profitability of the 1990s could be stalled by merger difficulties, potential re-regulation in railroad switching and terminal establishments, and a mid-1990s dip in the intermodal system of freight transportation. A dependency on the economic status of industries utilizing railroad transport, including coal, steel, and construction, could also contribute to any industry-wide fluctuation.*

Line-haul is defined as "the movement of freight between terminals." More generally, line-haul railroads are those that transport passengers or freight long distances on a network of tracks that disperse goods and passengers across the United States. Railroad switching and terminal establishments are primarily engaged in the furnishing of terminal facilities for these railroads, and in the movement of railroad cars between terminal yards, industrial sidings, and other local sites. Terminal companies do not necessarily operate any vehicles themselves, but may operate the stations and terminals.

In the mid-1990s, there were 541 railroad companies operating in the United States, generating $34.34 billion in operating revenues. Most of that business ($31.4 billion) was handled by Class 1 railroads, defined as those railroads with revenues of more than $95 million. The top 11 Class 1 railroads comprised only 2 percent of the railroad traffic in the United States, yet they accounted for 73 percent of the industry's mileage, 89 percent of its employees, and 91 percent of its freight revenues. Over 1.192 million cars and approximately 18,500 locomotives were operated between them. In the mid-1990s these top rail companies delivered over 1.2 trillion tons of cargo per day, with most of the volume in coal, grain, chemicals, and vehicles.

Top 10 MOST PRODUCTIVE RAILROADS IN THE U.S.

Ranked by: Operating revenue, in billions of dollars.

1. Burlington Northern Santa Fe, with $7.67 billion
2. Union Pacific Railroad, $6.07
3. CSX, $4.62
4. Norfolk Southern, $3.92
5. Consolidated Rail Corp., $3.84
6. Southern Pacific Rail, $2.94
7. Illinois Central Railroad, $0.59
8. CP Rail System/Soo Line Railroad, $0.55
9. Kansas City Southern, $0.47
10. CN North America/Grand Truck Western, $0.32

Source: *Recycling Today*, December, 1995, p. 66.

The 30 regional lines, by contrast, operated over 18,800 miles of track and brought in $1.55 billion in operating revenues. Smaller railroads that operate less than 350 miles of track are called shortline railroads; there were 500 of these nationwide in the mid-1990s operating a total 26,546 miles of track. Amtrak, the government-supported passenger rail system, was the only passenger carrier with national impact.

INDUSTRY OUTLOOK

The railroad industry suffered in the 1980s, as increased reliance on trucking and other modes of transportation and the perception of railroads as antiquated, contributed to slow growth. However, the advent of innovations such as double-stack containers, intermodal shipping, and computer-controlled dispatching have changed both perceptions and profits.

Development of high-technology tracking systems that aid crews in train turnover—resulting in tighter scheduling and dispatching—is closely tied to the railroads' increased profitability in the 1990s. This technology is essential to the railroad switching and terminal establishments for line-haul railroads, which are the connection points facilitating the movement of tons of goods on and off trains, and the assembly and tracking of those trains.

Another boon to the freight rail industry has been industry deregulation. The 1980's Staggers Rail Act reduced the Interstate Commerce Commission (ICC)'s regulation of rates and service, and in the following year, the ICC exempted all intermodal traffic from rate controls. In addition, the ICC exempted boxcar and trailer-on-flatcar traffic and the transport of some agricultural products, lumber, and transportation equipment. Industry analysts credited this loosening of regulations with rail companies' increased investment in equipment, especially intermodal containers.

Deregulation also spurred Class 1 railroads' sales of branch lines to smaller companies. In contrast to the mergers of the 1980s, which analysts say left the largest railroads weighted down by debt and property, the sales of the early 1990s helped the industry as a whole. Smaller lines were able to offer improved local service, while still maintaining connection to the larger lines' nationwide network of tracks. In addition, smaller railroads often hired non-union employees, who generally were unable to bargain for higher wages. Without union regulations, lines were also able to staff trains more lightly; they could rely on improved computer tracking and monitoring, which could be handled by a two-person crew. Shorter lines also had the advantage of being able to offer more personal service to customers.

With the merger of major railroad companies in the United States, railroad executives anticipate a potential bottleneck at terminals with some railroads not having easy access to switching. In 1997, the issue became

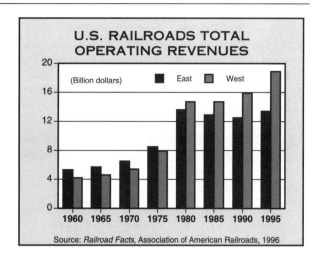

U.S. RAILROADS TOTAL OPERATING REVENUES

(Billion dollars) ■ East ▨ West

Source: *Railroad Facts*, Association of American Railroads, 1996

heated with the potential of some form of re-regulation coming to the industry.

Another important issue in the industry is the role of labor. Rail workers have long been unionized, and the unions have made making rail employees as a group one of the highest paid segments of the working population. Labor costs, including wages, accounted for 37 percent of all railroad operating costs in 1995 (as compared with 48 percent in 1982). But the increasing automation of trains, centralized dispatching, and company mergers, combined with companies' desire to cut operating costs as much as possible, have endangered several key employment positions. In addition, faster trains mean that crews, who are paid bonuses for miles traveled over a set limit, often earn bonuses of up to 70 percent of a day's wages for an eight- or ten-hour day. Companies are eager to cut these bonuses, but the power of the unions is strong.

In addition to the pressures applied by innovations and labor, the future of the rail industry is affected heavily by industries that produce the goods being shipped. Those industries relying most heavily on rail transportation for shipping their products include steel, coal, chemicals, pulp and paper, automobiles, construction, and agriculture. Coal alone makes up approximately 40 percent of rail shipments, so the coal industry's economic status has a strong effect on the fortunes of the railroads.

ORGANIZATION AND STRUCTURE

From the late 1980s to the early 1990s, the railroad industry began to pull out of the slump it had seen in the 1970s and 1980s. In 1995, railroads realized significant productivity gains with freight revenue ton-miles per employee rising to 7 million, up 11.1 percent over 1994 figures, and a dramatic 233 percent over 1980 totals of

211 million. In 1995, the industry's fleet expanded for the third year in a row to 69.4 million, up 7 percent from 1994 and twice the comparable 1980 level. Meanwhile, rail freight rates fell sharply and steadily. In 1995, revenue per-ton fell 16 percent to 2.401 cents. Nearly 70 percent of all rail freight was transported under contract relationships between railroads and shippers. Meanwhile, railroads would operate almost exclusively on privately owned rights-of-way, and would spend large sums of money on restoration of these rights-of-way, maintenance, and equipment investment.

An important innovation was the increase in intermodal transport, a system in which freight containers are attached to truck beds for shipments to rail yards, then transported by rail to a distribution "hub," where they are again picked up by trucks for the final leg of their journey. These containers can also be transported by ship to port locations where they are transferred to rail for the journey inland. Intermodal transport allows for both speed and low cost when transporting goods; due to decreased wind resistance from the lower-stacked cars, it cuts fuel consumption by 20 percent. More importantly, the system changed the relationship between rail and trucking companies—once intense rivals for the same business—by encouraging cooperation and new business collaboration for the benefit of both industries. Nevertheless, the intermodal trailer count fell 6.2 percent in the mid-1990s.

A side effect of intermodal shipping was the adoption of a hub-and-spoke network for shipping, in which fewer cities ("hubs") served as drop-off points for goods initially shipped by truck. This system reduced the number of stops that had to be made by a single train, speeding up travel time for many routes and reducing overall customer costs.

Another notable investment in new equipment came in the early 1980s, with the advent of double stack containers—boxcar containers that fit on a lowered platform and can be stacked one on top of the other, doubling the amount a single train can carry—that immediately improved the feasibility and profitability of rail transport.

WORK FORCE

The 11 largest Class 1 railroad companies, in addition to Amtrak, employed nearly 210,000 workers in 1995. Regional railroads employed 10,647 employees and shortlines, 13,269 employees. Although the early 1990s saw rail profits rise, corporate mergers and increased mechanization led to a decline in the number of rail employees during the same period. By the early 1990s,

most carriers were employing only two-person crews, with an engineer and a conductor controlling each train, the brake operator having become superfluous on most runs.

Each train is run by an engineer, who holds the highest rank on a train and is in charge of the train and its crew. The engineer checks the train for mechanical and safety problems before each run, starts and stops the train, and monitors its progress throughout a trip. Trained as "firers" (a term surviving from the days of steam locomotives) or assistant engineers, engineers must learn how to run and monitor all trains owned by their employer and must be familiar with tracks, signals, and hazards of each route.

All trains also employ a conductor who is responsible for the train crew and the passengers or freight. On freight trains, the conductor logs the contents of each freight car and ensures that their contents are deposited at their destinations along the route. On passenger trains, the conductor collects passenger fares, helps passengers with any needs or requests, and alerts the engineer when all passengers at a given stop have left the train. Conductors also act as an information conduit between the dispatchers, station managers, etc., and the engineer.

Some trains employ an assistant engineer ("fireman" or "firer"), who aids the engineer in running and monitoring the trains—this position is being phased out due to the increasing computerization and the mechanization of trains, terminals, and freight yards. Firers perform engine maintenance and repair and serve as emergency replacements for engineers. Brake operators (previously called "brakemen") maintain braking equipment and lights, and add and remove cars at station stops. Brake operators also are disappearing from trains due to railroad-union negotiations; they are being eliminated mainly through attrition and early-retirement incentives.

Railyard engineers oversee the movement of cars within the freight yard or terminal and the assembly of trains. Yard conductors oversee all yard employees, instructing them in assembling and disassembling trains and switching cars between tracks. Yard brakers (or "yard helpers") assist the conductor and do much of the physical labor of coupling and uncoupling cars. In addition to the yard crew, railroad terminals employ clerks, maintenance workers, and signalers and signal maintainers. Passenger terminals also employ station agents and ticket agents, who deal directly with the public.

RESEARCH AND TECHNOLOGY

The newest innovation in the railroad industry is EDI, or electronic data interchange, which allows the railways to track goods and trains more closely and quickly than in the past. The primary EDI system, ATCS (Advanced Train Control Systems), controls trains using telecommunications technology and computer tracking, allowing train crews to stay informed of all train operations, a development that can improve safety and reliability and reduce costs.

With ATCS, information gained from transponders attached to tracks at certain intervals and triggered by passing trains, is sent via fiber-optic cable or telephone line to a regional data center or directly to the switching yard to which a passing train is headed. This information, once gathered, allows switching establishments to react more quickly to changes on the line, as well as to assign incoming trains to certain tracks in the yard. Switching establishments, which may or may not be run by the railroads that use them, can use up to 100 track segments on which cars and locomotives are coupled and uncoupled, loaded and unloaded. In 1994, data was integrated into the U.S. and Canadian systems making it possible for a Canadian shipper to send freight out on a Canadian National or Canadian Pacific car all the way to Mexico City—without the car being opened—and know where the goods are anytime and anywhere.

Once industry standards are hammered out, some industry observers feel that ATCS will provide near-instantaneous data on car location, switching records, car scheduling, and other factors that affect the smooth synchronization of a vast network of trains. Of course, the up-front costs are great, but ATCS is one step toward further computerizing a large and complex industry.

Technology refinements in the utilization of intermodal containerized freight, the means by which containers can be interchanged between rail, seagoing, and trucking modes, resulted in railroads moving freight faster and more efficiently. Statistics from the Association of American Railroads indicated that the use of intermodal peaked in 1994 with 8.13 million trailers and containers in use, then slacked off in 1995 to 8.07 million. The engineering of double-stack trains, a means by which one container is literally stacked on top of another, also made it possible for a train to carry the equivalent of 200 trucks, thereby saving fuel and labor costs while improving efficiencies. Platforms on which the containers were secured provided a smoother ride for materials and products.

Other innovations include ISS (Interline Settlement System) and REN (Rate EDI Network), industry-wide standards of computerized data management that will manage revenue sharing among railroads when goods are shipped on more than one line, as is often the case, and speed billing and dispute resolution within the industry. An information system called Railinc, used

widely in the industry, already speeds customer service and tracking. Finally, it is predicted that the rail industry will take advantage of hand-held "slate" computers, which will allow crews to forward information to central schedulers "on the fly," or as it is taken down. All of this automation, based on smaller networked computer systems rather than large central mainframe machines, could lead to a continuing decentralization of control and information that will allow greater flexibility and improved response on the part of each company and the industry as a whole.

A major development affecting passenger rail service, and especially Amtrak, is high-speed rail passenger systems, which run at 125 miles or more per hour and bring train travel to a speed where it can compete with air travel over shorter distances, both in regard to cost and convenience. High-speed rail systems fall into two categories: steel-wheel-on-steel-rail and magnetic levitation systems. Among the more traditional wheel-on-rail trains, the fastest of which can reach 187 miles per hour, France's TGV train has been the most successful.

Maglev (magnetic levitation) technology, which uses magnetic forces to propel, brake, and control trains traveling up to 300 miles per hour, has been tested in Germany and Japan. The trains, which are separated from the tracks by a magnetic field, are not yet in commercial use. However, a planned maglev system that will connect the Orlando, Florida, airport and the Disney World complex is planned, with backing from American, German, and Japanese investors.

AMERICA AND THE WORLD

Regional trade agreements, railroad cooperation, railroad mergers, and transportation innovations have all impacted the growth and development of rail transportation. The U.S.-Canadian Free Trade Agreement, signed in 1988, resulted in Class 1 railroads on both sides of the border accelerating their connections into each others territory. The North American Free Trade Agreement (NAFTA), which diminished most trade barriers, and a wave of rail mergers in the United States in the mid-1990s further hastened this trend.

With trade between the United States and Canada forcing a north-south orientation, railroads shifted their east-west systems accordingly. Both shared track, railbeds, and operations on both sides of the border. U.S. railroads gained entry to Canada through interline agreements with Canadian railroads.

Rail traffic to Mexico started growing when the country first began easing trade barriers in the late 1980s, and reached new highs in the early 1990s with NAFTA. In the early 1990s, cargo volumes for Canadian railroads accounted for about one-quarter of the southbound export tonnage moving across the U.S. border. The pact particularly benefited U.S. producers of grain, automobiles, lumber, and other goods and Pacific Rim imports suited for transport by rail. American companies have worked with the Mexican national rail system, FNM (Ferrocarriles Nacionales de Mexico) to simplify border regulations and increase rail traffic.

ASSOCIATIONS AND SOCIETIES

ASSOCIATION OF AMERICAN RAILROADS
50 F St. NW
Washington, DC 20001
Phone: (202) 639-2100
Fax: (202) 639-2986

NATIONAL ASSOCIATION OF RAILROAD PASSENGERS
900 2nd St. NE, Ste. 308
Washington, DC 20002
Phone: (202) 408-8362
Fax: (202) 408-8287

NATIONAL ASSOCIATION OF RAILWAY BUSINESS WOMEN
c/o Pat Cohen
1121 Maplegrove Rd.
Duluth, MN 55811
Phone: (218) 722-0488

RAILWAY PROGRESS INSTITUTE
700 N. Fairfax St.
Alexandria, VA 22314
Phone: (703) 836-2332
Fax: (703) 548-0058

PERIODICALS AND NEWSLETTERS

PROGRESSIVE RAILROADING
Trade Press Publishing Co.
230 W Monroe, Rm. 2210
Chicago, IL 60606
Phone: (312) 629-1200
Monthly. $55.00 per year. Provides feature articles, news, new product information, etc. Relative to the railroad and rail transit industry.

RAILWAY AGE
Simmons-Boardman Publishing Corp.
345 Hudson St., 17 Fl.
New York, NY 10014-4502
Phone: (212) 620-7200
Fax: (212) 633-1165
Monthly. Free to railroad personnel; others, $35.00 per year.

TRAINS; THE MAGAZINE OF RAILROADING
Kalmbach Publishing Co.
PO Box 612
Waukesha, WI 53187-1612
Phone: (414) 796-8776
Fax: (414) 796-0126
Monthly. $34.95 per year.

UNITED STATES RAIL NEWS
Business Publishers, Inc.
951 Pershing Dr.
Silver Spring, MD 20910-4464
Phone: (800) 274-0122 or (301) 587-6300
Fax: (301) 585-9075
Biweekly. $390.00. Newsletter. Reports developments in all aspects of the rail transportation industry.

DATABASES

CITIBASE (CITICORP ECONOMIC DATABASE)
FAME Software Corp.
77 Water St., 9 Fl.
New York, NY 10005
Phone: (212) 898-7800
Fax: (212) 742-8956
Presents over 6,000 statistical series relating to business, industry, finance, and economics. Includes series from Survey of Current Business and many other sources. Time period is 1947 to date, with daily updates. Inquire as to online cost and availability.

DRI TRANSPORTATION COST FORECASTING
DRI/McGraw-Hill, Data Products Division
24 Hartwell Ave.
Lexington, MA 02173
Phone: (800) 541-9914 or (617) 863-5100
Provides 10-year forecasts, updated quarterly, of key expense items for U.S. railroads, trucking, and inland waterway transportation. Rail shipping rates are forecast for 11 major commodities. Inquire as to online cost and availability.

TRIS
National Research Council
2101 Constitution Ave. NW
Washington, DC 20418
Phone: (202) 334-3250
Fax: (202) 334-2003
Contains abstracts and citations to a wide range of transportation literature, 1968 to present, with monthly updates. Includes references to the literature of air transportation, highways, ships and shipping, railroads, trucking, and urban mass transportation. Formerly TRIS-ON-LINE. Inquire as to online cost and availability.

STATISTICS SOURCES

ANNUAL REPORT
National Railroad Passenger Corporation (Amtrak)
400 N. Capitol St.

Washington, DC 20001
Phone: (202) 906-3000

CARS OF REVENUE FREIGHT LOADED
Association of American Railroads
American Railroads Bldg.
50 F St. NW
Washington, DC 20001
Phone: (202) 639-2100
Weekly.

FREIGHT COMMODITY STATISTICS
Association of American Railroads
50 F St. NW
Washington, DC 20001
Phone: (202) 639-2301
Monthly.

NATIONAL TRANSPORTATION STATISTICS
Available from U.S. Government Printing Office
Washington, DC 20402
Phone: (202) 512-1800
Fax: (202) 512-2250
Annual. Issued by Bureau of Transportation Statistics, U.S. Department of Transportation. Provides data on operating revenues, expenses, employees, passenger miles (where applicable), and other factors for airlines, automobiles, buses, local transit, pipelines, railroads, ships, and trucks.

RAILROAD FACTS
Association of American Railroads
American Railroads Bldg.
50 F St. NW
Washington, DC 20001
Phone: (202) 639-2100
Annual.

GENERAL WORKS

OFFICIAL RAILWAY GUIDE. NORTH AMERICAN FREIGHT SERVICE EDITION
K-III Directory Corp.
424 W. 33rd St.
New York, NY 10001
Phone: (800) 221-5488 or (212) 695-5025
Phone: (212) 714-3157
Bimonthly. $119.00 per year.

FURTHER READING

Association of American Railroads. *Railroads Rip Bottleneck Scheme as Reregulation,* 16 October 1996.

Association of American Railroads. *Railroad Facts.* 1996 Edition.

Burke, Jack. "Rail Attacks Bottlenecks." *Traffic World,* 21 October 1996.

Burke, Jack. "UP Ready to Take Over SP." *Traffic World,* 9 September 1996.

"IC to Double Size of Chicago Bulk Terminal." *Rail Business Week,* 3 February 1997.

Johnson, Gregory S. "Widespread Delays in Railroad Service Worry Shippers." *Journal of Commerce,* 1 May 1996.

"Rail Intermodal Yard Greatly Increases NIT's Handling Facility." *The Virginia Maritimer,* June/July 1996.

Watson, Rip. "CSX, Conrail to Merge." *Journal of Commerce,* 10 October 1996.

REAL ESTATE AGENTS AND MANAGERS

SIC 6531

An increase in home sales and drops in interest rates through the mid-1990s helped the real estate industry realize 3.8 million home transactions in 1995. Several factors, including a strong move toward diversification of business activities and Internet utilization, contribute to an expected continuation of this strong showing.

Real estate agents and managers assist people who are purchasing, selling, leasing, financing and building places to live. The industry also includes agents and managers who work on commercial real estate, including high-rise office buildings, shopping centers, industrial plants, ranches, medical centers, museums, and theaters.

The real estate industry employs hundreds of thousands of full- and part-time workers in the United States, including real estate agents who assist buyers and sellers of property, mortgage brokers who assist with financing, leasing agents who lease residential and commercial real estate, property managers who manage the property of others, appraisers who analyze the fair market value of property, and developers who build new structures. In the early 1990s, the Census of Financial, Insurance and Real Estate Industries indicated that the area of real estate agents and managers incorporated 106,552 establishments, with revenues of almost $54 billion and 646,561 employees.

Top 10 LEADING REAL ESTATE MANAGERS

Ranked by: Tax-exempt assets in 1995, in millions of dollars.

1. Equitable Real Estate Investment Management Inc., with $11,043 million
2. Heitman/JMB, $10,879
3. RREEF Funds, $5,195
4. Prudential Asset Mgmt., $5,134
5. LaSalle Advertisers Ltd., $4,912
6. O'Connor, $4,389
7. Copley Real Estate Advisors, $4,289
8. Yarmouth Group Inc., $4,200
9. GE Investments, $4,193
10. TCW/Westmark, $3,247

Source: *Pensions & Investments,* October 2, 1995, p. 26.

The overall health of the real estate industry is closely intertwined with swings in the economy. As businesses grow, they generally acquire more real estate to expand their plants and hire more workers. The supply and demand of available homes, office buildings, and other real estate are strongly influenced by the availability of financing for developers who develop land into residential and business properties. Thus, during periods of tight credit and declining economic activity, real estate activity is low. Changes in tax laws and interest rates also have a great impact on the real estate industry.

INDUSTRY OUTLOOK

The real estate market can be strong in one part of the country and weak in another, as happened during the recession of the early 1990s. Massive worker layoffs during that recession resulted in a surplus of available commercial real estate and a decrease in rental rates. Many workers who lost their jobs were forced to sell their homes, and others were hesitant to purchase homes because of increased job insecurity. Consequently, home sales were depressed in some parts of the country.

Subsequent rises in home sales and drops in interest rates through the mid-1990s helped the real estate industry to recover. Agents were involved in the buying and selling of 3.8 million homes in 1995. But there also has been a strong move toward diversification of business activities, as well as toward providing services beyond those of the traditional agent/broker roles. Many of the largest real estate firms now offer their clients title insurance, mortgage loans, and similar extended services. The industry association, the National Association of Realtors, has begun entering into agreements with nations in eastern Europe, and has been expanding its outreach to first-time immigrant homebuyers within the United States. Brokers and agents who represent only buyers of real estate also have been growing in numbers and are now represented by the National Association of Exclusive Buyer Agents.

Real estate brokers also are exploring the world of high technology and reaping its benefits. Basic information about all of an agency's listings are routinely placed on office computers. In addition, real estate advertisements, complete with photographs and listing information, were routinely placed on Internet sites by the mid-1990s. The World Wide Web Site REALTOR.COM, sponsored by the National Association of Realtors, claimed to have online listings for over half a million homes in North America by 1997. Many less ambitious sites have been launched by individual real estate agencies.

ORGANIZATION AND STRUCTURE

Real estate is a service business involving a variety of professionals who act in concert to bring about the purchase, sale, financing, leasing or construction of property. It could involve residential real estate, commercial real estate, industrial property, agricultural land, or vacant lots.

Real estate brokers or agents generally earn their income from commissions on the purchase, sale, or leasing of real estate. In most states, a real estate broker holds an advanced license and manages an office of real estate agents. The agents have less experience and work under the supervision of a broker. When the agent earns a commission, it is usually split between the agent and the supervising broker.

Homeowners usually consult one or more real estate agents when trying to sell a home. The agents will then discuss the price at which the property might sell, develop their plans for marketing the property, outline the strengths and weaknesses of the property, and determine how the property compares to other homes on the market. The seller will then select one agent to market the property and represent the seller's interests when it comes to negotiating a contract of sale. The agent and the seller will sign a contract authorizing the agent to act on behalf of the seller and market the property, in exchange for a specified commission upon the sale of the property. If a buyer is not found for the property, the agent will not receive any commission.

Likewise, buyers of residential real estate generally contact one or more agents to scout neighborhoods for

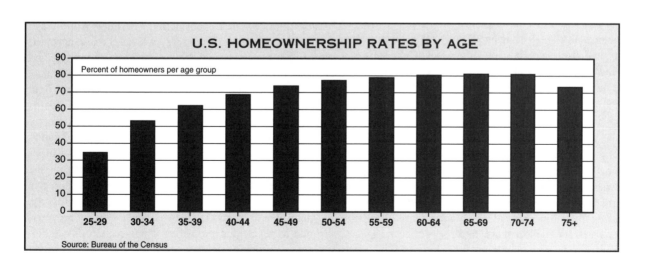

U.S. HOMEOWNERSHIP RATES BY AGE

Percent of homeowners per age group

Source: Bureau of the Census

homes fitting the buyers' requirements in terms of size, price, location and amenities. The agent then represents the buyer in negotiating a contract and assists in obtaining inspections of the property by experts, such as structural and termite inspectors, and may assist the buyer in obtaining a mortgage loan.

SPECIALISTS VARY

Some real estate agents are relocation specialists and work primarily to assist individuals who are relocating to another geographic area. They must have extensive knowledge of school facilities and other neighborhood attributes in order to properly serve their clients. They are sometimes paid by an employer that is relocating its employees.

Commercial real estate agents work in a similar fashion when the purchase or sale of commercial property is contemplated. This could include nearly any type of property used in a business. But their knowledge must include those things of special concern to businesses, including available housing for employees, school facilities for employees' children, and the availability of an appropriate labor force.

Leasing commercial real estate is another area in which many real estate agents are employed, particularly in major metropolitan regions. The leasing agent's purpose is to keep the building fully occupied, while obtaining the highest possible rental rates. This job requires the agent to have a thorough knowledge of the rental rates in the local market and to keep abreast of anything that may affect the market. Local laws affecting real estate development and rent control laws have significant impact on the real estate market, and agents must also be knowledgeable of any changes in such laws.

Leasing procedures vary, but the agent generally receives a commission based on the total value of the lease. The longer the lease term the higher the commission. Office leases generally are for longer time periods than residential leases, often having a term of three to fifteen years. The leasing agent must advertise the property and use every possible sales tool when leasing a brand new property, as it is important to the owner that the building be rented as quickly as possible without long exposure in the marketplace.

A large branch of the real estate industry involves managing property owned by others. Leasing commercial property is often one of the functions of a property manager. The modern-day property manager acts as an adviser and agent of the owner, and is primarily concerned with establishing rental rates, advertising and leasing the property, and negotiating leases. Property managers also collect rents, make sure that mortgages, taxes, insurance premiums and other bills are paid, act as

SIC 6530 - Real Estate Agents and Managers Establishments, Employment, and Payroll

	Estab- lish- ments	Mid- March Employ- ment	1st Q. Wages (annualiz. $ mil.)	Payroll per Empl. 1st Q. (annualiz.)	Annual Payroll ($ mil.)
1988	82,894	616,382	13,270.1	21,529	13,504.3
1989	70,224	567,121	12,954.4	22,842	13,169.7
%	-15.3	-8.0	-2.4	6.1	-2.5
1990	72,243	584,669	13,291.7	22,734	13,324.2
%	2.9	3.1	2.6	-0.5	1.2
1991	80,055	581,901	12,649.6	21,738	13,108.1
%	10.8	-0.5	-4.8	-4.4	-1.6
1992	92,086	637,222	14,173.2	22,242	14,973.8
%	15.0	9.5	12.0	2.3	14.2
1993	110,387	706,907	15,298.7	21,642	17,025.8
%	19.9	10.9	7.9	-2.7	13.7
% 88-93	33.2	14.7	15.3	0.5	26.1

Source: *County Business Patterns*, U.S. Department of Commerce, Washington, D.C., for 1988 through 1993. Payroll per employee is calculated using mid-March employment and 1st Quarter wages, annualized. Annual payroll, also shown, may not equal the annualized 1st Quarter wages. Rows headed by a percent sign (%) indicate change from the previous year. *na* stands for not available. The symbol (D) indicates that data are withheld by the source to avoid disclosure of competitive information. A dash (-) indicates that data are not available or cannot be calculated.

liaisons to tenants and make sure the building is maintained in good working order. They supervise and hire the building staff and may contract for janitorial, engineering, security and refuse services. They often do the bookkeeping for the property and prepare periodic financial reports for the owner. Owners of office buildings, shopping centers, apartments and other income-producing properties usually hire a real estate firm to manage the property.

The appraisal of real estate values is a specialized segment of the real estate industry. An appraisal might be done to determine the value of a home that an individual wants to sell, or it may be done at the request of a lending institution which is considering providing a mortgage loan to a prospective buyer. Appraisers use accepted methods to determine the value of a piece of property and generally express an opinion on the fair market value, insurable value, or investment value of the property. Real estate appraisers visit the property, search public records and interview those with knowledge about the property and the surrounding community, taking into consideration the structural quality and overall condition of the property. Any trends in real estate or imminent changes in the community that could influence the value of the property are also taken into account when appraising the property. Many appraisers specialize in particular types of property, such as residential properties, commercial office buildings, or shopping centers.

WORK FORCE

Every state and the District of Columbia require that real estate brokers and agents be licensed. They must complete educational courses in the fundamentals of real estate and pass a written examination. Appraisers of property financed by federally regulated lenders must be certified within their states.

The real estate industry employed 374,000 agents, brokers and appraisers nationwide in full- and part-time employment in the mid-1990s. Most of these people worked on a commission or fee basis rather than as employees. Many real estate agents begin working part-time because of the intermittent income the work provides. Though agents are essentially independent contractors, most are affiliated with a nationally known or local brokerage firm.

As sales commissions can be high on many properties, successful real estate agents can earn large amounts of money. However, only a small percentage of agents actually do so. The median weekly income for full-time agents, brokers and appraisers was $573 in the mid-1990s. The number of agents, brokers and appraisers employed was expected to change little or to grow slowly through 2005. However, due to the high turnover within the profession, there are generally many job openings in the industry.

There were approximately 261,000 real estate managers in the mid-1990s, most working for property management firms, development companies, banks, government agencies, and other entities. There also is a large group of self-employed developers, owner-managers of buildings, and operators of building management firms. No formal certification or licensing is required except for managers of federally subsidized housing, who must be state-certified. Many other managers complete training programs that include certification by the sponsoring

SIC 6530
Occupations Employed by SIC 653 - Real Estate Agents and Managers

Occupation	% of Total 1994	Change to 2005
Maintenance repairers, general utility	11.5	22.6
Property & real estate managers	10.2	31.7
Janitors & cleaners, incl maids	9.4	22.6
Secretaries, ex legal & medical	7.0	1.4
Sales agents, real estate	5.8	-0.1
General office clerks	5.1	-5.0
Bookkeeping, accounting, & auditing clerks	5.0	-16.4
Receptionists & information clerks	4.9	33.7
General managers & top executives	4.4	5.7
Real estate appraisers	3.6	11.4
Guards	3.2	0.3
Gardeners & groundskeepers, ex farm	3.2	0.3
Brokers, real estate	3.1	11.4
Real estate clerks	2.5	11.4
Financial managers	2.1	11.4
Marketing & sales worker supervisors	1.7	11.4
Service workers nec	1.3	11.4
Accountants & auditors	1.3	11.4
Clerical supervisors & managers	1.3	14.0
Typists & word processors	1.1	-44.3

Source: *Industry-Occupation Matrix*, Bureau of Labor Statistics. These data relate to one or more 3-digit SIC industry groups rather than to a single 4-digit SIC. The change reported for each occupation to the year 2005 is a percent of growth or decline as estimated by the Bureau of Labor Statistics. The abbreviation nec stands for 'not elsewhere classified'.

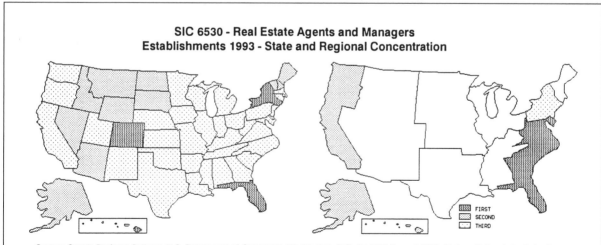

SIC 6530 - Real Estate Agents and Managers
Establishments 1993 - State and Regional Concentration

FIRST
SECOND
THIRD

Source: *County Business Patterns*, U.S. Department of Commerce, Washington, D.C., for 1988 through 1993. *States* with the darkest shading indicate those states which have proportionately more establishments, employment, or payrolls than would be indicated by the state's population. States with light shading are states with proportionately fewer establishments, less employment, and lower payrolls than population distribution. States shaded grey are within 15 percent of the state's population proportion in these categories. States for which no data are available are shown as average (grey). *Regions* are shaded to indicate absolute rank in the category. If no data for the category are available, establishment counts are used to shade the regions. Source of the data is the table on the facing page.

organization, such as the Institute of Real Estate Management (IREM).

Median annual earnings of all property and real estate managers were $22,600 in the mid-1990s. Growth in this field was expected to be average through 2005, but certain areas are likely to experience bigger growth. These include managers of office and retail space, particularly for restaurant, food, apparel, and specialized merchandise chains; managers of developments owned by community or homeowner associations; and managers of assisted living and retirement communities.

AMERICA AND THE WORLD

The U.S. real estate industry is tapping the market within the former Communist countries of eastern Europe, such as Russia and Hungary, where ownership of private property now is legal. Beginning in the early 1990s, the IREM began to enter into partnerships with real estate associations in those countries to help in training of real estate personnel and adoption of national standards. By mid-1996, there were 28 such partnerships in effect. The IREM also has partnership arrangements in Canada, Mexico, Singapore, and Spain. The National Association of Realtors is conducting similar activities in eastern Europe, and entered into agreements with five countries—Bulgaria, the Czech Republic, Hungary, Poland, and Russia—at its annual convention in 1996.

ASSOCIATIONS AND SOCIETIES

INSTITUTE OF REAL ESTATE MANAGEMENT
430 N Michigan Ave.
Chicago, IL 60611-4090
Phone: (312) 329-6000
Fax: (312) 661-0217

NATIONAL ASSOCIATION OF REAL ESTATE BROKERS
1629 K St. NW, No. 2, Ste. 602,
Washington, DC 20006
Phone: (202) 785-4477
Fax: (202) 785-1244

NATIONAL ASSOCIATION OF REALTORS
430 N Michigan Ave.
Chicago, IL 60611
Phone: (312) 329-8200
Fax: (312) 329-8576

SOCIETY OF INDUSTRIAL AND OFFICE REALTORS
777 14th St. NW, Ste. 400
Washington, DC 20005-3271
Phone: (202) 737-1150
Fax: (202) 737-3142

WOMEN'S COUNCIL OF REALTORS
430 N Michigan Ave.
Chicago, IL 60611
Phone: (312) 329-8483
Fax: (312) 329-3290

PERIODICALS AND NEWSLETTERS

THE JOURNAL OF REAL ESTATE TAXATION
Warren, Gorham and Lamont, Inc.
1 Penn Plz., 42 Fl.
New York, NY 10119-4098
Phone: (800) 950-1210 or (800) 950-1213
Fax: (212) 971-5113
Quarterly. $146.50 per year. Continuing coverage of the latest tax developments.

NATIONAL REAL ESTATE INVESTOR
Argus, Inc.
6151 Powers Ferry Rd. NW
Atlanta, GA 30339-2941
Phone: (800) 443-4969 or (404) 955-2500
Fax: (404) 955-0400
Monthly. $70.00 per year. Includes annual Directory. *Market surveys by city.*

REAL ESTATE ISSUES
American Society of Real Estate Counselors
430 N Michigan Ave
Chicago, IL 60611
Phone: (312) 329-8427
Fax: (312) 329-8881
Semiannual. Individuals, $27.00 per year; university faculty and students, $21.00 per year.

REAL ESTATE LAW JOURNAL
Warren, Gorham and Lamont, Inc.
1 Penn Plz., 42 Fl.
New York, NY 10119-4098
Phone: (800) 950-1210 or (800) 950-1213
Fax: (212) 971-5113
Quarterly. $141.50 per year. Continuing practical concerns of real estate law professionals. Covers timely issues.

REAL ESTATE TODAY
National Association of Realtors
430 N Michigan Ave.
Chicago, IL 60611
Phone: (312) 329-8458
Fax: (312) 329-5978
10 times a year. $38.00 per year.

DATABASES

BANKING INFORMATION SOURCE
UMI
620 S 3rd St.
Louisville, KY 40202-2475
Phone: (800) 626-2823 or (502) 583-4111
Fax: (502) 589-5572

Provides indexing and abstracting of periodical and other literature from 1982 to date, with weekly updates. Covers the financial services industry: banks, savings institutions, investment houses, credit unions, insurance companies, and real estate organizations. Emphasis is on marketing and management. Inquire as to online cost and availability. (Formerly FINIS: *Financial Industry Information Service.)*

STATISTICS SOURCES

FINANCE, INSURANCE, AND REAL ESTATE USA: INDUSTRY ANALYSES, STATISTICS, AND LEADING COMPANIES

Arsen J. Darnay, editor
Gale Research
835 Penobscot Bldg.
Detroit, MI 48226-4094
Phone: (800) 877-GALE or (313) 961-2242
Fax: (313) 961-6083
1994. $195.00. Contains industry statistical data and a listing of leading companies for each of 50 Standard Industrial Classification (SIC) 4-digit codes covering finance, insurance, and real estate. Includes banks, mortgage banks, securities dealers, commodity brokers, real estate companies, and related firms. Several indexes are provided.

NEW ONE-FAMILY HOUSES SOLD

Available from U.S. Government Printing Office
Washington, DC 20402
Phone: (202) 512-1800
Fax: (202) 512-2250
Monthly. $20.00 per year. Bureau of the Census Construction Report, C25. Provides data on new, privately-owned, one-family homes sold during the month and for sale at the end of the month.

ULI MARKET PROFILES

Urban Land Institute
625 Indiana Ave. NW, Ste. 400
Washington, DC 20004
Phone: (800) 321-5011 or (202) 624-7000
Fax: (202) 624-7140
Annual. $230.00. Provides real estate marketing data for residential, retail, office, and industrial sectors. Covers 76 U.S. metropolitan areas and 13 major foreign metropolitan areas.

U.S. HOUSING MARKETS

Lomas Mortgage USA
33300 5 Mile Rd., Ste. 202
Livonia, MI 48154
Phone: (800) 755-6269 or (313) 422-6100
Fax: (313) 397-2020
Quarterly. $180.00 per year. Includes eight interim reports. Provides data on residential building permits, apartment building completions, rental vacancy rates, sales of existing homes, average home prices, housing affordability, etc. All major U.S. cities and areas are covered.

GENERAL WORKS

RESEARCH IN REAL ESTATE

C. F. Sirmans, editor
JAI Press, Inc.
PO Box 1678
Greenwich, CT 06836-1678
Phone: (203) 661-7602
Fax: (203) 661-0792
Annual. $63.50.

MODERN REAL ESTATE

Charles H. Wurtzebach and Mike E. Miles
John Wiley & Sons, Inc.
605 3rd Ave.
New York, NY 10158-0012
Phone: (800) 526-5368 or (212) 850-6000
Fax: (212) 850-6088
1994. Fifth edition. Price on application.

QUESTIONS AND ANSWERS ON REAL ESTATE

Robert W. Semenow
Prentice-Hall
200 Old Tappan Rd.
Old Tappan, NJ 07675
Phone: (800) 922-0579
Fax: (800) 445-6991
1993. Tenth edition. Price on application.

REAL ESTATE

Larry E. Wofford and Terrance M. Clauretie
John Wiley and Sons, Inc.
605 3rd Ave.
New York, NY 10158-0012
Phone: (800) 526-5368 or (212) 850-6000
Fax: (212) 850-6088
1992. Third edition. Price on application.

FURTHER READING

Heath, Tracy, and Carrie King. "Brokers Speak Out: Sixty Professionals Tell Us How the Business is Changing." *National Real Estate Investor*, April 1996.

Lazich, Robert S., ed. *Market Share Reporter 1997.*Detroit: Gale Research 1997.

Litke, Ronald. "The Institute of Real Estate Management Delves into International Markets." *National Real Estate Investor*, September 1996.

Occupational Outlook Handbook, 1996-1997 Edition. Washington, DC: U.S. Department of Labor, 1996. Available from http://stats.bls.gov.

REALTOR.COM. National Association of Realtors, 1997. Available from http://www.realtor.net.

Timmons, Heather. "Realtors Looking Abroad for Growth Opportunities." *The American Banker*, 20 November 1996. ◄━

RESTAURANTS

SIC 5812

The *restaurant industry saw a steady increase in profits throughout the 1990s. By mid-decade, over half the adult population of the United States visited an eating place each day. While casual dining establishments experienced a decline in growth towards the end of the 1990s, fast-food venues posted sales of $98.4 billion starting in 1996. The restaurant industry provides more Americans with jobs than any other retail market, and is one of the country's most successful exports. Increased competition, new technologies, and fast-paced consumer lifestyles all point to continued growth and design innovations as eating and drinking places evolve to meet customer demands for convenience and value.*

In the late 1990s, the restaurant industry was relatively healthy compared to most other sectors of the retail trade. According to the National Restaurant Association, beginning in 1996, Americans spent about $308 billion at the nation's more than 400,000 eating and drinking establishments—an increase of 5 percent over the previous year. Competition increased and restaurants crowded the market in an effort to capitalize on the rapidly growing industry and still meet consumer demands for quality, convenience, and value. Indeed, in 1996 fast-food restaurants—the fastest growing sector of the industry—amassed $98.4 billion in sales, coming close to overtaking the long-time leading sector, full-service restaurants, which posted sales of $100.3 billion in the same year.

RESTAURANT CHAINS WITH THE HIGHEST SALES

Ranked by: Sales in 1994, in millions of dollars.

1. McDonald's (IL), with $25,987.0 million
2. Burger King (FL), $7,500.0
3. KFC (KY), $7,100.0
4. Pizza Hut (CA), $4,797.4
5. Taco Bell (CA), $4,500.0
6. Wendy's (OH), $4,200.0
7. Hardee's (NC, $3,670.0 (estimate)
8. Aramark, (PA), $3,200.0
9. 7-Eleven (TX), $2,900.0 (estimate)
10. Subway (CT), $2,799.0

Source: *Restaurants & Institutions*, Restaurants & Institutions 400 (annual), July 1, 1995, p. 62+.

FACTORS BEHIND INDUSTRY SUCCESS

Despite overall reduced consumer spending, restaurant and fast-food sales have grown steadily and industry profitability is up. The National Restaurant Association's *1996 Foodservice Industry Report* stated that from 1993 to 1996 "The industry has seen one of the strongest continuous growth periods since the mid- to late-1980s."

The buoyancy of the industry can be traced to a number of factors: women's increased role in the workplace has left them with less time to spend preparing food at home; the proliferation of fast-food and takeout eating places has broadened consumer choice and made eating places a convenient alternative to home-cooked food; and food prices have remained low since the early 1990s, enabling the industry to offer competitive prices. Restaurants' increasingly aggressive promotion of inexpensive, quality food has resulted in a shift of business from food stores to eating places. In the early 1990s, consumers spent 52 cents at restaurants and bars for every dollar spent in food stores, up from 34 cents in 1970. Fast food restaurants, in particular, create the impression of value with menus of low-priced items and specially priced meal packages. According to Standard & Poor's, "This combination approach helps restaurants boost volumes, including sales of high-margin items such as french fries and soft drinks."

COMPETITION SPURS CHANGES IN DESIGN

With the overall strength of the industry, and its concomitant growth, competition became increasingly fierce throughout the 1990s. Restaurants had to stake out a strong identity for themselves and pay closer attention to increasingly demanding consumers. In the mid-1990s, convenience became nearly as important to busy consumers as value. Consumer demand for convenience was clearly shown in the growth in the takeout segment of the industry. A report by the marketing research firm NPD Group Inc. indicated that by the mid-1990s, 21 billion takeout meals were purchased on a yearly basis, a 21 percent increase over the 17 billion of 1990.

This focus on convenience resulted in a hybrid of the traditional full-service restaurant and the fast-food outlet—the home-meal replacement segment (also known as "fast-casual"). Pioneered by Boston Chicken Inc.'s Boston Market chain, home-meal replacement offered fare reminiscent of home cooking—and higher in quality than the typical fast food—through a quick-service restaurant operation. Consumers could now take home meals closer in quality to that offered by casual dining houses.

The success of the home-meal replacement establishments led to the development of the restaurant/retail food concept. These venues, which also cater to the takeout crowd, typically look like markets and often offer a wide selection of meal possibilities—some of the gourmet variety—that the customer can combine as they wish and have the onsite chef prepare for takeout.

One of the hotter areas of the restaurant industry in the mid-1990s was the theme/entertainment restaurant sector. In some ways the popularity of such venues was also a matter of convenience, since customers could satisfy their appetites for food and entertainment at the same time. The popular music-oriented Hard Rock Cafe started the trend, and was followed by Planet Hollywood (movies), Rain-forest Cafe (tropical theme), and Official All-Star Cafe (sports). According to Katherine Paul, in an online article published by Streetnet, "Theme-based restaurants serve up side dishes of entertainment and, in many instances, branded merchandise, along with the food."

EFFECTS OF INCREASED COMPETITION

Meanwhile, the fast-food sector experienced something of a price war in the mid-1990s. McDonald's, Wendy's, and Taco Bell all at one time or another emphasized menu items under $1. These chains, along with others, also offered value meals to further entice frugal consumers. By the late 1990s, however, increased labor and beef costs were beginning to force the fast feeders to reevaluate their menus, according to an industry report by Bear, Stearns & Co. McDonald's introduced the Arch Deluxe in May 1996, touting it as part of an eventual line of "grown-up" menu items—including the Crispy Chicken Deluxe, the Grilled Chicken Deluxe, and the Fish Fillet Deluxe. Bear, Stearns & Co. believed the company's aim was to increase its customers' average check. In the initial months after its introduction, the Arch Deluxe achieved disappointing sales, but its appearance on the McDonald's menu guaranteed that fast-food companies would continue to seek ways to increase check averages.

By early 1997 packaged food companies began an exodus from the restaurant business in order to concentrate on their core operations. After Hershey, Sara Lee, and Ralston Purina jettisoned their restaurant operations, General Foods did the same in May 1995 when it spun off its Red Lobster, Olive Garden, and China Coast (now closed) restaurant chains to form the new public company, Darden Restaurants. Similarly, in early 1997, Pepsico announced that it would spin off its restaurants division—which included Pizza Hut, Kentucky Fried Chicken (KFC), and Taco Bell—into a publicly traded company. With Pepsico's exit, no U.S. packaged food company had a significant presence in the restaurant industry.

As the competition grew more intense in the 1990s, operators became more litigious, going to court in increasing numbers to protect their trademarks and trade dress. The easing of the burden of proof for companies filing trade dress litigation in March 1992 opened the gates for a flood of copycat suits. Defined as a business' defining overall appearance, trade dress is becoming more of a bone of contention between competing chains. Successful suits are extremely profitable and can put the competitor out of business. The Hard Rock Cafe, the Chicago-based Lettuce Entertain You Enterprises, Starbucks Coffee, and the Green Burrito are just a few of the many companies

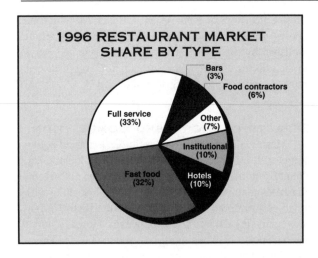

1996 RESTAURANT MARKET SHARE BY TYPE

- Bars (3%)
- Food contractors (6%)
- Full service (33%)
- Other (7%)
- Institutional (10%)
- Fast food (32%)
- Hotels (10%)

who have brought lawsuits against competitors, charging that their ideas have been plagiarized.

ORGANIZATION AND STRUCTURE

The classification of restaurant encompasses a wide variety of eating establishments, including five star gourmet restaurants, roadside cafes, fast-food joints, soda fountains, casual dining establishments, pizza parlors, hot dog stands, tea rooms, and oyster bars, among others. In 1996, full-service restaurants comprised the largest segment of the industry, with sales of $100.26 billion, or 33 percent of the total food service market, according to the National Restaurant Association. One of the strongest areas within this market was casual dining; that is, moderately priced dining houses offering a comprehensive menu at a reasonable price. Chains of casual dining houses, such as Olive Garden, Sizzler, Red Lobster, Ponderosa, TGI Fridays, and Ruby Tuesday had combined sales of $38.4 billion in 1996, up 36 percent from 1992. This sector of the industry began to experience a decline in growth in the mid-1990s as the segment matured, and consolidations began due to overbuilding.

In the late 1990s, fast-food restaurants were the second largest and fastest growing sector of the industry, posting sales of $98.4 billion (or 32 percent of total industry sales) starting in 1996. Over the preceding two decades this sector's success provided much of the entire industry's growth. Of the remaining sectors of the restaurant industry, 9.7 percent of total sales in 1996 came from in-house institutional service, 9.5 percent from eating places connected to hotels, 6.1 percent from food contractors, 3.0 percent from bars and taverns, 1.5 percent from commercial cafeterias, and less than 1 percent

each from social caterers and the sector that includes vendors of ice cream, custard, and yogurt.

The biggest companies operating restaurants include those operating single concept chains, like McDonald's, and those operating a number of different fast food businesses, such as Pepsico, which runs Pizza Hut, Kentucky Fried Chicken, and Taco Bell. Industry analysts are divided over whether diverse or specialized holdings make for a more successful food service company. An industry survey conducted by Standard & Poor's in the early 1990s concluded that "Multiplied chain ownership offers economies of scale, purchasing power, and cross-promotional opportunities, while sticking with a single concept may allow top management to be more focused."

Chain-owned restaurants in general have overtaken independently owned outlets in terms of number of units, possibly due to their greater stability and lower failure rate. This trend is likely to continue throughout the 1990s through mergers and acquisitions, according to the National Restaurant Association *Food Service Industry 2000* report.

WORK FORCE

The eating and drinking places industry is the largest employer in the U.S. retail business, providing 6.4 million jobs in the early 1990s, or a about a third of all retail jobs. Two-thirds of these jobs were in fast-food restaurants, where 70 percent of the workers were less than 21 years of age. In recent years, however, there has been a marked increase in the number of older workers, especially retirees, as operators adjust to a labor shortage. Restaurants are also reacting to this shortage by attempting to improve efficiency and productivity and by cutting back on counter service and increasing drive-throughs.

The level of employment in the industry grew rapidly during the 1980s and was two times greater in 1990 than in 1983. However, the rate of growth fell from a peak of 7 percent between 1973 and 1979 to 3.8 percent annually between 1979 and 1990. Between 1990 and 2005, it is projected to slow further to 1.9 percent, according to the Bureau of Labor Statistics. In the period up to 2005, the fastest growing sector of the industry, in terms of jobs, is projected to be managerial, which is expected to increase 41 percent. Still, in the year 2005, 83 percent of workers in the industry will be employed in service occupations, including food preparation and service.

At least 1 in 3 employees of eating places was employed part-time in the mid-1990s. In 1990, the average weekly hours of nonsupervisory employees in eating and drinking places was 25.2 hours. Women comprised over 56 percent of those employed in 1990, twice as many as in 1973. Nine out of ten workers were in nonsupervisory positions. Only 15 percent were members of labor unions or employee associations under formal labor-management agreements.

Payroll represents restaurant owners' second biggest expenditure after food. According to the National Restaurant Association, in the early 1990s, at full-menu, table service restaurants, 28.3 percent of every sales dollar was spent on payroll, plus another 4.5 percent on employee benefits. At limited-menu, table service restaurants, the figures were 25 percent and 3.2 percent, respectively. Limited-menu, no-table service restaurants spent 24.1 percent on wages and 2.8 percent on benefits, while cafeterias spent 31.1 percent on payroll and 4.3 percent on benefits.

The mid-1990s were a period of rising wages for workers in the eating place industry, according to the 1996 *Restaurant Industry Annual Review* by Schroder Wertheim & Co. Average wage rates grew 2.2 percent in 1994 over 1993 levels as competition in the industry increased the need for workers. Feeding this inflation was the decrease in 16 to 24 year-olds, the prime age range for basic staff/crew positions; from 1980 to 1995 the number of 16 to 24 year-olds fell by about 6 million. This labor squeeze will likely continue into the later part of the decade as the U.S. Bureau of the Census projected that the number of 16 to 24 year-olds would continue to fall in 1996 and 1997, only beginning modest increases in 1998.

In addition to the labor shortage, the industry is also beset by chronic high employee turnover. A survey conducted by the National Restaurant Association concluded that unless more permanent employees came to work in the industry, high worker turnover would continue. A U.S. Department of Labor study added that "the problem of labor turnover may be diminished by competitive pressure to reduce costs through greater use of offsite food preparation firms. Labor turnover has also been lowered by firms that offer employees improved training and occupational advancement opportunities. In addition, some firms are increasing wages and benefits to attract workers."

RESEARCH AND TECHNOLOGY

Technological change is sweeping the industry, most profoundly in the area of computerization, but also in the form of devices to facilitate and speed food preparation and service. There is still a way to go, however, before the industry reaches its full technological capacity.

Although all sectors of the industry have experienced computerization to a greater or lesser extent, "Computerized controls with a high degree of integration between order taking and dining, and various management and accounting functions are limited to some full-service establishments," according to a 1992 Bureau of Labor Statistics report. The most common dedicated computer systems used in the business in the early 1990s were programmed to transmit information from point of order taking to the kitchen and on to a microcomputer used by management. An electronic cash register/point of sale (ECR/POS) system transmitted customer orders to the kitchen where they were either printed out or displayed on a video display unit. The major input device in the system was a keyboard or touch screen unit, part of which was preprogrammed by the manufacturer, part of which was programmed at the restaurant in line with its specific needs.

Currently, hand-held terminals, which enable waitpersons to key in their orders at the table, are used to expedite service. Display screens that allow waitpersons to monitor the progress of their orders are also available. This data is also conveyed to a central microcomputer, which uses it to keep tabs on operations and to control inventory. A number of independent ECR/POS units can be networked using a powerful microcomputer.

In addition to simplifying restaurant operation, computers produce reports and maintain files. For example, says the U.S. Department of Labor report: "Menu item files are used to monitor keyboard operations and make changes in items or prices when needed. A labor file can produce numerous reports, including hours worked and different wage rates for each employee who may work at several different kinds of jobs during a pay period." Computers are especially useful in inventory control, allowing management to keep less stock and to be reminded when it runs low. In some systems, a list of the items needed to restore inventory is transmitted automatically to the supplier, whose computer is networked to the restaurant's.

Large restaurant chains have found the new super microcomputers useful for monitoring their various branches. Time-consuming daily or weekly polls of each outlet's business can be replaced by a direct hookup, which transmits the information automatically. These innovations save time, increase efficiency, and eliminate errors.

Despite these advances, the eating place sector of the food service industry remains relatively under-computerized. "Many tableservice establishments only use personal computers in their management and accounting operations. While three-fourths of the large tableservice restaurants use personal computers, less than two-fifths of the smaller tableservice restaurants and fast food restaurants have computers. [The latter] are most likely to use computers in preparing and dispensing food,'' said the U.S. Department of Labor report.

Apart from computers, technology is infiltrating the restaurant business in the form of food preparation devices such as microwave ovens, automatic dishwashers, food processors, automatic beverage dispensers, and other automated equipment. A new form of vacuum cooking called ``sous vide'' is generating a good deal of interest. Although it saves on labor costs and increases efficiency, the substantial investment in special equipment that it requires, as well as the exacting safety standards that need to be observed, will probably slow its diffusion through the industry at least until the end of the 1990s, according to the U.S. Department of Labor.

Technological advancements are not confined to the kitchen. A vibrating paging system for example, which costs about $5,000 and obviates the need to shout to a waiter when food is ready, was reporting great success in the early 1990s. Research has also shown that for fast-food restaurants eager to increase the volume and turnover of their drive-through trade, double drive-throughs are extremely successful. Restaurants on the west coast are experimenting with debit cards—specially coded automatic teller machine cards that are 8 to 15 seconds faster than cash transactions.

AMERICA AND THE WORLD

Eating establishments are one of North America's most successful exports. McDonald's, the chain with the largest foreign presence, had more than 4,000 outlets distributed throughout more than 59 countries in the early 1990s, with sales of $8.6 billion, or 31 percent of its total worldwide sales. Almost all of the industry leaders have a formidable overseas presence. Restaurants such as Pizza Hut, Kentucky Fried Chicken, Burger King, and Wendy's were gaining a significant foothold in western Europe and the emerging eastern European markets during the first half of the decade. The North American Free Trade Agreement is likely to increase investment opportunities for U.S. restaurant companies; it may also increase competition in the industry, as Canadian and Mexican chains begin to penetrate the U.S. market.

The majority of restaurant chains in the United States are owned by American citizens, although the number of ethnic restaurants operated by immigrants is increasing. Overseas, the fast-food restaurants with the strongest foreign presence are generally operated by natives of the countries in which they are situated, under a franchising agreement, although the parent companies retain ownership of a percentage of the foreign units.

ASSOCIATIONS AND SOCIETIES

NATIONAL ASSOCIATION OF RESTAURANT MANAGERS
5322 N. 78th Way
Scottsdale, AZ 85250
Phone: (800) 777-NARM

NATIONAL RESTAURANT ASSOCIATION
1200 17th St. NW
Washington, DC 20036
Phone: (202) 331-5900
Fax: (202) 331-2429

PERIODICALS AND NEWSLETTERS

CHEF
Talcott Communications Corp.
20 N Wacker Dr., Ste. 3230
Chicago, IL 60606
Phone: (312) 849-2220
Fax: (312) 849-2184
Monthly. $20.00 per year. Edited for executive chefs, food and beverage directors, caterers, banquet and club managers, and others responsible for food buying and food service. Special coverage of regional foods is provided.

COOKING FOR PROFIT
C P Publishing, Inc.
PO Box 267
Fond du Lac, WI 54936-0267
Phone: (414) 923-3700
Fax: (414) 923-6805
Monthly. $24.00 per year. The challenge of operations management in the food service industry.

THE CORNELL HOTEL AND RESTAURANT ADMINISTRATION QUARTERLY
Elsevier Science Publishing Co.
Cornell University School of Hotel Administration
PO Box 882,
Madison Square Sta.
New York, NY 10159
Phone: (212) 989-5800
Fax: (212) 633-3990
Quarterly. $112.00 per year.

FOODSERVICE EQUIPMENT AND SUPPLIES SPECIALIST
Cahners Publishing Co., Inc.
PO Box 5080
Des Plaines, IL 60017-5080
Phone: (800) 662-7776 or (708) 635-8800
Fax: (708) 635-6856
Monthly. $69.95 per year.

NATION'S RESTAURANT NEWS: THE NEWSPAPER OF THE FOOD SERVICE INDUSTRY

Lebhar-Friedman, Inc.
425 Park Ave.
New York, NY 10022
Phone: (212) 756-5000
Fax: (212) 838-9487
Weekly. $89.00 per year.

RESTAURANTS AND INSTITUTIONS

Cahners Publishing Co., Inc.
PO Box 5080
Des Plaines, IL 60017-5080
Phone: (800) 662-7776 or (708) 635-8800
Fax: (708) 299-8622
Biweekly. $104.95 per year. Features news, new products, recipes, menu concepts and merchandising ideas from the most successful foodservice operations around the U.S.

DATABASES

CITIBASE (CITICORP ECONOMIC DATABASE)

FAME Software Corp.
77 Water St., 9 Fl.
New York, NY 10005
Phone: (212) 898-7800
Fax: (212) 742-8956
Presents over 6,000 statistical series relating to business, industry, finance, and economics. Includes series from Survey of Current Business *and many other sources. Time period is 1947 to date, with daily updates. Inquire as to online cost and availability.*

STATISTICS SOURCES

BUSINESS STATISTICS

Available from U.S. Government Printing Office
Washington, DC 20402
Phone: (202) 512-1800
Fax: (202) 512-2250
Biennial. $20.00. Issued by Bureau of Economic Analysis, U.S. Department of Commerce. Shows annual data for 29 years and monthly data for a recent four-year period. Statistics correspond to the Survey of Current Business.

MONTHLY RETAIL TRADE: SALES AND INVENTORIES

Available from U.S. Government Printing Office
Washington, DC 20402
Phone: (202) 512-1800
Fax: (202) 512-2250
Monthly, with annual summary. $57.00 per year. Issued by Bureau of the Census, U.S. Department of Commerce. Includes Advance Monthly Retail Sales.

SURVEY OF CURRENT BUSINESS

Available from U.S. Government Printing Office
Washington, DC 20402
Phone: (202) 512-1800
Fax: (202) 512-2250
Monthly. $41.00 per year. Issued by Bureau of Economic Analysis, U.S. Department of Commerce. Presents a wide variety of business and economic data.

GENERAL WORKS

DIRECTORY OF FOODSERVICE DISTRIBUTORS

Chain Store Guide Information Services
3922 Coconut Palm Rd.
Tampa, FL 33619
Phone: (800) 925-2288 or (813) 664-6700
Fax: (813) 664-6810
Annual. $249.00. Covers distributors of food and equipment to restaurants and institutions.

FUNDAMENTALS OF PROFESSIONAL FOOD PREPARATION

Donald V. Laconi
John Wiley and Sons, Inc.
605 3rd Ave.
New York, NY 10158-0012
Phone: (800) 225-5945 or (212) 850-6000
Fax: (212) 850-6088
1995. $40.95.

FURTHER READING

Bear, Stearns & Co., Inc. "Restaurant Review - Industry Report." 24 October 1996.

Darnay, Arsen J., ed. *Market Share Reporter.* Detroit: Gale Research, 1997.

"Foodservice Industry Forecast 1996." *Restaurants USA,* December 1995.

Papiernik, Richard L. "Outlook: 1997." *Nation's Restaurant News,* 6 January 1997, 41.

Paul, Katherine. "Bon Appetit!" *Streetnet,* 8 October 1996. Available from http://www.streetnet.com/features.

Standard & Poor's Industry Surveys. New York: Standard & Poor's Corporation, April 1996, L51.

Tejada, Carlos. "Latest Restaurant Innovation Looks a Lot Like a Grocery." *Wall Street Journal,* 26 June 1996, B1. ◣

RETAIL DEPARTMENT STORES

SIC 5311

Faced with intense competition *from discount mass merchandisers and a sluggish, if stable, economy, department stores in the 1990s developed strategies to regain their niche in the retail market. The focus is shifting from appliances to home furnishings; from hardware to apparel. Department stores will have to differentiate themselves, and find the correct combination of service, customer responsiveness, and merchandise presentation in order to insure future growth. To compete with the discount superstores, the department stores will have to recreate the pleasant, almost entertaining experience they offered to shoppers originally.*

American department stores in 1996 had combined sales of $111 billion and 929,172 employees. For many retailers, 1996 was a favorable year. Economic conditions in the mid-1990s were much more difficult due to price cutting, higher interest rates, and a general economic slowdown. As firms entered 1997, overcapacity of retail space in comparison to the general U.S. population was not estimated to grow as fast as it did in the early 1990s. Stronger regional economies and better operating efficiencies due to advances in retailing and inventory technology should help the industry in the late 1990s.

The department store division of the retail industry was hit particularly hard in the early 1990s by discount retailers siphoning market share away, as well as by a drop in consumer spending. Sears, for example—one of the oldest and best-known department stores—was ousted from its number one position in sales by Wal-Mart and Kmart. In an attempt to regain their leadership position, many department stores tried to create a new identity that would attract customers.

Top 10 LEADING RETAIL STORES

Ranked by: Sales, in billions of dollars.

1. Wal-Mart Stores, with $82.2 billion
2. Kmart, $34.0
3. Sears, $29.5
4. Kroger Co., $23.0
5. Target, $21.3
6. J. C. Penney, $20.9
7. Jewel Food Stores, $18.4
8. Price/Costco Inc., $16.2
9. Safeway, $15.6
10. Home Depot, $12.5

Source: *Brandweek,* Superbrands: America's Top 2,000 Brands, October 9, 1995, p. 132+.

Department stores, along with other retailers, were quick to embrace advanced computer technology. The ability to centralize operations, have a complete and up-to-date status of inventory, and get an exact reading of items purchased are but a few pieces of information that can be generated by computerized point-of-sale systems. Retailers were able to reduce not only their paperwork, but also their lead time in updating stock. The usage of computer technology moved from a luxury to a necessity in order for any retailer to survive in the competitive market of the 1990s.

As of the mid-1990s, department stores changed their product mix somewhat from their traditional offerings. "White goods"—appliances such as stoves and refrigerators—were less emphasized to make room for more apparel items. Sears adopted the slogan, "Come see the softer side of Sears," emphasizing that power tools and lawn equipment were not the only items you would see in the store. J.C. Penney upgraded their store merchandising, emphasizing more apparel also.

INDUSTRY OUTLOOK

In 1996, department stores saw their business environment improve from the previous two years. The department stores have relied heavily on sales of women's clothing, which has always been an important focus in the push to increase store sales. The combination of better quality, higher fashion women's wear, and increased demand due to improved economic conditions in 1996 helped spur sales for department stores. Regionally, the increased economic activity in California and the Pacific Northwest also aided sales. Most large department stores have placed more emphasis on meeting the new purchasing trends—namely, that apparel, jewelry, and quality home furnishings play more of an important share of department store sales than the home improvement hard goods and home electronic products which were the focus in the past. Many department store retailers are also emphasizing their own private label brands, which have been significantly improved in quality and marketing. On the operations side, these companies generally have also taken advantage of improvements in retail automation that make their merchandising, accounting, inventory, and logistics functions more efficient and accurate.

One negative fact hanging over the industry—as well as the rest of the $3.2 trillion retail market—is that for the last 25 years, the amount of retail space per person in the United States increased by 450 percent. "It generally is agreed that the country is already overstored, so successful operators are the ones taking market share from others. The battle for market share continues to be fought largely on the pricing front," William G. Barr reported in *Value Line Investment Survey.*

However, the departure of the shop weary consumer continued to hurt department stores' sales. In sharp contrast to the retail heyday of the 1980s, consumers in the 1990s became more thrifty. Feeling financially strained, people tried to maintain their lifestyles on a smaller budget. Since consumer confidence remained relatively low, many retailers kept their markups just high enough to maintain their market share. As general economic conditions improved in 1996, confidence and the consumer's purchasing habits increased.

Changes in demographics in the early 1990s posed challenges to department store retailers. The rate of household formations slowed dramatically in the early 1990s, and in the next two decades the percentage of young adults was projected to decline. The fastest growing segment of the population, people between the ages of 45 and 54 years, was forecast to grow 46 percent between 1990 and 2000. In other words, the baby boomers, who "shopped till they dropped" during the 1980s, would reach middle age by the year 2000. This age shift should have far reaching ramifications for the marketing and merchandising direction of department stores. In addition, the 65 and older segment of the American population continued to grow quickly. This group tended to spend more on health care and leisure activities and less on goods like apparel.

In the early 1990s, research indicated that consumers no longer considered shopping "fun." According to the *Lieber/Yankelovitch Monitor,* the number of consumers who described shopping for clothes as fun dropped 4 percent from 1991 to 1992. Shopping was regarded as time consuming and frustrating. However, as economic conditions improved, interest rates trended downward, and personal income slowly rose, more and more shoppers extended themselves on credit, bucking the earlier trend of frugal shopping. A possible risk to the economy in general—and to department stores in particular—is that consumers might have had such a pent up demand for purchases in the early 1990s that they overextended their debt levels to the point that in 1996 consumers are holding record amounts of debt. If the Federal Reserve tightens money and raises interest rates this could dry up purchases that would have normally gone to department store retailers.

The long term forecast for department stores showed continued slow growth throughout the 1990s—as little as 1 to 2 percent in real terms. This projection was based largely on the simple fact that people were spending less. According to a Department of Labor projection, retail sales adjusted for inflation should show an average annual growth rate of 2.5 percent from 1990 to 2005, compared with a 3.5 percent annual rate posted during the preceding 15 years. The key for retailers during the 1990s was their ability to attract new customers, regain old customers, and make existing operations more productive. Creative merchandising and keeping up with the fashion trends of the day would be a crucial component to gaining sales.

In an attempt to attract more customers, department store executives questioned how best to present merchandise and market themselves to customers. Although it would be difficult for department stores to re-enter certain businesses, such as major appliances or hardware, the question remained as to what would be the most productive merchandise mix.

"I don't think department stores could really go back full-scale into toys, because Toys 'R' Us and the discounters have taken over the business. Besides, it's too seasonal, and department stores can't compete on a year-round basis," William N. Smith, vice president of Smith Barney, admitted in *Stores*. Consultant Walter Levy described department stores as becoming "large-space specialty stores," while retail analyst Fred Wintzer called them "apparel supermarkets." Wintzer continued, "I don't really see department stores going back into any of the product categories they have dropped. At this point, they must do everything they can to protect their men's, women's, and children's apparel business."

Yet Allen Questrom, CEO of Federated Department Stores, predicted that department stores would retain a major portion of market share for the fashion industry, despite the intense competition from discount retailers and the home shopping networks. Questrom commented in *Women's Wear Daily* that department stores offered the best one-stop shopping opportunities and attracted consumers by making shopping a pleasurable experience.

1995 U.S. LEADING DEPARTMENT STORE SALES

Source: *Chain Store Age*, Lebhar-Friedman, Inc., 1997

Analyst Bill Ress suggested in *Stores* that department stores broaden their appeal by being the best place "to facilitate lifestyle interests." For example, Ress projected that the decorative home would be among the best performing classifications in the 1990s. A business briefing in the *Wall Street Journal* confirmed this point, stating that consumers spent more on their homes than on clothes. Same store sales for home goods rose 6 percent in the mid-1990s, compared to 3 percent for apparel, according to *Retail Marketing Report*.

Whatever approach department stores decided to take with regard to merchandise mix, industry executives agreed that department stores also needed to differentiate themselves from each other. "If individually they can find a hole not being met by their competitors, they can grow," Wintzer affirmed in *Stores*. "Nordstrom has done it well with service; Saks has done it at the high end. And Macy's has done it by being a little more fashion-forward, a little trendier, while staying very promotional."

Phil Miller, vice president and chief financial officer of Saks Fifth Avenue, commented in the *Daily News Record* that department stores must keep pace with today's consumers. Miller added that retailers' redundancy in marketing, which contributed to consumer disinterest, had to change.

The correct combination of service, customer responsiveness, and merchandise presentation was critical to the future growth of department stores. They had to recreate the original pleasant, almost entertaining experience for shoppers if they were to find their space among the crowd of discount mass merchandisers.

ORGANIZATION AND STRUCTURE

Retail establishments primarily selling merchandise for personal or household consumption played a major role in the U.S. economy by providing more than 20 percent of all jobs in the private sector. Department stores always held a leadership position among "traditional" retailers. Yet the very definition of department stores changed within the industry, as many stores eliminated some of their individual departments. The new definition covered the traditional department stores, but also included the "multi-department soft goods stores with a fashion orientation, full markup policy, and operating in stores large enough to be a shopping center anchor," Penny Gill stated in *Stores*. Such stores included Lord & Taylor, Neiman-Marcus, and Saks Fifth Avenue.

Changes in how merchants sold their products and in how consumers shopped led to the creation of a new division of retailers—discount mass merchandisers. This category includes superstores and price clubs, which both cut into the market share of traditional retailers. Also known as off-price retailers, these stores feature a specialized merchandise line at discount prices. Superstores are large retail establishments offering discount prices on a limited product line with extensive complementary merchandise. Examples of superstores include Toys 'R' Us and Wal-Mart. Price clubs are a new type of superstore, with more retail floor space and a more extensive line of merchandise at more sharply discounted prices.

WORK FORCE

In 1996, approximately 10,000 department stores operated throughout the United States and employed more than two million people. Many of the industry's employees were under the age of 25 and worked part-time, evenings, and weekends. Over 40 percent of the people employed by department stores were retail sales workers—the people who "worked the floor" selling merchandise. Administrative support personnel were the next largest group, with 15 percent of total employment. These employees provided general office skills and bookkeeping tasks, in addition to some working as customer service representatives. No formal training was required for most sales and administrative support positions, although a high school education was preferred.

Management positions in department stores made up less than 7 percent of total employment. These positions included department managers, buyers, merchandise managers, store managers, and retail chain store area managers. A college degree became increasingly important for management positions, especially with large department stores. Companies preferred to hire people who earned a bachelor's degree in marketing or business to join their management training programs.

Hourly workers in department stores earned two-thirds the average pay of all workers in private industry. This lower wage might be due to the high proportion of part-time and less experienced workers. Few employees belonged to a union, and those who did generally received the same pay as nonunion workers. Department store jobs were projected to increase nearly 23 percent from 1990 to 2005; nearly as fast as the average for all industries. Large numbers of job openings will result primarily from the high turnover rate generally found in this industry.

RESEARCH AND TECHNOLOGY

Despite the sluggish retail forecast, department store companies continued to invest in technology—primarily because it became a necessity. Using computer technology, such as inventory management systems and point-of-sale bar code scanning, provided a tremendous advantage for stores trying to regain their competitive edge. Many stores gathered data from scanners at the point-of-sale (POS), which told managers their peak selling periods and allowed them to better shape work schedules. This data also showed managers exactly what products were selling, which helped in keeping the stores fully stocked and in forecasting upcoming selling trends.

For example, J.C. Penney implemented a state of the art, automated, merchandise replenishment system. This computerized program triggered orders based on projected sales demand so that stores were constantly stocked with basic merchandise items. Orders were processed every week instead of every two to four weeks. J.C. Penney also operated an information network based on seven large mainframe computers and 120,000 terminals, which processed about 700 million retail transactions annually.

Satellite networks also have entered the retail world. J.C. Penney was the first to use satellite transmission in its merchandising area with the introduction of its Direct Broadcast System (DBS) in 1985. Using one way video and two way audio, corporate buyers communicated with department managers during a broadcast session. The technology allowed buying procedures that previously took weeks to be reduced to just a few days.

In August 1993, R.H. Macy & Co, Inc. also began satellite broadcasting in each of its Macy's, Bullock's, and I. Magnin stores. The system allowed sales associates to discuss product introductions and new product developments with vendors. Each Macy store was equipped with a satellite receiving dish and decoder, a video monitor, and a VCR. Programming was linked directly to a satellite, sending a signal that was received and unscrambled at each store.

While most department stores upgraded and expanded their computer systems, Saks Fifth Avenue launched one of the most ambitious efforts in computer integration. The new system, implemented at the company's 63 stores, included hand held computers and scanning applications for bar codes. With its POS connection, inventory at all locations was upgraded constantly, making it possible to inform customers in minutes about the availability of a desired item located at any Saks store.

Sears made major financial commitments to implementing advanced computer technology a part of its restructuring plan. In 1990 Sears completed a major information systems (IS) reorganization and increased spending to accommodate growing networking needs. Sears also began using a public Electronic Data Exchange, making it easier for the company to communicate with other businesses.

New technologies projected for the retail industry include customer information management systems; open systems, where an architecture could accommodate several different kinds of hardware; and interactive promotional video displays.

AMERICA AND THE WORLD

Most department stores planned some sort of international expansion in the 1990s. With the completion of the North American Free Trade Agreement (NAFTA) in September 1992, many stores sought opportunities in both Canada and Mexico. According to a Coopers and Lybrand survey, retailers interested in Canada planned to open their own stores within that country. However, those interested in Mexico were more inclined to work through joint ventures or partnerships.

Some stores had already entered Mexico, and both J.C. Penney and Dillard Department Stores planned to anchor malls in Mexico City, Monterrey, and Guadalajara, Mexico. The Mexican malls were designed in a similar style to American malls, and Mexican retailers would occupy nearly half of the rental space. Sears also planned to enter the Mexican market with its Homelife furniture stores and the Japanese market with its auto supply stores. Saks Fifth Avenue also targeted Mexico, in addition to Asia and Europe, for expansion.

Another possible entry into the international arena might come through catalog sales and telemarketing. In this scenario, merchandise would be sold through a partnership with a third-party national. A special catalog would be created targeting international markets, and operations would be set up similar to catalog service companies in the United States. A licensed catalog sales program would place U.S. goods in foreign markets through a licensee with little risk to the American company. All sales would be concluded domestically, with the licensee responsible for transporting goods across borders. J.C. Penney began such a program in Bermuda and Aruba, and negotiations were ongoing in Russia, Iceland, Brazil, Panama, and Argentina for additional licensed catalog sales.

ASSOCIATIONS AND SOCIETIES

NATIONAL ASSOCIATION OF RETAIL DEALERS OF AMERICA
10 E. 22nd St.
Lombard, IL 60148
Phone: (708) 953-8950
Fax: (708) 953-8957

NATIONAL RETAIL FEDERATION
325 7th Ave. NW, Ste. 1000
Washington, DC 20004-2802
Phone: (202) 783-7971
Fax: (202) 737-2849

RETAIL, WHOLESALE AND DEPARTMENT STORE UNION
30 E. 29th St.
New York, NY 10016
Phone: (212) 684-5300
Fax: (212) 779-2809

PERIODICALS AND NEWSLETTERS

CHAIN STORE AGE
Lebhar-Friedman, Inc.
425 Park Ave.
New York, NY 10022
Phone: (212) 756-5000
Fax: (212) 756-5250
Monthly. $99.00 per year. Formerly Chain Store Age Executive with Shopping Center Age.

THE RETAIL MANAGEMENT LETTER
Management Facts Co.
Colony Farm Center
48153 Rupp
Plymouth, MI 48170-3304
Phone: (313) 459-1080
Monthly. $167.00 per year.

RETAILING TODAY
Robert Kahn and Associates
PO Box 249
Lafayette, CA 94549
Phone: (415) 254-4434
Fax: (415) 284-5612
Monthly. $54.00 per year. Newsletter. Written for retail chief executive officers and other top retail management.

STORES
National Retail Federation
Financial Executives Div.
325 7th St. NW, Ste. 1000
Washington, DC 20004-2802
Phone: (202) 783-7971
Fax: (202) 737-2849
Monthly. $49.00 per year.

DATABASES

***CITIBASE* (CITICORP ECONOMIC DATABASE)**
FAME Software Corp.
77 Water St., 9 Fl.
New York, NY 10005
Phone: (212) 898-7800
Fax: (212) 742-8956
Presents over 6,000 statistical series relating to business, industry, finance, and economics. Includes series from Survey of Current Business *and many other sources. Time period is 1947 to date, with daily updates. Inquire as to online cost and availability.*

STATISTICS SOURCES

MERCHANDISE AND OPERATING RESULTS OF DEPARTMENT AND SPECIALTY STORES

National Retail Federation
Financial Executives Div.
325 7th St. NW, Ste. 1000
Washington, DC 20004-2802
Phone: (202) 783-7971
Fax: (202) 737-2849
Annual. Members, $75.00; non-members, $150.00. Formerly National Retail Merchants Association.

MONTHLY RETAIL TRADE: SALES AND INVENTORIES

Available from U.S. Government Printing Office
Washington, DC 20402
Phone: (202) 783-3238
Monthly, with annual summary. $57.00 per year. Issued by Bureau of the Census, U.S. Department of Commerce. Includes Advance Monthly Retail Sales.

SALES IN 100 DEPARTMENT STORES

National Retail Federation
100 W. 31st St.
New York, NY 10001
Phone: (212) 244-8780
Fax: (212) 594-0487
Annual. Formerly National Retail Merchants Association.

GENERAL WORKS

DIRECTORY OF DEPARTMENT STORES

Chain Store Guide Information Services
3922 Coconut Palm Rd.

Tampa, FL 33619
Phone: (800) 925-2288 or (813) 664-6700
Fax: (813) 664-6810
Annual. $239.00.

NATIONAL RETAIL FEDERATION BUYER'S MANUAL

National Retail Federation
100 W. 31st St.
New York, NY 10001
Phone: (212) 244-8780
Fax: (212) 594-0487
$22.00. Formerly National Retail Merchants Association

THE RETAIL REVOLUTION: MARKET TRANSFORMATION, INVESTMENT, AND LABOR IN THE MODERN DEPARTMENT STORE

Barry Bluestone and others
Greenwood Publishing Group, Inc.
88 Post Rd.
W Westport, CT 06881
Phone: (800) 225-5800 or (203) 266-3571
Fax: (203) 222-1502
1980. $49.95.

FURTHER READING

Moukheiber, Zina. "Retailing—Annual Report on American Industry." *Forbes*, 13 January 1997.

"The Fortune 500—Retailing." *Fortune.* 28 April 1997.

Valueline. "Retail Store Industry." 21 February 1997. ◄►

RUBBER
PRODUCTS

SICs 3010, 3020, 3050, 3060

The recovery of the U.S. automobile industry was projected to fuel growth in industrial rubber products, which find more than half their end uses in cars. Other areas of growth were expected to be manufacturing, mining, construction, oil and natural gas, appliances, and agriculture.

The tire industry is a highly competitive commodities business dominated by a few tightly-run global players. Annual sales were estimated to have exceeded $12.5 billion in 1996, when the industry employed about 64,000 workers. According to the Rubber Manufacturers Association (RMA) (as quoted in *Rubber World,* January 1995) 1994 tire shipments established a new record, at 170 million replacement units and 58.2 million original equipment units. Those numbers were projected to rise to 172 million and 59.2 million, respectively, in 1995.

The rubber footwear industry consists primarily of two product areas. One area includes the waterproof footwear worn over shoes to protect them from inclement weather. Such products are often referred to as overshoes, rubbers, galoshes, and arctics. Also included in this area are rubber boots, which are not worn over shoes but protect the feet from mud and water. The second area consists of rubber soled canvas shoes, generally known as sneakers.

In the hoses and belts industry, more than 125 companies manufacture products that approached the $3 billion-a-year range entering the mid-1990s. Manufacturing companies range from a myriad of small shops filling niche markets all the way up to several firms producing broad product lines with sales approaching or exceeding $1 billion a year. The number of companies in the industry, however, actually dropped off from the late 1980s to the early 1990s because of the effects of restructuring and a move toward automation. These actions, though, helped the remaining players be more productive.

The gaskets and seals sector plays a vital role in the operation of many types of equipment. Three markets—transportation equipment, industrial equipment and machinery, and electrical equipment—account for more than 90 percent of total demand. Of this, sales to original equipment manufacturers (OEMs) account for about 40 percent of revenue, and aftermarket sales an additional 60 percent. Transportation equipment, including automobiles, is the largest OEM customer, accounting for 40 percent of total sales. The cyclical nature of the market resulting from such dependency on automobile sales has been offset by the relative stability of aftermarket demand for industry products. By 1996, U.S. shipments in the seals and gasket industry were estimated at $4.23 billion, about 72 percent higher than a decade earlier. Gaskets held the greatest share, at $1.38 billion, followed by molded seals, $801 million; shaft seals, $568 million; and compression packings, $116 million.

Molded, extruded, and lathe-cut goods are used in various machinery and equipment. End uses for these products exist in automobiles, oil and gas equipment,

Top 10 LARGEST CORPORATIONS IN THE RUBBER INDUSTRY

Ranked by: Revenue in 1995, in millions of dollars.

1. Goodyear Tire & Rubber Co., with $13,166 million
2. Premark International, $3,574
3. Rubbermaid, $2,344
4. M. A. Hanna, $1,957
5. Mark IV Industries Inc., $1,603
6. Raychem, $1,531
7. Cooper Tire & Rubber, $1,497
8. Foamex International, $1,269
9. A. Schulman, $1,035
10. Standard Products Co., $996

Source: *Fortune,* Fortune 500 Largest U.S. Corporations (annual), April 29, 1996, p. F-60.

appliances, farm equipment, and construction machinery. About 600 firms in the United States make molded, extruded, and lathe-cut goods. The market is fragmented due to the diversity of end uses and no single company has dominated the industry. The sector also faces strong foreign competition. The U.S. and Canadian market alone was estimated at $5.1 billion in 1993, with sales of about $5.8 billion by 1997. Total U.S. employment industry-wide is in the area of 50,000 people.

INDUSTRY OUTLOOK

According to *Modern Tire Dealer,* less than 20 firms were producing tires in the United States in the mid-1990s. Industrywide employment was estimated at 63,900 in 1996, with about 80 percent of these involved in production. Total tire shipments were estimated at $12.8 billion in 1996, up from $11.9 billion in 1990.

The rubber footwear industry in 1995 was made up of 62 companies with a total of 9,600 employees. Some of the companies manufactured rubber plastic footwear exclusively, while others maintained it as a modest or minor product line. By the end of 1995, 63,505 pairs of rubber, or plastic-soled, fabric-upper shoes had been manufactured with an overall shipment value of $521,866. Rubber or plastic protective footwear for that year saw 16,876 pairs of shoes produced at a shipment value of $253,792. By contrast, 1994 saw 61,280 pairs of fabric, rubber or plastic-soled shoes produced and shipped at a value of $599,154; 18,796 pairs of rubber or plastic protective footwear were produced and shipped

at a value of $276,956. By the end of 1996, shipments and subsequent shipment valuation decreased for both classes of footwear, with rubber, or plastic-soled, fabric-upper shoes valued at $404,081 for 60,757 pairs, and rubber or plastic protective overshoes valued at $212,601 for 14,866 pairs shipped.

Rubber hose shipments were expected to increase 3.5 percent a year during the mid-1990s, rising to $1.54 billion per year because of an increase in motor vehicle production and growth in other industrial and construction products. While showing steady growth, a lack of new applications and penetration by alternate materials were expected to keep the growth of rubber hose below the increases made by general industry. Imports, which have been felt in other rubber product markets, could limit growth in this industry sector as well. Commodity hose lines are the most likely to be affected by imports from southeast Asia. Conversely, domestic hose makers are projected to raise their export sales.

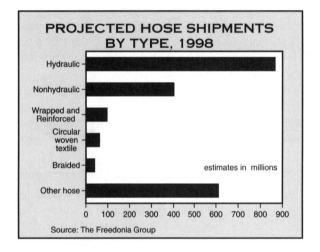

PROJECTED HOSE SHIPMENTS BY TYPE, 1998

Source: The Freedonia Group

The rubber belt market was estimated at $1.1 billion by 1996. Factors inducing growth were projected to include automobile sales and a growth in the sales of industrial equipment, two major belting markets. Both flat belting and V-belts were projected to enjoy robust growth in the mid-1990s. The latter category made up nearly two-thirds of belt sales and was expected to grow 4.5 percent a year to $735 million annually.

Replacement belt and hose sales are estimated to grow 2.4 percent from 1995 to 2000 as sales from these products are expected to steadily increase in that time period. The replacement belt industry is expected to top out at $340 million by the year 2000.

Manufacturers of molded seals, gaskets, and packings forecast the fastest growth—shipments totaled $801 million in 1992—because of the service the products provide in both static and dynamic sealing applications. Growth projections for molded seals alone called for annual increases of 7.1 percent—a $1.1 billion market in 1997. The advantages molded seals have over other seal types and an increase in durable goods production were seen as factors in growth potential. Also contributing to the growth was an effort underway to enact stricter fluid controls in the chemicals and petroleum industries.

OEM sales were projected to increase 7.3 percent a year through 1997, bringing this segment to $1.8 billion in sales. Replacement sales were estimated to climb to $2.5 billion in 1997, projecting an annual 6.4 percent increase annually. Areas expected to receive growth were transportation equipment servicing, manufacturing markets, and the utilities market. Though OEM sales were projected to grow at a more rapid pace, the aftermarket would still provide the majority of sales because of the broad base of existing machinery and equipment that would be serviced.

Shipments of lathe-cut goods were forecast to increase 5.7 percent a year. The segment also was expected to benefit from a stronger automotive market and rising spending on industrial equipment. Growth was, however, predicted to be confined by competition from other materials and imports.

ORGANIZATION AND STRUCTURE

The tire and inner tube industry depends chiefly on rubber suppliers for raw materials and automobile manufacturers for sales. Well over half of the world's production of rubber goes into the manufacture of automobile tires. The tire and inner tube industry is the largest element of the rubber industry group as a whole, constituting over 40 percent of that group's product sales. The rubber industry group is represented by the Rubber Manufacturers Association (RMA). The RMA members make up more than three-fourths of the dollar sales of the rubber industry group as a whole. One effort of the RMA has been the establishment of a Scrap Tire Management Council to promote environmentally proper disposition of scrap tires.

In the late 1980s, the tire and inner tube industry changed from one in which most leading companies were U.S.-owned to one in which 3 of the 4 largest companies are owned by French, Japanese, and Italian nationals. British interests have attempted, unsuccessfully, to acquire control of remaining leading American tire producers. Competition has become more severe and more international in scope. These ownership changes have been a part of a trend toward mergers of many of the major companies, resulting in larger but fewer independent companies in the top structure of the industry.

An important influence encouraging the purchases of American tire companies by foreign organizations has been the weaker dollar, which eliminated the price advantage for foreign companies when the dollar was stronger.

Much of the rubber and plastic footwear sold in the United States has been produced in other countries, largely due to lower production costs. Although sneakers represented a $5.5 billion industry in the United States in 1990, the value of rubber, or plastic-soled footwear produced and shipped within the United States was estimated at only $561,230 for that year.

Much of the structure of the hose and belting industry is organized around how the product gets to its end user—either in the original equipment (OE) or replacement market. Looking at the automotive market, the OE market is much more straightforward, as most of the products are sold directly to the auto makers. Sales to the aftermarket, though, are a bit more complicated, going through either a three-step or two-step distribution process. Hose and belt makers have had to ensure that their distribution system is getting the parts to the proper outlet in a timely fashion. Distribution also plays an important role in the industrial hose and belt markets. Many of these distributors also serve as fabricators, placing needed attachments and accessories onto the basic hose and belts for their final usage. The distributors in this sector also are more likely to play a role in OE accounts, especially for an account that needs to have local inventory. As for the aftermarket, a major portion of the business is sold through distribution sectors, although some hose and belt makers do sell some product directly to the end user.

The gasket and seal industry supports varied manufacturing and other industries, gaining its existence from the end use of its products rather than from the products themselves. Because of the industry's dependency on the health of the economy in general, the demand for gaskets, seals, and packings mirrors the cycles experienced by the makers of the durable goods that utilize such supplies. Makers of gaskets and seals are also influenced by their customers in areas such as product development, production processes, marketing, and pricing. With the large number of suppliers available, end users can bargain not only for better pricing, but for better service as well.

WORK FORCE

Opportunities for careers in the industry have generally been fewer than in other industries, largely because of severe competition resulting from many mergers and acquisitions, excess capacity, and the efforts of most companies in the industry to keep prices low to gain or maintain market share. Consequently, tire companies have sought to cut costs, eliminate plants, and resist pay increases. Nevertheless, some companies planned to increase prices and production capacity. Furthermore, at the top levels, opportunities have been created for business leaders to help organizations overcome losses or unsatisfactory profit margins.

In 1996 the tire and inner tube industry employed an estimated 78,000 workers, of which 80 percent were production workers. This was a 6 percent decline from 1990, a trend that was expected to continue throughout the remainder of the decade. The most plentiful jobs in the industry were in the production and maintenance areas. More technical activities are in the research and development, production planning and control, accounting and finance, and information systems functions. Career paths can proceed from production operator to supervisor, department head, and plant manager. Such lateral moves can be made as from production supervisor to production control technician. In 1996, the average tire industry production worker earned an estimated $19.74 per hour, up from $17.70 in 1991.

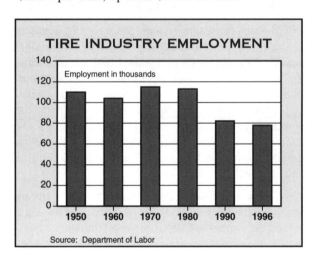

TIRE INDUSTRY EMPLOYMENT

Employment in thousands

Source: Department of Labor

U.S. employment in the rubber and plastics footwear industry decreased by 65 percent, between 1972 and 1987, caused in part by moves to lower cost suppliers overseas. Total employment had risen from 10,900 in 1987 to 11,700 in 1991, but continuously declined throughout the decade to an estimated low of 9,600 in 1996.

Total employment in the rubber and plastics hose and belting industry was estimated at 20,000 in 1995 and was expected to remain steady through 1998. Of those employed, about 16,200 were production workers earning about $12.08 an hour, according to government figures. Other occupations include chemists, product designers, engineers, and sales people. The average num-

ber of workers per factory has decreased over the years because of increased productivity traceable to improved processes and automation. In 1972, 19 hose and belt plants in the United States—about 21 percent of facilities—accounted for 76 percent of employment and 75 percent of shipments. A decade later, just 9 plants employed 500 workers or more, accounting for 44 percent of employment and 39 percent of shipments. The average number of workers per plant dropped from 354 in 1972 to 124 in 1987 to just 100 in 1995.

Total employment in 1994 in the gasket industry was about 35,100 according to the latest figures available from the U.S. government. The leading states in terms of employment were California, Illinois, Ohio, and Texas. The range of employment varied extensively, from factory workers producing the products, to chemists and engineers who develop the compounds and design, to the sales force that deals with OEM and aftermarket accounts. Estimated employment for 1995 was 38,000 workers. This was expected to increase by approximately 5.4 percent to reach an employment level of 37,000 by 1998. Of these 38,000 employees, 25,000 were production workers earning an average of $11.41 per hour in 1995. In 1998 the number of production workers is expected to increase by 5.2 percent to 26,300 employees earning and average of $12.23 per hour, an increase of 5.2 percent over the 1995 projected figures.

The mechanical rubber goods industry employed an estimated 51,400 workers in 1996. This was expected to reach an employment level of 52,200 by 1998. Of these 51,400 employees, 40,600 work in production and earn an average of $10.78 per hour. In 1998, the number of production workers is expected to increase by 4.2 percent to 41,700 workers earning $11.10 per hour, an increase of 4.5 percent over the 1995 projected figures.

RESEARCH AND TECHNOLOGY

Research and technology's emphasis has been on creating and improving the design and specifications of tire products to meet customers' needs. Though technical skills have always been applied to production methodology and cost controls, operating efficiency was a dominant objective in the 1980s and early 1990s because of the intense competition in that period.

Since the mid-1980s especially, when merger and acquisition activities have dominated the industry, the intensified competition has encouraged or required the tire producers to reduce costs so they could trim prices and survive with slimmer profit margins. To cut costs, producers have engaged in re-engineering or "downsizing," eliminating inefficient plants, and streamlining operations. These cost improvement activities have required the companies' technical staffs to design better production methods and apply computer techniques to save workers' time, speed processes, and improve quality.

The Shoe and Allied Trades Research Association (SATRA) has done a great deal of pioneering research, providing industry members with technology too costly for the smaller companies in the footwear business to develop on their own. For example, SATRA has developed beneficial concepts in the areas of ergonomics, color durability, the environment, materials standards, quality control, and computer applications like CAD/CAM, robotics, and bar coding.

In response to increasing imports, many makers of gaskets and seals took a proactive stance: cutting manufacturing costs, going to advanced production concepts such as computer-aided design, and after-uses that had the opportunity to provide greater than average growth. Examples of such applications are non-asbestos gasketing, or seals designed to reduce emissions in process industries. Industry participants also spent to improve product design. These actions helped the industry maintain steady growth since the early 1980s.

Despite their uses in highly complex applications, gasket and seal technology itself is more defined. Developments have come in the form of the new materials being used and demands from customers for longer lasting materials. One new type of material is an oil-resistant liquid-silicone-rubber (LSR) introduced by Dow Corning STI. Typical applications of this product are gaskets, O-rings, grommets, rollers and electrical components. These new silicones should extend ''hot-oil performance and high speed processing to manufacturers of automotive, off-highway, and industrial equipment''; according to *Mechanical Engineering*. The automobile industry demanded a new type of silicone due to rising temperatures in engine compartments, and the need for longer service-life in the automobile industry.

New techniques will continue to evolve. One such predicted growth area is liquid injection molding (LIM) using silicone rubber. This process was unveiled in the late 1970s amid much hype as to how it would simplify life for molders. According to early literature, the liquid material went directly into the machine and the finished product came out—supposedly eliminating the need for several secondary operations necessary with traditional rubber molding. While the reality of LIM didn't quite meet its promise when it was first introduced, improvements in its technology in the early 1990s increased its popularity. Molders of components for medical devices, especially, adopted the process, with many adding or expanding LIM capability. The draw for medical molders has been the ability to make a clean product—the finished component emerges virtually untouched—that meets tight tolerances.

Cellular manufacturing has also gained in prominence. In this process, molding and secondary finishing operations all take place in one ''cell,'' eliminating the necessity for the product to be moved to different areas of the plant. This improves quality, product flow, and efficiency, and helps reduce staffing requirements as well.

A new fully integrated system for high-yield molding of trimless/flashless parts is the industry's newest technology, developed by Hull/Finmac Inc. in Warminster, Pennsylvania, and Trimless/Flashless Design Inc. (TFD) in Chantilly, Virginia. The system is a combination of a 35-ton compression press and a unique modular mold, a first for the rubber industry. The system will reduce scrap rates and should eliminate most deflashing operations, improving speed and quality in molding natural or synthetic rubber.

AMERICA AND THE WORLD

Most of the leading companies have tire plants in several countries and sell their products in international markets. Since the latter part of the 1980s, the tire industry has also become much more multinational in ownership as many of the top tire companies in the United States were bought by foreign concerns. In fact, the multinational mergers and acquisitions have left few tire companies in the United States unaffiliated with foreign firms. Imports shrunk 9 percent from a high of 56 million units in 1995.

Global expansion is also an important force driving leading companies in the industry. ''Much of the logic behind the current activity is to supply the global automotive industry,'' according to the *European Rubber Journal*. Joint ventures, especially with Japanese-owned companies, also became prevalent. These helped U.S. firms gain business with both foreign automakers as well as transplant companies that make cars and other products in America.

ASSOCIATIONS AND SOCIETIES

INTERNATIONAL INSTITUTE OF SYNTHETIC RUBBER PRODUCERS
2077 S Gessner Rd., Ste. 133
Houston, TX 77063-1123
Phone: (713) 783-7511
Fax: (713) 783-7253

MALAYSIAN RUBBER BUREAU
1925 K St. NW, Ste. 204,
Washington, DC 20006
Phone: (202) 452-0544
Fax: (202) 659-5150

RUBBER MANUFACTURERS ASSOCIATION
1400 K St., NW
Washington, DC 20005
Phone: (800) 220-7622 or (202) 682-4800
Fax: (202) 682-4854

PERIODICALS AND NEWSLETTERS

***RUBBER AND PLASTICS NEWS: THE RUBBER
INDUSTRY'S INTERNATIONAL NEWSPAPER***
Crain Communications, Inc.
1725 Merriman Rd., Ste. 300
Akron, OH 44313-5251
Phone: (800) 678-9595 or (216) 836-9180
Fax: (216) 836-1005
Biweekly. $62.00 per year. Written for rubber product manufacturers.

RUBBER CHEMISTRY AND TECHNOLOGY
American Chemical Society Rubber Div.
University of Akron,
Akron, OH 44325-3801
Phone: (216) 972-7814
Fax: (216) 972-5269
Five times a year. $95.00 per year.

RUBBER WORLD
Lippincott and Peto, Inc.
PO Box 5485
Akron, OH 44313-0485
Phone: (216) 864-2122
Fax: (216) 864-5298
16 times a year. $29.00 per year.

DATABASES

***CITIBASE* (CITICORP ECONOMIC DATABASE)**
FAME Software Corp.
77 Water St., 9 Fl.
New York, NY 10005
Phone: (212) 898-7800
Fax: (212) 742-8956
Presents over 6,000 statistical series relating to business, industry, finance, and economics. Includes series from Survey of Current Business *and many other sources. Time period is 1947 to date, with daily updates. Inquire as to online cost and availability.*

DRI CHEMICAL FORECAST
DRI/McGraw-Hill, Data Products Division
24 Hartwell Ave.
Lexington, MA 02173
Phone: (800) 541-9914 or (617) 863-5100

Supply-demand and price forecasts are given quarterly and annually for over 120 U.S. chemical products. Quarterly forecasts generally extend three years, while annual forecasts cover five to ten years. Inquire as to online cost and availability.

STATISTICS SOURCES

BUSINESS STATISTICS
Available from U.S. Government Printing Office
Washington, DC 20402
Phone: (202) 512-1800
Fax: (202) 512-2250
Biennial. $20.00. Issued by Bureau of Economic Analysis, U.S. Department of Commerce. Shows annual data for 29 years and monthly data for a recent four-year period. Statistics correspond to the Survey of Current Business.

ENCYCLOPEDIA OF AMERICAN INDUSTRIES
Gale Research
835 Penobscot Bldg.,
Detroit, MI 48226-4094
Phone: (800) 877-GALE or (313) 961-2242
Fax: (800) 414-5043
1994. $500.00. Two volumes ($250.00 each). Volume one is Manufacturing Industries *and volume two is* Service and Non-Manufacturing Industries. *Provides the history, development, and recent status of approximately 1,000 industries. Includes statistical graphs, with industry and general indexes.*

RUBBER: PRODUCTION, SHIPMENTS, AND STOCKS
U.S. Bureau of the Census
Washington, DC 20233
Phone: (301) 763-4100
Annual. $1.00. Current Industrial Reports, MA-30A.

RUBBER STATISTICAL BULLETIN
International Rubber Study Group
York House, 8 Fl., Empire Way
Wembley, England HA9 OPA
Phone: 081 9 03 7727
Fax: 081 9 03 2848
Monthly. $280.00 per year.

GENERAL WORKS

RUBBER AND PLASTICS NEWS-RUBBICANA ISSUE
Crain Communications, Inc.
740 N. Rush St.
Chicago, IL 60611-2590
Phone: (312) 649-5200
Fax: (312) 280-3149
Annual. $65.00.

RUBBER RED BOOK
Communication Channels, Inc.
6151 Powers Ferry Rd. NW
Atlanta, GA 30339-2941
Phone: (800) 621-4709 or (404) 955-2500
Fax: (404) 955-0400

Annual. $79.95. Lists manufacturers and suppliers of rubber goods in U.S., Puerto Rico, and Canada.

FURTHER READING

Clifford, Mark J., Michael Shari, and Linda Himelstein. "Pangs of Conscience: Sweatshops Haunt U.S. Consumers." *Business Week,* 29 July 1996.

Darnay, Arsen J., ed. *Manufacturing USA.* Detroit: Gale Research, 1996.

Dun's Million Dollar Disc. Dun & Bradstreet, Inc., Fourth Quarter 1996.

Lazich, Robert S., ed. *Market Share Reporter.* Detroit: Gale Research, 1996.

"OE Market Share." *Modern Tire Dealer,* January 1996, 34.

Standard & Poor's Industry Surveys. New York: Standard & Poor's Corporation, 1996.

"Technology Focus: Oil Resistant Silicone." *Mechanical Engineering,* September 1996.

U.S. Bureau of the Census. *1995 Annual Survey of Manufactures.* Washington: GPO, 1997.

U.S. Bureau of the Census. *Current Industrial Reports.* Washington: GPO, 1996. Available from http://www.census.gov/cir/www/mq31a.html.

INDUSTRY SNAPSHOT

In 1996, more than 220 companies in the United States were involved in the manufacture of search and navigation systems and instruments. Together these companies generated $76.73 billion in sales and employed 501,700.

The search and navigation industry experienced declines in shipments in the early 1990s due to decreased defense budgets, the end of the Cold War, diminished commercial aircraft industry purchases, and a recessionary economy. Sharp reductions in the military-related expenditures that formed the backbone of industry profits hastened restructuring and globalization trends and continued to negatively impact the industry. Nevertheless, the United States was expected to continue leading the world in new technology in this market throughout the 1990s. The market will, however, be buoyed by increasing demand for these products from the civilian sector. Especially important will be those instruments relating to GPS and innovative automobile navigation and safety systems. The decrease in overall demand is expected to spur competitiveness as companies fight for market share and market niches. The export market is expected to be driven by orders from Russia, Singapore, China, South Korea, Canada, Turkey, and India as these countries upgrade existing aircraft radar and navigation systems rather than investing in new hardware.

ORGANIZATION AND STRUCTURE

With few exceptions, the principle suppliers of search and navigation equipment are the same contractors who comprise the larger U.S. aerospace industry. The search and navigation equipment industry accounted for about one-quarter of aerospace industry shipments ($129 billion) in the early 1990s, which in turn represented about two-thirds of the worldwide aerospace industry. Many of the largest and most recognizable corporations in the United States manufacture search and navigation industry products for the domestic and international defense and commercial markets.

Historically, the primary customer for industry products has been the U.S. government, particularly the Department of Defense, the Federal Aviation Authority, and the National Aeronautics and Space Administration. Industry sales to commercial establishments adhere to the traditional terms and conditions of the business marketplace, and products are evaluated in terms of competitive value for technical superiority, reputation, price, delivery schedule, financing, and reliability. Sales to the

SEARCH AND NAVIGATION EQUIPMENT

SIC 3812

The United States is the international leader in the development and manufacture of search and navigation instruments and systems. This industrial sector is one of the most technologically sophisticated in the domain of American business and manufacturing. Despite a steadily declining employment picture domestically, many of the industry's foremost companies are seeking to decrease their dependence on fluctuating U.S. government contracts and to tap the growth potential in newly flourishing export markets. Perhaps the preeminent technical development of recent years includes the production and continued enhancement of Global Positioning Systems (GPS)—a technology with great significance not only for the military, but for commercial and consumer markets as well. The civilian market for GPS is expected to exceed $8 billion by the year 2000, while major technological advances for all areas of the search and navigation industry will continue to occur at a rapid rate.

federal government, however, tend to follow a highly specialized and structured set of procedures.

GOVERNMENT PROCUREMENT

Funds for government search and navigation equipment contracts are authorized by Congress based on budget requests submitted by the executive branch for the agency or department requiring the equipment. Congress appropriates specific funding for programs on an annual basis, which often means that programs originally approved for development over several years are subject to adjustments or outright cancellation on a yearly basis. Contractors submit bids to government officials at bidding conferences attended by "prime" contractors—firms or consortia who submit the final integrated system directly to the end-user agency—and subcontractors who attend the conferences to seek out prime contractors with whom to team.

Contracts may be awarded to a single contractor in a "winner-take-all" competition or divided among several contractors or consortia as a percentage of the total awarded contract. Contracts may cover specific phases of the product development process: the concept/design or project definition stage, the prototype or demonstration/validation stage, or the execution or large-scale production stage. Government contracts are also awarded according to the method by which the contractor is paid. In "cost reimbursement" contracts, the contractor is paid for allowable or "allocable" costs such as engineering and manufacturing expenses, special tooling and test equipment costs, marketing and administrative expenditures, and the cost of the bid proposal itself. "Cost plus fixed fee" contracts involve payments to the contractor by the government of a preestablished fee regardless of the firm's actual final costs. Such contracts award contractors who deliver systems below the contracted price and penalize contractors who experience cost overruns. In "cost plus incentive fee" contracts, the government reimburses the contractor based on the firm's ability to meet certain targets such as cost guidelines, "mission success" parameters, and delivery time constraints. The average industry "win rate"—the ratio of contracts awarded to total contracts bid on—is about 25 percent in the aerospace and thus the search and navigation industry as a whole. Some firms, however, achieve win rates nearly twice as high.

Contractors are generally paid through periodic "progress payments" for work performed, with a final payment for remaining costs paid upon delivery of the product. Contracts may be extended through "replenishment" and "follow on" orders by the government customer and may be terminated without cause at the sole discretion of the government. Disputes regarding unpaid or overpaid amounts are handled by a Defense Contract Management District Termination Contracting Officer to whom settlement proposals are submitted by the contractor for claimed expenses and "termination costs." The Contracting Officer may award the contractor funds for work performed prior to the contract's termination or may require that the contractor reimburse funds paid out for canceled work.

The "monopsonic"—or single customer—nature of the government procurement market has led to a

SIC 3812 - Search and Navigation Equipment
General Statistics

Year	Companies	Establishments		Employment			Compensation		Production ($ million)			
		Total	with 20 or more employees	Total (000)	Production Workers (000)	Hours (Mil)	Payroll ($ mil)	Wages ($/hr)	Cost of Materials	Value Added by Manufacture	Value of Shipments	Capital Invest.
1982												
1983												
1984												
1985												
1986												
1987	920	1,084	508	369.4	158.8	314.3	12,373.0	14.21	12,208.3	24,738.7	36,266.8	1,439.0
1988				361.3	155.3	297.1	12,547.3	14.99	11,510.2	24,666.7	36,596.5	1,368.6
1989		895	502	339.5	140.8	276.7	12,445.3	14.99	10,874.7	23,924.5	35,295.4	1,366.9
1990				313.6	130.3	281.7	12,257.9	14.49	11,275.3	24,931.9	36,733.5	1,124.5
1991				279.8	112.3	258.0	11,630.7	14.08	11,401.5	23,672.3	36,213.4	829.9
1992	634	769	409	255.0	103.6	203.1	11,056.2	17.29	10,115.8	24,411.1	35,266.1	859.1
1993				225.1	88.5	170.8	10,123.0	18.79	8,844.2	24,031.3	33,546.2	706.1
1994				199.4	79.7	156.7	9,395.5	18.86	7,928.2	21,900.4	30,103.3	648.9
1995				177.3P	66.7P	138.8P	9,455.8P	19.07P	8,386.0P	23,165.1P	31,841.7P	471.7P
1996				151.6P	54.6P	115.2P	9,006.3P	19.76P	8,201.0P	22,654.1P	31,139.3P	344.8P
1997				125.9P	42.4P	91.6P	8,556.8P	20.45P	8,016.0P	22,143.1P	30,436.9P	217.9P
1998				100.2P	30.3P	68.1P	8,107.3P	21.14P	7,831.1P	21 632.0P	29,734.4P	91.0P

Sources: 1982, 1987, 1992 Economic Census; Annual Survey of Manufactures, 83-86, 88-91, 93-94. Establishment counts for non-Census years are from County Business Patterns; establishment values for 83-84 are extrapolations. 'P's show projections by the editors. Industries reclassified in 87 will not have data for prior years.

unique division of operations in the search and navigation industry: one set of rules and procedures for commercial clients and a second, completely segregated set of rules and procedures for government contracts. The purpose of the complex government procurement apparatus is to protect the government's interest in fair and reasonable prices, to eliminate contractor fraud, to ensure equal access by all bidders, and to guarantee that federal funds appropriated for government contracts reflect the economic and social priorities of the government. As a result, the process of bidding on federal contracts entails separate data collection and accounting procedures, conformance to supplier network requirements, adherence to hiring and personnel guidelines, and the disclosure of the contractor's corporate financial information to government auditors. These and other requirements regarding contractor certification and auditing and oversight conformance have resulted in historical labor costs for the industry three times higher for federal contracts (as a percentage of sales) than for equivalent commercial contracts.

PROCUREMENT AGENCIES

Several government agencies perform oversight and other procurement-related functions that directly affect search and navigation industry activities. The Defense Contract Audit Agency oversees expense, scheduling, and product performance reviews of industry contractors and specifies guidelines for planning and implementing federal contracts. The Government Accounting Office (GAO) and Office of Federal Procurement Policy of the Office of Management and Budget perform watchdog reviews of government contracts. "First tier" contractors—firms whose products are delivered directly to a prime contractor—may experience as many as 100 government audits in a single year for pricing, quality, and safety reviews. Similarly, an "operational readiness re-

view" administered by a defense department branch can involve as many as 50 auditors assigned to a single contractor plant at one time.

Establishments in the search and navigation industry can be classified in terms of their place in the product delivery hierarchy for government procurement contracts. The major prime contractors dominate the industry and are themselves the greatest source of competition for the subcontractors. The influence prime contractors have on subcontractors' profits is reflected in the announcement in the early 1990s by a major prime contractor, AlliedSignal Inc., that it planned to reduce its pool of 9,500 suppliers by 79 percent in just two years. Historically, about half of the worth of government contracts to prime contractors is channeled through subcontracts with firms supplying the "primes," and of this amount roughly 50 percent is divided between divisions of other prime contractors and the smaller subcontractors. Government procurement trends fluctuate between an emphasis on "single sourcing"—awarding whole contracts to a major prime contractor—and "multiple sourcing"—distributing procurement funds more evenly through the industry structure.

BUSINESS ENVIRONMENT

The unique nature of the government procurement environment entails business trends uncommon in other U.S. industries. Although industry profit rates as a percentage of sales have historically been less than for other industries, profits measured in terms of rate of return on investment are comparable to rates enjoyed by other manufacturing sectors. Search and navigation firms, like other defense sector businesses, may invest in plants and equipment at half the rate of firms in other industries because government contracts often reimburse firms for aging or obsolescent equipment, make available government-owned plants and equipment to the contractor, and

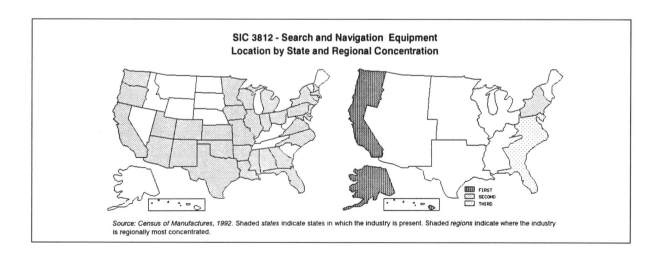

**SIC 3812 - Search and Navigation Equipment
Location by State and Regional Concentration**

FIRST
SECOND
THIRD

Source: Census of Manufactures, 1992. Shaded *states* indicate states in which the industry is present. Shaded *regions* indicate where the industry is regionally most concentrated.

offer no guarantee that the plant or equipment utilized for the procured product will ever be contracted for again. Moreover, government progress payments generally cover only ''certified costs'' and make few allowances for contractor investment in new facilities. Like members of other defense industries, search and navigation contractors require less working capital because they can rely on regular government progress payments instead of depending on unpredictable commercial revenues.

The search and navigation industry is subject to business risks not shared by other American industries. These include unusually high costs for obtaining skilled employees, intense domestic and international competition, the continual need to retrain employees and retool facilities, inevitable cost overruns resulting from untried technologies and advanced designs, and instability in the price of raw materials and supplies. Because defense-related products are driven by the requirement of continuing technological improvement and superiority, the rate of obsolescence for industry products is much higher and much more unpredictable than in other American industries.

PRODUCT GROUPS

Search and navigation products can be divided into two broad divisions and several subcategories. Search and detection systems and navigation and guidance systems and equipment ($31.76 billion in early 1990s shipments) constitute about 90 percent of the total search and navigation market and include the following product groups: light reconnaissance and surveillance systems; identification-friend-or-foe equipment; proximity fuses; radar systems and equipment; sonar search, detection, tracking, and communications equipment; specialized command and control data processing and display equipment; electronic warfare systems and equipment; and navigation systems and equipment, including navigational aids for aircraft, ships, and navigation applications.

The remaining 10 percent of the industry's market ($2.66 billion in the early 1990s) consists of aeronautical, nautical, and navigational instruments (excluding aircraft engine instruments) and includes the following product groups: flight and navigation sensors, transmitters, and displays; gyroscopes; airframe equipment instruments; thermocouple and thermocouple lead wire; nautical instruments; other aerospace flight instruments; and parts and components.

WORK FORCE

Employment by search and navigation industry firms declined steadily in the late 1980s and early 1990s. From 369,400 employees in 1987, industry employment fell to 314,000 in 1990 and to 220,400 in early 1993. Cutbacks in government defense contracts were the primary reason for these declines although companies with large ''backlogs'' of awarded but still uncompleted projects continued to hire despite diminished prospects for new contracts. By 1998, employment was expected to fall to about 100,000.

In 1996, approximately 34 percent of the industry's employees were classified as production workers. Establishments in four states—California, New York, Texas, and Florida—employed about 54 percent of the industry's workforce in the mid-1990s.

Average pay across all occupational categories was $38,491 in the early 1990s and average hourly earnings were $15.95. In 1996, hourly wages were estimated at $19.76 for the industry. The industry product groups with the highest concentration of employers in 1991 were: missile-borne and space vehicle systems and equipment with 45 establishments; specialized electronic and communication equipment with 44 employ-

SIC 3812 - Search and Navigation Equipment
Industry Data by State

| State | Establish-ments | Shipments | | | Employment | | | | Cost as % of Shipments | Investment per Employee ($) |
		Total ($ mil)	% of U.S.	Per Establ.	Total Number	% of U.S.	Per Establ.	Wages ($/hour)		
California	164	9,079.2	25.7	55.4	65,400	25.6	399	18.32	25.9	2,644
New York	72	3,873.1	11.0	53.8	22,300	8.7	310	21.32	25.0	4,184
Texas	50	2,864.5	8.1	57.3	23,000	9.0	460	14.31	25.1	3,643
Florida	55	2,667.3	7.6	48.5	18,700	7.3	340	12.18	28.4	4,540
Maryland	19	2,572.4	7.3	135.4	17,700	6.9	932	26.02	27.4	3,441
Massachusetts	49	2,490.8	7.1	50.8	16,300	6.4	333	18.81	37.3	2,472
New Jersey	46	2,281.2	6.5	49.6	15,100	5.9	328	21.88	37.6	3,497
Arizona	12	1,545.6	4.4	128.8	9,000	3.5	750	14.05	31.3	5,522
Virginia	13	1,371.7	3.9	105.5	8,800	3.5	677	12.28	22.2	6,193
Illinois	15	494.5	1.4	33.0	4,200	1.6	280	13.27	29.3	-

Source: 1992 *Economic Census*. The states are in descending order of shipments or establishments (if shipment data are missing for the majority). The symbol (D) appears when data are withheld to prevent disclosure of competitive information. States marked with (D) are sorted by number of establishments. A dash (-) indicates that the data element cannot be calculated; * indicates the midpoint of a range.

ers; and light reconnaissance and surveillance systems and equipment with 39 establishments.

Occupational categories employed in the industry included production workers such as machinists and assemblers, administrative support staff, administrators and executives, and engineers and other technical personnel. The industry employed a wide variety of engineering professionals—from aeronautical, civil, electrical, mechanical, quality assurance, and manufacturing engineers, to computer and digital systems, hardware, software, logistical, and algorithm systems engineers. Salaries for degreed engineers ranged between $18,000 and $78,000 per year depending on experience, professional specialization, job responsibilities, and other variables.

SIC 3812
Occupations Employed by SIC 381 - Search and Navigation Equipment

Occupation	% of Total 1994	Change to 2005
Electrical & electronics engineers	13.1	-9.2
Electrical & electronic equipment assemblers	5.8	-29.0
Electrical & electronic technicians,technologists	5.6	-29.0
Inspectors, testers, & graders, precision	4.7	-50.3
Engineering, mathematical, & science managers	4.1	-19.3
Industrial engineers, ex safety engineers	3.4	-21.8
Engineers nec	3.3	-14.8
Secretaries, ex legal & medical	3.3	-35.3
Production, planning, & expediting clerks	2.9	-29.0
Management support workers nec	2.7	-29.0
Electrical & electronic assemblers	2.7	-36.1
Blue collar worker supervisors	2.5	-38.8
Engineering technicians & technologists nec	2.5	-29.0
Systems analysts	2.4	13.7
Mechanical engineers	2.2	-21.8
Professional workers nec	2.1	-14.7
Managers & administrators nec	1.9	-29.0
Industrial production managers	1.5	-28.9
Administrative services managers	1.4	-43.2
Stock clerks	1.4	-42.3
General office clerks	1.3	-39.4
Assemblers, fabricators, & hand workers nec	1.2	-29.0
General managers & top executives	1.2	-32.6
Purchasing agents, ex trade & farm products	1.1	-28.9
Electromechanical equipment assemblers	1.1	-21.8
Drafters	1.1	-44.7
Accountants & auditors	1.1	-29.0
Clerical support workers nec	1.0	-43.2

Source: *Industry-Occupation Matrix*, Bureau of Labor Statistics. These data relate to one or more 3-digit SIC industry groups rather than to a single 4-digit SIC. The change reported for each occupation to the year 2005 is a percent of growth or decline as estimated by the Bureau of Labor Statistics. The abbreviation nec stands for 'not elsewhere classified'.

Because the search and navigation industry historically has been dependent on multi-million dollar, large-scale, limited duration government contracts, fluctuations in employment can be severe. In the early 1990s, for example, Hughes Aircraft Company released 60,000 workers in a single layoff. Layoffs of 8,000 workers or less, however, are more common.

RESEARCH AND TECHNOLOGY

Research and development (R&D) costs for new technology in the search and navigation industry are assumed by both the federal government and industry contractors. As the amount of R&D subsidized by the U.S. government decreased in the 1990s, industry firms either began to replace that support with company funds or simply reduced R&D investment.

Long-term R&D contracts made by industry firms with the federal government are often undertaken with no expectation of immediate profit. These so-called "loss contracts" sometimes involve the granting of exclusive data or technical rights to the contractor, which enable the firm to become the sole producer of the technology should it eventually reach a production phase. Unlike many other industries, search and navigation and other defense sectors are driven not only by intrinsic market competition but also by a government-sponsored national security mandate to produce technologies superior to future projected threats as well as existing ones.

NEW TECHNOLOGIES

Overall trends in search and navigation systems include increased reliability, "fault-tolerance" (i.e., ability to operate through system failures), and reduced size, cost, weight, and power consumption of system components. Specific innovations now operational or under development in the area of flight control and guidance include night-vision helmets for pilots in which flight instrument data are displayed on a visor; "three-dimensional" synthesized cockpit voices that help pilots visualize threats surrounding the aircraft; aircraft optical sensors that can imitate the processes of the human optic nerve for increased sensitivity and responsiveness to external threats; and windshear warning systems that can give pilots up to 90 seconds advance notice of dangerous conditions. Other advances include moving map displays projected onto the cockpit windscreen for navigation, voice-controlled avionics that respond to pilots' verbal commands, and on-board "Stormscope" systems that can detect lightning threatening commercial aircraft.

The major technological development in the field of search and navigation instruments is the growth of Global Positioning Systems (GPS) for the commercial and consumer markets. GPS originated with the U.S. Air Force and has been used by all branches of the military as guidance systems for troops, vehicles, and weapons. The system is dependent on 24 U.S. government supported satellites in six separate orbits around the earth. A GPS receiver measures the time interval between a satellite's high-frequency radio signal and its reception by the receiver on the ground. With this data the user can instantly acquire the latitude, longitude, and altitude of the receiver via electronic triangulation. Depending on a number of factors accuracy can range from 100 meters to less than a centimeter. By 1989 the civilian market for GPS instruments was $40 million. It quickly leapt to $1.2 billion by 1995 and is expected to top $8 billion by the end of the century. Although GPS systems are currently used primarily by marine and air vehicles, the greatest growth is predicted for the automobile market.

By late 1996, American automobile makers were offering GPS as an option on select vehicles. Like other GPS systems automobile navigators rely on satellite signals to plot the car's position and direction on an electronic road map stored in a computer memory. Industry observers predict that by the year 2000 automobile navigation systems will be a $1 billion industry and by 2005, 30 percent of all new cars will be equipped with this instrumentation. In 1995, 700,000 GPS devices were operating in Japanese cars, 20,000 in Europe, and 2,000 in the U.S.

Other electronic systems being tested for automobile applications are radar, intelligent cruise control, and night vision. Intelligent cruise control automatically decreases and automobile's speed as it approaches a slower moving vehicle. This system is expected to available in 1999 and is expected to sell for around $500. Also being developed are radar systems that will monitor a vehicle's blind spots for approaching automobiles and provide an visual warning signal in the side and rear view mirrors. An introductory date for these crash protection radar systems has not been announced but the price for the consumer is expected to be under $1000.

Early in 1996, the recommended continued support via the defense budget for the GPS satellite system and world wide availability of free C/A-code (commercial use) satellite signals.

AMERICA AND THE WORLD

The United States' global dominance in search and navigation is reflected in its export and import superiority relative to other leading nations. In 1992, the search and navigation industry exported about $2.1 billion in shipments. By contrast, Japan, the next leading exporting nation, shipped $301 million, followed by Canada ($213 million in shipments), the United Kingdom ($212 million), and France ($168 million). Similarly, while U.S. imports of search and navigation instruments and systems rose to $990 million in 1992, America's closest foreign competitors imported $196 million (Can-

ada), $111 million (the United Kingdom), and $107 million (Japan) in the early 1990s.

Historically, the U.S. search and navigation industry has experienced a trade surplus reflecting its advantage in developing advanced technology. In 1991, however, the U.S. trade surplus in search and navigation equipment declined for the first time—by more than 14 percent over 1990. This unprecedented decline reflected the weakness of the dollar overseas and the increasingly aggressive and competitive global search and navigation market.

FOREIGN MARKETS

Prior to an industry-wide slump in the early 1990s, the avionics product groups, which comprise the broad majority of the industry's products, experienced increased demand from democratizing Eastern European nations, growing industrial states in Southeast Asia, and Middle Eastern allies of the United States seeking military avionics upgrades. In the straitened climate of the early 1990s, demand for U.S. search and navigation equipment centered on radar equipment and parts (25 percent of U.S. industry exports) and avionics equipment for civil aircraft and space navigation applications (20 percent of industry exports). Potential export markets for U.S. search and navigation instruments include North Atlantic Treaty Organization (NATO) bases in Europe, which were being evaluated for possible conversion into dual-use civil/military facilities; South and Central American nations considering purchases of surveillance equipment for drug interdiction; and Middle Eastern allies reassessing their defense and avionics needs in the post-Gulf War environment.

Air traffic control systems represented the product group with the largest export growth potential for U.S. search and navigation firms. Although the U.S. domestic market was the largest air traffic control market in the world in the early 1990s, contracts for most of its systems and technology upgrades had already been awarded in 1992. U.S. search and navigation firms looked to anticipated upgrades of aging overseas air facilities and new airports planned in such nations as China, Mexico, Iran, Turkey, India, and the republics of the Commonwealth of Independent States (CIS), the former Soviet Union. Global air traffic control business, which was expected to center on radars, transponders, and integrated control systems, was estimated to total $6.3 billion in 1991 and grow to $14.4 billion by 2002. Air traffic control needs for the CIS was estimated at $12.5 billion alone in 1992.

JOINT VENTURES

The globalization of the search and navigation market offered the potential for enhanced efficiency, improved market access, and increased worldwide competition. Rationalization, standardization, and interoperability of technology and the growing number of international business arrangements resulted from an increasingly interlinked global marketplace for search and navigation equipment. Joint ventures, in which technologically superior U.S. manufacturers typically team up with less advanced foreign partner firms, are the most common industry business arrangement . Such cooperative ventures often hinge on the U.S. firm's willingness to surrender technology to the foreign producer in exchange for cheaper labor costs, larger markets, or some other "sweetener." In offset agreements, an exporter agrees to obtain domestic markets for the products of the purchaser, and in some cases the exporter is obliged to buy products within the purchasing nation equal to a certain percentage of the contract's value. Offset agreements may also require the production of the product in the purchasing country or some form of co-production under a licensing arrangement. Although some degree of joint venture or co-production between U.S. firms and other nations in the larger defense industry began in the early 1950s, the number, variety, and geographic breadth of such arrangements continues to grow.

ASSOCIATIONS AND SOCIETIES

INSTRUMENT SOCIETY OF AMERICA
67 Alexander Dr.
Research Triangle Park, NC 27709
Phone: (800) 334-6391 or (919) 549-8411
Fax: (919) 549-8288

SAMA
Group of Associations
225 Reinekers, Ste. 625
Alexandria, VA 23314
Phone: (703) 836-1360
Fax: (703) 836-6644

PERIODICALS AND NEWSLETTERS

CONTROL ENGINEERING: FOR DESIGNERS AND USERS OF CONTROL AND INSTRUMENTATION EQUIPMENT AND SYSTEMS WORLDWIDE
Cahners Publishing Co., Inc.
1350 E. Touhy Ave.
Des Plaines, IL 60018
Phone: (800) 662-7776 or (708) 635-8800
Fax: (708) 299-8622
14 times a year. $69.95 per year.

IAN: INSTRUMENTATION AND CONTROL NEWS
Chilton Co.
201 King of Prussia Rd.
Radnor, PA 19089
Phone: (800) 345-1214 or (215) 964-4000
Monthly. $35.00 per year.

ISA TRANSACTIONS
Instrument Society of America
67 Alexander Dr.
Research Triangle Park, NC 27709
Phone: (919) 549-8411
Quarterly. $75.00 per year.

REVIEW OF SCIENTIFIC INSTRUMENTS
American Institute of Physics
335 E. 45th St.
New York, NY 10017
Phone: (212) 661-9404
Semimonthly. $455.00 per year.

STATISTICS SOURCES

SELECTED INSTRUMENTS AND RELATED PRODUCTS
U.S. Bureau of the Census
Washington, DC 20233
Phone: (301) 763-4100
Annual. $1.00. Current Industrial Reports, MA-38B.

GENERAL WORKS

ADVANCES IN INSTRUMENTATION
Instrument Society of America
67 Alexander Dr.
Research Triangle Park, NC 27709
Phone: (919) 549-8411
Annual. Prices vary.

ISA PROCEEDINGS
Instrument Society of America
67 Alexander Dr.
Research Triangle Park, NC 27709
Phone: (919) 549-8411
Annual. $115.00.

FURTHER READING

Howes, Daniel. "High-Tech Cars Stall in the U.S." *Detroit News,* February 25, 1997.

Robinson, Edward A. "Soon Your Dashboard Will Do Everything Except Steer." *Fortune.* July 22, 1996.

Sedgwick, David. "Navigators Try to Locate Serious Market Niche." *Automotive News.* January 29, 1996.

Stevens, Tim. "GPS Comes Down to Earth." *Industry Week.* May 20, 1996.

SECURITY AND COMMODITY EXCHANGES

SIC 6231

Volume *trading will increase as securities exchanges continue to automate their operations, expand their automated networks globally, and offer extended trading hours. Many of the larger U.S. exchanges, including the New York Stock Exchange and the American Stock Exchange, offer after-hours trading. Like the stock exchanges, commodities exchanges are continuing to automate their trading systems. This automation will facilitate volume trading, and is apparent in the enormous increase in number of contracts traded on all U.S. commodity exchanges.*

This classification is divided into two distinct industries: stock exchanges and commodities exchanges. Each of these industries has its own structure, history, and participants. Modern securities exchanges in the United States are voluntary organizations organized for centralized trading. These organizations' constitutions, bylaws, rules, and regulations govern the members and their trading of issues listed by the exchange. These organizations do not themselves trade the listed securities. Rather, they provide the facilities for organized trading. Stock exchanges facilitate the marketability of their listed issues by providing the facilities required for high volume trade and by requiring the firms listed on the exchange to observe standards in accounting and reporting. These functions both make the issues accessible and enhance public confidence in the exchange and its listed securities.

Top 10 LARGEST CORPORATE INITIAL PUBLIC OFFERINGS

Ranked by: Amount, in billions of dollars.

1. Allstate Corp., with $2.1 billion
2. Conrail, $1.6
3. PacTel Corp., $1.4
4. Henley Group Inc., $1.3
5. Lyondell Petrochemical, $1.2
5. Coca-Cola Enterprises, $1.2
7. Nabisco Holdings Corp., $1.1
8. TIG Holdings Corp., $1.0
9. First Data Corp., $0.96
10. Dean Witter, $0.7

Source: *Wall Street Journal,* March 13, 1996, p. A3.

The Securities Exchange Act of 1934 regulates the trade of securities in the United States. This act created the Securities Exchange Commission (SEC) and required any brokers or dealers engaged in the exchange of securities, which makes use of any form of interstate commerce, to report these transaction to the SEC, unless the exchange was registered as a national securities exchange, was specifically exempted, or it was not practicable and necessary nor in the public interest for the protection of the investors to require such registration.

In addition to these formal exchanges, the over-the-counter market is also very significant. Over-the-counter transactions do not have a central market in which they are executed, but are negotiated over the phone or, more commonly, electronically. The National Association of

Securities Dealers (Nasdaq) automated quotation, in particular, has grown in importance, gaining market share of stock listings over the regular exchanges.

Bonds, too, are an exception. While various stock exchanges list bonds, they are traded primarily by bond houses and major commercial banks. The bond market is primarily institutional, with commercial banks as the primary investors. It is not heavily regulated, and there is no federal agency dedicated to overseeing the bond market other than the SEC.

Commodities exchanges are typically organizations which are owned by trading members and are organized to facilitate transactions between buyers and sellers of various commodities. These exchanges are regulated by three different acts. First, the Commodity Exchange Act of 1922 established the Commodity Exchange Commission which consisted of the U.S. Secretary of Commerce, Secretary of Agriculture, and the Attorney General. Second, the Commodity Exchange Act of 1936 attempted to limit fraud, manipulation, and excessive speculation. Finally, The Commodities Futures Trading Commission Act of 1974 created the Commodities Futures Trading Commission (CFTC) which succeeded the Commodity Exchange Commission.

INDUSTRY OUTLOOK

Commodities exchanges have come under recent pressure to implement stricter supervision. Critics argue that the commodities exchanges' structures permit more abuse by traders than other systems, that there are only limited alternatives, and that exchange members have a casual attitude towards trading violations. Supporters of the system, however, argue that the current system is strictly regulated, and the rules are strictly enforced.

In August 1996, the CFTC's Division of Enforcement established an Interactive Internet Enforcement Webpage. By December 1996, the same organization had completed a virtual open house on the World Wide Web; its website is http//www.cftc.gov. In February 1997, the CFTC approved final rules for fast-track approval of new contract and contract amendments.

Also in February 1997, the CFTC, along with other major exchanges in the United States, and their British counterparts took part in the first cross-border testing of market emergency coordination strategies. The occasion allowed such participating exchanges as the Chicago Mercantile Exchange (CME) and the New York Mercantile Exchange (NYMEX) a test scenario in which the default of a fictitious firm at an exchange in the United States caused a default at an exchange in England.

In March 1997, the CFTC announced that one year after the passage of the Declaration on Cooperation and Supervision of International Futures Exchanges and Clearing Organizations, six more international futures regulators had signed the declaration. They included the Comissao De Valores Mobiliarios (Brazil) , The Danish Financial Supervisory Authority, and the Malaysia Securities Commission, the Hungarian Banking and Capital Markets Supervisor , the Comissai de Mercado de Valores Mobiliarios (Portugal), and the Financial Supervisory Authority (Sweden).

According to the SEC 1995 Annual Report, almost 20 percent of its total investigations emerged out of investor complaints. The SEC in that year obtained court orders necessitating defendants to disgorge illicit profits of more than $994 million. In Commission-related cases, criminal authorities brought about 92 criminal indictments or information, in addition to 98 actual convictions in 1995. More than 42,000 inquiries and complaints were processed in 1995, up about 10 percent from 1994. Of the total number of complaints received in 1995, about half concerned broker-dealers, while the rest targeted issuers, mutual funds, banks, and other matters.

ORGANIZATION AND STRUCTURE

Securities exchanges are governed by the Securities Exchange Act of 1934 and regulated by the Securities and Exchange Commission (SEC). The SEC has three major responsibilities: ensuring the provision of full and fair disclosure of all material facts concerning securities offered for public investment, pursuing litigation for fraud when detected, and registering securities offered for public investment. The SEC's activities are similar to judicial proceedings. Appeals from its decisions are taken to the U.S. Court of Appeals. Structurally, the SEC is composed of five commissioners appointed by the President for five-year terms. No more than three of these commissioners may be from the same political party. The chairman is also designated by the President.

Commodities exchanges are regulated by the Commodities Futures Trading Commission subject to the Commodities Exchange Act of 1922. This act, along with its later amendments in 1936 and 1975, subjects commodities, commodity futures, and option trading to federal supervision and restricts trading to futures exchanges designated and licensed by the Commission. The regulatory organization, the Commodity Exchange Commission, was originally established by the Security Exchange Act of 1922 to supervise commodity exchange, but the Commission was succeeded by the Commodity Futures Trading Commission upon the passage of the Commodity Futures Trading Act of 1974.

In general, both the stock and commodities exchanges are governed by a board of directors which are elected from the membership of the exchange. In some cases, board members are also selected from outside the exchange's membership to represent the public. The members are individuals or other legal entities which own a ''seat'' on the exchange. Seats are generally acquired by purchasing existing seats from previous members. The individual exchanges derive their income from membership dues, listing fees, and specialized services. This income is used to cover the operational expenses of the exchange.

WORK FORCE

The securities and commodities exchanges in the United States employ a labor force of approximately 8,430 workers at locations across the country. These workers are hired and trained in a manner similar to other private industries. As reported in *The Wall Street Journal*, as part of its restructuring, the AMEX cut 50 jobs in 1996. According to the Bureau of Labor Statistics of the Department of Labor, the Securities/Commodities industry as a whole employed about 520,000 individuals in 1994, a gain of almost 100,000 jobs since the recession of the early 1990s.

RESEARCH AND TECHNOLOGY

The volume of securities and commodities transactions handled by contemporary exchanges has required automation of trading. The levels of exchange automation can be divided into three broad categories: order routing systems, quotation display systems, and order execution systems. A number of systems were implemented in the late 1980s and early to mid-1990s, including the New York Stock Exchange's Designated Order Turnaround system, Reuter's Instinet System, and the Chicago Mercantile Exchange's GLOBEX System.

The move to electronic trading systems has been universal. Not only are the major trading nations moving to greater automation, but also newly emerging economies. These nations are looking at the advanced electronic trading systems in the United States, Europe, and Japan and using these as models for their own systems. Several western stock markets have been transferring their technology to both emerging and established markets in order to facilitate global trade in securities and commodities.

AMERICA AND THE WORLD

Among the most important stock exchanges globally are the Paris Bourse, the Toronto Stock Exchange, the London Stock Exchange, the Tokyo Stock Exchange, and the Frankfurt Stock Exchange.

The Paris Bourse, or more formally, The Company of the Paris Bank, Exchange, Trade and Finance Brokers (Compagnie des Agents de Change de Paris), is one of the oldest stock exchanges in the world. The Bourse was recognized in 1724 by Louis XV. The modern Bourse began in 1801. Currently, the Bourse consists of three markets: the formal market, the curb market, and the unlisted market.

The Toronto Stock Exchange was founded in 1852 and has been the most important exchange in Canada since its merger with another exchange in 1934. In recent years, the range of traded securities has been greatly expanded. By the early 1990s, the Toronto Stock Exchange was one of the most important exchanges in North America.

The London Stock Exchange, founded in 1773, is one of the most important and best known exchanges in the world. The London Stock Exchange lists a large number of securities and participates directly in underwriting activities. In addition to this, there is some limited trade in options. The London Stock exchange does not operate on a daily settlement basis. Rather, there are bimonthly settlements, one near the middle and one near the end of each month. In 1996, the exchange introduced Sequal, an electronic trading system operating in real time. There were over 2,000 companies listed on the London Stock Exchange in 1995, with a market capitalization of over five trillion dollars.

The Tokyo Stock Exchange was founded in 1878. Despite its financial troubles in the late 1980s and early 1990s, a period in which the exchange lost nearly half of its value after its 1989 peak, the exchange is one of the most important in the world. The shares of approximately 1,700 companies are traded with an aggregate value of over three trillion dollars.

The Frankfurt Stock Exchange is the largest of the West German Bourse exchanges. The entire West German system, consisting of eight regional exchanges, had a market capitalization of $578 billion in December of 1995, making it the fourth largest in the world. The Frankfurt Stock Exchange accounts for 50 percent of the transactions in the German system. Although Frankfurt has not risen as financial center to rival London or New York, the wealth of the German economy has kept the exchange an important one globally.

Significant commodity exchanges are located throughout the world. Many of these organizations specialize in specific commodities, like the Potato Terminal Market in the Netherlands, the Tea Brokers' Association of London, and the Rubber Association of Singapore. Others are more generalized, like the Sydney Futures Exchange in Australia or the Vienna Commodity Exchange in Austria.

ASSOCIATIONS AND SOCIETIES

ASSOCIATION FOR INVESTMENT MANAGEMENT AND RESEARCH
5 Boar's Head Ln.
Charlottesville, VA 22903
Phone: (804) 977-6600
Fax: (804) 977-1103

ASSOCIATION OF PUBLICLY TRADED COMPANIES
1200 19th St. NW, Ste. 300
Washington, DC 20036
Phone: (202) 857-1114
Fax: (202) 223-4579
Formerly National Association of OTC Companies.

COMMODITY EXCHANGE
4 World Trade Center
New York, NY 10048
Phone: (212) 938-2900
Fax: (212) 432-1154

NATIONAL ASSOCIATION OF SECURITIES DEALERS
1735 K St. NW
Washington, DC 20006-1506
Phone: (202) 728-8000
Fax: (202) 293-6260

NATIONAL FUTURES ASSOCIATION
200 W. Madison St., Ste. 1600
Chicago, IL 60606-3447
Phone: (800) 621-3570 or (312) 781-1300
Fax: (312) 781-1467

SECURITIES INDUSTRY ASSOCIATION
120 Broadway
New York, NY 10271
Phone: (212) 608-1500
Fax: (212) 608-1604

SECURITY TRADERS ASSOCIATION
1 World Trade Ctr., Ste. 4511
New York, NY 10048
Phone: (212) 524-0484
Fax: (212) 321-3449

PERIODICALS AND NEWSLETTERS

BARRON'S: NATIONAL BUSINESS AND FINANCIAL WEEKLY
Dow Jones and Co., Inc.
200 Liberty St.
New York, NY 10281
Phone: (800) 416-3546 or (212) 416-2700
Fax: (212) 416-2829
Weekly. $129.00 per year.

CONSENSUS: NATIONAL FUTURES AND FINANCIAL WEEKLY
Consensus, Inc.
1737 McGee St.
Kansas City, MO 64108
Phone: (800) 383-1441 or (816) 471-3862
Fax: (816) 221-2045
Weekly. $365.00 per year. Newspaper. Contains news, statistics, and special reports relating to agricultural, industrial, and financial futures markets. Features daily basis price charts, reprints of market advice, and ''The Consensus Index of Bullish Market Opinion'' (charts show percent bullish of advisors for various futures).

CORPORATE FINANCING WEEK
Institutional Investor Newsletter Division
477 Madison Ave.
New York, NY 10022
Phone: (212) 224-3800
Fax: (212) 224-3493
Weekly. $1,495.00 per year. Newsletter for corporate finance officers. Emphasis is on debt and equity financing, mergers, leveraged buyouts, investment banking, and venture capital.

CRB FUTURES CHART SERVICE
Knight-Ridder Financial Publishing
30 S. Wacker Dr., Ste. 1820
Chicago, IL 60606
Phone: (800) 621-5271 or (312) 454-9116
Fax: (312) 454-0239
Weekly. $455.00 per year.

CRB FUTURES MARKET SERVICE
Commodity Research Bureau
Knight-Ridder Financial Publishing
30 S. Wacker Dr., Ste. 1820
Chicago, IL 60606
Phone: (800) 621-5271 or (312) 454-9116
Fax: (312) 454-0239
Weekly. $155.00 per year.

THE FINANCIAL POST
Financial Post Co.
333 King St. E
Toronto, ON, Canada M5A 4N2
Phone: (416) 350-6000
Fax: (416) 350-6301
Weekly. $130.00 per year. Provides Canadian business, economic, financial, and investment news. Features extensive price quotes from all major Canadian markets: stocks, bonds, mutual funds, commodities, and currencies.

FUTURES: NEWS, ANALYSIS, AND STRATEGIES FOR FUTURES, OPTIONS, AND DERIVATIVES TRADERS

Oster Communications, Inc.
219 Parkade
Cedar Falls, IA 50613
Phone: (800) 635-3931 or (319) 277-1271
Fax: (319) 277-5803
Monthly. $39.00 per year. Edited for institutional money managers and traders, brokers, risk managers, and individual investors or speculators. Includes special feature issues on interest rates, technical indicators, currencies, charts, precious metals, and hedge funds.

GOING PUBLIC: THE IPO REPORTER

Investment Dealer's Digest
2 World Trade Ctr., 18 Fl.
New York, NY 10048-0203
Phone: (212) 227-1200
Fax: (212) 432-1039
Weekly. $990.00 per year. Newsletter on current trends in the initial public offering (IPO) market. New and recent stock issues are profiled each week. Includes the "IPO 100 Index" and quotes aftermarket prices for each of the 100 stocks currently in the index.

INDIVIDUAL INVESTOR

Individual Investor's Group
333 7th Ave.
New York, NY 10001
Phone: (212) 843-2777
Monthly. $22.95 per year. Emphasis is on stocks selling for less than ten dollars a share. Includes a "Guide to Insider Transactions" and "New Issue Alert."

INVESTMENT DEALERS' DIGEST

Investment Dealers' Digest
2 World Trade Center, 18 Fl.
New York, NY 10048-0203
Phone: (212) 432-0045
Fax: (212) 432-1039
Weekly. $375.00 per year.

THE JOURNAL OF FUTURES MARKETS

John Wiley and Sons, Inc.
Journals Div.
605 3rd Ave.
New York, NY 10158-0012
Phone: (800) 526-5368 or (212) 850-6000
Fax: (212) 850-6088
Eight times a year. $396.00 per year.

MANAGED ACCOUNT REPORTS: THE CLEARING HOUSE FOR COMMODITY MONEY MANAGEMENT

Managed Account Reports, Inc.
220 5th Ave.
New York, NY 10001
Phone: (212) 213-6202
Fax: (212) 213-1870
Monthly. $299.00 per year. Newsletter. Reviews the performance and other characteristics of commodity trading advisors and their commodity futures funds or managed accounts. Includes tables and graphs.

OFFICIAL SUMMARY OF SECURITY TRANSACTIONS AND HOLDINGS

U.S. Securities and Exchange Commission
Available from U.S. Government Printing Office
Washington, DC 20402
Phone: (202) 512-1800
Fax: (202) 512-2250
Monthly. $115.00 per year. Lists buying or selling of each publicly held corporation's stock by its officers, directors, or other insiders.

SEC NEWS DIGEST

U.S. Securities and Exchange Commission, Public Reference Room
450 5th St. NW
Washington, DC 20549
Phone: (202) 942-0020
Daily.

SECURITIES WEEK

McGraw-Hill, Inc.
1221 Avenue of the Americas
New York, NY 10020
Phone: (800) 722-4726 or (212) 512-3145
Fax: (212) 512-2821
Weekly. $1,310.00 per year.

DATABASES

DISCLOSURE SEC DATABASE

Disclosure, Inc.
5161 River Rd.
Bethesda, MD 20816
Phone: (800) 843-7747 or (301) 951-1300
Fax: (301) 657-1962
Provides information from records filed with the Securities and Exchange Commission by publicly owned corporations, 1977 to present. Weekly updates. Inquire as to online cost and availability.

MJK COMMODITIES DATABASE

MJK Associates
Commodities Data Information Service
1885 Lindy Ave., Ste. 207-B
San Jose, CA 95131
Phone: (408) 456-5000
Fax: (408) 456-0302
Provides price, trading volume, and open interest data for a wide variety of commodities traded on futures markets in the U.S. and around the world (includes cash prices). In addition to daily updating of current prices, historical data is shown back to 1969. U.S. financial futures and stock index futures are covered. Inquire as to online cost and availability.

SECURITY APL QUOTE SERVER

DTN Wall Street and Security APL Security APL
Provides quotes for stocks from NYSE, AMEX, NASDAQ, OTC exchanges and for bonds traded at the NYSE and AMEX. Includes previous-day information for mutual and money market funds. Equity quotes are exchange-delayed 15 minutes. Futures are delayed 10 to 30 minutes. Market indexes and statistics are real-time. Fees: Free for non-business purposes. Subscription needed for more intensive use. URL: http://www.secapl.com/cgi-bin/qs

VALUE LINE CONVERTIBLE DATA BASE

Value Line Publishing, Inc.
220 E 42nd St.
New York, NY 10017
Phone: (212) 907-1500
Fax: (212) 661-2807
Provides online data for about 600 convertible bonds and other convertible securities: price, yield, premium, issue size, liquidity, and maturity. Information is current, with weekly updates. Inquire as to online cost and availability.

VICKERS ON-LINE

Vickers Stock Research Corp.
226 New York Ave.
Huntington, NY 11743
Phone: (800) 645-5043 or (516) 423-7710
Fax: (516) 423-7715
Provides detailed online information relating to insider trading and the securities holdings of institutional investors. Daily updates. Inquire as to online cost and availability.

STATISTICS SOURCES

FINANCE, INSURANCE, AND REAL ESTATE USA: INDUSTRY ANALYSES, STATISTICS, AND LEADING COMPANIES

Arsen J. Darnay, editor
Gale Research Inc.
835 Penobscot Bldg.
Detroit, MI 48226-4094
Phone: (800) 877-GALE or (313) 961-2242
Fax: (313) 961-6083
1994. $195.00. Contains industry statistical data and a listing of leading companies for each of 50 Standard Industrial Classification (SIC) 4-digit codes covering finance, insurance, and real estate. Includes banks, mortgage banks, securities dealers, commodity brokers, real estate companies, and related firms. Several indexes are provided.

NASDAQ FACT BOOK AND COMPANY DIRECTORY

Available from Hoover's, Inc.
1033 La Posada Dr., Ste. 250
Austin, TX 78752
Phone: (800) 486-8666 or (512) 374-4500
Fax: (512) 374-4501
Annual. $19.95. Published by the National Association of Securities Dealers, Inc. Contains statistical data relating to the Nasdaq Stock Market. Also provides corporate address, phone, symbol, stock price, and trading volume information for about 6,000 securities traded through the National Association of Securities Dealers Automated Quotation System (Nasdaq), including Small-Cap Issues. Includes indexing by Standard Industrial Classification (SIC) number.

STANDARD & POOR'S STOCK REPORTS: AMERICAN STOCK EXCHANGE

Standard & Poor's Corp.
25 Broadway
New York, NY 10004
Phone: (800) 221-5277 or (212) 208-8000
Fax: (212) 208-0040

Twice a week. Four looseleaf volumes. $1,325.00 per year (special library rates available). Provides two pages of financial details and other information for each corporation listed on the American Stock Exchange.

STATISTICAL ANNUAL: GRAINS, OPTIONS ON AGRICULTURAL FUTURES

Chicago Board of Trade
Education and Marketing Services Dept.
141 W. Jackson Blvd.
Chicago, IL 60604
Phone: (800) 572-3276 or (312) 435-3500
Annual. Includes historical data on Wheat Futures, Options on Wheat Futures, Corn Futures, Options on Corn Futures, Oats Futures, Soybean Futures, Options on Soybean Futures, Soybean Oil Futures, and Soybean Meal Futures.

STATISTICAL ANNUAL: INTEREST RATES, METALS, STOCK INDICES, OPTIONS ON FINANCIAL FUTURES, OPTIONS ON METALS FUTURES

Chicago Board of Trade
Education and Marketing Services Dept.
141 W. Jackson Blvd.
Chicago, IL 60604
Phone: (800) 572-3276 or (312) 435-3500
Annual. Includes historical data on GNMA CDR Futures, Cash-Settled GNMA Futures, U.S. Treasury Bond Futures, U.S. Treasury Note Futures, Options on Treasury Note Futures, NASDAQ-100 Futures, Major Market Index Futures, Major Market Index MAXI Futures, Municipal Bond Index Futures, 1,000-Ounce Silver Futures, Options on Silver Futures, and Kilo Gold Futures.

STOCKS, BONDS, BILLS, AND INFLATION YEARBOOK

Ibbotson Associates
225 N Michigan Ave., Ste. 700
Chicago, IL 60601-7676
Phone: (800) 758-3557 or (312) 616-1620
Fax: (312) 616-0404
Annual. $92.00. Provides detailed data from 1926 to the present on inflation and the returns from various kinds of financial investments, such as small-cap stocks and long-term government bonds.

UNITED STATES SECURITIES AND EXCHANGE COMMISSION ANNUAL REPORT

U.S. Government Printing Office
Washington, DC 20402
Phone: (202) 783-3238
Annual.

GENERAL WORKS

BUYING TREASURY SECURITIES: BILLS, NOTES, BONDS, OFFERINGS SCHEDULE, CONVERSIONS

Federal Reserve Bank of Philadelphia, Public Information Dept.
PO Box 66
Philadelphia, PA 19105-0066
Phone: (215) 574-6115
Revised as required. Free pamphlet. Provides clear definitions, information, and instructions relating to U.S. Treasury securities: short-term (bills), medium-term (notes), and long-term (bonds).

COMMODITY YEAR BOOK
Knight-Ridder Financial Publishing
30 S. Wacker Dr., Ste. 1820
Chicago, IL 60606
Phone: (800) 621-5271 or (312) 454-9116
Fax: (312) 454-0239
Annual. $70.00.

FINANCIAL MARKETS AND INSTITUTIONS
Emiel Owens
Macmillan Publishing Co.
200 Old Tappan Rd.
Old Tappan, NJ 07675
Phone: (800) 223-2336
Fax: (800) 445-6991
1995. Price on application.

INVESTING IN THE OVER-THE-COUNTER MARKETS: STOCKS, BONDS, IPOS
Alvin D. Hall
John Wiley and Sons, Inc.
605 3rd Ave.
New York, NY 10158-0012
Phone: (800) 225-5945 or (212) 850-6000
Fax: (212) 850-6088
1996. $27.95. Provides advice and information on investing in "unlisted" or NASDAQ (National Association of Securities Dealers Automated Quotation System) stocks, bonds, and initial public offerings (IPOs).

IRWIN BUSINESS AND INVESTMENT ALMANAC
Caroline Levine and Summer N. Levine, editors
Irwin Professional Publishing
1333 Burr Ridge Pky.
Burr Ridge, IL 60521
Phone: (800) 634-3966 or (708) 789-4000
Fax: (800) 926-9495
Annual. $75.00. A review of the previous year's business activity. Covers a wide variety of business and economic data: stock market statistics, industrial information, commodity futures information, art market trends, comparative living costs for U.S. metropolitan areas, foreign stock market data, etc. Formerly Business One Irwin Business and Investment Almanac.

SECURITIES MARKETS
Kenneth D. Garbade
McGraw-Hill
1221 Avenue of the Americas
New York, NY 10020
Phone: (800) 722-4726 or (212) 512-2000
1982. Price on application (Finance Series).

SECURITY ANALYSIS AND PORTFOLIO MANAGEMENT
Donald E. Fischer and Ronald L. Jordan
Prentice Hall
200 Old Tappan Rd.
Old Tappan, NJ 07675
Phone: (800) 922-0579
Fax: (800) 445-6991
1995. $68.00. Sixth edition.

SUPERTRADER'S ALMANAC AND CALENDAR BOOK
Market Movements, Inc.
5212 E. 69th Pl.
Tulsa, OK 74136-3402

Phone: (800) 878-7442 or (918) 493-2897
Fax: (918) 493-3892
Annual. $110.00. Explains technical methods for the trading of commodity futures, and includes data on seasonality, cycles, trends, contract characteristics, highs and lows, etc.

EDUCATION OF A SPECULATOR
Victor Niederhoffer
John Wiley and Sons, Inc.
605 3rd Ave.
New York, NY 10158-0012
Phone: (800) 225-5945 or (212) 850-6000
Fax: (212) 850-6088
1997. $29.95. An autobiography providing basic advice on speculation, investment, and the commodity futures market.

FUTURES MARKETS
J. Darrell Duffie
Prentice-Hall
200 Old Tappan Rd.
Old Tappan, NJ 07675
Phone: (800) 922-0579
Fax: (800) 445-6991
1989. $72.00.

GETTING STARTED IN FUTURES
Edgar K. Lofton
John Wiley and Sons, Inc.
605 3rd Ave.
New York, NY 10158-0012
Phone: (800) 225-5945 or (212) 850-6000
Fax: (212) 850-6088
1993. $18.95. Second edition. A general introduction to commodity and financial futures trading. Includes case studies and a glossary.

INSIDE THE FINANCIAL FUTURES MARKETS
Mark Powers and Mark Castelino
John Wiley and Sons, Inc.
605 3rd Ave.
New York, NY 10158-0012
Phone: (800) 225-5945 or (212) 850-6000
Fax: (212) 850-6088
1991. $55.00. Third edition.

FURTHER READING

The American Almanac 1996-1997, Washington: Statistical Abstract of the United States.

"Amex to Combine Offices, Cut Jobs in Restructuring." *Wall Street Journal*, 30 July 1996, 22.

"Amex Ready to Implement Revised Composite Index." *Wall Street Journal*, 23 December 1996, 2.

Commodities Futures Trading Commission. Available from http://www.cftc.gov.

Kansas, Dave. "The Amex Is Shrinking Despite Bull Market." *Wall Street Journal*, 9 January 1996: 1.

The LGT Guide to World Equity Markets 1996, London: Euromoney Publications PLC. ◄►

No longer wholly dependent on personal computer sales, the U.S. semiconductor industry provides components for a wide range of consumer and industrial electronics. Computers still account for a significant portion of the industry's sales, however. After growing 40 percent in 1995, the semiconductor industry was poised for ten years of extremely rapid growth according to industry analysts.

Preparing to enter the twenty-first century, the information technology sector accounted for 11 percent of the U.S. gross domestic product and one-fourth of the U.S. manufacturing output. U.S. semiconductor manufacturers supplied some 40 percent of the world's output of microchips. In the aggregate, U.S. chipmakers derived more than half of their sales from international markets. The semiconductor industry was one of the fastest growing sectors in the U.S. economy. With the rapid pace of technological advance in the semiconductor industry, a facility that commenced production in 1997 would be a mature factory by the year 2000, according to the Semiconductor Industry Association.

SEMI-CONDUCTORS AND RELATED DEVICES

SIC 3674

With *sales expected to hit $76.1 billion by 1999, the U.S. semiconductor industry can expect little deceleration through the late 1990s and modest competition from the Japanese ($57 billion with 26 percent of the market). Limits in computing capabilities will present problems in the next decade, but the interest in electronics—especially high-definition television—and the microchips that help them run will keep the industry fruitful through the turn of the century.*

 **TOP MEMORY CHIP MAKERS, 1995**

Ranked by: $26.0 billion in revenues.

1. Samsung, 13.2%
2. NEC, 9.7%
3. Hitachi, 9.6%
4. Toshiba, 7.2%
5. Hyundai, 7.2%
6. Texas Instruments, 6.8%
7. L.G. Semicon, 6.2%
8. Fujitsu, 4.7%
9. Mitsubishi, 4.6%
10. Micron Technology, 4.2%
11. Other, 26.0%

Source: *Purchasing,* March7, 1996, p. 64, from Dataquest Inc.

The overall chip market for 1996 declined 10.5 percent, however, reversing the previous three-year trend, according to World Semiconductor Trade Statistics. The fall in price of the most common memory unit, the DRAM, was the cause. Memory chip prices dropped 33 percent while microprocessors grew by 17.5 percent, according to *Electronic Business Today.* Due to decreased inventory levels caused by consumer spending, though, the global chip industry was expected to grow 13 percent in 1997. By 2000, with the semiconductor content of electrical equipment reaching 28 percent and with the emergence of new markets, industry analysts were optimistic that the semiconductor industry would double its sales.

INDUSTRY OUTLOOK

By the mid-1990s, the semiconductor industry had become one of the most explosive segments of the economy. The history of the semiconductor industry was cyclical, with semiconductor products having short life cycles caused primarily by rapid technological innovations and resulting in pricing pressures. The semiconductor industry—a $100 billion industry in 1995—was expected to be a $200 billion industry in 1997, and by 2000 grow into a $350 billion industry.

The demand for chips was driven not only by the increasing sales of PCs but also by the use of chips in consumer electronics, telecommunications, and networking. As inventory exceeded demand, DRAM prices started plummeting, creating an overall impact on the global chip market. After experiencing a growth rate of 45 percent in 1995, the cyclical trends caused the growth rate to decrease to 26 percent in 1996. Despite this fluctuation in the growth rate, the semiconductor industry continued to grow as the use of semiconductors as components in almost all industries continued to accelerate.

ORGANIZATION AND STRUCTURE

Sometimes referred to as "the crude oil of the information age," semiconductors are a pervasive but generally unseen aspect of everyday life. The tiny electronic circuits etched on chips of silicon are critical to the operation of virtually all electronics, from automatic coffee makers and antilock braking systems to cellular phones and supercomputers.

The computer industry is by far the largest market for semiconductors. In the early 1990s, sales to computer manufacturers and related enterprises accounted for 41 percent of overall sales of semiconductors in this country. Consumer electronics and the automotive industry are also significant consumers of semiconductors and related products. Sales to these two industries combined accounted for 25 percent of total sales during that same period.

WAFERS

Semiconductor chips are manufactured in "clean rooms" free of contaminating dust. In those facilities, thin, round silicon wafers are processed in batches. Chipmakers buy polished blank wafers from companies that specialize in growing silicon crystals, from which the wafers are cut. Each wafer is about half a millimeter thick. Microelectronics circuits are built up on the wafer layer by layer.

Circuit patterns—the collection of transistors, capacitors, and associated components and their interconnections—are inscribed on large glass plates called photomasks. The photomasks are later reduced and photolithographically projected onto the silicon wafers. Each mask comprises a total integrated circuit design.

Semiconductor companies design and manufacture primarily two types of products: integrated circuits (ICs) and discrete devices. A discrete semiconductor is an individual circuit that performs a single function affecting the flow of electrical current. For example, a transistor, one of the most common types of discrete devices, amplifies electrical signals; rectifiers and diodes generally convert alternating current into direct current; capacitors block the flow of alternating current at controlled levels; and resistors limit current flow and divide or drop current.

INTEGRATED CIRCUITS

Also called chips, integrated circuits are a collection of microminiaturized electronic components, such as transistors and capacitors, placed on a tiny rectangle of silicon. A single integrated circuit can perform the functions of thousands of discrete transistors, diodes, capacitors, and resistors. There are three basic types of integrated circuits currently produced by American semiconductor manufacturers: memory components, which are used to store data or computer programs; logic devices, which perform such operations as mathematical calculations; and components which combine the two. This latter category of integrated circuit is the most sophisticated and includes microprocessors, the computer "brain" which manipulates a wide range of data, and microcontrollers, which perform repetitive tasks.

The two largest selling types of memory integrated circuits are DRAMs and SRAMs. A DRAM (dynamic random access memories; pronounced DEE-ram) stores digital information and provides high-speed storage and retrieval of data. It is called a "dynamic" circuit because the data is stored in a temporary medium that allows it to fade and so must be constantly refreshed electronically.

SRAMs (static random access memories; pronounced ESS-rams) perform many of the same functions as DRAMs, but at higher speeds. Unlike DRAMs, they do not require constant electronic refreshing, hence the term "static." They also contain more electronic circuitry and are more expensive to produce than DRAMs.

Both of these integrated circuit products are manufactured in large quantities and are "process drivers." That is, the manufacturing processes used to produce them are constantly being refined, and those refinements often affect manufacturing processes of other products.

Two other important semiconductor memory products are EPROMs (erasable programmable read-only memories) and EEPROMs (electrically erasable read-only memories). EPROMs are used to store computer programs. Unlike older read-only memories (ROMs), which carried fixed programs, EPROMs are programmed by the customer. EEPROMs are easier and faster to update than EPROMs because they are programmed using electricity. While EPROMs are usually programmed only once, EEPROMs can be reprogrammed without removing them from their applications, so they can be updated virtually anytime.

ASICS

Most logic semiconductors are now customized products tailored to the specific needs of each customer. In fact, ASICS (application-specific integrated circuits) have become the most commonly manufactured non-microcomponent logic semiconductors.

There are four basic classes of ASICs, each with a different degree of customization of the chip: full-custom ASICs are designed from scratch; standard cells are designed by combining modular cells from a cell library; semi-custom chips are customized in only one or two areas; and programmable logic devices are programmed by blowing fuses in a device to alter the logic function. Because of high design costs and the often limited quantities produced, ASICs tend to be more expensive than integrated circuits built from off-the-shelf components. But because they combine several specialized functions on a single chip, they offer some important advantages: they are smaller, simpler, and fewer of them are needed; they allow for a greater degree of integration, which leads to more efficient use of circuitry; and, since they contain less circuitry, fewer interconnections are needed and overall performance is enhanced.

MICROPROCESSORS AND CONTROLLERS

Microprocessors (MPUs) are the central processing units in all microcomputer-based systems. These products perform a variety of tasks by manipulating data within a system and controlling input, output, peripherals, and memory devices.

The two major types of MPUs are CISCs (complex instruction set computing) and RISCs (reduced instruction set computing). Though CISCs used to be the basis for all MPU operations, RISCs became increasingly popular in the 1990s because of their faster operating speeds, their ability to run more sophisticated software, and their ability to deliver better graphics. MPUs are used in local area networks (linked personal computers and workstations; called LANs) and satellites. The latest generation of these circuits operate at speeds of 40 to 50 million cycles per second.

Microcontrollers (MCUs), which combine a microprocessor, memory circuits, and input/output circuitry, are used as embedded controllers in virtually every electronic product. They perform such repetitive tasks as controlling the antilock brake systems in automobiles.

WORK FORCE

Semiconductor jobs more than doubled from 115,200 workers in the early 1970s to 258,500 workers in 1996. According to the U.S. Department of Labor, the all-time high of almost 300,000 semiconductor workers in the mid-1980s was reached amidst a robust economy. However, from the mid-1980s to the early 1990s employment levels declined, in spite of a brief upsurge in the late 1980s. U.S. firms employed about half of their work force in facilities abroad, according to the Semiconductor Industry Association.

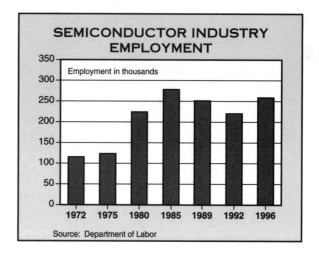

SEMICONDUCTOR INDUSTRY EMPLOYMENT

Employment in thousands

Source: Department of Labor

Within the United States, average hourly earnings for production workers in the semiconductor industry were $14.59 in 1995, 18 percent above the average for all manufacturing. According to the U.S. Department of Labor, this reflected in part, the higher skill and value added associated with the capital intensive processing steps and research and development (R&D) activities performed by U.S. semiconductor workers.

RESEARCH AND TECHNOLOGY

According to Dataquest, about one-third of U.S. semiconductor industry revenues is spent on technology development and capital; 14 percent of revenues is spent on R&D alone. Costs for new semiconductor fabrication facilities, a major capital consideration for many companies, range from $600 million to $900 million.

One emerging technology that could trigger a boom in semiconductor sales is high definition television (HDTV). HDTV produces pictures four to five times clearer than the standard television picture. In addition to commercial broadcast television, the first of which were expected by the mid-1990s, HDTV technology could also find applications in areas such as medical imaging and computer graphics. Since the sets require a huge number of semiconductors, they are expected to be a major new market for chipmakers.

Another emerging semiconductor technology expected to create important future markets was called "fuzzy logic." As *Standard & Poor's Industry Surveys* noted, "currently led by Japanese manufacturers, fuzzy logic allows microcontrollers to create gray areas between the yes/no, on/off choices of the binary world. The result is that engineers can design microprocessors that allow machinery to operate with gradual refinements."

With the unprecedented growth in the mid- to late 1990s, some believe the industry faces a slowdown due to the eventual breakdown of Moore's Law, according to *The Wall Street Journal*. Moore's Law, named after Intel's co-founder Gordon Moore, referred to the accumulation of transistors on microchips, doubling the computing capabilities on a single chip the same size every 18 months. Moore's Law was seen to reach its limits due to barriers imposed by quantum physics. According to *The Wall Street Journal*, the end of continued progress within the semiconductor industry was slated for the year 2010 by the U.S. Semiconductor Industry Association. This prompted American companies to initiate new research projects.

AMERICA AND THE WORLD

The United States has produced a trade deficit in semiconductors throughout the 1990s. In 1995, this deficit amounted to some $16 billion. Total U.S. imports were valued at $38 billion that year, compared with exports of $22 billion.

Japan is the world's largest producer of memory chips, but in the early 1990s its industry was in a severe slump and the country's overall economy was growing at only 1.5 percent. Consequently, there was a 6.3 percent drop in Japanese semiconductor sales.

In 1992 the market for North American chipmakers' products outgrew Japan's for the first time since the mid-1980s. The European market also grew, boosted by the weaker dollar. In fact, these factors led to an overall shift in worldwide market share for the semiconductor industry. North American companies' share increased to 30 percent in 1992, up from 28 percent the previous year. European firms held on to a steady 19 percent market share. Meanwhile, Japanese market share fell from 38 percent in 1991 to 33 percent in 1992. Many observers expect this trend to continue as companies in the United States and smaller countries grow rapidly and Japan struggles to regain its momentum.

The 1992 domestic industry rebound resulted in increased capital spending on the part of U.S. semiconductor manufacturers. By contrast, capital spending among Japanese companies dropped from the previous year's levels due to the difficult economic condition and overcapacity for DRAMs, a product niche the Japanese largely control.

In an effort to reduce costs and lower financial risks, Japanese chipmakers entered into alliances with foreign companies. Since 1989, Japan has entered into about 88 such alliances, ranging from manufacturing joint ventures to joint product development agreements. These alliances have focused primarily on HDTV chip development, microprocessor development, ASIC development, and computer-aided design projects.

In 1986, the United States and Japan entered into an agreement called the U.S.-Japan Semiconductor Agreement designed to eliminate the dumping of Japanese products in world markets and increase market access for foreign semiconductor manufacturers in the Japanese market. In 1991 the follow-on agreement to the 1986 agreement went into effect. The new agreement reflected U.S. expectations that more than 20 percent share of the Japanese market could be captured by foreign suppliers by the early 1990s through the efforts of government and industry.

While U.S. semiconductor companies were consolidating in the early 1990s, companies in the so-called dynamic Asian economies (DAEs) were expanding. DAE countries—South Korea, Taiwan, Hong Kong, China, Singapore, and Malaysia—dominated U.S. semiconductor imports in the early 1990s. Southeastern Asian markets present extensive opportunities for U.S. chip exporters as well, since most of the world's major electronics companies have established operations there, and more electronic products means more need for semiconductors. The re-establishment of trade relations with

Vietnam in the mid-1990s also presents U.S. companies with still another market to explore.

According to data compiled by the World Semiconductor Statistics organization, the European market for semiconductors was expected to grow by 7.7 percent in the early 1990s, making Europe approximately 19 percent of the world market. The European market was considered a battleground for competition among the global electronics giants. Both South Korean and Japanese semiconductor companies increased their presence in Europe, but American companies still held 44 percent of market share in the early 1990s.

In the late 1990s, America's market, including North and South America, remained as the world's largest market for the semiconductor industry, representing one-third of all sales. Chip sales were expected to grow 7.8 percent in 1996 to $50.6 billion, 9.2 percent in 1997, 15.7 percent in 1998, and 19.1 percent in 1999 as sales hit $76.1 billion, according to the Semiconductor Industry Association.

With nearly 26 percent of the chip market, Japan remained the second largest market for semiconductors. The Japanese market was expected to grow 10 percent in 1997, and by 1999 show a 15.8 percent growth as sales reached $57 billion. The fastest growing chip market, the Asia-Pacific, grew by 54.1 percent in 1995. By 1999 this market was expected to grow 23.3 percent to $53.4 billion. The Asia Pacific sector represented 20.9 percent of the world chip market, according to the Semiconductor Industry Association. The European market, which represented 20.5 percent of the world market, was expected to grow 18.7 percent in 1999 to $47.8 billion in sales.

ASSOCIATIONS AND SOCIETIES

COUNCIL ON SUPERCONDUCTIVITY FOR AMERICAN COMPETITIVENESS
1050 Thomas Jefferson St. NW
Washington, DC 20007
Phone: (202) 965-4070

ELECTRONIC INDUSTRIES ASSOCIATION
2001 Pennsylvania Ave., NW, Ste. 1100
Washington, Dc 20006
Phone: (202) 457-4900
Fax: (202) 457-4985
Includes a Solid State Products Committee.

IEEE ELECTRON DEVICES SOCIETY
c/o Institute of Electrical and Electronics Engineers
345 E. 47th St.
New York, NY 10017
Phone: (212) 705-7867
A society of the Institute of Electrical and Electronics Engineers.

IEEE SOLID STATE CIRCUITS COUNCIL
c/o Institute of Electrical and Electronics Engineers
345 E. 47th St.
New York, NY 10017
Phone: (212) 705-7867
A Council of the Institute of Electrical and Electronics Engineers.

THE INSTITUTE FOR INTERCONNECTING AND PACKAGING ELECTRONIC CIRCUITS (IPC)
7380 N. Lincoln Ave.
Lincolnwood, IL 60646
Phone: (708) 677-2850

JOINT ELECTRON DEVICE ENGINEERING COUNCIL
2001 Pennsylvania Ave. NW, Ste. 900
Washington, DC 20006
Phone: (202) 457-4971
Fax: (202) 457-4985
Affiliated with the Electronics Industries Association and concerned with the engineering of solid state devices.

SEMICONDUCTOR INDUSTRY ASSOCIATION
4300 Stevens Creek Rd., No. 721
San Jose, CA 95129
Phone: (408) 246-2711
Fax: (408) 246-2830
Members are producers of semiconductors and semiconductor products.

PERIODICALS AND NEWSLETTERS

CHANNEL
Semiconductor Equipment and Materials International (SEMI)
805 E. Middlefield Rd.
Mountain View, CA 94043-4080
Phone: (415) 964-5111

ECN: ELECTRONIC COMPONENT NEWS
Chilton Co.
201 King Prussia Rd.
Radnor, PA 19089
Phone: (800) 345-1214 or (215) 964-4000
Monthly. Free to qualified personnel; others, $50.00 per year.

ELECTRONIC COMPONENTS
1038 Leigh Ave., Ste. 100
San Jose, CA 95126-4155
Phone: (408) 295-4500

ELECTRONIC ENGINEERING TIMES
CMP Publications, Inc.
600 Community Dr.
Manhasset, NY 11030
Phone: (516) 562-5000

ELECTRONIC NEWS
Electronic News Publishing Corp.
488 Madison Ave.
New York, NY 10022
Phone: (800) 722-2346

IEEE MICRO
IEEE Computer Society
Institute of Electrical and Electronics Engineers, Inc.
10662 Los Vaqueros Cir.
Los Alamitos, CA 90720
Phone: (714) 821-8380
Bimonthly. $144.00 per year.

PAC/ASIA CIRCUIT NEWS
W.I.S.E. Ltd.
25 Wintergreen Hill
Danbury, CT 06811-4242
Phone: (203) 797-9103

SIBS: SEMICONDUCTOR INDUSTRY AND BUSINESS SURVEY
HTE Research, Inc.
400 Oyster Point Blvd., Ste. 220 South
San Francisco, CA 94080
Phone: (415) 871-4377
18 times a year. $495.00 per year. Tracks the activities of semiconductor firms worldwide.

SOLID STATE TECHNOLOGY
Penn Well Publishing Co.
14 Vanderventer Ave.
Port Washington, NY 11050
Phone: (516) 883-6200
Monthly. $60.00 per year. Covers fabrication, processing and production, assembly and testing of solid state devices and circuits.

SUPERCONDUCTOR WEEK
Atlantic Information Services
1050 17th St. NW, ste. 480
Washington, DC 20036
Phone: (202) 775-9008

STATISTICS SOURCES

SEMICONDUCTOR INDUSTRY TRADE STATISTICS SUBSCRIPTION
Semiconductor Industry Association
10201 Torre Ave., Ste. 275
Cupertino, CA 95014
Phone: (408) 973-9973
Monthly. $1,995.00 per year. Annual trade statistics compilation available at $300.00. Provides data on all world semiconductor markets including industry forecasts.

SEMICONDUCTORS, PRINTED CIRCUIT BOARDS, AND OTHER ELECTRONIC COMPONENTS
Available from U.S. Government Printing Office
Washington, DC 20402
Phone: (202) 783-3238
Annual. $1.00. Provides data on shipments: value, quantity, imports, and exports. (Bureau of the Census, Current Industrial Report No. MA-36Q).

WORLD SEMICONDUCTOR TRADE STATISTICS
Semiconductor Industry Association
4300 Stevens Creek Blvd.

San Jose, CA 95129
Phone: (408) 246-2711

GENERAL WORKS

CIRCUITREE
340 Martin Ave.
Santa Clara, CA 95050
Phone: (408) 986-1292

CIRCUITS ASSEMBLY
Miller Freeman, Inc.
2000 Powers Ferry Center, Ste. 450
Marietta, GA 30067
Phone: (404) 952-1303

D.A.T.A. DIGEST: DISCRETE SEMICONDUCTORS
D.A.T.A. Business Publishing
PO Box 6510
Englewood, CO 80155
Phone: (303) 799-0381
Fax: (303) 799-4082
Annual. $800.00 per year, including semiannual updates. Five volumes provide detailed specifications for transistors, diodes, thyristors, optoelectronics, and power semiconductors.

D.A.T.A. DIGEST: INTEGRATED CIRCUITS
D.A.T.A. Business Publishing
PO Box 6510
Englewood, CO 80155
Phone: (303) 799-0381
Fax: (303) 799-4082
Annual. $900.00 per year, including quarterly updates. Five volumes provide detailed specifications for linear ICs, memory ICs, digital ICs, interface ICs, and microprocessor ICs.

ELECTRONIC MARKET DATA BOOK—1994
2001 Pennsylvania Ave. NW
Washington, DC 20006
Phone: 202)457-4900

IC DATA FLASH SERVICE
D.A.T.A. Business Publishing
PO Box 6510
Englewood, CO 80155
Phone: (303) 799-0381
Fax: (303) 799-4082
Monthly. $495.00 per year. Provides schematics, specifications, and pricing for new microprocessors, memories, and other integrated circuits from Japanese manufacturers. Includes directory of distributors.

IC MASTER
(Integrated Circuits)
Hearst Business Communications, Inc.
645 Stewart Ave.
Garden City, NY 11530
Phone: (516) 785-7206
Annual. Semiannual supplements. List of over 575 manufacturers and distributors of integrated circuits. $145.00.

SEMICONDUCTOR INDUSTRY ASSOCIATION YEARBOOK/DIRECTORY

Semiconductor Industry Association
10201 Torre Ave., Ste. 275
Cupertino, CA 95014
Phone: (408) 973-9973
Biennial. $75.00. Provides information on key semiconductor issues.

SOLID STATE PROCESSING AND PRODUCTION BUYERS GUIDE AND DIRECTORY

Penn Well Publishing Co.
PO Box 21288
Tulsa, OK 74121
Phone: (800) 725-9764 or (918) 835-3161
Annual. $60.00.

SOLID STATE TECHNOLOGY PROCESSING AND PRODUCTION BUYERS GUIDE

Penn Well Publishing Co.
14 Vanderventer Ave.
Port Washington, NY 11050
Phone: (516) 883-6200
Annual. $60.00. Sourcebook of materials, equipment and services used in solid state devices and circuits.

SOLID STATE TECHNOLOGY

Penn Well Publishing Co.
1421 S. Sheridan Rd.
Tulsa, OK 74112
Phone: (918) 835-3161

SUPERCONDUCTOR INDUSTRY

Rodman Publishing Co.
17 S. Franklin Tpke.
PO Box 555
Ramsey, NY 07446
Phone: (201) 825-2552

FURTHER READING

Cohen, Warren. "Why the Chip Is Still the Economy's Champ." *U.S. News and World Report,* 25 March 1996.

Hamilton, David P., and Takahashi, Dean. "Scientists Are Battling to Surmount Barriers in Microchip Advances." *The Wall Street Journal,* 10 December 1996.

Hof, Robert D. and Port, Otis. "Silicon Goes from Peak to Peak." *Business Week,* 8 January 1996.

Moris, Francisco A. "Semiconductors: The Building Blocks of the Information Revolution." *U.S. Department of Labor,* 1996

Ristelhueber, Robert. "Semiconductor Makers See Brighter '97." *Electronic Business Today,* January 1997.

"Semiconductor Industry Report." *The American Stock Report,* February 1996.

SOFT DRINKS

SIC 2086

Pointing *to an aging U.S. population, changing consumer tastes, and an industry slump in the early 1990s, analysts have predicted a slow, steady decline for the soft drinks industry. Despite the real nature of these concerns, the soft drinks industry is on the upswing, owing largely to aggressive pursuit of overseas markets, and the introduction of new market segments within the industry. Although colas continue to lose market share in the United States, consumers have been very accepting of so-called "new age" beverages, which include bottled water products, all-natural sodas, as well as sports drinks, fruit juice drinks, flavored teas, and bottled coffees.*

Soft drinks have become intrinsically tied to the "American way of life," and the leading soft drink, Coca-Cola, is a virtual icon of American culture. Close to 500 soft drink manufacturers and bottling companies operate in the United States. According to the National Soft Drinks Association (NSDA), in 1995, the retail sale of soft drinks totaled more than $52 billion. In 1995, Americans consumed over 51 gallons of soft drinks per capita, a total of more than 13 billion gallons. Soft drinks accounted for more than 27 percent of Americans' beverage consumption. The U.S. market included nearly 450 different soft drinks.

Two companies, Coca-Cola and Pepsi-Cola, controlled nearly three-quarters of the U.S. soft drinks market, with each company producing 4 of the top 10 best-selling brands. Approximately 500 bottlers operate across the United States. Modern bottling plants can produce more than 2,000 soft drinks per minute on each line of operation. The soft drink industry employed more than 136,000 people nationwide.

Top 10 MOST PREFERRED SOFT DRINK BRANDS

Ranked by: Market share in 1995, in percent.

1. Coca-Cola Classic, with 20.0%
2. Pepsi-Cola, 15.4%
3. Diet Coke, 9.5%
4. Dr. Pepper, 6.0%
5. Mountain Dew, 5.6%
6. Diet Pepsi, 5.4%
7. Sprite, 4.9%
8. 7-Up, 2.7%
9. Diet Coke, caffeine-free, 1.9%
10. Diet Pepsi, caffeine-free, 1.1%

Source: *Beverage World*, March, 1996, p. 61.

There is more to America's soft drink industry than just the companies that provide consumers with their favorite refreshments, according to the NSDA. It's also a big part of the U.S. economy, buying products and services from many different industries, creating thousands of jobs, and contributing to worthwhile causes in local communities. According to the NSDA, bottlers and canners spend more than $65 billion annually purchasing supplies from 116 separate industries, accounting for 744,000 jobs across the United States in addition to the 136,000 people directly employed by the soft drink industry.

Soft drink flavorings are the number one product purchased, followed by metal cans in second place, and plastics used for packaging in third place. The soft drink industry also is a big buyer of corn syrup, advertising services, glass containers, boxes for shipping bottle caps, warehousing, fruits and vegetables, motor freight, carbonated water, sugar, and many other products and services that contribute to the manufacture of soft drinks. NSDA states that, each year, the soft drink industry pays $4.3 billion in payroll dollars, pays more than $1.0 billion in state and local taxes, and contributes more than $95 million to charities.

INDUSTRY OUTLOOK

The soft drink industry, after a slump in the early 1990s, finds itself doing well. One of the biggest reasons for this is the industry's expansion into fertile overseas markets. Innovative marketing strategies and timely new product introductions during the mid-1990s, caused U.S. consumption of soft drinks to improve. Consumers purchased higher volumes of both carbonated soft drinks and fruit beverages.

New age drinks were the best performers in the mid-1990s. Bottled water consumption reached 2.5 billion gallons in 1994, an increase of 10.4 percent over 1993. Sports drinks performed even better, with consumption reaching 391.1 million gallons in 1994, an increase of 11.4 percent over 1993.

Bottled water was seen as the best performing star of the soft drinks industry in the mid- to late 1990s. It's success was attributed to many factors including, ''A perception of a healthy, natural, good-for-you product,'' according to *Beverage World*. Given the concerns over municipal water, it was considered the only beverage

category that was driven because it was a tap water replacement. The bottled water industry saw many ''firsts'' in the mid-1990s. It was the first time that this industry ''topped 2.5 billion gallons, measured more than 10 gallons per capita, and totaled more than $3 billion in wholesale receipts,'' according to *Beverage World*. The sparkling water segment, however, was the only down spot in the industry, with dollar sales going down almost 10 percent according to *Beverage World*.

Bottled coffee was seen as the other rising trend of the 1990s. The well known coffee maker Starbucks Coffee Co. teamed up with Pepsico to produce Frappucino, the 1996 release of which was expected to be a challenging venture for the company, since cold bottled coffee is considered a tough sell to the beverage market. In spite of the failure of Maxwell House's Cappio, and Mazagran, a carbonated coffee drink from the Starbucks-Pepsi partnership, Frappuccino was seen as a drink that would succeed because of two reasons: 1) the Starbucks name brand, and 2) the fact that coffee has been the fastest growing beverage segment after carbonated drinks in the mid-1990s.

PACKAGING AND RECYCLING

Since 1989, soft drink container recycling has risen from 48.7 percent to more than 60.0 percent—a 23 percent increase. Nearly 48 billion soft drink containers were recycled in 1995. Soft drink containers account for less than 1 percent of the U.S. solid waste stream. Although beverage containers account for less than 20 percent of materials collected in most curbside programs, they generate up to 73 percent of total scrap revenue. Packaging innovations have lightened the weight of soft drink containers by an average of 30 percent since 1972. Nearly 78 percent of soft drinks are packaged, while the remaining 22 percent are dispensed from fountains. In 1995, 62.6 billion soft drinks were

SIC 2086 - Bottled & Canned Soft Drinks
Industry Data by State

| State | Establish-ments | Shipments | | | Employment | | | | Cost as % of Shipments | Investment per Employee ($) |
		Total ($ mil)	% of U.S.	Per Establ.	Total Number	% of U.S.	Per Establ.	Wages ($/hour)		
California	97	2,878.6	11.3	29.7	6,800	8.8	70	12.87	58.4	15,206
Texas	58	2,128.8	8.4	36.7	7,100	9.2	122	11.10	63.6	5,873
Florida	47	1,674.8	6.6	35.6	5,100	6.6	109	12.36	57.7	-
New York	56	1,489.1	5.9	26.6	4,200	5.4	75	14.73	66.6	8,048
Illinois	32	1,235.5	4.9	38.6	3,200	4.2	100	11.30	58.4	12,594
Michigan	26	1,013.9	4.0	39.0	1,900	2.5	73	13.08	58.4	8,684
Pennsylvania	45	1,011.5	4.0	22.5	3,500	4.5	78	10.97	59.4	13,143
New Jersey	27	975.1	3.8	36.1	2,300	3.0	85	15.91	53.4	6,696
Indiana	24	885.2	3.5	36.9	1,900	2.5	79	11.82	58.1	11,526
Tennessee	19	813.4	3.2	42.8	2,800	3.6	147	9.68	56.7	-

*Source: 1992 Economic Census. The states are in descending order of shipments or establishments (if shipment data are missing for the majority). The symbol (D) appears when data are withheld to prevent disclosure of competitive information. States marked with (D) are sorted by number of establishments. A dash (-) indicates that the data element cannot be calculated; * indicates the midpoint of a range.*

packaged in cans, 16.8 billion were packaged in PET bottles, and 3.6 billion were packaged in glass bottles.

BOTTLED AND CANNED SOFT DRINK SHIPMENTS

Billion dollars

Source: Department of Commerce   *estimate

ORGANIZATION AND STRUCTURE

Soft drink companies manufacture and sell beverage syrups and bases to bottling operations, which add sweeteners and/or carbonated water to produce the final product. Independent bottlers work under contract with various soft drink manufacturers and are allotted specific territories to serve. The manufacturers provide the bottlers with syrups and bases, but also with a variety of business services, including product quality control, marketing, advertising, engineering, and financial and personnel training. In turn, bottlers supply the required capital investment for land, buildings, machinery, equipment, trucks, bottles, and cases.

During the past few years, the number of independent bottlers declined as major soft drink manufacturers consolidated bottling operations by acquiring independent companies and combining them into one large operation. Both Coke and Pepsi have such arrangements. Coca-Cola Enterprises has become the world's largest soft drink bottler; production accounts for 55 percent of all the bottled and canned Coke products sold in the United States. The company operates in 37 states, Washington, D.C., and the U.S. Virgin Islands. Meanwhile, Pepsi's company-owned bottling operations have been responsible for 52 percent of its bottling volume. Both companies promoted the purchase of franchised bottling operations as a way of preparing for long-term strategic growth, domestically and internationally. As the economies of various countries have become more sophisticated and complex, so must soft drink manufacturers in their ability to produce, distribute, and market their products.

The soft drink distributers sells its product in two forms, packaged and fountain service. The packaged form of cans and bottles representes 75 percent of the total soft drink market. Fountain service, in which the soft drink product is dispensed and served in cups, typically in a restaurant or any location with a food service station, accounts for the remaining 25 percent of the market share.

WORK FORCE

According to *Ward's Business Directory of U.S. Public and Private Companies,* 292 soft drink manufacturers and bottling companies operated in the United States in the early 1990s, employing approximately 207,300 workers. At the turn of the decade there were 500 bottling operations in the United States employing about 136,000 workers. According to the U.S. Department of Labor, overall employment in food processing (which includes beverages) has been projected to decline 6 percent by the year 2005. Like other manufacturing industries, food processing has become less labor intensive, and occupational projections reflected this by predicting a decline in employment. According to *Manufacturing USA,* by the year 2000, employment for packaging and filling machine operations will drop 26.9 percent; industrial truck and tractor operators, 23.4 percent; freight stock and materials movers (by hand), 23.8 percent; and hand packers and packagers, 32.3 percent. Professional specialty occupations such as engineers and computer scientists have been expected to grow, which reflects the industry's continued emphasis on scientific research to improve food products and production processes. However, these jobs comprised a very small proportion of industry employment.

RESEARCH AND TECHNOLOGY

Advances in computer technology and automation have improved all aspects of the soft drink manufacturing industry from inventory control to "smart" vending machines. Those companies with computerized operations found both increased profitability and improved product quality. One example of a computerized system is a plant-wide automated measurement system used in some syrup manufacturing plants. Working with a personal computer, the automated system can measure nearly every important segment of beverage production, including syrup usage, Brix count (sugar percentage), and beverage carbonation. Other system checks include monitoring the purification system for failures, and checking the warehouse temperature for the precise dew point. "By keeping much closer control on all critical process variables, we (Abtex Beverage Corporation) have been able over time to significantly improve yields, while also increasing the quality and consistency of our product," reported Randy Mostert, Abtex production manager, in *Beverage World.*

Another technological advancement can be found on the user-end of the soft drink industry with the "smart" vending machines. These products use computerized components that keep track of stock supplies, sales patterns, breakdowns, and other conditions. "Bottlers are looking for ways to increase revenues and reduce their costs," Bill Astin, senior VP/sales and marketing at the Vendo Co., told *Beverage Industry.* "This improved technology allows them to do just that."

General Programming Inc. has introduced a wireless communications package called Vending Manager. This program allows vending machines to place orders as they are required, rather than have someone manually check the stock level. "Loss of sales from a stock-out situation or out-of order situations will be eliminated, as machines will immediately notify the dispatcher of their status," said H.O. Bransom, president of General Programming Inc., in *Beverage Industry.*

Claiming that it could be the wave of the future, Coca-Cola USA has already begun to test market their own version of the smart vending machine called the Generation II, manufactured by Royal Vendors. "With the GII, [collecting data] is as simple as plugging a hand-held computer into the vendor controller, or keying the LED readout to deliver the information for the route person . . . ," said Ray Steeley, president of Royal Vendors, in *Beverage Industry.*

The final outcome of computerized operations eventually will be the paperless warehouse, where computers, robotics, and electronic information transmission will control all operations. "Computer control gives instant information on the whereabouts of any material within the system," said Jim Larsen, VP of Eaton-Kenway, the company that installed a real-time management system (along with Operations Management Inc.) in Coca-Cola Enterprises Market Service Center in Cincinnati, Ohio, in 1991. "Those who use a real-time communications system in the warehouse also report better inventory control, faster truck check-in and check-out, better stock rotation in the distribution center and elimination of truck load errors," added Norand Corporation executive Tom Miller in *Beverage Industry.*

AMERICA AND THE WORLD

Soft drinks have been produced or consumed in nearly every corner of the world. Growing consumption trends can be attributed to rising disposable incomes, falling trade barriers, universal product acceptance, and a rising demand for American consumer goods. Both Pepsi-Cola and Coca-Cola have company-owned franchised bottling plants in more than 120 countries that

SIC 2086 - Bottled & Canned Soft Drinks
General Statistics

Year	Com-panies	Establishments		Employment			Compensation		Production ($ million)			
		Total	with 20 or more employees	Total (000)	Production Workers (000)	Hours (Mil)	Payroll ($ mil)	Wages ($/hr)	Cost of Materials	Value Added by Manufacture	Value of Shipments	Capital Invest.
1982	1,236	1,626	1,095	113.8	42.4	85.2	2,146.4	7.84	9,981.3	6,856.1	16,807.5	649.5
1983		1,555	1,057	112.3	41.5	85.1	2,244.8	8.24	10,248.5	7,086.1	17,320.8	680.5
1984		1,484	1,019	110.4	39.8	81.7	2,282.8	8.51	10,941.1	7,141.8	18,052.0	694.1
1985		1,414	980	105.8	37.2	77.8	2,344.8	9.10	11,830.7	7,587.2	19,358.2	720.8
1986		1,335	927	102.0	35.5	73.5	2,348.1	9.77	12,483.1	8,215.4	20,686.8	560.7
1987	818	1,190	787	95.6	35.4	71.5	2,276.7	10.45	13,461.0	8,573.7	22,006.0	569.2
1988		1,135	761	94.6	35.2	71.8	2,361.8	10.78	14,250.9	9,122.4	23,310.3	567.7
1989		1,027	697	88.7	33.4	67.7	2,190.5	10.98	14,146.0	8,898.4	23,002.1	507.8
1990		941	635	82.7	32.0	65.7	2,132.0	11.48	14,772.2	9,075.1	23,847.5	460.0
1991		913	623	81.7	31.9	66.8	2,210.3	11.85	15,644.3	9,554.8	25,191.1	548.5
1992	637	926	572	77.1	30.5	65.0	2,162.8	11.91	15,853.4	9,586.4	25,416.9	698.5
1993		886	560	78.6	31.6	68.1	2,228.1	11.66	15,779.6	10,228.4	25,997.6	616.2
1994		722P	458P	73.4	29.0	62.6	2,212.9	12.89	16,757.7	11,647.3	28,334.3	773.8
1995		648P	404P	68.1P	27.6P	59.4P	2,199.9P	13.24P	16,957.7P	11,786.3P	28,672.4P	606.0P
1996		574P	350P	64.5P	26.6P	57.6P	2,193.9P	13.64P	17,499.8P	12,163.1P	29,589.0P	604.2P
1997		500P	296P	60.9P	25.5P	55.7P	2,188.0P	14.04P	18,041.9P	12,539.9P	30,505.6P	602.3P
1998		426P	242P	57.2P	24.5P	53.8P	2,182.0P	14.44P	18,584.0P	12,916.6P	31,422.2P	600.5P

Sources: 1982, 1987, 1992 *Economic Census; Annual Survey of Manufactures,* 83-86, 88-91, 93-94. Establishment counts for non-Census years are from *County Business Patterns;* establishment values for 83-84 are extrapolations. 'P's show projections by the editors. Industries reclassified in 87 will not have data for prior years.

produce their respective brands within each country rather than exporting them from the United States.

Beverages that are exported from the United States include unsweetened bottled water, but these figures have remained relatively low as the worldwide market for bottled water has been dominated by a few well-established European producers. However, United States producers of sweetened water or New Age beverages have fared better in the export market. The international beverage market has seen the dominance and continued development of Coke and Pepsi in all parts of the world. These companies have taken their rivalry overseas and have been spending millions to develop new markets for their products. One market that Pepsi-Cola dominated has been Russia, controlling twice the market share of Coke. Establishing its presence in Russia during the Nixon administration, Pepsi gained entry into the country through a barter deal involving the exportation of vodka. By 1993, Pepsi-Cola controlled 4 percent of the market compared to Coke's 2 percent. The obvious market growth potential made this former Soviet state a prime target for an American invasion of the cola wars.

In April 1993, Coke announced the construction of a $15 million production plant and training facility near Moscow. These facilities will serve the kiosks that have been installed in various Russian communities. Coca-Cola owns these kiosks, which are shaped like giant Coke cans, and rents them to a wholesaler, who in turns employs local citizens to operate the small soda stands. The acceptance of Russian rubles instead of American dollars differentiates this enterprise from the other American operations in Russia. ''The idea,'' reported Laurie Hays in the *Wall Street Journal*, ''is that such transactions will help the economy firm up and ultimately put more money into the pockets of citizens—more money they can use to buy Coke.''

In the mid-1990s, Pepsico announced its plans to invest $500 million in Poland over a five year period of time, with $200 million expressly for the development of a Pepsi market among the country's 38 million consumers. This investment was the third such market development announcement made by Pepsi. The company previously committed to a $115 million, five-year investment plan for Hungary and a $750 million plan for Mexico.

With per-capita consumption second only to the United States, Mexico has been set up as another major battleground for the cola wars. The largest Pepsi bottler outside of the United States has been Grupo Embotellador de Mexico SA, or Gemex, located in Mexico City. Meanwhile, Fomento Economico Mexicano SA, or Femsa, owns the largest Coke franchise in the world and is located in Monterrey. Needless to say,

Pepsi has dominated Mexico City, while Coke has covered the southern Mexico market. With the assistance of market reforms enacted by Mexico's President Carlos Salinas de Gortari, both Coke and Pepsi have been working to compete in each other's established territories.

In the United States, imported unsweetened bottled waters, both still and carbonated, have continued to dominate their segment of the U.S. water and soft drink market. In the early 1990s, France was responsible for 60 percent of unsweetened water imports and 34 percent of all water and soft drink imports. Canada had 24 percent of the unsweetened water imports, mainly with Clearly Canadian, and 42 percent of carbonated soft drinks. Due to the cost of shipping and distribution, imported products generally have been more expensive than domestically produced drinks and can be found at the luxury end of the U.S. market.

ASSOCIATIONS AND SOCIETIES

NATIONAL SOFT DRINK ASSOCIATION
1101 16th St. NW
Washington, DC 20036
Phone: (202) 463-6732
Fax: (202) 463-6178

SOCIETY OF SOFT DRINK TECHNOLOGISTS
113 Heron Point Ln.
Hartfield, VA 23071
Phone: (804) 776-7315
Fax: (804) 776-9230
Members are professionals engaged in the technical areas of soft drink production.

PERIODICALS AND NEWSLETTERS

BEVERAGE DIGEST
Tomac & Co., Inc.
PO Box 238
Old Greenwich, CT 06870
Phone: (203) 358-8198
Fax: (203) 327-9761
Biweekly. $370.00 per year. Includes supplement. News pertaining to the soft drink industry including new products, marketing territory changes, acquisitions, legal cases, etc.

BEVERAGE INDUSTRY
Stagnito Publishing Co.
1935 Shermer Rd., Ste. 100
Northbrook, IL 60062
Phone: (708) 205-5660
Fax: (708) 205-5680
Monthly. Free to qualified personnel; others, $50.00 per year.

BEVERAGE WORLD: MAGAZINE OF THE BEVERAGE INDUSTRY
Keller International Publishing Corp.
150 Great Neck Rd.
Great Neck, NY 11021-3309
Phone: (516) 829-9210
Fax: (516) 829-5414
Monthly. $39.95 per year.

BEVERAGE WORLD PERISCOPE
Keller International Publishing Corp.
150 Great Neck Rd.
Great Neck, NY 11021-3309
Phone: (516) 829-9210
Fax: (516) 829-5414
Monthly. $35.00 per year. Newsletter.

LEISURE BEVERAGE INSIDER NEWSLETTER
Whitaker Newsletter, Inc.
PO Box 192
Fanwood, NJ 07023
Phone: (201) 889-6336
Fax: (908) 889-6339
Biweekly. $280.00 per year. For owners and managers of bottling operations. Covers soft drinks, juices.

STATISTICS SOURCES

IMPACT BEVERAGE TRENDS IN AMERICA
M. Shanken Communications, Inc.
387 Park Ave. S
New York, NY 10016
Phone: (212) 684-4224
Fax: (212) 684-5424
Annual. $695.00. Detailed compilations of data for various segments of the liquor, beer, and soft drink industries.

U.S. INDUSTRIAL OUTLOOK: FORECASTS FOR SELECTED MANUFACTURING AND SERVICE INDUSTRIES
Available from U.S. Government Printing Office
Washington, DC 20402
Phone: (202) 512-1800
Fax: (202) 512-2250
Annual. $37.00. (Replaced in 1995 by U.S. Global Trade Outlook.) Issued by the International Trade Administration, U.S. Department of Commerce. Provides basic data, outlook for the current year, and "Long-Term Prospects" (five-year projections) for a wide variety of products and services. Includes high technology industries.

- Gopher://gopher.umsl.edu:70/11/library/govdocs/usio94

GENERAL WORKS

SODA POPPERY: THE HISTORY OF SOFT DRINKS IN AMERICA
Stephen Tchudi
Simon and Schuster
200 Old Tappan Rd.
Old Tappan, NJ 07675
Phone: (800) 223-2336 or (800) 223-2348
Fax: (800) 445-6991
1986. $14.95.

FURTHER READING

"The 49th Annual Report on the American Industry." *Forbes,* 13 January 1997.

Browder, Seanna. "Starbucks Does Not Live By Coffee Alone." *Business Week,* 5 August 1996.

"The Economic Impact of the Industry." National Soft Drinks Association. Washington, D.C.

General Business File. University of Michigan Kresge Library Online Database. February 1997.

"More Fun Facts." National Soft Drinks Association. Washington, D.C.

Prince, Greg W. "In Hot Water." *Beverage World,* March 1995.

Sfiligoj, Eric. "The Big Get Smaller." *Beverage World,* January 1996.

———. "Bottled Water." *Beverage World,* May 1995.

———. "Fruit Beverages." *Beverage World,* May 1995.

———. "Soft Drinks." *Beverage World,* May 1995.

———. "Sports Drinks." *Beverage World,* May 1995.

———. "Time and Tide." *Beverage World,* October 1995.

Sfiligoj, Eric, and Greg W. Prince. "Reality Drinks." *Beverage World,* September 1994.

"Soft Drink Facts." National Soft Drinks Association. Washington, D.C.

Walsh, Matt. "Juice Wars." *Forbes,* 11 April 1994

SOFTWARE, PREPACKAGED

SIC 7372

The software industry is expected to remain strong through the turn of the century, as software has become as important to computer users as hardware: spending for these two components reached a one-to-one ratio by the latter half of the 1990s. Client/server networks are replacing mainframes and microcomputers within large corporations and are increasingly important as more and more individuals purchase PCs; this trend is opening up the market for new software to support these networks. But the fastest growing segment of the market is Internet and Intranet software, projected to be the biggest information technology trend through the end of the century.

Prepackaged software is one of the strongest and fastest growing industries in the United States, particularly for personal computers (PCs). Because the leading operating systems are manufactured in the United States, as well as many of the leading applications, American firms set the most important standards for packaged software.

In the mid-1990s, the United States manufactured about 45 percent of the $105 billion estimated total annual worth of the worldwide packaged software market, which was expected to grow to over $152 billion by 2000. In 1996, the market was estimated to have grown by 11.9 percent, a decline from 15.4 percent growth in 1995.

Since information and computer technology are central to industrialized economies, software sales grew in the 1990s even while the rest of the economy was in recession. Indeed, the industry has enjoyed double-digit growth for more than a decade, although this pace slowed somewhat through the mid-1990s. Moreover, competition has driven prices of software packages, especially those at the corporate level, downward. Discounts for corporate customers are especially deep in the areas of spreadsheet and word processing packages. As Paul Brainerd, president of Aldus Corp., noted in *Business Week,* ''There is the myth of the retail price and the reality of what major customers pay.''

 BEST-SELLING SOFTWARE BRANDS

Ranked by: Total sales, in millions of dollars.

1. Windows, Microsoft Office & Excel (Microsoft Corp.), with $5,266 million
2. Netware, WordPerfect & Perfect Office, (Novell Inc.), $2,003
3. Lotus 1-2-3, Lotus Notes & cc: Mail (Lotus Development Corp.),
4. $971 Photoship & PageMaker (Adobe Systems), $598
5. AutoCAD (Autodesk), $455

Source: *Brandweek,* Superbrands: America's Top 2,000 Brands, October 9, 1995, p. 124.

Because the maintenance and customization of software is a labor-intensive activity, a shortage of programmers developed as computers became an increasingly integral part of daily life, both at work and at home. This situation made prepackaged software, which can be purchased and used with little or no modification, doubly attractive. In 1972, when the packaged software industry was in its infancy, only seven cents were spent on packaged software for every dollar spent on hardware. Twenty years later, the ratio was about one to one.

Although International Business Machines Corporation (IBM) dominated the overall market, the leader of PC packaged software entering the mid-1990s was the Microsoft Corporation empire founded by Bill Gates. Microsoft was one of the largest software developers in the world, a status built initially on the strength of products such as Microsoft Disk Operating System (MS-DOS), a product it acquired, and further developed by the popularity of its Windows products, including Windows 95, Windows NT, and the Microsoft Office Suite.

INDUSTRY OUTLOOK

The prepackaged software industry is in a period of transition caused by the dominance of Microsoft, the rapid spread of graphic user interfaces, and the growing power of PCs. Microsoft controls increasingly large segments of the prepackaged software market, and many firms feel threatened by its economic position and its subsequent power to dictate standards.

Software prices continue to decline. List prices remained high, but discount software stores and mail-order firms often charge only 40 percent of the list price, and corporations that make volume purchases of programs can do so at even cheaper rates. Windows continues to shake up the software market, and, as the *Wall Street Journal* noted in the mid-1990s, the rate of growth in the number of new software users was declining, a set of circumstances that left software firms fighting over existing customers.

Due to the rapidly increasing power of smaller computers, client/server networks are replacing the

SIC 7372 - Prepackaged Software General Statistics

	Establish-ments	Employment (000)	Payroll ($ mil.)	Revenues ($ mil.)
1987	3,392	55.7	2,052.4	5,894.2*
1988	3,156	58.3	2,473.1	-*
1989	3,643	68.0	2,882.8	-*
1990	3,755	76.3	3,516.8	14,492.0
1991	3,786	87.2	4,083.0	12,607.0
1992	7,108	131.0	6,614.3	14,395.0
1993	6,970	142.4	7,373.2	16,733.0
1994	7,227P	149.1P	7,777.2P	16,684.5P
1995	7,898P	164.3P	8,686.0P	17,535.6P
1996	8,569P	179.4P	9,594.8P	18,386.7P

Sources: Data for 1982, 1987, and 1992 are from *Census of Service Industries*, Bureau of the Census, U.S. Department of Commerce. Revenue data are from the *Service Annual Survey* or from the Census. Revenue data from the Census are labelled with *. Data for 1988-1991 and 1993, when shown, are derived from *County Business Patterns* for those years from the Bureau of the Census. A P indicates projections made by the editor.

mainframe and minicomputers as the primary systems used by the government and large corporations. New operating systems and software for these networks are an increasingly important and competitive market. Client/server networks can become extremely complicated since they may have different platforms running different types of software. As a result, software companies that enter this market must stress service to a much larger extent than most did in the past.

As PCs and workstations grow similar in power, the Unix operating system is becoming increasingly important. Its power and communications abilities are signifi-

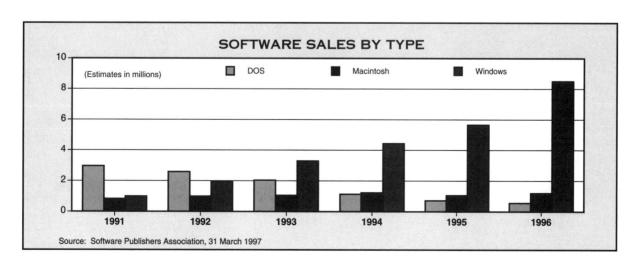

SOFTWARE SALES BY TYPE
(Estimates in millions) □ DOS ■ Macintosh ■ Windows

Source: Software Publishers Association, 31 March 1997

cant to users, and its position as a counterweight to Microsoft, which has little power in the Unix arena, is significant to software makers.

Corporate computer departments require a much higher level of support and service than do Microsoft's PC customers. Further, a line of computer firms using the Unix operating system is already serving that niche. The Unix companies such as IBM, Hewlett-Packard, and Sun Microsystems are experienced at dealing with corporate computer departments and have better corporate sales channels. As *Barron's* notes, "Microsoft also faces questions on how to provide Windows NT users with adequate service and support. While companies like IBM and H-P (Hewlett-Packard) have large in-house support staffs, Microsoft will have to rely on third parties to help customers with installation and maintenance problems." Some analysts feel these firms also have an advantage because Unix is an open operating system, while Windows NT is proprietary, giving its users less options. Windows NT needs powerful hardware and large amounts of memory to run, as much or more than the various versions of Unix.

Despite their competing sponsors, Windows NT and the various Unix operating systems share certain features. All use some form of graphic user interface. After the success of the Macintosh and Windows, it was clear that most consumers and businesses preferred the ease-of-use and other features of graphic interfaces. The new generation of operating systems are also able to use the 32-bit capabilities of more recent microprocessors, meaning that information can be dealt with in segments four times the size of the segments DOS used. Because so much money

had been invested in programs running on DOS, most of the new operating systems were expected to run DOS and Windows programs as well as newer applications.

An area of incredible growth, which caught even Microsoft by surprise, was the Internet. While it began in 1969 as a development project of the U.S. Department of Defense and had been used by scientists and researchers for years, in the 1990s the Internet began leaking into the lexicon of the general computer user. By the mid-1990s, through the proliferation of the World Wide Web (WWW), it had become a phenomenon. It had also developed into a medium for disseminating information ranked on the level of television and the printed word. With the Internet, whole new classes of software were born, including WWW servers and browsers, security systems known as fire walls, Web page development tools, and even new programming languages.

Netscape Communications Corporation took the market by storm by initially offering its browser software free. It was a shrewd tactic to gain market share and to make entry for its web server products. Distributions costs were low because the software could be downloaded from the Internet. Netscape's hold on the market still remained at more than 75 percent even a year after Microsoft released its Internet Server and the Internet Explorer browser.

Sun Microsystems released a programming language called Java, which also took the industry by storm. It enabled programmers to create small, easily portable applications called "applets" that could be run through

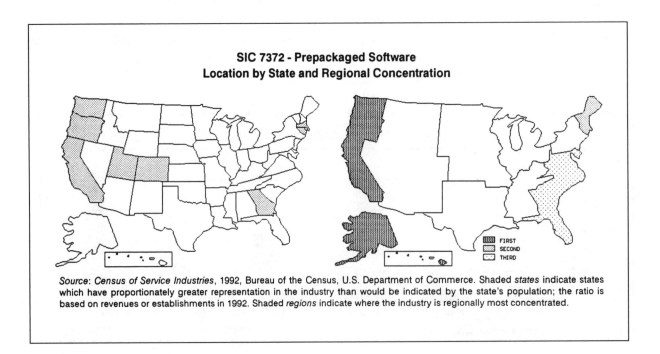

SIC 7372 - Prepackaged Software
Location by State and Regional Concentration

FIRST
SECOND
THIRD

Source: Census of Service Industries, 1992, Bureau of the Census, U.S. Department of Commerce. Shaded *states* indicate states which have proportionately greater representation in the industry than would be indicated by the state's population; the ratio is based on revenues or establishments in 1992. Shaded *regions* indicate where the industry is regionally most concentrated.

a Web browser. Because they run in conjunction with the browser, applets can be essentially universal to any hardware or software system. As long as the system can run a compliant browser, it can run the applet. Functions of applets might range from simple multimedia demonstrations to the user's PC to more complex applications, such as Corel Corporation's release of 1997 Java version of its WordPerfect program and Novell's Java-compliant version of NetWare.

Another application that emerged from Internet technology was the corporate "intranet"—a medium for private data sharing accessed through Internet software, but maintained for internal use only. As companies began developing and using Internet technology, they began finding ways to apply the same software to their networks. Intranets were relatively inexpensive and easy to implement, and like the Internet, intranet applications were platform independent. For companies that had computers using different operating systems on their networks, but had to share common information and applications, intranet software quickly became a valuable tool. According to *Datamation,* corporate intranets were going to be the biggest information technology trend in 1997.

ORGANIZATION AND STRUCTURE

Prepackaged software is the largest segment of the broader software industry. It is typically mass produced with standard functionalities that are expected to work across a given class of computers, e.g., PCs running Microsoft Windows 3.1 or later. With the emergence in the mid-1990s of the Internet as a viable consumer medium, mass-produced software may often be delivered without any packaging via Internet download, making "prepackaging" a bit of a misnomer for this industry.

There are three basic types of software: operating systems software, which controls how a computer operates; applications software, such as word processing or spreadsheet programs; and utility software, designed to perform support tasks for operating systems or applications. Many software companies sell products in each of these categories.

Software is also categorized by the type of computer on which it runs: mainframe, minicomputer, or PC. Many software companies concentrate on one of these markets, though some design products for more than one market. This varied attention is particularly true of firms that design networking software, which allows computers to communicate.

The software market for PCs exploded in the 1990s. In addition to operating systems and numerous utilities, many businesses and individuals bought PC software for applications such as spreadsheets, word processing, graphics and design, and desktop publishing. In addition, as PC hardware became more powerful, some applications formerly run on mainframe computers were being downsized for use on less costly PC networks.

Minicomputer and mainframe software still accounts for billions of dollars in sales annually, but software sales have been sluggish in these areas because applications are being run on less expensive workstations and PCs. The software for larger computers is based on the processing power of those systems and often costs tens of thousands of dollars. Much of it is not sold at all, but is rented or custom designed, and is therefore not classified as prepackaged software.

Software applications for larger computers tend to focus on accounting and database packages. Leading vendors include Computer Associates, Dun & Bradstreet, Oracle, DEC, and IBM.

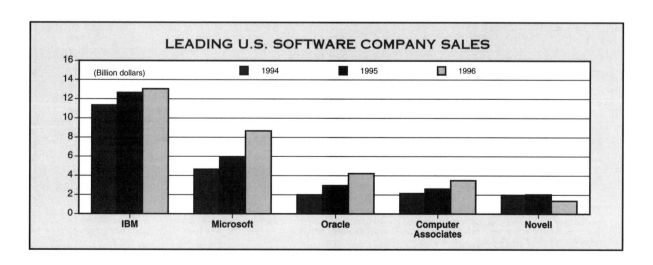

LEADING U.S. SOFTWARE COMPANY SALES

(Billion dollars) — 1994, 1995, 1996 — IBM, Microsoft, Oracle, Computer Associates, Novell

WORK FORCE

More than 206,300 people were employed in the prepackaged software industry in 1996, according to the Current Employment Statistics (CES) Survey conducted by the Bureau of Labor Statistics. This figure was up 13.4 percent from 1995 and demand for programmers was expected to continue to grow much faster than the average until at least 2005 as the use of computers expands. The average number of employees in the top 50 firms is about 1,850, many of whom are involved in marketing or management rather than programming, according to *Datamation*.

A full-time programmer earned, on average, about $22 an hour in 1996. Programmers' salaries vary widely, however. The highest earned more than $60,000 a year, while the lowest earned about $30,000 a year. In general, systems programmers are paid more than applications programmers.

Working conditions for programmers are generally good. Because of the large amount of attention required to do their jobs, most programmers work in quiet office settings and work alone. However, as labor trends change, programmers are working more an more out of their homes. The hours at some firms are the traditional nine-to-five, but from its earliest days, the PC software industry has been known for its long hours.

AMERICA AND THE WORLD

One of the major hurdles facing the global packaged software market was piracy. In 1996, it was estimated that more than $13 billion was lost worldwide to piracy, a 9 percent increase over the previous year. In certain areas of Eastern Europe and Latin America, piracy rates reached 97 percent; Vietnam and China were at 99 percent; while the United States had the lowest piracy rate in the world at 26 percent. However, the United States made strident efforts to help reduce piracy in hot spots around the world, especially in China.

During the mid-1990s the U.S. threatened to impose $2 billion in trade sanctions against China if they did crack down on piracy, which included not only computer software, but music and movies as well. After intense negotiations, China did agree to battle against piracy and shut down factories producing illegal software. The United States also sought to restrict trade with other countries that did not have proper policies and practices against piracy. This was done through an addition to the Omnibus Trade and Competitiveness Act of 1988, Section 182 or "Special 301," which required the U.S. to deny those countries that failed to meet intellectual property protection criteria fair access to their trade.

U.S. leads in many forms of computer and chip technology evaporated during the 1980s, but during mid-1990s, the country still held a formidable edge in software and supplied about 75 percent of software globally. In 1995, the United States accounted for about 45 percent of the global market, Western Europe held about 34 percent, and Japan came in around 10 percent.

Increases were also seen worldwide for U.S. software publishers. In 1996, according to the Software Publishers Association, Western Europe "continued to be the dominant international market for U.S. software publishers . . . especially in emerging product categories, such as e-mail." Japan broke the $1 billion mark and held over 70 percent of all revenue in the Asia Pacific region, making it the largest single country behind the United States. Latin America also saw a big increase with 28 percent gain over 1995.

SIC 7372 - Prepackaged Software
Industry Data by State

	Establishments			Employment			Payroll			Revenues - 1992 ($ mil.)			% change 87-92	
State	1987	1992	% of US 92	1987	1992	% of US 92	1987 ($ mil.)	1992 ($ mil.)	$ Per Empl. 92	Total ($ mil.)	Per Estab.	$ Per Empl. 92	Reve-nues	Pay-roll
California	730	1,421	59.1	12,281	36,529	74.6	472.5	2,144.5	58,708	6,843.6	4.8	187,347	428.9	353.9
Massachusetts	196	425	17.7	9,076	14,804	30.2	363.3	767.1	51,815	2,443.8	5.8	165,080	140.8	111.1
Texas	247	532	22.1	2,708	6,100	12.5	99.0	344.9	56,535	959.8	1.8	157,349	247.1	248.3
Washington	88	204	8.5	2,435	4,760	9.7	78.5	245.5	51,580	903.0	4.4	189,710	99.8	212.9
Illinois	177	315	13.1	2,652	5,985	12.2	102.8	301.3	50,347	800.1	2.5	133,686	184.9	193.1
New York	250	377	15.7	2,577	5,843	11.9	106.1	289.5	49,540	791.3	2.1	135,426	107.1	172.9
Ohio	102	217	9.0	2,537	3,636	7.4	88.6	161.4	44,377	697.2	3.2	191,762	216.1	82.2
Georgia	106	257	10.7	2,017	5,218	10.7	67.3	246.5	47,236	666.8	2.6	127,793	289.4	266.2
Utah	32	78	3.2	725	5,837	11.9	28.6	206.8	35,437	666.8	8.5	114,239	456.9	624.2
New Jersey	139	294	12.2	2,332	4,377	8.9	85.8	223.5	51,065	619.8	2.1	141,601	159.5	160.4

Source: Census of Service Industries, 1987 and 1992, Bureau of the Census, U.S. Department of Commerce. Data are sorted by 1992 revenues and, if revenues are unavailable, by establishments in 1992. (D) indicates that data are withheld by the source to avoid disclosure of competitive information. A dash (-) indicates that data are not available. Percentage changes between 1987 and 1992 are calculated using numbers that have *not* been rounded; hence they may not be reproducible from the values shown.

Japanese hardware makers led the charge into software in the early 1980s when prices for their hardware began falling. Leading firms such as Toshiba and Hitachi established software factories in which as many as 3,000 programmers wrote code for industrial applications and other software. The firms believed the factories would strengthen their advantages in low-cost, high-quality production. Japan quickly won large segments of the U.S. software market for video games, and by the mid-1980s, Japanese software makers sold software for airline reservation systems and banking.

Despite these successes, several factors held the Japanese prepackaged software industry back. Japanese software buyers, much as their American counterparts until the early 1970s, preferred custom software. This tepid domestic market retarded the growth of standardized, packaged software. Just as important, Japanese software developers were hurt by the cultural and language differences with the Western marketplace. Instruction manuals had to be translated, while the software programs themselves had to be switched to Roman characters and often rewritten entirely. Because of the large number of characters in the language, software developers faced inherent difficulties in processing information.

In the mid-1990s, Japan still lagged far behind the United States in software sales. Despite the ascendance of large software firms like Microsoft, a large amount of new U.S. software was created in smaller, independent software houses, while in Japan it was created under the auspices of large corporations. European software vendors remained far behind U.S. companies as well, though many found niches and continued to grow as mentioned earlier. Europe also worked on methods to speed and automate software writing.

nications, Computer Graphics, Computers in Education, Design Automation, Office Automation, Personal Computing, Robotics, Security and Privacy, and Software Engineering.

INFORMATION TECHNOLOGY ASSOCIATION OF AMERICA
1616 N. Fort Myer Dr., Ste. 1300
Arlington, VA 22209
Phone: (703) 522-5055
Fax: (703) 525-2279
Members are computer software and services companies. Maintains an Information Systems Integration Services Section. Formerly ADAPSO: The Computer Software and Services Industry Association.

INTERACTIVE DIGITAL SOFTWARE ASSOCIATION
919 18th St. NW, Ste. 210
Washington, DC 20006
Phone: (202) 833-4372
Fax: (202) 833-4431
Members are interactive entertainment software publishers concerned with rating systems, software piracy, government relations, and other industry issues.

OFFICE AUTOMATION SOCIETY INTERNATIONAL
5170 Meadow Wood Blvd.
Lyndhurst, OH 44124
Phone: (216) 461-4803
Fax: (216) 461-4803
Members are office automation professionals.

SPECIAL INTEREST GROUP ON SOFTWARE ENGINEERING
Association for Computing Machinery
1515 Broadway
New York, NY 10036
Phone: (212) 869-7440
Fax: (212) 869-0481
Concerned with the technology of software creation and evolution.

ASSOCIATIONS AND SOCIETIES

AMERICAN SOFTWARE ASSOCIATION
c/o ITAA
1616 N. Fort Meyer, Ste. 1300
Arlington, VA 22209-9998
Phone: (703) 522-5055
Fax: (703) 525-2279
Affiliated with the Association of Data Processing Service Organizations.

IEEE COMPUTER SOCIETY
1730 Massachusetts Ave. NW
Washington, DC 20036
Phone: (202) 371-0101
Fax: (202) 857-4799
A society of the Institute of Electrical and Electronics Engineers. Said to be the world's largest organization of computer professionals. Some of the specific committees are: Computer Commu-

PERIODICALS AND NEWSLETTERS

COMPUTER LANGUAGES
Elsevier Science
660 White Plains Rd.
Tarrytown, NY 10591-5153
Phone: (914) 524-9200
Fax: (914) 333-2444
Quarterly. $552.00 per year.

COMPUTERWORLD: NEWSWEEKLY FOR INFORMATION SYSTEMS MANAGEMENT
Computerworld, Inc.
PO Box 9171
Framingham, MA 01701-9171
Phone: (508) 879-0700
Fax: (508) 875-8931
Weekly. $48.00 per year.

DR. DOBB'S JOURNAL: SOFTWARE TOOLS FOR THE PROFESSIONAL PROGRAMMER

Miller Freeman, Inc.
411 Borel Ave.
San Mateo, CA 94402-3522
Phone: (415) 358-9500
Fax: (415) 358-9749
Monthly. $29.97 per year. A technical publication covering software development, languages, operating systems, and applications.

IEEE SOFTWARE

IEEE Computer Society
10662 Los Vacqueros Cir.
Los Alamitos, CA 90720-1264
Phone: (714) 821-8380
Fax: (714) 821-4010
Bimonthly. $305.00 per year. Covers software engineering, technology, and development. Affiliated with the Institute of Electrical and Electronics Engineers.

JOURNAL OF SOFTWARE MAINTENANCE: RESEARCH AND PRACTICE

Available from John Wiley & Sons, Inc.
Journals Div.
605 3rd Ave.
New York, NY 10158-0012
Phone: (800) 526-5368 or (212) 850-6645
Fax: (212) 850-6021
Bimonthly. $645.00 per year. Published in England by John Wiley & Sons Ltd. Provides international coverage of subject matter.

MANAGING AUTOMATION

Thomas Publishing Co.
5 Penn Plaza
250 W. 34th St.
New York, NY 10001
Phone: (800) 222-7900 or (212) 695-0500
Fax: (212) 629-1585
Monthly. Controlled circulation. Coverage includes software for manufacturing, systems planning, integration in process industry automation, computer integrated manufacturing (CIM), computer networks for manufacturing, management problems, industry news, and new products.

MICROSOFT SYSTEMS JOURNAL

Miller Freeman, Inc.
411 Borel Ave.
San Mateo, CA 94402-3522
Phone: (415) 358-9500
Fax: (415) 358-9865
Monthly. $50.00 per year. Produced for professional software developers using Windows, MS-DOS, Visual Basic, and other Microsoft Corporation products.

NETWORK COMPUTING: COMPUTING IN A NETWORK ENVIRONMENT

CMP Publications, Inc.
600 Community Dr.
Manhasset, NY 11030
Phone: (516) 562-5000
Fax: (516) 365-4601
Monthly. Controlled circulation.

PC WEEK: THE NATIONAL NEWSPAPER OF CORPORATE COMPUTING

Ziff-Davis Publishing Co.
10 Presidents Landing
Medford, MA 02155-5146
Phone: (800) 451-1032 or (617) 393-3700
Weekly. Free to qualified personnel; others, $195.00 per year.

SOFT.LETTER: TRENDS AND STRATEGIES IN SOFTWARE PUBLISHING

Jeffrey Tarter
17 Main St.
Watertown, MA 02172
Phone: (617) 924-3944
Fax: (617) 924-7288
Semimonthly. $345.00 per year. Newsletter on the software industry, including new technology and financial aspects.

SOFTWARE DIGEST RATINGS REPORT

National Software Testing Laboratories, Inc.
Plymouth Corporate Center
PO Box 1000
Plymouth Meeting, PA 19462
Phone: (800) 223-7093 or (610) 941-9600
Fax: (610) 941-9950
15 times a year. $445.00 per year. Critical evaluations of personal computer software.

SOFTWARE INDUSTRY BULLETIN

Digital Information Group
51 Bank St.
Stamford, CT 06901
Phone: (800) 255-0942 or (203) 348-2751
Fax: (203) 977-8310
Weekly. $395.00 per year. Newsletter. Covers financial, copyright, distribution, and other aspects of the software industry.

SOFTWARE LAW JOURNAL

Center for Computer Law
PO Box 3549
Manhattan Beach, CA 90266
Phone: (301) 544-7372
Quarterly. $97.50 per year.

SOFTWARE MAGAZINE

Sentry Publishing Co., Inc.
1 Research Dr., Ste. 400 B,
Westborough, MA 01581-3907
Phone: (508) 366-2031
Fax: (508) 366-4732
Monthly. Free to qualified personnel; others, $65.00 per year.

SOFTWARE PROTECTION: A JOURNAL ON THE LEGAL, TECHNICAL, AND PRACTICAL ASPECTS OF PROTECTING COMPUTER SOFTWARE

Law and Technology Press
4 Arbolado Ct.
Manhattan Beach, CA 90266-4937
Phone: (310) 544-0272
Fax: (310) 544-4965
Monthly. $225.00 per year.

DATABASES

BUSINESS SOFTWARE DATABASE
Information Sources, Inc.
PO Box 8120
Berkeley, CA 94707
Phone: (510) 525-6220
Fax: (510) 525-1568
Describes business software packages. Inquire as to online cost and availability.

COMPUTER DATABASE
Information Access Co.
362 Lakeside Dr.
Foster City, CA 94404
Phone: (800) 227-8431 or (415) 378-5000
Fax: (415) 378-5369
Provides online citations with abstracts to material appearing in about 150 trade journals and newsletters in the subject areas of computers, telecommunications, and electronics. Time period is 1983 to date, with weekly updates. Inquire as to online cost and availability.

GUIDE TO COMPUTER VENDORS
Systems for Business Accounting
Links to more than 800 hardware and software vendors o the world wide web. Includes a directory of several thousand computer companies, and a list of online computer magazines. When established: 1995. Fees: Free.

- URL: http://www.ronin.com/SBA

THE INTERNATIONAL PROGRAMMERS GUILD
Netshop International
Contains general and specific information about the guild. Time span: Current information. Updating frequency: Regularly. Fees: Free.

- URL: http: //www.ipgnet.com/ipghome.htm

MICROCOMPUTER ABSTRACTS [ONLINE]
Information Today, Inc.
143 Old Marlton Pke.
Medford, NJ 08055-8750
Phone: (609) 654-6266
Fax: (609) 654-4309
Contains abstracts covering a wide variety of personal and business microcomputer literature appearing in more than 90 journals and popular magazines. Time period is 1981 to date, with monthly updates. Formerly Microcomputer Index. *Inquire as to online cost and availability.*

MICROCOMPUTER SOFTWARE GUIDE ONLINE
R. R. Bowker
121 Chanlon Rd.
New Providence, NJ 07974
Phone: (800) 521-8110 or (908) 464-6800
Fax: (908) 665-6688
Provides information on more than 17,000 microcomputer software applications from more than 3,000 producers. Corresponds to printed Software Encyclopedia *, but with monthly updates. Inquire as to online cost and availability.*

PUBLIC HEARINGS ON SOFTWARE PATENTS
U.S. Patent and Trademark Office
Provides the complete transcripts of the PTO's two public hearings in 1994 on software patents. Includes prepared remarks from the hearings and e-mail comments. Fees: Free.

- URL: http://www.uspto.gov/hearings.html

STATISTICS SOURCES

SOFTWARE INDUSTRY FACTBOOK
Digital Information Group
51 Bank St.
Stamford, CT 06901
Phone: (800) 255-0942 or (203) 348-2751
Fax: (203) 977-8310
Annual. $395.00. Includes market research data and analysis.

SOFTWARE MARKET SURVEY
Sentry Market Research
1 Research Dr.
Westborough, MA 01581
Phone: (508) 366-2031
Fax: (508) 366-8104
Annual. $500.00. Provides installation data, growth projections, and dollars spent in each of 50 software categories. Comparative market share for each category is shown for previous five years.

GENERAL WORKS

COMPUTER INDUSTRY ALMANAC
Karen Juliussen and Egil Juliussen
Available from Hoover's, Inc.
1033 La Posada Drive, Ste. 250
Austin, TX 78752
Phone: (800) 486-8666 or (512) 374-4500
Fax: (512) 374-4501
Annual. $62.95. Published by Computer Industry Almanac, Inc. Analyzes recent trends in various segments of the computer industry, with forecasts, employment data and industry salary information. Includes directories of computer companies, industry organizations, and publications.

MANAGING SOFTWARE DEVELOPMENT PROJECTS: FORMULA FOR SUCCESS
Neal Whitten
John Wiley and Sons, Inc.
605 3rd Ave.
New York, NY 10158-0012
Phone: (800) 225-5945 or (212) 850-6000
Fax: (212) 850-6088
1995. $44.95. Second edition.

THE OTHER SIDE OF SOFTWARE: A USER'S GUIDE FOR DEFINING SOFTWARE REQUIREMENTS
Carolyn Shamlin
AMACOM, American Management Association
135 W. 50th St., 15 Fl.
New York, NY 10020-1201
Phone: (800) 262-9699 or (212) 903-8315
Fax: (212) 903-8168

1990. $22.95. Second edition. Explains how general management personnel can communicate effectively with computer personnel about software needs. First edition title: A User's Guide for Defining Software Requirements.

THE SOFTWARE BUSINESS
Meyer Solomon
Silicon Press
25 Beverly Rd.
Summit, NJ 07901
Phone: (908) 273-8919
Fax: (908) 273-6149
1991. $15.95.

FURTHER READING

"1997 Computer Industry Salary Survey." Datamasters, 1997. Available from http://www.datamasters.com/dm/survey.html.

Sanders, Jim, and Smiroldo, Diane. "More than $13 Billion Lost Worldwide to Software Piracy Join BSA/SPA Survey Reveals." Software Publishers Association, 18 December 1996. Available from http://www.spa.org/pres/pr_piracy95.htm.

"Worldwide Pacakged Software Revenue Grows 12 Percent as Market Reachs $105 Billion Mark." IDC Market Research. Available from http://www.idcresearch.com/f/hnr/wwsbns.htm.

SPORTING AND ATHLETIC GOODS

SIC 3949

The sporting goods industry continues to enjoy the general prosperity of the U.S. retail market, and a positive outlook for the industry is projected through the end of the 1990s. Sales for 1996 increased only slightly, but the market should remain strong due to increased interest in goods designed for niche markets, the growth in women's sports participation, a baby-boomer population committed to keeping physically fit, and expanding overseas markets.

INDUSTRY SNAPSHOT

Like other sectors of the U.S. economy, the sporting goods industry underwent substantial change in the mid-1990s. Computer technology linked sports equipment manufacturers more closely to retailers. The trends of globalization and restructuring transformed the organization of sporting good companies. Sports equipment makers pondered how to exploit the stunning growth of the Internet, and changing demographics and lifestyles affected the popularity of individual sports and past times.

Overall, the industry shared in the general prosperity of the U.S. economy. The three percent increase in U.S. wholesale sales of sports equipment recorded in 1996 was somewhat disappointing, but the outlook for the industry remained generally positive. While the American population was aging, much of the postwar baby-boom generation remained committed to staying physically fit. Growing numbers of women were becoming sports enthusiasts, and manufacturers were designing offerings specifically for their needs (rather than simply painting existing products in pastels). In general, companies were creating new demand by appealing to specific market segments (e.g. basketballs and backboards especially designed for children). Overseas markets were also a source of new demand because of expanding economies and liberalized trade regulations.

Top 10 BEST-SELLING SPORTING GOODS BRANDS

Ranked by: Total sales in 1995, in billions of dollars.

1. Nike, with $2.488 billion
2. Reebok, $2.160
3. Russell, $1.098
4. VF Corp., $.873
5. Tultex, $.844
6. Champion, $.602
7. Spakling, $.569
8. Coleman, $.554
9. Titleist/Foot-Joy, $.476
10. Adidas, $.473

Source: *Brandweek,* Superbrands: America's Top 2,000 Brands, October 9, 1995, p. 133.

Performance among the industry's numerous segments continued to vary significantly in the mid-1990s, as a sport's popularity waxed or waned depending on demographics, economics, marketing skill, and fads. The golf and fitness segments were doing well because of technologically improved products and new adherents among an aging population. After several years of spectacular growth, the in-line skating segment contracted significantly in 1996. Meanwhile, tennis sales were showing some improvement, although they were still below the levels of the mid-1980s.

INDUSTRY OUTLOOK

According to the annual survey of the Sporting Goods Manufacturers Association (SGMA), domestic shipments of sporting goods at the wholesale level were $15.2 billion in 1996, about 2.6 percent higher than the 1995 total. The increase compared with a 5.4 percent advance for 1995/1994, and an 11.6 percent jump in 1994/1993. The relatively slow advance in 1996 reflected a downturn in the in-line skating segment after several years of strong growth. Sports equipment makers generally remained upbeat about the industry's business prospects. The economy was doing well, demographic trends and healthy lifestyles were boosting demand in the over-40 age group, more women were playing sports, and enactment of the North American Free Trade Agreement and other pacts liberalizing trade boded well for overseas business.

The industry did face several challenges, however. In the short-term, consumer installment debt was on the rise; coupled with a general sense of job uncertainty, this could lead to tighter consumer spending. In the long term, there is concern that lack of free time and lack of motivation could hurt participation levels in some sports. Many sports were not attracting significant numbers of new enthusiasts, but were rather competing for participants against other sports.

Another challenge for equipment manufacturers was product liability costs. These expenses ran so high that manufacturers were discontinuing production of certain products. The number of football helmet manufacturers, for example, fell from 18 in 1970 to two in 1993.

For individual companies, the positives and negatives of the industry as a whole are often overshadowed by the environment in its particular segment. According to the SGMA survey, in 1996 shipments of golfing equipment rose five percent to an estimated $2.3 billion. Sales of clubs and balls have done best in the 1990s, rising at compound annual growth rates, respectively, of 13 percent and 10 percent during the 1991 to 1996 period. Golfing continued to attract older, more affluent players. In 1992, in fact, 30 percent of all golfers had incomes of $50,000 to $74,000, the highest proportion for any sport. They had the means to buy the technologically improved products that were introduced in the late 1980s and 1990s, such as clubs with graphite shafts, oversized heads, and beryllium copper facings. At Calla-

way, demand for Big Bertha metal oversized woods produced truly astonishing growth, as sales rose from $132 million in 1992 to $678 million in 1996.

Whether better clubs have actually helped the golfer's game is questioned by some observers, but there was little doubt they've done wonders for investors in golf club stocks. In January 1996, conglomerate American Brands bought Cobra Golf, makers of the King Cobra Titanium club that duels with Callaway's Big Bertha for the golfer's dollar. American paid $715 million for a company that had just $152 million in sales for the nine months ended September 30, 1995.

While some industry analysts predicted stagnation for the golfing equipment industry due to the increased demands on players' time from work and family, a slowdown has yet to be observed. In fact, the popularity and spectacular skill of Tiger Woods is attracting new, non-traditional enthusiasts to the game.

Tennis made a small comeback in 1996. According to the SGMA survey, sales for the segment rose to an estimated $245 million from $235 million a year before; sales of racquets and balls increased for the first time in four years. Nevertheless, overall sales were still down from the $300 million level of 1993. According to one study, the number of players fell by 500,000 through the early 1990s. While the sluggish economy and bad weather were partly responsible for the decline, it also appears that people are choosing other sports, like in-line skating or fitness training, rather than tennis.

The growth of in-line skating has been truly astonishing. According to one estimate, in-line skating participation grew 634 percent from 1987 to 1995. Naturally, the surge in popularity catapulted sales, which rose from nearly nothing to $725 million in 1995, according to the SGMA survey. Demand has been spurred by the interest in roller hockey, which has become one of the fastest growing sports in the country.

In 1996, however, the industry suffered an enormous setback, as sales declined 14 percent to $625 million. Some of the reasons offered for the industry's decline were overloaded inventories at the retail level, poor weather conditions, and a lack of exciting new products. The industry was also worried about the number of skaters injured and legislation limiting access to streets for in-line skating. Nevertheless, many in the industry were predicting a pick-up in sales for 1997, partly because of new product introductions, including hybrid soft-boot skates.

The desire of an aging American population to keep fit conveniently has supported sales of the fitness equipment segment. According to the SGMA survey, sales of fitness products totaled an estimated $2.07 billion in

1996, up from $1.93 billion in 1995 and compared with just $680 million in 1986. The most popular exercise in 1995 was using free weights, which replaced stationary bicycling for the number-one spot. Fitness walking, including treadmill use, was the most popular activity among women and seniors.

So-called "infomercials" and television shopping networks have also given a big boost to sales of fitness equipment. Sales of the abdominal exerciser reached over $200 million in 1996, although some observers think that the popularity of these machines has crested. The aero rider/glider was another product whose sales were propelled by the infomercial.

Basketball has benefited from increasing participation by women, spurred by the formation of professional women's leagues and the success of the women's team at the 1996 Olympics. Moreover, Title IX and other gender equity programs have encouraged more women to take up the game. Meanwhile, men aged 35 to 44 are playing the game in growing numbers. According to the SGMA, sales grew about three percent in 1996.

Sales in the baseball and softball segment have been lackluster, as participation rates stay flat or decline. Few adults played baseball, and some youngsters found soccer and in-line skating more entertaining. The Major League Baseball strike of 1994-95 and the cancellation of the World Series for the first time in 90 years certainly didn't help the game's appeal. Softball had also seen better days; participation dropped 16 percent between 1987 and 1996. One bright spot was women's fast pitch, whose image was enhanced by the excellent performance by the U.S. team in the 1996 Olympics.

Bowling equipment sales are also lackluster. More than 53 million people aged six or older bowled at least once in 1995, making it one of the largest participant sports. But league play, the traditional segment of the business, has been falling since the 1970s. Indeed, the decline in league play gained notoriety in 1995 when Harvard professor Robert Putnam linked it to a general drop in participation of all kinds of neighborhood- and community-level groups. Calling the syndrome "Bowling Alone," Putnam blamed it for the collapse of the democratic process. According to the SGMA survey, sales of bowling products declined five percent in 1995 to $215 million.

ORGANIZATION AND STRUCTURE

The sporting goods industry encompasses a wide variety of businesses and products, and there are hundreds of participants. Within a specific segment, how-

ever, a few large companies may dominate. In the mid-1990s, ownership of many sporting goods companies changed hands. Most notably, in 1996 Kohlberg, Kravis, Roberts & Co. acquired Spalding Sports Worldwide in a deal estimated at $1 billion the largest deal ever made in the sporting goods industry. Other companies, like Wilson Sporting Goods, consolidated and restructured their operations.

The sporting goods sector offers stunning success stories, as a new or substantially improved product, or even an entirely new sport, can capture the public's fancy and produce spectacular returns for the originator. But for every Rollerblade—a company that rode the in-line skate boom—there are dozens of failures. As John Riddle, president of the Sporting Goods Manufacturers Association told *Nation's Business,* "Having a good idea is ten percent of the trick, albeit no easy feat. The other 90 percent is in getting enough capital behind your product and marketing it correctly. A little luck never hurts either."

RESEARCH AND TECHNOLOGY

New technology plays a vital role in the sports market. Consumers are often driven to buy new equipment because of the real or perceived advantages of product introductions. On the other hand, tradition also has a hallowed place in sports, and participants have to feel comfortable that their equipment is in the historical spirit of the game. Additionally, innovative manufacturers can create substantially new sports through their products.

In some sports there have been revolutionary changes in equipment over the past 20 or 30 years. The traditional wooden tennis racket had pretty much stayed the same until the 1960s, when manufacturers began to redesign it in an effort to improve performance and ease of play. The introduction of durable metal and fiber-reinforced-composite rackets was followed by oversized and wide body models. More recently, finely balanced rackets that have shock- and vibration-damping handles and new string bed patterns for greater accuracy have been introduced. Compared with the classic wooden model that weighed 14 ounces and had a hitting area of 68 square inches, rackets sold in the early 1990s were 35 percent to 40 percent lighter, with the weight redistributed for better performance, and had a hitting area of 120 square inches.

In 1997, softball bats also received an upgrade. A division of Spalding was set to introduce the Fusion bat; a composite of aluminum and graphite, it was supposed to provide a lighter, faster swing. The SZ1-C from

Easton Sports, on the other hand, is made from a rare material used in Soviet MiG fighter jets. Meanwhile, Worth Inc. was expected to offer a new line of Cryogenic bats, which are first heated, then chilled to temperatures as low as -310 degrees.

Intriguingly, engineers have also had stunning successes in overhauling the humble bowling ball. Several new urethane and reactive resin bowling ball shells and complex inner core configurations—designed to vary the ball's rotation as it goes down the lane—have substantially altered the ball's hook as it approaches the pocket. This redesign could be related to the recent sharp rise in perfect games.

Smart entrepreneurs have also developed innovative products for niche markets. Passengers on cruise ships used to drive thousands of regulation golf balls into the sea. But in 1990 the International Maritime Organization banned the practice as part of its effort to protect sea life. Responding to opportunity, Patrick Kane of Bonita, California, developed a golf ball that flies almost as well as a traditional ball but is made of materials that decompose quickly and can be consumed safely by fish and other marine life. He told the *New York Times* that ''It's basically fish food . . . you can market it on the basis of sympathy for the environmentalists.''

The sporting goods industry is also working on improving its technology in the more mundane, but nonetheless important, areas of inventory and delivery systems. Better information systems allow manufacturers to keep retailers stocked in goods that are selling well and reduce their own inventories of slow-moving items. Manufacturers can also alert stores to overall sales patterns so that retailers can better react to market trends. Sporting goods companies have also worked to develop packaging that is more environmentally friendly.

AMERICA AND THE WORLD

In recent years, U.S. sporting goods companies have done well in overseas markets. According to the SGMA, total export sales for the entire sporting goods industry grew at an average rate of 25 percent per year in the 1995-1996 period. The top export market is Japan, followed by Germany, and the rest of Europe. Growth in traditional Asian markets like Japan, however, has been lackluster. In 1997, much interest centered on China, where entire industries can spring up almost overnight. For example, bowling has surged in popularity, and new lanes were being built at extraordinary rates. Some experts believed China could be the world's top bowling market by the year 2010.

The broad penetration of U.S. culture overseas has been a boon to the sporting goods industry. Often there is a dynamic interplay between the popularity of the American lifestyle, the star-quality of American athletes, and the marketing savvy of American industry. For example, the growing popularity of basketball among kids in Europe has been linked to the NBA's Shaquille O'Neal, whom they know solely through watching Pepsi commercials. U.S. sporting goods products are thus valued in some countries simply because they are made in the United States. Consumers believe they are participating in the American lifestyle by purchasing them. The perception that U.S. sporting goods are of unusually high quality in certain product categories has also spurred sales.

U.S. manufacturers were also eyeing South American markets. The restoration of democracy to many Latin American governments had been accompanied by better economic conditions, giving consumers more spending power. Moreover, a trend toward freer trade has been noted, as Argentina and Brazil have sharply reduced trade barriers to overseas goods. While Latin Americans have always been passionate about soccer, they have started to take up typically American sports like basketball and in-line skating, where U.S. companies hold an edge.

The manufacture of many sporting goods is labor-intensive, so U.S. companies have shifted much of their production to East Asia, where wage rates are generally lower. High-tech computer systems enable companies to institute global manufacturing programs that maximize efficiency. The move toward more open markets and reduced tariffs also accelerates the trend toward globalization. Thus companies can produce wherever efficiencies are greatest: the SGMA estimated in 1997 that 25 percent of all sporting goods emanate from China.

ASSOCIATIONS AND SOCIETIES

CENTER FOR SPORTS SPONSORSHIP
PO Box 280
Plainsboro, NJ 08536
Members are event originators, sanctioning bodies, and business firms involved with the sponsoring of athletic events.

SOCIETY OF RECREATION EXECUTIVES
PO Drawer 17148
Pensacola, FL 35222
Phone: (904) 477-7992
Members are corporate executives employed in the recreation and leisure industries.

SPORTS FOUNDATION
Lake Ctr. Plz. Bldg.
1699 Wall St.
Mount Prospect, IL 60056-5708
Phone: (708) 439-4000
Fax: (708) 439-0111
Seeks to stimulate interest in the development of new recreational activities and facilities through the promotion of sports and the sporting goods industry.

PERIODICALS AND NEWSLETTERS

ATHLETIC BUSINESS
Athletic Business Publications, Inc.
1842 Hoffman St., Ste. 201
Madison, WI 53704
Phone: (608) 249-0186
Fax: (608) 249-1153
Monthly. $36.00 per year. Published for those whose responsibility is the business of planning, financing and operating athletic/recreation/fitness programs and facilities.

ATHLETIC MANAGEMENT
College Athletic Administrator
438 W State St.
Ithaca, NY 14850-5220
Phone: (607) 272-0265
Fax: (607) 273-0701
Bimonthly. Free to qualified personnel. Formerly College Athletic Management.

MEDIA SPORTS BUSINESS
Paul Kagan Associates, Inc.
126 Clock Tower Pl.
Carmel, CA 93923
Phone: (408) 624-1536
Fax: (408) 625-3225
Monthly. $575.00 per year. Newsletter. Primary subject is broadcasting of sports events by national and regional cable and pay television systems.

SPORTS INDUSTRY NEWS: MANAGEMENT & FINANCE, REGULATION & LITIGATION, MEDIA & MARKETING
Game Point Publishing
PO Box 946
Camden, ME 04843
Phone: (207) 236-8346
Weekly. $244.00 per year. Newsletter. Covers ticket promotions, TV rights, player contracts, concessions, endorsements, etc.

DATABASES

PREDICASTS FORECASTS: INTERNATIONAL
Information Access Co.
362 Lakeside Dr.
Foster City, CA 94404
Phone: (800) 321-6388 or (415) 378-5000
Fax: (415) 358-4759
Provides online short-range and long-range industry and product forecasts for all countries of the world except the U.S.

Forecasts are abstracted from over 1,000 international sources. Time period is 1971 to date, with monthly updates. Inquire as to online cost and availability.

PREDICASTS FORECASTS: U.S.
Information Access Co.
362 Lakeside Dr.
Foster City, CA 94404
Phone: (800) 321-6388 or (415) 378-5000
Fax: (415) 358-4759
Provides numeric abstracts of a wide range of published forecasts relating to specific U.S. products, markets, and industries. Monthly updates. Time period is 1971 to date. Inquire as to online cost and availability.

PROMT: PREDICASTS OVERVIEW OF MARKETS AND TECHNOLOGY
Information Access Co.
362 Lakeside Dr.
Foster City, CA 94404
Phone: (800) 321-6388 or (415) 378-5000
Fax: (415) 358-4759
Companies, products, applied technologies and markets. U.S. and international literature coverage, 1972 to date. Daily updates. Inquire as to online cost and availability. Provides abstracts from more than 1,200 publications.

WILSONLINE: READERS' GUIDE ABSTRACTS
H. W. Wilson Co.
950 University Ave.
Bronx, NY 10452
Phone: (800) 367-6770 or (718) 588-8400
Fax: (718) 590-1617
Indexes and abstracts general interest periodicals, 1983 to date. Weekly updates. Inquire as to online cost and availability.

STATISTICS SOURCES

PREDICASTS FORECASTS
Information Access Co.
362 Lakeside Dr.
Foster City, CA 94404
Phone: (800) 321-6388 or (415) 358-4643
Fax: (415) 358-4759
Quarterly, with annual cumulation. $950.00 per year. Provides short-range and long-range forecasts of U.S. industry, product, service, economic, demographic, and financial data. Arranged according to Standard Industrial Classification (SIC) numbers, with projected annual growth rate given for each of the 50,000 series. Sources are over 500 publications issued by various organizations.

UNITED STATES CENSUS OF SERVICE INDUSTRIES
U.S. Bureau of the Census
Washington, DC 20233-0800
Phone: (301) 457-4100
Fax: (301) 457-3842
Quinquennial. Various reports available.

GENERAL WORKS

SPORTBIL
International Sport Summit
7315 Wisconsin Ave., Ste. 450 N
Bethesda, MD 20814
Phone: (212) 502-5306
Fax: (301) 718-0981
Annual. Price on application. A yearly review of the business of sport.

MARKET STRUCTURE OF SPORTS
Gerald W. Scully
University of Chicago Press
5801 Ellis Ave. 4 Fl.
Chicago, IL 60637
Phone: (800) 621-2736 or (312) 702-7700
Fax: (312) 702-9756
1995. $39.95.

WINNING IS THE ONLY THING: SPORTS IN AMERICA SINCE 1945.
Randy Roberts and James Olson
Johns Hopkins University Press
2715 N Charles St.
Baltimore, MD 21218-4319

Phone: (800) 537-5487 or (410) 516-6667
Fax: (410) 516-6998
1989. $12.95.

FURTHER READING

Broida, Rebecca. "In-Line Market Going Soft." *STN*, March 1997.

Geer, Carolyn. "Gold Mine or Sand Trap: If Golf is Such a Great Business, How Come the Number of Players and Rounds Has Been Dropping?" *Forbes*, 12 August 1996.

Hyman, Mark. "The New Bats of Summer." *Business Week*, 21 April 1997.

Murphy, Ian. "Bowling Industry Rolls Out Unified Marketing Plan." *Marketing News*, 20 January 1997.

Riddle, John. "State of the Industry Report." *Sporting Goods Manufacturers Association*, Available from http://www.sportlink.com.

"Super Show Exercises Options; Flood of Innovations Try to Appeal to the Time Pressed." *Discount Store News*, 3 March 1997.

STEEL WORKS AND BLAST FURNACES

SIC 3312

Faced with a competitive substitute materials market, high capital requirements, and environmental regulations, the steel industry is confronted with a difficult future. A strong economy and anti-dumping legislation—in addition to anticipated increased consumption by the automobile and construction industries—will see the industry through to 2000, but long-term prospects seem unfavorable.

INDUSTRY SNAPSHOT

The first steel mill in North America was built in the 1600s, making the industry one of the oldest in the country. By 1996, 79 U.S. steel companies employed about 171,000 people, shipped about $65 billion worth of products, and produced more than 103 million tons of steel. With domestic shipments rising nearly 3 percent, U.S. steel mills ran flat out for the fourth consecutive year. Low-cost producers continued to grab big pieces of the rich domestic market for conventional steel. The automotive industry alone consumed in excess of 11.2 million tons of steel in 1995, and U.S. companies exported 7.1 million tons. In particular, exports of hot-rolled steel to the Far East reversed the usual trend of imports from that region.

Despite its impressive size, the steel industry began declining in the mid-1970s and suffered a devastating depression between 1982 and 1986. After peaking in 1978 at over 137 million tons, U.S. steel production slipped to less than 90 million tons in 1991. Anemic market growth, expensive labor, increased production costs, and stagnant prices pummeled many manufacturers in the industry. In addition, the proliferation of foreign competition and the popularity of substitute materials, such as plastics and aluminum, gouged industry profits.

 Top 5 LEADING STEEL, COKE, AND COAL TAR CHEMICAL COMPANIES

Ranked by: Sales in 1995, in millions of dollars.

1. USX US Steel Group, with $6,456.0 million
2. Bethlehem Steel, $4,867.5
3. Inland Steel Industries, $4,781.5
4. LTV, $4,283.2
5. Armco, $1,559.9

Source: *ChemicalWeek*, ChemicalWeek 300 (annual), May 8, 1996, p. 57.

In response to a more competitive environment, the U.S. steel industry continued to restructure itself in the early 1990s. By 1993, new production techniques and facilities, as well as increased automation, had made U.S. steelmakers among the most productive in the world. Nevertheless, the economic slowdown in the late 1980s and early 1990s, coupled with the problems mentioned above, cast doubt on the future of most steelmakers. While more steel is being produced, the top seven companies reported a drop in the price per ton from $43 in 1995 to $25 in 1996. The likely glut in sheet steel, for instance, has forced companies to look for markets elsewhere, making each company a specialist in particular steel products.

INDUSTRY OUTLOOK

As a result of restructuring during the 1980s, U.S. steel companies in 1996 were the third most productive in the world. Manufacturers had dramatically reduced the average amount of labor required to produce one ton of steel from 11 manhours in the early 1980s to 3 manhours in the mid-1990s—less than both Japanese and European producers. At least one study estimated that pretax production costs in the United States were lower than costs in any other major steel producing nation, except Britain. Furthermore, exports, which have since slowed to 7 percent in 1995, had reached a peak of 8 percent of production in the early 1990s, despite a more than 5 percent decline in foreign demand since the late 1980s. At the same time, an upturn in the U.S. economy in 1995 and early 1996 buoyed domestic demand.

The success of domestic steelmakers against foreign dumping in the U.S. market also aided the industry. There were 84 anti-dumping suits filed with the U.S. Department of Commerce and the International Trade Commission by 12 U.S. companies in the early 1990s. The Commerce Department agreed with the charges and imposed severe duties on those importing countries identified in the suits. This development was expected to help increase domestic sales and prices in through the 1990s.

Despite successful restructuring and positive legislation, industry problems persisted in 1995. U.S. companies still faced massive capital investments in the 1990s, which were necessary to upgrade outdated operations. For instance, about 40 percent of the industry's coke ovens will need to be replaced at a cost of around $250 million each before the year 2000. In addition to capital requirements, substitute materials, such as glass, ceramics, aluminum, and plastics, continued to threaten steelmakers. The share of the beverage can market held by the steel industry, for example, fell from 100 percent in 1960 to 5 percent by 1995. By 1995, the typical passenger car contained 1,781 pounds of steel and 389 pounds of iron. In addition, the use of plastics increased to 245 pounds per vehicle from 195 pounds, while that of aluminum rose to 195.5 pounds from 130 pounds.

Environmental expenditures were also expected to increase through the 1990s. Stringent new amendments to the Clean Air Act were passed in 1990 and were expected to raise production costs. Some industry participants predicted dire consequences for the industry as a

1995-1996 U.S. STEEL INDUSTRY SHIPMENT GROWTH BY MARKET

Market	Percent
Electrical equipment	0.4
Packaging	3.1
Appliances and utensils	7.1
Industrial machinery	-10.6
Petroleum	9.1
Construction	10.4
Automotive	6.6
Service centers	7.7

Source: American Iron and Steel Institute, 1997

result of the new standards. As reported by *American Metals Market*, The American Iron and Steel Institute estimated that the industry's capital expenditures for cleaning up facilities over the last 20 years totaled $7.2 billion. Also, an average of 15 percent of the industry's total capital investment was earmaked for environmental improvement during 1995. Minimills were expected to suffer from provisions affecting electric power plants. Steelmakers hoped to offset some of these increases by boosting the use of recycled steel.

The new environmental regulations also made it easier to punish business executives for failing to have their companies comply with standards. For example, the maximum fine of $25,000 per day and one year in prison was increased to $250,000 per day for individuals, $500,000 per day for companies, and up to five years in prison for executives. The new amendments also allowed prosecutors to use circumstantial evidence, and increased the number of areas in which individuals could be held liable from 4 to 15.

THE FUTURE OF STEEL

Steel industry growth was expected to remain sluggish through 1997. The industry anticipated increased consumption by service centers, automobile manufacturers, and construction firms, at least in the short term. Oil and gas producers, on the other hand, while expected not to increase, did so by more than 100 percent in 1995. Demand from capital goods markets was also expected to increase slightly, and higher earnings for steelmakers were expected to result from long-awaited price increases, made possible by a recovering economy and anti-dumping legislation.

Integrated steelmakers, which were under severe profit pressure during the 1980s, were expected to reap the most benefits from increased prices. Nevertheless, analysts expected that minimills would continue to gain market share and significantly outperform integrated facilities throughout the 1990s. Minimills promised to pose a growing threat as they expanded their offerings to include flat-rolled sheet steel and large structural products—currently the domain of integrated producers. Furthermore, rapid advancements in minimill production technology were allowing this sector to compete with integrated manufacturers in a growing number of markets.

Direct steelmaking is the most likely long-term solution to problems caused by the capital-intensive nature of the integrated steelmaking process. Widespread implementation of the direct steelmaking process would also eliminate the need for coke ovens, many of which are badly in need of being rebuilt and have been the source for harmful emissions. One direct-process plant has been in operation since the late 1980s. Located in Pittsburgh, this experimental facility is capable of producing five tons of steel an hour. It uses a coal-based, continuous in-bath melting process that substitutes a single vessel for coke ovens, blast furnaces, and basic oxygen furnaces. This technique's energy requirements are about 20 percent lower than those of conventional steelmaking, which uses three separate processes. A second, larger experimental facility was completed in 1995, and several foreign competitors have built similar plants.

The quality of domestic steel has also risen in the last five years. One of the most visible examples of enhanced U.S. steel quality since the early 1980s has occurred in the auto market. Ford Motor Company, for instance, realized a drop in its rejection rate of steel. More significantly, steelmakers were increasingly gaining access to Japanese auto manufacturing plants in the United States that have traditionally maintained the highest quality standards. Nissan in Tennessee, Honda in Ohio, and AutoAlliance in Michigan (a Mazda/Ford venture) were all receiving nearly 100 percent of their steel from U.S. producers in the early 1990s.

ORGANIZATION AND STRUCTURE

Steel companies are involved in the manufacture of hot metal, pig iron, and silvery pig iron from iron ore, iron, steel scrap. They're also involved in converting pig iron, scrap iron, and scrap steel into steel as well as hot-rolling iron and steel into plates, sheets, strips, and bars. These end products are purchased by companies in other industries, which usually shape and manipulate the steel to create finished products.

Products offered by steelmakers are classified into five categories according to the manner in which they were processed and their chemical compositions. Carbon steels are used mostly for flat rolled products because of their high malleability. Machines, auto bodies,

ships, and building structures are made with this type of steel. In fact, carbon steels accounted for about 54 percent of all U.S. steel production in the 1990s. Alloy steels, which made up about 10 percent of the market, integrate elements into steel to enhance its physical properties. Corrosion resistance, greater strength, and increased conductivity are a few of the advantages offered by some alloys.

In comparison to carbon and alloy steels, stainless steels are highly resistant to rust and may be stronger or offer resistance to temperature changes. Accounting for 4.7 percent of the steel market volume, stainless steel is often used in pipes, tanks, and in the medical field. Tool steels and high-strength low alloy (HSLA) steels accounted for less than 1 percent of industry production, combined. They are used in applications in which strength and weight are critical.

INTEGRATED MANUFACTURERS VS. MINIMILLS

Steel manufacturers can be divided into two camps—traditional integrated mills and non-integrated "minimills." Integrated steel mills undertake every step of the steel making process. These facilities typically begin by converting mixtures of iron ore, limestone, and coke (made from coal) into molten iron using a blast furnace. Basic oxygen furnaces (BOFs) are next used to convert the molten iron into steel, which is then cast into ingots. Ingots are then shaped into slabs, billets, or blooms of steel.

Increasing numbers of integrated mills in the early 1990s were using a process called continuous casting to bypass the production of ingots and cast billets, slabs, and blooms directly from molten iron. Compared to the old ingot teeming process, continuous casting is less complicated and yields a superior product. In this process, molten steel from a furnace is quickly carried in a ladle directly to a refractory lined container, or tundish, at the top of the caster. The molten metal is then poured into the tundish, which feeds it continuously into the caster, the core of which is water-cooled mold open at both ends. When molten steel enters one end of the mold and cools, a "skin" of metal forms around a liquid core. The material leaves the other end of the machine and is further cooled by water sprays, solidifying the metal. Continuous casting cuts time, consumes less energy, and increases yield. It has been estimated that it cuts operating costs by about $30 a ton. Steelmakers next convert the finished, or semi-finished, steel into rolls, plates, bars, tubes, rails, or other more marketable products, especially for the auto industry, at a rolling mill. In 1995, every major U.S. manufacturer relied on continuous casting.

In the early 1990s, minimills, or non-integrated facilities, were using the same process as integrated mills with a few exceptions. Rather than process base materials—iron ore, coke, and limestone—minimills typically start with scrap iron or steel. The scrap, melted in an electric arc furnace (EAF), rather than a blast or basic oxygen furnace, is continuously cast into blooms and billets. Minimills typically produced fewer finished products than integrated mills. Although many manufacturers were broadening their offerings to include steel pipes, plates, and sheets, most minimills emphasized rods and bars used in light construction.

Minimills are capable of producing from 150,000 to 2 million tons of steel per year. In contrast, most integrated mills can generate 2 to 4 million tons per year. Minimills are also typically able to produce steel at a much lower cost than their larger cousins. Because minimills do not have to be located near supplies of raw ingredients, for instance, they are able to operate closer to their customers, thus reducing product transport costs. In addition, more minimills are located in the southern United States and benefit from less-expensive, nonunion labor. Integrated mills, on the other hand, employ union labor. Union contracts prevent integrated companies from reducing compensation costs when production declines due to downturns in demand. Furthermore, minimills are more likely to employ more advanced technology, such as continuous casting and EAFs, that reduce production costs and improve quality.

COMPETITIVE STRUCTURE

In the early 1990s, integrated steelmakers accounted for approximately 75 percent of U.S. steel industry production. At that time, the industry was relatively concentrated and imposed formidable entry barriers, such as high start-up costs and intense competition. The top 75 competitors in the industry, for instance, dominated over 90 percent of the market in the early 1990s, with about $55 billion in shipments. Furthermore, the top 6 firms in the industry accounted for about 40 percent of shipments, or $25 billion worth of product. In 1995, integrated steelmakers accounted for only 59.6 percent of U.S. steel production, with the top three accounting for 28.6 percent of the U.S. total.

On average, minimills realized about $500 in capital costs per ton of steel produced, while integrated mills incurred about $2,000 per ton. Likewise, during the mid-1980s and early 1990s, minimills generated about $32 in operating profit per ton of steel, compared to just $3 per ton for integrated mills. Minimills also shipped an average of 752 tons per employee during that period, compared with 381 tons per worker for integrated producers.

Service and distribution centers consumed 21 to 23 percent of U.S. steel production in 1995. The largest steel customer that built consumer products was the automobile industry, which used 13.5 million tons in 1995, or about 16 percent of total steel production. The construction industry purchased about 11.7 million tons of steel in 1995, and machinery manufacturers used about 2 million tons. Other large steel consumers included oil and gas companies with 2.7 million tons, container manufacturers with 3.8 million tons, and various commercial equipment producers with .7 million tons.

WORK FORCE

U.S. steel productivity nearly doubled between 1980 and the early 1990s. During the same period, the number of manhours required to produce a unit of steel plummeted more than threefold. These factors, combined with a reduction in demand since the late 1980s, dealt a lethal blow to many jobs in the industry. The trend toward automation was expected to maintain a trend toward fewer workers. Furthermore, workers worried that passage of the North American Free Trade Agreement (NAFTA) would have potentially devastating effects on laborers. Workers in the industry were concerned that producers would be drawn to the low-cost labor and reduced environmental liability offered in Mexico and consequently close numerous U.S. plants.

While overall steel employment was likely to decline through the 1990s, new positions were expected in the emerging minimill sector. In fact, employment growth at minimills rose by an average of 19 percent between the late 1980s and the early 1990s, while employment at integrated companies fell by 30 percent. It's expected that over 4 million tons of new minimill capacity should come online in 1997.

RESEARCH AND TECHNOLOGY

Rather than expanding production capacity, producers in the late 1980s and 1990s were relying on new technology to help achieve greater efficiency and quality. Because the overall global steel market has matured, companies in the mid-1990s could grow only by increasing market share, raising profit margins, or by developing new steel products.

In addition to continuous casting, thin-slab casting, and EAFs, companies were experimenting with a variety of new production techniques. For example, an array of devices were being employed in the early 1990s to help companies spot, map, describe, and classify defects in sheet steel that were as small as .02 inches in diameter. Strobe lights, laser beams, and artificial intelligence systems were all at work ensuring higher quality output. Furthermore, continuing advancements in alloys and steel coatings were allowing manufacturers to create new steel products that could compete with advanced plastics and ceramics.

Research within the industry has been conducted in several other areas, including: an electromagnetic braking system designed to improve surface quality of the sheet by reducing turbulence in the mold, which should result in fewer surface defects and allow for greater casting speed; a form of oxygen injection technique in blast furnaces to increase output and allow a decrease in the break-even volume for making steel in a blast furnace; and the utilization of information technology to allow companies to concentrate on steelmaking, rather than information management.

AMERICA AND THE WORLD

U.S. exports of steel reached 7.1 million tons in 1995, or 7 percent of total shipments. Despite moderate export growth and the comparative productivity of U.S. steelmakers, however, the U.S. steel industry still faces huge trade deficits. Imports in 1995, for instance, exceeded $8.3 billion, versus just $3.8 billion in exports. The only region in which the United States held a surplus was North America, where Canada and Mexico purchased over $2 billion of U.S. steel, versus about $1.8 billion which the United States bought from those two countries. The European Community (EC), on the other hand, sold $2.4 billion worth of steel to the United States and purchased only $309 million from domestic steelmakers. Significant deficits also existed with Japan, Asia, and South America. Domestic producers hoped that new anti-dumping legislation would reduce the imbalance.

Total global steel production rose to 760 million metric tons in 1995, and the total value of the world industry hovered around $315 billion. The EC produced the largest portion of global output, at 160 million metric tons. Japan, the second largest producer, generated 105 million metric tons of steel in 1995. The United States was third with 104.9 million metric tons, followed by China with 90 and Russia with 50, a significant drop since the early 1990s, when it was the top producer worldwide.

The International Iron and Steel Institute (ISI) estimates that world production will grow by about 32 million tons by the turn of the century. Most growth was expected to occur in developing nations. Asia, at least in the short term, offered the greatest likelihood of increased consumption.

ASSOCIATIONS AND SOCIETIES

INSTITUTE OF SCRAP RECYCLING INDUSTRIES
1627 K St. NW, Ste. 700
Washington, DC 2006
Phone: (202) 466-4050

PERIODICALS AND NEWSLETTERS

AMERICAN METAL MARKET
825 7th Ave.
New York, NY 10019
Phone: (212) 887-8550
Fax: (212) 887-8520
Daily. $460.00 per year. Provides daily news and pricing on the metals industry.

SCRAP PROCESSING AND RECYCLING
Institute of Scrap Recycling Industries
1627 K St. NW, Ste. 700
Washington, DC 20006
Phone: (202) 466-4050
Bimonthly. $18.00 per year. Formerly Scrap Age

STATISTICS SOURCES

IRON AND STEEL SCRAP. MINERAL INDUSTRY SURVEYS
U.S. Bureau of Mines
2401 E St. NW
Washington, DC 20241
Phone: (202) 634-1001
Monthly.

FURTHER READING

Baker, Stephen. ''Metals: Prognosis 1997.'' *Business Week* 13 January 1997.

Rudnitsky, Howard. ''Annual Report on American Industry: Metals.''*Forbes Magazine,* 13 January 1997.

Standard & Poor's Industry Surveys. New York: Standard & Poor's Corporation 21 November 1996.

SUGAR AND CONFECTIONERY PRODUCTS

SIC 2060

The value of U.S. candy and
confectionery exports in 1995 was about $527
million, a decrease of more than 3 percent from the
previous year. Exports to Canada and Mexico
accounted for about 64 percent of all U.S. candy
exports, while exports to South Korea and Japan
accounted for another 13 percent of export value.
Intense competition from within and without the
sugar industry, coupled with threats to remove
government subsidies, have created a cloud of
uncertainty with regard to the economic stability of
the industry for the rest of the decade.

The sugar cane industry is confined by the crop's growing conditions and the logistics of transporting sugar cane. United States production is limited to Florida, Hawaii, Louisiana, Texas and Puerto Rico. Mills that process the sugar cane into raw sugar must be located near cane plantations since cut sugar cane is too bulky and heavy to ship. Mills in this category process cane into crystals of raw sugar that can be transported in bulk, like grain, aboard ships or by land.

Sugar cane milling profitability in the United States depends on federal government subsidies and import controls. Since the late 1700s, producing raw sugar has been a lucrative business for growers and millers. Domestic sugar prices have been government-controlled and foreign imports severely limited. Some members of Congress, as well as numerous American agricultural policy critics, have been advocating less government involvement. They have been pushing for decreased price supports for domestic sugar cane as well as lifting or easing foreign sugar quotas.

Sugar beets are one of the world's main sugar sources and an important source of sugar for the United States. Reduced raw cane sugar imports hurt U.S. refiners in the 1980s, and the sugar industry turned to sugar beets to make up the difference. The United States processes more sugar from domestically-grown sugar beets than from domestically-grown sugar cane. Many cane refiners also invested in sugar beet processing firms in the 1980s as the sugar beet market share (including imports) climbed from 30 percent in the 1970s to 40 percent in 1988.

The U.S. cane sugar refining industry has been facing heavy competition and increased economic challenges, which make their viability into the year 2000 questionable. Manufacturers of beet sugar, high fructose corn syrup (HFCS), and artificial sweeteners have all taken a large share of the market away from cane sugar refiners. Ten out of 21 refineries closed between 1981 and 1990, according to *National Food Review. Journal of Commerce and Commercial* states an estimated 3,000 people were left jobless as a result.

The chocolate and cocoa products industry has traditionally been subject to significant fluctuations in demand. Chocolate products tend to be seasonal in nature, with demand increasing sharply during the holidays. In addition, several consumer trends have had an impact on demand. These include rising sales of premium-priced chocolates and the growing concern about the health risks associated with the consumption of such high-fat foods like chocolate. In 1995, the chocolate and cocoa products industry shipped $3.2 billion worth of products, a slight

Top 10 LEADING CANDY SUPPLIERS

Ranked by: Dollar sales in 1994 through civilian grocery, drug, and mass merchandisers.

1. Hershey Chocolate
2. M & M/Mars Inc.
3. Russell Stover
4. Nestle USA Inc.
5. E. J. Brach
6. Lifesavers Co.
7. Leaf North America
8. Private label (combined)
9. Storck USA LP
10. Tootsie Roll Industries Inc.

Source: *Military Market*, September, 1995, p. 46.

increase over 1990 figures, when products shipped totaled $3.0 billion. The number of establishments in the industry decreased from 186 in 1990 to 157 in the mid-1990s. The balance of trade for U.S. cocoa and chocolate has usually run at a deficit. In 1995, cocoa imports totaled $722 million, while exports totaled $39 million.

The American chewing gum industry has been marked by strong periods of growth and decline throughout the twentieth century. Since the 1970s, this industry has been growing at a faster pace overseas than within the United States. The industry's overall success has been the result of low manufacturing costs and aggressive marketing campaigns. As one of the best performers in the candy industry, chewing gum continues to be a favorite among American consumers. Sales of sugar and sugar-free gum continued to rise steadily since 1990. In 1996, there were 19 U.S. manufacturers in this industry.

Salted or dried peanuts account for about 53 percent of the snack-nut market. The rest of the snack-nut market is split among mixed nuts, cashews, walnuts, almonds, pistachios, and macadamia nuts. Salted or roasted sunflower seeds, pumpkin seeds, and other seeds are also included in this category. The industry shipped $2.8 billion worth of goods in 1995, up from $2.3 billion in 1990. Industry exports totaled 983 million tons in 1995. The number of establishments in the industry increased 13 percent since 1990, from 87 to 98 in 1995.

INDUSTRY OUTLOOK

Sugar and other agricultural supports continue to be criticized by members of Congress and other government officials. Although cuts in price supports are likely,

the government is unlikely to remove all supports. Sugar producers claimed that the federal sugar program protected U.S. consumers from wild swings in world prices. Critics say U.S. consumers spend an extra $1.4 billion annually because of the government program. The industry contends that figure should be about $200 million.

The U.S. sugar industry and its very powerful lobby claimed that 80 percent of the sugar in the United States is consumed by food processors, who did not pass drops in sugar prices on to consumers. They cited government reports that said, from 1982 to 1992, the average cost of sweeteners (cane sugar, beet sugar, and high fructose corn syrup) rose only about 9 percent, less than the rate of inflation, however prices for products containing sugar rose 54 percent. The chairman of the American Sugar Alliance also claimed that U.S. consumers pay 25 percent less for sugar than consumers in other developed nations and that the U.S. price for sugar was 10 percent less than the world average retail price. The American Sugar Alliance asserted that since the United States was not self-sufficient in sugar production, it imported 27 percent of its sugar in 1991 and that exporters of sugar to the United States received the same level of price supports as U.S. sugar cane producers.

The North American Free Trade Agreement promised to open up the sugar market to Mexico; however, rather than increasing overall import of sugar, it would probably reduce U.S. purchases from the Philippines or Caribbean nations. According to a *Monthly Review* article, "the industry is confronted with virtual extinction over the next decade," attributing the move to "policy decisions adopted in the boardrooms of a minuscule number of beverage companies with no consideration whatsoever for the millions of sugar workers and their families around the world." In other words, a shift to corn sweeteners and other sugar substitutes was to blame.

Soft drink manufacturers switched to high fructose corn syrup (HFCS) from liquid cane sugar in the 1980s, striking a severe blow to the sugar industry. To compensate for the losses, cane sugar refiners diversified, adding sugar beet processing operations and/or wet-milling operations to produce HFCS and other corn sweeteners. Beet sugar's share of the sugar market increased from 30 percent in the 1970s to 40 percent in the 1980s, and its market share continued to rise into the 1990s.

In addition to the rise in HFCS, there were other problems for cane sugar refiners. Domestic production of sugar cane dropped, and a strict quota on imported raw cane sugar was imposed by the federal government. The drop in availability of imported raw sugar was especially serious to the industry since sugar refineries in the United States processed more imported raw sugar than domestically-milled raw sugar.

Price, in addition to new product competition, plagued the cane sugar refining industry in the 1990s. Federal programs kept the price of domestic sugar higher than world market prices. In 1992, for example, when the world price of sugar was 10 cents a pound, the price in the United States was 21 cents a pound. The government also imposed a quota to prevent cheaper imported sugar from flooding the U.S. market. The United States continued to import some raw sugar, because it did not grow enough to meet U.S. demand. Additional problems with crops—drought years in Texas, storms in Florida, and freezing temperatures in Louisiana—in the mid-1990s further depressed yields.

High fructose corn syrup producers have been able to undercut the sugar market—both beet sugar and cane sugar—and make HFCS a cheaper alternative sweetening agent for processed foods. Americans consumed more corn syrup than refined sugar in the early 1990s, particularly in soft drinks. The beverage industry is said to be a primary force behind the demise of cane sugar production.

At least one market continued to prefer cane sugar to its competitors. Candy and pastry makers were not impressed with substitutes for refined cane sugar. They insisted that beet sugar was not suitable for their purposes and that they achieved better results with pure cane sugar. According to the U.S. government, cane sugar and beet sugar have the same chemical formula so refiners cannot claim any difference between them.

The adult health conscious market was seen as a major growth market for this industry. Nabisco Foods Group's Snackwell's brand of products pioneered a new era in this industry. The resounding success of Snackwell's motivated many manufacturers to join this era of new comparable products designed to placate consumers worried about the fat and calorie content in existing products. Hershey Foods Corporation and Mars Incorpo-

rated offered their new alternatives with the launch of Sweet Escapes and Milky Way Lite respectively. Other smaller companies were quick to join the growing fray as well. The market for sugar-free candies was valued at more than $50 million in the mid-1990s.

Demand for cocoa continues to increase worldwide. The decline in world output of cocoa and the increase in demand for chocolates in new markets such as China, Russia, and other emerging economies indicate the arrival of a long-awaited bull market in cocoa. Another area in which the demand for cocoa increased was the beverage industry. Of the 2,894 new product introductions in 1995, approximately one-half of the beverage products consisted of either cocoa, coffee, or tea.

In spite of the consistent demand for products in this industry, the gum sector of the candy industry exhibited major weaknesses, with 1995 dollar sales down by 7.1 percent and pound volume off by 4.5 percent from 1994 levels. Gum manufacturers continued to introduce new products, especially to cater to one of their biggest group of consumers—kids. It was found that kids make 270 visits to stores a year averaging 5.2 purchases a week. Therefore, gum manufacturers have spent a lot of money and time researching new products that would appeal to kids.

Another type of gum that was gaining popularity in the gum industry was smoking cessation products. In 1996, however, supermarket sales of these products were lagging behind sales at alternative formats, especially drug stores. According to sales figures from Chicago-based Information Resources Inc. in *Supermarket News,* food stores held 12 percent of the smoking cessation market, mass merchandisers held 20 percent of the market, and drug stores held a whopping 68 percent of the market.

Sale of processed nuts rose from 36 million pounds in 1990 to 42 million pounds in 1994, an increase of only

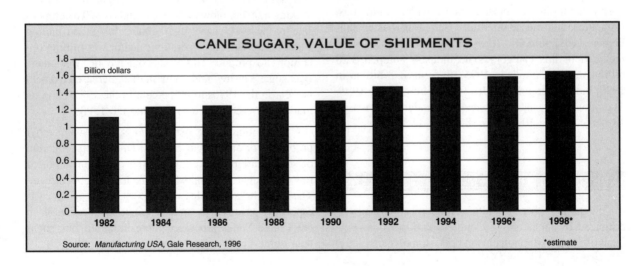

CANE SUGAR, VALUE OF SHIPMENTS

Billion dollars

Source: *Manufacturing USA,* Gale Research, 1996

*estimate

4 percent. The 1996 nut market was marked by fluctuations. The estimated peanut yield for 1997 was at 1.7 million tons. Growth in specialty nuts was the most encouraging in the market due to the greater interest in ethnic food and various-flavored nuts among consumers. Middle-aged consumers were the largest purchasers of processed nuts. Reduced-fat nuts appeared in the market in the mid-1990s and were expected to increase nut sales in supermarkets.

ORGANIZATION AND STRUCTURE

Sugar mills are located near the plantations on which sugarcane is grown and harvested. In many cases, these are operated by the plantations or as cooperatives by the owners of several sugarcane plantations. Mills run continuously, day and night, from fall until spring, when the last cane is harvested. To facilitate the constant milling, growers cultivate a variety of sugar cane that they can harvest throughout the season. The variety of cane available, however, depends on the soil and climate on a particular plantation.

The U.S. government has supported sugar prices for more than 200 years. In 1789, the federal government imposed an import tariff to raise revenue, and for the next 100 years, this sugar tariff yielded almost 20 percent of all import duties, the main source of government money before the Civil War. The Sugar Act of 1934 regulated domestic sugar production, imports, and prices. Import quotas were assigned to foreign sugar-growing countries. Price supports were applied sporadically during the 1970s, depending upon the price of sugar on the world market. Temporary suspensions of price controls in 1974 and 1980 resulted in increased sugar prices. Shortages soon followed and with that, sugar prices plummeted.

As a result, in the Agriculture and Food Act of 1981, the government agreed to purchase raw cane sugar and refined beet sugar for a specific price per pound if commercial prices were not high enough. In order to avoid payments, the government imposed tariffs to discourage imports, limit the supply of sugar, and therefore keep sugar prices level at or above the government's minimum price. Farmers claim to get no benefit from the subsidies. Industry claims are that United States consumers pay 28 percent less for sugar than consumers anywhere else worldwide, however, the United States price for sugar in 1995 was more than double the world price. Subsequent agricultural acts continued to provide price supports for sugar, keeping quotas low and prices high in the domestic market.

In recent decades, the United States imposed strict quotas on imports of foreign sugar, cutting imports 80 percent since 1975. The tariff on sugar imports in excess of the quota was also high enough to discourage imports. This quota created controversy regarding U.S. trade with developing nations. More than 110 countries grow sugar cane or sugar beets, and many of the developing nations have become dependent on sugar as a source of employment and income. In the early 1990s, the United States imported less than 1.5 million tons of sugar to make up the difference between the sugar cane produced domestically and the approximately 9 million tons used.

Price supports for sugar in the United States are provided in the form of nonrecourse loans, so that sugar growers can borrow money with the crop as collateral. The government sets the value of the crop-collateral at a minimum price per pound, guaranteeing that the sugar producer will receive at least that price, even if the commodity price drops. Loans are made to the processor because the raw sugarcane must be milled before being sold or stored. When the raw sugar is sold, the growers reportedly receive payment as well. In many cases the

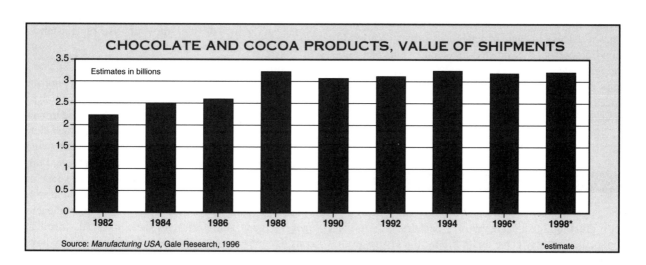

CHOCOLATE AND COCOA PRODUCTS, VALUE OF SHIPMENTS

Estimates in billions

Source: *Manufacturing USA*, Gale Research, 1996

*estimate

processor and the grower are the same concern. In 1996, to protest the United States policies surrounding subsidies, the Sugar Cane Growers Cooperative of Florida said it would decline $28,000 in government payments.

All cocoa beans processed by U.S. manufacturers must be imported, by direct purchase or through the services of a broker, as cocoa trees require a tropical climate to flourish. Growers are paid for the beans at market price, which is determined primarily by the quality and availability of the crop worldwide. A testament to cocoa's importance as a commodity is the existence of cocoa exchanges, similar to standard stock exchanges, in New York City, London, Hamburg, and Amsterdam. The beans are then processed to make chocolate liquor, which is in turn used to further manufacture such products as cocoa, chocolate syrup, and solid chocolate chips and baking bars. The chocolate liquor is also often sold to other manufacturers that combine it with additional ingredients to produce confections, bakery items, and dairy products.

The market for snack nuts has remained fairly level for a decade. Snack-food nuts have strong competition from potato chips, tortilla chips, pretzels, and microwave popcorn for the nation's snack dollars. The snack-nut and seed industry has handled its competition by introducing new flavors of seeds and nuts.

Manufacturers have also tried more creative packaging to expand their markets. But merchandising efforts for nut and seed snacks are minimal compared to those for potato chips. Manufacturers have also been pushing for more shelf space and displays in grocery stores. While salted snack nuts and seeds showed flat sales, many producers and distributors were optimistic about sales of dried nuts because of their nutritional value.

Price has been another factor working against the industry. About 20 to 25 percent of domestic peanuts are used for snack nuts. With peanut prices kept high by government quotas, restrictions against imports, and support prices, peanut snack manufacturers are somewhat restricted in their supplies and prices. While almond processors and processors of other nuts can buy foreign nuts, peanut processors must buy domestically-grown peanuts. A drought in 1990 sent peanut prices soaring, resulting in deep profit losses for peanut processors.

WORK FORCE

Sugar harvesters, called cane cutters, face one of the most grueling jobs imaginable. For decades, the Florida sugar cane industry came under fire for the severe, even slave-like conditions in which the cutters lived and for illegal practices concerning wages. A 1991 Congressional report accused the sugar cane industry of violating labor laws. In 1992, U.S. Sugar Corporation, one of the largest sugar concerns in Florida, agreed to a wage increase and other improvements. Farm-worker advocacy groups were hoping to win reforms for cane cutters working at other sugar companies. However, southern Florida producers were increasingly turning to machine cutting because of the historical controversy about the treatment of immigrant labor by the industry.

Employment in the fields and in the mills is seasonal, peaking between fall and spring. According to the Bureau of Labor Statistics, in 1990, total employment of production workers in the industry was 3,500 in July and 6,400 in November. One cooperative based in a single county in Florida reported employing about 900 people in 1996 on a payroll exceeding $26 million.

RESEARCH AND TECHNOLOGY

In an effort to compensate for lagging sales, a number of chocolate and cocoa-based companies have adopted technological solutions to increase efficiency and lower production costs. Part of the new technology includes the computerization of a number of production processes. While this has helped facilitate more efficient productivity, it also engendered a number of challenges. One of these was retraining employees who were familiar with only rudimentary chocolate making procedures.

Cocoa has become such an intrinsic and valuable part of the U.S. economy that efforts by industry and science are underway to better understand the bean itself. The American Cocoa Research Institute contributed $1.5 million to Penn State University's Molecular Biology of Cocoa program. The main objective of the program is to increase understanding of the biology, botany, and genetics of the cocoa plant. The objectives of the study include the study of disease resistance, quality, plant delivery, and tools.

Companies in the chewing gum industry are continually seeking ingredients and processes that can improve product quality and packaging. In the 1980s, new synthetic gum bases were developed to overcome the limitations of previously used natural ingredients. These new materials are aimed at increasing gum flavor, improving texture, and reducing stickiness. The environmental impact of the packaging used for chewing gum has been of considerable concern for companies in this industry. These companies rely on the wrappers and plastic packaging to keep gum fresh, yet these materials result in considerable waste. Scientists at gum companies have been evaluating and making changes to packaging and researching materials to meet future disposal and recycling requirements.

AMERICA AND THE WORLD

Although Europeans consume a great amount of candy, Europe continued to be a poor market for U.S. candy. High duties have kept U.S. candy out of the European Union (EU), although some American companies have invested in European candy companies and avoided the duties. U.S. companies face stiff competition from European confectioners, particularly Swiss chocolate producers, which are typically considered to market finer quality confections than American companies.

The value of U.S. candy imports in 1995 exceeded $1 billion. The EU provides most U.S. candy imports. In the early 1990s, Germany, the United Kingdom, Italy, the Netherlands, France, and Spain accounted for more than 40 percent of U.S. candy imports. Canada was the single most important source of candy imports, though, providing 24 percent. Mexico provided 4 percent of import value.

ASSOCIATIONS AND SOCIETIES

AMERICAN SUGAR ALLIANCE
1225 Eye St. NW, Ste. 505,
Washington, DC 20005
Phone: (202) 457-1437
Fax: (202) 408-0763
Members are domestic producers of sugar beets, sugarcane, and corn for syrup. Formerly U.S. Sweetener Producers Group.

AMERICAN SUGAR CANE LEAGUE OF THE U.S.A.
PO Drawer 938
Thibodaux, LA 70302
Phone: (504) 448-3707
Fax: (504) 448-3722

AMERICAN WHOLESALE MARKETERS ASSOCIATION
1128 16th St.
Washington, DC 20036
Phone: (202) 463-2124
Fax: (202) 467-0559

BAKERY, CONFECTIONERY AND TOBACCO WORKERS INTERNATIONAL
10401 Connecticut Ave.
Kensington, MD 20895
Phone: (301) 933-8600
Fax: (301) 946-8452

NATIONAL CANDY BROKERS ASSOCIATION
710 E. Ogden, Ste. 113
Naperville, IL 60563-2047
Phone: (708) 369-2406

NATIONAL CONFECTIONERS ASSOCIATION OF THE U.S.
7900 Westpark Dr., Ste. A-320
Mc Lean, VA 22102
Phone: (703) 790-5750
Fax: (703) 790-5752

NATIONAL CONFECTIONERY SALES ASSOCIATION OF AMERICA
4 Baxter Pl.
Pequannock, NJ 07440
Phone: (201) 696-7806
Fax: (201) 696-7806

RETAIL CONFECTIONERS INTERNATIONAL
1807 Glenview Rd., Ste. 204
Glenview, IL 60025
Phone: (708) 724-6120
Fax: (708) 724-2719

SUGAR ASSOCIATION, INC.
1101 15th St. NW, Ste. 600
Washington, DC 20005
Phone: (202) 785-1122
Fax: (202) 785-5019

UNITED STATES BEET SUGAR ASSOCIATION
1156 15th St. NW, Ste. 1019
Washington, DC 20005
Phone: (202) 296-4820

UNITED STATES CANE SUGAR REFINERS' ASSOCIATION
1000 Connecticut Ave. NW, Ste. 1106
Washington, DC 20036
Phone: (202) 331-1458
Fax: (202) 785-5110

PERIODICALS AND NEWSLETTERS

CANDY INDUSTRY
Advanstar Communications, Inc.
7500 Old Oak Blvd.
Cleveland, OH 44130
Phone: (800) 346-0085 or (216) 243-8100
Fax: (216) 891-2726
Monthly. $25.00 per year

CANDY MARKETER
Advanstar Communications, Inc.
7500 Old Oak Blvd.
Cleveland, OH 44130
Phone: (800) 346-0085 or (216) 843-8100
Fax: (216) 891-2726
Bimonthly. $25.00 per year.

CANDY WHOLESALER: THE MAGAZINE FOR CANDY AND TOBACCO AND SNACK FOOD DISTRIBUTORS
American Wholesalers Marketers Association
1128 16th St. NW
Washington, DC 20036
Phone: (202) 463-2124
Fax: (202) 467-0559
10 times a year. $36.00 per year.

CONFECTIONER: WHERE CONFECTIONERY AND SNACKS MEAN BUSINESS
American Publishing Corp.
17400 Dallas Pky., Ste. 125
Dallas, TX 75287-7305
Phone: (214) 250-3630
Fax: (214) 250-3733
Bimonthly. $30.00 per year. Covers a wide variety of topics relating to the distribution and retailing of candy and snacks.

FANCY FOOD
Talcott Communications Corp.
20 N. Wacker Dr., Ste. 3230
Chicago, IL 60606
Phone: (312) 849-2220
Fax: (312) 849-2184
Monthly. $28.00 per year. Emphasizes new specialty food products and the business management aspects of the specialty food and confection industries. Includes special issues on wine, cheese, candy, "upscale" cookware, and gifts.

GOURMET RETAILER
Sterling Southeast, Inc.
3301 Ponce de Leon Blvd., Ste. 300
Coral Gables, FL 33134-7273
Phone: (305) 893-8771
Monthly. $24.00 per year. Covers upscale food and housewares, including confectionery items, bakery operations, and coffee.

MANUFACTURING CONFECTIONER
Manufacturing Confectioner Publishing Co.
175 Rock Rd.
Glen Rock, NJ 07452
Phone: (201) 652-2655
Monthly. $35.00 per year.

SPOTLIGHT
National Confectionery Salesmen's Association of America, Inc.
1747 Pennsylvania Ave. NW, Ste. 1000
Washington, DC 20006
Phone: (202) 785-9500
Quarterly.

SUGAR BULLETIN
American Sugar Cane League of the U.S.A.
201 N. Canal Blvd.
Thibodauy, LA 70301
Phone: (504) 448-3707
Semimonthly. Free to member; non-members, $10.00 per year.

SUGAR JOURNAL: COVERING THE WORLD'S SUGAR INDUSTRY
Kriedt Enterprises Ltd.
129 S. Cortez St.
New Orleans, LA 70119-6118
Phone: (504) 482-3914
Fax: (504) 482-4205
Monthly. $33.00 per year. A monthly technical publication designed to inform sugar beet and cane farms, factories, and refineries throughout the world about the latest developments in the sugar industry.

THE SUGAR PRODUCER: REPRESENTING THE SUGAR BEET INDUSTRY IN THE UNITED STATES
Russell Jones, editor
Harris Publishing, Inc.
520 Park Ave.
Idaho Falls, ID 83402
Phone: (208) 524-7000
Fax: (208) 522-5241
Eight times a year. $8.00 per year. Supplies sugar beet growers with information to assist them in production of quality sugar beet crops.

DATABASES

CAB ABSTRACTS
CAB International North America
845 N Park Ave.
Tucson, AZ 85719
Phone: (800) 528-4841 or (602) 621-7897
Fax: (602) 621-3816
Contains 46 specialized abstract collections covering over 10,000 journals and monographs in the areas of agriculture, horticulture, forest products, farm products, nutrition, dairy science, poultry, grains, animal health, entomology, etc. Time period is 1972 to date, with monthly updates. Inquire as to online cost and availability. CAB Abstracts on CD-ROM also available, with annual updating.

CITIBASE (CITICORP ECONOMIC DATABASE)
FAME Software Corp.
77 Water St., 9 Fl.
New York, NY 10005
Phone: (212) 898-7800
Fax: (212) 742-8956
Presents over 6,000 statistical series relating to business, industry, finance, and economics. Includes series from Survey of Current Business and many other sources. Time period is 1947 to date, with daily updates. Inquire as to online cost and availability.

F & S INDEX
Information Access Co.
362 Lakeside Dr.
Foster City, CA 94404
Phone: (800) 321-6388 or (415-358-4643)
Fax: (415) 358-4759
Contains about four million citations to worldwide business, financial, and industrial or consumer product literature appearing from 1972 to date. Weekly updates. Inquire as to online cost and availability.

FOODS ADLIBRA
General Mills, Inc.
Technical Information Services
Foods Adlibra Publications
9000 Plymouth Ave.

N Minneapolis, MN 55427
Phone: (612) 540-4759
Fax: (612) 540-3166
Contains online citations, with abstracts, to the technical and business literature of food processing and packaging. New products and new ingredients are featured. Covers about 250 trade journals and 500 research journals from 1974 to date, with monthly updates. Inquire as to online cost and availability.

FSTA: FOOD SCIENCE AND TECHNOLOGY ABSTRACTS
International Food Information Service GmbH
Melibocusstrasse
52 D-6000 Frankfurt am Main 71, Germany
Phone: 4969- 6690070
Fax: 4969- 66900710
Provides worldwide online coverage of the literature of food technology and food production. Various types of publications are covered, including about 2,000 periodicals. Time period is 1969 to date, with monthly updates. Inquire as to online cost and availability.

STATISTICS SOURCES

AGRICULTURAL STATISTICS
Available from U.S. Government Printing Office
Washington, DC 20402
Phone: (202) 512-1800
Fax: (202) 512-2250
Annual. $21.00. Produced by the National Agricultural Statistics Service, U.S. Department of Agriculture. Provides a wide variety of statistical data relating to agricultural production, supplies, consumption, prices/price-supports, foreign trade, costs, and returns, as well as farm labor, loans, income, and population. In many cases, historical data is shown annually for 10 years. In addition to farm data, includes detailed fishery statistics.

ANNUAL SURVEY OF MANUFACTURES
Bureau of the Census, U.S. Department of Commerce
Available from U.S. Government Printing Office
Washington, DC 20402
Phone: (202) 512-1800
Fax: (202) 512-2250

SUGAR AND SWEETENER SITUATION AND OUTLOOK
Available from U.S. Government Printing Office
Washington, DC 20402
Phone: (202) 512-1800
Fax: (202) 512-2250
Quarterly. $14.00 per year. Issued by Economic Research Service, U.S. Department of Agriculture. Provides current statistical information on supply, demand, and prices.

UNITED STATES CENSUS OF MANUFACTURES
U.S. Bureau of the Census
Washington, DC 20233-0800
Phone: (301) 457-4100
Fax: (301) 457-3842
Quinquennial. Results presented in reports, tape, CD-ROM, and diskette files.

U.S. INDUSTRIAL OUTLOOK: FORECASTS FOR SELECTED MANUFACTURING AND SERVICE INDUSTRIES
Available from U.S. Government Printing Office
Washington, DC 20402
Phone: (202) 512-1800
Fax: (202) 512-2250
Annual. $37.00. (Replaced in 1995 by U.S. Global Trade Outlook.*) Issued by the International Trade Administration, U.S. Department of Commerce. Provides basic data, outlook for the current year, and "Long-Term Prospects" (five-year projections) for a wide variety of products and services. Includes high technology industries. Available on the world wide web at gopher://gopher.umsl.edu:70/11/library/govdocs/usio94*

FURTHER READING

Dorn, Chad A. "Nut Market Going 'Nutty in 1996." *Candy Industry,* October 1996.

———. "Candy Is More Than Dandy." *Prepared Foods,* 15 April 1996.

"The Expanding Market for Bulk Candy." *Candy Industry,* July 1996.

Graebner, Lynn. "Sugar Beet Industry Falls on Tough Times." *The Business Journal Serving Greater Sacramento,* 26 August 1996.

Ingram, Molly. "Glaze, Drizzle, Dip and Chip—Chocolate Does It All." *Bakery Production and Marketing,* 15 February 1996.

Malbin, Peter. "Butting Out: Retailers Are Caught in Swirl of Potential—and Problems—in Merchandising High-Priced Smoking Cessation Products." *Supermarket News,* 4 November 1996.

"Sugar Cane Growers Cooperative of Florida Rejects Payment from Federal Government." *PR Newswire,* 3 July 1996.

U.S. Department of Agriculture. "Sugar and Sweeteners— Summary." *M2 Presswire,* 20 December 1996.

SURGICAL AND MEDICAL INSTRUMENTS AND APPARATUS

SIC 3841

Development of a variety of new instruments and less-constrictive Food and Drug Administration regulations will offset increasing global competition and relatively unconcentrated manufacturers. One factor leading the industry towards favorable returns is the increasing market for minimally invasive devices, expected to significantly increase through the 1990s and 2000s.

While the first medical instruments of precision were used in the seventeenth century, surgery wasn't recognized as a definite branch of science until the eighteenth century. Rapid advances that took place in the twentieth century resulted in the evolution of a $28 billion U.S. surgical instrument industry by 1996. The U.S. maintains the most advanced surgical device industry in the world. Besides serving a critical role in the care of Americans' health, the medical and surgical instrument industry presently employs 102,000 individuals.

In the early 1990s, manufacturers continued to enjoy the fruits of their success. Revenues and profits increased at an average rate of over 9 percent in 1990, 1991, and 1992, and 1993. International demand for U.S. surgical and medical instruments continued to set new industry standards as 1996 revenues exceeded $10 billion. And, notwithstanding productivity gains, industry employment had grown at approximately 5 percent per year in the early 1990s. Substantial growth is anticipated for employment abroad in 1997 as a result of a recent effort by Congress to reform U.S. Food and Drug Administration (FDA) regulations.

Top 10 MOST PROFITABLE MEDICAL SUPPLIES COMPANIES

Ranked by: Profits per employee in 1995, in thousands of dollars.

1. St. Jude Medical, with $56.7 thousand
2. Medtronic, $37.4
3. Johnson & Johnson, $29.3
4. Guidant, $20.3
5. Pall, $19.9
6. Stryker Corp., 19.7
7. Baxter International, $19.1
8. Becton Dickinson, $14.3
9. Allergan, $13.3
10. Hillenbrand Industries, $9.1

Source: *Forbes*, Forbes 500s (annual), April 22, 1996, p. 294.

Despite an overall positive industry environment, medical instrument producers faced several hurdles going into the mid-1990s. Reduced availability of capital for research and development and a frustrating slowdown in FDA new product approvals were the major issues concerning competitors. Additionally, several segments of the industry appeared to be reaching maturity, indicating that overall profit growth might begin slowing in the future.

INDUSTRY OUTLOOK

As the industry's sales volume clambered past an impressive $28 billion, employment surged to over 102,000 in 1996. Success was partially attributable to massive industry investments, which amounted to about 6.5 percent of revenues in the early 1990s. The average investment for other U.S. industries was about 3.6 percent of sales. Medical device firms in the European Community and Japan, moreover, reinvested only 5 percent and 6 percent, respectively.

Leading growth in the 1990s was a promising new sphere of "minimally invasive" surgical instruments. These devices allowed surgeons to conduct complex operations without the pain, time, and expense associated with conventional procedures. Laparoscopic and endoscopic devices, for instance, involved the insertion of narrow tubes, called trocars, into a patient's abdomen. A laparoscope inserted into the tube is used to take pictures of the patient's inner organs, and miniature devices sent through the tube are used to perform complex surgical procedures. The market for minimally invasive devices was expected to explode in the 1990s and 2000s.

Another leading growth segment in the early 1990s was angioplasty catheters. In the early 1990s, about 400,000 angioplasty procedures were performed at a cost of $550 million compared with 184,000 such operations in the late 1980s and only 82,000 in the early 1980s. The procedure provided an important alternative to heart by-pass surgery in many cases.

Indeed, because of the changing dynamics of the health care market, cost-containment pressures were driving the growth of new money-saving procedures like angioplasty and laparoscopy. As purchasing decisions in the 1980s and 1990s shifted from physicians to hospitals and managed care facilities, producers were being forced to demonstrate the cost effectiveness of their products. Devices that could reduce hospital stays, increase labor productivity, and facilitate patient care in less expensive settings had become the dominant growth market by the mid-1990s.

Industry executives maintained an expectedly rosy outlook going into the mid-1990s, according to an early 1990s survey of 242 company presidents and CEOs in *Medical Device & Diagnostic Industry (MDDI)*. The survey indicated that 80 percent of respondents predicted that their business would improve in the very near future, while only 2 percent expected a decline. Eighty percent of the respondents believed that new product introduction and overall increased unit sales would spur growth, while 21 percent were relying on price growth to boost profits. About 66 percent of the respondents planned to increase research and development expenditures, while less than 1 percent planned a reduction.

CHALLENGES

Despite strong growth and optimism, competitors were facing significant obstacles to continued profitability as they entered the mid-1990s. Growing regulatory costs and barriers, decreased access to investment capi-

SIC 3841 - Surgical & Medical Instruments
General Statistics

Year	Companies	Establishments		Employment			Compensation		Production ($ million)			
		Total	with 20 or more employees	Total (000)	Production Workers (000)	Hours (Mil)	Payroll ($ mil)	Wages ($/hr)	Cost of Materials	Value Added by Manufacture	Value of Shipments	Capital Invest.
1982	760	859	312	56.9	38.5	74.3	999.5	6.97	1,252.5	2,884.8	4,084.5	230.2
1983		876	337	60.2	40.1	76.6	1,130.2	7.44	1,362.6	2,990.1	4,343.2	191.2
1984		893	362	61.3	39.7	77.3	1,215.5	7.78	1,529.4	3,155.6	4,629.6	219.1
1985		910	387	61.4	39.3	77.8	1,290.7	8.12	1,603.4	3,528.1	5,081.6	202.9
1986		950	390	62.6	39.4	79.3	1,386.2	8.66	1,814.7	3,575.2	5,346.8	217.2
1987	1,031	1,136	442	73.1	45.4	93.6	1,785.8	8.91	2,598.9	5,202.2	7,779.5	354.6
1988		1,137	460	75.7	46.7	93.1	1,918.5	9.57	2,668.3	5,683.2	8,258.6	384.8
1989		1,144	484	83.1	50.7	99.1	2,187.2	9.58	2,958.4	6,059.8	8,971.6	403.3
1990		1,127	498	86.0	53.8	104.2	2,433.8	9.81	3,219.0	7,077.5	10,261.6	468.7
1991		1,184	508	87.7	53.1	103.6	2,591.4	10.59	3,352.6	7,431.7	10,710.3	535.6
1992	1,216	1,340	551	98.2	58.5	113.1	3,095.3	10.86	4,063.5	9,397.8	13,384.9	688.8
1993		1,379	554	103.1	61.4	119.7	3,305.2	11.32	4,534.6	10,664.2	15,113.0	809.0
1994		1,387P	587P	100.5	60.0	119.1	3,403.6	11.52	4,480.7	10,272.2	14,811.6	624.4
1995		1,435P	610P	106.9P	63.1P	123.9P	3,565.5P	11.99P	4,731.9P	10,848.2P	15,642.1P	751.6P
1996		1,482P	633P	111.1P	65.2P	128.1P	3,781.0P	12.37P	5,033.0P	11,538.4P	16,637.4P	800.4P
1997		1,530P	655P	115.2P	67.3P	132.3P	3,996.5P	12.75P	5,334.1P	12,228.7P	17,632.6P	849.2P
1998		1,577P	678P	119.4P	69.4P	136.4P	4,212.0P	13.13P	5,635.2P	12,918.9P	18,627.9P	898.1P

Sources: 1982, 1987, 1992 *Economic Census*; *Annual Survey of Manufactures*, 83-86, 88-91, 93-94. Establishment counts for non-Census years are from *County Business Patterns*; establishment values for 83-84 are extrapolations. 'P's show projections by the editors. Industries reclassified in 87 will not have data for prior years.

tal, and increased competition in the health care industry all posed formidable challenges. Furthermore, some large segments, such as catheters, appeared to be entering a stage of maturity—meaning slower growth and reduced profit margins.

In an effort to offset some these industry problems, Congress loosened the collar on the FDA's regulations of the surgical and medical instruments industry—regulations many manufacturers felt dramatically slowed the introduction of new devices—in 1996. U.S. companies will no longer need FDA approval for products intended solely for the export market. This provision will undoubtedly ensure that Europe will become the industry testing ground for U.S. companies. Historically significant industry segments, such as catheters and syringes, will offer less profit potential as markets for those products mature and become more competitive. Market growth for leading-edge minimally invasive surgical tools and devices, however, will supplant profits from declining segments.

And although the growth attained in the 1970s and 1980s will likely wane, shipments are expected to grow at a healthy 6 percent per year (above inflation) through 1997. The market for endoscopic instruments, for example, was expected to grow from $550 million in the early 1990s to over $3 billion by 1996. Laparoscopic surgery, moreover, will likely account for 80 percent of all abdominal surgery performed by the turn of the century.

An aging population requiring more health care will augment overall growth. In addition, U.S. firms were well positioned to take advantage of emerging foreign markets going into the mid-1990s. Increased efficiency of the new FDA approval process should eventually diminish that industry hurdle, though possibly at a significant cost to competitors.

ORGANIZATION AND STRUCTURE

Major consumers of industry output in the early 1990s, in order of market size, included foreign consumers, the federal government, medical and health services, doctors and dentists, hospitals, individuals consumers, and drug companies. Over 20,000 medical device manufacturers were registered in the United States in 1996. Fewer than 1,500 of these firms, however, were engaged primarily in this industry.

The industry is relatively unconcentrated, partly because it is in a stage of growth and has not matured. However, unlike many other high-growth businesses, barriers to entry are significant. Companies often must incur huge start-up costs to cover research and product development costs. Furthermore, acute technical expertise is typically needed to develop proprietary knowledge necessary to differentiate products from others in the marketplace and to obtain approvals and patents. Companies that overcome these hurdles, however, often reap large profits if their products succeed.

FEDERAL REGULATION

An important dynamic influencing the industry's production and profitability is FDA regulation. The FDA is responsible for insuring that all products sold in the industry comply with federal safety standards. The FDA possesses the authority to recall products, temporarily suspend devices it deems high-risk, and impose monetary penalties for violations. Much of the FDA's export approval power over American medical devices was taken away by Congress in a 1996 amendment.

The 1990 Safe Medical Devices Act (SMDA), which defined procedures for bringing medical products to the market, is one of the most significant pieces of legislation governing producers. Among other stipula-

SIC 3841 - Surgical & Medical Instruments
Industry Data by State

| State | Establish-ments | Shipments | | | Employment | | | | Cost as % of Shipments | Investment per Employee ($) |
		Total ($ mil)	% of U.S.	Per Establ.	Total Number	% of U.S.	Per Establ.	Wages ($/hour)		
California	265	2,859.1	21.4	10.8	18,000	18.3	68	11.48	31.9	8,700
Connecticut	44	1,596.7	11.9	36.3	6,200	6.3	141	13.66	21.3	15,952
Massachusetts	91	1,331.9	10.0	14.6	9,300	9.5	102	11.36	28.0	5,452
Minnesota	65	676.7	5.1	10.4	5,300	5.4	82	11.09	21.8	8,453
New York	73	663.3	5.0	9.1	7,800	7.9	107	10.94	32.9	3,423
Pennsylvania	69	589.7	4.4	8.5	4,700	4.8	68	12.29	35.0	10,255
Florida	67	510.1	3.8	7.6	5,100	5.2	76	8.75	22.8	4,686
Texas	56	431.6	3.2	7.7	4,500	4.6	80	10.62	43.9	6,289
Missouri	35	408.3	3.1	11.7	3,600	3.7	103	10.73	33.7	2,944
Illinois	61	367.8	2.7	6.0	3,100	3.2	51	9.31	33.1	4,258

Source: 1992 *Economic Census*. The states are in descending order of shipments or establishments (if shipment data are missing for the majority). The symbol (D) appears when data are withheld to prevent disclosure of competitive information. States marked with (D) are sorted by number of establishments. A dash (-) indicates that the data element cannot be calculated; * indicates the midpoint of a range.

tions, the SMDA requires certain manufacturers to track patients that should be notified in the case of product failure; submit follow-up reviews for certain implants and devices; and, when applying for pre-market clearance, provide a summary of safety and effectiveness data for each device.

The FDA reviews medical devices under one of two procedures. Firms introducing completely new devices are required to submit a Product Marketing Application (PMA). The PMA must demonstrate the device's safety, as well as its diagnostic or therapeutic benefit. Detailed documentation of extensive animal and human tests must be provided to the FDA to support manufacturer claims. New devices resembling products already on the market are reviewed under a less stringent procedure called "501(k) pre-market notification." In 1992 about 2,500 new products were approved under the 501(k) procedure. Conversely, only 12 PMAs were approved that year.

WORK FORCE

Although a total of more than 21,000 companies were licensed to produce medical devices in the early 1990s, only about 1,200 of those firms were primarily engaged in producing surgical and medical instruments and apparatus. Those firms employed over 100,000 in the early 1990s. An undetermined number of workers were engaged in making products that fit this industry classification but were produced by companies primarily engaged in other industries.

Assemblers and fabricators comprised 14 percent of this industry's work force in the early 1990s. Inspectors, testers, and graders accounted for 3.4 percent of employment, and manufacturing supervisors made up 3.3 percent. Other blue collar manufacturing positions represented an additional 60 percent of the work force. Salespersons accounted for 6 percent of non-labor workers, while secretaries and clerical staff accounted for about 5 percent. Relatively high-paying engineering positions accounted for over 6 percent of the work force, while white collar managers and executives represented about 3.3 percent.

Fifteen percent of industry executives indicated a desire to move manufacturing facilities to foreign countries in the early 1990s, and many competitors were seeking increased productivity through automation. Despite these facts, employment prospects were positive going into the 1990s. The Bureau of Labor Statistics estimated that most occupations in the industry would grow significantly through 2000. Jobs for engineers, for instance, were expected to grow by 60 to 70 percent between 1990 and 2005. Sales and marketing positions,

SURGICAL INSTRUMENTS INDUSTRY EMPLOYMENT

Employment in thousands

Source: Department of Labor

moreover, were forecast to rise by more than 70 percent. Most management jobs will increase by around 40 percent by 2005.

Although blue collar production jobs will generally rise, the jump will be less substantial. Inspection, supervision, packaging, and shipping positions will rise by 30 to 50 percent by 2005. However, the number of jobs related to parts assembly, which account for about 18 percent the industry's work force, will stagnate or decline.

RESEARCH AND TECHNOLOGY

The medical and surgical device and apparatus industry is heavily driven by technological advances. In fact, much of the growth in U.S. health care expenditures which occurred during the 1960s, 1970s, and 1980s is attributable to the introduction of costly, high-tech equipment. For manufacturers that have devised new and better devices to help remedy ailments and illnesses, care providers have afforded an enthusiastic market. Life-saving procedures that were unheard of before 1970, such as angioplasty and coronary by-pass, were commonplace in the early 1990s. Industry profits were booming partially as a result of the increased demand for these new procedures.

Although U.S. producers already invested nearly 7 percent of their revenues into research and development in the early 1990s, industry executives indicated their intent to boost this figure in the mid-1990s. Furthermore, additional money for research was expected to flow from government sources. The Defense Reinvestment and Conversion Initiative developed in the early 1990s made available half a billion dollars for business partnerships designed to integrate America's high-tech defense industries into the civilian marketplace.

SIC 3841
Occupations Employed by SIC 384 - Medical Instruments and Supplies

Occupation	% of Total 1994	Change to 2005
Assemblers, fabricators, & hand workers nec	16.5	17.4
Sales & related workers nec	5.3	17.4
Inspectors, testers, & graders, precision	4.3	-17.8
Blue collar worker supervisors	3.3	-0.0
Precision assemblers nec	2.4	88.0
Secretaries, ex legal & medical	2.3	6.9
General managers & top executives	1.8	11.4
Traffic, shipping, & receiving clerks	1.8	13.0
Machine operators nec	1.7	-17.2
Electrical & electronic assemblers	1.7	5.7
Engineering technicians & technologists nec	1.6	17.4
Marketing, advertising, & PR managers	1.5	17.4
Hand packers & packagers	1.5	0.6
Sewing machine operators, non-garment	1.5	76.2
Mechanical engineers	1.5	29.3
Electrical & electronic equipment assemblers	1.5	17.4
Precision workers nec	1.5	5.7
Electrical & electronics engineers	1.4	49.1
Industrial production managers	1.4	17.4
Packaging & filling machine operators	1.3	17.4
Electrical & electronic technicians,technologists	1.3	17.4
Engineering, mathematical, & science managers	1.3	33.4
Bookkeeping, accounting, & auditing clerks	1.2	-11.9
Production, planning, & expediting clerks	1.2	17.4
General office clerks	1.2	0.2
Adjustment clerks	1.1	40.9
Machinists	1.1	-11.9
Managers & administrators nec	1.1	17.4

Source: *Industry-Occupation Matrix*, Bureau of Labor Statistics. These data relate to one or more 3-digit SIC industry groups rather than to a single 4-digit SIC. The change reported for each occupation to the year 2005 is a percent of growth or decline as estimated by the Bureau of Labor Statistics. The abbreviation nec stands for 'not elsewhere classified'.

Besides new product development, manufacturers were also concentrating on increased productivity going into the mid-1990s. A number of new flexible computer-integrated manufacturing techniques were being implemented. These techniques promised to synthesize manufacturing operations and promote international production standards. New information software had been developed, for instance, that helped device manufacturers integrate and manage software development, design changes, and testing data. The primary goal of such techniques was to reduce labor costs and increase productivity.

New and improved products in the early 1990s were numerous. Shape-memory polymers, for instance, are polyurethane-based polymers that can undergo and retain dramatic changes in hardness, flexibility, elasticity, and vapor permeability when exposed to heat. Among other uses, the resins were being used to form catheters that would remain stiff until inserted into the body. Similarly, new plastic springs offered an alternative to metal components in operations requiring resistance to corrosion and static charges.

AMERICA AND THE WORLD

Although the U.S. share of the entire global medical device market fell from 60 percent in 1980 to about 50 percent in the early 1990s, rapid expansion of global markets allowed domestic producers to sustain record export growth throughout that period. America's share of the world market was expected to decline to 40 percent by 2000, though export sales volume should rise steadily, even outpacing domestic growth.

The United States remained the world leader in medical device technology and maintained an especially dominant role in medical and dental instruments and supplies. This role was threatened, however, by an increasingly competitive global industry. Japanese and German producers had made significant strides in some market segments, such as high-tech electromedical equipment and some diagnostic machines. Furthermore, Japan plans to increase its investment in medical device research and development in an effort to catch up with capital expenditures made by their U.S. and German counterparts during the early 1990s.

Although Japan maintained the second largest market for medical devices in the world, the United States held a meager 12 percent share of that market in the early 1990s. Japan, in contrast, enjoyed relatively free access to American markets and accounted for over 20 percent of U.S. imports. Surgical and medical instrument imports into the United States in 1993, though, captured less than 9 percent of that market. The European Community delivered about 29 percent of U.S. imports in the early 1990s, Mexico and Canada sold 16 percent, and East Asian firms garnered about 14 percent of import revenues. Miscellaneous countries captured the remaining 20 percent. The largest buyer of U.S. goods was Canada, followed closely by Japan and Germany. Those three countries, combined with France and Mexico, consumed 50 percent of all industry exports.

Improving U.S. manufacturer prospects in the global instruments and apparatus market were two important international agreements that were hammered out in 1993. In July, seven major industrialized nations agreed to remove all inter-country tariffs on drugs and medical equipment, contingent on passage of the larger General Agreement on Trade and Tariffs (GATT). This development was expected to save U.S. medical industries $400 million per year. If the European Community agreed on a similar proposal, U.S. firms would benefit by only having to file for one permit to sell each product, rather than one for each of the 12 nations.

The second major agreement expected to boost sales was the North American Free Trade Agreement (NAFTA), which Congress passed in November of 1993.

NAFTA was expected to save companies in the industry $100 million annually from eliminated tariffs. In addition, investment restrictions on companies seeking to do business in Mexico were eliminated. The agreement also insured that the Mexican government, which made 70 percent of all national health care purchases, would open procurement processes to U.S. bidders.

ASSOCIATIONS AND SOCIETIES

AMERICAN SOCIETY FOR HEALTHCARE MATERIALS MANAGEMENT
c/o American Hospital Association
1 N. Franklin St.
Chicago, IL 60606
Phone: (312) 422-3840
Fax: (312) 422-3573
Members are involved with the purchasing and distribution of supplies and equipment for hospitals and other healthcare establishments. Affiliated with the American Hospital Association.

ASSOCIATION FOR THE ADVANCEMENT OF MEDICAL INSTRUMENTATION
3330 Washington Blvd., Ste. 400
Arlington, VA 22201
Phone: (800) 332-2264 or (703) 525-4890
Fax: (703) 276-0793
Members are engineers, technicians, physicians, manufacturers, and others with an interest in medical instrumentation.

HEALTH INDUSTRY DISTRIBUTORS ASSOCIATION
225 Reinekers Ln., No. 650
Alexandria, VA 22314-2875
Phone: (703) 549-4432
Fax: (703) 549-6495

HEALTH INDUSTRY MANUFACTURERS ASSOCIATION
1200 G St. NW, Ste. 4000
Washington, DC 20005
Phone: (202) 783-8700
Fax: (202) 783-8750

INSTRUMENT SOCIETY OF AMERICA
67 Alexander Dr.
Research Triangle Park, NC 27709
Phone: (800) 334-6391 or (919) 549-8411
Fax: (919) 549-8288

PERIODICALS AND NEWSLETTERS

BIOMEDICAL INSTRUMENTATION AND TECHNOLOGY
Hanley and Belfus, Inc.
210 S 13th St.,
Philadelphia, PA 19107
Phone: (215) 546-7293
Fax: (215) 790-9330
Bimonthly. Individuals, $72.00 per year; institutions, $96.00 per year.

HEALTH DEVICES ALERTS: A SUMMARY OF REPORTED PROBLEMS, HAZARDS, RECALLS, AND UPDATES
ECRI (Emergency Care Research Institute)
5200 Butler Pke.
Plymouth Meeting, PA 19462
Phone: (215) 825-6000
Fax: (215) 834-1275
Weekly. $695.00 per year. Newsletter containing reviews of health equipment problems.

HEALTHCARE PURCHASING NEWS
McKnight Medical Communications
2 Northfield Plz., Ste. 300
Northfield, IL 60093-1217
Phone: (800) 451-7838 or (708) 441-3700
Fax: (708) 441-3701
Monthly. $44.95 per year. Edited for personnel responsible for the purchase of medical, surgical, and hospital equipment and supplies. Features new purchasing techniques and new products. Includes news of the activities of two major purchasing associations, Health Care Material Management Society and International Association of Healthcare Central Service Materiel Management.

IAN: INSTRUMENTATION AND CONTROL NEWS
Chilton Co.
201 King of Prussia Rd.
Radnor, PA 19089
Phone: (215) 964-4000
Monthly. $35.00 per year.

DATABASES

EMBASE
Elsevier Science, Inc.
655 Avenue of the Americas
PO Box 945
New York, NY 10010
Phone: (212) 989-5800
Fax: (212) 633-3975
Worldwide medical literature, 1974 to present. Weekly updates. Inquire as to online cost and availability.

F-D-C REPORTS
FDC Reports, Inc.
5550 Friendship Blvd., Ste. 1
Chevy Chase, MD 20815
Phone: (301) 657-9830
Fax: (301) 656-3094
An online version of "The Gray Sheet" (medical devices), "The Pink Sheet" (pharmaceuticals), and "The Rose Sheet" (cosmetics). Contains full-text information on legal, technical, corporate, financial, and marketing developments from 1987 to date, with weekly updates. Inquire as to online cost and availability.

HEALTH DEVICES ALERTS [ONLINE]
ECRI
5200 Butler Pke.
Plymouth Meeting, PA 19462
Phone: (215) 825-6000
Fax: (215) 834-1275

Provides online reports of medical equipment defects, problems, failures, misuses, and recalls. Time period is 1977 to date, with weekly updates. Inquire as to online cost and availability.

STATISTICS SOURCES

SELECTED INSTRUMENTS AND RELATED PRODUCTS
U.S. Bureau of the Census
Washington, DC 20233
Phone: (301) 763-4100
Annual. $1.00.

GENERAL WORKS

ADVANCES IN INSTRUMENTATION AND CONTROL
Instrument Society of America
67 AlexanderDr.
Research Triangle Park, NC 27709
Phone: (800) 334-6391 or (919) 549-8411
Fax: (919) 549-8288
Annual. Prices vary.

GUIDE TO BIOTECHNOLOGY PRODUCTS, INSTRUMENTS, AND SERVICES
American Association for the Advancement of Science
1333 H St. NW, 8 Fl.
Washington, DC 20005-4792
Phone: (202) 326-6540
Fax: (202) 682-0816
Annual. $20.00. Formerly Guide to Scientific Instruments.

ISA DIRECTORY OF INSTRUMENTATION
67 AlexanderDr.
Research Triangle Park, NC 27709
Phone: (800) 334-6391 or (919) 549-8411
Fax: (919) 549-8288
Annual. $115.00.

FURTHER READING

Gianturco, Michael. "A Play on Catheterization." *Forbes,* 30 December 1996, 146.

Lane, Randall. "It's a Start." *Forbes,* 3 June 1996, 97-98.

Standard & Poor's Register CD. New York: McGraw-Hill Companies, Inc., 1997.

INDUSTRY SNAPSHOT

Since the invention of the telephone in 1877, the demand for telecommunication services has steadily ballooned. Even during the 1980s, when competition increased, wireline service sales grew at a rate of more than five percent annually and long-distance calling volume expanded by 12 percent. In 1995, total local service revenue exceeded $46 billion, and toll service revenues topped $83 billion. The wireless industry, as well, was effected by sweeping regulatory changes brought about by the Telecommunications Act of 1996. Aimed at removing segmentation between local phone service, long-distance service, wireless service, and cable television, the goal of the legislation was to decrease prices, improve services, drive still greater technological innovation, and create new business and more jobs for the United States. The eventual value of the wireless market alone is expected to reach over $36 billion by the year 2000.

TELECOM-MUNICATIONS

SICs 4810

In the mid-1990s, five of the top ten communications service providers in the world were U.S. firms. As the post-Telecommunications Act environment takes shape domestically, those industry leaders are clearly determined to maintain American dominance in the global telecommunications market through intense research and development efforts.

Such efforts are being focused on increasingly sophisticated and efficient digital, data transmission, and satellite technologies.

Top 10 **LARGEST CORPORATIONS IN THE TELE-COMMUNICATIONS INDUSTRY**

Ranked by: Revenue in 1995, in millions of dollars.

1. AT&T, with $79,609 million
2. GTE, $19,957
3. BellSouth, $17,886
4. MCI Communications Corp., $15,265
5. Sprint, $13,600
6. Bell Atlantic, $13,430
7. Ameritech Corp., $13,428
8. NYNEX, $13,407
9. SBC Communications, $12,670
10. U.S. West Media Group, $11,746

Source: *Fortune,* Fortune 500 Largest U.S. Corporations (annual), April 29, 1996, p. F-61+.

INDUSTRY OUTLOOK

TELECOMMUNICATIONS ACT OF 1996

The Telecommunications Act of 1996, signed into law February 8, 1996, swept away 62 years of regulation of the telecommunications industry. Local ''telcos,'' long-distance providers, wireless companies, and cable television operators would now be free to offer any and all telecommunications services.

Although full implementation of the legislation would require years, some commentators were already pronouncing it a failure by early 1997. Implementation along one track was stalled in October 1996 when the Eighth Circuit Court of Appeals, acting in a suit brought by several local telcos and state regulators, blocked the pricing provisions of Federal Communications Commission (FCC) rules on the terms on which the local companies were to open their networks to long-distance companies. This interconnection of telephone networks is one of the major provisions of the legislation.

LEGISLATION'S EFFECT ON BABY BELLS

Another major provision affecting the wireline telecommunications industry is that the Bell Operating Companies—also know as the Baby Bells—and any new local telephone network developers, must allow competition for local service using their local networks. They are also required to allow the resale of their services, much like long-distance service is resold by a great number of small long-distance companies, and they must provide the customers of these resellers the same type and quality of service that they provide their own customers.

The major benefit of the new regulations for the Baby Bells is freedom to enter the long-distance market once they have demonstrated that they have opened their local networks to viable competition. They will also be able to join with other companies, local or long-distance, to form subsidiaries to offer long-distance service jointly, again, after they have effective competition in their local markets. The goal is to provide "one stop shopping" for all telephone services.

UNIVERSAL AND VIDEO SERVICE

One of the goals of federal regulation continues to be universal service. Companies that provide service in a region must make it available to everyone at an affordable price, even in areas where the costs of providing the service are much higher. Companies that offer such service receive subsidies from a fund that under the new legislation will be supported by all interstate telecommunications providers.

Other provisions of the Act now allow telephone companies to offer video programming, allow Bells to manufacture telecommunications equipment, and other utility companies to offer telecommunications services through subsidiaries set up for that purpose.

MERGERS

A defining characteristic of the telecommunications industry in the late 1990s was the large number of mergers, acquisitions, and joint ventures. In anticipation of deregulation, many companies took steps to position themselves for the expected changes by joining with companies in other segments of the industry. For example, in 1994 American Telephone & Telegraph Co. (AT&T) acquired McCaw Cellular Communications, the largest cellular provider in the U.S. at the time. Altogether, 746 such transactions were announced in the industry between January 1994 and June 1996, with a value estimated at $110.7 billion. 72.4 percent were mergers of service providers, i.e., wireline, wireless, and cable TV operators. The rest involved equipment and software providers.

Probably the most significant merger announced in the first year after the passage of the Telecommunications Act was the acquisition of MCI, the second largest long-distance provider in the U. S., by British Telecommunications, which held a 90 percent share of the local and long-distance market in the U.K. and maintained network facilities in 30 countries. Besides creating another behemoth to stand beside AT&T, this merger indicated the increasingly global nature of the industry. Deutsche Telekom and France Telecom, German and French national telephone companies respectively, had already each acquired 10 percent of Sprint, the third largest long-distance provider in the U.S. More such international ventures were expected as the European market moved toward deregulation beginning in January 1998.

ORGANIZATION AND STRUCTURE

WIRELINE TELECOMMUNICATION SERVICES

The wireline telecommunication services industry includes firms that provide electronic communications using wire networks or fiber-optic lines. The massive U.S. wireline infrastructure incorporates 750,000 miles of aerial wire, 3.5 million miles of cable, and over 4.5 million miles of optical fiber. The Federal Communications Commission (FCC) reported that in July 1996 all the telephone companies together served 93.9 percent of U.S. households.

LONG DISTANCE CARRIERS AND LOCAL COMPANIES

Although the Telecommunications Act of 1996 removed legal barriers in general, in 1997 the industry was still largely divided into long-distance carriers and local telephone companies (telcos). Local telcos provide basic telephone services. They bring telephone access lines into homes, hook up new customers, and service local lines and equipment. Telcos also connect customers to long-distance carriers, and sometimes handle intrastate toll calls that are considered long-distance.

About 75 percent of all local telephone lines are serviced by the Bell Operating Companies (BOCs). They are called "Baby Bells," because they are the offspring of the 1984 AT&T divestiture. In addition to the regional BOCs, about 1,300 independent telcos provide local service. These companies range from tiny rural cooperatives with fewer than 1,000 lines to the giant independents, the largest being GTE.

Long-distance carriers provide national and international services via wire and fiber-optic lines. Their services often utilize satellite and microwave systems, as well. Long-distance carriers typically pay a hefty fee to have local carriers route long-distance calls to their lines. In fact, in 1995 the access revenues from interstate long-distance traffic totaled $22 billion.

CELLULAR, PAGING, AND PCS

The wireless telecommunications services industry in 1997 was comprised largely of cellular telephone and paging services, but a good number of Personal Communications Services networks (PCS) had been rolled out in major markets in 1996. These various services allow customers with mobile telephones to send (and receive) calls to (and from) people with landline phones, pagers, or hand-held wireless phones. Cellular service subscribers typically pay a monthly subscription fee plus an additional per-minute usage charge.

COMPETITIVE ACCESS PROVIDERS

In addition to the BOCs and independents, competitive access providers (CAPs) offer local telephone services. Started in 1992, CAPs typically furnish dedicated fiber-optic telephone lines that connect corporations and long-distance carriers. Because CAPs are not subject to the same pricing regulations with which the BOCs must comply, they can often deliver service to high-volume corporate customers at reduced rates. Although early on some observers feared that these companies would siphon off debilitating amounts of high margin business, the telcos have not suffered greatly from their presence.

RESEARCH AND TECHNOLOGY

Besides capital spending on labor-saving automation, U.S. wireline telecommunication service industry investments were targeted at several emerging technologies in the mid-1990s. The most important area of research and development was digital transmission. Both long-distance and local carriers were racing to develop and integrate new digital technology that would increase line capacity and speed, and allow the efficient transmission of data, voice, and video. ISDN deployment was being retarded by the lack of agreed standards in the United States. Telcos were also investing in other data transmission technologies, such as Switched Multimegabit Data Service (SMDS), frame relay, and asymmetric digital subscriber line (ASDL). These technologies, combined with advancing fiber-optic and ISDN efforts, were resulting in vast data transmission improvements.

An important element of the move to digital transmission was the development of a fiber-optic network, the basis of the much-touted "information superhighway." Fiber-optic networks can carry much more traffic than copper, making it much more suitable for the transport of large volumes of data and video. In 1995, long-distance carriers increased their deployment of fiber by 8 percent, with AT&T and MCI responsible for the bulk of the increase. The total deployment by

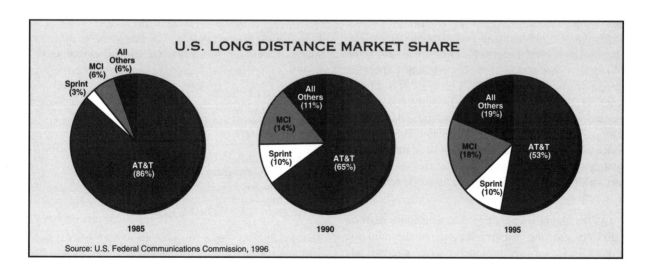

U.S. LONG DISTANCE MARKET SHARE

1985 — Sprint (3%), MCI (6%), All Others (6%), AT&T (86%)

1990 — All Others (11%), MCI (14%), Sprint (10%), AT&T (65%)

1995 — All Others (19%), MCI (18%), Sprint (10%), AT&T (53%)

Source: U.S. Federal Communications Commission, 1996

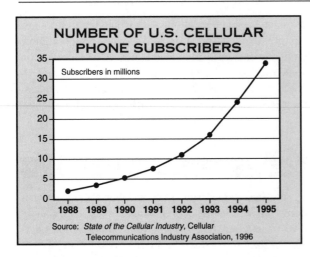

NUMBER OF U.S. CELLULAR PHONE SUBSCRIBERS

Subscribers in millions

Source: *State of the Cellular Industry*, Cellular Telecommunications Industry Association, 1996

long-distance carriers at this time was over 107,000 miles. The local service providers, led by BellSouth and GTE increased their deployment of fiber-optic cable by 18 percent in 1995, to a total of over 280,000 miles.

AMERICA AND THE WORLD

U.S. telecommunications service providers remained the most competitive in the world in the late-1990s. Technological experience, marketing know-how, and one of the least regulated communications environments in the industrialized world contribute to their global dominance. According to B. Holt Thrasher and Robert McNamara in *Telecommunications*, based on reported revenue for 1995, five of the top ten communications service providers and two of the top ten global communications equipment manufacturers in the world were U.S. companies.

But many nations were catching up to the United States, and some analysts believed that U.S. providers were missing the boat on several important new technologies. During the 1980s, for instance, Germany invested an average of $305 annually per telephone in its telecommunications infrastructure. Japan invested about $244 dollars per phone. The United States spent an average of only $218 per year. Likewise, U.S. investment in ISDN (Integrated Services Digital Network), the potentially vital global digital standard, lagged behind its major trading partners. On the other hand, U.S. wireline service providers were far ahead of most of their foreign counterparts in the transition to wireless telecommunications, which could eventually dominate landline services.

As the global wireless telecommunications markets heated up, growing at twice the rate of the domestic market, U.S. service providers were aggressively chasing foreign dollars. Overseas investment in the U.S. wireless industry was allowing many foreign competitors to participate in North American markets, and to form global partnerships with technological leaders. Despite extensive worldwide interaction between wireless services, major impediments to the creation of a seamless global network remained in the mid-1990s. Most notably, there was a lack of uniform technological and regulatory standards. However, industry organizations, such as the International Telecommunications Union (ITU), were working to develop such standards.

ASSOCIATIONS AND SOCIETIES

COMPETITIVE TELECOMMUNICATIONS ASSOCIATION
1140 Connecticut Ave., NW. Ste. 220
Washington, DC 20036
Phone: (202) 296-6650
Fax: (202) 296-7585

TELE-COMMUNICATIONS ASSOCIATION
701 N Haven Ave., Ste. 200
Ontario, CA 91724-4925
Phone: (909) 945-1122

TELECOMMUNICATIONS INDUSTRY ASSOCIATION
2001 Pennsylvania Ave. NW, Ste. 800
Washington, DC 20016-1813
Phone: (202) 457-4912
Fax: (202) 457-4939

PERIODICALS AND NEWSLETTERS

AT & T TECHNICAL JOURNAL
AT & T Bell Laboratories
600 Mountain Ave., Room 3C443
Murray Hills, NJ 07074
Phone: (800) 432-6600 or (908) 572-4834
Fax: (908) 582-4430
Bimonthly. $50.00 per year.

COMMUNICATIONS NEWS
American Society of Association Executives Communications Section
1575 Eye St. NW
Washington, DC 20005
Phone: (202) 626-2723
Fax: (202) 408-9635
Monthly. Membership.

FIBER OPTICS AND COMMUNICATIONS
Information Gatekeepers, Inc.
214 Harvard Ave.
Boston, MA 02134
Phone: (800) 323-1088 or (617) 232-3111
Fax: (617) 734-8562
Monthly. $545.00. Emphasis on the use of fiber optics in telecommunications.

NTQ: NEW TELECOM QUARTERLY—THE FUTURE OF TELECOMMUNICATIONS
Technology Futures, Inc.
11709 Boulder Ln.
Austin, TX 78726
Phone: (800) 835-3887 or (512) 258-8898
Fax: (512) 258-0087
Quarterly. $95.00 per year. Includes articles on trends in wireless telecommunications, fiber optics technology, interactive multimedia, online information systems, telephone systems, and telecommunications in general.

TELECOMMUNICATIONS
Horizon-House Pubications, Inc.
685 Canton St.
Norwood, MA 02060
Phone: (617) 769-9750
Fax: (617) 762-9230
Monthly. Free to qualified personnel; others, $75.00 per year. International coverage.

TELECOMMUNICATIONS WEEK
Business Research Publications, Inc.
817 Broadway, 3 Fl.
New York, NY 10003-4709
Phone: (800) 622-7237 or (212) 673-4700
Fax: (212) 475-1790
Weekly. $395.00 per year. Newsletter.

DATABASES

BELL ATLANTIC MEDIA RELATIONS AND PUBLIC ARCHIVES
Bell Atlantic Corp.
Provides information on telecommunications policies, as well as on the company Bell Atlantic. Documents include news releases, speeches, congressional testimony, company history, the 1994 Huber Report, FCC reports, and more. Time span: Current information. Updating frequency: As needed. Fees: Free. Gopher: ba.com URL: gopher://gopher.ba.com or http:// www.ba.com.

CSA ENGINEERING
Cambridge Scientific Abstracts
7200 Wisconsin Ave., Ste. 601
Bethesda, MD 20814
Phone: (800) 843-7751 or (301) 961-6750
Fax: (301) 961-6720
Provides the online version of Computer and Information Systems Abstracts, Electronics and Communications Abstracts, Health and Safety Science Abstracts, ISMEC: Mechanical Engineering Abstracts (Information Service in Mechanical Engineering) *and* Solid State and Superconductivity Abstracts. *Time period is 1981 to date, with monthly updates. Inquire as to online cost and availability.*

NATIONAL TELECOMMUNICATIONS AND INFORMATION ADMINISTRATION
U.S. Dept. of Commerce, National Telecommunications and Information Administration
Covers the U.S. government's telecommunication policies and the National Information Infrastructure. Includes full-text docu-ments, speeches, and testimony, as well as contact and explanatory information on NTIA programs and conferences. Time span: Current information. Updating frequency: Regularly. Fees: Free. Gopher: gopher.ntia.doc.gov URL: gopher:// gopher.ntia.doc.gov/ or http://www.ntia.doc.gov/ or http:// ntiaunix1.ntia.doc.gov

SEARCH THE CIX WEB SITE
Commercial Internet eXchange Association
Posts white papers, press releases, and articles on the Telecommunications Bill, online censorship, and other issues that affect the online community. When established: 1995. Updating frequency: Weekly. Fees: Free. URL: http://www.cix.org/ or http://www.cix.org/CIXInfo/

THE TELECOMMUNICATIONS LIBRARY
WilTel Network Services
LDDS WorldCom
Covers issues related to the technology and business of telecommunications. The site includes discussion boards, online magazines, directories, and other publications on communication issues, regulations, working papers, and market research reports. Time span: Current information. Updating frequency: As needed. Fees: Free to access the library; some documents are free. URL: http://www.wiltel.com/library/library.html E-mail: webmasteratswiltel.com

STATISTICS SOURCES

COMMUNICATION EQUIPMENT, AND OTHER ELECTRONIC SYSTEMS AND EQUIPMENT
U.S. Bureau of the Census
Washington, DC 20233-0800
Phone: (301) 457-4100
Fax: (301) 457-3842
Annual. Provides data on shipments: value, quantity, imports, and exports. (Current Industrial Reports, MA-36P.)

WIRELESS AND CABLE VOICE SERVICES: FORECASTS AND COMPETITIVE IMPACTS
Lawrence K. Vanston and Curt Rogers
Technology Futures, Inc.
11709 Boulder Ln.
Austin, TX 78726
Phone: (800) 835-3887 or (512) 258-8898
Fax: (512) 258-0087
1995. $495.00. Sponsored by the Telecommunications Technology Forecasting Group (telephone companies). Includes forecast data for prices, demand, and competitive factors.

GENERAL WORKS

COMMUNICATION TECHNOLOGY UPDATE
Focal Press
313 Washington St.
Newton, MA 02158
Phone: (800) 366-2665 or (617) 928-2500
Fax: (800) 446-6520 or (617) 933-6333
Annual. $32.95. A yearly review of developments in electronic media, telecommunications, and the Internet.

FUTURE TRENDS IN TELECOMMUNICATIONS
R. J. Horrocks
John Wiley and Sons, Inc.
605 3rd Ave.
New York, NY 10158-0012
Phone: (800) 225-5945 or (212) 850-6000
Fax: (212) 850-6088
1993. $89.95. Includes fiber optics technology, local area networks, and satellite communications. Discusses the future of telecommunications for the consumer and for industry.

MANAGING TO COMMUNICATE: USING TELECOMMUNICATIONS FOR INCREASED BUSINESS EFFICIENCY
M. P. Clark
John Wiley and Sons, Inc.
605 3rd Ave.
New York, NY 10158
Phone: (800) 225-5945 or (212) 850-6000
Fax: (212) 850-6088
1994. $34.95.

TELECOMMUNICATIONS
Warren Hioki
Prentice-Hall
200 Old Tappan Rd.
Old Tappan, NJ 07675

Phone: (800) 922-0579
Fax: (800) 445-6991
1995. $70.00. Second edition.

FURTHER READING

Statistics of Communications Common Carriers. Washington, DC: 1996. Available from http://www.fcc.gov/ccb/SOCC.zip

Garcia, D. Linda. "The Failure of Telecom Reform." *Telecommunications*, June 1996.

Girard, Kim. "Baby Bells Call in New Data Pipe Technology." *Computerworld,* August 26, 1996.

Healey, Jon. "Telecommnications Highlights." *Congressional Quarterly,* February 17, 1996.

Jackson, Susan, and Catherine Arnst. "Trench Warfare in Long Distance." *Business Week,* February 17, 1997.

Standard & Poor's Corporation. *Standard & Poor's Industry Surveys.* New York: 12 September 1996.

Thrasher, B. Holt, and Robert McNamara. "How Merger Mania Has Redefined the Communications Landscape." *Telecommunications,* October 1996.

TELEPHONE AND TELEGRAPH APPARATUS

SIC 3661

In *the wake of the deregulation of telecommunications industry in the United States in the 1980s, the business user faced a bewildering choice of services and equipment. Today, with the growing importance of voice, data, and text communication links for conducting everyday business, the industry still offers an immense product line; the key will be whether or not telecommunications companies can successfully target business users in specific markets for whom access to information and reliable communication links are vital. Moreover, with the advent of the Internet, there will be more opportunities for telephone and telegraph apparatus companies to target both business and residential consumers for their products.*

INDUSTRY SNAPSHOT

The telephone and telegraph apparatus industry shipped $24.6 billion worth of products in 1995, which was a 43 percent increase since 1990. The number of establishments in the industry stood at 528 in the mid-1990s, which was a 21 percent increase since 1990. In 1995, the United States imported $6.9 billion worth of telephone and telegraph equipment; exports totaled $5.7 billion.

Top 7 — TOP ISDN PROVIDERS

Ranked by: Percentage of lines that have ISDN service among regional bell operating companies.

1. Pacific Telesis, 83%
2. Ameritech, 81%
3. Bell Atlantic, 77%
4. BellSouth, 71%
5. Southwestern Bell, 66%
6. US West, 51%
7. NYNEX, 50%

Source: *Telecommunications*, March 1996, p. 22, from Bellcore.

INDUSTRY OUTLOOK

The real value of the United States' telecommunications system lies in its ability to access a wide range of users wherever they are located (Universal Service). This is the role of telephone switching systems. When large scale integrated circuits were perfected in the 1970s, it became technically feasible to develop a digital-switching network to replace the electronic network in central offices. Current state-of-the-art of central office technology has a digital switching network controlled by a programmable central processor. Most modern switching equipment, ranging from small Private Branch Exchange (PBXs) to large toll tandem switches that can handle thousands of trunks, use this technology. Further research was underway to develop even less costly switching systems capable of switching light streams rather than electrical pulses.

Before the arrival of microelectronics and stored program control private branch exchanges, large companies were reluctant to place switching systems on the premises to provide private branch exchange service. Centrex is a PBX-like service furnished by the local telephone company through equipment located in the central office. Centrex features allow direct inward dialing (DID) to a telephone number and direct outward dialing (DOD) from a number without operator intervention. For calls into the Centrex, the service is equivalent to individual line service. Outgoing calls differ from individual line service only in the requirement that the caller dials an individual access code (usually 9). Calls between stations in the Centrex group require four or five digits instead of the seven digits required for ordinary calls. An attendant position located on the customer's premises is linked to the central office over a separate circuit. Centrex service provides PBX features without locating a switching system on the user's premises.

The demand for Centrex service provided by the Regional Bell Operating Companies was expected to grow by 4 to 5 percent annually. Small business Centrex service (less than 100 lines) experienced 5 to 10 percent growth rates, while the intermediate to large line size segments experienced flat or negative growth rates. The distribution of the current 8 million-line Centrex installed base is as follows: less than 100 company lines, 1.4 million total lines; 100 to 399 company lines, 1 million total lines; 400 to 1,000 company lines, 1.55 million total lines; 1,000 or more company lines, 4.05 million total lines.

It was forecasted that sales of telephone products would grow 7.3 percent annually from $3.1 billion in 1992 to almost $4.1 billion in 1996. This category includes telephone sets, cordless telephones, and answering machines. The projected increase in this group was due primarily to a jump in market share for cordless phones from 41.9 percent in 1992 to 49.4 percent in 1996, and an expected growth in telephone answering

systems from 31.9 percent in 1992 to 36.7 percent in 1996. The market share for one- and two-line phones was forecasted to decline from 21.0 to 10.9 percent for single line units and 4.4 to 3.0 percent for two-line phones between 1992 and 1996.

In recent years, cordless telephones have gained wide consumer acceptance with an estimated 40 percent household penetration in the United States. Cordless phones are projected to account for 17 percent of the wireless communications equipment market by 1997. These instruments use a low-powered radio link between a base unit and the portable telephone. The latest generation of cordless telephones were multi button units that could be assigned to outside lines, intercom paths, or system features such as speed dial. The handset and base could talk on any of the channels, and the user could accept the channel with the best reception. Standard key features such as transfer and hold were activated from the cordless unit.

Telephone answering equipment, once provided exclusively by the LECs, were widely available from leading suppliers AT&T, Panasonic Co., and Sharp Corporation. Unit sales for this product reached the $14.5 million mark with manufacturers distributing stock primarily through mass merchants and electronic and appliance stores. The telephone answering machine market will continue to grow, but technological innovation was replacing the traditional stand-alone telephone answering machine connected to a telephone with integrated telephone answering devices. These units will include telephone answering devices incorporated into every piece

SIC 3661 - Telephone & Telegraph Apparatus
General Statistics

| Year | Companies | Establishments | | Employment | | | Compensation | | Production ($ million) | | | |
		Total	with 20 or more employees	Total (000)	Production Workers (000)	Hours (Mil)	Payroll ($ mil)	Wages ($/hr)	Cost of Materials	Value Added by Manufacture	Value of Shipments	Capital Invest.
1982	259	333	210	136.5	85.6	158.4	3,021.2	10.19	6,357.8	7,120.8	13,394.4	513.1
1983		342	219	128.0	81.3	149.5	3,124.4	10.84	6,789.6	6,725.8	13,527.2	592.1
1984		351	228	132.5	82.3	155.1	3,547.1	12.09	8,563.0	7,695.9	15,783.2	866.1
1985		359	237	130.5	75.6	143.3	3,524.9	12.08	8,928.3	8,502.9	17,775.0	725.7
1986		359	233	110.9	58.5	110.7	3,019.2	12.60	7,409.5	7,780.7	15,687.8	629.6
1987*	390	469	297	112.3	58.6	109.4	3,178.4	12.82	7,956.3	9,588.0	17,582.5	552.0
1988		448	284	111.7	57.2	107.5	3,458.4	13.37	8,756.7	9,195.1	17,901.1	625.1
1989		449	278	101.7	49.0	93.9	3,312.6	14.51	6,975.0	8,326.5	15,467.0	573.1
1990		433	273	94.0	46.5	91.8	3,421.2	14.48	7,606.3	9,619.4	17,297.3	592.7
1991		468	281	94.1	46.9	89.7	3,468.1	14.47	7,838.7	9,502.5	17,424.9	458.7
1992	479	544	315	91.0	44.7	87.4	3,741.4	14.95	8,153.5	12,463.1	20,498.3	614.8
1993		532	303	84.9	38.5	75.1	3,731.1	15.34	8,002.8	13,589.9	21,539.8	594.6
1994		535P	302P	86.1	41.2	78.6	3,576.6	15.46	9,638.6	14,435.7	23,471.8	781.3
1995		549P	305P	78.3P	35.6P	70.3P	3,779.8P	16.01P	9,402.3P	14,081.8P	22,896.4P	676.4P
1996		563P	308P	74.1P	32.9P	65.5P	3,845.1P	16.37P	9,767.2P	14,628.3P	23,785.0P	693.6P
1997		578P	311P	69.9P	30.2P	60.8P	3,910.3P	16.72P	10,132.1P	15,174.8P	24,673.6P	710.8P
1998		592P	314P	65.8P	27.5P	56.0P	3,975.6P	17.07P	10,497.0P	15,721.3P	25,562.1P	727.9P

Sources: 1982, 1987, 1992 *Economic Census*; *Annual Survey of Manufactures*, 83-86, 88-91, 93-94. Establishment counts are from *County Business Patterns* for non-Census years; establishment counts for 83-84 are extrapolations. * indicates that industry content changed in 87; earlier years use 77 SICs. 'P's mark projections.

of communications equipment from basic telephones to cordless integrated answering telephone devices to personal computer systems.

The market offers two categories of telephone sets: general purpose sets or corded phones and special purpose telephones, such as coin operated telephones. Leading suppliers AT&T, General Electric, and Conair Corp. distribute products primarily through electronics/appliance stores and mass merchant outlets. The price of general purpose sets is often a clue to quality. Many inexpensive instruments provide poor transmission quality and fail when dropped. At the high end of the scale, price usually is a function of features or looks. Two-line phone sets are expected to show only modest unit growth (3.9 percent) over the next several years with an overall decline in total dollar sales due to average price declines in manufacturer prices. Single-line phone sets will be replaced by feature phones with many more characteristics and capabilities than existing models.

The advent of the customer-owned coin operated telephone (COCOT) is another byproduct of divestiture that is confusing to many users. In the first few years following the dissolution of the Bell System, many private companies saw COCOTs as a potentially lucrative business. The companies that ventured into this market with less than adequate equipment, however, quickly discovered what the local exchange companies or LECs have long understood: the risks and administrative costs of coin telephones are high, and the companies that enter this market without understanding the hazards can lose large amounts. The two major risks are fraud and vandalism. These can be combatted with durable instruments and by building defenses into the telephone.

Key telephone systems (KTS) are not high-technology products compared to radio, satellite, and fiber optics, and they don't have the technical appeal of a PBX,

but they are the workhorses of American business. Like other customer premise products, KTSs have evolved from wired logic and electromechanical operation to stored program or firmware control. In the process, they adopted many features that were once the exclusive province of PBX. The difference between the PBX and the key system was indistinct enough that the industry used the term, ''hybrid,'' to describe one class of system that has elements of both.

The electronic key telephone system offers most of the features of a PBX, especially the hybrid version, which is a cross between a PBX and a key system. The distinction between the KTSs and PBXs is becoming more blurred as technology brings more intelligence to the KTS. Further blurring the trend between key systems and PBXs is the propensity of some manufacturers to make key telephone instrument lines compatible with PBX lines, allowing a company to grow out of its KTS and into a larger more sophisticated PBX.

Many organizations operate private telecommunications systems. These systems range in size from the federal telephone system, which is larger than the telecommunications systems in many countries, to small private branch exchanges (PBXs).

Nearly every business with more than 30 to 100 stations is in the market for a PBX, or its central office counterpart, Centrex (a service by the local phone companies where the guts of the system are located on the local phone company premise). PBXs are economical for some very small businesses that need features that most key systems do not provide such as restriction and least cost routing. They are also economical for very large businesses that have PBXs using central office switching systems of a size that rivals many metropolitan public networks. Most PBXs can be mounted in a cabinet on the business user's premises and can operate

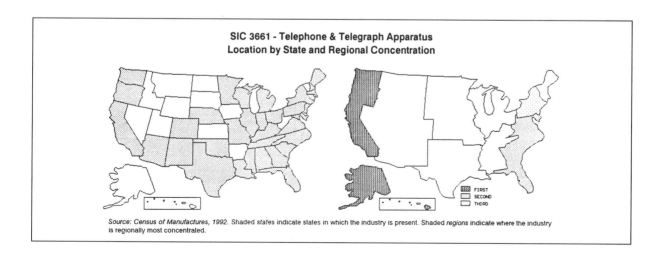

SIC 3661 - Telephone & Telegraph Apparatus
Location by State and Regional Concentration

FIRST
SECOND
THIRD

Source: Census of Manufactures, 1992. Shaded states indicate states in which the industry is present. Shaded regions indicate where the industry is regionally most concentrated.

without air conditioning in an ordinary office environment.

The office PBX increasingly controls private voice networks. As the network evolves into all-digital, so does the PBX in all but the low end systems of 100 stations or fewer, which remain analog. The advent of the T-1 carrier as the preferred transmission medium is the principle force driving the evolution of the PBX. The long distance carriers make it increasingly attractive for business users to bypass the local central office with T-1 trunks directly to the long distance carrier's central office. The cost of T-1 service for PBX lines is particularly advantageous when data transmission facilities parallel the route of voice. The integration of voice and data reduces the cost of access lines to the outside world.

Several converging forces have increased the importance of incoming call management systems. First, there is the increasing use of telemarketing. A telemarketing center typically has banks of 800-numbers with different numbers associated with different product lines or promotions, and different agents with access to various databases to handle callers' questions. A caller distribution system is needed in this case to direct incoming calls to the appropriate agent. Secondly, most incoming 800-calls are delivered via T-1 technology. With this technology, calls need to be routed to the appropriate party when they reach the customer premise. Finally, call distribution technology has advanced to the point where it is basically a merger of telephone and computer operations. Any organization with more than a few answering positions finds that the cost of some machine-controlled call distribution pays for itself quickly.

Call/voice processing systems accounted for 10.1 percent or $3.2 billion of all telecommunication and data equipment sales in the mid-1990s. This figure was up $329 million or 11.33 percent from 1992. Sales of U.S. call processing equipment were forecasted to grow at an annual compound rate of 21 percent between 1992 and 1998 to $8.2 billion. This category consists of uniform call distribution systems, call sequencers, automatic call distributors, and voice processing systems.

A uniform call distribution system (UCD), a standard feature of many PBXs, often significantly improves call handling. The stand-alone counterpart of a UCD is the call sequencer. This device may work with a PBX or key telephone system, or it may be connected directly to incoming lines. Unlike the UCD, a call sequencer does not direct calls, but alerts agents to the presence of incoming calls. The most sophisticated device is an automatic call distributor (ACD), which can either stand alone or integrate with a PBX. An ACD routes calls to the least busy agent to equalize the work load. The ACD administrator typically has a video display terminal that

presents call statistics in real time, and has many management tools that monitor and improve service and measure the agent's effectiveness. Any organization that has a large number of incoming calls targeted for service positions is a potential ACD user. This includes departments that handle mail orders, literary delivery, inquiries, field service, credit, and collections.

The marriage of computer and telecommunications technologies brought a family of equipment collectively known as voice processing systems to the market. Three classes of equipment comprise voice processing: voice mail, automated attendant, and voice response or audiotex equipment.

Over the last decade facsimile equipment (FAX) has become an indispensable business machine essential to the every day transactions of most businesses. The FAX machine works by scanning the printed page, encoding it, and transmitting a facsimile of the images in shades of black and white without identifying individual characters. Facsimile can convey both text and graphic information, source documents can be retransmitted without rekeying, and facsimile transmission is affected less by transmission errors than other types of data communication. Facsimile is also fast. Some facsimile machines also double as printers and copiers.

Like other types of telecommunications equipment, modems have become faster, cheaper, and smarter. The ready availability of inexpensive personal computers has expanded the demand for modems, and basically two types of modems exist in the market: dial-up modems and private line modems. Dial-up modems either plug into a personal computer slot, or are self contained devices that plug into the computers serial port. Many of the modem's features are designed to emulate a telephone. These features include: dial tone recognition, automatic tone and dial pulse dialing, monitoring call progress tones such as busy and reorder, automatic answer, and call termination. These items are priced on a commodity type basis and use the public network for the transmission of information. Private line modems work exclusively with voice and data private lines, and although it has the same functions as a dial-up modem, they are not as popular as their sister model the dial-up modem.

Many data applications, by nature, are incapable of fully using a data circuit. Rather than flowing in a steady stream, data usually flows in steady, short bursts with long, idle periods intervening. To make use of this idle capacity, data multiplexers are employed to collect data from multiple stations and combine it into a single, high-speed bit stream.

Data multiplexers come in two types: time division multiplexers (TDM) and statistical multiplexers (statmux). In a TDM, each station is assigned a time slot, and the multiplexer collects data from each station in turn. If a station has no data to send, its time slot goes unused. A statmux makes use of the idle time periods in a data circuit by assigning time slots to pairs of stations according to the amount of traffic they have to send. The multiplexer collects data from the terminal and sends it to the distant end, with the address of the receiving terminal minimizing idle times between transactions.

Analog or frequency division multiplexers are also available to divide a voice channel into multiple segments for data transmission. Their primary use is to connect multiple, slow-speed data terminals over voice channels. A concentrator is similar to a multiplexer except that it is usually a single-ended device which connects directly to a host computer. The primary application for multiplexers is in data networks that use asynchronous terminals. Since many of these items cannot be addressed and have no error correction capability, they are of limited use by themselves in remote locations. The multiplexer provides end-to-end error checking and correction and circuit sharing to support multiple terminals.

ORGANIZATION AND STRUCTURE

The telephone and telegraph equipment market is broken down into two broad categories: network equipment manufacturers, who sell telephone switching and switchboard equipment primarily to local and long distance phone companies; and end-user or terminal equipment manufacturers, who sell data and voice communications equipment, facsimile equipment, call/voice processing equipment, consumer communications electronics, private branch exchanges (PBX), and videoconferencing equipment to both large and small businesses and residential users.

WORK FORCE

There were 111,800 employed in the industry in 1995, an increase of 18 percent since 1990. Production workers in the industry totaled 59,600 in 1995, a 28 percent increase since 1990. Production workers' average hourly wages have decreased since 1990, from $14.48 to $13.30 in 1995.

Technological advances eliminated many of the traditional positions associated with the manufacture of telephone equipment and apparatus. A study by the U.S. Bureau of Labor anticipated a 51 percent decline in electrical and electronic assemblers between the years 1990 and 2005. This group accounted for 16.5 percent of the employees of manufacturers of telephone equipment and apparatus. A related group of electrical and electronic engineers, who accounted for 8.2 percent of the work force, was expected to grow by 5.7 percent over this time frame.

On the whole, there will be a substantial reengineering of the workflow in this industry, with many traditional jobs becoming automated and a downsizing in administrative and support staff. An increase of 17 percent was expected for computer programmers, and sales/marketing personnel would be needed to sell the products in a market driven by price/features.

RESEARCH AND TECHNOLOGY

All of the trends involving computers and communications ultimately converge at the desktop. Higher-

---

SIC 3661 - Telephone & Telegraph Apparatus
Industry Data by State

State	Establish-ments	Shipments			Employment				Cost as % of Shipments	Investment per Employee ($)
		Total ($ mil)	% of U.S.	Per Establ.	Total Number	% of U.S.	Per Establ.	Wages ($/hour)		
California	122	4,031.4	19.7	33.0	16,900	18.6	139	12.80	34.0	8,976
Massachusetts	28	2,531.1	12.3	90.4	10,700	11.8	382	18.85	39.0	9,411
Texas	43	1,841.3	9.0	42.8	8,100	8.9	188	14.65	39.7	5,815
Florida	32	937.1	4.6	29.3	5,900	6.5	184	13.00	24.3	4,373
Illinois	37	863.2	4.2	23.3	6,500	7.1	176	16.84	26.2	-
New Jersey	26	567.5	2.8	21.8	3,000	3.3	115	20.93	54.2	1,733
Minnesota	16	442.2	2.2	27.6	2,400	2.6	150	9.88	29.4	5,750
Georgia	17	315.9	1.5	18.6	1,700	1.9	100	14.36	51.0	4,882
Alabama	13	282.1	1.4	21.7	2,000	2.2	154	9.63	35.7	7,600
Virginia	15	242.4	1.2	16.2	1,900	2.1	127	10.63	45.8	5,211

Source: 1992 Economic Census. The states are in descending order of shipments or establishments (if shipment data are missing for the majority). The symbol (D) appears when data are withheld to prevent disclosure of competitive information. States marked with (D) are sorted by number of establishments. A dash (-) indicates that the data element cannot be calculated; * indicates the midpoint of a range.

SIC 3661
Occupations Employed by SIC 366 - Communications Equipment

Occupation	% of Total 1994	Change to 2005
Electrical & electronic assemblers	9.3	-22.9
Electrical & electronics engineers	7.6	9.6
Electrical & electronic equipment assemblers	7.2	-14.3
Electrical & electronic technicians,technologists	5.0	-14.3
Inspectors, testers, & graders, precision	4.5	-40.0
Assemblers, fabricators, & hand workers nec	4.0	-14.3
Sales & related workers nec	3.0	-14.3
Blue collar worker supervisors	2.5	-25.1
Secretaries, ex legal & medical	2.4	-22.0
Computer engineers	2.4	26.9
Engineering technicians & technologists nec	2.1	-14.3
Engineering, mathematical, & science managers	2.1	-2.7
Management support workers nec	2.0	-14.3
Electromechanical equipment assemblers	1.7	-5.8
Engineers nec	1.6	28.5
General managers & top executives	1.6	-18.7
Managers & administrators nec	1.5	-14.4
Mechanical engineers	1.4	3.7
Production, planning, & expediting clerks	1.4	-14.3
Systems analysts	1.3	37.0
Traffic, shipping, & receiving clerks	1.3	-17.6
Stock clerks	1.3	-30.4
Plant & system operators nec	1.2	-24.3
Drafters	1.2	-33.3
General office clerks	1.2	-27.0
Industrial production managers	1.2	-14.4
Marketing, advertising, & PR managers	1.2	-14.4
Purchasing agents, ex trade & farm products	1.1	-14.3

Source: Industry-Occupation Matrix, Bureau of Labor Statistics. These data relate to one or more 3-digit SIC industry groups rather than to a single 4-digit SIC. The change reported for each occupation to the year 2005 is a percent of growth or decline as estimated by the Bureau of Labor Statistics. The abbreviation nec stands for 'not elsewhere classified'.

speed processors, more powerful and higher capacity networks, and more flexible software and management systems are redefining the way we utilize communication products at our work space. While voice, video, and data communications have each evolved independently, they were starting to come together into a "multimedia" environment to make future communications more efficient, effective, and user-friendly.

While the personal computer revolution has been thoroughly documented over the past decade, the familiar telephone instrument found virtually everywhere has undergone a transformation of its own. This piece of communications equipment has been dramatically rethought, redesigned, and reequipped to accomplish a new role in the communications revolution. The standard telephone is becoming a voice terminal in a market where voice, video, and data applications are being formed into integrated communication systems.

The 1990s saw the emergence of Integrated Service Digital Network, or ISDN, as a mode of interfacing in this new communications environment. This interface is an important step toward achieving universal compatibility among different manufacturers.

In addition to the deployment of ISDN technology, an entirely new level of integration between telephones and computing is being developed on hardware and software systems called application programming interfaces, or APIs. APIs will enable the user to integrate his personal computer and voice terminal into one instrument. The personal computer's processing and memory-storage capabilities offer the potential for a new dimension of multimedia communications capabilities at the desktop. As this technology evolves, the basic telephone will be transformed from a stand-alone voice terminal to a device that integrates voice, data, text, fax, and video services. Eventually, push-button dial pads and handsets will be replaced by voice-activated terminals with integrated speaker and microphone capabilities.

The revolution in communications technology occurring at the desktop has also been taking place in the switched networks. Electromechanical switching will all but disappear by the year 2000. Around the mid-1990s, the country reached the crossover point between analog and digital switching with more than half the lines in the United States being served by digital central offices. The local exchange companies or LECs are basing their networks on ISDN technology, which uses circuit switched technology and it was estimated that most PBX manufacturers will retain circuit switching as well. The technology with the most intriguing future is photonic switching, estimated to be 1,000 times faster than present switching products. As fiber-optic cable extends to the desktops with a photonic switch in the network, users can link high-bandwidth facilities around the world presenting businesses with a myriad of communication opportunities for the future.

AMERICA AND THE WORLD

Historically, the United States has been the leader in telecommunications equipment technology and innovation. This factor was due primarily to the monopoly that AT&T (the Bell System) had on the nations' telephone system for the first 100 years of its existence. The breakup of the Bell System in 1984 created a new playing field for telecommunication equipment manufacturers worldwide. Since telephone technology is not drastically different from computer technology, and in fact, many of the same components and techniques are used in both, the race to compete in this market became a global endeavor. This factor coupled with the regulatory barriers harnessing the former Bell Operating Companies resulted in the United States losing this 100 year advantage almost overnight.

Although the United States is no longer the dominant manufacturer in the telecommunications equipment market, it is currently reestablishing itself as an international force. Despite an enormous trade deficit with Japan and other Far Eastern suppliers, the United States is the largest manufacturer of foreign-produced equipment in Japan. From 1987 to 1990, the United States had a trade surplus with Europe exceeding $700 million.

ASSOCIATIONS AND SOCIETIES

ARMED FORCES COMMUNICATIONS AND ELECTRONICS ASSOCIATION
4400 Fair Lakes Ct.
Fairfax, VA 22033
Phone: (800) 336-4583 or (703) 631-6100
Fax: (703) 631-4693

NORTH AMERICAN TELECOMMUNICATIONS ASSOCIATION
2000 M St. NW, Ste. 550
Washington, DC 20036
Phone: (202) 296-9800
Fax: (202) 296-4993
Members are manufacturers and suppliers of interconnect telephone equipment.

TELE-COMMUNICATIONS ASSOCIATION
701 N. Haven Ave., Ste. 200
Ontario, CA 91724-4925
Phone: (909) 945-1122

TELECOMMUNICATIONS INDUSTRY ASSOCIATION
2001 Pennsylvania Ave. NW, Ste. 800
Washington, DC 20006-1813
Phone: (202) 457-4912
Fax: (202) 457-4939

UNITED STATES TELEPHONE ASSOCIATION
Equipment Compatibility Committee
900 N. 19th St. NW, Ste. 800
Washington, DC 20006
Phone: (202) 835-3100
Fax: (202) 835-3198

PERIODICALS AND NEWSLETTERS

CELLULAR BUSINESS: JOURNAL OF CELLULAR TELECOMMUNICATIONS
Intertec Publishing Corp.
9800 Metcalf Ave.
Overland Park, KS 66212-2215
Phone: (800) 654-6776 or (913) 341-1300
Fax: (913) 967-1898
Monthly. Free to qualified personnel; others, $24.00 per year.

COMMUNICATIONS ENGINEERING AND DESIGN
Capital Cities-ABC, Inc.
600 S. Cherry St., Ste. 400
Denver, CO 80222
Fax: (303) 393-6654
Monthly. $48.00 per year.

ELECTRONICS NOW: TECHNOLOGY, AUDIO, VIDEO, COMPUTERS, PROJECTS
Gernsback Publications
500 Bi-county Blvd.
Farmingdale, NY 11735
Phone: (516) 293-3000
Fax: (516) 293-3115
Monthly. $19.97 per year. Formerly Radio Electronics.

IEEE TRANSACTIONS ON COMMUNICATIONS
Institute of Electrical and Electronics Engineers, Inc.
345 E. 47th St.
New York, NY 10017-2394
Phone: (800) 678-4333 or (212) 705-7900
Fax: (212) 752-4929
Monthly. Free to members; non-members, $130.00 per year.

LAND MOBILE RADIO NEWS
Phillips Business Information, Inc.
1201 7 Locks Rd., Ste. 300
Potomac, MD 20854
Phone: (800) 777-5006 or (301) 340-2100
Fax: (301) 424-4297
Weekly. $597.00. Newsletter emphasizing the rules and regulations of the Federal Communications Commission (FCC), particularly as applied to mobile radio communication systems. Formerly Industrial Communications.

TELECOMMUNICATIONS REPORTS
Business Research Publications, Inc.
1333 H St. NW
Washington, DC 20005
Phone: (800) 622-7237 or (202) 842-3006
Fax: (202) 842-1875
Weekly. Institutions, $795.00 per year; non-profit institutions, $545.00 per year. Regulatory newsletter.

TELECONNECT
Telcom Library, Inc.
Gerald A. Friesen, Inc.
12 W. 21st St.,
New York, NY 10010
Phone: (212) 691-8215
Monthly. $15.00 per year.

TELECONS
Applied Business Telecommunications
PO Box 5106
San Ramon, CA 94583
Phone: (510) 606-5150
Fax: (510) 606-9410
Bimonthly. $30.00 per year. Topics include teleconferencing, videoconferencing, distance learning, telemedicine, and telecommuting.

TELEPHONE ENGINEER AND MANAGEMENT: A TELECOMMUNICATIONS MAGAZINE
Advanstar Communications, Inc.
7500 Old Oak Blvd.
Cleveland, OH 44130
Phone: (800) 346-0085 or (216) 243-8100
Fax: (216) 891-2726
Semimonthly. $30.00 per year.

TWICE: THIS WEEK IN CONSUMER ELECTRONICS
Cahners Publishing Co.
249 W 17th St.
New York, NY 10011
Phone: (800) 662-7776 or (212) 645-0067
Fax: (212) 337-7066
28 times a year. $85.00 per year. Free to qualified personnel. Contains marketing and manufacturing news relating to a wide variety of consumer electronic products, including video, audio, telephone, and home office equipment.

DATABASES

PREDICASTS FORECASTS: INTERNATIONAL
Information Access Co.
362 Lakeside Dr.
Foster City, CA 94404
Phone: (800) 321-6388 or (415) 378-5000
Fax: (415) 358-4759
Provides online short-range and long-range industry and product forecasts for all countries of the world except the U.S. Forecasts are abstracted from over 1,000 international sources. Time period is 1971 to date, with monthly updates. Inquire as to online cost and availability.

PROMT: PREDICASTS OVERVIEW OF MARKETS AND TECHNOLOGY
Information Access Co.
362 Lakeside Dr.
Foster City, CA 94404
Phone: (800) 321-6388 or (415) 378-5000
Fax: (415) 358-4759
Companies, products, applied technologies and markets. U.S. and international literature coverage, 1972 to date. Daily updates. Inquire as to online cost and availability. Provides abstracts from more than 1,200 publications.

SCISEARCH
Institute for Scientific Information
3501 Market St.
Philadelphia, PA 19104
Phone: (800) 523-1850 or (215) 386-0100
Fax: (215) 386-2911
Broad, multidisciplinary index to the literature of science and technology, 1974 to present. Inquire as to online cost and availability. Coverage of literature is worldwide, with weekly updates.

STATISTICS SOURCES

ANNUAL SURVEY OF MANUFACTURES
Bureau of the Census, U.S. Department of Commerce
Available from U.S. Government Printing Office
Washington, DC 20402
Phone: (202) 512-1800
Fax: (202) 512-2250

COMMUNICATION EQUIPMENT, AND OTHER ELECTRONIC SYSTEMS AND EQUIPMENT
U.S. Bureau of the Census
Washington, DC 20233-0800
Phone: (301) 457-4100
Fax: (301) 457-3842
Annual. Provides data on shipments: value, quantity, imports, and exports. (Current Industrial Reports, MA-36P.)

ELECTRONIC MARKET DATA BOOK
Electronic Industries Association
2001 Pennsylvania Ave. NW
Washington, DC 20006-1813
Phone: (202) 457-4950
Fax: (202) 457-8779
Annual. Members, $75.00; non-member, $125.00.

RESEARCH AND DEVELOPMENT IN INDUSTRY
National Science Foundation
4201 Wilson Blvd.
Arlington, VA 22203
Phone: (703) 306-1234
Annual.

STANDARD & POOR'S INDUSTRY SURVEYS
Standard & Poor's Corp.
25 Broadway
New York, NY 10004
Phone: (800) 221-5277 or (212) 208-8000
Fax: (212) 412-0040
Weekly. $1,545.00 per year. Looseleaf service. Quarterly bound volumes, $875.00 per year. Discusses industry prospects and provides statistical tables.

GENERAL WORKS

ANALOG AND DIGITAL COMMUNICATION SYSTEMS
Martin S. Rodin
Prentice Hall
Rte. 9W
Englewood Cliffs, NJ 07632
Phone: (800) 922-0579 or (201) 592-2000
Fax: (201) 592-0696
1995. $75.00. Fourth edition.

COMMUNICATIONS OUTLOOK
Organization for Economic Cooperation and Development
OECD Publications and Information Center
2001 L St., Ste. 700
Washington, DC 20036
Phone: (202) 785-6323
Fax: (202) 785-0350

Annual. $32.00. Provides international coverage of yearly tele-communications activity. Includes charts, graphs, and maps.

CORPORATE INTERNET PLANNING GUIDE: ALIGNING INTERNET STRATEGY WITH BUSINESS GOALS

Richard J. Gascoyne and Koray Ozcubucku
Van Nostrand Reinhold
115 5th Ave.
New York, NY 10003
Phone: (800) 842-3636 or (212) 254-3232
Fax: (212) 254-9499
1997. $29.95. Provides administrative advice on planning, developing, and managing corporate Internet or intranet functions. Emphasis is on strategic planning.

TELEPHONE INDUSTRY DIRECTORY AND SOURCEBOOK

Phillips Publishing, Inc.
7811 Montrose Rd.
Potomac, MD 20854
Phone: (800) 722-9000 or (301) 340-2100
Fax: (301) 424-4297
Annual. $157.00. Lists telecommunications carriers, equipment manufacturers, distributors, agencies, and organizations.

FURTHER READING

Labate, John. ''Companies to Watch.'' *Fortune,* 21 March 1994.

''U.S. Call Processing Markets to Triple and Top $8 Billion.'' *Telephone IP News,* March 1994.

TOBACCO PRODUCTS

SIC 2100

In spite of several high-profile legal and government clashes in recent years, the tobacco industry continues to collect enormous profits from the sale of cigarettes. The industry has demonstrated a high degree of resilience in the face of increased awareness of the health risks involved in smoking, lawsuits holding tobacco manufacturers libel for smoking related illnesses, a decline in domestic tobacco usage, and higher federal taxes. The industry has maintained large profits in part by acquiring foreign processing plants and claiming a large segment of the lucrative international tobacco market. It has also capitalized on the cigar smoking trend of the mid-1990s.

The tobacco industry is one of the most powerful and controversial markets in the United States. In the early 1990s, the leading tobacco companies consistently posted total sales of more than $80 billion per year. Nevertheless, the industry has been besieged for years by smoking opponents who have drawn attention to the severe health risks associated with tobacco use. Critics have also accused tobacco producers of advertising to children in an effort to create a new generation of smokers; the "Joe Camel" advertising campaign—which features an eye-catching cartoon character who glamorizes smoking—was the center of intense debate for several years. These kinds of assaults led to a long-time slide in domestic tobacco consumption over the past three decades; the trend gradually stabilized in the mid-1990s, with the percentage of smokers in the American population holding at about 26 percent. Intense legal and legislative pressure in the late-1990s have continued to take toll on the overall sales and public image of the tobacco industry. Despite these problems, the tobacco industry has reaped huge profits from fiercely loyal domestic smokers and from vast foreign markets.

LARGEST CORPORATIONS IN THE TOBACCO INDUSTRY

Ranked by: Revenue in 1995, in millions of dollars.

1. Philip Morris Cos. Inc., with $53,139 million
2. American Brands, $5,905
3. Universal, $3,281
4. DiMon, $1,928
5. UST Inc., $1,300
6. Standard Commercial, $1,214

Source: *Fortune,* Fortune 500 Largest U.S. Corporations (annual), April 29, 1996, p. F-62.

INDUSTRY OUTLOOK

The tobacco industry faced many challenges in the 1980s and 1990s as the public became more concerned about tobacco-related health issues. The mid-1990s saw a flurry of legal activity as states sued companies to compensate state healthcare providers for the cost of treating tobacco related illnesses. In addition to the suits for smoking tobacco, smokeless tobacco producers were sued for injuries that plaintiffs claimed were caused by chewing tobacco. In 1996, President Clinton announced sweeping regulatory measures, which included the designation of the nicotine in tobacco as a drug, more stringent control of advertising, and efforts to keep tobacco away from minors. In 1997, state attorney generals and tobacco companies were working toward out-of-court settlements of anti-tobacco lawsuits in exchange for long-term regulation at the state and federal levels.

Perhaps a more disheartening development for tobacco companies in the early 1990s was their diminishing influence over federal lawmakers. In the past, through the combined efforts of the tobacco lobby and elected representatives from tobacco-growing states in the Southeast, manufacturers had been able to slow the rate of federally imposed cigarette taxes and mitigate—to a certain extent—federal legislation aimed at curbing cigarette use. But in the early 1990s, cigarette makers were assailed on several fronts with renewed energy. As *Business Week* noted, ''smokers are confronting an unprecedented rush to tax their cigs. Tobacco levies passed during the 1993 legislative sessions will provide 15 percent of new state tax revenue in fiscal 1994—even though cigarette taxes are less than two percent of state tax collections nationwide, according to the National Conference of State Legislatures. Several states, including Washington and New York, levy a tax above 50 cents a pack. Michigan voters recently approved raising the state's tax to 75 cents a pack to finance public education.''

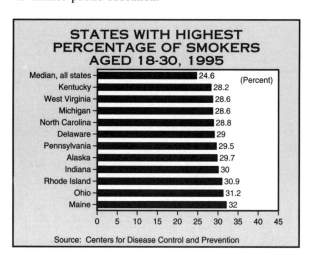

STATES WITH HIGHEST PERCENTAGE OF SMOKERS AGED 18-30, 1995

State	Percent
Median, all states	24.6
Kentucky	28.2
West Virginia	28.6
Michigan	28.6
North Carolina	28.8
Delaware	29
Pennsylvania	29.5
Alaska	29.7
Indiana	30
Rhode Island	30.9
Ohio	31.2
Maine	32

Source: Centers for Disease Control and Prevention

Over the long term, downward pressure on cigarette sales in the United States is likely to continue. In addition to taxes and regulatory restrictions, the increasing number of restrictions on where people can smoke, heightened awareness of the dangers of smoking, and the growing social stigma attached to the habit, are all expected to erode the market base for cigarettes. Faced with these formidable challenges, tobacco companies quickly sought to ameliorate their position, as they had frequently done in the past. The industry increasingly looked toward foreign markets to sell their traditional, higher-priced line of cigarettes. Toward this end, U.S. manufacturers were recording considerable success, tapping into a market in which sales tripled between 1985 and 1993.

Despite the fact that domestic consumption of tobacco products continued to trend downward in the 1990s, the major producers remained relatively unscathed. One reason for this success was due to the fact that manufacturers imported more inexpensive foreign tobacco to increase or maintain profit margins on cheaper cigarettes. Between 1989 and 1992, U.S. tobacco imports—the bulk of which were from Brazil, Zimbabwe, Argentina, Thailand, and Malawi—had more than doubled, while domestic output had risen only 26 percent.

Moreover, primarily because of increased smoking in Asia, worldwide tobacco consumption had jumped 75 percent in the 1970s and 1980s and was continuing to trend upward at 1 to 2 percent a year. Demand for so-called American-blend cigarettes, which tasted milder compared with the stronger and harsher cigarettes smoked in most of the rest of the world, was increasing—even in countries where overall demand was flat or down. Overseas demand for milder cigarettes, coupled with reduced trade barriers in important markets like Japan, helped U.S. cigarette exports to surge to 260 billion cigarettes in 1995, versus 100 billion in 1987 and 59 billion in 1985. Furthermore, with the implementation of the General Agreement on Tariffs and Trade (GATT) treaty in the mid-1990s, the tobacco industry was faced with less stringent import quotas. As a result, U.S. cigarette manufacturers began to buy more tobacco from outside the United States, and the overall tenor of the market brightened. U.S. imports of unmanufactured tobacco increased 20 percent between 1994 and 1996.

Despite their profitability in the foreign market, tobacco companies were concerned about the increasingly strong steps being taken to limit tobacco use. Dozens of localities around the country had passed measures that curtailed smoking in offices, restaurants, and other public places, and nationwide restrictions were being suggested by some in Congress. Studies that determined second hand cigarette smoke could cause lung cancer were gaining credence. States were suing the cigarette manufacturers to pick up their healthcare costs and were gaining significant court victories. In March 1997, bipartisan legislation was unveiled that would hike federal cigarette taxes 43 cents per pack to fund health insurance costs for children and to reduce the deficit.

RESURGENCE OF CIGARS

The cigar industry has experienced a boom in recent years thanks to increasing acceptance of cigar smoking among younger generations of the population, a resurgence in "cigar evenings," and the popularity of the Internet where cigars are being sold in record numbers. The magazine *Cigar Aficiando,* introduced in 1992, is generally credited with the upturn in the cigar industry. No longer a passion for older men alone, changing demographics find "twenty-something" men and women participating in cigar evenings and joining the 35-65 year old traditionalists in the purchase of premium cigars. Celebrities have also helped to add to the allure, adorning the cover of *Cigar Aficiando* and showing up frequently at soirees boasting "stogies."

Like other tobacco products, the sale of cigars had dropped off as Americans became increasingly concerned about the effects of tobacco smoking on health and fitness. In the mid-1970s, volume was more than 5.5 billion, and at the industry's peak in 1964, unit sales reached 9 billion cigars. The volume of cigar sales fell about five percent a year during a 15-year period, dropping to 2.2 billion units sold in 1991. Declines in volume have been offset by increases in prices and a growing market for premium cigars. Sales in dollars have risen to about $700 million in the early 1990s. In 1995 imports of premium cigars rose to 176.3 million units, an increase from 1994's level of 132.4 million. In 1996 imports increased to 294 million.

WORK FORCE

In 1995, the employment level of the tobacco industry stood at about 31,000, down more than 12,000 people from the previous decade. Throughout its history, the bulk of the industry's work force has been comprised of production workers, or those employees paid on an hourly basis to operate manufacturing machinery and to perform manual tasks in the production of cigarettes. Of the 31,000 total employees, 26,000 were employed as production workers. These workers, generally employed on a full-time basis, but averaging 11 percent fewer hours than production workers employed by all other manufacturing industries, earned $20.68 per hour, up from $9.23 per hour in 1980. Salaried employees, or those workers paid an annual salary for performing administrative, technical, or managerial duties, composed the balance of the industry's work force, earning an average of $47,915 per year.

SIC 2111
Occupations Employed by SIC 211 - Tobacco Products

Occupation	% of Total 1994	Change to 2005
Machine operators nec	12.3	-43.9
Helpers, laborers, & material movers nec	11.3	-36.3
Packaging & filling machine operators	7.3	-36.3
Industrial machinery mechanics	7.0	-29.9
Blue collar worker supervisors	5.5	-39.0
Sales & related workers nec	4.6	-36.3
Industrial truck & tractor operators	3.4	-36.3
Management support workers nec	3.4	-36.3
Machine feeders & offbearers	3.3	-42.6
Inspectors, testers, & graders, precision	2.5	-36.3
Freight, stock, & material movers, hand	2.3	-49.0
Precision food & tobacco workers nec	2.1	-30.0
Secretaries, ex legal & medical	2.0	-42.0
Science & mathematics technicians	1.4	-36.3
Maintenance repairers, general utility	1.3	-42.7
General managers & top executives	1.3	-39.5
Systems analysts	1.3	1.9
Industrial production managers	1.1	-36.2
Cooking, roasting machine operators	1.0	-29.9

Source: Industry-Occupation Matrix, Bureau of Labor Statistics. These data relate to one or more 3-digit SIC industry groups rather than to a single 4-digit SIC. The change reported for each occupation to the year 2005 is a percent of growth or decline as estimated by the Bureau of Labor Statistics. The abbreviation nec stands for 'not elsewhere classified'.

The average size of a cigarette manufacturing establishment, in terms of the number of employees per facility,

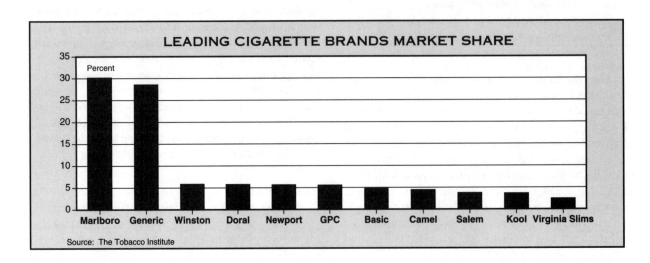

LEADING CIGARETTE BRANDS MARKET SHARE

Source: The Tobacco Institute

was enormous when compared to the average size of manufacturing establishments in all other manufacturing industries. In the early 1990s, the typical manufacturing establishment comprised 54 employees, 37 of whom were employed as production workers, while the cigarette industry averaged 2,277 employees per establishment, more than 42 times the size of all other manufacturing industries.

AMERICA AND THE WORLD

As legislation and taxation affecting the cigarette industry in the United States has become more commonplace, leading companies have increasingly turned to global opportunities. As *Newsweek* pointed out in 1994, "sixty percent of Philip Morris's sales already come from outside the United States; in the next decade it hopes to push its overseas profits closer to that 60 percent mark." By 1995, the company's overseas sales accounted for more than seventy percent of total sales, with overseas shipments accounting for 593 million units, compared to 222 million in the United States. This move to international markets is expected to be an expensive one; although American cigarette exports are growing 6 to 8 percent annually, tobacco companies recognize that establishing facilities in targeted countries is a priority. Plant construction or acquisition is expected to impact industry players for the next several years as a result.

Addressing the issue of foreign construction, *Forbes* pointed out in 1994 that "the tobacco companies have been buying every major Russian and Eastern European tobacco plant in sight. During 1995, Philip Morris modernized and expanded a manufacturing plant in the Czech Republic, began construction of a new plant in Lithuania, and undertook plant renovations in Russia and the Ukraine. The company also announced plans to increase capacity in Holland, upgrade its tobacco processing facility in Switzerland, and build a new factory in Kazakhstan. In 1996, Philip Morris acquired a 33 percent share of Poland's largest tobacco company, completed construction of a leaf-processing facility in Malaysia, and concluded an agreement under which a third party would contract-manufacture Marlboro cigarettes in China for the Chinese market. RJR has invested in plants in Hungary, Poland, Ukraine, and Russia, as well as manufacturing its brands through licensing agreements in about 20 other countries . . . In two to five years, company executives say, these new and recently acquired plants could gross up to $1 billion in sales for Philip Morris and $500 million for RJR. Both companies claim their Russian operations are already profitable." Smoking is on the rise in heavily-populated regions of the world such as Asia as well,

Cigarette Producers

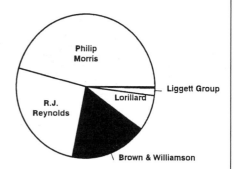

Shares are for 1995. Philip Morris produces Benson & Hedges and Marlboro; R.J. Reynolds produces Camel, Salem, and Winston; Brown & Williamson produces Kool and Raleigh; Lorillard produces Newport and True; Liggett Group produces Chesterfield and Eve.

Philip Morris	46.1%
R.J. Reynolds	25.7
Brown & Williamson	18.0
Lorillard	8.0
Liggett Group	2.2

Source: *U.S. News & World Report*, March 25, 1996, p. 17, from Maxwell Consumer Reports.

and "American companies must sell cheaper, less profitable smokes in the Third World, but margins will improve as those economies develop and prices rise."

Both in terms of supply and demand, the U.S. tobacco processing industry was increasingly looking abroad in the 1990s. The elimination of trade barriers and the rising popularity of lighter, American-blend cigarettes were expanding overseas markets. Following the fall of the Berlin Wall in 1989, new markets for U.S. exports sprung up in the former Soviet republics and in Eastern Europe. As international suppliers of tobacco, the processors were also selling tobacco grown overseas for cigarette manufacture in non-U.S. factories.

ASSOCIATIONS AND SOCIETIES

COUNCIL FOR TOBACCO RESEARCH - U.S.A.
900 3rd Ave.
New York, NY 10022
Phone: (212) 421-8885

NATIONAL ASSOCIATION OF TOBACCO DISTRIBUTORS

1199 N. Fairfax St., Ste. 701
Alexandria, VA 22314
Phone: (800) 642-6283 or (703) 683-8336
Fax: (703) 683-5987

RETAIL TOBACCO DEALERS OF AMERICA

107 E. Baltimore St.
Baltimore, MD 21202
Phone: (301) 547-6996
Fax: (301) 727-7533

TOBACCO ASSOCIATES

1725 K St. NW, Ste 512
Washington, DC 20006
Phone: (202) 828-9144

TOBACCO ASSOCIATION OF U.S.

3716 National Dr., Ste. 114
Raleigh, NC 27612
Phone: (919) 782-5151

TOBACCO INSTITUTE

1875 Eye St. NW, Ste. 800
Washington, DC 20006
Phone: (800) 424-9876 or (202) 457-4800
Fax: (202) 457-9350

TOBACCO MERCHANTS ASSOCIATION OF UNITED STATES

231 Clarksville Rd.
Princeton, NJ 08543
Phone: (609) 275-4900
Fax: (609) 275-8379

PERIODICALS AND NEWSLETTERS

BUREAU OF ALCOHOL, TOBACCO, AND FIREARMS QUARTERLY BULLETIN

Bureau of Alcohol, Tobacco, and Firearms
U.S. Department of the Treasury
Available from U.S. Government Printing Office
Washington, DC 20402
Phone: (202) 783-3238
Quarterly. $19.00 per year. Laws and regulations.

SMOKESHOP

BMT Publications, Inc.
7 Penn Plz.
New York, NY 10001
Phone: (800) 223-9638 or (212) 594-4120
Fax: (212) 714-0514
Monthly. $24.00 per year.

TOBACCO BAROMETER

Tobacco Merchants Association of the United States
PO Box 8019
Princeton, NJ 08543
Phone: (609) 275-4900
Monthly. Free. Guide to manufactured production, taxable re-movals, and tax-exempt removals for cigarettes, large cigars, chewing tobacco, snuff, and pipe tobacco.

SIC 2111
Occupations Employed by SIC 211 – Tobacco Products

Occupation	% of Total 1994	Change to 2005
Machine operators nec	12.3	-43.9
Helpers, laborers, & material movers nec	11.3	-36.3
Packaging & filling machine operators	7.3	-36.6
Industrial machinery mechanics	7.0	-29.9
Blue collar worker supervisors	5.5	-39.0
Sales & related workers nec	4.6	-36.6
Industrial truck & tractor operators	3.4	-36.3
Management support workers	3.4	-36.6
Machine feeders & offbearers	3.3	-42.6
Inspectors, testers, & graders	2.5	-36.3
Freight, stock, & material movers	2.3	-49.0
Secretaries, ex legal & medical	2.1	-30.0
Precision food/tobacco workers nec	2.0	-42.0
Science & mathematics technicians	1.4	-63.3
Maintenance repairers, general utility	1.3	-42.7
General managers & top executives	1.3	-39.5
Systems analysts	1.3	1.9
Industrial production managers	1.1	-36.2
Cooking & roasting machine operators	1.0	-29.9

Source: *Industry-Occupation Matrix*, Bureau of Labor Statistics. These data relate to one or more 3-digit SIC industry groups rather than to a single 4-digit SIC. The change reported for each occupation to the year 2005 is a percent of growth or decline as estimated by the Bureau of Labor Statistics. The abbreviation nec stands for 'not elsewhere classified'.

UNITED STATES DISTRIBUTION JOURNAL: THE NEWS PUBLICATION OF TOBACCO, CONFECTIONERY, GROCERY DISTRIBUTION

BMT Publications Inc. 7 Penn Plz.
New York, NY 10001
Phone: (212) 594-4120
Fax: (212) 714-0514
Monthly. $24.00 per year. Formerly United States Tobacco Journal.

STATISTICS SOURCES

MONTHLY STATISTICAL RELEASE: CIGARETTES AND CIGARS

Bureau of Alcohol, Tobacco, and Firearms
U.S. Treasury Dept.
1200 Pennsylvania Ave. NW
Washington, DC 20226
Phone: (202) 566-2000
Monthly.

TOBACCO SITUATION AND OUTLOOK

Available from U.S. Government Printing Office
Washington, DC 20402
Phone: (202) 783-3238
Fax: (202) 512-2233
Quarterly. $9.50 per year. Issued by the Economic Research Service of the U.S. Department of Agriculture. Provides current statistical information of supply, demand, and prices.

TOBACCO STOCKS REPORT
U.S. Dept. of Agriculture Marketing Service
14th St. and Independence Ave. SW
Washington, DC 20250
Phone: (202) 447-8999
Quarterly.

GENERAL WORKS

TOBACCO RETAILERS ALMANAC
Retail Tobacco Dealers of America
107 E. Baltimore St.
Baltimore, MD 21202
Phone: (301) 547-6996
Annual.

TOBACCO SCIENCE YEARBOOK
Lockwood Trade Journal Co., Inc.
130 W. 42nd St., 22nd Fl.
New York, NY 10036
Phone: (212) 391-2060
Annual. $20.00.

UNITED STATES DISTRIBUTION JOURNAL SUPPLIER DIRECTORY
BMT Publications Inc.
7 Penn Plz.
New York, NY 10001
Phone: (212) 594-4120
Fax: (212) 714-0514

Annual $10.00. Formerly United States Tobacco Journal Supplier Directory.

FURTHER READING

"Alcoholic Beverages and Tobacco." *Standard and Poor's Industry Surveys.* New York: McGraw Hill, January 1997.

American Cancer Society. *Cancer Facts & Figures—1997.* Available from http://www.cancer.org/97tobacc.html.

Edelman, Vladimir. "Blowing Smoke: The Cigar Renaissance." *Inc. Online,* 1 July 1996.

Flanagan, William G. "Cigar Madness." *Forbes,* 21 April 1997.

Forbes Annual Report on American Industry, 13 January 1997. Available from http://www.forbes.com/forbes/97/0113/5901160a.htm.

Greising, David and Catherine Yang. "Peace Talks in the Tobacco Wars?" *Business Week,* 10 February 1997, 88.

Lucke, James. "Kentucky Farmers Fear Tobacco Shortage May Harm State in World Markets." *Knight-Ridder/Tribune Business News,* 15 July 1996.

Simon, Howard. "US Tobacco Lights up Overseas," *Journal of Commerce,* 27 August 1996.

Walmac, Amanda. "Empty the Ashtray: Time is Running Out on Tobacco Stocks." *Money,* November. 1996.

TRAVEL AND TOURISM

SICs 4724, 4725

The travel industry represents a tremendously lucrative market with an estimated total value of up to $2 trillion, according to the World Tourist Organization. It is from this enormous market that U.S. travel agencies and tour operators earn their sizable revenues. Motivated by the closure in 1996 of the government sponsored U.S. Travel and Tourism Agency, private industry has filled the gap by funding the fledgling National Tourism Organization, whose avowed goal is to put the United States back on top of the international tourism market. The adoption of industry-wide computer automation and the broadening availability of ticket services via the Internet will continue to have a significant impact on the way travel agents and tour operators conduct their business throughout the end of the decade.

As retail outlets for the travel and tourism industry, travel agencies have benefitted from the explosive world-wide growth of this industry during the late twentieth century. While travel and tourism may not account for as high a percentage of the diversified U.S. economy as it does of other nation's economies, it is estimated that over $300 billion is spent on travel and tourism annually in the United States, with almost 30 percent (approximately $86 billion) passing through the over 30,000 travel agency locations across the country. According to a survey by *Lodging Hospitality,* four out of ten travelers now use travel agents to make their reservations. The type and purpose of travel, on the other hand, has shown a marked change over the years and has altered the entire structure of the travel agency industry in the United States. Business travel, which expanded enormously through the 1980s, has narrowly surpassed personal and pleasure travel in total annual sales. The tour operator—as distinct from the travel agency and generally considered a "wholesaler" of sorts—has traditionally attracted travelers who are looking for economy and the relative ease of travel afforded by being part of an organized group.

Top 10 TRAVEL AGENCIES WITH THE MOST AIR SALES

Ranked by: Air sales in 1995, in thousands of dollars.

1. American Express, with $7,300,000 thousand
2. Carlson Wagonlit, $2,426,947
3. Rosenbluth International, $1,800,000
4. BTI Americas, $1,634,933
5. Sato Travel, $1,107,141
6. Maritz Travel, $1,001,000
7. World Travel Partners, $505,000
8. Omega World Travel, $413,000
9. Travel & Transport, $381,000
10. Travel One, $355,000

Source: *Business Travel News,* Business Travel Survey (annual), May 27, 1996, p. 4.

U.S. transactions for non-domestic travel rose from $58.4 billion in 1994 to $61.1 billion in 1995. In 1994, 24 percent of business travelers and 8 percent of pleasure travelers used a travel agent for trips more than 100 miles away from home. Business use dropped one percent from the previous year. An estimated $55.6 billion was paid by U.S. travelers for passenger fares in 1994. In

1995, passenger fares were projected at $57.9 billion. In 1994, 47.4 million U.S. travelers went to foreign countries, while 42.9 million foreigners visited the United States. Foreign visitors to the U.S. declined from a peak in 1992 and U.S. visiting abroad continued to increase. Travel receipts from foreign visitors exceeded travel expenditures of U.S. travelers abroad for the same period. Travel to the United States is expected to grow 3 percent to 4 percent annually over the next few years. The increase will come largely from Asia and South America.

A record-breaking 48 million international arrivals have been predicted for 1998, and by 1999 nearly 50 million international arrivals are anticipated; this could cause total travel receipts to surpass the $100 billion mark. Foreign visitors generated more than $400 billion in business for the United States, making the tourism industry the nation's second largest employer. With a $20 billion trade surplus, it is considered the country's third largest exporting sector.

Travel is currently the second largest business in America, and by the year 2000, according to the American Society of Travel Agents, travel and tourism will be the number one industry in the United States. At present, 6.7 percent of the Gross National Product (GNP) is generated by travel, and a total of 6.3 million people are employed by the U.S. tourism industry. Tourism produced more jobs than any other industry except health and business. ASTA further states that 75 percent of all airline tickets and 95 percent of all cruise sales are sold through travel agents, with a total of $50 billion in national and international tickets sold through travel agents in 1996.

TRAVEL AGENCIES

There is a marked consistency in terms of products offered by travel agencies, a result of the industry's dependence on air travel. Airline tickets make up nearly 60 percent of a travel agency's business on average, more than all other "travel products" combined. Their attachment to the airline industry poses problems for some travel agencies, and so there has been an effort within the industry to decrease their dependence on airline ticket sales. With air travel continuing to increase, however, this dependency may be unavoidable. The remainder of a travel agency's business comes from cruise bookings (which make up 16 percent of total industry sales), hotel bookings (12 percent), car rentals (8 percent), and rail travel and other bookings (4 percent).

TOUR OPERATORS

According to the National Tour Association, the 2,678 tour operators in the United States and Canada

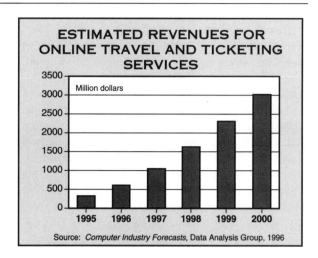

ESTIMATED REVENUES FOR ONLINE TRAVEL AND TICKETING SERVICES

Million dollars

Source: *Computer Industry Forecasts*, Data Analysis Group, 1996

supported almost 250,000 full-time equivalent employees in 1996. The total economic impact of the tour group industry in that same year was $11.6 billion, an 11.8 percent increase over 1995. Tour travelers accounted for $4.5 billion of the $11.6 billion. The amount of money spent by tour operators according to carrier was as follows: $215 million by air, $13 million by rail, and $221 million by cruise ships. The United States Tour Operators Association estimated the 1996 total impact of the broader U.S. tour operator industry much higher at $20 billion.

ORGANIZATION AND STRUCTURE

The travel agency industry is in a relatively constant state of transformation and growth. While no longer expanding at the explosive rate (almost 20 percent annually) of the early 1980s, the industry continues to grow in terms of total locations by nearly 6 percent every year.

REGIONAL DISTRIBUTION

Travel agencies can be found in virtually every community in the United States. The greatest share of travel agency locations has traditionally been in the eastern United States (30 percent), with the western United States close behind (28 percent); the South has 22 percent of the share, and the Midwest has 19 percent. Central city locations account for over 50 percent of the total, and the uneven growth of the 1980s—with the suburbs and small towns gaining disproportionate numbers of locations—has not only subsided but reversed itself. The share of rural and town locations has dropped quite significantly to 9 percent from nearly 12 percent in the late 1980s. With the emergence of Satellite Ticket Printers (STPs), automated ticket distribution machines have begun to replace branch offices altogether, a trend which may well continue.

CONSOLIDATION

The high level of consolidation activity in the travel agency industry is best assessed through the steep upturn in acquisitions. Almost a third of all agencies have acquired another agency already, and there are no signs of the buying spree slackening. When, in 1991, American Express Company purchased Lifeco of Houston, a firm whose airline ticket sales exceeded $1 billion annually, it provided a new scale for the already highly charged marketplace environment. This is not simply a case of the big feeding on the small; just as often the reverse applies. That is, many smaller agencies feel that they have much more to gain—in terms of access to the latest technological innovations, name credibility, and overall support—than they have to lose in giving up their autonomy; and, for this reason, they pursue buyers. Typically, the cost of purchasing an agency location is set at between 3 percent and 7 percent of its latest annual sales.

SMALLER AGENCIES

As much an impact as the industry's consolidation has had on its structure, it remains first and foremost an industry of small businesses. Even in the face of intensifying competition, single-location agencies still make up the vast majority of agency locations. In addition, they have successfully developed alternative business strategies to help them stay afloat. One common tactic is to seek out corporate clients. Eighty-nine percent of all agencies handle at least one corporate account. While only large agencies can manage the travel accounts of most medium-sized and large corporations, these accounts make up about 28 percent of all the corporations that use travel agencies. The rest (those with less than 100 employees) comprise a huge market for smaller agency services. The average number of corporate accounts an agency manages has dropped to 38 from a high of 43 in 1989, proof that small agencies have made inroads into the realm of business travel.

CONSORTIUMS

Membership in travel consortiums is seen as a way of benefitting from consolidation without ceding direct control of the business. Close to half of all U.S. travel agencies have become affiliated with a consortium of some sort. There are few signs of this trend slowing since business travel consortiums have begun to catch up to leisure travel consortiums in membership numbers. Through consortium membership, an agency develops close working relationships with other member-agencies. An increased purchasing power results in significantly higher override commissions from preferred suppliers, and in cheaper access to expensive services which foster office efficiency. These immediate paybacks,

however, are not the only focus. Many agencies feel consortiums, through annual meetings and newsletters, ensure that they remain up-to-date on broad developments in the industry. Consortiums also give travel agents a unified voice that increases their ability to influence supplier developments that affect them.

Largest U.S. Travel Agencies - 1995

Firms are ranked by gross sales in millions of dollars.

American Express	$ 8,700.0
Carlson Wagonlit Travel	4,500.0
RTI Americas	3,500.0
Rosenbluth International	2,500.0
Maritz Travel Co.	1,400.0
Liberty Travel	1,236.0
Sato Travel	942.2
Japan Travel Bureau Intl.	796.0
WorldTravel Partners	530.0
Travel One	435.0
Omega World Travel	428.0
Travel and Transport	424.0
Total Travel Management	398.0
VTS Travel Enterprises	375.2
Northwesterb Business Travel	347.2

Source: *Travel Weekly*, June 27, 1996, p. 14.

TRADE ASSOCIATIONS

Trade associations function as a coordinating mechanism that serve to integrate the industry. There are several large trade associations which act to influence government policy decisions on behalf of the travel complex as a whole; these associations also provide educational services for their members and promote the benefits of using travel agents. The largest of these trade associations, the American Society of Travel Agents (ASTA), is made up of American travel agents (comprising 50 percent of its membership), hotel operators, travel schools, cruise lines, and other travel industry members. Seventy to 75 percent of this not-for-profit organization's funding comes from its 27,000 member dues, the rest from an annual conference. Its total budget is $11 million. The second largest trade association, the Association of Retail Travel Agents (ARTA), has a much smaller membership of 3,000 travel agents, and a more specific agenda of promoting their interests.

While they provide services for travel agents, such associations are also important in legitimizing the trade

---

itself. Because only one state, Rhode Island, forces its travel agents to be licensed, an ASTA or ARTA membership offers assurance to both suppliers and consumers that an agent has some qualification beyond the easily obtainable agency accreditation, which is granted by the Airlines Reporting Corp. (ARC). In what has become a very technical field, there has been an increasing need for further standards of expertise, and educational bodies like the Institute of Certified Travel Agents (ICTA) have begun to serve a crucial role. The ICTA, a 16,000- member association that seeks to improve the level of competence within the industry, offers a course through which agents can become Certified Travel Counselors (CTC), a title which already carries significant weight within the industry. Another certification which has come into demand with the growth of corporate travel is the Certified Meeting Professional (CMP), which allows an individual to oversee every aspect of a business meeting.

The International Travel Agency Network, the other agency appointing body, is needed only if the suppliers do not do business with ARC, as is the case with several countries in Africa. Other important travel related associations include the Travel and Tourism Research Association and the Alliance of Independent Travel Agents.

SUPPLIER RELATIONSHIPS

Travel agencies rely entirely on commissions from their suppliers. Commissions, as a rule, are set at 10 percent of a booking, but slightly different arrangements can be made with each supplier. Airlines are the only suppliers who give significant commission overrides (marginally higher commissions) to agencies with which they have a preferred supplier relationship, whether negotiated through a consortium or through the agency itself.

The cruise line industry has undergone dramatic consolidation. Many companies have begun to formalize their communications systems. While most cruise line bookings are still made by phone, fax programs, which have been adopted by many companies, offer immediate confirmation of a reservation. What often slows the reservation process, however, are package deals for which an agent is often forced to wait for seating confirmations. Because of the cost of cruises, average commissions are quite high.

WORK FORCE

According to the *U.S. Occupational Outlook Handbook,* there were 122,000 travel agents in 1994, about 10 percent of which were self- employed. The American Society of Travel Agents (ASTA) and the Institute of Certified Travel Agents (ICTA) both offer self and group study courses. There are no federal licensing require-

ments, but nine states require some form of registration or certification. Employment of travel agents is expected to grow through 2005 primarily due to new agencies. The full impact of change in the industry has yet to be determined. The industry is sensitive to the economy, the perception of air safety, and political crises.

On average, travel agencies employ 6.5 employees in an office: one manager agent and 5.5 agents, the majority of whom are women. For those who are full-time employees receiving a straight salary (73 percent of all agents), the average incomes range from just over $12,000 for first-year agents to about $25,000 for agents with more than ten years of experience. Managers average $21,000 per year. A larger agency pays substantially more than a smaller one, with medians ranging from around $17,000 for inexperienced agents to approximately $32,000 for managers. Median salaries in 1994 were $21,300 with a range from $13,000 to $38,000 annually. ASTA noted that some suppliers pay a commission, usually 10 percent, but the majority of inside agents are salaried. Ranges given were $12,000 for entry level, $18,000 for agents with five years of experience, and about $23,000 for managers.

With greater economic pressures, though, agencies have been slowly turning away from straight salary compensation and moving toward compensation packages, which combine salary and commissions. Such plans are viewed as ways to ease the strain of flat revenues and rising salaries while bringing employee earnings in line with productivity. Agents paid in this manner (21 percent of all agents) tend to earn 6 to 11 percent more than their straight salary counterparts. Compensation packages have increased competition among agents, however, and concern for a friendly office environment has kept most agencies from resorting to paying commissions, which generally range from 25 to 30 percent of an agent's total earnings.

As agencies are revising their payment and benefit schemes, the actual work of an agent has become much more demanding over the years. Not only do agents have to learn complicated computer systems and cope with airline chaos, but they also must be a reliable source for travel guidance and advice. The growth in Certified Meeting Professionals and in-house agents in the corporate travel sector has been matched by the influence agents have on pleasure travelers. In fact, 51 percent of all leisure travelers seek travel agent counsel on their choice of destination.

RESEARCH AND TECHNOLOGY

A major development during the 1980s was the industry-wide adoption of automation. Virtually all agency locations in the United States became automated by the end of the decade, whereas only slightly more than half had been automated at the start of the decade. Cheaper, faster computer reservation systems like Sabre and Apollo (the two most widely used) have been vital in building and coordinating the vast and sophisticated complex of the 1990s.

Travel agencies have provided fertile ground for the application of cutting edge computer technology. Computer reservation systems (CRSs) are used by all but four percent of the industry. Of the five CRS vendors, Sabre has the largest market share of the industry at 35 percent; the other vendors include Apollo (23 percent), System One (20 percent), Pars (17 percent) and Data II (9 percent). Agents have become very comfortable in using their CRSs and have started to employ them in uses beyond airline bookings. More car rental companies and hotels can be accessed through CRSs than tour companies and cruises, and agents have responded by making the majority of both their car (68 percent) and hotel (53 percent) reservations by computer. The most important specialized software to appear in conjunction with CRSs is the fare-auditing scan that checks a system for better fares and/or routing. Such software has already given many large corporate agencies an invaluable marketing tool.

The emergence of Satellite Ticket Printer Networks (STPNs) and Electronic Ticket Delivery Networks (ETDNs) promises to have a major impact on travel agency ticket delivery. Starting in 1986, STPNs allowed agencies to set up ticket machines on client premises. The advent of third party ticketing networks, used by agencies who can't afford to establish networks themselves, has given agents the ability to issue tickets through their STPNs at a number of different locations. New networks are being developed which are essentially the same manner as STPNs but which are not agency-accredited by the Airlines Reporting Corp. (ARC). The ARC is expected to approve them, however, and many envision ticketing locations popping up in much the same as automated bank tellers machines. Without agency accreditation, though, ETDN vendors will neither sell tickets nor offer any kind of travel counseling.

ASSOCIATIONS AND SOCIETIES

AMERICAN SOCIETY OF TRAVEL AGENTS
1101 King St.
Alexandria, VA 22314
Phone: (703) 739-2782
Fax: (703) 684-8319

NATIONAL TOUR ASSOCIATION
546 E. Main St.
Lexington, KY 40596
Phone: (606) 226-4444
Fax: (606) 226-4404

TRAVEL AND TOURISM RESEARCH ASSOCIATION
10200 W. 44th Ave., Ste. 304
Wheat Ridger, CO 80033
Phone: (303) 940-6557
Fax: (303) 422-8894

TRAVEL INDUSTRY ASSOCIATION OF AMERICA
1100 New York Ave. NW, Ste. 450
Washington, DC 20005
Phone: (202) 408-8422
Fax: (202) 408-1255

PERIODICALS AND NEWSLETTERS

CONSUMER REPORTS TRAVEL LETTER
Consumers Union of the United States, Inc.
101 Truman Ave.
Yonkers, NY 10703-1057
Phone: (800) 221-7945 or (914) 378-2000
Fax: (914) 378-2903
Monthly. $37.00 per year. Newsletter with information on air fares, travel discounts, special hotel rates, etc.

TRAVEL HOLIDAY
Travel Publications, Inc.
28 W 23rd St.
New York, NY 10010
Phone: (800) 937-9241 or (212) 366-8700
Fax: (212) 366-8798
10 times a year. $12.97 per year.

TRAVEL PRINTOUT: RESEARCH NEWS FROM THE U.S.
TRAVEL DATA CENTER
U.S. Travel Data Center
1100 New York Ave. NW, Ste. 450-W
Washington, DC 20005-3934
Phone: (202) 408-1832
Fax: (202) 408-1255
Monthly. $75.00 per year. Newsletter. Covers trends in the U.S. travel industry.

TRAVEL SMART: PAY LESS, ENJOY MORE
Communications House
40 Beechdale Rd.
Dobbs Ferry, NY 10522-9989
Phone: (800) 327-3633 or (914) 693-8300
Monthly. $37.00 per year. Newsletter. Provides information and recommendations for travelers. Emphasis is on travel value and opportunities for bargains.

TRAVEL TRADE: THE BUSINESS PAPER OF THE
TRAVEL INDUSTRY
Travel Trade Publications
15 W. 44th St., 6 Fl.
New York, NY 10036
Phone: (212) 730-6600
Fax: (212) 730-7020
Weekly. $10.00 per year.

TRAVEL WEEKLY
Reed Travel Group
500 Plz. Dr.
Secaucus, NJ 07096
Phone: (800) 395-7333 or (201) 902-2000
Fax: (201) 902-1967
Twice a week. $29.00 per year. Includes cruise guides, a weekly "Business Travel Update," and special issues devoted to particular destinations and areas. Edited mainly for travel agents and tour operators.

DATABASES

CITIBASE (CITICORP ECONOMIC DATABASE)
FAME Software Corp.
77 Water St., 9 Fl.
New York, NY 10005
Phone: (212) 898-7800
Fax: (212) 742-8956
Presents over 6,000 statistical series relating to business, industry, finance, and economics. Includes series from Survey of Current Business *and many other sources. Time period is 1947 to date, with daily updates. Inquire as to online cost and availability.*

TOURISM OFFICES WORLDWIDE DIRECTORY
Lucas Internet
Contains contact information for more than 700 tourism offices around the world. The database is arranged alphabetically by country name. Time span: current information. Updating frequency: Continuous. Fees: Free. Gopher: gopher.nus.sg; Choose: NUS ftp servers/Miscellaneous/travel URL: http:// www.mbnet.mb.ca/lucas/travel or http://www.digimark.net/ rec-travel/

UNITED STATES INTERNATIONAL AIR TRAVEL STATISTICS
U.S. Dept. of Transportation, Center for Transportation Information Kendall Square
Cambridge, MA 02142
Phone: (617) 494-2429
Fax: (617) 494-3064
Provides detailed statistics on air passenger travel between the U.S. and foreign countries for both scheduled and charter flights. Time period is 1975 to date, with monthly updates. Inquire as to online cost and availability.

STATISTICS SOURCES

ECONOMIC REVIEW OF TRAVEL IN AMERICA
U.S. Travel Data Center
1100 New York Ave. NW, Ste. 450-W
Washington, DC 20005-3934
Phone: (202) 408-1832
Fax: (202) 408-1255
Annual. $70.00. Presents a statistical summary of travel in the U.S., including travel expenditures, travel industry employment, tax data, international visitors, etc.

IMPACT OF TRAVEL ON STATE ECONOMIES
U.S. Travel Data Center
1100 New York Ave. NW, Ste. 450-W
Washington, DC 20005-3934
Phone: (202) 408-1832
Fax: (202) 408-1255
Annual. $80.00. Contains data on travel spending and the travel industry in each U.S. state.

OUTLOOK FOR TRAVEL AND TOURISM
U.S. Travel Data Center
1100 New York Ave. NW, Ste. 450-W,
Washington, DC 20005-3934
Phone: (202) 408-1832
Fax: (202) 408-1255
Annual. $130.00. Contains forecasts of the performance of the U.S. travel industry, including air travel, business travel, recreation (attractions), and accomodations.

TRAVEL MARKET REPORT
U.S. Travel Data Center
1133 21st St. NW
Washington, DC 20036
Phone: (202) 293-1040

GENERAL WORKS

TOURISM: PRINCIPLES, PRACTICES, PHILOSOPHIES
Robert W. McIntosh and others
John Wiley and Sons, Inc.
605 3rd Ave.
New York, NY 10158-0012
Phone: (800) 526-5368 or (212) 850-6000
Fax: (212) 850-6088
1994. Seventh edition. Price on application. General review of the travel industry.

THE TOURISM SYSTEM: AN INTRODUCTORY TEXT
Robert C. Mill and Alastair M. Morrison
Prentice-Hall
200 Old Tappan Rd.
Old Tappan, NJ 07675
Phone: (800) 922-0579
Fax: (800) 445-6991
1992. $63.00. Second edition. General survey of travel marketing.

FURTHER READING

Dunfee, Thomas W. "Ethical Issues Confronting Travel Agents." *Journal of Business Ethics*, February 1996.

Gunther, Marc. "Travel Planning in Cyberspace." *Fortune*, September 9, 1996.

Jarrett, Ian. "Travel Agents Have Doubts About the Net." *Asian Business*, September 1996.

Johnstone, Helen. ''Internet Threatens Agents' Survival.'' *Asian Business,* September 1996.

Reamy, Lois Madison. ''Making the Most of Electronic Travel.'' *Institutional Investor,* April 1996.

U.S. Department of Commerce. Economics and Statistics Administration. Bureau of Economic Analysis. *Survey of Current Business,* July 1996.

U.S. Department of Labor. Bureau of Labor Statistics. *Occupational Outlook Handbook.* 1996-97 ed. Washington, DC: GPO, 1996. ━━

Approximately 362,288 interstate motor carriers were on file with the Office of Motor Carriers as of April 1996. Of these companies, 70 percent operate six or fewer trucks and 79 percent operate 28 or fewer trucks. Almost 5 percent (17,869 companies) were located in the Northwestern states of Washington, Idaho, Oregon, and Alaska. These companies employed about 9.3 million workers in 1995, up 32.1 percent from 1985. The number of commercial truck drivers for the time period 1985 to 1995 increased 18.5 percent. Some 2.9 million people had a main occupation of commercial truck driver, including linehaul, local, courier, government, etc., in 1995.

 LARGEST TRUCKING FIRMS

Ranked by: Sales in 1996, in millions of dollars.

1. United Parcel Service (OH), with $22,368 million
2. Yellow Corporation, $3,072
3. Roadway Express, $2,373
4. Consolidated Freightways, $2,146
5. J. B. Hunt Transport, $1,486

According to the American Trucking Association, the 5.5 billion tons of freight transported by intercity and local trucks in 1994 represented 55 percent of the total domestic tonnage shipped. Some 37 percent of the total tons shipped were general freight; 63 percent were bulk goods. Trucking's share of the nation's freight bill increased 78.9 percent in 1995 from 75.2 percent in 1985. Meanwhile, the truck fatal accident rate declined 39.5 percent during that 10-year time period, while the total miles driven by trucks increased 40.7 percent.

While the long-distance less-than-truckload (LTL) segment experienced decreased revenues in the early 1990s, regional LTL carriers experienced double digit growth by encroaching on the overnight delivery market once monopolized by small-package ground couriers. This trend was fueled by the widespread adoption of so-called ''zero-inventory'' production techniques by U.S. manufacturers, which entailed the creation of distribution centers or parts storage facilities within a delivery zone of two days or less in traveling distance from

TRUCKING AND COURIER SERVICES

SIC 4210

Increased internal competition for a static trucking services market, growing competition for freight dollars as a result of new rail technologies, and increased rail industry efficiency continued to restrict industry profits, weed out leveraged and marginal firms, and increase consolidation among industry leaders and surviving firms. The trucking and courier services industry looked to new truck tracking and information technologies, nontraditional markets such as express delivery of light freight, increased entree to intrastate markets, and general improvements in the U.S. economy to enhance industry revenues. The industry's ability to integrate new technologies and exploit global trends in freight transport conditioned its future strength.

manufacturers' sites. The growing emphasis on regional markets was also enhanced by the industry's need to retain drivers by offering them shorter hauls, the rail industry's increasing competitiveness in long-distance freight, and growing emphasis by shippers on on-time delivery guarantees. By the early 1990s, two-thirds of the total LTL market consisted of regional freight transport.

LEGISLATION

Despite federal deregulation of the trucking industry, regulation on the intrastate level continued in the early 1990s. In 1990, 28 states maintained strict regulatory control of trucking firms, and in 1991 Congress passed the Intermodal Surface Transportation Efficiency Act in an attempt to harmonize state regulations on interstate carriers. Congress also passed the International Registration Plan and International Fuel Tax Agreement, taking effect in 1996 and 1998 respectively, to allow truckers to avoid repetitive state-by-state vehicle registration requirements and fuel tax payments. The Clinton administration's gasoline and diesel fuel tax ratified in 1993 added 4.3 cents to per-gallon fuel costs, raising industry operating expenses by an estimated $3 billion annually.

Non-hazardous materials enforcement fell under the jurisdiction of the Federal Highway Administration's (FHWA) Office of Motor Carrier Safety at the U.S. Department of Transportation (DOT); hazardous materials regulations, DOT's Office of Hazardous Material Safety, and hazardous waste transportation, the Environmental Protection Agency (EPA). With increased federal emphasis on safety, truckers viewed safety compliance costs as a permanent part of doing business, recognizing that without careful and sustained attention from management, those costs could grow.

Additionally, several federal programs continued to affect the trucking industry's response to safety concerns. The Motor Carrier Safety Assistance Program, for example, gave the Federal Office of Motor Carrier Safety and relevant state agencies greater latitude in carrying out annual vehicle safety inspections. The resulting $6,000 to $9,000 per truck spent annually by the industry on maintenance and repair was expected to be offset by lower insurance premiums and cost savings derived from fleets maintained in optimal operating condition. The uniform national Commercial Drivers License mandated by the Commercial Motor Vehicle Safety Act of 1986 required truck drivers to pass a single-purpose driving competence exam and eliminated redundant state license requirements.

GROUND-BASED COURIER SECTOR

Although the ground courier market continued to grow in the early 1990s, its rate of growth began to slow. In late 1991 and early 1992, United Parcel Service's ground-based business declined for the first time since the 1940s. The major competitors in the ground courier industry continued to wage a fierce price war with each other and with the air courier industry. This battle resulted in lower rates for small package shippers but reduced earnings for firms in an industry already characterized by narrow profit margins.

The rapid spread of fax and e-mail technology in the 1980s and 1990s represented a significant source of competition for ground couriers (primarily in the same-day delivery niche) and was estimated to have cost the courier industry $75 million in lost business in 1990 alone. At the same time, the adoption of cost-saving ''just-in-time'' or zero-inventory management policies by many American businesses in the same period created a demand for truckers capable of providing same-day warehouse-to-customer transport of time-sensitive parts and manufacturing materials. Because of the quick-delivery, short-haul nature of many courier firms, this growing market represented a natural niche for the ground courier industry.

WORK FORCE

The trucking industry as a whole employed over 9.3 million people in 1995. That year there were 2.9 million truck drivers. Nearly 59 percent were employed in the wholesale/retail sector and 20 percent in the manufacturing sector. Only 23 percent employed were minorities and 4.5 percent were women. In total, $275.2 billion in annual wages were paid to employees throughout the trucking industry. Drivers operating heavy specialized trucks earned the highest annual salary in 1995 ($35,400). Tank drivers followed with an annual average wage of $35,300; refrigerated truck drivers, $35,100; LTL truck drivers, $33,600; truck-load (TL) truck drivers, $33,000; general cargo truck drivers, $33.200; and private fleet truck drivers earning to lowest average annual salary at $32,100.

Large LTL freight carriers with unionized employees often pay out 60 percent to 65 percent of their revenues in wages and benefits (including wages to independent drivers) compared with 40 percent to 45 percent in the mostly non-union TL segment. Long-distance truckers are usually paid by the mile and receive increases based on seniority. J. B. Hunt Transport, for example, paid its drivers as much as 27 cents per mile in addition to providing minimum mileage bonus programs, medical and dental insurance, and retirement and profit-sharing plans. Experienced drivers with seniority earned about 30 cents per mile in the early 1990s.

Fewer than 60 percent of new truck drivers lasted longer than four weeks on the job, and driver turnover rates (which rose as high as 100 percent for some firms) were considered to be among the most critical issues facing the industry. Besides bonuses, benefits, and higher pay, methods used to retain drivers included expanded use of husband and wife teams, "relay" driving in which routes normally handled by one driver are divided up, increased scheduling of short hauls, and equipment amenities designed to make the driver's job less taxing.

RESEARCH AND TECHNOLOGY

The areas of technology with the greatest potential impact on the nonlocal trucking industry are vehicle and freight tracking systems and information storage and interchange systems. Because these technologies enabled industry firms to increase productivity, enhance responsiveness to customers, and distinguish themselves from competitors, they played increasingly critical roles in the industry's profitability in the early 1990s.

Tracking technologies employ sophisticated computer systems to record the progress of freight from origin to destination and satellite technologies to provide precise fixes on fleet trucks. The use of bar code labels on freight packages and portable bar code scanners permitted industry firms to process extensive data on individual loads and monitor those loads' movements through the delivery network. Such electronic data interchange (EDI) systems allowed truckers to "capture" data automatically and permitted shippers to link up with a carrier's computer to access data on proof of delivery, invoices, shipment routing, and freight consolidation in "real time," with greater accuracy, and with reduced administrative paperwork and storage.

Handheld, portable laptop, and dashboard-mounted computers enable truckers to communicate with company computers, keep track of information on fuel taxes and fuel management performance, store navigational maps and information on truck stops and repair facilities, record departures and arrivals, send and receive messages, monitor vehicle speed and engine conditions, and register mileage or the results of trailer inspections.

Although satellite technology for vehicle tracking and navigation has been available since the early 1980s, active industry interest began only in 1987 when the first LTL carriers began installing satellite tracking equipment. These systems enabled trucking firms to locate trucks to accuracies of 300 yards by linking on-board computers with company dispatchers via specialized satellites. Less expensive "meteor burst" systems bounced VHF radio waves off meteor trails to obtain the same positioning coordinates offered by satellite signals.

Using satellite-based tracking equipment, C. R. England and Sons achieved 98 percent on-time performance in the early 1990s. Although satellite tracking systems can add as much as 2 percent to operating costs, 2,000 U.S. trucking fleets had 2-way satellite data links in 1992, and 30,000 trucks were equipped with position location systems. The number of trucks equipped with vehicle tracking equipment was expected to grow to 300,000 by the mid-1990s.

GROUND-BASED COURIER SECTOR

In its operations centers, shipping points, and package pickup and delivery trucks, the U.S. ground courier industry was transformed by mobile communications technology and electronic scanning, tracking, and billing technology. Faced with increasing competition from Federal Express in the late 1970s and early 1980s, industry leader UPS inaugurated a technology modernization program in the mid-1980s that transformed it into a technology-driven enterprise with a management information systems (MIS) staff of 4,000. In 1990, the United Parcel Service (UPS) began installing a cellular phone system in 50,000 of its fleet trucks that enabled customers to determine the exact status of their packages in real time for a cost of 75 cents. The $150 million system, called DIAD (Delivery Information Acquisition Device), utilized an electronic pen and clipboard device carried by the driver and was based on "image capture" software that recorded the customer's signature and the package's bar code data. When the driver attached the clipboard to an adaptor in the truck, the data was sent via UPS's "UPSNet" system to the company's main data center for customer access. Among other advantages, the system largely eliminated the problem of verifying illegible signatures, thereby tripling the number of next-day air deliveries made without errors, and enabling UPS to include an electronic "replica" of the recipient's signature when providing the shipper with a proof of delivery. In 1992, UPS introduced GroundTrac for electronically tracking packages passing through the UPS system. It also began investing in coded package labels capable of containing more data than existing bar code labels.

UPS also established a toll-free hot line that shippers could call to get a faxed sheet displaying the time and location of their package's delivery and the name of the person who signed for it. By 1996 this simple fax system had evolved into UPS's interactive home page on the World Wide Web through which customers could check the status of their shipments. Customers also could schedule pickups, get price estimates for shipping their packages, and make billing inquiries. By 1997, Federal Express's online system claimed more than 400,000 customers who generated over 60 percent of the company's two million-plus daily transactions. In January 1997 alone, more than 800,000 packages were tracked via the Web, and its Internet-based transactions were growing at the rate 10 to 12 percent a month.

Other advanced technology applications in the ground courier industry in the 1990s included parcel processing systems capable of sorting 20,000 packages per hour, and satellite-based computer systems that could locate courier fleet trucks to accuracies of 300 yards or better.

AMERICA AND THE WORLD

The United States and Canada trade more goods with each other than with any other economies, resulting in transportation costs—including trucking—of $4 billion to $7 billion a year. In 1989, Canada and the United States signed a trade agreement to promote cross-border commerce, which was expected to be further bolstered by the gradual implementation of NAFTA throughout the 1990s. The NAFTA agreement called for opening cross-border traffic in both the U.S. and Mexican border states by 1996. Other geographic and ownership access would be expanded by the year 2000, and virtually all access and investment restrictions on trucking companies would be lifted by 2003.

Prior to NAFTA, Mexican cross-border trucking was highly restricted. Mexico required foreign shippers to use Mexican drivers and Mexican equipment to handle shipments there. This forced U.S. shippers and carriers to form alliances with Mexican carriers. In response to the restrictions, the United States established an embargo in 1982 that limited Mexican access to U.S. markets. U.S. certificates of registration (CR) restricted Mexican carriers' access to a border zone generally ranging 10 to 25 miles north of the U.S. border. But just prior to NAFTA's passage some 4,354 Mexican carriers held CRs. Only three Mexican motor freight carriers, however, held broader authority and none held 48-state authority.

Amendments to Mexico's federal weights and measures law in 1994 were met with enthusiasm by U.S. truckers. The new law lowered Mexico's weight limit for trucks to just under 90,000 pounds for an 18-wheel tractor-trailer, only 10,000 pounds shy of U.S. limits. Trucks from Mexico had been weighing in excess of 140,000 to 160,000 pounds, an amount considered un-safe in the United States. Prior to the amendment, many Mexican vehicles weighing high amounts came across the border into the United States since resources to monitor all vehicles at border crossings were lacking.

With the advent of the European Union in 1992, U.S. carriers quickly established a presence to control the European leg of their shipments. European operators like steamship line Nedlloyd began offering land-based transportation in Europe and employed the services of U.S. trucking companies to provide the U.S. leg of the shipment. Nedlloyd Road Cargo signed such a contract with Consolidated Freightways's subsidiary Con-Way in 1992 to provide door-to-door LTL service between the United States and Europe, with Nedlloyd handling the European part of the venture. Carolina Freight opened an office in Rotterdam to provide faster service for its customers' European needs. Dutch-based motor carrier Bleckmann B.V. handled sales and marketing for Carolina's transportation services within the Dutch market, served as its general agent within the United Kingdom, and provided international trucking services within Europe. In 1993, Yellow Freight and The Royal Fran Maas group in Europe entered into an agreement to provide transatlantic LTL shipments.

ASSOCIATIONS AND SOCIETIES

AMERICAN TRUCKING ASSOCIATIONS
2200 Mill Rd.
Alexandria, VA 22314
Phone: (800) 282-5463 or (703) 838-1700
Fax: (703) 684-5720

NATIONAL MOTOR FREIGHT TRAFFIC ASSOCIATION
2200 Mill Rd.
Alexandria, VA 22314
Phone: (703) 838-1810
Fax: (703) 683-1094

NATIONAL PRIVATE TRUCK COUNCIL
66 Canal Ctr. Plz.
Alexandria, VA 22314
Phone: (703) 683-1300
Fax: (703) 683-1217

NATIONAL TANK TRUCK CARRIERS
2200 Mill Rd.,
Alexandria, VA 22314
Phone: (703) 838-1960
Fax: (703) 684-5753

PERIODICALS AND NEWSLETTERS

COMMERCIAL CARRIER JOURNAL

Chilton Co.
201 King of Prussia Rd.
Radnor, PA 19089-0110
Phone: (800) 695-1214 or (610) 964-4000
Fax: (610) 964-4512
Monthly. $40.00 per year.

FLEET OWNER

Intertec Publishing Corp.
707 Westchester Ave., Ste. 101
White Plains, NY 10604-3102
Phone: (800) 776-1246 or (919) 949-8500
Fax: (914) 287-6752
Monthly. Free to qualified personnel; others, $45.00 per year.

HEAVY DUTY TRUCKING: THE BUSINESS MAGAZINE OF TRUCKING

Newport Communications
PO Box W
Newport Beach, CA 92658
Phone: (714) 261-1636
Monthly. $54.00 per year.

LIFTING AND TRANSPORTATION INTERNATIONAL

Douglas Publications, Inc.
9607 Gayton Rd., Ste. 100
Richmond, VA 23233
Phone: (804) 741-6704
Fax: (804) 750-2399
Monthly. $65.00 per year. Covers specialized trucking, including oversized loads, cranes, hauling steel, heavy rigging, etc. Serves as the official publication of the Specialized Carriers and Rigging Association.

TRANSPORT TOPICS: NATIONAL NEWSPAPER OF THE TRUCKING INDUSTRY

American Trucking Associations, Inc.
2200 Mill Rd.
Alexandria, VA 22314-4677
Phone: (800) 282-5463 or (703) 838-1700
Fax: (800) 519-5272
Weekly. $59.00 per year.

DATABASES

DRI TRANSPORTATION COST FORECASTING

DRI/McGraw-Hill, Data Products Division
24 Hartwell Ave.
Lexington, MA 02173
Phone: (800) 541-9914 or (617) 863-5100
Provides 10-year forecasts, updated quarterly, of key expense items for U.S. railroads, trucking, and inland waterway transportation. Rail shipping rates are forecast for 11 major commodities. Inquire as to online cost and availability.

TRIS

National Research Council
2101 Constitution Ave. NW,
Washington, DC 20418

Phone: (202) 334-3250
Fax: (202) 334-2003
Contains abstracts and citations to a wide range of transportation literature, 1968 to present, with monthly updates. Includes references to the literature of air transportation, highways, ships and shipping, railroads, trucking, and urban mass transportation. Formerly TRIS-ON-LINE. Inquire as to online cost and availability.

STATISTICS SOURCES

AMERICAN TRUCKING TRENDS

American Trucking Associations, Inc.
2200 Mill Rd.
Alexandria, VA 22314
Phone: (800) 282-5463 or (703) 838-1700
Fax: (800) 519-5272
Annual. $20.00

CENSUS OF TRANSPORTATION

U.S. Government Printing Office
Washington, DC 20402
Phone: (202) 512-1800
Fax: (202) 512-2250
Quinquennial. Prices vary.

MONTHLY TRUCK TONNAGE REPORT

American Trucking Associations, Inc.
2200 Mill Rd.
Alexandria, VA 22314
Phone: (800) 282-5463 or (703) 838-1700
Fax: (800) 519-5272
Monthly. $35.00 per year.

MOTOR CARRIER ANNUAL REPORTS

American Trucking Associations, Inc.
2200 Mill Rd.
Alexandria, VA 22314
Phone: (800) 282-5463 or (703) 838-1700
Fax: (800) 519-5272
Annual. $400.00.

NATIONAL TRANSPORTATION STATISTICS

Available from U.S. Government Printing Office
Washington, DC 20402
Phone: (202) 512-1800
Fax: (202) 512-2250
Annual. Issued by Bureau of Transportation Statistics, U.S. Department of Transportation. Provides data on operating revenues, expenses, employees, passenger miles (where applicable), and other factors for airlines, automobiles, buses, local transit, pipelines, railroads, ships, and trucks.

GENERAL WORKS

AMERICAN MOTOR CARRIER DIRECTORY
K-III Information Co. Inc.
424 W. 33rd St.
New York, NY 10001
Phone: (800) 221-5488 or (212) 714-3100
Fax: (212) 714-3157
Semiannual. $287.00 per year. Lists all licensed Less Than Truckload (LTL) general commodity carriers in the U.S., includingspecialized motor carriers and related services.

FEDERAL CARRIERS REPORTS
Commerce Clearing House, Inc.
4025 W. Peterson Ave.
Chicago, Il 60646
Phone: (800) 248-3248 or (312) 583-8500
Biweekly. $935.00 per year. Looseleaf service. Four volumes. Federal rules and regulations for motor carriers, water carriers, and freight forwarders.

FURTHER READING

Bowman, Robert J. "Battling for Turf." *Distribution,* July 1996.

"Deliverance for UPS?" *Atlanta Business Chronicle* 18, no. 36 (2 February 1996): 6A.

Flanagan, William G. "Travel & Transport." *Forbes,* 1 January 1996.

"Follow the Flag of Convenience." *Economist* 342, no. 8005 (22 February 1997): 75.

Lee, Mie-Yun. "Are You Sure It's as Easy as Signed, Sealed and Delivered?" *Business First - Western New York* 12, no. 25 (1 April 1996): 17.

"Standard Trucking and Transportation Statistics, January/February 1997." ATA Statistics Department, American Trucking Association, Alexandria, VA.

Thurmond, Jeffery. "Shipping into the Next Century." *National Public Accountant* 41, no. 6 (June 96): 13.

Deep sea foreign transportation of freight is greatly affected by the global economy and international competition. United States companies in this industry compete with each other and with foreign carriers. Competition in the industry is heightened in part because of U.S. regulations that tend to make costs for U.S. shipowners higher than for ships bearing the flags of other nations. Many American-owned ships carry flags of nations with lower levels of expenses in order to stay competitive in the cargo transport business.

In 1995, U.S. merchant ships operating in the deep sea foreign transportation of freight carried a total of nearly $5.3 billion in cargo, according to the U.S. Bureau of Economic Analysis Survey of Current Business. Although tonnage of foreign merchandise trade had increased over previous years, rising costs and price competition still meant declining profits for U.S. shipowners. Some shipping firms received subsidies from the U.S. government to compensate for high U.S. flag operating costs. These subsidies fall under the Maritime Security Program in which steamships are made available to the U.S. Defense Department should the need arise.

In 1995 there were 343 active, privately-owned U.S. vessels of 1,000 gross tons and over engaged in deep sea transportation of freight, according to the U.S. Maritime Administration. Of that number, 129 were engaged in domestic trade and 128 were engaged in foreign trade. Another 48 privately-owned ships were leased to the U.S. Military Sealift Command, down from the 80 that were leased for use in its Desert Storm operation.

Deep sea domestic transportation of freight is part of a massive interrelated system of transport of manufactured and raw materials. Tank ships, which include tanker barges and liquified natural gas vessels, and bulk carriers, which include tug barges, comprised 100 of the total 129 privately owned U.S. flag merchant vessels operating in the domestic trade in 1995. Of these, 58 tankers and 4 bulk carriers operated on the coastal waters and 37 tankers and 1 bulk carrier operated on noncontiguous waters.

Although the health of the industry depends in large part on the health of the U.S. economy, domestic deep sea transportation plays an important role in the nation's private and public interests. The ocean going domestic vessels facilitate business between various areas of the country by providing relatively low-priced shipping service and is part of the vast network of trains, trucks, and inland water carriers that keeps the nation's commerce moving. The industry also supports millions of other jobs at shipbuilding yards, seaports, and terminals. In addition, the domestic waterborne shipping industry is

WATER TRANS-PORTATION OF FREIGHT

SICs 4410, 4420, 4430, 4440

Leading cargo-shipping companies in the United States have embraced a trend toward operating members of their fleets under the flag of another country. This trend is chiefly due to the fact that the high cost of insurance, maintenance, new vessel construction, operation, and safety regulations make it prohibitive to operate as a U.S. flag carrier when compared to foreign fleets. Industry analysts believe that by operating under the authority of other countries, American shipowners will cut labor costs by as much as 80 percent in the coming years.

Top North American Ports

Container ports are ranked by capacity in 20 foot equivalent units.

Long Beach	2,842,502
Los Angeles	2,555,344
New York/New Jersey	2,262,792
Oakland	1,549,886
San Juan	1,539,000
Seattle	1,479,076
Tacoma	1,092,087
Hampton Roads	1,077,848
Charleston	1,023,003
Honolulu	805,035

Source: *Purchasing*, June 6, 1996, p. 49, from American Association of Port Authorities.

also vital to national defense interests, as it has relieved rail congestion and provided transport of military equipment and supplies during periods of national emergency.

Much of the success of the U.S. deep sea domestic industry over the years has been reliant upon oil drilling in Alaska. Since the 1989 oil spill disaster involving the *Exxon Valdez* in Alaska's Prince William Sound, new laws aimed to prevent oil spills in U.S. waters have become a serious concern to U.S. shipping companies. The Oil Pollution Act of 1990 required that all oil products be conveyed in double-hulled ships in order to prevent a repeat of the *Exxon Valdez* spill. The law also required each carrier to provide a guarantee of financial responsibility in the event of a spill. Shipowners claimed that the law, as written, threatened the survival of domestic shipping.

Great Lakes shipping is a significant subset of the domestic water transportation industry. In 1995, there were 59 ships engaged in the transportation of domestic freight on the Great Lakes and upper St. Lawrence River. These ships also carried freight between U.S. and Canadian ports. Federal cabotage laws required that cargo shipped between U.S. ports be carried in ships built and registered in the United States, and owned and crewed by U.S. citizens. Ships of other maritime nations also sailed the Great Lakes-St. Lawrence Seaway.

The principal cargoes shipped on the Great Lakes-St. Lawrence Seaway are iron ore and coal. Freighters carry iron ore mined in Minnesota and Michigan to steel mills in Illinois, Indiana, Michigan, and Ohio. A single Great Lakes freighter can carry enough iron ore to produce the steel needed to build 87,000 automobiles. The second-largest cargo is coal, mined primarily in West Virginia, Kentucky, Pennsylvania, Ohio, and Illinois and shipped to utilities and factories in the upper Great Lakes states and Canada. Great Lakes freighters also carry low-sulfur Western coal shipped initially by rail to Superior, Wisconsin. The U.S. fleet typically hauls millions of tons of cargo annually during a nine-month navigation season. The principal cargoes of foreign transporters are wheat, barley, corn, and other grains from the Midwest and Canada that are destined primarily for European markets.

Nearly all of the U.S.-flagged ships engaged in freight transportation on the Great Lakes are members of the Lake Carriers Association, founded in 1880 and one of the oldest active trade organizations in the United States. In 1995, the Cleveland-based organization listed 14 members who owned 63 vessels. This included two steel companies that operated ore carriers. The fleet included 60 dry-bulk carriers and three double-hulled tankers. Their collective cargo capacity was more than 1.8 million tons.

INDUSTRY OUTLOOK

Despite the best intentions and stated policies of the U.S. government, American companies engaged in foreign deep sea transportation have been in trouble for many years. In the early 1990s, the Desert Storm confrontation with Iraq called for a gigantic shipping effort to bring American supplies and equipment to the Middle East. The military enlisted the services of the merchant marine for this task. It also used several dozen chartered transport ships it keeps fully loaded and ready. However, even these privately owned ships could not handle the demand of military shipments, and the U.S. was forced to turn to foreign transport to carry equipment and supplies. During the build-up of forces, almost half of the 200 ships carrying equipment to Saudi Arabia were foreign-owned.

Acknowledging the merchant marine's ineffectiveness during the Gulf War conflict and its overall age, an adviser to President Bill Clinton told the *Wall Street Journal* in late 1992 that the U.S. merchant marine "is on its last legs." He said that the fleet had dwindled to the point that 85 percent of U.S. exports were carried by foreign shipping lines. Government officials projected that if the merchant fleet continued to decline, by the end of the century the nation would not have the necessary sealift capacity to meet military needs. After years of debate, the U.S. Congress passed the Maritime Security Act in 1996 by an overwhelming margin. This act reformed outdated maritime regulations and ensured that privately owned merchant ships would be available to meet national security sealift requirements. It also established a program to provide participating carriers with $1 billion in operating assistance over 10 years.

Like the foreign fleet, the domestic fleet is a relatively old one, but shipowners are reluctant to replace their aging ships because of consistently low profit margins. In 1994, for example, 1 merchant vessel capable of carrying 7 gross tons and 1 tanker capable of hauling 17 gross tons were constructed, according to figures available from the U.S. Maritime Administration. No new ships were constructed in 1993, and in 1992, 3 merchants vessels with a total of 44 gross tons hauling capability, 1 cargo vessel capable to carry 32 gross tons, and 2 tankers with a hauling capability of 12 gross tons were constructed.

ORGANIZATION AND STRUCTURE

The U.S. deep sea fleet consists of three categories of service: liner, nonliner (or tramp), and tanker service.

Liner service includes regular, scheduled stops at ports along a designated route. The operators either own or charter the ships and must accept any legal cargo they are equipped to carry, unless it does not meet the minimum freight requirements. Liner service usually carries manufactured goods. Often, two or more carriers form ''conferences'' in order to regulate rates and competition along a route. All conference members must charge the same freight rates, although the laws of supply and demand may affect rates from one sailing to the next. Frequency of trips depends upon the demands for shipping along the route.

Nonliner, or tramp, service is scheduled individually by a customer who, in essence, is chartering the ship to carry its cargo. Tramps generally carry only one type of bulk cargo, usually a raw material such as coal, ores, grain, lumber, or sugar. On occasion, two shippers of the same commodity charter a ship jointly.

Merchant ships have become increasingly more specialized, especially during the last half of the twentieth century. Special ships were designed to carry bulk cement, coal, iron ore, liquefied natural gas, wood chips and pulp, refrigerated foods, and heavy equipment. These ships, operating as nonliner service, are often on long-term lease by one company. Because the ships are so expensive to build, the shipowner may require the

company to sign a long-term lease for most of the life of the vessel before beginning construction.

Tankers carry shipments of liquid cargoes, especially crude oil and petroleum products. Oil companies may own and operate their own tanker fleets and charter privately-owned ships as needed. Exxon Corporation owns one of the largest tanker fleets in the world and has a special department to oversee its operation.

The transport of oil in bulk began in the late 1880s. Tankers in the 100 years since then have changed dramatically, with more ship work handled by computers, thus cutting back on the size of the crew. The enormous size of the tankers of the modern era has also increased the risk of oil spills and the impact such spills can have on the environment. The infamous Alaskan oil spill in Prince William Sound by the *Exxon Valdez* served as a catalyst in the institution of stricter environmental regulations for tankers and other vessels.

A recent innovation in oil product shipment was the tug-barge. The bow of the tug fits into a notch in a barge weighing up to 20,000 tons and pushes the barge. This vessel was devised as a way to cut shipping costs on tanker routes from the Gulf of Mexico north along the eastern seaboard of the United States. The tug barge requires only a fraction of the crew needed aboard a tanker.

Domestic shipping includes coastwise, intercoastal, and noncontiguous services. Coastwise shipping refers to movement of cargo along the coastlines of the 48 contiguous states. This includes shipment of goods between the Atlantic and Gulf coasts. For the most part, tankers and ocean tug-barge systems carry petroleum and tramps carry dry bulk cargoes along this route.

Intercostal shipping includes movement of cargo between Gulf and Pacific ports, and between Atlantic and Pacific ports. Most traffic of this type consists of oil tankers carrying their cargo from Alaska to Gulf ports. Noncontiguous shipping includes service to Alaska, Hawaii, and U.S. territories and possessions. Outbound Alaskan shipping consists largely of petroleum products and crude oil; inbound service carries consumer goods for state residents. Hawaii and Puerto Rico rely on deep sea freight to transport goods in and out of their islands.

Several federal agencies promoted and regulated the U.S. merchant ships before the Maritime Administration (MARAD), part of the Department of Commerce, was given jurisdiction in 1950. The Merchant Marine Act of 1970 strengthened and expanded MARAD's function. It has brought the many facets of the merchant marine together in order to insure the strength of the industries involved, including shippers, shipbuilders, and shipowners, as well as the various unions in each of those industries. MARAD guarantees loans for shipbuilding as well as providing other subsidies and tax benefits for construction of new ships by fleet owners.

RESEARCH AND TECHNOLOGY

Foreign shipping benefited from a revolutionary improvement first introduced in domestic transport in 1956—containerization of freight as part of an integrated transportation system. Prior to this new design, cargo was lifted aboard either in separate packing crates or bundled on pallets. Container shipping, however, involved large containers that fit the chassis of a tractor trailer and that could be packed and sealed by the manufacturer, transported via truck to the ship terminal, removed from the truck chassis, and placed in the cargo hold of the ship with a large crane that was actually part of the ship. At its destination port, the container was lifted off the ship, placed on truck chassis, and driven to its ultimate destination. The containers could also be hauled by train if necessary. This innovation eliminated much of the handling that cargo once required; with this integrated system, it was handled once to pack it and once to unpack it, neither time by ship personnel, thus reducing the risk of damage and liability on the part of the shipowners.

Containerization led the way to Ro/Ro ships— Roll-on/Roll-off ships—with their gigantic cargo doors on the sides and stern that allow large vehicles or other large cargo to be driven or rolled on and off. Conversion to container ships was an expensive investment for shipowners, terminal operators, and port agencies. In the U.S. alone, between 1959 and 1973, the conversion costs were estimated at $7.5 billion dollars in containers, ships, and port facilities. The adoption of container ships also led to the establishment of new companies that bought containers and leased them to the shipowners, thus removing from the shipowners the complex problem of keeping track of the whereabouts of empty containers.

In recent years, American President, Sea-Land, and smaller independent shipping lines have installed sophisticated computers and information technology to provide shippers with access to information about their cargo, keep track of rates, and allow customs officers to screen cargo while the ship is still at sea.

The next decade may well be marked by the introduction of significantly faster shipping vessels. David L. Giles, an aeronautical engineer, has invented a new craft dubbed FastShip. The new breed of freighter would be 863 feet in length and marry jet-ski technology to a novel hull design 100 feet shorter than the conventional super-freighter. FastShip is estimated to cross the North Atlantic at speeds up to 40 knots in 3.5 days as compared to existing ocean service requiring seven to eight days. If successful, its biggest benefit will be delivering high value time sensitive (HVTS) cargo such as automobiles and automotive parts, pharmaceuticals, apparel and other consumer goods, on a door-to-door basis, in five to seven days as opposed to the current 14 to 35 days that existing services require. Japanese researchers are experimenting with ships driven by superconducting electromagnets and ships propelled by water jets and powered by gas turbine engines. Further in the future, a Techno-Superliner may be capable of traveling between Japan and the U.S. in three days.

ASSOCIATIONS AND SOCIETIES

AMERICAN BUREAU OF SHIPPING
2 World Trade Ctr., 106th Fl.
New York, NY 10048
Phone: (212) 839-5000
Fax: (212) 839-5130

AMERICAN INSTITUTE OF MERCHANT SHIPPING
1000 16th St. NW, Ste. 511
Washington, DC 20036
Phone: (202) 775-4399
Fax: (202) 659-3795

AMERICAN MARITIME ASSOCIATION
485 Madison Ave.
New York, NY 10022
Phone: (212) 319-9217

THE AMERICAN WATERWAYS OPERATORS
1600 Wilson Blvd., Ste. 1000
Arlington, VA 22209
Phone: (703) 841-9300

LAKE CARRIERS ASSOCIATION
614 Superior Ave. W
915 Rockeffeller Bldg.
Cleveland, OH 44113-1383
Phone: (216) 621-1107

NATIONAL ASSOCIATION OF MARINE SERVICES
5024-R Campbell Blvd.
Baltimore, MD 21236
Phone: (410) 931-8100
Fax: (410) 931-8111

NATIONAL ASSOCIATION OF STEVEDORES
2011 Eye St. NW, No. 601
Washington, DC 20006
Phone: (202) 296-2810
Fax: (202) 331-7479

PERIODICALS AND NEWSLETTERS

AMERICAN SHIPPER: PORTS, TRANSPORTATION AND INDUSTRY
Howard Publications, Inc.
33 S. Hogan St., Ste. 230
Jacksonville, FL 32201
Phone: (904) 355-2601
Monthly. $36.00 per year.

MARINE DIGEST AND TRANSPORTATION NEWS
Marine Publishing, Inc.
1201 1st Ave. S, No. 200
Seattle, WA 98124
Phone: (206) 682-3607
Fax: (206) 682-4023
Monthly. $28.00 per year. Formerly Marine Digest.

MARITIME REPORTER AND ENGINEERING NEWS
Maritime Activity Reports, Inc.
118 E. 25th St.
New York, NY 10010
Phone: (212) 477-6700
Monthly. Free to qualified personnel; others, $44.00 per year.

SEATRADE WEEK
Seatrade North America
Princeton Forrestal Village
125 Village blvd., Ste. 220
Princeton, NJ 08540-5703
Phone: (609) 452-9414

SEAWAY REVIEW
Harbor House Publishers, Inc.
221 Water St.
Boyne City, MI 49712
Phone: (616) 582-2814

SHIPPING DIGEST: FOR EXPORT AND TRANSPORTATION EXECUTIVES
Geyer-McAllister Publications, Inc.
51 Madison Ave.
New York, NY 10010
Phone: (212) 689-4411
Fax: (212) 683-7929
Weekly. $38.00 per year.

THE WATERWAYS JOURNAL
N. 4th St., Ste. 650
St. Louis, MO 63102
Phone: (314) 241-7354

WORKBOAT
Journal Publications
120 Tillson Ave., Ste. 201
PO Box 908
Rockland, ME 04841-00908

DATABASES

DRI TRANSPORTATION COST FORECASTING
DRI/McGraw-Hill
Data Products Div.
24 Hartwell Ave.
Lexington, MA 02173
Phone: (800) 541-9914 or (617) 863-5100
Provides ten-year forecasts, updated quarterly, of key expense items for U.S. railroads, trucking, and inland waterway transportation. Rail shipping rates are forecast for 11 major commodities.

OCEANIC ABSTRACTS ONLINE
Cambridge Scientific Abstracts
7200 Wisconsin Ave., 6th Fl.
Bethesda, MD 20814
Phone: (800) 843-7751 or (301) 961-6700
Fax: (301) 961-6720
Oceanographic and other marine-related technical literature, 1964 to present.

TRIS
National Research Council
2101 Constitution Ave. NW
Washington, DC 20418
Phone: (202) 334-3250
Fax: (202) 334-2003
Contains abstracts and citations to a wide range of transportation literature, 1968 to present, with monthly updates. Includes references to the literature of air transportation, highways, ships and shipping, railroads, trucking, and urban mass transportation. Formerly TRIS-ON-LINE.

WORLD SEA TRADE SERVICE
DRI/McGraw-Hill, Inc.
24 Hartwell Ave.
Lexington, MA 02173
Phone: (617) 861-7580

STATISTICS SOURCES

LLOYD'S REGISTER OF SHIPPING STATISTICAL TABLES
Lloyd's Register
17 Battery Pl.
New York, NY 10004
Phone: (212) 425-8050
Fax: (212) 363-9610
Annual. $120.00.

MARITIME TRANSPORT
Organization for Economic Cooperation and Development
2001 L St. NW
Washington, DC 20036-4910
Phone: (202) 785-6323
Fax: (202) 785-0350
Annual. $25.00. Review of the maritime transport industry for OECD member countries. Includes statistical information.

NATIONAL TRANSPORTATION STATISTICS
Available from U.S. Government Printing Office
Washington, DC 20402
Phone: (202) 783-3238
Annual. $17.00. Issued by Bureau of Transportation Statistics, U.S. Department of Transportation. Provides data on operating revenues, expenses, employees, passenger miles (where applicable), and other factors for airlines, automobiles, buses, local transit, pipelines, railroads, ships, and trucks.

REVIEW OF MARINE TRANSPORT
United Nations Conference on Trade and Development
Sales Section, Rm. DC2-853, Dept. 421
2 United Nations Plz.
New York, NY 10017
Phone: (800) 253-9646 or (212) 963-8302
Fax: (212) 963-3489
Annual. Price varies.

GENERAL WORKS

AMERICAN BUREAU OF SHIPPING RECORD
American Bureau of Shipping
2 World Trade Ctr., 106th Fl.
New York, NY 10048
Phone: (212) 839-5100
Fax: (212) 839-5130
Annual. $520.00 per year. Quarterly supplements.

BARGE FLEET PROFILE FOR THE MISSISSIPPI RIVER SYSTEM AND CONNECTED WATERWAYS
Leeper, Cambridge & Campbell, Inc.
1051 Marie Ave. W St.
Paul, MN 55118
Phone: (612) 454-0607

FEDERAL CARRIERS REPORTS
Commerce Clearing House, Inc.
4025 W. Peterson Ave.
Chicago, IL 60646
Phone: (800) 248-3248 or (312) 583-8500
Biweekly. $935.00 per year. Looseleaf service. Four volumes. Federal rules and regulations for motor carriers, water carriers, and freight forwarders.

JANE'S CONTAINERISATION DIRECTORY
Jane's Information Group
PO Box 1436
Alexandria, VA 22314-1651
Phone: (703) 683-3700
Fax: (703) 836-0029
Annual. $275.00. Formerly Jane's Freight Containers.

MARINE POLLUTION AND SAFER SHIPS
Drewry Shipping Consultants
11 Heron Quay

London E14 4JF
Phone: (71) 44 538-0191

MARITIME AFFAIRS—A WORLD HANDBOOK
Gale Research Inc.
835 Penobscot Bldg.
Detroit, MI 48226-4094
Phone: (800) 877-GALE or (313) 961-2242
Fax: (313) 961-6083
1992. $165.00. Second edition. Published by Longman. Discussion of international maritime law, shipping, natural resources, etc. Includes a directory of international maritime organizations and publications.

REGISTER OF SHIPS
Lloyd's Register
17 Battery Pl.
New York, NY 10004
Phone: (212) 425-8050
Fax: (212) 363-9610
Annual. $962.00. Three volumes. Formerly Lloyd's Register of Ships.

SHIP OPERATION AUTOMATION
Elsevier Science Publishing Co. Inc.
PO Box 882, Madison Square Sta.
New York, NY 10159
Phone: (212) 989-5800
Fax: (212) 633-3900
Two volumes. Vol. 3, $79.50; Vol. 4, $56.50. (Computer Applications in Shipping and Shipbuilding Series.)

FURTHER READING

Barnes, David. "Maritime Deregulation." *Traffic World* 10 March 1997.

Bergin, Sarah. "How Ocean Carriers are Staying Afloat." *Transportation & Distribution* February 1997.

Lake Carrier's Association. *1995 Annual Report, 1996 Objectives.* Cleveland: Lake Carrier's Association, 1996.

"Lykes in Critical Talks to Restructure Debt." *Traffic World* 12 February 1996.

"Sea-Land Breezing Along." *Distribution,* March 1997.

Thuermer, Karen E. "Ocean Carriers Turn to Bigger Ships, New Technology to Meet Customer Demands." *Traffic World,* 5 February 1996.

U.S. Department of Commerce.*Statistical Abstract of the United States. 1996* Washington: 1996.

INDUSTRY INDEX

The industry index lists four-digit U.S. Standard Industrial Classification (SIC) codes in numerical order with the classification reference following each code. The code is followed by the page number(s) in which the specific classification is discussed.

AGRICULTURAL PRODUCTION— CROPS

0111   Wheat 19, 21
0115   Corn 19, 21
0116   Soybeans 19-20
0119   Cash Grains NEC 19
0131   Cotton 20
0132   Tobacco 20
0133   Sugarcane and Sugar Beets 20
0139   Field Crops, Except Cash Grains, NEC 20
0161   Vegetables and Melons 20
0174   Citrus Fruits 20-21

AGRICULTURAL PRODUCTION— LIVESTOCK

0212   Beef Cattle, Except Feedlots 28, 29, 31-32
0213   Hogs 30, 33
0241   Dairy Farms 30-31, 32
0251   Broiler, Fryer, and Roaster Chickens 29-30, 32

FORESTRY

0811   Timber Tracts 269
0831   Forest Nurseries and Gathering of Forest Products 268
0851   Forestry Services 268

FISH AND MARINE PRODUCTS

0912   Finfish 253-255
0913   Shellfish 253
0919   Miscellaneous Marine Products 253

METAL MINING

1011   Iron Ores 375-376
1021   Copper Ores 376
1031   Lead and Zinc Ores 376
1041   Gold Ores 376-377
1044   Silver Ores 377
1061   Ferroalloy Ores, Except Vanadium 377
1094   Uranium-Radium-Vanadium Ores 377

COAL MINING

1221   Bituminous Coal and Lignite Surface Mining 156-159
1222   Bituminous Coal Underground Mining 156-159
1231   Anthracite Mining 158
1241   Coal Mining Services 156-159

OIL AND GAS EXTRACTION

1311   Crude Petroleum and Natural Gas 465-471
1381   Drilling Oil and Gas Wells 419-424
1382   Oil and Gas Field Exploration Services 419-424
1389   Oil and Gas Field Services, NEC 419-424

CONSTRUCTION

1521   General Contractors—Single-Family Houses 192, 193-194
1522   General Contractors—Residential Buildings, Other Than Single-Family 192, 194
1531   Operative Builders 192, 194
1541   General Contractors—Industrial Buildings and Warehouses 192
1542   General Contractors—Nonresidential Buildings, Other Than Industrial Buildings and Warehouses 192
1611   Highway and Street Construction, Except Elevated Highways 199, 200-201
1622   Bridge, Tunnel, and Elevated Highway Construction 199, 200, 201
1623   Water, Sewer, Pipeline, and Communications and Power Line Construction 200
1629   Heavy Construction, NEC 200

FOOD AND KINDRED PRODUCTS

2041   Flour and Other Grain Mill Products 257-259
2043   Cereal Breakfast Foods 127-129
2045   Prepared Flour Mixes and Doughs 128
2061   Cane Sugar, Except Refining 614-621
2062   Cane Sugar, Refining 614-621
2063   Beet Sugar 614-621
2064   Candy and Other Confectionery Products 615, 616, 617, 619
2066   Chocolate and Cocoa Products 616, 618
2067   Chewing Gum 615, 616, 618
2082   Malt Beverages 99-103
2084   Wines, Brandy, and Brandy Spirits 91-98
2085   Distilled and Blended Liquors 91-98
2086   Bottled and Canned Soft Drinks and Carbonated Beverages 588-593

TOBACCO PRODUCTS

2111   Cigarettes 644-649
2121   Cigars 645-646
2131   Chewing and Smoking Tobacco and Snuff 644-649

CLOTHING AND TEXTILES

2211   Broadwoven Fabric Mills, Cotton 203-208
2311   Men's and Boys' Suits, Coats, and Overcoats 50, 52
2321   Men's and Boys' Shirts, Except Work Shirts 50
2322   Men's and Boys' Underwear and Nightwear 51-52
2323   Men's and Boys' Neckwear 50-51, 52
2325   Men's and Boys' Separate Trousers and Slacks 52
2326   Men's and Boys' Work Clothing 51, 52-53
2329   Men's and Boys' Clothing, NEC 52-53
2331   Women's, Misses', and Juniors' Blouses and Shirts 58, 61
2335   Women's, Misses', and Juniors' Dresses 58, 60
2337   Women's, Misses', and Juniors' Suits, Skirts, and Coats 58, 60
2339   Women's, Misses', and Juniors' Outerwear, NEC 58
2341   Women's, Misses', Children's, and Infants' Underwear and Nightwear 58
2342   Brassieres, Girdles, and Allied Garments 58, 60

FURNITURE AND FIXTURES

2511   Wood Household Furniture, Except Upholstered 272
2512   Wood Household Furniture, Upholstered 272-273
2514   Metal Household Furniture 273
2515   Mattresses, Foundations, and Convertible Beds 273
2517   Wood Television, Radio, Phonograph, and Sewing Machine Cabinets 273
2519   Household Furniture, NEC 272

PAPER AND ALLIED PRODUCTS

2611   Pulp Mills 520-528
2621   Paper Mills 438-445
2631   Paperboard Mills 446-449

PRINTING AND PUBLISHING

2711   Newspapers: Publishing, or Publishing and Printing 409-414
2721   Periodicals: Publishing, or Publishing and Printing 457-464
2731   Books: Publishing, or Publishing and Printing 106-111
2752   Commercial Printing, Lithographic 514-519
2754   Commercial Printing, Gravure 514-519
2759   Commercial Printing, NEC 514-519

CHEMICALS AND ALLIED PRODUCTS

2812   Alkalies and Chlorine 139-140
2813   Industrial Gases 138, 141
2816   Inorganic Pigments 138-139
2819   Industrial Inorganic Chemicals, NEC 142, 143
2821   Plastics Materials, Synthetic Resins, and Nonvulcanized Elastomers 495-502
2833   Medicinal Chemicals and Botanical Products 365-370
2834   Pharmaceutical Preparations 481-488
2844   Perfumes, Cosmetics, and Other Toilet Preparations 450-456
2851   Paints, Varnishes, Lacquers, Enamels, and Allied Products 431-437
2861   Gum and Wood Chemicals 152
2865   Cyclic Organic Crudes and Intermediates and Organic Dyes and Pigments 149-150
2869   Industrial Organic Chemicals, NEC 147-153
2873   Nitrogenous Fertilizers 130-131
2874   Phosphatic Fertilizers 131
2875   Fertilizers, Mixing Only 132-133
2879   Pesticides and Agricultural Chemicals, NEC 133
2891   Adhesives and Sealants 8-13

PETROLEUM REFINING AND RELATED INDUSTRIES

2911   Petroleum Refining 472-480
2951   Asphalt Paving Mixtures and Blocks 72-73
2952   Asphalt Felts and Coatings 72-73

RUBBER AND MISCELLANEOUS PLASTICS PRODUCTS

3011   Tires and Inner Tubes 560-566
3021   Rubber and Plastics Footwear 560-566
3052   Rubber and Plastics Hose and Belting 560-566
3053   Gaskets, Packing, and Sealing Devices 560-566
3061   Molded, Extruded, and Lathe-Cut Mechanical Rubber Goods 560-566
3069   Fabricated Rubber Products, NEC 560-566
3081   Unsupported Plastics Film and Sheet 503-509
3082   Unsupported Plastics Profile Shapes 503-509
3083   Laminated Plastics Plate, Sheet, and Profile Shapes 503-509
3084   Plastics Pipe 503-509
3085   Plastics Bottles 503-509
3086   Plastics Foam Products 503-509
3088   Plastics Plumbing Fixtures 503-509
3089   Plastics Products, NEC 503-509

FOOTWEAR

3143   Men's Footwear, Except Athletic 261, 262
3144   Women's Footwear, Except Athletic 261-262, 264-265
3149   Footwear, Except Rubber, NEC 261

GLASS AND CONCRETE PRODUCTS

3221 Glass Containers 277, 278-279, 280-281
3229 Pressed and Blown Glass and Glassware, NEC 277, 297
3231 Glass Products, Made of Purchased Glass 277, 279
3271 Concrete Block and Brick 184-185, 187-189
3272 Concrete Products, Except Block and Brick 184-185, 187-189
3273 Ready-Mixed Concrete 184-185, 187-189
3274 Lime 185, 186-187
3275 Gypsum Products 185, 187

PRIMARY METAL INDUSTRIES

3321 Gray and Ductile Iron Foundries 323
3322 Malleable Iron Foundries 323
3324 Steel Investment Foundries 323

FABRICATED METAL PRODUCTS

3423 Hand and Edge Tools, Except Machine Tools and Handsaws 284
3425 Saw Blades and Handsaws 285
3429 Hardware, NEC 284-285
3441 Fabricated Structural Metal 371-374
3482 Small Arms Ammunition 216, 217, 219
3483 Ammunition, Except for Small Arms 216, 218, 219
3484 Small Arms 216, 218, 218

INDUSTRIAL AND COMMERCIAL MACHINERY AND COMPUTER EQUIPMENT

3534 Elevators and Moving Stairways 245-247
3552 Textile Machinery 350-351, 352, 353, 354
3554 Paper Industries Machinery 351, 352, 354
3555 Printing Trades Machinery and Equipment 351, 353
3556 Food Production Machinery 351, 353, 354-355
3559 Special Industry Machinery, NEC 350, 351, 352, 353-354
3561 Pumps and Pumping Equipment 338, 339, 340
3562 Ball and Roller Bearings 338, 339, 340
3563 Air and Gas Compressors 338-339, 340
3564 Industrial and Commercial Fans and Blowers and Air Purification Equipment 340
3568 Mechanical Power Transmission Equipment, NEC 339
3569 General Industrial Machinery and Equipment, NEC 339
3571 Electronic Computers 174-183
3577 Computer Peripheral Equipment, NEC 163-167
3579 Office Machines, NEC 415-418
3581 Automatic Vending Machines 344-345, 346, 347, 348
3861 Photographic Equipment and Supplies 489-494
3582 Commercial Laundry, Drycleaning, and Pressing Machines 345
3585 Air-Conditioning and Warm Air Heating Equipment and Commercial and Industrial Refrigeration Equipment 344, 345-346, 347-348
3586 Measuring and Dispensing Pumps 345, 346, 347
3589 Service Industry Machinery, NEC 345, 347

ELECTRONIC AND OTHER ELECTRICAL EQUIPMENT AND COMPONENTS

3621 Motors and Generators 405-408
3631 Household Cooking Equipment 70
3632 Household Refrigerators and Home and Farm Freezers 65
3633 Household Laundry Equipment 65, 67
3634 Electric Housewares and Fans 65
3635 Household Vacuum Cleaners 66
3639 Household Appliances, NEC 65, 39, 70
3641 Electric Lamp Bulbs and Tubes 238, 239, 214
3643 Current-Carrying Wiring Devices 238, 239, 242
3644 Noncurrent-Carrying Wiring Devices 238
3645 Residential Electric Lighting Fixtures 238, 240
3646 Commercial, Industrial, and Institutional Electric Lighting Fixtures 238, 240
3647 Vehicular Lighting Equipment 239, 241-242
3648 Lighting Equipment, NEC 239
3651 Household Audio and Video Equipment 76-79
3661 Telephone and Telegraph Apparatus 635-643
3674 Semiconductors and Related Devices 581-587

TRANSPORTATION EQUIPMENT

3711 Motor Vehicles and Passenger Car Bodies 394-395, 397-398, 399
3713 Truck and Bus Bodies 394, 395-396, 398, 399-400
3714 Motor Vehicle Parts and Accessories 396, 400-401
3721 Aircraft 43-49

MISCELLANEOUS MANUFACTURING INDUSTRIES

3812 Search, Detection, Navigation, Guidance, Aeronautical, and Nautical Systems, Instruments, and Equipment 567-573
3841 Surgical and Medical Instruments and Apparatus 622-628
3851 Ophthalmic Goods 425-430
3911 Jewelry, Precious Metal 328, 329
3949 Sporting and Athletic Goods, NEC 603-608
3961 Costume Jewelry and Costume Novelties, Except Precious Metal 327-328

TRANSPORTATION AND POSTAL SERVICES

4011 Railroads, Line-Haul Operating 536-541
4013 Railroad Switching and Terminal Establishments 536-541
4213 Trucking, Except Local 657-662
4311 United States Postal Service 510-513
4412 Deep Sea Foreign Transportation of Freight 663-668
4424 Deep Sea Domestic Transportation of Freight 663-668
4512 Air Transportation, Scheduled 36-42
4724 Travel Agencies 650-656
4725 Tour Operators 651

COMMUNICATIONS

4813 Telephone Communications, Except Radiotelephone 629-632
4832 Radio Broadcasting Stations 529-535

4833   Television Broadcasting Stations 529-535
4841   Cable and Other Pay Television Services 114-118

ELECTRIC AND GAS SERVICES
4911   Electric Services 229-234
4922   Natural Gas Transmission 229-234
4924   Natural Gas Distribution 229-234

RETAIL AND EATING PLACES
5251   Hardware Stores 283-285
5311   Department Stores 554-559
5812   Eating Places 548-553
5961   Catalog and Mail-Order Houses 121-125

BANKS AND EXCHANGES
6021   National Commercial Banks 81, 84
6022   State Commercial Banks 81, 84
6029   Commercial Banks, NEC 81, 84
6035   Savings Institutions, Federally Chartered 82, 85, 86
6036   Savings Institutions, Not Federally Chartered 82, 85, 86
6231   Security and Commodity Exchanges 574-580

INSURANCE AND OTHER BUSINESS SERVICES
6311   Life Insurance 313-330
6321   Accident and Health Insurance 305-312
6531   Real Estate Agents and Managers 542-547
7011   Hotels and Motels 299-304

7311   Advertising Agencies 13-18
7371   Computer Programming Services 169-173
7372   Prepackaged Software 594-602
7374   Computer Processing and Data Preparation and Processing Services 209-215

MOTION PICTURES
7812   Motion Picture and Video Tape Production 383-393
7819   Services Allied to Motion Picture Production 383-393
7822   Motion Picture and Video Tape Distribution 383-393
7829   Services Allied to Motion Picture Distribution 383-393
7832   Motion Picture Theaters, Except Drive-In 383-393
7841   Video Tape Rental 383-393

HEALTH SERVICES
8062   General Medical and Surgical Hospitals 288-295
8063   Psychiatric Hospitals 288-295
8069   Specialty Hospitals, Except Psychiatric 288-295

EDUCATIONAL AND MISCELLANEOUS SERVICES
8111   Legal Services 331-337
8211   Elementary and Secondary Schools 222, 223-224
8221   Colleges, Universities, and Professional Schools 222-223, 224, 225
8222   Junior Colleges and Technical Institutes 225
8711   Engineering Services 248-252
8721   Accounting, Auditing, and Bookkeeping Services 1-7
8742   Management Consulting Services 357-364

GENERAL INDEX

This index contains references to companies, associations, government agencies, and specific legislation cited in U.S. Industry Profiles. Citations are followed by the page number(s) in which the company, association, publication, agency, or legislative act is discussed.

A

A/C Flyer 49
ABA Bankers News 87
ABA Banking Journal 87
ABD-Aviation Buyer's Guide 49
Aberdeen's Concrete Journal: The Concrete Producer's Favorite Magazine 189
Aberdeen's Concrete Repair Digest: The Magazine for the Concrete Repair Specialist 189
ABI/INFORM 17, 41, 119, 311, 364
The Absolute Sound 78
Academy for Educational Development 226
Academy of Management, Division of Managerial Consultation 362
Academy of Motion Picture Arts and Sciences 389
Academy of Television Arts an d Sciences 533
Accident Facts 311
Accounting and Tax Database 5
Accounting Information Systems: Concepts and Practice For Effective Decision Making 6
Accounting Review 4
Accounting: The Basis for Business Decisions 6
Accounting Today: The Newspaper for the Accounting Professional 4
Accreditation Board for Engineering and Technology 249
Ace Hardware Corporation 285
ACI Directory 189
ACI Structural Journal 189
ACME 358
ACME: The Association of Management Consulting Firms 363
Acorn Computer Group Ltd. 175
Addison-Wesley 109
Adhesive and Sealant Council 11
Adhesives 12
Adhesives Age 11
Adhesives Age Directory 12

Adhesives and Sealants 12
Adhesives Manufacturers Association 11
Advanced Accounting 6
Advanced Materials and Processes 325, 379
Advances in Agronomy 26
Advances in Computers 182
Advances in Health Economics and Health Services Research 297
Advances in Instrumentation 573
Advances in Instrumentation and Control 628
Advances in Polymer Technology 501, 508
Advertiser and Agency Red Books Plus 17
Advertising Age-Leading National Advertisers 18
Advertising Age: National Expenditures in Newspapers 18
Advertising Age: The International Newspaper of Marketing 17
Advertising Agencies: What They Are, What They Do, How They Do It 17
Advertising Agency Business 18
Advertising Mail Marketing Association 513
Advertising Pure and Simple 18
Aeronautical Repair Station Association 47
Aerospace America 47
Aerospace/Defense Markets and Technology 48, 220
Aerospace Engineering Magazine 47
Aerospace Facts and Figures 49
Aerospace Industries Association of America 47
Aetna Inc. 317
Affiliated Dress Manufacturers 61
Affordable Employee Health Care: Options for a Model Benefits Plan 311
Aftermarket Fact Book 403
AGA American Gas 468
Agreement on Textiles and Clothing 50–51, 53, 61
Agribusiness Management 26
Agricola 135
Agricultural Outlook 24
Agricultural Research 24
Agricultural Research Institute 24
Agricultural Research Policy 26
Agricultural Statistics 26, 34, 260, 271, 621
Agricultural Waste Database 25
Agriculture and Food Act of 1981 617

Agriculture Council of America 24
Agriculture Fact Book 26
Agriculture Virtual Library 34, 270
Agronomy Journal 24
Agronomy News 24
AHA News 294
Air Carrier Financial Statistics Quarterly 42
Air Carrier Traffic Statistics Monthly 42
Air Conditioning and Refrigeration Institute (ARI) 346
Air Force Journal of Logistics 219
Air Market News 47
Air Products and Chemicals, Inc. 148
Air Transport Association of America 41
Air Transport World 41
Aircraft Transaction Listings 49
Airlines Reporting Corp. 653
Airport Activity Statistics of Certificated Route Air Carriers 42
Airport Business 41
Airport Press 41
Alcoholic Beverage Control 95, 101
All About Cable 119
All Operating Savings and Loan Associations; Selected Balance Sheet Data and Flow of Savings and Mortgage Lending Activity 89
Alliance of American Insurers 310, 317
Alliance of Independent Travel Agents 653
Alliance of Metalworking Industries 372
Alliance of Motion Picture and Television Producers 389, 533
Allied Signal, Inc. 569
Aluminum Association 372
Aluminum, Brick and Glass Workers International Union 281
Aluminum Industry 374
Aluminum Recycling Association 372
Aluminum Standards and Data 374
Aluminum Statistical Review 374
Amalgamated Clothing and Textile Workers Union 54, 61
America Online 117
America's Community Banker 87
America's Community Bankers 87
American Academy of Medical Administrators 293
American Academy of Optometry 428
American Accounting Association 3
American Advertising Magazine 17
American Airlines Inc. 36–37, 39
American Apparel Manufacturers Association 54, 60–61
American Architectural Manufacturers Association 373
American Association for Adult and Continuing Education 226
American Association for Textile Technology 206
American Association of Advertising Agencies 17, 531
American Association of Airport Executives 41
American Association of Cereal Chemists 129
American Association of Cosmetology Schools 455
American Association of Healthcare Consultants 293
American Association of Publishers 108
American Association of School Administrators 226
American Association of Textile Chemists and Colorists 206
American Automobile Association 401
American Automobile Manufacturers Association 401
American Automobile Manufacturers Association (AAMA) 394

American Banker 87
American Bankers Association 86
American Bar Association 334, 336
American Board of Medical Specialties 293
American Board of Ophthalmology 428
American Board of Opticianry 428
American Book-Trade Directory 112
American Booksellers Association 106
American Building Contractors Association 195
American Bureau of Metal Statistics 379
American Bureau of Shipping 666
American Bureau of Shipping Record 668
American Business Press (ABP) 462
American Chemical Society 144, 153
American Cloak and Suit Manufacturers Association 61
American Cocoa Research Institute 618
American College of Health Care Administrators 293
American College of Healthcare Executives 293
American College of Trial Lawyers 336
American Concrete Institute 186, 189
American Concrete Pressure Pipe Association 186
American Corn Millers' Federation 259
American Cotton Shippers Association 206
American Council of Life Insurance 317
American Council on Education 226
American Crop Protection 134
American Defense Preparedness Association 219
American Drug Index 369
American Farm Bureau Federation 24
American Firearms Industry 220
American Fisheries Society 255
American Forest and Paper Association 270, 442, 523, 525
American Foundrymen's Society 324
American Furniture Manufacturers Association 274
American Gas 235
American Gas Association 234, 397, 468
American Glass Review 281
American Hardware Manufacturers Association 286
American Health Care Association 293
American Home Products Corp. 482
American Hospital Association 293
American Hotel & Motel Association 299, 303
American Hotel & Motel Association (AHMA) 302
American Independent Refiners Association 477
American Institute of Aeronautics and Astronautics 47
American Institute of Baking 260
American Institute of Certified Public Accountants 2–3
American Institute of Merchant Shipping 666
American Insurance Association 310, 317
American Insurers Highway Safety Alliance 310
American Iron and Steel Annual Statistical Report 326
American Iron and Steel Institute 324, 610
American Jewelry Manufacturer 329
American Journal of Enology and Viticulture 97
American Journal of Nursing 294
American Journal of Ophthalmology 429
The American Lawyer 336
American Lighting Association 242
American Machinist 348, 355
American Managed Care and Review Association 293
American Manufacturers Association 58
American Maritime Association 666
American Medical Association 293
American Medical News 294
American Metal Market 373, 380, 613

American Mining Congress   378–379
American Motor Carrier Directory   662
American Nurses' Association   293
American Oil Chemists' Society Journal   144, 153
American Optometric Association   428
American Optometric Association Journal   429
American Optometric Association News   429
American Optometric Foundation   428
American Paint and Coatings Journal   436
American Painting Contractor   436
American Paper Institute   449
American Papermaker   444, 526
American Petroleum Institute   468, 477
American Petroleum Institute. Division of Statistics. Weekly Statistical Bulletin   469
American Pharmaceutical Association   486
American Postal Workers Union (APWU)   512
American Printer   518
American Public Gas Association   234
American Public Gas Association Newsletter   235
American Public Power Association   234
American Pulpwood Association   526
American Rifleman   220
American Road and Transportation Builders Association   198
American School and University: Facilities, Purchasing, and Business Administration   227
American School Board Journal   227
American Seafood Distributors Association   256
American Segmental Bridge Institute   186
American Shipper: Ports, Transportation and Industry   667
American Shoemaking   265
American Society for Contemporary Ophthalmology   428
American Society for Enology and Viticulture   96
American Society for Healthcare Materials Management   627
American Society for Testing and Materials   186
American Society of Agricultural Engineers   24
American Society of Agronomy   24
American Society of Animal Science   33
American Society of Brewing Chemists   103
American Society of Brewing Chemists Journal   103
American Society of Civil Engineers   188, 250–251
American Society of Civil Engineers. Proceedings   251
American Society of Civil Engineers: Transactions   252
American Society of CLU and CHFC   317
American Society of Magazine Editors   462
American Society of Mechanical Engineers   247, 251
American Society of Newspaper Editors   412
American Society of Perfumers   455
American Society of Travel Agents   651–652, 654
American Society of T.V. Cameramen and International Society of Videographers   389
American Software Association   599
American Sportscasters Association   533
American Statistics Index: A Comprehensive Guide and Index to the Statistical Publications of the United States Government Online   196
American Subcontractors Association   195
American Sugar Alliance   615, 619
American Sugar Cane League of the U.S.A.   619
American Supply and Machinery Manufacturers Association   342, 348, 355
American Textile Manufacturers Institute   205–206
American Tool, Die and Stamping News   286

American Trans Air Inc.   38, 40
American Trucking Associations   660
American Trucking Trends   403, 661
American Video Association   78
American Vocational Association   226
American Vocational Educational Research Association   226
The American Waterways Operators   666
American Wholesale Marketers Association   619
American Wine Society   97
American Women's Society of Certified Public Accountants   2
American Wood Preservers Institute   270
AMEX   576
Amoco Corporation   149
Amtrak   536
An Analysis of the Management Consulting Business in the U.S. Today   364
Analog and Digital Communication Systems   642
Anchor Glass Container Corporation   281
Andersen Consulting   360
Anheuser-Busch Companies, Inc.   99
Animal Health Yearbook   34
Annual Energy Review   161, 236, 470, 479
Annual Index to Motion Picture Credits   393
Annual Institute on Oil and Gas Law and Taxation   237
Annual Report   540
Annual Report of Postmaster General   513
Annual Review of Medicine: Selected Topics in the Clinical Sciences   297
Annual Review of Public Health   297
Annual Review of the Chemical Industry   145, 154
Annual Survey of Manufactures   135, 369, 430, 487, 621, 642
Annuity and Life Insurance Shopper   317
AOAC International   134
AOAC International Journal   135
APILIT   469, 478
APIPAT   470, 478
Apparel Industry Magazine   54, 62
Appliance   70
Appliance-Appliance Industry Purchasing Directory   71
Appliance Manufacturer   70, 243
Appliance Manufacturers Buyer's Guide   71
Appliance Parts Distributors Association   70
Appliance Service News   70
Approved Drug Products   487
Aquatic Sciences and Fisheries Abstracts Series (Online)   256
Architecture, Engineering and Construction Infocenter   196
Armed Forces Communications and Electronics Association   641
Armed Forces Journal International   220
Arthur Andersen   360
Arthur D. Little, Inc.   361
ASBC Newsletter   103
ASCE News   251
Ashland Oil, Inc.   148, 475
ASM International   379
Asphalt   74
Asphalt and Products   74
Asphalt Emulsion Manufacturers Association   73
Asphalt Institute   74
Asphalt Roofing Manufacturers Association   74
Asset and Liability Trends: All Operating Savings and Loan Associations by Type of Association and Area   89

Associated Builders and Contractors 195
Associated Corset and Brassiere Manufacturers 62
Associated Equipment Distributors 195, 202
Associated General Contractors of America 195
Associated Glass and Pottery Manufacturers 281
Associated Petroleum Employees Union 467
Association for Accounting Administration 3
Association for Computing Machinery 180
Association for Computing Machinery Journal 181
Association for Continuing Higher Education 226
Association for Investment Management and Research 577
Association for Suppliers of Printing and Publishing
  Technologies 518
Association for the Advancement of Medical
  Instrumentation 627
Association of America's Public Televised Stations 533
Association of American Publishers 111
Association of American Railroads 540
Association of Asphalt Paving Technologists 74
Association of Asphalt Paving Technologists-
  Proceedings 75
Association of Black CPA Firms 2
Association of Cinema and Video Laboratories 389
Association of Computer Users 180
Association of Consulting Chemists and Chemical
  Engineers 144, 153
Association of Consulting Management Engineers 358
Association of Data Communications Users 211
Association of Data Communications Users Newsletter 212
Association of Diesel Specialists 408
Association of Directory Publishers 125
Association of Edison Illuminating Companies 234
Association of Government Accountants 4
Association of Home Appliance Manufacturers 70
Association of Internal Management Consultants 358
Association of Iron and Steel Engineers 324
Association of Life Insurance Counsel 317
Association of Management Consultants 358
Association of Management Consulting Firms 358
Association of National Advertisers 17
Association of Official Analytical Chemists 134
Association of Operative Millers 260
Association of Paid Circulation Publications 513
Association of Publicly Traded Companies 577
Association of Retail Travel Agents 652
Association of Steel Distributors 324
Association of Trial Lawyers of America 336
AST Computer, Inc. 179
AT & T Technical Journal 632
AT&T 530, 630, 640
Athletic Business 607
Athletic Management 607
Atlantic States Marine Fisheries Commission 254
Audio 78
Audio Week: The Authoritative News Service of the Audio
  Consumer Electronics Industry 78
Audit Bureau of Circulations (ABC) 412, 462
Auditing 6
Auditing: An Integrated Approach 6
Auditing: Integrated Concepts and Procedures 6
Auto Mechanics Fundamentals 403
Auto Retail Report 402
Autocar and Motor 402
Automobile Insurance Losses, Collision, Comprehensive and
  Injury Coverages, Variations by Make and Series 310

Automotive Affiliated Representatives 401
Automotive Engineering Magazine 402
Automotive Engines: Theory and Servicing 408
Automotive Executive 402
Automotive Industries 402
Automotive Industries Insider 402
Automotive Industries Statistical Issue 403
Automotive Industry Data 403
Automotive News: Engineering, Financial, Manufacturing,
  Sales, Marketing, Servicing 402
Automotive Parts & Accessories Association 401
Automotive Recycling 402
Automotive Service Industry Association 401
Automotive Trade Association Executives 401
The Autoparts Report 403
Aviation Buyer's Guide 49
Aviation Daily 41
Aviation Digest: The News Magazine Edited for Aircraft
  Owners 47
Aviation Equipment Maintenance 48
Aviation Law Reports 49
Aviation Week and Space Technology 48

B

Baby and Junior: International Trade Magazine for
  Children's and Youth Fashions and Supplies 54, 62
Baby Bells 630
Bacon's Magazines Directories 464
Bain & Company 361
Baker & Taylor 111
Bakery, Confectionery and Tobacco Workers
  International 619
Bank Marketing 87
Bank Operating Statistics 89
Bank Profitability: Statistical Supplement-Financial
  Statements of Banks 89
Bank Rate Monitor: The Weekly Financial Rate Reporter 87
Banker's Round Table 87
The Bankers: The Next Generation 89
Bankers' Almanac 89
Bankers' Magazine 87
Banking Information Source 88, 546
BanxQuote Online 88
Barge Fleet Profile for the Mississippi River System and
  Connected Waterways 668
Barnes & Noble, Inc. 106–107
Barron's: National Business and Financial Weekly 206, 577
Basic Petroleum Data Book 470, 479
Bear, Stearns & Co. 549
Beaumont Methanol Corp. 149
Beef 33
Beer Institute 99, 103
Beer Marketer's Insights 103
Beer Statistics News 104
Being Digital 182
Bell Atlantic Media Relations and Public Archives 633
Bell Operating Companies 630
Bell South 116, 632
Best's Aggregates and Averages: Property-Casualty 319
Best's Review: Life-Health Insurance Edition 310
Best's Review. Property-Casualty Insurance 317
BESTLINK 311, 318
The Betrayed Profession: Lawyering at the End of the
  Twentieth Century 337

Better Vision Institute   428

Beverage Digest   592

Beverage Industry   592

Beverage World: Magazine of the Beverage Industry   593

Beverage World Periscope   593

BioBusiness   296

Biomedical Instrumentation and Technology   627

Biotechnology Information Center   25

Bituminous Coal Operators Association   160

Black Diamond   160

Blockbuster Entertainment Corp.   384

Blu-Book Directory: Hollywood's Most Comprehensive Entertainment Directory   393

Blue Cross & Blue Shield   305

Blue Cross and Blue Shield Association   310

The Blue Sheet: Health Policy and Biomedical Research   294

Blueprint   286

Body Fashions: Intimate Apparel   62

Book Industry Study Group   111

Book Industry Trends   112

Book Manufacturers Institute   111

Book Marketing Update   111

Book Publishing Career Directory   112

Book Publishing Report   111

Books in Print Online   126

Booz, Allen & Hamilton, Inc.   361

Borden Chemicals and Plastics Limited Partnership   148–149

Borders Group, Inc.   106–107

Boston Beer Company   99

Boston Chicken Inc.   549

Boston Consulting Group   361

Boston Market   549

Bowker Annual Library and Book Trade Almanac   112

Bowman's Accounting Report   5

Boxoffice   390

BPA International   462

Brady Bill   217

Brassey's Defense Yearbook   221

Breakfast Cereals and How They Are Made   129

Bretton Woods Committee   87

Brewers Almanac   104

Brewers Digest   103

Brewers' Association of America   103

British Petroleum   421

British Telecommunications   630

Broadcast Education Association   533

Broadcast Engineering: Journal of Broadcast Technology   533

Broadcast Investor: Newsletter on Radio-TV Station Finance   533

Broadcasting & Cable   118, 533

Broadcasting & Cable Yearbook   119, 535

Broadwoven Fabrics (Gray)

Broker World   318

Buena Vista Home Video   385

Builder   195

Builder and Contractor-Associated Builders and Contractors Membership Directory   197

Builders' Hardware Manufacturers Association   286

Building and Construction Trades Department-AFL-CIO   195

Building Material Retailer   195

Building Officials and Code Administrators International   195

Bulletin Board Systems for Business   214

Bureau of Alcohol, Tobacco and Firearms   95, 101

Bureau of Alcohol, Tobacco, and Firearms Quarterly Bulletin   97, 220, 648

Bureau of Labor   178

Bureau of Labor Statistics   73, 241, 551, 618

Bureau of Labor Statistics of the Department of Labor   576

Bureau of Wholesale Sales Representatives   54, 62

Burger King   552

Burlington Industries Equity Inc.   204

Business and Health   310

Business Insurance: News Magazine for Corporate Risk, Employee Benefit and Financial Executives   318

Business Journals of the United States: Historical Guides to the World's Periodicals and Newspapers   464

Business Products Industry Association   417

Business Software Database   601

Business Statistics   34, 49, 55, 63, 70, 98, 207, 221, 266, 275, 282, 304, 326, 349, 355, 449, 470, 519, 553, 565

Business Technology Association   417

Business Travel News   41

Buying Treasury Securities: Bills, Notes, Bonds, Offerings Schedule, Conversions   579

C

CA Search   11, 135, 144, 154

CAB Abstracts   25, 34, 270, 620

Cable and Station Coverage Atlas   120

Cable Telecommunications Association   118

Cable Television Administration and Marketing Society   118

Cable Television Consumer Protection and Competition Act of 1992   117

Cable Television Revenues   119

Cable TV Facts   119

Cable TV Financial Databook   120

Cable TV Programming: Newsletter on Programs for Pay Cable TV and Analysis of Basic Cable Networks   118

Cable TV Technology: Newsletter on Technical Advances, Construction of New Systems and Rebuild of Existing Systems   118

Cabletelevision Advertising Bureau   118

Cablevision Systems Corp.   115

Cablevision: The Analysis and Features Bi-Weekly of the Cable Television Industry   119

California Air Resources Board (CARB)   474

Canada/United States Free Trade Agreement   172

Canandaigua Wine Company   91

Candy Industry   619

Candy Marketer   619

Candy Wholesaler: The Magazine for Candy and Tobacco and Snack Food Distributors   620

Canon, Inc.   490

Cars of Revenue Freight Loaded   541

Casting Industry Suppliers Association   324

Casualty Actuarial Society   317

Casualty Actuarial Society Yearbook   319

Catalog Age   125

Cattleman   33

CDLA, The Computer Leasing and Remarketing Association   166

CEE News   243

Celebrity Directory: How to Reach Over 7,000 Movie-TV Stars and Other Famous Celebrities 393
Cellular Business: Journal of Cellular Telecommunications 641
Census of Manufactures 369
Census of Transportation 661
Center for Disease Control and Prevention 345
Center for Sports Sponsorship 606
Center on Education and Training for Employment 226
Cereal Chemistry 129
Certified Meeting Professional 653
Certified Travel Counselors 653
CFTC 575
Chain Store Age 558
Chamber of Commerce of the Apparel Industry 54, 62
Change: The Magazine of Higher Learning 227
Changing Medical Markets: The International Monthly Newsletter for Executives in the Healthcare and Biotechnology Industries 294
The Changing Structure of the U.S. Automotive Parts Industry 403
Channel 585
Chef 552
Chem-Bank 144, 154
Chemical Fabrics and Film Association 505
Chemical Management and Resources Association 144, 153
Chemical Manufacturers Association 144, 150, 153
Chemical Processing 144, 153
Chemical Regulation Reporter: A Weekly Review of Affecting Chemical Users and Manufacturers 145, 154
Chemical Substances Control 145, 154
Chemical Week 144, 153
Chemical Week-Buyer's Guide 145, 154
Chevron Corporation 149, 474–475
Chicago Mercantile Exchange 575–576
Chicago: The Lawyer's Magazine 336
Chilton's Automotive Marketing: A Monthly Publication for the Automotive Aftermarket 402
China Coast 549
Chrysler 396
Cinamerica 386
CircuiTree 586
Circuits Assembly 586
Circulation Council of DMA 462
Circulation Management 463
Circulation year 414, 534
CITIBASE (Citicorp Economic Database) 34, 48, 55, 63, 70, 88, 97, 104, 145, 154, 161, 207, 220, 236, 260, 266, 275, 281, 303, 325, 349, 355, 436, 444, 449, 470, 518, 527, 540, 553, 558, 565, 620, 655
Civil Engineering 251
Civil Engineering Database (CEDB) 252
Civil Engineering for the Plant Engineer 252
Civil Engineering Magazine 251
Civil Engineering Research Council 188
Civilian Manpower Statistics 221
Clean Air Act 140, 378
Clean Air Act Amendments of 1990 142, 148, 150, 232, 344, 420, 473, 517
Clean Water Act (CWA) 378
Clin-Alert 486
Clinton administration 39
Clothing Manufacturers of the U.S.A. 54, 62
Coal 160
Coal and Modern Coal Processing: An Introduction 162

Coal and Synfuels Technology 161
Coal Data 161
Coal Facts 162
Coal Information 162
Coal Law and Regulation 162
Coal Liquefaction Fundamentals 162
Coal Mining Newsletter 161
Coal Outlook 161
Coal Transportation Statistics 161
Coal Week 161
Coca-Cola Enterprises 590–591
College and University 227
Colorado School of Mines Quarterly 380
Columbia/HCA Healthcare Corporation 290
Columbia Pictures 386
Comcast 118
Comissai de Mercado de Valores Mobiliarios (Portugal) 575
Comissao De Valores Mobiliarios (Brazil) 575
Commercial Carrier Journal 661
Commodities Futures Trading Commission Act of 1974 575
Commodities Futures Trading Commission (CFTC) 575
Commodity Exchange 577
Commodity Exchange Act of 1922 575
Commodity Exchange Act of 1936 575
Commodity Exchange Commission 575
Commodity Year Book 374, 580
1994 Common Sense Initiative 110
Communication Equipment, and Other Electronic Systems and Equipment 633, 642
Communication Technology Update 633
Communications Engineering and Design 641
Communications News 212, 632
Communications Outlook 642
CommunicationsWeek 213
Company of the Paris Bank, Exchange, Trade and Finance Brokers (Compagnie des Agents de Change de Paris) 576
Compaq Computer Corp. 179
COMPENDEX PLUS 252
Competitive Telecommunicat ions Association 632
Composite Catalog of Oil Field Equipment and Services 424
The Composites and Adhesives Newsletter 11
CompuServe 117
Computer 181
Computer and Automated Systems Association of Society of Manufacturing Engineers 180
Computer and Business Equipment Manufacturers Association 417
Computer and Communications Industry Association 211
Computer and Mathematics Search 181
Computer Buyer's Guide and Handbook 167
Computer Communications: A Business Perspective 214
Computer Communications: Principles and Business Applications 214
Computer Communications Review 213
Computer Database 181, 214, 601
Computer Industry Almanac 182, 601
Computer Industry Report 213
Computer Languages 599
Computer Letter: Business Issues in Technology 181
Computer Parts and Supplies 167
Computer Phone Book Update 214
Computer Publishing and Advertising Report: The Biweekly Newsletter for Publishing and Advertising Executives in the Computer Field 111

Computer Reseller News: The Newspaper for Microcomputer Reselling   181

Computer Review   214

Computer Shopper: The Computer Magazine for Direct Buyers   181

Computers   182

Computers and Information Processing   182

Computers and Office and Accounting Machines   167, 182, 418

Computerworld: Newsweekly for Information Systems Management   213, 599

Computing Technology Industry Association   166

Concrete Producer News-Buyer's Guide   189

Concrete Products   189

Concrete Reinforcing Steel Institute   186

Concrete Technology   189

Confectioner: Where Confectionery and Snacks Mean Business   620

Conference of Casualty Insurance Companies   317

Conference of North East Governors   141

Consensus: National Futures and Financial Weekly   577

Consolidation   210

The Constitution of Glasses: A Dynamic Interpretation   282

Construction Contracting   197, 202

Construction Contracts and Specifications   197

Construction Equipment Distribution   202

Construction Industry Manufacturers Association   195, 202

Construction Law Adviser: Monthly Practical Advice for Lawyers and Construction Professionals   196

Construction Review   196

Construction Specifier: For Commercial and Industrial Construction   196

Consultants and Consulting Organizations Directory: CCOD Online   364

Consultants News   363

Consumer Bankers Association   87

Consumer Magazine and Agri-Media Rates and Data   464

Consumer Product Safety Commission   435

Consumer Reports Travel Letter   654

Consumption on the Woolen System and Worsted Combing   207

Contact Lens Council   426

Continental Cablevision Inc.   115

Control Engineering: For Designers and Users of Control and Instrumentation Equipment and Systems Worldwide   573

Cooking for Profit   552

Coors Brewing Company   99

Corn Annual   26

The Cornell Hotel and Restaurant Administration Quarterly   303, 552

Corning Incorporated   279

Corporate Financing Week   577

Corporate Internet Planning Guide: Aligning Internet Strategy with Business Goals   643

Corporation for Open Systems International   166

Cosmetic Ingredient Review   453

Cosmetic, Toiletries, and Fragrance Association   452, 455

Cotter & Company   285

Cotton Council International   206

Cotton Digest International   206

Cotton Incorporated   24, 203, 206

Council for Periodical Distributors Association   462

Council for the Advancement and Support of Education   226

Council for Tobacco Research-U.S.A.   647

Council of Consulting Organizations (CCO)   358

Council of Fashion Designers of America   54, 62

Council of Graduate Schools   226

Council of Insurance Agents and Brokers   317

Council on Family Health   369

Council on Superconductivity for American Competitiveness   585

Cox Communications   118

The CPA Journal   5

CPA Marketing Report   5

CPA Personnel Report   5

CPCU Society   317

CPI Purchasing Chemicals Yellow Pages   145, 154

CPI Purchasing: The Magazine About Buying for the Chemical and Process Industries   144, 153

CRB Futures Chart Service   577

CRB Futures Market Service   577

CRIS   25

Crop Production   26

Crop Protection Chemicals Reference   136

CSA Engineering   181, 252, 633

CSC/Index, Inc.   361

CSM   125

CTFA Newsletter   455

Current Business Reports: Monthly Wholesale Trade   330

Current Industrial Reports: Paint   436

Cutting Tool Engineering   286

Cyberia: Life in the Trenches of Hyperspace   214

D

Daily Variety: News of the Entertainment Industry   390

Danish Financial Supervisory Authority   575

Darden Restaurants   549

Data Channels   213

Data Communications   213

Data Communications-Buyers' Guide   214

D.A.T.A. Digest: Discrete Semiconductors   586

D.A.T.A. Digest: Integrated Circuits   586

Data Interchange Standards Association   211

Data Networking   214

Data Sources   167, 173, 214

Datamation   172, 213

Datapro Directory of Microcomputer Software   173, 214

Datapro Management of Data Communications   214

Datapro Reports on Office Automation   173

Datapro Reports on PC and LAN Communications   215

Dataquest, Inc.   172

Datatech   417

Davison's Textile Blue Book   207

Dealerscope Merchandising: The Marketing Magazine for Consumer Electronics and Major Appliance Retailing   70

DEC   176, 179

Decision-Making in Forest Management   271

Decorating Retailer   436

Decorative Laminate Products Association   500, 508

Defense   220

Defense & Economy World Report   220

Defense Contract Audit Agency   569

Defense Industry Report   220

Defense Marketing International   220

Defense Monitor   220

Defense Research and Trial Lawyers Association   336

Dell Computer Corporation   122, 179

Deloitte & Touche   360

Delphi Automotive Systems   396
Delta Air Lines, Inc.   36–37
Derwent Crop Protection File   135
Derwent Drug File   487
Design of Concrete Structures   189
Detroit Free Press   410
Detroit News   410
Deutsche Telekom   630
Diamond Shamrock, Inc.   475
Diesel Progress: Engines and Drives   408
Digest of Education Statistics   228
Direct Marketing Association   124
Directors Guild of America   389
*Directory of Business Information Resources: Associations,
   Newsletters, Magazines, Trade Shows*   464
Directory of Consumer Electronics   79
Directory of Department Stores   559
Directory of Fertilizer Plants in the United States   136
Directory of Foodservice Distributors   553
Directory of Home Furnishings Retailers   275
Directory of the Forest Products Industry   271
Directory of Value Added Resellers   167
Disability Insurance Training Council   310
Disclosure SEC Database   578
Distilled Spirits Council of the United States   94, 97
Distributed Computing   172
Division of Enforcement   575
DM News: The Newspaper of Direct Marketing   125
DNR   206
*Do-it-Yourself Retailing: Hardware, Home Centers,
   Lumberyards*   286
Doane's Agricultural Report   33
Domestic Mail Manual   513
Door and Hardware Institute   286
Doors and Hardware   286
The Dow Chemical Company   139, 148–149
Dow Corning STI   564
*Dr. Dobb's Journal: Software Tools for the Professional
   Programmer*   600
DRI Chemical Forecast   135, 145, 154, 501, 508, 565
DRI Financial and Credit Statistics   88
DRI Transportation Cost Forecasting   540, 661, 667
Drilling Magazine   423
Drug and Cosmetic Catalog   369
Drug and Cosmetic Industry   455
Drug, Chemical and Allied Trades Association   369
Drug Development Research   369, 486
Drug Information Association   369
Drug Information Fulltext   487
Drug Product Liability   369
Drug Topics   369, 486
DV: Digital Video   390

E

Early Warning Report   79, 392
Earth and Mineral Sciences   380
Eaton-Kenway   591
Ebsco Bulletin of Serials Changes   463
EC&M Electrical Products Yearbook (Electrical Construction
   and Maintenance)
EchoStar Communications Corp.   116
ECN: Electronic Component News   585
Economic Indicators   89
Economic Review of Travel in America   655

Economic Trends   296
*EDI News: The Executive Clearinghouse on Electronic Data
   Interchange*   213
EDI World   213
Edison Electric Institute   234
Editor and Publisher International Yearbook   414
*Editor and Publisher-The Fourth Estate: Spot News and
   Features About Newspapers, Advertisers and
   Agencies*   413
EDP Auditors Association   4
*EDP Weekly: The Leading Weekly Computer News
   Summary*   166
Education of a Speculator   580
Educational Administration Quarterly   227
Educational Marketer   227
Educational Media and Technology Yearbook   228
*Educational Record: The Magazine of Higher
   Education*   227
EEI Statistical Releases: Electric Output   236
E.I. du Pont de Nemours & Company   148
Electric Ideas Clearinghouse Bulletin Board System   236
Electric Lamps   244
Electric Power Monthly   236
*Electric Utility Week: The Electric Utility Industry
   Newsletter*   235
Electrical Apparatus Service Association   242
Electrical Construction and Maintenance (EC&M)
Electrical Contractor Magazine   243
Electrical Equipment Representatives Association   242
Electrical Generating Systems Association   242
Electrical World   235
Electronic Components   585
Electronic Data Interchange Association   212
Electronic Data Systems Corporation   210
Electronic Engineering Times   585
Electronic Industries Association   78, 585
Electronic Market Data Book   642
Electronic Market Data Book—1994   586
Electronic Media   391
Electronic News   585
Electronic Office: Management and Technology   173
*Electronics Now: Technology, Audio, Video, Computers,
   Projects*   78, 641
Elevator World   247
Embase   296, 429, 627
Encyclopedia of American Industries   349, 355, 445, 479,
   501, 508, 527, 565
Endangered Species Act of 1990   268, 439
Energy Information Administration   158, 377–378
Energy Information Association   230
Energy Management and Federal Energy Guidelines   479
Energy Management Report   469, 478
Energy Policy Act of 1992   234
Energy Science and Technology   161, 236, 470, 478
Energyline   161, 470, 478
Engine Manufacturers Association   408
Engineered Materials Abstracts online   501, 508
Engineering and Mining Journal (E&MJ)   380
ENR (Engineering News-Record)   251
Enron Corp.   231
Ente Nazionale Idrocarburi   477
Entertainment Marketing Letter   391
Environmental Protection Agency   110, 130, 133, 140, 150,
   239, 274, 278, 346, 435, 517, 658
EPRI Journal   235

Equipment Today 202
ERIC 227
Ernst & Young 360
Exploring Agribusiness 26
Exxon Corporation 148–149, 422, 475, 665
Eyecare Business: The Magazine for Progressive Dispensing 429

F

F & S Index 55, 63, 74, 236, 374, 494, 620
F-D-C Reports 296, 455, 487, 627
FAA Aviation Forecasts 42
FAA Statistical Handbook of Aviation 42, 49
Fabric Science 207
The Fabricator 373
Fabricators and Manufacturers Association International 373
Facts and Figures of the U.S. Plastics Industry 502, 509
Fairchild Fact File: Household Furniture and Bedding 275
Fairchild Fact File: Toiletries, Cosmetics, Fragrances, and Beauty Aids 456
Fairchild's Textile and Apparel Financial Directory 55, 63, 207
Fancy Food 620
FAO Fertilizer Yearbook 135
FAO Fishery Series 256
Farm Chemicals 135
Farm Chemicals Handbook 136
Fashion Merchandising: An Introduction 55, 64
Fashion Merchandising and Marketing 55, 64
Faulkner and Gray's Medicine and Health 294
Faulkner's Enterprise Networking 215
FCC 116
FDM: Furniture Design and Manufacturing 275
Federal Agriculture Improvement and Reform Act of 1996 (FAIR) 21, 30
Federal Alcohol Administration Act 95, 101
Federal Aviation Administration (FAA) 46
Federal Aviation Authority 567
Federal Carriers Reports 668
Federal Communications Commission 77, 94, 116, 387, 530, 630
Federal Deposit Insurance Corporation 83–84
Federal Deposit Insurance Corporation Improvement Act of 1991 85
Federal Energy Regulatory Commission 230
Federal Highway Administration 200–202
Federal Regulation of Energy 471, 479
Federal Reserve Act of 1913 84
Federal Reserve Bulletin 89
Federal Reserve System 83
Federal Trade Commission 94, 483, 531
Federation of Societies for Coatings Technology 436
Fedreral Carriers Reports 662
Fertilizer Facts and Figures 135
The Fertilizer Institute 134
Fertilizer Progress 135
Fiber Optics and Communications 632
The Film Journal: Trade Paper for Exhibitors of Motion Pictures 391
Film Quarterly 391
Finance, Insurance, and Real Estate USA: Industry Analyses, Statistics, and Leading Companies 89, 319, 547, 579
Financial Accounting Foundation 4
Financial Markets and Institutions 580

The Financial Post 577
Financial Reporting: An Accounting Revolution 6
Financial Statistics of Major Publicly Owned Electric Utilities in the U.S. 236
Financial Supervisory Authority (Sweden) 575
Fire, Casualty and Surety Bulletin 318
Fisheries of the United States 256
Fleet Owner 661
Flight Safety Foundation 47
Flour Milling Products 260
Folio: The Magazine for Magazine Management 463
Fomento Economico Mexicano SA 592
Food and Drug Administration 370, 452, 483, 488, 622
Food, Drug and Cosmetic Act 450
Food Safety Protection Act 133
FOODS ADLIBRA 620
Foodservice Equipment and Supplies Specialist 552
Footwear 266
Footwear Distributors and Retailers of America 265
Footwear Industries of America 261, 265
Footwear News 266
Ford 396
Foreign Operations Appropriations Act of 1990 269
Forest Industries 270
Forest Pro ducts and Wood Science: An Introduction 271
Forest Products Journal 270
Forest Products Society 270
Foundry Management and Technology 325
Fox Televisions Stations Group 532
Fragrance Foundation 455
France Telecom 630
Frankfurt Stock Exchange 576
''Freedom to Farm'' Bill 21
Freight Commodity Statistics 541
FSTA: Food Science and Technology Abstracts 621
Fuji 490
Fulfillment Management Association (FMA) 412, 462
Fundamental Accounting Principles 6
Fundamentals of Construction Estimating and Cost Accounting, with Computer Applications 197
Fundamentals of Professional Food Preparation 553
Furniture Design and Manufacturing: Source of Supply Directory Issue 276
Furniture/Today: The Weekly Business Newspaper of the Furniture Industry 275
Furniture World 275
Future Trends in Telecommunications 634
Futures Markets 580
Futures: News, Analysis, and Strategies for Futures, Options, and Derivatives Traders 578

G

Gale Database of Publications and Broadcast Media 119, 126, 413, 463, 534
Gale Directory of Publications and Broadcast Media 535
Gannett 410
Gas Data Book 236
Gas Digest: The Magazine of Gas Operations 469
Gas Facts: A Statistical Record of the Gas Utility Industry 236, 470
Gas Industries Magazine 235, 469
Gas Turbine World 408
Gateway 2000, Inc. 122
Gemological Institute of America 329

General Agreement on Tariffs and Trade   33, 57, 111, 172, 205, 507, 518, 626
General Agreement on Trade in Services   172
General Aviation Manufacturers Association   47
General Aviation Revitalization Act of 1994   45
General Aviation Statistical Databook, 1992 edition   49
General Electric Company   232, 406
General Foods   549
General Mills, Inc.   128
General Motors Corporation   233, 396, 530
General Programming Inc.   591
Generalized System of Preferences (GSP)   329
Generic Pharmaceutical Industry Association   486
GEOARCHIVE   380
Geophysical Directory   424
GEOREF   381
Georgia Gulf Corporation   148–149
Getting Started in Futures   580
Glass Association of North America   281
Glass Digest: Management Magazine Serving the Flat Glass, Architectural Metal and Allied Products Industry   281
Glass Magazine   281
Glass Packaging Institute (GPI)   278
Glass Science   282
Global Change Research Program   268
Global Positioning Systems   567
GLOBEX System   576
Going Public: The IPO Reporter   578
Gourmet Retailer   620
Government Accounting Office   569
Government Contractor   196
Grand Metropolitan PLC   94
Graphic Arts Monthly   518
Graphic Arts Monthly-Printing Industry Sourcebook   519
The Greatest Ever Bank Robbery: The Collapse of the Savings and Loan Industry   89
Green Burrito   549
Grupo Embotellador de Mexico SA   592
GTE   632
Guide to Biotechnology Products, Instruments, and Services   628
Guide to Computer Vendors   418, 601
Guide to Liability Insurance   311
Gummed Industries Association   11
Guns and Ammo   220
Guns: Finest in the Firearms Field   220

H

Haggar Corporation   52
Hard Rock Cafe   549
Hardware Age   286
Harmonized Tariff Schedule of the United States   61
Hay Group   361
HDS Network Systems Inc.   175
Health Alliance Alert   294
Health and Environment in America's Top-Rated Cities: A Statistical Profile   297
Health Care Competition Week   294
Health Care Construction Report   294
Health Care Costs   297
Health Care Financing Review   294
Health Care Strategic Management: The Newsletter for Hospital Strategies   294

Health Devices Alerts: A Summary of Reported Problems, Hazards, Recalls, and Updates   627
Health Devices Alerts online   627
Health Facilities Management   295
Health Industry Distributors Association   627
Health Industry Manufacturers Association   627
Health Industry Today: The Market Letter for Health Care Industry Vendors   295
Health Insurance Association of America   310
Health Insurance Company Financial Data   311
Health Insurance Reform Act of 1996   306
Health Insurance Statistics   311
Health Insurance Underwriter   310
Health Maintenance Organization   288
Health News Daily   295, 486
Health Planning and Administration   296
Healthcare Executive   295
Healthcare Financial Management   295
Healthcare Financial Management Association   293
Healthcare Financing Study Group   293
Healthcare Information Management   295
Healthcare Marketing Report   295
Healthcare Purchasing News   627
Heavy Duty Trucking   402
Heavy Duty Trucking: The Business Magazine of Trucking   661
Hershey Foods Corporation   549, 616
Hewitt Associates   361
Hewlett-Packard Co.   179
HFD (Home Furnishing Daily)
HG Digital Conference   77
High Performance Review: Definitive Magazine for Audiophiles and Music Lovers   79
History of Textiles   208
Hitachi Ltd.   179
HMAT (Hot Mix Asphalt Technology)
Hoechst Celanese Corporation   148
The Hollywood Reporter   391
Home Box Office (HBO)   387
Home Depot   285
Home Lighting and Accessories   243
Home Page of the Corporation for Public Broadcasting   534
Home Recording Rights Coalition   389
Home Shopping Network, Inc.   121
Hospital and Health Services Administration   295
Hospital Statistics   297
Hospitality Sales and Marketing Association International   303
Hospitals and Health Networks   295
Hotel and Motel Management   303
Hotel Employees and Restaurant Employees International Union   302
Household and Personal Products Industry: The Magazine for the Detergent, Soap, Cosmetics and Toiletry, Wax, Polish and Aerosol Industries   455
Household Audio and Video Equipment   79
Housing Starts   196
Hull/Finmac Inc.   564
Hungarian Banking and Capital Markets Supervisor   575
Hyatt Legal Services   332

I

IAN: Instrumentation and Control News   573, 627
IBM Journal of Research and Development   181

IC Data Flash Service   586
IC Master (Integrated Circuits)   586
ICIA Educational Technology Division   389
IEEE Computer Society   212, 599
IEEE Electron Devices Society   585
IEEE Industry Applications Magazine   243, 342
IEEE Micro   586
IEEE Software   600
IEEE Solid State Circuits Council   585
IEEE Transactions on Communications   641
Illuminating Engineering Society of North America   242
IMMAGE: Information on Mining, Metallurgy, and Geological Exploration   381
Impact Beverage Trends in America   98, 104, 593
Impact of Travel on State Economies   655
Impact: U.S. News and Research for the Wine, Spirits, and Beer Industries   97, 103
Imports and Exports of Fishery Products   256
In Focus   270
In-Plant Printer Including Corporate Imaging   518
Independent Bankers Association of America   87
Independent Coal Bargaining Alliance   160
Independent Computer Consultants Association   170
Independent Data Communications Manufacturers Assn.   212
Independent Electrical Contractors   242
Independent Petroleum Association of America   468, 478
Independent School   227
Index Group   361
Individual Investor   578
Industrial Association of Juvenile Apparel Manufacturers   54, 62
Industrial Distribution Association   342
Industrial Distribution: For Industrial Distributors and Their Sales Personnel   342
Industrial Equipment News   342
Infant and Juvenile Manufacturers Association   54, 62
Infinity Broadcasting   531
Information Bank Abstracts   18, 413
Information Industry Association   212
Information Sources: The Annual Directory of the Information Industry Association   215
Information Systems Audit and Control Association   4
Information Technology Association of America   180, 212, 599
Information Today: The Newspaper for Users and Producers of Electronic Information Services   213
Inside Job: The Looting of America's Savings and Loans   90
Inside the Financial Futures Markets   580
The Institute for Interconnecting and Packaging Electronic Circuits (IPC)   585
Institute of Certified Travel Agents   653
Institute of Electrical and Electronics Engineers   242
Institute of Electrical and Electronics Engineers; Broadcast, Cable and Consumer Electronics Society   390
Institute of Electrical and Electronics Engineers, Inc.   249
Institute of Gas Technology   234, 468
Institute of Internal Auditors   4
Institute of Management Accountants   4
Institute of Management Consultants   358, 363
Institute of Paper Science andTechnology   525
Institute of Real Estate Management   546
Institute of Scrap Recycling Industries   324, 613
Instrument Society of America   573, 627

Insurance Almanac: Who, What, When and Where in Insurance   311
The Insurance Forum: For the Unfettered Exchange of Ideas About Insurance   318
Insurance Information Institute   310
Insurance Journal   318
Insurance Law Review   319
Insurance News Network   311, 319
Insurance Periodicals Index online]   311, 319
Insurance Services Office   310
Insurance Statistics Yearbook   319
Integrated Services Digital Network (ISDN)   632
Intel   116
Interactive Digital Software Association   390, 599
Interactive Home   166
Interactive Multimedia Association   166
Intermodal Surface Transportation Efficiency Act of 1991   73, 198, 658
Internal Auditor   5
International Association of Clothing Designers   62
International Association of Electrical Inspectors   242
International Association of Lighting Management   242
International Business Machines Corporation   116, 175, 179, 210, 417, 595
International Communications Industries Association   390
International Data Corp.   176
International Energy Annual   470
International Hardware Distributors Association   286
International Institute of Synthetic Rubber Producers   564
International Iron and Steel Institute (ISI)   613
International Journal of Adhesion and Adhesives   11
International Journal of Mechanical Sciences   251
International Ladies' Garment Workers' Union   62
International Lead Zinc Research Organization   379
International Mail Manual   513
International Oil News   469
International Organization for Standardization   322
The International Programmers Guild   601
International Telecommunications Union (ITU)   632
International Teleproduction Society   390
International Television Association   390
International Trade Administration (ITA)   43
International Trade Commission   264, 610
International Travel Agency Network   653
International Wheat Council World Grain Statistics   26
Internet Computer Index   181
Internet Computing   181
Interstate Commerce Commission (ICC)   537
Interstate Natural Gas Association of America   235, 468
Interstate Producers Livestock Association   33
InterStudy Competitive Edge   297
InterStudy Quality Edge   297
Intimate Apparel Manufacturers Association   62
Intimate Fashion News   62
Introducing Computers: Concepts, Systems, and Applications   182
Introduction to Forest Science   271
Inventory of Power Plants in the United States   236
Investing in the Over-the-Counter Markets: Stocks, Bonds, IPOs   580
Investment Dealers' Digest   578
Iron and Steel Engineer   325
Iron and Steel Scrap. Mineral Industry Surveys   613
Iron and Steel Society   324
Irwin Business and Investment Almanac   580

ISA Directory of Instrumentation 628
ISA Proceedings (Instrument Society of America)
ISA Transactions (Instrument Society of America)
ITA 390

J

JAMA: The Journal of the American Medical
  Association 295
Jane's Containerisation Directory 668
Jane's Electronic Information System 221
Jewelers Board of Trade 329
Jewelers of America 329
Jewelers Security Alliance of the U.S. 329
Jewelers Vigilance Committee 329
Jewelers' Circular-Keystone 329
Jewelry Information Center 329
Jewelry Manufacturers Association 327, 329
Jim Beam Brands Co. 96
Jobson's Liquor Handbook: Statistics, Trends and Analysis
  for the Distilled Spirits Industry 98
Johnson & Johnson 482
Joint Electron Device Engineering Council 242, 585
Joint Industry Board of the Electrical Industry 243
JOM: Journal of Metals 380
Journal of Accountancy 5
Journal of Adhesion 11
Journal of Advertising Research 17
Journal of Agricultural and Food Information 24
Journal of Animal Science 33
Journal of Applied Mechanics 251
Journal of Applied Polymer Science 501, 508
Journal of Broadcasting and Electronic Media 533
Journal of Chemical Information and Computer
  Sciences 144, 153
Journal of Commerce and Commercial 104, 381
Journal of Data and Computer Communications 213
Journal of Elastomers and Plastics 501, 508
The Journal of Futures Markets 578
Journal of Heat Transfer 251
Journal of Higher Education 227
Journal of Hospitality and Leisure Marketing: The
  International Forum for Research, Theory and
  Practice 303
Journal of Imaging Science and Technology 493
Journal of International Hospitality, Leisure, and Tourism
  Management: A Multinational and Cross-Cultural Journal
  of Applied Research 303
Journal of Money, Credit and Banking 87
Journal of Pharmaceutical Marketing and Management 486
The Journal of Real Estate Taxation 546
Journal of Retail Banking 88
Journal of Risk and Insurance 310, 318
Journal of Software Maintenance: Research and
  Practice 600
Journal of Sustainable Agriculture 24
Journal of Sustainable Forestry 270
Journal of the American Society of CLU 318
Journal of Turbomachinery 252
JPT Journal of Petroleum Technology 423

K

Kagan Media Index 534

Kane's Beverage Week: The Newsletter of Beverage
  Marketing 97, 104
Kansas State University 23
Kellogg Company 127
Kentucky Fried Chicken (KFC) 549
Keystone Coal Industry Manual 162
Kiplinger Agriculture Letter 25
Kmart 416
Kodak 490
Kone 245
Kraft Foods 127

L

Lake Carriers Association 664, 666
Land Mobile Radio News 641
Large Animal Veterinarian: Covering Health and
  Nutrition 33
Law Office Economics and Management 336
Lawrence Livermore National Laboratory 280
The Lawyer's Almanac; An Encyclopedia of Information
  about Law, Lawyers, and the Profession 337
LC MARC: Serials 463
LD & A: (Lighting Design and Application)
LDB Interior Textiles 206
Lead and Zinc Statistics 381
Lead Industries Association 379
Lead Industry: Mineral Industry Surveys 381
League of Advertising Agencies 17
Leisure Beverage Insider Newsletter 593
Leisure Time Basic Analysis 392
Lender's Bagel Bakery 127
Leo Burnett 15
Lettuce Entertain You Enterprises 549
LEXIS Federal Banking Library 88
LEXIS-NEXIS 336
Lexmark International Inc. 417
Life Association News 318
Life Insurance Fact Book 319
Life Insurance in Estate Planning 319
Life Insurance Planning 318
Life Insurance Selling 318
The Lifetime Book of Money Management 320
Lifting and Transportation International 661
Light Metal Age 373
Lighting Research Institute 243
LIMRA International 317
LISA Online: Library and Information Science
  Abstracts 112
Literary Market Place: The Directory of the American Book
  Publishing Industry 112
Livestock and Poultry Situation and Outlook 34
Livestock Market Digest 33
Livestock Marketing Association 33
Livestock, Meat, Wool, Market News 34
Livestock Production Science 33
Livestock Slaughter 34
Livestock Weekly 34
L.L. Bean, Inc. 122, 125
Lloyd's Register of Shipping Statistical Tables 667
The Lodging and Food Service Industry 304
Loews Theatres 386
London Metal Exchange (LME) 375
London Stock Exchange 576
Los Angeles Times 409

Louis XV   576
Lumber Production and Mill Stocks   271
Lundberg Letter   469, 478
Lyondell Petrochemical Company   148–149

M

The Machine That Changed the World   403
Machinery Dealers National Association   348, 355
Macworld   181
Magazine and Bookseller: Mass Market Retailers and Publishers' Guide   463
Magazine Index   463
Magazine Publishers of America (MPA)   462
Magill's Cinema Annual   393
Major Home Appliance Industry Fact Book: A Comprehensive Reference on the United States Major Home Appliance Industry   70
Major Household Appliances   70
Malaysia Securities Commission   575
Malaysian Rubber Bureau   565
Malt Beverage Interbrand Competition Act   101
Malting and Brewing Science   104
Managed Account Reports: The Clearing House for Commodity Money Management   578
Management Accounting   5–6
Management Contents   5, 41, 48, 413, 463
Management Information Systems: A Study of Computer-Based Information Systems   182
Management of Healthcare Organizations   297
Management of Hotel and Motel Security   304
Managing Automation   600
Managing Office Technology   417
Managing Software Development Projects: Formula for Success   601
Managing to Communicate: Using Telecommunications for Increased Business Efficiency   634
Manufacturers Alliance for Productivity and Innovation   348, 355
Manufacturing Confectioner   620
Manufacturing Jewelers and Silversmiths of America   329
Marine Digest and Transportation News   667
Marine Pollution and Safer Ships   668
Maritime Administration (MARAD)   665
Maritime Affairs—A World Handbook   668
Maritime Reporter and Engineering News   667
Maritime Security Act in 1996   665
Maritime Security Program   663
Maritime Transport   667
Market Structure of Sports   608
Marketing and Advertising Reference Service   18, 392
Marketing Health Care into the Twenty-First Century: The Changing Dynamic   297
Marketing Management for the Hospitality Industry: A Strategic Approach   304
Marketing Newsletter   74
Mars Incorporated   616
Master Brewers Association of the Americas   103
Materials Business File   325, 374, 381, 501, 508
Matsushita   76
Maxwell House   589
MBAA Technical Quarterly   104
MCA/Universal   385
McCann-Erickson   16
McCaw Cellular Communications   630

McDonald's   549
MCI   630
McKinsey & Company, Inc.   361, 363
Mechanical Engineering   252
Media Industry Newsletter   17
Media Sports Business   607
Medicaid   290
Medical Care, Medical Costs: The Search for a Health Insurance Policy   297
Medical Group Management Association   293
Medical Group Management Journal   295
Medical Reference Services Quarterly   295
Medical Tribune: World News of Medicine and Its Practice   295
Medical Utilization Management   296
Medical World News: The Newsmagazine of Medicine   296
Medicare   290
Medline   296, 429
MedSearch America, Inc.   296
Menswear Retailers of America   54
Merchandise and Operating Results of Department and Specialty Stores   559
Merck and Company   482
Mergers   290
Messner, Vetere, Berger, Carey, and Schmetterer   15
Metadex (Metals Abstracts/Alloys Index)
Metal Center News   373, 380
Metal Statistics   374, 381
Metallurgia, The Journal of Metals Technology, Metal Forming and Thermal Processing   380
Metallurgical Transactions A: Physical Metallurgy and Materials Science   380
Metallurgical Transactions B: Process Metallurgy   380
Metalworking Digest   373
Methanex Corp.   148
Metlfax Magazine   373
Michie on Banks on Banking   90
Microcomputer Abstracts online   167, 601
Microcomputer Index (online)   214
Microcomputer Software Guide Online   601
Microsoft Corporation   116, 165, 595
Microsoft Systems Journal   600
Miller Brewing Company   99
Millers' National Federation   260
Milling and Baking News   260
Minerals, Metals, and Materials Society   379
Minerals Yearbook   74, 381
Mines Magazine   380
Mining and Metallurgical Society of America   379
Mining Machinery and Equipment   381
Mining Record   380
Minolta   490
Mintec   381
MJK Commodities Database   578
Mobil Corporation   422, 466, 475
Modern Accident Investigation and Analysis: An Executive Guide to Accident Investigation   312
Modern Brewery Age Blue Book   104
Modern Casting   325
Modern Healthcare: The Newsmagazine for Administrators and Managers in Hospitals and Other Healthcare Institutions   296
Modern Jeweler   329
Modern Medicine   296
Modern Metals   380

Modern Paint and Coatings 436
Modern Plastics Encyclopedia 502, 509
Modern Real Estate 547
Money, Banking, and the Economy 90
Monsanto Company 134
Monthly Energy Review 161, 471, 479
Monthly Retail Trade: Sales and Inventories 55, 63, 286, 553, 559
Monthly Statistical Release: Beer 104
Monthly Statistical Release: Cigarettes and Cigars 648
Monthly Statistical Release: Distilled Spirits 98
Monthly Truck Tonnage Report 661
Montreal Protocol 66
Moore's Law 584
Morningstar Variable Annuity/Life Performance Report 319
Mortgage Bankers Association of America 87
Mothers Against Drunk Drivers 94
Motion Picture Association of America 390
The Motion Picture Guide Annual 393
Motor Carrier Annual Reports 661
Motor Equipment Manufacturers Association 395, 401
Motor Vehicle Manufacturers Association of the United States 401
Motors and Generators 408
MTM Enterprises 387
Multichannel News 119
Multifiber Arrangement 50, 58, 61
Multimedia News 166
Mutual Advertising Agency Network 17
MVMA Motor Vehicle Facts and Figures 403

N

NAARS 5
Nabisco Foods Group 616
Narcotic Drugs: Estimated World Requirements 487
Nasdaq Fact Book and Company Directory 579
Nation's Restaurant News: The Newspaper of the Food Service Industry 553
National Academy of Opticianry 428
National Aeronautics and Space Administration 567
National Air Carrier Association 41
National Air Transportation Association 41
National Alliance of Stocking Gun Dealers 217
National Appliance Energy Conservation Act of 1987 66
National Appliance Parts Suppliers Association 243
National Appliance Service Association 70
National Asphalt Pavement Association 72, 74
National Asphalt Training Center II 72
National Association for Medical Equipment Services 293
National Association of Accountants 2
National Association of Aluminum Distributors 373
National Association of Boards of Pharmacy 486
National Association of Broadcasters 533
National Association of Casualty and Surety Executives 317
National Association of Catalog Showroom Merchandisers 125
National Association of Chemical Distributors 144, 153
National Association of Computer Consultant Businesses 170
National Association of Elevator Contractors 247
National Association of Elevator Contractors (NAEC) 246
National Association of Exclusive Buyer Agents 543
National Association of Flour Distributors 260
National Association of Health Underwriters 310

National Association of Home Builders of the United States 195
National Association of Independent Schools 226
National Association of Insurance Brokers 310
National Association of Letter Carriers (NALC) 512
National Association of Life Underwriters 317
National Association of Marine Services 666
National Association of Optometrists and Opticians 429
National Association of Pharmaceutical Manufacturers 369, 486
National Association of Printers and Lithographers 518
National Association of Professional Word Processing Technicians 172
National Association of Quick Printers 518
National Association of Railroad Passengers 540
National Association of Railway Business Women 540
National Association of Real Estate Brokers 546
National Association of Realtors 543, 546
National Association of Restaurant Managers 552
National Association of Retail Dealers of America 70, 558
National Association of Securities Dealers 575, 577
National Association of State Departments of Agriculture 24
National Association of Stevedores 666
National Association of Tobacco Distributors 648
National Association of Video Distributors 390
National Association of Wheat Growers 24
National Automatic Merchandising Association (NAMA) 347
National Automobile Dealers Association 401
National Automotive Parts Association 401
National Beer Wholesalers' Association 103
National Building Material Distributors Association 195
National Bulk Vendors Association (NBVA) 347
National Business Aircraft Association 47
National Cable Television Association 118
National Cable Television Institute 118
National Candy Brokers Association 619
National Catalog Managers Association 125
National Cattlemen's Association 31, 33
National Center for Education Statistics (NCES) 222
National Coal Association 160
National Committee for Quality Health Care 294
National Concrete Masonry Association 189
National Confectioners Association of the U.S. 619
National Confectionery Sales Association of America 619
National Constructors Association 195
National Corn Genome Initiative (NCGI) 23
National Corn Growers Association 23–24
National Cosmetology Association 455
National Cotton Council of America 206
National Council on Alcoholism and Drug Dependence 95
National Decorating Products Association 436
National Defense 220
National Defense Transportation Association 219
National Directory of Community Newspapers 414
National Drug Code Directory 370
National Economic Crossroads Transportation Efficiency Act of 1997 198
National Education Association 226
National Electrical Code (NEC) 239
National Electrical Contractors Association 243
National Electrical Manufacturers Association 243
National Elevator Industry, Inc. 247
National Elevator Industry, Inc. Newsletter 247

National Energy Security Act of 1992 239
National Farmers Union Washington Newsletter 25
National Federation of Press Women 413
National Fertilizer Solutions Association 134
National Fisheries Institute 253
National Five Digit Zip Code and Post Office Directory 513
National Formulary (NF) 367
National Foundation of the Chemically Hypersensitive 451
National Futures Association 577
National Glass Association 281
National Hardwood Lumber Association 270
National Highway System Designation Act of 1995 199
National Home Center News: The Newspaper for Retailers Serving Homeowners and Contractors 243
National Home Furnishings Association 275
National Housewares Manufacturers Association 70
National Independent Coal Leader: Dedicated to Safety in the Mining Industry 161
National Independent Coal Operators Association 160
National Industry Bycatch Coalition 254
National Institutes of Health (NIH) 484
National Interstate Council of State Boards of Cosmetology 455
National Jeweler 329
The National Law Journal: The Weekly Newspaper for the Profession 336
National Lawyers Guild 336
National Legal Aid and Defender Association 336
National Licensed Beverage Association-Members Directory 104
National Live Stock Producers Association 33
National Marine Fisheries Service 256
National Marine Fisheries Service (NMFS) 254
National Motor Freight Traffic Association 660
National Moving and Storage Association 275
National Newspaper Association 413
National Newspaper Index 413
National Optometric Association 429
National Paint and Coatings Association 432, 436
National Paper Trade Association 444, 449, 526
National Petroleum Council 468, 478
National Petroleum News-Market Facts 471, 479
National Petroleum News (NPN)
National Petroleum Refiners Association 478
National Pharmaceutical Council 369
National Pollutant Discharge Elimination System 378
National Pork Producers Council (NPPC) 30
National Post Office Mail Handlers, Watchmen, Messengers, and Group Leaders Division of Laborers' International Union of North America (Mail Handlers) 512
National Press Club 413
National Private Truck Council 660
National Propane Gas Association 235
National Public Accountant 5
National Ready Mixed Concrete Association 189
National Real Estate Investor 546
National Restaurant Association 548, 552
National Retail Federation 558
National Retail Federation Buyer's Manual 559
National Retail Hardware Association 285–286
National Rifle Association 217, 219
National Rural Letter Carriers' Association (NRLCA) 512
National School Boards Association 227
National Shellfisheries Association 256
National Shoe Retailers Association 265

National Society for the Study of Education Yearbook 228
National Society of Public Accountants 4
National Soft Drink Association 588, 592
National Tank Truck Carriers 660
National Telecommunications and Information Administration 633
National Tooling and Machining Association 286
National Tour Association 651, 654
National Tourism Organization 650
National Transportation Statistics 42, 541, 661, 668
National Underwriter Profiles 311
National Underwriter, Property and Casualty Edition 318
National University Continuing Education Association 226
National Wholesale Druggists' Association 486
Natural Gas 469
Natural Gas Monthly 471
Natural Gas Supply Association 468
Neckwear Association of America 51
Needle's Eye 54, 62
Netscape Communications Corporation 596
Network Computers Devices Inc. 175
Network Computing: Computing in a Network Environment 213, 600
Network World: The Newsweekly of User Networking Strategies 213
Networking Management: For MIS, Voice, Data, Video Professionals 213
New England Journal of Medicine 296
New Equipment Digest 342
New One-Family Houses Sold 547
New Steel: Mini and Integrated Mill Management and Technologies 325, 373
New World Communications 532
New York Coat and Suit Association 62
New York Mercantile Exchange (NYMEX) 575
New York Stock Exchange 409
New York Times Company 411
Newsinc 413
NewsInc.: The Business of Newspapers 413
NewsNet 41
Newspaper and Periodical Abstracts 413, 463
Newspaper Association of America 410
Newspaper Financial Executives Journal 413
The Newspaper Guild 413
Newspaper Preservation Act of 1970 409
Newspaper Rates and Data 414
Newspapers Online 414
NEXIS Service 41
Nielsen Media Research 530
Nielsen Scantrack U.S. 456
Nikon 490
Non-Ferrous Founders Society 324, 373
Non-Ferrous Metal Data 374
Non-Ferrous Metals Producers Committee 373, 379
Nonferrous Castings 326
Nonprescription Drug Manufacturers Association 486
Norand Corporation 591
North American Electric Reliability Council 230
North American Free Trade Agreement 21, 32, 50–51, 53, 57, 61, 65, 153, 172, 205, 240, 248, 264–265, 274, 324, 329, 342, 354, 388, 399, 416, 493, 500, 507, 518, 539, 615, 626
North American Steel Council (NASC) 324
North American Telecommunications Association 641

The Northern Miner: Devoted to the Mineral Resources Industry of Canada   380

NPD Group Inc.   549

NTIS Bibliographic Data Base   252

NTQ: New Telecom Quarterly—The Future of Telecommunications   633

Ortho Pharmaceutical   482

The Other Side of Software: A User's Guide for Defining Software Requirements   601

Otis Elevator Company   245–246

Outlook for Travel and Tourism   304, 655

Owens-Illinois Inc.   280

O

Occupational Safety and Health Act   142

Occupational Safety and Health Administration   72, 142, 150, 435, 517

Oce-Van der Grinten   490

Oceanic Abstracts Online   667

OECD Iron and Steel Industry   326

OECD Steel Market and Outlook   326

Of Counsel: The Legal Practice Report   337

Office Automation Report   172

Office Automation Society International   172, 599

Office Depot   416

Office of Federal Procurement Policy of the Office of Management and Budget   569

Office of Hazardous Material Safety   658

Office of Motor Carrier Safety   658

Office of the Comptroller of the Currency   82–83

Office of Thrift Supervision   84–85

Office Products Dealer Buying Guide and Directory   417

Official All-Star Cafe   549

Official Board Markets   449

Official Methods of Analysis of AOAC   136

Official Railway Guide. North American Freight Service Edition   541

Official Summary of Security Transactions and Holdings   578

Offshore Services and Equipment Directory   424

Ogilvy & Mather   15

Oil and Gas Alert   469

Oil and Gas Journal   235, 469, 478

The Oil and Gas Producing Industry in Your State   423, 471

Oil and Gas Tax Quarterly   235

Oil, Chemical and Atomic Workers   476

Oil, Chemical and Atomic Workers International Union   467

Oil Daily: Daily Newspaper of the Petroleum Industry   469, 478

Oil, Gas, and Petrochem Equipment   423

Oil Pollution Liability and Compensation Act of 1990   420, 466, 664

Oilfield Equipment   424

Oilfield Supply Industry Directory   424

Olive Garden   549

Omnibus Budget Reconciliation Act   466

OPEC   468

Operations Management Report   88

Ophthalmic Research Institute   429

Ophthalmology   429

Ophthalmology Times   429

Optical Industry Association   429

Optical Laboratories Association   429

Optical Society of America, Medical Optics Technical Group   429

Opticians Association of America   429

Optometric Management: The Business and Marketing Magazine for Optometry   429

Oracle Corp.   175

Orion Pictures Corporation   386

P

PAC/ASIA Circuit News   586

Pacific Gas and Electric Company   231, 233

Paint and Allied Products Annual Survey of Manufacturers   436

Paint and Coatings Industry   436

Paint, Varnish, and Lacquer   437

Painting and Decorating Contractors of America   436

Paper Age   444, 527

Paper Industry Management Association   444, 449, 526

Paperboard Packaging   449

Paperboard Packaging Council   449

Paperboard Packaging: Economic Review Issue   449

PaperChem Database   12, 270, 444, 527

Paramount   386

Paramount Pictures Corp.   383

Paramount Television Group   530

Parcel Shippers Association   513

Paris Bourse   576

Partnership for a New Generation of Vehicles (PNGV)   397

Pathfinder   181

PBS Online   534

PC Letter: The Insider's Guide to the Personal Computer Industry   166

PC Week: The National Newspaper of Corporate Computing   600

Pepsico   589, 592

Perfumer and Flavorist   455

Personal Communications Services (PCS)   631

Perspective   88

Perspectives on Radio and Television: Telecommunication in the United States   535

Petroleum Engineer International Drilling and Production Yearbook Issue   471, 479

Petroleum Equipment Institute   423

Petroleum Equipment Supplies Association   423

Petroleum Newsletter   469

Petroleum Supply Annual   471

Petroleum Supply Monthly   471

Pharmaceutical Engineering   369

Pharmaceutical Manufacturers Association   292

Pharmaceutical Manufacturers Association Annual Survey Report   487

Pharmaceutical Marketers Directory   370

Pharmaceutical Processing   369

Pharmaceutical Technology   369, 486

Photo Business   494

Photo Marketing   494

Photographic Manufacturers and Distributors Association   493

Photographic Society of America   493

Physician's Desk Reference   488

Physician's Desk Reference for Nonprescription Drugs   488

Pi Beta Alpha   111

PIRA   444, 449, 527

Pizza Hut   549

Planet Hollywood   549

Plastic Coatings and Film Association 505

Plastics Engineering 501, 508

Plastics Machinery and Equipment: For Those Who Select and Buy Plastics Processing Machinery and Equipment 501, 508

Plastics Technology: Machinery/Materials Systems for Maximum Productivity 501, 508

Plastics Technology Manufacturing Handbook and Buyer's Guide 502, 509

Platt's Oil Prices 470, 478

Plumbing Manufacturers Institute 505

PNI (Pharmaceutical News Index)

Pocketbook of Electric Utility Industry Statistics 236

Pollution Prevention Act of 1990 517

Ponderosa 550

Popular Photography Directory and Buying Guide Issue 494

Portfolio of Accounting Systems for Small and Medium-Sized Businesses 6

Portland Cement Association 186

Post-Tensioning Institute 186

Postal Bulletin 513

Postal Life: The Magazine for Postal Employees 513

Postal Reorganization Act of 1970 510

Postal World 513

Potato Terminal Market 577

Power and Communication Contractors Association 243

The Power Report on Automotive Marketing 403

The Practical Accountant: Accounting and Taxes in Everyday Practice 5

The Practical Lawyer 337

The Practical Real Estate Lawyer 337

Precast/Prestressed Concrete Institute 186

Predicasts Basebook 244, 445, 527

Predicasts Forecasts 167, 607

Predicasts Forecasts: International 430, 607, 642

Predicasts Forecasts: U.S. 48, 167, 444, 470, 487, 527, 607

Prescription Drug User Fee Act in 1992 485

Principles of Money, Banking and Financial Markets Basic 90

Printer Impressions 417

Printing Impressions 518

Printing Industries of America 517–518

Procter & Gamble Co. 530

Producers Guild of America 390

Professional Audiovideo Retailers Association 78, 390

Professional Builder and Remodeler 196

Professional Film and Video Equipment Association 78, 390

Professional Photographers of America 493

Progressive Railroading 540

PROMT: Predicasts Overview of Markets and Technology 119, 167, 325, 330, 342, 392, 418, 456, 607, 642

Property-Casualty Insurance Facts 311, 319

ProSales: For Dealers and Distributors Serving the Professional Contractor 196

PTN-Master Buying Guide and Directory (Photographic Trade News): Main Entrance to the Retail Photographic Market

Public Accounting Report 5

Public Hearings on Software Patents 601

Public Power 235

Public Power Directory 237

Public Power Weekly Newsletter 235

Public Service Electric and Gas Company 233

Publishers Directory: A Guide to new and Established Private and Special-Interest, Avant-Garde and Alternative, Organizational Association, Government and Institution Presses 112

Publishers, Distributors, and Wholesalers of the United States 112

Publishers Weekly: The International News Magazine of Book Publishing 111

Publishers' Auxiliary 413

Publishing Markets 111

Pulp and Paper 444, 527

The Pulp and Paper Industry in the OECD Member Countries 445, 528

Pulp and Paper Week 444, 527

Purchasing, Selection and Procurement for the Hospitality Industry 304

Q

Quad/Graphics, Inc. 518

Quality Value Convenience Channel 121

Quantum Chemical Corporation 148–149

Quarterly Coal Report 162

Quebecor Printing (USA) Corporation 518

Questions and Answers about the Electric Utility Industry 237

Questions and Answers on Real Estate 547

Quick Printing: The Information Source for Commercial Copyshops and Printshops 518

R

Radio Programming Profile 535

Radio World 534

Railroad Facts 541

Railway Age 540

Railway Progress Institute 540

Rainforest Cafe 549

Ralston Purina 549

The Rauch Guide to the U.S. Plastics Guide 502, 509

Reagan Administration 82

Real Estate 547

Real Estate Issues 546

Real Estate Law Journal 546

Real Estate Today 546

Recycled Paper News 444, 527

Red Lobster 549

Reebok International Ltd. 530

Reform of Health Care Systems: A Review of Seventeen OECD Countries 298

Register of Ships 668

Research and Development in Industry 642

Research in Real Estate 547

Research Institute for Fragrance Materials 453

Resolution Trust Corporation 84

Resource Conservation and Recovery Act (RCRA) 378

Restaurants and Institutions 553

Retail Confectioners International 619

The Retail Management Letter 558

The Retail Revolution: Market Transformation, Investment, and Labor in the Modern Department Store 559

Retail Tobacco Dealers of America 648

Retail, Wholesale and Department Store Union 558

Retailing Today 558

Reuter's Instinet System 576
Revenue and Cost Analysis Report 513
Review of Marine Transport 668
Review of Scientific Instruments 573
Risk Management 318
Road and Track 402
Rocky Mountain Coal Mining Institute 160
The Rose Sheet: Toiletries, Fragrances, and Skin Care 455
Royal Dutch/Shell Group 149
Royal Vendors 591
RTC Report (Resolution Trust Corporation)
*Rubber and Plastics News: The Rubber Industry's
  International Newspaper* 565
Rubber and Plastics-Rubbicana Issue 565
Rubber Association of Singapore 577
Rubber Chemistry and Technology 565
Rubber Manufacturers Association 560, 565
Rubber: Production, Shipments, and Stocks 565
Rubber Red Book 565
Rubber Statistical Bulletin 565
Rubber World 565
Ruby Tuesday 550

S

SAE Handbook (Society of Automotive Engineers)
Safe Medical Devices Act (SMDA) of 1990 624
Safe Money Report 88
Sales in 100 Department Stores 559
SAMA 573
Sara Lee 549
Savings Institutions Source Book 89
Schindler 245
Schlumberger Ltd. 421
School Business Affairs 227
*School Enrollment, Social and Economic Characteristics of
  Students* 228
School Planning and Management 227
Schroder Wertheim & Co. 551
Scisearch 48, 430, 642
Scrap Processing and Recycling 613
The Seagram Company Ltd. 94
Sealed Insulating Glass Manufacturers Association 281
Search the CIX Web Site 633
Seatrade Week 667
Seaway Review 667
SEC 575
SEC News Digest 578
Secretarial/Word Processing Service 173
Securities and Exchange Commission (SEC) 574–575
Securities Exchange Act of 1934 574
Securities Industry Association 577
Securities Markets 580
Securities Week 578
Security Analysis and Portfolio Management 580
Security APL Quote Server 578
Security Traders Association 577
Selected Instruments and Related Products 573, 628
Semiconductor Equipment & Materials Institute (SEMI) 354
Semiconductor Industry Association 585
Semiconductor Industry Association Yearbook/
  Directory 587
Semiconductor Industry Trade Statistics Subscription 586
*Semiconductors, Printed Circuit Boards, and Other
  Electronic Components* 586

Serials Review 463
Sharp Electronics Corp. 417
Ship Operation Automation 668
*Shipping Digest: For Export and Transportation
  Executives* 667
Shoe and Allied Trades Research Association (SATRA) 564
Short-Term Energy Outlook: Quarterly Projections 479
Shutterbug 494
SIBS: Semiconductor Industry and Business Survey 586
Silicon Graphics 116
SIMBA Report on Directory Publishing 125
Sizzler 550
Smokeshop 648
SMPTE Journal 391
Soap/Cosmetics/Chemical Specialties 455
Society for Imaging Science and Technology 493
Society of Automotive Engineers International 401
Society of Broadcast Engineers 533
Society of Cable Television Engineers 118
Society of Cosmetic Chemists 455
Society of Industrial and Office Realtors 546
Society of Mining, Metallurgy, and Exploration 379
Society of Motion Picture and Television Engineers 390
Society of Petroleum Engineers 423
Society of Plastics Engineers 500, 508
Society of Professional Management Consultants 358
Society of Recreation Executives 606
Society of Soft Drink Technologists 592
Society of the Plastics Industry 501, 508
Society of Wine Educators 97
Soda Poppery: The History of Soft Drinks in America 593
*Soft.Letter: Trends and Strategies in Software
  Publishing* 600
The Software Business 602
Software Digest Ratings Report 600
Software Industry Bulletin 600
Software Industry Factbook 601
Software Law Journal 600
Software Magazine 600
Software Market Survey 601
*Software Protection: A Journal on the Legal, Technical, and
  Practical Aspects of Protecting Computer Software* 600
Soil Science 135
Solar Car Corporation 397
Solid State Processing and Production Buyers Guide and
  Directory 587
Solid State Technology 586–587
Solid State Technology Processing and Production Buyers
  Guide 587
Sony Corp. 116, 383
Sound and Recording: An Introduction 79
The Southern Company 231
Southwest Airlines Co. 36–37, 39
Special Interest Group on Data Communication 212
Special Interest Group on Office Information Systems 212
Special Interest Group on Software Engineering 599
Sportbil 608
Sports Foundation 607
*Sports Industry News: Management & Finance, Regulation &
  Litigation, Media & Marketing* 607
Spotlight 620
Spring 630
Standard & Poor's 549
Standard & Poor's Industry Surveys 487, 642
Standard & Poor's Statistical Service 49, 487

Standard & Poor's Stock Reports: American Stock Exchange   579
Standard Periodical Directory   464
Starbucks Coffee Co.   549, 589
Station Representatives Association   533
Statistical Abstract of the United States   228
Statistical Annual: Grains, Options on Agricultural Futures   579
Statistical Annual: Interest Rates, Metals, Stock Indices, Options on Financial Futures, Options on Metals Futures   579
Statistical Trends in Broadcasting   534
Statistical Year Book of the Electric Utility Industry   236
Statistics of Paper, Paperboard and Wood Pulp   445, 449, 528
Statistics of World Trade in Steel   326
Steel Founders' Society of America   324
Steel Mill Products   326
Steel Service Center Institute   325
Steel Times International   325
Stereo Review   79
Stereophile: For the High Fidelity Stereo Perfectionist   79
Stocks, Bonds, Bills, and Inflation Yearbook   579
Stores   558
Streetnet   549
Stroh Brewing Company   100
The Subcontractor   196
Sugar Act of 1934   617
Sugar and Sweetener Situation and Outlook   621
Sugar Association, Inc.   619
Sugar Bulletin   620
Sugar Journal: Covering the World's Sugar Industry   620
The Sugar Producer: Representing the Sugar Beet Industry in the United States   620
Summers on Oil and Gas   471, 479
Sun Microsystems Inc.   175, 596
Superconductor Industry   587
Superconductor Week   586
Supertrader's Almanac and Calendar Book   580
Survey of Current Business   55, 63, 89, 98, 104, 207, 221, 266, 275, 282, 304, 326, 349, 355, 437, 445, 449, 519, 528, 553
Swift Textiles, Inc.   204
Switchboard   126
Sydney Futures Exchange   577
Synthetic Organic Chemicals: United States Production and Sales   154

T
Taco Bell   549
TAPPI   444, 526
TAPPI Journal   444, 527
Tariff Act of 1790   61
Tax Analysts   4, 336
Tax Analysts' Home Page   5
Tax Planning   6
Tax Reform Act of 1986   192
Taxation for Lawyers   337
TCI   118
Tea Brokers' Association of London   577
Tele-Communications Association   632, 641
Tele-Communications, Inc. (TCI)   115
Telecommunications   633–634
Telecommunications Act of 1996   116–117, 531, 629

Telecommunications Industry Association   632, 641
The Telecommunications Library   633
Telecommunications Reports   641
Telecommunications Week   633
Teleconnect   641
Telecons   641
Telematics and Informatics   214
Telephone Engineer and Management: A Telecommunications Magazine   642
Telephone Industry Directory and Sourcebook   643
Television and Cable Factbook   119, 535
Television Broadcast   534
Television Digest with Consumer Electronics   79, 119, 391, 534
Television Quarterly   534
Terra Industries, Inc.   148
Texas A&M   23
Texas Longhorn Breeders Association of America   33
Textile, Apparel, and Footwear Act of 1990   264
Textile Distributors Association   206
Textile Hi-Lights   54, 63
Textile Horizons: Providing Essential Reading for All Present and Future Decision Makers in Textiles and Fashion Worldwide   206
Textile Institute   54, 62, 206
Textile Research Journal   206
Textile Technology Digest online   55, 63, 207
Textile World   54, 63, 206
TGI Fridays   550
The Witch Doctors: Making Sense of the Management Gurus   364
Thomas Register Online   286, 343, 349, 355
Timber Bulletin   271
Time, Inc.   386
Time Warner   115–116, 118
Times Mirror Company   409
Timken Company   341
Titus   207
Tobacco Associates   648
Tobacco Association of U.S.   648
Tobacco Barometer   648
Tobacco Institute   648
Tobacco Merchants Association of United States   648
Tobacco Retailers Almanac   649
Tobacco Science Yearbook   649
Tobacco Situation and Outlook   648
Tobacco Stocks Report   649
Toiletries, Cosmetics and Fragrances   456
Tokyo Stock Exchange   576
Tooling and Production: The Magazine of Metalworking Manufacturing   286
Toronto Stock Exchange   576
Toshiba Corp.   179
Total Petroleum of North America   475
Tourism Offices Worldwide Directory   655
Tourism: Principles, Practices, Philosophies   655
The Tourism System: An Introductory Text   655
Trade & Industry Index   41, 414, 463
Trains; The Magazine of Railroading   540
Trans World Airlines, Inc.   39
Transport Topics: National Newspaper of the Trucking Industry   661
Travel and Tourism Research Association   653–654
Travel Holiday   654
Travel Industry Association of America   654

Travel Market Report   655
Travel Printout: Research News from the U.S. Travel Data Center   654
Travel Smart: Pay Less, Enjoy More   654
Travel Trade: The Business Paper of the Travel Industry   654
Travel Weekly   655
Trends in the Hotel Industry: USA Edition   304
Tri-Star   386
Tribune Broadcasting   532
Tribune Company   411
Trimless/Flashless Design Inc. (TFD)   564
TRIS   540, 661, 667
Truck Sales and Leasing   402
True Value Hardware   285
Tulsa (Petroleum Abstracts)
Tuned In: Radio World's Management Magazine   534
T.V. Broadcast Data Base   535
TV Link: Film & Television Website Archive   119, 392, 534
TV Technology   534
TWICE: This Week in Consumer Electronics   79, 391, 642
Type World: The Newspaper for Page Processing, Electronic Publishing, Typesetting and Graphic Communications   172

U

ULI Market Profiles   547
Ulrich's International Periodicals Directory Online   464
Ultramar Diamond Shamrock   475
Union Carbide Corporation   148
Union of Needletrades, Industrial and Textile Employees   52
Unisys   179
United Airlines Inc.   36–37, 39
United Furniture Workers of America Insurance and Pension Fund   275
United Garment Workers of America   54, 62
United Infants' and Children's Wear Association   54, 62
United Mine Workers Union   160
United Nations Disarmament Yearbook   221
United Press International   409
United States Beet Sugar Association   619
United States Cane Sugar Refiners' Association   619
United States Census of Agriculture   26
United States Census of Construction Industries   196
United States Census of Manufactures   145, 154, 349, 356, 621
United States Census of Mineral Industries   381
United States Census of Service Industries   535, 607
United States Distribution Journal Supplier Directory   649
United States Distribution Journal: The News Publication of Tobacco, Confectionery, Grocery Distribution   648
United States International Air Travel Statistics   655
United States Pharmacopeia and National Formulary   370
United States Rail News   540
United States Securities and Exchange Commission Annual Report   579
United States Telephone Association   641
United States Timber Production, Trade, Consumption, and Price Statistics   271
United States Tour Operators Association   651
United States Tuna Foundation   256
United Steelworkers of America   378
Universal Healthcare Almanac: A Complete Guide for the Healthcare Professional-Facts, Figures, Analysis   297
Universal Studios   383

Unocal   466
Update: The Executive's Purchasing Advisor   417
Upjohn   482
U.S. Advanced Battery Consortium (USABC)   397
The U.S. Apparel Industry: International Challenge-Domestic Response   56, 64
The U.S. Beer Market: Impact Databank Review and Forecast   104
U.S. Bureau of Labor   639
U.S. Bureau of Labor Statistics   68, 340
U.S. Bureau of Mines   187, 376
U.S. Bureau of the Census   339, 551
U.S.-Canada Free Trade Agreement   329
U.S. Census Bureau   431
U.S. Defense Department   663
U.S. Department of Agriculture   19, 29, 267
U.S. Department of Agriculture Market Wire Reports   25
U.S. Department of Commerce   180, 189, 339, 347, 351, 397, 610
U.S. Department of Defense   45, 339, 567
U.S. Department of Energy   66, 160, 231, 280, 397, 423, 442, 525
U.S. Department of Justice   531
U.S. Department of Labor   421, 551, 590
U.S. Department of Transportation   37, 200, 202
The U.S. Distilled Spirits: Impact Databank Market Review and Forecast   98
U.S. Food and Drug Administration   368
U.S. Forecasts   145, 154
U.S. Forest Service   267
U.S. Geological Survey   376
U.S. Glass, Metal, and Glazing   11, 281
U.S. Housing Markets   547
U.S. Industrial Outlook: Forecasts for Selected Manufacturing and Service Industries   12, 112, 135, 202, 244, 330, 337, 343, 364, 381, 392, 414, 430, 456, 464, 494, 593, 621
U.S. Information Agency   532
U.S. International Broadcasting Act of 1994   533
U.S.-Japan Semiconductor Agreement   584
U.S. Merchandise Trade: Selected Highlights   55, 63
U.S. Military Sealift Command   663
U.S. Office of Science and Technology   572
U.S. Pharmacopeia (USP)   367
U.S. Robotics   179
U.S. Sugar Corporation   618
U.S. Time Series   445, 527
U.S. Travel and Tourism Agency   650
U.S. West   116
U.S. Wheat Associates   24
The U.S. Wine Market: Impact Databank Review and Forecast   98
USA Today   410
Utility Automation   235

V

V & S Variety Stores   285
Value Line Convertible Data Base   579
Value of New Construction Put in Place   196
Viacom   386
Vickers On-Line   579
Video Business   79, 391
Video Cameras and Camcorders   79
Video Investor   391

Video Magazine 79, 391
Video Players-Recorders 79
Video Rating Guide for Libraries 391
Video Recorder Dealer Directory 79
Video Review 79, 391
Video Software Dealers Association 390
Video Store 80
Video Store: Tomorrow's Retailing Today 392
Video Systems: The Magazine for Video Professionals 392
Video Tape Recorders Market 80
Video Technology News 392
Video Week: Devoted to the Business of Program Sales and Distribution for Videocassettes, Disc, Pay TV and Allied News Media 392
Videography 392
Videos for Business and Training 392
Vienna Commodity Exchange 577
VITIS: Viticulture and Enology Abstracts online 98

W

WACA News 135
Wal-Mart Stores Inc. 416
Walden's Fiber and Board Report 449
Walt Disney Co. 383, 529
Walter Skinner's Oil and Gas International Year Book 237
Ward's Auto World 402
Ward's AutoInfoBank 403
Ward's Automotive Reports 402
Ward's Automotive Yearbook 403
Warner Bros. 383, 386
Washington Agricultural Record 25
Washington Health Record 296
Washington Post 412
The Waterways Journal 667
Weekly Coal Production 162
Weekly Petroleum Status Report 471, 479
Wendy's 549
Westinghouse Electric Company 531
Westinghouse Electric Corporation 232
Westlaw 336
Weyerhaeuser Timber Co. 267
Wheat Facts 26
Wheat Grower 25
Wheat Life 25
Wheaton Glass 281
Wholesale Drugs Magazine 487
WILSONLINE: Applied Science and Technology Abstracts 167, 182, 252, 349, 355, 501, 508
WILSONLINE: Art Index 494
WILSONLINE: Biological and Agricultural Index 25, 34
WILSONLINE: Education Index 227
WILSONLINE: Readers' Guide Abstracts 607
WILSONLINE: Wilson Business Abstracts 6, 364

WILSONLINE: Wilson Publishers Directory 112
Winchester 217
Wine and Spirits Guild of America 97
Wine and Spirits Wholesalers of America 97
Wine Enthusiast 97
Wine Institute 91, 97
The Wine Spectator 97
Wines and Vines Annual Statistical Issue 98
Wines and Vines: The Authoritative Voice of the Grape and Wine Industry 97
Winning is the Only Thing: Sports in America Since 1945. 608
Wireless and Cable Voice Services: Forecasts and Competitive Impacts 633
Wisconsin Brewing Co. 101
Women's Council of Realtors 546
Women's National Book Association 111
Women's Wear Daily: The Retailer's Daily Newspaper 63
Wood Products Manufacturers Association 270
Wood Technology-Equipment Catalog and Buyers' Guide 271
Wood Technology: Logging, Pulpwood, Forestry, Lumber, Panels 270
Workboat 667
World Factbook 221
World Market for Engines for Automobiles and Industrial Vehicles 424
World Metal Statistics 382
World Motor Vehicle Data 403
World Oil 423
World Resources Institute (WRI) 268
World Sea Trade Service 667
World Semiconductor Trade Statistics 586
World Surface Coatings Abstracts Online 12, 436
World Textiles 55, 63, 207
World Trade Organization 61, 172
Worldcasts: Product Edition 430
Wyse Technology Inc. 175

X
Xerox 490

Y
Yankelovich, Skelly and White/Clancy Shulman Inc. 361
Year-End Summary of the Electric Power Situation in the United States 237
Yearbook of Agriculture 26
Yearbook of Forest Products 271
Yellow Pages and Directory Report: The Newsletter for the Directory Publishing Industry 125
Young & Rubicam 16
Your Life Insurance Options 320